CW01638747

MANAGING INVESTMENT PORTFOLIOS

A DYNAMIC PROCESS

CFA Institute is the premier association for investment professionals around the world, with over 85,000 members in 129 countries. Since 1963 the organization has developed and administered the renowned Chartered Financial Analyst® Program. With a rich history of leading the investment profession, CFA Institute has set the highest standards in ethics, education, and professional excellence within the global investment community, and is the foremost authority on investment profession conduct and practice.

Each book in the CFA Institute Investment Series is geared toward industry practitioners along with graduate-level finance students and covers the most important topics in the industry. The authors of these cutting-edge books are themselves industry professionals and academics and bring their wealth of knowledge and expertise to this series.

MANAGING INVESTMENT PORTFOLIOS

A DYNAMIC PROCESS

Third Edition

John L. Maginn, CFA

Donald L. Tuttle, CFA

Dennis W. McLeavey, CFA

Jerald E. Pinto, CFA

WILEY

Managing Investment Portfolios: *A Dynamic Process, Third Edition*

Authorised reprint by Wiley India Pvt. Ltd., 4435-36/7, Ansari Road, Daryaganj, New Delhi-110002.

Copyright © 2007 by CFA Institute. All rights reserved

Published by John Wiley & Sons, Inc., Hoboken, New Jersey

No part of this book, including interior design, cover design, and icons, may be reproduced or transmitted in any form except with the permission of John Wiley & Sons, Inc., 111 River Street, Hoboken, NJ 07030, (201) 748-6011, fax (201) 748-6008, or online at http://www.wiley.com/go/permissions.

Limit of Liability/ Disclaimer of Warranty: The publisher and the author make no representations or warranties with respect to the accuracy or completeness of the contents of this work and specifically disclaim all warranties, including without limitation warranties of fitness for a particular purpose. No warranty may be created or extended by sales or promotional materials. The advice and strategies contained herein may not be suitable for every situation. This work is sold with the understanding that the publisher is not engaged in rendering legal, accounting, or other professional services. If professional assistance is required, the services of a competent professional person should be sought. Neither the publisher nor the author shall be liable for damages arising herefrom. The fact that an organization or website is referred to in this work as a citation and/or a potential source of further information does not mean that the author or the publisher endorses the information the organization or website may provide or recommendations it may make. Further, readers should be aware that Internet websites listed in this work may have changed or disappeared between when this work was written and when it is read.

TRADEMARKS: Wiley, the Wiley logo are trademarks or registered trademarks of John Wiley & Sons, Inc. and/or its affiliates, in the United States and other countries, and may not be used without written permission. All other trademarks are the property of their respective owners. Wiley Publishing, Inc. is not associated with any product or vendor mentioned in this book.

Wiley also publishes its books in a variety of electronic formats. Some content that appears in print may not be available in electronic books.

Reprint: 2017

Printed at: Bhushan Print Line

ISBN: 978-81-265-6444-6

CONTENTS

FOREWORD: NICE PORTFOLIOS AND THE UNKNOWN FUTURE

Peter L. Bernstein

In 1934, my father formed a small investment management firm based on his unshakeable conviction that the stock market had touched a historic bottom and great profitable opportunities were there for the picking. When friends would ask him how the business was going, he always replied, "We have some nice portfolios over there." I was a young boy at the time, and this repeated reference to "nice portfolios" led me to believe my father was in the business of selling briefcases and that kind of thing. What that had to do with the stock market was beyond me.

Years later, I went to work at my father's firm during one summer vacation from college. Then I began to appreciate what he was talking about when he kept referring to portfolios. I have been impressed ever since with my father's use of the word *portfolio* as early as 1934 and his emphasis on the portfolio in the investment process at this firm. Most investors of that time—and for many years to follow—looked at each equity holding and each bond without much regard to the interrelationships to other holdings or to the overwhelming importance of the whole relative to the parts.

It was not until 1952, in Harry Markowitz's immortal 14-page article, "Portfolio Selection," that the full meaning and significance of the portfolio was articulated for the first time. And few people took notice of what Markowitz had to say for many years to come. Even Milton Friedman, at Markowitz's oral exams for his PhD degree at Chicago, brushed off this work as neither economics nor mathematics, without in any way acknowledging the profound and far-reaching significance of Markowitz's achievement.

"Portfolio Selection" demonstrated that the riskiness of a portfolio depends on the covariance of its holdings, not on the average riskiness of the separate investments. This revelation was a thunderclap. No one had ever said that before, even those few who paid some attention to diversification. Investors had always bought and sold securities as individual items or perhaps grouped into separate buckets. For many, diversification was something for sissies, because diversification is an explicit statement that we do not know what the future holds. In time, however, Markowitz's emphasis on the portfolio would revolutionize the whole approach to the investment process, from security selection all the way to overall asset allocation.

Indeed, Markowitz was setting forth an even bigger vision. Before Markowitz, every work on investing, even the most serious such as Benjamin Graham's *Security Analysis*, focused on predicting returns, with risk as a secondary matter. Markowitz set risk at the heart of the investment process and emphasized the notion of the portfolio as the primary tool for maximizing the trade-off between risk and return. No wonder Bill Sharpe would exclaim, many years later, "Markowitz came along, and there was light!" [Burton, Jonathan, 1998. "Interview," *Dow Jones Asset Manager*, May/June.]

I have told the story above because it provides significance and meaning to the title of this book, *Managing Investment Portfolios*, which is the third in a series with this title dating all the way back to 1983. There are a zillion books whose title says, more or less, *How to Manage Your Investments*, but such works are valueless. They miss the entire point, encapsulated in that briefcase kind of vision I inherited from my father so many years ago. The whole is greater than the parts.

We can go further down this road. Many of these popular books ignore another point of the highest importance. If the portfolio is the primary tool for maximizing the risk/return trade-off, it plays that role because *risk is the dominant variable in the whole investment process* and the structure of the portfolio is where we make our risk management decisions. Return is an expectation, not a variable subject to our control. We obviously try to select attractive assets that we hope will promote our investment objectives, but we never know what the future holds. The best definition of risk I know was set forth a long time ago by Elroy Dimson of London Business School: Risk means more things can happen than will happen. The range of future outcomes is the impenetrable mystery all investors must face.

Investors must shape all portfolio decisions around that simple but powerful truth. If we do not know the future, decision errors and surprises are inevitable. As a result, managing investment portfolios is ultimately about managing risk, or preparing for uncertainty and unexpected outcomes.

By a happy coincidence, John Maginn and Donald Tuttle, who are among the authors of the opening contribution to this volume, were the editors of the first edition of *Managing Investment Portfolios* in 1983, to which I was also a contributor. At the end of their introductory chapter to the 1983 edition, "The Portfolio Management Process and Its Dynamics," Maginn and Tuttle set forth the fundamental principles of investing better than anyone else I know:

> *Portfolio management is the central work of investment management, and it is only in the context of a particular portfolio—and the realistic objectives of the particular portfolio beneficiary—that individual securities and specific investment decisions can be fully and correctly understood. And it is in the portfolio context that investors have learned to appreciate that their objective is not to manage reward but to control and manage risk. (page 23)*

Keep that paragraph in front of you as you read this book—and forever after.

In relation to this matter, this third edition is an improvement over the 1983 edition: It has an entire chapter, Chapter 9, explicitly devoted to risk management, a topic, the Preface assures us, that is "a discipline of immense importance in investment management." The 1983 edition discussed risk as just part of a chapter headed "Basic Financial Concepts: Return and Risk," by Keith Ambachtsheer and James Ambrose. Despite its broad coverage of the topic as set forth in its title, Ambachtsheer and Ambrose give return equal billing with risk and provide a heavier emphasis on measurement and implementation than on the essential character of risk and the manner in which it infuses every single investment decision.

In addition, Ambachtsheer and Ambrose employ the *Oxford Dictionary* definition of the word *risk*, which reads "chance of bad consequences . . . exposure to chance of injury or loss." This view is incorrect or at least incomplete. The ultimate derivation of the word is an old Italian word *risicare*, which means to dare. Recall Dimson's definition of risk as more things can happen than will happen. Dimson is really just using a fancy phrase to say we do not know what the future holds and that surprises are inevitable. But why do all the surprises have to be "bad consequences"? All investors have had moments (usually all too few) when decisions turned out to exceed their fondest expectations. By highlighting bad outcomes, we lose sight of the most significant feature of the risk/return trade-off that dominates all investment decisions. *Without risk, there is no expected positive return beyond the riskless rate of interest.* But if risk means the return runs the chance of turning out to be negative, risk also means the return could exceed the investor's expectations. Real life cuts both ways.

What would investing be like if there were no risks? Would markets be cornucopias of juicy returns available to any investor who chooses to play? Hardly. Under those conditions, everyone would rush in to grab the goodies while they last, and asset prices would soar to a point where the only return to expect is the riskless rate of interest. We cannot understand markets, grasp asset pricing principles, compose portfolios, define objectives, prepare investment policy statements, perform the intricacies of asset allocation, estimate expected returns, or execute trades in the marketplace without placing risk in the center of every one of these deliberations or actions.

One final observation is necessary before you begin to drink deep from the libations before you in this book. In financial markets, the price is the primary signal of value. The price may be too high or too low in some fashion, but price is the essential ingredient of a decision to buy or sell an asset. But whence the price? Prices are set by human beings making bids and offers, not by some impersonal mechanism. At the heart of the notion of investment risk-taking is a giant von Neumann-Morgenstern theory of games, in which no player can make a decision without taking into consideration what the other players are up to. The value of every asset at any moment does not depend on the economy, does not depend on interest rates, does not depend on any other familiar variable. It depends on what somebody else will pay for that asset at the moment some investor wants to liquidate it.

No wonder investing is a bet on an unknown future.

PREFACE

Managing Investment Portfolios now appears in its third edition, having served a worldwide readership of investment professionals through its first two. As before, the book's purpose is to survey the best of current portfolio management practice. Recognizing that portfolio management is an integrated set of activities, topic coverage is organized according to a well-articulated portfolio management decision-making process. This organizing principle—in addition to the breadth of coverage, quality of content, and meticulous pedagogy—continues to distinguish this book from other investment texts.

The book consists of 13 chapters. Each chapter covers one major area and is written by a team of distinguished practitioners and researchers. The authors have adopted a structured and modular presentation style, attempting to clearly explain and illustrate each major concept, tool, or technique so that a generalist practitioner, studying independently, can readily grasp it and use it. Illustrations are abundant and frequently include questions and answers. Terminology is consistent across individual chapters. Just as the book organizes chapters consistent with the portfolio management process, the individual chapters organize topic area knowledge logically, demonstrating processes that a practitioner can take to successfully address needs or tasks, e.g., the preparation of an investment policy statement for a client or the selection of an asset allocation that will help that client achieve his or her investment objectives. Within the unifying context of the portfolio management framework, the chapters thus complement and support each other. To further enhance understanding of the material, the publishers have made available the *Managing Investment Portfolios Workbook*—a comprehensive companion study guide containing challenging practice questions and solutions.

In more detail, chapter coverage is as follows:

Chapter 1 explains the portfolio management process and its cornerstone, the investment policy statement. The chapter describes an objectives-and-constraints framework for specifying key elements of investment policy. Basic concepts and vocabulary are introduced to give readers command of fundamentals at the outset of studying portfolio management.

Chapter 2 on managing individual investor portfolios takes a structured case-study approach to illustrating the formulation of an investment policy statement and the conduct of portfolio management on behalf of individual investors. The chapter covers the range of issues that distinguish private wealth management—from taxation to the interaction of personality and psychology with investment objectives.

Chapter 3 on managing institutional investor portfolios discusses portfolio management as applied to investors representing large pools of money such as pension funds, foundations, endowments, insurance companies, and banks. For each type of institutional investor, the chapter analyzes and illustrates the formulation of the elements of an appropriate investment policy statement.

Chapter 4 on capital market expectations provides a comprehensive and internationally attuned exposition of the formulation of expectations about capital market returns. The chapter offers a wealth of information on the variety of approaches, problems, and solutions in current professional practice.

Chapter 5 on asset allocation addresses the allocation of the investor's assets to asset classes. Strategic asset allocation integrates the investor's long-term capital market expectations (presented in Chapter 4) with the investor's return objectives, risk tolerance, and investment constraints from the investment policy statement (presented in Chapters 1, 2, and 3). Tactical asset allocation, reflecting shorter-term capital market expectations, is a distinct investment discipline that is also discussed in this chapter. The chapter digests many advances in the understanding and practice of asset allocation that have been made over the last decade.

Chapter 6 on fixed-income portfolio management provides a well-illustrated presentation of the management of fixed-income portfolios with varying investment objectives. The chapter also covers the selection of fixed-income portfolio managers.

Chapter 7 on equity portfolio management offers a detailed picture of current professional equity portfolio management practice. The authors cover the definition, identification, and implementation of the major approaches to equity investing. The chapter also discusses the problems of coordinating and managing a group of equity portfolio managers and selecting equity managers.

Chapter 8 on alternative investment portfolio management discusses the investment characteristics and possible roles in the portfolio of major alternative investment types. These include real estate, private equity and venture capital, commodities, hedge funds, managed futures, and distressed securities. The chapter also covers critical issues such as due diligence in alternative investment selection.

Chapter 9 on risk management surveys a discipline of immense importance in investment management. This chapter explains a framework for measuring, analyzing, and managing both financial and nonfinancial risks. The chapter is relevant not only to managing the risk of portfolios, but also to structuring an investment firm's overall operations and to evaluating the risks of companies that are prospects for investment or counterparties in financial transactions.

Chapter 10 on execution of portfolio decisions addresses the critical tasks of executing trades, measuring and controlling transaction costs, and effectively managing the trading function.

Chapter 11 on monitoring and rebalancing presents and illustrates two key activities in assuring that a portfolio continues to meet an investor's needs over time as investment objectives, circumstances, market prices, and financial market conditions evolve.

Chapter 12 on evaluating portfolio performance discusses performance measurement, attribution, and appraisal, addressing the questions: "How did the portfolio perform?" "Why did the portfolio produce the observed performance?" and "Is performance due to skill or luck?"

Chapter 13 on global investment presentation standards covers the accurate calculation and presentation of investment performance results as set forth in Global Investment Presentation Standards®, a set of standards that has been widely adopted worldwide.

Editorially directed from within CFA Institute, each chapter has been through several rounds of detailed external review by CFA charterholders to ensure that coverage is balanced, accurate, and clear. This intensive review process reflects the stated mission of CFA Institute *to lead the investment profession globally by setting the highest standards of ethics, education, and professional excellence.* We are confident you will find your professional education in investments enhanced through the study of *Managing Investment Portfolios.*

ACKNOWLEDGMENTS

It is often said that we stand on the shoulders of those that came before us. The *Managing Investment Portfolios* book has evolved over almost three decades, starting with a task force of six CFA charterholders who defined the investment management process that remains the cornerstone of this third edition. During this same period, the practice of portfolio management has made great strides. The authors and reviewers of the previous two editions blazed the trail that has been so ably and comprehensively updated and expanded by the authors of the chapters in this edition. We continue to be thankful for the role that so many have played in the evolution of this book and the practice of portfolio management.

Robert R. Johnson, CFA, managing director of the CFA and CIPM Programs Division at CFA Institute, initiated the revision project. We appreciate his support for the timely revision of this book. Christopher Wiese, CFA, director of curriculum projects at CFA Institute, helped prepare the glossary and made other contributions.

The Candidate Curriculum Committee provided invaluable input. We would especially like to thank Doug Manz, CFA, and Fredrik Axsater, CFA, for their advice on the curriculum relevancy of each chapter. Additional specialized input was received from CCC topic coordinators Jan Bratteberg, CFA (Alternative Investments), David Jordan, CFA (Equity), Leslie Kiefer, CFA (Private Wealth), Lavone Whitmer, CFA (Fixed Income), and Natalie Schoon, CFA (Economics).

The manuscript reviewers for this edition were as follows: Andrew Abouchar, CFA; Evan Ashcraft, CFA; Giuseppe Ballocchi, CFA; Donna Bernachi, CFA; Soren Bertelsen, CFA; DeWitt Bowman, CFA; Edward Bowman, CFA; Christopher Brightman, CFA; Ronald Bruggink, CFA; Terence Burns, CFA; Alida Carcano, CFA; Peng Chen, CFA; Robert Ernst, CFA; Jane Farris, CFA; Thomas Franckowiak, CFA; Jacques Gagne, CFA; Marla Harkness, CFA; Max Hudspeth, CFA; Joanne Infantino, CFA; David Jessop; Amaury Jordan, CFA; Lisa Joublanc, CFA; L. Todd Juillerat, CFA; Sang Kim, CFA; Robert MacGovern, CFA; Farhan Mahmood, CFA; Richard K.C. Mak, CFA; James Meeth, CFA; John Minahan, CFA; Edgar Norton, CFA; Martha Oberndorfer, CFA; George Padula, CFA; Eugene Podkaminer, CFA; Raymond Rath, CFA; Qudratullah Rehan, CFA; Douglas Rogers, CFA; Sanjiv Sabherwal; Alfred Shepard, CFA; Sandeep Singh, CFA; Zhiyi Song, CFA; Ahmed Sule, CFA; Karyn Vincent, CFA; Richard Walsh, CFA; and Thomas Welch, CFA. We thank them for their excellent work.

Fiona Russell, Ellen Barber, Elizabeth Collins, and Christine Kemper provided incisive copy editing that substantially contributed to the book's accuracy and readability. Maryann Dupes helped in marshalling CFA Institute editorial resources. Wanda Lauziere, the project manager for this revision, expertly guided the manuscript from planning through production and made indispensable contributions to all aspects of the revision.

John L. Maginn, CFA
Donald L. Tuttle, CFA
Dennis W. McLeavey, CFA
Jerald E. Pinto, CFA

INTRODUCTION

CFA Institute is pleased to provide you with this Investment Series covering major areas in the field of investments. These texts are thoroughly grounded in the highly regarded CFA Program Candidate Body of Knowledge (CBOK®) that draws upon hundreds of practicing investment professionals and serves as the anchor for the three levels of the CFA Examinations. In the year this series is being launched, more than 120,000 aspiring investment professionals will each devote over 250 hours of study to master this material as well as other elements of the Candidate Body of Knowledge in order to obtain the coveted CFA charter. We provide these materials for the same reason we have been chartering investment professionals for over 40 years: to improve the competency and ethical character of those serving the capital markets.

PARENTAGE

One of the valuable attributes of this series derives from its parentage. In the 1940s, a handful of societies had risen to form communities that revolved around common interests and work in what we now think of as the investment industry.

Understand that the idea of purchasing common stock as an investment—as opposed to casino speculation—was only a couple of decades old at most. We were only 10 years past the creation of the U.S. Securities and Exchange Commission and laws that attempted to level the playing field after robber baron and stock market panic episodes.

In January 1945, in what is today CFA Institute *Financial Analysts Journal*, a fundamentally driven professor and practitioner from Columbia University and Graham-Newman Corporation wrote an article making the case that people who research and manage portfolios should have some sort of credential to demonstrate competence and ethical behavior. This person was none other than Benjamin Graham, the father of security analysis and future mentor to a well-known modern investor, Warren Buffett.

The idea of creating a credential took a mere 16 years to drive to execution but by 1963, 284 brave souls, all over the age of 45, took an exam and launched the CFA credential. What many do not fully understand was that this effort had at its root a desire to create a profession where its practitioners were professionals who provided investing services to individuals in need. In so doing, a fairer and more productive capital market would result.

A profession—whether it be medicine, law, or other—has certain hallmark characteristics. These characteristics are part of what attracts serious individuals to devote the energy of their life's work to the investment endeavor. First, and tightly connected to this Series, there must be a body of knowledge. Second, there needs to be some entry requirements such as those required to achieve the CFA credential. Third, there must be a commitment to continuing education. Fourth, a profession must serve a purpose beyond one's direct selfish interest. In this case, by properly conducting one's affairs and putting client interests first, the investment professional can work as a fair-minded cog in the wheel of the incredibly productive global capital markets. This encourages the citizenry to part with their hard-earned savings to be redeployed in fair and productive pursuit.

As C. Stewart Sheppard, founding executive director of the Institute of Chartered Financial Analysts said, "Society demands more from a profession and its members than it does from a professional craftsman in trade, arts, or business. In return for status, prestige, and autonomy, a profession extends a public warranty that it has established and maintains conditions of entry, standards of fair practice, disciplinary procedures, and continuing education for its particular constituency. Much is expected from members of a profession, but over time, more is given."

"The Standards for Educational and Psychological Testing," put forth by the American Psychological Association, the American Educational Research Association, and the National Council on Measurement in Education, state that the validity of professional credentialing examinations should be demonstrated primarily by verifying that the content of the examination accurately represents professional practice. In addition, a practice analysis study, which confirms the knowledge and skills required for the competent professional, should be the basis for establishing content validity.

For more than 40 years, hundreds upon hundreds of practitioners and academics have served on CFA Institute curriculum committees sifting through and winnowing all the many investment concepts and ideas to create a body of knowledge and the CFA curriculum. One of the hallmarks of curriculum development at CFA Institute is its extensive use of practitioners in all phases of the process.

CFA Institute has followed a formal practice analysis process since 1995. The effort involves special practice analysis forums held, most recently, at 20 locations around the world. Results of the forums were put forth to 70,000 CFA charterholders for verification and confirmation of the body of knowledge so derived.

What this means for the reader is that the concepts contained in these texts were driven by practicing professionals in the field who understand the responsibilities and knowledge that practitioners in the industry need to be successful. We are pleased to put this extensive effort to work for the benefit of the readers of the Investment Series.

BENEFITS

This series will prove useful both to the new student of capital markets, who is seriously contemplating entry into the extremely competitive field of investment management, and to the more seasoned professional who is looking for a user-friendly way to keep one's knowledge current. All chapters include extensive references for those who would like to dig deeper into a given concept. The workbooks provide a summary of each chapter's key points to help organize your thoughts, as well as sample questions and answers to test yourself on your progress.

For the new student, the essential concepts that any investment professional needs to master are presented in a time-tested fashion. This material, in addition to university study and reading the financial press, will help you better understand the investment field. I believe that the general public seriously underestimates the disciplined processes needed for the best investment firms and individuals to prosper. These texts lay the basic groundwork for many of the processes that successful firms use. Without this base level of understanding and an appreciation for how the capital markets work to properly price securities, you may not find competitive success. Furthermore, the concepts herein give a genuine sense of the kind of work that is to be found day to day managing portfolios, doing research, or related endeavors.

The investment profession, despite its relatively lucrative compensation, is not for everyone. It takes a special kind of individual to fundamentally understand and absorb the teachings from this body of work and then convert that into application in the practitioner world. In fact, most individuals who enter the field do not survive in the longer run. The aspiring professional should think long and hard about whether this is the field for him- or herself. There is no better way to make such a critical decision than to be prepared by reading and evaluating the gospel of the profession.

The more experienced professional understands that the nature of the capital markets requires a commitment to continuous learning. Markets evolve as quickly as smart minds can find new ways to create an exposure, to attract capital, or to manage risk. A number of the concepts in these pages were not present a decade or two ago when many of us were starting out in the business. Hedge funds, derivatives, alternative investment concepts, and behavioral finance are examples of new applications and concepts that have altered the capital markets in recent years. As markets invent and reinvent themselves, a best-in-class foundation investment series is of great value.

Those of us who have been at this business for a while know that we must continuously hone our skills and knowledge if we are to compete with the young talent that constantly emerges. In fact, as we talk to major employers about their training needs, we are often told that one of the biggest challenges they face is how to help the experienced professional, laboring under heavy time pressure, keep up with the state of the art and the more recently educated associates. This series can be part of that answer.

CONVENTIONAL WISDOM

It doesn't take long for the astute investment professional to realize two common characteristics of markets. First, prices are set by conventional wisdom, or a function of the many variables in the market. Truth in markets is, at its essence, what the market believes it is and how it assesses pricing credits or debits on those beliefs. Second, as conventional wisdom is a product of the evolution of general theory and learning, by definition conventional wisdom is often wrong or at the least subject to material change.

When I first entered this industry in the mid-1970s, conventional wisdom held that the concepts examined in these texts were a bit too academic to be heavily employed in the competitive marketplace. Many of those considered to be the best investment firms at the time were led by men who had an eclectic style, an intuitive sense of markets, and a great track record. In the rough-and-tumble world of the practitioner, some of these concepts were considered to be of no use. Could conventional wisdom have been more wrong? If so, I'm not sure when.

During the years of my tenure in the profession, the practitioner investment management firms that evolved successfully were full of determined, intelligent, intellectually curious investment professionals who endeavored to apply these concepts in a serious and disciplined manner. Today, the best firms are run by those who carefully form investment hypotheses and test them rigorously in the marketplace, whether it be in a quant strategy, in comparative shopping for stocks within an industry, or in many hedge fund strategies. Their goal is to create investment processes that can be replicated with some statistical reliability. I believe those who embraced the so-called academic side of the learning equation have been much more successful as real-world investment managers.

THE TEXTS

Approximately 35 percent of the Candidate Body of Knowledge is represented in the initial four texts of the series. Additional texts on corporate finance and international financial statement analysis are in development, and more topics may be forthcoming.

One of the most prominent texts over the years in the investment management industry has been Maginn and Tuttle's *Managing Investment Portfolios: A Dynamic Process*. The third edition updates key concepts from the 1990 second edition. Some of the more experienced members of our community, like myself, own the prior two editions and will add this to our library. Not only does this tome take the concepts from the other readings and put them in a portfolio context, it also updates the concepts of alternative investments, performance presentation standards, portfolio execution and, very importantly, managing individual investor portfolios. To direct attention, long focused on institutional portfolios, toward the individual will make this edition an important improvement over the past.

Quantitative Investment Analysis focuses on some key tools that are needed for today's professional investor. In addition to classic time value of money, discounted cash flow applications, and probability material, there are two aspects that can be of value over traditional thinking.

First are the chapters dealing with correlation and regression that ultimately figure into the formation of hypotheses for purposes of testing. This gets to a critical skill that many professionals are challenged by: the ability to sift out the wheat from the chaff. For most investment researchers and managers, their analysis is not solely the result of newly created data and tests that they perform. Rather, they synthesize and analyze primary research done by others. Without a rigorous manner by which to understand quality research, not only can you not understand good research, you really have no basis by which to evaluate less rigorous research. What is often put forth in the applied world as good quantitative research lacks rigor and validity.

Second, the last chapter on portfolio concepts moves the reader beyond the traditional capital asset pricing model (CAPM) type of tools and into the more practical world of multifactor models and to arbitrage pricing theory. Many have felt that there has been a CAPM bias to the work put forth in the past, and this chapter helps move beyond that point.

Equity Asset Valuation is a particularly cogent and important read for anyone involved in estimating the value of securities and understanding security pricing. A well-informed professional would know that the common forms of equity valuation—dividend discount modeling, free cash flow modeling, price/earnings models, and residual income models (often known by trade names)—can all be reconciled to one another under certain assumptions. With a deep understanding of the underlying assumptions, the professional investor can better understand what other investors assume when calculating their valuation estimates. In my prior life as the head of an equity investment team, this knowledge would give us an edge over other investors.

Fixed Income Analysis has been at the frontier of new concepts in recent years, greatly expanding horizons over the past. This text is probably the one with the most new material for the seasoned professional who is not a fixed-income specialist. The application of option and derivative technology to the once staid province of fixed income has helped contribute to an explosion of thought in this area. And not only does that challenge the professional to stay up to speed with credit derivatives, swaptions, collateralized mortgage securities, mortgage backs, and others, but it also puts a strain on the world's central banks to provide oversight and the risk of a correlated event. Armed with a thorough grasp of the new exposures, the professional investor is much better able to anticipate and understand the challenges our central bankers and markets face.

I hope you find this new series helpful in your efforts to grow your investment knowledge, whether you are a relatively new entrant or a grizzled veteran ethically bound to keep up to date in the ever-changing market environment. CFA Institute, as a long-term committed participant of the investment profession and a not-for-profit association, is pleased to give you this opportunity.

Jeff Diermeier, CFA
President and Chief Executive Officer
CFA Institute
September 2006

CHAPTER 1

THE PORTFOLIO MANAGEMENT PROCESS AND THE INVESTMENT POLICY STATEMENT

John L. Maginn, CFA

Maginn Associates, Inc.
Omaha, Nebraska

Donald L. Tuttle, CFA

CFA Institute
Charlottesville, Virginia

Dennis W. McLeavey, CFA

CFA Institute
Charlottesville, Virginia

Jerald E. Pinto, CFA

CFA Institute
Charlottesville, Virginia

1. INTRODUCTION

This chapter introduces a book on managing investment portfolios, written by and for investment practitioners. In setting out to master the concepts and tools of portfolio management, we first need a coherent description of the portfolio management process. The **portfolio management process** is an integrated set of steps undertaken in a consistent manner to create and maintain an appropriate portfolio (combination of assets) to meet clients' stated goals. The process we present in this chapter is a distillation of the shared elements of current practice.

Because it serves as the foundation for the process, we also introduce the investment policy statement through a discussion of its main components. An **investment policy statement** (IPS) is a written document that clearly sets out a client's return objectives and risk tolerance over that client's relevant time horizon, along with applicable constraints such as liquidity needs, tax considerations, regulatory requirements, and unique circumstances.

The portfolio management process moves from planning, through execution, and then to feedback. In the planning step, investment objectives and policies are formulated, capital market expectations are formed, and strategic asset allocations are established. In the execution step, the portfolio manager constructs the portfolio. In the feedback step, the manager monitors and evaluates the portfolio compared with the plan. Any changes suggested by the feedback must be examined carefully to ensure that they represent long-run considerations.

The IPS provides the foundation of the portfolio management process. In creating an IPS, the manager writes down the client's special characteristics and needs. The IPS must clearly communicate the client's objectives and constraints. The IPS thereby becomes a plan that can be executed by any adviser or portfolio manager the client might subsequently hire. A properly developed IPS disciplines the portfolio management process and helps ensure against ad hoc revisions in strategy.

When combined with capital market expectations, the IPS forms the basis for a strategic asset allocation. **Capital market expectations** concern the risk and return characteristics of capital market instruments such as stocks and bonds. The **strategic asset allocation** establishes acceptable exposures to IPS-permissible asset classes to achieve the client's long-run objectives and constraints.

The portfolio perspective underlies the portfolio management process and IPS. The next sections illustrate this perspective.

2. INVESTMENT MANAGEMENT

Investment management is the service of professionally investing money. As a profession, investment management has its roots in the activities of European investment bankers in managing the fortunes created by the Industrial Revolution. By the beginning of the twenty-first century, investment management had become an important part of the financial services sector of all developed economies. By the end of 2003, the United States alone had approximately 15,000 money managers (registered investment advisers) responsible for investing more than $23 trillion, according to Standard & Poor's *Directory of Registered Investment Advisors* (2004). No worldwide count of investment advisers is available, but looking at another familiar professionally managed investment, the number of mutual funds stood at about 54,000 at year-end 2003; of these funds, only 15 percent were U.S. based.[1]

The economics of investment management are relatively simple. An investment manager's revenue is fee driven; primarily, fees are based on a percentage of the average amount of assets under management and the type of investment program run for the client, as spelled out in

[1] These facts are based on statistics produced by the Investment Company Institute and the International Investment Funds Association.

detail in the investment management contract or other governing document. Consequently, an investment management firm's size is judged by the amount of assets under management, which is thus directly related to manager's revenue, another measure of size. Traditionally, the value of an investment management business (or a first estimate of value) is determined as a multiple of its annual fee income.

To understand an investment management firm or product beyond its size, we need to know not only its investment disciplines but also the type or types of investor it primarily serves. Broadly speaking, investors can be described as institutional or individual. Institutional investors, described in more detail in Chapter 3, are entities such as pension funds, foundations and endowments, insurance companies, and banks that ultimately serve as financial intermediaries between individuals and financial markets. The investment policy decisions of institutional investors are typically made by investment committees or trustees, with at least some members having a professional background in finance. The committee members or trustees frequently also bear a fiduciary relationship to the funds for which they have investment responsibility. Such a relationship, if it is present, imposes some legal standards regarding processes and decisions, which is reflected in the processes of the investment managers who serve that market segment.

Beginning in the second half of the twentieth century, the tremendous growth of institutional investors, especially defined-benefit (DB) pension plans, spurred a tremendous expansion in investment management firms or investment units of other entities (such as bank trust divisions) to service their needs.[2] As the potentially onerous financial responsibilities imposed on the sponsors by such plans became more evident, however, the 1980s and 1990s saw trends to other types of retirement schemes focused on participant responsibility for investment decisions and results. In addition, a long-lasting worldwide economic expansion created a great amount of individual wealth. As a result, investment advisers oriented to serving high-net-worth individuals as well as mutual funds (which serve the individual and, to a lesser extent, the smaller institutional market) gained in relative importance.

Such individual investor–oriented advisers may incorporate a heavy personal financial planning emphasis in their services. Many wealthy families establish family offices to serve as trusted managers of their finances. **Family offices** are entities, typically organized and owned by a family, that assume responsibility for services such as financial planning, estate planning, and asset management, as well as a range of practical matters from tax return preparation to bill paying. Some family offices evolve such depth in professional staff that they open access to their services to other families (multifamily offices). In contrast to family offices, some investment management businesses service both individual and institutional markets, sometimes in separate divisions or corporate units, sometimes worldwide, and sometimes as part of a financial giant (American Express and Citigroup are examples of such financial supermarkets). In such cases, wrap-fee accounts packaging the services of outside investment managers may vie for the client's business with in-house, separately managed accounts, as well as in-house mutual funds, external mutual funds, and other offerings marketed by a brokerage arm of the business.

Investment management companies employ portfolio managers, analysts, and traders, as well as marketing and support personnel. Portfolio managers may use both outside research produced by **sell-side analysts** (analysts employed by brokerages) and research generated by in-house analysts—so-called **buy-side analysts** (analysts employed by an investment manager or institutional investor). The staffing of in-house research departments depends on the size

[2]A defined-benefit pension plan specifies the plan sponsor's obligations in terms of the benefit to plan participants. The plan sponsor bears the investment risk of such plans.

of the investment management firm, the variety of investment offerings, and the investment disciplines employed. An example may illustrate the variety of talent employed: The research department of one money manager with $30 billion in assets under management employs 34 equity analysts, 23 credit analysts, 3 hedge fund analysts, 12 quantitative analysts, 4 risk management professionals, 1 economist, and 1 economic analyst. That same company has a trading department with 8 equity and 8 bond traders and many support personnel. CFA charterholders can be found in all of these functions.

3. THE PORTFOLIO PERSPECTIVE

The portfolio perspective is this book's focus on the aggregate of all the investor's holdings: the portfolio. Because economic fundamentals influence the average returns of many assets, the risk associated with one asset's returns is generally related to the risk associated with other assets' returns. If we evaluate the prospects of each asset in isolation and ignore their interrelationships, we will likely misunderstand the risk and return prospects of the investor's total investment position—our most basic concern.

The historical roots of this portfolio perspective date to the work of Nobel laureate Harry Markowitz (1952). Markowitz and subsequent researchers, such as Jack Treynor and Nobel laureate William Sharpe, established the field of **modern portfolio theory** (MPT)—the analysis of rational portfolio choices based on the efficient use of risk. Modern portfolio theory revolutionized investment management. First, professional investment practice began to recognize the importance of the portfolio perspective in achieving investment objectives. Second, MPT helped spread the knowledge and use of quantitative methods in portfolio management. Today, quantitative and qualitative concepts complement each other in investment management practice.

In developing his theory of portfolio choice, Markowitz began with the perspective of investing for a single period. Others, including Nobel laureate Robert Merton, explored the dynamics of portfolio choice in a multiperiod setting. These subsequent contributions have greatly enriched the content of MPT.

If Markowitz, Merton, and other researchers created the supply, three developments in the investment community created demand for the portfolio perspective. First, institutional investing emerged worldwide to play an increasingly dominant role in financial markets. Measuring and controlling the risk of large pools of money became imperative. The second development was the increasing availability of ever-cheaper computer processing power and communications possibilities. As a result, a broader range of techniques for implementing MPT portfolio concepts became feasible. The third related development was the professionalization of the investment management field. This professionalization has been reflected in the worldwide growth of the professional accreditation program leading to the Chartered Financial Analyst (CFA®) designation.

4. PORTFOLIO MANAGEMENT AS A PROCESS

The unified presentation of portfolio management as a process represented an important advance in the investment management literature. Prior to the introduction of this concept in the first edition of this book, much of the traditional literature reflected an approach of selecting individual securities without an overall plan. Through the eyes of the professional, however, portfolio management is a *process*, an integrated set of activities that combine in a logical, orderly manner to produce a desired product. The process view is a *dynamic* and *flexible* concept that applies to all types of portfolio investments—bonds, stocks, real estate, gold, collectibles; to various organizational types—trust companies, investment counsel firms, insurance companies, mutual funds; to a full range of investors—individuals, pension plans, endowments, foundations, insurance companies, banks; and is independent of manager, location, investment philosophy, style, or approach. Portfolio management is a continuous and systematic process complete with feedback loops for monitoring and rebalancing. The process can be as loose or as disciplined, as quantitative or as qualitative, and as simple or as complex as its operators desire.

The portfolio management process is the same in every application: an integrated set of steps undertaken in a consistent manner to create and maintain appropriate combinations of investment assets. In the next sections, we explore the main features of this process.

5. THE PORTFOLIO MANAGEMENT PROCESS LOGIC

Three elements in managing any business process are planning, execution, and feedback. These same elements form the basis for the portfolio management process as depicted in Exhibit 1-1.

5.1. The Planning Step

The planning step is described in the four leftmost boxes in Exhibit 1-1. The top two boxes represent investor-related input factors, while the bottom two factors represent economic and market input.

5.1.1. Identifying and Specifying the Investor's Objectives and Constraints

The first task in investment planning is to identify and specify the investor's objectives and constraints. **Investment objectives** are desired investment outcomes. In investments, objectives chiefly pertain to return and risk. **Constraints** are limitations on the investor's ability to take full or partial advantage of particular investments. For example, an investor may face constraints related to the concentration of holdings as a result of government regulation, or restrictions in a governing legal document. Constraints are either **internal**, such as a client's specific liquidity needs, time horizon, and unique circumstances, or **external**, such as tax issues and legal and regulatory requirements. In Section 6, we examine the objective and constraint specification process.

5.1.2. Creating the Investment Policy Statement

Once a client has specified a set of objectives and constraints, the manager's next task is to formulate the investment policy statement. The IPS serves as the governing document for all investment decision making. In addition to objectives and constraints, the IPS may also cover a variety of other issues. For example, the IPS generally details reporting requirements, rebalancing guidelines, frequency and format of investment communication, manager fees, investment strategy, and the desired investment style or styles of investment managers. A typical IPS includes the following elements:

- A brief client description.
- The purpose of establishing policies and guidelines.

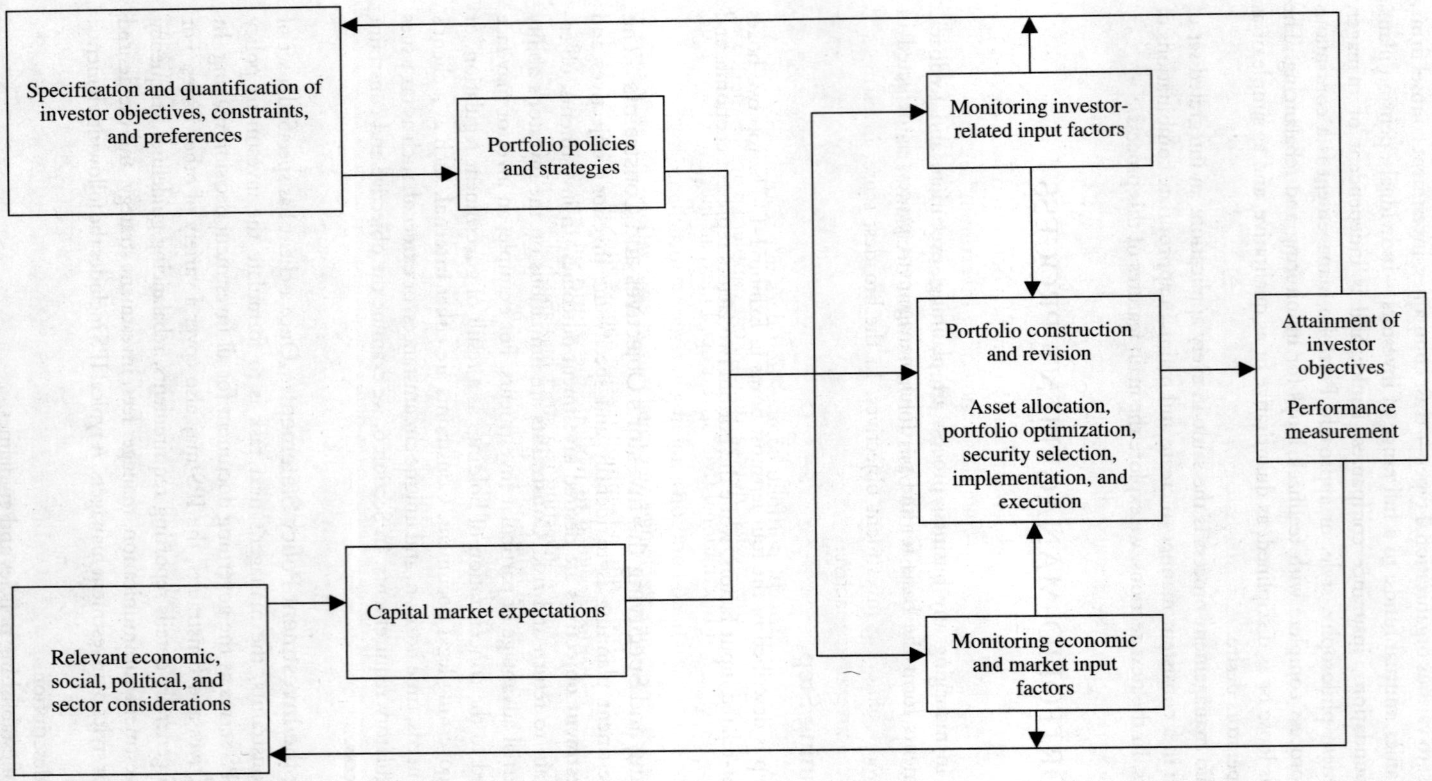

EXHIBIT 1-1 The Portfolio Construction, Monitoring, and Revision Process

- The duties and investment responsibilities of parties involved, particularly those relating to fiduciary duties, communication, operational efficiency, and accountability. Parties involved include the client, any investment committee, the investment manager, and the bank custodian.
- The statement of investment goals, objectives, and constraints.
- The schedule for review of investment performance as well as the IPS itself.
- Performance measures and benchmarks to be used in performance evaluation.
- Any considerations to be taken into account in developing the strategic asset allocation.
- Investment strategies and investment style(s).
- Guidelines for rebalancing the portfolio based on feedback.

The IPS forms the basis for the strategic asset allocation, which reflects the interaction of objectives and constraints with the investor's long-run capital market expectations. When experienced professionals include the policy allocation as part of the IPS, they are implicitly forming capital market expectations and also examining the interaction of objectives and constraints with long-run capital market expectations. In practice, one may see IPSs that include strategic asset allocations, but we will maintain a distinction between the two types.

The planning process involves the concrete elaboration of an **investment strategy**—that is, the manager's approach to investment analysis and security selection. A clearly formulated investment strategy organizes and clarifies the basis for investment decisions. It also guides those decisions toward achieving investment objectives. In the broadest sense, investment strategies are passive, active, or semiactive.

- In a **passive investment approach,** portfolio composition does not react to changes in capital market expectations (*passive* means "not reacting"). For example, a portfolio indexed to the Morgan Stanley Capital International (MSCI)-Europe Index, an index representing European equity markets, might add or drop a holding in response to a change in the index composition but not in response to changes in capital market expectations concerning the security's investment value. **Indexing,** a common passive approach to investing, refers to holding a portfolio of securities designed to replicate the returns on a specified index of securities. A second type of passive investing is a strict buy-and-hold strategy, such as a fixed, but nonindexed, portfolio of bonds to be held to maturity.
- In contrast, with an **active investment approach,** a portfolio manager will respond to changing capital market expectations. Active management of a portfolio means that its holdings differ from the portfolio's **benchmark** or comparison portfolio in an attempt to produce positive excess risk-adjusted returns, also known as positive **alpha.** Securities held in different-from-benchmark weights reflect expectations of the portfolio manager that differ from consensus expectations. If the portfolio manager's differential expectations are also on average correct, active portfolio management may add value.
- A third category, the **semiactive, risk-controlled active,** or **enhanced index approach,** seeks positive alpha while keeping tight control over risk relative to the portfolio's benchmark. As an example, an index-tilt strategy seeks to track closely the risk of a securities index while adding a targeted amount of incremental value by tilting portfolio weightings in some direction that the manager expects to be profitable.

Active investment approaches encompass a very wide range of disciplines. To organize this diversity, investment analysts appeal to the concept of investment style. Following Brown and Goetzmann (1997), we can define an **investment style** (such as an emphasis on growth stocks or value stocks) as a natural grouping of investment disciplines that has some predictive power in explaining the future dispersion in returns across portfolios. We will take up the discussion of investment strategies and styles in greater detail in subsequent chapters.

5.1.3. Forming Capital Market Expectations

The manager's third task in the planning process is to form capital market expectations. Long-run forecasts of risk and return characteristics for various asset classes form the basis for choosing portfolios that maximize expected return for given levels of risk, or minimize risk for given levels of expected return.

5.1.4. Creating the Strategic Asset Allocation

The fourth and final task in the planning process is determining the strategic asset allocation. Here, the manager combines the IPS and capital market expectations to determine target asset class weights; maximum and minimum permissible asset class weights are often also specified as a risk-control mechanism. The investor may seek both single-period and multiperiod perspectives in the return and risk characteristics of asset allocations under consideration. A single-period perspective has the advantage of simplicity. A multiperiod perspective can address the liquidity and tax considerations that arise from rebalancing portfolios over time, as well as serial correlation (long- and short-term dependencies) in returns, but is more costly to implement.

This chapter focuses on the creation of an IPS in the planning step and thereby lays the groundwork for the discussion in later chapters of tailoring the IPS to individual and institutional investors' needs. The execution and feedback steps in the portfolio management process are as important as the planning step and will receive more attention in subsequent chapters. For now, we merely outline how these steps fit in the portfolio management process.

5.2. The Execution Step

The execution step is represented by the "portfolio construction and revision" box in Exhibit 1-1. In the execution step, the manager integrates investment strategies with capital market expectations to select the specific assets for the portfolio (the **portfolio selection/composition decision**). Portfolio managers initiate portfolio decisions based on analysts' inputs, and trading desks then implement these decisions (**portfolio implementation decision**). Subsequently, the portfolio is revised as investor circumstances or capital market expectations change; thus, the execution step interacts constantly with the feedback step.

In making the portfolio selection/composition decision, portfolio managers may use the techniques of portfolio optimization. **Portfolio optimization**—quantitative tools for combining assets efficiently to achieve a set of return and risk objectives—plays a key role in the integration of strategies with expectations and appears in Exhibit 1-1 in the portfolio construction and revision box.

At times, a portfolio's actual asset allocation may purposefully and temporarily differ from the strategic asset allocation. For example, the asset allocation might change to reflect an investor's current circumstances that are different from normal. The temporary allocation may remain in place until circumstances return to those described in the IPS and reflected in the strategic asset allocation. If the changed circumstances become permanent, the manager must update the investor's IPS, and the temporary asset allocation plan will effectively become the new strategic asset allocation. A strategy known as tactical asset allocation also results in differences from the strategic asset allocation. **Tactical asset allocation** responds to changes in short-term capital market expectations rather than to investor circumstances.

The portfolio implementation decision is as important as the portfolio selection/composition decision. Poorly managed executions result in transaction costs that reduce performance. Transaction costs include all costs of trading, including explicit transaction costs, implicit transaction costs, and missed trade opportunity costs. **Explicit transaction costs** include commissions paid to brokers, fees paid to exchanges, and taxes. **Implicit transaction costs** include bid-ask spreads, the market price impacts of large trades, **missed trade opportunity costs** arising from price changes that prevent trades from being filled, and **delay costs** arising from the inability to complete desired trades immediately due to order size or market liquidity.

In sum, in the execution step, plans are turned into reality—with all the attendant real-world challenges.

5.3. The Feedback Step

In any business endeavor, feedback and control are essential elements in reaching a goal. In portfolio management, this step has two components: monitoring and rebalancing, and performance evaluation.

5.3.1. Monitoring and Rebalancing

Monitoring and **rebalancing** involve the use of feedback to manage ongoing exposures to available investment opportunities so that the client's current objectives and constraints continue to be satisfied. Two types of factors are monitored: investor-related factors such as the investor's circumstances, and economic and market input factors.

One impetus for portfolio revision is a change in investment objectives or constraints because of changes in investor circumstances. Portfolio managers need a process in place to stay informed of changes in clients' circumstances. The termination of a pension plan or death of a spouse may trigger an abrupt change in a client's time horizon and tax concerns, and the IPS should list the occurrence of such changes as a basis for appropriate portfolio revision.

More predictably, changes in economic and market input factors give rise to the regular need for portfolio revision. Again, portfolio managers need to systematically review the risk attributes of assets as well as economic and capital market factors (the chapter on capital market expectations describes the range of factors to consider in more detail). A change in expectations may trigger portfolio revision. When asset price changes occur, however, revisions can be required even without changes in expectations. The actual timing and magnitude of rebalancing may be triggered by review periods or by specific rules governing the management of the portfolio and deviation from the tolerances or ranges specified in the strategic asset allocation, or the timing and magnitude may be at the discretion of the manager. For example, suppose the policy allocation calls for an initial portfolio with a 70 percent weighting to stocks and a 30 percent weighting to bonds. Suppose the value of the stock holdings then grows by 40 percent, while the value of the bond holdings grows by 10 percent. The new weighting is roughly 75 percent in stocks and 25 percent in bonds. To bring the portfolio back into compliance with investment policy, it must be rebalanced back to the long-term policy weights. In any event, the rebalancing decision is a crucial one that must take into account many factors, such as transaction costs and taxes (for taxable investors). Disciplined rebalancing will have a major impact on the attainment of investment objectives. Rebalancing takes us back to the issues of execution, as is appropriate in a feedback process.

5.3.2. Performance Evaluation

Investment performance must periodically be evaluated by the investor to assess progress toward the achievement of investment objectives as well as to assess portfolio management skill.

The assessment of portfolio management skill has three components. **Performance measurement** involves the calculation the portfolio's rate of return. **Performance attribution** examines why the portfolio performed as it did and involves determining the sources of a portfolio's performance. **Performance appraisal** is the evaluation of whether the manager is doing a good job based on how the portfolio did relative to a benchmark (a comparison portfolio).

Often, we can examine a portfolio's performance, in terms of total returns, as coming from three sources: decisions regarding the strategic asset allocation, **market timing** (returns attributable to shorter-term tactical deviations from the strategic asset allocation), and **security selection** (skill in selecting individual securities within an asset class). However, portfolio management is frequently conducted with reference to a benchmark, or for some entities, with reference to a stream of projected liabilities or a specified target rate of return. As a result, relative portfolio performance evaluation, in addition to absolute performance measurement, is often of key importance.

With respect to relative performance we may ask questions such as, "Relative to the investment manager's benchmark, what economic sectors were underweighted or overweighted?" or "What was the manager's rationale for these decisions and how successful were they?" Portfolio evaluation may also be conducted with respect to specific risk models, such as multifactor models, which attempt to explain asset returns in terms of exposures to a set of risk factors.

Concurrent with evaluation of the manager is the ongoing review of the benchmark to establish its continuing suitability. For some benchmarks, this review would include a thorough understanding of how economic sectors and subsectors are determined in the benchmark, the classification of securities within them, and how frequently the classifications change. For any benchmark, one would review whether the benchmark continues to be a fair measuring stick given the manager's mandate.

As with other parts of the portfolio management process, performance evaluation is critical and is covered in a separate chapter. In addition, performance presentation is covered by the chapter on Global Investment Performance Standards (GIPS®). These topics play a central role in the portfolio management process.

5.4. A Definition of Portfolio Management

In sum, the process logic is incorporated in the following definition, which is the cornerstone for this book. **Portfolio management** is an ongoing process in which:

- Investment objectives and constraints are identified and specified.
- Investment strategies are developed.
- Portfolio composition is decided in detail.
- Portfolio decisions are initiated by portfolio managers and implemented by traders.
- Portfolio performance is measured and evaluated.
- Investor and market conditions are monitored.
- Any necessary rebalancing is implemented.

Although we have provided general insights into the portfolio management process, this book makes no judgments and voices no opinions about how the process should be organized, who should make which decisions, or any other process operating matter. How well the process works is a critical component of investment success. In a survey of pension fund chief operating officers, Ambachtsheer, Capelle, and Scheibelhut (1998) found that 98 percent of the respondents cited a poor portfolio management process as a barrier to achieving excellence in organizational performance. The organization of the portfolio management process of any investment management company should be the result of careful planning.

6. INVESTMENT OBJECTIVES AND CONSTRAINTS

As previously discussed, the IPS is the cornerstone of the portfolio management process. Because of the IPS's fundamental importance, we introduce its main components in this chapter. In subsequent chapters, we will create actual IPSs for individual and institutional investors. In this section, we return to the tasks of identifying and specifying the investor's objectives and constraints that initiate the planning step.

Although we discuss objectives first and then constraints, the actual process of delineating these for any investor may appropriately start with an examination of investor constraints. For example, a short time horizon affects the investor's ability to take risk.

6.1. Objectives

The two objectives in this framework, risk and return, are interdependent—one cannot be discussed without reference to the other. The risk objective limits how high the investor can set the return objective.

6.1.1. Risk Objective

The first element of the risk–return framework is the **risk objective** because it will largely determine the return objective. A 10 percent standard deviation risk objective, for example, implies a different asset allocation than a 15 percent standard deviation risk objective, because expected asset risk is generally positively correlated with expected asset return. In formulating a risk objective, the investor must address the following six questions:

1. *How do I measure risk?* Risk measurement is a key issue in investments, and several approaches exist for measuring risk. In practice, risk may be measured in absolute terms or in relative terms with reference to various risk concepts. Examples of absolute risk objectives are a specified level of standard deviation or variance of total return. The **variance** of a random variable is the expected value of squared deviations from the random variable's mean. Variance is often referred to as *volatility*. **Standard deviation** is the positive square root of variance. An example of a relative risk objective is a specified level of tracking risk. **Tracking risk** is the standard deviation of the differences between a portfolio's and the benchmark's total returns.

   Downside risk concepts, such as value at risk (VaR), may also be important to an investor. **Value at risk** is a probability-based measure of the loss that one anticipates will be exceeded only a specified small fraction of the time over a given horizon—for example, in 5 percent of all monthly holding periods. Besides statistical measures of risk, other risk exposures, such as exposures to specific economic sectors, or risk with respect to a factor model of returns, may be relevant as well.
2. *What is the investor's willingness to take risk?* The investor's stated willingness to take risk is often very different for institutional versus individual investors. Managers should try to understand the behavioral and, for individuals, the personality factors behind an investor's willingness to take risk. In the chapter on individual investors, we explore behavioral issues in reference to the investor's willingness to take risk.

3. *What is the investor's ability to take risk?* Even if an investor is eager to bear risk, practical or financial limitations often limit the amount of risk that can be prudently assumed. For the sake of illustration, in the following discussion we talk about risk in terms of the volatility of asset values:
   - In terms of spending needs, how much volatility would inconvenience an investor who depends on investments (such as a university in relationship to its endowment fund)? Or how much volatility would inconvenience an investor who otherwise cannot afford to incur substantial short-term losses? Investors with high levels of wealth relative to probable worst-case short-term loss scenarios can take more risk.
   - In terms of long-term wealth targets or obligations, how much volatility might prevent the investor from reaching these goals? Investors with high levels of wealth relative to long-term wealth targets or obligations can take more risk.
   - What are the investor's liabilities or pseudo liabilities? An institution may face legally promised future payments to beneficiaries (liabilities) and an individual may face future retirement spending needs (pseudo liabilities).
   - What is the investor's financial strength—that is, the ability to increase the savings/contribution level if the portfolio cannot support the planned spending? More financial strength means more risk can be taken.

4. *How much risk is the investor both willing and able to bear?* The answer to this question defines the investor's risk tolerance. **Risk tolerance,** the capacity to accept risk, is a function of both an investor's willingness and ability to do so. Risk tolerance can also be described in terms of **risk aversion,** the degree of an investor's inability and unwillingness to take risk. The investor's specific risk objectives are formulated with that investor's level of risk tolerance in mind. Importantly, any assessment of risk tolerance must consider both an investor's willingness and that investor's ability to take risk. When a mismatch exists between the two, determining risk tolerance requires educating the client on the dangers of excess risk taking or of ignoring inflation risk, depending on the case. In our presentation in this book, we assume that such education has taken place and that we are providing an appropriate risk objective in the IPS proposed to the client. When an investor's willingness to accept risk exceeds ability to do so, ability prudently places a limit on the amount of risk the investor should assume. When ability exceeds willingness, the investor may fall short of the return objective because willingness would be the limiting factor. These interactions are shown in Exhibit 1-2.

   An investor with an above-average ability to assume risk may have legitimate reasons for choosing a lower-risk strategy. In addition, an investor may face the pleasant situation of having an excess of wealth to meet financial needs for a long period of time. In these cases, the investor needs to have a clear understanding of the eventual consequences of the decision to effectively spend down excess wealth over time. As with any strategy, such a decision must be reevaluated periodically. In the case of a

EXHIBIT 1-2 Risk Tolerance

Willingness to	Ability to Take Risk	
Take Risk	Below Average	Above Average
Below Average	Below-average risk tolerance	Resolution needed
Above Average	Resolution needed	Above-average risk tolerance

high-net-worth investor who has earned substantial wealth from entrepreneurial risk taking, such an investor may now simply not want to lose wealth and may desire only liquidity to spend in order to maintain her current lifestyle.

5. *What are the specific risk objective(s)?* Just as risk may be measured either absolutely or relatively, we may specify both absolute risk and relative risk objectives. In practice, investors often find that quantitative risk objectives are easier to specify in relative than in absolute terms. Possibly as a consequence, absolute risk objectives in particular are frequently specified in qualitative rather than quantitative terms.

   What distinguishes the risk objective from risk tolerance is the level of specificity. For example, the statement that a person has a "lower-than-average risk tolerance" might be converted operationally into "the loss in any one year is not to exceed *x* percent of portfolio value" or "annual volatility of the portfolio is not to exceed *y* percent." Often, clients—particularly individual investors—do not understand or appreciate this level of specificity, and more general risk-tolerance statements substitute for a quantitative risk objective.
6. *How should the investor allocate risk?* This is how some investors frame capital allocation decisions today, particularly when active strategies will play a role in the portfolio. The question may concern the portfolio as a whole or some part of it. Risk budgeting disciplines address the above question most directly. After the investor has determined the *measure* of risk of concern to him (e.g., VaR or tracking risk) and the *desired total quantity of risk* (the overall **risk budget**), an investor using **risk budgeting** would allocate the overall risk budget to specific investments so as to maximize expected overall risk-adjusted return. The resulting optimal risk budgets for the investments would translate to specific allocations of capital to them.

6.1.2. Return Objective

The second element of the investment policy framework is the **return objective,** which must be consistent with the risk objective. Just as tension may exist between willingness and ability in setting the risk objective, so the return objective requires a resolution of return desires versus the risk objective. In formulating a return objective, the investor must address the following four questions:

1. *How is return measured?* The usual measure is **total return,** the sum of the return from price appreciation and the return from investment income. Return may be stated as an absolute amount, such as 10 percent a year, or as a return relative to the benchmark's return, such as benchmark return plus 2 percent a year. Nominal returns must be distinguished from real returns. **Nominal** returns are unadjusted for inflation. **Real** returns are adjusted for inflation and sometimes simply called *inflation-adjusted returns.* Also, pretax returns must be distinguished from post-tax returns. **Pretax** returns are returns before taxes, and **post-tax** returns are returns after taxes are paid on investment income and realized capital gains.
2. *How much return does the investor say she wants?* This amount is the **stated return desire.** These wants or desires may be realistic or unrealistic. For example, an investor may have higher-than-average return desires to meet high consumption desires or a high ending wealth target; for instance, "I want a 20 percent annual return." The adviser or portfolio manager must continually evaluate the desire for high returns in light of the investor's ability to assume risk and the reasonableness of the stated return desire, especially relative to capital market expectations.
3. *How much return does the investor need to achieve, on average?* This amount is the **required return** or **return requirement**. Requirements are more stringent than desires because

investors with requirements typically must achieve those returns, at least on average. An example of a return requirement is the average return a pension fund projects it must earn to fund liabilities to current and future pensioners, based on actuarial calculations. The compound rate of return that an individual investor must earn to attain the asset base needed for retirement is another example of a return requirement. A third example would be the return that a retired investor must earn on his investment portfolio to cover his annual living expenses. We illustrate these last two cases.

Suppose that a married couple needs £2 million in 18 years to fund retirement. Their current investable assets total £1.2 million. The projected future need (£2 million) incorporates expected inflation. The couple would need to earn (£2 million/£1.2 million)$^{1/18}$ – 1.0 = 2.88% per year after tax to achieve their goal. Every cash flow needs to be accounted for in such calculations. If the couple needed to liquidate £25,000 from the portfolio at the end of each year (keeping all other facts unchanged), they would need to earn 4.55 percent per year on an after-tax basis to have £2 million in 18 years (a financial calculator is needed to confirm this result). If all investment returns were taxed at 35 percent, 4.55 percent after tax would correspond to a 7 percent pretax required return [4.55/(1 – 0.35) = 7%].

A retiree may depend on his investment portfolio for some or all of his living expenses. That need defines a return requirement. Suppose that a retiree must achieve a 4 percent after-tax return on his current investment portfolio to meet his current annual living expenses. Thus, his return requirement on a real, after-tax basis is 4 percent per year. If he expects inflation to be 2 percent per year and a 40 percent tax rate applies to investment returns from any source, we could estimate his pretax nominal return requirement as (After-tax real return requirement + Expected inflation rate)/(1 – Tax rate) = (4% + 2%)/(1 – 0.40) = 10%.

In contrast to desired returns, which can be reduced if incongruent with risk objectives, large required returns are an important source of potential conflict between return and risk objectives. Other required return issues that are relevant to specific situations include the following:

- What are the needs and desires for current spending versus ending wealth?
- How do nominal total return requirements relate to expected rates of price inflation? If assets fund obligations subject to inflation, the return requirements should reflect expected rates of inflation.

4. *What are the specific return objectives?* The return objective incorporates the required return, the stated return desire, and the risk objective into a measurable annual total return specification. For example, an investor with a 5 percent after-tax, required, inflation-adjusted annual rate of return but above-average risk tolerance might reasonably set a higher than 5 percent after-tax, inflation-adjusted annual rate of return objective to maximize expected wealth.

   An investor's return objective should be consistent with that investor's risk objective. A high return objective may suggest an asset allocation with an expected level of risk that is too great in relation to the risk objective, for example. In addition, the anticipated return from the portfolio should be sufficient to meet wealth objectives or liabilities that the portfolio must fund.

   For investors with current investment income needs, the return objective should be sufficient to meet spending needs from capital appreciation and investment income: When a well-considered return objective is not consistent with risk tolerance, other adjustments may need to take place, such as increasing savings or modifying wealth objectives.

An investor delegating portfolio management to an investment manager will communicate a **mandate**—a set of instructions detailing the investment manager's task and how his performance will be evaluated—that includes a specification of the manager's benchmark. Because the manager's performance will be evaluated against the benchmark, the benchmark's total return is an effective return objective for the investment manager. These instructions may be part of the investment policy statement or, in the case of a portfolio with multiple managers, outlined in separate instructions for each mandate to each manager.

Although an **absolute return objective** (one independent of a reference return) is sometimes set (e.g., 8 percent), investors often specify a relative return objective. A **relative return objective** is stated as a return relative to the portfolio benchmark's total return (e.g., 1 percent higher than the benchmark).

Exhibit 1-3 illustrates the variation in return requirement and risk tolerance among various categories of investors—a subject we explore in detail in Chapters 2 and 3.

6.2. Constraints

The investor's risk and return objectives are set within the context of several constraints: liquidity, time horizon, tax concerns, legal and regulatory factors, and unique circumstances. Although all of these factors influence portfolio choice, the first two constraints bear directly on the investor's ability to take risk and thus constrain both risk and return objectives.

6.2.1. Liquidity A **liquidity requirement** is a need for cash *in excess of new contributions* (e.g., for pension plans and endowments) or *savings* (for individuals) at a specified point in

EXHIBIT 1-3 Return Requirements and Risk Tolerances of Various Investors

Type of Investor	Return Requirement	Risk Tolerance
Individual	Depends on stage of life, circumstances, and obligations	Varies
Pension plans (defined benefit)	The return that will adequately fund liabilities on an inflation-adjusted basis	Depends on plan and sponsor characteristics, plan features, funding status, and workforce characteristics
Pension plans (defined contribution)	Depends on stage of life of individual participants	Varies with the risk tolerance of individual participants
Foundations and endowments	The return that will cover annual spending, investment expenses, and expected inflation	Determined by amount of assets relative to needs, but generally above-average or average
Life insurance companies	Determined by rates used to determine policyholder reserves	Below average due to factors such as regulatory constraints
Non–Life insurance companies	Determined by the need to price policies competitively and by financial needs	Below average due to factors such as regulatory constraints
Banks	Determined by cost of funds	Varies

time. Such needs may be anticipated or unanticipated, but either way they stem from **liquidity events**. An example of a liquidity event is planned construction of a building in one year.

The liquidity requirement may reflect nonrecurring needs or the desire to hold cash against unanticipated needs (a safety or reserve fund). This requirement may be met by holding cash or cash equivalents in the portfolio or by converting other assets into cash equivalents. Any risk of economic loss because of the need to sell relatively less liquid assets to meet liquidity requirements is **liquidity risk**. (An asset that can be converted into cash only at relatively high total cost is said to be relatively less liquid.) Liquidity risk, therefore, arises for two reasons: an asset-side reason (asset liquidity) and a liability-side reason (liquidity requirements). Portfolio managers control asset selection but not liquidity requirements; as a result, in practice, managers use asset selection to manage liquidity risk. If the portfolio's asset and income base are large relative to its potential liquidity requirements, relatively less liquid assets can be held. A distinct consideration is liquidity requirements in relation to **price risk** of the asset—the risk of fluctuations in market price. Assets with high price risk are frequently less liquid, especially during market downturns. If the timing of an investor's liquidity requirements is significantly correlated with market downturns, these requirements can influence asset selection in favor of less risky assets. In many cases, therefore, consideration of both liquidity risk and price risk means that an investor will choose to hold some part of the portfolio in highly liquid and low-price-risk assets in anticipation of future liquidity requirements. Investors may also modify the payoff structure of a risky portfolio to address liquidity requirements using derivative strategies, although such modifications often incur costs. (**Derivatives** are contracts whose payoffs depend on the value of another asset, often called the *underlying asset*.)

6.2.2. Time Horizon

Time horizon most often refers to the time period associated with an investment objective. Investment objectives and associated time horizons may be short term, long term, or a combination of the two. (A time horizon of 10 years or more is often considered to be long term. Investment performance over the long term should average results over several market and business cycles.) A multistage horizon is a combination of shorter-term and longer-term horizons. An example of a multistage horizon is the case of funding children's education shorter term and the investor's retirement longer term.

Other constraints, such as a unique circumstance or a specific liquidity requirement, can also affect an investor's time horizon. For example, an individual investor's temporary family living arrangement can dictate that his time horizon constraint be stated in multistage terms. Similarly, an institutional investor's need to make an imminent substantial disbursement of funds for a capital project can necessitate a multistage approach to the time horizon constraint.

In general, relevant time horizon questions include the following:

- *How does the length of the time horizon modify the investor's ability to take risk?* The longer the time horizon, the more risk the investor can take. The longer the time horizon, the greater the investor's ability to replenish investment resources by increasing savings. A long-term investor's labor income may also be an asset sufficiently stable to support a higher level of portfolio risk.[3] Cash may be safe for a short-term investor but risky for a long-term investor who will be faced with continuously reinvesting.
- *How does the length of the time horizon modify the investor's asset allocation?* Many investors allocate a greater proportion of funds to risky assets when they address long-term as opposed

[3] See Campbell and Viceira (2002) for a discussion of this and the following point.

to short-term investment objectives. Decreased risk-taking ability with shorter horizons can thus constrain portfolio choice.

- *How does the investor's willingness and ability to bear fluctuations in portfolio value modify the asset allocation?* With a focus on risk, even an investor with a long-term objective may limit risk taking because of sensitivity to the possibility of substantial interim losses. The chance of unanticipated liquidity needs may increase during market downturns, for instance, because a market downturn may be linked to a decline in economic activity affecting income or other sources of wealth. An investor that often faces unanticipated short-term liquidity needs will usually favor investments with a shorter time horizon so as to limit the risk of loss of value.
- *How does a multistage time horizon constrain the investor's asset allocation?* The investment policy must be designed to accommodate all time horizons in a multistage horizon case. Such design will probably entail some compromise in the setting of objectives to attain short-, medium-, and long-term goals.

6.2.3. Tax Concerns A country's tax policy can affect important aspects of investment decision making for investors who reside there. **Tax concerns** arise for taxable investors because tax payments reduce the amount of the total return that can be used for current needs or reinvested for future growth. Differences between the tax rates applying to investment income and capital gains will influence taxable investors' choice of investments and their timing of sales. Estate taxes on wealth triggered by the investor's death can also affect investment decisions. Finally, tax policy changes that affect security prices affect both taxable and tax-exempt investors.

6.2.4. Legal and Regulatory Factors **Legal** and **regulatory factors** are external factors imposed by governmental, regulatory, or oversight authorities to constrain investment decision making. In the United Kingdom, for example, regulations issued by the Financial Services Authority (FSA) limit the concentration of holdings in debt and equity securities for U.K. mutual funds. Another example is the United States' Employee Retirement Income Security Act of 1974 (ERISA), as interpreted by regulatory agencies and the courts. ERISA limits the acquisition and holding of employer securities by certain pension plans. Some countries limit the use of certain asset classes in retirement accounts.

6.2.5. Unique Circumstances **Unique circumstances** are internal factors (other than a liquidity requirement, time horizon, or tax concern) that may constrain portfolio choices. For example, a university endowment may be constrained to avoid certain investments against which there may be ethical objections or social responsibility considerations. Similarly, an individual investor's portfolio choices may be constrained by circumstances focusing on health needs, support of dependents, and other circumstances unique to the particular individual. Investors may specify avoidance of nondomestic shares or derivatives. Portfolio choices may also be constrained by investor capability in terms of both human resources and financial resources such as time, interest, background, and technical expertise.

7. THE DYNAMICS OF THE PROCESS

One of the truly satisfying aspects of portfolio management as a professional activity is the underlying logic and the dynamism of the portfolio process concept. In a broad sense, the work of analysts, economists, and market strategists is all a matter of "getting ready." The work of portfolio management is the action: taking the inputs and moving step by step through the orderly process of converting this raw material into a portfolio that maximizes expected return relative to the investor's ability to bear risk, that meets the investor's constraints and preferences, and that integrates portfolio policies with expectational factors and market uncertainties. Portfolio management is where the payoff is, because this is where it all comes together. Of course, it is the end result of this process that is judged: the performance of the portfolio relative to expectations and comparison standards.

Professionalism is enhanced and practice improved by managing portfolios as a process that:

- Consists of the steps outlined in this book.
- Flows logically and systematically through an orderly sequence of decision making.
- Is continuous once put into motion with respect to a given investor.

This view approaches portfolio management not as a set of separate elements operating by fits and starts as intuition or inspiration dictates, but rather as an integrated whole in which every decision moves the portfolio down the process path and in which no decision can be skipped without sacrificing functional integrity.

8. THE FUTURE OF PORTFOLIO MANAGEMENT[4]

In the last few decades, portfolio management has become a more science-based discipline somewhat analogous to engineering and medicine. As in these other fields, advances in basic theory, technology, and market structure constantly translate into improvements in products and professional practices.

Among the most significant recent theoretical advances in investments is the recognition that the risk characteristics of the nontradable assets owned by an individual client, such as future earnings from a job, a business, or an expected inheritance, should be included in the definition of that client's portfolio. In the institutional area also, there is an increasing awareness and use of multifactor risk models and methods of managing risk.

Among the most significant market developments is the emergence of a broad range of new standardized derivative contracts—swaps, futures, and options. As active trading in these standardized products continues to develop, they make possible the creation of an infinite variety of customized investment products tailored to the needs of specific clients. As analysts continue to develop a more comprehensive view of risk, they also command a wider set of tools with which to manage it. In the subsequent chapters, we will encounter many of these concepts.

9. THE ETHICAL RESPONSIBILITIES OF PORTFOLIO MANAGERS

In this chapter, we have initiated a course of study that we hope will further the reader in his or her career as an investment professional. We select the term investment *professional* advisedly.

[4]This section on the future of portfolio management was contributed by Dr. Zvi Bodie.

The dictionary defines professional as "conforming to the standards of a profession." Every thoughtful person who has explored the subject has concluded that professional standards are of two types: standards of competence and standards of conduct. Merely drawing a livelihood from managing or advising on the investment of client monies is insufficient in itself to make an investment professional.

But verbal distinctions are not the most important point. The conduct of a portfolio manager affects the well-being of clients and many other people. The connection to individuals and their welfare is always present; it is no less important in those institutional contexts in which the portfolio manager may never meet the client. In the first years of the twenty-first century, press attention focused on abuses in the U.S. mutual fund industry such as late trading, abusive market timing, selective disclosure of information on portfolio holdings, and undisclosed payments for "shelf space" to gain placement on brokers' preferred lists.[5] Certain fund executives facilitated or participated in these activities for personal enrichment, at the expense of the well-being of their clients, the mutual fund shareholders. In truth, the docket of cases of professional misconduct is never empty, but the profession can and must work toward minimizing it. The portfolio manager must keep foremost in mind that he or she is in a position of trust, requiring ethical conduct toward the public, client, prospects, employers, employees, and fellow workers. For CFA Institute members, this position of trust is reflected in the Code of Ethics and Standards of Professional Conduct to which members subscribe, as well as in the professional conduct statement they submit annually. Ethical conduct is the foundation requirement for managing investment portfolios.

[5]The listing follows the enumeration of William H. Donaldson, CFA, chair of the U.S. Securities and Exchange Commission, in a speech to the Mutual Fund Directors Forum on January 7, 2004.

CHAPTER 2

MANAGING INDIVIDUAL INVESTOR PORTFOLIOS

James W. Bronson, CFA
Northern Trust Bank
Newport Beach, California

Matthew H. Scanlan, CFA
Barclays Global Investors
San Francisco, California

Jan R. Squires, CFA
CFA Institute
Hong Kong

1. INTRODUCTION

In the context of portfolio management, the terms *private client, high-net-worth investor,* and *individual investor* are used virtually interchangeably to reference the unique challenges of managing personal or family assets. Although a more precise definition of the individual investor is elusive, the basic need to properly manage one's financial affairs is self-evident, and the precedent for seeking professional management is well established. Indeed, Anglo-Saxon law has recognized the role of trustee, responsible for managing assets on behalf of others, as far back as the Middle Ages.

Private asset management has only recently begun to receive greater attention from the academic community and financial press. In contrast to large, tax-exempt institutional portfolios that are typically assumed to operate in perpetuity, the universe of private investors is heterogeneous, burdened by taxes, and less well suited to the simplifying assumptions of modern financial theory. Individual investors have diverse investment objectives, time horizons, and perceptions of risk, all subject to tax schedules that have varying degrees of stability and logic.

The increasing attention to private asset management reflects both a rising demand for financial services and an increased interest in empirical investor behavior. Net wealth in individually managed portfolios increased rapidly in the 1990s and beyond, creating a growth market for personalized financial services. At the same time, increased personal responsibility for investing retirement assets, evidenced by the growth in the self-directed segment of defined contribution pensions and savings plans, as well as the portability of fully vested retirement assets, has further increased the need for professional investment management at the individual level.

With the help of a case study, this chapter examines the portfolio management process for individual investors. The Ingers are typical of a successful multigenerational family, with most of their wealth generated by a family business. Now that a cash sale of the business is imminent, they must reassess their financial situation and set appropriate guidelines for their soon-to-be-large investment portfolio. The Ingers' goal is to create an investment policy statement (IPS) that recognizes their investment goals and constraints and then establishes consistent parameters for investing portfolio assets. The IPS should serve as the fundamental point of reference for both the Inger family and their investment advisers.

2. CASE STUDY

Victoria Jourdan, CFA, works for an investment firm that manages private client accounts. Both Jourdan and the Inger family reside in a politically stable country whose currency trades at a fixed exchange rate of 1:1 with the euro. Both real gross domestic product (GDP) growth and inflation average about 3 percent annually, resulting in nominal annual growth of approximately 6 percent.

The country in which the Ingers reside maintains a flat tax of 25 percent on all personal income and a net capital gains tax (based on the sale of price-appreciated assets) of 15 percent, with no distinction between short- and long-term holding periods. Also incorporated into the tax code is a wealth transfer tax. Any asset transfer between two parties, whether as a gift or family inheritance, is taxed at the flat rate of 50 percent.

The country maintains a national pension plan, but that plan's long-term viability has been called into question because of an unfavorable demographic trend toward older, retirement-age recipients. Public debate has grown about how to assure the financial security of future retirees, and among this debate's chief outcomes has been the creation of self-contributory, tax-advantaged investment accounts for individuals. Taxpayers may annually contribute up to €5,000 of *after-tax* income to a retirement saving account (RSA), which they then control. RSA investment returns are exempt from taxation, and participants may begin making tax-free withdrawals of any amount at age 62.

2.1. The Inger Family

Jourdan has been asked to manage the Inger family account, which is a new relationship for her firm. Jourdan observes that the Inger family has no stated investment policy or guidelines, and she arranges for a meeting with Peter and Hilda Inger, who have been married for 37 years, plus their two children, Christa and Hans, aged 25 and 30, respectively. Peter, Hilda, and Hans accept the invitation, but Christa, who currently resides a considerable distance away from her parents, cannot attend.

Peter Inger, 59, is a successful entrepreneur who founded a boat manufacturing business, IngerMarine, when he was 23 years old. He has worked compulsively to build the company into a producer of luxury pleasure boats sold worldwide, but he is now considering a business succession plan and retirement. Peter is eager to "monetize" his equity stake in IngerMarine and believes he will be able to sell his company within the next three months. He is already evaluating three separate bids that indicate probable proceeds, net of taxes on gains, of approximately €55 million to the Inger family in total. The four Inger family members are the sole IngerMarine shareholders, and any sale proceeds will accrue to the four family members in proportion to their percentage ownership in IngerMarine. Peter believes that everyone in his family is financially secure and wishes to preserve that security; he recognizes the family's need for a coherent investment plan.

Hilda Inger, 57, comes from a wealthy family. Since her marriage to Peter, she has been a housewife and mother to Christa and Hans. Hilda is the beneficiary of a trust established by her family. Throughout her lifetime, the trust will distribute to her an inflation-indexed annual payment (currently €75,000), which is taxed as personal income. At her death, payments will stop, and the trust's remaining assets will be transferred to a local charity.

Both Hans and Christa are unmarried. Hans currently works as a senior vice president at IngerMarine and specializes in boat design. Peter has tried to involve Christa in the family business but she has resisted, instead achieving moderate recognition and financial success as an artist. Christa has a 5-year-old son, Jürgen, whom she has chosen to raise alone.

The meeting with Peter, Hilda, and Hans and several telephone discussions with Christa result in the following financial and personal details for the Inger family.

2.2. Inger Family Data

Income (annual)	
Peter salary[a]	€500,000
Hans salary	100,000
Hilda trust payout	75,000
Christa (art sales)	50,000
Peter Personal Assets	
Home (fully paid for, held jointly with Hilda)	€1,200,000
IngerMarine company equity[b]	60,000,000
Diversified equity securities	750,000
Fixed income securities	1,000,000
Cash (money market fund)	1,000,000
Gold bullion	500,000
RSA[c]	50,000
Hilda Personal Assets	
IngerMarine company equity[b]	€1,200,000
Hans Personal Assets	
Home (net of mortgage)	€200,000
IngerMarine company equity[b]	2,400,000
Diversified equity securities	200,000
Cash (money market fund)	100,000

Christa Personal Assets	
IngerMarine company equity[b]	€1,200,000
Balanced mutual funds	75,000
Cash (money market fund)	25,000

[a]Peter expects to receive a fixed annual payment of €100,000 (taxable as income) from the IngerMarine pension plan, beginning five years from now.
[b]IngerMarine equity values are pretax market values; the equity has a zero cost basis for purposes of taxation on capital gains. The company stock pays no dividend.
[c]Beginning at age 62, Peter plans to take a fixed annual distribution of approximately €5,000 (tax exempt).

2.3. Jourdan's Findings and Personal Observations

Peter

Personality: Peter is a perfectionist and likes to maintain control. Now that he has attained financial success, he seems intent on preserving his wealth. He has consistently been averse to risk, leverage, and change, both in his company and in his personal life. IngerMarine has followed policies of low debt and slow growth, focusing on earnings stability. Like many of his countrymen, Peter holds a portion of his liquid assets in gold bullion. He believes that gold provides a viable hedge against catastrophic economic surprises and plans to maintain his current holding (€500,000) for the foreseeable future. By his own admission, Peter has been slow to adopt a succession plan—he has always believed that he was the best person to run IngerMarine. Although he now wants to sell IngerMarine and retire, in the past he resisted various purchase offers for the company.

Goals: Peter wants to maintain the standard of living that he and Hilda currently enjoy. In fact, he is actively investigating real estate for a second home, and he desires that the new home "make a statement." Hilda hopes the home will ultimately be featured in a magazine and anticipates that it will cost approximately €7 million.

Peter also wants to get to know his grandson better. Since Jürgen's birth, Peter has been estranged from his daughter, and he wants to restore the relationship. He would like to provide financial support for Jürgen's health- and education-related expenses, and he plans to begin a gifting program for Jürgen next year; the gifts will be €15,000 per year, increasing with inflation.

Peter has a passion for photography and anticipates purchasing a minority interest (€5 million) in *Exteriors,* a noted photography magazine. The purchase would reflect his desire to support the magazine's high-quality work and might also lead to a post-retirement consulting opportunity. Because the investment is unlikely to produce meaningful current income, Peter does not intend to make any additional investment in *Exteriors.* Finally, Peter also has a strong desire to ensure his family's financial security and feels he will have accumulated enough wealth through the sale of IngerMarine to realize this goal. He does not, however, have a formal estate plan for transferring assets to his children and grandchildren.

Hilda

Personality: Hilda has intentionally removed herself from the family business. She has been a major factor, however, in Peter's decision to retire and have a second home closer to their daughter and grandson. In light of the major changes about to take place, Hilda wants to become more knowledgeable and active in managing the family's wealth.

Goals: Hilda has a strong interest in interior design and two years ago founded a small, sole-proprietorship design company. She is eager to apply her talents to designing and building the Ingers' new home and desires complete freedom in determining the home's interior design. Her company currently operates on a breakeven basis, with revenues approximately matching expenses.

Hans

Personality: Hans appears to be somewhat of a gambler. He has always felt financially secure and is much more willing than his father Peter to engage in riskier investment opportunities. He sees his father as overly conservative and believes that IngerMarine would be in a more commanding position if Peter had only leveraged the company to expand production and marketing efforts. He drives a very expensive sports car.

Goals: Hans does not want to stay in the boat business and would prefer a career that allows him more free time. He has wanted to participate with college friends in various real estate projects, but his father has steadfastly refused to underwrite the investments. Consistent with his attitudes about risk, Hans prefers high-return investments, believing that he has enough time in his life to recover from any occasional losses. Although Hans is in no hurry to marry and have children, he believes he will ultimately do so and has been looking for a new, larger home, in the €500,000 to €700,000 price range. Finally, Hans is considering a minority investment (estimated to be €550,000, with no further investment planned) in a nightclub scheduled to open in his city.

Christa

Personality: Christa has been estranged from the family for several years. She has resisted pressure to enter the family business, deciding instead to pursue a career in art. She has also elected to raise her son Jürgen without family support, which has created tension within the family. She is very self-reliant but admits to having limited financial expertise. Her relations with the family have recently improved, and she is looking forward to increased contact with her parents.

Goals: Christa is hoping to take a more proactive role in her financial affairs. She recognizes the need for a coordinated family financial plan, yet she does not wish to rely solely on the family's wealth to provide for her son's future. She would like to move into a larger apartment that would afford her the opportunity to create a painting studio. Rents are expensive, however, and she needs an assured source of income so that she may focus on her art career.

3. INVESTOR CHARACTERISTICS

A distinguishing characteristic of private asset management is the wide range of personal concerns and preferences that influence the decision-making process. Often unaccounted for in traditional models of "rational investor" behavior, such factors as personality, life experiences, and personal circumstances can play an important role in determining the framework for addressing financial decisions. An investment approach that begins with consideration of the Ingers' biases, preferences, and perceptions of risk paves the way for a meaningful discussion of portfolio objectives and may result in a stronger, more enduring client relationship than if such consideration were not given.

3.1. Situational Profiling

Many useful attempts have been made to categorize individual investors by stage of life or by economic circumstance. Such "situational" profiling runs the risk of oversimplifying complex behavior and should be used with a measure of caution—individual investors are unique and likely to exhibit characteristics that cut across arbitrary lines of categorization. Nonetheless, situational profiling can serve as a useful first step in considering an investor's basic philosophy and preferences, facilitating the discussion of investment risk by anticipating areas of potential concern or special importance to the investor. Examples of situational profiling include approaches based on source of wealth, measure of wealth, and stage of life.

3.1.1. Source of Wealth Some classification schemes presume that the manner in which an individual investor has acquired wealth offers insight into that investor's probable attitude toward risk. Successful entrepreneurs, such as Peter Inger, who have created their wealth by personally taking business or market risks, are assumed to exhibit a higher level of risk tolerance than those who have been more passive recipients of wealth. "Self-made" investors may have greater familiarity with risk taking and a higher degree of confidence in their ability to recover from setbacks. Such self-made investors, however, often have a strong sense of personal control over the risks that they assume. Despite their demonstrated willingness to take entrepreneurial risk, they can be very reluctant to cede control to a third party or to accept investment volatility over which they have no influence. Peter's slowness to adopt a succession plan and his largely conservative investment decisions typify such behavior.

In contrast, more passive recipients of wealth may be associated with reduced willingness to assume risk. Such investors may have inherited their wealth; received a large, one-time payment; or simply accumulated savings during a period of secure employment. Because of the relatively passive nature of their wealth accumulation, these investors are assumed to have less experience with risk taking, less understanding of what taking risk means, and less confidence that they can rebuild their wealth should it be lost. Christa Inger may be an example of such an investor.

3.1.2. Measure of Wealth Given the subjective nature of financial well-being, it is difficult to categorize investors based on portfolio size (net worth). A portfolio that one individual considers large and ample to meet future needs may be insufficient in the eyes of another individual. All the same, it is not unreasonable to consider that investors who *perceive* their holdings as small may demonstrate lower tolerance for portfolio volatility than investors who perceive their holdings as large. A portfolio whose returns do not easily support the investor's lifestyle might be considered small. If the investor's ongoing needs are so well covered that succession and estate-planning issues have become important, the portfolio might be considered "large."

3.1.3. Stage of Life In life-stage classifications, investment policy, and particularly risk tolerance, are determined by one's progress on the journey from childhood to youth, adulthood, maturity, retirement, and death. Theoretically, a person's ability to accept risk should begin at a high level and gradually decline through his lifetime, while willingness to assume risk should be driven largely by cash-flow considerations (income versus expenses). The human financial condition is driven by additional factors, however, such as life experiences, living conditions, starting point on the scale of wealth, and personal abilities and ambitions. For the sake of illustration, an individual's investment policy can be viewed as passing through four general phases: foundation, accumulation, maintenance, and distribution.

During the *foundation* phase of life, the individual is establishing the base from which wealth will be created. This base might be a marketable skill, the establishment of a business, or the acquisition of educational degrees and certifications. During the foundation phase, the individual is usually young, with a long time horizon, which normally would be associated with an above-average tolerance for risk. Risk tolerance should certainly be above average in the foundation stage if the individual has inherited wealth. Lacking such wealth, the foundation phase may be the period when an individual's investable assets are at their lowest and financial uncertainty is at its highest. A young entrepreneur may have substantial expenses in establishing a business, resulting in a liquidity need that overrides all other considerations. Marriage and the arrival of children may create a desire for more rapid wealth accumulation that is not yet matched by either ability or willingness to assume risk.

Ironically, at the point in life when individuals should theoretically be ready to assume risk, many are either unwilling or unable to do so. Christa, because of her desired independence, has many of the financial stresses associated with the foundation phase and may still be building the foundation of her ultimate career as an artist. Her son Jürgen is in the earliest days of this phase as he begins his childhood education.

In the *accumulation* phase, earnings accelerate as returns accrue from the marketable skills and abilities acquired during the foundation period and gradually reach their peak. In the early years of the accumulation phase, income rises and investable assets begin to accumulate. Expenses also rise during this period, through the establishment of family, purchase of homes, and care and education of children. In the middle and later years of wealth accumulation, expenses typically begin to decline as children reach adulthood, educational needs are fulfilled, and home purchases are completed. Income generally continues to rise as the individual reaches peak productivity. If an individual's personal spending habits do not change, the gap between income and expenses may widen throughout the accumulation phase, allowing for an increase in savings.

Some individuals may forgo investing their growing wealth and instead increase spending on luxury items or perhaps make gifts to relatives or charities. For investors, however, the accumulation phase is characterized by increased risk tolerance, driven by their increasing wealth and a still long-term time horizon. Hans is in the early years of this phase and is clearly willing to assume high risk to achieve his wealth and lifestyle goals.

During the *maintenance phase*, the individual has moved into the later years of life and usually has retired from daily employment or the pressures of owning a business. This phase focuses on maintaining the desired lifestyle and financial security. Preserving accumulated wealth begins to increase in importance, while the growth of wealth may begin to decline in importance. Risk tolerance will begin to decline; not only is the individual's time horizon shortening but his confidence in the ability to replace capital or recover from losses is often diminished.

In the maintenance phase, investors will typically reduce exposure to higher-volatility asset classes, such as common stocks, and increase exposure to lower-volatility investments, such as intermediate-term bonds. Because the individual now has less time to recover from poor investment results, portfolio stability becomes increasingly important. In this phase, the challenge is to achieve a desired level of portfolio stability and maintain an exposure to risky assets sufficient to preserve the portfolio's purchasing power. Investors who become too conservative too soon after retirement may reach an elderly age with assets that have suffered significant declines in purchasing power. With the imminent sale of IngerMarine, Peter is about to enter the maintenance phase.

In the *distribution phase,* accumulated wealth is transferred to other persons or entities. For many, this phase begins when the individual is still reaping the benefits of the maintenance phase and retirement. For most, the phase involves a conscious decision to begin transferring wealth. Dealing with tax constraints often becomes an important consideration in investment planning, as investors seek to maximize the after-tax value of assets transferred to others. Although asset distribution may take place in the later stages of life, planning for such transfers can begin much earlier.

For individuals with substantial wealth, the distribution phase should be a well-planned program executed during the course of several years. Efficient wealth transfers take advantage of market conditions, tax laws, and various transfer mechanisms. An individual may consider various transfer strategies: He might establish trusts or foundations for heirs or charities, make outright gifts of cash or assets, modify the legal ownership structure of certain assets, and make advance provisions for care in the event of health problems and to pay wealth transfer taxes.

Although the progression from accumulation to distribution may be linear, it is not necessarily so. Individuals in the accumulation phase may become dissatisfied with a career choice and return to the foundation phase. Some may be forced to make such a move as demand for their skills diminishes. A sudden illness or accident may move an individual unexpectedly to the distribution phase.

In each of the above phases, personal circumstances are a driving force in how an individual responds to each cycle of life. The foundation phase will be different for those who enter life with a base of inherited wealth than it will for those who come from families of modest means. The distribution phase can become increasingly complicated for the very wealthy but remain quite basic for those with little wealth. Because of obligations and lifestyle, some investors never leave the accumulation phase. For others, the stress of an adverse life experience, such as living through an economic calamity or war, may override all phases and never allow them to properly match their willingness and ability to assume risk in a suitable investment program.

Situational assessments allow investment advisers to quickly categorize potential clients and explore investment issues likely to be of greatest importance to them. We must note, however, that investors seldom fall easily into just one category, and clearly a dynamic relationship exists among the above considerations. Peter and Hilda, for example, have a multigenerational planning perspective and a portfolio sufficiently large to maintain a long-term investment time horizon—their risk tolerance is not necessarily diminished because of their age. Although Hans may be moving into the accumulation phase, he clearly retains elements associated with the foundation phase (e.g., above-average risk tolerance). Similarly, Christa's circumstances most directly mirror the accumulation phase, although she has the financial ability to develop a long-term investment plan. Source-of-wealth considerations play an obvious role in the Inger family situation and are colored by stage-of-life issues. One recipient of inherited wealth (e.g., Hans) in a later life stage may view his or her portfolio as sufficiently large to assume additional risk, but a second recipient in an earlier stage (e.g., Christa), with less experience and lower confidence, may exhibit less willingness to take risk. The value of situational paradigms, therefore, lies more in their general insights into human behavior and less in their ability to fully interpret individual circumstances. Investment advisers should emphasize the *process* of gathering and assessing relevant situational information rather than the specific category in which an individual investor may fall. The adviser who recognizes familiar patterns is better able to anticipate areas of potential concern and to structure a discussion of portfolio policy in terms relevant to the client.

3.2. Psychological Profiling

A determinant of individual investing that has generally received less focus than other, more objective influences is the psychological process by which an individual establishes his or her investment preferences. Clearly, every individual brings to the investment decision-making process an objective set of financial circumstances, goals, and constraints that will strongly influence the set of investment alternatives from which he chooses. Yet underlying behavioral patterns and personality characteristics often also play an important role in setting individual risk tolerance and return objectives. Psychological profiling, sometimes referred to as personality typing, bridges the differences between *traditional finance* (economic analysis of objective financial circumstances) and what has come to be defined as *behavioral finance.*

3.2.1. Traditional Finance

Much of the standard history of economic and financial theory rests on the philosophy that financial market participants are rational, information-based investors with dispassionate objectives that maximize the expected utility of wealth.

In models of traditional, or standard, investment decision making, investors are assumed to:

- Exhibit risk aversion
- Hold rational expectations
- Practice asset integration

Risk aversion implies that investors with otherwise equivalent investment options will prefer the investment with the lowest volatility. They will choose an investment with a certain outcome over an investment with an uncertain outcome that has the same expected value.

Rational expectations assume that investors are coherent, accurate, and unbiased forecasters. Their forecasts will reflect all relevant information, and they will learn from their past mistakes.

Asset integration refers to the process by which investors choose among risky investments. Investors practice asset integration by comparing the portfolio return/risk distributions that result from combining various investment opportunities with their existing holdings. Assets are evaluated in the context of their impact on the aggregate investment portfolio, not as stand-alone investments.

As a consequence of the traditional assumptions about individual economic behavior, traditional models of the portfolio building process have historically relied on the following tenets:

- Asset pricing is driven by economic considerations such as production costs and prices of substitutes.
- Portfolios are constructed holistically, reflecting covariances between assets and overall objectives and constraints.

3.2.2. Behavioral Finance

A growing body of research points to differences in behavior caused by differences in how individuals approach uncertain situations. In these studies, psychological considerations appear to play an important role in guiding investor behavior, especially during periods of stress. Work done by Daniel Kahneman, Meir Statman, Richard Thaler, Robert Shiller, Amos Tversky, and others has firmly established the field of *behavioral finance,* and several investment firms currently incorporate behavioral finance as a cornerstone of their investment philosophy. These decision-making models attempt to incorporate the principles of behavioral finance, in which individual investors are recognized to:

- Exhibit loss aversion
- Hold biased expectations
- Practice asset segregation

Loss aversion is demonstrated when investors evaluate opportunities in terms of gain or loss rather than in terms of uncertainty with respect to terminal wealth. Faced with the choice between (1) a certain loss and (2) an uncertain outcome that might produce a smaller loss but whose expected value is a larger loss, investors are likely to exhibit loss aversion by choosing the uncertain alternative. Choosing the uncertain outcome actually demonstrates risk-seeking behavior—traditional finance predicts that investors, being risk averse, should choose the certain loss over an alternative whose expected loss is larger.

In their discussion of *prospect theory,* Kahneman and Tversky (1979) found that individuals place different weights on gains and losses. Their studies yielded evidence that most people are more distressed by prospective losses than they are pleased by the prospect of equivalent gains. Further, individuals responded differently to equivalent probabilistic scenarios, depending on whether the outcomes resulted in gains or losses. Kahneman and Tversky found that when subjects were presented with a choice between a sure gain of $500 or a 50/50 chance to either gain $1,000 or receive nothing at all, respondents overwhelmingly chose the "sure gain." Correspondingly, when another group was asked to choose between a sure loss of $500 or a 50/50 chance to lose either $1,000 or nothing at all, a majority gravitated to the uncertain alternative. It appears to be human nature to prefer an uncertain loss to a certain loss but to prefer a certain gain to an uncertain gain.

Biased expectations result from cognitive errors and misplaced confidence in one's ability to assess the future. Examples of cognitive errors include mistaking the skills of the average manager for those of a particular manager, overestimating the significance of low-probability events, and overestimating the representativeness of one asset compared with another asset.

Asset segregation is the evaluation of investment choices individually, rather than in aggregate. Related behavior includes reference dependence, in which economic behavior is shaped by the frame of reference or the context in which choices are presented, and mental accounting (organizing investments into separate psychological accounts depending on purpose or preference).

According to behavioral models of individual decision making, portfolio construction takes place under a more complex set of assumptions than those given previously:

- Asset pricing reflects both economic considerations, such as production costs and prices of substitutes, and subjective individual considerations, such as tastes and fears.
- Portfolios are constructed as "pyramids" of assets, layer by layer, in which each layer reflects certain goals and constraints.

Within this behavioral framework, individuals also have characteristics that either sharpen or blunt the human tendencies for risk avoidance. The process of *personality typing* seeks to identify and categorize these characteristics to facilitate the discussion of risk and risk tolerance. We emphasize, however, that the primary value of any personality typing approach is to provide both the investor and the manager with a framework for thinking about the influence of personality on investment decision making, not to neatly categorize investors into arbitrarily defined personality types.

3.2.3. Personality Typing Generally, all investors have unique, complex personality dimensions shaped by socioeconomic background, personal experience, and current wealth status. These diverse factors make it difficult to precisely categorize investors into types. Yet by combining studies of historical behavior with surveys and scenario analysis, we can broadly classify investors into types. Through personality typing, investment advisers can better understand the behavioral drivers that lead to an individual's goal-setting, asset allocation, and risk-taking decisions, and thus advisers can better manage client expectations and behavior.

Personality typing can assist investment advisers in determining an individual investor's propensity for risk taking and his decision-making style in seeking returns. By assigning values to the factors that successfully identify an individual's propensity to assume risk in the investment process, the adviser can obtain very useful information on the client's risk tolerance.

Generally, two approaches to personality classification exist. Often, the default option within investment firms is an ad hoc evaluation by the investment adviser, who categorizes the investor based on personal interviews and a review of past investment activity. Although experienced managers may claim proficiency in their ability to profile investor personalities, subjective assessments are difficult to standardize, and their terms often mean different things to different people. Even when the assessment is generally correct, the degree of an individual investor's risk tolerance is difficult to gauge.

Reflecting a discomfort with this ad hoc approach, a growing number of investment firms now employ short client questionnaires to gain insight into the investor's propensity to accept risk and the decision-making style used in pursuing investment returns. These questionnaires address investment topics but may also include self-evaluative statements that have no direct investment context. A hypothetical example of such a questionnaire is presented in Exhibit 2-1. The classification scheme blends the Bailard, Biehl, and Kaiser approach[1] with the analytical psychology of Carl Jung.[2] The questionnaire is representative but certainly not definitive or exhaustive; it is intended to reflect the process and content typically employed by investment firms and consultants engaged in more or less formal personality typing of clients.

The critical question that must be answered with respect to client questionnaires is whether the results consistently assign respondents to risk-taking and decision-making styles that explain the respondents' actual behavior. In addition, there must be a meaningful link between the survey results and the ultimate personality typing. To obtain the appropriate linkage between investor survey responses and ultimate investment behavior, a stratified sample can be drawn to replicate the overall demographic characteristics of investors. A stratified random sample involves independent sampling from subgroups that, when combined, represent a population's overall characteristics. Results from the sample questions (each question addresses a specific category of investor risk tolerance and decision-making style) are tabulated and used to identify systematic differences in decision-making style and risk tolerance. Continuing with the example from Exhibit 2-1, raw scores are portrayed across the two dimensions of decision-making style and risk tolerance. Based on these measures, four investment personality types are established. The types are consistent with distinct style/risk trade-offs and may provide predictive insight into an individual's ultimate investment behavior.

[1] See Bailard, Biehl, and Kaiser (1986).

[2] See, for example, Berens (2000).

EXHIBIT 2-1 Decision-Making Style and Risk Tolerance Questionnaire

Decision-Making Style Questions	Does Not Apply	Somewhat Applies	Generally Applies	Always Applies
1. I keep all my mail. I never throw anything out.	0	1	2	3
2. My favorite subject in school was mathematics.	0	1	2	3
3. I would rather sit in front of the television than organize one of my closets.	0	1	2	3
4. I would rather work by myself than in groups.	0	1	2	3
5. I consider myself to be independent.	0	1	2	3
6. When asked out to dinner or a movie, I generally organize the event.	0	1	2	3
7. I am bothered by people who don't work hard.	0	1	2	3
8. I never leave anything unfinished.	0	1	2	3
9. I generally drive very fast.	0	1	2	3
10. I enjoy competitive sports.	0	1	2	3
11. I rarely worry about finances.	0	1	2	3
12. I like seeing scary movies.	0	1	2	3
13. I am always eager to meet new people.	0	1	2	3
14. I sometimes become impatient waiting for an elevator.	0	1	2	3
15. People accuse me of having a "quick temper."	0	1	2	3

Risk Tolerance Questions	Does Not Apply	Somewhat Applies	Generally Applies	Always Applies
16. I become nervous when flying.	0	1	2	3
17. I don't like contact sports like football.	0	1	2	3
18. When arguing with friends, I am usually the one who concedes.	0	1	2	3
19. I never had a strong bond with my parents.	0	1	2	3
20. I wish I could be more expressive with my feelings.	0	1	2	3
21. I never raise my voice.	0	1	2	3
22. I don't like to discuss personal items with friends.	0	1	2	3
23. I like art.	0	1	2	3
24. I would classify my political beliefs as liberal.	0	1	2	3
25. I am not easily excitable.	0	1	2	3
26. I don't swim in the ocean.	0	1	2	3
27. I am afraid of public speaking.	0	1	2	3
28. If offered a bigger house, I would pass because I don't like the hassle of moving.	0	1	2	3
29. I have had many relationships with the opposite sex.	0	1	2	3
30. I often wear cutting-edge new fashions.	0	1	2	3
31. I will always take the initiative when others do not.	0	1	2	3

3.2.3.1. Cautious Investors Cautious investors are generally averse to potential losses. This aversion may be a consequence of their current financial situation or of various life experiences, but most exhibit a strong need for financial security. Cautious investors usually desire low-volatility investments with little potential for loss of principal. Although these individuals generally do not like making their own decisions, they are not easily persuaded by others and often choose not to seek professional advice. Cautious investors dislike losing even small amounts of money and seldom rush into investments. They often miss opportunities because of overanalysis or fear of taking action. Their investment portfolios generally exhibit low turnover and low volatility.

3.2.3.2. Methodical Investors This group relies on "hard facts." Methodical investors may intently follow market analysts or undertake research on trading strategies. Even when their hard work is rewarded, they typically remain on a quest for new and better information. Their reliance on analysis and database histories generally keeps them from developing emotional attachments to investment positions, and their discipline makes them relatively conservative investors.

3.2.3.3. Spontaneous Investors Spontaneous investors are constantly readjusting their portfolio allocations and holdings. With every new development in the marketplace, they fear a negative consequence. Although spontaneous investors generally acknowledge that they are not investment experts, they doubt all investment advice and external management decisions. They are overmanagers; their portfolio turnover ratios are the highest of any personality type. Although some investors in this group are successful, most experience below-average returns. Their investment profits are often offset by the commission and trading charges generated by second-guessing and frequent adjustment of portfolio positions. Spontaneous investors are quick to make decisions on investment trades and generally are more concerned with missing an investment trend than with their portfolio's level of risk.

3.2.3.4. Individualist Investors This group has a self-assured approach to investing. Individualists gain information from a variety of sources and are not averse to devoting the time needed to reconcile conflicting data from their trusted sources. They are also not afraid to exhibit investment independence in taking a course of action. Individualist investors place a great deal of faith in hard work and insight, and have confidence that their long-term investment objectives will be achieved.

An adviser can use questionnaire results to plot an investor's risk/style score, as Exhibit 2-2 illustrates. Clearly, the more extreme investor personality types will plot farther away from the center of the graph.

As mentioned earlier, a predictive link must exist from the questionnaire responses to the resulting personality typing that is derived, and to the subsequent investment behavior that occurs. If the correlation is high between the personality dimensions outlined in the questionnaire and the individual's ultimate portfolio selections, then the exercise has predictive value. If the results are uncorrelated, then the questionnaire must be revised. In the example above, a stratified sample of clients would complete the questionnaire, and the raw scores would be used to identify subgroups. Each subgroup would then be associated with a specific investment style. A "Methodical" subgroup might be expected to maintain a "value" equity portfolio of very stable stocks, along with a substantial commitment to highly rated fixed income securities.

Correlation analysis can be used to assess a questionnaire's usefulness. By assigning ranks to personality types (1 = Methodical, 2 = Cautious, 3 = Individualistic, 4 = Spontaneous)

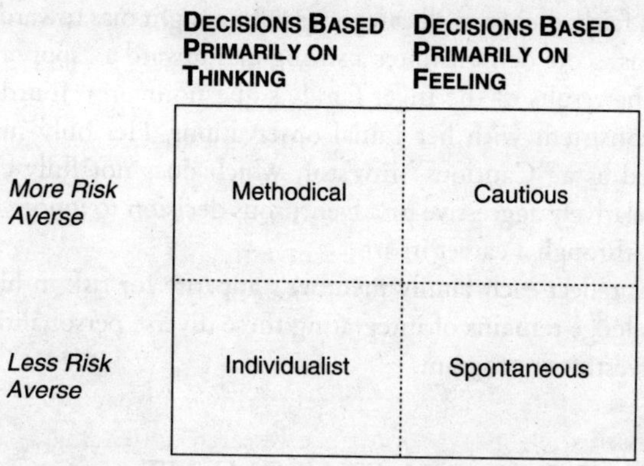

EXHIBIT 2-2 Personality Types

and to the riskiness of respondents' existing portfolios, standard statistical methods can be used to evaluate whether personality types are correlated with investor behavior, especially risk taking. If a significant positive correlation exists, the questionnaire may have predictive value and be of practical use to advisers. Note that because questionnaire design and analysis is a specialized area, advisers would be wise to have their classification scheme validated by a psychometrician; the style/risk personality typing example presented here should be viewed as only suggestive of those actually used in practice.

3.2.3.5. The Inger Family In trying to classify the Inger family using the above approach, Jourdan asks each family member to complete the investor style/risk survey. Based on their responses, Jourdan classifies the family members as shown in Exhibit 2-3.

The symbols represent each family member's composite survey score. The position of the symbol relative to the box represents the strength or polarization of the personality type. For

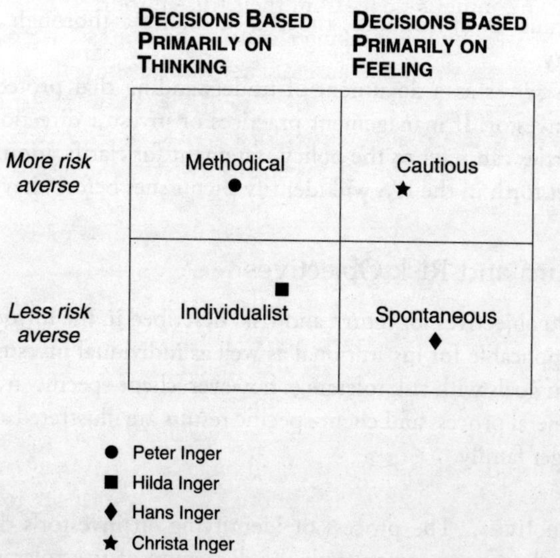

EXHIBIT 2-3 Inger Family Personality Types

example, Hilda scored fairly evenly in all categories with a slight bias toward an "individualist" personality, while Hans' score demonstrates a strong bias toward a "spontaneous" investor.

After reviewing the results of the Inger family's questionnaires, Jourdan notes that their scores are generally consistent with her initial observations. Her only mild surprise is that Christa was positioned as a "Cautious" investor, which does not fully coincide with what some would see as a relatively aggressive or adventurous decision to ignore the family business and support her child through a career in art.

The survey scores reflect each family member's appetite for risk in his or her individual portfolio, but the challenge remains of integrating these diverse personalities and goals into a coordinated family investment program.

4. INVESTMENT POLICY STATEMENT

The IPS is a client-specific summation of the circumstances, objectives, constraints, and policies that govern the relationship between adviser and investor. A well-constructed IPS presents the investor's financial objectives, the degree of risk he or she is willing to take, and any relevant investment constraints that the adviser must consider. It also sets operational guidelines for constructing a portfolio that can be expected to best meet these objectives while remaining in compliance with any constraints. Finally, the IPS establishes a mutually agreed-upon basis for portfolio monitoring and review.

Constructing an IPS is a dynamic process in which an individual and his or her investment adviser must identify and then reconcile investment objectives, portfolio constraints, and risk tolerance. The exercise should produce realistic investment goals and, equally important, a common vocabulary for adviser and investor to discuss risk and return.

The process of writing a thorough policy statement ultimately gives the individual investor greater control over his or her financial destiny. To the extent that drafting the IPS has been an educational process, the investor emerges better able to recognize appropriate investment strategies and no longer needs to blindly trust the investment adviser. Further, an IPS is portable and easily understood by other advisers. If a second opinion is needed, or if a new investment adviser must be introduced, the IPS facilitates a thorough review and ensures investment continuity.

Finally, the IPS serves as a document of understanding that protects both the adviser and the individual investor. If management practices or investor directions are subsequently questioned, both parties can refer to the policy statement for clarification or support. Ideally, the review process set forth in the IPS will identify such issues before they become serious.

4.1. Setting Return and Risk Objectives

Establishing portfolio objectives for return and risk, described in the introductory chapter, is a systematic process applicable for institutional as well as individual investor portfolios. As one reconciles investment goals with risk tolerance, however, client-specific investment parameters emerge. Both the general process and client-specific results are illustrated as Jourdan continues to work with the Inger family.

4.1.1. Return Objective The process of identifying an investor's desired and required returns should take place concurrently with the discussion of risk tolerance. In the end, the IPS must present a return objective that is attainable given the portfolio's risk constraints.

It is important at the outset to distinguish between a return requirement and a return desire. The former refers to a return level necessary to achieve the investor's primary or critical long-term financial objectives; the latter denotes a return level associated with the investor's secondary goals. In the case of Peter and Hilda, it appears that their current needs are being met by Peter's salary of €500,000. If IngerMarine is sold, they may *require* a return that replaces Peter's salary (a critical objective) and *desire* a return that will accommodate their major acquisitions and still leave their children financially secure (important but less critical objectives).

Return requirements are generally driven by annual spending and relatively long-term saving goals. Historically, these goals have often been classified as *income* requirements and *growth* requirements, with the presumption that portfolio income (dividends, interest, and rent) is used for current spending, and portfolio gains (from price appreciation) are reinvested for growth. Income needs, therefore, are met with income-producing securities, primarily bonds, and growth objectives are pursued with stocks and other equity-oriented investments.

Growth and *income* are intuitively appealing descriptors, and the terms remain in use. The terms are flawed, however, in that they blur the distinction between an investor's return requirements and risk tolerance. Portfolios classified as income oriented are typically biased toward a lower-risk, heavily fixed-income asset allocation. Conversely, growth-oriented portfolios are biased toward equities, with little direct consideration of risk tolerance.

Return requirements are often first presented in nominal terms, without adjustment for inflation. When an investor's current spending and long-term savings goals are expressed in terms of purchasing power, however, it becomes clear that even income-oriented portfolios require a considerable element of nominal growth.

As an alternative to growth and income, a *total return* approach to setting return requirements looks first at the individual's investment goals and then identifies the annual after-tax portfolio return necessary to meet those goals. That required return must then be reconciled with the individual's separately determined risk tolerance and investment constraints. With the notable exception of tax considerations, it is typically less important whether the total investment return stems from income or price appreciation.

When an investor's return objectives are inconsistent with his risk tolerance, a resolution must be found. If the investor's return objectives cannot be met without violating the portfolio's parameters for risk tolerance, he may need to modify his low- and intermediate-priority goals. Alternatively, he may have to accept a slightly less comfortable level of risk, assuming that he has the "ability" to take additional risk. An individual, for example, who discovers that his retirement goals are inconsistent with current assets and risk tolerance may have to defer the planned date of retirement, accept a reduced standard of living in retirement, or increase current savings (a reduction in the current standard of living).

If the investment portfolio is expected to generate a return that exceeds the investor's return objectives, there is the luxury of dealing with a surplus. The investor must decide whether to (1) protect that surplus by assuming less risk than she is able and willing to accept or (2) to use the surplus as the basis for assuming greater risk than needed to meet the original return goals, with the expectation of achieving a higher return.

To calculate the required return and to fully understand the cumulative effects of anticipated changes in income, living expenses, and various stage-of-life events, an adviser may wish to incorporate a cash-flow analysis. The cash-flow statement in Exhibit 2-4 simplistically highlights a five-year horizon for Peter and Hilda Inger based on information gleaned by Jourdan from interviews and background examination.

EXHIBIT 2-4 Peter and Hilda Inger Five-Year Cash-Flow Statement (in Euro)

	Current	1	2	3	4	5
Inflows						
Salary: Peter (taxed as income)	500,000					
Trust payment: Hilda[a] (taxed as income)	75,000	77,250	79,568	81,955	84,413	86,946
Pension: Peter[b] (taxed as income)	—	—	—	—	—	100,000
RSA: Peter[b] (tax-free)	—	—	—	5,000	5,000	5,000
Sale of company (taxed as gain)	—	61,200,000	—	—	—	—
Total inflows	575,000	61,277,250	79,568	86,955	89,413	191,946
Outflows						
Income tax (25%)	(143,750)	(19,313)	(19,892)	(20,489)	(21,103)	(46,737)
Gains tax (15%)		(9,180,000)				
Second home	—	(7,000,000)	—	—	—	—
Investment in magazine	—	(5,000,000)	—	—	—	—
Support for Jürgen[a]	—	(15,000)	(15,450)	(15,914)	(16,391)	(16,883)
Transfer tax on support payment (50%)		(7,500)	(7,725)	(7,957)	(8,196)	(8,442)
Living and miscellaneous expenses[a]	(500,000)	(515,000)	(530,450)	(546,364)	(562,754)	(579,637)
Total expenses	(643,750)	(21,736,813)	(573,517)	(590,724)	(608,444)	(651,699)
Net additions/ withdrawals	(68,750)	39,540,437	(493,949)	(503,769)	(519,031)	(459,753)

[a]Assumed to increase with inflation at 3 percent annually.
[b]Fixed annual payments.

Net cash flows for Peter and Hilda conveniently stabilize in Year 2 and decline in Year 5. Consequently, we can estimate their after-tax return objective in Exhibit 2-5 by dividing projected needs in Year 2 (€493,949) by their net investable assets at the end of Year 1 (€42.3 million). We find that $€493,949/€42,300,000 = 1.17\%$. Adding the current annual inflation rate of 3.00 percent to 1.17 percent results in an approximate after-tax nominal return objective of 4.17 percent. (*Note:* Strictly speaking, the inflation rate should be adjusted upward by the portfolio's average tax rate. For ease of presentation, we have simply added 3 percent inflation.)

4.1.2. Risk Objective

An individual's risk objective, or overall risk tolerance, is a function of both ability to take risk and willingness to take risk.

4.1.2.1. Ability to Take Risk Assessing an individual's ability to take risk is suited to quantitative measurement. It is generally the investment adviser who defines the terms of the

EXHIBIT 2-5 Peter and Hilda Inger Investable Assets, Net Worth, and Required Return

Investable Assets	Amount	Percent of Net Worth
Year 1 cash flow	€39,540,437	77%
Stock holdings	750,000	1
Fixed-income holdings	1,000,000	2
Cash equivalents	1,000,000	2
RSA account	50,000	0%
Total	€42, 340, 437	83%
Real Estate		
First home	€ 1,200,000	2%
Second home	7,000,000	14
Total	€ 8, 200, 000	16
Gold	€ 500,000	1
Net Worth	€51, 040, 437	100%
Required Return		
Distributions in Year 2	€ 493,949	= 1.17%
Divided by investable assets	€42, 340, 437	
Plus expected inflation	3%	= 4.17%

analysis and then must explain the results. Although approaches to the analysis will vary, all must address the following questions:

1. **What are the investor's financial needs and goals, both long term and short term?** An investor's ability to take risk is determined by his financial goals relative to resources and the time frame within which these goals must be met. If the investor's financial goals are modest relative to the investment portfolio, clearly she has greater ability, all else equal, to accommodate volatility and negative short-term returns.

   As the investment portfolio grows or as its time horizon lengthens, the ability to recover from intermediate investment shortfalls also increases. All else equal, longer-term objectives allow the investor greater opportunity to consider more-volatile investments, with correspondingly higher expected returns.

   Peter and Hilda Ingers' investment objectives are primarily short to intermediate term in nature:

   - Support for current lifestyle.
   - Construction of second home.
   - Investment in *Exteriors.*
   - Support for Jürgen's education.
   - Expansion of Hilda's design company.

   Longer term, Peter and Hilda wish to preserve the financial security that their family currently enjoys. Preserving purchasing power is apparently more important to them than creating further wealth.

2. **How important are these goals? How serious are the consequences if they are not met?**
Critical goals allow lower margin for error and reduce the portfolio's ability to accommodate volatile investments. Financial security and the ability to maintain current lifestyle are generally among the investor's highest priorities; luxury spending, however defined, is least critical.
Beyond assuring their financial security, the Ingers' investment goals appear *important* but perhaps not *critical.* The second home is important to both Peter and Hilda and will play a major role in defining their future lifestyle. Similarly, Peter's investment in *Exteriors* is not driven by economic need, but it will play an important role in his life after the sale of IngerMarine.
3. **How large an investment shortfall can the investor's portfolio bear before jeopardizing its ability to meet major short- and long-term investment goals?**
The limit of a portfolio's ability to accept risk is reached when the probability of failing to meet a high-priority objective becomes unacceptably high. The investment adviser can provide guidance with probability estimates and identify clearly unrealistic expectations, but the ultimate determination of "acceptable" will also depend on the investor's general willingness to accept risk.

4.1.2.2. Willingness to Take Risk In contrast to ability to take risk, investor willingness involves a more subjective assessment. No absolute measure of willingness exists, nor does any assurance that willingness will remain constant through time. Psychological profiling provides estimates of an individual's willingness to take risk, but final determination remains an imprecise science. It may, in fact, be necessary that investors have personal experience with significant losses as well as gains before a productive discussion of risk tolerance with them is possible.

Peter Inger's case illustrates both nuances in his willingness to take risk and a tension between willingness and ability. Peter's risk taking has clearly centered on the business risk of IngerMarine. He has retained ownership of the company for many years, demonstrating tolerance for business risks that he may feel he controls. In other areas, including company debt policy and expansion plans, Peter has shown less willingness to take risk. His personal debt policy and low-volatility investment portfolio also indicate a conservative approach to finances. When asked what he would consider to be bad portfolio performance, Peter at first answered, "Any loss greater than 5 percent is unacceptable." After being reminded of his ability to take risk, however, he revised his answer to no loss greater than 10 percent.

4.2. Constraints

The IPS should identify all economic and operational constraints on the investment portfolio. Portfolio constraints generally fall into one of five categories:

- Liquidity
- Time horizon
- Taxes
- Legal and regulatory environment
- Unique circumstances

4.2.1. Liquidity Liquidity refers generally to the investment portfolio's ability to efficiently meet an investor's anticipated and unanticipated demands for cash distributions. Two trading characteristics of its holdings determine a portfolio's liquidity:

- *Transaction costs.* Transaction costs may include brokerage fees, bid–ask spread, price impact (resulting, for example, from a large sale in a thinly traded asset), or simply the time and opportunity cost of finding a buyer. As transaction costs increase, assets become less "liquid" and less appropriate as a funding source for cash flows.
- *Price volatility.* An asset that can be bought or sold at fair value with minimal transaction costs is said to trade in a highly liquid market. If the market itself is inherently volatile, however, the asset's contribution to portfolio liquidity (the ability to meet cash-flow needs) is limited. Price volatility compromises portfolio liquidity by lowering the certainty with which cash can be realized.

Significant liquidity requirements constrain the investor's ability to bear risk. Liquidity requirements can arise for any number of reasons but generally fall into one of the following three categories:

1. *Ongoing expenses.* The ongoing costs of daily living create a predictable need for cash and constitute one of the investment portfolio's highest priorities. Because of their high predictability and short time horizon, anticipated expenses must be met using a high degree of liquidity in some portion of the investment portfolio.
2. *Emergency reserves.* As a precaution against unanticipated events such as sudden unemployment or uninsured losses, keeping an emergency reserve is highly advisable. The reserve's size should be client specific and might cover a range from three months to more than one year of the client's anticipated expenses. Individuals working in a cyclical or litigious environment may require a larger reserve than those in more stable settings. Although the timing of emergencies is by definition uncertain, the need for cash when such events do occur is immediate.
3. *Negative liquidity events.* Liquidity events involve discrete future cash flows or major changes in ongoing expenses. Examples might include a significant charitable gift, anticipated home repairs, or a change in cash needs brought on by retirement. As the time horizon to a major liquidity event decreases, the need for portfolio liquidity rises.

For the sake of completeness, positive liquidity events and external support should also be noted in the policy statement. In the case of a multigenerational family plan, positive liquidity events might include anticipated gifts and inheritance; the adviser should note, however, that inheritance planning is a sensitive and potentially divisive topic among family members.

Significant liquidity events facing the Ingers include the sale of IngerMarine and subsequent loss of Peter's salary, the purchase of a second home, and the investment in *Exteriors*. As the potential need for cash distributions increases, so too must the investment portfolio's commitment to assets that can be easily sold at predictable prices. Peter and Hilda have agreed on a normal liquidity reserve equal to two years of Peter's current salary ($2 \times$ €500,000) but will maintain an above-average reserve during their transition into retirement.

4.2.1.1. Illiquid Holdings To ensure that all parties have a complete understanding of portfolio liquidity, the IPS should specifically identify significant holdings of illiquid assets and describe their role in the investment portfolio. Examples might include real estate, limited partnerships, common stock with trading restrictions, and assets burdened by pending litigation.

The home or primary residence, often an individual investor's largest and most illiquid asset, presents difficult diversification and asset allocation issues. Unfortunately, this asset defies easy classification, having investment returns in the form of psychological and lifestyle benefits as well as the economic benefits of shelter and potential price appreciation.

The emotions attached to the primary residence will vary from individual to individual, and investment advisers must be sensitive to their clients' long-term view of the "home." Some investors may view their residence as part of their overall investment portfolio; others may view it as a "homestead" or sanctuary where life is lived, children are raised, and retirements are planned. Whether the primary residence is viewed objectively or with emotional attachment, the fact remains that it generally represents a significant percentage of an individual investor's total net worth. As such, the IPS should address the investment role of the primary residence.

It is not uncommon to exclude the residence from the asset allocation decision, under the premise that the home is a "sunk cost," a "legacy" or "private use" asset that is not actively managed as an investment. A similar approach treats the home as a long-term investment that will be used to meet equally long-term housing needs or estate-planning goals. Somewhat analogous to cash-flow matching or bond defeasance, the home and the investment goals that it offsets are removed from consideration in building the actively managed investment portfolio. Parents may, for example, wish to pass on to their children the wealth necessary to purchase a house and meet this goal through their own home ownership. Other investors may view the residence as a source of funding to meet future health care and housing costs.

Lifestyle changes often dictate selling a large, primary family residence and moving into a more manageable property or living arrangement (e.g., as an individual or couple matures, or as children move away to start their own lives and families). An increasingly popular option for older individuals in western Europe and the United States is to use the value of the primary residence to fund the costs of living in a managed care facility. Generally, these facilities provide members with progressive levels of health care and personal assistance, making it possible to continue living independently.

Alternatively, many individuals plan to retire in their primary residence. The IPS should recognize and discuss financial risks and liquidity issues created by a concentration of net worth in the investor's residence. Although the residence is typically considered to be a long-term, illiquid holding, it can also be the source of significant short-term losses and cash-flow problems. Financial engineers continue to develop products and techniques that allow individuals better access to their home equity (current market value, less any debt associated with the home) and better control over their exposure to fluctuations in property values. Some products, such as "reverse mortgages" and other annuity plans, have initially proven to be costly and illiquid. Newer financial vehicles are on the horizon, however, that may efficiently allow homeowners to "lock in" the current equity value of their home. In one such product (Robert Shiller's "macro securities"), hedges are built on the notion of swaps, in which two parties can exchange the returns of home appreciation for a static interest rate return.[3] Any decline in home value would be paid by the counterparty in exchange for the static rate of return.

Factoring the primary residence into a formal retirement plan is an uncertain proposition. Real estate returns vary with location, and the investor's holding period can be difficult to predict. Nonetheless, if the primary residence is treated as part of the investment portfolio, the

[3]See Shiller (2003).

adviser can use models for forecasting regional real estate inflation rates to approximate future values. Such models can be useful but will not capture the short-term dynamics of real estate markets.

4.2.1.2. The Inger Family It appears that Peter and Hilda can afford to build their second residence. Nonetheless, they should bear in mind that the two homes will constitute 16 percent of their net worth. Peter and Hilda's primary residence has a current market value of approximately €1.2 million and could serve in the future as a source of funds.

4.2.2. Time Horizon The investment time horizon has already been seen to play an important role in setting return objectives and defining liquidity constraints. No universal definition of *long-term* or *short-term* exists, however, and discussion is often left in relative rather than absolute terms. In many planning contexts, time horizons greater than 15 to 20 years can be viewed as relatively long term, and horizons of less than 3 years as relatively short term. Between 3 years and 15 years, there is a transition from intermediate to long term that different investors may perceive differently.

A second issue relating to the investment time horizon is whether the investor faces a single- or multistage horizon. Certain investor circumstances, such as an elderly investor with limited financial resources, are consistent with a single-stage time horizon. Given the unique nature and complexity of most individual investors' circumstances, however, the time horizon constraint most often takes a multistage form.

"Stage-of-life" classifications, as discussed earlier, often assume that the investment time horizon shortens gradually as investors move through the various stages of life. Although this assumption may often be true, it is not always. Once the primary investors' needs and financial security are secure, the process of setting risk and return objectives may take place in the context of multigenerational estate planning. The adviser's clients may be advanced in years yet be planning for their grandchildren; it may be the grandchildren's personal circumstances that determine the investment portfolio's goals and time horizon.

Peter and Hilda are extremely secure, assuming that the sale of IngerMarine is successful. They have expressed a desire to provide financial security for three generations and clearly have a long-term and probably multistage time horizon.

4.2.3. Taxes The issue of taxes is perhaps the most universal and complex investment constraint to be found in private portfolio management. Taxation of income or property is a global reality and poses a significant challenge to wealth accumulation and transfer. Although tax codes are necessarily country specific, the following general categories are widely recognized:

- *Income tax*. Income tax is calculated as a percentage of total income, often with different rates applied to various levels of income. Wages, rent, dividends, and interest earned are commonly treated as taxable income.
- *Gains tax*. Capital gains (profits based on price appreciation) resulting from the sale of property, including financial securities, are often distinguished from income and taxed separately. In many countries, the tax rate for capital gains is lower than the corresponding income tax; a minimum holding period between purchase and sale is sometimes required.
- *Wealth transfer tax*. A wealth transfer tax is assessed as assets are transferred, without sale, from one owner to another. Examples of wealth transfer taxes include "estate" or "inheritance" taxes paid at the investor's death and "gift" taxes paid on transfers made during the investor's lifetime.

- *Property tax*. Property tax most often refers to the taxation of real property (real estate) but may also apply to financial assets. Such taxes are generally assessed annually, as a percentage of reported value. Although straightforward in concept, property taxes present challenges with regard to valuation and compliance.

Taxation varies greatly across regions and continents, but marginal tax rates of 50 percent are not uncommon. With tax burdens of such magnitude, clearly the individual investor must approach investments and financial planning from an after-tax perspective. Exhibit 2-6 illustrates the degree of variation in top marginal tax rates that can exist internationally at a given point in time.

Taxes affect portfolio performance in two ways. When taxes are paid at the end of a given measurement period, portfolio growth is simply reduced by the amount of tax. When the same tax is assessed periodically throughout the measurement period, growth is further reduced: Funds that would otherwise compound at the portfolio growth rate are no longer available for investment. Exhibit 2-7 illustrates the effect of taxes on portfolio performance. In Example A, a periodic tax of 25 percent, similar to an annual income tax, is applied against investment returns over five years. In Example B, a tax of 25 percent is applied against the cumulative investment return at the end of a five-year holding period, similar to a capital gains tax. The difference in ending portfolio values demonstrates the benefit of deferring tax payments.

EXHIBIT 2-6 Top Marginal Tax Rates

Country	Income Tax	Gains Tax	Wealth Transfer Tax
Brazil	27.5%	15.0%	8.0%
Canada (Ontario)	46.4	23.2	0.0
Chile	40.0	17.0	25.0
China (PRC)	45.0	20.0	0.0
Egypt	32.0	0.0	0.0
France	48.1	27.0	60.0
Germany	42.0	50.0	50.0
India	30.0	20.0	0.0
Israel	49.0	25.0	0.0
Italy	43.0	12.5	0.0
Japan	37.0	26.0	70.0
Jordan	25.0	0.0	0.0
Korea	35.0	70.0	50.0
Mexico	30.0	30.0	0.0
New Zealand	39.0	0.0	25.0
Pakistan	35.0	35.0	0.0
Philippines	32.0	32.0	20.0
Russian Federation	35.0	30.0	40.0
South Africa	40.0	10.0	20.0
Taiwan	40.0	0.0	50.0
United Kingdom	40.0	40.0	40.0
United States	35.0	35.0	47.0

Note: Rates shown are subject to periodic change and do not fully reflect the complexity of the tax codes from which they were taken; additional regional taxes may also apply. This exhibit should not be used for tax planning purposes.
Source: "The Global Executive," Ernst & Young, 2005.

EXHIBIT 2-7 Effect of Taxes on Portfolio Performance
Example A: Periodic 25% Tax

Year	Beginning Value	Returns[a]	(Tax 25%)	Ending Value	Cumulative Gain
1	100,000	10,000	(2,500)	107,500	7,500
2	107,500	10,750	(2,688)	115,563	15,563
3	115,563	11,556	(2,889)	124,230	24,230
4	124,230	12,423	(3,106)	133,547	33,547
5	133,547	13,355	(3,339)	143,563	**43,563**

Example B: Cumulative 25% Tax

Year	Beginning Value	Returns[a]	Tax	Ending Value	Cumulative Gain
1	100,000	10,000	n/a	110,000	10,000
2	110,000	11,000	n/a	121,000	21,000
3	121,000	12,100	n/a	133,100	33,100
4	133,100	13,310	n/a	146,410	46,410
5	146,410	14,641	n/a	161,051	61,051
	Less 25% Tax		(15,263)	(15,263)	(15,263)
				145,788	**45,788**

[a]Annual return: 10 percent.

Tax strategies are ultimately unique to the individual investor and the prevailing tax code. Although the details of tax planning often involve complex legal and political considerations, all strategies share some basic principles.

4.2.3.1. Tax Deferral For the long-term investor, periodic tax payments severely diminish the benefit of compounding portfolio returns. Many tax strategies, therefore, seek to defer taxes and maximize the time during which investment returns can be reinvested. (Exhibit 2-7 demonstrated the value of tax deferral in general.) A portfolio strategy focusing on low turnover, for example, extends the average investment holding period and postpones gains taxes.

Loss harvesting, another tax reduction strategy, focuses on realizing capital losses to offset otherwise taxable gains without impairing investment performance. Low turnover and loss harvesting strategies are representative of a general portfolio policy that strives for a low rate of capital gains realization, resulting in deferred tax payments.

4.2.3.2. Tax Avoidance The ideal solution is to avoid taxes when legally possible.[4] A number of countries have introduced special purpose savings accounts, such as Peter Inger's RSA account, that may be exempt or deferred from taxation. Tax-exempt bonds may be available as alternative investment vehicles. Estate-planning and gifting strategies may allow the investor to reduce future estate taxes by taking advantage of specific tax laws.

Tax-advantaged investment alternatives typically come at a price, however, paid in some combination of lower returns, reduced liquidity, and diminished control.

- Tax-exempt securities typically offer lower returns or involve higher expenses (including higher transaction costs) relative to taxable alternatives, and they are attractive only

[4]The term *tax avoidance* is typically used in reference to the legal pursuit of tax efficient investment strategies; the term *tax evasion* typically describes an illegal attempt to circumvent tax liability.

when the following relationship holds (ignoring differential transaction costs): $R_{\text{Tax-free}} > [R_{\text{Taxable}} \times (1 - \text{Tax rate})]$.

- Liquidity is reduced in tax-sheltered savings accounts when a minimum holding period is required or when withdrawals are limited to specific purposes.
- The investor must often relinquish or share the direct ownership of assets placed in tax-advantaged partnerships or trusts.

4.2.3.3. Tax Reduction If taxes cannot be avoided entirely, opportunities may remain to reduce their impact. When income tax rates exceed the capital gains tax rate, as they do in a number of countries (see Exhibit 2-6), a portfolio manager may emphasize securities and investment strategies whose investment returns are recognized as gains rather than income (a portfolio "tilt," for example, toward low-dividend-paying stocks). Because the gains tax is assessed only at the time of sale, such strategies may also benefit from tax deferral as well as the lower tax rate. If only *net* gains are taxed, a policy to actively realize offsetting losses ("loss harvesting") will reduce reported gains. To achieve portfolio tax efficiency, a manager may use a variety of additional strategies, an increasing number of which are made possible through the use of derivatives.[5]

4.2.3.4. Wealth Transfer Taxes Wealth transfer strategies belong perhaps more to the world of tax- and estate-planning attorneys than to the realm of portfolio management. As a practical matter, however, investment advisers should have a working knowledge of estate-planning principles, as it is often the adviser who first recognizes the investor's need for estate planning and makes the necessary recommendation to seek legal counsel.

Multiple variables potentially influence the timing of personal wealth transfers, including the investor's net worth, time horizon, and charitable intentions, as well as the age, maturity, and tax status of the beneficiaries. Generally speaking, strategies for addressing wealth transfers focus on either the timing or the legal structure (partnerships, trusts, etc.) of the transfer. The possible legal structures for a wealth transfer are necessarily country specific. Timing of wealth transfers, however, involves the more universal principles of tax avoidance, tax deferral, and maximized compound returns.

Transfer at Death If the investor pursues no other strategy, a wealth transfer tax may be assessed at death (often referred to as an estate tax or death tax). In this scenario, the transfer tax has been deferred for as long as possible, retaining maximum financial flexibility for the individual and maximizing the final value of the investment portfolio. In a multigeneration estate plan, however, this strategy may not minimize transfer taxes.

Early Transfers Accelerated wealth transfers and philanthropic gifting may be desirable when the investor wishes to maximize the amount of his or her estate, after taxes, that is passed on to individuals or organizations. Early gifting of higher-growth assets into the hands of a younger generation may shelter the subsequent growth of those assets from transfer taxes when the investor ultimately dies. Logically, earlier transfers to younger beneficiaries offer the greatest tax deferral. Because assets transferred to children will quite possibly be taxed again when the children die, it may be advantageous to make gifts directly to grandchildren, effectively skipping a generation of transfer taxes. Note that some tax regimes may differentiate among

[5] See Brunel (2002).

recipients, taxing gifts made to family members, for example, at lower rates than gifts made to other parties.

The benefit of early wealth transfers is largely determined by tax codes and life expectancies. Additional issues to consider before making a permanent transfer include (1) the amount of retained wealth needed to ensure the financial security of the primary investor; (2) possible unintended consequences of transferring large amounts of wealth to younger, potentially less mature beneficiaries; and (3) the probable stability or volatility of the tax code. Early transfers implicitly assume that the current tax structure will remain relatively constant through time. If an early gift is made and the transfer tax is later abolished, refunds are unlikely.

4.2.4. Legal and Regulatory Environment In the context of portfolio management for individual investors, legal and regulatory constraints most frequently involve taxation and the transfer of personal property ownership. Legal and regulatory constraints vary greatly from country to country and change frequently. Achieving investment objectives within the constraints of a given jurisdiction frequently requires consultation with local experts, including tax accountants and estate-planning attorneys. Whatever a portfolio manager's level of legal and regulatory understanding, she must be careful to avoid giving advice that would constitute the practice of law (the role of a licensed attorney). To the extent that the manager is acting in a fiduciary capacity (e.g., employed as trustee of a trust), prudent investor rules may apply, depending on the legal jurisdiction.

4.2.4.1. Personal Trusts The use of trusts to implement investment and estate-planning strategies is well established in English and American law, and a basic familiarity with the vocabulary of trusts is often useful in other jurisdictions as well. A trust is a legal entity established to hold and manage assets in accordance with specific instructions.

The term *personal trust* refers to trusts established by an individual, who is called the *grantor*. The trust is a recognized owner of assets and can be subject to taxation in much the same manner that individuals are taxed. To form a trust, the creator (grantor) drafts a trust document defining the trust's purpose and naming a trustee who will be responsible for oversight and administration of the trust's assets. The trustee may or may not be the same person as the grantor. Many banks have trust departments that provide trustee services, including trust administration, investment management, and custody of assets. Trust companies are nonbank providers of trust services that have been granted trust powers by a government or regulatory body; these companies may or may not be owned by a bank.

The trust is funded when the grantor transfers legal ownership of designated assets to the trust. The assets of the trust can include a wide variety of items that the grantor owns, such as investment securities, residential or commercial real estate, farm or timber land, notes, precious metals, oil and gas leases, and collectibles. The valuation, marketability, and restrictions on sale of such assets can present challenges for the trustee trying to prudently manage the trust's holdings.

Personal trusts are not in and of themselves an investment strategy but rather an important tool for implementing certain aspects of an investment strategy (e.g., gifting). The appeal of personal trusts lies in the flexibility and control with which the grantor can specify how trust assets are to be managed and distributed, both before and after the grantor's demise. The two basic types of personal trusts, revocable and irrevocable, differ largely with respect to the issue of control. In a revocable trust, any term of the trust can be revoked or amended by the grantor at any time, including those terms dealing with beneficiaries, trustees, shares or interests, investment provisions, and distribution provisions. Revocable trusts are often used in place of a will or in combination with a will, because of their tax-planning efficiency and the generally lower legal expenses associated with transferring ownership of personal property at the time of the grantor's death. Because the grantor retains control over the trust's terms and assets, she also remains responsible for any tax liabilities, such as income and gains taxes, generated by the trust's assets; trust assets remain subject to any wealth transfer tax due after the grantor's demise (often referred to as *estate taxes* or *death taxes*). Upon the grantor's death, the trust can typically no longer be amended; in accordance with the terms of the trust, trust assets either continue under management by a trustee or are distributed outright to the trust's beneficiaries.

In an irrevocable trust, the terms of management during the grantor's life and the disposition of assets upon the grantor's death are fixed and cannot be revoked or amended. The creation of an irrevocable trust is generally considered to be an immediate and irreversible transfer of property ownership, and a wealth transfer tax, sometimes called a gift tax, may have to be paid when the trust is funded. U.S. tax treatment of irrevocable trusts is similar to the tax treatment of individuals. The trust, not the grantor, is responsible for tax liabilities generated by trust assets and for filing its own tax return. The grantor retains no control or ownership interest in the trust, and the trust's assets are no longer considered part of the grantor's estate.

The framework for investment decision making within a trust can vary significantly, but ultimate responsibility for investment oversight resides with the trustee (or co-trustees, if the trust document names multiple trustees). In revocable trusts, the trustee is often the grantor, who may or may not wish to personally manage the investment portfolio. As trustee of a revocable trust, the grantor may (1) appoint an investment manager, who then acts as an "agent" for the trustee; (2) amend the trust document to include a co-trustee with investment responsibility; or (3) manage the investment process directly. In the first two scenarios, the grantor may require that the agent or co-trustee obtain prior approval from the grantor before executing individual transactions. Requiring such prior approval can present difficulties from an investment management perspective, as no party has full authority to act. Upon the death of the grantor/trustee, the trust passes authority on to the successor trustee or co-trustees (named in the trust document), who then have responsibility for managing the assets according to the terms of the trust.

4.2.4.2. Family Foundations Civil law countries, as found in continental Europe, are characterized by the existence of family foundations. Similar to an irrevocable trust, the foundation is an independent entity, often governed by family members. Such foundations can be part of a multigeneration estate plan and often serve as a vehicle for introducing younger family members to the process of managing family assets.

There are many examples of trusts and foundations with customized terms of distribution. It is important to keep in mind, however, that trusts, foundations, and similar structures are only instruments with which to implement an underlying investment, estate-planning, or tax-saving strategy. Following are examples of how the Ingers might use such instruments:

- *Gifting to grandchildren.* Jürgen is currently too young to receive large, direct gifts, but an irrevocable trust might be established for his benefit. The trustee would disburse funds from the trust, in accordance with conditions specified in the trust document by the Ingers. The terms for distribution might limit early access, or allow funding only for specific purposes, such as education expenses. As previously mentioned, generation-skipping gifts may reduce wealth-transfer taxes.

- *Gifting to children.* Although the Ingers are eager to provide for the financial security of their children, they may be reluctant to entrust Hans and Christa with the management of large, unconditional transfers of family wealth. Christa does not seem to have the necessary investment skills or experience, and Hans's appetite for risk taking may leave his parents uneasy. As an alternative to direct transfers, the Ingers could create a trust or foundation and structure the terms of distribution such that lifetime support is assured. The trust or foundation might be instructed to distribute funds based on reasonable need, as defined by the Ingers, or as the children reach specific ages and stages of life.
- *Gifting with retained interest.* Various options exist for creating hybrid structures that provide immediate support for one party but ultimately distribute their assets to a second party. The Ingers might consider a trust in which they retain an ownership interest in any income generated by the trust but give up control over the trust's assets. All income would be distributed to Peter and Hilda, making them the income beneficiaries of the trust. When the income beneficiaries die or have no further claim on income, the trust's remaining assets will be distributed to remaindermen, which might be charities, foundations, or other individuals, including the Ingers' children. Such trusts are generally irrevocable and treated as a deferred gift to the remaindermen. Transfer taxes on the gift's present value may have to be paid at the time the trust is created. When the remainder beneficiaries are charities or foundations, such an arrangement may be referred to as a *charitable remainder trust.*

The conflicting needs and interests of income beneficiaries and remaindermen may present the trustee of an irrevocable trust with portfolio management challenges. Trust beneficiaries will often pressure the trustee to favor either current income or long-term growth, depending on their beneficial interest. Income beneficiaries will typically desire that the trustee seek to maximize current income through the selection of higher-income-producing assets. Remainderman beneficiaries will favor investments with long-term growth potential, even if this reduces current income. The trustee has the responsibility to consider the needs of both groups, under guidelines and criteria provided by the trust document. Although many older trust documents commonly define income as "interest, dividends, and rents," the trend is to adopt a total return approach, consistent with modern portfolio management, that allows distributions from realized capital gains as well as traditional "income" sources.

4.2.4.3. Jurisdiction Individual investors may enjoy a limited degree of flexibility in determining the jurisdiction in which their income and assets will be taxed. Some countries have both national and regional tax codes. By choosing to live in a region with low tax rates, the investor may be able to reduce his or her tax liability. Generally speaking, however, all investment returns (including "offshore" investments) are subject to taxation in the investor's country of citizenship or residence. The same is true for trusts, which are taxed in accordance with their "situs" (locality under whose laws the trust operates).

"Offshore" investments and trusts in "tax-friendly" countries typically offer some measure of enhanced privacy, asset protection, and estate-planning advantages, as well as possible opportunities to reduce tax liabilities. If tax reduction is the investor's only concern, however, an alternative domestic tax strategy may prove more efficient. Again, investors are generally required to declare and pay taxes on returns received from offshore investments, regardless of whether return data are disclosed by the host country.

4.2.5. Unique Circumstances Not surprisingly, individual investors often present their investment advisers with a wide range of unique circumstances that act to constrain portfolio choices. Such constraints might include guidelines for social or special-purpose investing, assets legally restricted from sale, directed brokerage arrangements, and privacy concerns. It is also appropriate to list here any assets held outside the investment portfolio and not otherwise discussed in the IPS.

In the Ingers' case, a unique circumstance exists in the self-imposed limitation on acceptable investments. In the 1960s, Peter and several of his friends lost money in equity investment schemes. Since that time, he has had a bias against putting his money in the stock market. Peter does feel quite comfortable with investments in real estate, however, and mentions that he has always been quite successful and comfortable investing in real estate projects. After several "educational" discussions, Peter still insists that he wants only a limited exposure to common stock investments.

4.2.6. Peter and Hilda Inger's Investment Policy Statement Using all of the information she has gathered about Peter and Hilda Inger, Jourdan formulates an IPS for them. Exhibit 2-8 displays the IPS.

EXHIBIT 2-8 Investment Policy Statement Prepared for Peter and Hilda Inger

I. Background: Peter and Hilda Inger own and operate IngerMarine, a producer of luxury pleasure boats sold worldwide. The Ingers are eager to convert their equity stake in IngerMarine to cash and have received bids indicating probable proceeds to Peter and Hilda of €52 million, net of taxes. They consider everyone in their family to be financially secure and wish to preserve that security.

The Ingers' family consists of their son Hans, daughter Christa, and grandson Jürgen. Hans is a senior vice president at IngerMarine, specializing in design. Christa is an artist and a single mother to Jürgen.

II. Return Objectives: Longer term, the Ingers wish to assure not only their own financial security and standard of living but that of their children as well. The investment portfolio must replace Peter's salary, which currently covers the couple's annual expenses and gifting. It should also provide a return sufficient to offset the effect of inflation (assumed to approximate 3 percent annually) on what will ultimately be their children's inheritance.

Required Return*:	1.17%
Expected Inflation:	3.00%
Return Objective:	4.17%

*Expected cash-flow requirement in Year 2 divided by investable assets (€493,949/€42,340,438).

III. Risk Tolerance:

Ability: Following the sale of IngerMarine, the Ingers' investment portfolio will be able to accommodate considerable volatility without endangering its ability to meet their financial objectives. Given Peter and Hilda's cash-flow circumstances, their likely wealth position after the IngerMarine sale, and their postretirement objectives, their ability to take risk appears to be "above average."

Willingness: The Ingers are relatively conservative by nature. Personality typing of the Ingers identifies Peter as "methodical" and Hilda as "individualist." Peter seems to have managed IngerMarine with a bias toward low debt and stable earnings rather than rapid expansion. The Ingers have historically held a large portion of their liquid assets in money market accounts. Furthermore, the Ingers do not want a portfolio value decline of more than 10 percent in nominal terms in any given 12-month period. Their willingness to take risk is generally "below average."

To reconcile the portfolio's considerable ability to accommodate risk and the Ingers' apparent preference for lower risk, their overall risk tolerance is described in this policy statement as "moderate" or "average."

IV. Constraints:

Liquidity

The Ingers have multiple short- to intermediate-term liquidity constraints:

- Construction of a second home (next one to three years): €7 million
- Probable investment in the magazine *Exteriors* (within one year): €5 million
- Emergency reserve: €1 million
- Annual expenses (estimated to rise with inflation): €500,000
- Annual support for grandson (estimated to rise with inflation): €15,000
- Illiquid holdings:
    - IngerMarine currently represents a disproportionately large and illiquid part of the Ingers' net worth.
    - After the sale of IngerMarine and the construction of their second home, the Ingers will have approximately 16 percent of their net worth committed to personal residences.

Time Horizon

Aside from the liquidity events listed above, the Ingers have a long-term, multistage time horizon.

Taxes

The Ingers are subject to their country's tax code and wish to pursue strategies that maximize the wealth passed on to their children.

Legal and Regulatory Environment

Any RSAs created by the Ingers must be managed in compliance with prevalent fiduciary standards for diversification and prudence.

Unique Circumstances

- The critical component of Peter and Hilda's retirement plan is the disposition of IngerMarine stock to a willing buyer. This situation should be continually monitored to ensure that the assumptions made in any plan remain valid.
- The Ingers' second home will represent an illiquid portion of their total net worth. They have discussed the possible risks and have decided to not consider the home as part of their actively managed investment portfolio. The second home will not carry a mortgage.
- Estate-planning considerations: (1) *Gifts to children.* The Ingers will consider various means of tax-efficiently securing their children's financial security, including outright gifts and the creation of special purpose trusts or foundations. (2) *Charitable gifts.* In addition to outright gifts, the Ingers will consider special-purpose trusts or foundations, naming selected charities as remaindermen and family members as income beneficiaries.
- The complex family changes that are about to occur suggest the need for increased flexibility in whatever investment strategy is adopted, to accommodate potentially frequent and abrupt shifts in attitudes and circumstances.
- The Ingers want only limited exposure to common stock investments.
- The Ingers want to maintain a fixed long-term holding of €500,000 in gold bullion.

5. AN INTRODUCTION TO ASSET ALLOCATION

In establishing a strategic asset allocation policy, the adviser's challenge is to find a set of asset-class weights that produce a portfolio consistent with the individual investor's return objective, risk tolerance, and constraints. This task must be completed from a taxable perspective, taking into consideration (1) after-tax returns, (2) the tax consequences of any shift from current portfolio allocations, (3) the impact of future rebalancing, and (4) asset "location." The issue of asset location results from the individual investor's ownership of both taxable and tax-deferred investment accounts—clearly, nontaxable investments should not be "located" in tax-exempt accounts.

In the balance of the chapter, we will illustrate the basic concepts of asset allocation for individual investors with a new case study, followed by a continuation of the Inger case. The chapter concludes with a discussion of probabilistic analysis, as applied to individual investor asset allocation and retirement planning.

5.1. Asset Allocation Concepts

This section illustrates how to arrive at an appropriate strategic asset allocation (or set of approximately equivalent allocations) through a process of elimination. As emphasized in the introductory chapter, investment objectives and constraints must be formulated prior to addressing asset allocation.

Example 2-1 introduces a new case study and provides the background information needed to establish asset allocation guidelines for a new private client, Susan Fairfax. The discussion then returns to Peter and Hilda Inger, formulating a strategic asset allocation appropriate to the Ingers' IPS.

EXAMPLE 2-1 Asset Allocation Concepts (1)

Susan Fairfax is president of Reston Industries, a U.S.-based company whose sales are entirely domestic and whose shares are listed on the New York Stock Exchange (NYSE). The following additional facts reflect her current situation:

- Fairfax is single and 58 years old. She has no immediate family, no debts, and does not own a residence. She is in excellent health and covered by Reston-paid health insurance that continues after her expected retirement at age 65.
- Her base salary of $500,000 a year, inflation protected, is sufficient to support her present lifestyle but can no longer generate any excess for savings.
- She has $2 million of savings from prior years held in the form of short-term instruments.
- Reston rewards key employees through a generous stock-bonus incentive plan, but the company provides no pension plan and pays no dividend.
- Fairfax's incentive plan participation has resulted in her ownership of Reston stock worth $10 million (current market value). The stock was received tax free but is subject to tax at a 35 percent rate (on entire proceeds) if sold. She expects to hold the Reston stock at least until her retirement.
- Her present level of spending and the current annual inflation rate of 4 percent are expected to continue after her retirement.
- Fairfax is taxed at 35 percent on all salary, investment income, and realized capital gains. Her composite tax rate is assumed to continue at this level indefinitely.

Fairfax's orientation is patient, careful, and conservative in all things. She has stated that an annual after-tax real total return of 3 percent would be completely acceptable to her, if it were achieved in a context whereby an investment portfolio created from her accumulated savings was unlikely to decline by more than 10 percent in nominal terms in any given 12-month period.

Working with Fairfax, HH Advisers (HH) created the following draft version of an IPS.

Investment Policy Statement for Susan Fairfax:
Overview

Ms. Fairfax is 58 years old and has seven years until her planned retirement. She has a fairly lavish lifestyle but few financial worries: Her salary pays all current expenses, and she has accumulated $2 million in cash equivalents from savings in previous years (the "Savings Portfolio"). Her health is excellent, and her employer-paid health insurance coverage will continue after retirement. She has sought professional advice to begin planning for her investment future, a future that is complicated by ownership of a $10 million block of company stock. The stock is listed on the NYSE, pays no dividends, and has a zero-cost basis for tax purposes. All salary, investment income (except interest on municipal bonds), and realized capital gains are taxed to Ms. Fairfax at a 35 percent rate. This tax rate and a 4 percent annual inflation rate are expected to continue into the future. Ms. Fairfax would accept a 3 percent real, after-tax return from the investment portfolio to be formed from her Savings Portfolio, if that return could be obtained with only modest downside risk (i.e., less than a 10 percent annual decline). She describes herself as being conservative in all things.

Objectives

- *Return requirement.* Ms. Fairfax's need for portfolio income begins seven years from now, when her salary stops on the day she retires. The interim return focus for her investment portfolio (to be created from the Savings Portfolio) should be on growing the portfolio's value in a way that provides protection against loss of purchasing power. Her 3 percent real, after-tax return preference implies a gross total return requirement of at least 10.8 percent, assuming her investments are fully taxable (as is the case now) and assuming 4 percent inflation and a 35 percent tax rate. For Ms. Fairfax to maintain her current lifestyle, she must generate \$500,000 $\times$ $(1.04)^7$, or \$658,000, in annual, inflation-adjusted income when she retires. If the market value of Reston's stock does not change, and if she has been able to earn a 10.8 percent return on the investment portfolio (or 7 percent nominal after-tax return = \$2,000,000 $\times$ $(1.07)^7$ = \$3,211,500), she should accumulate \$13,211,500 by retirement age. To generate \$658,000, a return on \$13,211,500 of approximately 5.0 percent is needed.
- *Risk Tolerance.* Ms. Fairfax has a below-average *willingness* to take risk, as evidenced by her statement that in any given year, she does not want to experience a decline of more than 10 percent in the value of the investment portfolio. This desire indicates that her portfolio should have below-average risk exposure to minimize its downside volatility. A below-average willingness is also suggested by her generally careful and conservative orientation. Her overall wealth position, however, suggests an above-average *ability* to take risk. Because of her preferences and the nondiversified nature of the total portfolio, an average to below-average risk tolerance objective is appropriate for the portfolio.

  It should be noted that truly meaningful statements about the risk of Ms. Fairfax's total portfolio are tied to assumptions about the volatility of Reston's stock (if it is retained) and about when and at what price the Reston stock will be sold. Because the Reston holding constitutes 83 percent of Ms. Fairfax's total portfolio, it will largely determine the large risk she is likely to experience as long as the holding remains intact.

Constraints

- *Time horizon.* Ms. Fairfax has a multistage time horizon. The first stage is the intermediate-term period, seven years, until her retirement. The second stage is relatively long term, representing Ms. Fairfax's life expectancy of perhaps 30 years or more. During the first stage, Ms. Fairfax should arrange her financial affairs in preparation for the balance of the second stage, a retirement period of indefinite length. Of the two horizons, the second horizon is the dominant one because it is during this period that her assets must fulfill their primary function of funding her expenses, in an annuity sense, in retirement.

- *Liquidity*. With liquidity defined either as income needs or as cash reserves to meet emergency needs, Ms. Fairfax's immediate liquidity requirement is minimal. She has $500,000 of salary available annually, health care costs are not a concern, and she has no planned needs for cash from the portfolio.
- *Taxes*. Ms. Fairfax's taxable income (salary, taxable investment income, and realized capital gains on securities) is taxed at a 35 percent rate. Careful tax planning and coordination of tax policy with investment planning is required. All else equal, investment strategies should seek to maximize after-tax income and defer the realization of taxable gains. Sale of the Reston stock will have sizeable tax consequences because Ms. Fairfax's cost basis is zero; special planning will be needed for this sale. Ms. Fairfax may want to consider some form of charitable giving, either during her lifetime or at death. She has no immediate family, and no other potential gift or bequest recipients are known.
- *Laws and regulations*. Ms. Fairfax should be aware of and abide by all laws and regulations relating to her "insider" status at Reston and her holding of Reston stock. Although no trust instrument is in place, if Ms. Fairfax's future investing is handled by an investment adviser, the responsibilities associated with the Prudent Person Rule will come into play, including the responsibility for investing in a diversified portfolio.
- *Unique circumstances and/or preferences*. Clearly, the value of the Reston stock dominates Ms. Fairfax's portfolio value. A well-defined exit strategy must be developed for the stock as soon as is practical and appropriate. If the stock's value increases, or at least does not decline before the holding is liquidated, Ms. Fairfax's present lifestyle can be sustained after retirement. A significant and prolonged setback for Reston Industries, however, could have disastrous consequences for the portfolio. Such circumstances would require a dramatic downscaling of Ms. Fairfax's lifestyle or generation of alternate sources of income to maintain her current lifestyle. A worst-case scenario might be characterized by a 50 percent drop in the market value of Reston's stock and a subsequent sale of the stock, with proceeds subject to a 35 percent tax. The net proceeds from such a sale would be $\$10,000,000 \times 0.5 \times (1 - 0.35) = \$3,250,000$. When added to the Savings Portfolio, Ms. Fairfax's total portfolio value would be $5,250,000. For this portfolio to generate $658,000 in income, a 12.5 percent return would be required.

Ms. Fairfax will need to seek legal estate-planning assistance, especially if she wishes to establish a gifting program.

Synopsis

The policy governing investments in Ms. Fairfax's Savings Portfolio shall emphasize realizing a 3 percent real, after-tax return from a mix of high-quality assets representing, in aggregate, no more than average, and preferably below average, risk. Ongoing attention shall be given to Ms. Fairfax's tax-planning and legal needs, her progress toward retirement, and the value of her Reston stock. The Reston stock holding is a unique circumstance of decisive significance; corporate developments should be monitored closely, and protection against the effects of a worst-case scenario should be implemented as soon as possible.

In setting asset allocation guidelines for Ms. Fairfax, one of the constraints that HH must address is her concern regarding negative portfolio returns. So-called "safety-first" rules[6] provide a means of reasonably approximating and controlling downside risk; HH uses the following safety-first guideline in establishing an asset allocation policy for Ms. Fairfax.

IF:

- The portfolio has an important or dominant equity component.
- The portfolio does not make significant use of options.
- The investment horizon for the shortfall risk concern is not short term.

THEN:

- The normal distribution may reasonably be used as an approximate model of portfolio returns.

Fama (1976) and Campbell, Lo, and MacKinlay (1997), for example, provide evidence about the normal distribution as applied to U.S. common stocks. A 2.5 percent probability of failing to meet a return threshold may be acceptable for many clients. For a normal distribution of returns, the probability of a return that is more than two standard deviations below the mean or expected return is approximately 2.5 percent. If the client is more (less) risk averse, the adviser can choose a larger (smaller) number for standard deviation. Therefore, if we subtract two standard deviations from a portfolio's expected return and the resulting number is above the client's return threshold, the client may find the resulting portfolio acceptable. If the resulting number is below the client's threshold, the portfolio may be unsatisfactory. Of course, the client may have other or different downside risk objectives than the two-standard-deviation approach we have used to illustrate this concept.

Once return and risk objectives and constraints have been established, an adviser sometimes will include a statement of the client's strategic asset allocation as part of the IPS. HH now turns to the task of establishing an appropriate strategic asset allocation for the investment portfolio to be created from Ms. Fairfax's existing savings (the "Savings Portfolio"). An HH analyst has developed the five potential asset allocations presented in Exhibit 2-9 and Exhibit 2-10. The analyst has commented that there is more uncertainty in the expectational data for real estate investment trusts (REITs) than for small- or large-cap U.S. stocks.

The process of selecting the most satisfactory from among several potential strategic asset allocations, both in the case of Susan Fairfax and for individual investors generally, consists of the following steps:

1. Determine the asset allocations that meet the investor's return requirements. In carrying out this step, the investment adviser should compare expected returns for the different asset allocations on a basis consistent with the IPS. The policy statement might, for example, set return requirements in real, after-tax terms. In that case, the adviser would adjust for the effects of taxes and expected inflation before deciding which allocations meet the investor's return requirement.
2. Eliminate asset allocations that fail to meet quantitative risk objectives or are otherwise inconsistent with the investor's risk tolerance. For example, an investor may have risk

[6]Elton, Gruber, Brown, and Goetzmann (2003) and DeFusco et al. (2004) discuss safety-first rules.

EXHIBIT 2-9 Proposed Asset Allocation Alternatives

Asset Class	Projected Total Return	Expected Standard Deviation	Allocation A	B	C	D	E
Cash equivalents	4.5%	2.5%	10%	20%	25%	5%	10%
Corporate bonds	6.0	11.0	0	25	0	0	0
Municipal bonds	7.2	10.8	40	0	30	0	30
Large-cap U.S. stocks	13.0	17.0	20	15	35	25	5
Small-cap U.S. stocks	15.0	21.0	10	10	0	15	5
International stocks (EAFE)	15.0	21.0	10	10	0	15	10
Real estate investment trusts (REITs)	10.0	15.0	10	10	10	25	35
Venture capital	26.0	64.0	0	10	0	15	5
Total			100%	100%	100%	100%	100%

Summary Data	Allocation A	B	C	D	E
Expected total return	9.9%	11.0%	8.8%	14.4%	10.3%
Expected after-tax total return	7.4%	7.2%	6.5%	9.4%	7.5%
Expected standard deviation	9.4%	12.4%	8.5%	18.1%	10.1%
Sharpe ratio	0.574	0.524	0.506	0.547	0.574

EXHIBIT 2-10 Asset Allocation Alternatives: Nominal and Real Expected Returns

Return Measure	Allocation A	B	C	D	E
Nominal expected return	9.9%	11.0%	8.8%	14.4%	10.3%
Expected real after-tax return	3.4%	3.2%	2.5%	5.4%	3.5%

objectives related to the expected standard deviation of return, worst-case return, or any of several other downside risk concepts (as is true for Fairfax). On a long-term basis, an individual investor will be unable to apply an asset allocation that violates a risk objective.

3. Eliminate asset allocations that fail to satisfy the investor's stated constraints. For example, an investor may have a liquidity requirement that is appropriately met by holding a certain level of cash equivalents, and allocations must satisfy that constraint. Unique circumstances may also make certain allocations unacceptable to the investor.
4. Evaluate the expected risk-adjusted performance and diversification attributes of the asset allocations that remain after Steps 1 through 3 to select the allocation that is expected to be most rewarding for the investor.

Example 2-2 applies these four steps to the Fairfax case.

EXAMPLE 2-2 Asset Allocation Concepts (2)

Step 1: Return Requirement: Fairfax has stated that she is seeking a 3 percent real, after-tax return. Exhibit 2-9 provides nominal, pretax figures, which HH must adjust for both taxes and inflation to determine which portfolios meet Fairfax's return guideline. A simple approach is to subtract the municipal bond return component from the stated return, then subject the resulting figure to a 35 percent tax rate and add back tax-exempt municipal bond income. This calculation produces a nominal, after-tax return, from which the expected 4 percent per year inflation rate is subtracted to arrive at the real, after-tax return. For example, Allocation A has an expected real after-tax return of 3.4 percent, calculated by $[0.099 - (0.072 \times 0.4)] \times (1 - 0.35) + (0.072 \times 0.4) - 0.04 = 0.034 = 3.4\%$.

Alternately, the return can be calculated by multiplying the taxable returns by their allocations, summing these products, adjusting for the tax rate, adding the result to the product of the nontaxable (municipal bond) return and its allocation, and deducting the inflation rate from this sum. For Allocation A, $[(0.045 \times 0.10) + (0.13 \times 0.2) + (0.15 \times 0.1) + (0.15 \times 0.1) + (0.1 \times 0.1)] \times (1 - 0.35) + (0.072 \times 0.4) - (0.04) = 0.035 = 3.5\%$.

Exhibit 2-10 presents the allocations' expected nominal returns—without adjustment for either inflation or taxes—and their expected real after-tax returns calculated by the first of the above approaches. From Exhibit 2-10, the HH analyst notes that Allocations A, B, D, and E meet Fairfax's real, after-tax return objective of 3 percent a year.

Step 2: Risk Tolerance: Fairfax has stated that a worst-case nominal return of −10 percent in any 12-month period would be acceptable. As discussed above, the expected return less two times the portfolio risk (expected standard deviation) is a reasonable baseline measure of shortfall risk. If the resulting number is above the client's threshold return level, the criterion is met. Two of the remaining four allocations—A and E—meet the risk tolerance criterion.

	Allocation				
Parameter	A	B	C	D	E
Expected return	9.9%	11.0%	8.8%	14.4%	10.3%
Exp. standard deviation	9.4%	12.4%	8.5%	18.1%	10.1%
Worst-case return	−8.9%	−13.8%	−8.2%	−21.8%	−9.9%

Step 3: Constraints: Portfolios A and E both meet the stated constraints of Fairfax and neither is eliminated in this step.

Step 4: Risk-Adjusted Performance and Diversification Evaluation: The recommended allocation is A. The allocations that are expected to meet both the minimum real, after-tax objective and the maximum risk tolerance objective are A and E. Both allocations have similar Sharpe ratios and expected real after-tax returns. Both A and E have large exposures to municipal bonds; Allocation E, however, has a large position in REIT stocks, whereas Allocation A's counterpart large equity allocation is to a diversified portfolio of large- and small-cap domestic stocks. Allocation A provides greater diversification through its large and small stock representation, as opposed to the specialized nature of REIT stocks. Furthermore, because of the great uncertainty in the expectational data for small- and large-cap stocks compared with REIT stocks, we can be more confident in selecting Allocation A that Fairfax's return and risk objectives will be met. Therefore, HH specifies Allocation A as Fairfax's strategic asset allocation.

The Susan Fairfax case in Examples 2-1 and 2-2 presented a process for selecting the strategic asset allocation most appropriate to her objectives and constraints. Example 2-3 contrasts the asset allocation problem of Peter and Hilda Inger to that of Fairfax.

EXAMPLE 2-3 Asset Allocation for Peter and Hilda Inger

To recap some important facts presented in the family's IPS, the Ingers have average risk tolerance in general but are relatively averse to common stock investments as a result of Peter's prior negative experience. Peter, however, has always been successful and comfortable investing in real estate projects (even those constituting greater overall risk than corresponding equity investments). Also, the Ingers do not wish to experience a loss greater than 10 percent, in nominal terms, in any given 12-month period. The Ingers' required return was calculated as their estimated disbursements, including taxes, beginning in Year 2, divided by their net worth at the end of Year 1 (€493,949/€42,340,438 = 1.17%). Adding expected annual inflation of 3 percent, the Ingers' stated return objective is 4.17 percent.

The critical component of Peter and Hilda's retirement plan is the disposition of IngerMarine stock to a willing buyer. If the sale is not realized, their investment objectives and the associated strategic asset allocation will both require review. We have discussed certain principles of asset allocation for individual investors and illustrated their application in previous examples. In terms of the IPS and asset allocation, what similarities and contrasts would an investment adviser observe in applying the methods used for Fairfax in Examples 2-1 and 2-2 to the Ingers? Among the key observations are the following:

- *Risk tolerance and return objective.* In consultation with the client, the investment adviser needs to develop an IPS prior to embarking on asset allocation. The client's risk tolerance and return objective are important parts of an IPS, and any asset allocation must be appropriate for these objectives. The Ingers want a chosen asset allocation to satisfy a downside risk constraint of −10 percent, just as in the Fairfax case. Yet, because the Ingers' objective of a 1.17 percent real, after-tax return is less than one half of Fairfax's in magnitude, all else being equal, we would expect a wider variety of asset allocations to satisfy the Ingers' requirements.
- *Asset class selection.* As with Fairfax, the Ingers' investment adviser must establish an appropriate set of asset classes. The asset classes in Exhibit 2-9 have a U.S. bias.

Eurozone equities and fixed-income asset classes for the Ingers would play a similar role to U.S. equities and U.S. fixed income classes for Fairfax, because the Ingers' consumption is in euros. U.S. equities represent a substantial proportion of the market value of world equities, and one might expect them to play a meaningful role in the Ingers' portfolio. The adviser would need to respect Peter's aversion to holding equities, however. On the other hand, because of Peter's prior experience and success with real estate projects, the Ingers might include more than one real estate investment asset type among those permissible for investment. The inclusion of a wide array of asset classes brings diversification benefits, as long as portfolio risk and expected return characteristics remain consistent with the investment policy statement. Emerging Markets, Commodities, and Private Capital Ventures are examples of asset classes that may be strong diversifiers but that also have higher volatility and less liquidity than traditional equity and fixed-income investments. Like Fairfax, the Ingers are taxable investors; if possible in their domestic market, the Ingers should probably also include tax-exempt investments as a permissible asset class.

- *Taxation and asset allocation simulation.* As in the Fairfax case, the Ingers' adviser should make an asset allocation decision in real, after-tax terms. This observation raises the point that expected after-tax returns for the Ingers will be computed using a tax rate different from Fairfax's, and such returns would incorporate their own expectations concerning future inflation rates.

  Taxes present one of the more vexing challenges in asset allocation for private wealth clients, because taxes depend heavily on the regulatory environment and the investor's unique set of financial circumstances. In modeling asset allocation scenarios, the adviser must address the question of whether to use after-tax return assumptions for individual asset classes or to instead use pretax assumptions and apply taxes to the resulting investment outcomes. Running simulations using after-tax return assumptions can be a daunting task—listed below are some of the hurdles in configuring asset allocation scenarios using after-tax estimates.
- *Location.* After-tax risk and return assumptions will be influenced by an investment's "location." After-tax returns on common stocks located in a tax-sheltered retirement account, for example, may differ distinctly from the return on common stocks located in an unsheltered account. Consequently, an adviser may need to break down the traditional asset classes into multiple, location-specific subclasses, each with its own risk and return profile.
- *Tax conventions.* Differing tax treatment of investment returns, depending for example on holding period or method of dissolution, may again create multiple risk and return characteristics for a given asset class. Securities held for a required minimum time period may be taxed at different, often more favorable rates. Assets ultimately gifted to charity or family members may be taxed favorably or not at all.
- *Investment instruments.* Investment securities whose tax characteristics are easily recognizable and predictable today may change dramatically over time, through legislative initiative or tax authority interpretations.

5.2. Monte Carlo Simulation in Personal Retirement Planning

We describe Monte Carlo simulation in detail in the chapter on asset allocation. Here, we focus on its applicability to personal retirement planning. With the introduction of

Monte Carlo simulation methodologies, the technology of retirement planning for individuals now rivals that of corporate pension planning. Monte Carlo analysis is computer and data intensive, so its availability for personal retirement planning at affordable cost is a direct result of the availability of inexpensive computing power. Such methodologies are now readily available to individual investors and their investment managers, from a variety of vendors.[7]

Monte Carlo simulation is the process by which probability "distributions" are arrayed to create path-dependent scenarios to predict end-stage results.[8] The methodology is useful when trying to forecast future results that depend on multiple variables with various degrees of volatility. Its use in projecting retirement wealth is valuable because the prediction of future wealth depends on multiple factors (investment returns, inflation, etc.), each with a unique distribution of probable outcomes. Monte Carlo simulation is generally superior to steady-state, or deterministic, forecasting because it incorporates the consequences of variability across long-term assumptions and the resulting path dependency effect on wealth accumulation. Merely using long-term averages for capital market returns or inflation assumptions oversimplifies their variability and leads to the clearly unrealistic implication of linear wealth accumulation. There is also an inherent assumption when using deterministic forecasting that performance in future periods will more or less replicate historical performance. Monte Carlo estimation, in contrast, allows for the input of probability estimates over multiperiod time frames and generates a probability distribution of final values rather than a single point estimate. This approach allows the investment adviser to view projections of possible best- and worst-case scenarios and leads to better financial planning over long time frames.

The ultimate objective of probabilistic approaches, such as Monte Carlo simulation, for investment planning is to improve the quality of managers' recommendations and investors' decisions. A brief look at the distinction between traditional deterministic analysis and probabilistic analysis reveals how the latter approach seeks to achieve that objective. In both approaches, the individual supplies a similar set of personal information, including age, desired retirement age, current income, savings, and assets in taxable, tax-deferred, and tax-exempt vehicles. In a deterministic analysis, single numbers are specified for interest rates, asset returns, inflation, and similar economic variables. In a Monte Carlo or probabilistic analysis, a probability distribution of possible values is specified for economic variables, reflecting the real-life uncertainty about those variables' future values.

Suppose an individual investor is 25 years away from her desired retirement age. A deterministic retirement analysis produces single-number estimates of outcomes for stated objectives, such as retirement assets and retirement income at the end of 25 years. Using the same inputs, a Monte Carlo analysis produces probability distributions for those objective variables by tabulating the outcomes of a large number (often 10,000) of simulation trials, each trial representing a possible 25-year experience. Each simulation trial incorporates a potential blend of economic factors (interest rates, inflation, etc.), in which the blending reflects the economic variables' probability distributions.

Consequently, whereas deterministic analysis provides a yes/no answer concerning whether the individual will reach a particular goal for retirement income, or perhaps retirement wealth,

---

[7]Wei Hu and Robert L. Young, CFA, of Financial Engines Inc., made important contributions to our presentation of Monte Carlo simulation for retirement planning in this section.

[8]Path dependency exists when the outcome in a given period is influenced or constrained by the outcomes of prior events.

mirroring a single set of economic assumptions, a Monte Carlo analysis provides a probability estimate, as well as other detailed information, that allows the investor to better assess risk (e.g., percentiles for the distribution of retirement income). Thus, Monte Carlo analysis is far more informative about the risk associated with meeting objectives than deterministic analysis. The investor can then respond to such risk information by changing variables under her control. An advisory module may present a range of alternative asset allocations and the associated probabilities for reaching goals and objectives.

A probabilistic approach conveys several advantages to both investors and their investment advisers. First, a probabilistic forecast more accurately portrays the risk–return trade-off than a deterministic approach. Until recently, advisers nearly exclusively used deterministic projections to inform their recommendations and communicate with their clients. Unfortunately, such projections cannot realistically model how markets actually behave. The probability of observing a scenario in which the market return is constant each year is effectively zero. Fundamentally, deterministic models answer the wrong question. The relevant question is not "How much money will I have if I earn 10 percent a year?" but rather "Given a particular investment strategy, what is the likelihood of achieving 10 percent a year?" By focusing on the wrong question, deterministic models can fail to illustrate the consequences of investment risk, producing, in effect, a misleading "return–return" trade-off in investors' minds whereby riskier strategies are always expected to produce superior long-term rewards.

In contrast, a probabilistic forecast vividly portrays the actual risk–return trade-off. For example, an investor considering placing a higher percentage of his portfolio in equities might be told that the average forecast return of the S&P 500 Index is 13 percent. Given an average forecast money market return of 5 percent, it may seem obvious that more equity exposure is desirable. This choice, however, should take into account the risk that the S&P 500 will not achieve its average return every year. Moreover, the median simulation outcome of the S&P 500, using the average return of 13 percent, is likely to be substantially lower because of return volatility. For example, a 20-year forecast of $1,000 invested in the S&P 500, using a riskless average return of 13 percent, yields ending wealth of $11,500. If a simulation is performed assuming normally distributed returns with an annual standard deviation of 20 percent, the median wealth after 20 years is only $8,400. In addition, a simulation-based forecast shows that there is substantial downside risk: The fifth percentile of wealth after 20 years is only approximately $2,000, even before adjusting for inflation.

A second benefit of a probabilistic approach is that a simulation can give information on the possible trade-off between short-term risk and the risk of not meeting a long-term goal. This trade-off arises when an investor must choose between lowering short-term volatility on one hand and lowering the portfolio's long-term growth because of lower expected returns on the other hand.

Third, as already discussed, taxes complicate investment planning considerably by creating a sequential problem in which buy and sell decisions during this period affect next-period decisions through the tax implications of portfolio changes. Through its ability to model a nearly limitless range of scenarios, Monte Carlo analysis can capture the variety of portfolio changes that can potentially result from tax effects.

Finally, an expected value of future returns is more complicated than an expected value of concurrent returns, even in the simplest case of independent and normally distributed returns. For concurrent returns, the expected portfolio return is simply the weighted sum of the individual expected returns, and the variance depends on the individual variances and covariances, leading to the benefits of diversification with lower covariances. In this case, the

$1 invested is simply divided among several investment alternatives. The future return case, however, involves a multiplicative situation; for example, the expected two-period return is the product of one plus the expected values of the one-period returns, leading to the importance of considering expected geometric return. As Michaud (1981) demonstrates, the expected geometric return depends on the horizon of the investment. The stochastic nature of the problem can be summarized by recognizing that the $1 invested now will then be reinvested in the next period and possibly joined by an additional $1 investment. This scenario clearly differs from the simple one-period case of spreading the dollar among several asset classes. Again, Monte Carlo analysis is well suited to model this stochastic process and its resulting alternative outcomes.

Monte Carlo simulation can be a useful tool for investment analysis, but like any investment tool, it can be used either appropriately or inappropriately. What should investors and managers know about a particular Monte Carlo product in order to be confident that it provides reliable information? Unfortunately, not all commercially available Monte Carlo products generate equally reliable results, so users should be aware of product differences that affect the quality of results.

First, any user of Monte Carlo should be wary of a simulation tool that relies only on historical data. History provides a view of only one possible path among the many that might occur in the future. As previously mentioned, it is difficult to estimate the expected return on an equity series using historical data, because the volatility of equity returns is large in relation to the mean. For example, suppose we are willing to assume that the expected return of the S&P 500 is equal to the average historical return. Annual data from 1926 through 1994 would yield an average return of 12.16 percent. Adding just five more years of data, however, would produce an average return of 13.28 percent. For a 20-year horizon, this relatively small adjustment in the input data would lead to a difference of more than 20 percent in ending wealth, given returns every year that were equal to the assumed average.

Second, a manager who wants to evaluate the likely performance of a client's portfolio should choose a Monte Carlo simulation that simulates the performance of specific investments, not just asset classes. Although asset class movements can explain a large proportion of, for example, mutual fund returns, individual funds can differ greatly in terms of their performance, fees, fund-specific risk, and tax efficiency. Failing to recognize these factors can yield a forecast that is far too optimistic. As an example of how much fees can affect performance, consider the case of a hypothetical S&P 500 index fund that charges an annual fee of 60 basis points; expected return is 13 percent with annual standard deviation of 20 percent and normally distributed returns, and capital gains are taxed at 20 percent. A Monte Carlo simulation shows that a $1,000 investment will grow to a median after-tax wealth of $6,200 after 20 years, if that fund pays no short-term distributions. In contrast, an investor with access to an institutional fund that charges only 6 basis points will see her after-tax wealth grow to a median of $6,800 after 20 years.

Third, any Monte Carlo simulation used for advising real-world investors must take into account the tax consequences of their investments. Monte Carlo simulation must and can be flexible enough to account for specific factors such as individual-specific tax rates, the different treatment of tax-deferred versus taxable accounts, and taxes on short-term mutual fund distributions. To understand the importance of short-term income distributions, take the previous example of the institutionally priced index fund. If the same fund were to pay half of its annual return as a short-term distribution taxed at a rate of 35 percent, the $6,800 median wealth after 20 years would shrink to just $5,600.

Certainly, no forecasting tool is perfect, and Monte Carlo simulation has drawbacks that create challenges in relying on it solely as a window to the future. Inputting distributions in determining probability outcomes for the simulations can be biased by historical perspective and the perceptions of the analyst. The process can be quite rigorous and still produce estimates that vary widely from actual results.

CHAPTER 3

MANAGING INSTITUTIONAL INVESTOR PORTFOLIOS

R. Charles Tschampion, CFA

CFA Institute
New York, New York

Laurence B. Siegel

The Ford Foundation
New York, New York

Dean J. Takahashi

Yale University
New Haven, Connecticut

John L.Maginn, CFA

Maginn Associates, Inc.
Omaha, Nebraska

1. OVERVIEW

The two broad classes of investors active in capital markets internationally are individual and institutional investors. **Institutional investors** are corporations or other legal entities that ultimately serve as financial intermediaries between individuals and investment markets. Frequently representing large pools of money, institutional investors have attained great importance—in many cases dominance—in financial markets worldwide. Institutional investors have also made important contributions to the advancement of investment knowledge and techniques, spurred by the challenges of effectively managing large amounts of money.

Today, advances in portfolio theory, performance pressures, and an ever-increasing array of new investment instruments surround the institutional portfolio manager and both test and enhance the manager's skills. As the manager meets these challenges and pressures, he or she should reflect that behind all investment portfolios lie "flesh and blood" individuals whose financial well-being is affected by the manager's actions. News reports remind us that ethical lapses occur, with serious consequences for both clients and errant portfolio managers. The client's interests must come first. As emphasized in this book's introduction, ethical conduct is the fundamental requirement for managing an institutional or any other type of portfolio.

This chapter presents the portfolio management process from the perspective of five different groups of institutional investors: pension funds, foundations, endowments, insurance companies, and banks. These five classes cover a wide spectrum of investment policy considerations and are well suited to illustrating the challenges and complexity of the institutional portfolio manager's tasks.

We have organized this chapter as follows. In Section 2 we present the background and investment setting of pension funds, which fall into two main types: defined benefit and defined contribution. For each of these types of pensions, we discuss the elements of formulating an investment policy statement (IPS)—the governing document for all investment decision making. We follow the same pattern of presentation for foundations and endowments in Section 3, insurance companies in Section 4, and banks in Section 5.

2. PENSION FUNDS

Pension funds contain assets that are set aside to support a promise of retirement income. Generally, that promise is made by some enterprise or organization—such as a business, labor union, municipal or state government, or not-for-profit organization—that sets up the pension plan. This organization is referred to as the **plan sponsor.**

Pension plans divide principally into one of two broad types, based on the nature of the promise that was made. They are either defined-benefit (DB) plans or defined-contribution (DC) plans. A **defined-benefit plan** is a pension plan that specifies the plan sponsor's obligations in terms of the benefit to plan participants. In contrast, a **defined-contribution plan** specifies the sponsor's obligations in terms of contributions to the pension fund rather than benefits to plan participants. There are also some hybrid types of plans (or *schemes*, as they often are called outside of North America), such as cash balance plans, that have characteristics of both DB and DC plans. A **cash balance plan** is a DB plan whose benefits are displayed in individual record-keeping accounts. These accounts show the participant the current value of his or her accrued benefit and facilitate portability to a new plan.

It is useful to understand the distinctions between DB and DC plans in greater detail. A DB plan sponsor promises the organization's employees or members a retirement income benefit based on certain defined criteria. For example, a worker may be promised that for every year employed by the company, he or she will receive a certain fixed money benefit each month. Alternatively, a plan sponsor might promise to pay a certain percentage of some factor related to the employee's pay (e.g., final year, average of final five years, average of top 5 of past 10 years). The sponsor might also promise to adjust benefit payments for those already retired in order to reflect price inflation. Additionally, the plan may have a whole list of other plan provisions dealing with early retirement supplements, surviving spouse benefits, and so forth.

All DB plans share one common characteristic: They are promises made by a plan sponsor that generate a future financial obligation or "pension liability." The nature and behavior of this liability is uncertain and often complex; consequently, setting investment policy for DB plans presents unique challenges.

The sponsor's promise for DB plans is made for the retirement stage—what the employee will be able to withdraw. In contrast, the promise for DC plans is made for the current stage—what the plan sponsor will contribute on behalf of the employee. This contribution promise at its most basic might be a fixed percentage of pay that is put into the plan by the employer. Alternatively, it could be a contribution based on a formula tied to the profitability of the sponsor. It could also be a promise to match a certain portion of a participant's own contributions into the plan.

DC plans encompass arrangements that are (1) pension plans, in which the contribution is promised and not the benefit, and (2) **profit-sharing plans,** in which contributions are based, at least in part, on the plan sponsor's profits. We can also classify as DC plans the miscellaneous individual, private business, and governmental tax-advantaged savings plans in which the benefit is not promised and in which participants typically make contributions to the plans (e.g., individual retirement accounts, or IRAs). The common elements of all these plans are (1) a contribution is made into an account for each individual participant, (2) those funds are invested over time, (3) the plans are tax deferred, and (4) upon withdrawal from the plan or reaching retirement, the participants receive the value of the account in either a lump sum or a series of payments.

The key differences between DC and DB plans are as follows:

- For DC plans, because the benefit is not promised, the plan sponsor recognizes no financial liability, in contrast to DB plans.
- DC plan participants bear the risk of investing (i.e., the potential for poor investment results). In contrast, in DB plans the plan sponsor bears this risk (at least in part) because of the sponsor's obligation to pay specified future pension benefits. DB plan participants bear early termination risk: the risk that the DB plan is terminated by the plan sponsor.
- Because DC plan contributions are made for individual participants' benefit, the paid-in contributions and the investment returns they generate legally belong to the DC plan participant.
- Because the records are kept on an individual-account basis, DC plan participants' retirement assets are more readily **portable**—that is, subject to certain rules, vesting schedules, and possible tax penalties and payments, a participant can move his or her share of plan assets to a new plan.[1]

From an investment standpoint, DC plans fall into two types:

- Sponsor directed, whereby much like a DB plan, the sponsor organization chooses the investments. For example, some profit-sharing plans (retirement plans in which contributions are made solely by the employer) are sponsor directed.
- Participant directed, whereby the sponsor provides a menu of diversified investment options and the participants determine their own personalized investment policy. Most DC plans are participant directed.

[1]Transfer of assets from a DB plan may be feasible; if so, it requires an actuary's calculations. For example, in Canada a terminated employee can request that the dollar value of his vested benefits in a DB plan (as determined by an actuary) be transferred to an individual registered retirement plan. In this context, **vested** means owned by the plan participant.

For a participant-directed DC plan, there is very little the institutional sponsor can do in the context of establishing a single investment policy allocation for the plans. Even for sponsor-directed DC plans, the investment policy is substantially less complex than for DB plans. We thus address DB plans first.

2.1. Defined-Benefit Plans: Background and Investment Setting

Defined-benefit plans have existed for a long time, with the first such corporate arrangement established in the United States by American Express in 1928. Today, the incidence of DB plans varies internationally, although in recent years the overall use of DC plans has been increasing. In the United States, DB plan assets stood at almost $2.5 trillion as of the end of 2000. Judging by both the number of plan participants and the aggregate amount of plan assets, however, in the United States, DC plans predominate. The increasing dominance of DC plans in the United States has been fueled chiefly by the growth of 401(k) plans in the corporate sector. In the United Kingdom, the DB model has traditionally dominated, accounting for approximately four fifths of all private-sector schemes (plans) as of 2001; however, the percentage of companies operating DB plans that are open to new members fell to 38 percent in 2004 from 56 percent in 2002.[2] Elsewhere in Europe, DB plans continue to follow the basic pension model as well, although DC plans are increasingly accepted. Japanese private pensions are overwhelmingly defined benefit, although Japanese companies now offer cash balance and DC plans as well.

Pension assets fund the payment of pension benefits (liabilities). Thus, a pension plan's investment performance should be judged relative to the adequacy of its assets with respect to funding pension liabilities, even if it also judged on an absolute basis. Understanding pension liabilities is important for knowledgeably setting investment policy.

The sponsor's plan actuary is a mathematician who has the task of estimating the pension liabilities. In addition to the specifics of defining benefits, the estimation of liabilities also involves projecting future workforce changes, determining wage and salary growth levels, estimating probabilities of early retirement elections, applying mortality tables, and other factors. The plan actuary's work provides the following key information to the plan sponsor.

First, an actuary will determine the liability's size and how its present value relates to the portfolio's existing asset size. The relationship between the value of a plan's assets and the present value of its liabilities is known as the plan's **funded status.** In a **fully funded plan,** the ratio of plan assets to plan liabilities is 100 percent or greater (a funded status of 100 percent or greater). The **pension surplus** equals pension plan assets at market value minus the present value of pension plan liabilities. In an **underfunded plan,** the ratio of plan assets to plan liabilities is less than 100 percent.

Three basic liability concepts exist for pension plans:

- *Accumulated benefit obligation (ABO).* The ABO is effectively the present value of pension benefits, assuming the plan terminated immediately such that it had to provide retirement income to all beneficiaries for their years of service up to that date (**accumulated service**). The ABO excludes the impact of expected future wage and salary increases.

[2] Sarah Veysey referencing a Mercer Human Resource Consulting study in her article, "Attraction Fading: Fewer U.K. Companies Keep DB Plans for New Members," *Pensions and Investments*, September 20, 2004, p. 40.

- *Projected benefit obligation (PBO).* The PBO stops the accumulated service in the same manner as the ABO but projects future compensation increases if the benefits are defined as being tied to a quantity such as final average pay. The PBO thus includes the impact of expected compensation increases and is a reasonable measure of the pension liability for a going concern that does not anticipate terminating its DB plan. Funding status is usually computed with respect to the PBO.
- *Total future liability.* This is the most comprehensive, but most uncertain, measure of pension plan liability. Total future liability can be defined as the present value of accumulated *and* projected future service benefits, including the effects of projected future compensation increases. This financial concept can be executed internally as a basis for setting investment policy.

An actuary's work will also determine the split of the plan liability between retired and active **lives** (employees). This distinction will indicate two important factors:

- Because retirees are currently receiving benefits, the greater the number of retired lives, the greater the cash flows out of the fund each month, and thus the higher the pension fund's liquidity requirement. The portion of a pension fund's liabilities associated with retired workers is the **retired-lives** part; that associated with active workers is the **active-lives** part.
- Because the same mortality table is being applied to both active and retired plan beneficiaries, a plan with a greater percentage of retirees generally has a shorter average life or duration of future pension liabilities.

We now turn to developing the investment policy statement elements for a DB plan.

2.1.1. Risk Objectives

In setting a risk objective, plan sponsors must consider plan status, sponsor financial status and profitability, sponsor and pension fund common risk exposures, plan features, and workforce characteristics, as shown in Exhibit 3-1. (Risk tolerance, to review, is the willingness and ability to bear risk.)

The points in Exhibit 3-1 deserve comment. In principle, an overfunded pension plan can experience some level of negative returns without jeopardizing the coverage of plan liabilities by plan assets because the plan surplus acts as a cushion. Thus, the sponsor's ability to assume investment risk in the plan increases with funded status, even though it may have no need to do so. An underfunded plan may increase the plan sponsor's willingness to take risk in an attempt to make the plan fully funded; however, all else equal, an underfunded plan has less ability to take risk because a funding shortfall already exists. Consequently, an underfunded plan must deemphasize its willingness to take risk.

If a plan is not fully funded, the plan sponsor has an obligation to make contributions to the plan. The sponsor's financial strength and profitability can affect the sponsor's ability and willingness to make such contributions when needed. When the sponsor is financially weak, it has a reduced ability to fund shortfalls that might occur from unfavorable investment experience.[3] Further, when the sponsor's operating results are highly correlated with pension

[3]Historically, in some countries such as Germany and the United Kingdom, DB pensions are not set up as separate entities and pension liabilities are set up as book reserves on a company's own balance sheet. In such cases, pension benefits are direct liabilities of the company. However, the European Union prescription that International Accounting Standards be adopted by 2005 (or 2007 in some cases) by companies listed within the EU is one of several forces at work reducing national differences.

EXHIBIT 3-1 Factors Affecting Risk Tolerance and Risk Objectives of DB Plans

Category	Variable	Explanation
Plan status	• Plan funded status (surplus or deficit)	Higher pension surplus or higher funded status implies greater risk tolerance.
Sponsor financial status and profitability	• Debt to total assets • Current and expected profitability	Lower debt ratios and higher current and expected profitability imply greater risk tolerance.
Sponsor and pension fund common risk exposures	• Correlation of sponsor operating results with pension asset returns	The lower the correlation, the greater risk tolerance, all else equal.
Plan features	• Provision for early retirement • Provision for lump-sum distributions	Such options tend to reduce the duration of plan liabilities, implying lower risk tolerance, all else equal.
Workforce characteristics	• Age of workforce • Active lives relative to retired lives	The younger the workforce and the greater the proportion of active lives, the greater the duration of plan liabilities and the greater the risk tolerance.

asset returns, the size of pension contributions may increase when the sponsor's operating results are weak.

Certain plan provisions may give participants options to speed up the disbursement of benefits, decreasing risk tolerance, all else equal. Older workforces mean shorter duration liabilities and higher liquidity requirements, implying lower risk tolerance in general. Also, for a plan with an older workforce, if the plan becomes underfunded, the company will have less time to generate and make contributions to the plan.

Example 3-1 illustrates some of these concepts.

EXAMPLE 3-1 Apex Sports Equipment Corporation (1)

George Fletcher, CFA, is chief financial officer of Apex Sports Equipment Corporation (ASEC), a leading producer of winter and water sports gear. ASEC is a small company, and all of its revenues come from the United States. Product demand has been strong in the past few years, although it is highly cyclical. The company has rising earnings and a strong (low debt) balance sheet. ASEC is a relatively young company, and as such its DB pension plan has no retired employees. This essentially active-lives plan has $100 million in assets and an $8 million surplus in relation to the projected benefit obligation. Several facts concerning the plan follow:

- The duration of the plan's liabilities (which are all U.S. based) is 20 years.
- The discount rate applied to these liabilities is 6 percent.

- The average age of ASEC's workforce is 39 years.

Based on the information given, discuss ASEC's risk tolerance.

Solution: ASEC appears to have above average risk tolerance, for the following reasons:

1. The plan has a small surplus (8 percent of plan assets); that is, the plan is overfunded by $8 million.
2. The company's balance sheet is strong (low use of debt).
3. The company is profitable despite operating in a cyclical industry.
4. The average age of its workforce is low.

The primary purpose of DB pension fund assets is to fund the payment of pension liabilities. DB plans share this characteristic with insurance companies and banks, as we shall later see. For all these investors, risk relative to liabilities is important and the asset/liability management (ALM) perspective on risk and on investing more generally is a primary concern. **Asset/liability management** is a subset of a company's overall risk management practice that typically focuses on financial risks created by the interaction of assets and liabilities; for given financial liabilities, asset/liability management involves managing the investment of assets to control relative asset/liability values. For a DB plan, one key ALM concept is the pension surplus, defined as pension assets at market value minus the present value of pension liabilities. DB plans may state a risk objective relative to the level of pension surplus volatility (i.e., standard deviation). Another kind of ALM risk objective relates to shortfall risk with respect to plan liabilities. (**Shortfall risk** is the risk that portfolio value will fall below some minimum acceptable level over some time horizon; it can be stated as a probability.) Shortfall risk may relate to achieving a:

- Funded status of 100 percent (or some other level) with respect to the ABO, PBO, or total future liability.
- Funded status above some level that will avoid reporting a pension liability on the balance sheet under accounting rules.
- Funded status above some regulatory threshold level. Examples (in the United States) include:
    - Levels under the Employee Retirement Income Security Act of 1974 (ERISA) that would trigger additional contribution requirements.
    - Levels under which the Pension Benefit Guaranty Corporation (PBGC) would require additional premium payments.[4]

Other goals that may influence risk objectives include two that address future pension contributions:

- Minimize the year-to-year volatility of future contribution payments.
- Minimize the probability of making future contributions, if the sponsor is currently not making any contributions because the plan is overfunded.

[4]The PBGC is a U.S. government agency that insures the vested DB pension benefits of beneficiaries of terminated DB plans. The premium rates charged by PBGC increase with the insured DB plan's level of unfunded vested benefits.

The risk considerations given on page 71 interact with each other extensively. For example, for a plan to maintain its funded status, the plan sponsor may need to increase contributions. Prioritizing risk factors is an integral part of establishing the sponsor's risk objectives. In addition to risk objectives relative to liabilities and contributions (which are characteristic of DB investment planning), sponsors may state absolute risk objectives, as with any other type of investing.

EXAMPLE 3-2 Apex Sports Equipment Corporation (2)

George Fletcher now turns to setting risk objectives for the ASEC pension plan. Because of excellent recent investment results, ASEC has not needed to make a contribution to the pension fund in the two most recent years. Fletcher considers it very important to maintain a plan surplus in relation to PBO. Because an \$8 million surplus will be an increasingly small buffer as plan liabilities increase, Fletcher decides that maintaining plan funded status, stated as a ratio of plan assets to PBO at 100 percent or greater, is his top priority.

Based on the above information, state an appropriate type of risk objective for ASEC.

Solution: An appropriate risk objective for ASEC relates to shortfall risk with respect to the plan's funded status falling below 100 percent. For example, ASEC may want to minimize the probability that funded status falls below 100 percent, or it may want the probability that funded status falls below 100 percent to be less than or equal to 10 percent. Another relevant type of risk objective would be to minimize the probability that ASEC will need to make future contributions.

In summary, plan funded status, sponsor financial status, plan features, and workforce characteristics influence risk tolerance and the setting of risk objectives. The plan sponsor may formulate a specific risk objective in terms of shortfall risk, risk related to contributions, as well as absolute risk.

2.1.2. Return Objectives A DB pension plan's broad return objective is to achieve returns that adequately fund its pension liabilities on an inflation-adjusted basis. In setting return objectives, the pension sponsor may also specify numerical return objectives. A pension plan must meet its obligations. For a DB pension plan, the *return requirement* (in the sense of the return the plan needs to achieve on average) depends on a number of factors, including the current funded status of the plan and pension contributions in relation to the accrual of pension benefits. If pension assets equal the present value of pension liabilities and if the rate of return earned on the assets equals the discount rate used to calculate the present value of the liabilities, then pension assets should be exactly sufficient to pay for the liabilities as they mature. Therefore, for a fully funded pension plan, the portfolio manager should determine the return requirement beginning with the discount rate used to calculate the present value of plan liabilities.[5] That discount rate may be a long-term government bond yield, for example.

[5] See Scanlon and Lyons (2006) for a detailed discussion of current issues related to return requirements.

The pension fund's stated return desire may be higher than its return requirement, in some cases reflecting concerns about future pension contributions or pension income:

- *Return objectives relating to future pension contributions.* The natural ambitious or "stretch target" of any DB plan sponsor is to make future pension contributions equal zero. A more realistic objective for most is to minimize the amount of future pension contributions, expressed either on an undiscounted or discounted basis.
- *Return objectives related to pension income.* Both U.S. generally accepted accounting principles (GAAP) and international accounting standards (IAS) incorporate accounting rules that address the recognition of pension expense in the corporate plan sponsor's income statement. The rules are symmetrical—that is, a well-funded plan can be in a position of generating negative pension expense (i.e. pension income). In periods of strong financial market performance, a substantial number of corporations will have pension income that is a measurable portion of total net income reported on the corporate plan sponsor's income statement. A sponsor in this position may have an objective of maintaining or increasing pension income.[6]

Just as risk tolerance increases with the duration of plan liabilities, in general, so may the stated return desire—within realistic limits. For example, if the plan has a young and growing workforce, the sponsor may set a more aggressive return objective than it would for a plan that is currently closed to new participants and facing heavy liquidity requirements.

It is worth noting that pension plan sponsors may manage investments for the active-lives portion of pension liabilities according to risk and return objectives that are distinct from those they specify for the retired-lives portion. Retired-lives benefits may be fixed in nominal terms—for example, based on a worker's final wages. For assets associated with such liabilities, return and risk objectives may be more conservative than for assets associated with liabilities for active lives, because active-lives liabilities will grow with inflation.

EXAMPLE 3-3 Apex Sports Equipment Corporation (3)

George Fletcher now addresses setting return objectives for ASEC. Because the plan is fully funded, Fletcher is proposing a return objective of 7.5 percent for the plan. Referring to the information in Examples 3-1 and 3-2, as well as to the above facts, answer the following questions:

1. State ASEC's return requirement.
2. State one purpose Fletcher might have in proposing a desired return of 7.5 percent.
3. Create and justify the return objective element of an investment policy statement for the ASEC pension plan.

Solution to Problem 1: The discount rate applied to finding the present value of plan liabilities is 6 percent. This discount rate is ASEC's return requirement.

[6] In considering whether to adopt this as an objective, however, a plan sponsor must recognize that pension income is based on the *expected* future return on pension assets. Many analysts exclude pension income from measures of core or underlying earnings.

Solution to Problem 2: Besides meeting pension obligations, Fletcher may have one of the following objectives in mind:

- To minimize ASEC's future pension contributions.
- To generate pension income (negative pension expense).

Solution to Problem 3: A statement such as the following is appropriate:

Return objectives. The primary return objective for the ASEC pension plan is to achieve a total return sufficient to fund its liabilities on an inflation-adjusted basis. The ASEC pension plan has a long-term growth orientation, with a total return objective of 7.5 percent per year.

Justification. In formulating a return objective for this essentially active-lives fund, considerations include:

- The return requirement is 6 percent. The objectives are consistent with achieving at least this level of return and with meeting pension liabilities.
- Because the plan has a long duration, little need for immediate liquidity, and a fully funded status, and because the sponsor's financial strength and profitability are strong, ASEC has above-average risk tolerance and can adopt an aggressive return objective. Thus a long-term growth orientation with a focus on capital appreciation, as well as a specific objective of 7.5 percent, appears to be appropriate.

In the next sections, we address the five broad categories of constraints.

2.1.3. Liquidity Requirement

A DB pension fund receives pension contributions from its sponsor and disburses benefits to retirees. The net cash outflow (benefit payments minus pension contributions) constitutes the pension's plan liquidity requirement. For example, a pension fund paying $100 million per month in benefits on an asset base of $15 billion, and receiving no sponsor pension contribution, would have an annual liquidity requirement of 8 percent of plan assets. During the year, the asset base would need to grow to $16.2 billion in order to meet the payout requirement without eroding the capital base. The following issues affect DB plans' liquidity requirement:

- The greater the number of retired lives, the greater the liquidity requirement, all else equal. As one example, a company operating in a declining industry may have an growing retired-lives portion placing increasing liquidity requirements on the plan.
- The smaller the corporate contributions in relation to benefit disbursements, the greater the liquidity requirement. The need to make contributions depends on the funded status of the plan. For plan sponsors that need to make regular contributions, young, growing workforces generally mean smaller liquidity requirements than older, declining workforces.
- Plan features such as the option to take early retirement and/or the option of retirees to take lump-sum payments create potentially higher liquidity needs.

EXAMPLE 3-4 Apex Sports Equipment Corporation (4)

Recall the following information from Example 3-1: ASEC is a relatively young company, and as such its DB pension plan has no retired employees. This essentially active-lives plan has $100 million in assets and an $8 million surplus in relation to the PBO. Several facts concerning the plan follow:

- The duration of the plan's liabilities (which are all U.S.-based) is 20 years.
- The discount rate applied to these liabilities is 6 percent.
- The average age of the workforce is 39 years.

Because of excellent recent investment results, ASEC has not needed to make a contribution to the pension fund in the most recent two years.

Based on the above information, characterize ASEC's current liquidity requirement.

Solution: ASEC currently has no retired employees and is not making pension contributions into the fund, but it has no disbursements to cover. Thus, ASEC has had no liquidity requirements recently. Given that the average age of ASEC's workforce is 39 years, liquidity needs appear to be small for the near term as well.

When a pension fund has substantial liquidity requirements, it may hold a buffer of cash or money market instruments to meet such needs. A pension fund with a cash balance can gain equity market exposure by holding stock index futures contracts, or bond market exposure by holding bond futures, if it desires.

2.1.4. Time Horizon The investment time horizon for a DB plan depends on the following factors:

- Whether the plan is a going concern or plan termination is expected.
- The age of the workforce and the proportion of active lives. When the workforce is young and active lives predominate, and when the DB plan is open to new entrants, the plan's time horizon is longer.

The overall time horizon for many going-concern DB plans is long. However, the horizon can also be multistage: for the active-lives portion, the time horizon is the average time to the normal retirement age, while for the retired-lives portion, it is a function of the average life expectancy of retired plan beneficiaries.

EXAMPLE 3-5 Apex Sports Equipment Corporation (5)

Based on the information from Example 3-4, characterize the time horizon for ASEC's pension plan.

Solution: On average, the plan participants are 39 years old and the duration of plan liabilities is 20 years. The "time to maturity" of the corporate workforce is a key strategic element for any DB pension plan. Having a younger workforce often means that the plan has a longer investment horizon and more time available for wealth compounding to occur. These factors justify ASEC's adopting a relatively long time horizon for as long as ASEC remains a viable going concern.

2.1.5. Tax Concerns Investment income and realized capital gains within private DB pension plans are usually exempt from taxation. Thus, investment planning decisions at the level of the plan itself can generally be made without regard to taxes. Although corporate contribution planning involves tax issues, as do plan terminations and the form of distributions to beneficiaries, DB pension fund investment planning usually does not. However, Example 3-6 illustrates a case in which tax considerations do arise.

EXAMPLE 3-6 Taxation and Return Objectives

In 1997, the U.K. government abolished a rule that had allowed pension funds to receive dividends gross of tax (tax free). Discuss the probable impact of the change on the prior return objectives of pension funds, given that pension schemes often invest in dividend-paying ordinary shares.

Solution: Total return on ordinary shares is the sum of capital appreciation and dividend yield. After the rule change, the after-tax total return became less than pretax total return for dividend-paying shares, so a given prior (pretax) return target became less effective at the margin in funding liabilities.

2.1.6. Legal and Regulatory Factors All retirement plans are governed by laws and regulations that affect investment policy. Virtually every country that allows or provides for separate portfolio funding of pension schemes imposes some sort of regulatory framework on the fund or plan structure. In the United States, corporate plans and multiemployer plans are governed by ERISA, although state and local government plans as well as union plans are not. State and local government plans are subject to state law and regulations that can differ from each other and also from ERISA. In the United States, union plans are subject to regulation under the Taft–Hartley Labor Act. An important attribute of ERISA is that it preempts state and local law, so that those plans that are subject to it must deal with only a single body of regulation. Both ERISA and state law and regulations generally specify standards of care that pension plan sponsors must meet in making investment decisions.

A pension plan trustee is an example of a **fiduciary**, a person standing in a special relation of trust and responsibility with respect to other parties (from the Latin word *fiducia*, meaning "trust"). A trustee is legally responsible for ensuring that assets are managed solely in the interests of beneficiaries (for a pension, the pension plan participants). Depending on legal jurisdiction, fiduciaries are subject to various legal standards of care as they execute their responsibilities. Beneficiaries may attempt to recover their losses from fiduciaries that fail to meet appropriate standards of care.

In Canada, pension funds are regulated at the provincial level, but the Ontario Pension Commission has arguably set the standard with an ERISA-like body of regulation. In the United Kingdom, recent years have seen the work of blue-ribbon panels such as the Free Commission and the Myner Commission become standards for guiding investment policy. European countries such as the Netherlands; Asia-Pacific nations including Australia, Japan, and Singapore; and Latin American countries such as Brazil, Chile, and Mexico are examples of countries having regulatory frameworks for employee pension and savings plans.

Historically, in some major developed markets, the pension plan structure does not involve having to deal with investment policy issues. For example, France has a state-run scheme requiring plan sponsor organizations to contribute. But apart from the countries where funded plans are not used, it is important for the institutional practitioner to understand and apply the law and regulations of the entity having jurisdiction when developing investment policy.

2.1.7. Unique Circumstances Although we cannot make general statements about unique circumstances, one constraint that smaller pension plans sometimes face relates to the human and financial resources available to the plan sponsor. In particular, investment in alternative investments (e.g., private equity, hedge funds, and natural resources) often requires complex due diligence. (**Due diligence** refers to investigation and analysis in support of an investment action or recommendation; failure to exercise due diligence may sometimes result in liability according to various laws.)

Another unique circumstance for a plan might be a self-imposed constraint against investing in certain industries viewed as having negative ethical or welfare connotations, or in shares of companies operating in countries with regimes against which some ethical objection has been raised. Such ethical investment considerations have played a role in the investment policy of many public employee pension plans and some private company and union pension plans. Australian and several European regulators require that pension funds disclose whether they include ethical criteria in their decision-making processes. In the United Kingdom, such legislation (imposed in 1999) contributed significantly to the growth of socially responsible investing in pension plans.

To conclude, Example 3-7 shows how Apex Sports Equipment might formulate an IPS that incorporates the analysis in Examples 3-1 through 3-5.

EXAMPLE 3-7 Apex Sports Equipment Corporation Defined-Benefit Plan Investment Policy Statement

Apex Sports Equipment Corporation (the "Company") operates in the recreation industry. The Company sponsors the Apex Sports Equipment Corporation Pension Plan (the "Plan"), the purpose of which is to accumulate assets in order to fund the obligations of the Plan. The Plan fiduciary is the Apex Sports Equipment Corporation Plan Investment Committee (the "Committee"). The Plan is an employer contributory defined-benefit pension plan covering substantially all full-time Company employees.

Purpose: The purpose of the investment policy statement (the "Policy") is to provide clear guidelines for the management of plan assets. This Policy establishes policies and guidelines for the investment practices of the Plan. The Committee has reviewed and, on

April 21, 2002, adopted this Policy. The Policy outlines objectives, goals, restrictions, and responsibilities in order that:

- The Committee, staff, investment managers, and custodians clearly understand the objectives and policies of the Plan.
- The investment managers are given guidance and limitations concerning the investment of the Plan's assets.
- The Committee has a meaningful basis for evaluating the investment performance of individual investment managers, as well as evaluating overall success in meeting its investment objectives.

The Plan shall at all times be managed in accordance with all state and federal laws, rules, and regulations including, but not limited to, the Employee Retirement Income Security Act of 1974 (ERISA).

Identification of Duties and Investment Responsibilities: The Committee relies on staff and outside service providers (including investment managers and bank custodians) in executing its functions. Each entity's role as fiduciary must be clearly identified to ensure clear lines of communication, operational efficiency, and accountability in all aspects of operation.

Investment Committee. The Committee is responsible for managing the investment process. The Committee, with the assistance of staff, monitors the performance of investments; ensures funds are invested in accordance with Company policies; studies, recommends, and implements policy and operational procedures that will enhance the investment program of the Plan; and ensures that proper internal controls are developed to safeguard the assets of the Plan.

Investment managers. Investment managers will construct and manage investment portfolios consistent with the investment philosophy and disciplines for which they were retained. They will buy and sell securities and modify the asset mix within their stated guidelines. The Committee believes that investment decisions are best made when not restricted by excessive limitations. Therefore, full discretion is delegated to investment managers to carry out investment policy within their stated guidelines. However, investment managers shall respect and observe the specific limitations, guidelines, attitudes, and philosophies stated herein and within any implementation guidelines, or as expressed in any written amendments. Investment managers are expected to communicate, in writing, any developments that may affect the Plan's portfolio to the Committee within five business days of occurrence. Examples of such events include, but are not limited to, the following:

- A significant change in investment philosophy.
- A change in the ownership structure of the firm.
- A loss of one or more key management personnel.
- Any occurrence that might potentially affect the management, professionalism, integrity, or financial position of the firm.

Bank custodian. The bank trustee/custodian(s) will hold all cash and securities (except for those held in commingled funds and mutual funds) and will regularly summarize these holdings for the Committee's review. In addition, a bank or trust depository arrangement will be used to accept and hold cash prior to allocating it to the investment manager and to invest such cash in liquid, interest-bearing instruments.

Investment Goals and Objectives: The Plan's overall investment objective is to fund benefits to Plan beneficiaries through a carefully planned and well-executed investment program.

Return objectives:

The overall return objective is to achieve a return sufficient to achieve funding adequacy on an inflation-adjusted basis. Funding adequacy is achieved when the market value of assets is at least equal to the Plan's projected benefit obligation as defined in Statement of Financial Accounting Standards No. 87, as calculated by the Plan's actuary. The Plan has a total return objective of 7.5 percent per year. In addition, the Plan has the following broad objectives:

- The assets of the Plan shall be invested to maximize returns for the level of risk taken.
- The Plan shall strive to achieve a return that exceeds the return of benchmarks composed of various established indexes for each category of investment, in which the weights of the indexes represent the expected allocation of the Plan's investments over a three- to five-year time horizon.

Risk objectives:

- The assets of the Plan shall be diversified to minimize the risk of large losses within any one asset class, investment type, industry or sector distributions, maturity date, or geographic location, which could seriously impair the Plan's ability to achieve its funding and long-term investment objectives.
- The Plan's assets shall be invested such that the risk that the market value of assets falls below 105 percent of the Plan's projected benefit obligation in a given year is 10 percent or less.

Constraints:

- The assets of the Plan shall maintain adequate liquidity to meet required benefit payments to the Plan's beneficiaries. The Plan currently and for the foreseeable future has minimal liquidity requirements.
- The Plan's assets shall be invested consistent with the Plan's long-term investment horizon.
- As a tax-exempt investor, the Plan shall invest its assets with a focus on total return without distinction made between returns generated from income and returns generated from capital gains.

Review Schedule: The Committee will review investment performance on a quarterly basis. This investment policy statement will be reviewed annually or more frequently as required by significant changes in laws or regulations, in the funded status of the Plan, or in capital market conditions.

Asset Allocation: The Committee believes that the level of risk assumed by the Plan is largely determined by the Plan's strategic asset allocation. The Committee has summarized the factors that should be considered in determining its long-term asset allocation as follows:

- The Plan's time horizon.
- The funded status of the Plan.
- The Company's financial strength.

In establishing the long-run asset allocation for the Plan, the Committee will consider conservative long-run capital market expectations for expected return, volatility, and asset class correlations. The Plan's strategic asset allocation will be set out by the Committee in a separate strategic asset allocation document.

Rebalancing: The Committee is responsible for the Plan's asset allocation decisions and will meet to review target allocations as required based on market conditions, but at least every three years. Until such time as the Committee changes target allocations, the portfolio must periodically be rebalanced as a result of market value fluctuations. The Committee has delegated to staff the duty of implementing such rebalancing. After the Plan has reached its target equity allocation, the equity allocation shall be rebalanced to its equity target on a quarterly basis using index-based vehicles. Specific investment manager allocations will be rebalanced back to target on an annual basis. Staff will report rebalancing activity to the Committee.

2.1.8. Corporate Risk Management and the Investment of DB Pension Assets

A DB pension plan can potentially so significantly affect the sponsoring corporation's financial performance that the study of DB pension asset investment in relation to pension and corporate objectives has developed into a wide-ranging literature. Practically, we can make several observations. From a risk management perspective, the two important concerns are:[7]

1. Managing pension investments in relation to operating investments.
2. Coordinating pension investments with pension liabilities.

To explain the first concern, in Exhibit 3-1 we identified the correlation between sponsor operating results and pension asset returns as one variable to monitor in assessing risk tolerance. We explained that the lower the correlation, the greater the risk tolerance, all else equal. Assuming that business and pension portfolio risks are positively correlated, a high degree of operating risk would tend to limit the amount of risk that a pension portfolio could assume, and vice versa. Although we are concerned with the IPS, our view will be more rounded if we look at the different perspective of building the pension portfolio. One question to address in that regard is whether the pension portfolio diversifies risk relative to the sponsor's operating activities. All else equal, a portfolio that diversifies sponsor operational risk increases the chance that, if the sponsor needs to increase contributions to support the payment of plan pension benefits, the sponsor will be in a position to do so. Consider a portfolio with actively managed equity holdings that overweight the telecommunications sector. Such

[7]See Haugen (1990). Coordinating pension liabilities with corporate liabilities has also been suggested as a risk management focus.

a portfolio would be less risky for a plan sponsor operating in the consumer staples sector, which has a relatively low correlation to telecom, than for one operating in a telecom-related technology sector (e.g., a supplier of digital subscriber line [DSL] equipment to telephone companies).

With respect to the second concern, coordination, the plan manager's objective is to increase the probability that pension plan assets will be sufficient to fund pension plan benefits with the minimal requirement for additional contributions by the corporate plan sponsor. For a fully funded pension plan, the goal is to maintain the plan's funded status (pension surplus) relative to plan liabilities. Although both stated concerns are consistent from a comprehensive risk management perspective, asset/liability management approaches to portfolio construction emphasize managing investments relative to liabilities. From an ALM perspective, the characterization of risk in the IPS needs to be stated in *relative* terms. The emphasis shifts from the expected volatility of pension *assets* to the expected volatility of pension *surplus* and to probabilities concerning expected levels of funded status over appropriate time frames. In practice, we can use tools such as simulation to explore whether specific portfolios can be expected to satisfy such relative risk objectives. The volatility of surplus is lower if changes in the value of plan assets are positively correlated with changes in the value of plan liabilities. Because pension plan liabilities are interest rate sensitive, pension plan sponsors emphasizing an ALM approach tend to make more intensive use of interest-rate-sensitive securities (in particular, bonds) than would otherwise be the case.

2.2. Defined-Contribution Plans: Background and Investment Setting

Two broad types of defined-contribution plans are those in which the investment of the assets is directed by the plan sponsor and those in which the investment is participant directed. Because setting investment policy for sponsor-directed plans is a simpler subset of the process for DB plans, here we will focus on participant-directed plans.

The principal investment issues for DC plans are as follows:

- *Diversification.* The sponsor must offer a menu of investment options that allows participants to construct suitable portfolios. For example, in the United States, Section 404(c) of ERISA establishes a safe harbor for DC plan sponsors against claims of insufficient or imprudent investment choice if the plan has (1) at least three investment choices diversified versus each other and (2) provision for the participant to move freely among the options. Sponsors of participant-directed DC plans frequently make available to participants sophisticated retirement planning tools such as Monte Carlo simulation to aid in decision making.
- *Company stock.* Holdings of sponsor-company stock should be limited to allow participants' wealth to be adequately diversified.

Even for participant-directed DC plans, the plan sponsor must have a written IPS. The IPS documents the manner in which the plan sponsor is meeting the fiduciary responsibility to have an adequate process for selecting the investment options offered to plan participants as well as for periodically evaluating those options; furthermore, the establishment of an IPS may be legally mandated. DC plans, however, call for quite different IPSs than do DB plans. A DC investment policy statement establishes procedures to ensure that a myriad of individual investor objectives and constraints can be properly addressed. This can best be seen in a sample statement, an example of which follows.

2.2.1. The Objectives and Constraints Framework In the DC setting, the plan sponsor does not establish objectives and constraints; rather, the plan participants set their own risk and return objectives and constraints. The plan sponsor provides educational resources, but the participant is responsible for choosing a risk and return objective reflecting his or her own personal financial circumstances, goals, and attitudes toward risk.

EXAMPLE 3-8 Participant Wanting to Make Up for Lost Time

A middle-aged man joined the participant-directed DC plan of BMSR five years ago. He had no previous retirement plan or asset base aside from home equity, and he states that he needs to take more risk than most people so that he can catch up. In fact, the participant's asset base, current income, and desired spending rate for retirement at age 65 all indicate that the participant needs a very high annual rate of return to deliver his desired retirement income.

1. Does the participant have a higher than average risk tolerance?
2. If the participant's risk objectives are not appropriate, would BMSR counsel him to change them?

Solution to Problem 1: No. This participant's ability to take risk is less than his willingness because of his small asset base and the limited time left until he needs to draw on his retirement assets; his risk tolerance is not above average.

Solution to Problem 2: BMSR would not counsel the participant because the plan is participant-directed. The employee needs to educate himself about the objectives and constraints framework as applied to individual investors.

EXAMPLE 3-9 Participant Early in Career

A 25-year-old plan participant joined BMSR recently. She is single and in good health. She has always been conservative and does not feel confident in her ability to choose funds for her retirement plan. She thinks that perhaps she should just put half in the money market fund and half in the large-capitalization value common stock fund. How do this participant's plan choices match her situation?

Solution: Given her investment time horizon, she may benefit by increasing her willingness to take risk to match her ability to take risk. She could adopt a more aggressive risk stance while increasing diversification by moving money from the money market fund to a bond fund and/or another equity fund (e.g., a growth-oriented fund). If her company offers an investor education program, this participant should attend so that she can explore the elements of assessing risk tolerance.

As mentioned, participants in DC plans bear the risk of investment results. As a consequence, an investment policy statement for a DC plan fulfills a much different role than an investment policy statement for a DB plan. For example, an IPS for a participant-directed DC plan is the governing document that describes the investment strategies and alternatives available to the group of plan participants characterized by diverse objectives and constraints. Such an IPS necessarily becomes an overall set of governing principles rather than an IPS for a specific plan participant. Example 3-10 provides sample excerpts from an investment policy statement for a participant-directed DC plan.

EXAMPLE 3-10 Investment Policy Statement for BMSR Company Defined-Contribution Plan

Purpose: The purpose of this investment policy statement is to assist the members of the Retirement Policy Committee (RPC) in effectively establishing, monitoring, evaluating, and revising the investment program established for the defined-contribution plan (the Plan) sponsored by the BMSR Company (BMSR). The authority for establishing this responsibility is by action of the BMSR board of directors at its March 26, 2002 meeting. The primary focuses of this investment policy statement are as follows:

- Clearly distinguish among the responsibilities of the RPC, the Plan participants, the fund managers, and Plan trustee/recordkeeper selected by the RPC.
- Provide descriptions of the investment alternatives available to Plan participants.
- Provide criteria for monitoring and evaluating the performance of investment managers and investment vehicles (funds) relative to appropriate investment benchmarks.
- Provide criteria for manager/fund selection, termination and replacement.
- Establish effective communication procedures for the fund managers, the trustee/recordkeeper, the RPC, and the Plan participants.

RPC Roles and Responsibilities: The RPC's responsibilities, in carrying out this investment policy statement, include:

- Monitoring the fund objectives and selecting specific funds to be offered to the Plan participants to provide sufficient diversification possibilities.
- Monitoring the investment performance, including fees, of funds made available to Plan participants and terminating and replacing funds when judicious and appropriate.
- Assuring ongoing communications with, and appropriate educational resources for, the Plan participants.
- Selecting, monitoring and, if necessary, recommending the replacement of the trustee/recordkeeper of the Plan.
- Assuring that the interest rate for Plan loans is in accordance with the provisions of the Plan.

Plan Participant Roles and Responsibilities: The responsibilities of plan participants include the allocation of Plan contributions and accumulations among the various fund choices made available and the obligation to educate themselves sufficiently in order to make appropriate allocations over their career or life span.

A participant's appropriate asset allocation is a function of multiple factors, including age, income, length of time before retirement, tolerance for risk, accumulation objectives, retirement income replacement objectives, and other assets. To permit participants to establish savings and investment strategies to suit their individual needs, the Plan offers a number of investment alternatives with varying return and risk characteristics.

The participant is best positioned to make the individual decision on how to allocate assets among the investment alternatives. As such, the investment direction of employees' elective deferrals and contributions made by BMSR will be each individual participant's responsibility. It is also each individual participant's responsibility to reallocate assets among funds as personal circumstances change.

To help address the factors mentioned above, BMSR will provide information to participants regarding the investment alternatives and basic principles of investing. However, the dissemination of information and the provision of investment alternatives by BMSR do not constitute advice to participants.

The return/risk concept is basic to investments. Over time, investment alternatives offering higher expected returns will exhibit higher risk (i.e., volatility of returns or of principal values). The Plan offers a variety of investment choices in order to provide participants the opportunity to select return/risk strategies that meet their savings and investment objectives and to adequately diversify.

ERISA 404(c) Compliance: BMSR intends to comply with ERISA Section 404(c) regulations, by, among other things, offering a broad, diversified range of investment choices; allowing transfers of funds between investment choices at least once every 90 days; and providing sufficient investment information to participants on a regular basis.

Selection of Investment Alternatives: The RPC's role is to provide participants with an array of investment choices with various investment objectives that should enable participants to invest according to their varying investment needs. The investment choices offered should represent asset classes with different risk and return characteristics and with sufficient diversification properties. The following asset classes have the investment characteristics currently desired:

- Money market instruments
- Intermediate-term fixed-income instruments
- Intermediate-term Treasury inflation-indexed securities
- Equity
  - Large-cap growth
  - Large-cap blend/core
  - Large-cap value
  - Mid-cap blend/core
  - Small-cap blend/core
  - International
- Life-cycle mutual funds (funds customized for various retirement dates)

The criteria for selection and for replacement of funds include the following:

- The array of investment options should be chosen with the goal of permitting participants to diversify their investments and to align the risk of their investments to their risk tolerance.
- The funds must have reasonable fees, including adviser fees, 12(b)-1 fees, and other fees.
- Every fund must have a clearly articulated and explained investment strategy, accompanied by evidence that the strategy is followed over time.
- The funds' time-weighted returns and volatility of returns over at least the three (and preferably five) prior years must compare favorably with the performance of a passively managed index with the same style (e.g., large-cap growth). This is the primary performance criterion.
- Funds selected must:
    - Be managed by a bank, insurance company, investment management company, or investment advisor (as defined by the Registered Investment Advisers Act of 1940) that has had significant assets under management for at least 10 years and has exhibited financial stability throughout that period.
    - Provide historical quarterly performance calculated on a time-weighted basis and reported net and gross of fees
    - Provide performance evaluation reports that illustrate the risk–return profile of the manager relative to passive indexes and other managers of like investment style
    - Clearly articulate the investment strategy to be followed and document that the strategy has been successfully executed over time.
- Transfers among investment funds are permitted on at least a quarterly basis, thus fulfilling an ERISA 404(c) requirement.

Monitoring Investment Performance: The RPC will monitor each fund's return and risk performance on a quarterly basis relative to appropriate investment benchmarks. In the event a fund over a five-year time frame

- Underperforms a passively managed (index) fund with similar objectives (i.e., same style) or, alternatively,
- Ranks worse than the fiftieth percentile in terms of investment performance relative to funds with similar investment objectives,

the RPC will review the fund to determine whether its performance has resulted from the fund manager, the style of management, or market volatility, and decide whether the fund should be eliminated from the menu of possible investment choices. The RPC will also consider the fund's performance over periods of more than five years, if available, before making a decision.

As noted above, the RPC will evaluate each fund's performance using a five-year time horizon. The RPC realizes that most investments go through cycles; therefore, at any given time a fund may encounter a time period in which the investment objectives are not met or when a fund fails to meet its expected performance target. The fund's performance should be reported in terms of an annualized time-weighted rate of return. As noted above, the returns should be compared to appropriate market indexes and to peer group universes for the most recent five-year (or longer) period.

In light of the evaluation of each fund's performance, the RPC has the authority to recommend the replacement or elimination of an investment objective or fund if, in the opinion of the RPC, the investment objective or fund does not, or is not expected to, meet the specified performance criteria; is no longer suited to the needs of the Plan participants; or if, in the sole opinion of the RPC, a more appropriate investment choice exists.

EXAMPLE 3-11 BMSR Committee Decision

A member of the RPC committee for BMSR is concerned about the small-cap growth fund. During the last two years, this fund has ranked in the top half of small-cap growth funds and has outperformed a passively managed small-cap growth benchmark. However, the fund has dropped in value far more than the overall market. The concerned member suggests that the RPC replace the fund. Do the IPS criteria support this suggestion?

Solution: According to IPS guidelines, investment performance must be evaluated over time horizons longer than two years. The IPS also specifies a comparison to a passively managed benchmark with the same style rather than to the overall market. For these reasons, the IPS cannot support the suggestion that the fund be eliminated.

2.3. Hybrid and Other Plans

During the 1990s, many employers concluded that neither the traditional DB nor DC plan structure exactly met their pension plan objectives. Hybrid plans began to emerge that combined the features of DB and DC plans.[8] Examples of hybrid plans include cash balance plans, pension equity plans, target benefit plans, and floor plans. These plans sought to combine some of the most highly valued features of a DC plan (such as portability, administrative ease, and understandability by participants) with the highly valued features of a DB plan (such as benefit guarantees, years of service rewards, and the ability to link retirement pay to a percentage of salary). In this section, we discuss cash balance plans as one example of a hybrid plan as well as another important type of plan, the employee stock ownership plan (ESOP).

A cash balance plan is a DB plan, in that the employer bears the investment risk. To employees, however, it looks like a DC plan because they are provided a personalized statement showing their account balance, an annual contribution credit, and an earnings credit. The contribution credit is a percentage of pay based on age, while the earnings credit is a percentage

[8]In 1985 only 1 percent of Fortune 100 companies offered a hybrid plan; by 2002 that fraction had grown to 33 percent. See Scanlan and Lyons (2006, p. 38).

increase in the account balance that is typically tied to long-term interest rates. In reality, the account balance is hypothetical because, unlike in a DC plan, the employee does not have a separate account. Some plans allow investment choices among fixed-income and equity-based options, which introduces investment risk for the employee.

Cash balance plans usually are not start-up plans but rather are traditional DB plans that have been converted in order to gain some of the features of a DC plan. Some of these plans have come under criticism as being unfair to older workers with many years of service, who may have accrued higher retirement benefits under the DB plan than the cash balance plan offers. In response to this criticism, some companies have offered a "grandfather" clause to older workers, allowing them to choose between joining a new cash balance plan or continuing with an existing traditional DB plan.

Finally, most developed countries allow for retirement or other savings plans that encourage employees to become stockholders of their employer. These plans may be complex qualified plans that purchase stock in a DC pension plan with pretax money, or they may be simple savings plans that allow employees to buy stock personally with their after-tax pay. The acronym ESOP refers to an employee *stock* ownership plan (in the United States) or employee *share* ownership plan (United Kingdom). These are DC plans that invest all or the majority of plan assets in employer stock. ESOPs are DC plans because the contribution is set as a percentage of employee pay. The final value of the plan for the employee will depend on the vesting schedule, the level of contributions, and the change in the per-share value of the stock.

Although ESOPs all share the common goal of increasing employee ownership in a company, they vary widely from country to country in terms of regulation. Some ESOPs may sell stock to employees at a discount from market prices, while others may not. Some require employee contribution; others prohibit such. Some ESOP trusts may borrow to purchase large amounts of employer stock, while others must rely solely on contributions.

In addition to encouraging ownership of one's employer, ESOPs have been used by companies to liquidate a large block of company stock held by an individual or small group of people, avoid a public offering of stock, or discourage an unfriendly takeover by placing a large holding of stock in the hands of employees via the ESOP trust. Apart from his or her investment in the ESOP, a plan participant may have a major investment of human capital in the company by virtue of working for that company. Should the company fail, the participant might see the value of the ESOP investment plummet at the same time that he or she becomes unemployed. An important concern for ESOP participants is that their overall investments (both financial and human capital) reflect adequate diversification.[9]

3. FOUNDATIONS AND ENDOWMENTS

Foundations and endowments provide vital support for much of today's philanthropic and charitable activities. **Foundations** are typically grant-making institutions funded by gifts and investment assets. **Endowments,** on the other hand, are long-term funds generally owned by operating nonprofit institutions such as universities and colleges, museums, hospitals, and other organizations involved in charitable activities.

Although both are created by donations, foundations and endowments usually develop differently over time. Private foundations typically are created and funded by a single donor to

[9]Many 401(k) plans, especially large ones, have company stock as an investment option. For participants in such plans, similar issues arise.

fund philanthropic goals. The investment portfolio provides the dominant source of revenue, and the purchasing power of its corpus is either maintained or eventually given away. In the United States, tax law essentially mandates minimum levels of annual spending for some types of foundations. By donating cash and securities, many of the world's great industrialists and financiers have created foundations that bear their name (e.g., the Ford, Rockefeller, and Gates foundations). Endowments, by contrast, are often built up over time by many individual gifts to the endowed institution. Spending distributions are determined by the beneficiary institution, supplementing other revenue sources such as tuition, grants, fees, or gifts for current use. Prominent endowments, such as those of Harvard, Yale, and Princeton universities, have grown along with their institutions over centuries.

In Sections 3.1 and 3.2, we discuss the investment objectives and constraints of foundations and endowments, respectively.

3.1. Foundations: Background and Investment Setting

Foundations provide essential support of charitable activity. In broad terms, four types of foundations exist: independent, company sponsored, operating, and community.[10] Exhibit 3-2 briefly describes the principal types of foundations in the United States, as distinguished by their purpose, sources of funds, and annual spending requirements.[11] Independent foundations, also referred to as private or family foundations, are grant-making organizations funded by an individual donor and generally required to pay out a minimum of 5 percent of assets annually. Company-sponsored foundations tend to have a short-term investment focus to facilitate philanthropic funding from the corporation to grantees. Operating foundations, much like endowments, provide income to support specific programs. Community foundations draw upon broad support for donations to fund a variety of grants. Most of the following discussion relates to independent (private and family) foundations, which represent the majority of investment assets in the foundation sector.

The most noteworthy aspect of foundations is that they can vary widely in their investment goals and time horizons. For example, a foundation may be the primary or even sole source of funding for a charitable program. In such a case, a stable, reliable flow of funds is extremely important because the program has few alternative sources of funding to make up the shortfall. However, many foundations give funding for numerous independent projects or programs for only a few years at most. Because such foundations are generally not those projects' primary means of support, the funded programs can handle drops in spending by the foundation relatively easily because funding reductions are less likely to critically disrupt their operations. Often, a foundation's mission may address a problem with a limited time horizon or an urgent need (e.g., a need resulting from a natural disaster or an environmental emergency).

Another distinctive characteristic of the foundation sector, in contrast to endowments, is that most private and family foundations must generate their entire grant-making and operating budget from their investment portfolio for the following reasons: These institutions generally do not engage in fund-raising campaigns; they may not receive any new contributions from the donor; and they do not receive any public support. These unique conditions help to guide the investment approach taken by foundations. In addition, as mentioned earlier,

[10]Community foundations are a prominent type of public charity (meeting tax code tests for public support) in the United States and are used to represent public charities as a group.

[11]The international links at the Association of Charitable Foundations (www.acf.org.uk/linksinter.htm) are good starting points for researching the diversity of foundations worldwide.

EXHIBIT 3-2 Types of Foundations in the United States

Foundation Type	Description	Source of Funds	Decision-Making Authority	Annual Spending Requirement
Independent foundation (private or family)	Independent grant-making organization established to aid social, educational, charitable, or religious activities.	Generally an individual, family, or group of individuals.	Donor, members of donor's family, or independent trustees.	At least 5% of 12-month average asset value, plus expenses associated with generating investment return.
Company-sponsored foundation	A legally independent grant-making organization with close ties to the corporation providing funds.	Endowment and/or annual contributions from a profit-making corporation.	Board of trustees, usually controlled by the sponsoring corporation's executives.	Same as independent foundation.
Operating foundation	Organization that uses its resources to conduct research or provide a direct service (e.g., operate a museum).	Largely the same as independent foundation.	Independent board of directors.	Must use 85% of interest and dividend income for active conduct of the institution's own programs. Some are also subject to annual spending requirement equal to 3.33% of assets.
Community foundation	A publicly supported organization that makes grants for social, educational, charitable, or religious purposes. A type of public charity.	Multiple donors; the public.	Board of directors.	No spending requirement.

private and family foundations are subject to a payout requirement that mandates a minimum level of spending, while university endowments and many other nonprofit institutions face no such requirement.

3.1.1. Risk Objectives

Because foundations' goals differ somewhat from those of traditional DB pension funds and other asset pools, foundations can have a higher risk tolerance. Pension funds have a contractually defined liability stream (the pension payments expected to be made to retirees); in contrast, foundations have no such defined liability. The desire to keep spending whole in real terms, or to grow the institution, is simply that: a desire. Foundation investment policy can thus be more fluid or creative, and arguably more aggressive, than pension fund policy.

It is also acceptable, if risky, for foundations to try to earn a higher rate of return than is needed to maintain the purchasing power of assets—in essence, seeking to make as much money as possible. Such behavior makes it possible for the institution to increase its grant making over time because the funding needs of organizations supported by foundations are essentially unbounded.

3.1.2. Return Objectives

Foundations differ in their purposes, and so vary in their return objectives. Some foundations are meant to be short lived; others are intended to operate in perpetuity. For those foundations with an indefinitely long horizon, the long-term return objective is to preserve the real (inflation-adjusted) value of the investment assets while allowing spending at an appropriate (either statutory or decided-upon) rate. Such a policy, if successful, keeps spending constant in real terms, on average over time, achieving what is sometimes called intergenerational equity or neutrality: an equitable balance between the interests of current and future beneficiaries of the foundation's support.[12]

If we look at the 5 percent annual spending minimum for foundations as a benchmark and add 0.3 percent as a low-end estimate of investment management expenses (i.e., the cost of generating investment returns), we thus have calculated that the fund must generate a return of 5.3 percent, plus the inflation rate, to stay even in real terms. We can use 5.3 percent plus the expected inflation rate as a starting point for setting the return objective of a foundation. If the expected inflation rate is 2 percent, the minimum return requirement will be 7.3 percent. This additive formulation of the return objective is intuitive but approximate. The most precise formulation is multiplicative, which accounts for the effect of compounding in a multiperiod setting and results in a higher requirement. For our example, the multiplicative calculation is $(1.05)(1.003)(1.02) - 1.0 = 0.0742$, or 7.42 percent.

3.1.3. Liquidity Requirements

A foundation's liquidity requirements are anticipated or unanticipated needs for cash in excess of contributions made to the foundation. Anticipated needs are captured in the periodic distributions prescribed by a foundation's spending rate. In the United States, the spending policy of private foundations is dictated, at least as concerns the 5 percent annual minimum, by the Tax Reform Act of 1969 and subsequent amendments. Expenses associated with management of the foundation's investments do not count toward the payout requirement, so one must add this cost (conservatively, 0.3 percent annually) to the minimum that the foundation is required to spend. "Overhead" associated with grant making—for example, the salaries of program officers and other executives—does count toward the payout requirement.

To avoid erosion in the portfolio's real value over time, many foundations try to spend only the minimum or else set a maximum that only slightly exceeds the minimum. In addition, to avoid large fluctuations in their operating budget, foundations may use a smoothing rule. A **smoothing rule** averages asset values over a period of time in order to dampen the spending rate's response to asset value fluctuation.

[12]Think of a school that spends so much on scholarships in the current time frame that the endowment becomes depleted. A generation hence, the school will be in a poor financial position to give scholarships or otherwise compete for good students and professors. Under such a policy, intergenerational neutrality is clearly defeated. The underlying philosophy is that a long-lived foundation, or endowment, should not favor one particular generation of would-be recipients over another. A similar tension exists in certain types of trusts that must balance the interests of life-income beneficiaries and remaindermen (who receive the trust corpus after the death of the income beneficiaries).

The U.S. Internal Revenue Service (IRS) allows carryforwards and carrybacks, within limits, so that a foundation may avoid being penalized for underspending by spending more than 5 percent of assets in a subsequent year. Conversely, as a result of overspending in prior years, a foundation may be allowed to underspend in a subsequent year. Carryforwards and carrybacks not only make smoothing rules workable but also allow a foundation to make a large grant in a single year without compromising the long-run soundness of its investment program.

The 5 percent payout requirement for private and family foundations, combined with the desire to maintain the portfolio's value in real terms, can be daunting. Foundation executives may disagree about whether the 5 percent spending requirement motivates an aggressive investment policy or a conservative one. Clearly, motivation refers to willingness to bear risk, but ability to bear risk must also be considered in determining a foundation's risk tolerance.

It is prudent for any organization to keep some assets in cash as a reserve for contingencies, but private and family foundations need a cash reserve for a special reason: They are subject to the unusual requirement that spending in a given fiscal year be 5 percent or more of the 12-month average of asset values *in that year*. One cannot, of course, know what this amount will be in advance, so one cannot budget for it. Instead, a well-managed foundation places some (say 10 percent or 20 percent) of its annual grant-making and spending budget in a reserve. This reserve may simply be in the form of not spending budgeted money until the year is mostly over and the 12-month average of asset values is known with greater certainty. In an "up" year for markets, this method may cause a rush of grants to be paid by the foundation at the end of the year, to avoid spending less than the minimum required amount. A year-end rush should be more acceptable to the foundation than the alternative that would occur without a reserve—overspending in flat or "down" market years.

3.1.4. Time Horizon The majority of foundation wealth resides in private and other foundations established or managed with the intent of lasting into perpetuity. Our discussion has thus focused on strategies for preserving capital in real terms after spending. Some institutions, however, are created to be "spent down" over a predefined period of time; therefore, they pursue a different strategy, exhibiting an increasing level of conservatism as time passes. All else equal, investors often assume that a longer time horizon implies a greater ability to bear risk because a longer horizon affords them more time to recoup losses.

3.1.5. Tax Concerns In the United States, income that is not substantially related to a foundation's charitable purposes may be classified as **unrelated business income** and be subject to regular corporate tax rates. For instance, a museum gift shop that sells artwork has business income related to its purposes; if it sells motorcycles, it has unrelated business income. Income from real estate is taxable as unrelated business income if the property is debt financed, but only in proportion to the fraction of the property's cost financed with debt.

In the United States, a private foundation must estimate and pay quarterly in advance a tax (currently set at 2 percent) on its net investment income. **Net investment income** includes dividends, interest, and capital gains, less the foundation's expenses related directly to the production of such income. The excise tax may be reduced to 1 percent if the charitable distributions for the year equal or exceed both 5 percent and the average of the previous five years' payout plus 1 percent of the net investment income. In creating this requirement, Congress hoped that foundations would translate their tax savings into increased charitable activities.

3.1.6. Legal and Regulatory Factors Foundations may be subject to a variety of legal and regulatory constraints, which vary by country and sometimes by type of foundation. As one example, in the United States, the Internal Revenue Code (Section 4944) addresses private foundations, imposing a graduated series of excise taxes if a private foundation invests in a manner that jeopardizes the carrying out of its tax-exempt purposes. In the United States, many states have adopted the Uniform Management of Institutional Funds Act (UMIFA) as the primary legislation governing any entity organized and operated exclusively for educational, religious, or charitable purposes. We will present some of the details of UMIFA that concern investing activities when we address endowments.

3.1.7. Unique Circumstances A special challenge faces foundations that are endowed with the stock of one particular company and that are then restricted by the donor from diversifying. The asset value of such an institution is obviously subject to the large market fluctuations attendant to any one-stock position.

With the permission of the donor, some institutions have entered into swap agreements or other derivative transactions to achieve the payoffs of a more diversified portfolio. Such a strategy achieves the donor's goal of retaining voting rights in the stock, while providing the foundation with a more stable asset value. Other institutions simply tolerate the fluctuations associated with a single-stock position.

Against the background of investment objectives and constraints for foundations, Example 3-12 illustrates how all these elements come together in an investment policy statement.

EXAMPLE 3-12 The Fund for Electoral Integrity

A group of major foundations has endowed a new organization, the Fund for Electoral Integrity, to supervise elections and political campaigns in countries undergoing a transition to democracy. The fund is headquartered in a developing country. It has received initial grants of $20 million, with $40 million expected to be received in further grants over the next three years. The fund's charter expressly decrees that the fund should spend itself out of existence within 10 years of its founding rather than trying to become a permanent institution. Determine and justify appropriate investment policy objectives and constraints for the Fund for Electoral Integrity.

Solution

Risk Objective

Although the fund has a 10-year life, it is receiving donations over a period of years and it is also constantly spending money on programs. Thus, it can be assumed to have a five-year investment horizon on average and should *initially* adopt a conservative or below-average risk profile (a standard deviation of annual returns in the range of 5 percent to 7 percent).[13] Over the life of the fund, the risk objective should gradually

[13] The standard deviation of annual returns on intermediate-term bonds typically falls in this range.

migrate to an even more conservative profile (standard deviation of 3 percent to 5 percent). The relatively short time horizon calls for a below-average risk tolerance. Both the risks inherent in markets and the fund's risk tolerance may change, so it is important to periodically review the investment policy and the portfolio from a risk management perspective. In making their investment recommendations, the board and investment committee should take the following into account:

- Market risk (fluctuation in asset values).
- Liquidity risk.
- Political, regulatory, and legal risks.
- Operations and control risks.
- Any other risks that the board and investment committee deem relevant.

Return Objective

The fund's broad return objective is to earn the highest inflation-adjusted return consistent with the risk objective. At inception, the fund's return objective is to equal or better the total return of an average five-year maturity U.S. Treasury note portfolio over a rolling four-year period.

Constraints

Liquidity. The fund must pay out roughly $6 million annually for 10 years.
Time horizon. The fund has a 10-year time horizon.
Tax concerns. The fund is a tax-exempt organization in the country in which it is organized.
Regulatory factors. No special legal or regulatory factors impinge on the organization's ability to invest as it chooses.
Unique circumstances. The fund has no constraints in the sense of prohibited investments.

3.2. Endowments: Background and Investment Setting

Endowments play a critical role in the vitality and success of today's charitable activity. As the long-term investment portfolios of nonprofit operating institutions, endowments provide a significant amount of budgetary support for universities, colleges, private schools, hospitals, museums, and religious organizations.

The term *endowment* has taken on two related but distinct meanings. As commonly understood, an endowment is simply the long-term investment portfolio of a charitable organization. Legally and formally, however, the term *endowment* refers to a permanent fund established by a donor with the condition that the fund principal be maintained over time. In contrast to private foundations, endowments are not subject to a specific legally required spending level.

Donors establish true endowments by making gifts with the stipulation that periodic spending distributions from the fund be used to pay for programs and that the principal value of the gift be preserved in perpetuity. Thus, true endowments are funds permanently restricted in terms of spending. Many schools and nonprofit organizations will supplement true endowments with voluntary savings in the form of quasi-endowments, sometimes referred to as funds functioning as endowments (FFEs). Although designated as long-term financial capital, quasi-endowments have no spending restrictions; the institution may spend such funds completely. Because endowments are owned by nonprofit organizations, they generally are exempt from taxation on investment income derived from interest, dividends, capital gains, rents, and royalties.

Typically, the large investment pools commonly referred to as endowments consist of a variety of individual funds, including true endowments and FFEs. Each endowment fund is established with a specific indenture detailing the conditions and intended uses of the gifts. Although many endowment funds are unrestricted, meaning that endowment spending can be used for the general purposes of the beneficiary institution, others are restricted so that monies can be spent only for specified purposes. For instance, one restricted fund might support a professorship, while another fund might support student financial aid. Spending from these funds must be kept distinct and support only the specified use—money from a professorship endowment, for example, cannot be used to provide student aid.

Endowments are a vital source of funding for many charitable programs, and spending distributions should be substantial to support such programs' needs. Large fluctuations in year-to-year spending can disrupt the endowed institution's operating budget, finances and staffing. Therefore, spending distributions should be stable and reliable. Because donors establish endowment funds with the intention of funding an activity in perpetuity, recipient institutions generally operate with the fiduciary intent of preserving the fund's purchasing power. The nonprofit should not count on new gifts to supplement endowment funds whose value has been eroded by spending beyond investment returns. In summary, endowments should provide substantial, stable, and sustainable spending distributions.

Historically, prior to the 1970s, income provided the basis for determining an endowment's spending distributions. Institutions invested their endowments primarily in stocks, bonds, and cash, and they spent the dividend and interest income. Unfortunately, in following such policies, endowment spending was not tied to the investment portfolio's total return after inflation. Institutions skewed portfolios toward high-yielding fixed-income instruments at the expense of equities in order to increase current endowment spending. Although high-quality bonds typically make their promised nominal payments, unanticipated inflation reduces those payments' real values below anticipated levels. Furthermore, shifts toward higher-yielding assets allowed increased portfolio spending but decreased an endowment's ability to generate adequate inflation-adjusted long-term returns.

Educated and encouraged by a seminal Ford Foundation report published in 1969, many endowed institutions adopted a new approach to determining spending based on the concept of total return.[14] As codified by UMIFA in 1972, income and capital gains (realized and unrealized) are now included in determining total return in the United States. Freed from the strictures of yield, institutions could determine endowment-spending levels as a percentage of an endowment's market value.

Today, most endowed institutions determine spending through policies based on total return as reflected in market values. A spending rule, by defining the amount of the distribution from the endowment available for spending, helps instill discipline into the budgeting and financial management process. A balanced budget is not a meaningful achievement if it results from pulling from the endowment whatever is needed to cover a deficit.

Spending is typically calculated as a percentage, usually between 4 percent and 6 percent of endowment market value (endowments are not subject to minimum spending rates as are

[14]See Cary and Bright (1969) for more information.

private foundations in the United States).[15] In calculating spending, endowments frequently use an average of trailing market values rather than the current market value to provide greater stability in the amount of money distributed annually. In computing such an average, the endowment manager may adjust historical market values to reflect inflation. A common, simple rule might call for spending 5 percent of the average of the past three years' ending market values of the endowment. One problem with this rule is that it places as much significance on market values three years ago as it does on more recent outcomes. Even if endowment values were relatively stable for the last two years, an extraordinary return three years ago could force a dramatic change in spending this year. A more refined rule might use a geometrically declining average of trailing endowment values adjusted for inflation, placing more emphasis on recent market values and less on past values. Examples of spending rules include the following:

- *Simple spending rule.* Spending equals the spending rate multiplied by the market value of the endowment at the beginning of the fiscal year.

$$\text{Spending}_t = \text{Spending rate} \times \text{Ending market value}_{t-1}$$

- *Rolling three-year average spending rule.* Spending equals the spending rate multiplied by the average market value of the last three fiscal year-ends.

$$\text{Spending}_t = \text{Spending rate} \times (1/3)\left[\text{Ending market value}_{t-1} + \text{Ending market value}_{t-2} + \text{Ending market value}_{t-3}\right]$$

- *Geometric smoothing rule.* Spending equals the weighted average of the prior year's spending adjusted for inflation and the product of the spending rate times the market value of the endowment at the beginning of the prior fiscal year. The smoothing rate is typically between 60 and 80 percent.

$$\text{Spending}_t = \text{Smoothing rate} \times [\text{Spending}_{t-1} \times (1 + \text{Inflation}_{t-1})] + (1 - \text{Smoothing rate}) \times (\text{Spending rate} \times \text{Beginning market value}_{t-1})$$

Because most endowed institutions complete their budget planning process well before the endowment market value at the beginning of a fiscal year becomes known, it may be advisable to calculate spending from an endowment value based on a date in advance of the final budget process. The geometric smoothing rule description reflects this approach and uses the prior year's beginning, rather than ending, endowment market value.

3.2.1. Risk Objectives An endowment's investment risk should be considered in conjunction with its spending policy and in the context of its long-term objective of providing a significant, stable, and sustainable stream of spending distributions. Spending policies with smoothing or averaging rules can dampen the transmission of portfolio volatility to spending distributions, allowing the institution to accept short-term portfolio volatility while striving for high long-term investment returns necessary to fund programs and maintain purchasing

[15]According to Swensen (2000), 90 percent of endowments spend between 4 percent and 6 percent of endowment market value annually.

power. Endowments that do not use a smoothing rule may have less tolerance for short-term portfolio risk. Investment portfolios with very low volatility, or investment risk, usually provide low expected returns, which increases the risk of failing to achieve the endowment's goals of significant, stable, and sustainable spending. Low investment risk does not equate to low risk for meeting endowment objectives.

An institution's risk tolerance depends on the endowment's role in the operating budget and the institution's ability to adapt to drops in spending. If endowment income represents only a small portion of the budget, poor investment returns may have little impact on the bottom line. However, modest drops in endowment value may have serious consequences if endowment income contributes a large part of overall revenues. If the same market forces affect both its donor base and its endowment, an institution that relies heavily on donations for current income may see donations drop at the same time as endowment income. Large fixed expenditures such as debt service can aggravate damage inflicted by drops in endowment income.

On a short-term basis, an endowment's risk tolerance can be greater if the endowment has experienced strong recent returns and the smoothed spending rate is below the long-term average or target rate. In such a case, the endowment value could drop and spending might still increase the following year. However, endowment funds with poor recent returns and a smoothed spending rate above the long-term average run the risk of a severe loss in purchasing power. High spending rates can aggravate the erosion of the endowment's corpus at the same time that institution comes under pressure to cut operating expenses.

Because of the assumed positive relation between risk and return, a high required return objective and a willingness to meet relatively high spending needs often imply a high willingness to accept risk. However, short-term performance pressures will indicate a low willingness to accept risk. Despite their long-term investment mandate, endowment managers often come under pressure to perform well over relatively short-term time horizons for several reasons. Poor investment results may lead to reductions in the level of endowment spending. In addition, investment staff and trustees with oversight responsibility are evaluated formally or informally on relatively short time frames—often yearly. Many large endowments are highly visible; supporters and peers closely scrutinize their annual performance. Endowed institutions thus need to objectively assess and, if necessary, enhance their actual tolerance for short-term volatility before pursuing investment strategies that really are consistent with only a very long-term investment horizon.

3.2.2. Return Objectives Endowments have high return objectives, reflecting the goal of providing a significant, stable, and sustainable flow of income to operations. Endowments typically provide vital support of ongoing operations and programs, and distributions from endowment to operations should be as large as practical. An endowment manager must thus balance this objective of providing substantial resources to programs with the need to provide a stable flow. Erratic and volatile endowment distributions are unsuitable for programs with permanent staff or recurring expenses. Furthermore, an endowment must balance significant and stable spending objectives with the imperative to provide sustainable support—in other words, endowment funds should maintain their long-term purchasing power after inflation.

Endowments often need to generate relatively high long-term rates of return in order to provide a substantial flow of spending to institutions affected by rates of inflation above those of the general economy. The growth of higher education expenses in the United States is a case in point. Inflation for U.S. higher education expenses has been generally above that for the broad economy such as the gross domestic product (GDP) deflator or for consumers as measured by the U.S. Consumer Price Index (CPI). Since 1960, annual inflation for colleges and universities, as measured by the Higher Education Price Index (HEPI), averaged approximately 1 percentage point more than the CPI or the GDP deflator.[16] A major factor for this higher inflation rate is the difficulty of increasing faculty productivity without impairing the quality of education. For instance, colleges and universities cannot simply improve efficiency by increasing class size or student-to-faculty ratios. Because faculty compensation typically constitutes a majority portion of higher education operating budgets, many of the costs associated with increasing salaries cannot be offset by efficiency gains. In order to maintain long-term support of an academic program, therefore, a higher-education institution must increase spending over time to adjust for inflation that is higher than the CPI or the GDP deflator.

The objective of providing a significant, stable, and sustainable flow of funds to support operating programs provides a useful framework for evaluating investment and spending policies. We may ask questions such as: How do the trade-offs of expected risk and returns relate to meeting endowment objectives? What spending policy makes sense for the institution? What long-term rate of spending can the portfolio support without unduly risking impairment of purchasing power? Conventional mean–variance analysis can help to suggest appropriate asset allocations. Computer simulations using Monte Carlo techniques can be extremely helpful in comparing and assessing investment and spending policies and their ability to meet endowment objectives. Monte Carlo techniques use random numbers to develop multiple, simulated time-series of annual returns given a portfolio's risk and return characteristics. Applying the spending rule to each time series, we can evaluate the interaction of investment choices and spending policy.

Monte Carlo simulations illustrate the effect of investment and spending policies on the likelihood that an endowment will provide a stable and sustainable flow of operating funds for an institution. How do various portfolios and spending rules affect the risk that the endowment will need to severely cut back on spending in the short term? How should the endowment's board set spending policies so as to support the objective of preserving the real purchasing power of the endowment? To answer these questions, an endowment must quantify risk measures. A severe drop in support for the operating budget might be defined as a real reduction of 10 percent from year to year. The risk of a dramatic decline in endowment purchasing power might be defined as the probability of more than a 50 percent real decline over a 50-year horizon. The specific pain threshold or downside risk tolerance would depend on the endowment's role with respect to operations and the endowed institution's ability to adapt to endowment spending declines.

Simulations can demonstrate several key aspects of the interaction of investment and spending policies on managing endowment risk. First, the endowment's spending rate must be lower than its expected rate of return in order to preserve purchasing power long term. For example, if an endowment has a 6 percent simple spending rate and 6 percent expected real returns with 12 percent annual standard deviation of returns, the probability that its purchasing power will fall by more than 50 percent over a 50-year period is 41 percent, according to Monte Carlo simulation. With the same portfolio return of 6 percent and a 5 percent simple spending rate, the long-term risk of such purchasing power impairment falls to 19 percent.

If returns had no volatility, an endowment could set spending at a rate that equated to the real return—that is, the nominal return net of inflation. Returns above spending would

[16]According to Research Associates of Washington.

be reinvested to compensate for inflation, and the endowment would retain its purchasing power. With the introduction of volatility, however, the endowment's long-term purchasing power would be impaired more than 40 percent of the time according to the simulations. In order to achieve its objective of maintaining purchasing power, an endowment must keep its long-term average spending rate below its long-term expected real return.

From simulations, we can also observe that the risk of short-term disruptive spending may be reduced with a smoothing rule. For instance, there is a 17 percent risk of a 10 percent real drop in spending in any year with a simple 5 percent spending rule for an endowment with a 6 percent expected real return and 12 percent annual standard deviation of returns. With the same portfolio, a 70/30 smoothing rule (70 percent of last year's spending and 30 percent of 5 percent of last year's endowment market value) would reduce the risk of a short-term spending drop from 17 percent with a simple 5 percent rule to less than 3 percent.

Finally, a low-volatility, low-return portfolio increases the risk of an endowment failing to meet its objectives. For example, an endowment with a 5 percent spending target, a 70/30 smoothing rule, and a portfolio with a 5 percent real return and a 9 percent annual standard deviation of returns would lose half its purchasing power 34 percent of the time at the end of 50 years. Low investment risk does not equate to low risk of purchasing power impairment.

In summary, an endowment must coordinate its investment and spending policies. An endowment's returns need to exceed the spending rate to protect against a long-term loss of purchasing power. Calculating the return objective as the sum of the spending rate, the expected inflation rate, and the cost of generating investment returns can serve as a starting point for determining an endowment's appropriate return objective (analogous to the approach previously discussed for foundations). As is clear from Monte Carlo analysis in a multiperiod setting, however, an endowment may need to set its return objective higher than the above starting point in order to preserve its purchasing power. In addition, an endowed institution should adopt a spending policy that appropriately controls the risk of long-term purchasing power impairment and dampens short-term volatility in spending distributions. Unlike foundations, endowments are not subject to specific payout requirements. The endowment can set a long-term spending rate consistent with its investment approach. Furthermore, spending policies can include a smoothing rule, which gradually adjusts to changes in endowment market values, to dampen the effects of portfolio volatility on spending distributions.

3.2.3. Liquidity Requirements

The perpetual nature and measured spending of true endowments limit their need for liquidity. They must, however, have cash to make spending distributions, to meet capital commitments, and to facilitate portfolio-rebalancing transactions. In addition to gifts, an endowment's investment yield, the normal sale of securities, and maturation of bonds meet much of its need for cash. Although the typical endowment maintains more liquidity than required, managers of quasi-endowments should monitor the potential for major capital projects, such as a planned capital outlay for the construction of a building.

In general, endowments are well suited to invest in illiquid, nonmarketable securities given their limited need for liquidity. Care and discipline should be exercised in valuing nonmarketable investments because endowments must use accurate market values estimates to determine spending, calculate performance, and establish unit values for funds entering and exiting pooled endowment portfolios.

3.2.4. Time Horizon

In principle, endowment time horizons are extremely long term because of the objective of maintaining purchasing power in perpetuity. Annual draws for spending, however, may present important short-term considerations, because endowments often use yearly market values to determine spending, and each annual withdrawal of capital has its specific time horizon. Such considerations, as well as planned decapitalizations (reductions in capital, e.g., to fund large projects) for quasi-endowments, may suggest a multistage time horizon, in certain cases.

3.2.5. Tax Concerns

Although taxation may vary by domicile internationally, taxes are not a major consideration for endowments in general. In the United States, for example, endowments owned by nonprofit organizations are exempt from taxation on investment income derived from interest, dividends, capital gains, rents, and royalties. Under certain circumstances, unrelated business taxable income (UBTI) from operating businesses or from assets with acquisition indebtedness may be subject to tax. In addition, a portion of dividends from non-U.S. securities may be subject to withholding taxes that cannot be reclaimed or credited against U.S. taxes.

3.2.6. Legal and Regulatory Factors

In the United States, few laws and regulations exist regarding the management and conduct of endowment funds. Most states have adopted UMIFA as the primary governing legislation for endowments. First promulgated in 1972, UMIFA authorizes a broad range of investments for endowments. It also allows for the delegation of investment responsibility to external advisors and managers, as well as for wide discretion in setting the compensation for such services.

An endowed institution's governing board must "exercise ordinary business care and prudence" in dealing with investments. UMIFA explicitly authorizes institutions to spend endowment investment gain as well as income. Endowment spending must, however, respect any use restriction imposed by the donor, and it should not include principal when an endowment fund's market value falls below its historical book value. In other words, only income may be spent when an endowment's market value is less than its original gift value.[17] This requirement can lead to disruptive spending patterns, particularly for new funds or funds with market value at or near book value. To maintain normal spending patterns, institutions may consider an accounting reclassification or transfer of unrestricted FFE to fulfill balance sheet requirements that the market value of an endowment fund not fall below its historical book value.

At the federal level, U.S. endowed institutions must comply with tax and securities laws and reporting requirements. To achieve and maintain tax-exempt status under Section 501(c)(3) of the U.S. Internal Revenue Code, an institution must ensure that no part of its net earnings inure or accrue to the benefit of any private individual. The code provides for intermediate sanctions in the form of excise taxes against individuals in a position to exercise substantial authority who engage in "excess benefit transactions" whereby they receive unreasonably high compensation or inappropriately derive private benefit from the tax-exempt organization. With little governmental oversight, endowed institutions must develop, maintain, and enforce clear guidelines and policies to prohibit improper behavior and manage conflicts of interest.

3.2.7. Unique Circumstances

Endowments vary widely in their size, governance, and staff resources, and thus in the investment strategies that they can intelligently and practically pursue. Endowments range from the very small, providing financial aid for a day care center, to

[17] A few states supplement UMIFA with this fiduciary standard of preserving the purchasing power of endowment values.

the very large, supporting a major university. The responsibility of managing the endowment might fall to an unsophisticated board or to a collection of individuals knowledgeable about investments. Likewise, the investment staff responsible for managing and administering the endowment may be nonexistent or consist of many highly paid and experienced professionals. This wide variety in expertise and resources suggests that an endowment's specific circumstances may constrain the types of investments its board should consider.

Many large endowments have been leaders in adopting investments in alternative investments, such as private equities, real estate, natural resources, and absolute return strategies. These investments often require significant staff time and expertise to find, evaluate, select, and monitor. Because the active management component of returns in these alternative, less-efficient markets is extremely important to long-term success, endowments should have significant resources and expertise before investing in nontraditional asset classes.

Often, alternative investment funds in the United States will seek exemption from registration under the Investment Company Act of 1940 and accept capital commitments only from investors who are Qualified Purchasers. Generally, endowments must have at least $25 million of investments to qualify. In some instances, investments are placed privately without Securities and Exchange Commission (SEC) registration and are limited to accredited investors with assets in excess of $5 million. Thus, the resources and size of an endowment or foundation can dictate its universe of potential investments.

Some endowed institutions develop ethical investment policies that become constraints to help ensure that portfolio investment activity is consistent with the organization's goals and mores. These policies can guide portfolio managers in voting shareholder proxies on issues of social or political significance. In certain circumstances, such as apartheid in South Africa, ethical investment policies have been used in an attempt to foster change through shareholder resolutions and divestment. Other examples of socially responsible investing include the application of exclusion criteria related to child labor, gambling, tobacco, firearms, and violation of human rights. In Example 3-13, we show how investment objectives and constraints come together in the formulation of an investment policy statement for an endowment.

EXAMPLE 3-13 The City Arts School

The City Arts School (CAS) is an independent private school educating 500 children from 9th through 12th grade. Founded in 1920, it is located in a modest-sized city in the northeastern United States with a diverse socioeconomic and racial population. CAS has an outstanding reputation and draws students from the city and surrounding suburban communities. The school has an excellent program in the performing and visual arts; in addition, it offers a broad and innovative curriculum with small class sizes.

CAS has an annual operating budget of approximately $10 million, more than 90 percent of which goes to salaries and benefits for teachers and a small administrative staff. With conservative fiscal management, the school has built and maintained a fine campus over the years without the use of debt. Due to the limited availability of adjacent land or other space, the school is unlikely to expand in the foreseeable future. CAS's inflation rate has averaged 1 percent above that of the economy in general.

CAS has an endowment of \$30 million, composed of \$10 million for general unrestricted support, \$10 million for financial aid, \$5 million of small funds with various donor-specified use restrictions, and \$5 million of unrestricted funds functioning as endowment.

The CAS board consists of 15 elected directors, each serving three-year terms. In addition, the head of the school serves on the board *ex officio*. The board delegates responsibility for investing the endowment to an investment committee that includes at least three board members as well as other members of the CAS community who can offer investment expertise and guidance. Investments are monitored and implemented by the school's business and operations manager.

Proposed Statement of Endowment Goals: The goal of the CAS Endowment (and funds that the board has designated as endowment) is to provide significant, stable, and sustainable funding to support the school's annual operating budget and specific donor-designated programs. Endowment funds will be invested with the objective of earning high, long-term returns after inflation without undue risk of permanently impairing the long-term purchasing power of assets or incurring volatile short-term declines in asset values or annual spending flows.

Spending Policy for Endowment: The goal of the CAS Endowment spending policy is to provide a sustainable, stable annual source of income from the endowment to the operating budget of CAS. The spending policy helps provide financial discipline to the school by providing a clear, unequivocal amount of annual funding from the endowment consistent with sustainable long-term operations.

Spending from the endowment (and funds designated as endowment by the board) shall be determined by a spending rule that smoothes the volatility of spending from year to year using a weighted-average formula. The formula takes into account spending from the prior year as well as the endowment's current market value. Spending for a fiscal year shall be calculated by adding 70 percent of the prior year's spending amount to 30 percent of the endowment market value at the beginning of the prior fiscal year times the policy spending rate of 4.5 percent.

$$\begin{aligned}\text{Spending for fiscal year } t = {} & 70\% \\ & \times [\text{Spending for fiscal year } (t-1)] + 30\% \times [4.5\% \\ & \times \text{Endowment market value at beginning of fiscal year } (t-1)]\end{aligned}$$

Adjustments will be made to incorporate the effects of new gifts, additions, or fund decapitalizations. Spending from new gifts or additions to the endowment in their first year shall be at the same rate as other endowment funds adjusted pro rata to reflect the partial year of inclusion in the endowment.

Given these goals for the endowment, specify appropriate objectives and constraints.

Solution:

Return objectives. The goal of the CAS Endowment is to provide a significant annual distribution to support the school's programs while maintaining the fund's long-term purchasing power. In general, inflation for the school runs about 1 percent above that of the economy. Therefore, in order to maintain the fund's purchasing power with a 4.5 percent spending rate, net of investment management expenses the portfolio must generate a long-term return greater than 5.5 percent above a broad measure of inflation such as the U.S. CPI.

Risk objectives. CAS must address two primary risks in investing its endowment. As discussed above, CAS must protect the endowment's long-term purchasing power by generating real returns above spending. In the short term, the CAS Endowment should produce a reliable and somewhat stable flow of funding for programs. This short-term risk is tempered by CAS's spending rule, which smoothes distributions with a geometric moving average spending rate. In addition, endowment spending is not a very large part of the school's annual budget (less than 14 percent of revenues). Endowment spending could fall by as much as 20 percent and the impact on the budget would be less than 3 percent of revenues. CAS is debt free and has an above-average risk tolerance.

Liquidity. Only a small percentage of the fund, approximately 4 or 5 percent, is spent each year, and the fund's historical gift value should remain invested and not spent. A portion of the CAS Endowment pool, however, is composed of funds functioning as endowment. The board, in extraordinary circumstances, may decide to spend the FFE because the monies are not permanently restricted.

Time horizon. Endowment funds have an extremely long time horizon because they are expected to support activities in perpetuity.

Tax concerns. CAS is a tax-exempt organization, and returns on its investments are not taxed in most circumstances. The school should carefully consider any investment or gift that generates UBTI, because such an item could dramatically increase tax-reporting requirements.

Legal and regulatory factors. CAS's investments have very few legal and regulatory constraints. The school should, however, take precautions to avoid conflicts of interest, or the perception of conflicts, involving committee or board members. In addition to being poor and wasteful management, inappropriate transactions with individuals in a supervisory role may lead to sanctions and penalties under IRS regulations. In general, the school's financial and investment activities are under the purview of the state attorney general. Trustees are expected to act prudently, consistent with standards of sound business practice.

Unique circumstances. CAS is a small school with limited administrative and investment resources. Its endowment portfolio, although meaningful to the school and its operations, is not of sufficient scale to support dedicated internal investment staffing. All investments should be managed externally. CAS should view skeptically any investment that requires extensive monitoring, a close long-term relationship with external investment managers, or a high degree of sophisticated expertise to manage properly. Similarly, CAS should be wary of investments that require a high degree of active management skill to generate satisfactory returns. The school does not have the resources to identify, evaluate, and monitor the top managers in specialized investment areas. Furthermore, the size of its portfolio will not support a diversified investment program in nontraditional alternatives such as private equity. Even an aggressive allocation of 20 percent would amount to only $6 million, barely enough to make a single commitment to a top-tier private equity investment fund.

The investment committee has a relatively high turnover, with members serving only three-year terms. CAS runs the risk that new committee members renounce some long-term investments and act hastily to liquidate or pull support from worthy but underperforming investments. This risk is greatest with volatile, unconventional investments that may require patience, fortitude, and a contrarian mindset to endure difficult market environments.

4. THE INSURANCE INDUSTRY

The economic significance of the insurance industry lies in its unique role as an absorber of personal and business risks. By providing financial protection, the industry plays a key role in a country's economic growth and development. Because of the risk aspects of the business and the contractual obligations to policyholders, the insurance industry's traditional investment practices have been characterized as conservative. As we will discuss later, however, insurers have shown increasing risk tolerance in recent years.

The insurance industry is complex but can be divided into three broad product categories: life insurance, health insurance, and property and liability insurance. For purposes of considering investment policy, it is sufficient to narrow the categories to life and non–life (casualty) insurance companies. This division is consistent with the major classifications established by the insurance regulatory bodies and some, if not most, taxing authorities in the world's industrialized countries.

Insurance companies, whether life or casualty, are established either as **stock companies** (companies that have issued common equity shares) or as **mutuals** (companies with no stock that are owned by their policyholders). Mutuals traditionally have played a major role in certain segments of the insurance industry, but stockholder-owned companies are now the primary form of entry into the industry. Many of the major mutual insurance companies in the United States, Canada, the United Kingdom, and continental Europe have completed or are in the process of **demutualizing** (converting to stock companies). Although the investment operations of mutual and stock companies differ only slightly, the differences between life and non–life insurers are substantial, as we illustrate in the following sections.

4.1. Life Insurance Companies: Background and Investment Setting

Exposure to interest rate–related risk is one major characteristic of life insurers' investment setting. Besides fixed-income portfolio gains and losses related to interest rate changes, many life insurance company liabilities such as annuity contracts are interest rate sensitive. In addition, insurers also face the risk of disintermediation, which often becomes acute when interest rates are high.[18]

One type of disintermediation occurs when policyholders borrow against the accumulated cash value in insurance products such as ordinary life insurance.[19] U.S. life insurance companies experienced unprecedented disintermediation in the early 1980s. As interest rates reached record high levels (in the mid to high teens) during that period, policyholders took advantage of the option to borrow some or all of the accumulated cash value in their policies at the below-market policy loan rates (generally 5 to 9 percent) that were contractually defined in their insurance policies. The policy loan feature has long been considered an important life insurance policy provision. In the 1980s, the true cost of this option became clear to the

[18] **Disintermediation** occurs when individuals withdraw funds from financial intermediaries for deposit or investment in other financial intermediaries or investments offering a higher return (yield).

[19] **Ordinary life insurance** (also called **whole life insurance**) is a type of policy that typically provides level death benefits for the whole of the insured's life. The premium is typically a level amount determined by such factors as the insured's sex and age at the time the policy is issued, and the cash value is based on the insurer's estimate of the expected return on the investments that fund policy reserves. In contrast, **term life insurance** provides death benefits for a specified length of time and accumulates little or no cash values.

EXHIBIT 3-3 Analysis of Life Insurance Purchases in the United States: Selected Years, 1978–2002

	Percentage of Dollar Amount of Life Insurance Purchases			
Policy Type	1978	1988	1999	2002
Term life	52%	40%	57%	69%
Whole life	45	30	13	10
Universal life	NA	20	11	9
Variable life	NA	9	19	12
Other	3	1	0	0
Total	100%	100%	100%	100%

NA = not applicable.
Source: Life Insurance Fact Book (1979, 1989, 2000) and *ACLI Survey* (2003).

industry, as cash available for investment at the then prevailing double-digit interest rates was siphoned off in part to fund policy loans. When interest rates are high, insurers also face another type of disintermediation: the risk that policyholders will surrender their cash value life insurance policies for their accumulated cash values, in order to reinvest the proceeds at a higher interest rate. As a result of these forces, insurers face marketplace pressures to offer competitive cash value accumulation rates or **credited rates** (rates of interest credited to a policyholder's reserve account).

These developments have made the liabilities of life insurers more interest rate sensitive than before and have tended to shorten the duration of liabilities. Policyholders are now more prone to exercise their option to surrender a life insurance policy or annuity contract as they seek the most competitive credited rates and/or policy benefits. Surrender rates triggered by interest rate changes are more difficult to predict than mortality rates and thus are the more critical variable for many interest-sensitive life insurance products. Shorter liability durations have necessitated the shortening of the duration of life insurance company portfolios, or at least those segments designed to fund these interest rate–sensitive product liabilities.

Universal life, variable life, and variable universal life represent the insurance industry's response to disintermediation.[20] Companies developed these products to offset the competitive appeal of buying term insurance and investing the difference between term insurance premiums and the often higher premiums of ordinary life insurance policies. These new products provide life insurance buyers with a viable means of purchasing varying amounts of insurance protection along with an opportunity to save or invest at rates that vary with capital market and competitive conditions.

Exhibit 3-3 illustrates the growth of new individual life insurance forms in the United States, based on data provided by the American Council of Life Insurers.

[20]**Universal life** provides premium flexibility, an adjustable face amount of death benefits, and current market interest rates on the savings element. The universal life policyholder pays a specified amount for the insurance protection desired and can deposit funds in a savings account, for a fee. **Variable life insurance (unit-linked life insurance)** is a type of ordinary life insurance for which death benefits and cash values are linked to the investment performance of a policyholder-selected pool of investments held in a so-called separate account. **Variable universal life (flexible-premium variable life)** combines the flexibility of universal life with the investment choice flexibility of variable life.

As the increase in term life insurance purchases demonstrates, there is a trend toward unbundling insurance risk management and investment management. To attract customers, each of the new policy forms must offer competitive rates of return.

4.1.1. Risk Objectives

An insurance company's primary investment objective is to fund future policyholder benefits and claims. Because of the economic importance of the insurance industry, the investment portfolio of an insurer (life or non–life) is looked upon from a public policy viewpoint as a quasi-trust fund. Accordingly, conservative fiduciary principles limit the risk tolerance of an insurance company investment portfolio. Confidence in an insurance company's ability to pay benefits as they come due is a crucial element in the economy's financial foundation. Therefore, insurance companies are sensitive to the risk of any significant chance of principal loss or any significant interruption of investment income.

To absorb some modest loss of principal, U.S. life insurance companies are required to maintain an asset valuation reserve, a reserve established by the National Association of Insurance Commissioners (NAIC). Companies use specific NAIC-developed "quality tests" for each class of invested assets to determine the annual contributions to, and maximum amounts of, the reserve. The maximum reserve rates establish a substantial margin for absorbing investment losses. With a growing portfolio, however, a life company's asset valuation reserves may be inadequate. Surplus is thus vulnerable to write-downs if significant losses occur.[21]

Insurance regulators worldwide have been moving toward risk-based capital (RBC) requirements to assure that companies maintain adequate surplus to cover their risk exposures relating to both assets and liabilities. In the United States, RBC calculations are somewhat complex and attempt to allocate surplus in proportion to the asset and liability risk exposures of each insurance company. By subtracting the risk-based capital required from each company's total surplus, the regulators can estimate whether the company's surplus is sufficient. In addition, applying GAAP to both mutual and stock insurance companies requires the use of market valuation for most classes of assets and thus has increased balance sheet volatility. Absent a requirement that life insurance liabilities be marked to market, however, accounting statement implications may affect a company's risk tolerance in ways that are inconsistent with a market-based-valuation perspective of the company's risk exposure.

Asset/liability risk considerations figure prominently in life insurers' risk objectives, not only because of the need to fund insurance benefits but also because of the importance of interest rate–sensitive liabilities. Examples of such liabilities are annuities and deposit-type contracts, such as guaranteed investment contracts (GICs) and funding agreements (stable-value instruments similar to GICs).

The two aspects of interest rate risk are valuation concerns and reinvestment risk:

- *Valuation concerns*. In a period of changing interest rates, a mismatch between the duration of an insurance company's assets and that of its liabilities can lead to erosion of surplus. Life insurance companies are particularly sensitive to the losses that can result during periods of rising interest rates from holding assets with an average duration that exceeds the average duration of liabilities. (Adding to insurers' concerns is the fact that the risk of

[21]The excess of losses on assets over the assets' valuation reserve is a direct reduction in surplus. A **valuation reserve** is an allowance, created by a charge against earnings, to provide for losses in the value of the assets. **Surplus** is the net difference between the total assets and total liabilities of an insurance company; it is equivalent to policyholders' surplus for a mutual insurance company and stockholders' equity for a stock company.

disintermediation is greatest in such interest rate environments.) In these situations, the existence of valuation reserves alone may be insufficient to prevent a write-down of surplus, possibly creating a capital adequacy problem. Consequently, valuation concerns tend to limit insurers' risk tolerance.

- *Reinvestment risk*. For many life insurance companies, especially those competing for annuity business, yet another risk factor can be significant—reinvestment risk. **Reinvestment risk** is defined as the risk of reinvesting coupon income or principal at a rate less than the original coupon or purchase rate. For annuity contracts on which no interest is paid until maturity (the terminal date) of the contract, the guarantee rate typically includes the insurance company's best estimate of the rate(s) at which interest payments will be reinvested. If a company does not carefully manage its asset and liability durations, an unexpected decline in interest rates can jeopardize the profitability of these contracts. Thus, controlling reinvestment risk is also an important risk objective.

Asset/liability management (ALM) is the foundation for controlling both interest rate risk and liquidity for a life insurance company. Risk objectives addressing the mismatch of the duration of assets and liabilities are common.

Credit risk is also important in meeting insurance promises:

- *Credit risk*. Credit risk represents another potential source of income loss for insurance companies, although credit analysis has long been considered one of the industry's strengths. Insurers seek to control this risk through broad diversification and seek adequate compensation for taking risk in terms of the expected return or interest rate spread when investing in various asset classes. Risk objectives may relate to losses caused by credit risk.[22]

Another risk consideration relates to uncertainty in the timing of receipt of cash flows:

- *Cash-flow volatility*. Loss of income or delays in collecting and reinvesting cash flow from investments is another key aspect of risk for which life insurance companies have low tolerance. Compounding (interest on interest) is an integral part of the reserve funding formula and a source of surplus growth. Actuaries assume that investment income will be available for reinvestment at a rate at least equal to an assumed (minimum return) rate. Controlling cash-flow volatility is thus a risk objective.

Despite the above four risk-related considerations, competition has modified the traditional conservatism of life insurance companies, motivating them to accept and manage varying degrees of risk in pursuit of more competitive investment returns.

4.1.2. Return Objectives

Historically, a life insurance company's return requirements have been specified primarily by the rates that actuaries use to determine policyholder reserves,

[22]Recent changes in GAAP have further complicated the management of credit risk by U.S. insurance companies. The Financial Accounting Standard 115 and subsequent interpretative documents require a permanent write-down of the value of securities that have experienced an "Other Than Temporary Impairment" (OTTI). This type of impairment in value is defined as an unrealized loss that results from the decline in the market value of a security below its cost for an extended period of time. This Standard has been controversial and most likely will undergo additional modification because it does not allow for any subsequent write-up in value if the credit quality of the issuer improves and is so recognized in the market value. Also, declines in market value below cost that are caused by an increase in interest rates may require a permanent write-down under the current interpretation of FAS 115.

that is, accumulation rates for the funds held by the company for future disbursement.[23] In effect, the rate either continues as initially specified for the life of the contract or may change to reflect the company's actual investment experience, according to the contract terms. Interest is then credited to the reserve account at the specified rate; this rate can thus be defined as the minimum return requirement. If the insurer fails to earn the minimum return, its liabilities will increase by an accrual of interest that is greater than the increase in assets. The shortfall is reflected in a decrease in surplus or surplus reserves, assuming the simplest case. The insurer, in short, desires to earn a positive net interest spread, and return objectives may include a desired net interest spread. (The **net interest spread** is the difference between interest earned and interest credited to policyholders.) Reserve funding adequacy is monitored carefully by management, regulatory commissions, and insurance rating agencies such as A.M. Best, as well as through the claims paying rating services initiated by Moody's Investors Service, Standard & Poor's Corporation, and Fitch Ratings.

In the mid to late 1980s, Japanese life insurance companies issued policies that guaranteed what proved to be unsustainable reserve crediting rates—and guaranteed those rates for as long as 10 years. With the sharp decline in interest rates, stock prices, and real estate values during the 1990s in Japan, these companies sustained unprecedented losses and consequent erosion of the surplus of the Japanese life insurance industry. These events provided an important lesson regarding the setting of return objectives, crediting rates, and guarantee periods in a volatile investment environment.

In the United States, with whole-life insurance policies, the minimum statutory accumulation rate for most life insurance contracts ranges between 3 and 5.5 percent. Thus, in the higher interest rate environment of the 1970s and 1980s, the spread between life insurance companies' return on new investments and even the return on their entire portfolio exceeded the minimum returns by a widening margin. But as growing investor sophistication and competition in insurance markets led to higher credited rates, and as interest rates declined in the 1990s and early 2000s, the net interest spread narrowed quickly and dramatically. As a result, U.S. regulators have permitted minimum statutory accumulation rates to be reduced.

Consistently above-average investment returns should and do provide an insurance company with some competitive advantage in setting premiums. Life insurance companies have found that an improvement as small as 10 basis points (0.10 percent) in the total portfolio yield improves their competitive position and profitability significantly. Portfolio yields for most life portfolios, however, are more similar than different, as Exhibit 3-4 shows. To a large extent, this similarity reflects the role regulation plays in constraining the asset mix and quality characteristics of every life insurance company portfolio and the historical evolution of portfolio asset allocation in that regulatory environment.

Some companies have experimented with using total return rather than interest rate spread to measure their investment portfolios' performance and their products' profitability. When only the asset side of a balance sheet reflects market volatility, it is difficult to use total return measures. To the extent that comprehensive fair market value accounting standards are developed in the future, they will greatly enhance asset/liability management and performance and profitability measurement on a total return basis.

For companies selling annuity and guaranteed investment contracts, competitive investment returns have become necessary and spread margins are narrow. The annuity segment

[23]**Policyholder reserves** are a balance sheet liability for an insurance company; they represent the estimated payments to policyholders, as determined by actuaries, based on the types and terms of the various insurance policies issued by the company.

EXHIBIT 3-4 Portfolio Yields of U.S. Life Insurance Companies: Selected Years, 1975–2004

		Major Life Insurance Companies		
	Industry Rate	Prudential	Lincoln National	AXA Equitable-NY
1975	6.44%	6.47%	6.98%	6.22%
1985	9.87	9.07	8.49	8.72
1995	7.90	7.47	7.87	6.88
2000	7.40	6.41	6.93	6.70
2004	5.93	5.55	5.82	6.23

Note: Portfolio yield equals the ratio of net investment income (after expenses and before income taxes) to mean cash and invested assets.

Source: Life Insurance Fact Book (2001); *Best's Insurance Reports* (2005).

EXHIBIT 3-5 Reserves for Annuities and Guaranteed Investment Contracts for the U.S. Life Insurance Industry: Selected Years, 1970–2002

	Percentage of Total Reserves
1970	26.6%
1980	45.4
1990	66.7
2002	64.6

Source: *Life Insurance Fact Book* (2003).

of the life insurance business has accounted for approximately two thirds of total industry reserves for more than a decade (see Exhibit 3-5).

For these lines of business, competition comes from outside as well as from within the industry. These competitive pressures create a dilemma for insurance companies. While insurance companies are required to control risk, many companies feel compelled to mismatch asset/liability durations or downgrade the credit quality of their investments in an attempt to achieve higher returns for competitive reasons.

Segmentation of insurance company portfolios has promoted the establishment of subportfolio return objectives to promote competitive crediting rates for groups of contracts. The major life insurance companies find themselves specifying return requirements by major line of business, the result being that a single company's investment policy may incorporate multiple return objectives.

Another dimension of return objectives for life insurance companies relates to the need to grow surplus to support expanding business volume. Common stocks, equity investments in real estate, and private equity have been the investment alternatives most widely used to achieve surplus growth. Life companies establish return objectives for each of these classes of equity investments to reflect historical and expected returns. Many life insurance companies are evaluating a variety of capital appreciation strategies, as well as financial leverage, to supplement the narrowing contribution to surplus from the newer product lines that are more competitive and have lower profit margins.

4.1.3. Liquidity Requirements

Traditionally, life insurance companies have been characterized as needing minimal liquidity. Except during the depression of the 1930s and the disintermediation of the early 1980s, annual cash inflow has far exceeded cash outflow. Thus, the need to liquidate assets has been negligible, reflecting the growing volume of business, the longer-term nature of liabilities, and the rollover in portfolio assets from maturing securities and other forms of principal payments. However, volatile interest rate environments and the ever-increasing importance of annuity products require that life companies pay close attention to their liquidity requirements. Otherwise, insurers may be forced to sell bonds at a loss to meet surrenders of insurance policies in periods of sharply rising interest rates. In assessing their liquidity needs, insurers must address disintermediation and asset marketability risk.

- *Disintermediation.* In the United States, on four different occasions in the past 40 years (1966, 1970, 1974, and 1979–1981), inflation and high interest rates have forced life insurance companies to take measures to accommodate extraordinary net cash outflows. Initially, policy loan drains in conjunction with heavy forward commitment positions forced some remedial but temporary changes in investment strategies. Likewise, the trend of policy surrenders caused (1) actuaries to reevaluate and reduce their estimates of the duration of liabilities and (2) portfolio managers to reduce the average duration of the portfolio and in some cases add to liquidity reserves.

  In a period of rising interest rates, a mismatch between the duration of an insurance company's assets and its liabilities can create a net loss if the assets' duration exceeds that of the liabilities. If disintermediation occurs concurrently, the insurer may need to sell assets at a realized loss to meet liquidity needs. Thus, an asset/liability mismatch can exacerbate the effects of disintermediation.
- *Asset marketability risk.* The marketability of investments is important to insure ample liquidity. Life insurance companies have traditionally invested some portion of their portfolios in less liquid investments, such as private placement bonds, commercial mortgage loans, equity real estate, and venture capital. Increasingly, liquidity considerations are constraining the percentage invested in these asset classes. Also, forward commitment activity has been slowed by liquidity considerations. Such commitments represent agreements by life insurance companies to purchase private placement bonds or mortgages, with part or all of the settlement typically delayed from 6 to 18 months. The traditional stability and growth of cash flow fostered this practice in the 1960s and 1970s, but volatile interest rates and disintermediation have undermined the predictability of life companies' cash flow. Forward committing has thus waned in importance in recent years.

The growth and development of the derivatives market has broadened the life insurance industry's ability to manage interest rate risk and reduced companies' need to hold significant liquidity reserves. Many companies also maintain lines of credit with banks for added liquidity.

4.1.4. Time Horizon

Life insurance companies have long been considered the classic long-term investor. Traditionally, portfolio return objectives have been evaluated within the context of holding periods as long as 20 to 40 years. Most life insurance companies have traditionally sought long-term maturities for bond and mortgage investments. In addition, life companies have found equity investments (real estate, common stocks, convertible securities, and venture capital) attractive because of their capital appreciation potential and inflation (purchasing power) risk protection.

One reason that life insurance companies have traditionally segmented their portfolios is the recognition that particular product lines or lines of business have unique time horizons and return objectives. For example, group annuities are generally written with maturities of 2 to 10 years. Therefore, many, if not most, of the assets funding those products have comparable maturities (or, more accurately, durations).

ALM practices have tended to shorten the overall investment time horizon of the typical life insurance company. Today, portfolio segments have differing time horizons, reflected in each segment's investment policies.

4.1.5. Tax Concerns

Unlike pension funds and endowments, insurance companies are tax-paying rather than wholly or partially tax-exempt investors. As commercial enterprises, they are subject to income, capital gains, and other types of taxes in the countries where they operate. The types and application of taxes differ by country, but in all cases, taxes mean that insurance companies must focus on after-tax returns in their investment activities.

In a very simplified context, life insurance companies' investment income can be divided into two parts for tax purposes: the policyholders' share (that portion relating to the actuarially assumed rate necessary to fund reserves) and the corporate share (the balance that is transferred to surplus). Under present U.S. law, only the latter portion is taxed.

One very important tax consideration being watched carefully by the U.S. life insurance industry relates to the tax treatment of the so-called inside buildup of cash values under a life insurance policy or annuity. The deferral of taxes on the accumulation of cash values within a life insurance contract has been a long-standing characteristic of such products. In the United States, Congress periodically reassesses the tax deferral of such inside buildup for life and annuity products. Tax law changes that would reduce or eliminate the tax deferral granted to the inside buildup would create significant competitive issues for the life insurance industry.

4.1.6. Legal and Regulatory Factors

Insurance is a heavily regulated industry. In the United States, state rather than federal regulation prevails. The lack of uniformity of state regulation and the cost of meeting the unique requirements imposed by 50 different states impose costs on insurers. Currently, state regulation pervades all aspects of an insurance company's operations—permitted lines of business, product and policy forms, authorized investments, and the like. The NAIC, whose membership includes regulators from all 50 states, promulgates insurance industry accounting rules and financial statement forms. In 1999, the U.S. Congress passed the Financial Modernization Act, which essentially removed barriers to entry for banks, insurance companies, and investment brokerage firms that dated back to the Great Depression of the 1930s. Regulation of financial institutions in the United States is now more closely aligned with prevailing regulation in many other parts of the world. In Canada, regulation is federal, except for those companies doing business only within a specific province. At either level—federal or provincial—Canadian regulation is as pervasive as U.S. regulation. In Japan, the Ministry of Finance regulates insurance companies, while in the United Kingdom, the Department of Trade is the responsible governmental authority.

The relevant insurance department or ministry audit procedures ensure compliance with the regulations of the state or country where the company is domiciled. In most cases, these regulations are the primary constraint affecting investment policy. Important concepts related to regulatory and legal considerations include eligible investments, the prudent investor rule, and valuation methods.[24]

- *Eligible investments.* Insurance laws determine the classes of assets eligible for investment and may specify the quality standards for each asset class. In the United States, for example, many states' insurance laws require that for a bond issue to be eligible for investment, its interest coverage ratio (earnings plus interest divided by interest) must meet minimum standards over a specified time period (e.g., 1.5 times coverage over each of the past five years) or minimum credit ratings. Generally, regulations specify the percentage of an insurance company's assets that may be invested in a specific class of eligible assets. For example, in the United States, most states limit the value (at cost) of life companies' common stock holdings to no more than 20 percent of total admitted assets. Non-U.S. investments are also limited to some extent as a percentage of admitted assets in most states.
- *Prudent investor rule.* Although the scope of regulation is extensive, it is important to note that the prudent investor concept has been adopted in some U.S. states. Replacing traditional "laundry lists" of approved investments with prudent investor logic simplifies the regulatory process and allows life insurance companies much needed flexibility to keep up with the ever-changing array of investment alternatives. New York's leadership in this area is important because, traditionally, regulations of this state have been the model for insurance regulation in the United States. Despite a major effort in the mid-1990s, however, no model law or universal investment standards have been adopted by all U.S. states.
- *Valuation methods.* In the European Union, International Accounting Standards specify a set of valuation procedures. In the United States, uniform valuation methods are established and administered by the NAIC. In fact, the NAIC's *Security Valuation Book*, published at the end of each year, compiles the values or valuation bases to be used by insurance companies for portfolio securities. This book is the source of the valuation data listed in Schedule D of the annual statement that each company files with the insurance departments of the states in which it operates. Schedule D is an inventory of all bond and stock holdings at year-end and a recap of the year's transactions.

In summary, regulation has a profound effect on both the risk and return aspects of a life insurance company portfolio, primarily because it constrains two critical aspects of portfolio management—asset allocation and the universe of eligible investments.

4.1.7. Unique Circumstances

Each insurance company, whether life or non–life, may have unique circumstances attributable to factors other than the insurance products it provides. These idiosyncrasies may further modify portfolio policies. The company's size and the sufficiency of its surplus position are among the considerations influencing portfolio policy.

To conclude, we provide a sample investment policy statement. Although the format and content of investment policy statements are unique to each insurance company, Example 3-14 represents a typical IPS for a stock life insurance company.[25]

[24]The scope of regulation is not limited to these areas. Many life insurance and annuity products have investment features. In the United States and the European Union, life insurance companies are subject to anti-money-laundering regulation to prevent the use of such products for illegal purposes.

[25]A stock life insurance company is organized as a corporation owned by stockholders.

EXAMPLE 3-14 Investment Policy Statement for a Stock Life Insurer

ABC Life Insurance Company ("the Company") underwrites and markets life insurance and annuity products. The Company is licensed to do business in all 50 U.S. states. In recent years, the Company has expanded its operations outside the United States and now is licensed and doing business in one Asian and two European countries. The Company's total assets exceed $15 billion; the Company has surplus of more than $1 billion. Competition in its markets is increasing both from traditional insurance company competitors and more recently, from other financial institutions, such as banks and mutual funds. In response to this increased competition, the Company must take more risk and establish higher return objectives for its investment portfolio so as to maintain an adequate margin (spread) between its investment portfolio return and the weighted-average rates of return being credited to its interest-rate-sensitive life insurance policies and annuity contracts. The Company's investment objectives may be defined in terms of its return and risk objectives for each of the portfolio segments (for example, its real estate portfolio). The statement below reflects a common set of objectives that applies in whole or in part to each of the respective portfolio segments. Policy statements exist for each segment that contain details on segment-specific risk and return specifications. Capital market and insurance market conditions shape the achievement of these policy objectives.

Investment Philosophy: The assets of the Company should be invested to provide for the payment of all contractual obligations to policyholders and to contribute to the growth of surplus over the long-term. Therefore, the investment strategy will be based on prudent investment principles within the context of applicable insurance regulations. The strategy will seek to achieve the appropriate balance among: providing investment income to enhance profitability; maintaining liquidity and generating cash flow to meet all obligations; funding policyholder reserves within pricing strategies; and growing the value of surplus over time, thereby contributing to the Company's future growth.

Investment Goals, Objectives, and Constraints: The Company's investment goals and objectives will be stated in terms of return expectations and requirements and risk tolerance. The constraints under which the investment portfolio will be managed include liquidity considerations, time horizon, regulatory restrictions, tax considerations and unique requirements.

Return Objectives

The return objectives of the Company are twofold: (1) earn a sufficient return to fund all policyholder liabilities and match or exceed the expected returns factored into the pricing of the Company's various products, and (2) contribute to the growth of surplus through capital appreciation. The return objectives will be stated in terms of meeting or exceeding projected needs related to investment income, product pricing spreads, and total return. The return requirements may vary by portfolio segments that have been established for certain product lines or groupings of product lines.

Risk Tolerance

The risk tolerance of the Company is based on the competitive requirements of various product lines, asset/liability management factors, risk-based capital considerations, rating agency parameters and the responsibility to fulfill all short-term and long-term obligations to policyholders. Interest rate risk and credit (default) risk need to be monitored and managed to support the competitive position of the Company while providing for its long-term viability. The risk parameters may vary by segment.

Investment Constraints

The Company's investment constraints are defined in terms of the following factors, all or some of which may apply to specific portfolio segments:

Liquidity. The portfolio will be managed to meet the liquidity requirements so as to pay all benefits and expenses in a timely manner. Investment cash flows will be a primary source of liquidity, so as to minimize the need to hold lower yielding cash reserves. In addition, publicly traded securities will provide an additional source of liquidity.

Time horizon. The Company is a long-term investor and will establish duration targets for the portfolio and any product segments based on appropriate asset/liability management specifications.

Tax. Income tax considerations determine the mix of investments that provides the most favorable after-tax returns. From time to time, operating conditions or corporate tax planning requirements may mandate the realization or postponement of capital gains.

Regulatory. All investments must qualify under the insurance code of the state in which the Company is domiciled and the nondomestic insurance companies' regulations in the countries in which the Company operates.

Unique circumstance. The Company may invest in less liquid private placement bonds, commercial mortgage loans, real estate and private equity to enhance returns so long as liquidity requirements are not compromised.

Review schedule. This policy statement will be reviewed at least annually by the board of directors and is subject to modification based on significant changes in insurance or tax regulations as well as significant changes in the Company's financial position and/or capital- or insurance-market conditions.

Asset allocation. The Company's strategic allocation is designed to identify and authorize the strategies for achieving the objectives specified by the investment policy statement. The strategic asset allocation also recognizes the constraints (both regulatory and self-imposed) specified in the investment policy statement. The selection of authorized asset classes and their allocation percentages are recognized as key determinants of the success of the Company's investment activities. The strategic asset allocation will be set out in a separate document.

Rebalancing. Changes in market values and market conditions require periodic portfolio rebalancing on at least a quarterly (and in some cases a more frequent) basis. Cash flow, insofar as it is available, will be used to rebalance. It should be recognized that some asset classes, such as private placement bonds, private equity, commercial mortgage loans, and real estate, are less liquid than publicly traded securities. Therefore, under most conditions, these asset classes should not be allowed to exceed the target allocations specified in the strategic asset allocation.

Investment responsibilities. The board of directors is responsible for overseeing the invested assets and the investment process of the Company. The board will rely on both Company employees and/or external investment service providers for the ongoing management of the investment portfolio. Because of the number of parties involved, each entity's role must be identified to ensure operational efficiency, clear lines of communication and accountability in all aspects of the management of the investment portfolio of the Company.

Board of directors. The board of directors approves the investment policy statement and asset allocation at least annually. At least quarterly, the board will review the performance of the investment portfolio and review and approve all transactions for that quarter.

Investment Management Committee. The Investment Management Committee will be composed of investment and financial officers of the Company. They will have ongoing responsibility for the management of the investment portfolio. On a quarterly basis, the Investment Management Committee will review investment performance and cash flow requirements with the board of directors. On an annual basis, or when either the Company's financial condition or capital market conditions change, the Investment Management Committee will review the investment policy statement and asset allocation and recommend changes to the board.

External investment advisers. With the approval of the board of directors, the Investment Management Committee may retain external investment consultants and advisors to assist in the management of the investment portfolio or subparts thereof. All external investment advisors will be expected to manage all or any part of the portfolio in conformity with the investment policy statement and asset allocation.

Custodian. The Investment Management Committee is authorized to retain the services of a regulated bank or trust company to safeguard the cash and invested assets of the Company. The custodian will also be responsible for the payment and collection of all investment funds.

4.2. Non–Life Insurance Companies: Background and Investment Setting

The second broad insurance category is the non–life (casualty) sector, which includes but is not limited to health, property, liability, marine, surety, and workers' compensation insurance. For purposes of considering investment policy, these non–life companies are really quite similar even though the products they sell are rather diverse. The investment policies of a non–life company differ significantly from those of a life insurance company, however, because the liabilities, risk factors, and tax considerations for non–life companies are distinctly different from those for life companies. For example:

- Non–life liability durations tend to be shorter, and claim processing and payments periods are longer, than for life companies.
- Some (but not all) non–life liabilities are exposed to inflation risk, although liabilities are not directly exposed to interest rate risk as those of life insurance companies.
- In general, a life insurance company's liabilities are relatively certain in value but uncertain in timing, while a non–life insurance company's liabilities are relatively uncertain in both

value and timing, with the result that non–life insurance companies are exposed to more volatility in their operating results.

As detailed in this section, the investment policies and practices of non–life insurance companies in the United States are evolving, with changes brought on by both operating considerations and new tax laws. In fact, tax planning has dominated the investment policy of non–life companies for decades, reflecting the cyclical characteristics of this segment of the insurance industry. For reasons described in the following pages, asset/liability management is receiving increased attention.

A unique aspect of the casualty insurance industry is what is often described as the "long tail" that characterizes the industry's claims reporting, processing, and payment structure.[26] Whereas life insurance is heavily oriented toward products sold to or for individuals, commercial customers account for a very large portion of the total casualty insurance market. The long tail nature of many types of liability (both individual and commercial) and casualty insurance claims arises from the fact that months and years may pass between the date of the occurrence and reporting of the claim and the actual payment of a settlement to a policyholder. Many casualty industry claims are the subject of lawsuits to determine settlement amounts. Furthermore, some of these claims require expert evaluation to determine the extent of the damages—for example, a fire in a major manufacturing plant or damage to an oceangoing vessel. Thus, the liability structure of a casualty insurance company is very much a function of the products that it sells and the claims reporting and settlement process for those types of products.

From an asset/liability management perspective, most casualty insurance companies traditionally have been classified as having relatively short-term liabilities, even though the spectrum of casualty insurance policies covers a wide range of liability durations. One of the primary factors that limits the duration of a non–life company's assets is the so-called **underwriting (profitability) cycle,** generally averaging three to five years. These cycles typically result from adverse claims experience and/or periods of extremely competitive pricing. They often coincide with general business cycles and, in the low part of the cycle, frequently require companies to liquidate investments to supplement cash flow shortfalls.

Estimating the duration of a casualty insurance company's liabilities introduces a different set of issues than with life insurance liabilities. Using multiscenario and multifactor models, casualty actuaries attempt to capture (1) the underwriting cycle, (2) the liability durations by product line, and (3) any unique cash outflow characteristics. For non–life companies, business cycles and not interest rate cycles, per se, determine a company's need for liquidity through appropriate durations and maturities of assets.

4.2.1. Risk Objectives

Like life insurance companies, casualty insurance companies have a quasi-fiduciary role; thus, the ability to meet policyholders' claims is a dominant consideration influencing investment policy. The risks insured by casualty companies, however, are less predictable. In fact, for companies exposed to catastrophic events—such as hurricanes, tornadoes, and explosions—the potential for loss may be significantly greater. Furthermore, casualty policies frequently provide replacement cost or current cost coverage; thus inflation adds to the degree of risk. In setting risk objectives, casualty companies must consider both cash-flow characteristics and the common stock-to-surplus ratio.

[26]"Long tail" refers to the possibly long time span between the liability-triggering event and the filing of a claim related to it.

- *Cash-flow characteristics.* Not surprisingly, cash flows from casualty insurance operations can be quite erratic. Unlike life insurance companies, which historically have been able to project cash flows and make forward commitments, casualty companies must be prepared to meet operating cash gaps with investment income or maturing securities. Therefore, for the portion of the investment portfolio relating to policyholder reserves, casualty companies have low tolerance for loss of principal or diminishing investment income. Investment maturities and investment income must be predictable in order to directly offset the unpredictability of operating trends.

  Interestingly, no regulations require casualty insurance companies to maintain an asset valuation reserve, although risk-based capital requirements have been established in the United States. Regulators and rating agencies closely monitor the ratio of a casualty insurance company's premium income to its total surplus. Generally, this ratio is maintained between 2-to-1 and 3-to-1.
- *Common stock-to-surplus ratio.* Inflation worldwide has further reduced investment risk tolerance among many casualty insurers. In fact, volatile stock market conditions in the 1970s persuaded many casualty companies to reduce the percentage of surplus invested in common stock. Until then, it was not uncommon for a casualty insurance company to hold common stock investments equal to or greater than its total surplus. Regulators in the United States forced several major companies to liquidate large portions of their common stock holdings near the end of the 1974 bear market because of significant erosion of surplus. This liquidation impaired these companies' ability to increase volume and, in some cases, their ability to provide sufficient financial stability for existing volume of business.

  Essentially, the regulators gave such companies the option of reducing common stock holdings or of temporarily ceasing or curtailing the issuance of new policies. Needless to say, this experience reduced casualty companies' risk tolerance for the portion of the investment portfolio related to surplus. Unlike the life insurance industry, the casualty industry has almost no absolute limits imposed by regulation (in the United States, some states do limit commons stocks as a percentage of surplus). However, many casualty companies have adopted self-imposed limitations restricting common stocks at market value to some significant but limited portion (frequently one half to three quarters) of total surplus. During the bull market of the 1990s, many companies modified those self-imposed limits. Nevertheless, the attention paid to stock market risk exposure has prevented a repeat of the mid-1970s experience.

4.2.2. Return Objectives

Historically, most casualty insurance companies have not implicitly taken investment earnings into account when calculating premiums, in striking contrast to the accumulation rates long factored into life insurance premiums. For this reason, casualty insurance companies were once thought to be operating as if they were two separate organizations—an insurance company and an investment company operating a balanced fund (a fund holding a mixture of bonds and stocks). However, times have changed and the investment and operating functions are much more closely coordinated now. Factors influencing return objectives include competitive pricing policy, profitability, growth of surplus, tax considerations, and total return management.

- *Competitive policy pricing.* Low insurance policy premium rates, due to competition, provide an incentive for insurance companies to set high desired investment return objectives. The flip side is that high investment returns may induce insurance companies to lower their policy rates, even though a high level of returns cannot be sustained. In the late 1970s and early 1980s, for example, many casualty insurance companies, especially the larger ones, took advantage of the high interest rates being earned on new investments to lower insurance premiums or to delay the normal passthrough of cost increases to their customers. As a result of this strategy, casualty insurance premiums lagged the otherwise high rate of inflation that characterized the early 1980s. Once interest rates began to fall, projections of high investment returns became suspect. The operating margin decline that many casualty insurance companies experienced in the mid-1980s resulted, in part, from the mispricing of their products because of expected returns that did not materialize. The low interest rate and weak stock market environment of 2000 through 2002 reinforced the perception that insurers cannot rely on investment returns to cover underwriting losses and that underwriting quality and profitable pricing are important. Thus any influence of competitive policy pricing on a casualty company's return objectives needs to be assessed in light of well-thought-out capital market assumptions and the insurance company's ability to accept risk.

- *Profitability.* Investment income and the investment portfolio return are primary determinants of continuing profitability for the typical casualty company and, indeed, the industry. The underwriting cycle influences the volatility of both company and industry earnings. Return requirements for casualty companies are not framed in reference to a crediting rate for their policies; rather, casualty insurance portfolios are managed to maximize return on capital and surplus to the extent that prudent asset/liability management, surplus adequacy considerations, and management preferences will allow.

  Given the underwriting uncertainties inherent in the casualty insurance business, investment income obviously provides financial stability for the insurance reserves. In fact, investment earnings are expected to offset periodic underwriting losses (claims and expenses in excess of premium income) from the insurance side of the company. Most casualty insurance products are priced competitively, and thus casualty premium rates are generally not sufficiently ample or flexible to eliminate the loss aspects of the underwriting cycle. The insurance industry measures underwriting profitability using the "combined ratio," the percentage of premiums that an insurance company spends on claims and expenses. Over the past 25 years, the combined ratio for U.S.-based non–life insurance companies has been above 100 percent, reflecting underwriting losses, in over 60 percent of the years.
- *Growth of surplus.* An important function of a casualty company's investment operation is to provide growth of surplus, which in turn provides the opportunity to expand the volume of insurance the company can write. As mentioned earlier, the risk-taking capacity of a casualty insurance company is measured to a large extent by its ratio of premiums to capital and surplus. Generally, companies maintain this ratio between 2-to-1 and 3-to-1, although many well capitalized companies have lower ratios. Casualty companies have invested in common stocks, convertible securities, and alternative investments to achieve growth of surplus. These investments' return and marketability characteristics fit well within the industry's underwriting cycles.
- *Tax considerations.* Over the years, non–life insurance companies' investment results have been very sensitive to the after-tax return on the bond portfolio and to the tax benefits, when they exist, of certain kinds of investment returns. In the United States, these returns have included dividend income (through the exclusion of a portion of the dividends received by one corporation on stock issued by another corporation), realized long-term capital gains, and tax-exempt bonds. U.S. casualty insurance companies have historically favored the latter, especially when underwriting is profitable, to achieve the highest after-tax return. For many casualty companies, the flexibility to shift between taxable and tax-exempt bonds

has long been an important consideration as a key element of managing and optimizing after-tax income through the operating loss carryback and carryforward provisions of the U.S. tax code. Most companies have maintained some balance of taxable and tax-exempt bonds in their portfolios, shifting that mix as tax considerations warranted. Recent changes in the tax laws have diminished most of the tax benefits available to casualty insurance companies. Outside of the United States, tax-exempt securities for insurance companies either do not exist or are more limited in supply. For non-U.S. insurance companies, therefore, taxes are even more of a constraint.

- *Total return management*. Active bond portfolio management strategies designed to achieve total return, rather than yield or investment income goals only, have gained popularity among casualty insurance companies, especially large ones. Because GAAP and statutory reporting require that realized capital gains and losses flow through the income statement, the decline in interest rates and increase in bond prices since 1982 have encouraged casualty insurance portfolio managers to trade actively for total return in at least some portion of their bond portfolios.

One of the most interesting characteristics of casualty insurance companies is that their investment returns vary significantly from company to company. This variation reflects (1) the latitude permitted by insurance regulations; (2) differences in product mix, and thus in the duration of liabilities; (3) a particular company's tax position; (4) the emphasis placed on capital appreciation versus the income component of investment return; and (5) the strength of the company's capital and surplus positions. Exhibit 3-6 illustrates this contrast.[27]

4.2.3. Liquidity Requirements

Given the uncertainty of the cash flow from casualty insurance operations, liquidity has always been a paramount consideration for non–life companies, in sharp contrast with life insurance companies which face relatively certain cash flows, excluding policy loans and surrenders. In addition to its use in meeting cash flow needs, liquidity has also been a necessary adjunct of a casualty company's variable tax position. Historically, casualty companies have found it necessary to liquidate portions of their bond portfolios to increase tax-exempt income during periods of underwriting profits and to increase taxable income during periods of underwriting losses. Liquidity remains a necessity for casualty companies, providing portfolio flexibility under changing tax, underwriting, and interest rate conditions.

EXHIBIT 3-6 Pretax Portfolio Yields of U.S. Casualty Insurance Companies: Selected Years, 1975–2004

	Allstate	CNA Financial	State Farm	Travelers
1975	5.1%	5.3%	5.5%	7.3%
1985	6.8	9.7	8.2	7.2
1995	6.0	6.4	5.7	5.9
2000	5.5	6.4	6.0	6.8
2004	5.3	4.3	4.6	5.5

Source: *Best's Insurance Reports* (2005).

[27] Because insurers' portfolios are heavily weighted toward fixed income, the variation in yields for four major companies shown in Exhibit 3-6 provides evidence for variation in total returns (data for which are not readily available).

To meet its liquidity needs, the typical casualty company does several things related to the marketability and maturity schedule of its investments. Quite often it maintains a portfolio of short-term securities, such as commercial paper or Treasury bills, as an immediate liquidity reserve. In addition, it may also hold a portfolio of readily marketable government bonds of various maturities; maintain a balanced or laddered maturity schedule to ensure a sufficient rollover of assets; match some assets against seasonal cash-flow needs; or concentrate some portion of its bond portfolio in higher-quality bonds that are generally more marketable. Needless to say, such attention to maturity and marketability complements the limited risk tolerance and further modifies the return objectives of casualty insurers.

4.2.4. Time Horizon The time horizon of casualty insurance companies is a function of two primary factors. First, the durations of casualty liabilities are typically shorter than those of life insurance liabilities. Second, underwriting cycles affect the mix of taxable and tax-exempt bond holdings. Because the tax-exempt yield curve in the United States tends to be more positively sloped than the taxable curve, casualty companies find that they must invest in longer maturities (15 to 30 years) than the typical life company to optimize the yield advantage offered by tax-exempt securities (see Exhibit 3-7).

Differences in the average maturity of bond portfolios between casualty and life insurance companies may also reflect the companies' willingness to accept interest rate risk via asset/liability duration mismatches and trade at least some portion of their portfolios through a market or underwriting cycle.

In terms of common stock investments, casualty companies historically have been long-term investors, with growth of surplus being the primary return objective of their portfolios' stock portion. As noted earlier, realized gains and losses flow through the income statement. Currently, the long-term equity investor status of the industry has been modified by objectives related to current reported earnings that have in turn led to some additional turnover in the common stock portfolio and more active management of the total portfolio.

4.2.5. Tax Concerns Tax considerations are a very important factor in determining casualty insurance companies' investment policy. Prior to changes in the tax law in 1986, U.S. casualty insurance companies operated under a relatively simple and straightforward set

EXHIBIT 3-7 Comparison of Average Maturity of Bond Portfolios of Selected U.S. Non–life and Life Insurance Companies: Year-End 2004

Company	Average Maturity of Bond Portfolio (years)
Casualty	
Allstate	13
CNA Financial	14
State Farm	7
Travelers	7
Life	
AXA Equitable-NY	11
Lincoln National	9
Prudential	8

Source: Best's Insurance Reports (2005).

of tax provisions. Under those laws, their investment policy was directed toward achieving the appropriate balance between taxable and tax-exempt income on one hand, and taking advantage of the lower capital gains tax rate and corporate dividend exclusion, where possible, on the other.

As a result of the 1986 changes, tax-exempt bond income became subject to tax for U.S. casualty insurance companies. Applying the current tax provisions requires a series of calculations to determine the net tax being levied on tax-exempt bond income. Because the equations must factor in both the operating profit or loss characteristics of the casualty company and alternative minimum tax provisions of the code, a computer model is generally needed to determine the appropriate asset allocation, if any, between tax-exempt and taxable securities for both new purchases and existing holdings. The complexities and implications of the taxation of tax-exempt bond income for casualty companies are beyond the scope of this chapter.

As in the life insurance industry, casualty insurers are likely to be subjected to further tax code modification, which increases uncertainty for the investment manager as to the tax consequences of certain portfolio activities or alternatives when measured over a long time horizon. Tax considerations also shape the investment policy of non-U.S. casualty insurance companies. Portfolio managers typically work closely with the companies' tax advisers to measure and monitor the tax implications of various portfolio strategies.

4.2.6. Legal and Regulatory Factors

Although the insurance industry in general is heavily regulated, casualty company investment regulation is relatively permissive. On the one hand, classes of eligible assets and quality standards for each class are specified just as they are for life companies. In the United States, New York state law, which is considered the most restrictive, requires that assets equal to 50 percent of unearned premium and loss reserves combined be maintained in "eligible bonds and mortgages." Beyond these general restrictions, however, casualty insurance companies are permitted to invest the remainder of their assets in a relatively broad array of bonds, mortgages, stocks, and real estate, without restriction as to the amount invested in any particular asset class (except in certain states that limit common stock and/or real estate holdings).

A casualty company is not required to maintain an asset valuation reserve. In essence, then, the surplus of a casualty company reflects the full impact of increases and decreases in the market value of stocks. The United States, however, has recently established risk-based capital regulations for the casualty industry. U.S. risk-based capital regulations for casualty insurers specify the minimum amount of capital that an insurer must hold as a function of the size and degree of the asset risk, credit risk, underwriting risk, and off-balance-sheet risk that the insurer takes.[28]

4.2.7. Determination of Portfolio Policies

As in the case of life insurance companies, casualty companies' limited investment risk tolerance is the dominant factor in determining their investment policy. Because of contractual liabilities and difficulty in forecasting the cash flow from insurance operations, casualty companies seek some degree of safety from the assets offsetting insurance reserves. Indeed, casualty companies' willingness to assume investment

[28]**Asset risk** addresses fluctuation in market value. **Credit risk** addresses probability of default. **Underwriting risk** arises from underestimating liabilities from business already written or inadequately pricing current or prospective business. **Off-balance-sheet risk** addresses the risk from items not reflected in the balance sheet.

risk with the assets offsetting surplus has been moderated, or is at least subject to more careful management, as a result of market volatility in recent years.

Over and above liquidity needs, which are clearly important, casualty insurance companies develop a significant portfolio of stocks and bonds and generate a high level of income to supplement or offset insurance underwriting gains and losses. Capital appreciation also builds the surplus base and supports additional investment in the business. The structure of a casualty company's bond portfolio between taxable and tax-exempt securities depends on the company's underwriting experience and current tax policy. A casualty company's investment and business operating policies and strategies must be closely coordinated given the volatility of both the capital markets and the casualty insurance markets.

To conclude, we provide a sample investment policy statement. The format and content of investment policy statements are of course unique to each insurance company; however, Example 3-15 details an investment policy statement for a typical casualty insurance company.

EXAMPLE 3-15 Investment Policy Statement for a Casualty Insurance Company

Cornish Casualty Insurance Company ("the Company") underwrites auto and homeowners insurance. The company is licensed to do business in all 50 U.S. states. In recent years, the Company's business has been growing steadily, and its board of directors has approved a strategic plan for increasing its growth rate and profitability. The Company's total assets exceed $5 billion, and its surplus approaches $2 billion. The company is facing increased competition in its markets from companies selling auto and homeowners insurance through the Internet, as well as from other direct sellers. This competitive environment has focused the board and management's attention on increasing the after-tax return on the bond portfolio and enhancing the growth of surplus. The company's chief investment officer (CIO) has been asked to revise the Company's investment policy statement to reflect the changes that will be necessary to meet the new growth targets. The CIO has revised the return and risk objectives for the overall portfolio and various portfolio segments. Following are the investment objectives and constraints under which the Company's investment portfolio will be managed.

Investment Philosophy: The assets of the Company should be invested to provide for the payment of all contractual obligations to policyholders and to contribute to the growth of surplus over the long term. Therefore, the investment strategy will be based on prudent investment principles within the context of applicable insurance regulations. The strategy will seek to achieve the appropriate balance among: providing investment income to enhance profitability; maintaining liquidity and generating cash flow to meet all obligations; and growing the value of assets over time, thereby contributing to the Company's ability to write additional business and grow premium income.

Investment Goals, Objectives, and Constraints: The Company's investment goals and objectives will be stated in terms of return expectations and requirements and risk tolerance. The constraints under which the investment portfolio will be managed include liquidity considerations, time horizon, regulatory restrictions, tax considerations and unique requirements.

Return Objectives

The return objectives of the Company are threefold: (1) earn a sufficient return to fund all policyholder liabilities, (2) support the competitive pricing of all products, and (3) contribute to the growth of surplus through capital appreciation. The return objectives will be measured in terms of meeting or exceeding projections of investment income and total return.

Risk Tolerance

The risk tolerance of the Company is based on the competitive requirements of various product lines, risk- based capital considerations, and the responsibility to fulfill all short-term and long-term obligations to policyholders. Credit (default) risk and stock market risk need to be monitored and managed so as to support the competitive position of the Company while providing for its long-term viability.

Investment Constraints

The Company's investment constraints can be defined in terms of the following factors:

Liquidity. The portfolio will be managed to meet the liquidity requirements to pay all benefits and expenses in a timely manner. Investment cash flows will be a primary source of liquidity, to minimize lower yielding cash reserves. In addition, publicly traded securities will provide an important additional source of liquidity.

Time horizon. The Company is a long-term investor but will adjust the average maturity of the bond portfolio in line with the relative attractiveness of the after tax return on taxable versus tax-exempt bonds.

Tax. Tax considerations determine the optimal allocation within the bond portfolio between taxable and tax-exempt bonds. Tax considerations may also play a role in the realization of gains and losses for both the bond and stock portfolios.

Regulatory. All investments must qualify under the insurance law of the state in which the Company is domiciled.

Unique circumstances. Private placement bonds are not authorized and investments in commercial mortgage loans and real estate are limited, due to liquidity considerations.

Review schedule. This policy statement will be reviewed at least annually by the board of directors and is subject to modification based on significant changes in insurance or tax regulations as well as significant changes in the Company's financial position and/or capital or insurance market conditions.

[Other parts of the investment policy statement are omitted.]

5. BANKS AND OTHER INSTITUTIONAL INVESTORS

The final type of institutional investor that we discuss in detail is banks.

5.1. Banks: Background and Investment Setting

Banks are financial intermediaries involved in taking deposits and lending money. Nearly everywhere, however, the scope of banks' activities has evolved and widened over time, although distinct regional and national traditions remain. Western Europe and Canada follow the model of universal banking, in which traditional banking (involving deposit-taking and lending), securities underwriting, and insurance (in Europe) are organized under one corporate roof.[29] In this universal banking model, banks can provide one-stop shopping for financial services. In contrast to this model, in the twentieth century the United States and Japan evolved regulatory separations between commercial banking and investment banking (security underwriting) activities. Gradually, this separation has eroded in the United States, as highlighted by the 1998 merger of Citicorp (a holding company that included Citibank) and Travelers Group (a holding company that included Travelers Insurance and Salomon Smith Barney) and by the Gramm–Leach–Bliley Act of 1999, which permits affiliations under a financial holding company structure. Nevertheless, important differences in regulatory constraints and business structures persist among banks internationally.

Banks' liabilities consist chiefly of time and demand deposits[30] (as much as 90 percent of total liabilities and capital for smaller banks) but also include purchased funds and sometimes publicly traded debt. The asset side of the balance sheet consists of loan and securities portfolios as well as an assortment of other assets. For Federal Deposit Insurance Corporation (FDIC)-insured U.S. commercial banks as of the end of 2002, loans and leases represented on average 58 percent of assets. Loans may include real estate, commercial, individual, and agricultural loans. Securities represented 19 percent of total assets; other assets (trading accounts, bank premises and fixed assets, and other real estate owned) were 14 percent; and cash and federal funds represented 5 percent and 4 percent, respectively.

Traditionally, a bank's portfolio of investment securities has been a residual use of funds after loan demand has been met. The securities portfolio nevertheless plays a key role in managing a bank's risk and liquidity positions relative to its liabilities. Consequently, a bank's asset/liability risk management committee (ALCO) is generally in charge of overseeing the bank's securities portfolio. Exhibit 3-8 sets a context for understanding a bank's ALCO's concerns. Although banks have fee and other noninterest sources of income, and, of course, noninterest expenses, interest revenues, and costs are the chief financial variables affecting bank profitability. The quantity, duration, and credit quality of both the loan and securities portfolio affects a bank's interest revenues. On the market-value balance sheet, interest rate risk affects the market value of net worth representing the value of equity claims on the bank. Observing the bank's financial performance, the ALCO can make needed changes in assets and liabilities.

Some more detail is helpful. Among the profitability measures that the ALCO will monitor are the following:

- The **net interest margin,** already mentioned, equals net interest income (interest income minus interest expense) divided by average earning assets. Net interest margin is a summary measure of the net interest return earned on income-producing assets such as loans and bonds.[31]

[29]**Bancassurance** is the term that has developed to describe the sale of insurance by banks. As of 2004, more than 50 percent of life insurance is sold through banks in Spain, France, and Italy, and about 20 percent is sold through banks in the United Kingdom and Germany. Although banks in Japan have been permitted to sell insurance products since 2002 and in the United States since 1999, banks constitute a minor share of the insurance market in these countries.

[30]A **time deposit** is a deposit requiring advance notice prior to a withdrawal; a **demand deposit** is one that can be drawn upon without prior notice, such as a checking account.

[31]Earning assets include all assets that generate explicit interest income (plus lease receipts) but exclude discount instruments such as acceptances.

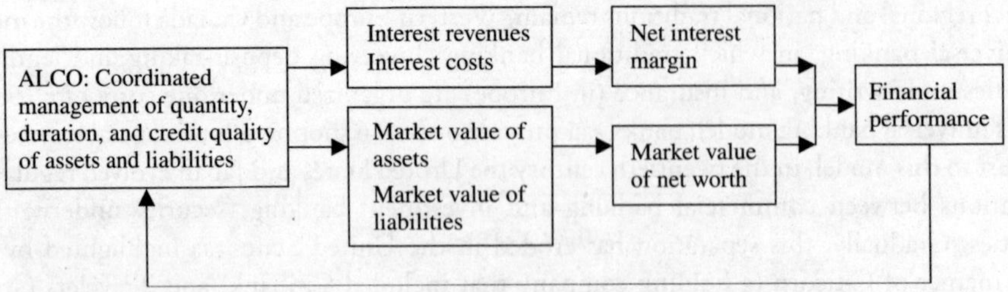

EXHIBIT 3-8 Elements of the ALM Process

- The **interest spread** equals the average yield on earning assets minus the average percent cost of interest-bearing liabilities. The interest spread is a measure of the bank's ability to invest in assets yielding more than the cost of its sources of funding.

Because both interest income and interest expense fluctuate in response to interest rate changes, net interest margin and interest spread are key indicators of a bank's ability to profitably manage interest rate risk. Among the risk measures the ALCO will monitor are the following:

- The **leverage-adjusted duration gap** is defined as $D_A - kD_L$, where D_A is the duration of assets, D_L is the duration of liabilities, and $k = L/A$, the ratio of the market value of liabilities (L) to the market value of assets (A). The leverage-adjusted duration gap measures a bank's overall interest rate exposure. For a positive interest rate shock (unexpected increase in rates), the market value of net worth will decrease for a bank with a positive gap; be unaffected for a bank with a zero gap (an immunized balance sheet); and increase for a bank with a negative gap.[32]
- Position and aggregate Value at Risk (VaR) are money measures of the minimum value of losses expected over a specified time period (e.g., a day, a quarter, or a year) at a given level of probability (often 0.05 or 0.01). As a result of risk-based capital regulatory initiatives internationally, nearly all banks track this measure of exposure to large losses.
- Credit measures of risk may include both internally developed and commercially available measures such as CreditMetrics.

A bank's securities portfolio plays an important role in achieving its financial performance objectives. According to one survey, banks' objectives in managing securities portfolios include the following, listed in order of importance[33]:

- *To manage overall interest rate risk of the balance sheet*. In contrast to business, consumer, and mortgage loans, bank-held securities are negotiable instruments trading in generally liquid markets that can be bought and sold quickly. Therefore, securities are the natural adjustment mechanism for interest rate risk. For example, if the duration of equity is higher than desired, a bank can shorten it by shortening the maturity of its securities portfolio.

---

[32]The change in the market value of net worth for an interest rate shock is approximately equal to the leverage-adjusted duration gap times the size of the bank (measured by A) times the size of the interest rate shock. Bankers also use other gap concepts in measuring interest rate risk. See Koch and MacDonald (2003).

[33]BAI Foundation (1995).

EXHIBIT 3-9 U.S. Commercial Banks: Investment Securities Weights (Trading Account Not Included): Year-End 2003

Asset Class	All Commercial Banks
U.S. Treasury securities	5.2%
U.S. government agency and corporate securities	68.8
Municipal securities	8.3
Other domestic debt securities	10.6
Non-U.S. debt securities	5.2
Equities	1.8

Source: www.financialservicesfacts.org.

- *To manage liquidity.* Banks use their securities portfolios to assure adequate cash is available to them. The rationale for selling securities to meet liquidity needs is again the ready marketability of securities.
- *To produce income.* Banks' securities portfolios frequently account for a quarter or more of total revenue.
- *To manage credit risk.* The securities portfolio is used to modify and diversify the overall credit risk exposure to a desired level. Banks frequently assume substantial credit risk in their loan portfolios; they can balance that risk by assuming minimal credit risk in their securities portfolio. Additionally, they can use the securities portfolio to diversify risk when the loan portfolio is not adequately diversified.

Banks also use their securities portfolios to meet other needs. For example, in the United States, banks must hold (pledge) government securities against the uninsured portion of deposits (an example of a **pledging requirement**—i.e., a required collateral use of assets).

Just as a bank's liabilities are interest-rate sensitive (as is its loan portfolio, on the asset side), a bank's security portfolios consist almost exclusively of fixed-income securities. This characteristic, as well as the bias toward low-credit risk holdings, is reinforced by regulatory constraints on securities holdings. Exhibit 3-9 gives the average asset class weights of U.S. commercial banks' securities portfolios (because of rounding, weights do not sum to exactly 100). We note that Exhibit 3-9 does not show off-balance-sheet derivatives used to manage interest rate and credit risk.

The major trend in banks' securities holdings during the past 10 years or more has been the decline in holdings of tax-exempt bonds and the increase in holdings of mortgage-backed securities, which are included under corporate securities in the above exhibit.

5.1.1. Risk Objectives

As already emphasized, banks' risk objectives are dominated by ALM considerations that focus on funding liabilities. Therefore, risk relative to liabilities, rather than absolute risk, is of primary concern. Although banks would like to earn high interest margins, they must not assume a level of risk that jeopardizes their ability to meet their liabilities to depositors and other entities. Overall, banks have below-average risk tolerance as concerns the securities portfolio.

5.1.2. Return Objectives

A bank's return objectives for its securities portfolio are driven by the need to earn a positive return on invested capital. For the interest-income part of return, the portfolio manager pursues this objective by attempting to earn a positive spread over the cost of funds.

5.1.3. Liquidity Requirements

A bank's liquidity position is a key management and regulatory concern. Liquidity requirements are determined by net outflows of deposits, if any, as well as demand for loans.

5.1.4. Time Horizon

A bank's time horizon for its securities portfolio reflects its need to manage interest rate risk while earning a positive return on invested capital. A bank's liability structure typically reflects an overall shorter maturity than its loan portfolio, placing a risk management constraint on the time horizon length for its securities portfolio. This time horizon generally falls in the three- to seven-year range (intermediate term).

5.1.5. Tax Concerns

Banks' securities portfolios are fully taxable. In the United States prior to 1983, the full amount of interest used to finance the purchase of tax-exempt securities was tax deductible, and banks were major buyers of municipal bonds. Since 1986, such deductions have been completely disallowed for the purchase of most municipal bonds, and U.S. banks' portfolios have been concentrated in taxable securities. In the United States since 1983 securities gains and losses affect net operating income. Thus realized securities losses decrease reported operating income, while securities gains increase reported operating income. According to some observers, this accounting treatment creates an incentive not to sell securities showing unrealized losses, providing a mechanism by which earnings can be managed.

5.1.6. Legal and Regulatory Factors

Regulations place restrictions on banks' holdings of common shares and below-investment-grade risk fixed-income securities. To meet legal reserve and pledging requirements banks may need to hold substantial amounts of short-term government securities. Risk-based capital (RBC) regulations are a major regulatory development worldwide affecting banks' risk-taking incentives. RBC requirements restrain bank risk-taking by linking the formula for required capital to the credit risk of the bank's assets, both on and off balance sheet. To illustrate this type of regulation, following the Basel Accord, since 1993 bank assets have been placed in one of four risk categories involving risk weights of 0 percent, 20 percent, 50 percent, and 100 percent, respectively.[34] A risk weight of 100, for example, applies to most bank loans. That weight means that 100 percent of the loan is subject to the baseline minimum 8 percent capital requirement. Under Basel II, proposed for implementation in 2006, banks will place assets in risk-exposure categories involving weights of 0 percent, 20 percent, 50 percent, 100 percent, and 150 percent, respectively. In contrast to the original Basel Accord, Basel II accounts for credit-quality differences within a given security type.

5.1.7. Unique Circumstances

There are no common unique circumstances to highlight relative to banks' securities investment activities. That situation stands in contrast to banks' lending activities, in which banks may consider factors such as historical banking relationships and community needs, which may be viewed as unique circumstances.

Example 3-16 excerpts the investment policy statement of a hypothetical small commercial bank. We incorporated this chapter's investment objectives and constraints framework in its

[34]The Basel Accord, sponsored by the Bank for International Settlements, applies to the banks of a group of major industrialized countries.

format, and we included a section on authorized investments that typically is found in such documents. The IPS excerpts cover many of the major topics that would be included in an IPS for a typical U.S. commercial bank (referred to as the "Bank").

EXAMPLE 3-16 Investment Policy Statement for a Commercial Bank

Purpose: The purpose of the investment policy statement (IPS) is to set forth the policies and procedures that govern the administration of all the Bank's investment activities. The Bank's Money Market Account is subject to additional constraints set forth in a later section of the IPS.

Responsibility: The Bank's board of directors (the "Board") is responsible for formulating and implementing investment policies. The Board delegates authority for making specific investments to the Bank's officers ("Management") designated in Exhibit A attached to this IPS, for investments consistent with this IPS. The Board also appoints an investment committee (the "Committee") to act as a liaison between the Board and Management and to carry out the following functions:

1. Monitor and review all investment decisions for compliance with the IPS and with federal and state regulations.
2. Review the IPS and recommend changes to it to the Board when appropriate.

Investment Objectives and Constraints: The primary purposes of the investment portfolio are to provide liquidity and to control the overall interest rate and credit risk exposures of the Bank. The portfolio will convert excess cash resulting from net deposit inflows and/or slack loan demand into earning assets. The portfolio will be drawn down when needed to meet net deposit outflows, loan demand, or other contingencies.

Return requirements. The Bank will attempt to earn an average positive spread over the cost of funds.

Risk Objectives:

- Because of the need to be able satisfy depositor and other liabilities at short notice and taking account of the typical characteristics of its loan portfolio, the Bank's tolerance for interest rate, credit, and liquidity risk in its securities portfolio is below average.
- The yield on investments is secondary to liquidity and safety of principal.
- To limit the risk of loss as a result of an individual issuer default, the Bank will maintain adequate diversification in its holdings.

Tax. As a taxable corporation the Bank will appraise taxable and tax-exempt investments on an after-tax basis.

Regulatory. All investments must qualify under state and federal banking regulations governing the investment activities of the Bank.

Unique Circumstances. None.

Authorized Investments: The following investments are legally permitted by Federal Regulations and authorized by the Board:

1. U.S. Treasury securities.
2. U.S. government agency and agency-guaranteed securities.
3. Certificates of deposit and bankers acceptances:

   a. Insured CDs. Negotiable and nonnegotiable CDs of any domestic commercial bank or savings and loan association may be purchased.
   b. Uninsured CDs. Investment in excess of $100,000 in the CDs of a single domestic bank may be made only in those banks shown on the Approved List (Exhibit B).
   c. Eurodollar CDs. Investments may be made only in such CDs issued by banks on the Approved List.
   d. Yankee CDs. Investments may be made only in such CDs issued by banks on the Approved List.
   e. Banker's acceptances. Investments are limited to accepting banks on the Approved List.
   f. Federal funds sold. Sales of federal funds may be made only to those institutions on the Approved List.
   g. Repurchase agreements (repos).
      i. The term shall not exceed 30 days, although a continuous agreement (remaining in effect until cancelled) is allowed.
      ii. The securities acceptable for purchase under a repo are those issued by the U.S. Treasury and agencies of the U.S. government.
      iii. The institutions with which repos may be made are limited to those on the Approved List.
   h. Reverse repurchase agreements (reverse repos). Reverse repos may be used so long as no more than 40 percent of the funds so obtained are used to purchase additional securities.

Maturity of Investments: To control the risk of loss resulting from an increase in the level of interest rates, Management is restricted to investments that mature within five years. This restriction does not apply to securities repurchased under the provisions of a repurchase agreement.

Diversification Requirements:

1. U.S. Treasury and agency securities. These may be held in unlimited quantities.
2. Securities not guaranteed by the U.S. Government, its agencies, or instrumentalities are subject to an overall maximum 10 percent commitment at cost.

Unauthorized Transactions:

1. Short sales.
2. Adjusted trades. The Bank may not hide an investment loss by an adjusted trade—that is, selling a security at a fictitiously high price to a dealer and simultaneously buying another overpriced security from the same dealer.

[Exhibits and other sections omitted.]

5.2. Other Institutional Investors: Investment Intermediaries

As we define the term, *institutional investors* are financial intermediaries in various legal forms with relatively large amounts of money to invest. The institutional investors previously discussed in this chapter (pension plans, foundations, endowments, insurance companies, and banks) have well-defined purposes besides investing. Banks take deposits and make loans, for example; pension plans have the specific purpose of providing retirement income.

Investment companies constitute another type of institutional investor that is important in financial markets. Investment companies include such investment vehicles as mutual funds (open-end investment companies), closed-end funds (closed-end investment companies), unit trusts, and exchange-traded funds. All these vehicles represent pooled investor funds invested in equity and fixed-income markets. Investment companies are pure investment vehicles in the sense that they have no other corporate purpose besides investing. We might aptly call them investment intermediaries. Each investment company selects its specific investment objectives and describes objectives, constraints, and costs in legally prescribed formats (e.g., a prospectus) and draws in funds from investors who are attracted to it for various portfolio purposes. Commodity pools serve similar purposes, but in futures rather than equity and fixed-income markets. Hedge funds are another type of investment vehicle that falls under the rubric of institutional investors. Hedge funds differ from investment companies in that they market to other institutional investors and to high-net-worth individuals exclusively; in addition, they are subject to fewer regulations.

One cannot generally characterize the investment objects and constraints of a given type of investment intermediary with the expectation that it will apply to all members of the group. Mutual funds, for example, cover the range of equity and fixed-income investment styles; one cannot characterize the return requirement and risk tolerance of "a mutual fund" in general, as we have done for other institutional investors such as life insurers. Readers who may be involved in managing equity or fixed-income mutual funds will find relevant guidance in the chapters on equity portfolio management and fixed-income portfolio management, respectively.

Nonfinancial corporations (i.e., businesses), although not financial intermediaries, are major investors in **money markets** (markets for fixed-income securities with maturities of one year or less) to manage their cash positions. "Cash," of course, includes "liquid cash" such as funds held in demand deposits and very short-term money market securities, and "long-term" or "core" cash, which is invested in longer-term money market instruments. These investments are part of the corporate function of cash management, which typically falls under the responsibilities of an organization's corporate treasurer. For most companies, liquidity and safety of principal are paramount investment considerations in cash management. Companies with very large cash positions will actively manage the composition of the cash position relative to anticipated cash needs (including seasonal needs), nondomestic currency needs, and tax concerns. Cash management is an important function for all the institutional investors previously discussed as well as for governmental units.[35]

[35] See Kallberg and Parkinson (1993) for more on cash management.

CHAPTER 4

CAPITAL MARKET EXPECTATIONS

John P. Calverley
American Express Bank
London, England

Alan M. Meder, CFA
Duff & Phelps Investment Management Co.
Chicago, Illinois

Brian D. Singer, CFA
UBS Global Asset Management
London, England

Renato Staub
UBS Global Asset Management
Chicago, Illinois

1. INTRODUCTION

A noted investment authority has written that the "fundamental law of investing is the uncertainty of the future."[1] Yet investors have no choice but to forecast at least elements of the future because nearly all investment decisions look toward it. Specifically, investment decisions incorporate the decision maker's expectations concerning factors and events believed to affect investment values. The decision maker finally integrates these views into expectations about the risk and return prospects of individual assets and groups of assets.

[1] Peter L. Bernstein in the foreword to Rapaport and Mauboussin (2001), p. xiii.

The particular concern of this chapter is **capital market expectations** (CME): the investor's expectations concerning the risk and return prospects of asset classes, however broadly or narrowly the investor defines those asset classes. Capital market expectations are an essential input to formulating a strategic asset allocation. For example, if an investor's investment policy statement specifies and defines eight permissible asset classes, the investor will need to have formulated long-term expectations concerning those asset classes to develop a strategic asset allocation. The investor may also act on short-term expectations. Capital market expectations are expectations about classes of assets, or **macro expectations.** By contrast, **micro expectations** are expectations concerning individual assets. Micro expectations are key ingredients in security selection and valuation. Insights into capital markets gleaned during CME setting should help in formulating accurate micro expectations in security selection and valuation.

One theme of this chapter is that a disciplined approach to expectations setting will be rewarded. Therefore, much of the chapter is devoted to explaining a widely applicable expectations-setting process. A second theme of this chapter is that skillful economic analysis can contribute to expectations setting. That theme is supported by the observation that securities markets trade claims on the cash flows of the business sector and that other markets reflect the macro economy, too.

The chapter is organized as follows: Section 2 presents a general framework for developing capital market expectations and alerts the reader to the range of problems and pitfalls that await the investor or analyst in this arena. Section 3 then turns to describing the range of tools, both formal and judgmental, that an analyst may use in expectations setting. Section 4 covers economic analysis as applied to formulating capital market expectations.

2. ORGANIZING THE TASK: FRAMEWORK AND CHALLENGES

In this section, we provide a guide to collecting, organizing, combining, and interpreting information. After illustrating the process, we turn to a discussion of typical problems and challenges to formulating the most informed judgments possible.

2.1. A Framework for Developing Capital Market Expectations

The following is a framework for a disciplined approach to setting CME:

1. *Specify the final set of expectations that are needed, including the time horizon to which they apply.* The analyst needs to understand the specific objectives of the analysis in order to work efficiently toward them. To make this step even more concrete, the analyst should write the questions that need to be answered. Accomplishing this step requires the analyst to formulate his or her specific needs in terms of a relevant set of asset classes that are of concern, giving appropriate regard to the constraints of the client. In many cases, the investor's investment policy statement may provide guidance in this task. For example, for a taxable investor with a 10-year time horizon, the portfolio manager would develop long-term after-tax expectations for use in developing a strategic asset allocation.
2. *Research the historical record.* Most forecasts have some connection to the past. For many markets, the historical record contains useful information on the investment

characteristics of the asset, suggesting at least some possible ranges for future results. Beyond the raw historical facts, the analyst should seek to identify the factors that affect asset class returns and to understand the what, when, where, why, and how of these return drivers. The analyst will then have a better sense of the information mosaic that he or she will need to piece together to arrive at well-informed conclusions.

3. *Specify the method(s) and/or model(s) that will be used and their information requirements.* The investor, capital market analyst, or unit responsible for developing capital market expectations (as the case may be) should be explicit about the method(s) and/or model(s) that will be used and should be able to justify the selection. Information requirements (economic and financial market data needs, for example) depend on the decision about method(s).
4. *Determine the best sources for information needs.*
5. *Interpret the current investment environment using the selected data and methods, applying experience and judgment.* The analyst should be sure that he or she is working from a common set of assumptions in interpreting different elements of the investment and economic scene so that the analyst's conclusions are mutually consistent. The analyst often needs to apply judgment and experience to interpret apparently conflicting signals within the data.
6. *Provide the set of expectations that are needed, documenting conclusions.* These are the analyst's answers to the questions set out in Step 1. The answers should be accompanied by the reasoning and assumptions behind them.
7. *Monitor actual outcomes and compare them to expectations, providing feedback to improve the expectations-setting process.*

Disciplined capital market expectations setting requires experience and expertise in investments and economics. Large asset managers may have a research unit—for example, an economics unit—with responsibility for developing capital market expectations. Through superior forecasts, such asset managers seek to better control risk and improve the results of actively managed accounts in particular. The development of capital market expectations is **beta research** (research related to systematic risk and returns to systematic risk). As such, it is usually centralized so that the CME inputs used across all equity and fixed-income products are consistent. By contrast, **alpha research** (research related to capturing excess risk-adjusted returns by a particular strategy) is typically conducted within particular product groups with the requisite investment-specific expertise. For institutional investors, professional consultants are a resource for systematically developed capital market expectations. Consultants' assistance may be given in the course of asset allocation reviews or asset/liability planning studies. Institutional investors may develop capital market expectations in-house, although they will usually be aware of the perspectives of professional consultants and peers. Most individual investors rely on their investment adviser or other external source for guidance in setting capital market expectations, as they often do not have expertise in this area. Yet an adviser may incorporate the client's perspectives on capital markets prospects, as the portfolio is run on the client's behalf and the client must be comfortable with the inputs to constructing the portfolio.

The first step in the framework for developing CME requires that analysts set boundaries to focus their attention on the expectations most relevant for their investment situation. Otherwise, effort is wasted. Even pared down to the minimum needs, the scope of the expectations-setting process can be quite challenging. As Example 4-1 illustrates, there is a direct relationship between the number and variety of permissible asset class alternatives and the scope of the expectations-setting task facing the manager.

EXAMPLE 4-1 Capital Market Expectations Setting: Information Requirements (1)

Consider the tasks facing two investment managers, John Pearson and Michael Wu.

Pearson runs U.S. balanced separately managed accounts (SMAs) for high-net-worth individuals within a bank trust department. The mandates of these accounts restrict investments to U.S. equities, U.S. investment-grade fixed-income instruments, and prime U.S. money market instruments. These balanced accounts have an investment objective of long-term capital growth and income. In contrast, Wu is the chief investment officer of a large Hong Kong–based, internationally focused asset manager that uses the following types of assets within its investment process:

Equities	Fixed Income	Alternative Investments
Hong Kong equities	Eurozone sovereign debt	Eastern Europe venture capital
Eurozone equities[2]	U.S. government debt	New Zealand timber assets
U.S. large-cap equities		U.S. apartment properties
U.S. small-cap equities		
Canadian large-cap equities		

Note: Venture capital is equity investment in private companies.

Wu runs SMAs with generally long-term time horizons and global tactical asset allocation (GTAA) programs. Compare and contrast the information and knowledge requirements of Pearson and Wu.

Solution: Pearson's in-depth information requirements relate to U.S. equity and fixed-income markets. By contrast, Wu's information requirements relate not only to U.S. and non-U.S. equity and fixed-income markets, but also to three alternative investment types with nonpublic markets, located on three different continents. Wu's need to be current on political, social, economic, and even trading-oriented operational details worldwide is more urgent than Pearson's. Given their respective investment time horizons, Pearson's focus is on the long term while Wu needs to focus not only on the long term but also on near-term disequilibria among markets (as he runs GTAA programs). One challenge that Pearson has in U.S. fixed-income markets that Wu does not face is the need to cover corporate as well as government debt securities. Nevertheless, Wu's overall information and knowledge requirements are clearly more demanding than Pearson's.

In the next example, the balanced fund manager from Example 4-1 specifies the final set of expectations needed and the time frame for those expectations.

[2]The **Eurozone** is the region of countries using the euro as a currency. As of the beginning of 2006, the Eurozone consisted of Austria, Belgium, Finland, France, Germany, Greece, Ireland, Italy, Luxembourg, the Netherlands, Portugal, and Spain. The list is expected to expand over time.

EXAMPLE 4-2 Capital Market Expectations Setting: Information Requirements (2)

Following the practice of his employer, Pearson uses the results of constrained mean–variance optimization (MVO) and information from clients' investment policy statements to develop strategic asset allocations for the balanced accounts.

Pearson is now addressing the first step in the framework given in the text for a client whose investment time horizon is five years. What set of final expectational data does Pearson need?

Solution: Pearson needs the following final set of expectations:

- Expected U.S. broad market annual equity total return over a five-year horizon.
- Expected U.S. investment-grade bond annual total return over a five-year horizon.
- Standard deviation of annual returns of U.S. broad market equities.
- Standard deviation of annual returns of U.S. investment-grade bonds.
- Correlation of annual U.S. stock and U.S. bond returns.

In total, Pearson needs two expected returns, two standard deviations, and one correlation for the MVO.

Steps 2 and 3 in the expectations-setting process involve understanding the historical performance of the asset classes and researching their return drivers. The analyst can approach these tasks by collecting macroeconomic and market information (e.g., asset returns) by:

- Geographic area (e.g., domestic, nondomestic, or some subset—for example, a single international area) or
- Broad asset class (e.g., equity, fixed income, or real estate).

The finer classifications depend on the characteristics of the task and the orientation of the investor. For equities, one approach would be to further classify by economic sector, possibly making style-related (e.g., market-capitalization) distinctions. A fixed-income investor might distinguish between governmental and corporate sectors and make further credit distinctions. For example, an industry rotation equity strategist might formulate expectations on domestic equities as follows:

Economic Sector (e.g., technology manufacturers)

Industry (e.g., computer equipment manufacturers)

Subindustry (e.g., microchip component manufacturers)

EXAMPLE 4-3 Historical Analysis

As Peter L. Bernstein (2004) has written, forecasters who make predictions without regard to past experience have no benchmarks to distinguish between what is new about their expectations and what may be a continuation of past experience. Dimson, Marsh, and Staunton (2006), in a rigorous study covering the 106-year period from 1900 to 2005, found that equities achieved higher annualized geometric mean real returns than did bonds or bills in 17 major national markets. It would be appropriate for an analyst forecasting that bonds would outperform equities over some (probably shorter-term) horizon to supply supporting analysis that recognizes the tension between the forecast and past long-term experience.

In Step 3, the analyst also needs to be sensitive to the fact that the effectiveness of forecasting approaches and relationships among variables may be related to the investor's time horizon. As an example, a discounted cash flow approach to developing equity market expectations is usually considered to be most appropriate to long-range forecasting.

The fourth step involves determining the best sources for information needs. Executing this step well requires that the analyst research the quality of alternative data sources. Factors such as data collection principles and definitions, error rates in collection, calculation formulas, and for asset class indices, qualities such as investability, correction for free float, turnover in index constituents, and biases in the data are relevant. The cost of data may also be relevant. In short, analysts must understand everything they can about the data they will use for analysis. Using flawed or misunderstood data is a recipe for faulty analysis. Furthermore, analysts should constantly be alert to new, superior sources for their data needs.

Besides taking care with data sources, the analyst must select the appropriate data frequency. For instance, long-term data series should not be used for setting short-term trading expectations or evaluating short-term volatility. Daily series are of more use for setting shorter-term capital market expectations. Quarterly or annual data series are useful for setting long-term capital market expectations.

The fifth step involves interpreting the current investment environment using the selected data and methods, applying experience and judgment. In the sixth step, we take all of our analyses of the economic and market environment into forward-looking views on capital markets, developing any required quantitative forecasts. In other words, the questions formulated in Step 1 are answered in Step 6. Economic analysis may work itself into quantitative forecasts in a variety of ways depending on the investor's selection of methodology. Top-down investment approaches often use economic analysis more intensively than bottom-up approaches. Example 4-4 illustrates several ways an analyst's relative optimism or pessimism concerning a market might be reflected in quantitative forecasts.

EXAMPLE 4-4 Incorporating Economic Analysis into Expected Return Estimates

Michael Wu has gathered information on consensus expectations in equity and fixed-income markets. On the basis of his economic analysis, Wu is optimistic relative to the consensus on the prospects for Hong Kong equities. However, Wu is pessimistic relative to the consensus on the prospects for U.S. large-cap equities. Depending on the model chosen, Wu's views might be reflected in his quantitative expectations in several ways, including the following:

- **Historical Mean Return with Adjustments.** If Wu takes a historical mean return as his baseline for each asset class, he may make an upward adjustment to that mean for Hong Kong equities and a downward adjustment for U.S. large-cap equities.
- **Risk Premium Approach.** Wu may frame his analysis in terms of the equity risk premium (the expected return on equities in excess of the long bond expected return). After translating his views into equity risk premium estimates for Hong Kong and U.S. large-cap equities, his return expectation for each asset class is the expected equity risk premium in each market plus the long bond expected return in each market (which he can estimate directly from the term structure of interest rates).
- **Discounted Cash Flow (DCF) Model Estimates.** Wu may use his economic analysis to forecast the growth rates of corporate profits for the United States and Hong Kong and input those forecasts into a DCF model solved for the required return on equities in each country.
- **Implied Market Estimates of Expected Return with Adjustment.** Making use of a world market benchmark and a methodology known as the Black–Litterman model, Wu may infer the equilibrium expected returns on asset classes as reflected by their values in the allocated world market benchmark. Wu can then incorporate his own views on Hong Kong and U.S. large-cap equities using a procedure specified by Black–Litterman.[3]

For a Hong Kong–based client, Hong Kong dollar returns are relevant, so Wu will also need to make exchange rate forecasts to arrive at his conclusions.

Finally, we want to use experience to improve the expectations-setting process. We measure our previously formed expectations against actual results to assess the level of accuracy that the expectations-setting process is delivering. Generally, good forecasts are:

- Unbiased, objective, and well researched.
- Efficient, in the sense of reducing the magnitude of forecast errors to a minimum.
- Internally consistent.

Internal inconsistency can take a number of forms. For example, domestic bond and domestic equity expectations developed by different analysts using different inflation projections would not be internally consistent. A restructuring of a portfolio based on those expectations would, at least in part, merely reflect an unresolved difference in assumptions. In some cases, inconsistent forecasts may result in conclusions that are implausible or impossible. Example 4-5 illustrates inconsistent statistical forecasts.

[3]The Black–Litterman model is discussed further in Chapter 5.

EXAMPLE 4-5 Inconsistency of Correlation Estimates: An Illustration

Frequently, the expected correlations between asset classes form part of the final expectational data that an analyst needs. If the number of asset classes is n, the analyst will need to estimate $(n^2 - n)/2$ distinct correlations (or the same number of distinct covariances). In doing so, the analyst must be sure that his or her estimates are consistent. For example, consider the correlation matrix for three assets shown in Exhibit 4-1.

EXHIBIT 4-1 Inconsistent Correlations

	Market 1	Market 2	Market 3
Market 1	1	−1	−1
Market 2	−1	1	−1
Market 3	−1	−1	1

According to Exhibit 4-1, the estimated correlation between each asset and each other asset is −1. These estimates are internally inconsistent but, in fact, not possible. If Markets 1 and 2 are perfectly negatively correlated and Markets 2 and 3 are as well, then Markets 1 and 3 should be perfectly positively correlated rather than perfectly negatively correlated.

Other cases of an inconsistent correlation matrix are not so obvious.[4]

As a result of the final feedback step, we may be able to identify and correct weaknesses in our expectations-setting process or methods.

2.2. Challenges in Forecasting

A range of problems can frustrate analysts' expectations-setting efforts. Expectations reflecting faulty analysis or assumptions may cause a portfolio manager to construct a portfolio that is inappropriate for the client. At the least, the portfolio manager may incur the costs of changing portfolio composition without any offsetting benefits. On the principle that forewarned is forearmed, the following sections provide guidance on the points where special caution is warranted. The discussion focuses on problems in the use of data and on analyst mistakes and biases.

2.2.1. Limitations of Economic Data

The analyst needs to understand the definition, construction, timeliness, and accuracy of any data used, including any biases. The time lag

[4]What may look like a viable correlation matrix at first inspection is not necessarily feasible. In a three-asset case, it is feasible for all pairwise correlations to be −0.50; however, it can be shown that correlations that are all equal to −0.51 are not feasible (i.e., are inconsistent). Correlations must be consistent for variances to be nonnegative.

with which economic data are collected, processed, and disseminated can be an impediment to their use. Although in some highly developed markets some economic data may be reported with a lag as short as one week, other important data may be reported with a lag of more than a quarter. The International Monetary Fund sometimes reports macroeconomic data for developing economies with a lag of two years or more. Older data for a variable increase the uncertainty concerning the current state of the economy with respect to that variable.

Furthermore, one or more official revisions to the initial values are common. In effect, measurements are made with error, but the direction and magnitude of the error are not known at the time the data are initially publicized.

Definitions and calculation methods change too. For example, the sampling procedures and calculation methods for the U.S. Consumer Price Index for All Urban Consumers (CPI-U) used by the Bureau of Labor Statistics (BLS) have changed in significant ways since the series was first published. In 1983, for example, the BLS shifted to a flow-of-services model for pricing owner-occupied housing, based on the costs that would be associated with renting such housing. In 1991, the BLS began the introduction of hedonic or regression-based quality adjustments to prices to reflect any increases in quality and features of various consumption items.

EXAMPLE 4-6 A Change in Focus from GNP to GDP

In the late 1980s, expanding international trade caused economists to favor the use of gross domestic product (GDP) over gross national product (GNP). Basically, GDP measures production within national borders regardless of whether the labor and property inputs are domestically or foreign owned. In contrast, GNP makes an adjustment to GDP equal to the receipts of factor income from the rest of the world to the country, less the payments of factor income from a country to the rest of the world. This change in preference reflected the fact that product subcomponents, such as automobile parts, were being created in various regions of the world. Thus, measuring economic activity according to what nation was responsible for activities in various regions of the world was becoming more difficult and less useful than being able to measure what was being made within a nation or particular region. Consistent with this observation, the United Nations System of National Accounts (known as UNSNA, or SNA for short) emphasizes GDP.

An analyst must realize that suppliers of indices of economic and financial data periodically **rebase** these indices, meaning that the specific time period used as the base of the index is changed. A rebasing is not a substantive change in the composition of an index. It is more of a mathematical change. Analysts constructing a data series should take care that data relating to different bases are not inadvertently mixed together.

2.2.2. Data Measurement Errors and Biases

Analysts need to be aware of possible biases in data measurement of series such as asset class returns. Errors in data series include the following:

- *Transcription errors.* These are errors in gathering and recording data. Such errors are most serious if they reflect a bias.
- *Survivorship bias.* Survivorship bias arises when a data series reflects only entities that have survived to the end of the period. For example, a share index may be based on companies that trade on an exchange. Such companies are often delisted (removed from trading on the exchange) after events such as bankruptcy filings and mergers. Shares of bankrupt companies may trade elsewhere after delisting. Do reported returns on a share index reflect post-delisting returns? If not, the return series will probably convey an overly optimistic picture of the real-time investment returns from owning all listed shares. Without correction, statistics derived from series subject to survivorship bias can be misleading in the forward-looking context of expectations setting.[5]
- *Appraisal (smoothed) data.* For certain assets without liquid public markets, appraisal data are used in lieu of market price transaction data. Appraised values tend to be less volatile than market-determined values for the identical asset would be. The consequences are (1) the calculated correlations with other assets tend to be smaller in absolute value than the true correlations, and (2) the true standard deviation of the asset is biased downward. This concern has been raised particularly with respect to alternative investments such as real estate.

EXAMPLE 4-7 Smoothed Data: The Case of Alternative Investments (1)

The perception of alternative investments is that they yield high returns with low risk and that they barely correlate with traditional asset classes. At least in some cases, this perception results from the uncritical use of flawed historical statistics because alternative assets are not traded on exchanges with continuously observable markets. First, risk is underestimated. Consider the following analogy: A bat is flying through a dark tunnel. While it is in the tunnel, you cannot see it. The bat may exit from the tunnel at about the same height it entered the tunnel, as shown.

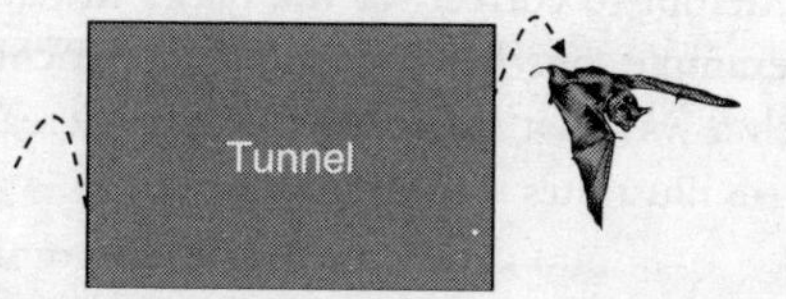

Source: Staub (2005). © 2006 UBS Global Asset Management (Americas) Inc. All rights reserved.

However, the bat's flight within the tunnel, if it could be viewed, would be seen to go up and down:

[5]See Brown, Goetzmann, and Ross (1995).

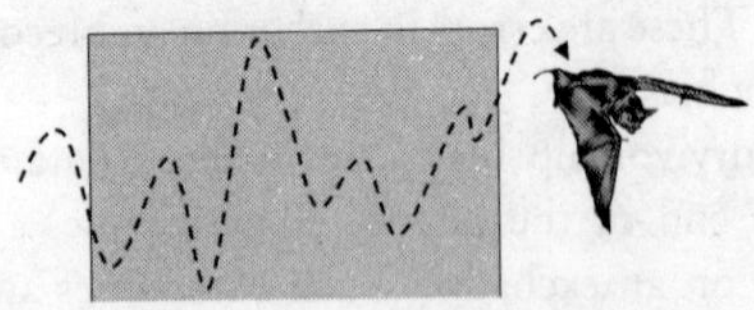

Source: Staub (2005). © 2006 UBS Global Asset Management (Americas) Inc. All rights reserved.

In this analogy, the time in the tunnel corresponds to the time between trades (or fund valuations) and the bat's height of flight corresponds to the true price of the asset. In measuring the bat's height only at the points of entry and exit from the tunnel, we would underestimate the real volatility of price. Asset liquidity corresponds to the end of the tunnel, when the true price is first clearly visible. In the context of venture capital, for instance, the end of the tunnel is analogous to the initial public offering date.

Data for alternative investments tend to overly smooth return variation because they are often appraisal based rather than transaction based. Many indices, such as those for real estate, private equity, and natural resources, were created with a focus on measuring return rather than risk. Unfortunately, these indices have been used to derive risk and correlation estimates that are biased downward. For alternative investments, the issue is not only whether the past is a good indicator of the future, but also whether the past is even correctly recorded.

As an illustration, consider the quarterly returns on the S&P 500 between 1981 and 1999, which include the crash of 1987. The period contains 18 negative quarters and has an annual standard deviation of returns of 16.1 percent. Venture capital also represents equity claims, but on less seasoned and riskier companies. Nevertheless, based on venture economics data, the index-based quarterly venture capital returns over the same period are considerably smoother. Venture capital also seems unaffected by the crash, with a reported 5.2 percent return in the fourth quarter of 1987. Only six negative quarters are reported. The reported annual standard deviation of returns is 9.1 percent, and correlation with the S&P 500 is 0.28.

The analyst can attempt to correct for the biases in data sets (when a bias-free data set is not available). For example, one heuristic approach to correcting for smoothed data is to rescale the data in such a way that their dispersion is increased but the mean of the data is unchanged. Example 4-8 illustrates this idea.

EXAMPLE 4-8 Smoothed Data: The Case of Alternative Investments (2)

How might an analyst address the biases resulting from smoothed data? To continue with the case of venture capital return data, one approach would be to rescale the reported data so that dispersion is increased but the mean is unchanged. The point is that the larger the rescaling, the larger the number of negative quarterly returns, because the frequency distribution is centered in the same place but there is more probability in the tails as dispersion is larger. For example:

- The venture returns rescaled by a factor of 1.4 provide 18 negative quarters—that is, as many as the S&P 500. The estimated standard deviation of the rescaled data is 13 percent.
- The venture returns rescaled by a factor of 4.1 provide 36 negative quarters, which is twice as many as the S&P 500. The estimated standard deviation of the rescaled data is 37 percent.
- The venture returns rescaled by a factor of 4.4 provide 38 negative quarters, 2.1 times as many as the S&P 500. The estimated standard deviation of the rescaled data is 40 percent.

Using these data in conjunction with other analyses, one might propose risks of 43 percent for early-stage venture capital, 34 percent for late-stage venture capital, 29 percent for leveraged buyouts (largely debt-financed purchases of established companies), and 20 percent for distressed debt (the debt of companies that are under financial distress or in or near bankruptcy).[6]

The key is to model the risks of alternative investments as if they were frequently traded, focusing not on statistical observations but on the underlying fundamental and economic drivers of returns.

2.2.3. The Limitations of Historical Estimates

With justification, analysts frequently look to history for information in developing capital market forecasts. But although history is usually a guide to what we may expect in the future, the past cannot be simply extrapolated to produce future results uncritically. A historical estimate should be considered a starting point for analysis. The analysis should include a discussion of what may be different from past average results going forward. If we do not see any such differences, we may want to project the historical estimates into the future (perhaps after making certain technical adjustments). However, making such projections without raising the question of differences is questionable. Changes in the technological, political, legal, and regulatory environments, as well as disruptions such as wars and other calamities, can alter risk–return relationships. Such shifts are known as changes in **regime** (the governing set of relationships) and give rise to the statistical problem of **nonstationarity** (meaning, informally, that different parts of a data series reflect different underlying statistical properties). For example, the shifts in U.S. central bank policy in 1980 began a period of declining and subsequently stable inflation that is widely recognized as representing a break with the past. Also, disruptive events in a particular time period may boost volatilities in a manner that is simply not relevant for the future. However, extending a dataset to the distant past increases the chance of including irrelevant data. The well-informed analyst tracks the range of events that can indicate an important change in a time series. Statistical tools are available to help identify such changes or turning points.[7]

[6] See Chapter 8 for a discussion of these alternative investments.
[7] See Hamilton (1994).

When many variables are considered, a long data series may be a statistical necessity. (For example, to calculate a historical covariance matrix, the number of observations must exceed the number of variables). If we could be assured of stationarity, going back farther in time to capture a larger sample should increase the precision with which population parameters of a return distribution are estimated.[8] Related to that point, using larger samples may reduce the sensitivity of parameter estimates to the starting and ending dates of the sample. In practice, using a long data series may involve a variety of problems. For instance:

- The risk that the data cover multiple regimes increases.
- Time series of the required length may not be available.
- In order to get data series of the required length, the temptation is to use high-frequency data (weekly or even daily). Data of high frequency are more sensitive to asynchronism across variables.[9] As a result, high-frequency data tend to produce lower correlation estimates.

Researchers have concluded that the underlying mean returns on volatile asset classes such as equities are particularly difficult to estimate from historical data.[10] Using high-frequency data is of no help in increasing the accuracy of mean return estimates.

A practical approach to deciding whether one should use the whole of a long data series is to answer two questions. The first question is: Is there is any fundamental reason to believe that the entirety of the series' time period is no longer relevant? If there is, the next question to answer is: Do the data support that hypothesis? Texts on time-series and regression analysis offer a variety of means to assess objectively whether there is a break in a time series. If the answers to both questions are yes, one should use only that part of the time series that appears to be relevant to the present.

EXAMPLE 4-9 Using Regression Analysis to Identify a Change in Regime

The effects of specific events on a time series (e.g., the announcement by a central bank of a new monetary policy) can be most simply modeled in a regression framework using a dummy explanatory variable $z(t)$, where $z(t) = 0$ for t before the intervention (change) date and $z(t) = 1$ for t at and subsequent to the intervention date. This dummy variable approach models a simple shift in the mean of the dependent variable.

2.2.4. Ex Post Risk Can Be a Biased Measure of Ex Ante Risk

In interpreting historical prices and returns over a given sample period for their relevance to current decision making, we need to evaluate whether asset prices in the period reflected the possibility of a

[8] According to sampling theory, the precision of the estimate of the population mean is proportional to $1/\sqrt{(\text{number of observations})}$.

[9] **Asynchronism** is a discrepancy in the dating of observations that occurs because stale (out-of-date) data may be used in the absence of current data.

[10] See Luenberger (1998).

very negative event that did not materialize during the period. Looking backward, we are likely to underestimate *ex ante* risk and overestimate *ex ante* anticipated returns.[11] For example, suppose that bond prices anticipate a small chance of a central bank policy change that would be very negative for inflation and bond returns. When investors become aware that the risk has passed, bond prices should show strong gains. *Ex post* realized bond returns are high although *ex ante* they were lower. Because the bank policy change did not occur, it may be overlooked as a risk that was faced by bond investors at the time. An analyst reviewing the record might conclude that bonds earn high returns in excess of the short-term interest rate.[12] Similarly, a high *ex post* U.S. equity risk premium may reflect fears of adverse events that did not materialize and may be a poor estimate of the *ex ante* risk premium.[13] Only the *ex ante* risk premium is important in decision making.

2.2.5. Biases in Analysts' Methods

Analysts naturally search for relationships that will help in developing better capital market expectations. Among the preventable biases that the analyst may introduce in such work are the following:

- *Data-mining bias*. Data-mining bias is introduced by repeatedly "drilling" or searching a dataset until the analyst finds some statistically significant pattern. Such patterns cannot be expected to be of predictive value. It is almost inevitable that the analyst will find some statistically significant relationship by mining the data: Using a given sample, if we examine 50 different variables as predictors of the equity risk premium and set a 10 percent significance level in our tests, we would expect five variables to appear significant by random chance alone. The absence of an explicit economic rationale for a variable's usefulness is one warning sign of a data-mining problem: no story, no future.[14]
- *Time-period bias*. Time-period bias relates to results that are time period specific. Research findings are often found to be sensitive to the selection of starting and/or ending dates. As one example, the small-cap stock effect in U.S. stock returns has been found to be largely concentrated in the nine-year period 1975 to 1983, when as a group, small-cap stocks outperformed large-cap equities by 19.6 percent per year. Excluding the 1975 to 1983 period, a given investment in large-cap equities in 1926 would have grown by the end of 2001 to an amount that was 20 percent greater than the amount resulting from an equal initial investment in small-cap equities.[15]

How might the analyst avoid the mistake of using a variable in a forecasting mode that historical analysis has suggested as useful but which is actually irrelevant? The analyst should scrutinize the variable selection process for data-mining bias and be able to provide an economic rationale for the variable's usefulness in a forecasting mode. A further practical check is to examine the forecasting relationship out of sample (i.e., on data other than those

---

[11]That situation of biased measurement has been called the "generalized peso problem" or the "peso problem." The name comes from an explanation for the fact that forward markets for the Mexican peso in the mid-1970s consistently underpredicted the U.S. dollar/peso exchange rate. The explanation is that traders feared that the Mexican government would devalue the peso from its peg.

[12]This explanation has been offered by Bekaert, Hodrick, and Marshall (2001) along with time-varying term premiums for anomalies in the term structure of interest rates noted by Campbell and Shiller (1991).

[13]See Goetzmann and Jorion (1999) and references therein.

[14]See McQueen and Thorley (1999).

[15]See Siegel (2002, pp. 134–135).

used to estimate the relationship). For example, the available data period could be split into two subperiods. If the forecasting relationship estimated from the first period does not hold similarly when tested using data from the second subperiod, the variable may not be useful as a forecaster.

2.2.6. The Failure to Account for Conditioning Information We observed above that the analyst should ask whether there are relevant new facts in the present when forecasting the future. Where such information exists, the analyst should condition his or her expectations on it.

We can take the case of estimating mean returns. Long-run mean returns and risk involve an averaging over many different economic and market conditions. Prospective returns and risk for an asset as of today are conditional on the specific characteristics of the current marketplace and prospects looking forward. That fact explains the role of economic analysis in expectations setting: We should not ignore any relevant information or analysis in formulating expectations. Indeed, the use of unconditional expectations can lead to misperceptions of risk, return, and risk-adjusted return.

Consider an asset class that has a beta of 0.80 in economic expansions and 1.2 in recessions (with respect to a world market portfolio). If we make the assumptions in Exhibit 4-2 on the market return and the risk-free rate, the asset class's expected return is 10 percent in an expansion versus 4.4 percent in a recession and its true unconditional expected return is 0.5(10%) + 0.5(4.4%) = 7.2%. The asset class fairly rewards risk in both expansions and recessions [alpha = 0.5(0%) + 0.5(0%) = 0%]. The asset class would appear to have a beta of 0.5(0.8) +0.5(1.2) = 1.0 in a regression. Given this unconditional beta, the expected return according to the CAPM would be 8 percent.

Comparing the unconditional expected return using the unconditional beta of 1.0, the asset class appears to inadequately reward risk (alpha = −0.8 percent) although we know from the analysis presented that the asset class fairly rewards risk.[16] How would an analyst avoid drawing the wrong conclusion? The analyst would need to uncover through research that the asset class's systematic risk varies with the business cycle. The analyst would then condition his or her forecasts on the state of the economy to formulate the most accurate expectations.

EXHIBIT 4-2 Misvaluation from Using an Unconditional Benchmark

	Expansion	Recession	Unconditional Expectation
Risk-free rate	2%	2%	2%
Exp. return on market	12%	4%	8%
β_i	0.80	1.20	1.0
$E(R_i)$	2% + 0.8(12% − 2%) = 10%	2% +1.2(4% − 2%) = 4.4%	True: 7.2% Using β_i = 1.0: 2% + 1.0(8% − 2%) = 8%
α_i	0%	0%	7.2% − 8% = −0.8%

Note: An expansion and a recession are assumed to be equally likely.

[16]Note that Ferson and Schadt (1996) developed a method to estimate conditional alpha.

2.2.7. Misinterpretation of Correlations In financial and economic research, the analyst should take care in interpreting correlations. When a variable A is found to be significantly correlated with a variable B, there are at least three possible explanations:

- A predicts B.
- B predicts A.
- A third variable C predicts A and B.

Without the investigation and modeling of underlying linkages, relationships of correlation cannot be used in a predictive model. For example, suppose A relates to natural disasters in quarter t and B represents property insurer claims in quarter $t+1$. One can discern on the basis of simple economic reasoning a cause-and-effect link from A to B. Supporting that conclusion, no plausible feedback linkage exists from B to A: A is truly an exogenous variable (an **exogenous variable** is determined outside the system, in contrast to an **endogenous variable,** which is determined within the system). One might consider using A as one predictor of B, but the reverse—using claims in $t+1$ to predict natural disasters in $t+2$—would not be fruitful (although the observed correlation by itself would not tell you that).

As the third bullet point represents, there may be no predictive relationship between A and B; the relationship between A and B is conditional on the presence of the variable C, and the correlation between A and B is spurious.

Another surprise that might be in store: A and B could have a strong but *nonlinear* relationship but have a low or zero correlation.[17]

Suppose that one has a plausible model of an underlying causal link to support the use of a variable as a predictor. Are there any more powerful tools to apply to establish the variable's usefulness than simple correlation? Multiple-regression analysis may be one such tool. For example, suppose we have a model that suggests B predicts A but we need to eliminate C as mediating the relationship between A and B (as in the third bullet point above). We can estimate the following regression:

$$A = \beta_0 + \beta_1 B + \beta_2 C + \varepsilon$$

The variable C in this regression is a control variable. The coefficient β_1 represents the effect of B on A after accounting for the effect of the control variable C on A. The coefficient β_1 reflects the **partial correlation** between A and B. If the estimated value of β_1 is significantly different from 0 but β_2 is not significantly different from 0 (based on t-tests), we have a piece of evidence in support of the proposition that B predicts A. The multiple-regression framework supports the introduction of multiple control variables. The analyst may also use time-series analysis. For example, with sufficiently long time series, we can regress A on lagged values of itself, lagged values of B, and lagged values of control variables, and test the null hypothesis that all the coefficients on the lagged values of B jointly equal 0. If we can reject the null hypothesis, the variable B may be useful in predicting A.[18]

---

[17]For example, consider $B = A^2$ (A raised to the second power indicates a nonlinear association). The variable B increases with increasing values of A when A is above 0. But consider negative values of A. As A increases from -100 to 0, B decreases. The correlation between A and B is zero, although the relationship between them is so precise that it can be expressed in a mathematical equation.

[18]This would be a test of "predictive causality," known as Granger causation. See Granger (1969) and Diebold (2004).

EXAMPLE 4-10 Causality Relationships

That one event follows another is not sufficient to show that the first event caused the second. For example, a decrease in the number of new accountants following an increase in tax rates would be **association without cause-and-effect relationship**. But seasonal incoming tax receipts probably bear a **direct cause-and-effect relationship** to the needs of governments to borrow funds in some months versus others. If an increase in income tax rates causes individuals to be more concerned with minimizing taxes, one might discern an **indirect cause-and-effect relationship** between the tax rate increase and a subsequent jump in sales of tax preparation software.

2.2.8. Psychological Traps Hammond, Keeney, and Raiffa (1998) formulated several psychological traps that are relevant to our discussion because they can undermine the analyst's ability to make accurate and unbiased forecasts.

The **anchoring trap** is the tendency of the mind to give disproportionate weight to the first information it receives on a topic. In other words, initial impressions, estimates, or data anchor subsequent thoughts and judgments. For instance, in an investment committee in which several different perspectives on capital market returns are presented, the first presentation may tend to function as an anchor for discussion and its lead-off position might give it an edge in being adopted. The analyst can try to address this trap by consciously attempting to avoid premature conclusions.

The **status quo trap** is the tendency for forecasts to perpetuate recent observations—that is, to predict no change from the recent past. If inflation has been rising at a double-digit rate for several recent periods, it is a natural tendency to forecast a similar increase in the next period. In a decision-making context, because doing something other than maintaining the status quo (risking an error of commission) may lead to increased work and regret if the decision is wrong, doing nothing (risking an error of omission) becomes the easy and oft-preferred alternative. The status quo trap may be overcome with rational analysis used within a decision-making process.

The **confirming evidence trap** is the bias that leads individuals to give greater weight to information that supports an existing or preferred point of view than to evidence that contradicts it. The tendency to seek out information that supports an existing point of view also reflects this bias. Several steps may be taken to help ensure objectivity:

- Examine all evidence with equal rigor.
- Enlist an independent-minded person to argue against your preferred conclusion or decision.
- Be honest about your motives.

The **overconfidence trap** is the tendency of individuals to overestimate the accuracy of their forecasts. Many people do not admit or attempt to measure the possibility of failure in predicting uncertain events. In similar fashion, we tend to believe that most people share our particular views. The overconfidence trap would be reflected in admitting too narrow a range of possibilities or scenarios in forecasting. A good practice to prevent this trap from undermining the forecasting endeavor is to widen the range of possibilities around the primary target forecast.

The **prudence trap** is the tendency to temper forecasts so that they do not appear extreme, or the tendency to be overly cautious in forecasting. In a decision-making context, it is the tendency to be cautious when making decisions that could be potentially expensive or damaging to the decision maker's career. To avoid the prudence trap, an analyst is again wise to widen the range of possibilities around the target forecast. In addition, the most sensitive estimates affecting a forecast should be carefully reviewed in light of the supporting analysis.

The **recallability trap** is the tendency of forecasts to be overly influenced by events that have left a strong impression on a person's memory. Often, forecasts are overly influenced by the memory of catastrophic or dramatic past events. For example, investors' memory of the stock market crash of 1929 has sometimes been cited as a depressing influence on equity valuation levels for as long as three decades following the crash. To minimize the distortions of the recallability trap, analysts should ground their conclusions on objective data and procedures rather than on personal emotions and memories.

EXAMPLE 4-11 Traps in Forecasting

Cynthia Casey is a Canada-based investment adviser with a clientele of ultra-high-net-worth individuals. The Canadian equity allocation of client Philip Lasky's portfolio had favorable risk-adjusted performance from 1999 to 2001 but nevertheless lost 20 percent of its year-end 2000 value by the end of 2001. In a phone call prior to a quarterly portfolio review at the end of 2001, Lasky expressed the thought that the pain of the recent and continuing bear market had made him very cautious about investing in the stock market. Although his equity allocation results with Casey showed healthy appreciation over the entire period he had invested with her, his conversation dwelled mostly on the experience of the past year. Lasky told Casey that he had read a variety of financial reports containing predictions by investment notables on the equity risk premium ranging from near zero to 6 percent. During the call, he repeated to Casey, sometimes inaccurately, the arguments of the most bearish prognosticator. At the time of the call, Casey was preparing to share with clients relatively optimistic forecasts for Canadian equities, developed with an assistant who was well grounded in capital market analysis. Perceiving that Lasky and many of her other clients held more pessimistic viewpoints and that she might lose their trust if her own viewpoint turned out to be wrong, after the phone call, Casey decided to revise downward some of the economic growth assumptions she had previously made.

Critique the forecasts of (1) Lasky and (2) Casey with respect to psychological traps in forecasting.

Solutions:

1. In focusing on the most recent period only and predicting a continuation of the most recent trend, Lasky may have fallen into the status quo trap. The pain of the bear market may have overinfluenced his thinking about the present (recallability

trap). Furthermore, in sharing the viewpoint of the most bearish prognosticator, Lasky may be falling into the confirming evidence trap.

2. By trimming her assumptions to be more conservative without real supporting analysis, Casey may have fallen into the prudence trap.

2.2.9. Model Uncertainty The analyst usually encounters at least two kinds of uncertainty in conducting an analysis: **model uncertainty** (uncertainty concerning whether a selected model is correct) and **input uncertainty** (uncertainty concerning whether the inputs are correct). For example, suppose an analyst takes the equity risk premium of U.K. equities to be the realized value of the return of U.K. equities over U.K. bonds over the past 50 years. The analyst's model might be described as follows: "The *ex ante* U.K. equity risk premium was, is, and will be equal to some constant number μ." If the model is far off the true state of affairs, the analyst's forecast will also be off. (The sampling error in the estimate of μ using 50 years of data would constitute the input error in this approach.) To take another example, if the analyst uses a monetarist model for forecasting future inflation, the analyst faces uncertainty concerning whether that model is correct. In some cases, the analyst may gauge model uncertainty by observing the variation in results that comes from shifting between the several most promising models.

Input uncertainty and model uncertainty in particular often make it hard to confirm the existence of capital market anomalies (inefficiencies); some valuation model usually underlies the identification of an inefficiency. **Behavioral finance** (the theory that psychological variables affect and often distort individuals' investment decision making) has offered explanations for many perceived capital market anomalies. Kurz, Jin, and Motolese (2005) argue that many of these apparent anomalies could represent equilibria resulting from the actions of investors who use competing models but process and act on information rationally.[19]

3. TOOLS FOR FORMULATING CAPITAL MARKET EXPECTATIONS

The following sections introduce a range of tools that have been used in professional forecasting of capital market returns. Although an analyst may have distinct preferences among these approaches, familiarity with all these major tools will be helpful in addressing the widest variety of forecasting problems according to their particular characteristics.

3.1. Formal Tools

Formal tools are established research methods amenable to precise definition and independent replication of results. The information provided by well-chosen formal tools applied to sound data can help the analyst produce accurate forecasts.

[19]That is, apparent anomalies could represent a *rational belief equilibrium* in the sense of Kurz (1994).

3.1.1. Statistical Methods

Statistical methods relevant to expectations setting include **descriptive statistics** (methods for effectively summarizing data to describe important aspects of a dataset) and **inferential statistics** (methods for making estimates or forecasts about a larger group from a smaller group actually observed).

The simplest approach to forecasting is to use past data to directly forecast future outcomes of a variable of interest.

3.1.1.1. Historical Statistical Approach: Sample Estimators[20]

Suppose an investor uses the FTSE 100 as his benchmark for U.K. large-cap equity allocations. The investor could use the mean return on the FTSE 100 over some selected sample period as his forecast of the long-run expected return on U.K. large-cap equities. If future returns over the selected time horizon reflect the same probability distribution as past returns (because the time series is **stationary**—that is, the parameters that describe the return-generating process are unchanged), the resulting estimate will be useful. For example, in a mean–variance framework, the analyst might use:

- The sample arithmetic mean total return or sample geometric mean total return as an estimate of the expected return.
- The sample variance as an estimate of the variance.
- Sample correlations as estimates of correlations.

One decision point relates to the choice between an arithmetic mean and a geometric mean. The arithmetic mean return (which is always used in the calculation of the sample standard deviation) best represents the mean return in a single period. The geometric mean return of a sample represents the compound rate of growth that equates the beginning value to the ending value of a data series. The geometric mean return represents multiperiod growth more accurately than the arithmetic mean return. The geometric mean return is always lower than the arithmetic mean return for a risky variable. The differences between the arithmetic mean and the geometric mean in historical estimates of the equity risk premium can be substantial.[21] Both approaches are used in current practice.

Dimson, Marsh, and Staunton (2006) presented authoritative evidence on asset returns in 17 countries for the 106 years 1900 to 2005. Exhibit 4-3 excerpts their findings.

An analyst using a historical statistical approach would use historical data such as those given in Exhibit 4-3 as the basis for forecasts. Alternatively, using a historical statistical approach for the equity risk premium and a current term-structure estimate for the expected return on bonds (e.g., a yield to maturity on a zero-coupon government bond), the expected return on equities could be estimated as their sum.

[20]A **sample estimator** is a formula for assigning a unique value (a **point estimate**) to a population parameter.

[21]Looking forward to later discussion, the arithmetic historical equity risk premium would be calculated as the difference between the arithmetic mean return on the proxy for equities and the arithmetic mean return on long-term bonds. The geometric mean can be approximated as the difference between the geometric mean return on the proxy on equities ($R_{G,e}$) and the geometric mean return on long-term bonds ($R_{G,b}$), or more precisely, as $(1 + R_{G,e})/(1 + R_{G,b})$. In practice, the geometric mean calculation produces a lower estimate for the equity risk premium than does the arithmetic mean calculation.

EXHIBIT 4-3 Real (Inflation-Adjusted) Equity and Bond Returns: Seventeen Major Markets, 1900–2005

Country	Equities		Bonds	
	Arithmetic Mean Equity Return	Standard Deviation of Return	Arithmetic Mean Bond Return	Standard Deviation
Australia	9.2%	17.6%	2.2%	13.3%
Belgium	4.6	22.1	0.6	12.2
Canada	7.6	16.8	2.5	10.5
Denmark	6.9	20.3	3.7	11.8
France	6.1	23.2	0.7	13.2
Germany	8.0	32.6	0.7	15.8
Ireland	7.0	22.1	2.2	14.9
Italy	6.5	29.1	−0.4	14.4
Japan	9.3	30.0	1.5	20.6
Netherlands	7.2	21.3	1.8	9.5
Norway	7.1	27.0	2.4	12.4
South Africa	9.5	22.6	2.3	10.5
Spain	5.9	21.9	2.1	12.0
Sweden	10.1	22.6	3.2	12.6
Switzerland	6.3	19.7	2.9	7.9
United Kingdom	7.4	20.0	2.3	13.9
United States	8.5	20.2	2.4	9.9

Source: Dimson, Marsh, and Staunton (2006), Tables 20, 24, 28, 32, 36, 40, 44, 48, 52, 56, 60, 64, 68, 72, 76, 80, and 84. German data exclude 1922–1923.

3.1.1.2. Shrinkage Estimators **Shrinkage estimation** involves taking a weighted average of a historical estimate of a parameter and some other parameter estimate, where the weights reflect the analyst's relative belief in the estimates. This "two-estimates-are-better-than-one" approach has desirable statistical properties that have given it a place in professional investment practice. The term *shrinkage* refers to the approach's ability to reduce the impact of extreme values in historical estimates. The procedure has been applied to covariances and mean returns.

A **shrinkage estimator** of the covariance matrix is a weighted average of the historical covariance matrix and another, alternative estimator of the covariance matrix, where the analyst places the larger weight on the covariance matrix he or she believes more strongly in.[22] Why are analysts often not satisfied with using the historical sample covariance matrix? Basically, because investment data series are relatively short and samples often reflect the nonrecurring peculiarities of a historical period. The sample covariance matrix is perfectly well suited for *summarizing* an observed dataset and has the desirable (large-sample) property of unbiasedness. Nevertheless, a shrinkage estimator is a superior approach for estimating the population covariance matrix for the medium- and smaller-size datasets that are typical in finance.

A shrinkage estimator approach involves selecting an alternative estimator of the covariance matrix, called a **target covariance matrix.** For example, an analyst might believe that a

[22]This method is usually presented in terms of covariances rather than correlations for technical reasons. Either covariance or correlation can be used in MVO. Stein (1956) introduced shrinkage estimates.

particular model relating asset class returns to a particular set of return drivers or systematic risk factors has some validity. The asset classes' estimated betas or factor sensitivities in such a model can be used to estimate the asset classes' covariances. To consider one number in the covariance matrix, suppose that the estimated covariance between domestic shares and bonds is 48 using the factor model and 80 using a historical estimate, and assume further that the optimal weights on the model and historical estimates are 0.75 and 0.25, respectively. The shrinkage estimate of the covariance would be $0.75(48) + 0.25(80) = 56$. There is a systematic way to determine the optimal weights on the two estimates that the analyst can obtain from the investment literature on this topic.[23]

A surprising fact concerning the shrinkage estimator approach is that any choice for the target covariance matrix will lead to an increase (or at least not a decrease) in the efficiency of the covariance estimates versus the historical estimate. The improvement will be greater if a plausible target covariance matrix is selected. If the target covariance matrix is useless in improving the accuracy of the estimate of covariance, the optimal weight on the historical estimate would be calculated as 1. One reasonable choice for the target covariance matrix would be a factor-model-based estimate of the covariance matrix, following the lead of Ledoit and Wolf (2003). Another choice for the target covariance matrix would be a covariance matrix based on assuming each pairwise covariance is equal to the overall average covariance.[24]

EXAMPLE 4-12 Adjusting a Historical Covariance

Cynthia Casey has estimated the covariance between Canadian equities and U.S. equities as 230 using historical data. Using a factor model approach based on a proxy for the world market portfolio, she estimates the covariance as 190. Casey takes a shrinkage estimator approach to estimating covariances and determines that the optimal weight on the historical estimate is 0.30.

1. Calculate the shrinkage estimate of the covariance between U.S. and Canadian equities.
2. Describe the theoretical advantage of a shrinkage estimate of covariance compared to a raw historical estimate.

Solution to Problem 1:

$$0.30(230) + 0.70(190) = 202.$$

Solution to Problem 2: The shrinkage estimate should be more accurate, given that the weights are chosen appropriately.

[23] Ledoit and Wolf (2003) give a simple formula for the optimal weights. The criterion their formula satisfies is that the weights minimize the mean square error in the resulting estimate.

[24] An identity matrix or a scalar multiple of it is considered a serviceable choice when the researcher has no insight into an intuitive target for the covariance matrix.

A shrinkage estimator of mean returns involves taking a weighted average of each historical mean return and some other target constant—for example, the overall (grand) mean historical return across assets. Given five assets with sample mean returns of 4 percent, 6 percent, 7 percent, 8 percent, and 10 percent, respectively, and a weight of 80 percent on the sample mean, we would calculate the overall mean return as 7 percent and the shrinkage estimate of the first asset's return as 0.8(4%) +0.2(7%) = 4.6%.

3.1.1.3. Time-Series Estimators **Time-series estimators** involve forecasting a variable on the basis of lagged values of the variable being forecast and often lagged values of other selected variables.

Time-series methods have been found useful in developing particularly short-term forecasts for financial and economic variables. Time-series methods have been notably applied to estimating near-term volatility, given persuasive evidence of variance clustering (particularly at high frequencies, such as daily and weekly) in a number of different markets, including equity, currency, and futures markets.[25] **Volatility clustering** is the tendency for large (small) swings in prices to be followed by large (small) swings of random direction. Volatility clustering captures the idea that some markets represent periods of notably high or low volatility. Robert F. Engle shared the 2003 Nobel Prize in Economics in part for the development of time-series models that can accurately capture the property of volatility clustering.[26]

One of the simplest specifications in this broad class of models was developed within a division at J. P. Morgan that was later established as the RiskMetrics Group. This model specifies that the volatility in period t, σ_t^2, is a weighted average of the volatility in the previous period, σ_{t-1}^2, and the squared value of a random "noise" term, ε_t^2. The expression is

$$\sigma_t^2 = \beta\sigma_{t-1}^2 + (1-\beta)\varepsilon_t^2 \tag{4-1}$$

with $0 < \beta < 1$. The coefficient β measures the rate of decay of the influence of the value of volatility in one period on future volatility, and the rate of decay is exponential. The higher β is, the more volatility in one period "remembers" what happened in the past and the more it clusters.

To illustrate using $\beta = 0.94$, we will suppose that the standard deviation of returns in $t = 11$ is 10 percent, so $\sigma_{11}^2 = 0.10^2 = 0.01$. The noise term is $\varepsilon_{12} = 0.05$, so $\varepsilon_{12}^2 = 0.05^2 = 0.0025$. The prediction for $t = 12$ is therefore:

$$\begin{aligned}\sigma_{12}^2 &= 0.94\sigma_{11}^2 + 0.06\varepsilon_{12}^2 \\ &= 0.94(0.01) + 0.06(0.0025) \\ &= 0.00955\end{aligned}$$

implying that $\sigma_{12} = \sqrt{0.00955} = 0.0977$, or 9.77 percent. Intuitively, the high weight on σ_{11}^2 means that it had a strong effect on σ_{12}^2. However, on occasion, the noise term will take on an extreme value and cause volatility to shift quite a bit. In a similar vein to this approach to variance estimation, the correlation matrix has also been estimated with some success using exponentially weighted historical observations.[27]

[25] See Drost and Nijman (1993) and references therein.

[26] Such models are called autoregressive conditional heteroskedasticity (ARCH) time-series models. The Nobel Prize was shared with Clive W.J. Granger, who developed methods for analyzing cointegrated time series (informally, time series with common trends).

[27] For more details on models of volatility clustering, see Bollerslev, Engle, and Nelson (1994).

3.1.1.4. Multifactor Models A **multifactor model** is a model that explains the returns to an asset in terms of the values of a set of return drivers or risk factors.

The structure of a multifactor model, if the analyst believes that K factors drive asset returns, is as follows:

$$R_i = a_i + b_{i1}F_1 + b_{i2}F_2 + \cdots + b_{iK}F_K + \varepsilon_i \tag{4-2}$$

where

R_i = the return to asset i
a_i = an intercept term in the equation for asset i
F_k = the return to factor k, $k = 1, 2, \ldots, K$
b_{ik} = the sensitivity of the return to asset i to the return to factor k, $k = 1, 2, \ldots, K$
ε_i = an error term with a zero mean that represents the portion of the return to asset i not explained by the factor model. The error term is assumed to be uncorrelated with each of the K factors and to be uncorrelated with the error terms in the equations for other assets.

This structure has been found useful for modeling asset returns and covariances among asset returns. Multifactor models are useful for estimating covariances for the following reasons:

- By relating the returns on all assets to a common set of return drivers, a multifactor model simplifies the task of estimating covariances: Estimates of covariances between asset returns can be derived using the assets' factor sensitivities.
- When the factors are well chosen, a multifactor model approach may filter out noise (i.e., random variation in the data specific to the sample period).
- Such models make it relatively easy to verify the consistency of the covariance matrix, because if the smaller factor covariance matrix is consistent, so are any covariances computed on the basis of it.

In the balance of this section, we illustrate a top-down structured approach to using factor models in estimating the covariance matrix. In this approach, we model factors as portfolios of securities and start from a simple two-factor model at the most aggregated level.

Assume that two factors, a global equity factor and a global bonds factor, drive the returns of all assets in the investable universe. In this case, we start the modeling process with a covariance matrix for global equity and global bonds (we will refer to it in this discussion as the *equity–bonds covariance matrix*). A standard deviation of 14 percent for global equity and 4 percent for global bonds and a correlation between them of 0.30 imply the covariance matrix shown in Exhibit 4-4. In Exhibit 4-4, 0.0196 is the variance for global equity, 0.0016 is the variance for global bonds, and 0.0017 is the covariance between global equity and global bonds. The covariance between global equity and global bonds is the product of their standard deviations times the correlation between them, or (0.14)(0.04)(0.30) = 0.0017 to

EXHIBIT 4-4 Factor Covariance Matrix

	Global Equity	Global Bonds
Global Equity	0.0196	0.0017
Global Bonds	0.0017	0.0016

four decimal places; for global equity variance, $0.0196 = (0.14)^2$; for global bonds variance, $0.0016 = (0.04)^2$.

This is a **factor covariance matrix,** as it contains the covariances for the factors assumed to drive returns. In order to derive the **asset covariance matrix** (the covariance matrix for the asset classes or markets under consideration), we need to know how each of the markets responds to factor movements. We measure the responsiveness of markets to factor movements by the markets' **factor sensitivities** (also known as **factor betas** or **factor loadings**), represented by the quantities b_{ik} in Equation 4-2. If Market 1 moves by 110 basis points in response to a 100 basis point move of global equities, the corresponding factor sensitivity is 1.10. In addition, every market has some risk that is not explained by the factors. This is called the market's idiosyncratic or residual risk and is represented by the residual variance, $\text{Var}(\varepsilon_i)$ for market i. It is assumed that the residuals are uncorrelated.

Exhibit 4-5 shows hypothetical statistics for five securities markets.

Judged by its factor sensitivities, Market A is an equity market, with zero sensitivity to global bonds and a positive sensitivity to global equity. The zero sensitivity to global bonds does not mean that Market A is uncorrelated with global bonds, although it does mean that its partial correlation with bonds (the correlation after removing the influence of the other markets) is zero and that global bonds are not one of Market A's return drivers.[28]

In the case we are examining, we are assuming that the return of market i, M_i, is as follows:

$$M_i = a_i + b_{i1}F_1 + b_{i2}F_2 + \varepsilon_i, i = 1 \text{ to } 5$$

We compute the markets' variances and covariance using Equations 4-3a and 4-3b, respectively:

$$M_{ii} = b_{i1}^2\text{Var}(F_1) + b_{i2}^2\text{Var}(F_2) + 2b_{i1}b_{i2}\text{Cov}(F_1, F_2) + \text{Var}(\varepsilon_i), \text{ for } i = 1 \text{ to } 5 \quad (4\text{-}3a)$$

where M_{ii} is the variance of market i;

$$M_{ij} = b_{i1}b_{j1}\text{Var}(F_1) + b_{i2}b_{j2}\text{Var}(F_2) + (b_{i1}b_{j2} + b_{i2}b_{i1})\text{Cov}(F_1, F_2) \text{ for } i = 1 \text{ to } 5,$$

$$j = 1 \text{ to } 5, \text{ and } i \neq j \quad (4\text{-}3b)$$

where M_{ij} is the covariance of market i with market j.

EXHIBIT 4-5 Hypothetical Statistics for Five Markets

	Sensitivities		
	Global Equity	Global Bonds	Residual Risk
Market A	1.10	0	10.0%
Market B	1.05	0	8.0%
Market C	0.90	0	7.0%
Market D	0	1.03	1.2%
Market E	0	0.99	0.9%

Source: Staub (2006).

[28]Through the positive covariance (and correlation) between global equity and global bonds, Market A is still positively correlated with global bonds, although moderately.

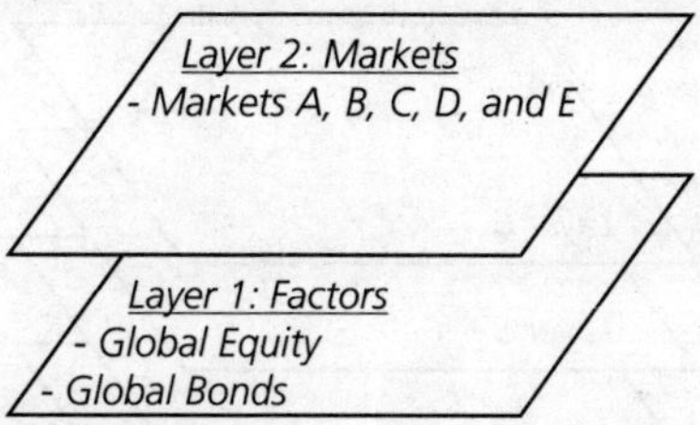

EXHIBIT 4-6 A Two-Layer Factor Approach
Source: Staub (2006). © 2006 UBS Global Asset Management (Americas) Inc. All rights reserved.

For example, suppose we want to compute the covariance between Markets A and B. Using Equation 4-3b (with $i = 1$ for Market A and $j = 2$ for Market B), we calculate that:

$$M_{12} = (1.1)(1.05)(0.0196) + (0)(0)(0.0016) + [(1.10)(0) + (0)(1.05)](0.0017) = 0.0226$$

Because both Market A and Market B have zero sensitivity to the global bonds factor, their correlation is explained only through their sensitivities to the global equity factor. Equations 4-3a and 4-3b are basic formulas for using multifactor models to estimate asset class covariance.

Note that establishing the consistency of the equity–bonds covariance matrix would not be a challenge, because it has only four entries. If the equity–bonds covariance matrix is consistent, then the covariance matrix for the markets calculated using Equations 4-3a and 4-3b will be consistent, even if many markets are involved so that consistency might be hard to check directly. The ability to establish consistency efficiently is a significant advantage of a multifactor model approach.

The above example, illustrated in Exhibit 4-6, is a two-layer structure with the factors on the first layer and the markets to be modeled on the second and final layer.[29]

In practice, a two-layer approach is not sufficient to accurately model interrelationships with the level of detail needed. Consider expanding the set of markets from securities markets to real estate markets, including U.S. real estate sectors—apartment, industry, office, and retail. These are mutually fairly highly correlated but have moderate or weak correlations with most other markets.

In the case of these real estate sectors, we would require new factor layers to model co-movements that are unrelated to the movement of factors in the prior layer. To meet our needs, the two-layer approach must be replaced by a multilayer approach, as illustrated in Exhibit 4-7 on page 154.

In a layer immediately below the U.S. real estate sectors, we would introduce U.S. real estate as a whole as a factor. The total number of layers would depend on the final set of markets whose covariance structure we wanted to model.[30]

3.1.2. Discounted Cash Flow Models **Discounted cash flow models** (DCF models) express the idea that an asset's value is the present value of its (expected) cash flows. Formally,

[29]The two-layer concept goes back to Grinold and Kahn (1995), who employ it for stock modeling. For more details, see p. 58f.
[30]See Staub (2006) for more details.

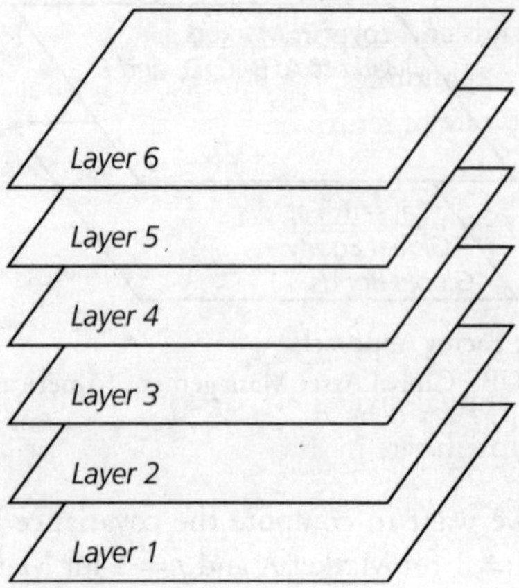

EXHIBIT 4-7 A Multilayer Factor Approach
Source: Staub (2006). © 2006 UBS Global Asset Management (Americas) Inc. All rights reserved.

the value of an asset using a DCF approach is as follows:[31]

$$V_0 = \sum_{t=1}^{\infty} \frac{CF_t}{(1+r)^t} \tag{4-4}$$

where

V_0 = the value of the asset at time $t = 0$ (today)
CF_t = the cash flow (or the expected cash flow, for risky cash flows) at time t
r = the discount rate or required rate of return

For simplicity, we represent the discount rate in Equation 4-4 as the same for all time periods—a flat term structure of discount rates.

Analysts use DCF models in expectations setting both for traditional securities markets and for alternative investment markets where the investment (e.g., private equity or real estate) generates cash flows.

DCF models are a basic tool for establishing the intrinsic value of an asset based on fundamentals (e.g., its projected cash flows) and its fair required rate of return. DCF models have the advantage of being forward looking. They do not address short-run factors such as current supply-and-demand conditions, so practitioners view them as more appropriate for setting long-term rather than short-term expectations. That said, asset prices that are disconnected from fundamentals may reflect conditions of speculative excess that can reverse abruptly.[32]

3.1.2.1. Equity Markets Analysts have frequently used the **Gordon (constant) growth model** form of the dividend discount model, solved for the required rate of return, to formulate

[31]If the asset trades in an integrated market, the future cash flows of the asset are to be translated into the home currencies of investors.

[32]See Calverley (2004) for a discussion of **bubbles** (episodes in which asset market prices move to extremely high levels in relation to estimated intrinsic value).

the long-term expected return of equity markets. The Gordon growth model assumes that there is a long-term trend in dividends and corporate earnings, which is a reasonable approximation for many developed country economies.[33] The expression for the Gordon growth model solved for $E(R_e)$, the expected rate of return on equity, is:

$$E(R_e) = \frac{D_0(1+g)}{P_0} + g = \frac{D_1}{P_0} + g \tag{4-5}$$

where

D_0 = the most recent annual dividend per share
g = the long-term growth rate in dividends, assumed equal to the long-term earnings growth rate
P_0 = the current share price

According to the Gordon growth model, share price should appreciate at a rate equal to the dividend growth rate. Therefore, in Equation 4-5, the expected rate of return is composed of two parts: the dividend yield (D_1/P_0) and the capital gains (or appreciation) yield (g).

The quantity g can be estimated most simply as the growth rate in **nominal gross domestic product** (nominal GDP), a money measure of the goods and services produced within a country's borders.[34] Nominal GDP growth can be estimated as the sum of the estimated real growth rate in GDP plus the expected long-run inflation rate. A more advanced analysis can take account of any perceived differences between the expected growth of the overall economy and that of the constituent companies of the particular equity index that the analyst has chosen to represent equities. The analyst can use:

Earnings growth rate = GDP growth rate + Excess corporate growth (for the index companies)

where the term *excess corporate growth* may be positive or negative depending on whether the sectoral composition of the index companies is viewed as higher or lower growth than that of the overall economy.[35] If the analyst has chosen a broad-based equity index, the excess corporate growth adjustment, if any, should be small. Exhibit 4-8 presents the real GDP growth rates for selected countries.

In the United States and other major markets, share repurchases have become an important means for companies to distribute cash to shareholders. Grinold and Kroner (2002) provided a restatement of the Gordon growth model that takes explicit account of repurchases. Their model also provides a means for analysts to incorporate expectations of valuation levels through the familiar price-to-earnings ratio (P/E). The **Grinold–Kroner model,** which is based on elaborating the expression for the expected single-period return on a share, is:[36]

$$E(R_e) \approx \frac{D}{P} - \Delta S + i + g + \Delta PE \tag{4-6}$$

33 See Jagannathan, McGrattan, and Scherbina (2000).

34 See Diermeier (1990) and Singer and Terhaar (1997) for a theoretical analysis of this relationship.

35 See Grinold and Kroner (2002), p. 12.

36 See Grinold and Kroner (2002) for a derivation. Ibbotson and Chen (2003) presented a broadly similar analysis of the sources of equity returns but did not model stock repurchases.

EXHIBIT 4-8 Average Annual Real GDP Growth Rates: 1980–2004 (in percent)

Country	Time Period 1980–1989	1990–1999	2000–2004
Australia	3.4%	3.3%	3.2%
Canada	3.0	2.4	3.0
Denmark	2.2	2.3	1.5
France	2.1	1.8	2.1
Germany	1.9	1.3	1.0
Italy	2.4	1.5	1.3
Japan	3.9	1.7	1.5
Netherlands	2.0	3.0	1.3
Sweden	2.4	1.8	2.6
Switzerland	1.8	1.1	1.4
United Kingdom	2.4	2.1	2.8
United States	3.1	3.1	2.6

Source: OECD, Datastream, Bloomberg.

where

$E(R_e)$ = the expected rate of return on equity
D/P = the expected dividend yield
ΔS = the expected percent change in number of shares outstanding
i = the expected inflation rate
g = the expected real total earnings growth rate (not identical to the EPS growth rate in general, with changes in shares outstanding)
ΔPE = the per period percent change in the P/E multiple

The term ΔS is negative in the case of net positive share repurchases, so $-\Delta S$ is a positive **repurchase yield** in such cases.

Equation 4-6 consists of three components: an expected income return, an expected nominal earnings growth return, and an expected repricing return (from expected P/E expansion or contraction).

- Expected income return: $D/P - \Delta S$
- Expected nominal earnings growth return: $i + g$
- Expected repricing return: ΔPE

The expected nominal earnings growth return and the expected repricing return constitute the expected capital gains.

The Grinold–Kroner model can be used not only in expectations setting, but also as a tool to analyze the sources of historical returns. For example, the S&P 500 achieved a compound growth rate of 10.7 percent per year over the 76-year period 1926 to 2001 (corresponding to an equity premium of 5.3 percent).[37] Following the Grinold–Kroner analysis, the sources of this return were as follows:

[37]The *equity risk premium* was defined by the authors as the mean return on the S&P 500 less the mean 10-year U.S. Treasury bond return over this period.

- 4.4 percent from income
- 4.8 percent from nominal earnings growth (consisting of 1.7 percent real earnings growth and 3.1 percent annual inflation)
- 1.5 percent from repricing

As a check, 4.4% +4.8% + 1.5% = 10.7%. Repricing return was a volatile contributor to total return. The growth of the P/E from 10.2 in 1926 to 30.6 in 2001 represented a compound annual growth rate of 1.5 percent. However, the P/E of 10.2 in 1926 was actually somewhat above the P/E in 1981: Most of the repricing return was concentrated in the 20 years leading up to the ending date of 2001.

EXAMPLE 4-13 The Grinold–Kroner Forecast of the U.S. Equity Risk Premium

The details of the Grinold–Kroner (GK) forecast of the U.S. equity risk premium (as of early 2002) are instructive. Their forecast horizon was 10 years.

Expected income return. The forecast dividend yield was 1.75 percent (somewhat above the then-current yield of 1.4 percent but below the historical mean of over 4 percent for 1926 to 2001). The repurchase yield was forecast to be 0.5 percent, down from the 1 to 2 percent rate of the 1990s, which was viewed as an unusual period. The expected income return was therefore 1.75% +0.5% = 2.25%.

Expected nominal earnings growth return. Economic theory suggests that the real GDP growth rate is the sum of labor productivity growth and labor supply growth. GK took the historical 2 percent per year U.S. labor productivity growth rate as their forecast. Using a U.S. population growth forecast of 0.8 percent and assuming a 0.2 percentage point increase in the labor force participation rate, the forecast of the labor supply growth rate was 1 percent per year. The overall real GDP growth estimate of 2% +1% = 3% was within the 2.7 percent to 3.6 percent range of forecasts by economists. Viewing the S&P 500 companies as having a slightly higher growth profile than the overall economy, GK added a 0.5 percent excess corporate growth return for a 3.5 percent real earnings growth return estimate. GK expected an inflation rate of 2.5 percent, 0.3 percentage points above the contemporaneous consensus estimate of economists (viewed by GK as slightly optimistic). Thus, the expected nominal earnings growth return was 3.5% +2.5% = 6%.

Expected repricing return. This component was perhaps the hardest to forecast. Viewing the contemporaneous P/E of 28 as a slight overreaction to the positive factors of decreased inflation, technological advances (positive productivity shocks), and an expected increase in growth rates from globalization, over a 10-year horizon, GK forecast downward repricing equal to −0.75 percent per year.

The GK forecast of the expected return on U.S. equities was therefore 2.25% +6% − 0.75% = 7.5%. Subtracting the 10-year government bond yield of 5 percent, the GK forecast of the U.S. equity risk premium was 2.5 percent.

The 2.5 percent estimate put GK in a middle position between the predictions of the "risk premium is dead" and the "rational exuberance" camps.

EXAMPLE 4-14 Forecasting the Return on Equities Using the Grinold–Kroner Model

Cynthia Casey employs the Grinold–Kroner model in forecasting long-term developed market equity returns. Casey makes the following forecasts:

- A 2.25 percent dividend yield on Canadian equities, based on the S&P/TSE Composite Index.
- A repurchase yield of 1 percent for Canadian equities.
- A long-term inflation rate of 2 percent per year.
- Long-term corporate real earnings growth at 4 percent per year, based on a 1 percentage point premium for corporate growth over her expected Canadian GDP growth rate of 3.0 percent.
- An expansion rate for P/E multiples of 0.25 percent per year.

Based only on the information given, determine the expected rate of return on Canadian equities consistent with Casey's assumptions.

Solution: Using Casey's assumptions and Equation 4-6, the expected rate of return on Canadian equities should be 9.5 percent, calculated as:

$$E(R_e) \approx 2.25\% - (-1.0\%) + 2.0\% + 4.0\% + 0.25\% = 9.5\%$$

DCF model thinking has provided various methods for evaluating stock market levels. The best known of these is the Fed model, which asserts that the stock market is overvalued if the market's current earnings yield (earnings divided by price) is less than the 10-year Treasury bond yield.[38] The earnings yield is the required rate of return for no-growth equities and is thus a conservative estimate of the expected return for equities. The intuition of the Fed model is that when the yield of T-bonds is greater than the earnings yield of stocks (a riskier investment than T-bonds), stocks are overvalued.

3.1.2.2. Fixed-Income Markets The DCF model is a standard tool in the pricing of fixed-income instruments. In many such markets, bonds are quoted in terms of the single discount rate (the yield to maturity, or YTM) that equates the present value of the instrument's promised cash flows to its market price. The yield to maturity of a bellwether (reference) instrument for a bond market segment is a readily available first approximation of the market expected return for the asset segment at a time horizon equal to the maturity of the instrument.[39] The YTM

[38]This model was developed by the U.S. Federal Reserve System (the Fed), the central bank of the United States.

[39]If the bond is callable, a downward adjustment would generally need to be made. **Yield to worst** (the yield assuming the bond is called at the earliest opportunity) is sometimes used as a conservative estimate in such cases.

calculation makes the strong assumption that as interest payments are received, they can be reinvested at an interest rate that always equals the YTM. Therefore, the YTM of a bond with intermediate cash flows is an estimate of the expected rate of return on the bond that is more or less plausible depending on the level of the YTM. If a representative zero-coupon bond is available at the chosen time horizon, its YTM would be a superior estimate.

3.1.3. The Risk Premium Approach The **risk premium approach** expresses the expected return on a risky asset as the sum of the risk-free rate of interest and one or more risk premiums that compensate investors for the risky asset's exposure to sources of **priced risk** (risk for which investors demand compensation). Investors would avoid purchasing assets offering inadequate expected compensation for priced risk; the lower demand should lead to lower asset prices until the point is reached at which the compensation for risk is adequate. The risk premium approach (sometimes called the **build-up approach**) is most often applied to estimating the required return in equity and bond markets.[40] In the following discussion, we assume that assets are fairly priced so that an asset's required return is also an investor's expected return.[41]

3.1.3.1. A General Expression Following our verbal definition of the risk premium approach, a formal expression for the expected return on a risky asset is

$$E(R_i) = R_F + (\text{Risk premium})_1 + (\text{Risk premium})_2 + \cdots + (\text{Risk premium})_K \quad (4\text{-}7)$$

where $E(R_i)$ is the asset's expected return and R_F denotes the risk-free rate of interest.

3.1.3.2. Fixed-Income Premiums The expected bond return, $E(R_b)$, can be built up as the real rate of interest plus a set of premiums:

$$\begin{aligned} E(R_b) = {} & \text{Real risk-free interest rate} + \text{Inflation premium} + \text{Default risk premium} \\ & + \text{Illiquidity premium} + \text{Maturity premium} + \text{Tax premium} \end{aligned}$$

- The **real risk-free interest rate** is the single-period interest rate for a completely risk-free security if no inflation were expected. In economic theory, the real risk-free rate reflects the time preferences of individuals for current versus future real consumption.
- The **inflation premium** compensates investors for expected inflation and reflects the average inflation rate expected over the maturity of the debt plus a premium (or discount) for the probability attached to higher inflation than expected (or greater disinflation). The sum of the real risk-free interest rate and the inflation premium is the **nominal risk-free interest rate,** often represented by a governmental Treasury bill YTM.[42]

[40] For more discussion on equity risk premiums, see Arnott and Bernstein (2002), Grinold and Kroner (2002), and Ilmanen (2003).

[41] If there is a mispricing, then the expected return would differ from the required return by a capital appreciation or depreciation component reflecting the convergence to fair value over some time frame.

[42] Technically, 1 plus the nominal rate equals the product of 1 plus the real rate and 1 plus the inflation rate. As a quick approximation, however, the nominal rate is equal to the real rate plus an inflation premium. In this discussion, we focus on approximate additive relationships to highlight the underlying concepts.

- The **default risk premium** compensates investors for the possibility that the borrower will fail to make a promised payment at the contracted time and in the contracted amount. This itself may be analyzed as the sum of the expected default loss in yield terms plus a premium for the nondiversifiable risk of default.[43]
- The **illiquidity premium** compensates investors for the risk of loss relative to an investment's fair value if the investment needs to be converted to cash quickly.[44]
- The **maturity premium** compensates investors for the increased sensitivity, in general, of the market value of debt to a change in market interest rates as maturity is extended, holding all else equal. The difference between the interest rate on longer-maturity, liquid Treasury debt and that on short-term Treasury debt reflects a positive maturity premium for the longer-term debt (and possibly different inflation premiums as well).
- A **tax premium** may also be applicable to certain classes of bonds in some tax jurisdictions.[45]

For example, consider the expected return on a five-year Treasury instrument traded in a developed market when the real risk-free interest rate is 1.5 percent per year, the expected inflation rate over that horizon is 2.5 percent per year, and a one-year Treasury instrument has a yield to maturity of 4 percent per year. Suppose that the five-year Treasury instrument is priced to yield 5 percent. What is the source of the 5 percent to 4 percent spread? As government debt does not have default risk, the longer-term instrument does not bear a default risk premium. Nor does it have an illiquidity premium or differ in taxation from the one-year instrument. The spread would be accounted for as a 1 percent maturity premium.

EXAMPLE 4-15 The Long-Term Real Risk-Free Rate

The real risk-free rate is compensation for forgoing current consumption in exchange for certain future consumption. Historical real cash rates exhibit high volatility and differ through time and between countries. We distinguish between the current real rate (driven by cyclical factors) and the long-term real rate assumption (based on sustainable equilibrium conditions). In a free economy, the real rate equilibrates the productivity of the economy and society's time preference for consumption. On a forward-looking basis, we can form opinions about the size of the real rate by analyzing societal consumption time preferences and studying the economy's productivity. For developed countries, a range for the long-term real risk-free rate is 2.0 percent to 2.8 percent. Obviously, variation around this estimate has been and is likely to be substantial, but 2.4 percent is an indication of central tendency over the long term.

[43] See Elton, Gruber, Agrawal, and Mann (2001) for empirical support for such an analysis.

[44] Some writers refer to the *illiquidity* premium as the *liquidity* premium (where "lack of liquidity" is understood).

[45] For example, in the United States, bonds issued by private corporations are generally tax disadvantaged relative to bonds issued by the federal government, and a tax premium would compensate corporate bondholders. See Elton, Gruber, Agarwal, and Mann (2001) for evidence on the tax premium.

EXAMPLE 4-16 The Real Interest Rate and Inflation Premium in Equilibrium

The expected return to any asset or asset class has at least three components: the real risk-free rate, the inflation premium, and the risk premium. In equilibrium and assuming fully integrated markets, the real risk-free rate should be identical for all assets globally. Similarly, from the frame of reference of any individual investor, the inflation premium should be the same for all assets. For investors with different base currency consumption baskets, different inflation premiums are required to compensate for different rates of depreciation of investment capital.

The inflation premium is the compensation for the depreciation of invested principal because of *expected* price inflation. In equilibrium, we use the inflation rate that each market is using to compensate it for the loss of purchasing power.

EXAMPLE 4-17 The Risk Premium: Some Facts

The term *risk premium* is often used to refer to the total premium above the nominal default-risk-free interest rate. Some points to keep in mind:

- In comparing risk premium estimates, the analyst should make sure that a common benchmark for the risk-free rate is being used; if not, the estimates should be adjusted to a common risk-free-rate reference point.
- Some analysts do not view illiquidity as a kind of risk and may refer to an illiquidity premium in addition to the risk premium when estimating the required return on an illiquid asset.
- Modeling any risk premium requires an assessment of the degree of capital market integration. Capital market integration will be discussed in Section 3.1.4.

Examples 4-15, 4-16, and 4-17 provide some information on the real risk-free interest rate, including long-term levels. The inflation premium is typically a more volatile element of the yield of bonds. In standard discussions of term-structure theory, the term structure of interest rates for default-free government bonds can provide an estimate of inflation expectations. Furthermore, in markets with active issuance of inflation-indexed bonds, the yield spread at a given maturity of conventional government bonds over inflation-indexed bonds of the same maturity may be able to provide a market-based estimate of the inflation premium at that horizon. The analyst can use market yield data and credit ratings (or other credit models) to estimate the default risk premium by comparing the yields on bonds matched along other dimensions but differing in default risk. An analogous approach may be applied to estimating the other premiums.

3.1.3.3. The Equity Risk Premium The **equity risk premium** is the compensation required by investors for the additional risk of equity compared with debt (debt has a prior claim on the cash flows of the company). An estimate of the equity risk premium directly supplies an estimate of the expected return on equities through the following expression:

$$E(R_e) = \text{YTM on a long-term government bond} + \text{Equity risk premium} \quad (4\text{-}8)$$

where "long-term" has usually been interpreted as 10 or 20 years. (In many markets, bonds with maturities longer than 10 years are not available or actively traded.) As long as one is consistent with the choice of maturity in defining the equity risk premium, either choice is feasible. Equation 4-8 has been called the **bond-yield-plus-risk-premium method** of estimating the expected return on equity. From Equation 4-8, we also see that the *equity risk premium in practice is specifically defined as the expected excess return over and above a long-term government bond yield.*

A historical analysis has often been used as a point of departure in estimating the equity risk premium. Exhibit 4-9 gives the *ex post* data for the 106 years from 1900 to 2005. The standard deviation column represents the volatility in the difference between equity returns and bond returns on a year-by-year basis.

From Exhibit 4-9, we can draw the following conclusions:

- The geometric mean historical equity risk premium ranged from a low of 1.8 percent (Switzerland) to a high of 6.2 percent (Australia) with an average of 4.0 percent.

EXHIBIT 4-9 Historical Equity Risk Premiums around the World: 1900–2005

	Annual Realized Equity Risk Premium Relative to Long Bond Returns			
Country	Geometric Mean	Arithmetic Mean	Standard Error	Standard Deviation
Australia	6.2%	7.8%	1.8%	18.8%
Belgium	2.6	4.4	2.0	20.1
Canada	4.2	5.7	1.7	17.9
Denmark	2.1	3.3	1.6	16.2
France	3.9	6.0	2.2	22.3
Germany (ex-1922/3)	5.3	8.3	2.7	27.4
Ireland	3.6	5.2	1.8	18.4
Italy	4.3	7.7	2.9	29.7
Japan	5.9	10.0	3.2	33.1
Netherlands	3.9	5.9	2.1	21.6
Norway	2.6	5.3	2.7	27.4
South Africa	5.4	7.0	1.9	19.3
Spain	2.3	4.2	2.0	20.2
Sweden	5.2	7.5	2.2	22.3
Switzerland	1.8	3.3	1.7	17.5
United Kingdom	4.1	5.3	1.6	16.6
United States	4.5	6.5	2.0	20.2
World average	4.0	5.1	1.5	15.0

Source: Dimson, Marsh, and Staunton (2006), Table 11. See this source for the details of the equity and bond series used.

- The arithmetic mean historical equity risk premium ranged from a low of 3.3 percent (Denmark and Switzerland) to a high of 10.0 percent (Japan) with an average of 5.1 percent.
- As measured by the standard error (which applies to the arithmetic mean), for most markets there is considerable sampling error in the sample mean estimate of the (presumed unchanging) population mean equity risk premium. Consider the United States, with a standard error of 2 percent. Under a normality assumption, one could be only 68 percent confident that the population mean is between 4.5 percent (6.5%–2.0%) and 8.5 percent (6.5% + 2.0%).
- The standard deviation column shows that there is a great amount of variation in the annual return difference between equities and bonds.

The size of *ex ante* equity risk premiums in international markets and the interpretation of the historical record for the purposes of estimating them have been the source of a lively, continuing, and unresolved debate. Grinold and Kroner (2002) and Dimson, Marsh, and Staunton (2002, 2006) provide useful observations on the issues raised.

3.1.4. Financial Market Equilibrium Models

Financial equilibrium models describe relationships between expected return and risk in which supply and demand are in balance. In that sense, equilibrium prices or equilibrium returns are fair if the equilibrium model is correct.

Equilibrium approaches to setting capital market expectations include the Black–Litterman approach and the international CAPM–based approach presented in Singer and Terhaar (1997). The Black–Litterman approach reverse-engineers the expected returns implicit in a diversified market portfolio, combining them with the investor's own views in a systematic way that takes account of the investor's confidence in his or her views.[46] This approach is discussed at greater length in Chapter 5.

Singer and Terhaar (1997) proposed an equilibrium approach to developing capital market expectations that involves calculating the expected return on each asset class based on the international capital asset pricing model (ICAPM),[47] taking account of market imperfections that are not considered by the ICAPM.[48]

Assuming that the risk premium on any currency equals zero—as it would be if purchasing power parity relationships hold—the ICAPM gives the expected return on any asset as the sum of:

- The (domestic) risk-free rate and
- A risk premium based on the asset's sensitivity to the world market portfolio and expected return on the world market portfolio in excess of the risk-free rate.

Equation 4-9 is the formal expression for the ICAPM:

$$E(R_i) = R_F + \beta_i[E(R_M) - R_F] \tag{4-9}$$

[46]See Black and Litterman (1991, 1992). The notion of using reverse optimization to infer expected returns was first described in Sharpe (1974).

[47]ICAPM has also been used as an acronym for the intertemporal capital asset pricing model developed by Merton (1973). In this presentation, ICAPM refers to the international capital asset pricing model.

[48]See also Terhaar, Staub, and Singer (2003). The specific suggestion of this approach is to use the factor-model-based estimate of the covariance matrix presented in Section 3.1.1.4.

where

$E(R_i)$ = the expected return on asset i given its beta
R_F = the risk-free rate of return
$E(R_M)$ = the expected return on the world market portfolio
β_i = the asset's sensitivity to returns on the world market portfolio, equal to $\text{Cov}(R_i, R_M)/\text{Var}(R_M)$

An important question concerns the identification of an appropriate proxy for the world market portfolio. Based on the criteria of Brinson, Diermeier, and Schlarbaum (1986, p.17), the analyst can define and use the **global investable market** (GIM). The GIM is a practical proxy for the world market portfolio consisting of traditional and alternative asset classes with sufficient capacity to absorb meaningful investment.[49]

Equation 4-9 implies that an asset class risk premium, RP_i, equal to $E(R_i) - R_F$, is a simple function of the world market risk premium, RP_M, equal to $E(R_M) - R_F$:[50]

$$\text{RP}_i = \frac{\sigma_i}{\sigma_m}\rho_{i,M}(\text{RP}_M)$$

Moving the market standard deviation of returns term within the parentheses, we find that an asset class's risk premium equals the product of the Sharpe ratio (RP_M/σ_M) of the world market portfolio, the asset's own volatility, and the asset class's correlation with the world market portfolio:

$$\text{RP}_i = \sigma_i\rho_{i,M}\left(\frac{\text{RP}_M}{\sigma_M}\right) \qquad (4\text{-}10)$$

Equation 4-10 is one of two key equations in the Singer–Terhaar approach. The Sharpe ratio in Equation 4-10 (i.e., RP_M/σ_M) is the expected excess return per unit of standard deviation of the world market portfolio. The world market portfolio's standard deviation represents a kind of risk (systematic risk) that cannot be avoided through diversification and that should therefore command a return in excess of the risk-free rate. An asset class's risk premium is therefore the expected excess return accruing to the asset class given its global systematic risk (i.e., its beta relative to the world market portfolio).

Equation 4-10 requires a market Sharpe ratio estimate. Singer and Terhaar (1997, pp. 44–52) describe a complete analysis for estimating it. As of the date of their analysis, 1997, they recommended a value of 0.30 (a 0.30 percent return per 1 percent of compensated risk). Goodall, Manzini, and Rose (1999, pp. 4-10) revisited this issue on the basis of different macro models and recommended a value of 0.28. For this exposition, we adopt a value of 0.28. In fact, the Sharpe ratio of the global market could change over time with changing global economic fundamentals.

To illustrate Equation 4-10, suppose that an investor predicts that the standard deviation of Canadian bonds will be 7.0 percent per year and that their correlation with the GIM is 0.54. Then, with our estimate of the market Sharpe ratio, we would estimate the risk premium as

$$7\% \times 0.54 \times 0.28 = 1.06\%$$

[49] See Brinson, Diermeier, and Schlarbaum (1986) for more details.

[50] The expression is derived as follows: $\text{RP}_i = \beta_i(\text{RP}_M) = [\text{Cov}(R_i, R_M)/\sigma_M^2](\text{RP}_M) = (\sigma_i\ \sigma_M\rho_{iM}/\sigma_M^2)(\text{RP}_M) = \sigma_i\rho_{iM}(\text{RP}_M/\sigma_M)$, where we have used the fact that $\text{Cov}(R_i, R_M) = \sigma_i\sigma_M\rho_{iM}$.

For Canadian equities, with a standard deviation of 17 percent and a 0.70 correlation with the GIM, we would estimate the equity risk premium as

$$17\% \times 0.70 \times 0.28 = 3.33\%$$

The Singer–Terhaar approach recognizes the need to account for market imperfections that are not considered by the ICAPM. We will consider two market imperfections: illiquidity and market segmentation.

In the discussion of bonds, we defined the illiquidity premium as compensation for the risk of loss relative to an investment's fair value if the investment needs to be converted to cash quickly. The ICAPM assumes **perfect markets** (markets without any frictional costs, where all assets trade in liquid markets). Thus, we need to add an estimated illiquidity premium to an ICAPM expected return estimate as appropriate. The ICAPM was formulated with developed securities markets such as the Canadian bond and equity markets in mind, and the Singer–Terhaar approach would not add an illiquidity premium to ICAPM expected return estimates for Canadian stocks and bonds.

However, the illustrated risk premium estimates for Canadian bonds and equities (1.06 percent and 3.33 percent, respectively) are those that would hold if Canadian bond and equity markets were perfectly integrated with other world asset markets. **Market integration** means that there are no impediments or barriers to capital mobility across markets. Barriers include not only legal barriers, such as restrictions a national emerging market might place on foreign investment, but also cultural predilections and other investor preferences. If markets are perfectly integrated, all investors worldwide participate equally in setting prices in any individual national market. Market integration implies that two assets in different markets with identical risk characteristics must have the same expected return. **Market segmentation** means that there are some meaningful impediments to capital movement across markets. Although many barriers to international capital flows have come down, some do persist and a number of asset markets are in practice at least partially segmented across national borders. The more a market is segmented, the more it is dominated by *local* investors. When markets are segmented, two assets in different markets with identical risk characteristics may have different expected returns. If an asset in a segmented market appears undervalued to a nondomestic investor *not* considering barriers to capital mobility, *after* such barriers are considered, the investor may not actually be able to exploit the opportunity.

Most markets lie between the extremes of perfect market integration and complete market segmentation. A home-biased perspective or partial segmentation is perhaps the best representation of most markets in the world today. We need first to develop an estimate of the risk premium for the case of complete market segmentation. With such an estimate in hand, the estimate of the risk premium for the common case of partial segmentation is just a weighted average of the risk premium assuming perfect market integration and the risk premium assuming complete segmentation, where the weights reflect the analyst's view of the degree of integration of the given asset market.

To address the task of estimating the risk premium for the case of complete market segmentation, we must first recognize that if a market is completely segmented, the market portfolio in Equations 4-9 and 4-10 must be identified as the *individual local market.* Because the individual market and the reference market portfolio are identical, $\rho_{i,M}$ in Equation 4-10 equals 1. (For example, if Canadian equities were a completely segmented market, the reference market portfolio and the individual market portfolio would each be a broad-based index for Canadian equities, and the correlation of such an index with itself would of course be 1.) The value of 1 for correlation is the maximum value, so all else being equal, the risk premium for the completely segmented markets case is higher than that for the perfectly integrated markets case and equal to the amount shown in Equation 4-11:

$$RP_i = \sigma_i \left(\frac{RP_M}{\sigma_M} \right) \tag{4-11}$$

This is the second key equation in the Singer–Terhaar approach. Assuming that Canadian bonds and equities trade in completely segmented markets, we would calculate respective risk premiums of:[51]

$$7\% \times 0.28 = 1.96\%$$

and

$$17\% \times 0.28 = 4.76\%$$

Taking the degree of integration as 0.8 for both Canadian equities and bonds, our final risk premium estimates would be as follows:

- $RP_{CdnFI} = (0.8 \times 1.06\%) + (0.2 \times 1.96\%) = 1.24\%$
- $RP_{Cdnequities} = (0.8 \times 3.33\%) + (0.2 \times 4.76\%) = 3.62\%$

Thus, assuming a risk-free rate of 4 percent, we would estimate the expected returns on Canadian bonds and equities as the sum of the risk-free rate and the relevant risk premium, as follows:

- Canadian bonds: $E(R_{CdnFI}) = 4\% + 1.24\% = 5.24\%$
- Canadian equities: $E(R_{Cdnequities}) = 4\% + 3.62\% = 7.62\%$

To summarize, to arrive at an expected return estimate using the Singer–Terhaar approach, we take the following steps:

- Estimate the perfectly integrated and the completely segmented risk premiums for the asset class using the ICAPM.
- Add the applicable illiquidity premium, if any, to the estimates from the prior step.
- Estimate the degree to which the asset market is perfectly integrated.
- Take a weighted average of the perfectly integrated and the completely segmented risk premiums using the estimate of market integration from the prior step.[52]

The analyst needs to develop estimates of the degree of integration of an asset market, but as a starting point, research has suggested that developed market equities and bonds are approximately 80 percent integrated. To give a flavor of the variation that might be expected, research has also indicated that U.S. and U.K. real estate is approximately 70 percent integrated; real estate in France, Germany, the Netherlands, and Switzerland is 60 percent integrated; emerging market equities and bonds are about 65 percent integrated; and at the

[51] For simplicity, we are assuming that the Sharpe ratios of the GIM and the local market portfolio (used in Equation 4-11) are the same.

[52] Alternatively, we can substitute the Sharpe ratio of the "typical" local investor's investment portfolio for the GIM portfolio in Equation 4-10 and use the correlation of the asset class under consideration with that typical local portfolio.

low end of integration are assets such as timber at 50 percent (United States, Australia) or 40 percent (Argentina, Brazil, Chile, Uruguay). Currency and cash markets are 100 percent integrated.[53]

Another task for the analyst is estimating the illiquidity premium for an asset class. Estimating this premium for alternative investments presents a great challenge. Many such investments cannot be traded at all for some time (i.e., are **locked up,** as might be the case for early-stage venture capital). Rebalancing to a target allocation is not feasible during the lockup period and is relatively costly afterward.

EXAMPLE 4-18 Justifying Capital Market Forecasts

Samuel Breed, CIO of a university endowment, is presenting the capital market expectations shown in Exhibit 4-10 to the endowment's board of trustees.

EXHIBIT 4-10 Capital Market Projections

Asset Class	Proxy	Projected 5-Year Annual Return	Projected Standard Deviation
Equities			
1. Large-cap U.S. equity	S&P 500	8.8%	16.5%
2. Small/mid-cap U.S. equity	Russell 2500	9.8	22.0
3. Ex-U.S. equity	MSCI EAFE	9.2	20.0
Fixed Income			
4. Domestic fixed income	LB Aggregate	4.7	4.5
5. Non-U.S. fixed income	Citi Non-U.S. Govt.	4.6	9.5
Other Assets			
6. U.S. real estate	NCREIF	7.6	14.0
7. Private equity	VE Post Venture Cap.	12.0	34.0
8. Cash equivalents	90-day T-bill	3.3	1.0
Inflation	CPI-U	2.6	1.4

Correlations:	**1**	**2**	**3**	**4**	**5**	**6**	**7**	**8**
1. Large-cap U.S. equity	1.0							
2. Small/mid U.S. equity	0.85	1.0						
3. Ex-U.S. equity	0.74	0.61	1.0					
4. Domestic fixed income	0.27	0.20	0.21	1.0				
5. Non-U.S. fixed income	0.03	−0.03	0.22	0.32	1.0			
6. U.S. real estate	0.64	0.52	0.47	0.20	0.03	1.0		
7. Private equity	0.63	0.57	0.63	0.20	0.10	0.45	1.0	
8. Cash equivalents	−0.10	−0.15	−0.25	0.30	−0.05	−0.06	0.07	1.0

[53] See Staub (2005).

Assume the following:

- The Sharpe ratio of the global investable market portfolio (GIM) is 0.28, and its standard deviation is 7 percent.
- The beta of private equity with respect to the GIM is 3.3, and the beta of small/mid-cap U.S. equity is 2.06.

William Smyth, a trustee, questions various projections for private equity, as follows:

A. "I have seen volatility estimates for private equity based on appraisal data that are much smaller than the one you are presenting, in which the volatility of private equity is much larger than that of small/mid-cap U.S. equity. Your volatility estimate for private equity must be wrong."
B. "The premium of private equity over small/mid-cap U.S. equity is not justifiable because they both represent ownership interests in U.S. business."
C. "Using the ICAPM, the forecast correlation between private equity returns and small/mid-cap U.S. equity returns is lower than your estimate indicates."

1. Evaluate whether Smyth's Comment A is accurate.
2. Evaluate whether Smyth's Comment B is accurate.
3. Evaluate whether Smyth's Comment C is accurate.

Solution to Problem 1: Smyth's Comment A is not accurate. Although private equity and small-cap stocks both represent ownership interests, private equity is not traded and appraisal data will tend to underestimate volatility.

Solution to Problem 2: Smyth's Comment B is not accurate. One justification for a higher expected return for private equity is that it has a lockup period and should therefore bear an illiquidity premium.

Solution to Problem 3: Smyth's Comment C is accurate. According to elementary portfolio theory, the correlation between two assets is given by $\beta_1\beta_2\sigma_M^2/\sigma_1\sigma_2$. Thus, the correlation between private equity and small/mid-cap U.S. equity is equal to $(3.3)(2.06)(7\%)^2/(34\%)(22\%) = 0.45$, which is lower than the estimate of 0.57 given in Exhibit 4-10.

The illiquidity premium for an alternative investment should be positively related to the length of the investment's lockup period or illiquidity horizon. How can the amount of the illiquidity premium be estimated? One estimation approach uses the investment's **multiperiod Sharpe ratio** (MPSR), which is based on the investment's multiperiod wealth in excess of the wealth generated by the risk-free investment (i.e., compounded return over compounded cash return). The relevant MPSR is one calculated over a holding period equal to the investment's lockup period. There would be no incentive to invest in an illiquid alternative investment unless its MPSR—its risk-adjusted wealth—were at least as high as the MPSR of the market portfolio at the end of the lockup period. Suppose that an alternative investment has a lockup period of eight years and its ICAPM-given required rate of return is 12 percent but its MPSR is below that of the GIM—say, 0.67—at an eight-year horizon. If increasing its expected return to 20 percent makes the alternative investment's MSPR equal 0.67 at the eight-year horizon, then the estimate of the illiquidity premium is 20% − 12% = 8%.[54]

Example 4-19 illustrates the Singer–Terhaar approach. In the example, for simplicity's sake, the ICAPM betas are used to develop covariance estimates.

EXAMPLE 4-19 Setting CME Using the Singer–Terhaar Approach

Zimmerman Capital Management (ZCM) is developing a strategic asset allocation for a small U.S. foundation that has approved investment in the following five asset classes: U.S. equities, U.S. fixed income, non-U.S. equities, non-U.S. fixed income, and U.S. real estate. The foundation limits nondomestic assets to no more than 12 percent of invested assets.

- The final set of expectations needed consists of the expected returns, standard deviations, and all distinct pairwise covariances of U.S. equities, U.S. fixed income, non-U.S. equities, non-U.S. fixed income, and U.S. real estate. The investment time horizon is 10 years.
- A risk premium approach will be taken to developing expected return estimates following the methodology of Singer and Terhaar. Historical estimates of standard deviations will be used, and ICAPM betas will be used to develop estimates of covariances.
- Exhibit 4-11 supplies the standard deviation estimates and gives relevant inputs for other quantities needed. In addition, ZCM has gathered the following facts and estimates:
  - The Sharpe ratio of the GIM is estimated to be 0.28.
  - The standard deviation of the GIM is estimated to be 7 percent.
  - The risk-free rate of interest is 3 percent.
- Equities and bonds are assumed to be 80 percent integrated, and U.S. real estate is assumed to be 70 percent integrated.

EXHIBIT 4-11 Equilibrium Approach to Risk Premium Estimation

Asset Class	Standard Deviation	Correlation with GIM	Premium to Equate Sharpe Ratio at Illiquidity Horizon
U.S. equities	15.7%	0.85	0 %
U.S. fixed income	3.8	0.75	0
Non-U.S. equities	15.6	0.80	0
Non-U.S. fixed income	9.1	0.70	0
U.S. real estate	11.5	0.50	0.30

[54]See Staub and Diermeier (2003) for more details.

Based on the information given, address the following problems:

1. Calculate the expected returns on U.S. equities, U.S. fixed income, non-U.S. equities, non-U.S. fixed income, and U.S. real estate. Make any needed adjustments for illiquidity.
2. Show the calculation of the covariance between U.S. equities and U.S. fixed income.
3. Critique the following statement: "The ZCM risk premium estimates are low, given that the foundation has a very strong home-country bias, reflected in its limitation of nondomestic assets to no more than 12 percent of the portfolio."

Solution to Problem 1: To calculate the expected return for an asset class, we take the following steps. First, we calculate the risk premium of the asset class for two distinct cases: full integration and complete segmentation. In the calculation for either case, we take care to add any applicable illiquidity premium. Second, we average the two estimates of the risk premium for an asset class by weighting the full integration estimate by the assumed degree of integration and the complete segmentation estimate by (1 – Assumed degree of integration). The result of this step is our informed estimate of the asset class's risk premium. Finally, adding the risk premium estimate to the risk-free rate yields our estimate of the expected return on the asset class.

Step 1. Using Equation 4-10, we find that in the fully integrated case,

$$RP_{\text{U.S.equities}} = 15.7\% \times 0.85 \times 0.28 = 3.74\%$$

$$RP_{\text{U.S.FI}} = 3.8\% \times 0.75 \times 0.28 = 0.80\%$$

$$RP_{\text{non-U.S.equities}} = 15.6\% \times 0.80 \times 0.28 = 3.49\%$$

$$RP_{\text{non-U.S.FI}} = 9.1\% \times 0.70 \times 0.28 = 1.78\%$$

$$RP_{\text{U.S.RE}} = (11.5\% \times 0.50 \times 0.28) + 0.30\% = 1.61\% + 0.30\% = 1.91\%$$

Using Equation 4-11, we find that in the fully segmented case,

$$RP_{\text{U.S.equities}} = 15.7\% \times 0.28 = 4.4\%$$

$$RP_{\text{U.S.FI}} = 3.8\% \times 0.28 = 1.06\%$$

$$RP_{\text{non-U.S.equities}} = 15.6\% \times 0.28 = 4.37\%$$

$$RP_{\text{non-U.S.FI}} = 9.1\% \times 0.28 = 2.55\%$$

$$RP_{\text{U.S.RE}} = (11.5\% \times 0.28) + 0.30\% = 3.22\% + 0.30\% = 3.52\%$$

Note that we added an illiquidity premium of 0.3 percent to the ICAPM-derived premium estimates for real estate.

Step 2. We now weight each asset class's fully integrated and segmented premiums according to the assumed degree of integration.

$$RP_{\text{U.S.equities}} = (0.8 \times 3.74\%) + (0.2 \times 4.4\%) = 3.87\%$$

$$RP_{\text{U.S.FI}} = (0.8 \times 0.80\%) + (0.2 \times 1.06\%) = 0.85\%$$

$$RP_{non-U.S.equities} = (0.8 \times 3.49\%) + (0.2 \times 4.37\%) = 3.67\%$$

$$RP_{non-U.S.FI} = (0.8 \times 1.78\%) + (0.2 \times 2.55\%) = 1.93\%$$

$$RP_{U.S.RE} = (0.7 \times 1.91\%) + (0.3 \times 3.52\%) = 2.39\%$$

Step 3. The expected return estimates are as follows:

$$E(R_{U.S.equities}) = 3\% + 3.87\% = 6.87\%$$

$$E(R_{U.S.FI}) = 3\% + 0.85\% = 3.85\%$$

$$E(R_{non-U.S.equities}) = 3\% + 3.67\% = 6.67\%$$

$$E(R_{non-U.S.FI}) = 3\% + 1.93\% = 4.93\%$$

$$E(R_{U.S.RE}) = 3\% + 2.39\% = 5.39\%$$

Solution to Problem 2: Based on Equation 4-3b with one factor, the covariance between any two assets in a one-beta model (such as the ICAPM) is equal to the product of each asset's beta with respect to the market times the variance of the market. The needed betas can be calculated as:

$$\beta_{U.S.equities} = (15.7\% \times 0.85)/7\% = 1.91$$

$$\beta_{U.S.FI} = (3.8\% \times 0.75)/7\% = 0.41$$

and the covariance between U.S. equities and U.S. fixed income returns as:

$$\text{Cov(U.S.equities, U.S.FI)} = 1.91 \times 0.41 \times (7\%)^2$$

$$= 38.37 \text{(in units of percent squared)}$$

Solution to Problem 3: Although the client is correct about the foundation's home-country bias, the point being made is not correct. The equilibrium risk premium is determined by all investors, reflected in the overall degree of integration estimates.

3.2. Survey and Panel Methods

The **survey method** of expectations setting involves asking a group of experts for their expectations and using the responses in capital market formulation. If the group queried and providing responses is fairly stable, the analyst in effect has a panel of experts and the approach can be called a **panel method.** These approaches are based on the straightforward idea that a direct way to uncover a person's expectations is to ask the person what they are.

The oldest continuous survey of expectations is the so-called Livingston Survey, initiated in 1946 by Joseph Livingston, a Philadelphia journalist, and managed since 1990 by the Federal Reserve Bank of Philadelphia, part of the U.S. Federal Reserve System. The survey covers real U.S. GDP growth, Consumer Price Index (CPI) and Producer Price Index (PPI) inflation, the unemployment rate, and 3-month T-bill and 10-year T-bond yields. In the United States, Welch surveyed financial economists for their views about the short- and

EXHIBIT 4-12 Consensus Expectations of U.S. Financial Economists of the 30-Year U.S. Equity Risk Premium

	2001 Survey	1998 Survey
Mean	5.5%	7.1%
Median	5.0	7.0
Interquartile range	4%–7%	6%–8.4%

Source: Welch (2000, 2001).

long-term (30-year) equity risk premium in 1998 and 2001.[55] The results of the two Welch surveys for the 30-year equity risk premium are summarized in Exhibit 4-12.

A 2002 survey of global bond investors by Schroder Salomon Smith Barney found an average equity risk premium in the range of 2 percent to 2.5 percent, while a Goldman Sachs survey of global clients recorded a mean long-run equity risk premium of 3.9 percent.[56] Such surveys may be sensitive to the professional identity of the respondents. Lally, Roush, and Van Zijl (2004) found the predictions of practitioners for the New Zealand equity risk premium significantly higher than those of academics.[57] Besides direct questions on capital market expectations, for certain equity markets, there are commercial surveys of analysts' forecasts of long-term earnings growth rates that implicitly contain an equity market forecast given a DCF valuation model.

EXAMPLE 4-20 Short-Term Consumer Spending in the United Kingdom

Bryan Smith is researching the 6- to 12-month expectations for consumer spending in the United Kingdom as of the middle of 2003. One piece of evidence he gathers is changes in consumer sentiment in the United Kingdom as measured by the Economic Optimism Index, shown in Exhibit 4-13.

Interpret Exhibit 4-13 as it relates to the probable path of consumer spending.

Solution: Based on the reading at December 2003 of the U.K. Consumer Optimism Index, it appears that consumers are considerably more optimistic than in December 2002. Rising consumer optimism is a reflection of consumers feeling secure about their income stream and future. Rising consumer optimism suggests that near-term consumer spending will increase.

[55] See Welch (2000) and Welch (2001). The 1998 survey had 226 respondents, while the 2001 survey had 510. Graham and Harvey (2001) report a survey of 10-year forecasts of the U.S. equity risk premium by chief financial officers, but their survey question was not specific about whether an arithmetic or geometric mean estimate was sought.

[56] See Ilmanen, Byrne, Gunasekera, and Minikin (2002) and O'Neill, Wilson, and Masih (2002).

[57] The median forecast was 7.0 percent for practitioners and 5.5 percent for academics.

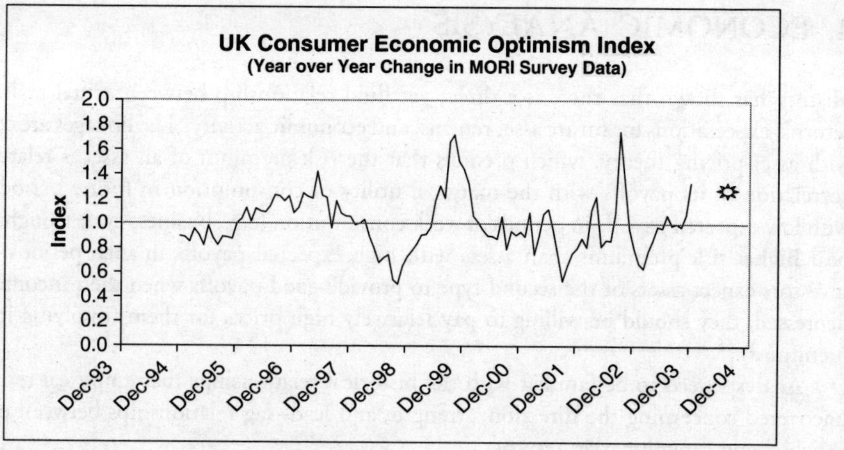

EXHIBIT 4-13 *Note*: Based on an index created from U.K. Consumer Optimism MORI survey data.
The asterisk represents the forecast target for 2004 as of mid-2003.

3.3. Judgment

In a disciplined expectations-setting process, the analyst should be able to factually explain the basis and rationale for forecasts. Quantitative models such as equilibrium models offer the prospect of providing a non-emotional, objective rationale for a forecast. The expectations-setting process nevertheless can give wide scope to applying judgment—in particular, economic and psychological insight—to improve forecasts. In forecasting, numbers, including those produced by elaborate quantitative models, must be evaluated.

EXAMPLE 4-21 Judgment Applied to Correlation Estimation

William Chew's firm uses a multifactor model to develop initial correlation forecasts that are then challenged by professionals within the capital markets unit. Based on U.S. historical data including periods of high inflation, Chew finds that the model forecasts a correlation between U.S. equity and U.S. bonds in the range of 0.40 to 0.45. Based on empirical evidence, Chew believes that the correlation between equity and bond returns is higher in high-inflation periods than in low-inflation periods. His firm's chief economist forecasts that in the medium term, U.S. inflation will be low, averaging less than 3 percent per annum. In light of that forecast, Chew has decided that he will recommend a judgmental downward adjustment of the correlation to 0.30.

Other investors who rely on judgment in setting capital market expectations may discipline the process by the use of devices such as checklists. In any case, investment experience, the study of capital markets, and intelligence are requisites for the development of judgment in setting capital market expectations.

4. ECONOMIC ANALYSIS

History has shown that there is a direct yet fluid relationship between actual realized asset returns, expectations for future asset returns, and economic activity. The linkages are consistent with asset-pricing theory, which predicts that the risk premium of an asset is related to the correlation of its payoffs with the marginal utility of consumption in future periods. Assets with low expected payoffs in periods of weak consumption (e.g., business cycle troughs) should bear higher risk premiums than assets with high expected payoffs in such periods. Because investors expect assets of the second type to provide good payoffs when their income may be depressed, they should be willing to pay relatively high prices for them (implying lower risk premiums).[58]

Analysts need to be familiar with the historical relationships that empirical research has uncovered concerning the direction, strength, and lead–lag relationships between economic variables and capital market returns.

The analyst who understands which economic variables may be most relevant to the current economic environment has a competitive advantage, as does the analyst who can discern or forecast a change in trend or point of inflection in economic activity. Inflection points often present unique investment opportunities at the same time that they are sources of latent risk. Questions that may help the analyst assess points of inflection include the following:

- What is driving the economy in its current expansion or contraction phase?
- What is helping to maintain economic growth, demand, supply, and/or inflation rates within their current ranges?
- What may trigger the end of a particular trend?

The economic output of many economies has been found to have cyclical and trend growth components. Trend growth is of obvious relevance for setting long-term return expectations for asset classes such as equities. Cyclical variation affects variables such as corporate profits and interest rates, which are directly related to asset class returns and risk. In the following sections, we address business cycles and trend growth.

4.1. Business Cycle Analysis

In business cycle analysis, two cycles are generally recognized: a short-term **inventory cycle,** typically lasting 2 to 4 years, and a longer-term **business cycle,** usually lasting 9 to 11 years. Evidence for both these cycles goes back two centuries or more, but they are very far from working like clockwork. In particular, they can be disrupted by major shocks, including wars and shifts in government policy. Also, both the duration and amplitude of each phase of the cycle, as well as the duration of the cycle as a whole, vary considerably and are hard to predict.

Cycles mark variation in economic activity, so we should be clear on how that variation is measured. The chief measurements of economic activity are as follows:

- *Gross domestic product (GDP).* GDP is a calculation of the total value of final goods and services produced in the economy during a year. The main expenditure components are consumption, investment, change in inventories, government spending, and exports

[58]See Cochrane (1999a, 1999b).

less imports. The total value of goods and services can change because the quantities of goods and services change and/or because their prices change. To focus on increases in the quantity (output) of goods and services produced—which are directly associated with increases in the standard of living—rather than on price-driven increases in the value of output, economists focus on **real GDP** (reflecting an adjustment for changes in prices during the period). For brevity's sake in our discussion, GDP is understood as referring to "real GDP" unless otherwise stated.

- *Output gap.* The **output gap** is the difference between the value of GDP estimated as if the economy were on its trend growth path (sometimes referred to as **potential output**) and the actual value of GDP. A positive output gap opens in times of recession or slow growth. When a positive output gap is open, inflation tends to decline. Once the gap closes, inflation tends to rise. When GDP is above its trend value, the economy is under inflationary pressure. Many macroeconomists consider the output gap as the key measure of real activity for policy making because it provides information about future inflationary pressures as well as an output objective. However, because changing demographics and technology affect the economy's trend path, real-time estimates of the output gap can sometimes be quite inaccurate.
- *Recession.* In general terms, a **recession** is a broad-based economic downturn. More formally, a recession occurs when there are two successive quarterly declines in GDP.

The following sections discuss the inventory cycle and the business cycle in more detail.

4.1.1. The Inventory Cycle Economists have found evidence of a short-term inventory cycle, lasting 2 to 4 years. The **inventory cycle** is a cycle measured in terms of fluctuations in inventories. The inventory cycle is caused by companies trying to keep inventories at desired levels as the expected level of sales changes.

In the up phase of the inventory cycle, businesses are confident about future sales and are increasing production. The increase in production generates more overtime pay and employment, which tends to boost the economy and bring further sales. At some point, there is a disappointment in sales or a change in expectations of future sales, so that businesses start to view inventories as too high. In the recent past, a tightening of monetary policy has often caused this inflection point. It could also be caused by a shock such as higher oil prices. Then, business cuts back production to try to reduce inventories and hires more slowly (or institutes layoffs). The result is a slowdown in growth.

It usually takes a year or two for business to correct inventory levels after an inflection point. A good indicator of the inventory position is the inventory/sales ratio. Exhibit 4-14 shows the inventory/sales ratio for the United States over the period 1974 to 2004. Note that the historical data series was discontinued in 2001 but the new series (shown in light gray), with slightly different coverage, shows the same pattern. When the inventory/sales ratio has moved down, the economy is likely to be strong in the next few quarters as businesses try to rebuild inventory, as in early 2004. Conversely, when the ratio has moved sharply up, as in 2000, a period of economic weakness can be expected. Note that while this indicator has been trending down because of improved techniques such as "just in time" inventory management, the 2- to 4-year inventory cycle is still evident.

In the late 1990s, it was argued that improved and computerized techniques of inventory control would make the inventory cycle obsolete. In fact, the 2001 recession saw one of the steepest inventory corrections on record. The reason seems to have been that excess inventories were more visible more quickly than in the past, and businesses rapidly cut back production.

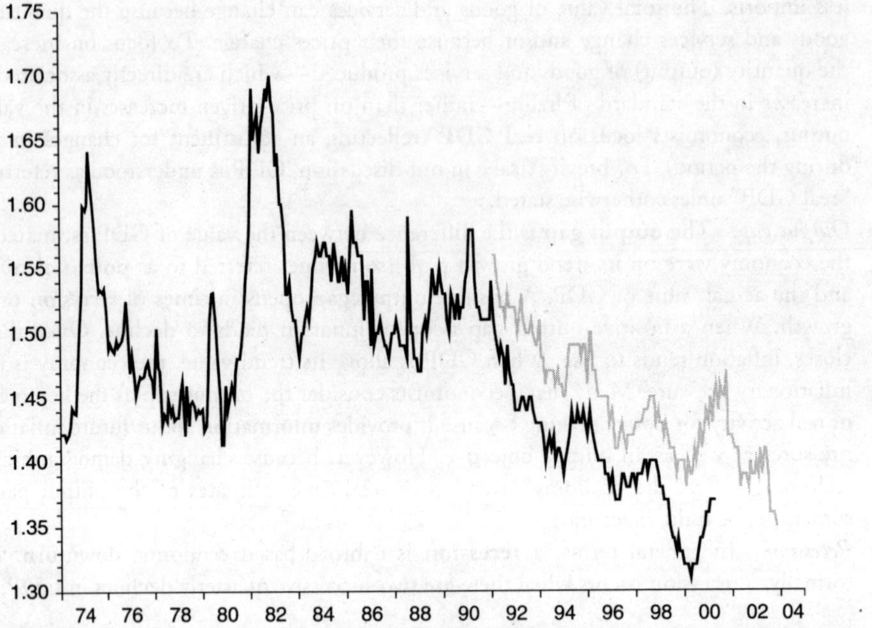

EXHIBIT 4-14 U.S. Inventory/Sales Ratios
Source: DATASTREAM

4.1.2. The Business Cycle In addition to the inventory cycle, there is evidence of a longer cycle, often lasting 9 to 11 years, called the business cycle. The **business cycle** represents fluctuations in GDP in relation to long-term trend growth. A typical business cycle has five phases: initial recovery, early upswing, late upswing, slowdown, and recession (see Exhibit 4-15).

Initial Recovery. This is usually a short phase of a few months in which the economy picks up from its slowdown or recession. Generally, confidence is rising among businesses, although consumer confidence may still be at low levels since unemployment is still high. In the initial recovery phase, there are often stimulatory economic policies from the government in the form of lower interest rates or a budgetary deficit. The business cycle recovery is usually supported by a simultaneous upswing in the inventory cycle, which is sometimes the main cause of the recovery. Inflation will still be falling in the initial recovery phase. The output gap is still large.

Capital market effects: Government bond yields may continue to come down through this phase in anticipation of a further decline in inflation but are likely to be bottoming. Stock markets may rise strongly at this point because fears of a longer recession (or even a depression) dissipate. Cyclical assets—and riskier assets, such as small stocks, higher-yield corporate bonds, and emerging market equities and bonds—attract investors and perform well.

Early Upswing. After the initial recovery period, confidence is up and the economy is gaining some momentum. This is the healthiest period of the cycle, in a sense, because economic growth can be robust without any signs of overheating or sharply higher inflation. Typically, there is increasing confidence, with consumers prepared to borrow and spend more as unemployment starts to fall. Concurrently, businesses build inventories and step up investment in the face of strong sales and increased capacity use. Higher operating levels allow many businesses to enjoy lower unit costs, so that profits rise rapidly.

Capital market effects: A key question is how long it will take before inflation starts to become a problem. Short rates are moving up at this time as the central bank starts to withdraw the stimulus put in place during the recession. Longer bond yields are likely to be stable or rising slightly. Stocks are still trending up. This phase usually lasts at least a year and often several years if growth is not too strong and the output gap closes slowly.

Late Upswing. At this stage of the cycle, the output gap has closed and the economy is in danger of overheating. Confidence is high; unemployment is low. The economy may grow rapidly. Inflation starts to pick up, with wages accelerating as shortages of labor develop.

Capital market effects: Typically, interest rates are rising as the monetary authorities become restrictive. Any heavy borrowing puts pressure on the credit markets. Central banks may aim for a "soft landing," meaning a period of slower growth to cool the economy but not a major downturn. Bond markets anxiously watch this behavior, and bond yields will usually be rising as a result of changed expectations. Stock markets will often rise but may be nervous too, depending on the strength of the boom. Nervous investors mean that equities are volatile.

Slowdown. At this point, the economy is slowing, usually under the impact of rising interest rates. The economy is especially vulnerable at this juncture to a shock, which can turn a "soft landing" into a recession. Business confidence starts to waver. Despite the slowdown, inflation often continues to rise. The slowdown is exacerbated by the inventory correction as companies try to reduce their inventory levels. This phase may last just a few months, as in the United States in 2000, or it may last a year or more, as in the United States in 1989 to 1990.

Capital market effects: Short-term interest rates are high and rising at first but then may peak. Bonds top out at the first sign of a slowing economy and then rally sharply (yields fall). The yield curve often inverts. The stock market may fall, with interest-sensitive stocks such as utilities and financial services performing best.

Recession. A recession is conventionally defined as two successive quarterly declines in GDP. There is often a large inventory pullback and sometimes a large decline in business investment. Consumer spending on big-ticket items such as cars usually declines (although the U.S. 2001 recession was an exception). Once the recession is confirmed, central banks ease monetary policy, but only cautiously at first. Recessions typically last six months to a year. Both consumer and business confidence decline. Profits drop sharply. In a severe recession, the financial system may be stressed by bad debts, making lenders extremely cautious. Often, recessions are punctuated by major bankruptcies, incidents of uncovered fraud, or a financial crisis. Unemployment can rise quickly, putting downward pressure on inflation.

Capital market effects: Short-term interest rates drop during this phase, as do bond yields. The stock market usually starts to rise in the later stages of the recession, well before the recovery emerges.

Exhibit 4-15 summarizes the characteristics of the five phases of the business cycle.

The description given of business cycles is a stylized one. Each cycle is different because of specific events and trends that fall outside the stylized business cycle framework. Trends that

EXHIBIT 4-15 Five Phases of the Business Cycle

Phase	Economy	Fiscal and Monetary Policy	Confidence	Capital Markets
1. Initial recovery	Inflation still declining	Stimulatory fiscal policies	Confidence starts to rebound	Short rates low or declining; bond yields bottoming; stock prices strongly rising
2. Early upswing	Healthy economic growth; inflation remains low		Increasing confidence	Short rates moving up; bond yields stable to up slightly; stock prices trending upward
3. Late upswing	Inflation gradually picks up	Policy becomes restrictive	Boom mentality	Short rates rising; bond yields rising; stocks topping out, often volatile
4. Slowdown	Inflation continues to accelerate; inventory correction begins		Confidence drops	Short-term interest rates peaking; bond yields topping out and starting to decline; stocks declining
5. Recession	Production declines; inflation peaks		Confidence weak	Short rates declining; bond yields dropping; stocks bottoming and then starting to rise

have affected the business cycle from the 1990s through the early 2000s include the growing importance of China in world markets, the aging of populations, and the deregulation of markets. Events such as a petroleum or financial crisis can abruptly take the economy to the next phase of the business cycle or intensify the current phase.

EXAMPLE 4-22 The Yield Curve, Recessions, and Bond Maturity

The yield spread between the 10-year T-bond rate and the 3-month T-bill rate has been found internationally to be a predictor of future growth in output.[59] The observed tendency is for the yield spread to narrow or become negative prior to recessions. Another way of saying the same thing is that the yield curve tends to flatten or become inverted prior to a recession. Effects that may explain a declining yield spread include the following: (1) Future short-term rates are expected to fall, and/or (2) investors' required premium for holding long-term bonds rather than short-term bonds has fallen. At least,

[59] See Estrella and Mishkin (1998).

the link between an expected decline in short-term rates from expected lower loan demand and declining output growth is economically somewhat intuitive.

When the yield spread is expected to narrow (the yield curve is moving toward inversion), long-duration bonds should outperform short-duration bonds. On the other hand, a widening yield spread (e.g., an inverted yield curve moving to an upward-sloping yield curve) favors short-duration bonds.

4.1.3. Inflation and Deflation in the Business Cycle **Inflation** simply means rising prices, while **deflation** means falling prices. At any given time, some prices are rising and others are falling. Thus, investors look at indices of prices to discern the overall trend. Consumer price indices, calculated from a basket of goods and services based on consumers' spending patterns, are commonly watched. Another set of price indices that are closely watched are the GDP and consumer expenditure deflators, which are inflation indices used to adjust or deflate the nominal series for inflation.

Inflation is linked to the business cycle, tending to rise in the late stages of a business cycle and to decline during recessions and the early stages of recovery. However, the analyst also needs to note any long-term trends in inflation in formulating capital market expectations.

EXAMPLE 4-23 Inflation, Disinflation, and Deflation

Today, people expect prices of goods and services and of investment assets to trend up over time. However, during most of the nineteenth century and through the twentieth

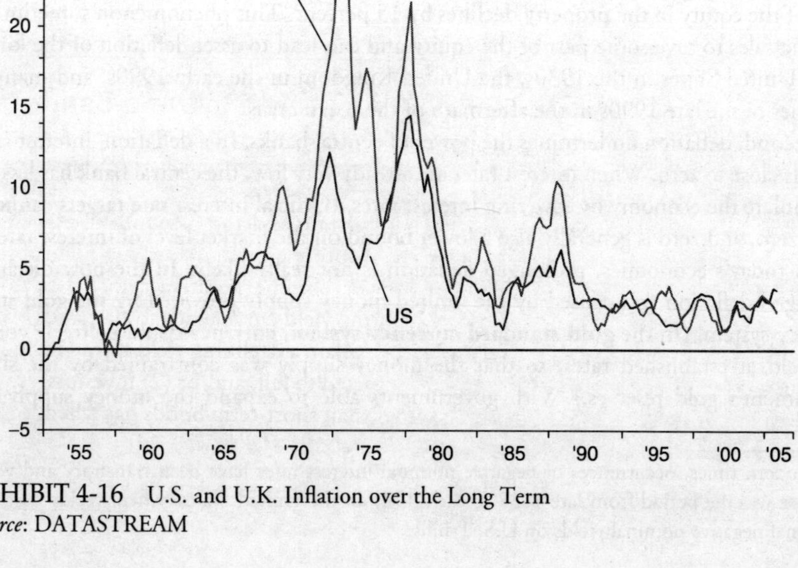

EXHIBIT 4-16 U.S. and U.K. Inflation over the Long Term
Source: DATASTREAM

century prior to the 1960s, price inflation was negligible. Indeed, the price level in the United Kingdom fell for a large part of the nineteenth century. In the United States, the main period of inflation occurred during the Civil War (1861–1865). Prices dropped for long periods otherwise. However, from the late 1950s until the late 1970s, inflation gradually accelerated almost everywhere, reaching over 10 percent in the United States and over 30 percent in the United Kingdom for brief periods. Then from about 1979, a period of disinflation set in as inflation gradually retreated back toward zero. Exhibit 4-16 illustrates the inflation rates in the United States and the United Kingdom since the 1950s.

Central bank orthodoxy for dealing with inflation rests on three principles:

- Central banks' policy-making decisions must be independent of political influence. If political pressure is brought to bear on central banks, they may be too loose in their monetary policy and allow inflation to gradually accelerate.
- Central banks should have an inflation target, both as a discipline for themselves and as a signal to the markets of their intentions. An inflation target also serves to anchor market expectations.
- Central banks should use monetary policy (primarily interest rates) to control the economy and prevent it from either overheating or languishing in a recession for too long.

By the end of the twentieth century, inflation had been defeated almost everywhere. All the major countries enjoyed inflation below 3 percent, and only a handful of emerging countries suffered from double-digit inflation. The challenge is to keep inflation low without succumbing to deflation.

Deflation is a threat to the economy for two main reasons. First, it tends to undermine debt-financed investments. If the price of a debt-financed asset (e.g., new equipment or a house) declines in value, the value of the "equity" in the asset (i.e., the difference between the asset's value and the loan balance) declines at a leveraged rate. For example, if the value of a property financed with a 67 percent loan-to-value mortgage then declines by 5 percent, the value of the equity in the property declines by 15 percent. This phenomenon sometimes leads to panic sales to save some part of the equity and can lead to asset deflation of the kind seen in the United States in the 1930s, the United Kingdom in the early 1990s, and many Asian countries in the late 1990s in the aftermath of the Asian crisis.

Second, deflation undermines the power of central banks. In a deflation, interest rates fall to levels close to zero. When interest rates are already very low, the central bank has less leeway to stimulate the economy by lowering interest rates. (Official interest rate targets cannot drop below zero, and zero is generally also a lower bound on the market level of interest rates.)[60]

In today's economies, prolonged deflation is not really likely. In the now distant past, prolonged deflation was caused by the limited money supply provided by the gold standard currency system. (In the **gold standard currency system,** currency could be freely converted into gold at established rates, so that the money supply was constrained by the size of a government's gold reserves.) With governments able to expand the money supply to any

[60] In modern times, occurrences of negative nominal interest rates have been transitory and very rare. One case was the period from late 1938 to early 1941 in the United States, when weekly data showed occasional negative nominal yields on U.S. T-bills.

desired degree, there is really no reason for deflation to last long. Nevertheless, even today, weak periods within the business cycle can still bring short periods of deflation, even if the upswing phases produce inflation.

Example 4-24 looks at some of the considerations that might enter into a short-term inflation forecast.

EXAMPLE 4-24 An Inflation Forecast for Germany

Early in 2004, Hans Vermaelen, a capital market analyst, has the task of making an inflation forecast for Germany over the next 6 to 12 months. Vermaelen gathers the following inputs and outputs:

Inputs:

1. A survey of manufacturers, asking them whether they expect to see price declines for the products they sell in order to stay globally competitive in light of a then-strengthening euro.
2. Information on German manufacturing orders and consumer price inflation.
3. Data inputs for a multifactor model including the following variables:
    - Prices of commodities
    - Prices for labor
    - Wholesale and producer price measures

Outputs:

1. The survey of manufacturers indicates that manufacturers are passing some price increases to German customers without meeting strong resistance. After initially lowering export product prices to maintain market share in the face of a rising euro, German manufacturers are now passing price increases on to their international customers, thereby restoring their profit margins.
2. Current year-over-year annual inflation of 1.1 percent is below the average annual rate of 1.5 percent experienced over the past 10 years and over the past 10 quarters. Manufacturing orders have increased at a 3 percent average rate over the past year. However, over the past quarter, manufacturing orders have increased at a 6.9 percent year-over-year rate. Exhibit 4-17 graphs inflation and manufacturing orders.
3. The multifactor model indicates a positive correlation between the inflation rate and manufacturing orders and a negative correlation between a strengthening local currency (euro) and inflation.

Based on the above information, Vermaelen forecasts that inflation will increase to a 1.5 percent rate over the next 6 to 12 months. Critique Vermaelen's forecast.

Solution: The manufacturing orders have been increasing recently at a 6.9 percent year-over-year rate versus a 3 percent average rate over the past year. This fact suggests

EXHIBIT 4-17 Inflation Pressure in Germany
Note: The asterisk represents a forecast target of 1.5 percent inflation for 2004.

that the German economy is strengthening rapidly. At the same time, the survey of manufacturers indicates that they are having success at passing along price increases to customers. These factors suggest an increase in inflation from the recent 1.1 percent rate. Overall, it is reasonable to forecast a return to the recent average trend inflation rate of 1.5 percent.

Inflation tends to accelerate in the later stages of the business cycle, when the output gap has been closed. Inflation decelerates when, during a recession or in the early years afterward, there is a large output gap putting downward pressure on prices. As a result, the rate of inflation will decelerate to a low level and **deflation** (an increase in the purchasing power of a unit of currency) becomes possible.[61] Resistance to reduction in wages is a counterweight to deflationary pressures. Except in the worst circumstances, such as in the United States in the early 1930s, the rate of annual deflation is likely to be limited to about 2 percent, with wages holding steady.

During a recession, with falling inflation and interest rates, bonds generally post capital gains (for some bonds, deteriorating credit can offset such gains). In a strong upswing, bond yields will rise as investors fear that central banks will not hold inflation on target, resulting in capital losses to bondholders.

The impact of the inflation cycle on equities is more complex. In theory, as long as inflation stays near its expected or equilibrium level, the inflation rate is not very important. Higher inflation should be reflected in higher profits, so stocks will rise to compensate. However, signs that inflation is moving out of equilibrium indicate a potential threat because

[61] The most extreme instances of deflation in the past 100 years occurred in the years surrounding the Great Depression (in particular, in the period 1926 to 1933).

EXHIBIT 4-18 Inflation/Deflation Effects on Asset Classes

	Cash	Bonds	Equity	Real Estate/ Other Real Assets
Inflation at or below expectations	Short-term yields steady or declining. **[Neutral]**	Yield levels maintained; market in equilibrium. **[Neutral]**	Bullish while market in equilibrium state. **[Positive]**	Cash flow steady to rising slightly. Returns equate to long-term average. Market in general equilibrium. **[Neutral]**
Inflation above expectations	Bias toward rising rates. **[Positive]**	Bias toward higher yields due to a higher inflation premium. **[Negative]**	High inflation a negative for financial assets. Less negative for compa-nies/industries able to pass on inflated costs. **[Negative]**	Asset values increasing; increased cash flows and higher expected returns. **[Positive]**
Deflation	Bias toward 0% short-term rates. **[Negative]**	Purchasing power increasing. Bias toward steady to lower rates (may be offset by increased risk of potential defaults due to falling asset prices). **[Positive]**	Negative wealth effect slows demand. Especially affects asset-intensive, commodity-producing (as opposed to commodity-using), and highly levered companies. **[Negative]**	Cash flows steady to falling. Asset prices face downward pressure. **[Negative]**

rising inflation could mean that the central banks need to act to slow the economy. Falling inflation, or possible deflation, is a problem because it threatens a recession and a decline in asset prices.

Exhibit 4-18 shows how changes in the inflation (deflation) rate affect the relative attractiveness of asset classes.

4.1.4. Market Expectations and the Business Cycle

The description of a typical business cycle may suggest that forming capital market expectations for the short and medium terms is relatively straightforward. If the investor can identify the current phase of the cycle and correctly predict when the next phase will begin, he or she should be able to make money easily. Unfortunately, it is not that simple for several interrelated reasons.

First, the phases of the business cycle vary in length and amplitude. Recessions can be steep, and downturns (such as in the 1930s and, to a lesser extent, the early 1980s) can be frightening. Recessions can be short-lived affairs with only a small decline in output and only a modest rise in unemployment. Sometimes, the weak phase of the cycle does not even involve a recession but merely a period of slower economic growth or a "growth recession." A period of economic growth below trend will open up the output gap. A mild downturn, or growth recession, is most likely if the trend rate of growth of the economy is relatively rapid. For example, China—with a trend rate of annual growth of about 8 percent as of the early 2000s—will see unemployment rise and inflation decline if growth is only 5 to 6 percent. For the main industrial economies, with trend rates of annual growth of 2 to 4 percent, a mild downturn is more likely than a recession if some or all of the following conditions hold:

- The upswing was relatively short or mild.
- There was no bubble or severe overheating in the stock market or property market.
- Inflation is relatively low, so the central bank is willing to cut interest rates quickly.
- The world economic and political environments are positive.

EXAMPLE 4-25 The 1980–1982 and 2001 U.S. Recessions

The U.S. downturn in 1980 to 1982 was particularly severe. Inflation had reached 12 to 14 percent in early 1980, partly due to a rise in oil prices. The Board of Governors of the Federal Reserve System under its new chairman, Paul Volcker, was determined to eradicate inflation. The Fed kept interest rates high in 1982. In contrast, the 2001 recession was relatively mild. There had been a stock market bubble, but commercial property prices were not inflated and banks were in good shape. Because inflation was low, the Fed was willing to cut interest rates very rapidly.

The 2001 recession is instructive on the limitations of economic data, which are backward looking and often revised. After the terrorist attack of September 11, 2001 on the World Trade Center, much commentary focused on the risk that it would lead to a recession. In fact, the revised GDP data show that the economy had been in a recession since early in 2001 and began to come out of it starting in October 2001. At the time, it was clear that the economy was weak and therefore growing at less than the trend rate, so bond yields fell and the stock market declined.

4.1.5. Evaluating Factors That Affect the Business Cycle For the purposes of setting capital market expectations, we need to focus business cycle analysis on four areas:

1. Consumers.
2. Business.
3. Foreign trade.
4. Government activity, both **monetary policy** (concerning interest rates and the money supply) and **fiscal policy** (concerning taxation and governmental spending).

Consumer spending amounts to 60 to 70 percent of GDP in most large developed economies and is therefore typically the most important business cycle factor.

Business investment has a smaller weight in GDP than consumer spending but is more volatile.

Foreign trade is an important component in many smaller economies, for which trade is often 30 to 50 percent of GDP. However, for the large economies, such as the United States and Japan, foreign trade is typically only around 10 to 15 percent of GDP and correspondingly less important. The same range holds true for the European Union (EU) in relation to trade outside the EU (although between countries within the EU, trade generally represents a higher percentage of GDP).

Finally, government policy can influence the business cycle. There are three motivations for government to intervene in the cycle. First, both the government and monetary authorities may try to control the cycle to mitigate severe recessions and also, on occasion, to moderate economic booms. Second, the central bank monetary authorities often have an inflation target and they will consciously try to stimulate or constrain the economy to help meet it. Third, because incumbent politicians prefer to hold elections during economic upswings, they may try to influence fiscal and/or monetary policy to achieve this end.

4.1.5.1. Taking the Pulse of Consumers The principal sources of data on consumer spending are retail sales, miscellaneous store sales data, and consumer consumption data. Like most data, consumer spending can be erratic from month to month and can be affected by unusual weather or holidays (such as New Year celebrations).

By far the most important factor affecting consumption is consumer income after tax, which depends on wage settlements, inflation, tax changes, and employment growth. Employment growth is often closely watched because data are usually available on a very timely basis. Most countries have some particular series that analysts scrutinize. In the United Kingdom, besides the unemployment rate, the British Retail Consortium (BRC) retail sales survey is closely watched. In the United States, the monthly nonfarm payrolls as well as the weekly new unemployment claims are regular market movers when they diverge from expectations.

If the household savings rate remained constant, then changes in income would exactly predict changes in spending. But the savings rate does change over time, influenced generally by consumer confidence in future jobs and income and also by changes in asset prices. Consumer confidence survey data are also watched closely as indicators of whether consumers are likely to raise or lower their savings rates.

4.1.5.2. Taking the Pulse of Business Data on business investment and spending on inventories reveal recent business activity. As already mentioned, both tend to be relatively volatile so that it is not uncommon for business investment to fall by 10 to 20 percent or more during a recession and to increase by a similar amount during strong economic upswings. Data for inventories need careful interpretation, however. A report of rising inventories may mean that businesses are very confident of sales and are spending on inventories ahead of expected sales. This would normally be the case in the early stages of an inventory cycle upswing and is bullish for economic growth. But at the late stage of the inventory cycle, a rise in inventories may be involuntary because sales are lower than expected. Such news would be negative.

Some of the most useful data on business are surveys. A particularly useful one is the purchasing managers index (PMI) published for several decades by the Institute of Supply Management (ISM) in the United States (formerly the National Association of Purchasing

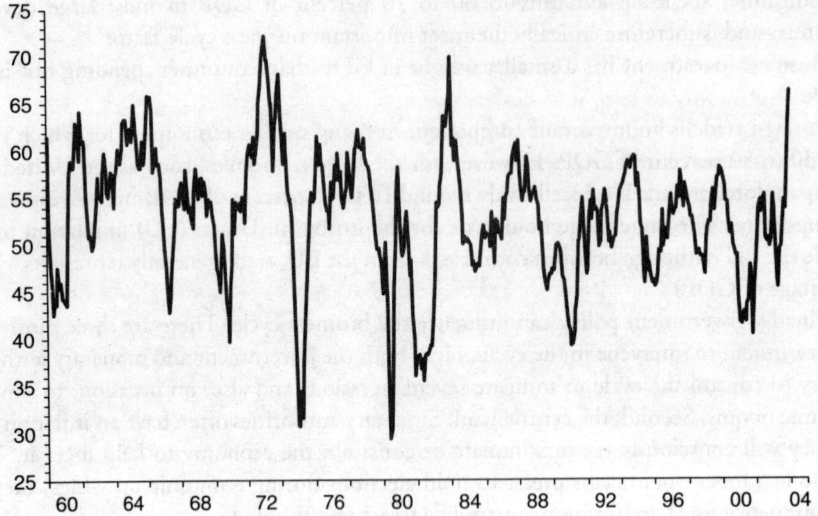

EXHIBIT 4-19 U.S. ISM PMI Manufacturing
Source: DATASTREAM

Managers). The PMI is one of the best indicators of the U.S. economy. In the 1990s, the ISM added a survey of nonmanufacturing companies, which is beginning to acquire a useful track record. In recent years, most developed countries have developed PMIs using a similar methodology. Exhibit 4-19 presents U.S. PMI manufacturing data for the years 1959 to 2004.

The PMI is based on answers to a series of questions about the company's position, including production plans, inventories, prices paid, prices received, and hiring plans. Each component is reported as well as an overall index. The indices are calibrated so that 50 should be the breakeven point for manufacturing growth. These surveys are particularly useful because of their timeliness.

4.1.5.3. Monetary Policy Monetary policy is sometimes used as a mechanism for intervention in the business cycle. For example, monetary policymakers may switch to stimulative measures (increasing money supply growth and/or lowering short-term interest rates) when the economy is weak and restrictive measures (decreasing money supply growth and/or raising short-term interest rates) when the economy is in danger of overheating. If unemployment is relatively high and there is spare capacity, then a rate of GDP growth higher than the trend rate will be tolerated for a while. This scenario is typical of the recovery and early upswing phases of the business cycle. In the late upswing phase, the economy is threatening to overheat and monetary authorities will restrict money supply to slow growth. If they get it wrong and a recession emerges, then they will cut rates sharply to restore growth. Finally, if a major financial crisis threatens the financial system, they will also cut rates sharply and flood the economy with liquidity, as was seen in the United States in 1987, 1998, and 2001.

The key variables watched by monetary authorities are as follows:

- The pace of economic growth.
- The amount of excess capacity still available (if any).
- The level of unemployment.
- The rate of inflation.

In recent times, the common means for the largest central banks to effect monetary policy has been setting short-term interest rates to levels that are meant to control inflation without inhibiting economic growth. Central banks often see their role as smoothing out the growth rate of the economy to keep it as near as possible to its long-term sustainable trend rate—in effect, neither too hot nor too cold. A change in short-term interest rates affects the economy through a number of different mechanisms, which vary in their effects at different times.

Lower rates encourage more borrowing by consumers and businesses. Lower interest rates also usually result in higher bond and stock prices. These in turn encourage consumers to spend more and encourage businesses to invest more. From an international trade perspective, lower interest rates usually lower the exchange rate and therefore stimulate exports.

The effect of a cut in interest rates also depends on the absolute level of interest rates, not just the direction of change. For example, suppose that interest rates have been raised from 3 to 6 percent to deal with inflation and then, in response to a recession, are lowered to 4 percent. The lowering of interest rates might stimulate the economy, but interest rates are still higher than where they started. In other words, what matters is not whether interest rates have most recently been moved up or down but where they stand in relation to their average or "neutral" level. It is common to think of this "neutral" level as a point of interest rate equilibrium within the economy. The concept of the neutral level of interest rates is an important one, though in reality, it is impossible to identify precisely. Conceptually, the argument is that a neutral level of short-term interest rates should include a component to cover inflation and a real rate of return component. For example, in the United States, if inflation is targeted at 2 percent and the economy is growing at 2 percent, many economists argue that the neutral level of interest rates is about 4 percent.

4.1.5.3.1. The Taylor Rule One way to assess the central bank's stance and to predict changes is through the so-called **Taylor rule**.[62] In essence, this rule links a central bank's target short-term interest rate to the rate of growth of the economy and inflation. A simple approach to this rule (giving equal weights to GDP growth and inflation) is given by the following Taylor rule equation:

$$R_{\text{optimal}} = R_{\text{neutral}} + [0.5 \times (\text{GDPg}_{\text{forecast}} - \text{GDPg}_{\text{trend}}) + 0.5 \times (I_{\text{forecast}} - I_{\text{target}})] \quad \text{(4-12)}$$

where

R_{optimal} = the target for the short-term interest rate
R_{neutral} = the short-term interest rate that would be targeted if GDP growth were on trend and inflation on target
$\text{GDPg}_{\text{forecast}}$ = the GDP forecast growth rate
$\text{GDPg}_{\text{trend}}$ = the observed GDP trend growth rate
I_{forecast} = the forecast inflation rate
I_{target} = the target inflation rate

The Taylor rule gives the optimal short-term interest rate as the neutral rate plus an amount that is positively related to the excess of the forecasts of GDP and inflation growth rates above their trend or target values. For example, assume that a current short-term rate of 4 percent is the neutral rate. Thus, if the United States is forecast to achieve its 2 percent trend rate of growth and 2 percent inflation target, then the Fed would be happy with the federal funds

[62] See Taylor (1993).

rate at the neutral rate of 4 percent. At 4 percent, the Fed would expect that the GDP growth and inflation rates would remain at trend or targeted levels. The Taylor rule then states that if the forecast GDP growth rate and/or the forecast inflation rate are above the trend or target level, short-term interest rates need to be raised by *half* the difference between the forecast and the trend or target. Conversely, GDP growth and/or inflation rates below trend or target would motivate the Fed to lower the fed funds rate. (The **federal funds rate,** or **fed funds rate** for short, is the interest rate on overnight loans of reserves [deposits] at the Fed between Federal Reserve System member banks.)[63] The intuition in this last case is that when GDP forecast growth is below trend, lowering the interest rate will stimulate output by lowering corporations' cost of capital. When forecast inflation is below target, lowering the interest rate will help the inflation rate return to target through its stimulative effect on the money supply.

EXAMPLE 4-26 A Taylor Rule Calculation

Assume the following scenario:

- The neutral value of the short-term interest rate is 3.5 percent.
- The inflation target is 2.5 percent.
- The GDP trend rate of growth is 3 percent.

If the inflation forecast is 4 percent and the forecast for GDP growth is 1 percent, what is the optimal short-term interest rate?

Solution: According to the Taylor rule,

$$\begin{aligned} R_{\text{optimal}} &= R_{\text{neutral}} + [0.5 \times (\text{GDPg}_{\text{forecast}} - \text{GDPg}_{\text{trend}}) + 0.5 \times (I_{\text{forecast}} - I_{\text{target}})] \\ &= 3.5\% + [0.5(1.0\% - 3.0\%) + 0.5(4.0\% - 2.5\%)] \\ &= 3.5\% + (-1.0\% + 0.75\%) \\ &= 3.5\% - 0.25\% \\ &= 3.25\% \end{aligned}$$

The GDP growth forecast by itself implies that the short-term interest rate should lowered by 1 percentage point, because GDP growth is under trend. Partially offsetting the effect of below-trend GDP growth is the interest rate increase implied by above-target inflation. Net, the Taylor rule implies that the central bank should lower short-term rates by 25 bps to 3.25 percent.

[63]According to U.S. law, Federal Reserve System member banks are required to hold reserves at the Fed equal to a fraction of the deposits with the banks. In the Eurozone, banks have broadly similar requirements that relate to holding reserves at national central banks.

Historically, the Taylor rule has provided a reasonably accurate description of central banks' behavior.

4.1.5.3.2. Money Supply Trends Trends in the money supply can be a good indicator of monetary conditions and of the trend of the economy. Over the long run, there is a reasonably stable relationship between the growth in money supply and the growth in nominal GDP (inflation plus real growth). If money growth is particularly strong in relation to nominal GDP, chances are that growth will accelerate in the near future and that inflation may eventually accelerate.

4.1.5.3.3. What Happens When Interest Rates Reach Zero? All the discussion so far has been about central banks' manipulation of interest rates to affect the economy. But what happens if the economy is weak and interest rates have fallen to zero? This is often the situation in periods of deflation. An important lesson of the Japanese experience in the 1990s is that it is appropriate to cut interest rates aggressively during an economic downturn, if inflation is not at high levels, in order to kick-start an economic recovery before deflation sets in.

Once interest rates are at zero, further monetary stimulus requires new types of measures. First, the central bank can push cash (bank "reserves") directly into the banking system. Japan tried this approach in recent years with limited success because there was still no desire to borrow or lend. A second possibility is to devalue the currency. The third option is to promise to hold short-term interest rates low for an extended period. The United States used this approach in 2003, as did the Bank of Japan. It may not work if the markets think that rates will soon rise, indicating an expected economic recovery. The final option is for the central bank to buy assets directly from the private sector. This option has the effect of putting money directly into people's hands and driving down yields on these assets. The Bank of Japan has been buying government bonds for several years, driving 10-year bond yields below 1 percent at times. It has also bought small amounts of stocks and could buy property or overseas assets.

Given that deflation removes some of the central bank authorities' ability to effect monetary policy, central banks prefer to target a low positive rate of inflation, retaining flexibility in using interest rates to affect the business cycle.

EXAMPLE 4-27 Monetary Policy in the Eurozone Compared with the United States in 2001

Both Europe and the United States saw a sharp economic slowdown in 2001. The Fed responded by cutting the fed funds rate from 6.50 percent to 1.75 percent during 2001. In contrast, the European Central Bank (ECB), the central bank for the Eurozone, cut interest rates from 4.75 percent to 3.50 percent, a much less aggressive move. The reasons for these different responses were twofold:

- In 2001, U.S. CPI inflation stood at 2.6 percent, well within the Fed's likely informal target range of 1 to 3 percent inflation. Coincidentally, the Eurozone also had inflation of 2.6 percent in mid-2001, but this rate was above the explicit target range of 0 to 2 percent.

- In the United States, unemployment rose rapidly during 2001 from about 4 percent to nearly 6 percent, opening an output gap in the economy. In contrast, Eurozone unemployment was constant at 8 percent for most of 2001, rising only slightly at the end of the year. Hence, the ECB welcomed the slowdown as a way to put downward pressure on inflation.

4.1.5.4. Fiscal Policy **Fiscal policy** means manipulating the budget deficit to influence the economy. Governments increase spending or cut taxes to stimulate the economy and cut spending or raise taxes to slow the economy. In analyzing fiscal policy, or the so-called "fiscal stance," it is crucial to remember two points. First, an analyst should focus on the *changes* in the government budgetary deficit, not its level. For example, although the Japanese budget deficit has been running at around 8 percent of GDP for many years (as of 2005), it has not been a continuous stimulus to the economy. But if the deficit rose to 10 percent, that increase could represent a stimulus. Conversely, a reduction in the deficit would represent a tighter policy.

Second, it is only changes in the deficit due to *deliberate changes* in government fiscal policy that matter. The budget deficit will constantly change in response to the economy without any change in fiscal policy. During recessions, the deficit tends to rise because tax revenues fall and government spending on unemployment benefits increases. In contrast, when the economy grows strongly, the budget deficit naturally falls.

4.1.5.4.1. Linkages with Monetary Policy It is useful to consider the overall mix of fiscal and monetary policy. If fiscal and monetary policies are both tight, then the situation is unambiguous and the economy is certain to slow. Similarly, if both monetary policy and fiscal policy are expansionary, then the economy can be expected to grow. However, monetary and fiscal policies are sometimes at odds with one another. These situations create opportunities for investors as well as risks.

The fiscal/monetary mix usually shows up in the shape of the yield curve. Exhibit 4-20 illustrates the four possibilities. When both fiscal and monetary policies are loose, the yield curve tends to be steeply upward sloping. When fiscal policy is tightened while monetary policy remains loose, bond yields tend to fall and the yield curve comes back to a more moderate upward slope.

If monetary and fiscal policies are both tight, the yield curve is typically inverted. Finally, when monetary policy is tight but fiscal policy is loose, the yield curve tends to be flat.

4.2. Economic Growth Trends

The economic growth trend is the long-term growth path of GDP. The long-term growth path reflects the average growth rate around which the economy cycles. The differences between

EXHIBIT 4-20 Policy Mix and the Yield Curve

		Fiscal Policy	
		Loose	Tight
Monetary Policy:	**Loose**	Yield curve steep	Yield curve moderately steep
	Tight	Yield curve flat	Yield curve inverted

economic trends and cycles need to be understood. Economic trends exist independently of the cycle but are related to it. Business cycles take the economy through an alternating sequence of slow and fast growth, often including recessions and economic booms.

Economists are concerned with a variety of trends besides the economic growth trend, because that trend is determined by other economic trends, such as population growth and demographics, business investment and productivity, government structural policies, inflation/deflation, and the health of banking/lending processes.

Trends are more easily forecast than cycles, but there are always uncertainties. In practice, it is often difficult to know which trends are most important. Moreover, some trends or changes in trends are by definition not open to forecasting. These are often called *shocks.* Examples include wars that cause market dislocations, abrupt changes in government tax or trade policies, and the sudden collapse in an asset market or in an exchange rate. Often, these abrupt changes in trend affect the overall paradigm of capital market expectations. One example of a paradigm-changing shock was the revelation of accounting irregularities at Enron and other U.S. companies in 2002. Investors' perceptions both of the reliability of companies' earning statements and of corporate leaders' attitudes profoundly shifted. Changes in regulations reinforced these shifts. In contrast, other trends such as demographics are usually very much in the background because they change only very gradually.

While shocks are not forecastable, investors do try to assess the risk that they will occur. Unrest in the Middle East may push up the price of oil as well as "safe haven" investments such as gold, the Swiss franc, and U.S. government bonds. If a particular tax change is being considered, markets may partially anticipate it in the pricing of such assets. Some events do come unexpectedly, and they are the ones likely to have the greatest impact as investors struggle to understand their implications.

EXAMPLE 4-28 Cycles and Trends: An Example

Consider the following hypothetical passage describing the German economy in late 2003:

- "After a recession in the first half of 2003, the German economy picked up. Starting in the third quarter, it grew at 1.5 percent annualized in the second half of the year. Exports led the way, and business investment picked up. Consumer spending stabilized after declining in 2002.
- Significant progress on labor market reforms and pension reforms by the government, as well as increased sales to China, boosted confidence. The construction sector is the only one remaining in the doldrums after the post-unification building boom (in 1990) and the ending of special tax incentives in the late 1990s. The German economy minister welcomed the upturn in economic growth and expressed optimism that growth would accelerate to an above-trend 2.5 percent in 2004."

These two statements contain information about the economy. The first refers to the business cycle, while the second describes other economic trends. The final sentence is a mixture of cycle and trend information. It provides the government forecast for economic growth in the following year (cyclical information) but also implies an estimate for the long-term average rate of growth that the German economy is believed capable of achieving (2.5 percent per year).

The expected trend rate of economic growth is a key input in discounted cash flow models of expected return. First, a country with a higher trend rate of growth may offer equity investors a particularly good return. Second, a higher trend rate of growth in the economy allows actual growth to be faster before there is a danger of inflation.

The trend rate of growth of the economy is usually thought not to change much over time. Indeed, for the United Kingdom, historically the first industrial economy, it would appear that GDP has had a 2 percent to 2.5 percent trend growth rate for two hundred years with very little variation. However, most countries have had periods of faster and slower trend growth during their development. Emerging countries naturally can more easily have faster growth as they catch up with the leading industrial countries. But the more developed they become, the more likely it is that their growth will slow. This effect has been very obvious in the case of Japan. After Japan's GDP grew at an annual average rate of 11 percent in the 20 years leading up to 1973, growth in the next 17 years averaged only 3.9 percent and then fell to 1.6 percent between 1990 and 2003.

4.2.1. Consumer Impacts: Consumption and Demand

Consumers can be counted upon as the largest source of aggregate economic growth in both developed and developing economies. It is interesting to note that although consumers spend more in response to perceived increases in their wealth due to a "wealth effect," overall consumer consumption is quite stable over the business cycle. Milton Friedman (1957) developed an explanation for this stability in his permanent income hypothesis. The **permanent income hypothesis** asserts that consumers' spending behavior is largely determined by their long-run income expectations. Temporary or unexpected (or one-time) events such as benefiting from an inheritance might temporarily increase an individual's demand for items that might not ordinarily be purchased, but overall spending patterns remain largely determined by long-run expectations. However, if an unexpected event (e.g., winning the lottery) produced an ongoing series of incoming cash flows, it would be expected to permanently alter an individual's spending patterns since the flows would be ongoing and could be depended upon over the long term.

In similar fashion, when temporary events reduce the income flows of consumers, individuals typically reduce the amount they save to maintain their long-term spending patterns. Only when income disruptions occur over the long term may individuals capitulate and reduce their consumption—out of necessity. Thus, consumer trends are usually stable or even countercyclical over a business cycle. When incomes rise the most (during the cyclical expansion phase), spending increases less than income rises. When incomes fall as an economy's growth slows or declines, consumption falls only a fraction and usually only for a relatively short period of time.

4.2.2. A Decomposition of GDP Growth and Its Use in Forecasting

The simplest way to analyze an economy's aggregate trend growth is to split it into:

- Growth from changes in employment (growth from labor inputs).
- Growth from changes in labor productivity.

For longer-term analysis, growth from changes in employment is broken down further into growth in the size of the potential labor force and growth in the actual labor force participation rate (e.g., more or fewer women or older people working; "growth" can be positive or negative).

For example, annual U.S. GDP growth used to be thought of as likely to average 2.5 percent over the long term. This number results from adding a 1 percent growth in the

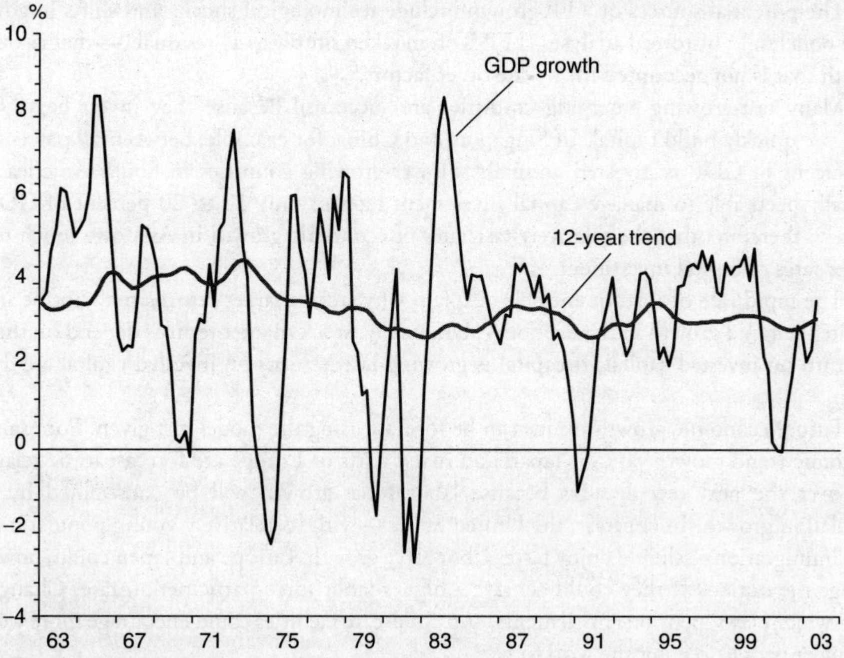

EXHIBIT 4-21 U.S. Business Cycles and Economic Trend Growth
Source: DATASTREAM/G26H

potential labor force, a 0.5 percent growth in labor force participation, and a 1 percent annual growth in labor productivity.

During the late 1990s, there were signs that productivity had risen perhaps to around 2.5 percent annually, so estimates of trend growth were raised to about 4 percent or somewhat less. In contrast, the figures for many developing countries would be closer to 2 percent potential labor force growth, 1 percent growth in labor force participation, and 3 to 4 percent growth in labor productivity, suggesting that annual growth could average 6 to 7 percent over a long period. Exhibit 4-21 shows the U.S. economic trend growth since 1960.

A more sophisticated approach to economic trend growth estimation breaks down the growth in labor productivity into two components, just as growth from labor inputs was analyzed into two components. Productivity increases come from investment in equipment or new machines (growth from capital inputs) and from **growth in total factor productivity** (TFP growth), known also as technical progress and resulting from increased efficiency in using capital inputs.

To summarize, with this approach, the trend growth in GDP is the sum of the following:

- Growth from labor inputs, comprising:
  - Growth in potential labor force size and
  - Growth in actual labor force participation, plus
- Growth from labor productivity, comprising:
  - Growth from capital inputs and
  - TFP growth (i.e., growth from increase in the productivity in using capital inputs).

The potential sources of TFP growth include technological shocks and shifts in government policies. In historical analyses, TFP is often taken simply as a "residual"—that is, output growth that is not accounted for by the other factors.[64]

Many fast-growing emerging countries are successful because they invest heavily and therefore quickly build capital. In Singapore and China, for example, between 30 percent and 40 percent of GDP is invested annually. Slower-growing countries in South America have typically been able to manage capital investment rates of only 15 to 20 percent of GDP. It is likely, therefore, that the relatively fast rates of economic growth in Asia owe much to the higher rates of capital investment.

The rapid rate of investment helps explain why stock market returns may not be strong despite the rapid growth in the economy. Ultimately, stock market returns depend on the rate of return on invested capital. If capital is growing fast, returns on invested capital are driven down.

Future economic growth trends can be forecast using the model just given. For example, economic trend growth rates in Japan and many parts of Europe are forecast to be relatively low over the next few decades because labor force growth will be constrained by slow population growth. In contrast, the United States—with its relatively young population and high immigration—should enjoy faster labor force growth. Europe and Japan could, however, change the outlook if they could achieve a higher labor force participation rate. Changes to employment laws, pension entitlements, and child-care facilities could encourage more women and older people to enter the workforce.

Trend growth will also be boosted if investment is stronger. For example, the surge in economic growth in the United States in the 1990s was partly linked to higher investment. The combination of an economic boom, higher stock market valuations, and a high level of investment in new opportunities in computers and networking in turn boosted overall productivity. Opinions still differ as to how much of the increase in productivity was due to "more machines" and how much was due to greater TFP. Part of the problem is how to value the machines, since computer prices have been falling sharply while their power increases.

By 2005, Europe had not seen a comparable surge in productivity. Investment has not been as strong, and various rigidities seem to be in the way of raising TFP. For example, in the United Kingdom, planning (zoning) restrictions on new large shops on the scale of Wal-Mart in the United States may have limited the scope of retailing efficiencies. Continental European labor laws, which restrict redundancies, or layoffs, also may have made companies move relatively slowly in "delayering" bureaucracies by using the advantages of networking.

EXAMPLE 4-29 Forecasting GDP Trend Growth

Cynthia Casey is reviewing a consultant's forecast that Canadian GDP will grow at a long-term 3.5 percent annual rate. According to Casey's own research, a 3.2 percent growth rate is more realistic. Casey and the consultant agree on the following assumptions:

- The size of the Canadian labor force will grow at 1 percent per year based on population projections.

[64]This component is known as the Solow residual estimate of TFP growth.

- Labor force participation will grow at 0.25 percent per year.
- Growth from capital inputs will be 1.5 percent per year.

Determine the reason for the discrepancy between Casey's forecast and the consultant's forecast.

Solution: Casey and the consultant agree on three of the four components of GDP growth, so the reason for the discrepancy in their GDP growth forecasts must be disagreement about the value of the fourth component, total factor productivity growth. For Casey to arrive at a 3.2 percent growth rate estimate, she must be assuming that total factor productivity growth will be $3.2\% - (1\% + 0.25\% + 1.5\%) = 0.45\%$. By contrast, the consultant is predicting that total factor productivity growth will be $3.5\% — (1\% + 0.25\% + 1.5\%) = 0.75\%$. Thus, the consultant is more optimistic than Casey about GDP growth from increases in the productivity in using capital inputs.

4.2.3. Government Structural Policies

Government structural policies refer to government policies that affect the limits of economic growth and incentives within the private sector. Government policies affect economic growth trends in profound ways. In the first three quarters of the twentieth century, governments increasingly intervened in the economy in most countries. This intervention often took the form of outright government ownership of large enterprises, combined with labor market and product market regulation. Starting in the 1980s, the trend to privatization led by former Prime Minister Thatcher in Britain substantially reduced the amount of government ownership in most economies. However, the trend toward heavy government regulation of the economy, other than through direct ownership, remains a powerful one.

The following are elements of a pro-growth government structural policy:

1. *Fiscal policy is sound*. Fiscal policy is sometimes used to influence the business cycle and can play a useful role. For example, decreasing a budget surplus (or increasing a budget deficit) may be a justifiable economic stimulus during a recession. But countries that regularly run large deficits tend to have one or more of three potential problems. First, a government budget deficit often brings a current account deficit (the so-called "twin deficits" problem), which means that the country must borrow abroad. Eventually, when the level of foreign debt becomes too high, that borrowing must be scaled back. This usually requires a large and potentially destabilizing devaluation of the currency. Second, if the deficit is not financed by borrowing, it will ultimately be financed by printing money, which means higher inflation. Third, the financing of the deficit takes resources away from private sector investment, and private sector investment is usually more productive for the country as a whole. It is for all these reasons that investors prefer to see governments hold the budget deficit close to zero over the long term.
2. *The public sector intrudes minimally on the private sector*. According to economic theory, a completely unfettered competitive market would probably supply too little in the way of public goods, such as national defense, and too much in the way of goods with negative externalities, such as goods whose manufacture pollutes the environment.[65]

[65] A **public good** is a good that is not divisible and not excludable (a consumer cannot be denied it); because of these properties, a public good cannot be priced or traded. An **externality** is a result of a transaction or process that spills over to the public.

However, the thrust of economic theory is that the marketplace usually provides the right incentives to individuals and businesses and leads to an efficient allocation of scarce resources. Recognizing this, many countries have privatized government-owned businesses over the last few decades and reduced regulations affecting business. The most damaging regulations for business tend to be labor market rules (e.g., restricting hiring and firing) because such regulations tend to raise the **structural level of unemployment** (the level of unemployment resulting from scarcity of a factor of production); however, such regulations are also the most difficult to lift.

3. *Competition within the private sector is encouraged*. Competition is important for trend growth because it drives companies to be more efficient and therefore boosts productivity growth. In the last several decades, the reduction of trade tariffs and barriers has been very important in increasing competition in the goods sector. Recent advances in networking technologies have spread that competition into the service sector. Another positive government policy is openness to foreign investment. However, note that competition makes it more difficult for companies to earn high returns on capital and thus can work against high stock market valuations.
4. *Infrastructure and human capital development are supported*. Projects supporting these goals may be in partnership with the private sector. Building health and education infrastructure has important economic benefits.
5. *Tax policies are sound*. Governments provide a range of goods, including defense, schools, hospitals, and the legal system. They also engage in a certain amount of redistribution of income directly, through pensions and welfare programs. As a result, developed country governments typically collect between 30 percent and 50 percent of GDP in taxes. According to economic theory, taxes distort economic activity by reducing the equilibrium quantities of goods and services exchanged. A decrease in total societal income and efficiency is the cost of redistributing wealth to the least well-off. As a result, investors often look with skepticism on governments that impose high overall tax burdens. Sound tax policy involves simple, transparent, and rarely altered tax rates; low marginal tax rates; and a very broad tax base.

4.3. Exogenous Shocks

Exogenous shocks are events from outside the economic system that affect its course. These could be short-lived political events, changes in government policy, or natural disasters, for example. How do shocks contrast with economic trends? Over time, trends in an economy are likely to stay relatively constant. As such, they should already be discounted in market expectations and prices. Exogenous shocks may have short-lived effects or drive changes in trends. They are typically not built into prices or at most are only partially anticipated.

Most shifts in trends are likely to come from shifts in government policies, which is why investors closely watch both specific measures and the overall direction of government policy (e.g., consumer friendly, business friendly, export friendly).

The biggest impact occurs when there is new government or a major institutional shift. For example, a major fiscal law that prevents the government from borrowing beyond certain limits can be a very effective constraint on excessive spending. A decision to make the central bank more independent or to enter a currency union could have a major impact on the economy. Such government-induced impacts typically are swiftly felt.

Some shocks do not affect trends but are felt in a more immediate or short-term manner. While they are often negative, they are not always so. In 1986, the unexpected breakup of an Organization of Petroleum Exporting Countries (OPEC) meeting without an agreement to cut production led to a sharp decline in oil prices. This event played an important role in keeping inflation low for several years after that. The fall of the Berlin wall triggered German reunification and a "peace dividend" for governments as they cut defense spending.

The creation and assimilation of new products, markets, and technologies provide a positive, longer-term impact on economic trends. Too often, analysts focus on shorter-term benefits, under-appreciating the evolving nature of the technologies and the scope of their effects. For example, the evolution of communication technologies from the telegraph, telephone, phonograph, wireless (cellular and satellite), and Internet has been a source of great positive economic impact. These gains show up in TFP growth.

Shocks cannot be forecast in general. But there are two types of economic shock that periodically affect the world economy and often involve a degree of contagion, as problems in one country spread to another. Oil shocks are important because a sharp rise in the price of oil reduces consumer purchasing power and also threatens higher inflation. Financial shocks, which can arise for a variety of reasons, threaten bank lending and therefore economic growth.

4.3.1. Oil Shocks

Crises in the Middle East regularly produce spikes in oil prices. Military conflicts that led to declines in world production of oil occurred in 1973 to 1974, 1979, 1980, 1990, and 2003 to 2004. Even though oil is a smaller input to the world economy now than it was in the 1970s, a sudden rise in prices affects consumers' income and reduces spending. Inflation rates also rise, though here the effect is ambiguous. Although inflation moves up initially, the contractionary effect of higher oil prices restricts employment and opens up an output gap so that, after a period, inflation slows to below the level where it otherwise might have been.

There have also been episodes of declining oil prices, most notably in 1986 and again in 1999. These tend to have the effect of extending the economic upswing because they contribute to lower inflation. Low oil prices and low inflation boost economic growth that can contribute to overheating, as was seen in the United States in 1987 and again in 1999 to 2000. Dependence on Middle East oil remains high, and the sources of political instability in the region remain numerous.

4.3.2. Financial Crises

Periodic financial crises affect growth rates either directly through bank lending or indirectly through their effect on investor confidence. In the last few decades, events in emerging markets have been the cause of several crises. The Latin American debt crisis of 1982, the Mexican currency crisis of 1994, the Asian financial crisis of 1997, and the Russian crisis of 1998 are examples. The last was particularly important because it threatened both financial markets and investment banks with widespread collapse. The reason was a possible domino effect due to the subsequent collapse of Long-Term Capital Management (LTCM), a large U.S. hedge fund. Most of LTCM's positions had been based on expectations of declining risk spreads. When the Russian crisis sent those spreads upward, it triggered a crisis. Among central banks, the U.S. Federal Reserve's response to these emerging market crises was particularly proactive. The Fed injected liquidity into the system, thereby reducing U.S. interest rates and moderating the impact on financial institutions.

There have been other financial crises. Banks are always potentially vulnerable after a major decline in asset prices, particularly property prices, as in the United States in the early 1990s. In that case, the Fed's response was to keep interest rates low for a prolonged period to provide sufficient liquidity to ensure that the payment system could continue. That action would have been more difficult in a world of low inflation or deflation. Financial crises are therefore potentially more dangerous in a low interest rate environment.

4.4. International Interactions

In general, the dependence of any particular country on international interactions is a function of its relative size and its degree of specialization. Large countries with diverse economies, such as the United States, tend to be less influenced by developments elsewhere than small countries, such as Chile, whose production depends significantly on a few commodities like copper. Increasing globalization of trade, capital flows, and direct investment means that practically all countries are increasingly affected by international interactions.

4.4.1. Macroeconomic Linkages

Countries' economies are directly affected by changes in the foreign demand for their exports. This is one way that the business cycle in one country can affect that in others. But there are other international linkages (other than trade) at work, such as those resulting from cross-border direct business investment. The United States has often been the leader in such investment. As a result, an economic slowdown in the United States frequently makes companies worldwide more cautious about investment and hiring.

However, the U.S. economy and the economies of other developed countries are clearly not perfectly integrated. For example, continental Europe did not suffer a recession in 1990 despite the U.S. recession because the stimulative effects of German reunification outweighed the negative effects of the U.S. slowdown. Similarly, while the United States and most other countries suffered a weak economy in the first half of 2003, China's economy boomed under the influence of stimulative monetary and fiscal policies.

4.4.2. Interest Rate/Exchange Rate Linkages

One of the linkages of most concern to investors involves interest rates and exchange rates.

Sometimes, short-term interest rates are affected by developments in other countries because one central bank pursues a formal or informal exchange rate link with another currency. Some governments *unilaterally* peg their currencies firmly or loosely to one of the major currencies, usually the U.S. dollar or the euro. This strategy is much less common now than it was before the Asian crisis in 1997, but it is still practiced in several countries in Asia (notably China, Hong Kong, and Malaysia) and by members of the Gulf Cooperation Council (Saudi Arabia, Kuwait, Bahrain, Qatar, the United Arab Emirates, and the Sultanate of Oman). Also, various countries in Eastern and Central Europe peg to the euro.

The countries that follow this strategy find two benefits. First, domestic business has some reassurance that exchange rates are not going to fluctuate wildly. Second, by pegging the exchange rate, a "pegged" country often hopes to control inflation. This consideration was important in Europe under the Exchange Rate Mechanism (an exchange rate regime established in preparation for the introduction of the euro) and was also the reason for Argentina's convertibility plan, which tied the peso to the dollar in the early 1990s but collapsed amidst a severe economic crisis in 2001.

If a country is following such an exchange rate policy, then the level of interest rates will depend on overall market confidence in the peg. A high degree of confidence in the exchange rate peg means the interest rate differential can converge to near zero. For example, the Hong Kong dollar has been pegged to the U.S. dollar. Interest rate differentials were near zero in 2000 to 2001 after an uncertain period in 1997 to 1999, when Hong Kong interest rates were periodically much higher than those in the United States because of the handover of sovereignty to China. But if the markets see the peg policy as unsustainable, then investors will demand a substantial interest differential.

If a country is known to be linking its currency to another, then bond yields of the weaker currency are nearly always higher. Hence, in Europe, Polish bond yields bear a spread over euro bond yields. If the expectation were that the zloty/euro exchange rate would remain broadly the same as its current level over the long term, then bond yields in Poland would converge with those in the Eurozone for bonds of equal credit risk. An expectation of a stable exchange rate might be justified by a belief in the Polish government's determination to maintain parity or by a perception that inflation and the competitiveness outlook for Poland obviate the need for a devaluation. If, however, markets anticipate a devaluation at some stage before Poland joins the euro, then a bond yield spread should remain in place.

Even if countries are not trying to link their currencies, bond yields can diverge substantially between countries. For example, if one country's exchange rate is severely undervalued and is expected to rise substantially against another country's, then bond yields in the first country will be lower than they would otherwise be in relation to the other country.

Exchange rates can be over- or undervalued, requiring an offset from bond yields, for a number of reasons, such as government action on *short-term* interest rates. For example, the Exchange Rate Mechanism was maintained as long as it was by using high short-term interest rates to limit speculation against currencies.

Misvaluation can also happen when bond yields reflect a particularly strong economy. In 1984, U.S. bond yields averaged 12.5 percent despite an annual inflation of 4 percent. These high real and nominal rates were due to the combination of the increasing U.S. budget deficit, a strong private sector economy, and a tightening monetary policy. In comparison, Germany had bond yields of 8 percent with an annual inflation of 2.5 percent. Hence, investors in the United States could enjoy real yields 3 percent above those seen by investors in German bonds: 8.5% real U.S. yield $-$5.5% real German yield = 3% excess real yield difference in favor of the United States. This yield difference was enough to take the dollar up substantially in 1983 to 1985, leaving the bond markets in some degree of equilibrium, although the U.S. dollar was then viewed as overvalued.

Obviously, *nominal* bond yields vary between countries according to those countries' different inflation outlooks and other factors. It is sometimes thought that *real* bond yields ought to be similar in different countries because international capital flows will equalize them. However, movements in exchange rates to under- or overvalued levels can compensate for different real bond yields. Although real yields can and often do vary among countries, they tend to move together. In the example above from 1984, bond yields in both the United States and Germany were comparatively high in relation to inflation and overall historical experience.

The key factor linking bond yields (especially real bond yields) is world supply and demand for capital or the perceptions of supply and demand. Take the example of the collapse of world bond markets and the sharp rise in bond yields in 1994. These events seem to have been partly due to a perception that synchronized world growth would force short- and long-term interest rates up as the demand for world savings exceeded the supply. Since in the end, the demand has to equal the supply, interest rates everywhere rose to choke off demand and/or stimulate more supply. Similarly, in 2001, bond yields fell everywhere as private demand for capital dropped off in the face of a world slowdown.

4.4.3. Emerging Markets

There are some special considerations in setting capital market expectations for emerging countries. Here, we outline some of the key differences from major economies and look briefly at country risk analysis techniques and data sources that analysts use in evaluating emerging markets.

4.4.3.1. Essential Differences between Emerging and Major Economies

Emerging countries are engaged in a catch-up process. As a result, they need higher rates of investment than developed countries in physical capital and infrastructure and in human capital. But many emerging countries have inadequate domestic savings and therefore rely heavily on foreign capital. Unfortunately, managing the consequent foreign debt often creates periodic crises, dealing a major blow to investors in emerging stocks and bonds.

Very often, emerging countries have a more volatile political and social environment than developed countries. In comparison with developed countries, emerging countries tend to have a relatively large percentage of people with low income and few assets and a relatively small middle class with its typically major stake in political and economic stability.

Most emerging countries need major structural reform to unlock their potential, which can be difficult to achieve in a volatile political environment. The potential for growth is often blocked by governments protecting vested interests. As a result, the International Monetary Fund (the IMF, an international organization entrusted with fostering global monetary and financial stability) and the World Bank (a group of five international organizations responsible for providing finance to developing countries) have often placed conditions on aid both to manage the risk of crises and to promote growth. For countries within an IMF program, analysts often focus closely on a country's progress in meeting the targets.

Even the largest emerging countries are relatively small in world terms, and their economies are often concentrated in a few areas such as particular commodities or in a narrow range of manufactured goods. Others rely heavily on oil imports and are thus vulnerable to fluctuation in oil prices or are dependent on continuing capital inflows.

4.4.3.2. Country Risk Analysis Techniques Investors in emerging bonds focus on the risk of the country being unable to service its debt (make promised payments of interest and principal). Investors in stocks need to assess the growth prospects of emerging countries as well as their vulnerability to surprises. A common approach is to use a checklist of various economic and financial ratios and a series of qualitative questions. Following are six questions that country risk analysis seeks to answer, with suggestions for data to analyze and points to look for.

1. **How sound is fiscal and monetary policy?**
   If there is one single ratio that is most watched in all emerging market analysis, it is the ratio of the fiscal deficit to GDP. Most emerging countries have deficits and are engaged in a perpetual struggle to reduce them. Deficits are a major cause of slow growth and frequently a factor in serious crises. A persistent ratio above 4 percent is regarded with concern. The range of 2 to 4 percent is acceptable but still damaging. Countries with ratios of 2 percent or less are doing well.

   If the fiscal deficit is large for a sustained period, the government is likely to build up significant debt. In developing countries, governments usually borrow in the short term from domestic lenders in local currency and from overseas in foreign currency. The Argentinean crisis in 2001 was essentially the result of too much government debt. For a developing country, the level of debt that would be considered too high is generally lower than for developed countries. Countries with a ratio of debt of more than about 70 to 80 percent of GDP are extremely vulnerable.
2. **What are the economic growth prospects for the economy?**
   The most successful countries in Asia have been able to grow at annual rates of 6 to 8 percent on a sustained basis. Others have achieved a respectable rate of 4 to 6 percent per annum. Annual growth rates of less than 4 percent generally mean that the country is catching up with the industrial countries slowly, if at all. It also means that, given

some population growth, per capita income is growing very slowly or even falling, which is likely to bring political stresses.

Investors usually welcome a wave of reform because it will typically boost economic growth and the stock market. But growth may slow down after that unless there is further reform or new opportunities are opened up. One of the best indicators of the structural health of an economy is the Economic Freedom Index, published by a consortium of research institutes around the world (www.freetheworld.com). This index consists of a range of indicators of the freedoms enjoyed by the private sector, including tax rates, tariff rates, and the cost of setting up companies. Countries such as the United States, Singapore, and Hong Kong have scored well. The index has been found to have a broad positive correlation with economic growth.

3. **Is the currency competitive, and are the external accounts under control?** Managing the currency has proven to be one of the most difficult areas for governments. If the exchange rate swings from heavily undervalued to seriously overvalued, there are negative effects on business confidence and investment. Moreover, if the currency is overvalued for a prolonged period, the country is likely to be borrowing too much, creating a large current account deficit and a growing external debt.

   The size of the current account deficit is a key measure of competitiveness and the sustainability of the external accounts.[66] Any country with a deficit persistently greater than 4 percent of GDP is probably uncompetitive to some degree. Current account deficits need to be financed. If the deficits are financed through debt, servicing the debt may become difficult. A combination of currency depreciation and economic slowdown will likely follow. The slowdown will also usually cut the current account deficit by reducing imports. Note, however, that a small current account deficit on the order of 1 to 3 percent of GDP is probably sustainable, provided that the economy is growing. A current account deficit is also more sustainable to the extent that it is financed through foreign direct investment rather than debt, because foreign direct investment creates productive assets.

4. **Is external debt under control?** External debt means foreign currency debt owed to foreigners by both the government and the private sector. It is perfectly sensible for countries to borrow overseas because such borrowing serves to augment domestic savings. But borrowing needs to be kept within reasonable bounds or lenders will begin to question its sustainability. The resulting reluctance to lend new money may lead to an exodus of capital as money invested in local bonds and stocks flows out.

   Analysts watch several measures of debt burden. The ratio of foreign debt to GDP is one of the best measures. Above 50 percent is dangerous territory, while 25 to 50 percent is the ambiguous area. Another important ratio is debt to current account receipts. A reading above 200 percent for this ratio puts the country into the danger zone, while a reading below 100 percent does not.

[66] To briefly review accounting for cross-border flows, the **balance of payments** (an accounting of all cash flows between residents and nonresidents of a country) consists of the **current account,** dominated by the trade balance (reflecting exports and imports), and the **financial account,** consisting of portfolio flows (from security purchases and sales—e.g., bonds and equities) and **foreign direct investment** (FDI) by companies (e.g., Toyota Motor Corporation building an automobile assembly plant in the United States), as well as flows such as borrowing from and deposits with foreign banks. The sum of the current account and the financial account, or the **overall trade balance,** should be zero.

5. **Is liquidity plentiful?**

   By liquidity, we mean foreign exchange reserves in relation to trade flows and short-term debt. Traditionally, reserves were judged adequate when they were equal in value to three months' worth of imports. However, with the vastly greater importance of debt and capital flows, we now relate reserves to other measures. An important ratio is reserves divided by short-term debt (debt maturing in less than 12 months). A safe level is over 200 percent, while a risky level is under 100 percent.

   Excess short-term borrowing is present in most emerging market crises. This is partly a result of the fact that countries often find it more difficult to borrow longer-term in the period leading up to the crisis. But if the country borrows too much, even short-term lending eventually stops and the country is typically in crisis very quickly thereafter.

6. **Is the political situation supportive of the required policies?**

   If the economy of the country is healthy, with fast growth, rapid policy liberalization, low debt, and high reserves, then the answer to this question matters less. Poor political leadership is unlikely to create a crisis. However, if the economic indicators and policy are flashing warning signals, the key issue becomes whether the government will implement the necessary adjustment policies. Cutting the budget deficit, which usually requires some combination of higher taxes and lower spending, is always painfully difficult, especially if the economy is weak already. Other key policy changes are reforms such as privatization and the ending of monopolies.

In summary, the evaluation of emerging economies uses many of the same tools as the evaluation of developed countries but places a greater emphasis on the balance of payments, debt, liquidity, and politics. The analysis pays off because despite serious risks caused by political instability and periodic crises, many emerging countries grow faster than developed countries and offer good investment opportunities. Since the Asian crisis in 1997, investors are much more conscious of the potential risks, which include market declines, fixed or quasi-fixed exchange rates, major recessions, and contagion. The worst losses have been suffered in the countries that turned out to be the weakest politically.

4.5. Economic Forecasting

Having reviewed some practical basics of macroeconomics for the investment analyst with many real-world illustrations, we can now indicate some of the disciplines that the analyst can apply to economic forecasting. Often, analysts consider the implications of a variety of approaches, which will often raise questions that lead to productive analysis and insight. We may distinguish at least three distinct approaches:

- Econometric models, the most formal and mathematical approach to economic forecasting.
- Leading indicators: variables that have been found to lead (precede) turns in the economy.
- Checklists, requiring the subjective integration of the answers to a set of relevant questions.

In the following sections, we address each of these approaches in turn.

4.5.1. Econometric Modeling **Econometrics** is the application of quantitative modeling and analysis grounded in economic theory to the analysis of economic data.[67] Whereas generic

[67]There are also quantitative approaches reflecting **unstructured modeling**—that is, modeling without a theory on the underlying structure—such as vector autoregression (VAR), that may be appropriate for certain types of economic forecasting. See Diebold (2004) for an introduction to VAR.

data analysis can involve variables of all descriptions (possibly including economic, security characteristic, demographic, and statistical variables), econometric analysis focuses on economic variables, using economic theory to model their relationships.

Econometric models vary from small models with just one equation or perhaps a handful of equations to large, complex models with hundreds of equations. However, they all work in essentially the same way. A model is created of the economy based on variables suggested by economic theory. Optimization (frequently the least-squares criterion from regression analysis) using historical data is used to estimate the parameters of the equations. The estimated system of equations is used to forecast the future values of economic variables, with the forecaster supplying values for the exogenous variables. For example, such a model may require the forecaster to enter an exchange rate, an interest rate, and commodity prices. But the model then uses the estimated past relationships to forecast the future.

A very simple model is presented in the following series of equations:

1. GDP growth = function of (Consumer spending growth and Investment growth)
2. Consumer spending growth = function of (Consumer income growth lagged one period and Interest rate*)
3. Investment growth = function of (GDP growth lagged one period and Interest rate*)
4. Consumer income growth lagged one period = Consumer spending growth lagged one period

Here, the asterisk (*) denotes an exogenous variable. So, with this four-equation model estimated on past data and with the actual data for the variables lagged one period, together with the modeler's exogenous forecasts for the interest rate, the model will solve for GDP growth in time in the current period. Note that the final equation asserting that consumer income growth is always identical to consumer spending growth assumes a static relationship between these two variables.

Additional variables make a model more complex, more realistic, but often more difficult to construct, estimate, and interpret. Most models will incorporate variables such as government spending, employment, the savings rate, money supply, exports, and imports. However, it is by no means certain that larger models are superior to smaller models. Also, different models have different structures, and these structures reflect the views of the modeler both in what variables are included and in how they interrelate with one another. Monetarist models, for example, rely heavily on money-supply-related variables and relationships.

Econometric models are widely regarded as very useful for simulating the effects of changes in certain variables. For example, they can be useful for assessing the impact of a 10 percent rise in oil prices or a rise in income tax rates or a faster growth rate in trading partners on consumer demand.[68] Econometric models have several limitations. First, econometric models require the user to find adequate measures for the real-world activities and relationships to be modeled, and these measures may not be available. Variables may also be measured with error. Relationships among the variables may change over time because of changes in the structure of the economy; as a result, the econometric model of the economy may be misspecified.

In practice, therefore, skillful econometric modelers use a great deal of personal judgment in arriving at forecasts. Very often, the first run of the model will generate a forecast that the

[68]Mehra and Peterson (2005) found that in the United States a 10 percent increase in oil prices is associated with the level of consumer spending at the end of six quarters being 0.80 percent to 1.60 percent lower than it otherwise would be.

modelers do not believe. So they will go back and change some of the exogenous variables to arrive at a forecast they do believe. The great merit of the econometric approach, however, is that it constrains the forecaster to a certain degree of consistency and also challenges the modeler to reassess prior views based on what the model concludes.

In practice, model-based forecasts rarely forecast recessions well, although they have a better record in anticipating upturns. For example, the U.S. economic upswing that gathered pace in the second half of 2003 was well forecast by econometric models.

4.5.2. Economic Indicators **Economic indicators** are economic statistics provided by government and established private organizations that contain information on an economy's recent past activity or its current or future position in the business cycle. **Lagging economic indicators** and **coincident indicators** are indicators of recent past and current economic activity, respectively. A **leading economic indicator** (LEI) is a variable that varies with the business cycle but at a fairly consistent time interval before a turn in the business cycle. Most analysts' greatest interest is leading indicators because they may provide information about upcoming changes in economic activity, inflation, interest rates, and security prices.

Leading indicator–based analysis is the simplest forecasting approach to use because it requires following only a limited number of variables. The indicators are best thought of as early signs of probable events to come.

Many private sector forecasters try to gain an edge in identifying the factors that best predict the path of the economy and use their own proprietary indicators. Nevertheless, a good place to start for most investors is the leading indicators published by national governments or, in some countries, by established private organizations such as the Conference Board in the United States.

Analysts may use both individual LEIs and composite LEIs, reflecting a collection of economic data releases that are combined to give an overall reading. Composite LEIs combine these releases using weights based on an analysis of their forecasting usefulness in past cycles. They can also be combined in a so-called **diffusion index,** which measures how many indicators are pointing up and how many down. For example, if 7 out of 10 are pointing upward, then the odds are that the economy is accelerating.

We review a selection of LEIs, both individual and composite, by geographic region:

Worldwide:[69]

- OECD Composite Leading Indicators (CLI) (www.oecd.org). The Organization for Economic Cooperation and Development (OECD) is a Paris-headquartered organization comprising 23 member countries. The OECD publishes CLI on Friday of the first full week of each month (these releases relate to information on production two months earlier). The indices are based on a range of variables (5 to 11 for each country), such as share prices, industrial production data, building permits, and monetary data that may have predictive value for the course of the business cycle. A Total OECD Composite Leading Indicator is published, as well as indices for the 23 member countries and for seven regions:
  - Big Four European Countries (France, Germany, Italy, and the United Kingdom).
  - Eurozone.
  - G-7 (Canada, France, Germany, Italy, Japan, the United Kingdom, and the United States).

[69]See *Guide to Economic Indicators*, 5th ed. (*The Economist,* 2003).

- EU-25 (the 25 members of the European Union plus Denmark, Sweden, and the United Kingdom).[70]
- OECD-Europe (the EU-25 countries plus Norway, Switzerland, and Turkey).
- Total OECD countries (OECD-Europe plus Canada, Mexico, the United States, Australia, and Japan).
- NAFTA (Canada, Mexico, and the United States).

The OECD publishes the six-month rate of change (annualized) in the monthly index numbers. Some analysts follow the six-month rate of change series more closely than the monthly index numbers because it may filter out the meaningless variation (noise) in the monthly numbers.[71]

Europe: Selected indicators include the following:

- **Eurozone Harmonized Index of Consumer Prices** (HICP) (http://epp.eurostat.cec.eu.int). Eurostat, the statistical office of the EU, publishes a composite index of inflation in the Eurozone. The European Central Bank (ECB) developed this index for use in inflation targeting, and indices standardized on the ECB methodology have been developed for individual EU countries. Inflation indices are not in general viewed as leading indicators. However, because of the ECB's strong focus on inflation containment, an unexpected increase in this index may presage events such as an interest rate increase.
- **German Industrial Production** (www.destatis.de). The Statistiches Bundesamt Deutschland (German Federal Office of Statistics) publishes in the second week of each month an index of German industrial production relating to production data two months earlier. Germany is Europe's largest economy and has frequently ranked among the top two exporters in the world. (As of 2004, its largest export partners were France, 10.3 percent; the Unites States, 8.8 percent; the United Kingdom, 8.3 percent; Italy, 7.2 percent; the Netherlands, 6.2 percent; Belgium, 5.6 percent; Austria, 5.4 percent; and Spain, 5 percent.)[72] This series is closely watched as a leading indicator for the German and Eurozone economies.
- The **German IFO Business Survey** (www.ifo.de) and the **French Monthly Business Survey** (www.insee.fr), both released during the fourth week of the month being surveyed, are influential surveys of German and French business executives, respectively. Analysts focus on the answers to the forward-looking component of these series (a six-month-ahead time frame for the German series and a three-month-ahead time frame for the French series) for indications of Eurozone industrial production over the next several months. France is the Eurozone's second-largest economy.

Asia Pacific: Selected indicators include the following:

- The **Tankan Survey** of the Bank of Japan (www.boj.or.jp). Japan's central bank's detailed quarterly survey of business, published at the start of April, July, and October and in mid-December, is a rich source for information on Japanese business conditions and the expectations of business executives. Japan has been ranked among the world's three largest economies and has been the world's largest producer of foreign direct investment.

---

[70]As of the beginning of 2005, the European Union has 25 members, subject to national ratification in some cases. The number of countries in the EU may change from time to time.

[71]See Baumohl (2005), p. 328.

[72]See www.cia.org.

Furthermore, the Japanese yen is one of the world's most important currencies: The Bank of Japan has the world's largest reserves of foreign currency and gold, and the bank has frequently been active in foreign exchange markets. As of the end of 2004, the major export partners of Japan were the United States, 22.7 percent; China, 13.1 percent; South Korea, 7.8 percent; Taiwan, 7.4 percent; and Hong Kong, 6.3 percent. Japan's largest import partners were China, 20.7 percent; the United States, 14 percent; South Korea, 4.9 percent; Australia, 4.3 percent; Indonesia, 4.1 percent; Saudi Arabia, 4.1 percent; and the UAE, 4 percent.

- **China Industrial Production** (www.stats.gov.cn). China's National Bureau of Statistics (NBS) releases monthly data on industrial production usually four weeks after the month being surveyed. These data are measures of the value added by light industry (mainly producing consumer goods) and heavy industry (producing durable goods such as factory equipment and automobiles). Baumohl (2005) provides a critique of the reliability of these data. Valuing the Chinese currency (called the renminbi or yuan) on a purchasing power parity basis (defined in Section 4.6.9.1), as of 2005, China ranked as the world's second-largest economy.

South America:

- **Brazil Industrial Production** (www.ibge.gov.br). The Brazilian Institute for Geography and Statistics releases monthly data on industrial production approximately 40 days after the end of the month surveyed. This series is probably the closest watched by analysts. As of the end of 2004, Brazil represented more than 40 percent of South America's total GDP. With an estimated population of over 185 million as of 2005, Brazil is also by far the most populous South American country. As of 2004, Brazil's major export partners were the United States, 20.8 percent; Argentina, 7.5 percent; the Netherlands, 6.1 percent; China, 5.6 percent; Germany, 4.1 percent; and Mexico, 4 percent. Its major import partners were the United States, 18.3 percent; Argentina, 8.9 percent; Germany, 8.1 percent; China, 5.9 percent; Nigeria, 5.6 percent; and Japan, 4.6 percent.

North America:[73]

- The Conference Board's **Index of Leading Economic Indicators** (www.globalindicators.org). The Conference Board is a private, nonprofit, New York City-headquartered research organization that took over the management of this series from the U.S. Commerce Department in 1995. The Conference Board releases this monthly series three weeks after the end of the month reported upon, as well as coincident and lagging indices. Exhibit 4-22 shows the 10 components of the U.S. leading indicator index, which is normally quoted as a weighted index but is also available as a diffusion index. The Conference Board also publishes indices for Australia, France, Germany, Japan, Korea, Mexico, Spain, and the United Kingdom, researching the best indicators to use for each country. The United States is the world's largest economy. As of 2004, the United States' largest exporting partners were Canada, 23 percent; Mexico, 13.6 percent; Japan, 6.7 percent; the United Kingdom, 4.4 percent; and China, 4.3 percent. Its largest importing partners were Canada, 17 percent; China, 13.8 percent; Mexico, 10.3 percent; Japan, 8.7 percent; and Germany, 5.2 percent.

[73]This example draws on Baumohl (2005).

In a given index, the component factors are inversely related to the standard deviation of the month-to-month changes in each component. They are used to equalize the volatility of the contribution from each component and are "normalized" to sum to 1. When one or more of the components are missing, the other factors are adjusted proportionately to ensure that the total continues to sum to 1.

As Exhibit 4-22 shows, the Conference Board's LEI index consists of seven nonfinancial and three financial components (numbers 7, 8, and 9). Of particular note is number 5, provided by the Institute of Supply Management (ISM), which is a professional organization of purchasing managers. This release comes out on the first business day of each month and so is one of the earliest pieces of information on the business cycle available in a given month. This release receives more attention than number 3, also from the ISM. Because capital goods orders are more sensitive to the business cycle than consumer goods, the release of number 5 is often a market-moving event. Another interesting component is number 7, the S&P 500 Index, which historically has been a good leading indicator of the stock market.

In contrast with the release of some of its individual components, the release of the LEI index is rarely a market-moving event because some of its components are already public.

Traditionally, the general rule was that three consecutive months of increases, or three consecutive months of decreases, signaled an upturn or downturn in the economy within

EXHIBIT 4-22 U.S. Composite Indices: Components and Standardization Factors

Leading Index	Factor
1. Average weekly hours, manufacturing	0.1946
2. Average weekly initial claims for unemployment insurance	0.0268
3. Manufacturers' new orders, consumer goods and materials	0.0504
4. Vendor performance, slower deliveries diffusion index	0.0296
5. Manufacturers' new orders, non-defense capital goods	0.0139
6. Building permits, new private housing units	0.0205
7. Stock prices, 500 common stocks	0.0309
8. Money supply, M2	0.2775
9. Interest rate spread, 10-year Treasury bonds less federal funds	0.3364
10. Index of consumer expectations	0.0193
Coincident Index	
1. Employees on nonagricultural payrolls	0.5186
2. Personal income less transfer payments	0.2173
3. Industrial production	0.1470
4. Manufacturing and trade sales	0.1170
Lagging Index	
1. Average duration of unemployment	0.0368
2. Inventory/sales ratio, manufacturing and trade	0.1206
3. Labor cost per unit of output, manufacturing	0.0693
4. Average prime rate	0.2692
5. Commercial and industrial loans	0.1204
6. Consumer installment credit to personal income ratio	0.1951
7. Consumer price index for services	0.1886

Source: Conference Board, www.globalindicators.org.

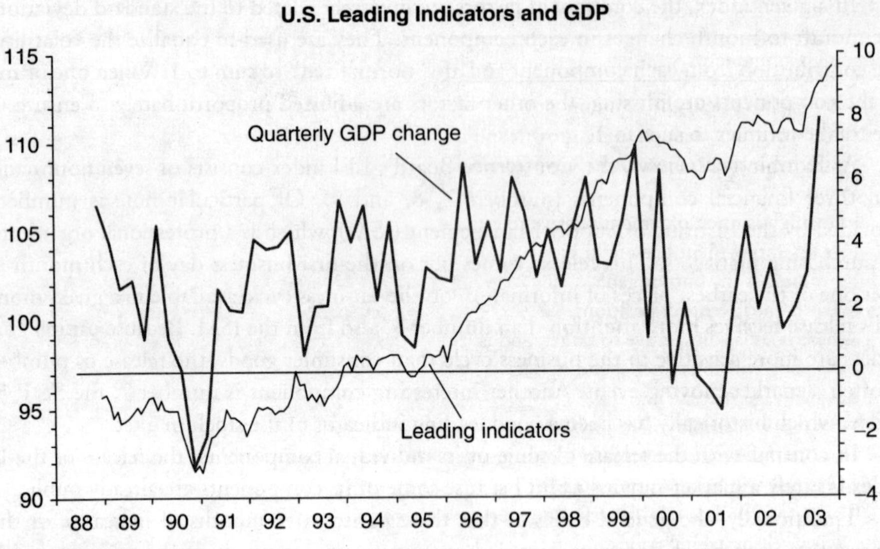

EXHIBIT 4-23 U.S. Leading Indicators and GDP
Source: DATASTREAM

three to six months. The Conference Board and others have also indicated other rules for interpreting changes in the index.

Exhibit 4-23 plots the composite LEI against quarterly GDP changes. The U.S. LEI index gave a somewhat ambiguous signal ahead of the 1990 recession but performed much better in the most recent cycle. In the late 1990s, it correctly showed that the Asian crisis was not threatening a U.S. downturn. Then, in 2000, it peaked in January and began to turn down in February (which would have been reported in March). By midyear, it was clearly falling, well before there was general agreement that the economy was slowing. In 2003, it picked up strongly in May (reported in June) and continued to rise rapidly, correctly signaling a strong recovery.

4.5.3. Checklist Approach

Formally or informally, many forecasters consider a whole range of economic data to assess the future position of the economy. Checklist assessments are straightforward but time-consuming because they require looking at the widest possible range of data. The data may then be extrapolated into forecasts via objective statistical methods, such as time-series analysis, or via more subjective or judgmental means. An analyst may then assess whether the measures are in an equilibrium state or nearer to an extreme reading.

Inflation reports provided by many central banks or through the minutes of central bank meetings give an idea of the range of indicators that may be included in checklists related to preparing general economic forecasts.

Exhibit 4-24 is an example of a checklist for evaluating economic growth. In effect, the forecaster asks a series of questions about likely components of spending and then, aggregating the information gathered, reaches a conclusion about the outlook for the economy. Such an approach involves a substantial amount of subjective judgment as to what is important in the economy.

Example 4-30 is a simple illustration of the checklist approach.

EXHIBIT 4-24 Checklist for Economic Growth

Spending Components	Focus
1. Where in the cycle is the economy now?	Aggregate activity
• Review previous data on GDP growth and its components (consumer spending, business investment, inventories, net exports, and government spending).	Aggregate activity
• How high is unemployment relative to estimates of "full employment"?	Consumer
• Has unemployment been falling?	Consumer
• How large is the output gap?	Business
• What is the inventory position?	Business
• Where is inflation relative to target, and is it threatening to rise?	Inflation
2. How strong will consumer spending be?	Consumer
• Review wage/income patterns.	Consumer
• How fast will employment grow?	Consumer
• How confident are consumers? Consumer confidence indices.	Consumer
3. How strong will business spending be?	Business
• Review survey data (e.g., purchasing managers indices).	Business
• Review recent capital goods orders.	Business
• Assess balance sheet health of companies.	Business
• Assess cash flow and earnings growth trends.	Business
• Has the stock market been rising?	Business
• What is the inventory position? Low inventory/sales ratio implies GDP strength.	Business
4. How strong will import growth be?	Government
• Exchange rate competitiveness and recent movements.	Government
• Strength of economic growth elsewhere.	Government
5. What is the government's fiscal stance?	Government
6. What is the monetary stance?	Central Bank
• Review recent changes in interest rates.	Central Bank
• What do real interest rates tell us?	Central Bank
• What does the Taylor rule tell us?	Central Bank
• Monetary conditions indices (i.e., trends in asset prices and exchange rate).	Central Bank
• Money supply indicators.	Central Bank
7. Inflation	Inflation
• How fast is inflation rising, or are prices falling?	Inflation

EXAMPLE 4-30 An Analyst's Forecasts

As a capital market analyst at a large money management firm, Charles Johnson has developed a list of six broad questions for evaluating the economy. The questions are given below with his responses for his own national market. The current inflation rate is 2 percent per year.

A. Is consumer spending increasing or decreasing? *Johnson*: Consumer spending is increasing at a lackluster rate of 0.75 percent per annum.

B. Are business conditions and fundamentals growing stronger or weakening? *Johnson*: Based on recent values of manufacturers' new orders for consumer goods and materials and non-defense capital goods, business demand is weakening.

C. What is the consensus forecast for the GDP growth rate over the next year? *Johnson*: The median forecast from a survey of economists is that GDP will decline from a 3.5 percent to a 3.0 percent annual growth rate.

D. Are government programs and fiscal policy becoming more restrictive or expansive? *Johnson*: Political support for a stimulative fiscal policy is absent; fiscal policy will be neutral.

E. Is monetary policy neutral, tightening, or loosening? *Johnson*: Monetary policy is neutral.

F. Is inflation in a steady state (state of equilibrium)? *Johnson*: The current inflation rate of 2 percent is close to a steady state value.

Based on the information given, what conclusions will Johnson reach concerning:

1. Inflation over the next six months?
2. Short-term interest rates?

Solution to Problem 1: Based on the expected slow growth in consumer demand and weakening business demand, inflation should remain muted over the next six months.

Solution to Problem 2: Reduced aggregate economic activity and stable inflation should allow for stable to falling interest rates.

The subjectivity of the checklist approach is perhaps its main weakness. The checklist's strength is its flexibility. It allows the forecaster to take changes in the structure of the economy into account quickly by changing the variables or the weights assigned to variables within the analysis. The next section summarizes the three chief approaches.

4.5.4. Economic Forecasting Approaches: Summary of Strengths and Weaknesses

Exhibit 4-25 summarizes the advantages and disadvantages of forecasting using econometric models, leading indicators, and checklists.

4.6. Using Economic Information in Forecasting Asset Class Returns

Movements in economic variables play a key role in forming investors' expectations. Although some investors, such as pure bottom-up stock pickers or fully hedged arbitrage specialists, do not care much about the way that economic developments move markets, it is important for most investors. In this section, we look at how the principal asset classes are moved by different economic variables.

4.6.1. Cash and Equivalents

Cash managers make money through selection of the maturity of the paper in their portfolio or, if permitted by investment policy, by taking credit risk. Longer maturities and lower credit ratings reward the extra risk with higher expected returns. Managers lengthen or shorten maturities according to their expectations of where

EXHIBIT 4-25 Advantages and Disadvantages of Three Approaches to Economic Forecasting

Advantages	Disadvantages
Econometric Models Approach	
• Models can be quite robust with many factors used that can approximate reality. • Once models are built, new data may be collected and consistently used within models to quickly generate output. • Provides quantitative estimates of the effects on the economy of changes in exogenous variables.	• Most complex and time-consuming to formulate. • Data inputs and relationships not easy to forecast and not static. • Requires careful analysis of output. • Rarely forecasts recessions well.
Leading Indicator–Based Approach	
• Usually intuitive and simple in construction. • May be available from third parties. • May be tailored for individual needs. • A literature exists on the effective use of various third-party indicators.	• Historically, has not consistently worked, as relationships between inputs are not static. • Can provide false signals.
Checklist Approach	
• Limited complexity. • Flexible: allows structural changes to be easily incorporated.	• Subjective. • Time-consuming. • Complexity has to be limited due to the manual nature of the process.

interest rates will go next. Normally, longer-maturity paper will pay a higher interest rate than shorter-maturity paper, even if overnight interest rates are expected to remain the same, because the risk of loss is greater for the longer-term paper if this expectation is not fulfilled. If further rises in rates are expected over time, then 6- and 12-month paper should offer even higher rates than shorter-term paper.

The overnight interest rate is targeted by the central bank and will normally vary only slightly from the target set. For example, in the United States, the Federal Reserve's target for the fed funds rate along with open market operations usually ensures the overnight interest rate is close to the target. (**Open market operations** are the purchase or sale by a central bank of government securities, which are settled using reserves, to influence interest rates and the supply of credit by banks.) Occasional variations are due normally to liquidity factors, especially close to year-end or during unusual market turbulence. In other countries, the target rate may be the repo rate (repurchase rate), as in the Eurozone, where the European Central Bank conducts open market operations.

At any given time, the yield curve of interest rates of a particular security (e.g., Treasury bills or interest rate futures) reflects the market's expectations of rates over that period. The money manager is trying to be ahead of others in correctly forecasting those levels. In practice, this means forecasting both the behavior of the economy and the reaction of the central bank to that behavior. It also means understanding what the markets currently anticipate and distinguishing between future data surprises and what is already factored into expectations (i.e., likely to have no effect on the market). Money managers therefore spend a great deal of time in so-called "central bank watching."

EXAMPLE 4-31 Central Bank Watching and Short-Term Interest Rate Expectations

At the beginning of 2000, the U.S. stock market bubble peaked and the economy was strong. At this point, one-month U.S. interest rates stood at about 5.7 percent per annum, with the six-month yield about 40 basis points higher at 6.1 percent per annum. Interest rates had already moved up in 1999, but the market was expecting the Federal Reserve to announce additional small increases in rates to help slow the economy and avoid rising inflation. A money manager might have been tempted to buy the longer-term paper, given its higher yield. However, the Federal Reserve raised interest rates faster than expected, with the fed funds rate moving up from 5.5 percent to 6.5 percent by June 2000. The best place to be was therefore at the short end of the curve, because by May 2000, one-month paper could be bought to yield 6.5 percent per annum and six-month paper could be bought to yield 6.8 percent per annum. During periods of rising short-term rates, keeping maturities short is a good strategy.

Early summer 2000 turned out to be the peak for U.S. interest rates, and rates were cut sharply in 2001 when the U.S. economy went into recession. In November 2000, shortly before the markets began to expect that the Fed would cut interest rates sharply, six-month rates of 6.7 percent per annum were available, just above one-month rates of 6.5 percent per annum. In the first months of 2001, the Fed cut rates rapidly and one-month yields plummeted to 4 percent per annum by May 2001 with an average yield of only just over 5 percent per annum.

Consider a manager who, during the summer of 2000, correctly anticipated the actions of the Fed in 2001. For such a manager, contrast the appropriateness of the following two strategies:

1. An investment strategy of rolling over one-month paper.
2. An investment strategy of buying longer-maturity paper (in this case, six-month paper).

Solution: The second strategy is superior, as it would lock in the higher yields for six months in a declining interest rate environment. By contrast, the first strategy counts on interest rates rising, not declining. The first strategy would produce higher returns only if interest rates rose.

4.6.2. Nominal Default-Free Bonds

Nominal default-free bonds are conventional bonds that have no (or minimal) default risk. Conventional government bonds of developed countries are the best example. Thus, our focus is on the government yield curve. One way to think of the yield on a government bond is that it reflects the expected future short-term

Treasury bill yields over the same horizon. Another approach, which is more useful for longer-term bonds, is to break down the yield into at least two components. First, the so-called real bond yield is determined by the growth rate of GDP and the supply and demand for capital. Second, yields are affected by forecast inflation over the investment period. For default-risk-free bonds, the credit spread or default risk premium is zero. Investors may thus assess whether bonds are cheap or expensive according to their view on whether the markets are too optimistic or too pessimistic based on real yields and inflation.

Historically, taking the period 1900 to 2000, the average annual real return on long-term government bonds above inflation was 1.6 percent for the United States and 1.3 percent for the United Kingdom.[74] However, there is some evidence that investors underestimated inflation during several periods, including the world wars and the peacetime inflation of the 1960s and 1970s. Hence, a better estimate of the *ex ante* expectations for annual returns above inflation (i.e., real yields) is 2 to 4 percent.

The investor then needs to forecast the inflation rate over the long term. For example, if 10-year bonds yield 5 percent and inflation is forecast at 2 percent, then the investor is hoping to receive approximately a 3 percent real return. If his or her judgment is that annual inflation is likely to be only 0.5 percent or perhaps that deflation will occur, then these bonds will be particularly attractive. Conversely, if inflation is thought likely to accelerate—for example, to 6 percent—then the bonds are very unattractive because they will not compensate for this higher inflation rate and will likely fall below par value during their lifetime as market yields rise.

For investors buying and selling long-term bonds over a shorter time period, the emphasis is on how bond yields will respond to developments in the business cycle and changes in short-term interest rates. News of stronger economic growth usually makes bond yields rise (prices fall) because it implies greater demand for capital and perhaps higher inflation too. Changes in short-term rates have less predictable effects on bond yields. More often than not, a rise in short-term rates will lead to a rise in longer-term bond yields. However, a rise in rates will sometimes be expected to slow the economy, and bond yields could fall as a result. If bond markets expect that central banks will exactly achieve their inflation objectives, then bond yields should not change on inflation expectations but nevertheless could go up and down according to changes in short rates (with higher short rates making bonds less attractive in relative terms).

As bond investors look toward the long-term picture, they must carefully assess the future effects of inflation, which erodes the future purchasing power of the yields earned on their fixed-income investments. In the 1970s, bond investors in the United States and most major countries suffered severe losses in real terms because of unexpected inflation. Yields in the 1960s were at single-digit levels, and yet inflation in the following 15 years moved up into double digits. In the 1980s, after this bad experience, investors were apprehensive of a new surge in inflation and therefore demanded higher yields (a higher inflation premium). Hence, yields were often 4 to 6 percent above recorded inflation—much higher than normal. As of early 2005, with inflation very low, U.S. bond investors have begun to believe not only that inflation will stay low, but also that there is a risk of deflation. Thus, as inflation fears declined during the 1990s, the inflation premium in bond yields likewise declined, reducing overall nominal yields. In recent years, the inflation premium embedded in bond yields fell further, to unusually low levels in the first half of 2003, when deflation fears reached a high point and bond yields registered as little as 1 to 2 percent above recorded inflation.

[74]See Dimson, Marsh, and Staunton (2002).

4.6.3. Defaultable Debt **Defaultable debt** is debt with some meaningful amount of credit risk—in particular, most corporate debt. For corporate debt, such as certificates of deposit and bonds, the spread over Treasuries represents at least in part the market's perception of default risk.[75] Individual securities move in response to particular corporate circumstances, but the market as a whole responds primarily to changes in short-term rates and changes in the business cycle. During a business cycle, spreads tend to rise during a recession because companies are under stress from both weak business conditions and, typically, higher interest rates. Sometimes, borrowing from banks or in the commercial paper market becomes more difficult too, so that companies can be severely squeezed. Default rates typically rise during recessions. Investors demand higher rates to pay for the uncertainties and possible surprises, such as fraud. In contrast, during periods of strong economic growth, spreads narrow as fears of default decline.

4.6.4. Emerging Market Bonds **Emerging market debt** refers here to the sovereign debt of nondeveloped countries. So far, we have considered only government issues and regarded them as virtually risk-free from a credit point of view. Almost all of the main industrial country governments, the members of the OECD area, are AAA rated by the rating agencies and likely to remain so. Japan is the main exception (rated AA), with its rapidly rising debt/GDP ratio an increasing concern. In practice, even in Japan, rising debt is more likely to lead to a bout of inflation than an outright default, as long as governments can control monetary policy and therefore can ultimately print money to pay off debts. Emerging market bonds, as an asset class, are different in that the country is borrowing in a foreign currency. The government therefore cannot simply inflate its way out of a problem in servicing the debt, and so the risk of default is correspondingly higher. Assessing this risk, using what is known as country risk analysis, involves a large array of economic and political factors. Much of country risk analysis comes down to predicting policy moves and therefore often hinges on politics—that is, whether a government has the power to follow the necessary policies to stabilize the economy. Emerging market bonds are usually analyzed by developed market investors in terms of their spread over domestic Treasuries compared to similarly rated domestic corporate debt.

4.6.5. Inflation-Indexed Bonds Many governments now issue bonds linked to inflation, so in principle, we can directly observe the market's forecast of inflation by comparing the yield of these indexed bonds with the yield on similarly dated conventional bonds. Examples of this important class of bonds are Treasury inflation-protected securities (TIPS) in the United States and Index-linked gilts (ILGs) in the United Kingdom. These provide a fixed coupon (the real portion) plus an adjustment equal to the change in consumer prices. In principle, indexed bonds are the perfect risk-free asset because, unlike conventional bonds, they entail no risk from unexpected inflation. However, the yield on indexed bonds still changes over time, and in practice it varies with three economic factors.

First, the yield goes up and down with the real economy and particularly with the level of short-term interest rates. If real yields generally are high because the economy is strong, then real yields on TIPS and ILGs will be higher. Second, yields fall if inflation accelerates because these securities are more attractive when inflation is volatile. In other words, their value in hedging against inflation risk is higher. Finally, as with all assets, the yield can vary

[75] Other factors, such as differences in taxation or the presence or absence of a call provision, can also account for part of this spread.

EXHIBIT 4-26 The Macroeconomy and the Yield Curve

Economic Observation	Effect on Bond Yields (real interest rates)
Economic growth rising (falling)	Rise (fall)
Inflation expectations rising (falling)	Rise (fall)
Investor demand rising (falling)	Fall (rise)

according to institutional supply and demand. In practice, tax effects and the limited size of the market (particularly for TIPS in the United States) may also distort the real yield; thus, investors usually find it worthwhile to forecast all three components (real yield, inflation, and supply and demand).

The yield-related relationships that affect indexed fixed-income securities directly parallel the relationships in place with respect to non-inflation-adjusted bonds, albeit on a less pronounced basis. In shorthand form, they can be shown as in Exhibit 4-26.

4.6.6. Common Shares

To relate economic analysis to common equity valuation, it is useful to think of economic factors, first, in the way that they affect company earnings and, second, in the way that they affect interest rates, bond yields, and liquidity. The two views combined provide a forecast for the equity markets and can lead to new investor ideas and trading activity. Particular economic factors will also affect the outlook for specific companies—for example, the price of oil or the demand for airline travel. Here, we focus on the impact on the overall stock market.

4.6.6.1. Economic Factors Affecting Earnings In the long term, the trend growth in aggregate company earnings is mainly determined by the trend rate of growth of the economy. A faster-growing economy is likely to show faster average earnings growth, while a slower economy is correlated with slower earnings growth. The trend rate of growth of an economy is dependent on labor force growth, the level of investment, and the rate of labor productivity growth. Variations in growth rates among countries are usually due to past overinvestment, government overregulation or political instability, or the bursting of a major asset price bubble.

EXAMPLE 4-32 Economic Return Drivers: Energy and Transportation

Willem DeVries is researching the macroeconomic return drivers of the energy and transportation industries. He has gathered the information in Exhibit 4-27 from a U.S. investment manager's research report.

Using only the information given, compare and contrast the macroeconomic return drivers of the energy and transportation industries.

Solution: The larger positive correlations between GDP and the transportation industry's sales, earnings, and dividends compared to the corresponding correlations for the energy industry are an indication that transportation companies are more procyclical.

EXHIBIT 4-27 Correlations of GDP, Inflation, and Interest Rates with Industry Sales, Earnings, and Dividends[76]

	Energy Industry			Transportation Industry		
	GDP	Inflation	Interest Rates	GDP	Inflation	Interest Rates
Sales	+0.10	+0.77	+0.78	+0.58	+0.75	+0.74
Earnings	+0.13	+0.66	+0.67	+0.81	+0.26	+0.25
Dividends	+0.16	+0.03	+0.05	+0.65	−0.03	−0.08

Sales for the energy and transportation industries are approximately equally positively related to inflation and interest rates. However, earnings are less positively correlated with inflation and interest rates for the transportation industry. Transportation companies appear to be less able to pass through to customers the increased costs of higher inflation and interest rates. These observations should be helpful when one is using economic factors to draw inferences on future industry fundamentals.

Over the shorter term, the share of profits in GDP varies with the business cycle and is influenced by a variety of factors, including final sales, wages, capacity utilization, and interest rates.

During a recession, earnings are depressed because of reduced sales and a set amount of fixed costs. Capacity utilization is typically low. In severe recessions, earnings can disappear altogether for many companies. Other companies, less affected by the cycle (e.g., food companies), may see very little change in earnings. Companies that can maintain earnings growth through recessions receive high market valuations from investors.

During the early stages of an economic upswing, earnings recover strongly. One reason is the rise in capacity utilization and increasing employment. Many costs stay the same while volume rises, which brings large increases in profits. Wage awards usually remain modest because of continuing relatively high unemployment, so that most of the productivity gains flow straight into profits. A second factor is often the efficiency gains made during the recession that become evident when output rises. A leaner, fitter company emerges from recession as some of the fat built up during the growth years, including both obvious waste and "luxury" projects, is cut out.

Later in the economic upswing, wage growth starts to quickly rise, profits contract, and earnings growth slows. Some companies, generally the ones with large fixed costs and a pronounced sales cycle, are more sensitive to the business cycle than others. These are called **cyclical stocks.** Examples include car manufacturers and chemical producers.

Example 4-33 shows an analyst methodically organizing the economic analysis to formulate an answer to a client's question on the equity risk premium.

[76]Analysis excerpted from a Duff & Phelps Investment Management Co. study of the 1,000 largest U.S. companies over 1990–2003, using annual data.

EXAMPLE 4-33 Researching U.S. Equity Prospects for a Client

In the beginning of 2004, Michael Wu has one of his regular quarterly meetings with an institutional client for whom he manages a U.S. equity portfolio. The economic forecasts of Wu's firm covering the next 12 to 18 months are consistent with the client's view that short-term interest rates will be increasing from 3.0 percent to 3.5 percent while long-term government bonds will return 5.5 percent. The client views U.S. equities as currently slightly overvalued. The client is not optimistic about long-term prospects for U.S. equities either and states to Wu that the long-term U.S. equity risk premium will be in the range of 1.0 percent to 2.5 percent. The client asks Wu to help him decide, based on economic analysis, whether a 1.0 percent or 2.5 equity risk premium is more likely.

Wu summarizes his firm's research in Exhibit 4-28.

Using only the information in Exhibit 4-28, address the following problems:

1. State and justify a long-term expected return for equities within the client's guidelines.
2. Comment on whether the economic data support the client's belief that the equity market is overvalued.

Solution to Problem 1: The consumer and business sectors are critical for corporate profits, and the long-term forecast strengths of these sectors are a positive for U.S.

EXHIBIT 4-28 Current and Expected Economic/Market Trends: United States

	Expected Economic Trends/ Impact Forecast		
Category	Short-term (1 year)	Long-term (<1 year)	Comments on Economic Measures and Categories
Macro-economy	$E_{(Trend)}$: Slowing GDP growth $E_{(Economic\ Impact)}$: Negative: Growth slowing from 4% to a lower rate	Average growth [3.1% annual GDP growth] $E_{(Trend)}$: Stable $E_{(Economic\ Impact)}$: Neutral	High current economic growth rate is due to fiscal and monetary stimuli and is not sustainable. Overall economic growth rate to slow to a lower 3.1% rate beyond 1-year time horizon.
Consumer	$E_{(Trend)}$: Improving consumer spending $E_{(Economic\ Impact)}$: Positive	$E_{(Trend)}$: Stable $E_{(Economic\ Impact)}$: Positive	Looking forward, stabilization in employment patterns and personal income will aid the consumer component of the economy.

(*continued*)

EXHIBIT 4-28 *(continued)*

Category	Expected Economic Trends/ Impact Forecast: Short-term (1 year)	Long-term (<1 year)	Comments on Economic Measures and Categories
Business	$E_{(Trend)}$: Stable $E_{(Economic\ Impact)}$: Neutral	$E_{(Trend)}$: Stable $E_{(Economic\ Impact)}$: Positive	The low base against which current results are being compared has aided profit and sales growth rate comparisons. Productivity growth has been aided by the weak employment (hiring) practices of the past few years. As employment rises, profit and productivity increases will diminish. Export-oriented businesses will be in the best position over the next few years as the U.S. dollar is expected to decline further. Sales and profits showing signs of strength but are being compared to weak prior year results.
Central bank	Economic strength and fiscal deficits likely to put pressure on short-term interest rates; slightly higher inflation $E_{(Trend)}$: Declining stimulation $E_{(Economic\ Impact)}$: Negative	$E_{(Trend)}$: Stable $E_{(Economic\ Impact)}$: Neutral Short-term rates and inflation rate will stabilize near long-term average rates	Monetary stimulus expected to be reduced in light of the increased economic strength. The stronger economy will place upward pressure on short-term interest rates and on the rate of inflation near-term, but short-term interest rates and inflation are expected to quickly stabilize near their long-term average rates.

EXHIBIT 4-28 *(continued)*

Category	Expected Economic Trends/ Impact Forecast: Short-term (1 year)	Long-term (<1 year)	Comments on Economic Measures and Categories
Government	$E_{(\text{Trend})}$: Stable measures $E_{(\text{Economic Impact})}$: Positive	$E_{(\text{Trend})}$: Weakening $E_{(\text{Economic Impact})}$: Negative	Fiscal stimulus (i.e., deficit spending and tax cuts) is giving a current boost to GDP. More work must be done to cut the budget deficit and to deal with a declining dollar. The U.S. government needs to deal with the problem of increasing long-term transfer payment costs.

Note: Expected economic trends are denoted by $E_{(\text{Trend})}$, while expected economic impact is denoted by $E_{(\text{Economic Impact})}$.

equities. The central bank appears to be a neutral factor long-term. Although the government sector is a negative, it is not expected to push inflation and interest rates above their long-term averages. Overall, a 2.5 percent equity risk premium, at the upper end of the client's range, appears to be justified by the positive economic outlook, which would lead to a forecast of an 8.0 percent arithmetic average return on equities. (A long government bond expected return of 5.5% + expected equity risk premium of 2.5% = 8.0% expected equity return over the forecast period.)

Solution to Problem 2: By contrast to the long-term forecasts, the short-term economic forecasts of decelerating growth and increasing interest rates might constitute a negative for short-term equity returns. However, the analyst would need to evaluate whether current market prices incorporate this information before concurring in the client's assessment.

4.6.6.2. The P/E Ratio and the Business Cycle The price-to-earnings ratio of a stock market is the price that the market is willing to pay for the earnings of that market. During the business cycle, the P/E ratio tends to be high and rising when earnings are expected to rise. For example, the P/E would be high in the early stages of an economic recovery, or when interest rates are low and the return on fixed-rate investments such as cash or bonds is less attractive. Conversely, P/Es are likely to be low and falling if the outlook for earnings worsens (e.g., in an economic slump). Nevertheless, P/Es of cyclical companies may be above their own historical means during economic downturns as investors anticipate a sharp future earnings recovery when the economy turns up (a phenomenon known as the Molodovsky effect).

P/Es vary over longer periods too. In general, they are lower for an economy stuck on a slower growth path. During the 1990s, P/E ratios were at relatively high levels (e.g., multiples greater than 20 in the United States). At the time, some saw this situation as reflecting the benign economic influences of falling inflation, relatively low interest rates, fast productivity and profits growth, and a relatively stable economy. Another view was that these valuations were too high and would decline in the future, and this view has been borne out since 2000.

High inflation rates tend to depress P/E ratios. Inflation can distort the economic meaning of reported earnings, leading investors to value a given amount of reported earnings less during inflationary periods, which tends to lower observed P/Es during those periods. Consequently, comparisons of current P/E with past average P/E that do not control for differences in inflation rates may be suspect.[77]

4.6.6.3. Emerging Market Equities Empirical evidence points to *ex post* equity risk premiums for emerging markets that are on average higher and more volatile than those in developed markets. *Ex post,* emerging market equity risk premiums in U.S. dollar terms appear to be positively correlated with expansion phases in G-7 economies as proxied by industrial production.[78] Transmission channels for G-7 macroeconomic fluctuations to developing economies include trade (demand for many of the goods produced by emerging countries, such as natural resources, is procyclical), finance, and direct sectoral linkages. In addition to evaluating linkages, the analyst needs to do considerable country and often sector-specific research to appraise the prospects for equity investments in a particular emerging country.

4.6.7. Real Estate

Ling and Naranjo (1997, 1998) identify growth in consumption, real interest rates, the term structure of interest rates, and unexpected inflation as systematic determinants of real estate returns. Interest rates are linked with a number of factors that affect the supply and demand for real estate, such as construction financing costs and the costs of mortgage financing. In general, lower interest rates are net positive for real estate valuation, resulting in lower capitalization rates.

In Example 4-34, an analyst with a one-year horizon applies a checklist approach to economic forecasting in modifying baseline historical capital market forecasts. The set of asset classes includes real estate.

EXAMPLE 4-34 Modifying Historical Capital Market Expectations

Cortney Young is an investment analyst in a firm serving an international clientele. Young's firm has developed the baseline forecasts shown in Exhibit 4-29 for six asset classes that are particularly relevant for U.K.-focused portfolios. The forecasts are based on a recent part of the historical record of the asset classes. Young is currently working on establishing capital market expectations for mean return and standard deviation of returns for these six asset classes based on a one-year horizon; she focuses first on the U.K. equities, U.K. intermediate-term bonds, U.K. long-term bonds, and U.K. real estate.

[77] For more details, see Bodie, Kane, and Marcus (2001).
[78] See Salomons and Grootveld (2003).

EXHIBIT 4-29 Baseline Forecasts

Asset Class	Mean Annual Returns (in percent)	Standard Deviation of Returns (in percent)
U.K. equities	9.72	15.3
Non-U.K. equities	8.94	11.6
U.K. intermediate-term bonds	3.60	6.5
U.K. long-term bonds	4.42	7.7
International bonds	4.81	8.3
U.K. real estate	12.63	8.7

Young's economic analysis leads her to the conclusions on the U.K. economy shown in Exhibit 4-30.

EXHIBIT 4-30 Economic Conclusions

Economic Category	Economic Conclusion
Consumers	Consumer spending is expected to be stronger over the next year with very positive effects for the U.K. economy.
Business	Business spending, revenues, and profits are expected to show solid growth in year-over-year results over the next 12 months.
Government	Tax policies are stable. Government is currently a source of moderate economic stimulation.
Central bank	It is anticipated that the Bank of England (the central bank) will want to hold short-term interest rates steady over the next year. The inflation target is 2 percent.
Inflation rates	The inflation rate is expected to increase to 2.2 percent per year over the next year.
Other/unique	The U.K. economy is expected to outperform other major economies over the next 12 months. The growth of the real estate sector will moderate.

1. Explain the expected impact on U.K. asset classes of each of Young's economic conclusions.
2. Demonstrate and justify the direction of judgmental modifications that Young might make to the baseline forecasts of her firm.

Solution to Problem 1: Young reaches the conclusions shown in Exhibit 4-31.

Solution to Problem 2: The arrows in Exhibit 4-32 indicate the direction of adjustment to the baseline forecasts.

The growth outlook for consumers and businesses is a strong positive for U.K. equities. The steady central bank, government, and inflation outlooks suggest below-average or at least unchanged volatility. The outlook of steady interest rates is neutral for intermediate- and long-term bonds, but the uncertainty about the economy overheating suggests an increase in risk. Real estate's returns should decrease from the high baseline forecast. The break with the past trend growth should translate into higher risk for real estate.

EXHIBIT 4-31 Market/Asset Class Conclusions

Economic Conclusion	Market/Asset Class Impact
Consumers	Consumers are creating a positive investment environment for corporate profits and therefore for U.K. equities and credit quality. However, if spending rises much more steeply than anticipated, we might expect upward pressure on both short-term and long-term interest rates that would be a negative for bonds and real estate.
Business	The economic conclusion is a positive for U.K. equities and bonds via improved credit quality. However, predicted business growth may put upward pressure on wages, costs, and inflation rates.
Government	The government sector conclusion is a slight positive for the economy at this time.
Central bank	The expected steady interest rate environment is a positive factor for the U.K. investment market. If the economy expands too quickly, there may be pressure from the central bank for higher interest rates looking out 12 months.
Inflation rates	The current stable inflation picture should have a positive impact on the economy and on the financial assets we are comparing in this analysis.
Other/unique	Returns to U.K. real estate should moderate from unusually high rates.

EXHIBIT 4-32 Modifications to Capital Market Forecasts for U.K. Asset Classes

Asset Class	Average Annual Returns	Average Annual Standard Deviation
U.K. equities	↑	↓ or →
Intermediate bonds	→	↑
Long-term bonds	→	↑
Real estate	↓	↑

4.6.8. Currencies

The exchange rate between two countries reflects the balance of buyers and sellers. One major reason for buying and selling foreign currencies is to facilitate trade in goods and services (exports and imports). If a country begins to import more, the currency will tend to depreciate (all else being equal). Hence, considerable attention is usually paid to determining a competitive exchange rate at which the trade balance—or, more broadly, the current account balance (which includes services and transfers)—is zero. Governments and central banks are often concerned with maintaining a competitive exchange rate and may try to do so by buying or selling foreign currencies or by raising or lowering interest rates.

However, trade is only one motive for purchases and sales of foreign currency and it has become relatively less important. The other motive is international flows of capital. Companies wishing to invest in a country are likely to be buyers of the currency as they bring in capital to build assets. Strong domestic economic growth and an opening of new industries to foreign ownership are two possible drivers of a rise in foreign direct investment that will likely push up a currency too. The liberalization of capital flows and the increasing trend toward global diversification mean that there may also be inflows to buy local stocks, bonds, or short-term instruments, including deposits. These flows can be volatile and may quickly reverse. The foreign direct investment is likely to be more stable.

Portfolio flows may be influenced by the growth of the economy or by domestic interest rates. When interest rates are high, inflows are likely to be higher and the currency value rises. Conversely, falling interest rates often weaken a currency. However, the link between interest rates and the currency sometimes works the other way. This is because investors may see higher interest rates as slowing the economy. If a currency departs from the level that equilibrates trade for a long time, the resulting deficits or surpluses may eventually become too large for capital flows to finance. Among the major currencies, there are often prolonged over- and undervaluations around a long-term equilibrium level. For this reason, many governments in emerging countries use some combination of capital controls and currency management (pegs, currency boards, managed floats, etc.) to try to keep the currency competitive. This approach tends to lead to stability for extended periods punctuated by periodic sudden, large movements.

EXAMPLE 4-35 A Currency Example

Between 1990 and July 1997, the Bank of Thailand managed the Thai baht in a narrow range. Over time, a gradual loss of competitiveness through higher inflation pushed the current account deficit up to 8 percent of GDP, financed by strong capital inflows. In 1996, the economy slowed and capital inflows faltered, prompting speculation that the baht might fall. The central bank intervened heavily to defend the baht in early 1997 but by midyear had exhausted its reserves and was forced to float the currency. Within a few months, the baht halved in value and other currencies in the region were also under pressure. The Asian crisis of 1997 had begun.

Forecasting exchange rate movements is widely viewed as especially difficult. For this reason, some investors try to fully hedge currency exposure. Others see opportunities in currency forecasting because of the volatility of many exchange rates and the highly liquid markets. The following sections review the major approaches to exchange rate forecasting.

4.6.9. Approaches to Forecasting Exchange Rates

There are four broad approaches to forecasting exchange rates, and most forecasters probably use a combination of them all.

4.6.9.1. Purchasing Power Parity

Purchasing power parity (PPP) asserts that movements in an exchange rate should offset any difference in the inflation rates between two countries.[79] PPP reflects the idea that exchange rates should find a level that keeps different countries broadly competitive with each other.

To illustrate PPP, suppose that over a five-year period, Canadian prices are forecast to increase by 10.41 percent (equal to 2 percent annual inflation) while Eurozone prices are forecast to show 15.93 percent growth (equal to 3 percent annual inflation). Over the five-year period, the Canadian–Eurozone inflation differential is 10.41% − 15.93% = −5.52%. PPP would predict that the Canadian dollar will appreciate against the euro by approximately the same percentage. For example, if the exchange rate is C\$1.3843 per euro, PPP would predict an exchange rate of approximately (1 − 0.0552) × (C\$1.3843per euro) = C\$1.3079 per euro.

PPP in broad terms does seem to be useful in the long run—say, over periods of five years or longer. Furthermore, governments and central banks take PPP very seriously in their approach to exchange rates because periods of under- or overvaluation of a currency may lead to sudden exchange rate instability or be destabilizing for business.

However, with the huge rise in capital flows over the last three decades, exchange rates can depart from PPP levels for long periods of time. PPP is often not a useful guide to the direction of exchange rates in the short or even medium run (up to three years or so). There are also times when factors other than PPP dominate exchange rate movements. This usually happens when a large current account deficit is opening up and the markets question whether a growing deficit can be financed. Markets then focus on what level of the currency is needed to correct the deficit.

4.6.9.2. Relative Economic Strength The **relative economic strength forecasting approach** focuses on investment flows rather than trade flows. It suggests that a strong pace of economic growth in a country creates attractive investment opportunities, increasing the demand for the country's currency and causing it to appreciate. Sometimes, demand comes from a higher short-term deposit rate in that country combined with an expectation that the currency will stay the same or appreciate. More recently, the focus has been on the pace of economic growth and the existence of attractive investment opportunities in general.

When interest rates are relatively high in a country, capital moves into that country and, as a result, the currency strengthens. Even if investors begin to see the exchange rate as overvalued in some long-term sense, they may still be content if they feel the extra yield compensates for that overvaluation. However, once the exchange rate reaches an excessive level, they will question whether the high yield is enough to justify the likely exchange rate depreciation.

What is the role of short rates? There is little question that short-term interest rates can influence exchange rates but primarily over a short-term time horizon. The level of short-term interest rates influences the extent to which speculators are willing to bet against a currency. If interest rates in a particular country are especially high, speculators are less likely to short that currency because that currency will probably strengthen as a result of the higher interest rates. Similarly, very low interest rates on Japanese yen in recent years have periodically encouraged investors to borrow yen to fund other investments (a so-called carry trade).

It can be helpful to combine the PPP and relative strength approaches. The relative strength approach indicates the response to news on the economy but does not tell us anything about the level of exchange rates. The PPP approach indicates what level of the exchange rate can be regarded as a long-term equilibrium. By combining the two, we can generate a more complete theory.

[79]The definition refers to relative PPP, the form of PPP most economists are concerned with. See Solnik and McLeavey (2004) for further details.

4.6.9.3. Capital Flows The **capital flows forecasting approach** focuses on expected capital flows, particularly long-term flows such as equity investment and foreign direct investment (FDI). Inflows of FDI into a country increase the demand for the country's currency, all else being equal.

From 1999 onward, there was considerable focus on this approach because of the surprising strength of the dollar versus the euro. This situation coincided with a clear increase in long-term flows from the Eurozone to the United States, especially FDI and U.S. equities. This capital was being attracted into the United States by the boom in the domestic economy and the attractiveness of equity assets, particularly in the Internet and technology sectors, until at least 2001.

Note that long-term capital flows may have the effect of reversing the usual relationship between short-term interest rates and the currency. This is explained by the fact that a cut in short-term rates would be expected to boost economic growth and the stock markets, thereby making long-term investments more attractive. In this environment, central banks face a dilemma. Whereas they might want to raise interest rates to respond to a weak currency that is threatening to stimulate the economy too much and boost inflation, the effect may actually be to push the currency lower. Hence, the effectiveness of monetary policy is much reduced.

This appeared to be a problem for the Eurozone at times during 2001. As the economy slowed, the ECB was reluctant to cut interest rates because of rising inflation and a weak currency. The inaction seemed to make the currency weaker. Similarly, the Fed's aggressive cutting in the first half of 2001 pushed the dollar higher, which attracted capital and thus reduced the impact of lower interest rates in stimulating the economy.

4.6.9.4. Savings–Investment Imbalances The **savings–investment imbalances forecasting approach** explains currency movements in terms of the effects of domestic savings–investment imbalances on the exchange rate. Although it is not easy to use for forecasting, this approach can sometimes help with understanding why currencies depart from equilibrium for long periods. It starts from the fact that the current account deficit of a country is the sum of its government deficit and private sector deficit. For example, in the United States in 2004, the current account deficit was estimated at about 6 percent of GDP, with the government deficit at about 5 percent and the private sector deficit at about 1 percent. In contrast, Japan had a current account surplus of 4 percent of GDP, with a government deficit of 8 percent balanced by a private sector surplus of 12 percent of GDP. So, in Japan, the private sector was financing the government deficit as well as an outflow of capital.

However, if the private-sector or government currency-related trends change, then the current account position must change too and the exchange rate moves to help achieve that. Suppose that an economy suddenly begins to expand rapidly, driven by a new government budget deficit or bullish entrepreneurs. If domestic savings do not change, there will be excess demand for capital as investment tries to exceed savings. The only way that investment can exceed savings in reality is for foreign savings to be used, since the accounts have to balance. But this solution requires a deficit on the current account of the balance of payments.

So, where does this deficit on the current account come from? Some of it may arise simply because imports are strong due to the buoyant economy or because exports are weak as companies focus on the domestic market. But if that is not enough, the exchange rate needs to rise. If capital flows are attracted to the country, either due to high interest rates or due to attractive expected returns on investments, then the exchange rate will indeed rise as needed.

Because trade takes time to adjust, the exchange rate will frequently depart far from generally accepted equilibrium rates for prolonged periods, typically two to four years. Eventually, the rising currency will widen the current account deficit sufficiently and the domestic currency may start to decline. Of course, it needs to stay reasonably strong as long as domestic investment exceeds savings.

If the economy becomes weak enough at this point and domestic investments no longer exceed domestic savings, then the currency will also weaken. To return to a current account surplus, the exchange rate may need to drop to a level well below its equilibrium rate. Hence, there is a risk that the currency could swing sharply to an undervalued position.

EXAMPLE 4-36 The USD/Euro Exchange Rate, 1999–2004

The euro was first established as a currency at the beginning of 1999. To the surprise of nearly everyone, it started trading weakly, its value against the U.S. dollar falling from about US$1.17 to a low of US$0.82 in late 2000. But beginning in 2001 and accelerating in 2002 to 2004, the dollar fell. In 2004, the euro reached US$1.37. On a PPP basis, the euro probably lies in the range of US$1.10 to US$1.20. So, in the course of five years, the exchange rate cycled around that level. These swings can be considered according to the three explanations below.

1. **Relative economic strength.** This approach explains why the dollar rose strongly in 1999 to 2000, with faster economic growth and consequent higher interest rates in the United States. In 2001, the fact that the U.S. economy was weaker than that of the Eurozone helps to explain why the dollar peaked and went sideways during that year. The explanation breaks down in 2002 to 2003, however. Despite the superior performance of the U.S. economy over the Eurozone in 2002 and beyond, the dollar retraced its path all the way back to its starting point.
2. **Capital flows.** This approach explains more about the dollar's recent moves. The dollar's strength in 1999 to 2000 was matched by massive long-term inflows into the United States in the form of foreign direct investment and equity purchases. In 2001, these flows fell off rapidly, though there were still large inflows into U.S. bonds. The current account deficit had expanded by then as a result of the strong dollar, so the capital flows were no longer large relative to the necessary inflow to finance the deficit. Hence, the dollar's decline.
3. **Savings–investment imbalances.** During 1999 to 2000, the U.S. economy grew very rapidly with pressure to reduce domestic savings and increase investment. Households reduced savings, encouraged by low and falling unemployment and the rising stock prices. Businesses cut savings because they saw major new investment opportunities. The result was a soaring U.S. dollar opening up the current account deficit, further encouraged by the inflow of capital described above. In 2001 to 2002, the private sector deficit was slashed drastically as companies cut back on borrowing and spending. The government cut taxes and shifted the government accounts from surplus to deficit. But the dollar still fell back against the euro because the current account deficit needed to be in the 4 to 6 percent range to balance the internal savings balances. Hence, the

dollar fell back from its still-overvalued position and nosed into undervalued territory.

This approach, if correct, suggests that the dollar's weakness (at least in 2004 to 2005) may be limited by the continued large government borrowing requirement and low private savings. Beyond 2005, however, the dollar could reach past lows if either the government makes a major effort to reduce the budget deficit or an economic slowdown prompts increased private savings.

4.6.10. Government Intervention Since the developed world moved to floating rates in the early 1970s, periodic attempts have been made to control exchange rates. However, economists and the markets have been skeptical about whether governments really can control exchange rates with market intervention alone because of three factors. First, the total value of foreign exchange trading, in excess of US$1 trillion *daily*, is large relative to the total foreign exchange reserves of the major central banks combined. Second, many people believe that market prices are determined by fundamentals and that government authorities are just another player. Third, experience with trying to control foreign exchange trends is not encouraging in the absence of capital controls. Unless governments are prepared to move interest rates and other policies, they cannot expect to succeed.

4.7. Information Sources for Economic Data and Forecasts

Having presented economic analysis for capital market expectations setting, we can indicate several fruitful sources for gathering economic data. The sources we present link to many other useful resources.

The main sources of leading indicators are the Conference Board and national sources. Most other economic data also come from national statistical sources, such as central banks and government statistical offices. Some survey data come from other organizations, such as the Institute of Supply Management. Useful international sources include the OECD, IMF, and World Bank. A list of websites is provided below.

Forecasts from econometric models are published by governments. The OECD publishes forecasts twice a year in its *Economic Outlook* reports. The IMF publishes forecasts, and various private sector forecasters also publish forecasts, though these are sometimes proprietary. Exhibit 4-33 summarizes some sources for researching U.S. markets.

EXHIBIT 4-33 A Selection of Data Sources for Researching U.S. Markets

Categories of Economic Interest	Factor Measures	Data Use LT	Data Use ST	Data Source
Economic fundamentals	Measures of economic output/growth (e.g., GDP, industrial production)	✓		www.bea.gov
	General price level stability	✓		Bloomberg

(*continued*)

EXHIBIT 4-33 *(continued)*

Categories of Economic Interest	Factor Measures	Data Use LT	Data Use ST	Data Source
Consumers	Employment/ unemployment	√		Bloomberg
	Measures of consumption/income	√		www.bea.gov
	Measures of savings, investment, and leverage	√		
	Measures of sentiment	√		U. of Michigan Survey
Business	Measures of profitability	√		www.bea.gov
	Measures of productivity	√		Federal Reserve Bank
	Industry price level stability	√	√	Internal or third-party research; Trade pub.
	Capacity utilization rates		√	
Central bank	Measures of monetary policy	√	√	www.stls.frb.org
	General price level stability (inflation)	√	√	Bloomberg
	Assessment of central bank independence		√	Internal analysis
Government	Fiscal policy	√	√	Congressional Budget Office/Bloomberg
	Assessment of exchange rate stability/trends	√	√	Internal/www.wto.org
	Measures of political stability	√		Internal analysis
	Assessment of legal system's ability to protect assets (including intangible assets) and ability to settle disputes (due process)	√		Internal analysis
Economic technical factors	Capital flows		√	Internal/third-party research
	Sector/industry supply and demand		√	Trade publications

EXHIBIT 4-33 *(continued)*

Categories of Economic Interest	Factor Measures	Data Use LT	Data Use ST	Data Source
Market fundamentals	Rates of return	√	√	Relative (industry) internal research; Third-party research; Trade publications
	Valuation trends (e.g., equity P/E multiples)	√	√	
	Asset class price volatility			
	Large-cap equities	√		
	Corporate bonds vs. overall market	√	√	
	Short sovereign debt	√		
	Exchange rate movements	√		
Market technical factors	Ratio of advances/declines in equity market		√	Reuters
	Corporate bond issuance (market yield)		√	Internal research
Other: unique; social; political	Demographic influences	√	√	Internal/third-party
	Seasonal patterns of consumption	√	√	Third-party/Trade pub.
	Current account trends; net exports versus imports	√	√	Bloomberg

Some additional useful resources include the following:

www.imf.org

www.worldbank.org

www.oecd.org

www.federalreserve.gov

www.ecb.int

www.bankofengland.co.uk

www.boj.or.jp/en (the English site for the Bank of Japan)

www.bis.org

www.nber.org (the web site of the National Bureau of Economic Research, the U.S. organization that dates business cycles; it contains useful data and research on past business cycles)

CHAPTER 5

ASSET ALLOCATION

William F. Sharpe

Stanford University and Financial Engines, Inc.
Palo Alto, California

Peng Chen, CFA

Ibbotson Associates
Chicago, Illinois

Jerald E. Pinto, CFA

CFA Institute
Charlottesville, Virginia

Dennis W. McLeavey, CFA

CFA Institute
Charlottesville, Virginia

1. INTRODUCTION

For investors, selecting the types of assets for a portfolio and allocating funds among different asset classes are major decisions. A 70/30 stock/bond portfolio has a different expected return, risk, and cash flow pattern than a 30/70 stock/bond portfolio. Which asset allocation is more appropriate for a particular investor will depend on how well the allocation's characteristics match up with the investment objectives and circumstances described in the investor's investment policy statement (IPS). This chapter covers the principles of determining an appropriate asset allocation for an investment client. The questions we will address include the following:

- How does asset allocation function in controlling risk?
- What are the major approaches to asset allocation and the strengths and weaknesses of each?
- How should asset classes be defined, and how can one evaluate the benefits from including additional asset classes?
- What are the pitfalls in asset allocation according to practice?
- What are the current choices in optimization?
- How may a portfolio manager use prior investment experience in selecting an asset allocation?
- What are the special considerations in determining an asset allocation for individual and institutional investors?

We have organized this chapter as follows: Sections 2 and 3 orient the reader about the role of asset allocation. As the discussion points out, two types of asset allocation—strategic and tactical—have developed into distinct disciplines. Sections 4 through 7 explain the strategic asset allocation process from the selection of asset classes to optimization and implementation, and Sections 8 and 9 focus on strategic asset allocation for individual and institutional investors, respectively. Finally, Section 10 presents tactical asset allocation.

2. WHAT IS ASSET ALLOCATION?

Asset allocation is a process and a result. Strategic asset allocation, the focus of the first part of this chapter, is an integrative element of the planning step in portfolio management. In **strategic asset allocation,** an investor's return objectives, risk tolerance, and investment constraints are integrated with long-run capital market expectations to establish exposures to IPS-permissible asset classes. The aim is to satisfy the investor's investment objectives and constraints. Thus, strategic asset allocation can be viewed as a process with certain well-defined steps. Performing those steps produces a set of portfolio weights for asset classes; we call this set of weights the strategic asset allocation (or the **policy portfolio**).[1] Thus, strategic asset allocation may refer to either a process or its end result.

A second major type of asset allocation is **tactical asset allocation** (TAA), which involves making short-term adjustments to asset-class weights based on short-term expected relative performance among asset classes. We can better understand the contrasts between strategic and tactical asset allocation if we first cover some basic notions concerning strategic asset allocation.

Exhibit 5-1 gives an example of a strategic asset allocation or policy portfolio. Frequently, the policy portfolio is specified as target percentages for each asset class and a range of permissible values, as shown in the exhibit. Stating a range of permissible values is a risk management device. Because allocations outside the range may have substantially different

[1]The term *policy portfolio* sometimes refers to a strategic asset allocation that ignores an investor's liabilities. The term need not have that connotation, and we do not use it that way in this reading.

EXHIBIT 5-1 A Strategic Asset Allocation (Policy Portfolio)

Asset Class	Target Allocation	Permissible Range
1 Domestic equities	50%	46–54%
2 International equities	10	9–11
3 Cash equivalents	2	0–5
4 Domestic intermediate-term bonds	25	22–28
5 Domestic long-term bonds	8	6–10
6 International bonds	5	3–7

risk characteristics from the policy portfolio, the portfolio must be rebalanced if an asset-class weight moves outside the permissible range. (The setting of such ranges is discussed in Chapter 11.)

Strategic asset allocation is the first element of the portfolio management process to focus on selecting investments. It is a bridge to the execution step of portfolio management but at the broad level of asset classes. Strategic asset allocation is a starting point for portfolio construction and a step of the portfolio management process on which many investors expend considerable thought and effort. Institutional and individual investors often consider it a central element of the investment process. Why do they do so? What role does strategic asset allocation play in relation to risk? We address these questions next.

2.1. The Role of Strategic Asset Allocation in Relation to Systematic Risk

A continuing debate surrounds strategic asset allocation's relative importance, compared with security selection and timing, for producing investment results in practice. Irrespective of that debate (addressed in a subsequent section), strategic asset allocation fulfills an important role as a discipline for aligning a portfolio's risk profile with the investor's objectives.

For the investor, strategic asset allocation is pivotal in executing investment plans. Economically, why is this so? Why should the allocation of funds to asset classes command so much attention among professional investors?

A keystone of investment analysis is that systematic risk is rewarded. In the long run, investors expect compensation for bearing risk that they cannot diversify away. Such risk is inherent in the economic system and may relate, for example, to real business activity or to inflation. In the long run, a diversified portfolio's mean returns are reliably related to its systematic risk exposures. Conversely, measuring portfolio risk begins with an evaluation of the portfolio's systematic risk, because systematic risk usually accounts for most of a portfolio's change in value in the long run. Groups of assets of the same type (e.g., debt claims) that are relatively homogeneous (e.g., domestic intermediate-term bonds) should predictably reflect exposures to a certain set of systematic factors. Distinct (and well-differentiated) groups of assets should have distinct exposures to factors and/or exposures to different factors. These observations suggest a key economic role of strategic asset allocation: *The strategic asset allocation specifies the investor's desired exposures to systematic risk.*[2]

Adopting and implementing a strategic asset allocation is an effective way to exercise control over systematic risk exposures. As Example 5-1 illustrates, less disciplined approaches may offer investment managers incentives to take risks that conflict with the investor's interests.

[2]We might say *net* exposures to risk in the sense of netting out the risk exposures of the investor's liabilities (if any).

EXAMPLE 5-1 Making Asset Allocation a "Horse Race"

Sanjiv Singh is chief investment officer (CIO) of The Canadian Endowment for the Fine Arts. CEFA has a strategic asset allocation with a weight of 60 percent in equities and 40 percent in bonds. William Smith, a trustee of the endowment, recently suggested to Singh that CEFA replace its strategic asset allocation with a "horse race" or "equal balanced managers" system. According to this approach, as explained by Smith, the trustees would decide only on an asset-class-mix benchmark. For example, the trustees might specify a benchmark with weights of 50 percent on the S&P/TSX Composite Index for Canadian equities, 10 percent on the MSCI Europe Index, and 40 percent on the RBC Capital Markets Canadian Bond Market Index. According to Smith, the trustees could then hire a number of outside investment managers, initially giving them equal amounts of money to manage. The managers would be expected to hold the three component asset classes of the benchmark, but each manager would have substantial freedom to diverge from the 50/10/40 benchmark weights according to his or her judgment. At CEFA's annual review, the trustees would compare each manager's performance with the benchmark and with each other, based on mean returns earned. Managers that performed relatively well would be given more money to manage, at the expense of managers that performed relatively poorly (who might be fired).

Explain the relative merits of strategic asset allocation and the horse race system as approaches to controlling CEFA's systematic risk exposures.

Solution: Strategic asset allocation is superior to the horse race system as a method for controlling the endowment's systematic risk exposures. Using strategic asset allocation, the trustees maintain maximum control over the risk exposures of the endowment's funds. The policy portfolio reflects what the trustees believe is the best asset mix for CEFA to achieve its return objectives given its risk tolerance. In contrast, the horse race system creates incentives for the investment managers to take on a higher level of risk than is appropriate for the endowment. The managers have the incentive to greatly overweight the highest-expected-return asset class in order to finish first in the race, particularly if they are lagging other managers. The resulting portfolio will tend to be less diversified and have higher risk than the policy portfolio.

Strategic asset allocation provides an important set of benchmarks for an investor. It indicates the appropriate asset mix to be held under long-term or "normal" conditions. It also suggests the investor's long-run or "average" level of risk tolerance. The investor may also want to consider reacting to shorter-term forecasts as discussed in the next section.

2.2. Strategic versus Tactical Asset Allocation

Having introduced the basic themes of strategic asset allocation, we are in a position to understand the contrasts between strategic asset allocation and tactical asset allocation.

Strategic asset allocation sets an investor's desired long-term exposures to systematic risk. We have emphasized that the expectations involved in strategic asset allocation are long term. "Long term" has different interpretations for different investors, but five years is a reasonable minimum reference point. Tactical asset allocation involves making short-term adjustments to asset-class weights based on short-term predictions of relative performance among asset classes. TAA can subsume a range of approaches, from occasional and ad hoc adjustments to frequent and model-based adjustments. In practice, TAA often refers to investment disciplines involving short-term (such as quarterly or monthly) adjustments to the proportions invested in equities, bonds, and cash.[3] Taking as the benchmark the policy portfolio invested in passively managed indexes for the asset classes, TAA creates active risk (variability of active returns—i.e., portfolio returns minus benchmark returns). In exchange for active risk, the manager using TAA hopes to earn positive active returns that sufficiently reward the investor after deducting expenses. TAA is an active investment strategy choice that has evolved into a distinct professional money management discipline. This chapter discusses strategic asset allocation first, then tactical asset allocation (Section 10).

Strategic asset allocations are reviewed periodically or when an investor's needs and circumstances change significantly. Among institutional investors, regular annual reviews are now commonplace. Ad hoc reviews and changes to strategic asset allocation in response to the news items of the moment may lead to less thoughtful decisions. Example 5-2 describes the nature of the capital market expectations involved in strategic asset allocation.

EXAMPLE 5-2 Expectations and the Policy Portfolio

John Stevenson is an analyst reporting to CIO Sanjiv Singh. Stevenson strongly believes that domestic equities will underperform international equities during the next six months. He has presented to Singh a detailed analysis in support of his view. Both asset classes are part of the endowment's policy portfolio. Stevenson suggests that Singh ask CEFA's trustees to convene a special meeting before the regularly scheduled strategic asset allocation review for the purpose of revising downward the weight of domestic equities in the endowment's policy portfolio. Based on the information provided, is such a special meeting appropriate?

Solution: No. The policy portfolio should be revised only to account for changes in the investor's *long-term* capital market forecasts, not to reflect short-term forecasts. If the endowment expected domestic equities to underperform international equities during the next six months, with no implications for long-term relationships, the policy portfolio should not change.

2.3. The Empirical Debate on the Importance of Asset Allocation

In a prior section, we observed that strategic asset allocation plays a pivotal role in establishing exactly the systematic risk exposures that an investor wants. Because of its planning and risk management functions, strategic asset allocation clearly deserves the thought and attention it receives in practice. One might also ask, how important is strategic asset allocation relative to other investment decisions in determining investment results in practice? This empirical question has obvious relevance for budgeting resources effectively.

[3]The discipline is often called *global tactical asset allocation* when executed for asset classes in many country markets.

Not surprisingly, how we interpret and measure "importance" affects any conclusions. A classic and frequently cited empirical study is Brinson, Hood, and Beebower (1986). These authors interpreted the importance of asset allocation as *the fraction of the variation in returns over time* attributable to asset allocation, based on regression analysis. In a regression, total variation is the sum of squared deviations from the mean and the fraction of total variation accounted for by the regression is the coefficient of determination or R-squared. This approach takes the perspective of a single portfolio over time. Brinson et al. concluded that asset allocation explained an average 93.6 percent of the variation of returns over time for 91 large U.S. defined benefit pension plans. The range was 75.5 percent to 98.6 percent, and the study period was 1974 to 1983. A pension fund's policy portfolio was assumed to be the average asset allocation during the study period. On average, timing and security selection explained $100 - 93.6 = 6.4\%$.[4] Furthermore, the contributions of timing and security selection to active returns were on average negative, suggesting that resources invested in these activities were not rewarded on average. Two similar studies followed: Brinson, Singer,and Beebower (1991) updated the average percent of variation explained to 91.5 percent for U.S. plans for the period 1977–87, and Blake, Lehmann, and Timmermann (1999) investigated asset allocation in the United Kingdom. Examining more than 300 medium-size to large actively managed U.K. defined-benefit pension schemes for the period 1986–94, Blake et al. concluded that asset allocation accounted for approximately 99.5 percent of the variation in plan total returns. These studies' results concerning the relative importance of strategic asset allocation reflect at least in part pension funds' typical investment emphasis. Pension funds frequently emphasize strategic asset allocation. We expect asset allocation to explain a high proportion of a given fund's returns over time if that fund's discipline is to consistently adhere to its strategic asset allocation and limit the scope of security selection (i.e., limit deviations of security holdings in an asset class relative to weights of securities in the asset class's passive benchmarks).

An alternative perspective is asset allocation's importance in explaining the *cross-sectional variation of returns*—that is, the proportion of the variation *among* funds' performance explained by funds' different asset allocations. In other words, to what degree do differences in asset allocation explain differences in rates of return over time for a group of investors?

The degree of diversity among asset allocations must affect the cross-sectional importance of asset allocation that we will find after the fact. For example, if all balanced funds continuously rebalance to a 60/40 stock/bond allocation, then asset allocation will explain precisely none of their return differences. If the investor group is quite diverse in its asset allocations and does not engage in active management, then asset allocation will explain a substantial amount of cross-sectional differences in return; but if that group were composed of very active investors, asset allocation would explain relatively less. Ibbotson and Kaplan (2000) found that asset allocation explained about 40 percent of the cross-sectional variation in mutual fund returns, using 10 years of data (April 1988 to March 1998) for 94 U.S. balanced mutual funds. The remaining 60 percent was explained by factors such as asset-class timing, style within asset classes, security selection, and fees.[5] The cross-sectional percentage of variation explained, 40 percent, was much lower than the median time-series result, 87.6 percent, for the mutual funds. Forty percent, however, is sufficiently large to suggest that those investors in practice significantly differentiate themselves from peers through asset allocation. In other results,

[4]In this study, timing was defined as altering the investment mix weights away from the policy allocation. Security selection refers to selecting individual securities within an asset class.

[5]However, the authors did not examine these other components' individual contributions to cross-sectional explanatory power.

Ibbotson et al. concluded as did earlier researchers that after expenses, the sample pension funds and balanced funds were not adding value through timing and security selection.

The research discussed above was empirical—that is, focused on actual performance records. By contrast, Kritzman and Page (2003) explored asset allocation versus security selection in terms of the hypothetical potential to affect terminal wealth. What should investors emphasize if they are skillful, asset allocation or security selection? What should they avoid if they lack skill? The authors found that active security selection lead to greater potential dispersion in final wealth than did varying asset allocation. They thus concluded that skillful investors have the potential to earn higher incremental returns through security selection than through asset allocation. Skill as a security selector may be highly valuable. Kritzman and Page also note that security selection's potentially higher incremental returns come at the cost of greater risk; thus, not only the investor's skill but his risk aversion must be considered.

What are the practical messages of these studies? Investors need to keep in mind their own specific risk and return objectives and establish a strategic asset allocation that is expected to satisfy both. Sidestepping strategic asset allocation finds no support in the empirical or normative literature. When investors decide whether and to what degree they will engage in active investment approaches, they must objectively assess not only the supply of opportunities (the informational efficiency of markets) but the costs and the skills and information they bring to the task relative to all other market participants. A note of caution consistent with the empirical part of the literature discussed: Because investors in the aggregate are the market and costs do not net out across investors, the return on the average actively managed dollar should be less than the return on the average passively managed dollar, after costs (Sharpe 1991).

3. ASSET ALLOCATION AND THE INVESTOR'S RISK AND RETURN OBJECTIVES

An investor's risk and return objectives may be described in a number of distinct ways, both quantitative and qualitative. The approach we choose in characterizing those objectives determines the type of analysis we perform, the way we model return and risk, and, ultimately, our recommendations. The next subsection outlines the major choice that we face in overall approach. The focus then moves to concepts that will help us to accurately describe an investor's return and risk preferences and the behavioral considerations that may play a role in setting objectives.

3.1. Asset-Only and Asset/Liability Management Approaches to Strategic Asset Allocation

As discussed in the chapter on managing institutional portfolios, insurers, defined-benefit (DB) pension plans, and certain other institutional investors face streams of significant future liabilities. Controlling the risk related to funding future liabilities is a key investment objective for such investors, who frequently take an asset/liability management approach to strategic asset allocation.

In the context of determining a strategic asset allocation, the **asset/liability management (ALM) approach** involves explicitly modeling liabilities and adopting the optimal asset allocation in relationship to funding liabilities.[6] For example, a DB pension plan may want to maximize the future risk-adjusted value of pension surplus (the value of pension assets minus the present value of pension liabilities).[7] Investors other than those with significant future liabilities may adopt an ALM approach by treating future needs (such as for income) as if they were liabilities; we call those needs "quasi-liabilities." Ziemba (2003) discusses this approach for individual investors; the method he describes involves setting penalties for failing to meet annual income needs and specifying a numerical value for the investor's risk tolerance.[8]

In contrast to ALM, an **asset-only (AO) approach** to strategic asset allocation does not explicitly involve modeling liabilities. In an AO approach, any impact of the investor's liabilities on policy portfolio selection is indirect (e.g., through the level of the return requirement). Compared with ALM, an AO approach affords much less precision in controlling risk related to the funding of liabilities.

One example of an AO approach to strategic asset allocation is the Black–Litterman (1991, 1992) model. This model takes a global market-value-weighted asset allocation (the "market equilibrium portfolio") as the default strategic asset allocation for investors. The approach then incorporates a procedure for deviating from market capitalization weights in directions that reflect an investor's views on asset classes' expected returns as well as the strength of those views. For example, the weights in a globally diversified index provide a starting point for the investor's policy portfolio weights irrespective of the investor's liabilities (if any). In a later section, we illustrate a simple AO mean–variance approach to strategic asset allocation. However, mean–variance analysis has also been used in ALM approaches to strategic asset allocation, as we will illustrate later.[9]

In a subsequent section we will discuss ALM approaches to asset allocation in more detail. ALM strategies run from those that seek to minimize risk with respect to net worth or surplus (assets minus liabilities) to those that deliberately bear surplus risk in exchange for higher expected surplus, analogous to the trade-off of absolute risk for absolute mean return in an AO approach. We may also describe ALM approaches as either static or dynamic.

To take the risk dimension first, the earliest-developed ALM approaches were at the risk-minimizing end of the spectrum. These strategies are cash-flow matching (also known as exact matching) and immunization (also known as duration matching). A **cash-flow matching** approach structures investments in bonds to match (offset) future liabilities or quasi-liabilities. When feasible, cash flow matching minimizes risk relative to funding liabilities. An **immunization** approach structures investments in bonds to match (offset) the weighted-average duration of liabilities.[10] Because duration is a first-order approximation of interest rate risk, immunization involves more risk than does cash-flow matching with respect to funding liabilities. To improve the risk-control characteristics of an immunization approach

[6] A **liability** is a financial obligation.

[7] See Sharpe (1990).

[8] The objective function is to maximize the expected value of [Final wealth – (Accumulated penalized shortfalls/Risk tolerance)]. The solution approach is a technique known as *stochastic programming*.

[9] Examples include the mean–variance surplus optimizations of Leibowitz and Henriksson (1988) and Sharpe and Tint (1990); Leibowitz and Henriksson (1989), which incorporates shortfall constraints; and Elton and Gruber (1992), which focuses on the mean and variance of period-by-period changes in net worth.

[10] Besides matching the weighted-average duration of liabilities, the investments in bonds must satisfy other conditions, including having the same present value as the liabilities being immunized. See Fabozzi (2004b, Chapter 4) and Waring (2004a) for more information on these techniques.

relative to shifts in the yield curve, portfolio managers often match the convexity as well as the duration of liabilities. Highly risk-averse approaches such as immunization remain important for investors such as banks and life insurers. ALM approaches permitting higher risk levels include those specifying the satisfaction of liabilities as constraints under which the best asset allocation will be chosen, as well as those incorporating an objective function that includes a penalty for failing to satisfy liabilities.

The second dimension concerns static versus dynamic approaches, and the contrast between them is important for understanding current practice in ALM investing. A **dynamic approach** recognizes that an investor's asset allocation and actual asset returns and liabilities in a given period affect the optimal decision that will be available next period. The asset allocation is further linked to the optimal investment decisions available at all future time periods. In contrast, a **static approach** does not consider links between optimal decisions at different time periods, somewhat analogous to a driver who tries to make the best decision as she arrives at each new street without looking further ahead. This advantage of dynamic over static asset allocation applies both to AO and ALM perspectives. With the ready availability of computing power, institutional investors that adopt an ALM approach to strategic asset allocation frequently choose a dynamic rather than a static approach. A dynamic approach, however, is more complex and costly to model and implement.[11] Nonetheless, investors with significant future liabilities often find a dynamic approach to be worth the cost.

How do the recommended strategic asset allocations resulting from AO and ALM approaches differ? The ALM approach to strategic asset allocation characteristically results in a higher allocation to fixed-income instruments than an AO approach. Fixed-income instruments have prespecified interest and principal payments that typically represent legal obligations of the issuer. Because of the nature of their cash flows, fixed-income instruments are well suited to offsetting future obligations.

What types of investors gravitate to an ALM approach? In general, the ALM approach tends to be favored when:

- The investor has below-average risk tolerance.
- The penalties for not meeting the liabilities or quasi-liabilities are very high.
- The market value of liabilities or quasi-liabilities are interest rate sensitive.
- Risk taken in the investment portfolio limits the investor's ability to profitably take risk in other activities.
- Legal and regulatory requirements and incentives favor holding fixed-income securities.
- Tax incentives favor holding fixed-income securities.[12]

Exhibit 5-2 reflects practical experience with the concerns and typical asset allocation approaches of the various investor types covered in earlier chapters.

Both AO and ALM approaches have appropriate roles in strategic asset allocation depending on the investor's circumstances and needs.

[11]Among the complexities of dynamic ALM modeling are the random components of liabilities in many cases (e.g., pension benefits). Monte Carlo simulation is used in dynamic ALM modeling with multivariate risks.

[12]An ALM approach may incorporate equities, however. For example, after assuring the funding of liabilities, the investor might optimally invest some part of excess assets in equities. For a topical discussion on the variety of approaches to ALM, see Denmark (2005).

EXHIBIT 5-2 Characteristic Liability Concerns of Various Investors

Type of Investor	Type of Liability (Quasi-Liability)	Penalty for Not Meeting	Asset Allocation Approach in Practice
Individual	Taxes, mortgage payments (Living expenses, wealth accumulation targets)	Varies	AO most common ALM
Pension plans (defined benefit)	Pension benefits	High, legal and regulatory	ALM AO
Pension plans (defined contribution)	(Retirement needs)	Varies	Integrated with individual's asset allocation approach
Foundations and endowments	Spending commitments, Capital project commitments	High	AO ALM
Life insurance companies	Death proceeds, annuity payments, return guarantees on investment products	Very high, legal and regulatory	ALM
Non–life insurance companies	Property and liability claims	Very high, legal and regulatory	ALM
Banks	Deposits	Very high, legal and regulatory	ALM

3.2. Return Objectives and Strategic Asset Allocation

Investors have both qualitative and quantitative investment objectives. Qualitative return objectives describe the investor's fundamental goals, such as to achieve returns that will:

- Provide an adequate retirement income (for an individual currently in the workforce).
- Maintain a fund's real purchasing power after distributions (for many endowments and foundations).
- Adequately fund liabilities (for investors such as pension plans and insurance companies).
- Exceed the rate of inflation in the long term (from the prospectus of an inflation-protected bond fund).

We can often concretely determine whether a qualitative objective has been satisfied. For example, we can determine whether a university endowment's investment program has preserved real purchasing power after distributions by reference to the endowment's asset values and a published cost-of-higher-education inflation index. But investors also benefit by formulating quantitative (numerical) goals that reflect the return and risk levels perceived to be appropriate for achieving the qualitative objectives. In an AO approach, the concern is for absolute returns and absolute risk. In an ALM approach, it is for net returns (net of the return or growth rate of liabilities) and risk with respect to funding liabilities. Given a set of capital market expectations, numerical objectives offer great practical help in determining specific asset allocations for final consideration.

Because strategic asset allocation involves meeting an investor's long-term needs, precise statements of numerical return objectives must take account of the effects of compounding.

Consider a foundation's simple additive return objective equal to the spending rate plus the expected inflation rate. This objective aims to preserve the portfolio's real purchasing power after making distributions. If the spending rate is 5 percent and expected inflation is 4 percent, for example, the return requirement would be stated as 9 percent, using an additive return objective. To expect to preserve purchasing power, however, the fund must earn $(1.05)(1.04) - 1.0 = 0.092$ or 9.2 percent, 20 basis points higher than the additive return requirement. The higher the spending and inflation rates, the higher the discrepancy between the additive objective and the need. Through compounding, the practical effect of this divergence increases the greater the number of periods. Further, if we specify that the cost of earning investment returns is 0.30 percent of beginning assets, then we need to earn $(1.05)(1.04)(1.003) - 1.0 = 0.0953$ or 9.53 percent to preserve the portfolio's purchasing power after distributions. We would then have a return objective of 9.53 percent.[13] Thus a careful specification of the numerical return objective should reflect the costs of earning investment returns and inflation as well as their compound effects through time.

EXAMPLE 5-3 CEFA's Return Objective

CEFA's trustees have established a policy that calls for annually spending 4 percent of the prior 12-quarter moving average of the portfolio's market value. The trustees have asked Singh to revise the statement of CEFA's return objective to reflect the 4 percent spending rate, a forecast of 2 percent in the long-run inflation rate represented by the consumer price index (CPI), and a 40-basis-point cost of earning investment returns.

Singh makes the following calculation: $(1.04)(1.02)(1.004) - 1 = 0.065$ or 6.5 percent. He drafts the following statement for the trustees to consider:

"The investment objective of the Canadian Endowment for the Fine Arts is to maintain the endowment's real purchasing power after distributions. To attain this objective, the targeted annual rate of return is 6.5 percent, reflecting a spending rate of 4 percent, an expected inflation rate of 2 percent, and a 40-basis-point cost of earning investment returns."

Chapter 3 notes that an additive formulation of a return objective can serve as a starting point. Because additive formulations provide an intuitive wording of a return objective, such formulations are common in actual investment policy statements. The differences between additive and multiplicative formulations can be essentially negligible for low levels of spending rates and inflation. Nevertheless, portfolio managers should prefer the multiplicative formulation for strategic asset allocation purposes; managers should also observe the distinction between compound and arithmetic mean rates of growth.

[13] Some entities count investment management expenses in spending and the spending rate. If it were explicitly stated that the spending rate of 5 percent included the cost of earning investment returns, then the return objective would be $(1.05)(1.04) - 1.0 = 9.2\%$.

If an investor's return requirement is based on the compound rate of return needed to achieve a goal, the corresponding arithmetic mean one-period return needed to achieve that goal will be higher than the return requirement stated as a compound rate of return. The differences between the arithmetic mean and compound rate of growth (geometric mean) are approximately 13, 50, and 113 basis points for portfolio standard deviations of returns of 5 percent, 10 percent, and 15 percent, respectively.[14] Thus, if an investor requires an 8 percent compound growth rate to reach an investment objective, with a 5 percent standard deviation of portfolio returns the investor will need to achieve an 8.13 percent arithmetic mean return to achieve his or her goal. The main point is that if the investor states an arithmetic mean annual return objective based on a compound growth rate calculation, the investor's return objective should reflect an appropriate upward adjustment from the compound growth rate.

Often, an investor's time horizon is multistage, reflecting periods with foreseeably distinct needs. For example, an individual investor's retirement often marks the end of an accumulation stage. Multistage horizons present a challenge to strategic asset allocation. A dynamic model most accurately captures the effects of a multistage time horizon on strategic asset allocation. Using a static asset allocation model (such as the mean–variance model), however, we can incorporate multistage effects approximately. For example, we can reflect an investor's average return and risk requirements (for the remaining stages) in the return and risk objectives that guide the strategic asset allocation. The investor should be ready to update the strategic asset allocation to reflect significant shifts in return and risk requirements with the passage of time.

3.3. Risk Objectives and Strategic Asset Allocation

In addition to the investor's return objectives, the investor's risk tolerance enters into creating a policy portfolio. As with return objectives, both qualitative and quantitative risk objectives are important.

Many practitioners will qualitatively evaluate an investor's risk tolerance as below average, average, or above average, based on the investor's willingness and ability to take risk. To apply a quantitative approach to asset allocation, however, we must quantify an investor's attitude to risk. The most precise way to do so is to measure the investor's numerical risk aversion, R_A. Numerical risk aversion can be measured in an interview or questionnaire in which the investor expresses preferences among sets of choices involving risky and certain returns. Risk aversion is the inverse of risk tolerance: A lower value of risk aversion means a higher tolerance for risk. To give approximate guidelines for the scale we will use, an R_A of 6 to 8 represents a high degree of risk aversion (i.e., a low risk tolerance), while an R_A of 1 to 2 represents a relatively low degree of risk aversion (i.e., a high risk tolerance).[15] A mean–variance investor will evaluate an asset allocation (mix) m using Equation 5-1:

$$U_m = E(R_m) - 0.005 R_A \sigma_m^2 \tag{5-1}$$

where

U_m = the investor's expected utility for asset mix m
$E(R_m)$ = expected return for mix m

[14]These numbers are based on the following approximate relationship: $R_G \approx E(R) - 0.5\sigma^2$, where R_G is the compound growth rate, $E(R)$ is the arithmetic mean return, σ^2 is the variance of return, and all the terms are stated in decimal form rather than percent.

[15]See Ziemba (2003, p. 6). An R_A of zero represents indifference to risk (risk neutrality).

R_A = the investor's risk aversion

σ_m^2 = variance of return for mix m

In Equation 5-1, $E(R_m)$ and σ_m are expressed as percentages rather than as decimals.[16]

We can interpret the investor's expected utility for asset mix m, U_m, as the asset mix's risk-adjusted expected return for the particular investor. The quantity $0.005R_A\sigma_m^2$ is a risk penalty that is subtracted from the allocation's expected return to adjust it for risk. The risk penalty's size depends on the investor's risk aversion, R_A, and on the standard deviation of the asset mix, σ_m. The more risk averse the investor, the greater the penalty subtracted from expected return. To illustrate the expression *risk-adjusted expected return,* suppose that a moderately risk-averse investor ($R_A = 4$) is choosing between the strategic asset allocations given in Exhibit 5-3. For that investor,

$$\begin{aligned} U_m &= E(R_m) - 0.005R_A\sigma_m^2 \\ &= E(R_m) - 0.005(4)\sigma_m^2 \\ &= E(R_m) - 0.02\sigma_m^2 \end{aligned}$$

The risk-adjusted expected return of Asset Allocation A is $U_A = E(R_A) - 0.02\sigma_A^2 = 9.7\% - 0.02(15.0\%)^2 = 9.7\% - 4.5\% = 5.2\%$; that of Asset Allocation B is $U_B = E(R_A) - 0.02\sigma_A^2 = 7\% - 0.02(10\%)^2 = 7\% - 2\% = 5.0\%$. The investor should prefer A to B because of A's higher risk-adjusted expected return.

Another way an investor can quantify his risk tolerance is in terms of an acceptable level of volatility as measured by standard deviation of return. For example, an investor who is uncomfortable with the volatility associated with a standard deviation of return of 12 percent or higher could eliminate Asset Allocation A from consideration.

Still another way for an investor to quantify risk is in terms of **shortfall risk,** the risk that a portfolio's value will fall below some minimum acceptable level during a stated time horizon. The risks that a retiree's assets will fall below the amount needed to supply an adequate retirement income, or that a DB plan's assets will be less than the present value of plan liabilities, are examples of shortfall risk. When shortfall risk is an important concern for an investor, an appropriate shortfall risk objective improves the description of the investor's attitude to risk. Shortfall risk is one example of the larger concept of **downside risk** (risk relating to losses or worse than expected outcomes only). Downside risk concepts include not

EXHIBIT 5-3 Strategic Asset Allocation Choices

	Investor's Forecasts	
Allocation	Expected Return	Standard Deviation of Return
A	9.7%	15%
B	7.0	10

[16]See Bodie, Kane, and Marcus (2004, p. 168) for this expression. A standard expression for a mean–variance investor's expected utility is $U_m = E(R_m) - 0.50R_A\sigma_m^2$, where expected return and standard deviation are stated in decimal form and 0.5 is a scaling factor. Dividing 0.5 by 100 to get 0.005 in the text expression ensures that we can express expected return and standard deviation as percentages.

only shortfall risk but concepts such as **semivariance** and **target semivariance** that also may be applied in asset allocation and are discussed in statistical textbooks (as well as defined in the glossary).

The oldest shortfall risk criterion is Roy's safety-first criterion. Roy's safety-first criterion states that the optimal portfolio minimizes the probability over a stated time horizon that portfolio return, R_P, will fall below some threshold level R_L that the investor insists on meeting or exceeding. The safety-first optimal portfolio *maximizes* the safety-first ratio (SFRatio):

$$\text{SFRatio} = \frac{E(R_P) - R_L}{\sigma_P} \tag{5-2}$$

Equation 5-2 gives the distance from the expected return to the shortfall level in the numerator. The denominator converts the result into units of the portfolio's standard deviation of return. If a portfolio's expected return were many standard deviations above the threshold return, the chance that the threshold would be breached would be relatively small.[17] There are two steps in choosing among risky portfolios using Roy's criterion (assuming normality):

1. Calculate each portfolio's SFRatio.
2. Choose the portfolio with the highest SFRatio.

If there is an asset offering a risk-free return for the time horizon being considered, and if R_L is less than or equal to that risk-free rate, then it is safety-first optimal to be fully invested in the risk-free asset. Holding the risk-free asset in this case eliminates the chance that the threshold return is not met. Example 5-4 illustrates a use of Roy's safety-first criterion.

EXAMPLE 5-4 Applying Roy's Safety-First Criterion in Asset Allocation

An investment adviser is counseling Aimeé Goddard, a client who recently inherited €1,200,000 and has above-average risk tolerance ($R_A = 2$). Because Goddard is young and one of her purposes is to fund a comfortable retirement, she wants to earn returns that will outpace inflation in the long term. Goddard expects to liquidate €60,000 of the portfolio in 12 months, however, to make the down payment on a house. If that need arises, she states that it is important for her to be able to take out the €60,000 without invading the initial capital of €1,200,000. Exhibit 5-4 shows three alternative strategic asset allocations.

[17]The expression does not depend on the normal distribution; it holds under the same general conditions as Chebyshev's inequality (see Elton, Gruber, Brown, and Goetzmann, 2003). We can associate a precise probability of not meeting the return with a given level of this expression, however, if we assume the normal distribution. Note too that if we substitute the risk-free rate R_F for R_L, we obtain the Sharpe ratio. The highest-Sharpe-ratio portfolio is the one that minimizes the probability of a return below the risk-free rate.

EXHIBIT 5-4 Strategic Asset Allocation Choices for Goddard

	Investor's Forecasts	
Asset Allocation	Expected Return	Standard Deviation of Return
A	10.00%	20%
B	7.00	10
C	5.25	5

Address the following questions:

1. Based only on Goddard's risk-adjusted expected returns for the asset allocations, which asset allocation would she prefer?
2. Given Goddard's desire not to invade the €1,200,000 principal, what is the shortfall level, R_L?
3. According to Roy's safety-first criterion, which of the three allocations is the best?
4. Recommend a strategic asset allocation for Goddard.

Solution to Problem 1: Using Equation 5-1,

$$U_m = E(R_m) - 0.005R_A\sigma_m^2$$

$$= E(R_m) - 0.005(2)\sigma_m^2$$

$$= E(R_m) - 0.01\sigma_m^2$$

So Goddard's risk-adjusted returns for Asset Allocations A, B, and C are as follows:

$$U_A = E(R_A) - 0.01\sigma_A^2 = 10.0\% - 0.01(20\%)^2 = 10.0\% - 4.0\% = 6.0\%$$

$$U_B = E(R_B) - 0.01\sigma_B^2 = 7.0\% - 0.01(10\%)^2 = 7.0\% - 1.0\% = 6.0\%$$

$$U_C = E(R_C) - 0.01\sigma_C^2 = 5.25\% - 0.01(5\%)^2 = 5.25\% - 0.25\% = 5.0\%$$

Goddard would be indifferent between A and B based only on their common perceived risk-adjusted expected return of 6 percent.

Solution to Problem 2: Because €60,000/€1,200,000 is 5.0 percent, for any return less than 5.0 percent Goddard will need to invade principal if she liquidates €60,000. So $R_L = 5$ percent.

Solution to Problem 3: To decide which of the three allocations is safety-first optimal, we need to calculate the ratio $[E(R_P) - R_L]/\sigma_P$:

$$\textit{Allocation A}: (10 - 5)/20 = 0.25$$

$$\textit{Allocation B}: (7 - 5)/10 = 0.20$$

$$\textit{Allocation C}: (5.25 - 5)/5 = 0.05$$

Allocation A, with the largest ratio (0.25), is the best alternative according to Roy's safety-first criterion.

Solution to Problem 4: Both A and B have the same perceived risk-adjusted expected return, but Allocation A is superior according to Roy's safety-first criterion: Allocation A has a smaller probability of not meeting the threshold 5 percent return than Allocation B. Therefore, A would be the recommended strategic asset allocation.

In Example 5-4 we used a shortfall risk constraint to identify the asset allocation with the *smallest* probability of not meeting a threshold return level. We could calculate that, in Example 5-4, the selected asset allocation (Asset Allocation A) has a probability of about 33 percent of not meeting a 5 percent recent threshold, under a normality assumption. This result suggests another shortfall risk approach. An investor could also specify a given maximum probability of not meeting a return threshold. That probability can be translated into a standard deviation test, if we assume a normal distribution of portfolio returns. For example, suppose that a 2.5 percent probability of failing to meet a return threshold is acceptable. Given a normal distribution of returns, the probability of a return that is more than two standard deviations below the expected return is approximately 2.5 percent. Therefore, if we subtract two standard deviations from a portfolio's expected return and the resulting number is above the client's return threshold, the resulting portfolio passes that shortfall risk test. If the resulting number falls below the client's threshold, the portfolio does not pass that shortfall risk test. Shortfall probability levels of 5 percent and 10 percent translate into 1.65 and 1.28 standard deviations below the mean, respectively, under a normality assumption.

Shortfall risk in relation to liabilities is a key focus of ALM approaches to asset allocation. An AO approach can also easily incorporate shortfall risk in a variety of ways. Besides specifying a shortfall risk–related objective such as Roy's safety-first criterion, an investor can optimize using a one-sided, downside risk concept rather than a symmetric one such as variance, or by adding a shortfall risk constraint to an optimization based on variance.

3.4. Behavioral Influences on Asset Allocation

Standard finance views investors as rational decision makers and is based on the axioms of economic utility theory. Behavioral finance, grounded in psychology, focuses on describing individuals' observed economic behavior. By far the majority of research in asset allocation has been in the context of standard finance. Advisers of individual investors in particular, however, may better understand their clients' investment goals, needs, and reactions to proposed asset allocations if they become familiar with behavioral finance tenets such as loss aversion, mental accounting, and regret avoidance.

Behavioral finance asserts that most investors worry more about avoiding losses than acquiring gains. According to behavioral finance, most individuals are risk seekers when faced with the prospect of a substantial loss.[18] If the adviser establishes that a client is loss averse, one approach may be to incorporate an appropriate shortfall risk constraint or objective in the asset allocation decision. Managing assets with such a constraint or objective should reduce the

[18]This discussion reflects the insights of the area of behavioral finance theory known as **prospect theory.** The term *prospect theory* comes from the analysis of decision making under risk in terms of choices among prospects. For more details, see the chapter on managing individual investor portfolios and see Tversky (1990).

chance that the client finds himself facing the prospect of a substantial loss. An ALM approach may be appropriate for such clients as well.

If the investor displays mental accounting the investor will place his total wealth into separate accounts and buckets. Each bucket is associated with a different level of risk tolerance depending on a purpose the investor associates with it, such as speculation or a building a fund for college expenses. Such an investor looks at his portfolio narrowly in pieces rather than as one fund. The money's source may affect how an individual invests: An investor may be more likely to invest in a risky venture with cash is drawn from a windfall gain rather than from salary. The standard finance approach to asset allocation involves determining an optimal asset allocation for the total portfolio, typically reflecting an overall, blended measure of a client's risk tolerance. That asset allocation would generally be different than the overall asset allocation implied by summing the asset allocations an investor would choose for each bucket individually, and it could be perceived as inappropriate by the client.

Some writers have suggested meeting mental accounting on its own terms by adopting a multistrategy or goal-based asset allocation procedure.[19] For example, Brunel (2003) recommends an asset allocation framework in which asset allocations are developed for four buckets individually: liquidity, income, capital preservation, and growth. In principle, the number and kind of buckets could be adapted to the needs of each client individually, although at greater cost. A multistrategy approach has greater complexity than the standard finance approach of developing one strategic asset allocation for the client, because it involves many optimizations rather than just one. Furthermore, developing a set of asset allocations for stand-alone portfolios ignores the correlations between assets across portfolios; the resulting overall asset allocation may fail to use risk efficiently. Advisers may need to discuss the advantages of adopting a broad frame of reference in asset allocation.

Behavioral finance asserts that investors are sensitive to regret, the pain that comes when a decision turns out to have been a bad one. The fear of regret may play a role in actual asset allocation decisions in at least two ways. First, it may be a psychological factor promoting diversification.[20] Second, regret avoidance may limit divergence from peers' average asset allocation if the investor is sensitive to peer comparisons.[21]

EXAMPLE 5-5 Behavioral Biases in Asset Allocation

Joseph Gowers, CFA is a financial planner serving high-net-worth individuals. He is discussing strategic asset allocation with May Smith. Smith is 30 years old and in good health. With her formal education behind her, she has begun a promising career in management. She describes herself as ambitious and ready to take calculated

[19] See Shefrin and Statman (2000), Brunel (2003), and Nevins (2004).

[20] For example, Harry M. Markowitz was quoted in Zweig (1998) as follows concerning investing for retirement: "I should have computed the historical covariances of the asset classes and drawn an efficient frontier. Instead, I visualized my grief if the stock market went way up and I wasn't in it—or if it went way down and I was completely in it. My intention was to minimize my future regret. So I split my contribution fifty-fifty between bonds and equities."

[21] Regret avoidance may also play a role in the implementation of a strategic asset allocation—for example, in some investors' desire to establish the positions in risky asset classes gradually.

risks. She intends to retire at age 60. She also supplies the following facts and comments:

- Smith has no substantial debts and has $150,000 saved from salary and bonuses.
- Smith's $150,000 portfolio is currently invested 80 percent in equity mutual funds and 20 percent in bond mutual funds.
- Besides a checking account to meet her regular expenses, Smith keeps a "rainy day" fund of $25,000 in a separate checking account at her bank. She views both accounts as separate from her investment portfolio because the accounts are for current and potential liquidity needs.
- As a result of an inheritance, she will receive $3 million very shortly. The inheritance was the motivation for seeking professional investment counsel.
- Smith's plan was to set aside $500,000 of the $3 million inheritance for speculative common stock investments and invest the balance of $2.5 million conservatively in short-term tax-exempt bonds.
- Smith views a $500,000 speculative stock investment as her chance to "score big."
- Smith views the $2.5 million she intended to invest conservatively as permanently securing a comfortable retirement; she considers the investment of that money the single most important economic decision she will ever make.
- Smith has told Gowers that she is extremely unlikely ever to inherit a meaningful amount of money again and would forever be disappointed if she suffered a serious loss to the $2.5 million.

Based only on the above information, address the following:

1. Compare the consistency of the risk tolerance implied by Smith's current asset allocation with that implied by the asset allocation that would result if Smith's $3,000,000 inheritance were invested according to her plan.
2. Discuss the behavioral biases in Smith's approach to investing her inheritance.
3. Evaluate whether Smith's intended approach is likely to make efficient use of risk by incorporating information about correlations.

Solution to Problem 1: Ignoring the $25,000 rainy day fund, Smith currently has an aggressive 80/20 stock/bond asset allocation. Stocks represent $120,000 and bonds represent $30,000. Post-inheritance, her expected investable portfolio is $\$150,000 + \$3,000,000 = \$3,150,000$. If her intended postinheritance investments are executed, her allocation to stocks will be $(\$120,000 + \$500,000)/\$3,150,000 = 0.197$, or 19.7 percent. Her bond allocation will be $(\$30,000 + \$2,500,000)/\$3,150,000 = 0.803$, or 80.3 percent. This asset allocation is far more conservative than her current one It appears that the risk tolerance level is inconsistent between her current and intended asset allocations.

Solution to Problem 2: Smith's approach reflects mental accounting, specifically setting up separate buckets for wealth, each serving a specific purpose and each invested independently. She views $500,000 as targeted for growth and $2.5 million as targeted for capital preservation. A second bias in her intended asset allocation is regret avoidance; she is focused on the disappointment that will result if she does not preserve a once-in-a-lifetime inheritance.

Solution to Problem 3: Smith's asset allocation is a mental-accounting approach rather than one that optimizes the overall asset allocation taking account of correlations between assets. Her approach is unlikely to result in an efficient strategic asset allocation.

4. THE SELECTION OF ASSET CLASSES

An asset class is a group of assets with similar attributes. The selection of asset classes as inputs to a strategic asset allocation is an important decision, with long-term effects on a portfolio's returns and risk. The selection must be from the set of asset classes permitted by the investment policy statement (the IPS-permissible asset classes). In practice, the set of IPS-permissible asset classes has considerable variation, reflecting regulatory and other constraints that affect the portfolio. For example, banks and life insurance companies are frequently subject to regulatory restrictions limiting investment in common equity. Before turning to asset-class selection, however, we must discuss how to effectively specify an asset class. For investors subject to regulation, such specifications may be ready-made. Many investors, however, can increase their control over risk by specifying asset classes skillfully.

4.1. Criteria for Specifying Asset Classes

A basic principle is that asset-class specification should support the purposes of strategic asset allocation. For example, if a manager lumps together very different investments such as real estate property and common equities into an asset class called *equities,* asset allocation becomes less effective in diversifying and controlling risk. Furthermore, the investor needs a logical framework for examining the not infrequent claims by sponsors of new investment products that their product is a new asset class rather than an investment strategy. If the product is accepted as an asset class, it will become a part of strategic asset allocations and tend to be more widely held than otherwise. Following are five criteria that will help in effectively specifying asset classes:

1. *Assets within an asset class should be relatively homogeneous.* Assets within an asset class should have similar attributes. In the example just given, defining equities to include both real estate and common stock would result in a nonhomogeneous asset class.
2. *Asset classes should be mutually exclusive.* Overlapping asset classes will reduce the effectiveness of strategic asset allocation in controlling risk and also introduce problems in developing asset-class return expectations. For example, if one asset class for a U.S. investor is domestic common equities, then world equities ex-U.S. is more appropriate as an asset class than world equities including U.S. equities.
3. *Asset classes should be diversifying.* For risk-control purposes, an included asset class should not have extremely high expected correlations with other asset classes or with a linear combination of the other asset classes. Otherwise, the included asset class will be effectively redundant in a portfolio because it will duplicate risk exposures already present. In general, a pairwise correlation above 0.95 is undesirable.

   The criticism of relying on pairwise correlations is that an asset class may be highly correlated with some linear combination of other asset classes even when the pairwise correlations are not high.[22] Kritzman (1999) proposed a criterion to assess a proposed asset class's diversifying qualities that is superior to relying on pairwise correlations: For each current asset class, find the linear combination of the other asset classes that minimizes tracking risk with the proposed asset class. (Tracking risk is defined as the square root of the average squared differences between the asset class's returns and the combination's returns.) Similarly find the minimum tracking risk combination of current asset classes for the proposed asset class and qualitatively judge whether it is sufficiently high based on the current asset classes' tracking risk levels. For example, if the tracking risks for existing asset classes are 18 percent, 12 percent, and 8 percent, a proposed asset class with a 15 percent tracking risk should be diversifying.

4. *The asset classes as a group should make up a preponderance of world investable wealth.* From the perspective of portfolio theory, selecting an asset allocation from a group of asset classes satisfying this criterion should tend to increase expected return for a given level of risk. Furthermore, including more markets expands the opportunities for applying active investment strategies, assuming the decision to invest actively has been made.
5. *The asset class should have the capacity to absorb a significant fraction of the investor's portfolio without seriously affecting the portfolio's liquidity.*[23] Practically, most investors will want to be able to reset or rebalance to a strategic asset allocation without moving asset-class prices or incurring high transaction costs.

Traditional asset classes include the following:

- *Domestic common equity.* Market capitalization sometimes has been used as a criterion to distinguish among *large-cap, mid-cap*, and *small-cap domestic common equity* as asset classes.
- *Domestic fixed income.* Maturity sometimes has been used to distinguish among *intermediate-term* and *long-term domestic bonds* as asset classes. Recently, inflation protection has been used to distinguish between *nominal bonds* and *inflation-protected bonds* as asset classes.
- *Nondomestic (international) common equity.* Developed market status sometimes has been used to distinguish between *developed market equity* and *emerging market equity.*
- *Nondomestic fixed income.* Developed market status sometimes has been used to distinguish between *developed market fixed income* and *emerging market fixed income.*
- *Real estate.* The term *alternative investments* is now frequently used to refer to all risky asset classes excluding the four listed above. Alternative investments include real estate, private equity, natural resources, commodities, currencies, and the investment strategies represented by hedge funds. The usage is convenient, but such groups should be broken out as separate asset classes alongside real estate because alternative assets are far from homogeneous.

[22]We can illustrate this assertion as follows. Suppose the returns to three assets are denoted by X, Y, and Z, respectively, and we are considering making Asset Z available for investment. We are unaware of the fact that Z is an exact linear combination of X and Y (i.e., $Z = aX + bY$, where a and b are constants and not both zero). Because a weighted combination of X and Y replicates Z, Asset Z is redundant. We observe that Z has a moderate pairwise correlation of 0.5 with X as well as with Y (furthermore, assume a moderate -0.5 correlation between X and Y). The stated correlations, although not particularly large, are consistent with Z being a redundant asset in the sense mentioned. See Gujarati (2003, pp. 359–60) for details.

[23]The statement of this criterion follows Kritzman (1999) closely.

- *Cash and cash equivalents*. Later in this chapter, we will explore why a manager sometimes will initially exclude cash and cash equivalents when choosing the optimal asset allocation.

In addition to regulatory constraints, if any, we must examine tax concerns to determine what asset classes to use in strategic asset allocation. Tax-exempt bonds, where available, generally play no role in strategic asset allocation for tax-exempt institutional investors because these bonds' pricing and yields reflect demand from taxable investors. For high-net-worth individuals and taxable institutional investors such as banks and non-life insurers, however, tax-exempt bonds are an appropriate fixed-income asset class, when they are available to the investor. Other considerations besides taxes may also be important. Some assets such as private equity play no role for investors of modest means or with limited due diligence capabilities.

EXAMPLE 5-6 Are Inflation-Protected Bonds an Asset Class?

Bonds with payments linked to inflation indexes (inflation-protected or inflation-indexed bonds) were probably first issued by the Commonwealth of Massachusetts in 1780 and in modern times by Finland (1945), followed by Israel and Iceland in the 1950s, Brazil, Chile, and Columbia in the 1960s, Argentina and United Kingdom in the 1970s, Australia and Mexico in the 1980s, and Canada, Sweden, New Zealand, the United States, and Turkey more recently.[24]

U.S. Treasury inflation-indexed securities (usually called TIPS) were introduced in 1997. TIPS have a so-called capital-indexed design. That design provides for a fixed real coupon rate with the principal adjusted for inflation or deflation (however, the U.S. Treasury guarantees full payment of the original face value regardless of whatever deflation may occur). Inflation is measured by changes in the U.S. consumer price index (CPI).

Consider the following reasons that have been put forward in support of viewing TIPS as a separate asset class:

Reason A. TIPS returns of all maturities (10 years to 30 years) are strongly correlated with each other (Roll 2004).

Reason B. TIPS have a low correlation with nominal bonds and equities. From 1997 to 2003, long-term TIPS had correlations with long-term nominal bonds in the range of 0.5 to 0.8 (Roll 2004).

Reason C. The economics of TIPS is distinct from the economics of nominal bonds. Volatility of TIPS depends on volatility of real interest rates, whereas the volatility of conventional bonds depends on the volatility of nominal rates. Because it reflects the volatility of inflation, the volatility of nominal rates is generally greater then the volatility of real rates.

[24] See Shiller (2003) for the early history of such bonds.

Reason D. TIPS offer investors inflation and deflation protections that complement those of nominal bonds, whether fixed or floating coupon, as Exhibit 5-5 illustrates.

EXHIBIT 5-5 Protection against Inflation and Deflation

	Coupon	Principal
Nominal fixed-coupon bonds	Deflation protected Inflation unprotected	Deflation protected Inflation unprotected
Nominal floating-coupon bonds	Deflation unprotected Inflation protected	Deflation protected Inflation unprotected
TIPS	Deflation unprotected Inflation protected	Deflation protected (partial) Inflation protected

Reason E. To the extent the CPI reflects employment costs, TIPS can be effective in hedging pension benefits that incorporate salary increases.

Appraise the validity of each of Reasons A through E above.

Solution: All the reasons are valid.

A. High within-group correlations are consistent with the criterion that assets within an asset class should be relatively homogeneous.
B. These levels of correlation are consistent with the criterion that asset classes should be diversifying.
C. This economic argument provides one rationale to explain the level of historical correlations given in B. Differing economics provides some confidence that the observed level of correlations is not an anomaly.
D. This argument also makes sense. TIPS permit increased flexibility in meeting investor goals affected by inflation or deflation.[25]
E. This point identifies a concrete application of the point made in D and is thus also a valid argument.

4.2. The Inclusion of International Assets (Developed and Emerging Markets)

In the prior section, we stated that asset classes as a group should make up a preponderance of world investable wealth. According to that criterion, nondomestic (international) assets have a place in the lineup of *permissible* asset classes for many investors. This section addresses the further question of justifying *investment* in a specific class of international assets.

An objective criterion based on mean–variance analysis can help an investor decide whether he can improve on his existing portfolio by adding a positive holding in nondomestic

[25] Put another way, TIPS help *complete the market*, a finance expression indicating that the existence of TIPS increases the available set of payoff patterns.

equities or bonds or any other asset class. Suppose an investor holds a portfolio p with expected or mean return $E(R_p)$ and standard deviation of return σ_p. The investor then gains the opportunity to add another asset class to his portfolio. Can the investor achieve a mean–variance improvement by expanding his portfolio to include a positive position in the asset class? To answer this question, we need three inputs:

1. The Sharpe ratio of the asset class.
2. The Sharpe ratio of the existing portfolio.
3. The correlation between the asset class's return and portfolio p's return, $\text{Corr}(R_{new}, R_p)$.

Adding the asset class (denoted *new*) to the portfolio is optimal if the following condition is met:[26]

$$\frac{E(R_{new}) - R_F}{\sigma_{new}} > \left(\frac{E(R_p) - R_F}{\sigma_p}\right) \text{Corr}(R_{new}, R_p) \qquad (5\text{-}3)$$

This expression says that in order for the investor to gain by adding the asset class, that asset class's Sharpe ratio must exceed the product of the existing portfolio's Sharpe ratio and the correlation of the asset class's rate of return with the current portfolio's rate of return. If Equation 5-3 holds, the investor can combine the new investment with his or her prior holdings to achieve a superior efficient frontier of risky assets (one in which the tangency portfolio has a higher Sharpe ratio).[27] Note that although the expression may indicate that we can effect a mean–variance improvement at the margin by adding a positive amount of a new asset, it offers no information about how much of the new asset to add.

EXAMPLE 5-7 A Foundation Decides to Add an Asset Class

Wilhelm Schmidt is CIO of a German charitable foundation invested in European equities and bonds. The portfolio has a Sharpe ratio of 0.15. Schmidt is considering adding U.S. equities to the existing portfolio. U.S. equities, as represented by the Russell 3000 Index, have a predicted Sharpe ratio of 0.18; the predicted correlation with existing portfolio is 0.7. Explain whether the foundation should add U.S. equities to its existing portfolio.

Solution: (Sharpe ratio of existing portfolio) × (Correlation of U.S stocks with the existing portfolio) = (0.15)(0.70) = 0.105. The foundation should add U.S. equities if their predicted Sharpe ratio exceeds 0.105. Because Schmidt predicts a Sharpe ratio of 0.18 for U.S. equities, the foundation should add them to the existing portfolio.

In Example 5-7, even if the correlation between the foundation's existing portfolio and U.S. equities were +1.0, so that adding U.S. equities had no potential risk-reduction benefits,

[26] See Blume (1984) and Elton, Gruber, and Rentzler (1987).

[27] Of course, the condition is an inequality. We use *equation* to refer to all numbered formulas or conditions for simplicity.

Equation 5-3 would indicate that the class should be added because the condition for adding the asset class would be satisfied, because $0.18 > 0.15(1.0)$. For any portfolio, we can always effect a mean–variance improvement at the margin by adding an investment with a higher Sharpe ratio than the existing portfolio. This result is intuitive: The higher-Sharpe-ratio investment will mean–variance dominate the existing portfolio in a pairwise comparison. Prior to using the Equation 5-3 criterion, the investor should check whether distribution of the proposed asset class's returns is pronouncedly non-normal. If it is, the criterion is not applicable.

When investing in international assets, investors should consider the following special issues:

- *Currency risk.* Currency risk is a distinctive issue for international investment. Exchange rate fluctuations affect both the total return and volatility of return of any nondomestic investment. Investors in nondomestic markets must form expectations about exchange rates if they decide not to hedge currency exposures. Currency risk as measured by standard deviation may average half the risk of the corresponding stock market and twice the risk of the corresponding bond market.[28]
- *Increased correlations in times of stress.* Investors should be aware that correlations across international markets tend to increase in times of market breaks or crashes.[29]
- *Emerging market concerns.* Among the concerns are limited free float of shares (shares available in the marketplace), limitations on the amount of nondomestic ownership, the quality of company information, and pronounced non-normality of returns (an issue of concern in using a mean–variance approach to choose an asset allocation).

Many researchers believe U.S. investors underinvest in nondomestic markets, a phenomenon called home country bias. One explanation suggested for this tendency is investors' relative lack of familiarity with nondomestic markets. Indexing to an asset class, however, provides an efficient way to deal with any lack of familiarity.

4.3. Alternative Investments

At the beginning of the 1990s, real estate was the other major asset class besides fixed income and equity that investors would list as an asset class for the investable portfolio. Many investors now group real estate along with a range of disparate nontraditional investments, such as private equity and hedge funds of all descriptions, as alternative investments. Exhibit 5-6 gives historical data on the mean returns, volatilities, and correlations of four traditional asset classes (from a U.S. perspective) and four alternative asset classes: private equity, real estate, natural resources, and hedge funds. The statistics for alternative asset classes show distinct relationships within the group and between the individual alternative asset classes and traditional asset classes. For example, the correlations of real estate with private equity, natural resources, and hedge funds were 0.32, −0.46, and −0.18, respectively. Real estate had a correlation of 0.02 with U.S. equity; the correlations of U.S. equity with private equity, natural resources, and hedge funds were 0.18, 0.43, and 0.68, respectively. These

[28] See Solnik and McLeavey (2004, pp. 471–472).

[29] Increased market volatility during such times will by itself tend to produce upwardly biased estimated correlations; after correcting for that bias, however, evidence remains that correlations increase during times of stress. See Solnik and McLeavey (2004, Chapter 9).

EXHIBIT 5-6 Mean Returns, Volatilities, and Correlations: U.S. Traditional and Alternative Asset Classes, 1981–2003

	Mean Return	Volatility	Correlation 1	2	3	4	5	6	7	8
1. U.S. equity	12.3%	15.4%	1.00							
2. Ex-U.S. equity	9.9	18.8	0.71	1.00						
3. U.S. fixed income	10.1	6.7	0.25	0.12	1.00					
4. Ex-U.S. fixed income	9.9	5.9	0.22	0.30	0.74	1.00				
5. Private equity	15.7	15.3	0.18	0.40	−0.23	0.13	1.00			
6. Real estate	7.8	5.5	0.02	0.34	−0.05	0.21	0.32	1.00		
7. Natural resources	15.3	10.3	0.43	0.38	0.09	0.08	0.34	−0.46	1.00	
8. Hedge funds	17.4	7.2	0.68	0.55	0.22	0.19	0.20	−0.18	0.46	1.00

Note: Natural Resources series covers the 1987–2003 period.
Source: UBS Global Asset Management.

data suggest that *alternative investments* is a label of convenience for a quite heterogeneous array of investments that may more appropriately be treated as distinct asset classes. The highest correlation of an alternative asset class with a traditional asset class, 0.68 for hedge funds with U.S. equity, was still well below the level (1.0) at which no diversification benefits would exist. In summary, at least these data suggest potentially meaningful diversification benefits from exposure to alternative asset classes. One concern for many investors, however, is the availability of resources to directly or indirectly research investment in these groups. Information for publicly traded equities and bonds is more widely available than for private equity, for example, and indexed investment vehicles for alternative asset groups are often lacking. Thus, some investors may face an internal resource constraint limiting investment in alternative assets. Furthermore, the fees and related expenses incurred in many alternative investments are often relatively steep.

5. THE STEPS IN ASSET ALLOCATION

In establishing a strategic asset allocation, an investment manager must specify a set of asset-class weights to produce a portfolio that satisfies the return and risk objectives and constraints as stated in the investment policy statement. With the specification and listing of the IPS-permissible asset classes in hand, our focus is on understanding the process for establishing and maintaining an appropriate asset allocation. Most organizations undertake this process regularly in **asset allocation reviews.** This section outlines the steps to follow during the review process.[30]

The procedure outlined includes liabilities in the analysis. An asset-only approach can be considered a special case in which liabilities equal zero.

[30]The steps laid out in Exhibit 5-7 roughly follow the portfolio construction, monitoring, and revision process laid out in Exhibit 1-1 in Chapter 1. The process in Exhibit 5-7 is truncated, however, because it terminates with the asset allocation decision, implementation, and evaluation rather than proceeding to the optimization of each of the subportfolios (e.g., of fixed income, equity, real estate).

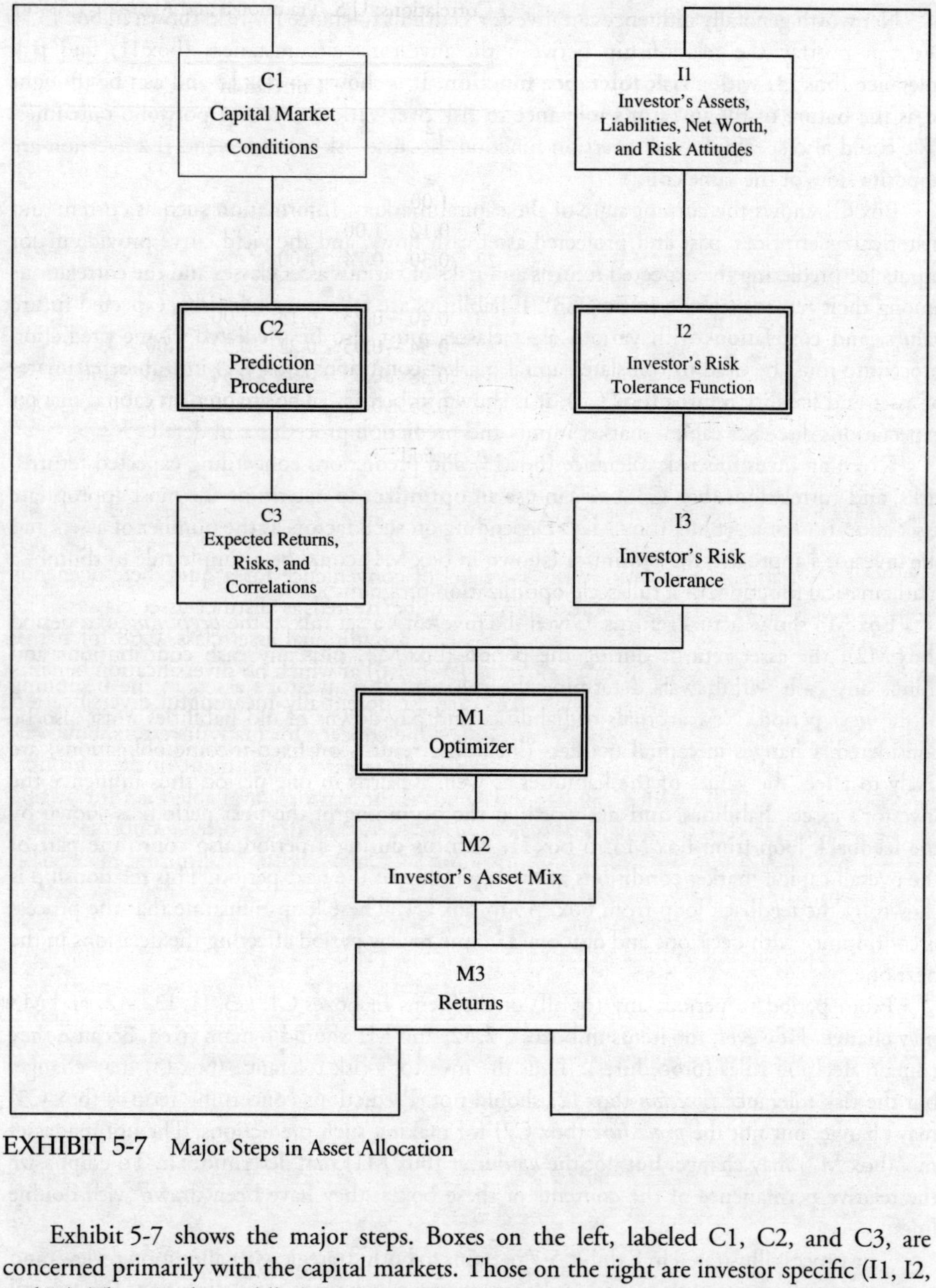

EXHIBIT 5-7 Major Steps in Asset Allocation

Exhibit 5-7 shows the major steps. Boxes on the left, labeled C1, C2, and C3, are concerned primarily with the capital markets. Those on the right are investor specific (I1, I2, and I3). Those in the middle (M1, M2, and M3) bring together aspects of the capital markets and the investor's circumstances to determine the investor's asset mix and its performance. The asset allocation review process begins at the top of the diagram and proceeds downward. Then the outcomes (M3) provide feedback to both the capital market–and investor-related steps at the next asset allocation review.

Box I1 shows factors that determine risk tolerance—the current values of assets and, if applicable, liabilities (or quasi-liabilities); net worth (assets minus liabilities); and the investor's innate attitude to risk (conservatism).

Net worth generally influences an investor's current tolerance for risk, shown in box I3.[31] We can portray the relationship between the investor's circumstances (box I1) and risk tolerance (box I3) with a **risk tolerance function.** It is shown in box I2 and can be thought of as the nature of the investor's tolerance to risk over various levels of portfolio outcomes. (We could also speak of a risk-aversion function, because risk tolerance and risk aversion are opposite sides of the same coin.)

Box C1 shows the current state of the capital markets. Information such as current and historical asset prices, past and projected asset cash flows, and the yield curve provide major inputs for predicting the expected returns and risks of various asset classes and the correlations among their returns (shown in box C3). If liabilities are relevant, their risks, expected future values, and correlations with various asset classes must also be predicted. Some prediction procedure must be used to translate capital market conditions (box C1) into these estimates of asset and liability returns (box C3); it is shown in box C2. The chapter on capital market expectations discusses capital market inputs and prediction procedures in detail.

Given an investor's risk tolerance (box I3) and predictions concerning expected returns, risks, and correlations (box C3), we can use an **optimizer** to determine the most appropriate asset allocation or asset mix (box M2). Depending on such factors as the number of assets and the investor's approach, the optimizer (shown in box M1) could be a simple rule of thumb, a mathematical function, or a full-scale optimization program.

Box M3 shows actual returns. Given the investor's asset mix at the *beginning* of a period (box M2), the asset returns during the period (box M3) plus any cash contributions and minus any cash withdrawals determine the values of the investor's assets at the beginning of the *next* period. New accruals of liabilities and pay-downs of old liabilities must also be considered. Changes in capital markets (including returns on fixed-income obligations) are likely to affect the values of the liabilities as well. Returns in one period thus influence the investor's assets, liabilities, and net worth at the beginning of the next period, as shown by the feedback loop from box M3 to box I1. Returns during a period also constitute part of the overall capital market conditions at the beginning of the next period. This relationship is shown by the feedback loop from box M3 to box C1. These loops illustrate that the process is continuous, with decisions and outcomes in one review period affecting the decisions in the next one.

From period to period, any (or all) of the items in boxes C1, C3, I1, I3, M2, and M3 may change. However, the items in boxes C2, I2, and M1 should remain fixed, because they contain decision rules (procedures). Thus the investor's risk tolerance (box I3) may change, but the risk tolerance *function* (box I2) should not. Predictions concerning returns (box C3) may change, but not the *procedure* (box C2) for making such predictions. The optimal asset mix (box M2) may change, but not the *optimizer* (box M1) that determines it. To emphasize the relative permanence of the contents of these boxes, they have been drawn with double lines.

The process illustrated in Exhibit 5-7 pertains to both strategic asset allocation reviews and tactical asset allocation if the investor chooses to actively manage asset allocation. For tactical asset allocation, the focus is on the impact of capital market conditions on short-term capital market expectations (box C3), possibly resulting in short-term asset allocation adjustments. The main attention is on the prediction procedure (C1) in a competitive marketplace. By

---

[31] Even when the investor's risk tolerance function is such that changes in net worth do not change his or her risk tolerance, we can still show a link between box I1 and box I3 because new circumstances (or even the process of aging) may alter an investor's risk attitudes.

contrast, a strategic asset allocation considers only the effects, if any, of capital market conditions on long-term capital market expectations.

When all the steps discussed in the previous section are performed with careful analysis (formal or informal), the process may be called **integrated asset allocation.** This term is intended to indicate that all major aspects have been included in a consistent manner. If liabilities are relevant, they are integrated into the analysis. If they are not, the procedure still integrates aspects of capital markets, the investor's circumstances and preferences, and the like. Moreover, each review is based on conditions at the time—those in the capital markets and those of the investor. Thus the process is dynamic as well as integrated.

In the next section, we discuss the optimizer (box M1): the procedure we use to select an asset allocation for an investor.

6. OPTIMIZATION

A critical step in strategic asset allocation is the procedure we use for converting the inputs to a specific recommended strategic asset allocation. Much of the research by practitioners and academics alike has focused on developing and refining a variety of procedures. Many of the most important established procedures have a quantitative flavor, reflecting not only the advances of modern portfolio theory but also the need for many institutional investors to document relatively objective procedures. Some investment advisers, particularly those serving an individual investor clientele, may use a qualitative approach based on experience. In fact, nearly all professional investors apply judgment in making recommendations. In the following, we examine the major procedures in use today, beginning with one of the most well established.

6.1. The Mean–Variance Approach

Mean–variance analysis provided the first, and still important, quantitative approach to strategic asset allocation. As with all approaches that we will discuss, a strategic asset allocation suggested by mean–variance analysis should be subjected to professional judgment before adoption.

6.1.1. The Efficient Frontier

According to mean–variance theory, in determining a strategic asset allocation an investor should choose from among the efficient portfolios consistent with that investor's risk tolerance. Efficient portfolios make efficient use of risk; they offer the maximum expected return for their level of variance or standard deviation of return.

Efficient portfolios plot graphically on the **efficient frontier,** which is part of the **minimum-variance frontier** (MVF). Each portfolio on the minimum-variance frontier represents the portfolio with the smallest variance of return for its level of expected return. The graph of a minimum-variance frontier has a turning point (its leftmost point) that represents the **global minimum-variance** (GMV) portfolio. The GMV portfolio has the smallest variance of all minimum-variance portfolios. The portion of the minimum-variance frontier beginning with and continuing above the GMV portfolio is the efficient frontier. Exhibit 5-8 illustrates these concepts using standard deviation (the positive square root of variance) for the *x*-axis because the units of standard deviation are easy to interpret.

Once we have identified an efficient portfolio with the desired combination of expected return and variance, we must determine that portfolio's asset-class weights. To do so, we use

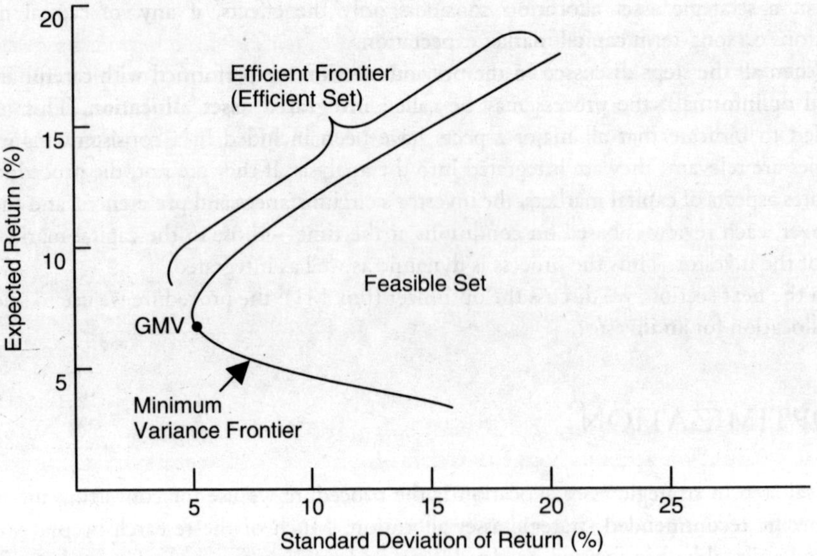

EXHIBIT 5-8 The Efficient Frontier

mean–variance optimization (MVO).[32] There is a structure to minimum-variance frontiers and consequently to the solutions given by optimizers. Understanding that structure not only makes us more-informed users of optimizers but can also be helpful in practice.

6.1.1.1. The Unconstrained MVF The simplest optimization places no constraints on asset-class weights except that the weights sum to 1. We call this form an **unconstrained optimization,** yielding the unconstrained minimum-variance frontier. In this case, the Black (1972) two-fund theorem states that the asset weights of any minimum-variance portfolio are a linear combination of the asset weights of any other two minimum-variance portfolios. In an unconstrained optimization, therefore, we need only determine the weights of two minimum-variance portfolios to know the weights of any other minimum-variance portfolio.

For example, in a three-asset-class optimization, if we determine that one minimum-variance portfolio has weights (80 percent, 15 percent, 5 percent) with an expected return of 10.5 percent and that a second has weights (40 percent, 40 percent, 20 percent) with an expected return of 7.4 percent, we can trace out the entire minimum-variance frontier.[33] To find the weights of the minimum-variance portfolio with an expected return of 9.57 percent, for example, we specify the equation

$$9.57 = 10.5w + 7.4(1 - w)$$

[32]MVOs come in many varieties. Besides special-purpose software, Microsoft Excel with the Solver add-in is a powerful tool for computing the minimum-variance frontier as described in a variety of books and Web-available sources. For example, see Benninga (2000) for financial modeling with Excel.

[33]The expression (80%, 15%, 5%) is a compact way of indicating that the weights on the first, second, and third asset classes are 80 percent, 15 percent, and 5 percent, respectively.

where w is the weight in the 10.5%-expected-return portfolio and $(1 - w)$ is the weight in the 7.4%-expected-return portfolio. We find that $w = 0.70$ and $(1 - w) = 0.30$. For each asset class, we use 0.70 and 0.30 to take a weighted average of the asset class's weights in the two minimum-variance portfolios; doing so gives us the weight of the asset class in the 9.57 percent expected-return portfolio:

$$\begin{aligned} \text{Weight of Asset Class 1:} &\quad 0.70(80\%) + 0.30(40\%) = 68.00\% \\ \text{Weight of Asset Class 2:} &\quad 0.70(15\%) + 0.30(40\%) = 22.50\% \\ \text{Weight of Asset Class 3:} &\quad 0.70(5\%) + 0.30(20\%) = 9.50\% \end{aligned}$$

We check that 68% + 22.5% + 9.5% = 100%. To summarize, after determining the asset-class weights and expected returns of two minimum-variance portfolios, we took a desired expected return level (9.57 percent), which we set equal to a weighted average of the expected returns on the two portfolios. This equation had a unique solution, giving two weights (0.70 and 0.30). We applied those two weights to the known asset-class weights of the two minimum-variance portfolios to find the weights of the 9.57 percent expected-return portfolio (68.0 percent, 22.5 percent, 9.5 percent).

6.1.1.2. The Sign-Constrained MVF: The Case Most Relevant to Strategic Asset Allocation The Black theorem is helpful background for the case of optimization that is most relevant to practice, MVO, including the constraints that the asset-class weights be non-negative and sum to 1. We call this approach a **sign-constrained optimization** because it excludes negative weights, and its result is the sign-constrained minimum-variance frontier. A negative weight would imply that the asset class is to be sold short. In a strategic asset allocation context, an allocation with a negative asset-class weight would generally be irrelevant. Accordingly, we focus on sign-constrained optimization. In addition to satisfying non-negativity constraints, the structure we describe here also applies when we place an upper limit on one or more asset-class weights.

The constraint against short sales restricts choice. By the nature of a sign-constrained optimization, each asset class in a minimum-variance portfolio is held in either positive weight or zero weight. But an asset class with a zero weight in one minimum-variance portfolio may appear with a positive weight in another minimum-variance portfolio at a different expected return level. This observation leads to the concept of corner portfolios.

Adjacent **corner portfolios** define a segment of the minimum-variance frontier within which (1) portfolios hold identical assets and (2) the rate of change of asset weights in moving from one portfolio to another is constant. As the minimum-variance frontier passes through a corner portfolio, an asset weight either changes from zero to positive or from positive to zero. The GMV portfolio, however, is included as a corner portfolio irrespective of its asset weights.

Corner portfolios allow us to create other minimum-variance portfolios. For example, suppose we have a corner portfolio with an expected return of 8 percent and an adjacent corner portfolio with expected return of 10 percent. The asset weights of *any* minimum-variance portfolio with expected return between 8 and 10 percent is a positive weighted average of the asset weights in the 8 percent and 10 percent expected-return corner portfolios. *In a sign-constrained optimization, the asset weights of any minimum-variance portfolio are a positive linear combination of the corresponding weights in the two adjacent corner portfolios that bracket it in terms of expected return (or standard deviation of return).* The foregoing statement is the key observation about the structure of a sign-constrained optimization; we may call it the **corner portfolio theorem.** Corner portfolios are generally relatively few in number. Knowing the

EXHIBIT 5-9 U.K. Institutional Investor Capital Market Expectations

	Asset Class	Expected Return	Standard Deviation	Correlation 1	2	3	4	5	6
1	U.K. Equities	10.0%	15%	1.00					
2	Ex-U.K. Equities	8.0	12	0.76	1.00				
3	Intermediate Bonds	4.0	7	0.35	0.04	1.00			
4	Long-Term Bonds	4.5	8	0.50	0.30	0.87	1.00		
5	International Bonds	5.0	9	0.24	0.36	0.62	0.52	1.00	
6	Real Estate	7.0	10	0.30	0.25	−0.05	−0.02	0.20	1.00

composition of the corner portfolios allows us to compute the weights of any portfolio on the minimum-variance frontier.

We can illustrate these concepts using the data in Exhibit 5-9, which gives hypothetical inputs to a sign-constrained optimization. A U.K. institutional investor is developing a strategic asset allocation among six asset classes: domestic (U.K.) equities, international (ex-U.K.) equities, domestic intermediate- and long-term bonds, international bonds, and real estate. The investor cannot sell securities short or buy on margin. Later we illustrate the effects of changing the expectations for the asset classes in Exhibit 5-9.

Exhibit 5-10 illustrates the efficient frontier based on the expectations in Exhibit 5-9. Only the efficient portion of the minimum-variance frontier is relevant for the investor's asset allocation decision.

Exhibit 5-10 shows that in this case, seven corner portfolios provide the information needed to trace the efficient frontier. Exhibit 5-11 provides information on their composition.[34]

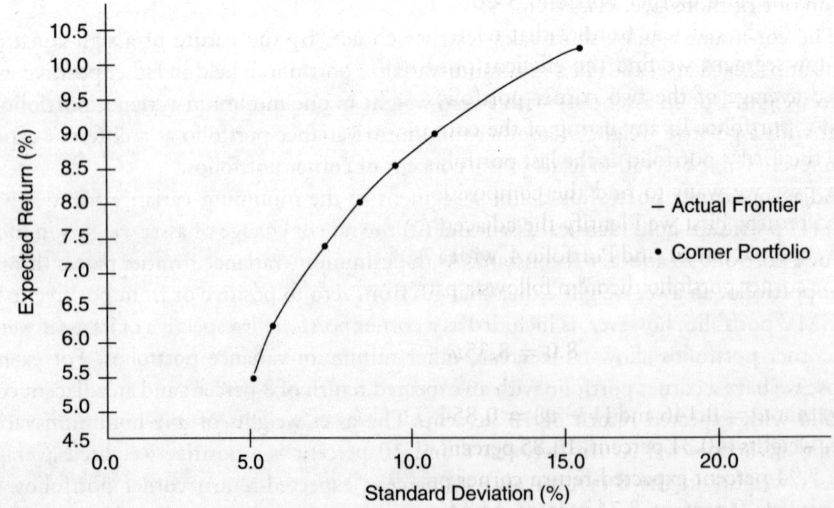

EXHIBIT 5-10 An Efficient Frontier Showing Corner Portfolios

[34]Various algorithms are available for computing the weights of the corner portfolios and the sign-constrained minimum-variance frontier more generally. The first was Markowitz's (1959) critical

EXHIBIT 5-11 U.K. Institutional Investor Corner Portfolios

Corner Portfolio Number	Expected Return	Standard Deviation	Sharpe Ratio	Asset Class (Portfolio Weight) 1	2	3	4	5	6
1	10.00%	15.00%	0.53	100.00%	0.00%	0.00%	0.00%	0.00%	0.00%
2	8.86	11.04	0.62	61.90	0.00	0.00	0.00	0.00	38.10
3	8.35	9.80	0.65	40.31	13.85	0.00	0.00	0.00	45.83
4	7.94	8.99	0.66	32.53	14.30	0.00	0.00	8.74	44.44
5	7.30	7.82	0.68	19.93	21.09	16.85	0.00	0.00	42.13
6	6.13	5.94	0.70	0.00	26.61	37.81	0.00	0.00	35.58
7	5.33	5.37	0.62	0.00	13.01	59.94	0.00	0.00	27.06

We also report the corner portfolios' expected returns and standard deviations of returns, as well as their Sharpe ratios (a measure of risk-adjusted performance) assuming a 2 percent risk-free rate.

Corner Portfolio 1 represents a portfolio 100 percent invested in the highest-expected-return asset class, U.K. equities. The highest-expected-return asset class generally appears as the first corner portfolio. Moving along the efficient frontier from Corner Portfolio 1 to lower levels of expected return, we reach Corner Portfolio 2, which contains real estate. Any efficient portfolio with expected return between that of Corner Portfolio 1 (i.e., 10.00 percent) and that of Corner Portfolio 2 (i.e., 8.86 percent) holds U.K. equities and real estate, because Corner Portfolio 2 does, and such an "in-between" portfolio would be a weighted average of Corner Portfolio 1 and Corner Portfolio 2. Corner Portfolio 3, with an expected return of 8.35 percent, contains ex-U.K. equities in addition to U.K. equities and real estate. Therefore, any efficient portfolio with expected return between that of Corner Portfolio 2 (i.e., 8.86 percent) and that of Corner Portfolio 3 (i.e., 8.35 percent) holds U.K. equities, ex-U.K. equities, and real estate, because Corner Portfolio 3 does. Each pair of adjacent corner portfolios defines a segment of the efficient frontier that relates to a specific interval for expected returns, and within the segment we find the efficient portfolio for a given level of expected return as a weighted average of the two corner portfolios defining the segment. Corner Portfolio 7 is the GMV portfolio. In any listing of the corner portfolios of an efficient frontier, we always include the GMV portfolio as the last portfolio.

Suppose we want to find the composition of the efficient portfolio with an 8 percent expected return. First we identify the adjacent corner portfolios as Portfolio 3, with an 8.35 percent expected return, and Portfolio 4, with a 7.94 percent expected return. The arithmetic in using the corner portfolio theorem follows a pattern familiar from the Black theorem example:

$$8.0 = 8.35w + 7.94(1 - w)$$

We find that $w = 0.146$ and $(1 - w) = 0.854$. The 8.35 percent expected-return corner portfolio has weights (40.31 percent, 13.85 percent, 0 percent, 0 percent, 0 percent, 45.83 percent) and the 7.94 percent expected-return corner portfolio has weights (32.53 percent, 14.30 percent, 0 percent, 0 percent, 8.74 percent, 44.44 percent). An efficient portfolio with an 8 percent

line algorithm; see Sharpe (2000) and www.stanford.edu/~wfsharpe/for details. We thank Michael Kishinevsky for providing us with a spreadsheet based on the critical-line algorithm that reports corner portfolio weights.

expected return will have weights of 0.146 × (40.31%, 13.85%, 0%, 0%, 0%, 45.83%) + 0.854 × (32.53%, 14.30%, 0%, 0%, 8.74%, 44.44%) = (33.67%, 14.23%, 0%, 0%, 7.46%, 44.64%).[35] The 8 percent-expected-return efficient portfolio includes U.K. equities (33.67 percent), ex-U.K. equities (14.23 percent), international bonds (7.46 percent), and real estate (44.64 percent); intermediate and long-term bonds are not in the portfolio.

What is the standard deviation of return on the 8 percent expected-return efficient portfolio? We know that it must lie between 9.80 percent (the standard deviation of the 8.35 percent expected-return corner portfolio) and 8.99 percent (the standard deviation of the 7.94 percent expected-return corner portfolio). Using the correlations from Exhibit 5-9, we could compute the standard deviation exactly using expressions for portfolio variance given in any investment text. We can also find the approximate standard deviation of the 8 percent expected-return efficient portfolio by taking a weighted average of the adjacent corner portfolios' standard deviations of 9.80 percent and 8.99 percent, using the weights of 0.146 and 0.854 computed earlier: 0.146(9.80) + 0.854(8.99) = 9.1%. The efficient frontier bows out toward the left as shown in Exhibit 5-10, reflecting less-than-perfect positive correlation between corner portfolios. As a result, the actual standard deviation of the 8 percent expected-return efficient portfolio will be slightly less than 9.11 percent. The linear approximation just illustrated provides a quick approximation (and upper limit) for the standard deviation; we also can apply this approximation in other cases in which we calculate efficient portfolios using the corner portfolio theorem.

EXAMPLE 5-8 Identifying Asset-Class Weights in Efficient Portfolios

Using the information given in Exhibit 5-11, answer the following questions:

1. What is the maximum weight of long-term bonds in any portfolio on the efficient frontier?
2. What are the asset-class weights in an efficient portfolio with an expected return of 7 percent?
3. Which asset class is most important in the 7 percent expected-return efficient portfolio?
4. Explain your answer to Part 3.

Solution to Problem 1: The maximum weight of long-term bonds is 0 percent because long-term bonds do not appear with a positive weight in any of the corner portfolios, and any efficient portfolio can be represented as a weighted average of corner portfolios.

Solution to Problem 2: First we identify the adjacent corner portfolios as Corner Portfolio 5 (with a 7.30 percent expected return) and Corner Portfolio 6 (with a 6.13 percent

[35]The compact notation 0.146× (40.31%, 13.85%, 0%, 0%, 0%, 45.83%) means that we multiply each element in the parenthetical list (vector) by 0.146.

expected return). From the corner portfolio theorem, it follows that

$$7.0 = 7.30w + 6.13(1 - w)$$

We find that $w = 0.744$ and $(1 - w) = 0.256$. The detailed arithmetic follows:

Weight of U.K. equities	$0.744(19.93\%) + 0.256(0\%)$	$= 14.83\%$
Weight of ex-U.K. equities	$0.744(21.09\%) + 0.256(26.61\%)$	$= 22.50\%$
Weight of intermediate bonds	$0.744(16.85\%) + 0.256(37.81\%)$	$= 22.22\%$
Weight of long-term bonds	$0.744(0\%) + 0.256(0\%)$	$= 0\%$
Weight of international bonds	$0.744(0\%) + 0.256(0\%)$	$= 0\%$
Weight of real estate	$0.744(42.13\%) + 0.256(35.58\%)$	$= 40.45\%$

As an arithmetic check, $14.83\% + 22.50\% + 22.22\% + 0\% + 0\% + 40.45\% = 100\%$.

Solution to Problem 3: Real estate (Asset Class 6) with a weight of more than 40 percent appears as the dominant holding in the 7 percent expected-return efficient portfolio.

Solution to Problem 4: Real estate is the first or second most important holding in all but the first corner portfolio. Because of its forecasted low correlations with other asset classes (including negative correlations with domestic bonds), real estate brings strong risk-reduction benefits, given this investor's estimates for the MVO inputs. Identifying the asset classes in the GMV portfolio gives a useful indication of the asset classes whose combination of standard deviations and correlations effectively diversify risk. Here those classes are ex-U.K. equities, intermediate-term bonds, and real estate.

As mentioned earlier, investors sometimes place an upper limit on one or more asset-class weights in addition to constraining asset-class weights to be non-negative. For example, the sign-constrained efficient portfolios represented by Exhibit 5-11 and discussed in Example 5-8 have relatively high weights on real estate. If the investor were uncomfortable with a weight on real estate above 15 percent, we could rerun the optimization with a new constraint limiting real estate holdings to no more than 15 percent. The result would be the efficient frontier subject to the new set of constraints, and again it would be represented by a set of corner portfolios.

6.1.2. The Importance of the Quality of Inputs

A limitation of the mean–variance approach is that its recommended asset allocations are highly sensitive to small changes in inputs and, therefore, to estimation error. In its impact on the results of a mean–variance approach to asset allocation, estimation error in expected returns has been estimated to be roughly 10 times as important as estimation error in variances and 20 times as important as estimation error in covariances.[36] Best and Grauer (1991) demonstrate that a small increase in the expected return of one of the portfolio's assets can force half of the assets from the portfolio. Thus *the most important inputs in mean–variance optimization are the expected returns.* Unfortunately, mean returns are also the most difficult input to estimate.

[36]See Ziemba (2003, p. 12).

The following example illustrates the extreme weights that may result from MVO and shows the limitations of using unadjusted historical return distribution parameter estimates as inputs. Exhibit 5-12 presents the historical average annual return, standard deviation, and correlation coefficients across five equity markets from 1992 to 2003. Using these as inputs for MVO, Exhibit 5-13 presents the resulting optimal allocations along the frontier. The *y*-axis shows the asset-class weights in a particular portfolio on the efficient frontier. The *x*-axis runs from 0 to 100 percent and identifies the efficient portfolio by standard deviation: The position of 0 represents the standard deviation of the GMV portfolio and the position of 100 the standard deviation of the highest-mean-return asset class, the Dow Jones Global Index (DJGI) Americas, which is the rightmost point on the efficient frontier without short sales. The position of 50 percent is the midpoint in terms of standard deviations between the GMV portfolio and DJGI Americas. We see that the efficient frontier is dominated by two asset classes: U.K. equity for very low risk efficient portfolios (towards 0 on the *x*-axis) and Americas equity for moderate and high risk efficient portfolios (towards 100 on the *x*-axis). Neither Europe ex-U.K. equity nor Japan equity enter into any efficient portfolio.

Practically, the investor should conduct sensitivity analysis with an emphasis on the effects of different expected return estimates. Another approach, which we present later, involves using the concept of the resampled efficient frontier. Using any approach, we need to apply professional judgment in evaluating results. Chapter 4 provides more information on formulating quality capital market expectations.

6.1.3. Selecting an Efficient Portfolio In his IPS, the investor formulates risk and return objectives. The risk objective reflects the investor's risk tolerance (his capacity to accept risk as a function of both his willingness and ability). If the investor is sensitive to volatility of returns, the investor may quantify his risk objective as a capacity to accept no greater than a

EXHIBIT 5-12 Historical Average Annual Return, Standard Deviation, and Correlation Coefficients: 1992–2003[37]

	Average Return	Standard Deviation	Corr. w/DJGI Americas TR	Corr. w/DJGI Asia Pacific ex-Japan TR	Corr. w/DJGI Europe ex-U.K.	Corr. w/DJGI Japan TR USD	Corr. w/DJGI U.K. TR USD
DJGI Americas TR	11.87%	18.83%	1.000	0.641	0.747	0.393	0.778
DJGI Asia Pacific ex-Japan TR	11.21	37.03	0.641	1.000	0.584	0.444	0.599
DJGI Europe ex-U.K.	11.04	21.58	0.747	0.584	1.000	0.369	0.768
DJGI Japan TR USD	3.19	33.66	0.393	0.444	0.369	1.000	0.351
DJGI U.K. TR USD	9.58	17.41	0.778	0.599	0.768	0.351	1.000

Note: TR = total return, USD = in U.S. dollar terms.

[37] Correlations are calculated using monthly data.

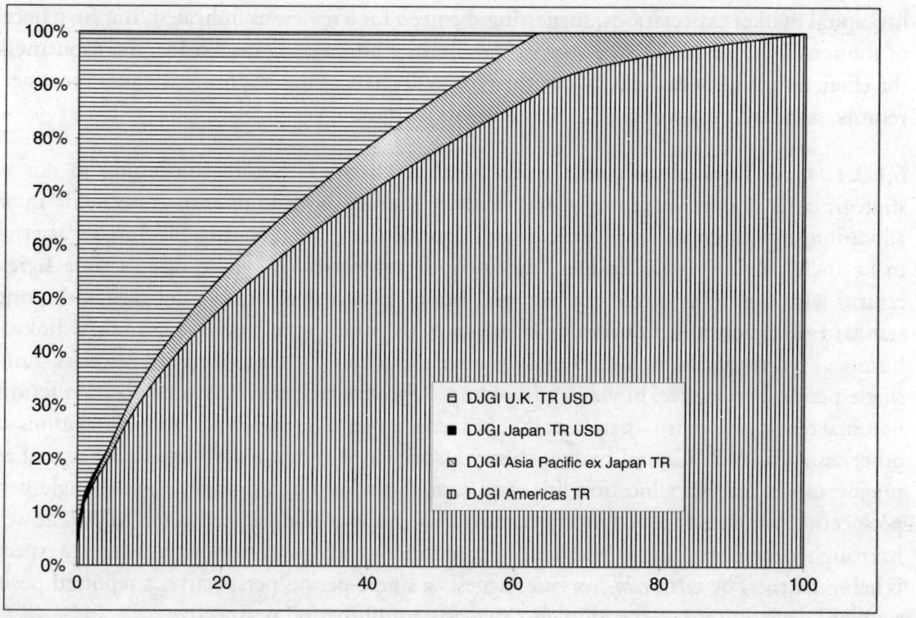

EXHIBIT 5-13 Efficient Portfolio Weights Using Raw Historical Mean Returns
Note: On the *x*-axis, zero represents the GMV portfolio's standard deviation and 100 represents the highest-mean-return asset class's standard deviation. The *y*-axis shows asset class weights. The in-figure legend is a key to regions, starting from the topmost at the zero-SD point; Asia Pacific ex-Japan appears only near zero on the *x*-axis

9 percent average standard deviation of return, for example. Given this type of information, how might an investor use MVO to select an asset allocation?

Let us use the data in Exhibit 5-11 and the results of Example 5-8 to frame our discussion. Suppose the investor's return objective is 7 percent a year. The 7 percent expected-return efficient portfolio identified in Example 5-8 has a standard deviation of return of less than 7.82 percent (7.82 is the standard deviation of Corner Portfolio 5 that lies above it), so it satisfies the risk objective. The 7 percent expected-return efficient portfolio also has the highest Sharpe ratio among the risk-objective-consistent portfolios that satisfy the investor's return objective. Another efficient portfolio to consider is that represented by the fourth corner portfolio with an expected return of 7.94 percent and a standard deviation (8.99 percent) just within the allowable range. That portfolio includes exposure to an additional asset class, international bonds, as do the other efficient portfolios with expected returns above 7.30 percent up to and including 7.94 percent. Indeed, efficient portfolios with expected returns ranging from 7.00 percent to 7.94 percent are all consistent with the stated risk and return objectives, and we could compute the weights of any of those portfolios using the information from Exhibit 5-11. In some cases, we may have additional information from the IPS that permits us to narrow the choices or select the most appropriate choice.

The results of a mean–variance optimizer may prompt an investor to revise his saving and spending plans, or reconsider his return and risk objectives in light of his circumstances. For example, suppose the investor's return objective was 8.25 percent in the case just examined, with all else unchanged. No efficient portfolio exists that is consistent with the investor's stated 8.25 percent return objective, his risk objective of a standard deviation of 9 percent or less, and his capital market expectations, suggesting the need for a review as indicated. But first, because of the sensitivity of MVO to errors in the inputs, the investor should test the robustness of the efficient frontier asset-class allocations to small changes in the point estimates for expected returns, standard deviations, and expected correlations.

6.1.3.1. Cash Equivalents and Capital Market Theory Before continuing to our next strategic asset allocation example, we need to address the role of cash equivalents in asset allocation. Practice varies concerning cash equivalents (e.g., Treasury bills) as an asset class to be included in MVO. From a multiperiod perspective, T-bills exhibit a time series of returns with variability, as do equities, and can be included as a risky asset class with positive standard deviation and nonzero correlations with other asset classes. Optimizers linked to historical return databases always include a series such as T-bills as a risky asset class. From a single-period perspective, buying and holding a T-bill to maturity provides a certain return in nominal terms—a return, therefore, that has zero standard deviation and zero correlations with other asset classes.[38] Capital market theory associated with concepts such as the capital asset pricing model, capital allocation line, and capital market line originally took a single-period perspective, which is retained in this reading. The multiperiod perspective in MVO, however, has roughly equal standing in practice.[39] From the context, it will be obvious which perspective is being taken. The term *risk-free rate* suggests a single-period perspective; a reported positive standard deviation for cash equivalents suggests a multiperiod perspective.

When we assume a nominally risk-free asset and take a single-period perspective, mean–variance theory points to choosing the asset allocation represented by the perceived tangency portfolio *if the investor can borrow or lend at the risk-free rate*. (Borrowing in this context means using margin to buy risky assets, resulting in a negative weight on the risk-free asset.) The tangency portfolio is the perceived highest-Sharpe-ratio efficient portfolio. The investor would then use margin to leverage the position in the tangency portfolio to achieve a higher expected return than the tangency portfolio, or split money between the tangency portfolio and the risk-free asset to achieve a lower risk position than the tangency portfolio. The investor's portfolio would fall on the **capital allocation line,** which describes the combinations of expected return and standard deviation of return available to an investor from combining his or her optimal portfolio of risky assets with the risk-free asset. Many investors, however, face restrictions against buying risky assets on margin. Even without a formal constraint against using margin, a negative position in cash equivalents may be inconsistent with an investor's liquidity needs. Leveraging the tangency portfolio may be practically irrelevant for many investors.

We can illustrate the issue using our example of an investor with a 7 percent return objective. The perceived highest-Sharpe-ratio efficient portfolio in our example, the tangency portfolio, is close to Corner Portfolio 6 in Exhibit 5-11, assuming a 2 percent risk-free rate (see the column on Sharpe ratios in that exhibit). However, Corner Portfolio 6, with an expected return of 6.13, does not satisfy the investor's return objective. By assumption, the investor cannot use margin. Therefore, the investor cannot use the tangency portfolio to meet his or her return objective. Instead, the investor should choose a portfolio to the right of the tangency point on the efficient frontier.

For a different investor, if the tangency portfolio's expected return exceeds the return objective, the investor might combine the tangency portfolio and the 2 percent risk-free asset

[38]An inflation-indexed discount instrument, if available, would serve a similar role in an analysis performed in real terms.

[39]Note that treating cash equivalents as risky does not overcome the limitations of MVO as a static approach.

to achieve an optimal portfolio. Thus the investor might first check the tangency portfolio's expected return to see whether it exceeds his or her return objective. If so, combining the tangency portfolio with the risk-free asset may be optimal.

Suppose an investor has a short-term liquidity need that is funded appropriately using cash equivalents. Pragmatically, the investor might set aside an amount equal to the present value of the need, then separately determine an appropriate efficient allocation for the balance of his or her wealth. If the money set aside for the liquidity need earns 1.5 percent annually, for example, we use a 1.5 percent discount rate to determine present value.

To illustrate, suppose an investor sets aside 7.5 percent of assets in cash equivalents to meet a one-year-ahead liquidity need. The investor can then perform an MVO over risky assets as in Exhibit 5-11 and apply that allocation to the 92.5 percent balance of his or her total funds. For example, if the investor's total wealth is \$2 million and the investor needs \$150,000 (7.5 percent of \$2 million) to meet the future liquidity need (i.e., \$150,000 is the present value of that need), a 65 percent allocation to equities and 35 percent allocation to bonds will require $0.65(\$2,000,000 - \$150,000) = \$1,202,500$ and $0.35(\$2,000,000 - \$150,000) = \$647,500$, respectively. We "take off the table" the cash equivalents targeted to meet the liquidity requirement in this example. Hence, the return objective (which generally relates to longer-term horizons) must be determined against the remaining asset base of $\$2,000,000 - \$150,000 = \$1,850,000$. (The investor may still allocate some part of that remaining asset base to cash equivalents.)

In Example 5-9, a different investor formulates different expectations about the asset classes in Exhibit 5-9. Note that a change in inputs produces eight corner portfolios rather than seven.

EXAMPLE 5-9 A Strategic Asset Allocation for Ian Thomas

Ian Thomas is a 53-year-old comptroller for a City of London broker. In excellent health and planning to retire in 12 years, Thomas expects pension income from two sources to supply approximately 60 percent of his annual retirement income needs.

The trustees of one of Thomas's favorite charities have approached him for a £150,000 gift that would permit construction to begin on a new building. With his two children now established independently; a home free and clear of debt; an annual salary of £170,000; and a net worth of £2.75 million from savings, investment, and inheritance, Thomas considers himself financially secure. Because of his prospect for a substantial pension, he feels well positioned to make a £150,000 gift to the charity. He has notified the trustees that he will make the £150,000 gift in six months (in a new tax year). Thomas intends to fund the gift entirely from his savings; the charity has requested that the gift be in cash or cash equivalents rather than other securities. His £2.75 million net worth amount includes the £240,000 value of his home. To the extent he undertakes additional real estate investment, he will include the £240,000 as part of the total real estate allocation; he holds the balance of his net worth in securities.

Advised by a financial planner, Thomas has created an IPS. Thomas generally feels comfortable taking thought-out risks and is optimistic about his own and the economy's future. Thomas has shown a definite bias towards equities in his prior investing. Working with his adviser, he has agreed on a set of capital market expectations.[40] The current risk-free rate is 2 percent. Thomas has access to a six-month bank deposit that earns 2 percent.

The following summarizes some key information about Thomas:

Objectives:

- **Return objective.** The return objective is to earn an average 8.5 percent annual return.[41]
- **Risk objectives.** Given his substantial assets and the length of the first stage of his time horizon, Thomas has above-average willingness and ability to take risk, quantified as a capacity to accept a standard deviation of return of 18 percent or less.

Constraints:

- **Liquidity requirements.** Thomas has minimal liquidity requirements outside the planned £150,000 gift.
- **Time horizon.** His investment horizon is multistage, with the first stage being the 12 years remaining to retirement and the second being his retirement years.
- **Tax considerations.** Thomas holds £2.51 million of securities in taxable accounts.[42]

Thomas states that he does not want to borrow (use margin) to purchase risky assets. No substantive relevant legal and regulatory factors or unique circumstances affect his decisions.

The IPS specifies that Mr. Thomas's assets "... shall be diversified to minimize the risk of large losses within any one asset class, investment type, geographic location, or maturity date, which could seriously impair Mr. Thomas's ability to meet his long-term investment objectives." It further states that investment results will be evaluated based on absolute risk-adjusted performance and performance relative to benchmarks given elsewhere in the IPS. Exhibit 5-14 lists Thomas's capital market expectations (in

EXHIBIT 5-14 Thomas's Capital Market Expectations

	Asset Class	Expected Return	Standard Deviation	Correlation 1	2	3	4	5	6
1	U.K. Equities	11.00%	20.0%	1.00					
2	Ex-U.K. Equities	9.00	18.0	0.76	1.00				
3	Intermediate Bonds	4.00	7.0	0.35	0.04	1.00			
4	Long-Term Bonds	4.75	8.0	0.50	0.30	0.87	1.00		
5	International Bonds	5.00	9.5	0.24	0.36	0.62	0.52	1.00	
6	Real Estate	7.00	14.0	0.35	0.25	0.11	0.07	0.12	1.00

[40] In relation to the institutional investor's forecasts in Exhibit 5-9, Thomas's forecasts for the standard deviations of equities, including real estate, are higher; real estate's correlations with intermediate and long-term bonds are also higher, reducing real estate's diversification potential.

[41] We do not present the cash flow considerations that underlie Thomas's return objective, but the return objective is determined on his wealth excluding the cash equivalents set aside to cover his liquidity requirement.

[42] £2,750,000 (net worth) − £240,000 (value of home) = £2,510,000 (securities in taxable accounts).

nominal terms), and Exhibit 5-15 gives results from the sign-constrained MVO based on the inputs in Exhibit 5-14.

EXHIBIT 5-15 Corner Portfolios based on Thomas's Capital Market Expectations

Corner Portfolio Number	Expected Return	Standard Deviation	Sharpe Ratio	Asset Class (Portfolio Weight)					
				1	2	3	4	5	6
1	11.00%	20.00%	0.45	100.00%	0.00%	0.00%	0.00%	0.00%	0.00%
2	10.09	16.84	0.48	77.35	0.00	0.00	0.00	0.00	22.65
3	9.67	15.57	0.49	63.56	6.25	0.00	0.00	0.00	30.19
4	7.92	11.08	0.53	36.19	4.05	0.00	0.00	30.48	29.28
5	6.47	8.21	0.54	11.41	8.29	0.00	31.31	22.36	26.63
6	5.73	7.04	0.53	0.00	17.60	40.67	11.99	6.77	22.96
7	5.43	6.66	0.52	0.00	16.16	60.78	0.00	3.52	19.54
8	4.83	6.33	0.45	0.00	8.34	77.04	0.00	1.17	13.45

Note: Risk-free rate = 2 percent.

1. Based on mean–variance analysis, perform the following tasks.

    A. Determine the strategic asset allocation that is most appropriate for Thomas.
    B. Justify your answer to Part A.
    C. State the amount of net new investment or disinvestment in real estate.

2. Appraise the effectiveness of ex-U.K. equities in diversifying risk given Thomas's expectations.
3. Identify the corner portfolio most likely to be the tangency portfolio and explain its appropriateness for Thomas in selecting an optimal strategic asset allocation.

To make his risk preferences more precise, Thomas undergoes an interview in which he is asked to express preferences among sets of choices involving risky and certain returns. As a result, Thomas's measured risk aversion, R_A, is ascertained to equal 3.

4. Determine the most appropriate asset allocation for Thomas given his measured risk aversion and his return objective, if Thomas had to choose only one portfolio from the eight corner portfolios given in Exhibit 5-15. Contrast that asset allocation to the strategic asset allocation chosen as optimal in Part 1A.

Solution to Problem 1A: The efficient portfolio that satisfies Thomas's return and risk objectives must lie on the portion of the efficient frontier represented between Corner Portfolio 3 (with 9.67 expected return) and Corner Portfolio 4 (with 7.92 percent expected return). Based only on the information given and the IPS, the recommended portfolio is the one that just meets his 8.5 percent return objective. From the corner portfolio theorem, it follows that:

$$8.50 = 9.67w + 7.92(1 - w)$$

We find that the weight on Corner Portfolio 3 is $w = 0.331$ and the weight on Corner Portfolio 4 is $(1 - w) = 0.669$. Therefore,

Weight of U.K. equities	$0.331(63.56\%) + 0.669(36.19\%)$	$= 45.25\%$
Weight of ex-U.K. equities	$0.331(6.25\%) + 0.669(4.05\%)$	$= 4.78\%$
Weight of intermediate bonds	$0.331(0\%) + 0.669(0\%)$	$= 0\%$
Weight of long-term bonds	$0.331(0\%) + 0.669(0\%)$	$= 0\%$
Weight of international bonds	$0.331(0\%) + 0.669(30.48\%)$	$= 20.39\%$
Weight of real estate	$0.331(30.19\%) + 0.669(29.28\%)$	$= 29.58\%$

As an arithmetic check, $45.25\% + 4.78\% + 0\% + 0\% + 20.39\% + 29.58\% = 100\%$.

Solution to Problem 1B: The recommended portfolio:

- Is efficient (i.e., it lies on the efficient frontier).
- Is expected to satisfy his return requirement.
- Is expected to meet his risk objective.
- Has the highest expected Sharpe ratio among the efficient portfolios that meet his return objective.
- Is the most consistent with the IPS statement concerning minimizing losses within any one investment type.

The standard deviation of the recommended asset allocation must be less than that of the third corner portfolio, 15.57, demonstrating that the portfolio meets his risk objective. [More precisely, the standard deviation of the recommendation is slightly less than $0.331(15.57) + 0.669(11.08) = 12.57$, the linear approximation.] Thomas is also concerned with absolute risk-adjusted performance. We see from Exhibit 5-15 that the Sharpe ratio increases as we move from Corner Portfolios 1 through 5, and the recommended portfolio is closer to Corner Portfolio 5 than any other efficient portfolio satisfying Thomas's return objective.

Solution to Problem 1C: The amount Thomas needs to set aside today is the present value of £150,000 at 2 percent for one-half of one year: $(£150{,}000)/(1.02)^{0.5} = £148{,}522$. The recommended portfolio has a pound allocation to real estate of $29.58\% \times (£2{,}750{,}000 - £148{,}522) = £769{,}517$. Netting the value of his home, £ 240,000, the recommended net new investment in real estate is £529,517.

Solution to Problem 2: Despite the fact that ex-U.K. equities have the second-highest standard deviation of return (18 percent), ex-U.K. equities appear with substantial weight in the efficient portfolio that has the smallest standard deviation of return, the GMV portfolio, as well as in other expected low-risk, efficient portfolios. Thus ex-U.K. equities appear to be an effective risk diversifier.

Solution to Problem 3: The tangency portfolio is the efficient portfolio with the highest Sharpe ratio. Corner Portfolio 5, with the highest Sharpe ratio (0.54) among the corner portfolios, is most likely to be the tangency portfolio. Because it has an expected return below Thomas's return objective, however, and Thomas does not want to use margin, he can ignore that portfolio in determining his strategic asset allocation.

Solution to Problem 4: We determine the risk-adjusted expected returns of the corner portfolios using the expression for risk-adjusted expected return of asset mix m, U_m, where $E(R_m)$ is the mix's expected return, R_A is Thomas's measured risk aversion, and σ_m^2 is the mix's variance of return:

$$\begin{aligned} U_m &= E(R_m) - 0.005R_A\sigma_m^2 \\ &= E(R_m) - 0.005(3)\sigma_m^2 \\ &= E(R_m) - 0.015\sigma_m^2 \end{aligned}$$

Corner Portfolio 1 $U_1 = 11.00 - (0.015)(20.00)^2 = 5.0$

Corner Portfolio 2 $U_2 = 10.09 - (0.015)(16.84)^2 = 5.8$

Corner Portfolio 3 $U_3 = 9.67 - (0.015)(15.57)^2 = 6.0$

Corner Portfolio 4 $U_4 = 7.92 - (0.015)(11.08)^2 = 6.1$

Corner Portfolio 5 $U_5 = 6.47 - (0.015)(8.21)^2 = 5.5$

Corner Portfolio 6 $U_6 = 5.73 - (0.015)(7.04)^2 = 5.0$

Corner Portfolio 7 $U_7 = 5.43 - (0.015)(6.66)^2 = 4.8$

Corner Portfolio 8 $U_8 = 4.83 - (0.015)(6.33)^2 = 4.2$

The corner portfolio with the highest risk-adjusted expected return is Corner Portfolio 4. It does not meet Thomas's 8.5 percent return objective, however. Corner Portfolio 3, with an expected return of 9.67 percent, has the highest risk-adjusted expected return among the corner portfolios that meet his return objective. *If we limit the choices to the eight corner portfolios*, Corner Portfolio 3 is optimal; the strategic asset allocation it represents has approximate weights of 64 percent in U.K. equities, 6 percent in ex-U.K. equities, and 30 percent in real estate.

Note that the strategic asset allocation chosen as optimal in Part 1A lies between Corner Portfolio 3 and Corner Portfolio 4. To evaluate the risk-adjusted expected return of the strategic asset allocation selected in Part 1A, we could use the linear approximation of 12.57 for its standard deviation mentioned in the solution to Part 1B: $8.50 - (0.015)(12.57)^2 = 6.13$. Because the approximation 12.57 is a slight overestimate, the portfolio's risk-adjusted expected return is somewhat above 6.13. The strategic asset allocation selected in Part 1A has a very slightly higher risk-adjusted expected return than either Corner Portfolio 3 or 4 (which is 6.08 to two decimal places).

In Example 5-9, Part 1A, the recommended strategic asset allocation was an efficient portfolio that was expected to *just* meet the return objective. With different capital market expectations and risk-free rates, however, that will not always be the case. For example, the expected return of the highest-Sharpe-ratio efficient portfolio (the tangency portfolio) may exceed the return objective, and if so, it may be optimal for the investor to hold the highest-Sharpe-ratio efficient portfolio in combination with the risk-free asset (as suggested in a capital allocation line analysis). On the other hand, as in Example 5-10, the highest-Sharpe-ratio efficient portfolio's expected return may be below the return objective. Assuming that margin is not allowed, in such cases the highest-Sharpe-ratio portfolio is not optimal for the investor.

EXAMPLE 5-10 A Strategic Asset Allocation for CEFA

CIO Sanjiv Singh is considering the recommendation for CEFA's policy portfolio that he will present at the next meeting of the endowment's trustees. CEFA was established to provide funding to museums in their acquisitions programs as well as to make grants to foster education and research into the fine arts. Its portfolio currently has a value of C$80 million. Although CEFA's long time horizon implies an above-average ability to take risk, its trustees are conservative. Reflecting their below-average willingness to take risk, the trustees have set a relatively conservative spending rate of 4 percent and have expressed a concern about downside risk. Overall, they have characterized CEFA's risk tolerance as average. The following summarizes some key information about CEFA:

Objectives: The overall investment objective of the Canadian Endowment for the Fine Arts is to maintain the endowment's real purchasing power after distributions.

Return Objectives

1. CEFA's assets shall be invested to maximize returns for the level of risk taken.
2. CEFA's assets shall be invested with the objective of earning an average 6.5 percent annual return, reflecting a spending rate of 4 percent, an expected inflation rate of 2 percent, and a 40-basis-point cost of earning investment returns.[43]

Risk Objectives

1. CEFA's portfolio should be structured to maintain diversification levels that are consistent with prudent investment practices.
2. CEFA has a capacity to accept a standard deviation of return of 12 percent or less.
3. CEFA's portfolio should be constructed with consideration of minimizing the probability that the annual portfolio return will fall below CEFA's spending rate.

CEFA has minimal liquidity needs. The IPS further specifies the following permissible asset classes:

- Canadian equities
- Ex-Canada equities
- Canadian bonds (traditional)
- Government of Canada real return bonds (GCRRB)
- International bonds
- Money market instruments rated at least Prime-1 by Moody's Investors Service, A-1+ by Standard & Poor's, or R-1 (middle) by Dominion Bond Rating Service

Exhibit 5-16 gives Singh's capital market forecasts, which the trustees have approved. Cognizant of the sensitivity of mean–variance analysis to expected return estimates, Singh will present to the trustees his approach in developing the Canadian equity expected return estimate of 9.5 percent. Singh employed a variation of the

[43]The calculation is $(1.04)(1.02)(1.004) - 1 = 0.065$ or 6.5 percent.

EXHIBIT 5-16 CEFA's Capital Market Expectations

Asset Class	Expected Return (%)	Standard Deviation (%)	Correlations 1	2	3	4	5
1 Canadian Equities	9.50	18	1.00				
2 Ex-Canada Equities	7.40	15	0.65	1.00			
3 Canadian Bonds	3.80	7	0.25	0.40	1.00		
4 GCRRB	2.70	6	−0.15	0.30	0.75	1.00	
5 International Bonds	4.00	9	0.20	0.45	0.60	0.50	1.00

Gordon growth model expression as given in Grinold and Kroner (2002):

$$r \approx \frac{D}{P} - \Delta S + i + g + \Delta PE$$

where r is the expected rate of return on equity, D/P is the expected dividend yield (expected per-share dividend, D, divided by price per share, P), ΔS is the expected percent change in number of shares outstanding, i is the expected inflation rate, g is the expected real earnings (not earnings per share) growth rate, and ΔPE is the per-period percent change in the P/E multiple. ΔS is negative in the case of net positive share repurchases, so $-\Delta S$ is the "repurchase yield." The term $D/P - \Delta S$ represents the income return, $i + g$ represents the earnings growth return, and ΔPE represents the repricing return.

Singh forecasts a 2.25 percent dividend yield on Canadian equities, based on the S&P/Toronto Stock Exchange Composite Index and a repurchase yield of 1 percent. He forecasts the long-run inflation rate at 2 percent per year. Singh's forecast of real earnings growth is 4 percent, based on a 1-percentage-point premium for corporate growth over his expected Canadian GDP growth rate of 3.0 percent. Singh forecasts a very minor expansion in P/E multiples of 0.25 percent. Thus his expected return prediction is

$$r \approx 2.25\% - (-1.0\%) + 2.0\% + 4.0\% + 0.25\% = 9.5\%$$

Using a similar process Singh developed forecasts for international (ex-Canada) equities. A consultant developed other forecasts for Singh using economic forecasts and approaches that Singh approved. Singh uses the T-bill yield of 2.3 percent for the risk-free rate.

Exhibit 5-17 gives results from the sign-constrained MVO based on the inputs in Exhibit 5-16.

EXHIBIT 5-17 Corner Portfolios Based on CEFA's Capital Market Expectations

Corner Portfolio Number	Expected Return	Standard Deviation	Sharpe Ratio	Asset Class (Portfolio Weight) 1	2	3	4	5
1	9.50%	18.00%	0.400	100.00%	0.00%	0.00%	0.00%	0.00%
2	8.90	15.98	0.413	71.52	28.48	0.00	0.00	0.00
3	8.61	15.20	0.415	67.63	26.30	0.00	0.00	6.07
4	7.24	11.65	0.424	49.46	16.55	23.05	0.00	10.93
5	5.61	7.89	0.419	39.85	1.01	0.00	47.75	11.38
6	5.49	7.65	0.417	38.86	0.00	0.00	50.00	11.14
7	3.61	5.39	0.244	12.94	0.00	0.00	84.60	2.45

Note: Risk-free rate = 2.3 percent.

In consultation with the trustees, Singh has adopted Roy's safety-first criterion for implementing the shortfall risk objective. The safety-first criterion aims to minimize the probability that the portfolio return falls below a threshold level R_L; the safety-first optimal portfolio maximizes the ratio $[E(R_p) - R_L]/\sigma_P$. The higher this ratio for a portfolio, the smaller the probability that the portfolio's return will fall below the threshold level at a given time horizon.

1. Determine and justify the overall most appropriate strategic asset allocation for CEFA using mean–variance analysis.

A trustee has suggested that CEFA adopt the sole objective of minimizing the level of standard deviation of return subject to meeting its return objective.

2. Determine the most appropriate strategic asset allocation if CEFA adopts the trustee's suggested objective.

Solution to Problem 1: Note that we need not consider the portion of the efficient frontier beginning at and extending below Corner Portfolio 5, because the portfolios on it do not satisfy CEFA's 6.5 percent return objective.

Corner Portfolio 4 meets CEFA's return objective and risk objectives. It also appears to be the approximate tangency portfolio, with a higher expected Sharpe ratio than neighboring corner portfolios. This asset allocation appears to be optimal for CEFA; it involves an allocation of approximately 49 percent to Canadian equities, 17 percent to ex-Canadian equities, 23 percent to Canadian bonds, and 11 percent to international bonds. The IPS states a concern for shortfall risk below the spending rate. To evaluate the downside risk of Corner Portfolio 4 according to Roy's safety-first criterion, we compute $(7.24\% - 4\%)/11.65\% = 0.28$. Corner Portfolio 4's standard deviation is near the maximum acceptable to CEFA, so the trustees would not consider higher-standard-deviation portfolios. They might consider lower-standard-deviation portfolios that meet CEFA's return objective, however.

Thus, another portfolio that we might consider is the portfolio that minimizes standard deviation subject to meeting the return objective. To minimize risk *without lowering the Sharpe ratio*, we can combine the tangency portfolio with T-bills to choose a portfolio on CEFA's capital allocation line. (We would lower the Sharpe ratio if we combined Corner Portfolio 4 with Corner Portfolio 5.)

The tangency portfolio (Corner Portfolio 4) has an expected return of 7.24 percent, and the risk-free asset (T-bills) has a nominally certain return of 2.3 percent. Thus to establish the allocation to Corner Portfolio 4 and T-bills, we solve:

$$6.50 = 7.24w + 2.3(1 - w)$$

We find that the weight on Corner Portfolio 4 is $w = 0.85$ and the weight on T-bills is $(1 - w) = 0.15$. Therefore, the optimal allocation that minimizes risk is

Weight of Canadian equities	0.85(49.46%)	=	42.04%
Weight of ex-Canada equities	0.85(16.55%)	=	14.07%
Weight of Canadian bonds	0.85(23.05%)	=	19.59%
Weight of international bonds	0.85(10.93%)	=	9.29%
Weight of T-bills			15.0%

As an arithmetic check, 42.04% + 14.07% + 19.59% + 9.29% + 15.0% = 100%, ignoring rounding. This portfolio has an expected return of 6.5 percent and a standard deviation of return of 9.9 percent (0.85× the tangency's portfolio's standard deviation = 0.85 × 11.65% = 9.90%). As mentioned, it has the same Sharpe ratio as Corner Portfolio 4. The deciding factor is shortfall risk. To evaluate this asset allocation's shortfall risk, we compute (6.5 − 4)/9.9 = 0.25. Because 0.25 is below the value of 0.28 for Corner Portfolio 4, Corner Portfolio 4 (the tangency portfolio) gives the recommended asset allocation for CEFA.

Solution to Problem 2: If the trustee's suggestion were accepted, the portfolio 15 percent invested in T-bills and 85 percent invested in Corner Portfolio 4 (discussed in Part 1) would be optimal for CEFA; that asset allocation meets CEFA's return objective with minimum standard deviation of return.

6.1.4. Extensions to the Mean–Variance Approach

The mean–variance approach has proven readily adaptable to incorporate a number of concerns suggested by practice. Exhibit 5-18 reviews some of these variations on the model under three groupings.

6.2. The Resampled Efficient Frontier

Experience with MVO has often shown that the composition of efficient portfolios is very sensitive to small changes in inputs. Because forecasting returns, volatilities, and correlations is so difficult and subject to substantial estimation error, what confidence can we have that MVO will suggest the best asset allocations for investors?

EXHIBIT 5-18 Selected Extensions to the Mean–Variance Approach

Concern	Adaptation	Source
A. Downside risk	1. Mean–semivariance	Markowitz (1959)
	2. MVO with shortfall constraint	Leibowitz and Henriksson (1989)
	3. MV Surplus Optimization	Leibowitz and Henriksson (1988) Sharpe and Tint (1990) Elton and Gruber (1992)
	4. Safety-first criterion	Roy (1952)
B. Tracking risk relative to benchmark	5. MVO with constraints on asset weights relative to benchmark	Ad hoc practice
	6. Mean–Tracking Error (MTE) Optimization[a]	Roll (1992)
	7. Mean–Variance–Tracking Error (MVTE) optimization[b]	Chow (1995)
C. Changing correlations in times of stress	8. MVO with adjusted correlation matrix	Chow et al. (1999)

[a]This approach optimizes mean return against tracking error (tracking risk) rather than variance.
[b]This approach adds a tracking risk penalty to the MV objective function.

Generally, we have little confidence in the results of a single MVO. In practice, professional investors often rerun an optimization many times using a range of inputs around their point estimates to gauge the results' sensitivity to variation in the inputs. The focus, as mentioned earlier, should be on mean return inputs. Although sensitivity analysis is certainly useful, it is ad hoc. Some researchers have sought to address the problem of MVO's input sensitivity by taking a statistical view of efficiency. Jobson and Korkie (1981) first suggested a statistical perspective, and Michaud (1989, 1998) and Jorion (1992) developed it further.

The Michaud approach to asset allocation is based on a simulation exercise using MVO and a data set of historical returns. Using the sample values of asset classes' means, variances, and covariances as the assumed true population parameters, the simulation generates sets of simulated returns and, for each such set (simulation trial), MVO produces the portfolio weights of a specified number of mean–variance efficient portfolios (which may be called *simulated efficient portfolios*). Information in the simulated efficient portfolios resulting from the simulation trials is integrated into one frontier called the resampled efficient frontier.[44] Generally, a simulated efficient portfolio with a mean return, for example, of 7.8 percent would not match up exactly by mean return with a simulated efficient portfolio from another simulation trial. Numbering simulated efficient portfolios by return rank from lowest to highest, one approach to this problem of integration is to associate simulated efficient portfolios of equivalent return rank. Michaud defines a **resampled efficient portfolio** for a given return rank as the portfolio defined by the average weights on each asset class for simulated efficient portfolios with that return rank. For example, the fifth-ranked resampled efficient portfolio is defined by the average weight on each of the asset classes for the fifth-ranked simulated efficient portfolios in the individual simulation trials. Averaging weights in this fashion preserves the property that portfolio weights sum to 1, but has been challenged on other grounds.[45] The set of resampled efficient portfolios represents the **resampled efficient frontier**.[46]

The portfolios resulting from the resampled efficient frontier approach tend to be more diversified and more stable through time than those on a conventional mean–variance efficient frontier developed from a single optimization. If at least one draw from an asset class's assumed distribution of returns is sufficiently favorable to the asset class so that it appears in a simulated efficient portfolio, the asset class will be represented in the resampled efficient frontier. This observation explains the fact that most or all asset classes are typically represented in the resampled efficient frontier. On the other hand, the resampled efficient frontier approach has been questioned on ground such as the lack of a theoretical underpinning for the method and the relevance of historical return frequency data to current asset market values and equilibrium.[47]

6.3. The Black–Litterman Approach

Fischer Black and Robert Litterman developed another quantitative approach to dealing with the problem of estimation error, which we recall is most serious when it concerns expected returns. Two versions of the Black–Litterman approach exist:

1. *Unconstrained Black–Litterman (UBL) model*. Taking the weights of asset classes in a global benchmark such as MSCI World as a neutral starting point, the asset weights are

[44] The term "resampled" refers to the use of simulation.

[45] See Scherer (2002).

[46] Resampled efficiency is a U.S. patent–protected procedure with worldwide patents pending. New Frontier Advisors, LLC, is the exclusive worldwide licensee.

[47] See Scherer (2002) for a review and critique of the field.

adjusted to reflect the investor's views on the expected returns of asset classes according to a Bayesian procedure that considers the strength of the investor's beliefs. We call this unconstrained Black–Litterman model, or UBL model, because the procedure does not allow non-negativity constraints on the asset-class weights.

2. *Black–Litterman (BL) model*. This approach reverse engineers the expected returns implicit in a diversified market portfolio (a process known as **reverse optimization**) and combines them with the investor's own views on expected returns in a systematic way that takes into account the investor's confidence in his or her views.[48] These view-adjusted expected return forecasts are then used in a MVO with a constraint against short sales and possibly other constraints.

The UBL model is a direct method for selecting an asset allocation. It usually results in small or moderate deviations from the asset-class weights in the benchmark in intuitive ways reflecting the investor's different-from-benchmark expectations. Because the UBL model is anchored to a well-diversified global portfolio, it ensures that the strategic asset allocation recommendation is well diversified. In practice, the UBL model is an improvement on simple MVO because the absence of constraints against short sales in the UBL model usually does not result in unintuitive portfolios (e.g., portfolio with large short positions in asset classes), a common result in unconstrained MVO.

Nevertheless, investors often formally want to recognize such constraints in optimization. As a result, the second version of the Black–Litterman approach, the BL model, is probably more important in practice, and will be the chief focus of this section. Although the BL model could be considered a tool for developing capital market expectations for the range of asset classes in a global index such as MSCI World, employed with MVO with short sale constraints it also may be viewed as an asset allocation process with two desirable qualities:

1. The resulting asset allocation is well diversified.
2. The resulting asset allocation incorporates the investor's views on asset-class returns, if any, as well as the strength of those views.

In the language of the model, a view is an investor forecast on an asset class's return, whether stated in absolute or relative terms. (For instance, "Canadian equities will earn 8 percent per year" is an absolute view, and "Canadian equities will outperform U.S. equities by 1 percent per year" is a relative view.) With each view, the investor also provides the information related to the confidence he has in the view.

A practical goal of the BL model is to create stable, mean–variance-efficient portfolios which overcome the problem of expected return sensitivity. The set of expected asset-class returns used in the BL model blends equilibrium returns and the investor's views, if he or she has any. The equilibrium returns are the set of returns that makes the efficient frontier pass through the market weight portfolio. They can be interpreted as the long-run returns provided by the capital markets. The equilibrium returns represent the information that is built into capital market prices and thus reflects the "average" investor's expectations. A major advantage of this approach is that its starting point is a diversified portfolio with market capitalization portfolio weights, which is optimal for an uninformed investor using the mean–variance approach. Exhibit 5-19 shows the steps in BL model.

[48] The notion of using reverse optimization to infer expected returns was first described in Sharpe (1974). See Sharpe (1985), pp. 59–60 for further details.

EXHIBIT 5-19 Steps in the BL Model

Step	Description	Purpose
1	Define equilibrium market weights and covariance matrix for all asset classes	Inputs for calculating equilibrium expected returns
2	Back-solve equilibrium expected returns	Form the neutral starting point for formulating expected returns
3	Express views and confidence for each view	Reflect the investor's expectations for various asset classes. The confidence level assigned to each view determines the weight placed on it.
4	Calculate the view-adjusted market equilibrium returns	Form the expected return that reflects both market equilibrium and views
5	Run mean–variance optimization	Obtain efficient frontier and portfolios

In Section 6.1.2 on the importance of inputs to mean–variance optimization, we presented a case in which we applied MVO to five equity classes using raw historical statistics as our expectations for the future. The resulting efficient portfolios were concentrated in two assets, U.K. equity and Americas equity. In the balance of this section, we show that the BL model results in better diversified portfolios using the same data as a starting point.[49]

The first step in the BL model is to calculate the equilibrium returns, because the model uses those returns as a neutral starting point. Because we cannot observe equilibrium returns, we must estimate them based on the capital market weights of asset classes and the asset-class covariance matrix. The estimation process can be thought of as a "back-solving" of the mean–variance optimization. In the traditional MVO, the investor uses expected returns and the covariance matrix to derive the optimal portfolio allocations. In the BL model, the investor assumes the market-capitalization weights are optimal (given no special insights) and then uses those weights and the covariance matrix to solve for the expected returns. By the nature of the procedure, these are the expected returns that would make the portfolio represented by the capital market weights mean–variance efficient.

To pick up the example using five equity markets, the first task is to calculate the assets' capitalization weights. Exhibit 5-20 presents the equity market weights of five major markets across the world reported by Dow Jones Global Index at the end of 2003.

Example 5-11 shows the selection of an asset allocation that is consistent with the Black–Litterman approach.

EXHIBIT 5-20 DJGI Market Weights, December 2003

	DJGI Americas	DJGI Asia Pacific ex-Japan	DJGI Europe/Africa ex-U.K. and South Africa	DJGI Japan	DJGI U.K.
Dollar weight	$12,362,002	$1,269,324	$3,703,025	$2,238,885	$2,161,903
Percentage weight	56.9%	5.8%	17.0%	10.3%	9.9%

[49]We do not show the mathematics of the Black–Litterman model. See Idzorek (2002) for an introduction.

EXAMPLE 5-11 An Asset Allocation for an Investor with No Views

John Merz is not a professional investor and is reticent in expressing any opinion about future asset returns. Merz has average risk tolerance.

1. If Merz were constrained to invest only in the five asset classes given in Exhibit 5-20, what would be his optimal asset allocation?
2. How would your answer to Part 1 change if Merz had below-average risk tolerance?

Solution to Problem 1: According to the Black–Litterman approach, Merz should invest in the five asset classes in the proportional market-value weights given in Exhibit 5-20, approximately:

- 57 percent DJGI Americas.
- 6 percent DJGI Asia Pacific ex-Japan.
- 17 percent DGJI Europe/Africa ex-U.K. and South Africa.
- 10 percent DJGI Japan.
- 10 percent DJGI U.K.

Solution to Problem 2: Following the Black–Litterman approach, Merz would still hold the five asset classes in market-value weights because he holds no views on the asset classes. He would combine that portfolio with the risk-free asset to lower the overall risk, however.

We use the capitalization weights combined with the covariance matrix (computable with data given for correlations and standard deviations in Exhibit 5-12 in Section 6.1.2). We combine the covariance matrix with the capitalization weights in Exhibit 5-20 to find equilibrium expected returns, shown in Exhibit 5-21.[50]

EXHIBIT 5-21 Historical Average and Market Equilibrium Returns, 1992–2003

	Historical Average Return (H)	Standard Deviation	Equilibrium Return (E)	E − H
DJGI Americas TR	11.87%	18.83%	9.49%	−2.38%
DJGI Asia Pacific ex-Japan TR	11.21	37.03	12.66	1.45
DJGI Europe/Africa ex-U.K. and S. Africa TR	11.04	21.58	9.58	−1.46
DJGI Japan TR USD	3.19	33.66	9.91	6.72
DJGI U.K. TR USD	9.58	17.41	8.39	−1.19

[50]The equilibrium return vector (Π) can be calculated using the formula $\Pi = \delta \Sigma w$, where δ is the risk-aversion level of the market portfolio, Σ is the covariance matrix, and w is the vector of market weights.

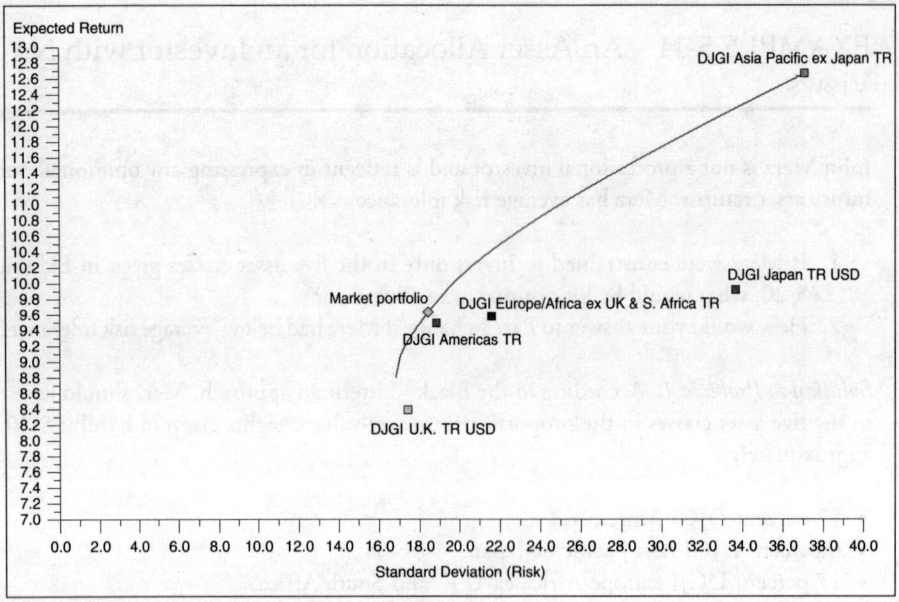

EXHIBIT 5-22 Efficient Frontier with Equilibrium Returns

Exhibit 5-22 shows the efficient frontier with the equilibrium returns based on the back-solved equilibrium returns. Notice that the efficient frontier passes through the portfolio with market-value weights. Exhibit 5-23 shows that all five assets enter in efficient portfolios at some level of standard deviation of return, in contrast to the MVO using historical mean returns shown in Exhibit 5-13. The efficient allocations along the frontier are also much more diversified compared with those resulting from the MVO using historical mean returns. This observation is key, because the investor will use these equilibrium returns as a starting point for mean return estimates.

Incorporating equilibrium returns has two major advantages. First, combining the investor's views with equilibrium returns helps dampen the effect of any extreme views the investor holds that could otherwise dominate the optimization. The result is generally better-diversified portfolios than those produced from a MVO based only on the investor's views, regardless of the source of those views. Second, anchoring the estimates to equilibrium returns ensures greater consistency across the estimates.

Having established the equilibrium returns, the next step is to express market views and confidence for those views. Suppose the investor has the following two relative views:

1. U.K. equity return will be the same as the return on "European equity" (shorthand for DJGI Europe/Africa ex-U.K. and South Africa). Exhibit 5-21 shows that this view contrasts with an underperformance of 1.46 percent (9.58–11.04) for U.K. equities during the 1992–2003 period.
2. Asian equity will outperform Japanese equity by 2 percent. From Exhibit 5-21 we see that this view contrasts with an outperformance of 8.02 percent (11.21 − 3.19) during the 1992–2003 period.

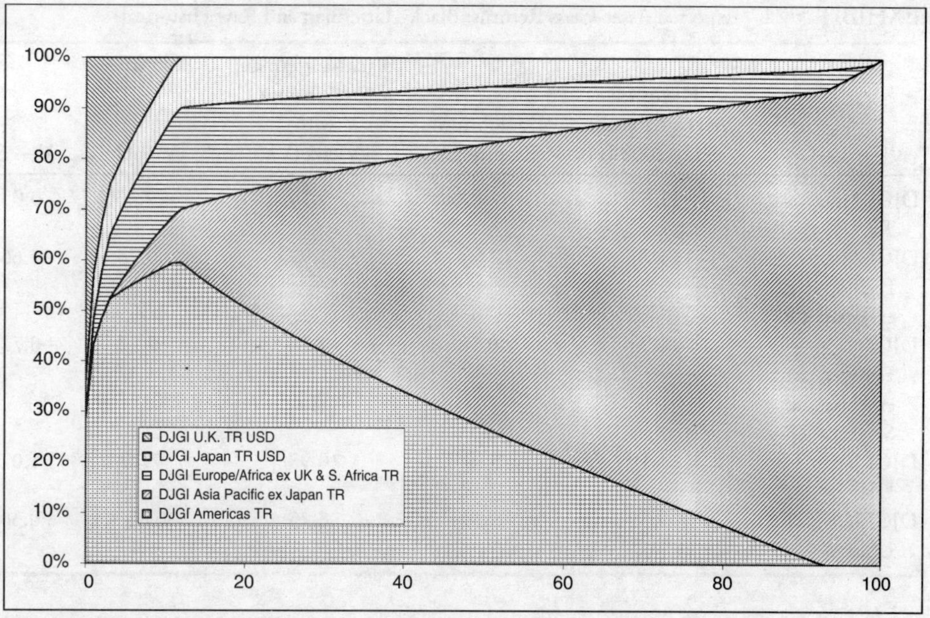

EXHIBIT 5-23 Efficient Portfolio Weights with Equilibrium Returns
Note: On the *x*-axis, zero represents the GMV portfolio's standard deviation and 100 represents the highest-mean-return asset class's standard deviation. The *y*-axis shows asset class weights. The in-figure legend is a key to regions, starting from the topmost at the zero-SD point.

We express the confidence levels for these views as variances. The smaller the variance, the greater the precision of one's view, and the greater one's confidence. We assume the variance for both views is 0.001, which would represent a high level of confidence.

Exhibit 5-24 presents historical, equilibrium, and Black–Litterman view-adjusted returns. The equilibrium returns are based on current market prices and so reflect investors' expectations about the future. Looking backward, we see that Asian equities outperformed Japan equities by a huge 8.02 percent. Looking forward, the market weights imply a much smaller difference, 2.75 percent (12.66 − 9.91).

The investor's two precise views are intuitively reflected in the Black–Litterman view-adjusted returns. Europe is expected to outperform U.K. equity by 1.19 percent (9.58 − 8.39) according to equilibrium returns. After imposing the view that U.K.'s equity return will equal the European equity return, the expected return difference is only 0.06 percent (8.81 − 8.75). Similarly, after imposing the second view, Asian equity now is expected to outperform Japanese equity by only 1.01 percent, in contrast to the 2.75 percent equilibrium difference. Although neither of the two views concerns DJGI Americas, the Black–Litterman value of DJGI Americas at 9.54 percent is different from the equilibrium return at 9.49 percent. Ripple effects through all return estimates are typical of the Black–Litterman process.

The Black–Litterman view-adjusted returns yield the efficient frontier shown in Exhibit 5-25. The market portfolio lies close to but no longer exactly on the efficient frontier.

Exhibit 5-26 shows the portfolio weights of efficient portfolios moving upward on the efficient frontier from the GMV portfolio. The view on Japan relative to Asia was more favorable than equilibrium (Exhibit 5-23) and thus much higher weights for Japan (and smaller weights for Asia) appear in Exhibit 5-26 than in Exhibit 5-23. The favorable view on

EXHIBIT 5-24 Expected Asset-Class Returns: Black–Litterman and Raw Historical

	Historical Average Return, 1992–2003 (H)	Equilibrium Return (E)	Black–Litterman: Equilibrium with Views (V)	V − H	V − E
DJGI Americas TR	11.87%	9.49%	9.54%	−2.33%	0.05%
DJGI Asia Pacific ex-Japan TR	11.21	12.66	11.99	0.78	−0.66
DJGI Europe/Africa ex-U.K. and S. Africa TR	11.04	9.58	8.81	−2.23	−0.77
DJGI Japan TR USD	3.19	9.91	10.98	7.79	1.07
DJGI U.K. TR USD	9.58	8.39	8.75	−0.83	0.36

the United Kingdom relative to Europe has caused Europe to drop out of the efficient frontier. Thus differences in efficient portfolio weights relative to equilibrium reflect the investor's views in the intuitively expected directions.

Comparing Exhibit 5-26 with Exhibit 5-13 (repeated on the following page), we see that the efficient frontier using Black–Litterman view-adjusted returns represents much better-diversified portfolios than does the efficient frontier that results from using raw historical mean returns.

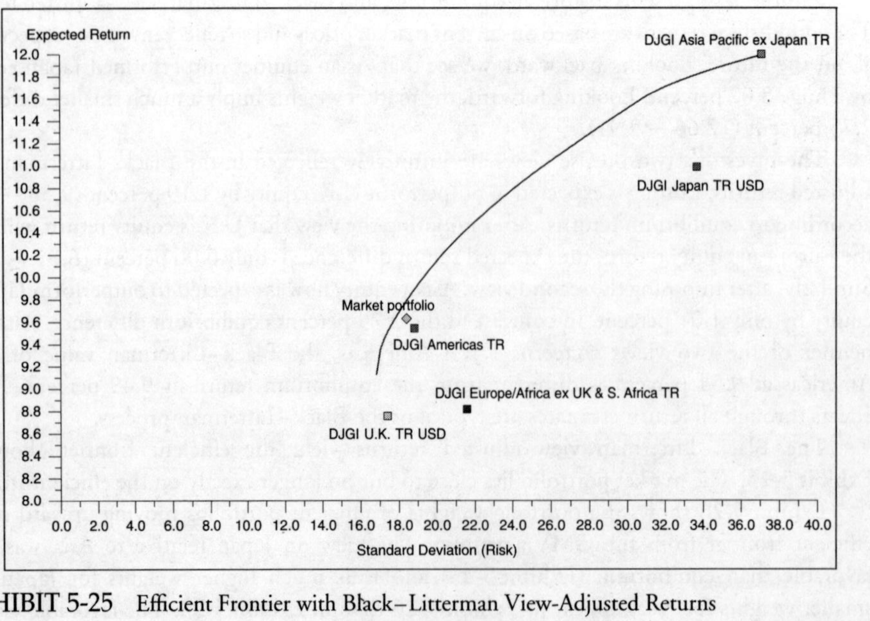

EXHIBIT 5-25 Efficient Frontier with Black–Litterman View-Adjusted Returns

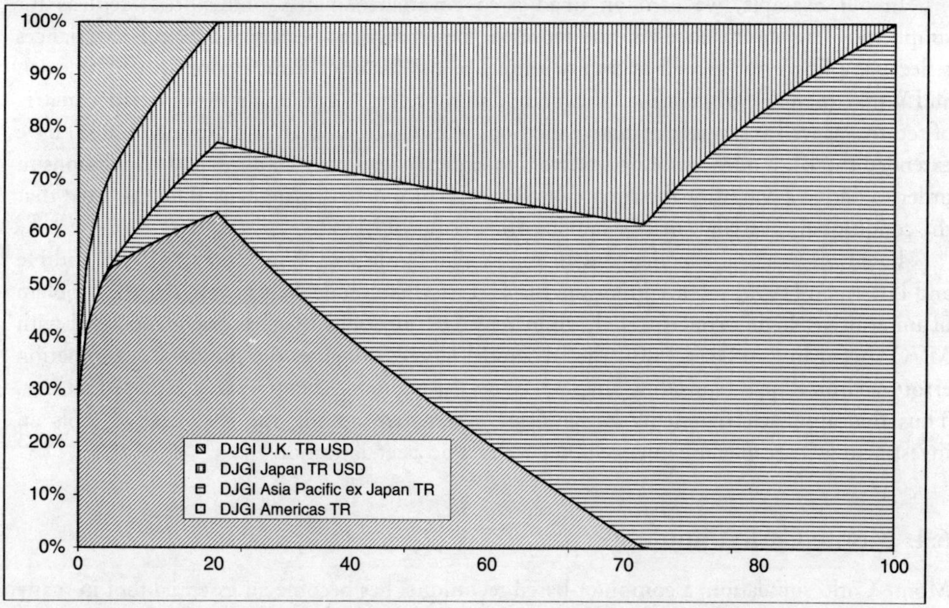

EXHIBIT 5-26 Efficient Portfolio Weights with Black–Litterman View-Adjusted Returns
Note: On the *x*-axis, zero represents the GMV portfolio's standard deviation and 100 represents the highest-mean-return asset class's standard deviation. The *y*-axis shows asset class weights. The in-figure legend is a key to regions, starting from the topmost at the zero-SD point.

EXHIBIT 5-13 (Repeated) Efficient Portfolio Weights Using Raw Historical Mean Returns
Note: On the *x*-axis, zero represents the GMV portfolio's standard deviation and 100 represents the highest-mean-return asset class's standard deviation. Asia Pacific ex-Japan appears only near zero on the *x*-axis. The *y*-axis shows asset class weights. The in-figure legend is a key to regions, starting from the topmost at the zero-SD point; Asia Pacific ex-Japan appears only near 0 level on the *x*-axis.

In our example, we used an unadjusted covariance matrix of historical returns for simplicity. This approach does not represent best practice, because historical covariances reflect sampling error as well as events unique to the historical time period used. Litterman and Winkelmann (1998) outlined the method they prefer for estimating the covariance matrix of returns, as well as several alternative methods of estimation. Qian and Gorman (2001) have extended the BL model, enabling investors to express views on volatilities and correlations in order to derive a conditional estimate of the covariance matrix of returns. They asserted that the conditional covariance matrix stabilizes the results of MVO.

Based on practical experience with the model, Bevan and Winkelmann (1998) and He and Litterman (1999) reported that the Black–Litterman model helps overcome the problem of unintuitive, highly concentrated, input-sensitive portfolios that has been associated with MVO. According to Lee (2000), the BL model largely mitigates the problem of estimation error-maximization by spreading any such errors throughout the entire set of expected returns. Thus this approach represents a significant alternative among the quantitative tools an investment adviser may use in developing a strategic asset allocation.

6.4. Monte Carlo Simulation

Monte Carlo simulation, a computer-based technique, has become an essential tool in many areas of investments. In its application to strategic asset allocation, Monte Carlo simulation involves the calculation and statistical description of the outcomes resulting in a particular strategic asset allocation under random scenarios for investment returns, inflation, and other relevant variables. The method provides information about the range of possible investment results from a given asset allocation over the course of the investor's time horizon, as well as the likelihood that each result will occur.

Monte Carlo simulation contrasts to and complements MVO. Standard MVO is an analytical methodology based on calculus. By contrast, Monte Carlo simulation is a statistical tool. Monte Carlo simulation imitates (simulates) an asset allocation's real-world operation in an investments laboratory, where the investment adviser incorporates his best understanding of the set of relevant variables and their statistical properties.

Using Monte Carlo simulation, an investment manager can effectively grapple with a range of practical issues that are difficult or impossible to formulate analytically. Consider taxes and rebalancing to a strategic asset allocation for a taxable investor. We can readily calculate the impact of taxes during a single time period. Also, in a single-period setting as assumed by MVO, rebalancing is irrelevant. In the multiperiod world of most investment problems, however, the portfolio will predictably be rebalanced, triggering the realization of capital gains and losses. Given a specific rebalancing rule, different strategic asset allocations will result in different patterns of tax payments (and different transaction costs too). Formulating the multiperiod problem mathematically would be a daunting challenge. We could more easily incorporate the tax-rebalancing interaction in a Monte Carlo simulation.

We will examine a simple multiperiod problem to illustrate the use of Monte Carlo simulation, evaluating the range of outcomes for wealth that may result from a strategic asset allocation (and not incorporating taxes).

The value of wealth at the terminal point of an investor's time horizon is a criterion for choosing among asset allocations. Future wealth incorporates the interaction of risk and return. The need for Monte Carlo simulation in evaluating an asset allocation depends on whether there are cash flows into or out of the portfolio over time. For a given asset allocation with no cash flows, the sequence of returns is irrelevant; ending wealth will be path independent (unrelated to the sequence or path of returns through time). We could find expected terminal wealth and percentiles of terminal wealth analytically.[51] Investors save to and spend from their portfolios, however, so the more typical case is that terminal wealth is path dependent (the sequence of returns matters) because of the interaction of cash flows with returns earned. With terminal wealth path dependent, an analytical approach is not feasible but Monte Carlo simulation is. Example 5-12 applies Monte Carlo simulation to evaluate a strategic asset allocation of an investor who regularly withdraws from his portfolio.

EXAMPLE 5-12 Monte Carlo Simulation for a Retirement Portfolio with a Proposed Asset Allocation

Edward Renshaw has sought the advice of an investment adviser concerning his retirement portfolio. At the end of 2003, he is 65 years old and holds a portfolio valued at $1 million. Renshaw would like to withdraw $50,000 a year to supplement the corporate pension he has begun to receive. Given his health and family history, Renshaw believes he should plan for a retirement lasting 20 years. He is also concerned about passing along to his two children at least the portfolio's current value when he dies. Consulting with his adviser, Renshaw has expressed this desire quantitatively: He wants the median value of his bequest to his children to be worth no less than his portfolio's current value of $1 million. The median is the most likely outcome. The asset allocation of his retirement portfolio is currently 50/50 U.S. equities/U.S. intermediate-term government bonds. Renshaw and his adviser have decided on the following set of capital market expectations:

- U.S. equities: expected return 12.4 percent, standard deviation 20.4 percent.
- U.S. intermediate-term government bonds: expected return 5.6 percent, standard deviation 5.7 percent.
- Predicted correlation between U.S. equities and U.S. intermediate-term government bond: 0.042.
- Long-term inflation rate: 3.1 percent.

With the current asset allocation, the expected return on Renshaw's retirement portfolio is 8.9 percent with a standard deviation of 10.6 percent. Exhibit 5-27 gives the results of the Monte Carlo simulation.[52]

Based on the information given, address the following:

1. Justify the choice of presenting ending wealth in terms of real rather than nominal wealth in Exhibit 5-27.
2. Is the current asset allocation expected to satisfy Renshaw's investment objective?

---

[51]Making a plausible statistical assumption such as a lognormal distribution for ending wealth.

[52]Note that the *y*-axis in this figure is a logarithmic scale. The quantity $1,000,000 is the same distance from $100,000 as $10,000,000 is from $1,000,000, because $1,000,000 is 10 times $100,000 just as $10,000,000 is 10 times $1,000,000. $100,000 is 10^5 and $1,000,000 is 10^6. In Exhibit 5-27, a distance halfway between the $100,000 and $1,000,000 hatch marks is $10^{5.5} = \$316,228$.

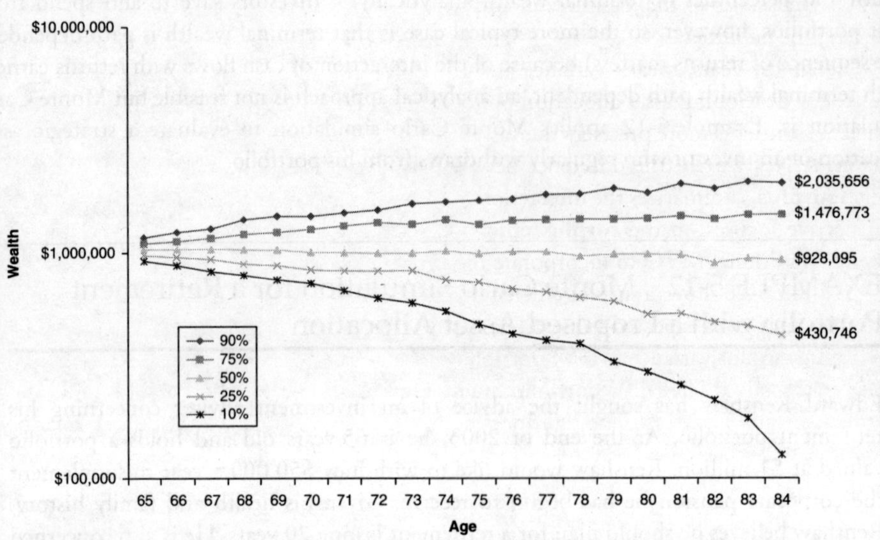

EXHIBIT 5-27 Monte Carlo Simulation of Ending Wealth with Annual Cash Outflows

Solution to Problem 1: Renshaw wants the median value of his bequest to his children to "be worth no less than his portfolio's current value of $1 million." We need to state future amounts in terms of today's values (i.e., in real dollars) to assess their worth relative to $1 million. Exhibit 5-27 thus gives the results of the Monte Carlo simulation in real dollar terms.

Solution to Problem 2: From Exhibit 5-27 we see that the median terminal value of the retirement portfolio in real dollars is less than the initial value of $1 million. Therefore, the most likely bequest is less than the amount Renshaw has specified that he wants. The current asset allocation is not expected to satisfy all his investment objectives.

An investor seeking an adviser's help often has an existing portfolio, and we can use a Monte Carlo simulation to evaluate it relative to the investor's goals. We can run the simulation at the individual security level or the asset-class level. The risk–return characteristics at the asset-class level are more stable than at the individual security level. Consequently, to evaluate a strategic asset allocation over a long time horizon, Monte Carlo simulation at the asset-class level is usually more appropriate.

6.5. Asset/Liability Management

Up to this point we have discussed optimization in the context of an asset-only approach to asset allocation. In many cases, however, an asset portfolio is meant to fund a specified liability schedule (funding a liability means being able to pay the liability when it comes due). Such cases call for an ALM approach. Using an ALM approach, asset allocation must consider the risk characteristics of the liabilities in addition to those of the assets, because the focus is on funding the liabilities.

For many years, mean–variance analysis in its various developments has been a tool of choice for developing asset allocation policy. Earlier we presented the efficient frontier. That efficient frontier is more precisely the "asset-only" efficient frontier, because it fails to consider liabilities. **Net worth** (the difference between the market value of assets and liabilities), also called **surplus,** summarizes the interaction of assets and liabilities in a single variable. The ALM perspective focuses on the **surplus efficient frontier.** Mean–variance surplus optimization extends traditional MVO to incorporate the investor's liabilities.

Exhibit 5-28 shows a surplus efficient frontier. The *x*-axis represents the standard deviation and the *y*-axis gives expected values. The leftmost point on the surplus efficient frontier is the minimum surplus variance (MSV) portfolio, the efficient portfolio with the least risk from an ALM perspective. The MSV portfolio might correspond to a cash flow matching strategy or an immunization strategy. The rightmost point on the surplus efficient frontier represents the highest-expected-surplus portfolio. Similar to traditional MVO, the highest-expected-surplus portfolio typically consists of 100 percent in the highest-expected-return asset class. In fact, at high levels of risk, the asset allocations on the surplus efficient frontier often resemble high-risk asset-only efficient portfolios. Exhibit 5-28 plots the investor's liability as a point with positive standard deviation but negative expected value (because the investor owes the liability and so effectively has a short position).

The investor must choose a policy portfolio on the surplus efficient frontier. Investors with low risk tolerance may choose to bear minimal expected surplus risk and thus select the MSV portfolio. Other investors might choose to bear some greater amount of surplus risk with the expectation of greater ending surplus. Understanding "beta" to loosely mean compensated risk, we can call this choice the surplus beta decision. If we evaluate surplus risk relative to the

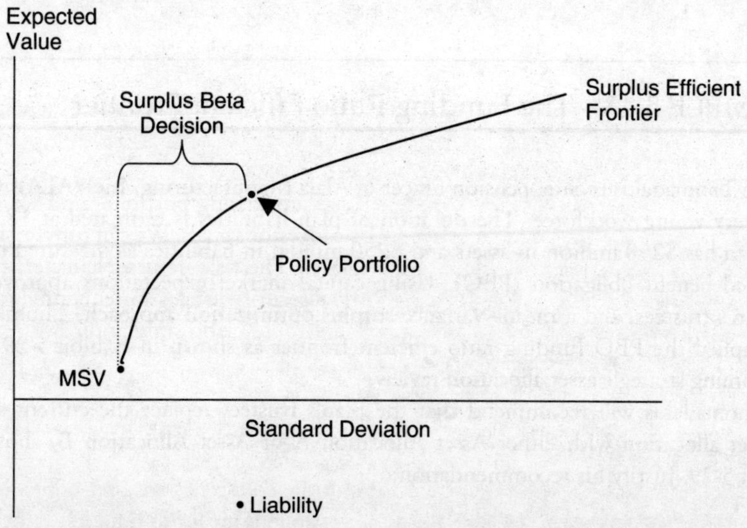

EXHIBIT 5-28 Surplus Efficient Frontier

risk of the MSV portfolio, we can measure the surplus beta decision in terms of the increment of risk accepted above the risk of the MSV portfolio.[53]

The estimation error problems of traditional MVO also apply to surplus optimization. The techniques that help mitigate these problems in traditional MVO, such as resampling and the Black–Litterman model, can be used in this context as well.

6.5.1. An ALM Example: A Defined-Benefit Pension Plan

For a DB pension plan, net worth is called pension surplus. The **funding ratio,** calculated by dividing the value of pension assets by the present value of pension liabilities, measures the relative size of pension assets compared with pension liabilities.[54] Some countries state requirements pertaining to pension plan contributions in terms of the funding ratio:

- If the funding ratio exceeds 100 percent, then the pension fund is overfunded.
- If the funding ratio is less than 100 percent then the pension fund is underfunded.
- If the funding ratio equals100 percent, then the pension fund is exactly fully funded.

Effectively managing a pension fund's surplus is often taken to be the plan sponsor's goal. If surplus is positive, the sponsor can finance future liability accruals, at least in part, by drawing on the surplus. If the present value of liabilities exceeds the value of assets (i.e., a negative surplus or unfunded liability exists), however, the sponsor must make up the asset shortfall through future contributions from the sponsor's assets or investment earnings. Surplus increases with plan contributions and investment earnings and decreases with plan withdrawals or investment losses. A pension plan's surplus is thus a logical variable for optimization.

Example 5-13 illustrates a variation on the surplus efficient frontier that appears not infrequently; in that example, the efficient frontier is stated in terms of the funding ratio.

EXAMPLE 5-13 The Funding Ratio Efficient Frontier

George Thomadakis is chief pension officer of Alaia Manufacturing, Inc. (ALA), which has a very young workforce. The duration of plan liabilities is estimated at 18 years. The plan has $250 million in assets and $250 million in liabilities as measured by the projected benefit obligation (PBO). Using capital market expectations approved by the plan's trustees, and a mean–variance surplus optimization approach, Thomadakis has graphed the PBO funding ratio efficient frontier as shown in Exhibit 5-29 for a forthcoming strategic asset allocation review.

Thomadakis will recommend that the plan's trustees replace the current strategic asset allocation with either Asset Allocation A or Asset Allocation B, shown in Exhibit 5-29. Justify his recommendation.

[53] See Barton Waring (2004b) for more details on this type of analysis.

[54] The funding ratio has also been referred to as the **funded ratio** or **funded status.**

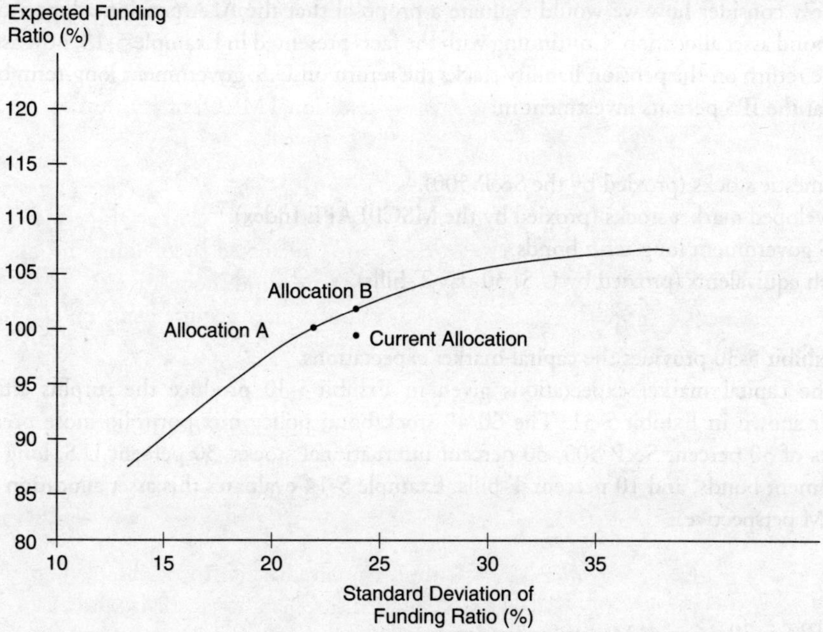

EXHIBIT 5-29 PBO Funding Ratio Efficient Frontier: 18-Year Time Horizon

Solution: The current strategic asset allocation is expected to maintain a 100 percent funding ratio with expected volatility of 25 percent a year at an 18-year time horizon. Allocation A is expected to result in the same 100 percent funding ratio as the current strategic asset allocation but with less risk (the standard deviation of A is approximately 22 percent, below the current allocation's 25 percent level). Allocation B is expected to result in a higher than 100 percent funding ratio with the same risk as the current asset allocation. Both A and B lie on the efficient frontier, but the current asset allocation is not efficient. Thus both A and B are superior to the current asset allocation; in deciding between the two, the trustees must determine whether lower risk or a higher expected funding ratio is more important.

Continuing with the example of the ALA pension plan, suppose that the expected return on plan assets and plan liabilities are 7.8 percent and 5 percent, respectively. A liability return is the change in value of a liability, just as an asset return is the change in value of an asset.

- The forecast of pension assets at a one-year horizon is ($250 million) × 107.8% = $269.5 million.
- The forecast of pension liabilities is $250 million × 105% = $262.5 million.
- The forecast of surplus is $269.5 million − $262.5 million = $7 million, which we could also compute directly as $250 million × (7.8% − 5%).
- The forecast of the funding ratio is $269.5 million/$262.5 million = 1.027, or 102.7 percent.
- Making projections for underfunded and overfunded pension follows the same computational pattern.

Now consider how we would evaluate a proposal that the ALA pension adopt a 60/40 stock/bond asset allocation. Continuing with the facts presented in Example 5-13, now assume that the return on the pension liability tracks the return on U.S. government long-term bonds and that the IPS permits investment in:

- Domestic stocks (proxied by the S&P 500).
- Developed market stocks (proxied by the MSCI EAFE Index).
- U.S government long-term bonds.
- Cash equivalents (proxied by U.S. 30-day T-bills).

Exhibit 5-30 provides the capital market expectations.

The capital market expectations given in Exhibit 5-30 produce the surplus efficient frontier shown in Exhibit 5-31. The 60/40 stock/bond policy mix portfolio more precisely consists of 30 percent S&P 500, 30 percent international stocks, 30 percent U.S. long-term government bonds, and 10 percent T-bills. Example 5-14 evaluates this asset allocation from an ALM perspective.

EXHIBIT 5-30 Capital Market Expectations

	Expected Return	Standard Deviation	Corr. w/S&P 500 TR	Corr. w/MSCI EAFE TR	Corr. w/U.S. LT Govt. TR	Corr. w/U.S. 30 Day T-Bill TR
S&P 500 TR	10%	20%	1.00			
MSCI EAFE TR	10	25	0.59	1.00		
U.S. LT Govt TR	5	10	0.12	0.08	1.00	
U.S. 30-Day T-Bill TR	3	3	−0.03	−0.11	0.23	1.00

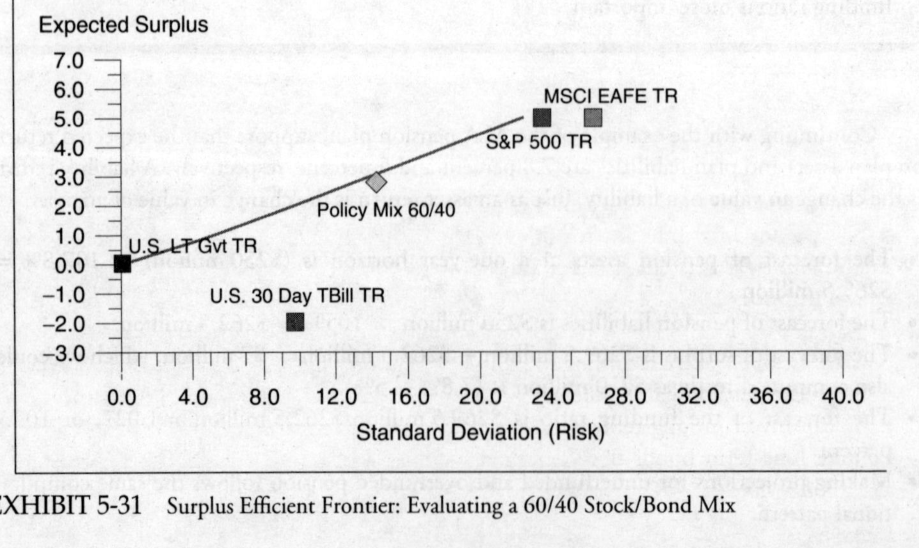

EXHIBIT 5-31 Surplus Efficient Frontier: Evaluating a 60/40 Stock/Bond Mix

EXAMPLE 5-14 The Surplus Efficient Frontier

Exhibit 5-32 shows the asset-class weights in the efficient portfolios running from the MSV portfolio to the highest-expected-return surplus efficient portfolio for the ALA pension fund.

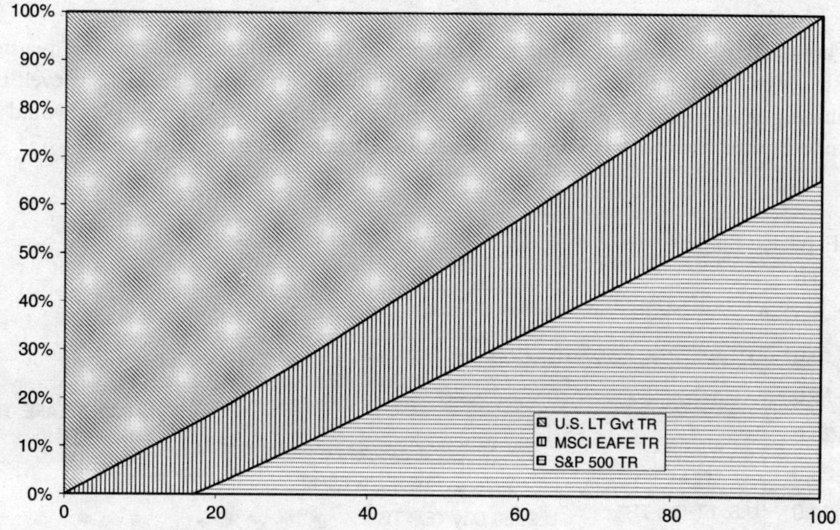

EXHIBIT 5-32 Surplus Efficient Frontier: Portfolio Weights
Note: On the *x*-axis, zero represents the GMV portfolio's standard deviation and 100 represents the highest-mean-return asset class's standard deviation.

1. Appraise the surplus efficiency of the proposed 60/40 policy mix.
2. Justify the absence of T-bills in surplus efficient portfolios for the ALA pension.

Solution to Problem 1: The 60/40 asset allocation is almost but not exactly surplus efficient: It lies just below the surplus efficient frontier. The proposed 60/40 asset allocation includes a 10 percent weighting in T-bills. As Exhibit 5-32 shows, U.S. T-bills do not enter into any surplus efficient portfolio; including T-bills in the policy mix accounts at least in part for the 60/40 portfolio not appearing on the surplus efficient frontier.

Solution to Problem 2: According to Exhibit 5-32, no surplus efficient portfolio includes T-bills. The pension liability behaves as a long-term bond, by assumption. Intuitively, if we can invest in long-term bonds, we can completely negate surplus risk. By itself, holding long-term bonds is riskier than holding T-bills, but relative to the pension liability, T-bills are riskier. The MSV portfolio is 100 percent long-term bonds. If we want to move from the MSV portfolio to higher-expected-surplus portfolios, we logically require equities with a 10 percent expected return, not T-bills.

EXAMPLE 5-15 Interpreting the Surplus Efficient Frontier

Thomadakis is interested in the performance of the 60/40 asset allocation if pension assets were \$200 million rather than \$250 million. With plan assets at that level, the funding ratio would be 80 percent (\$200 million/\$250 million), so the plan would be underfunded. Exhibit 5-33 depicts the surplus efficient frontier in that case.

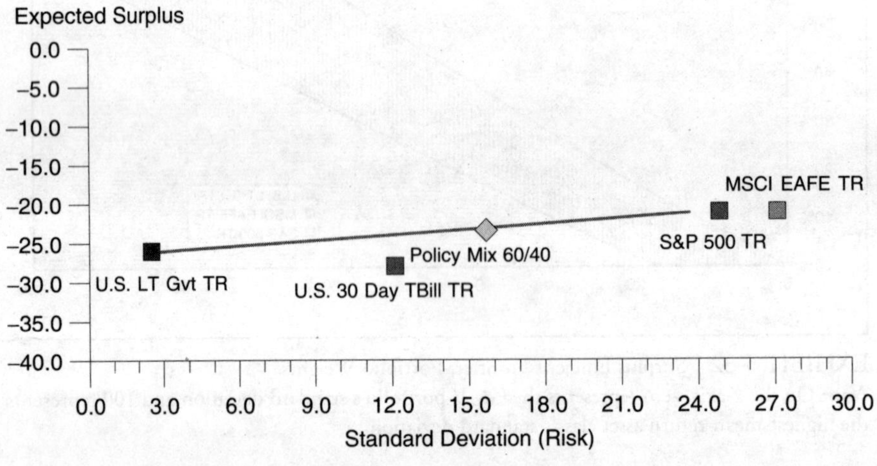

EXHIB!T 5-33 Surplus Efficient Frontier: 80 Percent Funding Ratio

Based on Exhibit 5-33, address the following.

1. Contrast the position of the surplus efficient frontier with an 80 percent funding ratio to its position with a 100 percent funding ratio.
2. Appraise the surplus efficiency of the 60/40 strategic asset allocation.

Solution to Problem 1: The MSV portfolio's expected surplus is now negative, and the MSV portfolio has positive risk rather than zero risk. All surplus efficient portfolios have negative expected surplus. Because the plan is currently only 80 percent funded, one year's expected positive asset returns are expected to be insufficient to make up the funding shortfall whatever the risk assumed. (This fact implies that the pension plan sponsor will probably need to make additional contributions in the future to help make up the funding shortfall.) The MSV portfolio has positive risk because a \$200 million,

100 percent position in long-term bonds cannot completely offset the liability, which is effectively a $250 million short position in long-term bonds.

Solution to Problem 2: The 60/40 allocation appears to be surplus efficient at an 80 percent funding ratio because it lies on the surplus efficient frontier.

6.5.2. Asset/Liability Modeling with Simulation Managers often use Monte Carlo simulation together with surplus optimization (or sometimes standard mean–variance optimization) to provide more detailed insight on the performance of asset allocations under consideration. Simulation is particularly important for investors with long time horizons, because the MVO or surplus optimization is essentially a one-period model. Monte Carlo simulation can help confirm that the recommended allocations provide sufficient diversification and to evaluate the probability of funding shortfalls (requiring contributions), the likelihood of breaching return thresholds, and the growth of assets with and without disbursements from the portfolio.

A simple asset allocation approach that blends surplus optimization with Monte Carlo simulation follows these steps:[55]

- Determine the surplus efficient frontier and select a limited set of efficient portfolios, ranging from the MSV portfolio to higher-surplus-risk portfolios, to examine further.
- Conduct a Monte Carlo simulation for each proposed asset allocation and evaluate which allocations, if any, satisfy the investor's return and risk objectives.
- Choose the most appropriate allocation that satisfies those objectives.

Below we elaborate on the steps.

Step 1 The first step in the three-step ALM employs the model presented in Sharpe (1990).[56] The objective function is to maximize the risk-adjusted future value of the surplus (or net worth). Formally, in a mean–variance context, doing so amounts to maximizing the difference between the expected change in future surplus and a risk penalty. The risk penalty is a function of the variance of changes in surplus value and the investor's risk tolerance (or risk aversion).

$$U_m^{\text{ALM}} = E(\text{SR}_m) - 0.005 R_A \sigma^2(\text{SR}_m) \tag{5-4}$$

where

U_m^{ALM} = the surplus objective function's expected value for a particular asset mix m, for a particular investor with the specified risk aversion

$E(\text{SR}_m)$ = expected surplus return for asset mix m, with surplus return defined as (Change in asset value − Change in liability value)/(Initial asset value)

$\sigma^2(\text{SR}_m)$ = variance of the surplus return for the asset mix m[57]

R_A = risk-aversion level

[55]The approach illustrated reflects the input of R. Charles Tschampion, CFA.

[56]We state the expression consistently with Equation 5-1.

[57]Given the return on assets (AR) and the return on liabilities (LR), with A_0 and L_0 the market value of assets and liabilities, we could calculate surplus variance using $\sigma^2(\text{SR}) = \sigma^2(\text{AR}) + \sigma^2(\text{LR}) \times (L_0/A_0)^2 - 2\rho(\text{AR, LR}) \times \sigma(\text{AR}) \times \sigma(\text{LR}) \times (L_0/A_0)$.

EXHIBIT 5-34 Expectation Concerning Surplus Return

	Investor's Forecasts	
Asset Allocation	Expected Surplus Return	Standard Deviation of Surplus Return
A	5.0%	12%
B	0.5	8

In Equation 5-4, $E(\text{SR})$ and $\sigma(\text{SR})$ are expressed as percentages rather than as decimals. A set of proposed efficient portfolios may be found by incrementing the risk-aversion parameter from 0 (highest expected surplus asset allocation) upwards; we might also include the immunizing or cash flow matching portfolio as a traditional risk-minimizing choice.[58]

Suppose an insurance company with a risk-aversion level of 6 is deciding between the two asset allocations shown in Exhibit 5-34.

With a risk aversion of 6, the insurer has objective function:

$$U_m^{\text{ALM}} = E(\text{SR}_m) - 0.005R_A\sigma^2(\text{SR}_m)$$

$$= E(\text{SR}_m) - 0.005(6)\sigma^2(\text{SR}_m)$$

$$= E(\text{SR}_m) - 0.03\sigma^2(\text{SR}_m)$$

For Asset Allocation A, $U_A^{\text{ALM}} = E(SR_A) - 0.03\sigma^2(\text{SR}_A) = 5.0 - 0.03(12)^2 = 5 - 4.32 = 0.68$. For Asset Allocation B, $U_B^{\text{ALM}} = E(\text{SR}_B) - 0.03\sigma^2(\text{SR}_B) = 0.5 - 0.03(8)^2 = 0.5 - 1.92 = -1.42$. Because 0.68 is greater than -1.42, the insurer should prefer Allocation A.

Step 2 Before conducting a Monte Carlo simulation, we need to project pension payments and specify the rule for making contributions. Exhibit 5-35 is an example of a projection of pension payments that could enter into a Monte Carlo simulation.

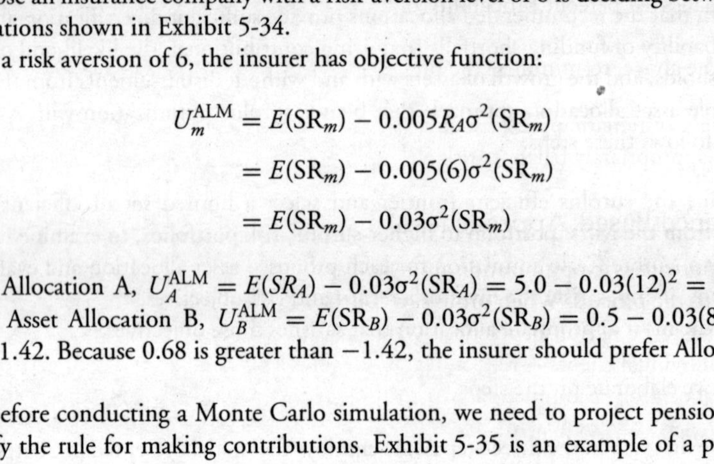

EXHIBIT 5-35 Projected Pension Payments

[58] In practice, a restriction against short sales of an asset class would make the procedure more complex.

The Monte Carlo simulation produces a frequency distribution for the future values of the asset mix, plan liabilities, and net worth or surplus. In a broad sense, the second step is a process of simulating how a particular asset allocation may perform in funding liabilities given the investor's capital market expectations.

Simulated results for portfolio returns are typically reported in inflation-adjusted terms and represent the probability of achieving actual real return levels for different time periods. Projected benefit payments are also reported in today's dollars. Therefore, all simulations regarding ending wealth values have been adjusted for inflation.

Step 3 This step may involve the investor's professional judgment as well as quantitative criteria. One example of quantitative criteria is as follows:

- Median funded ratio after 20 years equals at least 100 percent.
- No more than a 10 percent probability of a funded ratio less than 90 percent in any one year.
- Subject to the above, to minimize the present value of pension contributions.

Employing a systematic process such as that given will help in selecting a strategic asset allocation that appropriately balances risk and return.

6.6. Experience-Based Approaches

Quantitative approaches to optimization are a mainstay of strategic asset allocation because they add discipline to the process. When professionally executed and interpreted, such approaches have been found to be useful in practice. Many investment advisers, however—particularly those serving individual clients—rely on tradition, experience, and rules of thumb in making strategic asset allocation recommendations. Although these approaches appear to be ad hoc, their thrust often is consistent with financial theory when examined carefully. Furthermore, they may inexpensively suggest asset allocations that have worked well for clients in the broad experience of many investment advisers. In this section, we describe some of the most common experience-based approaches and ideas concerning asset allocation.

1. *A 60/40 stock/bond asset allocation is appropriate or at least a starting point for an average investor's asset allocation.* From periods predating modern portfolio theory to the present, this asset allocation has been suggested as a neutral (neither highly aggressive nor conservative) asset allocation for an average investor.[59] The equities allocation is viewed as supplying a long-term growth foundation, the fixed-income allocation as supplying risk-reduction benefits. If the stock and bond allocations are themselves diversified, an overall diversified portfolio should result.
2. *The allocation to bonds should increase with increasing risk aversion.* We can illustrate this idea with the example of the Vanguard LifeStrategy® Funds, which offer four choices of relatively fixed asset allocations stated to be appropriate for investors with different risk tolerances, investment objectives, and time horizons, as shown in Exhibit 5-36.[60]

   An increased allocation to fixed income on average should tend to lower the portfolio's interim volatility over the investor's time horizon. Conservative investors highly value low volatility.

[59]As one example, Mellon Capital Management's *Capital Communications* (Summer 2000) describes a 60/40 stock/bond mix as the neutral asset allocation for "normal" market conditions.

[60]Vanguard provides a questionnaire for investors to assess their risk tolerance.

EXHIBIT 5-36 Asset Allocation of the Vanguard LifeStrategy Funds

LifeStrategy Fund (risk profile)	Stocks	Bonds	Short-Term Fixed Income
Income fund (conservative)	20%	60%	20%
Conservative growth fund (moderate)	40	40%	20%
Moderate growth fund (moderately aggressive)	60	40%	0%
Growth fund (aggressive)	80	20%	0%

EXHIBIT 5-37 Life-Cycle Investment Guide to Asset Allocation

Investor Age Range	Stocks	Real Estate	Bonds	Cash
20s	65%	10%	20%	5%
30s to 40s	55	10	30	5
50s	45	12	38	5
60+	25	15	50	10

Source: Malkiel (2004).

3. *Investors with longer time horizons should increase their allocation to stocks.* One idea behind this rule of thumb is that stocks are less risky to hold in the long run than the short run, based on past data. This idea, known as time diversification, is widely believed by individual and institutional investors alike. Theoreticians who have explored the concept have found that conclusions depend on the assumptions made—for example, concerning utility functions and the time series properties (independence/non-independence) of returns, among other assumptions.[61]
4. *A rule-of-thumb for the percentage allocation to equities is 100 minus the age of the investor.* This rule of thumb implies that young investors should adopt more aggressive asset allocations than older investors. For example, it would recommend a 70/30 stock bond allocation for a 30-year-old investor. Exhibit 5-37 offers an example of this principle, if not the above rule of thumb precisely.

For young investors, an aggressive portfolio may be more appropriate because they have a longer time frame to make up any losses as markets fluctuate, and because young investors have a lifetime of earnings from employment ahead of them. For many investors, the present value of those future earnings may be relatively low risk and uncorrelated with stock market returns, justifying higher risk in their financial portfolio. We return to this subject in a later section.

The investment practitioner should be familiar with the entire range of asset allocation approaches, including the widely held ideas discussed above.

7. IMPLEMENTING THE STRATEGIC ASSET ALLOCATION

Strategic asset allocation is part of the *planning* step in portfolio management, and in this chapter we have focused on how to choose an appropriate strategic asset allocation. Managers

[61] See Ross (1999) for an analysis of the critique on time diversification begun by Samuelson (1963).

also must be familiar with the implementation choices such decisions will create, however. In the following we briefly discuss those choices.

7.1. Implementation Choices

For each asset class specified in the investor's strategic asset allocation, the investor will need to select an investment approach. At the broadest level, the choice is among:

- Passive investing.
- Active investing.
- Semi-active investing or enhanced indexing.
- Some combination of the above.

A second choice concerns the instruments used to execute a chosen investment approach.

- A passive position can be implemented through:
  - A tracking portfolio of cash market securities—whether self-managed, a separately managed account, an exchange-traded fund, or a mutual fund—designed to replicate the returns to a broad investable index representing that asset class.
  - A derivatives-based portfolio consisting of a cash position plus a long position in a swap in which the returns to an index representing that asset class is received.
  - A derivatives-based portfolio consisting of a cash position plus a long position in index futures for the asset class.
- Active investing can be implemented through:
  - A portfolio of cash market securities that reflects the investor's perceived special insights and skill and that also makes no attempt to track any asset-class index's performance.
  - A derivatives-based position (such as cash plus a long swap) to provide commodity-like exposure to the asset class plus a market-neutral long–short position to reflect active investment ideas.
- Semiactive investing can be implemented through (among other methods):
  - A tracking portfolio of cash market securities that permits some under- or overweighting of securities relative to the asset class index but with controlled tracking risk.
  - A derivatives-based position in the asset class plus controlled active risk in the cash position (such as actively managing its duration).

The IPS will often specify particular indexes or benchmarks for each asset class. Such a specification is useful not only for performance evaluation but for guiding passive investment, if that approach is chosen.

The selection of investment approaches for asset classes specified in the strategic asset allocation is an early-stage planning decision. The factors that may affect this decision include the investor's return requirements and risk objective; the perception of informational efficiency (availability of profitable active investment opportunities); the investor's self-perception of investment skill; costs; and peer practice.

7.2. Currency Risk Management Decisions

Whether using passive or active investing, if any money is allocated to a nondomestic asset class, the investor's portfolio will be exposed to **currency risk**—the volatility of the home-currency value of nondomestic assets that is related to fluctuations in exchange rates. Therefore, the investor must decide what part of the net exposures to currencies to hedge (eliminate). The hedging decision affects the expected return and volatility characteristics of the portfolio. Hedging can be managed passively, i.e., not incorporating views on currency returns, or managed actively, when the investor has definite forecasts about currency returns and the desire to exploit them tactically. The asset allocation and hedging decisions can be optimized jointly, but in practice the currency risk hedging decision is frequently subordinated to the asset allocation decision—that is, currency exposures are optimized or selected subsequent to determination of the asset allocation. Often, this type of subordination accompanies delegation of the currency management function to a **currency overlay manager**—a specialist in currency risk management operating in currency forward and other derivatives markets to establish desired currency exposures. If asset returns and currency returns are correlated, however, there will be efficiency losses relative to joint optimization.[62] In many cases, the IPS will give instructions on policy with respect to currency hedging.

7.3. Rebalancing to the Strategic Asset Allocation

What does *rebalancing* mean? We should distinguish between (1) changes to the policy portfolio itself because of changes in the investor's investment objectives and constraints, or because of changes in his or her long-term capital market expectations and (2) adjusting the actual portfolio to the strategic asset allocation because asset price changes have moved portfolio weights away from the target weights beyond tolerance limits. Although *rebalancing* is used sometimes to refer to the first type of adjustments, in industry practice rebalancing usually refers to (2) and thus we should know some basic facts about it in that sense.[63]

Rebalancing may be done on a calendar basis (such as quarterly) or on a percentage-of-portfolio basis. Percentage-of-portfolio rebalancing occurs when an asset-class weight first passes through a rebalancing threshold (also called a trigger point). For example, in Exhibit 5-1 we stated the target allocation to equities as 50 percent with a permissible range of 46 percent to 54 percent. The end points 46 percent and 54 percent are rebalancing thresholds. When a threshold is breached, the asset-class weight may be rebalanced all the way back to the target weight (50 percent), or to some point between the target weight and the threshold that has been passed, according to the discipline the investor has established. A variety of approaches exist for setting the thresholds. Although some investors set them in an ad hoc fashion, disciplined approaches exist that consider the investor's risk tolerance, the asset's volatility correlations with other asset classes, and transaction costs.[64] The percentage-of-portfolio approach done in a disciplined fashion provides a tighter control over risk than calendar-basis rebalancing. The chapter on monitoring and rebalancing provides more information on these topics.

[62] See Clarke and Kritzman (1996) and references therein for technical details and Solnik and McLeavey (2004) for a general introduction to currency risk management.

[63] Perold and Sharpe (1988) called such a rebalancing approach a constant-mix strategy. We discuss the Perold–Sharpe theory of adjusting asset mix between a risky and a safe asset class in the chapter on monitoring and rebalancing.

[64] See Masters (2003) for an example.

8. STRATEGIC ASSET ALLOCATION FOR INDIVIDUAL INVESTORS

What characteristics of individual investors distinguish them from other investors in ways that may affect the strategic asset allocation decision? Individual investors are taxable and must focus on after-tax returns. Tax status distinguishes individual investors from tax-exempt investors (such as endowments) and even other taxable investors such as banks, which are often subject to different tax schedules than individual investors. Other, inherent rather then external, differences exist, however. Asset allocation for individual investors must account for:

- The part of wealth flowing from current and future labor income, and the changing mix of financial and labor-income-related wealth as a person ages and eventually retires.
- Any correlation of current and future labor income with financial asset returns.
- The possibility of outliving one's resources.

As discussed in a prior section, psychological factors may also play a role. Behavioral finance points to a variety of issues that individual investors and their advisers face when determining the asset allocation. In the next sections, however, we focus on the three concerns mentioned above.

8.1. Human Capital

An individual investor's ability and willingness to bear risk depends on:

- Personality makeup.
- Current and future needs.
- Current and anticipated future financial situation, considering all sources of income.

As Malkiel (2004) states in *A Random Walk Down Wall Street*, "The risks you can afford to take depend on your total financial situation, including the types and sources of your income exclusive of investment income." Earning ability is important in determining capacity for risk. People with high earning ability can take more risk because they can more readily recoup financial losses than lower-earning individuals.[65] A person's earning ability is captured by the concept of human capital.

Human capital, the present value of expected future labor income, is not readily tradable. In addition to human capital, an individual has **financial capital,** which consists of more readily tradable assets such as stocks, bonds, and real estate. Human capital is often an investor's single largest asset. Young investors generally have far more human capital than financial capital. With little time to save and invest, their financial capital may be very small. But young investors have a long work life in front of them, and the present value of expected future earnings is often substantial.

The following example illustrates the importance of human capital at young ages and its declining importance as retirement approaches. Our hypothetical investor is 25 years old,

[65]Educational attainments and working experience are the two most significant factors in determining a person's earning ability.

makes \$50,000 per year, and has \$100,000 of current investments with a 5 percent annual real return. Human capital is estimated using Equation 5-5.

$$\text{Human capital}(t) = \sum_{j=t}^{T} \frac{I_j}{(1+r)^{(j-t)}} \qquad (5\text{-}5)$$

where

t = current age
I_j = expected earnings at age j
T = life expectancy
r = discount rate[66]

We then follow the growth of human and financial capital until retirement at age 65. Exhibits 5-38 and 5-39 illustrate the magnitudes and relative proportions of financial capital and human capital for a hypothetical investor from age 25 to age 65.

From Exhibit 5-38 we observe that when the investor is 25 years old, his human capital far outweighs his financial capital. Human capital is estimated to be approximately \$900,000 and represents about 90 percent of the total wealth (human plus financial capital), while financial capital is only \$100,000. As the investor gets older, the investor will continue to make savings contributions and earn positive returns, so his or her financial capital will increase. At age 65, human capital decreases to zero, while the financial portfolio peaks above \$1 million.[67]

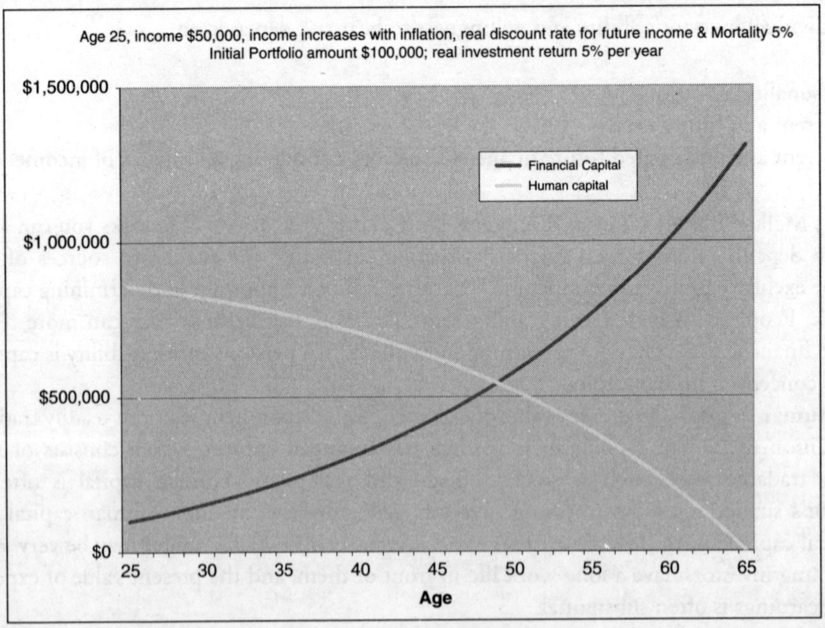

EXHIBIT 5-38 Financial Capital and Human Capital Trends as Investor Ages

[66]The discount rate should be adjusted to the risk level of the person's labor income. For simplicity, we assume it is 3 percent after inflation.

[67]In this example, we ignore any corporate or governmental retirement benefits after retirement.

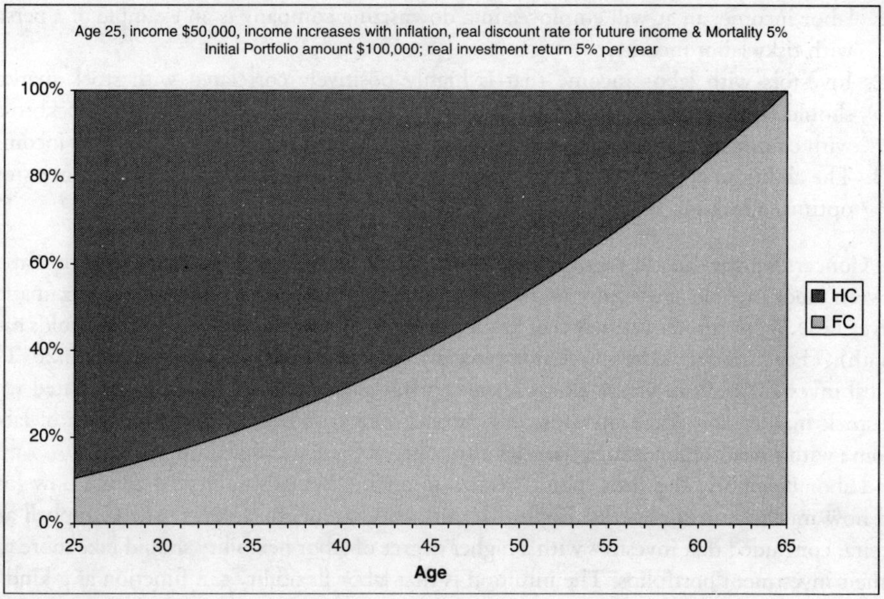

EXHIBIT 5-39 Financial Capital and Human Capital Relative to Total Wealth

Human capital's importance is often underestimated. Using the 1992 Survey of Consumer Finances, Lee and Hanna (1995) estimated that the ratio of financial assets to total wealth including human capital was 1.3 percent for the median household in the United States—for half of the households, financial assets represented less than 1.3 percent of total wealth. For 75 percent of households, financial assets represented less than 5.7 percent of total wealth, while for 90 percent of households it was 17.4 percent or less. Thus for most households studied, wealth was chiefly in the form of human capital.

8.1.1. Asset Allocation and Human Capital Strategic asset allocation concerns the asset mix for financial capital. Nevertheless, for individual investors, strategic asset allocation must also consider human capital as Merton (2003) has emphasized. When our perspective incorporates human capital, we see the logic in the traditional professional advice on asset allocation for individuals: that the appropriate strategic asset allocation varies with age or lifecycle.

According to theory, asset allocation advice crucially depends on whether labor income and human capital are both considered. Ignoring human capital, individuals should optimally maintain constant portfolio weights throughout their life given certain assumptions, including assumptions about the investor's risk aversion (Samuelson 1969, Merton 1969).[68] When we do take labor income into account, individuals appear to optimally change their asset allocation in ways related to their life cycle and characteristics of their labor income. In *Strategic Asset Allocation: Portfolio Choice for Long-Term Investors* (2002), Campbell and Viceira reached several intuitive theoretical conclusions:

1. Investors with safe labor income (thus safe human capital) will invest more of their financial portfolio into equities. A tenured professor is an example of a person with safe

[68]The investor must be assumed to have what is known as constant relative risk aversion (CRRA). See Elton, Gruber, Brown, and Goetzmann (2003) for a description of CRRA.

labor income; an at-will employee in a downsizing company is an example of a person with risky labor income.

2. Investors with labor income that is highly positively correlated with stock markets should tend to choose an asset allocation with less exposure to stocks. A stockbroker with commission income is an example of a person who has that type of labor income.
3. The ability to adjust labor supply (high labor flexibility) tends to increase an investor's optimal allocation to equities.

Concerning the second point above, Davis and Willen (2000) estimated the correlation between labor income and equity market returns in the U.S., using the Current Occupation Survey (a U.S. government survey that randomly samples about 60,000 U.S. households each month). They found that the correlation typically lies in the interval from −0.10 to 0.20. The typical investor need not worry about his or her human capital being highly correlated with the stock market. For some investors (e.g., stockbrokers), however, the correlation of labor income with stock market returns is a definite concern for asset allocation.

Labor flexibility, the third point, relates to an individual's ability to adjust how long and how much he or she works. Bodie, Merton, and Samuelson (1992), like Campbell and Viceira, concluded that investors with a higher degree of labor flexibility should take more risk in their investment portfolios. The intuition is that labor flexibility can function as a kind of insurance against adverse investment outcomes; for example, working longer hours or retiring later can help offset investment losses. Younger investors typically have such flexibility. Hanna and Chen (1997) took account of human capital in using simulation to explore the optimal asset allocation for individual investors with varying time horizons. Assuming human capital is risk free (which increases the capacity for bearing risk), they concluded that for most investors with long horizons, an all-equity portfolio is optimal.

A concrete illustration will help us understand the life-cycle relatedness of an individual's asset allocation. We present a simple case in which future labor income is certain—that is, human capital is a risk-free asset. Later we comment on the effects of risky human capital on asset allocation.

Assume that only two asset classes are available: stocks and bonds. The investor can invest financial capital (FC) in these two financial assets; human capital (HC) constitutes the balance of wealth and has effectively bond-like investment characteristics. If the investor's inherent risk appetites remain constant through time, the investor's optimal allocation of total wealth between the risky and risk-free assets will remain constant during his lifetime, all else equal.

Continuing with our investor from Exhibit 5-38, we assume that a 50/50 stock/bond strategic asset allocation for total wealth (financial and human capital) is optimal. Now compare the appropriate asset allocation for the investor at 25, 55, and 65 years old. Without considering human capital, the investor would optimally maintain a 50/50 stock/bond strategic asset allocation throughout his life.

Taking human capital into account, however, the 25-year-old investor should choose a 100 percent stock asset allocation for his financial capital because he already has 95 percent of his total wealth (represented by his human capital) effectively invested in bonds. Investing 100 percent of his financial capital in stocks is the closest he can get his total portfolio to the target 50/50 asset allocation without using leverage (borrowing money to buy stocks). As shown in Exhibit 5-40, at age 55, his total wealth consists of 50 percent financial capital and 50 percent human capital. With that split, his optimal strategic asset allocation for financial capital is 100 percent stocks, because he thereby achieves the target 50/50 allocation for his total wealth. After age 55, the allocation to stocks declines, reaching 50 percent at retirement at age 65 when human capital effectively reaches zero.

EXHIBIT 5-40 Changing Optimal Asset Allocations from Age 25 through Retirement

	Age 25 FC: 5% Total Wealth HC: 95% Total Wealth	Age 55 FC: 50% Total Wealth HC: 50% Total Wealth	Age 65 FC:100% Total Wealth HC: 0% Total Wealth
Overall asset allocation maintaining a fixed 50/50 strategic asset allocation for FC	FC: 50/50 Stocks/Bonds HC: 100% Bonds **Overall AA: 2.5/97.5 Stocks/Bonds**	FC: 50/50 Stocks/Bonds HC: 100% Bonds **Overall AA: 25/75 Stocks/Bonds**	FC: 50/50 Stocks/Bonds HC: n/a **Overall AA: 50/50 Stocks/Bonds**
Recommended FC asset allocation considering human capital	**FC: 100/0 Stocks/Bonds** HC: 100% Bonds Overall AA: 5/95 Stocks/Bonds	**FC: 100/0 Stocks/Bonds** HC: 100% Bonds Overall AA: 50/50 Stocks/Bonds	**FC: 50/50 Stocks/Bonds** HC: n/a Overall AA: 50/50 Stocks/Bonds

Note: FC is financial capital, HC is human capital

In this simple example, we have illustrated that an investor would logically allocate more to stocks as a young person than as an old person. The result comes from the declining proportion of total wealth represented by human capital as the investor ages and the assumed risk characteristics of human capital. Although investment adviser frequently suggest that individuals follow a life-cycle-related asset allocation strategy, empirical studies suggest that only a small minority of investors actually adjust their asset allocations accordingly.[69]

In the above example we assumed human capital is risk free. In reality, for most individuals future labor income is neither certain nor safe. Most people face the risk of losing their job or being laid off. Uncertainty in labor income makes human capital a risky asset. How do we incorporate risky human capital into asset allocation?

We first need to establish the risk and return characteristics of the individual's human capital. Risky human capital may have two components: a component correlated with stock market returns and a component uncorrelated with stock market returns. The two types affect the asset allocation decision differently.

When the investor's labor income is risky but not correlated with the stock market, the investor's optimal strategic asset allocation over time follows by and large the same pattern as the case where the investor's human capital is risk free—so long as the risk of human capital (i.e., income variance over time) is small. This effect occurs because the investor's human capital does not add to his or her stock market exposure. When the risk of uncorrelated human capital is substantial, however, the investor's optimal allocation to stocks is less than it would be otherwise, all else equal.

By contrast, when a large part of an investor's human capital is correlated with the stock market, the appropriate strategic asset allocation involves a much higher allocation to bonds at young ages. For example, some large part of an equity portfolio manager's human capital is positively correlated with stock market returns. Portfolio managers earn more and have greater job security when the stock market does well. This investor should prefer an asset allocation with reduced exposure to stocks because part of the investor's human capital is implicitly

[69]For example, see Ameriks and Zeldes (2001).

invested in the stock market. Nevertheless, because the share of wealth represented by human capital declines with age, the correlated-human-capital factor favoring bonds should become less important as the portfolio manager approaches retirement. Contrary to the risk-free human capital case, the appropriate allocation to stocks at this later life stage may be greater than when the portfolio manager is younger.

In summary, to effectively incorporate human capital in developing the appropriate asset allocation, an individual's investment adviser must determine (1) whether the investor's human capital is risk-free or risky and (2) whether the human capital's risk is highly correlated with the stock market. Advisers should keep in mind the following themes:

- Investors should invest financial capital assets in such a way as to diversify and balance out their human capital.
- A young investor with relatively safe human capital assets and/or greater flexibility of labor supply has an appropriate strategic asset allocation with a higher weight on risky assets such as stocks than an older investor. The allocation to stocks should decrease as the investor ages. When the investor's human capital is risky but uncorrelated with the stock market, the optimal allocation to stocks may be less but still decreases with age.
- An investor with human capital that has high correlation with stock market returns should reduce the allocation to risky assets for financial assets and increase the allocation to financial assets that are less correlated with the stock market.[70]

8.2. Other Considerations in Asset Allocation for Individual Investors

The human life span is finite but uncertain. As human beings we face both mortality risk and longevity risk.

Mortality risk is the risk of loss of human capital if an investor dies prematurely. Of course, it is the investor's family that bears the effects of mortality risk. Life insurance has long been used to hedge this risk. Mortality risk may suggest the holding of a liquidity reserve fund but otherwise plays no explicit role in strategic asset allocation.

Longevity risk is the risk that the investor will outlive his or her assets in retirement. In the United States, 65-year-old women have about an 81 percent chance of living to age 80; for men, the chance is 68 percent. When combined with the life expectancy of a spouse, the odds reach about 91 percent that at least one person in a married couple aged 65 will live to age 80. For a broader sense of the potential longevity risk, Exhibit 5-41 illustrates survival probabilities of 65-year-olds in the United States. The "joint" column shows the probability that at least one person in a married couple will survive to age 80, 85, 90, 95, and 100. The next column shows the probability that an individual will survive to the various ages. For married couples, in more than 78 percent of the cases, at least one spouse will still be alive at age 85.

Like mortality risk, longevity risk is independent of financial market risk. In contrast to mortality risk, however, the investor bears longevity risk directly. Longevity risk is also related to income needs and so logically should be directly related to asset allocation, unlike mortality risk. But many investment retirement plans ignore longevity risk. For example,

[70]For example, alternative assets with low correlation to the stock market (commodities, hedge funds, etc.) can be very attractive for these investors.

EXHIBIT 5-41 Probability of 65-Year-Olds Living to Various Ages (U.S. data)

Age	Joint	Individual	Male	Female
80	90.6%	74.0%	68.0%	80.6%
85	78.4	56.8	49.3	65.3
90	57.0	36.3	29.5	44.5
95	30.9	17.6	13.4	23.0
100	11.5	6.0	4.2	8.6

Source: 1996 U.S. Annuity 2000 Mortality Table (Society of Actuaries).

many such approaches assume that the investor needs to plan only to age 85. Although 85 years is approximately the life expectancy for a 65-year-old individual in many countries, life expectancy is only an average. Approximately half of U.S. investors currently age 65 will live past age 85; for a married couple, the odds of one spouse surviving beyond age 85 are more than 78 percent. If investors use an 85-year life expectancy to plan their retirement income needs, many of them will outlive their personal retirement resources (other than government and corporate pensions).

Longevity risk cannot be completely managed through asset allocation. One reaction to this risk might be to bear greater investment risk in an effort to earn higher long-term returns. If the investor can tolerate additional risk, this approach may be appropriate. Such a strategy reduces longevity risk only in expectation, however; the higher mean return may not be realized and the investor may still outlive his resources.

In fact, exposure to longevity risk offers no potential reward, and investors should be willing to pay a premium to transfer it just as they transfer property and liability exposures through homeowners insurance.[71] Transferring longevity risk in whole or in part to an insurer through an annuity contract may be rational. Insurers can profitably accept longevity risks by (1) spreading the risks among a large group of annuitants and (2) making careful and conservative assumptions about the rate of return earned on their assets. A life annuity type of instrument should be considered for many retirement plans. A **life annuity** guarantees a monthly income to the annuitant for the rest of his life. Life annuities may have one of three forms:[72] In a **fixed annuity,** the periodic income payments are constant in amount; in a **variable annuity,** the payments vary depending on an underlying investment portfolio's returns; and an **equity-indexed annuity** provides a guarantee of a minimum fixed payment plus some participation in stock market gains, if any. In an asset allocation, we would include the value of a fixed annuity as a risk-free asset and that of a variable annuity as a risky holding (looking through to the underlying portfolio's composition for a more precise classification). An equity-indexed annuity resembles a risk-free asset plus a call option on stock returns. Purchasing an annuity, however, is a product choice quite distinct from the strategic asset allocation decision.

[71] Living a long life is desirable from many aspects; we are only focusing on the financial aspect of longevity.

[72] See Rejda (2005).

EXAMPLE 5-16 Critique of an Asset Allocation Approach for Individual Clients

Ridenour Associates is an investment management firm focused on high-net-worth individuals.

As a preliminary step to asset allocation, twice a year Ridenour develops three or four economic scenarios in-house. The senior staff assigns probabilities and generates return forecasts for domestic stocks, domestic bonds, and cash equivalents (the only asset types the firm uses); then expected values are computed for each asset category.

The staff develops a table containing a range of possible strategic asset allocations. Each allocation selected for the table has the highest three-year expected return among those allocations expected to have a 90 percent probability of achieving a specific minimum annual return. In consultation with the client, the Ridenour portfolio manager will choose one or two minimum return thresholds and then discuss the associated recommended asset allocations. If one or both recommended allocations appear to satisfy the client's other return and risk objectives, then a selection will be made from those choices. Ridenour repeats this process approximately every six months, when new allocations are developed. Exhibit 5-42 shows the current list.

EXHIBIT 5-42 Ridenour Associates' Recommended Asset Allocations (June 1, 2005)

Minimum Annual Return (90% Probability)	Anticipated 3-Year Compound Annual Return	Recommended Asset Allocation		
		Cash	Bonds	Stocks
−6%	12.0%	10%	30%	60%
−4	11.0	20	40	40
−2	10.0	30	40	30
0	9.0	50	30	20
2	8.5	60	30	10
4	8.0	70	20	10
6	7.5	80	15	5

Discuss the strengths and weaknesses of Ridenour's asset allocation approach.

Solution: Ridenour's approach has the following strengths and weaknesses:

Strengths

- The process is explicit and relatively straightforward.
- It offers clients a fairly wide range of choice across the risk–return spectrum, and permits allocations to be selected and varied according to client needs and preferences.
- It forces client interaction to take place at least twice a year, providing recurring opportunity for discussion, education, and updating.

Weaknesses

- Ridenour's approach employs only three classes of domestic securities. It excludes tax-exempt bonds from consideration, although in certain countries such bonds may play a role in the portfolios of high-net-worth investors, who generally are subject to high tax rates. The process also excludes asset classes such as international securities that may offer diversification benefits.
- The approach fails to give differentiated attention to human capital considerations. Young wealthy clients may want their exposure to equities to exceed the 60 percent maximum Ridenour allows.
- The three-year time horizon for assessing asset allocations is artificial. The horizon must be chosen with reference to each client's needs and circumstances. In addition, twice-a-year revision of three-year forecasts may result in excessive trading and high transaction costs.

9. STRATEGIC ASSET ALLOCATION FOR INSTITUTIONAL INVESTORS

The basic principles of optimization do not vary depending on the type of investor we are considering. The results and recommendations can only be as good as our inputs and model choices, however. In recommending a strategic asset allocation, we should seek a comprehensive picture of the investor's characteristics and choose our models and inputs appropriately. The following sections introduce institutional investors' characteristics and concerns as they affect strategic asset allocation. We discuss five major kinds of institutional investors: defined-benefit plans, foundations, endowments, insurance companies, and banks.

9.1. Defined-Benefit Plans

Pension plan sponsors use a variety of methods to select an asset allocation, with a strong focus on ALM techniques. Whatever approach they choose, plan sponsors typically face a range of constraints motivated by regulatory and liquidity concerns.

1. *Regulatory constraints*. The United States, the United Kingdom, Canada, the Netherlands, and Australia generally rely on the prudent person concept rather than limitations on asset-class holdings in their oversight of pension investing.[73] Nevertheless, the restriction on Canadian pension funds' holding of non-Canadian investments valued at cost to no more than 30 percent of assets is an example of a regulatory *maximum*. Denmark requires pension funds to have 60 percent at a *minimum* invested in domestic debt. Another example of a regulatory constraint is a set of "basket clauses," which place percentage limits for the aggregate holdings of certain illiquid or alternative investments

[73]See Davis (1995). A percentage limitation on investment in the sponsoring company's stock is common in these countries, however.

(venture capital, hedge funds, emerging market securities, etc.). Regulatory constraints are intended to promote safety and diversification and to discourage conflicts of interest (e.g., by limitations on self-investment).

2. *Liquidity constraints.* A fund may have sufficiently high liquidity requirements that it must limit its percentage of illiquid assets (e.g., private debt, private equity, or real estate).

Just as for any other investor, a strategic asset allocation for a pension fund should meet the investor's return objective and be consistent with the fund's risk tolerance. In a prior section, we used defined-benefit plans to illustrate an ALM approach to asset allocation. From an ALM perspective, the following are desirable characteristics for an asset allocation:

- The risk of funding shortfalls is acceptable.
- The anticipated volatility of the pension surplus is acceptable. Low pension surplus volatility is generally associated with asset allocations whose duration approximately matches the duration of pension liabilities, because pension liabilities behave similarly to bonds as concerns interest rate sensitivity.
- The anticipated volatility of the contributions is acceptable.
- An asset-only approach to a pension fund's strategic asset allocation was traditionally, and remains, a choice in professional investment practice. From an asset-only perspective, a reasonable starting point is the efficient asset allocation with the lowest standard deviation of return that meets the specified return objective of the pension fund.

In either an ALM or AO approach, if pension liabilities are fixed in nominal terms, inflation is not a concern. Otherwise, the adviser needs to consider how much inflation protection the asset allocation is expected to afford. Many pension sponsors attempt to use investments such as equities that represent real claims on the economy to at least

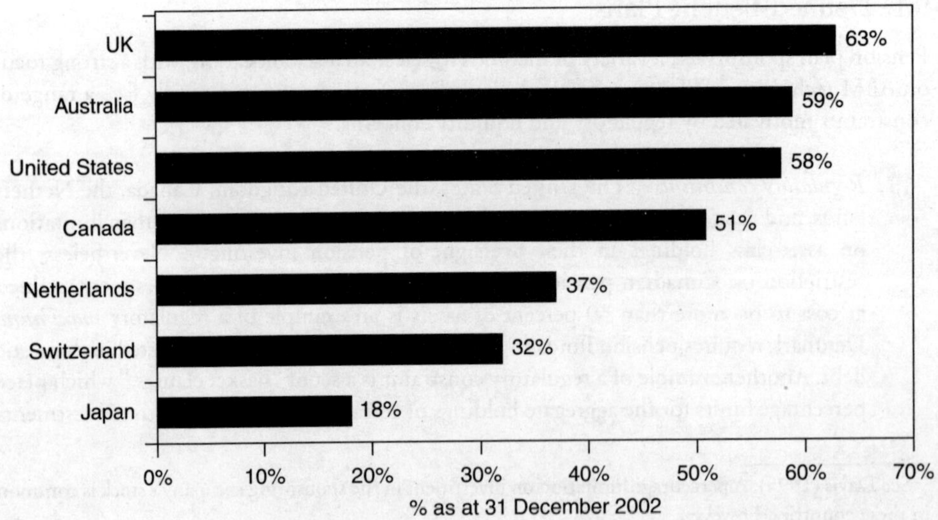

EXHIBIT 5-43 Total Equities (Domestic and International) as a Proportion of Institutional Pension Fund Assets, December 31, 2002
Source: Memorandum (March 2004), Watson Wyatt Canada.

partially offset the pension plan's exposure to higher wage and salary costs from inflation and productivity gains. Pensions in Australia, Canada, the United Kingdom, and the United States traditionally have given stocks a major role. In certain continental European countries and in Japan, however, bond investments have traditionally played the major role, consistent with a risk-averse ALM concept of pension investing. Exhibits 5-43 and 5-44 show these country differences.

Exhibit 5-45 shows pension asset allocations in Canada and the United States, two countries where pension plans on average have an equity bias. The greater allocation to

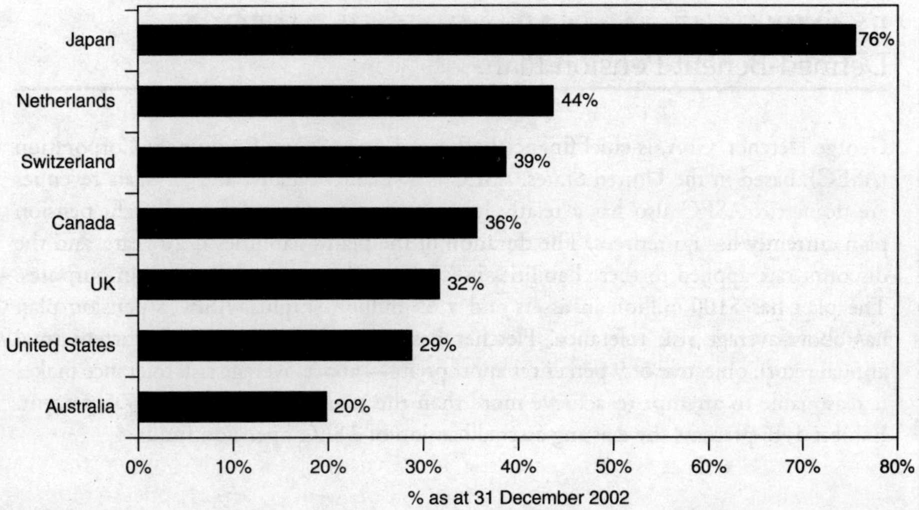

EXHIBIT 5-44 Total Bonds (Domestic and International) as a Proportion of Institutional Pension Fund Assets, December 31, 2002
Source: Memorandum (March 2004), Watson Wyatt Canada.

EXHIBIT 5-45 Asset Allocations of Canadian and U.S. Pension Funds, December 31, 2002

	Canadian Pension Funds[a]	U.S. Pension Funds
Domestic equities	25%	49%
Nondomestic equities	26	9
Domestic bonds	33	28
Nondomestic bonds	3	1
Real estate	4	3
Cash	2	6
Other	5	4
Alternatives	2	
Total	100%	100%

[a]These data are for the top 100 pension funds in Canada and exclude the Canada Pension Plan (CPP) and the Québec Pension Plan (QPP). These funds account for approximately 65 percent of the market excluding CPP and QPP.
Source: Memorandum (March 2004), Watson Wyatt Canada.

non-Canadian equities in Canada is logical, because Canadian equity markets total less than one-tenth the size of U.S. markets. In the United Kingdom, which also has an equities orientation in pension asset allocation, real estate investment has tended to play a substantially larger role than in Canada or the United States.

Example 5-17 illustrates how to evaluate a set of allocations in light of a pension plan's risk and return objectives.

EXAMPLE 5-17 Asset Allocation for the ASEC Defined-Benefit Pension Plan.

George Fletcher, CFA, is chief financial officer of Apex Sports Equipment Corporation (ASEC), based in the United States. ASEC is a small company, and all of its revenues are domestic. ASEC also has a relatively young staff, and its defined-benefit pension plan currently has no retirees. The duration of the plan's liabilities is 20 years, and the discount rate applied to these liabilities is 7.5 percent for actuarial valuation purposes. The plan has $100 million in assets and a $5 million surplus. ASEC's pension plan has above-average risk tolerance. Fletcher has concluded that ASEC's current total annual return objective of 9 percent is appropriate—above-average risk tolerance makes it reasonable to attempt to achieve more than the return requirement of 7.5 percent. Exhibit 5-46 presents the existing asset allocation of ASEC's pension fund.

EXHIBIT 5-46 Original ASEC Strategic Asset Allocation

Asset Class	Allocation
Large-cap U.S. equities	50%
Small-cap U.S. equities	10
U.S. 30-day Treasury bills	10
U.S. intermediate-term bonds (5-year duration)	20
U.S. long-term bonds (20-year duration)	10
Total	100%
Risk-free rate	5.0%
Expected total portfolio return (annual)	9.0%
Standard deviation (annual)	13.0%
Sharpe ratio	0.31

The ASEC pension oversight committee now requests that Fletcher research additional asset classes to include in the strategic asset allocation. The board tells him not to consider U.S. venture capital or real estate at this time. Fletcher conducts his research and concludes that both developed and emerging international markets offer diversification benefits. He constructs the four possible asset allocations shown in Exhibit 5-47.

EXHIBIT 5-47 Proposed Strategic Asset Allocations for ASEC

Asset Class	Allocation A	B	C	D
Large-cap U.S. equities		35%	35%	50%
Small-cap U.S. equities		15	10	10
International developed market equities		15	10	
International emerging market equities		5	5	
U.S. 30-day Treasury bills		15		20
U.S. intermediate-term bonds (5-year duration)		15		20
U.S. long-term bonds (20-year duration)	100%		40	
Expected return (annual)	7.0%	9.5%	9.0%	8.5%
Standard deviation (annual)	8.0%	13.5%	11.5%	12.0%
Sharpe ratio	0.25	0.33	0.35	0.29

Based on the above information, recommend and justify two of these four asset allocations in Exhibit 5-47 for final consideration. The selections must:

- Meet the pension plan's return objective.
- Be consistent with the pension plan's risk tolerance.
- Improve on the original asset allocation's expected risk-adjusted performance.
- Have acceptable surplus volatility (the risk caused by a mismatch between plan assets and plan liabilities).
- Provide inflation protection.

Solution: Justification exists for recommending either Asset Allocation B or Asset Allocation C as best for achieving the three objectives simultaneously. The justification for choosing B or C might address the following points.

1. *Meets the return objective*. The board's return objective is 9 percent. Only Allocations B and C have expected returns satisfying this long-term return objective.
2. *Consistent with risk tolerance*. As judged by the standard deviation of return compared with that of the original asset allocation, all four allocations in Exhibit 5-47 are acceptable.
3. *Risk-adjusted performance*. The Sharpe ratio is a common barometer of risk-adjusted performance; it estimates an investment's or portfolio's expected excess return per unit of risk. Asset Allocation C has a higher Sharpe ratio than that of the original portfolio (0.35 versus 0.31) and the highest Sharpe ratio of any allocation shown in Exhibit 5-47. Allocation B is the only other alternative with a higher Sharpe ratio than the original asset allocation. The difference between the Sharpe ratios for B and C is small.
4. *Acceptable surplus volatility*. Allocations A and C include long-term U.S. bonds with 20-year duration, which may make these allocations more closely match the stated duration of ASEC's liabilities (20 years) than the other allocations do. Closely matching the duration of assets and liabilities should reduce pension-surplus volatility. Therefore, some may view a strategy of matching bonds with

20-year duration to the 20-year-duration liabilities as appropriate because it may minimize surplus volatility.

5. *Inflation protection.* Ongoing pension liabilities contain uncertainty in both the amount and timing of the cash outlay, because of factors such as varying future inflation and interest rates. In this context, Allocation A, which consists of 100 percent bonds, is not diversified and offers no protection against the risk that inflation will increase plan liabilities through inflation-related wage and benefit increases. Allocation C, which consists 40 percent in 20-year duration bonds and 60 percent in equities, is a better choice than A. Allocation B, which is 70 percent invested in a diversified portfolio of U.S. and non-U.S. equities, may provide even more protection than Allocation C against the erosion of values.

In summary, the above considerations clearly point to a selection from Asset Allocation B or C.

9.2. Foundations and Endowments

We can consider foundations and endowments together, because they frequently share many characteristics as generally tax-exempt long-term investors with various spending commitments. These investors must generate a high long-term rate of return in order to provide a substantial spending flow as well as to compensate for inflation. For endowments that support institutions such as universities, the relevant inflation rates have generally exceeded those of the overall economy. Historically, fixed-income investments such as bonds or cash have not provided meaningful returns above inflation. In order to generate the high returns necessary to fund meaningful spending distributions, most endowments invest predominantly in equities or equity-like investments. Equities have been viewed as supplying the long-term growth bias, with bonds playing a role in diversification.[74]

Fiduciaries of endowments and foundations should focus on developing and adhering to appropriate long-term investment and asset allocation policies. Low-cost, easy-to-monitor, passive investment strategies are often their primary approach to implementing a strategic asset allocation. The institution's investment policy and approach should be understood and embraced by the organization's governing body to ensure steady and disciplined execution of the program through the markets' cycles and vicissitudes.

Because of limited resources to fund the costs and complexities of due diligence, small endowments have a constrained investment opportunity set compared with large endowments. Furthermore, the constrained opportunity set may preclude participation in high-return opportunities in some alternative asset classes. The National Association of College and University Business Officers reports that on June 30, 2004, endowments with more than $1 billion of assets were on average more than 28 percent invested in alternative assets. In comparison, endowments with between $50 million and $100 million were on average less than 7 percent invested in alternative assets. These small endowments had an average 22 percent allocation to fixed-income assets, compared with the 15 percent held by large endowments.[75]

---

[74]Swensen (2000, p. 54) provides a clear statement of this viewpoint.

[75]See www.ncccs.cc.nc.us/Resource Development/docs/Endowment%20study/02 SummaryofFindings.pdf.

Example 5-18 reviews the construction of an investment policy statement for a foundation and addresses the formulation of an appropriate strategic asset allocation in light of the IPS.

EXAMPLE 5-18 Asset Allocation for the Help for Students Foundation

The Help for Students Foundation (HFS) exists to provide full scholarships to U.S. universities for gifted high school graduates who otherwise would be denied access to higher education. Additional facts concerning the organization are as follows:

- Per-student full scholarship costs, which have been rising rapidly for many years, were $30,000 this year and are expected to grow at least 4 percent annually for the indefinite future.
- The market value of HFS's investment assets is $300 million, currently allocated as shown below:
    - 35 percent to long-maturity U.S. Treasury bonds,
    - 10 percent to a diversified portfolio of corporate bond issues,
    - 10 percent to U.S. bank certificates of deposit (CDs), and
    - 45 percent to large-cap, income-oriented U.S. stocks.
- HFS's entire annual administrative costs are paid for by supporters' donations.
- An amount equal to 5 percent of the year-end market value of HFS's investment portfolio must be spent annually in order to preserve the foundation's existing tax-exempt status under U.S. law.

The IPS currently governing trustee actions, unchanged since its adoption in the early 1960s, reads as follows:

> *The Foundation's purpose is to provide university educations for as many deserving individuals as possible for as long as possible. Accordingly, investment emphasis should be on the production of income and the minimization of market risk. Because all expenses are in U.S. dollars, only domestic securities should be owned. It is the Trustees' duty to preserve and protect HFS's assets while maximizing its grant-making ability and maintaining its tax-exempt status.*

After a long period in which board membership was unchanged, new and younger trustees are now replacing retiring members. As a result, many aspects of HFS's operations are under review, including the principles and guidelines that have shaped past investment decision-making. Referring to the above facts, address the following tasks:

1. Identify four shortcomings of the existing IPS and explain why these policy aspects should be reviewed.
2. Create a new IPS for the foundation. In your response, be specific and complete with respect to investment objectives and constraints.
3. Using the policy created in Part 2 above, revise HFS's existing asset allocation and justify the resulting asset mix. You must choose from the following asset classes in constructing your response (calculations are not required).

Asset Class	Expected Total Return
Cash equivalents	4%
Medium- and long-term government bonds	7
Real estate	8
Large- and small-cap U.S. equities	10
International equities (EAFE)	12

Solution to Problem 1: Shortcomings of HFS's existing IPS, and an explanation of why these policy aspects should be reviewed, are as follows:

- The statement's "emphasis... on the production of income and the minimization of market risk" is inappropriate. The return objective should focus on total (expected) return rather than on its components. Furthermore, the return focus should be on enhancing either real total return or nominal return to include protection of purchasing power. Either maximization of return for a given level of (nondiversifiable) risk or minimization of risk for a given level of return is a more appropriate objective statement than the current one.
- The existing IPS does not specify important constraints normally included, such as time horizon, liquidity, tax considerations, legal and regulatory considerations, and unique needs.
- It is unclear whether the IPS of the early 1960s has been subjected to periodic review. The new statement should be reviewed at regular intervals (e.g., annually), and this review requirement should be specific in the IPS.
- It is unclear whether the four asset classes in which the foundation is now invested represent the only classes considered. In any event, the asset-mix policy should permit inclusion of more asset classes, including alternative investments.
- The IPS should specify the limits within which HFS's manager(s) may tactically allocate assets.
- The limitation of holding "only domestic securities" because "all expenses are in U.S. dollars" is inappropriate. At a minimum, non-U.S. investment, with some form of currency exchange risk hedge, should be considered when the return–risk trade-off for these securities exceeds that on domestic securities.

Solution to Problem 2: A statement such as the following is appropriate:

Objectives

- ***Return requirement.*** In order to maintain its ability to provide inflation-adjusted scholarships and its tax-exempt status, HFS requires a real rate of return of 4 percent. The appropriate definition of inflation in this context is the 4 percent rate at which full scholarship cost per student is expected to increase.
- ***Risk tolerance.*** Given its very long time horizon, HFS has the ability to take moderate risk, with associated volatility in returns, in order to maintain purchasing power, as long as no undue volatility is introduced into the flow of resources to cover near-term scholarship payments.

Constraints

- ***Liquidity requirements.*** Given the size of HFS's assets and the predictable nature of its annual cash outflows, its liquidity needs can be easily ascertained and met. A systematic plan for future needs can be constructed and appropriate portfolio investment built to meet these planned needs.
- ***Time horizon.*** The foundation has a potentially infinite time horizon. A three-to-five year cycle of investment policy planning with reviews should be put into place.
- ***Tax considerations.*** Maintenance of HFS's tax-exempt status, including the 5 percent minimum spending requirement, should receive ongoing attention. The foundation's tax status should be examined and reviewed annually in connection with its annual audit report.
- ***Legal and regulatory considerations.*** Foundation trustees and others involved in investment decision making should understand and obey applicable state law and adhere to the prudent person standard.
- ***Unique circumstances.*** There are no significant circumstances not already considered under objectives and other constraints.

Solution to Problem 3: In designing a revised asset allocation, the board should assume long-term historical risk and correlation measures for each of the five asset classes. Some adjustments may be necessary, however, such as for the positive risk and correlation bias of real estate resulting from the use of appraisal value in calculating real estate returns.

Given the answers to Parts 1 and 2 and the expected returns given in the statement of Part 1, increased investment in common stock, including large- and small-cap domestic equities and international equities, and in real estate (for its inflation hedging and diversification attributes) is warranted. Bank CDs should be minimized or eliminated; with no pressing liquidity needs, HFS can minimize its cash equivalent holdings. One appropriate allocation that includes both the current target (required) and possible future range (not required) is as follows:

Asset Class	Future Range	Current Target
Cash equivalents	0–5%	2%
Medium- and long-term (U.S.) Government bonds	20–35	30
Real estate	0–10	8
Large- and small-cap U.S. equities	30–50	40
International equities (EAFE)	5–20	20

Equity securities make up 60 percent of the total in this allocation, an appropriate mix given the relatively moderate spread between fixed-income and equity expected returns.

9.3. Insurance Companies

An insurer's strategic asset allocation must complement and coordinate with the insurer's operating policy. Investment portfolio policy thus seeks to achieve the most appropriate mix of assets (1) to counterbalance the risks inherent in the mix of insurance products involved and (2) to achieve the stated return objectives. The insurer must consider numerous factors in arriving at the appropriate mix, the most important of which are asset/liability management concerns, regulatory influences, time horizons, and tax considerations.

Insurers are taxable enterprises, in contrast to defined-benefit pension plans, endowments, and most foundations. Therefore, insurers focus on after-tax return and risk. Like defined-benefit plans, however, insurers face contractual liabilities to insureds. As a result, an ALM approach to strategic asset allocation is generally chosen. ALM considerations include yield, duration, convexity, key rate sensitivity, value at risk, and the effects of asset risk on capital requirements given the spread of risk-based capital regulation.[76] Public policy frequently views insurance portfolios as quasi-trust funds, further stressing the importance of managing risk.

We have discussed the ALM approach to strategic asset allocation in earlier sections; however, portfolio segmentation is a distinctive feature of life insurers' investment activities that we have not addressed previously. **Portfolio segmentation** is the creation of subportfolios within the general account portfolio, according to the product mix for each individual company. In this approach, the insurer groups liabilities according to the product line of business or segment. (Some insurers segment by individual product line; others group similar lines according to such characteristics as duration.) Portfolios are then constructed by segment in such a way that the most appropriate securities fund each product segment. An asset type's appropriateness is measured on at least three bases: expected return, interest rate risk (duration), and credit risk characteristics. Each of these factors is evaluated relative to the competitive, actuarial, and statutory characteristics of the product line(s) being funded. Each segment has its own return objective, risk parameters, and liquidity characteristics.

Most life insurance companies in the United States and Canada have adopted some form of portfolio segmentation. Prior to segmentation, the return on invested assets in the general account was required to be allocated proportionately to various lines of insurance business (whole life, annuities, group, and so on).[77] Compared with that method, portfolio segmentation offers the following advantages:

Segmentation:

- Provides a focus for meeting return objectives by product line.
- Provides a simple way to allocate investment income by line of business.
- Provides more accurate measurement of profitability by line of business. For example, the insurer can judge whether its returns cover the returns it offers on products with investment features such as annuities and guaranteed investment contracts (GICs).[78]
- Aids in managing interest rate risk and/or duration mismatch by product line.

---

[76]Value at risk is an estimate of the loss that we expect to be exceeded with a given level of probability over a specified time period e distribution of a portfolio's ending values over some specified time horizon.

[77]Allocation has generally been on the basis of the ratio of each line's reserves to total reserves. Companies use one of two methods for determining the investment yield by line of business. The **investment year method** credits the cash available for investment from a particular line of business with the new money rate (average yield for new investments in that year). The portfolio method allocates return to line of business on the basis of the cumulative investment return of the entire portfolio (not distinguishing among years). Statutorily, all general account assets of a life insurance company back all liabilities. For reporting purposes only, however, insurers can divide their general account portfolios into segments by line of business.

[78]A **guaranteed investment contract** is a debt instrument issued by insurers, usually in large denominations, that pays a guaranteed, generally fixed interest rate for a specified time period.

- Assists regulators and senior management in assessing the suitability of investments.
- The portfolio segmentation approach establishes multiple asset allocations that are each appropriate for the product lines associated with the segments. Most life insurance companies have found that too many segments create span of control and suboptimization problems. Thus, most companies use relatively few segments. Furthermore, the optimization of the total portfolio is the ultimate controlling factor for determining the asset allocation for each segment and the portfolio as a whole.

Another development affecting insurers has been the expansion of their opportunity set. Exhibit 5-48 illustrates the evolution of the asset classes in which life insurers invest.

Compared with the past, insurers now make use of a much wider array of investment vehicles. The individual entries in Exhibit 5-48 deserve comment.

Fixed-income investments constitute the majority holding of most life and non-life insurers. Casualty insurance companies traditionally maintain a bond portfolio to offset insurance reserves, with capital and surplus funds invested largely in common stocks. As previously mentioned, insurance companies are sensitive to cash flow volatility and reinvestment risk, and fixed-income investments are made with these concerns in mind, as well as the expected compensation for bearing these risks. Insurance companies traditionally have been buyers of investment-grade bonds (Baa/BBB or higher), with emphasis on Baa/BBB and A quality bonds. Many insurers, especially large companies, occasionally purchase bonds of Ba/BB quality or below. Because of the importance of private placement bonds in life insurance company portfolios, credit analysis has long been considered one of the industry's strengths.

EXHIBIT 5-48 Assets in Which Life Insurance Companies Invest

Traditional	Contemporary
Bonds	Bonds
Domestic (Aaa/AAA–Baa/BBB)	Domestic
	• Aaa/AAA–Ba/BB quality
	• Junk bonds
	• Residential mortgage backed
	• Commercial mortgage backed
	• Asset backed
	• Collateralized bond obligations
	• Collateralized loan obligations
	Nondomestic
	• Hedged
	• Unhedged
Mortgage loans: residential	Mortgage loans: commercial and residential
Stocks: common and preferred	Common and preferred stocks: domestic and international
Equity real estate	Equity real estate
Other: venture capital	Venture capital
	Hedge funds
	Derivative investments
	• Futures
	• Options
	• Interest rate swaps

Source: Mutual of Omaha Companies.

In recent years, many insurance companies have included some exposure to high-yield, below-investment-grade (junk) bonds. Further, historical default rates support an expectation for the realization of a significant net yield advantage over U.S. Treasuries from a diversified portfolio of junk bonds over the holding period. This projected advantage, typically anywhere from 300 to 600 basis points (net), is well in excess of the spreads over Treasuries available from Baa/BBB securities and even mortgage loans. In the United States, there are generally regulatory constraints on junk bond holdings. For example, in New York, regulations limit junk bonds to 20 percent of assets for those insurance companies doing business in that state. Also, the default rates on junk bonds, which exceeded 10 percent in the early 1990s and again in the early 2000s, have tempered some of the life insurance industry's enthusiasm for this asset class.

In addition to credit quality, insurers must also consider bonds' taxability. In the United States, bonds issued by states and municipalities are generally exempt from taxation at the federal level (state bonds are also exempt also from state taxes, and municipal bonds from municipal and state taxes, in general). For tax reasons, non-life insurers have often been major purchasers of such tax-exempt bonds.

For a life insurance company, the selection of bond maturities is substantially dictated by its need to manage the interest rate risk exposure arising from asset/liability duration mismatch. Consequently, life insurers typically structure the bond portfolio's maturity schedule in line with the estimated liability cash outflows, at least in the short and intermediate term.

Insurers hold equity investments for several reasons. Life insurers market a variety of products such as variable annuities and variable life insurance policies that may be linked to equity investments. Insurers then hold equity investments in the separate account(s) associated with those products. Another important function of the investment operation is to provide growth of surplus to support the expansion in insurance volume; common stocks, equity investments in real estate, and venture capital have been the investment alternatives most widely used to achieve surplus growth. Surplus adequacy is a growing concern for the life insurance industry. Companies are looking at more-aggressive capital appreciation-oriented strategies as well as financial leverage to supplement the narrowing contributions to surplus from the newer product lines. At the same time, concerns regarding valuation risk (discussed earlier) have led most life insurers to limit common stock holdings (at market value) as a percentage of surplus rather than as a percentage of assets as specified in the statutes.

Insurers (particularly life insurers) generally maintain limited liquidity reserves; most life insurers depend on their fixed-income portfolio's maturity schedule and their ability to control interest rate risk to assure that surrenders and/or policy loans can be funded with little or no loss of principal income. Casualty insurers, especially those with relatively short duration liabilities, tend to have higher liquidity requirements than other insurers.

Example 5-19 provides an example of an asset allocation for a stock life insurer (a life insurer organized as a corporation owned by shareholders).

EXAMPLE 5-19 An Asset Allocation for a Stock Life Insurer

ABC Life is a hypothetical stock life insurer. The following asset allocation would not be unusual for a stock life insurer. The allocation reflects regulatory constraints operative in the United States.

	Target	Permissible Range
Cash Equivalents	2%	1–5%
Public Bonds	35	30–40
Government	2	0–5
Corporate	15	10–20
Mortgage backed	8	4–12
Residential	5	2–8
Commercial	3	0–6
Asset backed	5	2–8
International	5	2–8
Private Placement Bonds	32	27–37
Corporate	20	15–25
Asset backed	10	5–15
International	2	0–4
Public Common Stocks	10	5–15
Large cap	5	2–8
Small cap	3	1–5
International	2	0–4
Private Equity	5	0–10
Venture capital	2	0–4
Buyout	3	0–5
Commercial Mortgage Loans	10	5–15
Apartment	4	2–6
Industrial	3	1–5
Office	3	1–5
Retail Mortgage Loans	2	0–5
Real Estate	4	0–6
Commercial	4	0–6
Residential	0	0–0
International	0	0–0
Land	0	0–0

9.4. Banks

Banks are financial intermediaries with a traditional focus on taking deposits and lending money. As such, they are taxable investors with predominantly short- and intermediate-term liabilities.

Although we can view a bank's strategic asset allocation from the perspective of all bank assets including loans, real estate (including bank premises) and so forth, a bank's securities portfolio is subject to a distinct set of regulations and is traditionally treated separately.

As discussed in the chapter on managing institutional investor portfolios, a bank's securities portfolio plays an important role in (1) managing the balance sheet's overall interest rate risk, (2) managing liquidity (assuring adequate cash is available to meet liabilities), (3) producing income, and (4) managing credit risk. The first concern is the most important and dictates an ALM approach to asset allocation. Banks' portfolios of loans and leases are generally not very liquid and may carry substantial credit risk. Therefore, a bank's securities portfolio plays a balancing role in providing a ready source of liquidity and in offsetting loan-portfolio credit risk.

As with the portfolios of insurers, public policy usually views bank portfolios as quasi-public trust funds. Thus banks typically face detailed regulatory restrictions on maximum holdings of asset types, often stated as a percentage of capital. In turn, the risk of assets affects banks' costs through the operation of risk-based capital rules.

EXAMPLE 5-20 An Asset Allocation for a Commercial Bank

William Bank is a hypothetical U.S. commercial bank. Although a more detailed breakdown of asset classes would be more realistic, the asset allocation presented below shows the typical emphasis on high-credit-quality debt instruments. The target percentages are stated as a percentage of the securities portfolio, for consistency with the presentation elsewhere, but regulatory guidelines are as a percentage of capital (capital stock and surplus plus undivided profits).

Investment Portfolio Asset Type	Target	Regulatory Guideline
U.S. Treasury bonds	10%	No limitation
Agency obligations	65	No limitation
Tax-exempt general obligations	3	No limitation
Tax-exempt other	5	<4% of capital,>Baa/BBB
Corporate bonds	12	<10% of capital,>Baa/BBB
Money-market preferred stock	5	<15% of capital

10. TACTICAL ASSET ALLOCATION[79]

Tactical asset allocation (TAA) involves deliberately underweighting or overweighting asset classes relative to their target weights in the policy portfolio in an attempt to add value. TAA is active management at the asset-class level. Thus in a top-down perspective, TAA would follow the strategic asset allocation decision and stand one level above decisions about how to manage money within an asset class. TAA can be conducted independently of the within-class investment decisions by using derivative securities, a cost-efficient means for changing asset-class exposures. In that case, TAA can be described as an overlay strategy.

TAA is based on short-term expectations and perceived disequilibria. We know from prior discussion that strategic asset allocation reflects the investor's long-term capital market

[79]This section was contributed by Robert D. Arnott.

expectations. That concept is logical because strategic asset allocation concerns meeting the investor's long-term objectives. The investor's short-term views may well differ from his long-term views, however. TAA involves tactical bets to exploit those differences. Economically speaking, it seeks to exploit transitory deviations of asset-class values from their expected long-term relationships. An investor may make occasional tactical weight adjustments in some circumstances or may have an ongoing and more systematic program of tactical adjustments. Both can be described as tactical asset allocation. TAA can be managed in-house or delegated to one of the many professional investment managers who run TAA programs.

TAA is frequently based on the following three principles:

1. *Market prices tell explicitly what returns are available.* Cash yields reveal the immediate nominal return accorded short-term investors. The yield to maturity of T-bills is the nominal reward for holding them to maturity. Thus, at least for this and similar pure discount instruments, investors have *objective knowledge* of prospective returns. Although prices yield less direct information about prospective return for other asset classes, we can at least make educated estimates. For example, we could use dividend yield plus growth rate to estimate the return to equities. Inevitably, reality will not quite match these expectations. Nevertheless history suggests that simple objective measures provide a useful, objective guide to future rewards.

   As an illustration, Exhibit 5-49 demonstrates one method for constructing return expectations (many others are in industry use as well). Almost any investment we might choose has three components to return: income, growth in income, and changing valuation levels (changes in the value that the market assigns to each dollar of income). For the last 77 years, U.S. stocks delivered a real return, over and above inflation, of nearly 7 percent. This return consisted of 4.2 percent from yield, a growth rate in dividends that was 1.2 percent above the rate of inflation, and 1.5 percent from a tripling in the price/dividend ratio (a 70 percent decline in dividend yields). Looking to the future, can we count on continued expansion in the price/dividend ratio? Doing so

EXHIBIT 5-49 Long-Term Return Attribution for U.S. Equities

	January 1926–September 2003	As of September 2003
Average dividend yield	4.2%	1.8%
Growth in real dividends	1.2	1.2
Change in valuation levels[80]	1.5	0.0
Real stock return	6.9	3.0
Less average real bond yield	2.1	2.4
Less bond valuation change[81]	−0.3	0.0
Real bond return	1.8	2.4
Return differential	5.1	0.6

[80] Yields went from 5.1 percent to 1.6 percent, representing a 1.5 percent annual increase in the price/dividend valuation level.

[81] Bond yields fell during this period, and real yields on reinvestment were also poor during much of this span.

would be dangerous, because the ratio could as easily go the other way. Can we count on 4.2 percent from income? Not when the current market yield is 1.8 percent as of this writing. This method thus suggests a 3 percent real return as one possible starting point for expectations of U.S. equity returns.

2. *Relative expected returns reflect relative risk perceptions.* When investors perceive more risk, they demand payment for assuming it. If expected equity returns are particularly high compared with bond expected returns, the market is clearly according a substantial risk premium to stocks. It does so when investors in general are uneasy with the outlook for stocks. In the 20 years following the deepest point of the Great Depression of the 1920s, equity dividend yields were significantly higher than the yields on bonds. Apprehensive of a replay of the depression, stockholders demanded a compensatory premium. Ultimately, the markets rewarded those investors willing to bear equity risk. Conversely, as recently as 1981, demoralized U.S. bond investors priced those securities to reflect their unprecedented volatility amid fears of rebounding inflation.

In the mid- to late 1990s, investors embraced the concept that stocks had little risk when measured over the long-term, which lowered their perception of equity risk. Many investors greatly increased their stock holdings without regard to their investment time horizons. As stock prices rose and the risk premium of stocks declined, so the prospects of future rewards from stocks declined as well. The subsequent bursting of the stock market bubble in March 2000 was merely the effect of the market reestablishing an appropriate risk premium for what is still the riskier asset class.

Exhibit 5-50 illustrates the link between risk and reward in U.S. markets for the last 30 years. It shows how the risk premium that is delivered for investing in stocks rather than bonds varies through time, in line with the relative volatility of stocks over bonds. The volatility is calculated as the mean absolute deviation of global stock total returns divided by the mean absolute deviation of global bond total returns during the prior five years.

In 1988, the global equity risk premium dipped below normal levels and remained low for most of the next decade. At the same time, the global volatility ratio rose, and these two measures diverged until the volatility and risk premium again converged in

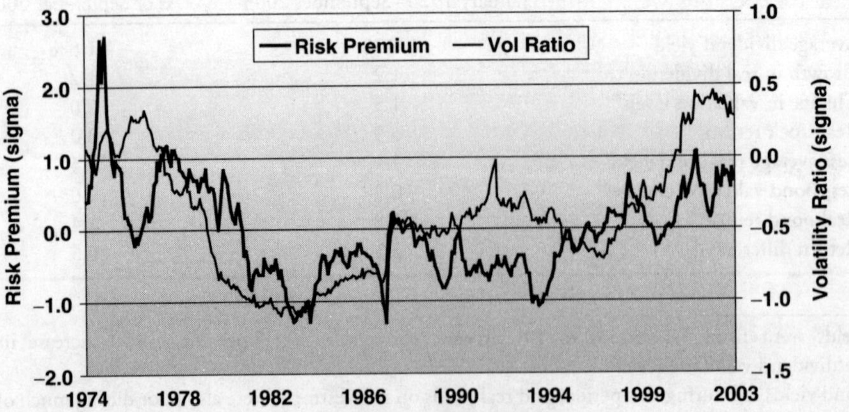

EXHIBIT 5-50 Volatility Ratio vs. Equity Risk Premium

the mid-1990s. In the long term, these measures tend to track one another. In the short term, they provide information when they diverge.

If relative expected returns reflect relative risk perceptions and those perceptions do not have a solid economic basis, overweighting the out-of-favor asset class can be fruitful. To illustrate such an analysis, the period just subsequent to the end of 2003 saw the volatility ratio rise in line with, albeit somewhat faster than, the equity risk premium. This implies that the equity risk premium, although still high by historical standards, may be at least partially explained by a higher than usual volatility ratio, and hence it is not as bullish an indicator for equities as it would be otherwise. The equity risk premium is best viewed in the context of the relative risk of global markets, not in isolation.

3. *Markets are rational and mean reverting.* If the TAA manager can identify departures from equilibrium in the relative pricing of asset classes, the manager may try to exploit them with knowledge that departures from equilibrium compress a proverbial spring that drives the system back towards balance. If 6 percent bonds produce zero return over a certain year (by declining in price enough to offset the coupon), they then offer a higher yield in subsequent years to a prospective holder. Because this process is inherently finite, these bonds, short of default, will eventually produce their promised returns. Bond price changes, moving cyclically, exhibit negative annual serial correlation, a characteristic prized by contrarian tactical asset allocators.

In the same way, differences between expected return on equities and realized return persist over time, but only if earnings growth estimates are inaccurate. They typically are inaccurate, of course, but the law of large numbers provides more confidence in estimating returns of asset classes than individual securities. Similarly, aggregated reported earnings are more meaningful than earnings reported on a company-by-company basis, because the most egregious earnings manipulations are tempered by results from more-truthful peers. Similar to bond yield for bonds, earnings yields on stocks provide an effective (if approximate) valuation measure of future stock returns.

The above three principles address the returns that an investor may expect the markets to deliver when they function rationally and tend toward fair value. The suggested tactical asset allocation decisions were contrarian in nature. The tactical asset allocator should be aware that if a rule for trading leads to superior performance, investors on the losing side of the trades may eventually stop playing; market prices will then adjust to reflect changes in supply and demand, and a trading rule may cease to work. Furthermore, the tactical asset allocator should be aware that deviations from fair value based on historical analysis could persist if the economic environment has changed. Factors such as

- changes in assets' underlying risk attributes,
- changes in central bank policy,
- changes in expected inflation, and
- position in the business cycle

need to be considered in evaluating relative valuations, because they can either mark changes in return regimes or otherwise explain current pricing. A U.S. TAA manager (managing a mix of U.S. stocks, U.S. bonds, and cash) might specify one weighting of relative value and business cycle variables during periods of expansionary Federal Reserve policy (indicated by Fed discount rate decreases) and another weighting during periods of restrictive Fed policy. Fed policy changes could mark periods in which the relationships between stocks and bonds differ. Besides relative value and business cycle variables, some TAA managers use technical/sentiment variables in assessing future asset-class prospects. Price momentum is an example of a technical/sentiment indicator. It is not contradictory that an asset could exhibit momentum at a short time horizon and mean reversion at another, longer, time horizon.

Risk and costs deserve close attention. TAA may decrease or increase the absolute risk level of the investor's overall portfolio, depending on manager skill, the type of TAA discipline involved, and the direction of markets during the time period considered. Relative to the strategic asset allocation, however, TAA is a source of tracking risk. To manage that risk, in practice, TAA managers often are limited to making adjustments within given bands or tactical ranges around target asset-class weights. As an example, the tactical range could be the target weight ± 5 percent or ± 10 percent of portfolio value. With a ± 10 percent tactical range and a 60 percent target for equities, the TAA manager could weight equities within a range of 50 percent to 70 percent. At least one study has found that within-asset-class active management is a much greater source of risk relative to the strategic asset allocation than the selection of tactical weights.[82]

TAA must overcome a transaction-costs barrier to be advantageous. The potential benefits of any tactical adjustment must be examined on an after-costs basis.

Example 5-21 illustrates in a simplified setting the basic mechanics of a TAA program. Example 5-22 presents several more advanced concepts.

EXAMPLE 5-21 Global Tactical Asset Allocation Adjustments

Georgina Henry is chief investment officer of the Glenmore University Endowment (GUE) based in Canada. GUE's strategic asset allocation is as follows, where percentages refer to proportions of the total portfolio:

Global Equities		70%
Canadian equities	30%	
U.S. equities	30	
European equities	10	
Global Fixed Income		30%
Canadian bonds	20	
U.S. bonds	10	

Exhibit 5-51 gives Henry's asset-class expectations.

[82]See Ammann and Zimmerman (2001).

EXHIBIT 5-51 Total Return Expectations for Asset Classes

Asset Class	Long-Term	Short-Term
Global equities	*A*	*B*
Canadian equities	10%	12%
U.S. equities	8	8
European equities	7	7
Global fixed income	*C*	*D*
Canadian bonds	5%	6%
U.S. bonds	5	3

GUE runs a top-down global tactical asset allocation program that first looks at the overall allocation between global equities and global fixed income, and then at the asset allocation within global equities and global fixed income. Assume that the risk characteristics of asset classes are constant.

1. Calculate the long-term and short-term return expectations for global equities (*A* and *B*, respectively) and global fixed income (*C* and *D*, respectively).
2. Determine and justify the changes in portfolio weights (relative to the policy portfolio target weights) that would result from a global tactical asset allocation program.

Solution to Problem 1: Canadian equities, U.S. equities, and European equities represent respectively 30%/70% = 0.4286, 30%/70% = 0.4286, and 10%/70% = 0.1429 of global equities. Therefore, for global equities,

$$A = (0.4286 \times 10\%) + (0.4286 \times 8\%) + (0.1429 \times 7\%) = 8.7143\%, \text{or } 8.71\%$$
$$B = (0.4286 \times 12\%) + (0.4286 \times 8\%) + (0.1429 \times 7\%) = 9.5714\%, \text{or} 9.57\%$$

Global equities' short-term expected return at 9.57 percent is above the long-term expectation of 8.71 percent because Canadian equities are expected in the short term to outperform their long-term expected return. Canadian bonds and U.S. bonds represent respectively 20%/30% = 0.6667 and 10%/30% = 0.3333 of global fixed income. Therefore, for global fixed income,

$$C = (0.6667 \times 5\%) + (0.3333 \times 5\%) = 5\%$$
$$D = (0.6667 \times 6\%) + (0.3333 \times 3\%) = 5\%$$

Global fixed income's short-term expected return at 5 percent equals its long-term expectation. Within global fixed income, however, Canadian bonds are expected short-term at 6 percent to outperform their long-term expected return while U.S. bonds are expected short term at 3 percent to underperform their long-term expected return.

Solution to Problem 2: The results in Part 1 suggest three actions:

- Because global equities appear undervalued compared with global fixed income in the short term, increase the weight on global equities from 70 percent and decrease the weight on global fixed income from 30 percent. The justification is that the short-term expected return on global equities is higher than its long-term expectation, while the short-term expected return on global fixed income is unchanged from its long-term expectation.

- Within global equities, overweight Canadian equities versus their target weight of 30 percent and decrease the weight on U.S. and European equities. Although the short-term expected return on U.S. and European equities are unchanged from their long-term expectations, Canadian equities are expected to outperform short term.
- Within the new global fixed-income allocation, overweight Canadian bonds and underweight U.S. bonds, reflecting their short-term expected performance.

EXAMPLE 5-22 A Tactical Asset Allocation Decision

William Davenport is the chief investment officer of an endowment that is invested 45 percent in U.S. equities, 15 percent in non-U.S. developed market equities, and 40 percent in U.S. Treasury Inflation-Indexed Securities (often called TIPS). The endowment annually reviews its strategic asset allocation. Its IPS authorizes tactical ranges of ± 10 percent in each asset class. Based on his own past observations and his reading of the investment literature, Davenport believes the following:

- U.S. monthly equity returns are less sensitive to the U.S. business contractions than monthly equity returns in European markets and Japan. That is, in U.S. recessions, U.S. equities' returns may actually be relatively better than equity market returns in Europe and Japan.
- An increase in the yield of a 1-year Treasury note indicates a decrease in the probability of a recession in one year's time.

Based on a decrease in the yield of U.S. 1-year T-notes, Davenport has suggested a 55/5/40 U.S. equities/developed market equities/TIPS tactical asset allocation.

1. Evaluate whether the recommended tactical asset allocation is feasible.
2. Appraise the logic of the recommendation.
3. Evaluate the additional information that should be considered before adopting Davenport's recommendation.

Solution to Problem 1: Davenport's TAA suggestion is just within the tactical ranges allowed by the endowment's IPS. Therefore, the suggestion is feasible.

Solution to Problem 2: If Davenport's beliefs are correct, the decrease in the T-note yield indicates an increase in the probability of a U.S. recession in one year. If a recession occurs, he expects U.S. stocks to outperform non-U.S. equities. Therefore, shifting funds from non-U.S. to U.S. equities is logical.

Solution to Problem 3: The following information should be assessed:

- The costs of the tactical adjustment in relation to the expected benefits.
- The increase in tracking risk and the change in expected absolute risk in relation to the expected benefits.
- The economic logic of Davenport's beliefs. If they have an economic logic, it is more likely that relationships based on past observations will hold for the future.
- The strength of the expected relationships. Davenport is suggesting making the maximum permissible allocation to U.S. equities. After the adjustment, the portfolio may be less well diversified than previously. Is the size of the bet justified?
- The presence of any factor such as a change in the risk attributes of assets that may make past relationships fail to hold in the future.

CHAPTER 6

FIXED-INCOME PORTFOLIO MANAGEMENT

H. Gifford Fong

Gifford Fong Associates
Lafayette, California

Larry D. Guin, CFA

Murray State University
Murray, Kentucky

1. INTRODUCTION

Over the past 25 years, fixed-income portfolio management has moved from a sleepy backwater of the investment arena to the cutting edge of investment thought. Once, managers in the field concentrated on earning an acceptable yield to maturity and used a few relatively simple measures to control risk in the portfolio. Today, the portfolio manager has a stunning array of new tools at his disposal, capable of measuring and explaining the smallest variations in desired performance while simultaneously controlling risk with a variety of quantitative tools. This chapter examines the results of that revolution in fixed-income portfolio management.

It is not our purpose to examine in great detail the analytical "tools of the trade"; these techniques are covered extensively elsewhere. Our focus is broader and emphasizes the effective construction of a fixed-income portfolio and related risk issues. The fixed-income portfolio management process and the major themes in managing the fixed-income portion of a portfolio receive the emphasis in this chapter.

The chapter begins with a short review in Section 2 of the framework used for managing fixed-income portfolios. A fixed-income portfolio manager may manage funds against a bond market index or against the client's liabilities. In the former approach, the chief concern is performance relative to the selected bond index; in the latter, it is performance in funding the payment of liabilities. Managing funds against a bond market index is covered in Section 3 while management against liabilities (asset/liability management or ALM) is covered in Section 4. The chapter then addresses other fixed-income strategies, including derivative-enabled strategies, in Section 5, while international bond investing and selecting a fixed-income manager are the subjects of Sections 6 and 7, respectively.

2. A FRAMEWORK FOR FIXED-INCOME PORTFOLIO MANAGEMENT

To make our discussion easier to follow, let us revisit the four activities in the investment management process:

1. Setting the investment objectives (with related constraints).
2. Developing and implementing a portfolio strategy.
3. Monitoring the portfolio.
4. Adjusting the portfolio.

These four steps as they apply to fixed-income portfolio management are shown in Exhibit 6-1. For ease of illustration, Exhibit 6-1 breaks the second activity (developing and implementing a portfolio strategy) into its individual parts and combines the third and fourth activities (monitoring and adjusting the portfolio).

As can be seen in Exhibit 6-1, the basic features of the investment management process are the same for a fixed-income portfolio as for any other type of investment. Risk, return, and constraints are considered first. If the client is a taxable investor, portfolio analysis must be done on an after-tax basis and considerations of the tax-efficient placement of fixed-income assets come to the fore. For any type of client, the fixed-income portfolio manager must agree with the client on an appropriate benchmark, based on the needs of the client as expressed in the investment policy statement or the investor's mandate to the portfolio manager.

Broadly, there are two types of investor based on investment objectives. The first type of investor does not have liability matching as a specific objective. For example, a bond mutual fund has a great deal of freedom in how to invest its funds because it does not have a set of liabilities that requires a cash-flow stream to satisfy them. The fund receives money from investors and provides professional expertise in investing this money for them, but the fund is not guaranteeing investors a certain rate of return. An investor (and manager) not focused on liability matching will typically select a specific bond market index as the benchmark for the portfolio; the portfolio's objective is to either match or exceed the rate of return on that index. In other words, the bond market index serves as the benchmark for the portfolio.

The second type of investor has a liability (or set of liabilities) that needs to be met. For example, some investors create a liability by borrowing money at a stated rate of interest, thereby leveraging the portfolio. Other investors have a liability as a result of legal promises that have been made, such as the payouts under a defined-benefit pension plan. Some investors may have quasi-liabilities represented by their retirement needs, and these can be treated as liabilities in context of portfolio management. The investor with liabilities will measure success by whether the portfolio generates the funds necessary to pay out the cash outflows associated with the liabilities. In other words, meeting the liabilities is the investment objective; as such, it also becomes the benchmark for the portfolio.

Later, we will examine in detail managing funds to ensure that the investor's liabilities are met. But for now, let us concentrate on managing the portfolio against a bond market index.

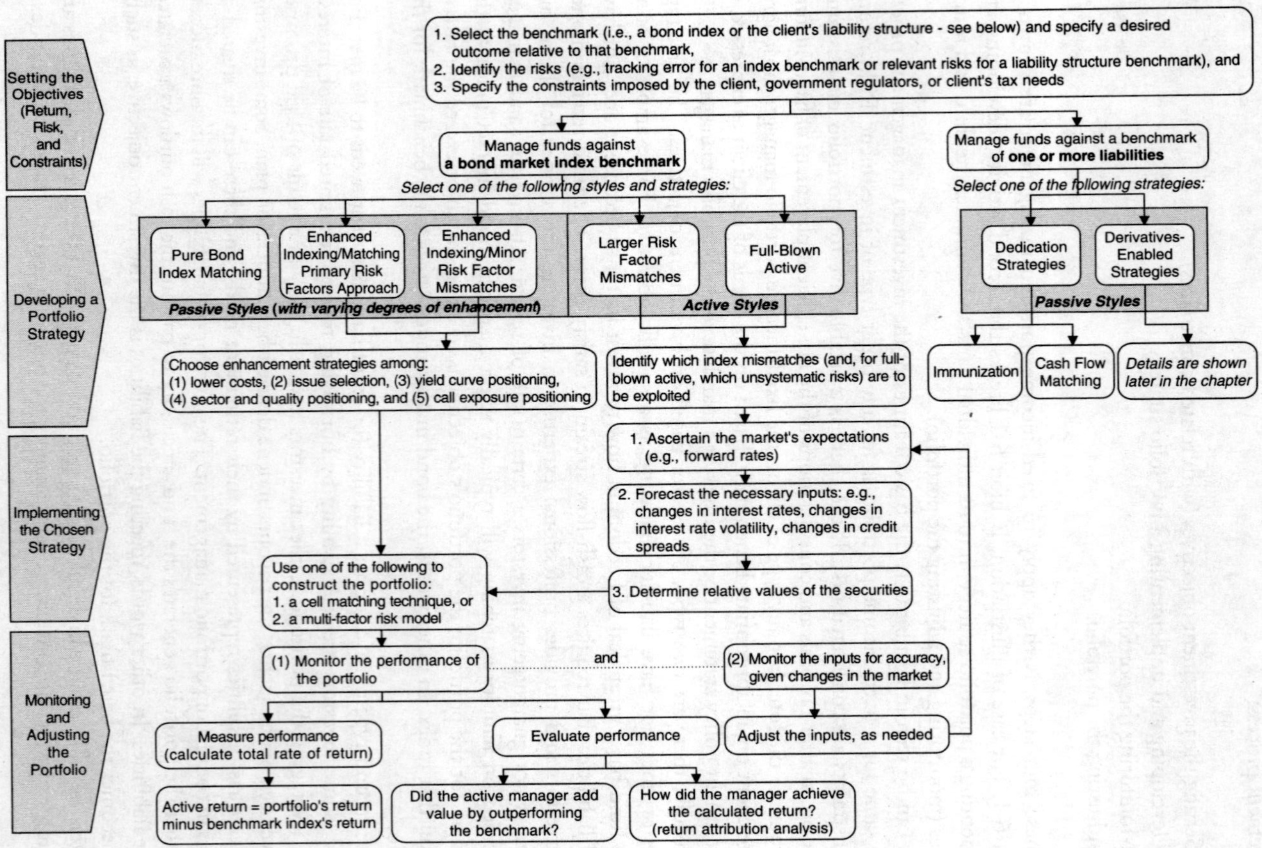

EXHIBIT 6-1 Fixed-Income Portfolio Management Process

3. MANAGING FUNDS AGAINST A BOND MARKET INDEX

This section addresses fixed-income portfolio management from the perspective of an investor who has no liabilities and who has chosen to manage the portfolio's funds against a bond market index (as shown in Exhibit 6-1).

A passive management strategy assumes that the market's expectations are essentially correct or, more precisely, that the manager has no reason to disagree with these expectations—perhaps because the manager has no particular expertise in forecasting. By setting the portfolio's risk profile (e.g., interest rate sensitivity and credit quality) identical to the benchmark's risk profile and pursuing a passive strategy, the manager is quite willing to accept an average risk level (as defined by the benchmark's and portfolio's risk profile) and an average rate of return (as measured by the benchmark's and portfolio's return). Under a passive strategy, the manager does not have to make independent forecasts and the portfolio should very closely track the benchmark index.

An active management strategy essentially relies on the manager's forecasting ability. Active managers believe that they possess superior skills in interest rate forecasting, credit valuation, or in some other area that can be used to exploit opportunities in the market. The portfolio's return should increase if the manager's forecasts of the future path of the factors that influence fixed-income returns (e.g., changes in interest rates or credit spreads) are more accurate than those reflected in the current prices of fixed-income securities. The manager can create small mismatches (enhancement) or large mismatches (full-blown active management) relative to the benchmark to take advantage of this expertise.

When the major decision to manage funds against a benchmark index has been made, the next step is to select one or more appropriate investment strategies. Strategies can be grouped along a spectrum, as explained in the next section.

3.1. Classification of Strategies

Volpert (2000, pp. 85–88) provided an excellent classification of the types of fixed-income strategies relevant to this discussion.[1] Exhibit 6-1, in the shaded group of boxes next to "developing a portfolio strategy" shows these five types of strategies based on a scale that ranges from totally passive to full-blown active management. The types can be explained as follows:

1. *Pure bond indexing (or full replication approach).* The goal here is to produce a portfolio that is a perfect match to the benchmark portfolio. The pure bond indexing approach attempts to duplicate the index by owning all the bonds in the index in the same percentage as the index. Full replication is typically very difficult and expensive to implement in the case of bond indices. Many issues in a typical bond index (particularly the non-Treasuries) are quite illiquid and very infrequently traded. For this reason, full replication of a bond index is rarely attempted because of the difficulty, inefficiency, and high cost of implementation.

[1]Note that the terms "investment style" and "investment strategy" are often used interchangeably in the investment community. In this chapter, we use the term "style" as the more general term (i.e., either active or passive). An investment style may encompass many different types of strategies, which are implementation techniques or methodologies for achieving the portfolio's objective.

2. *Enhanced indexing by matching primary risk factors.*[2] This management style uses a sampling approach in an attempt to match the primary index risk factors and achieve a higher return than under full replication. **Primary risk factors** are typically major influences on the pricing of bonds, such changes in the level of interest rates, twists in the yield curve, and changes in the spread between Treasuries and non-Treasuries.
   - By investing in a sample of bonds rather than the whole index, the manager reduces the construction and maintenance costs of the portfolio. Although a sampling approach will usually track the index less closely than full replication, this disadvantage is expected to be more than offset by the lower expenses.
   - By matching the primary risk factors, the portfolio is affected by broad market-moving events (e.g., changing interest rate levels, twists in the yield curve, spread changes) to the same degree as the benchmark index. The portfolio manager may try to enhance the portfolio's return using bonds that are perceived to be undervalued, for example.
3. *Enhanced indexing by small risk factor mismatches.*[3] While matching duration (interest rate sensitivity), this style allows the manager to tilt the portfolio in favor of any of the other risk factors. The manager may try to marginally increase the return by pursuing relative value in certain sectors, quality, term structure, and so on. The mismatches are small and are intended to simply enhance the portfolio's return enough to overcome the difference in administrative costs between the portfolio and the index.
4. *Active management by larger risk factor mismatches.* The difference between this style and enhanced indexing is one of degree. This style involves the readiness to make deliberately larger mismatches on the primary risk factors than in Type 3—definitely active management. The portfolio manager is now actively pursuing opportunities in the market to increase the return. The manager may overweight A rated bonds relative to AA/Aaa rated bonds, overweight corporates versus Treasuries, position the portfolio to take advantage of an anticipated twist in the yield curve, or adjust the portfolio's duration slightly away from the benchmark index's duration to take advantage of a perceived opportunity. The objective of the manager is to produce sufficient returns to overcome this style's additional transaction costs while controlling risk.
5. *Full-blown active management.* Full-blown active management involves the possibility of aggressive mismatches on duration, sector weights, and other factors.

The following sections offer further information and comments on these types of management.

3.2. Indexing (Pure and Enhanced)

We begin by asking the obvious question: "Why should an investor consider investing in an indexed portfolio?" Actually, several reasons exist for bond indexing.

- Indexed portfolios have lower fees than actively managed accounts. Advisory fees on an indexed portfolio may be only a few basis points, whereas the advisory fees charged by

[2] Factor matching is considered a implementation choice for indexing by other some authorities.
[3] *Small* here is used to refer to the size of the mismatch and not the level of risk.

active managers typically range from 15 to 50 bps. Nonadvisory fees, such as custodial fees, are also much lower for indexed portfolios.

- Outperforming a broadly based market index on a consistent basis is a difficult task, particularly when one has to overcome the higher fees and costs associated with active management.
- Broadly based bond index portfolios provide excellent diversification. The most popular U.S. bond market indices each have a minimum of 5,000 issues and a market value measured in the trillions of dollars. The indices contain a wide array of maturities, sectors, and qualities.[4] The diversification inherent in an indexed portfolio results in a lower risk for a given level of return than other less diversified portfolios.

3.2.1. Selection of a Benchmark Bond Index: General Considerations Once the decision has been made to index, important follow-up questions remain: "Which benchmark index should I choose? Should the benchmark index have a short duration or a long duration?" At the risk of oversimplifying, you should choose the index containing characteristics that match closely with the desired characteristics of your portfolio. The choice depends heavily on three factors:

1. *Market value risk*. The market value risk of the portfolio and benchmark index should be comparable. Given a normal upward-sloping yield curve, a bond portfolio's yield to maturity increases as the maturity of the portfolio increases. Does this mean that the total return is greater on a long portfolio than on a short one? Not necessarily. According to the expectations theory of term structure, a rising yield curve means that investors believe interest rates will likely increase in the future. Because a long duration portfolio is more sensitive to changes in interest rates, a long portfolio will likely fall more in price than a short one. In other words, as the maturity and duration of a portfolio increases, the market risk increases. For investors who are risk averse, the short-term or intermediate-term index may be more appropriate as a benchmark index than the long index.
2. *Income risk*. The portfolio and benchmark should provide comparable assured income streams. Many investors (e.g., foundations and retirees) prefer portfolios that generate a high level of income while conserving principal. Investing in a long portfolio can lock in a dependable income stream over a long period of time and does not subject the income stream to the vagaries of fluctuating interest rates. If stability and dependability of income are the primary needs of the investor, then the long portfolio is the least risky and the short portfolio is the most risky.
3. *Liability framework risk*. This risk should be minimized. In general, it is prudent to match the investment characteristics (e.g., duration) of assets and liabilities, if liabilities play any role. The choice of an appropriate benchmark index should reflect the nature of the liabilities: Investors with long-term liabilities should select a long index.[5] Of course, bond investors that have no liabilities have much more latitude in the choice of a benchmark because of the lack of this restriction.

[4]"Qualities" refers to the default risk of the bonds. This can be measured by the bonds' rating, for example, Standard & Poor's/Moody's Investor Services AAA/Aaa, AA/Aa, A, BBB/Baa, and so on.

[5]Management of a portfolio against liabilities is covered in detail in Section 4.

EXAMPLE 6-1 Illustrations of Benchmark Selection

Trustworthy Management Company specializes in managing fixed-income investments on an indexed basis. Some of the indices they consider as possible benchmarks are as follows:

- Merrill Lynch 1–3-Year Corporate Bond Index
- Lehman Brothers Corporate High-Yield Bond Index
- Lehman Brothers Corporate Intermediate Bond Index
- Merrill Lynch Long-Term Corporate Bond Index

All of the above include U.S. corporate debt, and all except Lehman Brothers Corporate High-yield Bond Index include only debt issues rated investment grade, which means they are rated Baa or higher. The duration of the Merrill Lynch 1–3-Year Corporate Bond Index is short, the duration of the two Lehman Brothers indices is medium, and the duration of the Merrill Lynch Long-Term Corporate Bond Index is long.

Of the above, which index(es) would be suitable as a benchmark for the portfolios of the following clients?

1. A highly risk-averse investor who is sensitive to fluctuations in portfolio value.
2. An educational endowment with a long investment horizon.
3. A life insurer that is relying on the fixed-income portfolio being managed by the Trustworthy Management Company to meet short-term claims.

Solution to Problem 1: Because the investor is quite risk averse, an index with a short or intermediate duration would be appropriate to limit market value risk. Of the short and intermediate duration indices listed above, the Lehman Brothers Corporate High-yield Bond Index is not suitable because it invests in less-than-investment-grade bonds. Accordingly, either the Merrill Lynch 1–3-Year Corporate Bond Index or the Lehman Brothers Corporate Intermediate Bond Index could be selected as the benchmark.

Solution to Problem 2: Given the endowment's long-term horizon, the Merrill Lynch Long-Term Corporate Bond Index, which has the longest duration of the indices given, is an appropriate benchmark.

Solution to Problem 3: For a company issuing life insurance policies, the timing of outlay (liabilities) is uncertain. However, because the insurer is relying on the portfolio to meet short-term liabilities, stability of market value is a concern, and the insurer would desire a portfolio with a low level of market risk. Therefore, Merrill Lynch 1–3-Year Corporate Bond Index, a short duration index, is an appropriate benchmark.

To build an indexed portfolio, the manager begins by selecting a broadly diversified bond market index that will serve as the benchmark for the portfolio. Fortunately, a wide variety of these is available. A well-constructed bond market index will have the same exposure to risks

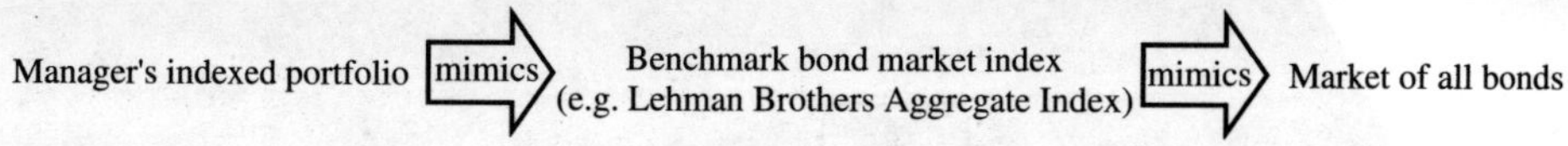

EXHIBIT 6-2 Indexing

as a portfolio that contains available fixed-income securities trading in the marketplace. The index may contain only a sample of all the marketplace's bonds; but if the characteristics and risk exposure are the same, the index will match the performance of the larger portfolio made up of all bonds.

However, although the bond market index may serve as a realistic benchmark portfolio, it is not a real portfolio. It exists only on paper or, more accurately, in a computer system somewhere. Therefore, a portfolio manager cannot invest directly in the index. The manager must construct her own portfolio that mimics (closely tracks) the characteristics of the index (and the market). That is, as Exhibit 6-2 illustrates, the bond market index is constructed to mimic the overall market and the manager's portfolio is constructed to mimic the bond market index. In this way, the manager's portfolio will also mimic the overall market.

3.2.2. Risk in Detail: Risk Profiles

The identification and measurement of risk factors plays a role both in benchmark selection and in a major benchmark construction.

The major source of risk for most bonds relates to the **yield curve** (the relationship between interest rates and time to maturity). Yield curve changes include (1) a parallel shift in the yield curve (an equal shift in the interest rate at all maturities), (2) a **twist** of the yield curve (movement in contrary directions of interest rates at two maturities), and (3) other curvature changes of the yield curve. Among the three, the first component (yield curve shift) typically accounts for about 90 percent of the change in value of a bond.

In assessing bond market indices as potential benchmark candidates, the manager must examine each index's **risk profile,** which is a detailed tabulation of the index's risk exposures. After all, if the portfolio manager is going to create (and invest in) a portfolio that mimics the benchmark index, the portfolio needs to contain the same exposures to various risks as the benchmark index. The manager needs to know: "How sensitive is the benchmark's return to changes in the level of interest rates (**interest rate risk**), changes in the shape of the yield curve (**yield curve risk**), changes in the spread between Treasuries and non-Treasuries (**spread risk**), and various other risks?"

Bonds are subject to a wide variety of risks, as illustrated in Exhibit 6-3.

Having obtained a clear grasp of the chosen benchmark's risk exposures, the portfolio manager can then use the risk profile in constructing an effective indexed portfolio. A completely effective indexed portfolio will have the exact same risk profile as the selected benchmark. The portfolio manager may use various techniques, perhaps in combination, to align the portfolio's risk exposures with those of the benchmark index.

A **cell-matching technique** (also known as **stratified sampling**) divides the benchmark index into cells that represent qualities that should reflect the risk factors of the index. The manager then selects bonds (i.e., sample bonds) from those in each cell to represent the entire cell taking account of the cell's relative importance in the benchmark index. The total dollar amount selected from this cell may be based on that cell's percentage of the total. For example, if the A rated corporates make up 4 percent of the entire index, then A rated bonds will be sampled and added until they represent 4 percent of the manager's portfolio.

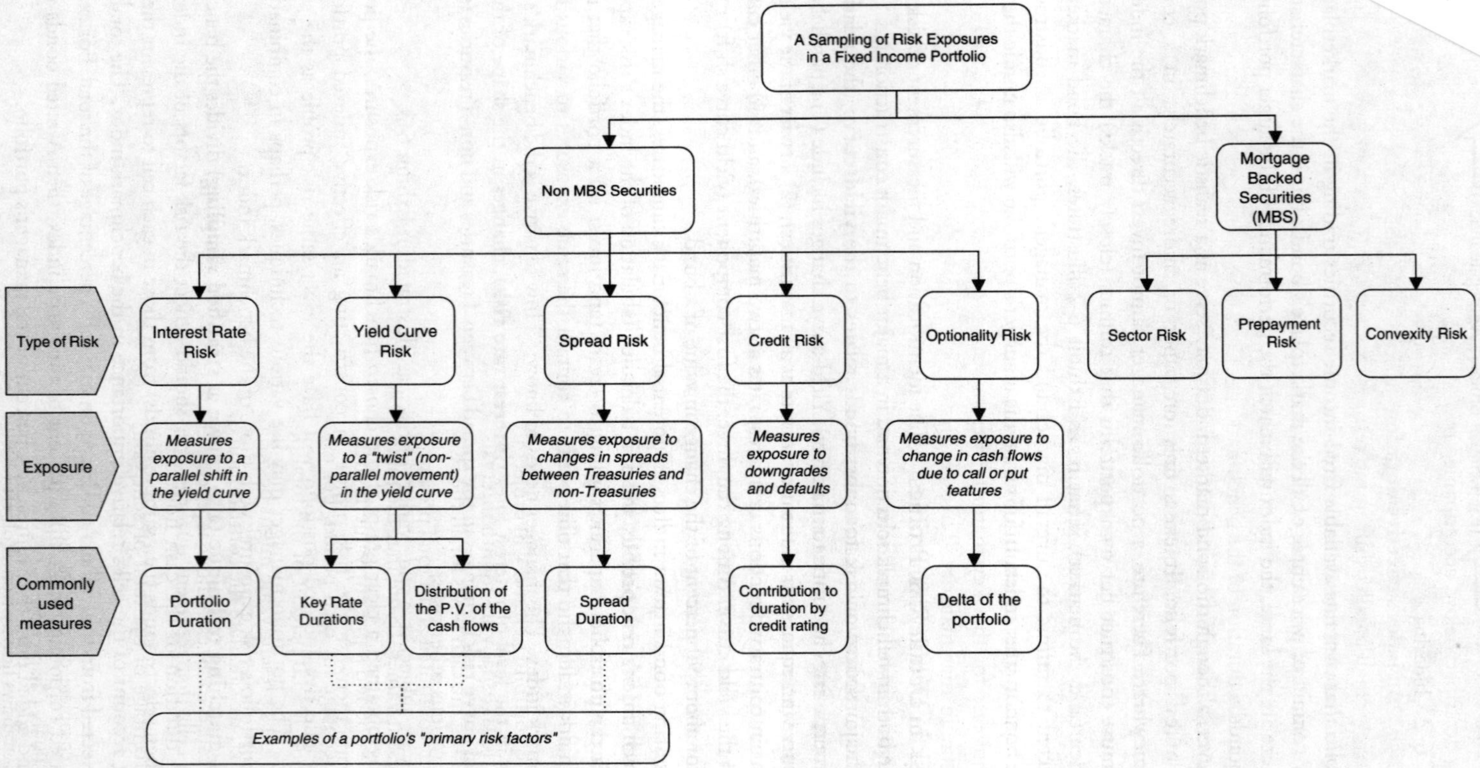

EXHIBIT 6-3 Typical Risk Exposures

A **multifactor model technique** makes use of a set of factors that drive bond returns.[6] Generally, portfolio managers will focus on the most important or primary risk factors. These measures are described below, accompanied by practical comments.[7]

1. *Duration.* An index's **effective duration** measures the sensitivity of the index's price to a relatively small parallel shift in interest rates (i.e., interest rate risk). (For *large* parallel changes in interest rates, a convexity adjustment is used to improve the accuracy of the index's estimated price change. A **convexity adjustment** is an estimate of the change in price that is not explained by duration.) The manager's indexed portfolio will attempt to match the duration of the benchmark index as a way of ensuring that the exposure is the same in both portfolios. Because parallel shifts in the yield curve are relatively rare, duration by itself is inadequate to capture the full effect of changes in interest rates.
2. *Key rate duration and present value distribution of cash flows.* Nonparallel shifts in the yield curve (i.e., yield curve risk), such as an increase in slope or a twist in the curve, can be captured by two separate measures. **Key rate duration** is one established method for measuring the effect of shifts in key points along the yield curve. In this method, we hold the spot rates constant for all points along the yield curve but one. By changing the spot rate for that key maturity, we are able to measure a portfolio's sensitivity to a change in that maturity. This sensitivity is called the **rate duration.** We repeat the process for other key points (e.g., 3 years, 7 years, 10 years, 15 years) and measure their sensitivities as well. Simulations of twists in the yield curve can then be conducted to see how the portfolio would react to these changes. Key rate durations are particularly useful for determining the relative attractiveness of various portfolio strategies, such as bullet strategies with maturities focused at one point on the yield curve versus barbell strategies where maturities are concentrated at two extremes. These strategies react differently to nonparallel changes in the yield curve.

   Another popular indexing method is to match the portfolio's present value distribution of cash flows to that of the benchmark. Dividing future time into a set of non-overlapping time periods, the **present value distribution of cash flows** is a list that associates with each time period the fraction of the portfolio's duration that is attributable to cash flows falling in that time period. The calculation involves the following steps:

   a. The portfolio's creator will project the cash flow for each issue in the index for specific periods (usually six-month intervals). Total cash flow for each period is calculated by adding the cash flows for all the issues. The present value of each period's cash flow is then computed and a total present value is obtained by adding the individual periods' present values. (Note that the total present value is the market value of the index.)
   b. Each period's present value is then divided by the total present value to arrive at a percentage for each period. For example, the first six-month period's present value might be 3.0 percent of the total present value of cash flows, the second six-month period's present value might be 3.8 percent of the total present value, and so forth.
   c. Next, we calculate the contribution of each period's cash flows to portfolio duration. Because each cash flow is effectively a zero-coupon payment, the time period is the duration of the cash flow. By multiplying the time period times the period's percentage of the total present value, we obtain the duration contribution of each

[6]For a more complete coverage of how multifactor risk models are used in portfolio construction, see Fabozzi (2004b, Chapter 3).
[7]This discussion draws heavily from Volpert (2000).

period's cash flows. For example, if we show each six-month period as a fractional part of the year (0.5, 1.0, 1.5, 2.0, etc.), the first period's contribution to duration would be 0.5 × 3.0%, or 0.015. The second period's contribution would be 1.0 × 3.8%, or 0.038. We would continue for each period in the series.

d. Finally, we add each period's contribution to duration (0.015 + 0.038 + . . .) and obtain a total (3.28, for example) that represents the bond index's contribution to duration. We then divide each of the individual period's contribution to duration by the total. The resulting distribution might look as follows:

   Period 1 = 0.46 percent
   Period 2 = 1.16 percent
   Period 3 = 3.20 percent
   . . ., etc.

   It is this distribution that the indexer will try to duplicate. If this distribution is duplicated, nonparallel yield curve shifts and "twists" in the curve will have the same effect on the portfolio and the benchmark portfolio.

3. *Sector and quality percent*. To ensure that the bond market index's yield is replicated by the portfolio, the manager will match the percentage weight in the various sectors and qualities of the benchmark index.
4. *Sector duration contribution*. A portfolio's return is obviously affected by the duration of each sector's bonds in the portfolio. For an indexed portfolio, the portfolio must achieve the same duration exposure to each sector as the benchmark index. The goal is to ensure that a change in sector spreads has the same impact on both the portfolio and the index.

   The manager can achieve this by matching the amount of the index duration that comes from the various sectors, i.e., the sector duration contribution.
5. *Quality spread duration contribution*. The risk that a bond's price will change as a result of spread changes (e.g., between corporates and Treasuries) is known as spread risk. A measure that describes how a non-Treasury security's price will change as a result of the widening or narrowing of the spread is **spread duration.** Changes in the spread between qualities of bonds will also affect the rate of return. The easiest way to ensure that the indexed portfolio closely tracks the benchmark is to match the amount of the index duration that comes from the various quality categories.
6. *Sector/coupon/maturity cell weights*. Because duration only captures the effect of small interest rate changes on an index's value, convexity is often used to improve the accuracy of the estimated price change, particularly where the change in rates is large. However, some bonds (such as mortgage-backed securities) may exhibit negative convexity, making the index's exposure to call risk difficult to replicate. A manager can attempt to match the convexity of the index, but such matching is rarely attempted because to stay matched can lead to excessively high transactions costs. (Callable securities tend to be very illiquid and expensive to trade.)

   A more feasible method of matching the call exposure is to match the sector, coupon, and maturity weights of the callable sectors. As rates change, the changes in call exposure of the portfolio will be matched to the index.
7. *Issuer exposure*. Event risk is the final risk that needs to be controlled. If a manager attempts to replicate the index with too few securities, event risk takes on greater importance.

The degree of success of an indexer in mimicking the returns on a benchmark is measured by tracking risk.

3.2.3. Tracking Risk **Tracking risk** (also known as **tracking error**) is a measure of the variability with which a portfolio's return tracks the return of a benchmark index. More specifically, tracking risk is defined as the standard deviation of the portfolio's active return, where the active return for each period is defined as

Active return = Portfolio's return − Benchmark index's return

Therefore,

Tracking risk = Standard deviation of the active returns

EXAMPLE 6-2 Calculating Tracking Risk

A portfolio's return and its benchmark's return are shown in Columns 2 and 3 of Exhibit 6-4. To calculate the standard deviation over the 10 periods, we calculate the active return for each period (in Column 4) and find the average active return (i.e., total return of 0.90 percent divided by 10 = 0.090 percent). We then subtract the average (or mean) active return from each period's active return and square each of the differences (Column 5). We add the values in Column 5 and divide the total by the number of sample periods minus one (i.e., 0.00829 percent/9), then take the square root of that value: $\sqrt{\frac{0.00829(\%)^2}{9}}$. The tracking risk is 0.30350 percent, or a little more than 30 bps.

EXHIBIT 6-4 Calculating Tracking Risk

Period Return (1)	Portfolio Return (2)	Benchmark Return (3)	Active Return (AR) (4)	$(AR - Avg.\ AR)^2$ (5)
1	12.80%	12.60%	0.200%	0.00012%[8]
2	6.80	6.50	0.300	0.00044
3	0.80	1.20	−0.400	0.00240
4	−4.60	−5.00	0.400	0.00096
5	4.00	4.10	−0.100	0.00036
6	3.30	3.20	0.100	0.00000
7	5.40	5.10	0.300	0.00044
8	5.40	5.70	−0.300	0.00152
9	5.10	4.60	0.500	0.00168
10	3.70	3.80	−0.100	0.00036

Average active return per period: 0.090%
Sum of the squared deviations: $0.00829(\%)^2$
Tracking risk: 0.30350%

[8] For Period 1, the calculation for the fifth column is $(0.200\% - 0.090\%)^2$ or $(0.000121\%)^2$.

Assume that the tracking risk for a portfolio is calculated to be 30 bps. Statistically, the area that is one standard deviation either side of the mean captures approximately two-thirds of all the observations if portfolio returns approximately follow a normal distribution. Therefore, a tracking risk of 30 bps would indicate that, in approximately two-thirds of the time periods, the portfolio return will be within a band of the benchmark index's return plus or minus 30 bps. The smaller the tracking risk, the more closely the portfolio's return matches, or tracks, the benchmark index's return.

Tracking risk arises primarily from mismatches between a portfolio's risk profile and the benchmark's risk profile.[9] The previous section listed seven primary risk factors that should be matched closely if the tracking risk is to be kept to a minimum. Any change to the portfolio that increases a mismatch for any of these seven items will potentially increase the tracking risk. Examples (using the first five of the seven) would include mismatches in the following:

1. *Portfolio duration.* If the benchmark's duration is 5.0 and the portfolio's duration is 5.5, then the portfolio has a greater exposure to parallel changes in interest rates, resulting in an increase in the portfolio's tracking risk.
2. *Key rate duration and present value distribution of cash flows.* Mismatches in key rate duration increase tracking risk. In addition, if the portfolio distribution does not match the benchmark, the portfolio will be either more sensitive or less sensitive to changes in interest rates at specific points along the yield curve, leading to an increase in the tracking risk.
3. *Sector and quality percent.* If the benchmark contains mortgage-backed securities and the portfolio does not, for example, the tracking risk will be increased. Similarly, if the portfolio overweights AAA securities compared with the benchmark, the tracking risk will be increased.

EXHIBIT 6-5 Contribution to Spread Duration

	Portfolio			Benchmark		
Sector	% of Portfolio	Spread Duration	Contribution to Spread Duration	% of Portfolio	Spread Duration	Contribution to Spread Duration
Treasury	22.60%	0.00%	0.00%	23.20%	0.00%	0.00%
Agencies	6.80	6.45	0.44	6.65	4.43	0.29
Financial Institutions	6.20	2.87	0.18	5.92	3.27	0.19
Industrials	20.06	11.04	2.21	14.20	10.65	1.51
Utilities	5.52	2.20	0.12	6.25	2.40	0.15
Non-U.S. Credit	6.61	1.92	0.13	6.80	2.02	0.14
Mortgage	32.21	1.10	0.35	33.15	0.98	0.32
Asset Backed	0.00	0.00	0.00	1.60	3.20	0.05
CMBS	0.00	0.00	0.00	2.23	4.81	0.11
Total	100.00%		3.43%	100.00%		2.77%

[9]Ignoring transaction costs and other expenses, the only way to completely eliminate tracking risk is to own all the securities in the benchmark. Even after all significant common risk factors are considered, it is possible to have some residual issue specific risk.

4. *Sector duration contribution.* Even though the sector percentages (e.g., 10 percent Treasuries, 4 percent agencies, 20 percent industrials) may be matched, a mismatch will occur if the portfolio's industrial bonds have an average duration of 6.2 and the benchmark's industrial bonds have an average duration of 5.1. Because the industrial sector's contribution to duration is larger for the portfolio than for the benchmark, a mismatch occurs and the tracking risk is increased.
5. *Quality spread duration contribution.* Exhibit 6-5 shows the spread duration for a 60-bond portfolio and a benchmark index based on sectors. The portfolio's total contribution to spread duration (3.43) is greater than that for the benchmark (2.77). This difference is primarily because of the overweighting of industrials in the 60-bond portfolio. The portfolio has greater spread risk and is thus more sensitive to changes in the sector spread than the benchmark is, resulting in a larger tracking risk.

The remaining two factors are left for the reader to evaluate.

EXAMPLE 6-3 Interpreting and Reducing Tracking Risk

John Spencer is the portfolio manager of Star Bond Index Fund. This fund uses the indexing investment approach, seeking to match the investment returns of a specified market benchmark, or index. Specifically, it seeks investment results that closely match, before expenses, the Lehman Brothers Global Aggregate Bond Index. This index is a market-weighted index of the global investment-grade bond market with an intermediate-term weighted average maturity, including government, credit, and collateralized securities. Because of the large number of bonds included in the Lehman Brothers Global Aggregate Bond Index, John Spencer uses a representative sample of the bonds in the index to construct the fund. The bonds are chosen by John so that the fund's (1) duration, (2) country percentage weights, and (3) sector- and quality- percentage weights closely match those of the benchmark bond index.

1. The target tracking risk of the fund is 1 percent. Interpret what is meant by this target.
2. Two of the large institutional investors in the fund have asked John Spencer if he could try to reduce the target tracking risk. Suggest some ways for achieving a lower tracking risk.

Solution to Problem 1: The target tracking risk of 1 percent means that the objective is that in at least two-thirds of the time periods, the return on the Star Bond Index Fund is within plus or minus 1 percent of the return on the benchmark Lehman Brothers Global Aggregate Bond Index. The smaller the tracking risk, the more closely the fund's return matches the benchmark's index return.

Solution to Problem 2: The target tracking risk could be reduced by choosing the bonds to be included in the fund so as to match the fund's duration, country percentage weights, sector weights, and quality weights to those of the benchmark, and to minimize the following mismatches with the benchmark:

1. Key rate distribution and present value distribution of cash flows.
2. Sector duration contribution.
3. Quality spread duration contribution.
4. Sector, coupon, and maturity weights of the callable sectors.
5. Issuer exposure.

3.2.4. Enhanced Indexing Strategies Although there are expenses and transaction costs associated with constructing and rebalancing an indexed portfolio, there are no similar costs for the index itself (because it is, in effect, a paper portfolio). Therefore, it is reasonable to expect that a perfectly indexed portfolio will underperform the index by the amount of these costs. For this reason, the bond manager may choose to recover these costs by seeking to enhance the portfolio's return. Volpert (2000) has identified a number of ways (i.e., index enhancement strategies) in which this may be done:[10]

1. *Lower cost enhancements*. Managers can increase the portfolio's net return by simply maintaining tight controls on trading costs and management fees. Although relatively low, expenses do vary considerably among index funds. Where outside managers are hired, the plan sponsor can require that managers re-bid their management fees every two or three years to ensure that these fees are kept as low as possible.
2. *Issue selection enhancements*. The manager may identify and select securities that are undervalued in the marketplace, relative to a valuation model's theoretical value. Many managers conduct their own credit analysis rather than depending solely on the ratings provided by the bond rating houses. As a result, the manager may be able to select issues that will soon be upgraded and avoid those issues that are on the verge of being downgraded.
3. *Yield curve positioning*. Some maturities along the yield curve tend to remain consistently overvalued or undervalued. For example, the yield curve frequently has a negative slope between 25 and 30 years, even though the remainder of the curve may have a positive slope. These long-term bonds tend to be popular investments for many institutions, resulting in an overvalued price relative to bonds of shorter maturities. By overweighting the undervalued areas of the curve and underweighting the overvalued areas, the manager may be able to enhance the portfolio's return.
4. *Sector and quality positioning*. This return enhancement technique takes two forms:

   a. Maintaining a yield tilt toward short duration corporates. Experience has shown that the best yield spread per unit of duration risk is usually available in corporate securities with less than five years to maturity (i.e., short corporates). A manager can increase the return on the portfolio without a commensurate increase in risk by tilting the portfolio toward these securities. The strategy is not without its risks, although these are manageable. Default risk is higher for corporate securities, but this risk can be managed through proper diversification. (**Default**

[10] See Volpert (2000, pp. 95–98).

risk is the risk of loss if an issuer or counterparty does not fulfill contractual obligations.)

b. Periodic over- or underweighting of sectors (e.g., Treasuries vs. corporates) or qualities. Conducted on a small scale, the manager may overweight Treasuries when spreads are expected to widen (e.g., before a recession) and underweight them when spreads are expected to narrow. Although this strategy has some similarities to active management, it is implemented on such a small scale that the objective is to earn enough extra return to offset some of the indexing expenses, not to outperform the index by a large margin as is the case in active management.

5. *Call exposure positioning*. A drop in interest rates will inevitably lead to some callable bonds being retired early. As rates drop, the investor must determine the probability that the bond will be called. Should the bond be valued as trading to maturity or as trading to the call date? Obviously, there is a crossover point at which the average investor is uncertain as to whether the bond is likely to be called. Near this point, the actual performance of a bond may be significantly different than would be expected, given the bond's **effective duration**[11] (duration adjusted to account for embedded options). For example, for premium callable bonds (bonds trading to call), the actual price sensitivity tends to be less than that predicted by the bonds' effective duration. A decline in yields will lead to underperformance relative to the effective duration model's prediction. This underperformance creates an opportunity for the portfolio manager to underweight these issues under these conditions.

EXAMPLE 6-4 Enhanced Indexing Strategies

The Board of Directors of the Teachers Association of a Canadian province has asked its chairman, Jim Reynolds, to consider investing C$10 million of the fixed-income portion of the association's portfolio in the Reliable Canadian Bond Fund. This index fund seeks to match the performance of the Scotia Capital Universe Bond Index. The Scotia Capital Universe Bond Index represents the Canadian bond market and includes more than 900 marketable Canadian bonds with an average maturity of about nine years.

Jim Reynolds likes the passive investing approach of the Reliable Canadian Bond Fund. Although Reynolds is comfortable with the returns on the Scotia Capital Universe Bond Index, he is concerned that because of the expenses and transactions costs, the actual returns on the bond fund could be substantially lower than the returns on the index. However, he is familiar with the several index enhancement strategies identified by Volpert (2000) through which a bond index fund could minimize the underperformance relative to the index. To see if the fund follows any of these strategies, Reynolds carefully reads the fund's prospectus and notices the following.

> *"Instead of replicating the index by investing in over the 900 securities in the Scotia Capital Universe Bond Index, we use stratified sampling. The fund consists of about 150 securities.*

[11] See Fabozzi (2004b, p. 235).

> *... We constantly monitor the yield curve to identify segments of the yield curve with the highest expected return. We increase the holdings in maturities with the highest expected return in lieu of maturities with the lowest expected return if the increase in expected return outweighs the transactions cost. Further, the fund manager is in constant touch with traders and other market participants. Based on their information and our in-house analysis, we selectively overweight and underweight certain issues in the index."*

1. Which of the index enhancement strategies listed by Volpert are being used by the Reliable Canadian Bond Fund?
2. Which additional strategies could the fund use to further enhance fund return without active management?

Solution to Problem 1: By investing in a small sample of 150 of over 900 bonds included in the index, the fund is trying to reduce transactions costs. Thus, the fund is following lower cost enhancements. The fund is also following yield curve positioning enhancement by overweighting the undervalued areas of the curve and underweighting the overvalued areas. Finally, the fund is following issuer selection enhancements by selectively over- and underweighting certain issues in the index.

Solution to Problem 2: The fund could further attempt to lower costs by maintaining tight controls on trading costs and management fees. Additional strategies that the fund could use include sector and quality positioning and call exposure positioning.

3.3. Active Strategies

In contrast to indexers and enhanced indexers, an active manager is quite willing to accept a large tracking risk, with a large positive active return. By carefully applying his or her superior forecasting or analytical skills, the active manager hopes to be able to generate a portfolio return that is considerably higher than the benchmark return.

3.3.1. Extra Activities Required for the Active Manager

Active managers have a set of activities that they must implement that passive managers are not faced with. After selecting the type of active strategy to pursue, the active manager will:

1. *Identify which index mismatches are to be exploited.* The choice of mismatches is generally based on the expertise of the manager. If the manager's strength is interest rate forecasting, deliberate mismatches in duration will be created between the portfolio and the benchmark. If the manager possesses superior skill in identifying undervalued securities or undervalued sectors, sector mismatches will be pursued.
2. *Extrapolate the market's expectations (or inputs) from the market data.* As discussed previously, current market prices are the result of all investors applying their judgment to the individual bonds. By analyzing these prices and yields, additional data can be obtained. For example, forward rates can be calculated from the points along the spot rate yield curve. These forward rates can provide insight into the direction and level that investors believe rates will be headed in the future.

3. *Independently forecast the necessary inputs and compare these with the market's expectations.* For example, after calculating the forward rates, the active manager may fervently believe that these rates are too high and that future interest rates will not reach these levels. After comparing his or her forecast of forward rates with that of other investors, the manager may decide to create a duration mismatch. By increasing the portfolio's duration, the manager can profit (if he or she is correct) from the resulting drop in the yield curve as other investors eventually realize that their forecast was incorrect.
4. *Estimate the relative values of securities in order to identify areas of under- or overvaluation.* Again, the focus depends on the skill set of the manager. Some managers will make duration mismatches while others will focus on undervalued securities. In all cases, however, the managers will apply their skills to try and exploit opportunities as they arise.

3.3.2. Total Return Analysis and Scenario Analysis

Before executing a trade, an active manager obviously needs to analyze the impact that the trade will have on the portfolio's return. What tools does the manager have in his or her tool bag to help assess the risk and return characteristics of a trade? The two primary tools are total return analysis and scenario analysis.

The **total return** on a bond is the rate of return that equates the future value of the bond's cash flows with the full price of the bond. As such, the total return takes into account all three sources of potential return: coupon income, reinvestment income, and change in price. **Total return analysis** involves assessing the expected effect of a trade on the portfolio's total return given an interest rate forecast.

To compute total return when purchasing a bond with semiannual coupons, for example, the manager needs to specify (1) an investment horizon, (2) an expected reinvestment rate for the coupon payments, and (3) the expected price of the bond at the end of the time horizon given a forecast change in interest rates. The manager may want to start with his prediction of the most likely change in interest rates.[12] The semiannual total return that the manager would expect to earn on the trade is:

$$\text{Semiannual total return} = \left(\frac{\text{total future dollars}}{\text{full price of the bond}}\right)^{\frac{1}{n}} - 1$$

where n is the number of periods in the investment horizon.

Even though this total return is the manager's most likely total return, this computation is for only one assumed change in rates. This total return number does very little to help the manager assess the risk that he faces if his forecast is wrong and rates change by some amount other than that forecast. A prudent manager will never want to rely on just one set of assumptions in analyzing the decision; instead, he or she will repeat the above calculation for different sets of assumptions or scenarios. In other words, the manager will want to conduct a **scenario analysis** to evaluate the impact of the trade on expected total return under all reasonable sets of assumptions.

Scenario analysis is useful in a variety of ways:

1. The obvious benefit is that the manager is able to assess the distribution of possible outcomes, in essence conducting a risk analysis on the portfolio's trades. The manager

[12] We use the term *interest rates* rather generically here. For non-Treasury issues, the manager would likely provide a more detailed breakdown, such as the change in Treasury rates, the change in sector spreads, and so on.

may find that, even though the expected total return is quite acceptable, the distribution of outcomes is so wide that it exceeds the risk tolerance of the client.

2. The analysis can be reversed, beginning with a range of acceptable outcomes, then calculating the range of interest rate movements (inputs) that would result in a desirable outcome. The manager can then place probabilities on interest rates falling within this acceptable range and make a more informed decision on whether to proceed with the trade.
3. The contribution of the individual components (inputs) to the total return may be evaluated. The manager's a priori assumption may be that a twisting of the yield curve will have a small effect relative to other factors. The results of the scenario analysis may show that the effect is much larger than the manager anticipated, alerting him to potential problems if this area is not analyzed closely.
4. The process can be broadened to evaluate the relative merits of entire trading strategies.

The purpose of conducting a scenario analysis is to gain a better understanding of the risk and return characteristics of the portfolio before trades are undertaken that may lead to undesirable consequences. In other words, scenario analysis is an excellent risk assessment and planning tool.

3.4. Monitoring/Adjusting the Portfolio and Performance Evaluation

Details of monitoring and adjusting a fixed-income portfolio (with its related performance evaluation) are essentially the same as other classes of investments. Because these topics are covered in detail in other chapters of this book, this chapter will not duplicate that coverage.

4. MANAGING FUNDS AGAINST LIABILITIES

We have now walked our way through the major activities in managing fixed-income investment portfolios. However, in doing so, we took a bit of a shortcut. In order to see all the steps at once, we only looked at one branch of Exhibit 6-1—the branch having to do with managing funds against a bond market index benchmark. We now turn our attention to the equally important second branch of Exhibit 6-1—managing funds against a liability, or set of liabilities.

4.1. Dedication Strategies

Dedication strategies are specialized fixed-income strategies that are designed to accommodate specific funding needs of the investor. They generally are classified as passive in nature, although it is possible to add some active management elements to them. Exhibit 6-6 provides a classification of dedication strategies.

As seen in Exhibit 6-6, one important type of dedication strategy is immunization. **Immunization** aims to construct a portfolio that, over a specified horizon, will earn a predetermined return regardless of interest rate changes. Another widely used dedication strategy is **cash-flow matching,** which provides the future funding of a liability stream from the coupon and matured principal payments of the portfolio. Each of these strategies will be more fully developed in the following sections followed by a discussion of some of the extensions based on them.

There are four typical types (or classes) of liabilities that can be identified. These are shown in Exhibit 6-7.

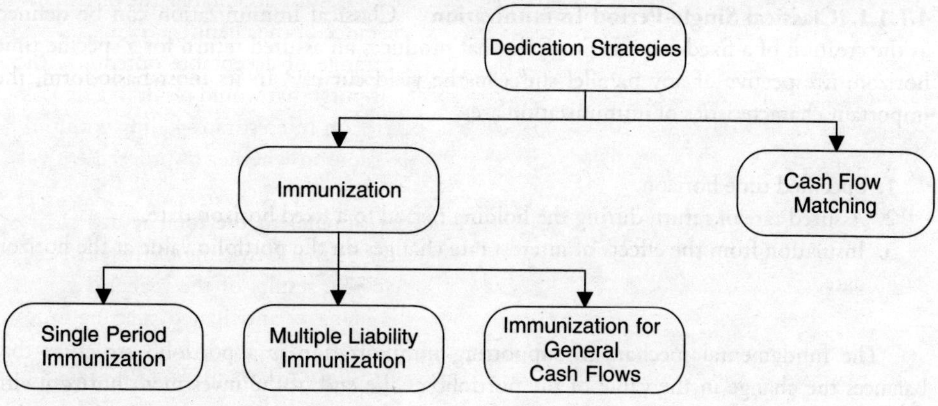

EXHIBIT 6-6 Dedication Strategies

EXHIBIT 6-7 Classes of Liabilities

Amount of Liability	Timing of Liability	Example
Known	Known	A principal repayment
Known	Unknown	A life insurance payout
Unknown	Known	A floating rate annuity payout
Unknown	Unknown	Postretirement health care benefits

Obviously, the more uncertain the liabilities, the more difficult it becomes to use a passive dedication strategy to achieve the portfolio's goals. For this reason, as liabilities become more uncertain, managers often insert elements of active management. The goal of this action is to increase the upside potential of the portfolio while simultaneously generating a set of cash flows that are believed to be the minimum necessary to pay the anticipated liabilities. Examples of these more aggressive strategies, such as active/passive combinations, active/immunization combinations, and contingent immunization, are discussed later.

4.1.1. Immunization Strategies Immunization is a popular strategy for "locking in" a guaranteed rate of return over a particular time horizon. As interest rates increase, the decrease in the price of a fixed-income security is usually at least partly offset by a higher amount of reinvestment income. As rates decline, a security's price increase is usually at least partly offset by a lower amount of reinvestment income. For an arbitrary time horizon, the price and reinvestment effects generally do not exactly offset each other: The change in price may be either greater than or less than the change in reinvestment income. The purpose of immunization is to identify the portfolio for which the change in price is exactly equal to the change in reinvestment income at the time horizon of interest. If the manager can construct such a portfolio, an assured rate of return over that horizon is locked in. The implementation of an immunization strategy depends on the type of liabilities that the manager is trying to meet: a single liability (e.g., a guaranteed investment contract), multiple liabilities (a defined-benefit plan's promised payouts), or general cash flows (where the cash flows are more arbitrary in their timing).

4.1.1.1. Classical Single-Period Immunization Classical immunization can be defined as the creation of a fixed-income portfolio that produces an assured return for a specific time horizon, irrespective of any parallel shifts in the yield curve.[13] In its most basic form, the important characteristics of immunization are:

1. Specified time horizon.
2. Assured rate of return during the holding period to a fixed horizon date.
3. Insulation from the effects of interest rate changes on the portfolio value at the horizon date.

The fundamental mechanism supporting immunization is a portfolio structure that balances the change in the value of the portfolio at the end of the investment horizon with the return from the reinvestment of portfolio cash flows (coupon payments and maturing securities). That is, immunization requires offsetting price risk and reinvestment risk. To accomplish this balancing requires the management of duration. Setting the duration of the portfolio equal to the specified portfolio time horizon assures the offsetting of positive and negative incremental return sources under certain assumptions, including the assumption that the immunizing portfolio has the same present value as the liability being immunized.[14] Duration-matching is a minimum condition for immunization.

EXAMPLE 6-5 Total Return for Various Yields

Consider the situation that a life insurance company faces when it sells a guaranteed investment contract (GIC). For a lump sum payment, the life insurance company guarantees that a specified payment will be made to the policyholder at a specified future date. Suppose that a life insurance company sells a five-year GIC that guarantees an interest rate of 7.5 percent per year on a bond-equivalent yield basis (3.75 percent every six months for the next 10 six-month periods). Also suppose that the payment the policyholder makes is $9,642,899. The value that the life insurance company has guaranteed the policyholder five years from now is thus $13,934,413. That is, the **target value** for the manager of the portfolio of supporting assets is $13,934,413 after five years, which is the same as a target yield of 7.5 percent on a bond-equivalent basis.

Assume that the manager buys $9,642,899 face value of a bond selling at par with a 7.5 percent yield to maturity that matures in five years. The portfolio manager will not be assured of realizing a total return at least equal to the target yield of 7.5 percent, because to realize 7.5 percent, the coupon interest payments must be reinvested at a minimum rate of 3.75 percent every six months. That is, the accumulated value will depend on the reinvestment rate.

[13] Any yield curve shift involves a change in the interest rate either up or down by the same amount at all maturities. The classical theory of immunization is set forth by Reddington (1952) and Fisher and Weil (1971).

[14] See Fabozzi (2004b) for further details.

To demonstrate this, suppose that immediately after investing in the bond above, yields in the market change, and then stay at the new level for the remainder of the five years. Exhibit 6-8 illustrates what happens at the end of five years.[15]

EXHIBIT 6-8 Accumulated Value and Total Return after Five Years: Five-Year, 7.5 Percent Bond Selling to Yield 7.5 Percent

Investment horizon (years)	5
Coupon rate	7.50%
Maturity (years)	5
Yield to maturity	7.50%
Price	100.00000
Par value purchased	$9,642,899
Purchase price	$9,642,899
Target value	$13,934,413

After Five Years

New Yield	Coupon	Interest on Interest	Bond Price	Accumulated Value	Total Return
11.00%	$3,616,087	$1,039,753	$9,642,899	$14,298,739	8.04%
10.50	3,616,087	985,615	9,642,899	14,244,601	7.96
10.00	3,616,087	932,188	9,642,899	14,191,175	7.88
9.50	3,616,087	879,465	9,642,899	14,138,451	7.80
9.00	3,616,087	827,436	9,642,899	14,086,423	7.73
8.50	3,616,087	776,093	9,642,899	14,035,079	7.65
8.00	3,616,087	725,426	9,642,899	13,984,412	7.57
7.50	3,616,087	675,427	9,642,899	13,934,413	7.50
7.00	3,616,087	626,087	9,642,899	13,885,073	7.43
6.50	3,616,087	577,398	9,642,899	13,836,384	7.35
6.00	3,616,087	529,352	9,642,899	13,788,338	7.28
5.50	3,616,087	481,939	9,642,899	13,740,925	7.21
5.00	3,616,087	435,153	9,642,899	13,694,139	7.14
4.50	3,616,087	388,985	9,642,899	13,647,971	7.07
4.00	3,616,087	343,427	9,642,899	13,602,414	7.00

Source: Fabozzi (2004b, p. 109).

If yields do not change and the coupon payments can be reinvested at 7.5 percent (3.75 percent every six months), the portfolio manager will achieve the target value. If market yields rise, an accumulated value (total return) higher than the target value (target yield) will be achieved. This result follows because the coupon interest payments can be reinvested at a higher rate than the initial yield to maturity. This result contrasts with what happens when the yield declines. The accumulated value (total return) is then less than the target value (target yield). Therefore, investing in a coupon bond

[15]For purposes of illustration, we assume no expenses or profits to the insurance company.

with a yield to maturity equal to the target yield and a maturity equal to the investment horizon does not assure that the target value will be achieved.

Keep in mind that to immunize a portfolio's target value or target yield against a change in the market yield, a manager must invest in a bond or a bond portfolio whose (1) duration is equal to the investment horizon and (2) initial present value of all cash flows equals the present value of the future liability.

4.1.1.2. Rebalancing an Immunized Portfolio Textbooks often illustrate immunization by assuming a one-time instantaneous change in the market yield. In actuality, the market yield will fluctuate over the investment horizon. As a result, the duration of the portfolio will change as the market yield changes. The duration will also change simply because of the passage of time. In any interest rate environment that is different from a flat term structure, the duration of a portfolio will change at a different rate from time.

How often should a portfolio be rebalanced to adjust its duration? The answer involves balancing the costs and benefits of rebalancing. On the one hand, more frequent rebalancing increases transactions costs, thereby reducing the likelihood of achieving the target return. On the other hand, less frequent rebalancing causes the duration to wander from the target duration, which also reduces the likelihood of achieving the target return. Thus, the manager faces a trade-off: Some transactions costs must be accepted to prevent the duration from straying too far from its target, but some mismatch in the duration must be lived with, or transactions costs will become prohibitively high.

4.1.1.3. Determining the Target Return Given the term structure of interest rates or the yield curve prevailing at the beginning of the horizon period, the assured rate of return of immunization can be determined. Theoretically, this **immunization target rate of return** is defined as the total return of the portfolio, assuming no change in the term structure. This target rate of return will always differ from the portfolio's present yield to maturity unless the term structure is flat (not increasing or decreasing), because by virtue of the passage of time, there is a return effect as the portfolio moves along the yield curve (matures). That is, for an upward-sloping yield curve, the yield to maturity of a portfolio can be quite different from its immunization target rate of return while, for a flat yield curve, the yield to maturity would roughly approximate the assured target return.

In general, for an upward-sloping yield curve, the immunization target rate of return will be less than the yield to maturity because of the lower reinvestment return. Conversely, a negative or downward-sloping yield curve will result in an immunization target rate of return greater than the yield to maturity because of the higher reinvestment return.

Alternative measures of the immunization target rate of return include the yield implied by a zero coupon bond of quality and duration comparable with that of the bond portfolio and an estimate based on results of a simulation that rebalances the initial portfolio, given scenarios of interest rate change.

The most conservative method for discounting liabilities—the method resulting in the largest present value of the liabilities—involves the use of the **Treasury spot curve** (the term structure of Treasury zero-coupon bonds).

A more realistic approach utilizes the yield curve (converted to spot rates) implied by the securities held in the portfolio. This yield curve can be obtained using a curve-fitting methodology.[16] Because spreads may change as well as the term structure itself, the value of the liabilities will vary over time.

4.1.1.4. Time Horizon The **immunized time horizon** is equal to the portfolio duration. Portfolio duration is equal to a weighted average of the individual security durations where the weights are the relative amounts or percentages invested in each.

A typical immunized time horizon is five years, which is a common planning period for GICs and allows flexibility in security selection because there is a fairly large population of securities to create the necessary portfolio duration. Securities in the portfolio should be limited to high-quality, very liquid instruments, because portfolio rebalancing is required to keep the portfolio duration synchronized with the horizon date.

4.1.1.5. Dollar Duration and Controlling Positions **Dollar duration** is a measure of the change in portfolio value for a 100 bps change in market yields.[17] It is defined[18] as:

$$\text{Dollar duration} = \text{Duration} \times \text{Portfolio value} \times 0.01$$

A portfolio's dollar duration is a weighted average of the dollar durations of the component securities.

EXAMPLE 6-6 Calculation of Dollar Duration

We have constructed a portfolio consisting of three bonds in equal par amounts of $1,000,000 each. The initial values and durations are shown in Exhibit 6-9. Note that the market value includes accrued interest.

EXHIBIT 6-9 Initial Durations of a Three-Bond Portfolio

Security	Price	Market Value	Duration	Dollar Duration
Bond 1	104.013	1,065,613	5.025	53,548
Bond 2	96.089	978,376	1.232	12,054
Bond 3	103.063	1,034,693	4.479	46,343
Average				37,315

[16]See Vasicek and Fong (1982).

[17]Dollar duration is a traditional term in the bond literature; the concept applies to portfolios denominated in any currency. A related concept is the price value of a basis point (PVBP), also known as the dollar value of a basis point (DV01). The PVBP is equal to the dollar duration divided by 100.

[18]The use of the term "duration" in this chapter (and in the equation) is consistent with Fabozzi (2004a, p. 228), who defines it as "the approximate percentage change in price for a 100 basis point change in rates." Taking a concept known as **Macaulay duration** (the percentage change in price for a *percentage change* in yield) as a baseline calculation measure, a tradition also exists for referring to "duration" as used in the equation as "modified duration" because it is equal to Macaulay duration modified to obtain a measure of price sensitivity for a change in the *level* of yields.

The dollar duration of this portfolio is \$37,315, which is calculated as:

$$\text{Portfolio Dollar Duration} = \frac{0.01}{3}[(1,065,613)(5.025) + (978,376)(1.232) + (1,034,693)(4.479)] = \$37,315$$

In a number of ALM applications, the investor's goal is to reestablish the dollar duration of a portfolio to a desired level. This rebalancing involves the following steps:

1. Move forward in time and include a shift in the yield curve. Using the new market values and durations, calculate the dollar duration of the portfolio at this point in time.
2. Calculate the **rebalancing ratio** by dividing the original dollar duration by the new dollar duration. If we subtract one from this ratio and convert the result to a percent, it tells us the percentage amount that each position needs to be changed in order to rebalance the portfolio.
3. Multiply the new market value of the portfolio by the desired percentage change in Step 2. This number is the amount of cash needed for rebalancing.

EXAMPLE 6-7 Rebalancing Based on the Dollar Duration

We now move forward one year and include a shift in the yield curve. The portfolio values at this point in time are given in Exhibit 6-10:

EXHIBIT 6-10 Durations of a Three-Bond Portfolio after One Year

Security	Price	Market Value	Duration	Dollar Duration
Bond 1	\$99.822	\$1,023,704	4.246	\$43,465
Bond 2	98.728	1,004,770	0.305	3,063
Bond 3	99.840	1,002,458	3.596	36,049
Average				\$27,526

The portfolio dollar duration has changed from \$37,315 to \$27,526. Our requirement is to maintain the portfolio dollar duration at the initial level. To do so, we must rebalance our portfolio. We choose to rebalance using the existing security proportions of one-third each.

To calculate the rebalancing ratio, we divide the original dollar duration by the new dollar duration:

$$\$37,315/\$27,526 = 1.356$$

Rebalancing requires each position to be increased by 35.6 percent. The cash required for this rebalancing is calculated as

$$\begin{aligned}\text{Cash Required} &= 0.356 \times (\$1,023,704 + 1,004,770 + 1,002,458)\\ &= \$1,079,012\end{aligned}$$

One possible method of maintaining the original portfolio dollar duration is changing the weight of a particular security (referred to as a *controlling position*) to adjust the dollar duration. In our example, we could use Bond 2 as our controlling position. This security has the shortest duration, so by selling a portion of this bond position, we would in effect lengthen our portfolio duration. The Bond 2 position must be reduced by approximately 87 percent in order to bring the portfolio dollar duration back to its original value.

Controlling positions may also consist of derivatives.

4.1.1.6. Spread Duration Spread duration is a measure of how the market value of a risky bond (portfolio) will change with respect to a parallel 100 bps change in its spread above the comparable benchmark security (portfolio). Spread duration is an important measurement tool for the management of spread risk. Spreads do change and the portfolio manager needs to know the risks associated with such changes.

A characteristic of bonds with **credit risk** (risk of loss because of credit events such as default or downgrades in credit ratings)—sometimes called "spread product"—is that their yield will be higher than a comparable risk-free security. The large spectrum of bond products available in the marketplace leads to differing types of spread duration. The three major types are:

1. **Nominal spread,** the spread of a bond or portfolio above the yield of a certain maturity Treasury.
2. **Static spread** or **zero-volatility spread,** defined as the constant spread above the Treasury spot curve that equates the calculated price of the security to the market price.
3. **Option-adjusted spread** (OAS), the current spread over the benchmark yield minus that component of the spread that is attributable to any embedded optionality in the instrument.

The spread duration of a portfolio is calculated as a market weighted average of the spread durations of the component securities. A portfolio that includes non-Treasury securities will have a spread duration that is different from the portfolio duration.

A bond index will have an overall spread duration as will each sector within the index. The manager can calculate the effect on the portfolio of a change in sector spreads. The effect due to a change in sector spreads is in addition to the effect that is implied by a general increase or decrease in interest rates.

EXAMPLE 6-8 Portfolio Immunization

The Managers of Reliable Life Insurance Company are considering hiring a consultant to advise them on portfolio immunization. Following are some of the statements that were made during these presentations:

1. A great thing about immunization is that it is a set-and-forget strategy. That is, once you have immunized your portfolio, there is no subsequent work to be done.
2. The immunization target rate of return is less than yield to maturity.
3. If a portfolio is immunized against a change in the market yield at a given horizon by matching portfolio duration to horizon, the portfolio faces no risk except for default risk.
4. The liquidity of securities used to construct an immunized portfolio is irrelevant.
5. In general, the entire portfolio does not have to be turned over to rebalance an immunized portfolio. Furthermore, rebalancing need not be done on a daily basis.

Critique the above statements.

Solution:

1. This statement is incorrect. One needs to rebalance the portfolio duration whenever interest rates change and as time elapses since the previous rebalancing.
2. This statement is only true if the yield curve is upward sloping. If the yield curve is downward sloping, then this statement is not true as the immunization target rate of return would exceed the yield to maturity because of the higher reinvestment return.
3. The statement is incorrect. The portfolio described would be exposed to the risk of a change in interest rates that results in a change in the shape of the yield curve.
4. The statement is incorrect because immunized portfolios need to be rebalanced, the liquidity of securities used to construct an immunized portfolio is a relevant consideration. Illiquid securities involve high transaction costs and make portfolio rebalancing costly.
5. The statement is correct. The entire portfolio does not have to be turned over to rebalance it because shifting a small set of securities from one maturity range to another is generally enough. Also, to avoid excessive transactions costs, rebalancing is usually not done on a daily basis, which could involve excessive transaction costs.

4.1.2. Extensions of Classical Immunization Theory Classical immunization theory is based on several assumptions:

1. Any changes in the yield curve are parallel changes, that is, interest rates move either up or down by the same amount for all maturities.
2. The portfolio is valued at a fixed horizon date, and there are no interim cash inflows or outflows before the horizon date.

3. The target value of the investment is defined as the portfolio value at the horizon date if the interest rate structure does not change (i.e., there is no change in forward rates).

Perhaps the most critical assumption of classical immunization techniques is the first one concerning the type of interest rate change anticipated. A property of a classically immunized portfolio is that the target value of the investment is the lower limit of the value of the portfolio at the horizon date if there are parallel interest rate changes.[19] According to the theory, if there is a change in interest rates that does not correspond to this shape-preserving shift, matching the duration to the investment horizon no longer assures immunization.[20] Non-shape-preserving shifts are the commonly observed case.

Exhibit 6-11 illustrates the nature of the portfolio value, given an immunized portfolio and parallel shifts in rates. The curve **aa′** represents the behavior of the portfolio value for various changes in rates, ranging from a decline to an increase as shown on the horizontal axis. Point $\mathbf{V}_0$ on line **tt′** is the level of the portfolio value assuming no change in rates. As we note above, an immunized portfolio subjected to parallel shifts in the yield curve will provide at least as great a portfolio value at the horizon date as the assured target value, which thus becomes the minimum value. Therefore, if the assumptions of classical theory hold, immunization provides a minimum-risk strategy.

Exhibit 6-12 illustrates the relationship between the value of a classically immunized portfolio and interest rate changes when interest rates do not shift in a parallel fashion. Depending on the shape of the nonparallel shift, either the relationship shown in (a) or that shown in (b) will occur. This exhibit shows the possibility (in cases *d* and *e*) that the value of a classically immunized portfolio can be less than the target. The important point is that merely matching the duration of the portfolio to the investment horizon as the condition for immunization may not prevent significant deviations from the target value.

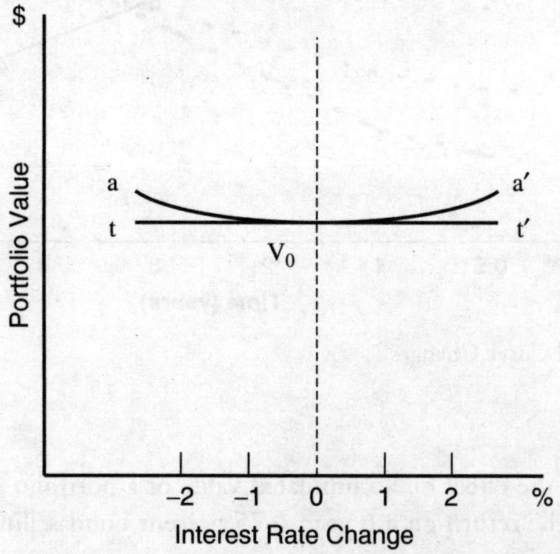

EXHIBIT 6-11 Changes in Portfolio Value Caused by Parallel Interest Rate Changes for an Immunized Portfolio

[19] See Fisher and Weil (1971) and Fabozzi (2004b).

[20] For a more complete discussion of these issues, see Cox, Ingersoll, and Ross (1979).

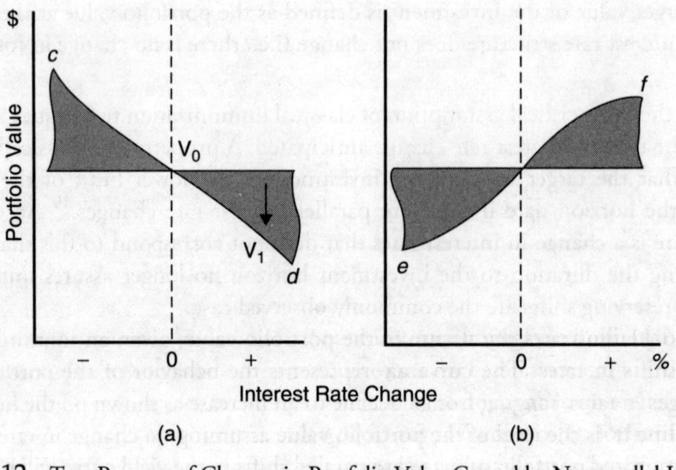

EXHIBIT 6-12 Two Patterns of Changes in Portfolio Value Caused by Nonparallel Interest Rate Shifts for an Immunized Portfolio
Source: Gifford Fong Associates.

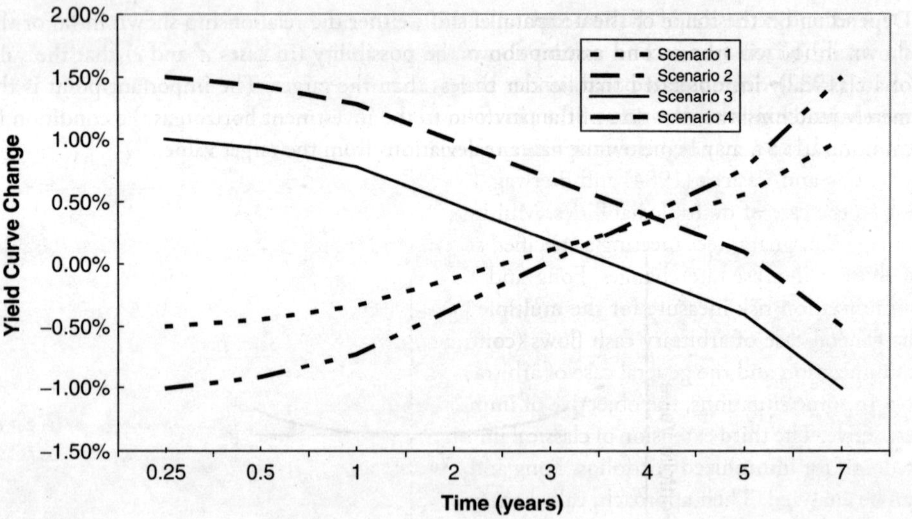

EXHIBIT 6-13 Yield Curve Changes

As an example of the effect on accumulated value of a portfolio given nonparallel yield curve shifts, consider the return on a 6 year, 6.75 percent bond selling to yield 7.5 percent. Our horizon remains at 5 years.

The four yield curve changes shown in Exhibit 6-13 below are applied to the existing yield curve. For example, Scenario 1 twists the existing yield curve by reducing the 3-month rate by 50 bps and increasing the 7-year rate by 100 bps. Intermediate points on the yield curve are linearly interpolated between the end points. The total return is then calculated and displayed in Exhibit 6-14.

EXHIBIT 6-14 Total Return after Yield Curve Change

Scenario	Coupon	Interest on Interest	Price of the Bond	Accumulated Value	Total Return
Scenario 1	$3,375,000	$572,652	$9,999,376	$13,947,029	7.519%
Scenario 2	3,375,000	547,054	10,025,367	13,947,421	7.519
Scenario 3	3,375,000	679,368	9,894,491	13,948,860	7.522
Scenario 4	3,375,000	728,752	9,847,756	13,951,508	7.525

A natural extension of classical immunization theory is to extend the theory to the case of nonparallel shifts in interest rates. Two approaches have been taken. The first approach has been to modify the definition of duration so as to allow for nonparallel yield curve shifts, such as **multifunctional duration** (also known as **functional duration** or key rate duration). The second approach is a strategy that can handle any arbitrary interest rate change so that it is not necessary to specify an alternative duration measure. This approach, developed by Fong and Vasicek (1984), establishes a measure of immunization risk against any arbitrary interest rate change. The immunization risk measure can then be minimized subject to the constraint that the duration of the portfolio equals the investment horizon, resulting in a portfolio with minimum exposure to any interest rate movements. This approach is discussed later in the section.

A second extension of classical immunization theory applies to overcoming the limitations of a fixed horizon (the second assumption on which immunization depends). Marshall and Yawitz (1982) demonstrated that, under the assumption of parallel interest rate changes, a lower bound exists on the value of an investment portfolio at any particular time, although this lower bound may be below the value realized if interest rates do not change.

Fong and Vasicek (1984) and Bierwag, Kaufman, and Toevs (1979) extended immunization to the case of multiple liabilities. Multiple liability immunization involves an investment strategy that guarantees meeting a specified schedule of future liabilities, regardless of the type of shift in interest rate changes. Fong and Vasicek (1984) provided a generalization of the immunization risk measure for the multiple liability case. Moreover, it extends the theory to the general case of arbitrary cash flows (contributions as well as liabilities). Multiple liability immunization and the general case of arbitrary cash flows are discussed later in the chapter.

In some situations, the objective of immunization as strict risk minimization may be too restrictive. The third extension of classical immunization theory is to analyze the risk and return trade-off for immunized portfolios. Fong and Vasicek (1983) demonstrated how this trade-off can be analyzed. Their approach, called *return maximization,* is explained later in this chapter.

The fourth extension of classical immunization theory is to integrate immunization strategies with elements of active bond portfolio management strategies. The traditional objective of immunization has been risk protection, with little consideration of possible returns. Leibowitz and Weinberger (1981) proposed a technique called **contingent immunization,** which provides a degree of flexibility in pursuing active strategies while ensuring a certain minimum return in the case of a parallel rate shift. In contingent immunization, immunization serves as a fall-back strategy if the actively managed portfolio does not grow at a certain rate.

Contingent immunization is possible when the prevailing available immunized rate of return is greater than the required rate of return. For example, if a firm has a three-year investment horizon over which it must earn 3 percent and it can immunize its asset portfolio at 4.75 percent, the manager can actively manage part or all of the portfolio until it reaches the safety net rate of return of 3 percent. If the portfolio return drops to this safety net level, the portfolio is immunized and the active management is dropped. The difference between the 4.75 percent and the 3 percent safety net rate of return is called the **cushion spread** (the difference between the minimum acceptable return and the higher possible immunized rate).

If the manager started with a \$500 million portfolio, after three years the portfolio needs to grow to

$$P_I\left(1+\frac{s}{2}\right)^{2T} = \$500\left(1+\frac{0.03}{2}\right)^{2x3} = \$546.72$$

where dollar amounts are in millions and

P_I = initial portfolio value

s = safety net rate of return

T = years in the investment horizon

At time 0, the portfolio can be immunized at 4.75 percent, which implies that the required initial portfolio amount, where dollar amounts are in millions, is

$$\frac{\text{Required terminal value}}{\left(1+\frac{i}{2}\right)^{2T}} = \frac{\$546.72}{\left(1+\frac{0.0475}{2}\right)^{2x3}} = \$474.90$$

The manager therefore has an initial dollar safety margin of \$500 million − \$474.90 million = \$25.10 million.

If the manager invests the entire \$500 million in 4.75 percent, 10-year notes at par and the YTM (yield to maturity) immediately changes, what will happen to the dollar safety margin?

If the YTM suddenly drops to 3.75 percent, the value of the portfolio will be \$541.36 million. The initial asset value required to satisfy the terminal value of \$546.72 million at 3.75 percent YTM is \$489.06 million so the dollar safety margin has grown to \$541.36 million − \$489.06 million = \$52.3 million. The manager may therefore commit a larger proportion of her assets to active management.

If rates rise so that the YTM is now 5.80 percent, the portfolio value will be \$460.55 million and the initial asset value required will be \$460.52 million. The dollar safety margin has gone to zero, and thus the portfolio must be immunized immediately.

Another example of the use of immunization as an adjunct to active return strategies is described by Fong and Tang (1988). Based on option valuation theory, a portfolio strategy can systematically shift the proportion between an active strategy and an immunized strategy in a portfolio to achieve a predetermined minimum return while retaining the potential upside of the active strategy.

4.1.2.1. Duration and Convexity of Assets and Liabilities In order for a manager to have a clear picture of the **economic surplus** of the portfolio—defined as the market value of assets minus the present value of liabilities—the duration and convexity of both the assets and liabilities must be understood. Focusing only on the duration of a company's assets will not give a true indication of the total interest rate risk for a company.

As an example, assume that a company's assets and liabilities have the characteristics shown in Exhibit 6-15.

EXHIBIT 6-15 Balance Sheet Characteristics of a Company (Dollar amounts in millions)

	Market Value	Present Value	Economic Surplus	Duration
Assets	$500	—	$100	4
Liabilities	—	$400	—	7

EXHIBIT 6-16 Interest Rate Scenarios (Dollar amounts in millions)

	Approximate Market Value	Present Value	Economic Surplus
A. When Rates Increase by 100 bps			
Assets	$480	—	$108
Liabilities	—	$372	—
B. When Rates Decrease by 100 bps			
Assets	$520	—	$ 92
Liabilities	—	$428	—

We can consider two interest rate scenarios, up 100 bps and down 100 bps, with results shown in Exhibit 6-16 in Panels A and B, respectively.

The economic surplus of the company has increased as rates rise. This increase is a result of the mismatch in duration between the assets and liabilities.

Convexity also plays a part in changes in economic surplus. If liabilities and assets are duration matched but not convexity matched, economic surplus will be exposed to variation in value from interest rate changes reflecting the convexity mismatch.

The manager must continuously monitor the portfolio to ensure that asset and liability durations and convexities are well matched. If the duration/convexity mismatch is substantial, the portfolio should be rebalanced to achieve a closer match.

4.1.2.2. Types of Risk As the market environment changes, the portfolio manager faces the risk of not being able to pay liabilities when they come due. Three sources of this risk are interest rate risk, contingent claim risk, and cap risk.

Interest rate risk. Because the prices of most fixed-income securities move opposite to interest rates, a rising interest rate environment will adversely affect the value of a portfolio. If assets need to be sold to service liabilities, the manager may find a shortfall. Interest rate risk is the largest risk that a portfolio manager will face.

Contingent claim risk. When a security has a contingent claim provision, explicit or implicit, there is an associated risk. In a falling rate environment, the manager may have lucrative coupon payments halted and receive principal (as is the case with mortgage-backed securities when the underlying mortgages prepay principal). The loss of the coupons is bad enough but now the principal must be reinvested at a lower rate. In addition, the market value of a callable security will level out at the call price, rather than continuing upwards as a noncallable security would.

Cap risk. An asset that makes floating rate payments will typically have caps associated with the floating rate. The manager is at risk of the level of market rates rising while the asset returns are capped. This event may severely affect the value of the assets.

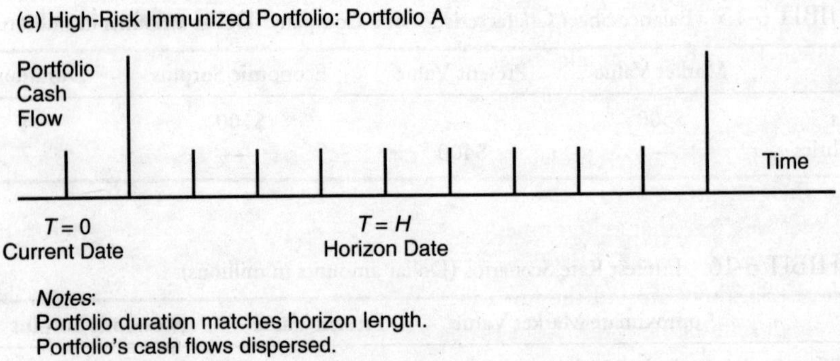

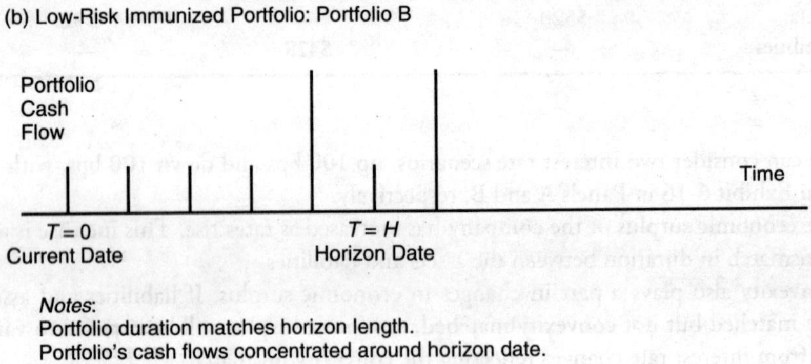

EXHIBIT 6-17 Illustration of Immunization Risk Measure
Source: Fabozzi (2004b, p. 123).

4.1.2.3. Risk Minimization for Immunized Portfolios The Fong and Vasicek (1984) extension of classical immunization theory produced an immunized portfolio with a minimum exposure to any arbitrary interest rate change. One way of minimizing immunization risk is shown in Exhibit 6-17.

The spikes in the two panels of Exhibit 6-17 represent actual portfolio cash flows. The taller spikes depict the actual cash flows generated by securities at maturity, whereas the smaller spikes represent coupon payments. Both Portfolio A and Portfolio B are composed of two bonds with durations equal to the investment horizon. Portfolio A is, in effect, a **barbell portfolio**—a portfolio made up of short and long maturities relative to the horizon date and interim coupon payments. Portfolio B, however is a **bullet portfolio**—the bond maturities are very close to the investment horizon.

If both portfolios have durations equal to the horizon length, both portfolios are immune to parallel rate changes. When interest rates change in an arbitrary nonparallel way, however, the effect on the value of the two portfolios differs—the barbell portfolio is riskier than the bullet portfolio.

Suppose, for instance, short rates decline while long rates go up. Both the barbell and bullet portfolios would realize a decline of the portfolio value at the end of the investment horizon below the target investment value, because they would experience a capital loss in addition to lower reinvestment rates.

The decline would be substantially higher for the barbell portfolio, however, for two reasons. First, the barbell portfolio experiences the lower reinvestment rates longer than the bullet portfolio does. Second, more of the barbell portfolio is still outstanding at the end of the investment horizon, which means that the same rate increase causes much more of a capital loss. In short, the bullet portfolio has less exposure to changes in the interest rate structure than the barbell portfolio.

It should be clear that reinvestment risk determines immunization risk. *The portfolio that has the least reinvestment risk will have the least immunization risk.* When there is a high dispersion of cash flows around the horizon date, as in the barbell portfolio, the portfolio is exposed to high reinvestment risk. When the cash flows are concentrated around the horizon date, as in the bullet portfolio, the portfolio is subject to minimal reinvestment risk. In the case of a pure discount instrument maturing at the investment horizon, immunization risk is zero because, with no interim cash flows, reinvestment risk is absent. Moving from pure discount instruments to coupon payment instruments, the portfolio manager is confronted with the task of selecting coupon-paying securities that provide the lowest immunization risk—if the manager can construct a portfolio that replicates a pure discount instrument that matures at the investment horizon, immunization risk will be zero.

Recall that the target value of an immunized portfolio is a lower bound on the terminal value of the portfolio at the investment horizon if yields on all maturities change by the same amount. If yields of different maturities change by different amounts, the target value is not necessarily the lower bound on the investment value.

Fong and Vasicek (1984) demonstrated that if forward rates change by any arbitrary function, the relative change in the portfolio value depends on the product of two terms.[21] The first term depends solely on the structure of the investment portfolio, while the second term, denoted M^2, is a function of interest rate movement only. The second term characterizes the nature of the interest rate shock. It is an uncertain quantity and, therefore, outside the control of the manager. The first term, however, is under the control of the manager, as it depends solely on the composition of the portfolio. The first term can be used as a measure of immunization risk because when it is small, the exposure of the portfolio to any interest rate change is small. The immunization risk measure M^2 is the variance of time to payment around the horizon date, where the weight for a particular time in the variance calculation is the proportion of the instrument's total present value that the payment received at that time represents.[22] The immunization risk measure may be called the **maturity variance;** in effect, it measures how much a given immunized portfolio differs from the ideal immunized portfolio consisting of a single pure discount instrument with maturity equal to the time horizon.

Given the measure of immunization risk that is to be minimized and the constraint that the duration of the portfolio equals the investment horizon, the optimal immunized portfolio can be found using **linear programming** (optimization in which the objective function and constraints are linear). Linear programming is appropriate because the risk measure is linear in the portfolio payments.

The immunization risk measure can be used to construct approximate confidence intervals for the target return over the horizon period and the target end-of-period portfolio value. A

---

[21]The Fong and Vasicek (1984) result is derived by expansion of the terminal portfolio value function into the first three terms of a Taylor series.

[22]The measure is $M^2 = \sum_{j=1}^{m}(s_j - H)^2 C_j P_0(s_j)/I_0$, where s_j is the time at which payment C_j is made, H is the horizon date, $P_0(s_j)$ is the present value of the payment(s) made at time s_j, and I_0 is initial portfolio value.

confidence interval represents an uncertainty band around the target return within which the realized return can be expected with a given probability. The expression for the confidence interval is:

$$\text{Confidence interval} = \text{Target return} \pm (k)(\text{Standard deviation of target return})$$

where k is the number of standard deviations around the expected target return. The desired confidence level determines k. The higher the desired confidence level, the larger k, and the wider the band around the expected target return.

Fong and Vasicek (1983) demonstrated that the standard deviation of the expected target return can be approximated by the product of three terms:[23] (1) the immunization risk measure, (2) the standard deviation of the variance of the one-period change in the slope of the yield curve,[24] and (3) an expression that is a function of the horizon length only.[25]

4.1.3. Multiple Liability Immunization

Immunization with respect to a single investment horizon is appropriate where the objective of the investment is to preserve the value of the investment at the horizon date. This objective is appropriate given that a single liability is payable at, or a target investment value must be attained by, the horizon date. More often, however, there are a number of liabilities to be paid from the investment funds and no single horizon that corresponds to the schedule of liabilities. A portfolio is said to be immunized with respect to a given liability stream if there are enough funds to pay all the liabilities when due, even if interest rates change by a parallel shift.

Bierwag, Kaufman, and Toevs (1979) demonstrate that matching the duration of the portfolio to the average duration of the liabilities is not a sufficient condition for immunization in the presence of multiple liabilities. Instead, the portfolio payment stream must be decomposable in such a way that each liability is separately immunized by one of the component streams; there may be no actual securities providing payments that individually match those of the component payment streams.

Fong and Vasicek (1984) demonstrate the conditions that must be satisfied to assure multiple liability immunization in the case of parallel rate shifts. The necessary and sufficient conditions are:

1. The (composite) duration of the portfolio must equal the (composite) duration of the liabilities.[26]
2. The distribution of durations of individual portfolio assets must have a wider range than the distribution of the liabilities.[27]

[23]The derivation is based on the assumption that the immunization risk measure of an optimally immunized portfolio periodically rebalanced decreases in time in approximate proportion to the third power of the remaining horizon length.

[24]This term can be estimated empirically from historical yield changes.

[25]The expression for the third term for the standard deviation of the expected target return of a single-period liability immunized portfolio is $(7H)^{-1/2}$, where H is the length of the horizon.

[26]The duration of the liabilities is found as follows: $[(1)\,PVL_l + (2)\,PVL_2 + \cdots + (m)PVL_m]$/(Total present value of liabilities) where PVL_t = present value of the liability at time t and m = time of the last liability payment.

[27]More specifically, the mean absolute deviation of the portfolio payments must be greater than or equal to the mean absolute deviation of the liabilities at each payment date.

An implication of the first condition is that to immunize a liability stream that extends 30 years, it is not necessary to have a portfolio with a duration of 30. The condition requires that the manager construct a portfolio so that the portfolio duration matches the weighted average of the liability durations. This fact is important because in any reasonable interest rate environment, it is unlikely that a portfolio of investment-grade coupon bonds could be constructed with a duration in excess of 15. Yet for corporate pension funds retired lives, the liability stream is typically a diminishing amount. That is, liabilities in the earlier years are the greatest, and liabilities toward the 30-year end are generally lower. Taking a weighted average duration of the liabilities usually brings the portfolio duration to something manageable, say, 8 or 9.

The second condition requires portfolio payments to bracket (be more dispersed in time than) the liabilities. That is, the portfolio must have an asset with a duration equal to or less than the duration of the shortest-duration liability in order to have funds to pay the liability when it is due. And the portfolio must have an asset with a duration equal to or greater than the longest-duration liability in order to avoid the reinvestment rate risk that might jeopardize payment of the longest duration. This bracketing of shortest- and longest-duration liabilities with even shorter- and longer-duration assets balances changes in portfolio value with changes in reinvestment return.

To understand why the portfolio payments have to be more spread out in time than the liabilities to assure immunization, consider the case of a single investment horizon in which immunization is achieved by balancing changes in reinvestment return on coupon payments with changes in investment value at the investment horizon. The same bracketing of each liability by the portfolio payments is necessary in the multiple liability case, which implies that the payments have to be more dispersed in time than the liabilities. Thus, managers selecting securities to be included in the portfolio must not only keep track of the matching of duration between assets and liabilities but also maintain a specified distribution for assets in the portfolio.

The two conditions for multiple liability immunization assure immunization against parallel rate shifts only. Reitano (1991) has explored the limitations of the parallel shift assumption.[28] He has also developed models that generalize the immunization of multiple liabilities to arbitrary yield curve shifts. His research indicates that classical multiple period immunization can mask the risks associated with nonparallel yield curve shifts and that a model that protects against one type of yield curve shift may expose a portfolio to other types of shifts.

Fong and Vasicek (1984) also addressed the question of the exposure of an immunized portfolio to an arbitrary interest rate change and generalize the immunization risk measure to the multiple liability case. Just as in the single investment horizon case, they find that the relative change in the portfolio value if forward rates change by any arbitrary function depends on the product of two terms: a term solely dependent on the structure of the portfolio and a term solely dependent on the interest rate movement.

An optimal immunization strategy is to minimize the immunization risk measure subject to the constraints imposed by these two conditions (and any other applicable portfolio constraints). Constructing minimum-risk immunized portfolios can then be accomplished by the use of linear programming.

Approximate confidence intervals can also be constructed in the multiple liability case. The standard deviation of the expected target return is the product of the three terms indicated in the section on risk minimization.[29]

[28] See also Reitano (1992) for a detailed illustration of the relationship between the underlying yield curve shift and immunization.

[29] See Fong and Vasicek (1983). The expression for the third term in the multiple liability case is a function of the dates and relative sizes of the liabilities, as well as the horizon length.

4.1.4. Immunization for General Cash Flows In both the single investment horizon and multiple liability cases, we have assumed that the investment funds are initially available in full. What if, instead, a given schedule of liabilities to be covered by an immunized investment must be met by investment funds that are not available at the time the portfolio is constructed?

Suppose a manager has a given obligation to be paid at the end of a two-year horizon. Only one-half of the necessary funds, however, are now available; the rest are expected at the end of the first year, to be invested at the end of the first year at whatever rates are then in effect. Is there an investment strategy that would guarantee the end-of-horizon value of the investment regardless of the development of interest rates?

Under certain conditions, such a strategy is indeed possible. The expected cash contributions can be considered the payments on hypothetical securities that are part of the initial holdings. The actual initial investment can then be invested in such a way that the real and hypothetical holdings taken together represent an immunized portfolio.

We can illustrate this using the two-year investment horizon. The initial investment should be constructed with a duration of 3. Half of the funds are then in an actual portfolio with a duration of 3, and the other half in a hypothetical portfolio with a duration of 1. The total stream of cash inflow payments for the portfolio has a duration of 2, matching the horizon length. This match satisfies a sufficient condition for immunization with respect to a single horizon.

At the end of the first year, any decline in the interest rates at which the cash contribution is invested will be offset by a corresponding increase in the value of the initial holdings. The portfolio is at that time rebalanced by selling the actual holdings and investing the proceeds together with the new cash in a portfolio with a duration of 1 to match the horizon date. Note that the rate of return guaranteed on the future contributions is not the current spot rate but rather the forward rate for the date of contribution.

This strategy can be extended to apply to multiple contributions and liabilities, which produces a general immunization technique that is applicable to the case of arbitrary cash flows over a period. The construction of an optimal immunized portfolio involves quantifying and then minimizing the immunization risk measure. Linear programming methods can then be used to obtain the optimal portfolio.

4.1.5. Return Maximization for Immunized Portfolios The objective of risk minimization for an immunized portfolio may be too restrictive in certain situations. If a substantial increase in the expected return can be accomplished with little effect on immunization risk, the higher-yielding portfolio may be preferred in spite of its higher risk.

Suppose that an optimally immunized portfolio has a target return of 8 percent over the horizon with a 95 percent confidence interval at ± 20 bps. Thus, the minimum-risk portfolio would have a 1 in 40 chance of a realized return less than 7.8 percent. Suppose that another portfolio less well-immunized can produce a target return of 8.3 percent with a 95 percent confidence interval of ± 30 bps. In all but one case out of 40, on average, this portfolio would realize a return above 8 percent compared with 7.8 percent on the minimum-risk portfolio. For many investors, the 8.3 percent target-return portfolio may be the preferred one.

The required terminal value, plus a safety margin in money terms, will determine the minimum acceptable return over the horizon period. As already mentioned, the difference between the minimum acceptable return and the higher possible immunized rate is known as the cushion spread. This spread offers the manager latitude in pursuing an active strategy. The greater the cushion spread, the more scope the manager has for an active management policy.

Fong and Vasicek's (1983) approach to the risk/return trade-off for immunized portfolios maintains the duration of the portfolio at all times equal to the horizon length. Thus, the portfolio stays fully immunized in the classical sense. Instead of minimizing the immunization risk against nonparallel rate changes, however, a trade-off between risk and return is considered. The immunization risk measure can be relaxed if the compensation in terms of expected return warrants it. Specifically, the strategy maximizes a lower bound on the portfolio return. The lower bound is defined as the lower confidence interval limit on the realized return at a given confidence level.

Linear programming can be used to solve for the optimal portfolio when return maximization is the objective. In fact, parametric linear programming can be employed to determine an efficient frontier for immunized portfolios analogous to those in the mean–variance framework.

4.2. Cash-Flow Matching Strategies

Cash-flow matching is an alternative to multiple liability immunization in asset/liability management. Cash-flow matching is an appealing strategy because the portfolio manager need only select securities to match the timing and amount of liabilities. Conceptually, a bond is selected with a maturity that matches the last liability, and an amount of principal equal to the amount of the last liability is invested in this bond. The remaining elements of the liability stream are then reduced by the coupon payments on this bond, and another bond is chosen for the next-to-last liability, adjusted for any coupon payments received on the first bond selected. Going back in time, this sequence is continued until all liabilities have been matched by payments on the securities selected for the portfolio. Linear programming techniques can be employed to construct a least-cost cash-flow matching portfolio from an acceptable universe of bonds.

Exhibit 6-18 provides a simple illustration of this process for a five-year liability stream.

Exhibit 6-19 provides a cash-flow analysis of sources and application of funds of a portfolio being used to cash-flow match a series of remaining liabilities falling due on 31 December of 2004 to 2018. In the first row for 2004, the previous cash balance of €0 indicates that the previous liability was exactly met by maturing principal and coupon payments. Principal payments of €1,685, coupon payments of €2,340, and €13 from an account that accumulates interest on reinvested payments, suffice to meet the liability due year-end 2004 ($€1,685 + €2,340 + €13 = €4,038$). (The interest account reflects interest on payments expected to be received in advance of the liability that the payments will fund.) The last column in the exhibit shows the excess funds remaining at each period, which are reinvested at an assumed 1.2 percent reinvestment rate supplied by the portfolio manager. The more excess cash, the greater the risk of the strategy, because the reinvestment rate is subject to uncertainty.

4.2.1. Cash-Flow Matching versus Multiple Liability Immunization

If all the liability flows were perfectly matched by the asset flows of the portfolio, the resulting portfolio would have no reinvestment risk and, therefore, no immunization or cash-flow match risk. Given typical liability schedules and bonds available for cash-flow matching, however, perfect matching is unlikely. Under such conditions, a minimum immunization risk approach should be as good as cash-flow matching and likely will be better, because an immunization strategy would require less money to fund liabilities. Two factors contribute to this superiority.

First, cash-flow matching requires a relatively conservative rate of return assumption for short-term cash and cash balances may be occasionally substantial. By contrast, an immunized portfolio is essentially fully invested at the remaining horizon duration. Second, funds from

Assume: 5-year liability stream. Cash flow from bonds is annual.

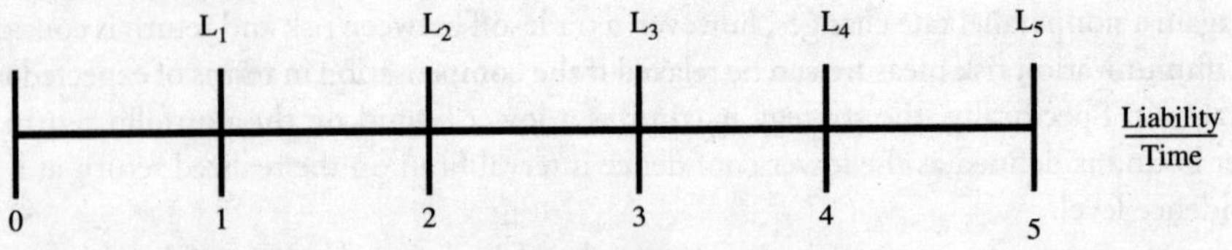

Step 1 – Cash flow from Bond A selected to satisfy L_5
Coupons = A_c ; Principal = A_p and $A_c + A_p = L_5$

Unfunded liabilities remaining:

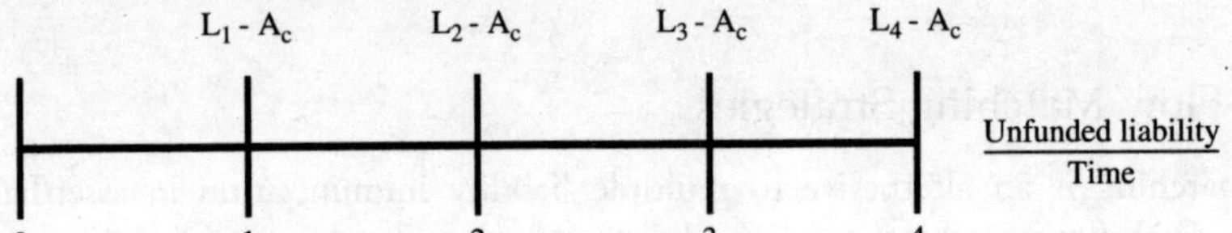

Step 2 – Cash flow from Bond B selected to satisfy $L_4 - A_c$
Coupons = B_c ; Principal = B_p and $B_c + B_p = L_4 - A_c$

Unfunded liabilities remaining:

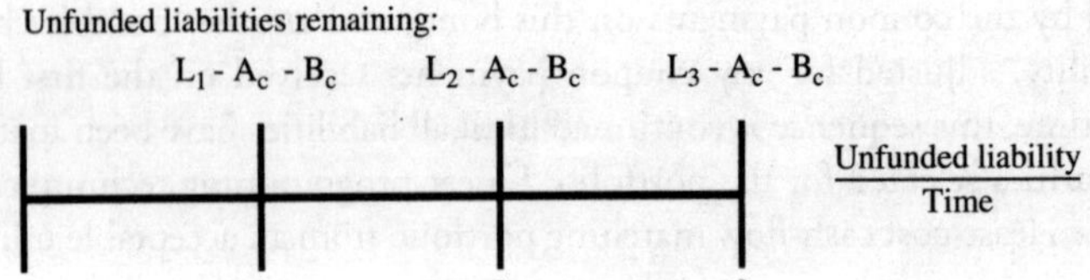

Step 3 – Cash flow from Bond C selected to satisfy $L_3 - A_c - B_c$
Coupons = C_c ; Principal = C_p and $C_c + C_p = L_3 - A_c - B_c$

Unfunded liabilities remaining:

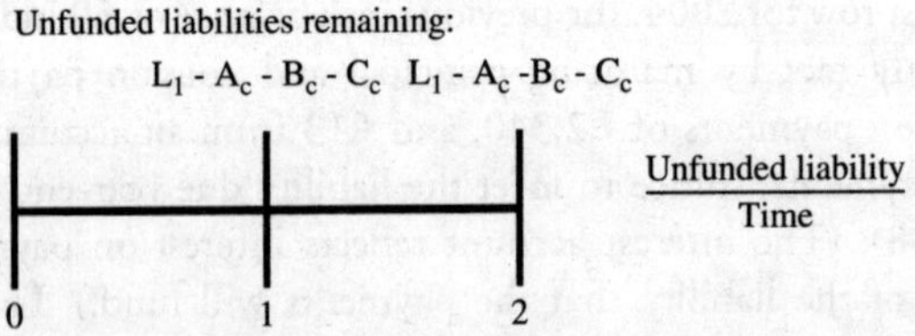

Step 4 – Cash flow from Bond D selected to satisfy $L_2 - A_c - B_c - C_c$
Coupons = D_c ; Principal = D_p and $D_c + D_p = L_2 - A_c - B_c - C_c$

Unfunded liabilities remaining:

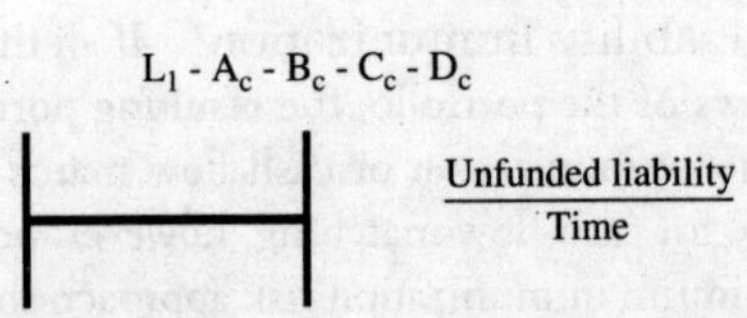

Step 5 – Select Bond E with a cash flow of $L_1 - A_c - B_c - C_c - D_c$

EXHIBIT 6-18 Illustration of Cash Flow Matching Process
Source: Fabozzi (2004b, p.123)

EXHIBIT 6-19 Cash-Flow Analysis of Sample Portfolio for Cash-Flow Matching
Reinvestment Rate: 1.2 percent; Evaluation Date: December 31, 2003

Year End (Dec 31)	Previous Cash Balance	Principal Payments	Coupon Payments	Interest on Reinvestment of Payments	Liability Due	New Cash Balance
2004	€ 0	€ 1,685	€ 2,340	€ 13	(€4,038)	€ 0
2005	0	1,723	2,165	13	(3,900)	0
2006	0	1,805	1,945	12	(3,762)	0
2007	0	1,832	1,769	23	(3,624)	0
2008	0	1,910	1,542	22	(3,474)	0
2009	0	1,877	1,443	10	(3,330)	0
2010	0	2,081	1,072	21	(3,174)	0
2011	0	2,048	950	14	(3,012)	0
2012	0	1,996	847	7	(2,850)	0
2013	0	3,683	768	9	(2,582)	1,878
2014	1,878	0	611	25	(2,514)	0
2015	0	1,730	611	5	(2,346)	0
2016	0	1,733	440	5	(2,178)	0
2017	0	1,756	233	15	(2,004)	0
2018	0	1,740	157	3	(1,900)	0

a cash flow–matched portfolio must be available when (and usually before) each liability is due, because of the difficulty in perfect matching. Because the reinvestment assumption for excess cash for cash-flow matching extends many years into the future, a conservative interest rate assumption is appropriate. An immunized portfolio needs to meet the target value only on the date of each liability, because funding is achieved by a rebalancing of the portfolio.

Thus, even with the sophisticated linear programming techniques used, in most cases cash-flow matching will be technically inferior to immunization. Cash-flow matching is easier to understand than multiple liability immunization, however; this ease of use occasionally supports its selection in dedication portfolio strategies.

4.2.2. Extensions of Basic Cash-Flow Matching

In basic cash-flow matching, only asset cash flows occurring prior to a liability date can be used to satisfy the liability. The basic technique can be extended to allow cash flows occurring both before and after the liability date to be used to meet a liability.[30] This technique, called **symmetric cash-flow matching,** allows for the short-term borrowing of funds to satisfy a liability prior to the liability due date. The opportunity to borrow short-term so that symmetric cash matching can be employed results in a reduction in the cost of funding a liability.

A popular variation of multiple liability immunization and cash-flow matching to fund liabilities is one that combines the two strategies. This strategy, referred to as **combination matching** or **horizon matching,** creates a portfolio that is duration-matched with the added constraint that it be cash-flow matched in the first few years, usually the first five years. The advantage of combination matching over multiple liability immunization is that liquidity needs are provided for in the initial cash-flow matched period. Also, most of the curvature

[30] See Fabozzi, Tong, and Zhu (1991).

of yield curves is often at the short end (the first few years). Cash-flow matching the initial portion of the liability stream reduces the risk associated with nonparallel shifts of the yield curve. The disadvantage of combination matching over multiple liability immunization is that the cost to fund liabilities is greater.

4.2.3. Application Considerations

In applying dedication strategies, the portfolio manager must be concerned with universe selection, optimization, monitoring, and transaction costs.

4.2.3.1. Universe Considerations Selection of the universe for construction of a single period immunized portfolio or a dedicated portfolio is extremely important. The lower the quality of the securities considered, the higher the potential risk and return. Dedication assumes that there will be no defaults, and immunization theory further assumes that securities are responsive only to overall changes in interest rates. The lower the quality of securities, the greater the probability that these assumptions will not be met. Further, securities with embedded options such as call options or prepayments options (e.g., mortgage-backed securities) complicate and may even prevent the accurate measurement of cash flow, and hence duration, frustrating the basic requirements of immunization and cash-flow matching. Finally, liquidity is a consideration for immunized portfolios, because they must be rebalanced periodically.

4.2.3.2. Optimization Optimization procedures can be used for the construction of immunized and cash flow–matched portfolios. For an immunized portfolio, optimization typically takes the form of minimizing maturity variance subject to the constraints of matching weighted average duration and having the necessary duration dispersion (in multiple-liability immunization). For cash-flow matching, optimization takes the form of minimizing the initial portfolio cost subject to the constraint of having sufficient cash at the time a liability arises. Further considerations such as average quality, minimum and maximum concentration constraints, and, perhaps, issuer constraints may be included. Throughout the process, it is critical to establish realistic guidelines and objectives. Accurate pricing is important because optimization is very sensitive to the prices of the securities under consideration. Because there are many inputs and variations available, the optimization process should be approached iteratively, with a final solution that is the result of a number of trials.

4.2.3.3. Monitoring Monitoring an immunized or cash flow–matched portfolio requires periodic performance measurement. For a bullet portfolio, performance monitoring may take the form of regular observations of the return to date linked with the current target return and annualized. This return should fluctuate only slightly about the original target return.

The performance of a multiple liability immunized plan can be monitored most easily by comparing the current market value of the assets with the present value of the remaining liabilities. The current internal rate of return on the immunized portfolio should be used to discount the remaining liabilities. (This rate is used because it is the expected rate of return that is necessary to provide sufficient cash flow to fund the liabilities.) These two quantities should track one another closely. It may also be useful to monitor the estimated standard deviation of the terminal value of the fund to make sure that it falls more or less uniformly to zero as the horizon date approaches.

4.2.3.4. Transactions Costs Transactions costs are important in meeting the target rate for an immunized portfolio. They must be considered not only in the initial immunization (when the immunized portfolio is first created) but also in the periodic rebalancing necessary to avoid duration mismatch.

5. OTHER FIXED-INCOME STRATEGIES

Whether managing against a bond market index or against a pool of liabilities, there are a range of combinations and alternatives that fixed-income managers might pursue in search of enhanced performance.

5.1. Combination Strategies

Although we have explained a number of basic portfolio strategies, the range of portfolio strategies really represents a continuum. At various phases during an interest rate cycle, a particular strategy may be most appropriate, but more often than not, a mix of alternatives is best for part or all of the cycle.

When decision makers have strong convictions, a one-strategy approach may be optimal; in the more likely case of uncertainty, strategy combinations may produce the best expected risk/return trade-off. A trade-off, for example, might be to tie a portion of the portfolio's risk and return to some baseline portfolio whose performance over the long term should provide satisfactory results, and actively manage the remaining portion. Retaining an active component preserves the opportunity for superior performance.

Two of the most popular combination strategies are active/passive and active/immunization. An **active/passive combination** allocates a core component of the portfolio to a passive strategy and the balance to an active component. The passive strategy would replicate an index or some sector of the market. In the active portion, the manager is free to pursue a return maximization strategy (at some given level of risk). A large pension fund might have a large allocation to a core strategy, consisting of an indexed portfolio, with additional active strategies chosen on the margin to enhance overall portfolio returns.

An **active/immunization combination** also consists of two component portfolios: The immunized portfolio provides an assured return over the planning horizon while the second portfolio uses an active high-return/high-risk strategy. The immunized portfolio is intended to provide an assured absolute return source. An example of an active immunization strategy is a surplus protection strategy for fully funded pension plan in which the liabilities are immunized and the portion of assets equal to the surplus is actively managed.

5.2. Leverage

Frequently, a manager is permitted to use leverage as a tool to help increase the portfolio's return. In fact, the whole purpose of using leverage is to magnify the portfolio's rate of return. As long as the manager can earn a return on the investment of the borrowed funds that is greater than the interest cost, the portfolio's rate of return will be magnified. For example, if a manager can borrow €100 million at 4 percent (i.e., €4 million interest per year) and invest the funds to earn 5 percent (i.e., €5 million return per year), the difference of 1 percent (or €1 million) represents a profit that increases the rate of return on the entire portfolio.

5.2.1. Effects of Leverage

As we have just seen, the purpose of using leverage is to potentially magnify the portfolio's returns. Let us take a closer look at this magnification effect with the use of an example.

EXAMPLE 6-9 The Use of Leverage

Assume that a manager has $40 million of funds to invest. The manager then borrows an additional $100 million at 4 percent interest in the hopes of magnifying the rate of return on the portfolio. Further assume that the manager can invest all of the funds at a 4.5 percent rate of return. The return on the portfolio's components will be as follows:

	Borrowed Funds	Equity Funds
Amount invested	$100,000,000	$40,000,000
Rate of return @4.5%	4,500,000	1,800,000
Less interest expense @4.0%	4,000,000	0
Net profitability	500,000	1,800,000
Rate of return on each component	$\frac{\$500,000}{\$100,000,000} = 0.50\%$	$\frac{\$1,800,000}{\$40,000,000} = 4.50\%$

Because the profit on the borrowed funds accrues to the equity, the rate of return increases from 4.5 percent in the all-equity case to 5.75 percent when leverage is used:

$$\frac{\$1,800,000 + \$500,000}{\$40,000,000} = 5.75\%$$

Even though the net return on the borrowed funds is only 50 bps, the return on the portfolio's equity funds is increased by 125 bps (5.75%–4.50%) because of the large amount of funds borrowed. The larger the amount of borrowed funds, the larger the magnification will be.

Leverage cuts both ways however. If the manager cannot invest the borrowed money to earn at least the rate of interest, the leverage will serve as a drag on profitability. For example, in the illustration above, if the manager can only earn a 3.50 percent rate on the portfolio, the portfolio's net return will be 2.25 percent, which is 125 bps less than the unleveraged return. Exhibit 6-20 shows the portfolio return at various yields on the invested funds (and for varying levels of borrowed funds).

Two relationships can be seen in Exhibit 6-20:

1. The larger the amount of borrowed funds, the greater the variation in potential outcomes. In other words, the higher the leverage, the higher the risk.
2. The greater the variability in the annual return on the invested funds, the greater the variation in potential outcomes (i.e., the higher the risk).

Let us now examine the expressions for the returns on borrowed and equity components of a portfolio with leverage. Let us also develop the expression for the overall return on this portfolio.

Suppose that:

E = Amount of equity
B = Amount of borrowed funds
k = Cost of borrowing
r_F = Return on funds invested

EXHIBIT 6-20 Portfolio Returns at Various Yields

	Annual Rate of Return on Portfolio's Equity Funds				
Borrowed Funds	2.50%	3.50%	4.50%	5.50%	6.50%
$60,000,000	0.25%	2.75%	5.25%	7.75%	10.25%
80,000,000	−0.50	2.50	5.50	8.50	11.50
100,000,000	−1.25	2.25	5.75	9.25	12.75
120,000,000	−2.00	2.00	6.00	10.00	14.00
140,000,000	−2.75	1.75	6.25	10.75	15.25

$$
\begin{aligned}
R_B &= \text{Return on borrowed funds} \\
&= \text{Profit on borrowed funds/Amount of borrowed funds} \\
&= B \times (r_F - k)/B \\
&= r_F - k
\end{aligned}
$$

As expected, R_B equals the return on funds invested less the cost of borrowing.

$$
\begin{aligned}
R_E &= \text{Return on equity} \\
&= \text{Profit on equity/Amount of equity} \\
&= E \times r_F/E \\
&= r_F
\end{aligned}
$$

As expected, R_E equals the return on funds invested.

$$
\begin{aligned}
R_P &= \text{Portfolio rate of return} \\
&= (\text{Profit on borrowed funds} + \text{Profit on equity})/\text{Amount of equity} \\
&= [B \times (r_F - k) + E \times r_F]/E \\
&= r_F + (B/E) \times (r_F - k)
\end{aligned}
$$

For example, assume equity is €100 million and €50 million is borrowed at a rate of 6 percent per year. If the investment's return is 6.5 percent, portfolio return is 6.5% + (€50/€100)(6.5% – 6.0%) = 6.75%.

5.2.2. Repurchase Agreements

Managers may use a variety of financial instruments to increase the leverage of their portfolios. Among investment managers' favorite instruments is the repurchase agreement (also called a repo or RP). A **repurchase agreement** is a contract involving the sale of securities such as Treasury instruments coupled with an agreement to repurchase the same securities on a later date. The importance of the repo market is suggested by its colossal size, which is measured in trillions of dollars of transactions per year.

Although a repo is legally a sale and repurchase of securities, the repo transaction functions very much like a collateralized loan. In fact, the difference in selling price and purchase price is referred to as the "interest" on the transaction.[31] For example, a manager can borrow $10 million overnight at an annual interest rate of 3 percent by selling Treasury securities valued at $10,000,000 and simultaneously agreeing to repurchase the same notes the following day for $10,000,833. The payment from the initial sale represents the principal amount of the loan; the excess of the repurchase price over the sale price ($833) is the interest on the loan.

[31]The repo "interest" should not be confused with the interest that is accruing on the security being used as loan collateral. The borrower is entitled to receive back the security that was put up as collateral as well as any interest paid or accrued on this instrument.

In effect, the repo market presents a low-cost way for managers to borrow funds by providing Treasury securities as collateral. The market also enables investors (lenders) to earn a return above the risk-free rate on Treasury securities without sacrificing liquidity.

Term to maturity. RP agreements typically have short terms to maturity, usually overnight or a few days, although longer-term repos of several weeks or months may be negotiated. If a manager wants to permanently leverage the portfolio, he may simply "roll over" the overnight loans on a permanent basis by entering the RP market on a daily basis.

Transfer of securities (with related costs). Obviously, the buyer of the securities would like to take possession (or delivery) of the securities. Otherwise, complications may arise if the seller defaults on the repurchase of the securities. Also, if delivery is not insisted on, the potential exists for an unscrupulous seller to sell the same securities over and over again to a variety of buyers. Transfer agreements take a variety of forms:

- Physical delivery of the securities. Although this arrangement is possible, the high cost associated with physical delivery may make this method unworkable, particularly for short-term transactions.
- A common arrangement is for the securities to be processed by means of credits and debits to the accounts of banks acting as clearing agents for their customers (in the United States, these would be credit and debits to the banks' Federal Reserve Bank accounts). If desired, the banking system's wire transfer system may be used to transfer securities electronically in book-entry form from the seller (the borrower of funds) to the buyer (or lender of funds) and back later. This arrangement may be cheaper than physical delivery, but it still involves a variety of fees and transfer charges.
- Another common arrangement is to deliver the securities to a custodial account at the seller's bank. The bank takes possession of the securities and will see that both parties' interests are served; in essence, the bank acts as a trustee for both parties. This arrangement reduces the costs because delivery charges are minimized and only some accounting entries are involved.
- In some transactions, the buyer does not insist on delivery, particularly if the transaction is very short term (e.g., overnight), if the two parties have a long history of doing business together, and if the seller's financial standing and ethical reputation are both excellent.

Default risk and factors that affect the repo rate. Notice that, as long as delivery is insisted on, a repo is essentially a secured loan and its interest rate does not depend on the respective parties' credit qualities. If delivery is not taken (or is weakly secured), the financial stability and ethical characteristics of the parties becomes much more important.

A variety of factors will affect the repo rate. Among them are:

1. *Quality of the collateral*. The higher the quality of the securities, the lower the repo rate will be.
2. *Term of the repo.* Typically, the longer the maturity, the higher the rate will be. The very short end of the yield curve typically is upward sloping, leading to higher yields being required on longer-term repos.

3. *Delivery requirement*. If physical delivery of the securities is required, the rate will be lower because of the lower default risk; if the collateral is deposited with the bank of the borrower, the rate is higher; if delivery is not required, the rate will be still higher. As with all financial market transactions, there is a trade-off between risk and return: The greater control the repo investor (lender) has over the collateral, the lower the return will be.
4. *Availability of collateral*. Occasionally, some securities may be in short supply and difficult to obtain. In order to acquire these securities, the buyer of the securities (i.e., the lender of funds) may be willing to accept a lower rate. This situation typically occurs when the buyer needs securities for a short sale or to make delivery on a separate transaction. The more difficult it is to obtain the securities, the lower the repo rate.
5. *Prevailing interest rates in the economy*. The federal funds rate is often used to represent prevailing interest rates in the United States on overnight loans.[32] As interest rates in general increase, the rates on repo transactions will increase. In other words, the higher the federal funds rate, the higher the repo rate will be.
6. *Seasonal factors*. Although minor compared with the other factors, there is a seasonal effect on the repo rate because some institutions' supply of (and demand for) funds is influenced by seasonal factors.

The preceding sections demonstrate the motivation for managers to borrow money and discuss a major instrument used to raise this money—the repurchase agreement. Borrowed money often constitutes a single liability and, therefore, a single benchmark. Other managers are faced with multiple liabilities—managers of defined-benefit plans, for example. Regardless of whether the benchmark is single or multiple, a variety of investment strategies are available to the manager to satisfy the goal of generating cash flows to meet these liabilities. Let us now examine some of those strategies.

5.3. Derivatives-Enabled Strategies

Fixed-income securities and portfolios have sensitivities to various factors. These sensitivities are associated with return and risk characteristics that are key considerations in security selection and portfolio management. Factors include duration and convexity as well as additional factors for some securities such as liquidity and credit. We can call these sensitivities ***factor exposures,*** and they provide a basis for understanding the return and risk characteristics of an investment.

The use of derivatives can be thought of as a means to create, reduce, or magnify the factor exposures of an investment. This modification can make use of basic derivatives such as futures and options in addition to combinations of factor exposures such as structured products.

In the following sections, we will review interest risk measurement and control and some of the most common derivatives used for such purposes, such as interest rate futures, interest rate swaps, credit options, credit swaps, and collateralized debt obligations.

5.3.1. Interest Rate Risk

The typical first-order source of risk for fixed-income portfolios is the duration or sensitivity to interest rate change. Conveniently, portfolio duration

[32] The federal funds rate is the interest rate on an unsecured overnight loan (of excess reserves) from one bank to another bank.

is a weighted average of durations of the individual securities making up the portfolio:

$$\text{Portfolio duration} = \frac{\sum_{i=1}^{n} D_i \times V_i}{V_P}$$

where

D_i = duration of security i
V_i = market value of security i
V_P = market value of the portfolio

In the course of managing a portfolio, the portfolio manager may want to replace one security in the portfolio with another security while keeping portfolio duration constant. To achieve this, the concept of dollar duration or the duration impact of a one dollar investment in a security can be used. Dollar duration is calculated using

$$\text{Dollar duration} = \frac{D_i \times V_i}{100}$$

where V_i = market value of the portfolio position if held; the price of one bond if not held.

To maintain the portfolio duration when one security is being exchanged for another, the dollar durations of the securities being exchanged must be matched. This matching can be accomplished by comparing the dollar durations of each side and thereby determining the necessary par value of the new bond. Specifically,

$$\text{New bond market value} = \frac{DD_O}{DD_N} \times 100$$

where

DD_O = dollar duration of old bond
DD_N = dollar duration of new bond

EXAMPLE 6-10 Maintaining Portfolio Duration in Changing Portfolio Holdings

A portfolio manager wants to exchange one bond issue for another that he believes is undervalued. The existing position in the old bond has a market value of 5.5 million dollars. The bond has a price of \$80 and a duration of 4. The bond's dollar duration is therefore 5.5 million × 4/100 or \$220,000.

The new bond has a duration of 5 and a price of \$90, resulting in a dollar duration of 4.5 (\$90 × 5/100) per bond. What is the par value of the new bond need to keep the duration of the portfolio constant?

Solution: The amount of the new bond required to keep the portfolio constant is \$4.889 million (\$220,000/4.5 × 100) and the required par value would be \$5.432 million (4.889/0.90).

Although duration is an effective tool for measuring and controlling interest rate sensitivity, it is important to remember that there are limitations to this measure. For example, the accuracy of the measure decreases as the magnitude of the amount of interest rate change increases.

Duration is one measure of risk, related to sensitivity to interest rate changes. The following sections address statistical risk measures.

5.3.2. Other Risk Measures The risk of a portfolio can be viewed as the uncertainty associated with the portfolio's future returns. Uncertainty implies dispersion of returns but raises the question, "What are the alternatives for measuring the dispersion of returns?"

If one assumes that portfolio returns have a normal (bell-shaped) distribution, then standard deviation is a useful measure. For a normal distribution, standard deviation has the property that plus and minus one standard deviation from the mean of the distribution covers 68 percent of the outcomes; plus and minus two standard deviations covers 95 percent of outcomes; and, plus and minus three standard divisions covers 99 percent of outcomes. The standard deviation squared (multiplied by itself) results in the variance of the distribution.

Realistically, the normality assumption may not be descriptive of the distribution, especially for portfolios having securities with embedded options such as puts, call features, prepayment risks, and so on.

Alternative measures have been used because of the restrictive conditions of a normal distribution. These have focused on the quantification of the undesirable left hand side of the distribution—the probability of returns less than the mean return. However, each of these alternatives has its own deficiency.

1. **Semivariance** measures the dispersion of the return outcomes that are below the target return.
   Deficiency: Although theoretically superior to the variance as a way of measuring risk, semivariance is not widely used in bond portfolio management for several reasons:[33]
   - It is computationally challenging for large portfolios.
   - To the extent that investment returns are symmetric, semivariance is proportional to variance and so contains no additional information. To the extent that returns may not be symmetric, return asymmetries are very difficult to forecast and may not be a good forecast of future risk anyway. Plus, because we estimate downside risk with only half the data, we lose statistical accuracy.
2. **Shortfall risk** (or risk of loss) refers to the probability of not achieving some specified return target. The focus is on that part of the distribution that represents the downside from the designated return level.
   Deficiency: Shortfall risk does not account for the magnitude of losses in money terms.
3. **Value at risk** (VaR) is an estimate of the loss (in money terms) that the portfolio manager expects to be exceeded with a given level of probability over a specified time period.
   Deficiency: VaR does not indicate the magnitude of the very worst possible outcomes.

Unfortunately, a universal and comprehensive risk measure does not exist. Each alternative has its merits and limitations. It is important to keep in mind that the portfolio will have multiple risk exposures (factors) and the appropriate risk measures will vary with the particular requirements of the portfolio.

[33]See Kahn (1997).

5.3.3. Bond Variance vs. Bond Duration The expected return of a portfolio is the weighted average of the expected returns of each individual security in the portfolio. The weight is calculated as the market value of each security as a percentage of the market value of the portfolio as a whole. The variance of a portfolio is determined by the weight of each security in the portfolio, the variance of each security, and the covariance between each pair of securities.

Two major problems are associated with using the variance or standard deviation to measure bond portfolio risk.

1. The number of the estimated parameters increases dramatically as the number of the bonds considered increases. The total number of variances and covariances that needs to be estimated can be found as follows:

$$\text{Number of bonds} \times (\text{Number of bonds} + 1)/2$$

   If a portfolio has 1,000 bonds, there would be 500,500 [i.e., 1,000 × (1,000 + 1)/2] different terms to be estimated.

2. Accurately estimating the variances and covariances is difficult. Because the characteristics of a bond change as time passes, the estimation based on the historical bond data may not be useful. For instance, a bond with five years to maturity has a different volatility than a four-year or six-year bond. Besides the time to maturity factor, some securities may have embedded options, such as calls, puts, sinking fund provisions, and prepayments. These features change the security characteristics dramatically over time and further limit the use of historical estimates.

Because of the problems mentioned above, it is difficult to use standard deviation to measure portfolio risk.

We now turn our attention to a variety of strategies based on derivatives products. A number of these derivatives products are shown in Exhibit 6-21 and are explained in the following sections.

5.3.4. Interest Rate Futures A **futures contract** is an enforceable contract between a buyer (seller) and an established exchange or its clearinghouse in which the buyer (seller) agrees to take (make) delivery of something at a specified price at the end of a designated period of time. The "something" that can be bought or sold is called the **underlying** (as in *underlying asset* or *underlying instrument*). The price at which the parties agree to exchange the underlying in the future is called the **futures price.** The designated date at which the parties must transact is called the **settlement date** or **delivery date.**

When an investor takes a new position in the market by buying a futures contract, the investor is said to be in a long position or to be long futures. If, instead, the investor's opening position is the sale of a futures contract, the investor is said to be in a short position or to be short futures.

Interest rate futures contracts are traded on short-term instruments (for example, Treasury bills and the Eurodollars) and longer-term instruments (for example, Treasury notes and bonds). Because the Treasury futures contract plays an important role in the strategies we discuss below, it is worth reviewing the nuances of this contract. The government bond futures of a number of other countries, such as Japan and Germany, are similar to the U.S. Treasury futures contract.

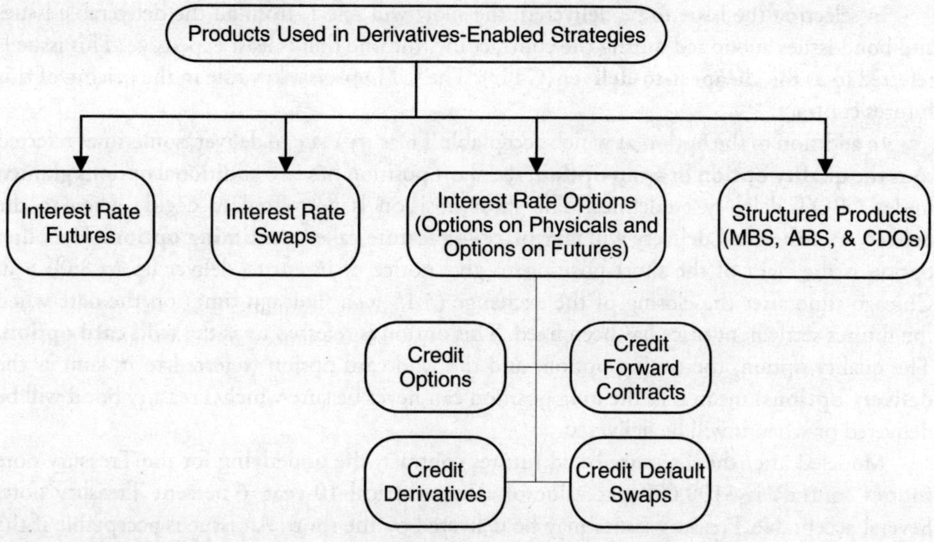

EXHIBIT 6-21 Derivatives-Enabled Strategies

The 30-year Treasury bond and 10-year U.S Treasury note futures contracts are both important contracts. The 30-year contract is an important risk management tool in ALM; the 10-year U.S. Treasury note futures contract has become more important than the 30-year contract in terms of liquidity. The U.S. Treasury ceased issuing its 30-year bond in 2002 but reintroduced it in 2006. The following discussion focuses on the 30-year bond futures contract, which shares the same structure as the 10-year note futures contract.

The underlying instrument for the Treasury bond futures contract is \$100,000 par value of a hypothetical 30-year, 6 percent coupon bond. Although price and yield of the Treasury bond futures contract are quoted in terms of this hypothetical Treasury bond, the seller of the futures contract has the choice of several actual Treasury bonds that are acceptable to deliver. The Chicago Board of Trade (CBOT) allows the seller to deliver any Treasury bond that has at least 15 years to maturity from the date of delivery if not callable; in the case of callable bonds, the issue must not be callable for at least 15 years from the first day of the delivery month. To settle the contract, an acceptable bond must be delivered.

The delivery process for the Treasury bond futures contract makes the contract interesting. In the settlement month, the seller of a futures contract (the short) is required to deliver to the buyer (the long) \$100,000 par value of a 6 percent, 30-year Treasury bond. No such bond exists, however, so the seller must choose from other acceptable deliverable bonds that the exchange has specified.

To make delivery equitable to both parties, and to tie cash to futures prices, the Chicago Board of Trade has introduced **conversion factors** for determining the invoice price of each acceptable deliverable Treasury issue against the Treasury bond futures contract. The conversion factor is determined by the CBOT before a contract with a specific settlement date begins trading. The conversion factor is based on the price that a deliverable bond would sell for at the beginning of the delivery month if it were to yield 6 percent. The conversion factor is constant throughout the trading period of the futures contract. The short must notify the long of the actual bond that will be delivered one day before the delivery date.

In selecting the issue to be delivered, the short will select, from all the deliverable issues and bond issues auctioned during the contract life, the one that is least expensive. This issue is referred to as the **cheapest-to-deliver** (CTD). The CTD plays a key role in the pricing of this futures contract.

In addition to the option of which acceptable Treasury issue to deliver, sometimes referred to as the **quality option** or **swap option,** the short position has two additional options granted under CBOT delivery guidelines. The short position is permitted to decide when in the delivery month actual delivery will take place—a feature called the **timing option.** The other option is the right of the short position to give notice of intent to deliver up to 8:00 P.M. Chicago time after the closing of the exchange (3:15 P.M. Chicago time) on the date when the futures settlement price has been fixed. This option is referred to as the **wild card option.** The quality option, the timing option, and the wild card option (referred to in sum as the **delivery options**) mean that the long position can never be sure which Treasury bond will be delivered or when it will be delivered.

Modeled after the Treasury bond futures contract, the underlying for the Treasury note futures contract is $100,000 par value of a hypothetical 10-year, 6 percent Treasury note. Several acceptable Treasury issues may be delivered by the short. An issue is acceptable if the maturity is not less than 6.5 years and not greater than 10 years from the first day of the delivery month. The delivery options granted to the short position are the same as for the Treasury bond futures contract.

5.3.4.1. Strategies with Interest Rate Futures The prices of an interest rate futures contract are negatively correlated with the change in interest rates. When interest rates rise, the prices of the deliverable bonds will drop and the futures price will decline; when interest rates drop, the price of the deliverable bonds will rise and the futures price will increase. Therefore, buying a futures contract will increase a portfolio's sensitivity to interest rates, and the portfolio's duration will increase. On the other hand, selling a futures contract will lower a portfolio's sensitivity to interest rates and the portfolio's duration will decrease.

There are a number of advantages to using futures contracts rather than the cash markets for purposes of portfolio duration control. Liquidity and cost effectiveness are clear advantages to using futures contracts. Furthermore, for duration reduction, shorting the contract (i.e., selling the contract) is very effective. In general, because of the depth of the futures market and low transaction costs, futures contracts represent a very efficient tool for timely duration management.

Various strategies can use interest rate futures contracts and other derivative products, including the following.

5.3.4.1.1. Duration Management A frequently used portfolio strategy targets a specific duration target such as the duration of the benchmark index. In these situations, futures are used to maintain the portfolio's duration at its target value when the weighted average duration of the portfolio's securities deviate from the target. The use of futures permits a timely and cost-effective modification of the portfolio duration.

More generally, whenever the current portfolio duration is different from the desired portfolio duration, interest rate futures can be an effective tool. For example, interest rate futures are commonly used in interest rate anticipation strategies, which involve reducing the portfolio's duration when the expectation is that interest rates will rise and increasing duration when the expectation is that interest rates will decline.

To change a portfolio's dollar duration so that it equals a specific target duration, the portfolio manager needs to estimate the number of future contracts that must be purchased or sold.

$$\text{Portfolio's target dollar duration} = \text{Current portfolio's dollar duration without futures} + \text{Dollar duration of the futures contracts}$$

$$\text{Dollar duration of futures} = \text{Dollar duration per futures contract} \times \text{Number of futures contracts}$$

The number of futures contracts that is needed to achieve the portfolio's target dollar duration then can be estimated by:

$$\begin{aligned}\text{Approximate number of contracts} &= \frac{(D_T - D_I)P_I}{\text{Dollar duration per futures contract}} \\ &= \frac{(D_T - D_I)P_I}{D_{CTD}P_{CTD}} \times \frac{D_{CTD}P_{CTD}}{\text{Dollar duration per futures contract}} \\ &= \frac{(D_T - D_I)P_I}{D_{CTD}P_{CTD}} \times \text{Conversion factor for the CTD bond}\end{aligned}$$

where

D_T = target duration for the portfolio
D_I = initial duration for the portfolio
P_I = initial market value of the portfolio
D_{CTD} = the duration of the cheapest-to-deliver bond
P_{CTD} = the price of the cheapest-to-deliver bond

Notice that if the manager wishes to increase the duration, then D_T will be greater than D_I and the equation will have a positive sign. Thus, futures contracts will be purchased. The opposite is true if the objective is to shorten the portfolio duration. It should be kept in mind that the expression given is only an approximation.

EXAMPLE 6-11 Duration Management with Futures

A U.K.-based pension fund has a large portfolio of British corporate and government bonds. The market value of the bond portfolio is £50 million. The duration of the portfolio is 9.52. An economic consulting firm that provides economic forecasts to the pension fund has advised the fund that the chance of an upward shift in interest rates in the near term is greater than the market currently perceives. In view of this advice, the pension fund has decided to reduce the duration of its bond portfolio to 7.5 by using a futures contract priced at £100,000 that has a duration of 8.47. Assume that the conversion factor for the futures contract is 1.1.

1. Would the pension fund need to buy futures contracts or sell?
2. Approximately, how many futures contracts would be needed to change the duration of the bond portfolio?

Solution to Problem 1: Because the pension fund desires to reduce the duration, it would need to sell futures contracts.

Solution to Problem 2:

D_T = target duration for the portfolio = 7.5

D_I = initial duration for the portfolio = 9.52

P_I = initial market value of the portfolio = £50 million

D_{CTD} = the duration of the cheapest-to-deliver bond = 8.47

P_{CTD} = the price of the cheapest-to-deliver bond = £100,000

Conversion factor for the cheapest-to-deliver bond = 1.1

$$\text{Approximate number of contracts} = \frac{(D_T - D_I)P_I}{D_{CTD}P_{CTD}} \times \text{Conversion factor for the CTD bond}$$

$$= \frac{(7.5 - 9.52) \times 50{,}000{,}000}{8.47 \times 100{,}000} \times 1.1 = -131.17.$$

Thus, the pension fund would need to sell 131 futures contracts to achieve the desired reduction in duration.

5.3.4.1.2. Duration Hedging Fixed-income portfolios are commonly used for purposes of asset/liability management in which portfolio assets are managed to fund a specified set of liabilities. In the case of immunization, the use of duration is critical. The matching of the portfolio duration to the duration of liabilities to be funded by the portfolio is a form of hedging. Offsetting (reducing) the interest rate exposure of a cash position in a portfolio is also a form of hedging. Whenever an interest rate exposure must be reduced, futures can be used to accomplish the hedge. The following discussion reviews several important issues in hedging an existing bond position.

Hedging with futures contracts involves taking a futures position that offsets an existing interest rate exposure. If the hedge is properly constructed, as cash and futures prices move together any loss realized by the hedger from one position (whether cash or futures) will be offset by a profit on the other position.

In practice, hedging is not that simple. The outcome of a hedge will depend on the relationship between the cash price and the futures price both when a hedge is placed and when it is lifted. The difference between the cash price and the futures price is called the **basis.** The risk that the basis will change in an unpredictable way is called **basis risk.**

In some hedging applications, the bond to be hedged is not identical to the bond underlying the futures contract. This kind of hedging is referred to as **cross hedging.** There may be substantial **basis risk** in cross hedging, that is, the relationship between the two instruments may change and lead to a loss. An unhedged position is exposed to **price risk,** the risk that the cash market price will move adversely. A hedged position substitutes basis risk for price risk.

Conceptually, cross hedging requires dealing with two additional complications. The first complication is the relationship between the cheapest-to-deliver security and the futures contract. The second is the relationship between the security to be hedged and the cheapest-to-deliver security.

The key to minimizing risk in a cross hedge is to choose the right **hedge ratio.** The hedge ratio depends on exposure weighting, or weighting by relative changes in value. The purpose of a hedge is to use gains or losses from a futures position to offset any difference between the target sale price and the actual sale price of the asset. Accordingly, the hedge ratio is chosen with the intention of matching the volatility (specifically, the dollar change) of the futures contract to the volatility of the asset. In turn, the factor exposure drives volatility. Consequently, the hedge ratio is given by:

$$\text{Hedge ratio} = \frac{\text{Factor exposure of the bond (portfolio) to be hedged}}{\text{Factor exposure of hedging instrument}}$$

As the formula shows, if the bond to be hedged has greater factor exposure than the hedging instrument, more of the hedging instrument will be needed.

Although it might be fairly clear why factor exposure is important in determining the hedge ratio, *exposure* has many definitions. For hedging purposes, we are concerned with exposure in absolute money terms. To calculate the dollar factor exposure of a bond (portfolio), one must know the precise time at which exposure is to be calculated as well as the price or yield at which to calculate exposure (because higher yields generally reduce dollar exposure for a given yield change).

The relevant point in the life of the bond for calculating exposure is the point at which the hedge will be lifted. Exposure at any other point is essentially irrelevant, because the goal is to lock in a price or rate only on that particular day. Similarly, the relevant yield at which to calculate exposure initially is the target yield. Consequently, the "factor exposure of the bond to be hedged" referred to in the formula is the dollar duration of the bond on the hedge lift date, calculated at its current implied forward rate. The dollar duration is the product of the price of the bond and its duration.

The relative price exposures of the bonds to be hedged and the cheapest-to-deliver bond are easily obtained from the assumed sale date and target prices. In the formula for the hedge ratio, we need the exposure not of the cheapest-to-deliver bond, but of the hedging instrument, that is, of the futures contract. Fortunately, knowing the exposure of the bond to be hedged relative to the cheapest-to-deliver bond and the exposure of the cheapest-to-deliver bond relative to the futures contract, the relative exposures that define the hedge ratio can be easily obtained as follows:

$$\text{Hedge ratio} = \frac{\text{Factor exposure of bond to be hedged}}{\text{Factor exposure of futures contract}}$$

$$= \frac{\text{Factor exposure of bond to be hedged}}{\text{Factor exposure of CTD bond}} \times \frac{\text{Factor exposure of CTD bond}}{\text{Factor exposure of futures contract}}$$

Considering only interest rate exposure and assuming a fixed yield spread between the bond to be hedged and the cheapest-to-deliver bond, the hedge ratio is

$$\text{Hedge ratio} = \frac{D_H P_H}{D_{CTD} P_{CTD}} \times \text{Conversion factor for the CTD bond}$$

where D_H = the duration of the bond to be hedged and P_H = the price of the bond to be hedged. The product of the duration and the price is the dollar duration.

Another refinement in the hedging strategy is usually necessary for hedging nondeliverable securities. This refinement concerns the assumption about the relative yield spread between the cheapest-to-deliver bond and the bond to be hedged. In the discussion so far, we have assumed that the yield spread is constant over time. In practice, however, yield spreads are not in constant over time. They vary with the maturity of the instruments in question and the level of rates, as well as with many unpredictable factors.

A hedger can use regression analysis to capture the relationship between yield levels and yield spreads. For hedging purposes, the variables are the yield on the bond to be hedged and the yield on the cheapest-to-deliver bond. The regression equation takes the form:

$$\text{Yield on bond to be hedged} = a + b\,(\text{Yield on CTD bond}) + \text{Error term}$$

The regression procedure provides an estimate of b, called the **yield beta,** which is the expected relative change in the two bonds. The error term accounts for the fact that the relationship between the yields is not perfect and contains a certain amount of noise. The regression will, however, give an estimate of a and b so that, over the sample period, the average error is zero. Our formula for the hedge ratio assumes a constant spread and implicitly assumes that the yield beta in the regression equals 1.0.

The formula for the hedge ratio can be revised to incorporate the impact of the yield beta by including the yield beta as a multiplier.

$$\text{Hedge ratio} = \frac{D_H P_H}{D_{CTD} P_{CTD}} \times \text{Conversion factor for the CTD bond} \times \text{Yield beta}$$

The effectiveness of a hedge may be evaluated after the hedge has been lifted. The analysis of hedging error can provide managers with meaningful insights that can be useful subsequently.

The three major sources of hedging error are incorrect duration calculations, inaccurate projected basis values, and inaccurate yield beta estimates. A good valuation model is critical to ensure the correct calculation of duration, especially for portfolios containing securities with embedded options.

5.3.5. Interest Rate Swaps

An **interest rate swap** is a contract between two parties (counterparties) to exchange periodic interest payments based on a specified dollar amount of principal (**notional principal amount**). The interest payments on the notional principal amount are calculated by multiplying the specified interest rate times the notional principal amount. These interest payments are the only amounts exchanged; the notional principal amount is only a reference value.

The traditional swap has one party (**fixed-rate payer**) obligated to make periodic payments at a fixed rate in return for the counter party (**floating-rate payer**) agreeing to make periodic payments based on a benchmark floating rate.

The benchmark interest rates used for the floating rate in an interest rate swap are those on various money market instruments: Treasury bills, the London Interbank Offered Rate (LIBOR), commercial paper, bankers' acceptances, certificates of deposit, the federal funds rate, and the prime rate.

5.3.5.1. Dollar Duration of an Interest Rate Swap

As with any fixed-income contract, the value of a swap will change as interest rates change and dollar duration is a measure of interest-rate sensitivity. From the perspective of the party who pays floating and receives fixed, the interest rate swap position can be viewed as:

Long a fixed-rate bond + Short a floating-rate bond

This means that the dollar duration of an interest rate swap from the perspective of a floating-rate payer is just the difference between the dollar duration of the two bond positions that make up the swap:

$$\text{Dollar duration of a swap} = \text{Dollar duration of a fixed-rate bond} - \text{Dollar duration of a floating-rate bond}$$

The dollar duration of the fixed-rate bond chiefly determines the dollar duration of the swap because the dollar duration of a floating-rate bond is small.

5.3.5.2. Applications of a Swap to Asset/Liability Management An interest rate swap can be used to alter the cash-flow characteristics of an institution's assets or liabilities so as to provide a better match between assets and liabilities. More specifically, an institution can use interest rate swaps to alter the cash-flow characteristics of its assets or liabilities: changing them from fixed to floating or from floating to fixed. In general, swaps can be used to change the duration of a portfolio or an entity's surplus (the difference between the market value of the assets and the present value of the liabilities).

Instead of using an interest rate swap, the same objectives can be accomplished by taking an appropriate position in a package of forward contracts or appropriate cash market positions. The advantage of an interest rate swap is that it is, from a transaction costs standpoint, a more efficient vehicle for accomplishing an asset/liability objective. In fact, this advantage is the primary reason for the growth of the interest rate swap market.

5.3.6. Interest Rate Options Interest rate options can be written on cash instruments or futures. Several exchange-traded option contracts have underlying instruments that are debt instruments. These contracts are referred to as **options on physicals.** In general, however, **options on futures** have been far more popular than options on physicals. Market participants have made increasingly greater use of over-the-counter (OTC) options on Treasury and mortgage-backed securities.

Besides options on fixed-income securities, there are OTC options on the shape of the yield curve or the yield spread between two securities (such as the spread between mortgage passthrough securities and Treasuries or between double-A rated corporates and Treasuries). A discussion of these option contracts, however, is beyond the scope of this section.

An option on a futures contract, commonly referred to as a **futures option,** gives the buyer the right to buy from or sell to the writer a designated futures contract at the strike price at any time during the life of the option. If the futures option is a call option, the buyer has the right to purchase one designated futures contract at the strike price. That is, the buyer has the right to acquire a long futures position in the designated futures contract. If the buyer exercises the call option, the writer of the call acquires a corresponding short position in the futures contract.

A put option on a futures contract grants the buyer the right to sell one designated futures contract to the writer at the strike price. That is, the option buyer has the right to acquire a short position in the designated futures contract. If the buyer exercises the put option, the writer acquires a corresponding long position in the designated futures contract.

5.3.6.1. Options and Duration The price of an interest rate option will depend on the price of the underlying instrument, which depends in turn on the interest rate on the underlying instrument. Thus, the price of an interest rate option depends on the interest rate on the underlying instrument. Consequently, the interest-rate sensitivity or duration of an interest rate option can be determined.

The duration of an option can be calculated with the following formula:

$$\text{Duration for an option} = \text{Duration of underlying instrument} \times \text{(Price of underlying)/(Price of option instrument)}$$

As expected, the duration of an option depends on the duration of the underlying instrument. It also depends on the price responsiveness of the option to a change in the underlying instrument, as measured by the option's **delta.** The leverage created by a position in an option comes from the last ratio in the formula. The higher the price of the underlying instrument relative to the price of the option, the greater the leverage (i.e., the more exposure to interest rates for a given level of investment).

The interaction of all three factors (the duration of the underlying, the option delta, leverage) affects the duration of an option. For example, all else equal, a deep out-of-the-money option has higher leverage than a deep in-the-money option, but the delta of the former is less than that of the latter.

Because the delta of a call option is positive, the duration of an interest rate call option will be positive. Thus, when interest rates decline, the value of an interest rate call option will rise. A put option, however, has a delta that is negative. Thus, duration is negative. Consequently, when interest rates rise, the value of a put option rises.

5.3.6.2. Hedging with Options The most common application of options is to hedge a portfolio. There are two hedging strategies in which options are used to protect against a rise in interest rates: **protective put** buying and **covered call** writing. The protective put buying strategy establishes a minimum value for the portfolio but allows the manager to benefit from a decline in rates. The establishment of a floor for the portfolio is not without a cost. The performance of the portfolio will be reduced by the cost of the put option.

Unlike the protective put strategy, covered call writing is not entered into with the sole purpose of protecting a portfolio against rising rates. The covered call writer, believing that the market will not trade much higher or much lower than its present level, sells out-of-the-money calls against an existing bond portfolio. The sale of the calls brings in premium income that provides partial protection in case rates increase. The premium received does not, of course, provide the kind of protection that a long put position provides, but it does provide some additional income that can be used to offset declining prices. If, on the other hand, rates fall, portfolio appreciation is limited because the short call position constitutes a liability for the seller, and this liability increases as rates go down. Consequently, there is limited upside potential for the covered call writer. Covered call writing yields best results if prices are essentially going nowhere; the added income from the sale of options would then be obtained without sacrificing any gains.

Options can also be used by managers seeking to protect against a decline in reinvestment rates resulting from a drop in interest rates. The purchase of call options can be used in such situations. The sale of put options provides limited protection in much the same way that a covered call writing strategy does in protecting against a rise in interest rates.

Interest rate **caps**—call options or series of call options on an interest rate to create a cap (or ceiling) for funding cost—and interest rate **floors**—put options or series of put options on an interest rate—can create a minimum earning rate. The combination of a cap and a floor creates a **collar.**

Banks that borrow short term and lend long term are usually exposed to short-term rate fluctuation. Banks can use caps to effectively place a maximum interest rate on short-term borrowings; specifically, a bank will want the **cap rate** (the exercise interest rate for a cap) plus the cost of the cap to be less than its long-term lending rate. When short-term rates increase, a bank will be protected by the ceiling created by the cap rate. When short-term rates decline, the caps will expire worthless but the bank is better off because its cost of funds has decreased. If they so desire, banks can reduce the cost of purchasing caps by selling floors, thereby giving up part of the potential benefit from a decline in short-term rates.

On the opposite side, a life insurance company may offer a guaranteed investment contract that provides a guaranteed fixed rate and invest the proceeds in a floating-rate instrument. To protect itself from a rate decline while retaining the benefits from an interest rate increase, the insurance company may purchase a floor. If the insurance company wants to reduce the costs of purchasing a floor, it can sell a cap and give up some potential benefit from the rate increase.

5.3.7. Credit Risk Instruments

A given fixed-income security usually contains several risks. The interest rate may change and cause the value of the security to change (interest rate risk); the security may be prepaid or called (**option risk**); and the value of the issue may be affected by the risk of defaults, credit downgrades, and widening credit spreads (credit risk). In this section, we will focus on understanding and hedging credit risk.

Credit risk can be sold to another party. In return for a fee, another party will accept the credit risk of an underlying financial asset or institution. This party, called the **credit protection seller,** may be willing to take on this risk for several reasons. Perhaps the credit protection seller believes that the credit of an issuer will improve in a favorable economic environment because of a strong stock market and strong financial results. Also, some major corporate events, such as mergers and acquisitions, may improve corporate ratings. Finally, the corporate debt refinancing caused by a friendlier interest rate environment and more favorable lending rates would be a positive credit event.

There are three types of credit risk: default risk, credit spread risk, and downgrade risk. Default risk is the risk that the issuer may fail to meet its obligations. **Credit spread risk** is the risk that the spread between the rate for a risky bond and the rate for a default risk-free bond (like U.S. treasury securities) may vary after the purchase. **Downgrade risk** is the risk that one of the major rating agencies will lower its rating for an issuer, based on its specified rating criteria.

5.3.7.1. Products That Transfer Credit Risk

Credit risk may be represented by various types of credit events, including a credit spread change, a rating downgrade, or default. A variety of derivative products, known as **credit derivatives,** exist to package and transfer the credit risk of a financial instrument or institution to another party. The first type of credit derivatives we examine are credit options.

5.3.7.1.1. Credit Options

Unlike ordinary debt options that protect investors against interest rate risk, credit options are structured to offer protection against credit risk. The triggering events of credit options can be based either on (1) the value decline of the underlying asset or (2) the spread change over a risk-free rate.

1. *Credit Options Written on an Underlying Asset*. **Binary credit options** provide payoffs contingent on the occurrence of a specified negative credit event.

In the case of a binary credit option, the negative event triggering a specified payout to the option buyer is default of a designated reference entity. The term *binary* means that there are only two possible scenarios: default or no default. If the credit has not defaulted by the maturity of the option, the buyer receives nothing. The option buyer pays a premium to the option seller for the protection afforded by the option.

The payoff of a binary credit option can also be based on the credit rating of the underlying asset. A credit put option pays for the difference between the strike price and the market price when a specified credit event occurs and pays nothing if the event does not occur. For example, a binary credit put option may pay the option buyer $X - V(t)$ if the rating of Bond A is below investment-grade and pay nothing otherwise, where X is the strike price and $V(t)$ is the market value of Bond A at time t. The strike price could be a fixed number, such as \$200,000, or, more commonly, expressed as a spread (**strike spread**) that is used to determine the strike price for the payoff when the credit event occurs.

EXAMPLE 6-12 Binary Credit Option

The manager of an investment-grade fixed-income fund is concerned about the possibility of a rating downgrade of Alpha Motors, Inc. The fund's holding in this company consists of 5,000 bonds with a par value of \$1,000 each. The fund manager doesn't want to liquidate the holdings in this bond, and instead decides to purchase a binary credit put option on the bond of Alpha Motors. This option expires in six months and pays the option buyer if the rating of Alpha Motors' bond on expiration date is below investment grade (Standard & Poor's/Moody's BB/Ba or lower.) The payoff, if any, is the difference between the strike price and the value of the bond at expiration. The fund paid a premium of \$130,000 to purchase the option on 5,000 bonds.

1. What would be the payoff and the profit if the rating of Alpha Motors' bond on expiration date is below investment grade and the value of the bond is \$870?
2. What would be the payoff and the profit if the rating of Alpha Motors' bond on expiration date is investment grade and the value of the bond is \$980?

Solution to Problem 1: The bond is in the money at expiration because its rating is below investment grade. The payoff on each bond is \$1,000 – \$870 = \$130. Therefore, the payoff on 5,000 bonds is 5,000 × \$130 = \$650,000. The profit is \$650,000 – \$130,000 = \$520,000.

Solution to Problem 2: The bond is out of the money at expiration because its rating is above investment grade. The payoff on each bond is zero. The premium paid of \$130,000 is the loss.

2. *Credit Spread Options*. Another type of credit option is a call option in which the payoff is based on the spread over a benchmark rate. The payoff function of a credit spread call option is as follows:

$$\text{Payoff} = \text{Max}[(\text{Spread at the option maturity} - K) \times \text{Notional amount} \times \text{Risk factor}, 0]$$

where K is the strike spread, and the risk factor is the value change of the security for a one basis point change in the credit spread. Max[A, B] means "A or B, whichever is greater."

5.3.7.1.2. Credit Forwards **Credit forwards** are another form of credit derivatives. Their payoffs are based on bond values or credit spreads. There are a buyer and a seller for a credit forward contract. For the buyer of a credit forward contract, the payoff functions as follows:

$$\text{Payoff} = (\text{Credit spread at the forward contract maturity} - \text{Contracted credit spread}) \times \text{Notional amount} \times \text{Risk factor}$$

If a credit forward contract is symmetric, the buyer of a credit forward contract benefits from a widening credit spread and the seller benefits from a narrowing credit spread. The maximum the buyer can lose is limited to the payoff amount in the event that the credit spread becomes zero. In a credit spread option, by contrast, the maximum that the option buyer can lose is the option premium.

Example 6-13 illustrates the payoff of credit spread forward, and Example 6-14 contrasts binary credit options, credit spread options, and credit spread forwards.

EXAMPLE 6-13 Evaluating the Payoff of a Credit Spread Forward

The current credit spread on bonds issued by Hi-Fi Technologies relative to same maturity government debt is 200 bps. The manager of Stable Growth Funds believes that the credit situation of Hi-Fi Technologies will deteriorate over the next few months, resulting in a higher credit spread on its bonds. He decides to buy a six-month credit spread forward contract with the current spread as the contracted spread. The forward contract has a notional amount of $5 million and a risk factor of 4.3.

1. On the settlement date six months later, the credit spread on Hi-Fi Technologies' bonds is 150 bps. How much is the payoff to Stable Growth Funds?
2. How much would be the payoff to Stable Growth Funds if the credit spread on the settlement date is 300 bps?
3. How much is the maximum possible loss to Stable Growth Funds?
4. How much would be payoffs in Parts 1, 2, and 3 above to the party that took the opposite side of the forward contract?

Solutions: The payoff to Stable Growth Funds would be:

$$\text{Payoff} = (\text{Credit spread at the forward contract maturity} - 0.020) \times \$5 \text{ million} \times 4.3$$

1. $\text{Payoff} = (0.015 - 0.020) \times \$5{,}000{,}000 \times 4.3 = -\$107{,}500$, a loss of \$107,500.
2. $\text{Payoff} = (0.030 - 0.020) \times \$5{,}000{,}000 \times 4.3 = \$215{,}000$.

3. Stable Growth Funds would have the maximum loss in the unlikely event of the credit spread at the forward contract maturity being zero. So, the worst possible payoff would be $(0.000 - 0.020) \times \$5,000,000 \times 4.3 = -\$430,000$, a loss of \$430,000.
4. The payoff to party that took the opposite side of the forward contract, that is, the party that took the position that credit spread would decrease, would be:

Payoff = (0.020 − Credit spread at the forward contract maturity) × \$5,000,000 × 4.3

The payoffs to this party would be the opposite of the payoffs to Stable Growth Fund. So, the payoffs would be a gain of \$107,500 in Part 1, a loss of \$215,000 in Part 2, and a maximum possible gain of \$430,000 in Part 3. Because there is no limit to the increase in credit spread, the maximum possible loss for this party is limitless.

EXAMPLE 6-14 Binary Credit Option, Credit Spread Option, and Credit Spread Forward

The portfolio manager of a fixed-income fund is concerned about possible adverse developments in three of the bond holdings of the fund. The reason for his concern is different for the three bond holdings. In particular, he is concerned about the possibility of a credit rating downgrade for Company X, the possibility of a credit default by Company Y, and the possibility of a widening credit spread for Company Z. The portfolio manager contacts a credit derivative dealer. The dealer tells him that his firm offers several credit instruments, some of which are given below.

For each of the following, indicate if it could be used to cover one or more of the three risks the portfolio manager is concerned about.

1. A binary credit put option with the credit event specified as a default by the company on its debt obligations.
2. A binary credit put option with the credit event specified as a credit rating downgrade.
3. A credit spread put option where the underlying is the level of the credit spread.
4. A credit spread call option where the underlying is the level of the credit spread.
5. A credit spread forward, with the credit derivative dealer firm taking a position that the credit spread will decrease.

Solutions:

1. The fixed-income fund could purchase this put option to cover the risk of a credit default by Company Y.
2. The fixed-income fund could purchase this put option to cover the risk of a credit rating downgrade for Company X.

3. This option is not useful to cover any of the three risks. A credit spread put option where the underlying is the level of the credit spread is useful if one believes that credit spread will decline.
4. The fixed-income fund could purchase this credit spread call option where the underlying is the level of the credit spread to cover the risk of an increased credit spread for Company Z.
5. The fixed-income fund could enter into this forward contract to cover the risk of an increased credit spread for Company Z. The dealer firm would take a position that the credit spread will decrease, while the fixed-income fund would take the opposite position.

5.3.7.1.3. Credit Swaps A number of different products can be classified as credit swaps, including credit default swaps, asset swaps, total return swaps, credit-linked notes, synthetic collateralized bond obligations, and basket default swaps. Among all credit derivative products, the **credit default swap** is the most popular and is commonly recognized as the basic building block of the credit derivative market. Therefore, we focus our discussion on credit default swaps.

A credit default swap is a contract that shifts credit exposure of an asset issued by a specified **reference entity** from one investor (protection buyer) to another investor (protection seller). The protection buyer usually makes regular payments, the swap premium payments (default swap spread), to the protection seller. For short-dated credit, investors may pay this fee up front. In the case of a **credit event,** the protection seller compensates the buyer for the loss on the investment, and the settlement can take the form of either physical delivery or a negotiated cash payment equivalent to the market value of the defaulted securities. The transaction can be schematically represented as in Exhibit 6-22.

Credit default swaps can be used as a hedging instrument. Banks can use credit default swaps to reduce credit risk concentration. Instead of selling loans, banks can effectively transfer credit exposures by buying protections with default swaps. Default swaps also enable investors to hedge nonpublicly traded debts.

Credit default swaps provide great flexibility to investors. Default swaps can be used to express a view on the credit quality of a reference entity. The protection seller makes no upfront investment to take additional credit risk and is thus able to leverage credit risk exposure. In most cases, it is more efficient for investors to buy protection in the default swap market than selling or shorting assets. Because default swaps are negotiated over the counter, they can be tailored specifically toward investors' needs.

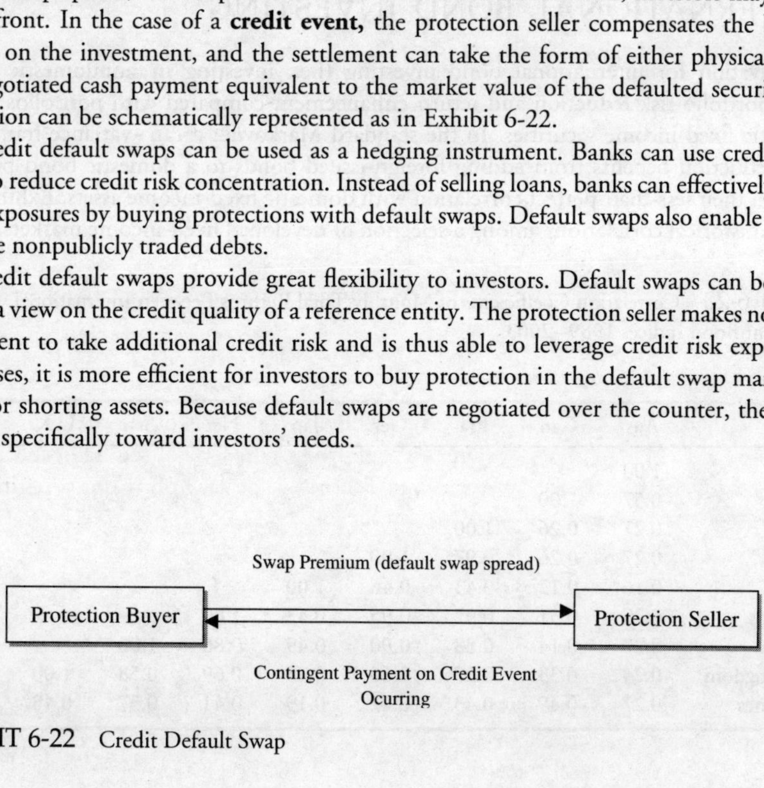

EXHIBIT 6-22 Credit Default Swap

EXAMPLE 6-15 Credit Default Swap

We Deal Inc., a dealer of credit derivatives, is quite bullish on the long-term debt issued by the governments of three countries in South America. We Deal decides to sell protection in the credit default swap market on the debt issued by these countries. The credit event in these transactions is defined as the failure by the borrower to make timely interest and/or principal payments. A few months later, the government of Country A defaults on its debt obligations, the rating of debt issued by Country B is lowered by Moody's from Baa to Ba because of adverse economic developments in that country, and the rating of debt issued by Country C is upgraded by Moody's from Baa to A in view of favorable economic developments in that country. For each of the countries, indicate whether We Deal suffers a loss.

Solution: In the protection sold by the dealer, the credit event was defined as the failure by the borrower to make timely interest and/or principal payments. This credit event occurred only in the case of Country A. Therefore, the dealer is likely to have suffered a loss only in the protection sold for Country A.

In the next section we broaden our view of fixed-income portfolio management by examining selected issues in international bond investing.

6. INTERNATIONAL BOND INVESTING

The motivation for international bond investing (i.e., investing in nondomestic bonds) includes portfolio risk reduction and return enhancement compared with portfolios limited to domestic fixed-income securities. In the standard Markowitz mean–variance framework, the risk reduction benefits from adding foreign-issued bonds to a domestic bond portfolio result from their less-than-perfect correlation with domestic fixed-income assets. Exhibit 6-23 illustrates historical correlations among a selection of developed fixed-income markets.

EXHIBIT 6-23 Correlation Coefficients of Monthly Total Returns Between International Government Bond Indices 1989–2003

In US$

	Aus	Can	Fra	Ger	Jap	Net	Swi	U.K.	U.S.
Australia	1.00								
Canada	0.57	1.00							
France	0.27	0.26	1.00						
Germany	0.27	0.26	0.97	1.00					
Japan	0.16	0.12	0.43	0.46	1.00				
Netherlands	0.28	0.31	0.97	0.95	0.43	1.00			
Switzerland	0.20	0.14	0.88	0.90	0.49	0.86	1.00		
United Kingdom	0.24	0.33	0.67	0.66	0.35	0.69	0.58	1.00	
United States	0.27	0.49	0.43	0.42	0.19	0.41	0.37	0.48	1.00

(continued)

In local currency (*continued*)

	Aus	Can	Fra	Ger	Jap	Net	Swi	U.K.	U.S.
Australia	1.00								
Canada	0.70	1.00							
France	0.45	0.46	1.00						
Germany	0.48	0.52	0.86	1.00					
Japan	0.25	0.27	0.20	0.29	1.00				
Netherlands	0.43	0.42	0.86	0.74	0.12	1.00			
Switzerland	0.34	0.35	0.61	0.68	0.27	0.55	1.00		
United Kingdom	0.51	0.59	0.67	0.71	0.24	0.58	0.53	1.00	
United States	0.63	0.71	0.56	0.62	0.26	0.46	0.47	0.57	1.00

The highest correlation was observed among the European markets because of the common monetary policy of the European Central Bank and introduction of the euro in 1999, which resulted in a larger, more liquid and integrated European bond market. The correlation coefficients are the lowest among countries with the weakest economic ties to each other. When returns are converted to U.S. dollars, the correlation coefficients reflect the impact of currency exchange rates on international investment. For example, the correlation coefficient between U.S. and U.K. returns is 0.57 in local currency terms and only 0.48 in U.S. dollar terms.

Overall, local currency correlations tend to be higher than their U.S. dollar equivalent correlations. Such deviations are attributed to currency volatility, which tends to reduce the correlation among international bond indices when measured in U.S. dollars.

In summary, the low-to-moderate correlations presented in Exhibit 6-23 provide historical support for the use of international bonds for portfolio risk reduction. Expanding the set of fixed-income investment choices beyond domestic markets should reveal opportunities for return enhancement as well.

If the investor decides to invest in international fixed-income markets, what directions and choices may be taken? Clearly, certain issues in international bond investing, such as the choice of active or passive approaches, as well as many fixed-income tools (e.g., yield curve and credit analysis), are shared with domestic bond investing. However, international investing raises additional challenges and opportunities and, in contrast to domestic investing, involves exposure to **currency risk**—the risk associated with the uncertainty about the exchange rate at which proceeds in the foreign currency can be converted into the investor's home currency. Currency risk results in the need to formulate a strategy for currency management. The following sections offer an introduction to these topics.

6.1. Active versus Passive Management

As a first step, investors in international fixed-income markets need to select a position on the passive/active spectrum. The opportunities for active management are created by inefficiencies that may be attributed to differences in tax treatment, local regulations, coverage by fixed-income analysts, and even to differences in how market players respond to similar information. The active manager seeks to add value through one or more of the following means: bond market selection, currency selection, duration management/yield curve management, sector selection, credit analysis of issuers, and investing outside the benchmark index.

- **Bond market selection.** The selection of the national market(s) for investment. Analysis of global economic factors is an important element in this selection that is especially critical when investing in emerging market debt.
- **Currency selection.** This is the selection of the amount of currency risk retained for each currency, in effect, the currency hedging decision. If a currency exposure is not hedged, the return on a nondomestic bond holding will depend not only on the holding's return in local currency terms but also on the movement of the foreign/domestic exchange rate. If the investor has the ability to forecast certain exchange rates, the investor may tactically attempt to add value through currency selection.
- **Duration management/yield curve management.** Once a market is chosen and decisions are made on currency exposures, the duration or interest rate exposure of holding must be selected. Duration management strategies and positioning along the yield curve within a given market can enhance portfolio return. Duration management can be constrained by the relatively narrow selection of maturities available in many national markets; however, growing markets for fixed-income derivatives provide an increasingly effective means of duration and yield curve management.
- **Sector selection.** The international bond market now includes fixed-income instruments representing a full range of sectors, including government and corporate bonds issued in local currencies and in U.S. dollars. A wide assortment of coupons, ratings, and maturities opens opportunities for attempting to add value through credit analysis and other disciplines.
- **Credit analysis of issuers.** Portfolio managers may attempt to add value through superior credit analysis, for example, analysis that identifies credit improvement or deterioration of an issuer before other market participants have recognized it.
- **Investing in markets outside the benchmark.** For example, benchmarks for international bond investing often consist of government-issued bonds. In such cases, the portfolio manager may consider investing in nonsovereign bonds not included in the index to enhance portfolio returns. This tactic involves a risk mismatch created with respect to the benchmark index; therefore, the client should be aware of and amenable to its use.

Relative to duration management, the relationship between duration of a foreign bond and the duration of the investor's portfolio including domestic and foreign bonds deserves further comment. As defined earlier, portfolio duration is the percentage change in value of a bond portfolio resulting from a 100 bps change in rates. Portfolio duration defined this way is meaningful only in the case of a domestic bond portfolio. For this duration concept to be valid in the context of international bond investments, one would need to assume that the interest rates of every country represented in the portfolio simultaneously change by 100 bps. International interest rates are not perfectly correlated, however, and such an interpretation of international bond portfolio duration would not be meaningful.

The duration measure of a portfolio that includes domestic and foreign bonds must recognize the correlation between the movements in interest rates in the home country and each nondomestic market. Thomas and Willner (1997) suggest a methodology for computing the contribution of a foreign bond's duration to the duration of a portfolio.

The Thomas–Willner methodology begins by expressing the change in a bond's value in terms of a change in the foreign yields, as follows:

$$\text{Change in value of foreign bond} = \text{Duration} \times \text{Change in foreign yield} \times 100$$

From the perspective of a Canadian manager, for example, the concern is the change in value of the foreign bond when domestic (Canadian) rates change. This change in value can be determined by incorporating the relationship between changes in domestic (Canadian) rates and changes in foreign rates as follows:

$$\text{Change in value of foreign bond} = \text{Duration} \times \text{Change in foreign yield given a change in domestic yield} \times 100$$

The relationship between the change in foreign yield and the change in Canadian yield can be estimated empirically using monthly data for each country. The following relationship is estimated:

$$\Delta y_{\text{foreign}} = \alpha + \beta \Delta y_{\text{domestic}}$$

where

$\Delta y_{\text{foreign}}$ = change in a foreign bond's yield in month t
$\Delta y_{\text{domestic}}$ = change in domestic (Canadian) yield in month time t
$\beta = \text{correlation}(\Delta y_{\text{foreign},t}, \Delta y_{\text{domnestic},t}) \times \sigma_{\text{foreign}}/\sigma_{\text{domestic}}$

The parameter β is called the **country beta.** The duration attributed to a foreign bond in the portfolio is found by multiplying the bond's country beta by the bond's duration in local terms, as illustrated in Example 6-16.

EXAMPLE 6-16 The Duration of a Foreign Bond

Suppose that a British bond portfolio manager wants to invest in German government 10-year bonds. The manager is interested in the foreign bond's contribution to the duration of the portfolio when domestic interest rates change.

The duration of the German bond is 6 and the country beta is estimated to be 0.42. The duration contribution to a British domestic portfolio is $2.52 = 6 \times 0.42$. For a 100 bps change in U.K. interest rates, the value of the German bond is expected to change by approximately 2.52 percent.

Because a portfolio's duration is a weighted average of the duration of the bonds in the portfolio, the contribution to the portfolio's duration is equal to the adjusted German bond duration of 2.52 multiplied by its weight in the portfolio.

6.2. Currency Risk

For the investor in international bonds, fluctuations in the exchange rate between domestic and foreign currencies may decrease or increase the value of foreign investments when converted into the investor's local currency. In particular, when a foreign currency depreciates against the investor's home currency (i.e., a given amount of the foreign currency buys less of the home currency) a currency loss occurs, but when it appreciates, a currency gain occurs.

In order to protect the value of international investments from adverse exchange rate movements, investors often diversify currency exposures by having exposure to several currencies. To the extent depreciation of one currency tends to be associated with appreciation of another—i.e., currency risks are less than perfectly correlated—a multi-currency portfolio has less currency risk than a portfolio denominated in a single currency.

The standard measure of the currency risk effect on foreign asset returns involves splitting the currency effect into (1) the expected effect captured by the **forward discount** or **forward premium** (the forward rate less the spot rate, divided by the spot rate; called the forward discount if negative) and (2) the unexpected effect, defined as the unexpected movement of the foreign currency relative to its forward rate. Every investor in the foreign markets can either remain exposed to this currency risk or hedge it. The investor may also have access to and may consider investing in **currency-hedged instruments,** which neutralize the currency exposure while maintaining the exposure to local bond price changes.

The bond investor should be aware of a basic result in economics concerning the forward discount/premium called covered interest rate parity as it suggests an approach to comparing (fully) hedged returns across international bond markets.

6.2.1. Interest Rate Parity

Interest rate parity (IRP) states that the forward foreign exchange rate discount or premium over a fixed period should equal the risk-free interest rate differential between the two countries over that period to prevent the opportunity for arbitrage profits using spot and forward currency markets plus borrowing or lending. Furthermore, as the interest rate differential between two countries changes, so should the forward discount or premium. To explain further, let the forward discount or premium, f, be given by:

$$f = (F - S_0)/S_0$$

where

F = forward exchange rate (stated as domestic currency/foreign currency)
S_0 = spot exchange rate (stated as domestic currency/foreign currency)

The currency quotation convention used—domestic currency/foreign currency—called **direct quotation,** means that from the perspective of a investor in a foreign asset an increase in the spot exchange rate is associated with a currency gain from holding the foreign asset.

According to IRP,[34]

$$f \approx i_d - i_f$$

where i_d and i_f are, respectively, the domestic and foreign risk-free interest rates over the time horizon associated with the forward exchange rate. For example, suppose the investor is based in the Eurozone and the available 1-year risk-free interest rate, at $i_d = 3.0$ percent, is lower than the 1-year U.S. risk-free interest rate, at $i_f = 4.5\%$. Thus, the interest rate differential is $i_d - i_f = 3.0\%–4.5\% = -1.5\%$. The spot exchange range is €0.8000 per dollar. According to IRP, the no-arbitrage forward exchange rate is €0.7880 per dollar because the resulting forward discount is $(0.7880 - 0.8000)/0.8000 = -1.5\%$. If the Eurozone investor makes a U.S. dollar bank deposit, the higher interest earned is offset by a currency loss.

6.2.2. Hedging Currency Risk

The decision on how much currency risk to hedge—from none to all—is important because currency movements can have a dramatic effect on the investor's return from international bond holdings. To illustrate the issue, Exhibit 6-24 shows the fluctuations in the U.S.–Australian dollar exchange rate over the period January 1993 to January 2004.

[34]For more details, including an explanation of the approximation, see Solnik and McLeavey (2004, Chapters 1 and 2).

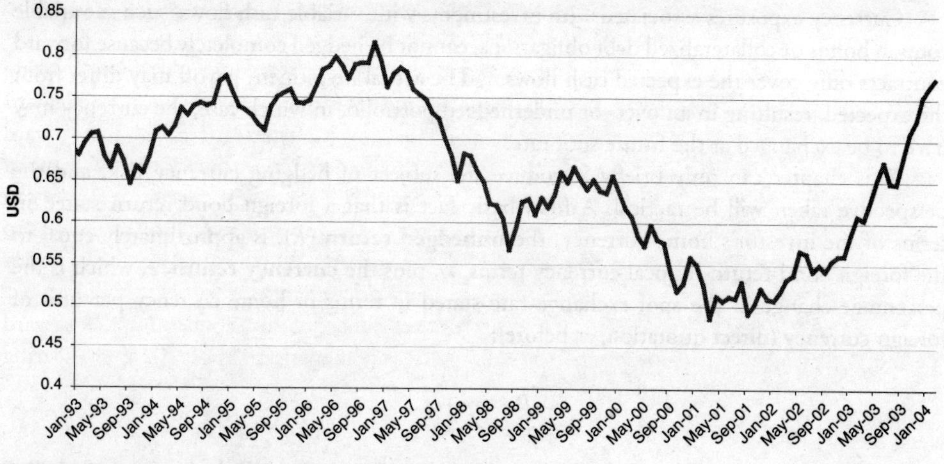

EXHIBIT 6-24 U.S. Dollars per Australian Dollars

During the period of a falling Australian dollar (1997 to mid-2001), hedged Australian investment positions generated higher returns in terms for U.S. investors than similar unhedged positions. From mid-2001 to the start of 2004, the trend reversed—the Australian currency appreciated—and hedged investments underperformed. Hedged and unhedged international investments with Australian dollar exposure generated drastically different returns in 2000 and 2003. Therefore, investors must carefully examine the decision to hedge and be familiar with hedging methods.

The three main methods of currency hedging are:

1. Forward hedging
2. Proxy hedging
3. Cross hedging

Forward hedging involves the use of a forward contract between the bond's currency and the home currency. **Proxy hedging** involves using a forward contract between the home currency and a currency that is highly correlated with the bond's currency. The investor may use proxy hedging because forward markets in the bond's currency are relatively undeveloped, or because it is otherwise cheaper to hedge using a proxy. In the context of currency hedging, **cross hedging** refers to hedging using two currencies other than the home currency and is a technique used to convert the currency risk of the bond into a different exposure that has less risk for the investor. The investment policy statement often provides guidance on permissible hedging methods.

The most popular hedging approach is forward hedging. For example, a German investor may be holding a position in Canadian bonds that is expected to pay C$5 million at maturity in nine months. Forward contracts are used to lock in the current value of a currency for future delivery. To hedge this position, therefore, the investor enters a forward agreement to purchase euros nine months from today at a forward rate of €1.20 per Canadian dollar. By entering the forward agreement and arranging the receipt of €6 million = C$5 million × 1.20€/C$ nine months from now, the investor is hedging against fluctuations in the euro/Canadian dollar exchange rate over the next nine months.

Currency exposures associated with investments with variable cash flows, such as variable coupon bonds or collateralized debt obligations, cannot be hedged completely because forward contracts only cover the expected cash flows.[35] The actual investment payoff may differ from the expected, resulting in an over- or underhedged portfolio, in which case, the currency may have to be exchanged at the future spot rate.

This chapter can only briefly introduce the subject of hedging currency risk, and the perspective taken will be tactical. A first, basic fact is that a foreign bond return stated in terms of the investor's home currency, the **unhedged return** (R), is approximately equal to the foreign bond return in local currency terms, r_l, plus the **currency return,** e, which is the percentage change in the spot exchange rate stated in terms of home currency per unit of foreign currency (direct quotation, as before):

$$R \approx r_l + e$$

If the investor can hedge fully with forward contracts, what return will the investor earn? The (fully) **hedged return,** HR, is equal to the sum of r_l plus the forward discount (premium) f, which is the price the investor pays (receives) to hedge the currency risk of the foreign bond. That is,

$$HR \approx r_l + f$$

If IRP holds, f is approximately equal to the interest rate differential, so that

$$HR \approx r_l + f \approx r_l + (i_d - i_f) = i_d + (r_l - i_f)$$

In other words, the hedged bond return can be viewed as the sum of the domestic risk-free interest rate (i_d) plus the bond's local risk premium (its excess return in relation to the local risk-free rate) of the foreign bond. If we compare the fully hedged return of international bond issues from different national markets, the expected difference in their fully hedged returns will reflect only the differences in their local risk premia. This idea provides an easy way to compare the hedged yields of bonds in different markets, as illustrated in Example 6-17.

EXAMPLE 6-17 Comparing Hedged Returns Across Markets

Suppose a U.K. investor is making a choice between same maturity (and credit risk) Japanese and Canadian government bonds. Currently, 10-year yields on government bonds in Japan and in Canada are 2.16 percent and 3.40 percent, respectively. Short-term interest rates are 1.25 percent and 1.54 percent in Japan and Canada, respectively. Assume that IRP holds. Contrast the expected fully hedged returns on 10-year Japanese and Canadian government bonds.

[35] A **collateralized debt obligation** is a securitized pool of fixed-income assets.

Solution: The Japanese government bond's local risk premium is 0.91% = 2.16% − 1.25%, and the Canadian government bond's local risk premium is 1.86% = 3.40% − 1.54%. Because the local risk premium on the Canadian bond is higher, its expected fully hedged return will be higher as well.

Example 6-17 contrasted the hedged yields of two bonds. In Example 6-18, the investor chooses hedging with forwards over leaving an investment unhedged based on a comparison of the interest rate differential with the expected currency return.

EXAMPLE 6-18 To Hedge or Not with a Forward Contract (1)

A U.S. fixed-income fund has substantial holdings in euro-denominated German bonds. The portfolio manager of the fund is considering whether to leave the fund's exposure to the euro unhedged or fully hedge it using a dollar–euro forward contract. Assume that the short-term interest rates are 4 percent in the United States and 3.2 percent in Germany. The fund manager expects the euro to appreciate against the dollar by 0.6 percent. Assume that IRP holds. Explain which alternative has the higher expected return based on the short-term interest rates and the manager's expectations about exchange rates.

Solution: The interest rate differential between the dollar and the euro is 4 − 3.2 = 0.8%. Because this differential is greater than the expected return on euro of 0.6 percent, a forward hedged investment is expected to result in a higher return than an unhedged position.

Example 6-19 examines the tactical decision to hedge or not based on the expected **excess currency return,** which is defined as the expected currency return in excess of the forward premium or discount.

EXAMPLE 6-19 To Hedge or Not with a Forward Contract (2)

David Marlet is the portfolio manager of a French fund that has substantial holdings in the U.K. pound-denominated British government bonds. Simon Jones is the portfolio manager of a British fund that has large holdings in euro-denominated French government bonds. Both the portfolio managers are considering whether to hedge their portfolio exposure to the foreign currency using a forward contract or leave the exposure unhedged. Assume that the short-term interest rates are 3.2 percent in France and 4.7 percent in the United Kingdom and that the forward discount on the pound is $4.7 - 3.2 = 1.5\%$. Marlet and Jones believe that the U.K. pound, the currency associated with the higher interest rate, will depreciate less relative to the euro than what the forward rate between the two currencies would indicate assuming interest rate parity.

1. Should Marlet use a forward contract to hedge the fund's exposure to the British pound?
2. Should Jones use a forward contract to hedge the fund's exposure to the euro?

Solutions: Both portfolio managers expect that the pound will depreciate less than 1.5 percent.

1. If Marlet were to hedge using a forward contract, he would be locking in a currency return of −1.5 percent; that is, a 1.5 percent loss on currency. By remaining unhedged, however, he expects the loss on currency to be less than 1.5 percent. Based on expected returns alone, he should not hedge the currency risk using a forward contract.
2. The situation of Jones, the portfolio manager of the British fund, is exactly the opposite of the portfolio manager of the French fund. If Jones were to hedge using a forward contract, he would be locking in a currency return of 1.5 percent, that is, a 1.5 percent gain on currency. Jones expects the gain on currency to be less than 1.5 percent if he does not hedge. Therefore, Jones should hedge the currency risk. Because Jones's anticipated return on currency (less than 1.5 percent) is below the interest rate differential (1.5 percent), the currency risk should be hedged.

6.3. Breakeven Spread Analysis

One consideration in active international bond portfolio selection is bond and country yield advantages. Breakeven spread analysis can be used to quantify the amount of spread widening required to diminish a foreign yield advantage. Breakeven spread analysis does not account for exchange rate risk, but the information it provides can be helpful in assessing the risk in seeking higher yields. Yield relationships can change because of a variety of factors. Furthermore, even a constant yield spread across markets may produce different returns. One reason is that prices of securities that vary in coupon and maturity respond differently to changes in yield: Duration plays an important role in breakeven spread analysis. Also, the yield advantage of investing in a foreign country may disappear if domestic yields increase and foreign yields decline.

EXAMPLE 6-20 Breakeven Spread Analysis

Suppose the spread between Japanese and French bonds is 300 bps, providing Japanese investors who purchased the French bond with an additional yield income of 75 bps per quarter. The duration of the Japanese bond is 7. Let W denote the spread widening.

With a duration of 7, the price change for the Japanese bond will be seven times the change in yield. (For 100 bps change yield in yield, the price change for the Japanese bond will be 7 percent.)

$$\text{Change in Price} = 7 \times \text{ Change in yield}$$

$$\text{Change in Price} = 7 \times W$$

Assuming that the increase in price caused by the spread widening will be 0.75 percent, the yield advantage of French bonds:

$$0.75\% = 7 \times W$$

Solving for the spread widening, W,

$$W = 0.1071\% = 10.71 \text{ bps}$$

Thus, a spread widening of 10.71 bps because of a decline in the yields in Japan would wipe out the additional yield gained from investing in the French bond for that quarter. A change in interest rates of only 10.71 bps in this case would wipe out the quarterly yield advantage of 75 bps.

Note that the breakeven spread widening analysis must be associated with an investment horizon (3 months in Example 6-20) and must be based on the higher of the two countries' durations. The analysis ignores the impact of currency movements.

The ability to choose individual sectors and/or securities varies considerably across the globe. For the developed countries, the same type of analysis for each of the respective fixed-income markets is appropriate. For the developing countries, such external influences as specific country or worldwide economic factors are relatively more important.

Emerging market security selection is especially limited. The resulting liquidity variation must be taken into account, which results in many countries limiting the choice to benchmark government bonds. In all cases, the details on settlements, taxation, and regulatory issues are important. Finally, as one builds a portfolio, the effects of currency positions adds a critical dimension. Use of derivative products has enabled more flexibility but is usually available only at notional amounts in the tens of millions of dollars at a minimum.

6.4. Emerging Market Debt

Emerging markets comprise those nations whose economies are considered to be developing and are usually taken to include Latin America, Eastern Europe, Africa, Russia, the Middle East, and Asia excluding Japan. Emerging market debt (EMD) includes sovereign bonds (bonds issued by a national government) as well as debt securities issued by public and private companies in those countries.

Over the past 10 years, emerging market debt has matured as an asset class and now frequently appears in many strategic asset allocations. Because of its low correlation with domestic debt portfolios, EMD offers favorable diversification properties to a fixed-income portfolio. EMD has played an important role in **core-plus** fixed-income portfolios. Core-plus is a label for fixed-income mandates that permit the portfolio manager to add instruments with relatively high return potential, such as EMD and high-yield debt, to core holdings of investment-grade debt.[36]

6.4.1. Growth and Maturity of the Market Although emerging market governments have always borrowed to meet their needs, the modern emerging markets debt sector originated in the 1980s when the Mexican financial crisis led to the creation of a secondary market in loans to that country. The Brady plan, which followed soon thereafter, allowed emerging country governments to securitize their outstanding external bank loans. A liquid market for these securities (called Brady bonds) soon followed. As a result of debt securitization, the majority of emerging market debt risk has now shifted from the banks to the private sector. The market has grown rapidly to its current substantial size—the International Monetary Fund (2005, p. 268) estimates the total size of the emerging external debt market in 2006 to be approximately $3.3 trillion.

The proportion of emerging market countries that are rated as investment grade has risen to about 40 percent of the countries represented in the emerging market indices. Mexico, for example, can now borrow almost as cheaply as the U.S. government. The quality of emerging market sovereign bonds has increased to the point that they now have frequencies of default, recovery rates, and ratings transition probabilities similar to corporate bonds as well as similar ratings. As a result, the spread of emerging market debt over risk-free rates has narrowed considerably.

The EMD market has also shown remarkable resiliency. During the Asian crisis of the late 1990s, the price of Asian debt fluctuated over wide ranges, but the market rebounded impressively, offering rates of return that exceeded those of many developed countries' equity markets in the post-crisis period. The market has dealt with crises in Latin America, Southeast Asia, and Russia with relatively little damage to investors, with the notable exception of the large Russian default in 1998.

Since 1992, the standard index in emerging markets has been the Emerging Markets Bond Index Plus (EMBI+). Although the index emphasizes the inclusion of highly liquid bonds, its main disadvantage is the lack of diversification in the securities that make up the index. An overwhelming percentage of the index (58 percent) is in Latin American securities, with Brazil and Mexico making up 37 percent of the total.

6.4.2. Risk and Return Characteristics Emerging market debt frequently offers the potential for consistent, attractive rates of return. Sovereign emerging market governments possess several advantages over private corporations. They can react quickly to negative economic events by cutting spending and raising taxes and interest rates (actions that may make it more difficult for private corporations in these countries to service their own debt). They also have access to lenders on the world stage, such as the International Monetary Fund and the World Bank. Many emerging market nations also possess large foreign currency reserves, providing a shock absorber for bumps in their economic road. Using these resources, any adverse situation can be rapidly addressed and reversed.

Risks do exist in the sector however—volatility in the EMD market is high. EMD returns are also frequently characterized by significant negative skewness. Negative skewness is the potential for occasional very large negative returns without offsetting potential on the upside.

[36]For example, a core-plus manager might be officially benchmarked to the Lehman Aggregate Bond Index, but invest a fraction of the portfolio (perhaps up to 25 percent) outside the benchmark.

An instance of an extreme negative event is the massive market sell-off that occurred from August 1997 to September 1998.

Other risks abound. Emerging market countries frequently do not offer the degree of transparency, court-tested laws, and clear regulations that developed market countries do. The legal system may be less developed and offer less protection from interference by the executive branch than in developed countries. Also, developing countries have tended to over borrow, which can damage the position of existing debt. If a default of sovereign debt occurs, recovery against sovereign states can be very difficult. Also, little standardization of covenants exists among various emerging market issuers. Sovereign debt also typically lacks an enforceable seniority structure, in contrast to private debt.

6.4.3. Analysis of Emerging Market Debt Just as with any credit analysis, an investor in EMD securities must determine the willingness and ability of the issuers to pay their debt obligations. This analysis begins with a look at the country's fundamentals: the source of government revenues, fiscal and monetary policies, current debt levels, and willingness of the country's citizens to accept short-term sacrifices in order to strengthen the country's long-term economic situation. For example, consider the Russian default in 1998. A great deal of money was lent to Russia before its economic and financial collapse. Yet, even a cursory examination would have shown that the country had no experience in collecting taxes, had an extremely weak economic infrastructure, and was dependent on a single commodity (energy) for its revenues. Investors either forgot the fundamentals or chose to ignore them. Historically, the largest returns have come from countries with strong fundamentals, usually characterized by an export-oriented economy and a high savings rate.

In evaluating EMD, the risk of default remains a critical consideration, particularly when private debt is concerned. Investors should not simply accept a bond rating as the final measure of the issue's default risk. In some countries, the financial strength of a large company may be greater than that of the sovereign government. The underlying assets for the company can be quite valuable and may justify a high credit rating. However, the credit rating for the company debt will not be higher than that of sovereign debt. This restriction on private debt ratings creates opportunities for astute investors to purchase high-quality debt at prices below fair market value.

Whether investing in established or emerging markets, investment in foreign assets, while providing diversification benefits, carries the same types of risk of domestic investments plus some additional risks associated with converting the foreign investment cash flows into domestic currency. Political risk and currency risk are major sources of uncertainty for portfolios with international exposures. And, changes in liquidity and taxation may be additional sources of risk.

Political risk or **geopolitical risk** includes the risk of war, government collapse, political instability, expropriation, confiscation, and adverse changes in taxation. A common political risk is the uncertainty that investors will be able to convert the foreign currency holdings into their home currency as a result of constraints imposed by foreign government policies or political actions of any sort.

Sovereign governments may impose restrictions on capital flows, change rules, revise taxes, liberalize bankruptcy proceedings, modify exchange rate regimes, and create new market regulations, all of which add an element of uncertainty to financial markets by affecting the performance and liquidity of investments in those countries.

Political crises during the 1990s in Europe, Southeast Asia, Russia, Latin America, and the Middle East highlight the increasing global links among political risks. Today's political risks are often subtle, arising not only from legal and regulatory changes and government transitions but also from environmental issues, foreign policies, currency crises, and terrorism. Nevertheless, diversification among international securities is one means to controlling the effect of political risk on the investment performance. However, investments in countries with close economic and political links would afford less than investments in countries with looser links.

Investors in EMD face default risk as does any investor in debt. Sovereign EMD bears greater credit risk than developed market sovereign debt, reflecting less-developed banking and financial market infrastructure, lower transparency, and higher political risk in developing countries. Rating agencies issue sovereign ratings that indicate countries' ability to meet their debt obligations. Standard & Poor's investment-grade sovereign rating of BBB– and Moody's Baa3 are given to the most creditworthy emerging markets countries. Increased transparency and availability of reliable foreign market data are valued in the marketplace and directly linked to foreign capital inflow. For example, some evidence indicates that U.S. investors in the early 2000s moved out of smaller markets and markets with low and declining credit ratings to countries with more transparent financial markets, open economies, and better inflation performance.[37]

In the next section, we turn our attention to the final topic of this chapter, selecting a fixed-income portfolio manager.

7. SELECTING A FIXED-INCOME MANAGER

When funds are not managed entirely in-house, a search for outside managers must be conducted. Because the average institutional fixed-income portfolio has approximately 85 percent of the assets managed actively and 15 percent indexed, we focus our attention here on the selection of an active manager.

Active return and active risk (tracking risk) are intricately linked. The typical range for tracking risk in large fixed-income institutional portfolios is between 40 and 120 bps with the upper end of the range typically including a high-yield component and the lower end being more typical for core managers. Because active management fees typically range from 15 to 50 bps (plus custodial fees), it is clear that outperforming the benchmark on a net-of-fees basis is a challenging and difficult task.

The due diligence for selection of managers is satisfied primarily by investigating the managers' investment process, the types of trades the managers are making, and the manager's organizational strengths and weaknesses. The key to better performance is to find managers who can produce consistent positive style-adjusted alphas. Then, the portfolio can be constructed by optimizing the combination of managers in order to maximize the variety of styles and exposures contributed by each manager.

7.1. Historical Performance as a Predictor of Future Performance

Is a fixed-income manager's historical performance a good predictor of future performance? Studies indicate some evidence of persistence of overperformance by some managers relative to their peers over short periods of time. However, over long periods of time (15 years or more) and when fund fees and expenses are factored in, the realized alpha of fixed-income

[37] See Burger and Warnock (2003).

managers has averaged very close to zero and little evidence of persistence exits. So it is clear that selecting a manager purely on the basis of historical performance is not a good approach to manager selection.

7.2. Developing Criteria for the Selection

The value of due diligence is found in the details; a fundamental analysis of the manager's strategy must be conducted. Here are some of the factors that should be considered:

1. *Style analysis.* In large part, the active risk and return are determined by the extent to which the portfolio differs from the benchmark's construction—particularly with regard to overweighting of sectors and duration differences. An analysis of the managers' historical style may prove helpful in explaining the types of biases and quality of the views reflected in the portfolio weighting have affected a portfolio's overall performance.

   For example, consider a style analysis of an individual core-plus manager. The analysis may demonstrate a significant style weight to MBS and high-yield bonds (consistent with the core-plus strategy), coupled with a persistent and large underweighting of investment-grade securities (relative to the Lehman Aggregate). Also, the manager may make consistent duration bets across the portfolio by investing in bonds with a longer duration than the benchmark. Under the right conditions, this approach could certainly lead to larger returns, but it will also likely lead to higher active risk. A close examination of the results should yield some insight into the manager's skill in using this approach.
2. *Selection bets.* If an active manager believes that she possesses superior credit or security analysis skills, she may frequently deviate from the weights in the normal portfolio. By forecasting changes in relative credit spreads and identifying undervalued securities, the manager may attempt to increase the active return of the portfolio. The manager's skill in this approach may be measured by decomposing the portfolio's returns.
3. *The organization's investment process.* The investor needs to be intimately familiar with the investment process of the manager's organization. What research methods are used by the organization? What are the main drivers of alpha? How are decisions regarding changes in the portfolio made? A manager is often only as good as the support staff. Before selection, the plan sponsor needs to spend quite a bit of time asking questions of several key people in the organization.
4. *Correlation of alphas.* The historical correlations of alpha across managers should also be examined. Many managers exhibit similarities in their management of a portfolio. If multiple managers are to be used, obviously the plan sponsor will prefer to low to high correlation among managers' alphas to control portfolio risk.

7.3. Comparison with Selection of Equity Managers

Selecting a fixed-income manager has both similarities with and differences from the selection of an equity manager.

1. In both cases, a consultant is frequently used to identify a universe of suitable manager candidates (because of the consultants' large databases).
2. In both sectors, the available evidence indicates that past performance is not a reliable guide to future results.

3. The same qualitative factors are common to both analyses: philosophy of the manager and organization, market opportunity, competitive advantages, delegation of responsibility, experience of the professionals, and so on.
4. Management fees and expenses are vitally important in both areas, because they often reduce or eliminate the alpha that managers are able to earn gross of expenses. If anything, fees are more important in the fixed-income area, because fixed-income funds have a higher ratio of fees to expected outperformance. There is some evidence that fixed-income managers with the highest fees have the lowest information ratios (i.e., ratio of expected alpha to volatility of alpha), so the avoidance of high fees is clearly a defensible strategy.

Although limited space prevents discussion for all the relevant items here, Example 6-21 illustrates some of the key areas that should be investigated in a complete due diligence analysis.

EXAMPLE 6-21 Due Diligence Questionnaire for a U.S. Fixed-Income Portfolio

When conducting a search for managers, organizations will typically ask portfolio managers to submit answers to a wide variety of questions as part of the due diligence process. The following questionnaire illustrates the types of information typically asked of candidate managers:

1. Organization:
   a. History (key events and date).
   b. Structure.
   c. Ownership.
   d. Number of employees (last three years).
   e. Awards/ratings.
   f. Flagship products and core competencies.
   g. Timeline of products/product development.
   h. Total assets, total fixed-income assets, and total core-plus assets.
   i. Significant client additions/withdrawals in last three years.
   j. Current lawsuits for investigations.
   k. Policy on market timing, excessive trading, and distribution fee arrangements.
   l. Form ADV, Parts 1 and 2.
2. Product (Provide information based on a similar or composite portfolio):
   a. Inception date.
   b. Investment philosophy.
   c. Nonbenchmark sectors and exposure to these sectors via commingled fund or direct investment.

d. Return objective.
e. Gross and net-of-fee performance versus the Lehman Brothers Aggregate Bond Index.
    - Annualized returns for the quarter, year-to-date, 1 year, 3 years, 5 years, 10 years, and since inception.
    - Annual returns for 1 through 10 years.
    - Monthly returns for 1 through 5 years.
f. Quantitative analysis—metrics such as:
    - Volatility, tracking risk, information ratio, Sharpe ratio, and so on.
g. Sector allocation vs. the Lehman Brothers Aggregate Bond Index, quarterly for the past three years.
h. Portfolio characteristics vs. the Lehman Brothers Aggregate Bond Index, quarterly for the past three years.
    - Duration, average quality, average maturity, average yield, and so on.
i. Permitted security types, including a statement on the use of short positions, derivative products, and leveraging.
j. Description of any constraints/limits:
    - Frequency of subscription/redemption.
    - Cash limits.
k. Average number of total holdings.
l. Total management fees and additional fees, if any.
m. Asset value data provider.
n. Administrator, custodian, auditor, advisers for commingled funds, if any.
o. Growth of assets under management of this product.
p. Top clients by assets under management utilizing this product.
q. Three current client references.

3. Risk management:
    a. Philosophy and process.
    b. Portfolio risk monitoring.
    c. Limits on single positions, regions/countries, industries/sectors, and so on.
4. Investment personnel:
    a. Structure of investment team.
    b. Responsibilities.
    c. Bios of key personnel.
    d. Significant team departures in last five years.
    e. Additional products managed by same manager or management team.
    f. Compensation structure of investment team.
    g. Tenure of investment team.
    h. A description of the client service resources that will be made available.

5. Investment process:
   a. Decisions by committee or by manager.
   b. Quantitative or fundamental analysis.
   c. Top-down or bottom-up approach.
   d. Use of internal and external research.
   e. Universal securities.
   f. Main alpha drivers/sources of value added.
   g. Significant changes in investment process over last 10 years or since inception.
   h. Process driven or people driven fund management.
   i. Sell discipline.
   j. Best execution trading policy.
6. Reporting capabilities:
   a. Sample monthly and quarterly reports.
   b. Online reporting/download capability.

CHAPTER 7

EQUITY PORTFOLIO MANAGEMENT

Gary L. Gastineau

ETF Consultants LLC
Summit, New Jersey

Andrew R. Olma, CFA

Barclays Global Investors
San Francisco, California

Robert G. Zielinski, CFA

Japan Advisory
Tokyo, Japan

1. INTRODUCTION

Equities constitute a significant part of many investment portfolios' value. For numerous investors, the decision of how to invest the equity allocation among competing investment approaches ranks second in importance only to the decision of how much of the portfolio to allocate to equities in the first place.

This chapter presents a broad overview of equity portfolio management organized as follows: Section 2 summarizes the role of equities in investors' portfolios. Sections 3 through 6 introduce and discuss three broad approaches to equity investing and their subdisciplines. Section 7 discusses managing a portfolio of managers so that the overall equity allocation achieves the investor's purposes. Section 8 presents the important subject of identifying, selecting, and contracting with equity portfolio managers. Section 9 discusses structuring equity research and security selection.

2. THE ROLE OF THE EQUITY PORTFOLIO

Equities represent a significant source of wealth in the world today. As of September 30, 2004, the aggregate market value of the equities in the Morgan Stanley Capital International All Country World Index (MSCI ACWI) was more than $19 trillion, of which almost half represented markets outside the United States.[1] Furthermore, nearly 5 percent of the $19 trillion total, equal to a market value of nearly $950 billion, represented emerging markets.

This vast pool of equity assets is held in both individual and institutional portfolios. Exhibit 7-1 shows the equity allocation weighting for institutional clients in various markets.[2] Both domestic and international equities play a large role in these portfolios—domestic equities are in the investor's home markets; international equities are outside those markets. Exhibit 7-1 makes clear that international equities constitute differing proportions of the

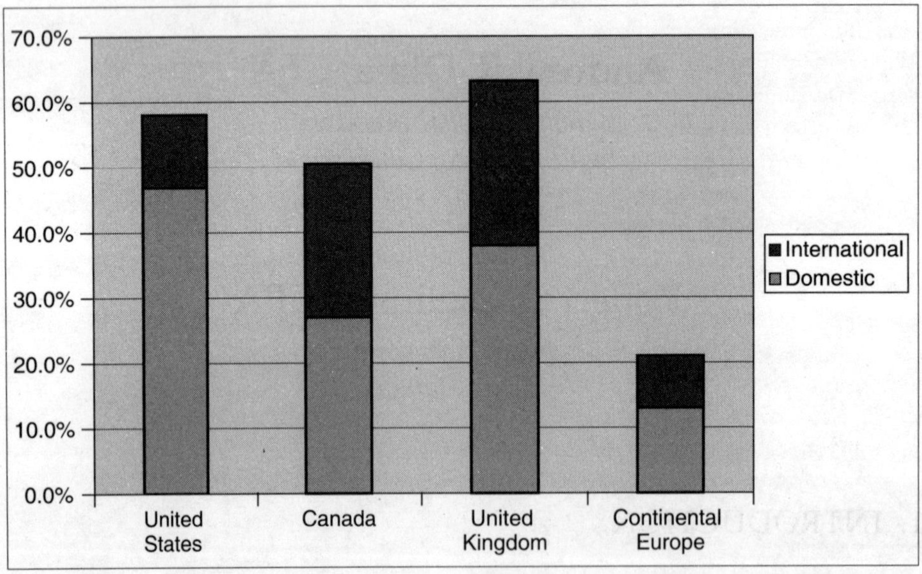

EXHIBIT 7-1 Equity Allocations for Institutional Investors
Source: Greenwich Associates, 2003.

[1]This index covers 49 developed and emerging markets and is intended to represent approximately 85 percent of each country's equity market value.

[2]According to a 2003 survey by the Pension Fund Association in Japan, covering 1,316 Japanese pension plans, the average allocations to domestic and international equities were 28.2 percent and 15.1 percent, respectively (43.3 percent in total). Although focusing on corporate pension plans rather than all institutional investors as in Exhibit 7-1, this survey suggests that Japanese equity allocations tend to be smaller than those in North American and U.K. markets, but larger than those in continental Europe. The survey is available at www.pfa.or.jp.

average equity portfolio in different countries. These differences probably reflect, at least in part, differences in the market capitalizations (values) of investors' home equity markets in relation to a global portfolio of equities: The larger the domestic market's global weight, the more we might expect investors to emphasize that market. Different attitudes and investment constraints may also affect these international differences.

Investing across multiple markets also offers diversification benefits, because no one market fully captures all global economic factors. Furthermore, many companies located outside of an investor's home market have no exact home-market equivalent, regardless of whether the domestic market is small or as large and diverse as in the United States.

Most investors worry about inflation, and inflation hedging ability is a sought-after characteristic. Informally, an asset is an **inflation hedge** if its returns are sufficient on average to preserve purchasing power during periods of inflation. More formally stated, an inflation hedge's nominal returns tend to be highly correlated with inflation rates. As residual real claims on businesses, common equities should offer superior protection against unanticipated inflation compared with conventional bonds. This phenomenon is so because companies' earnings tend to increase with inflation, whereas payments on conventional bonds are fixed in nominal terms. Nevertheless, companies do face challenges in coping with inflation. Reported earnings often overstate their real economic value to varying degrees. Corporate income taxes and capital gains tax rates are typically not inflation indexed, so inflation can cut into investors' after-tax real returns unless share prices fully reflect (through lower prices) the interaction of inflation and taxation. Furthermore, individual equities differ in their sensitivities to inflation because of industry, competitive, and other types of factors. Companies' abilities to raise output prices and revenues to keep pace with increases in input prices vary inversely with the amount of price competition in their markets. Yet the historical record indicates that the very long-run real return on stocks in the United States has been relatively insensitive to realized inflation rates, in contrast to bonds, whose returns have been negatively related to inflation.[3] Evidence from many markets indicates that using long measurement periods (longer than annual), equities on average do have value as an inflation hedge.[4] That fact has been an argument for equity investment not only for investors with general inflation concerns but also for defined-benefit plan sponsors, which may be exposed through the terms of the pension benefit formula to increasing nominal wage and salary costs.

Finally, equities' comparatively high historical long-term real rates of return have been important in establishing the widely held perspective that they play a growth role in a portfolio. Exhibit 7-2, showing historical real rates of return on equity, is taken from a Dimson, Marsh, and Staunton (2006) survey of capital market returns internationally. Their analysis shows that during the 106 years from 1900 to 2005, the long-term real rates of return to equities have exceeded that of bonds in all 17 countries listed in Exhibit 7-2.[5]

For all the reasons discussed, many successful long-term investors have had an equity bias in their asset allocation, diversifying with instruments such as bonds to obtain an

---

[3]See Siegel (2002) p. 195. Siegel examined 30-year holding periods from 1871 to 2001. Equities have not been effective inflation hedges, however, for the short-term (Siegel 2002) or in periods of high (4.00 percent to 7.99 percent) or extraordinary inflation (8.00 percent and above). See Ibbotson and Brinson (1987).

[4]See Boudoukh and Richardson (1993), focusing on U.S. data; Ely and Robinson (1997) for an international focus; and Luintel and Paudyal (2006), focusing on U.K. data.

[5]See Dimson, Marsh, and Staunton (2006) for data on historical bond returns.

EXHIBIT 7-2 Equity Real Rates of Return, 1900–2005

Country	Mean Geometric	Mean Arithmetic	Standard Deviation
Australia	7.7%	9.2%	17.6%
Belgium	2.4	4.6	22.1
Canada	6.2	7.6	16.8
Denmark	5.2	6.9	20.3
France	3.6	6.1	23.2
Germany (excludes 1922–1923)	3.1	8.2	32.5
Ireland	4.8	7.0	22.1
Italy	2.5	6.5	29.1
Japan	4.5	9.3	30.0
The Netherlands	5.3	7.2	21.3
Norway	4.3	7.1	27.0
South Africa	7.3	9.5	22.6
Spain	3.7	5.9	21.9
Sweden	7.8	10.1	22.6
Switzerland	4.5	6.3	19.7
United Kingdom	5.5	7.4	20.0
United States	6.5	8.5	20.2
World	5.7	7.2	17.2

Source: Dimson, Marsh, and Staunton (2006).

acceptable level of risk and/or income. In the next sections we discuss how investors approach equity investment.

3. APPROACHES TO EQUITY INVESTMENT

There are a number of different approaches to managing equity portfolios, each of which we will discuss in more detail later in this chapter.

In **passive management,** the investor does not attempt to reflect his investment expectations through changes in security holdings. The dominant passive approach is **indexing,** which involves investing in a portfolio that attempts to match the performance of some specified benchmark. Although passive in the sense of not incorporating the investor's expectations concerning securities, indexed portfolios are anything but passive in implementation. When a stock is added to or dropped from an index, or when the weight of a given stock changes because of a corporate action (such as a share buyback, or a **secondary offering**—an offering after the initial public offering of securities), the portfolio must be adjusted. Pioneered in the 1970s, indexing has quickly grown to the point that in the United States alone has more than $1 trillion in institutional indexed equities. Today, indexed portfolios often function as the core holding in an investor's overall equity allocation.

Another approach is **active management,** which historically is the principal way that investors have managed equity portfolios. An active manager seeks to outperform a given **benchmark portfolio** (the portfolio against which the manager's performance will be evaluated). The manager does this by identifying which stocks she thinks will perform comparatively well versus the benchmark portfolio, buying or holding those, and avoiding stocks she believes will underperform the benchmark. Despite indexing's growing popularity during the last few decades, active equity management still accounts for the overwhelming majority of equity assets managed.

The final approach is **semiactive management** (also called **enhanced indexing** or **risk-controlled active management**) and is in reality a variant of active management. In a semiactive portfolio, the manager seeks to outperform a given benchmark, as do active managers in general. A semiactive portfolio manager, however, worries more about tracking risk than an active manager does and will tend to build a portfolio whose performance will have very limited volatility around the benchmark's returns.

Exhibit 7-3 compares the typical expected active return, tracking risk, and information ratio for successful (first-quartile) practitioners of these three different approaches. **Active return** is the portfolio's return in excess of the return on the portfolio's benchmark. **Tracking risk,** the annualized standard deviation of active returns, measures **active risk** (risk relative to the portfolio's benchmark).[6]

The **information ratio** equals a portfolio's mean active return divided by tracking risk and represents the efficiency with which a portfolio's tracking risk delivers active return.

What can we infer from Exhibit 7-3 about how an investor in each of these categories views equity market informational efficiency? Investors who believe that an equity market is efficient will usually favor indexing because they think that equity research will not provide a sufficient increment in return to overcome their research and transaction costs. Active investors believe that the equity market is often inefficient and that good research will allow them to outperform the market net of all costs. Enhanced indexers fall somewhere between the two, believing that they can extract information about companies that has not been imbedded in stock prices, but attempting to do so in a way that limits tracking risk.

Within any of these three broad investment approaches, the investor needs to define the investment universe from which to select common stock. Considerations such as fund size and investment horizon affect the desired minimal level of holdings' liquidity. Tax concerns particularly concern individual and taxable corporate investors. Social concerns (e.g., corporate performance in matters such as governance and ethics, environment, workplace conditions,

EXHIBIT 7-3 Indexing, Enhanced Indexing, and Active Approaches: A Comparison

	Indexing	Enhanced Indexing	Active
Expected active return	0%	1% – 2%	2%+
Tracking risk	<1%	1% – 2%	4% + r
Information ratio[a]	0	0.75	0.50

[a]Estimated values expected of first-quartile portfolio managers.
Source: Authors' estimates.[7]

[6]**Tracking risk** has also been called **tracking error** and **tracking error volatility.**

[7]An information ratio (IR) of 0.50 is frequently viewed as distinguishing top-quartile active equity managers. For a summary of empirical results, see Grinold and Kahn (2000), p. 131. Jorion (2002), Table 4, finds that the first quartile of enhanced index funds is close to 0.75. The IR that distinguishes a top-quartile manager may change over time, however, and more research is needed on the distribution of IRs.

product safety and impact, and human rights) may matter to any type of investor. The mandates that clients give their investment managers will reflect these constraints.

4. PASSIVE EQUITY INVESTING

Passive investment philosophy has its roots in the history of equity indexing. The first indexed portfolio, launched in 1971 by Wells Fargo, was created for a single pension fund client. In 1973, Wells Fargo organized a commingled index fund for trust accounts. In 1976, Wells Fargo combined the funds, using capitalization-weighted S&P 500 Index as the template for the combined portfolios. By 1981, Wells Fargo had established a fund designed to track the broader market of companies outside the S&P 500. By holding these two funds in market cap weights, an investor could effectively capture the return of the U.S. equity market. Indexed investments became available for individual investors too. John Bogle at The Vanguard Group, Inc., launched the first broad-market index fund for retail investors in 1975.

Several early advocates of indexing were influential in establishing indexing as a major investment approach. Burton Malkiel called for "A New Investment Instrument" in the first edition of his best seller, *A Random Walk Down Wall Street* (1973). He wrote, "What we need is a no-load, minimum-management-fee mutual fund that simply buys the hundreds of stocks making up the broad stock-market averages and does no trading from security to security in an attempt to catch the winners." Other early advocates included Paul Samuelson (1974) and Charles D. Ellis in "The Loser's Game" (1975), one of the most widely cited papers in the literature of both finance and tennis. Ellis marshaled some simple facts illustrating that the institutionalization of the equity markets in the 1960s and early 1970s had made it probable that the *average* institutional investment manager would typically underperform the market as measured by a representative index. According to Ellis, the increased institutional share of the market left too little stock in the hands of nonprofessional investors for amateurs to fill the ranks of underperformers by themselves. Given the costs of trading, administrative expenses, and management fees as well, average active institutional investors inevitably would underperform the unmanaged market indices over time. In his classic article "The Arithmetic of Active Management," William F. Sharpe (1991) explains why the average investor cannot hope to beat a comprehensive equity index. His argument is unassailably clear and simple: "If 'active' and 'passive' management styles are defined in sensible ways, it *must* be the case that

- Before costs, the return on the average actively managed dollar will equal the return on the average passively managed dollar and
- After costs, the return on the average actively managed dollar will be less than the return on the average passively managed dollar."

History has generally proven Ellis and Sharpe right. Appropriately designed performance studies have generally found that the *average* active institutional portfolio fails to beat the relevant comparison index after expenses.[8] Frequently, the difference in performance has been found to be close to the average expense disadvantage of active management.[9] Therefore,

[8]Equity mutual funds have been perhaps the most intensively and rigorously researched institutional equity segment. See Daniel, Grinblatt, Titman, and Wermers (1997) and the references therein for equity mutual funds for empirical findings, as well as Ennis (2005).
[9]See Daniel et al.

compared with the average actively managed fund that has similar objectives, a well-run indexed fund's major advantage is expected superior long-term net-of-expenses performance because of relatively low portfolio turnover and management fees (often 0.10 percent of assets or less). For tax-sensitive investors, indexing's often relatively high tax efficiency (i.e., post-tax returns that are close to pre-tax returns) is appealing. That tax efficiency comes from turnover that is usually low compared with active investing.

Indexing has advantages in a broad range of equity market segments. The relatively high informational efficiency of prices in large-cap equity markets favors indexing. In typically less efficient market segments, such as small cap, the supply of active investment opportunities may be larger but transaction costs are higher. Indexing is also a logical choice to gain exposure to markets with which an investor may be unfamiliar (e.g., an overseas market), because active investing when one may be at an informational disadvantage is usually ill advised.

To thoroughly understand the implementation of indexing, we need to discuss the construction and maintenance of equity indices. The way indices are created, selected, and used may be passive investing's weakest link.

4.1. Equity Indices

Investment performance is undeniably important to an equity portfolio manager, whether he takes an active or passive investment approach. It makes little difference how well a manager can identify great companies, make long-term earnings estimates, or forecast the economy, if his investment performance is consistently inferior. Equity portfolio managers frequently evaluate their performance against equity benchmark indices designed to show how the overall stock market or some subsector of the market has performed.[10]

The benchmark is not just about measuring asset-class performance. A well-chosen benchmark index for a portfolio manager also represents that manager's investment "neighborhood." If a manager's benchmark is the S&P 500, he is unlikely to be investing in Russian stocks. Investors find it easier to manage their aggregate portfolios if an index well captures the investment universe of their investment managers, and to compartmentalize managers for the purposes of comparison with peers.

In addition to their role as portfolio management benchmarks, stock indices are also used to measure the returns of a market or market segment, as the basis for creating an index fund, to study factors that influence share price movements, to perform technical analysis, and to calculate a stock's systematic risk (or beta).

Four choices determine a stock index's characteristics: the boundaries of the index's universe, the criteria for inclusion in the index, how the stocks are weighted, and how returns are calculated. The first choice, the boundaries of the stock index's universe, is important in determining how well the index represents a specific population of stocks. The greater its number of stocks and the more diversified by industry and size, the better the index will measure broad market performance. A narrower universe will measure performance of a specific group of stocks. The second choice, the criteria for inclusion, establishes any specific characteristics desired for stocks within the selected universe. The third, the weighting of the stocks, is usually a choice among price weighting, value (or float) weighting, or equal weighting. The fourth choice, computational method, includes variations such as price only and total return series that include the reinvestment of dividends. Only total return series capture the two sources of equity returns, capital appreciation and dividends.

[10] See the chapter on performance evaluation for details and alternative approaches to evaluation.

4.1.1. Index Weighting Choices Probably the greatest differences among indices covering similar universes lie in how the index components are weighted. The three basic index weighting methods are price weighting, value (or float) weighting, and equal weighting.

- **Price weighted.** In a **price-weighted index,** each stock in the index is weighted according to its absolute share price. In other words, the index is simply the sum of the share prices divided by the adjusted number of shares in the index (adjustments are for the purpose of ensuring that the index value does not change merely because of stock splits or changes in index components since the base or launch date of the index). *The performance of a price-weighted index represents the performance of a portfolio that simply bought and held one share of each index component.*
- **Value weighted** (or **market-capitalization weighted).** In a **value-weighted index** (also called a **market-capitalization weighted index** or a **market capitalization index),** each stock in the index is weighted according to its market cap (share price multiplied by the number of shares outstanding). *The performance of a value-weighted index would represent the performance of a portfolio that owns all the outstanding shares of each index component.* A given percentage change in a value-weighted index is equal to the change in the total value of all included companies. A value-weighted index self-corrects for stock splits, reverse stock splits, and dividends because such actions are directly reflected in the number of shares outstanding and price per share for the company affected.

  A subcategory of the value-weighted method involves adjustment of market cap weights for each issue's **floating supply of shares** or **free float**—the number of shares outstanding that are actually available to investors. The resulting index is called a **free float–adjusted market capitalization index,** or **float-weighted index** for short. Float adjustments usually exclude corporate cross-holdings, large holdings by founding shareholders, and government holdings of shares in partly privatized companies.[11] The weight of a stock in a float-weighted index equals its market-cap weight multiplied by a free-float adjustment factor (a number between 0 and 1 representing the fraction of shares that float freely). A float-weighted index is concerned with the *investable* market values of equity issues—the market values actually available to be held by the public. *The performance of a float-weighted index represents the performance of a portfolio that buys and holds all the shares of each index component that are available for trading.* Thus, the (total) return of a float-weighted index will represent the return to the average dollar invested passively in the index's securities (ignoring costs). If the index securities are the manager's investment universe, such a float-weighted index represents a plausible performance benchmark for him. With the changeover of Standard & Poor's principal U.S. indices (the S&P 500, the S&P MidCap 400 Index, and the S&P SmallCap 600 Index) and the principal Japanese index (TOPIX) to float weighting, all major value-weighted indices are now free-float adjusted.

  For brevity, in the text discussion we will use "value-weighted/float-weighted indices" to refer to value-weighted indices without float adjustment (sometimes called for emphasis *full* market-cap indices) and value-weighted indices with float adjustment as a group.
- **Equal weighted.** In an equal-weighted index, each stock in the index is weighted equally. *The performance of an equal-weighted index represents the performance of a portfolio in which*

[11] For instance, in Example 7-1 given later, two stocks (Wal-Mart and Microsoft) have substantial free-float adjustments. In both cases, substantial shareholdings of founding executives, their heirs, or foundations that they established are expected never to be liquidated.

the same amount of money is invested in the shares of each index component. Equal-weighted indices must be rebalanced periodically (e.g., monthly, quarterly, or annually) to reestablish the equal weighting, because varying individual stock returns will cause stock weights to drift from equal weights.

These different weighting schemes can lead to a number of biases. A price-weighted index is biased towards the highest-priced share. For example, a stock with a price of €50 will have twice the weight in a price-weighted index as a stock with a price of €25. Therefore, a 10 percent increase in the higher-priced stock will have the same effect on the index as a 20 percent increase in the lower-priced stock. The absolute level of a share price is an arbitrary figure, however, because a company can change its share price through a stock split, a stock dividend, or a reverse split. It makes no sense to invest money merely in proportion to an absolute share price, which is what such an index would dictate. Some price-weighted averages, such as the Nikkei 225 for Japanese equities, systematically reduce the weighting of very high-priced stocks to minimize such arbitrary distortion of the index by very high-priced shares.

A price-weighted index's main advantage lies in the simplicity of its construction. Straightforwardly, the share prices are added up and then divided by the number of shares in the index adjusted to maintain continuity in the series, taking account of stock splits and additions/deletions of components. Stock price data series are also easier to obtain historically than market value series. Consequently, price-weighted index series can go back far into the past. Price-weighted indices can be created with a rich, if sometimes hypothetical, history. The oldest and most widely followed equity index, the Dow Jones Industrial Average, is calculated this way. When that index was first published in 1896, the weighting choices most index users prefer today were impractical.

A value-weighted index is biased toward the shares of companies with the largest market capitalizations. In other words, a 10 percent share price increase for a large-cap company would affect the index more than would a 10 percent share price increase for a smaller company. Such an index excels at conveying the effect of a change in companies' total value, or aggregate investor wealth. Float adjustments to capitalization weights exclude shares that are unavailable to investors, making float-weighted indices most representative of the range of securities and weights that public investors as a group can buy and hold. The bias towards large market cap issues in value-weighted/float-weighted indices, however, means that such indices will tend to be biased toward:

- Large and probably mature companies.
- Overvalued companies, whose share prices have already risen the most.

Arnott (2005) argues that even if pricing errors are random, the largest-cap stocks are more likely to incorporate positive pricing errors than negative pricing errors. Arnott, Hsu, and Moore (2005) have suggested the weighting of component securities by fundamentals (adjusting the market cap of components downward or upward when price-to-fundamentals metrics such as price-to-earnings ratios [P/Es] are high or low, respectively) as a means of addressing such biases.[12] Another criticism of value-weighted/float-weighted indices is that a portfolio based on such an index may be concentrated in relatively few issues and, hence,

[12]See Arnott, Robert D., Jason Hsu, and Philip Moore, "Fundamental Indexation." *Financial Analysts Journal,* vol. 61, no. 2 (March/April) 2005:83–99.

less diversified than most actively managed portfolios.[13] Furthermore, because of regulatory or other restrictions on maximum holdings, indexing to some concentrated indices may be infeasible. Although controversy exists (as on many investment issues), float-weighting is generally regarded as today's gold standard for indexing portfolios because it facilitates the minimization of tracking risk and portfolio turnover, and because it results in indices that well represent asset-class performance.

In an equal-weighted index, all stocks are treated the same. Small companies have the same weight in the index as very large companies. An equal-weighting methodology introduces a small-company bias because such indices include many more small companies than large ones. Moreover, to maintain equal weighting, this type of index must be rebalanced periodically. Frequent rebalancing can lead to high transaction costs in a portfolio tracking such an index. Another limitation of equal-weighted indices as indexing benchmarks is that not all components in such an index may have sufficiently liquid markets to absorb the demand of indexers.

Example 7-1 contrasts the various types of indices.

EXAMPLE 7-1 A Problem of Benchmark Index Selection

Stephen Alcorn is a portfolio manager at Amanda Asset Management, Inc. (AAM). At the end of 2002, a wealthy client engaged Alcorn to manage $10,000,000 for one year in an active **focused** (concentrated) equity style. The investment management contract specified a symmetric incentive fee of $10,000 per 100 basis points (bps) of capital appreciation relative to that of an index of the stocks selected for investment.[14] (*Symmetric* means that the incentive fee will reduce the investment management fee if benchmark-relative performance is negative.) In an oversight, the contract leaves open the method by which the benchmark index will be calculated. Alcorn invests in shares of Eastman Kodak Company, McDonald's Corporation, Intel Corporation, Merck & Co., Wal-Mart Stores, and Microsoft Corporation, achieving a 15.9 percent price return for the year. Exhibit 7-4 gives information on the six stocks.

EXHIBIT 7-4 Equity Market Data for the Shares of Six Companies

	Share Price Dec 31, 2002	Share Price Dec 31, 2003	Price Change	Market Value of Shares Dec 31, 2002 (millions)	Market Value of Shares Dec 31, 2003 (millions)	Free Float Factor
Kodak	$35.04	$24.85	−29.1%	$ 10,056	$ 7,132	1
McDonald's	16.08	24.09	49.8	20,406	30,570	1
Intel	15.57	31.36	101.4	101,703	204,844	1
Merck	53.58	45.10	−15.8	119,216	100,348	1
Wal-Mart	50.51	53.05	5.0	221,992	233,154	0.6
Microsoft	25.85	27.37	5.9	277,060	293,352	0.85
Total				$750,433	$869,400	

[13] See Bernstein (2003).

[14] To simplify the calculations, the problem is stated in terms of capital appreciation. In practice, the incentive fee would usually be stated in terms of total return.

Using only the information given, address the following:

1. For each of the six shares, explain the price-only return calculation on the following indices for the period December 31, 2002 to December 31, 2003:

   i. Price-weighted index
   ii. Value-weighted index
   iii. Float-weighted index
   iv. Equal-weighted index

2. Recommend the appropriate benchmark index for calculating the performance incentive fee on the account and determine the amount of that fee.

Solution to Problem 1:

i. As Exhibit 7-5 illustrates, the value of the price-weighted index on December 31, 2002 is found by adding the six share prices as of that date and dividing by 6: 196.63/6 = 32.77. As of December 31, 2003, the value of the index is 205.82/6 = 34.30. Thus the one-year return is (34.30 − 32.77)/32.77 = 0.047, or 4.7 percent. At December 31, 2002, the index gives a 53.58/196.63 = 27.2 percent weight to Merck and a 50.51/196.63 = 25.7 percent weight to Wal-Mart, the highest-priced shares.

EXHIBIT 7-5 Price-Weighted Index

	Share Price Dec 31, 2002	Share Price Dec 31, 2003	Price Change	Percentage of Index Dec 31, 2002	Contribution to Return
Kodak	$ 35.04	$ 24.85	−29.1%	17.82%	−5.19%
McDonald's	16.08	24.09	49.8	8.18	4.07
Intel	15.57	31.36	101.4	7.92	8.03
Merck	53.58	45.10	−15.8	27.25	−4.31
Wal-Mart	50.51	53.05	5.0	25.69	1.28
Microsoft	25.85	27.37	5.9	13.15	0.78
Total	$196.63	$205.82	4.7%	100%	4.7%
Index	32.77	34.30			

ii. A value-weighted index is calculated by multiplying the share price by the number of shares outstanding to arrive at each company's market value, then summing these values to create an index. As Exhibit 7-6 shows, such an index would have risen by 15.9 percent in 2003, because it would have had almost 14 percent of assets in Intel, which doubled, and only 1 percent in Kodak, which fell by the largest amount. Note that for real world value-weighted indices, if X is the total market values of the index components, the index vendor will normalize X by dividing it by the total market value as of some baseline date, and multiply that result by some value such as 100 to represent the starting index value. In the case of Exhibit 7-6 data, for example, if December 31, 2002 were chosen as the starting date and 100 as the beginning value, then an index vendor would give the index value as of December 31, 2002 as 100, and its value as of December 31, 2003 as $(869,400/750,433) \times 100 = 115.85$.

EXHIBIT 7-6 Value-Weighted Index

	Market Value of Shares Dec 31, 2002 (millions)	Market Value of Shares Dec 31, 2003 (millions)	Value Change	Percentage of Index Dec 31, 2002	Contribution to Return
Kodak	$ 10,056	$ 7,132	−29.1%	1.34%	−0.39%
McDonald's	20,406	30,570	49.8	2.72	1.36
Intel	101,703	204,844	101.4	13.55	13.74
Merck	119,216	100,348	−15.8	15.89	−2.51
Wal-Mart	221,992	233,154	5.0	29.58	1.48
Microsoft	277,060	293,352	5.9	36.92	2.18
Index	$750,433	$869,400	15.9%	100%	15.9%

iii. A float-weighted index is calculated the same way as a value-weighted index, except that the market value is adjusted by a float factor that represents the fraction of shares outstanding actually available to investors. As shown in Exhibit 7-7, the market values are identical to those given in Exhibit 7-6 for the value-weighted index except for Wal-Mart and Microsoft, which have free-float factors below 1.0. A free-float index would have risen by 18.1 percent in 2003, or a bit over 2 percentage points more than a simple value-weighted index. The pickup results from the fact that the effect of Wal-Mart and Microsoft's relatively poor performance in 2003 decreases because of their smaller weights after adjusting for free float.

EXHIBIT 7-7 Float-Weighted Index

	Market Value Dec 31, 2002 (millions)	Market Value Dec 31, 2003 (millions)	Value Change	Percentage of Index Dec 31, 2002	Contribution to Return
Kodak	$ 10,056	$ 7,132	−29.1%	1.62%	−0.47%
McDonald's	20,406	30,570	49.8	3.29	1.64
Intel	101,703	204,844	101.4	16.40	16.63
Merck	119,216	100,348	−15.8	19.23	−3.04
Wal-Mart	133,195	139,892	5.0	21.48	1.07
Microsoft	235,501	249,349	5.9	37.98	2.24
Index	$620,077	$732,135	18.1%	100.00%	18.1%

iv. An equal-weighted index assumes an equal investment in each of the six stocks. Its performance would be the average performance of the six stocks over the year, or 19.5 percent. In Exhibit 7-8, the base value of each of the six components on December 31, 2002 is $100/6 = 16.67$. The value of a component shown for

December 31, 2003 is found by multiplying its December 31, 2002 value by 1 plus the return over the year. For Kodak, for example, 16.67(1 − 0.291) = 11.82 on December 31, 2003. The weights of the components would then be rebalanced to 16.67 to reestablish equal weighting.

EXHIBIT 7-8 Equal-Weighted Index

	Index Dec 31, 2002	Index Dec 31, 2003	Price Change	Percentage of Index Dec 31, 2002	Contribution to Return
Kodak	16.67	11.82	−29.1%	16.67%	−4.85%
McDonald's	16.67	24.97	49.8	16.67	8.3
Intel	16.67	33.57	101.4	16.67	16.90
Merck	16.67	14.04	−15.8	16.67	−2.63
Wal-Mart	16.67	17.50	5.0	16.67	0.83
Microsoft	16.67	17.65	5.9	16.67	0.98
Index	100	119.55	19.5%	100%	19.5%

Solution to Problem 2: A float-weighted index of the six shares is the recommended benchmark index because it represents the return to the average dollar invested passively in the six stocks, reflecting the supply of shares actually available to the public. Because the portfolio underperformed that index by 220 basis points, AAM management fees should be reduced by (220/100) × \$10,000 = \$22,000. Exhibit 7-9 summarizes the dispersion of active returns for the various ways in which the benchmark index might be calculated. The manager greatly outperformed a price-weighted index of the six shares, matched a value-weighted index, and underperformed float-weighted and equal-weighted indices.

EXHIBIT 7-9 Summary of Weighting Method Results

Weighting Method	Index Return	Active Return to Benchmark
Price-weighted	4.7%	11.2%
Value-weighted	15.9	0.0
Float-weighted	18.1	−2.2
Equal-weighted	19.5	−3.6

4.1.2. Equity Indices: Composition and Characteristics of Major Indices

A large number of stock price indices exist for measuring share performance on a global, regional, country, and sector basis. The sector category includes indices designed to reflect results for large stocks, small stocks, growth stocks, value stocks, and specific industries.

Exhibit 7-10 compares some of the major stock market indices. The exhibit first gives facts on indices within the currently very small group of major price-weighted and equal-weighted equity indices. The list of important value-weighted/float-weighted indices is very long: even giving summary facts on them would run to many pages. Exhibit 7-10 thus covers

EXHIBIT 7-10 Some Representative Equity Indices Worldwide

	Representing	Number of Stocks	Weighting of Index	Special Characteristics	Drawbacks/Comments
Dow Jones Industrial Average	U.S. blue chip companies	30	Price weighted	The oldest and most widely followed U.S. equity index	30 stocks chosen by *Wall Street Journal* editors; large, mature blue chip companies.
Nikkei Stock Average	Japanese blue chip companies	225	Modified price weighted	Originally formulated by Dow Jones & Company, using essentially the same method as the DJIA	Also known as the Nikkei 225. There is a huge variation in share price levels of the component companies, and some high-priced shares are weighted at a fraction of their share price. Some component stocks are illiquid.
Value Line Arithmetic Composite Index	Equities traded in U.S. markets	Approximately 1,700	Equal weighted	Represents the performance of the stocks covered in the *Value Line Investment Survey*	A well-known equal-weighted index. The Value Line Geometric Composite Index is based on the same stocks but calculates index changes using a geometric rather than arithmetic mean.
S&P TSX Composite	Broad market cap stocks listed on the Toronto Stock Exchange	Varies	Float weighted	Very comprehensive index	Widely used Canadian equities benchmark.
CAC 40	French blue chip companies	40	Float weighted	Chosen from the 100 largest market cap stocks on the Paris Bourse (Euronext Paris)	
DAX 30	German blue chip companies	30	Float weighted	Published by the Frankfurt Stock Exchange	Widely used German equities benchmark.
TOPIX	All listed companies on the Tokyo Stock Exchange 1st Section	Varies	Value weighted[15]	Includes all stocks listed on the TSE 1st Section, which represents about 93% of the market value of all equities in Japan	The index contains a large number of very small, illiquid stocks, making it difficult to replicate exactly.
FTSE 100	The 100 largest publicly traded stocks on the London Stock Exchange	100	Float weighted	A large-cap index, pronounced "Footsie 100"	There are also a FTSE Mid 250 for mid-cap stocks and a small-cap index.

[15]The TOPIX became float weighted in three stages: October 2005, February 2006, and June 2006.

EXHIBIT 7-10 (*continued*)

	Representing	Number of Stocks	Weighting of Index	Special Characteristics	Drawbacks/Comments
Russell 3000	The 3,000 largest stocks in the United States by market cap	3,000 selected on the last trading day of May. The new composition becomes effective on the last Friday in June.	Float weighted and value weighted available	Very comprehensive index	The Russell indices are reconstituted annually based on market cap data as of the last day of May. Widely used institutional benchmark.
Russell 1000	The 1,000 largest stocks in the Russell 3000	1,000 on the day the new composition is determined	Float weighted	A large-cap index	Competes with the S&P 500 as a large-cap benchmark.
Russell 2000	The smallest 2,000 stocks in the Russell 3000 Index	2,000 on the day the new composition is determined	Float weighted	A small-cap index	The many U.S. small-cap index funds tracking this index and the consequent annual reconstitution costs and possible tax consequences make this a relatively high-cost benchmark for a U.S. small-cap index fund.
S&P 500	Predominantly large-cap companies representative of the U.S. stock market	500	Float-weighted	Membership determined by a committee of S&P employees	Its popularity with indexers causes new components to earn average positive abnormal returns on the announcement that they are joining the index.[16]
MSCI Index Family	Separate series for individual developed and emerging markets; regions, world developed markets—MSCI World; and All Country World (developed and emerging markets)—MSCI ACWI	Varies	Float weighted	Most widely used global index family. The MSCI World ex U.S., ex Japan (MSCI Kokusai), ex U.K., and ex EMU, are some indices used as benchmarks for nondomestic equities in various markets.	Other major families of global benchmark indices are published by FTSE, Dow Jones, and S&P/ Citigroup.

[16]See Lynch and Mendenhall (1997) and Malkiel and Radisich (2001) for more information and a discussion of competing explanations for this phenomenon.

indices that are discussed in text examples, examples from each of the world's six largest equity markets (which are, in alphabetical order: Canada, France, Germany, Japan, the United Kingdom, and the United States), and an example of a global index family.[17]

The first entry is the oldest equity index, the Dow Jones Industrial Average. Interestingly, the DJIA consists of only 30 companies, but since its creation in 1896 it has had a total of more than 100 different constituents. As leading companies of their time go into decline, they are routinely taken out of the index. Many disappeared long ago. General Electric is the only one of the original 12 constituents in the DJIA currently in the index, and it has been in and out of the DJIA a few times over the years. One moral of DJIA's story for equity investors is that if an investor holds a single stock long enough, he is about as likely to lose most or all of his money as to accumulate great wealth. The history of changes in the Dow's composition is one of the best arguments for diversification.

An indexer's choice of index to track has important consequences. Committee-determined indices tend to have lower turnover than those reconstituted regularly according to an algorithm. Thus, indexing on the former type of index may have transaction cost and tax advantages. However, indices (and index funds based on them) that are not reconstituted regularly may drift away from the market segment they are intended to cover. The indexer should also be aware of liquidity differences among the component securities of the various indices that cover the same market segment. For example, liquidity and relatively adequate float are criteria for selection to the S&P SmallCap 600 Index but not the Russell 2000 Index. On the other hand, investing in less liquid shares may allow the indexer to capture an illiquidity premium. In choosing the index to replicate, a fund must evaluate the trade-off between differences in transaction costs and differences in return premiums among the indices.

4.2. Passive Investment Vehicles

Having described the array of equity indices, in the following sections we describe specific passive investment vehicles. The major choices are:

- Investment in an indexed portfolio.
- A long position in cash plus a long position in futures contracts on the underlying index, when such markets are available and adequately liquid.
- A long position in cash plus a long position in a swap on the index. (That is, in the swap the investor pays a fixed rate of interest on the swap's notional principal and in return receives the return on the index.)

4.2.1. Indexed Portfolios

The three most important categories of indexed portfolios are:

1. Conventional index mutual funds.
2. Exchange-traded funds (ETFs), which are based on benchmark index portfolios.
3. Separate accounts or pooled accounts, mostly for institutional investors, designed to track a benchmark index.

The most obvious difference between conventional index mutual funds and ETFs is that shareholders in mutual funds usually buy shares from the fund and sell them back to the fund

[17]The country weights in the MSCI World Index as of September 30, 2005, were used to select the six largest equity markets worldwide.

at a net asset value determined once a day at the market close.[18] ETF shareholders buy and sell shares in public markets anytime during the trading day. Dealers can create and redeem ETF shares with in-kind deposits and withdrawals at each day's market close.

The principal difference between index mutual funds and exchange-traded funds on the one hand, and indexed institutional portfolios, on the other hand, is cost. Indexed institutional portfolios managed as separate accounts with a single shareholder or, increasingly, as pooled accounts, are extremely low-cost products. Depending on the nature of the securities used in the portfolio, total annual expenses may be as low as a few basis points. Occasionally, where securities with an active lending market are involved, the revenue from securities lending can equal or exceed total portfolio management and custody expenses.[19]

Conventional index mutual funds vary greatly in their cost structure. Elton, Gruber, and Busse (2004) examined and compared the expenses and performance of all conventional S&P 500 mutual funds continuously available in the United States from 1996 to 2001. A large part of the difference in performance among these funds came from differences in the funds' expense ratios, but other significant differences affected performance as well. For example, funds use securities lending as a source of income to varying degrees. The difference between the best-performing S&P 500 fund and the worst-performing fund for that six-year period was an average of 209 bps (2.09 percent) a year. Clearly, S&P 500 index funds and index portfolio managers are sometimes not the "commodities" they are often thought to be. Other differences among index funds become apparent when exchange-traded funds are added to the range of choices.

At least four economically significant differences separate conventional index mutual funds from exchange-traded funds (which in the United States are currently all index funds):[20]

1. Shareholder accounting at the fund level can be a significant expense for conventional mutual funds in some markets, but ETFs do not have fund level shareholder accounting.
2. Exchange-traded funds generally pay much higher index license fees than conventional funds.
3. Exchange-traded funds are often much more tax-efficient than conventional funds in many markets, including the United States.
4. Users of exchange-traded funds pay transaction costs including commissions to trade them, but for their ongoing shareholders, ETFs provide inherently better protection from the cost of providing liquidity to shareholders who are selling fund shares.

To the extent that a fund has a large number of small shareholders, shareholder record-keeping will be a significant cost reflected in the fund's expense ratio. Some funds attempt to cope with this cost and to allocate it to the shareholders who are responsible for it by charging a maintenance fee for accounts below a certain size and/or by offering funds with a lower

[18] A few funds in the United States and all funds in some countries make more-frequent net asset value calculations: once an hour in some cases, and almost continuously in others.

[19] Securities lending is a common practice in most equity and fixed-income markets around the world. The securities lender typically receives cash equal or slightly greater in value than the securities lent. The lender invests this cash and typically shares the interest with the securities borrower. In some cases, when a security has great value in the lending market because it is popular with short sellers, the securities lender may keep all the interest and even receive an additional premium for lending the securities.

[20] As of mid-2005, U.S. ETFs were all index funds, although a few actively managed ETFs exist outside of the United States. In mid-2005, some actively managed U.S. ETFs were in the planning stages.

expense ratio to very large investors. For example, Vanguard imposes a periodic fee on certain small accounts; the Vanguard Admiral share class (offered to investors who buy more than \$250,000 worth of shares in a fund) typically has a 6 bps (0.06 percent) lower expense ratio than Vanguard's Investor share class.[21] Exchange-traded funds have no shareholder accounting at the fund level, so their expense ratios are typically lower than conventional mutual fund expense ratios for funds linked to comparable indices. Brokers who carry these shares for investors may levy inactivity fees on ETF shareholders if they trade rarely, and of course there are transaction costs associated with buying and selling ETF shares in the marketplace.

Another important difference between index mutual funds and exchange-traded funds is that, at least in the United States, exchange-traded funds are usually more tax efficient in the sense that they are less likely than mutual funds to make taxable capital gains distributions. At the investor level, mutual fund buyers are affected by a fund's cost basis for its positions, which may differ quite a bit from the positions' current values. As a result, at the time of purchase an investor may buy into a potential tax liability if the positions show a gain.

At the fund level, the most significant tax difference between conventional funds and ETFs is in the process by which fund shares are redeemed. A traditional mutual fund will usually experience a tax event from selling portfolio securities when holders of a significant number of shares redeem their positions for cash. Unlike a traditional mutual fund that will ordinarily sell stocks inside the fund and pay cash to a fund shareholder who is redeeming shares, the redemption mechanism for an exchange-traded fund is usually "in kind" in the sense of being an exchange of shares. The fund typically delivers a basket of the fund's portfolio stocks to a redeeming dealer who has turned in shares of the fund for this exchange. In the United States, this transaction is not taxable from the fund's perspective, and there is no distributable gain on the redemption. Occasionally, a conventional fund—particularly a non-index fund—will deliver stock in kind to a large redeeming shareholder; but most conventional funds offer limited opportunities to redeem fund shares by delivering portfolio stock in kind. The in-kind creation and redemption process of ETFs also insulates long-term ETF shareholders from the costs of supplying liquidity to traders, a persistent problem with mutual funds in a number of markets.[22]

Turning to indexed institutional portfolios, a relatively small number of quantitatively oriented investment management organizations manage the majority of the money in such indexed accounts. The same organization may manage institutional portfolios, conventional funds, and ETFs. Management of these different portfolios may be assigned to separate groups of managers or integrated, with the portfolio management and trading functions consolidated in a single indexing group. Investment management firms' aggressiveness in implementing index composition changes varies, and in fact may vary from one type of account to another within the same firm. Indeed, index fund managers have sometimes come under scrutiny for failing to implement anticipated index composition changes aggressively because of their concern for minimizing tracking risk. The issue arises because changes to indexes are often predictable or announced in advance of the effective date, but index funds may not effect the forthcoming changes as soon as they are foreseeable because of a concern with minimizing tracking risk relative to the current index components. In the interim, arbitrageurs may trade

[21]Vanguard and other managers also offer even lower expense ratio share classes to "institutional" investors.

[22]In the United States, the inconsistent application of deadlines for accepting mutual fund buy and sell orders has been a related problem for long-term mutual fund shareholders.

on the basis of the anticipated changes, affecting prices and causing an implicit loss to index fund investors.[23]

If an index contains less than, say, 1,000 stocks, and the stocks are liquid, the index fund manager will usually attempt to manage the portfolio with **full replication** of the index—that is, every issue in the index will be represented in the portfolio, and each portfolio position will have approximately the same weight in the fund as in the index. As the number of issues in the index passes 1,000, it is increasingly likely that the manager will construct the portfolio using either **stratified sampling** (also called **representative sampling**) or **optimization.** In some cases, the preferred method depends on portfolio size and the availability of active trading in an index basket by means of portfolio trades. For example, an indexer may use full replication for a large fund (e.g., an ETF) tracking the Russell 2000, making use of standard Russell 2000 basket trades, but may choose optimization for smaller, separately managed accounts indexed to the same index.

Full replication, where the number and liquidity of the issues permit using it, should result in minimal tracking risk. Apart from minimizing tracking risk, a full replication portfolio based on a value-weighted (or float-weighted) index has the advantage of being self-rebalancing because the stock weights in the portfolio will mirror changes in the index weights resulting from constantly changing stock prices. Self-rebalancing is a desirable characteristic because it implies that trading is needed only for the reinvestment of dividends and to reflect changes in index composition. Full replication is the most common procedure for indices such as the S&P 500 that are composed of highly liquid securities.

Typically, the return on a full replication index fund may be less than the index return by an amount equal to the sum of:

- The cost of managing and administering the fund.
- The transaction costs of portfolio adjustments to reflect changes in index composition.
- The transaction costs of investing and disinvesting cash flows, and
- In upward-trending equity markets, the drag on performance from any cash positions.[24]

Attempting to fully replicate an index containing a large proportion of illiquid stocks will usually result in an index portfolio that underperforms the index.[25] This phenomenon occurs because indices do not have to bear transaction costs but a real portfolio does. These transaction costs include brokerage commissions, bid–offer spreads, taxes, and the market impact of trades (the effect of large trades on the market price).[26] There are two ways to build an index-tracking portfolio using a subset of stocks in the index: stratified sampling and optimization. Skillful use of these techniques should permit a portfolio manager to index successfully to even a very broad index containing illiquid securities.

Using stratified sampling, a portfolio manager divides the index along a number of dimensions (e.g., market capitalization, industry, value, and growth), creating multidimensional cells. Each index stock is placed into the cell that best describes it. For instance, a simple

[23]See Chen, Noronha, and Singal (2006).

[24]In the long run, we expect equity returns to exceed the returns on cash, justifying the inclusion of this factor.

[25]Nevertheless, superior tax reclaims (of withheld taxes) on large international index funds can deliver a significant boost to performance relative to most international indices, which use conservative assumptions on tax reclaims.

[26]Taxes are levied on transactions in some countries. For example, a stamp duty of 0.50 percent is paid on the value of each stock purchase in the United Kingdom.

cell structure could focus on market cap and industry. A manager trying to build a portfolio mimicking the TOPIX index would then place a stock such as Toyota into a cell that is defined by automobile stocks with market cap greater than ¥5 trillion. Next, she would characterize all stocks in the index in this way and determine the weight of each cell in the index by totaling the market cap for all stocks in that cell. The manager would then build a portfolio by selecting a random sample of stocks from each cell and ensuring that the sum of the weights of the stocks purchased from each cell corresponds to the cell's weight in the index.

For example, suppose that a cell contains 2 percent of the weight of the index and that two stocks chosen to represent the cell have index weights of 0.3 percent and 0.5 percent, leaving a balance of 2.0% − 0.8% = 1.2%. By overweighting each security by 1.2%/2 = 0.6 percentage points (i.e., holding them in weights of 0.3% + 0.6% = 0.9% and 0.5% + 0.6% = 1.1%), the index fund can achieve the same exposure to the cell factors as the index.[27] Stratified sampling allows the manager to build a portfolio that retains the basic characteristics of the index without having to buy all of the stocks in the index. Generally speaking, the greater the number of dimensions and the finer the divisions, the more closely the portfolio will resemble the index.

Sometimes an index with relatively few components or with a few heavily weighted components is not naturally compliant with regulatory requirements for fund diversification (which often place maximums on how much of the portfolio may be invested in any one issuer). In such cases, stratified sampling techniques may be used to create an index fund variation loosely based on the non-diversification-compliant index. In the United States, the relevant diversification requirements are the rules for Regulated Investment Company (RIC) diversification in Sub-Chapter M of the Internal Revenue Code. In the European Union, the appropriate rules cover Undertakings for Collective Investment in Transferable Securities (UCITS). As of early 2006, the EU member states were considering adoption of modifications to the UCITS requirements that would allow index funds with an EU passport (approved for offering in all EU jurisdictions) to hold up to 20 percent of assets in one security if the index called for such.[28] Increasingly, ETF issuers and index publishers who develop indices specifically for the ETF market are designing indices to be inherently RIC-compliant in the United States and UCITS-compliant in Europe. If the fund can replicate the index and comply with local diversification requirements simultaneously, a fund analyst can better evaluate the fund's portfolio manager and the fund management process.

Another technique commonly used to build portfolios containing only a subset of an index's stocks is optimization. Optimization is a mathematical approach to index fund construction involving the use of:

- A multifactor risk model, against which the risk exposures of the index and individual securities are measured.
- An objective function that specifies that securities be held in proportions that minimize expected tracking risk relative to the index subject to appropriate constraints.

The multifactor model might include factors such as market capitalization, beta, and industry membership, as well as macroeconomic factors such as interest rate levels. The

[27]This simple approach to weight adjustment has been used in practice. A more precise approach would be to increase the securities weights so as to maintain their relative proportion of 0.3/0.5 = 0.6: weights of 0.75 percent and 1.25 percent for the first and second securities, respectively (0.75%/1.25% = 0.60 and 0.75% + 1.25% = 2%).

[28]EU member states could increase the limit to 35 percent under exceptional market circumstances.

objective function seeks to match the portfolio's risk exposures to those of the index being tracked. An advantage of optimization compared with stratified sampling is that optimization takes into account the covariances among the factors used to explain the return on stocks. The stratified sampling approach implicitly assumes the factors are mutually uncorrelated.

Optimization has several drawbacks as an approach to indexation. First, even the best risk models are likely to be imperfectly specified. That is, it is virtually impossible to create a risk model that exactly captures the risk associated with a given stock, if only because risks change over time and risk models are based on historical data. Furthermore, the optimization procedure seeks to maximally exploit any risk differences among securities, even if they just reflect sampling error (this is the problem known as overfitting the data). Even in the absence of index changes and dividend flows, optimization requires periodic trading to keep the risk characteristics of the portfolio lined up with those of the index being tracked. As a result of these limitations, the predicted tracking risk of an optimization-based portfolio will typically understate the actual tracking risk. That said, indexers have found that the results of an optimization approach frequently compare well with those of a stratified sampling approach, particularly when replication is attempted using relatively few securities. With either stratified sampling or optimization, the indexer may fully replicate (purchase in index-weight proportions) the largest stocks and create an optimized/sampled portfolio for the rest.

EXAMPLE 7-2 Passive Portfolio Construction Methods

An investment manager has been given a mandate for managing a Russell 2000 index fund for a moderate-size foundation. The manager must choose either full replication or optimization for managing the portfolio. Recommend the most appropriate method for constructing this index portfolio.

Solution: Optimization is the most appropriate method. Each of the techniques for building an index portfolio has strengths and weaknesses. Generally, when the index contains highly liquid stocks, full replication is usually the preferred index construction method. Apart from minimizing tracking risk, a full replication portfolio has the advantage of being self-rebalancing (given that it is based on a value- or float-weighted index). That said, the Russell 2000 is dominated by smaller-cap companies, and replication may not be the most cost effective choice given the costs of transacting in small-cap issues.

Stratified sampling and optimization are preferred when a portfolio manager wishes to track an index containing a large number of stocks, particularly stocks that are more difficult and costly to trade. In this case, however, stratified sampling is not under consideration. Therefore, the pension plan should use optimization to construct the index portfolio.

4.2.2. Equity Index Futures

Institutional indexed portfolios and conventional indexed mutual funds, which date back to the 1970s, are the earliest index products and are probably the most familiar to investors. In the 1980s, two additional indexing products, **portfolio trades** (also known as **basket trades** or **program trades**) and **stock index futures,** arrived.

These products grew in tandem because they were closely related; the success of each was closely linked to the success of the other. A portfolio trade is simply a basket of securities traded as a basket or unit, whereas a traditional security trade is done one share issue at a time. A portfolio trade is made when all of the stocks in the basket—most commonly, the components of an index—are traded together under relatively standardized terms.

In the United States, the most popular trading basket by far is the S&P 500 basket. In the early 1980s, trading in such baskets increased dramatically in conjunction with the introduction of S&P 500 index futures contracts on the Chicago Mercantile Exchange (CME). By the end of that decade, trading in S&P 500 portfolios accounted for a growing share of trading in U.S. securities, and the notional value of trading in the S&P 500 futures contract regularly surpassed the notional value of trading in the underlying securities. The e-mini S&P 500 futures contract, with a notional value of 50 times the value of the S&P 500 (compared with 250 times for the standard S&P 500 contract), became a very liquid vehicle favored by traders in the early 2000s.[29] Trading in these index instruments interacted and found a variety of applications. Trading index securities as a basket and exchanging the stock basket for the futures contract on the index—a transaction called an **Exchange of Futures for Physicals**—permits sharp reductions in transaction costs.[30] Using an EFP, a futures position can be translated into a portfolio position. The product interchangeability through the EFP process facilitates risk-management transactions for many participants in the securities markets.

Although the S&P 500 portfolios are still the largest such standardized portfolios, trading in a variety of other index baskets and futures contracts has grown significantly throughout the world. Among the most liquid stock index futures contracts are those on the FTSE 100, the Nikkei 225, the CAC 40, and DAX 30.[31]

The limited life of a futures contract and the fact that the most active trading in the futures market is in the nearest expiration contract means that a futures position must be rolled over periodically to maintain appropriate market exposure. Trading a basket of stocks can be relatively cumbersome at times, particularly on the short side where any uptick rule occasionally impedes basket transactions. (**Uptick rules** require that a short sale must not be on a downtick relative to the last trade at a different price.)[32] Exchange-traded funds generally are exempt from the uptick rule for short sales. This fact, and their lack of an expiration date, has made ETFs instruments of choice for many indefinite-term portfolio hedging and risk management applications.

4.2.3. Equity Total Return Swaps

Conceptually, equity swaps resemble the more widely known fixed-income and currency swaps. The distinct feature of an equity swap is that at least one side of the transaction receives the total return of either an equity instrument or, more commonly, an equity index portfolio. The other side can be either another equity

[29] The e-mini futures contracts trade on CME's Globex electronic trading system.

[30] In an EFP, one party buys cash market assets and sells futures contracts, and the opposite party sells the cash market assets and buys futures contracts. For example, a long position in equity futures can be exchanged for a long position in a portfolio of securities representative of the index composition. The counterparties privately set the prices, quantities, and other terms of the transaction.

[31] The CME launched futures on equity style indices in 1995, but they did not develop a useful amount of liquidity. See Hill (2003).

[32] A **tick** is the smallest possible price movement of a security. Uptick and downtick in this context refer to any up- or down-price change, whatever the size.

instrument or index or an interest payment. The most common nonequity swap counter payments are U.S. dollar London Interbank Offered Rate (LIBOR) for equity swaps based on U.S. securities, or LIBOR in the appropriate currency for equity swaps based on non-U.S. stocks.

Equity swaps enjoyed a brief and intense popularity in the United States as a way for high-tax bracket investors to achieve diversification, by exchanging the return on a single stock or an undiversified stock basket for the return on a broad stock market index. Changes in U.S. tax law, however, sharply curtailed this application. Today, most equity swap applications are motivated by differences in the tax treatment of shareholders domiciled in different countries or by the desire to gain exposure to an asset class in asset allocation. The tax-oriented applications focus primarily on differences in tax treatment accorded domestic and international recipients of corporate dividends in many countries. Dividend withholding taxes, and an often cumbersome process for obtaining appropriate relief from part of the withholding tax, give many cross-border investors an incentive to use an equity total return swap. They receive the total return of a nondomestic equity index in return for an interest payment to a counterparty that holds the underlying equities more tax-efficiently. Although many cross-border tax differences have been reduced, as long as tax differences persist, equity swaps can provide significant tax-saving opportunities to many large cross-border investors.

Equity swaps have another important application: asset allocation transactions. A manager can use equity swaps to rebalance portfolios to the strategic asset allocation. Total costs to rebalance by trading the underlying securities may exceed the cost of an equity swap. Consequently, effecting the asset allocation change with a swap is often more efficient. Equity swaps are used in tactical asset allocation for similar reasons.

5. ACTIVE EQUITY INVESTING

The active equity portfolio manager's primary job is to deliver the best possible performance relative to the benchmark's performance working within the risk and other constraints specified in the client's mandate. To add value, the active manager must sharpen information, investment insights, and investment tools to the point at which he has a distinct competitive advantage over his peers. Investment tools include the area of equity valuation models, a subject of study in itself.[33] The following sections on active investing focus on macro choices of orientation and strategy that distinguish the different approaches to active equity investing.

Indexing, discussed earlier, sprang from the efficient markets theory initiated in academia during the 1960s. In the subsequent three decades, however, academic and practitioner research identified a variety of possible opportunities for active management. These developments have reinvigorated active management, allowing portfolio managers to justify the higher expenses of active management compared with passive management. Furthermore, demand for performance in excess of broad market averages has been and probably will continue to be a regular feature of both the individual and institutional investor landscape. That said, many investment managers offer a range of equity investment products from active to passive to suit the differing interests of a broad spectrum of investors.

5.1. Equity Styles

To understand the landscape of active equity portfolio management today, we must discuss the concept of equity styles. Most broadly, an **investment style** is a natural grouping of investment

[33]See Stowe, Robinson, Pinto, and McLeavey (2002).

disciplines that has some predictive power in explaining the future dispersion of returns across portfolios.[34] As we will discuss in detail later, a traditional equity style contrast is between **value** (focused on paying a relatively low share price in relation to earnings or assets per share) and **growth** (focused on investing in high-earnings-growth companies) disciplines. **Market oriented** is often specified as an intermediate grouping for investment disciplines that cannot be clearly categorized as value or growth. Furthermore, the market-capitalization segment(s) in which an equity investor operates is frequently specified in describing an investor's style.

Style plays roles in both risk management and performance evaluation. If an equity portfolio manager adopts a specific style and is evaluated relative to a benchmark that reflects that style, then investors who hire the manager can readily determine whether she is talented or is just earning the generic returns to a style, which might be more inexpensively obtained by indexing on an appropriate equity **style index** (an index intended to reflect the average returns to a given style). Certain categories of stocks (e.g., value stocks) can outperform the overall market for years. A mediocre value stock investor might be beating a broad market benchmark consistently while actually underperforming his chosen style as represented by a benchmark for a value style.

Identifying true talent became an important issue with the emergence of the pension fund consultant in the 1980s. Pension fund consultants are hired to identify good portfolio managers, track their performance, and recommend their replacement if necessary. To accomplish this, the consultants partition managers according to the style that each follows. In this environment, an active equity portfolio manager who claims he follows no definable style automatically excludes himself from consideration by many pension funds and other institutional accounts.

The groundbreaking work in style and performance measurement was done by Nobel Laureate William F. Sharpe (1988, 1992). Sharpe set out to explain U.S. equity mutual funds' returns in terms of their exposures to the four asset classes into which he divided the U.S institutional equity universe: large-cap value, large-cap growth, medium cap, and small cap. Exhibit 7-11 reproduces Sharpe's original diagram. The horizontal lines divide total market cap into the fraction accounted for by large-cap, mid-cap, and small-cap equities; the vertical line divides large-cap equities into equal halves of large-cap value and large-cap growth.

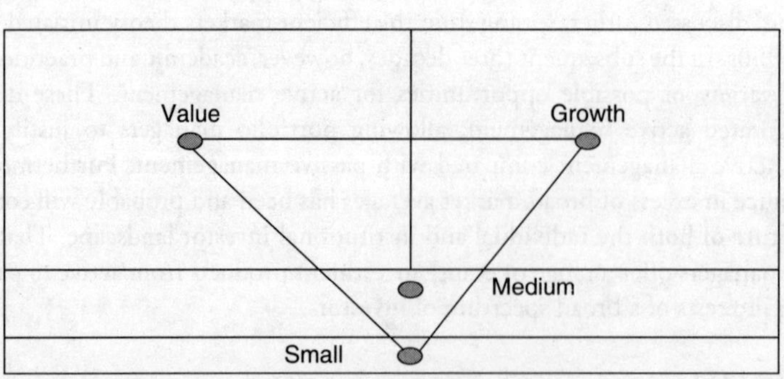

EXHIBIT 7-11 Composition of Four Domestic Equity Classes
Source: Sharpe (1992)

[34]See Brown and Goetzmann (1997).

Sharpe's purpose was to define style to facilitate performance measurement and to reflect the distinct and useful differences in the way active portfolio managers structured their portfolios. As he observed in 1992:

> *Much has been written about both the small-stock and the value/growth phenomena. While the terms value and growth reflect common usage in the investment profession, they serve only as convenient names for stocks that tend to be similar in several respects. As is well known, across securities there is significant positive correlation among: book/price, earnings/price, low earnings growth, dividend yield and low return on equity. Moreover, the industry compositions of the value and growth groups differ (e.g., companies with high research budgets tend to have low book values relative to their stock prices).*

Thus style distinctions recognize the similarities and differences among active equity managers. The contrast between value and growth stocks is fuzzy, however, particularly when we categorize stocks in a forward-looking sense rather using historical data. Almost any stock can be categorized as cheap or expensive depending on one's expectations for the future. Fuzziness in the growth–value contrast coincides with a movement in some quarters to give portfolio managers greater flexibility to use a wide range of techniques and instruments to add value wherever they perceive it lies.[35]

EXAMPLE 7-3 Same Stock, Different Opinions

Value and growth investors have opposite views on the best way to invest, and they thus tend to reach different conclusions about a stock. In 2004, one example was the Eastman Kodak Company ("Kodak"), the world's largest photography company and one of the oldest members of the DJIA.

For most of its history, Kodak was a growth company. It had a dominant market share in photographic films, photographic paper, and cameras. Its only real rival has been Fuji Photo of Japan. Kodak's earnings, dividends, and cash flow were strong throughout its history. The company was unsuccessful in its attempts to diversify out of photography, however, and in recent years has suffered from the rapid growth of digital cameras. In 2003, its share price fell approximately 28 percent, primarily because digital cameras caused its sales of film and paper to collapse. The company announced sweeping job cuts, slashed its dividend, and came out with a plan to focus on digital imaging.

A growth investor would simply dismiss Kodak's stock as a potential investment. The company has not increased its sales in a decade, and those sales are expected to fall further as demand for film and photo paper continues to decline. Its earnings will be under pressure from restructuring charges and its new strategic investments. Although Kodak is trying to find a niche in the digital imaging market, its strategic repositioning may be too late. In contrast to the film business, the digital imaging market has many competitors.

[35]Bernstein (2003).

A value investor, however, would point to the fact that Kodak was trading on a P/E of 12.4x versus 20x for the DJIA, that its shares fell 28 percent in 2003 versus an approximate 25 percent gain for the DJIA, and that it still had one of the strongest brand names in the world, similar in public recognition to those of Coca-Cola and Sony. Although Kodak is struggling to make the transition to digital photography, it is a technologically advanced company with an excellent distribution network. For a value investor, Kodak might be a buy.

5.1.1. Value Investment Styles All else being equal, value investors are more concerned about buying a stock that is deemed relatively cheap in terms of the purchase price of earnings or assets than about a company's future growth prospects. They may make several possible arguments to justify buying such stocks. One is that companies' earnings may have a tendency to revert to a mean value; if valuation multiples for a set of stocks are depressed because of recent earnings problems, an investor in those stocks may benefit from reversion to the mean in earnings accompanied by expansion in P/Es. The flip side of the argument is that investments in stocks that are relatively expensive expose the investor to the risk of contractions in multiples and in earnings. Value investors often believe that investors inherently overpay for "glamour" stocks—those seen as having particularly good growth prospects—while neglecting those with less favorable prospects.

All of these arguments presume that investors as a whole do not accurately judge forward-looking risk and return prospects, and so this line of thinking relates closely to the behavioral argument that investors overreact to bad news and thus provide opportunities for value investors. In contrast, Fama and French (1996) suggest that stocks that are cheap in terms of assets—in particular, stocks having a relatively high ratio of book value of equity to market value of equity (equivalent to a *low* price-to-book ratio, or P/B)—have a higher risk of financial distress and thus offer higher expected returns as fair compensation for that risk.[36] Empirically, most studies have found that in the long run a value style may earn a positive return premium relative to the market.[37] Evidence on this phenomenon is still evolving, however. For example, using U.S. data from 1980 through 2001, Phalippou (2004) found that the extra return to value is concentrated in the smallest 7 percent of equities by market value. That segment is relatively illiquid. Various commentators have suggested that, in general, value investors may earn a return premium for supplying liquidity to the market, buying when short-term excess supply causes shares to decline.

The main risk for a value investor is that he has misinterpreted a stock's cheapness. The stock may be cheap for a very good economic reason that the investor does not fully appreciate. Value investors also face the risk that the perceived undervaluation will not be corrected within the investor's investment time horizon. Questions that the value investor should ask include the following:

- How long is it expected to take to for price to rise to reflect the shares' perceived higher intrinsic value?

[36]They postulate that distress risk is highly correlated across firms so that it is nondiversifiable and commands a premium.

[37]See Bodie, Kane, and Marcus (2005).

- What **catalyst** (triggering event or change) will make the price rise?
- Is the expected time frame for the price to correct acceptable?

The value investing style has at least three substyles: **low P/E, contrarian,** and **high yield.**[38] A low P/E investor will look for stocks that sell at low prices to current or normal earnings. Such stocks are generally found in industries categorized as defensive, cyclical, or simply out-of-favor. The investor buys on the expectation that the P/E will at least rise as the stock or industry recovers. A contrarian investor will look for stocks that have been beset by problems and are generally selling at low P/Bs, frequently below 1. Such stocks are found in very depressed industries that may have virtually no current earnings. The investor buys on the expectation of a cyclical rebound that drives up product prices and demand. A yield investor focuses on stocks that offer high dividend yield with prospects of maintaining or increasing the dividend, knowing that in the long run, dividend yield has generally constituted a major portion of the total return on equities.[39]

5.1.2. Growth Investment Styles In contrast to value investors, who are more concerned with price, growth investors are more concerned with earnings. Their underlying assumption is that if a company can deliver future growth in earnings per share and its P/E does not decline, then its share price will appreciate at least at the rate of EPS growth. Growth investors generally will pay above-market earnings multiples for companies that have superior growth rates. They also tend to invest in companies in growth industries, such as (during the decade ending in 2005) technology, health care, and consumer products. Growth stocks have high sales growth relative to the overall market and tend to trade at high P/Es, P/Bs, and price-to-sales ratios (P/Ss). The major risk facing growth investors is that the forecasted EPS growth does not materialize as expected. In that event, P/E multiples may contract at the same time as EPS, amplifying the investor's losses.

The growth style has at least two substyles: **consistent growth** and **earnings momentum.** Companies with consistent growth have a long history of unit-sales growth, superior profitability, and predictable earnings. They tend to trade at high P/Es and be the leaders in consumer-oriented businesses. An example of such a growth stock as of 2005 is Dell, Inc. Companies with earnings momentum have high quarterly year-over-year earnings growth (e.g., EPS for the first quarter of 2006 represents a large increase over EPS for the first quarter of 2005). Such companies may have higher potential earnings growth rates than consistent growth companies, but such growth is likely to be less sustainable. Some growth investors also include price momentum indicators such as relative strength indicators in their investment disciplines, relying on possible patterns of price persistence for certain (usually relatively short) time horizons.[40] (**Relative strength indicators** compare a stock's performance during a specific period either to its own past performance or to the performance of some group of stocks.)

The growth investor who buys a stock at a premium to the overall market is counting on the market to continue paying a premium for the earnings growth that a company has been providing and may continue to deliver. During an economic expansion, earnings growth is abundant—even in the depressed stocks preferred by a value investor—which *may* cause this premium to above-average growth to shrink or vanish. By contrast, when companies with

[38] See Christopherson and Williams (1997) for this classification.
[39] See Siegel (2002) for a popular account and details of these substyles focused on the U.S. experience.
[40] See Chan, Jegadeesh, and Lakonishok (1999) for a discussion of price persistence and reversal.

positive earnings momentum become scarce, as in a slowing economy, earnings growth becomes a scarce resource commanding a higher price, and growth investors may do relatively well.[41]

5.1.3. Other Active Management Styles Market-oriented investors do not restrict themselves to either the value or growth philosophies. The term *market-oriented style* (also sometimes called a **blend** or **core** style) gathers an eclectic group of approaches, with the common element that the valuation metrics of market-oriented portfolios resemble those of a broad market index more than those of a value or growth index, averaged over a full market cycle.[42] Market-oriented investors may be willing to buy stocks no matter where they fall on the growth/value spectrum, provided they can buy a stock below its perceived intrinsic value. They might use a discounted cash-flow model or other discipline to estimate intrinsic value. Market-oriented style investors might buy a stock with a high P/E provided the price can be justified through future growth expected in EPS. They might also buy a depressed cyclical issue provided that they foresee some recovery in product pricing in the future. The potential drawback of a market-oriented active style is that if the portfolio achieves only marketlike returns, indexing or enhanced indexing based on a broad equity market index will likely be the lower-cost and thus more effective alternative.

Among the recognized subcategories of market-oriented investors are **market-oriented with a value bias, market-oriented with a growth bias, growth-at-a-reasonable-price,** and **style rotators**. As the names imply, value bias and growth bias investors tilt their portfolios toward value and growth respectively, but not so distinctively as to clearly identify them as value or growth investors. They typically hold well-diversified portfolios. Growth-at-a-reasonable-price investors favor companies with above-average growth prospects that are selling at relatively conservative valuation levels compared with other growth companies. Their portfolios are typically somewhat less well diversified than those of other growth investors. Style rotators invest according to the style that they believe will be favored in the marketplace in the relatively near term.

Another characteristic often used in describing the style of equity investors is the typical market capitalization of the issues they hold. **Small-capitalization equity investors** (also called **small-cap** or **small-stock investors**) focus on the lowest market-capitalization stocks in the countries in which they invest. (**Micro-cap** is sometimes used to characterize investors in the lowest capitalization range within the small-cap segment.) The underlying premise of this style is that more opportunity exists to find mispriced stocks through research in the small-cap universe than in the less numerous and more intensely researched universe of large-cap blue chip firms.[43] Another rationale is that smaller companies tend to have better growth prospects (if their business model is sound) because their business is starting from a smaller base and their product line tends to be more focused. Also, the chance of earning a very high rate of return on one's money is much better if the starting market capitalization is small. Small-cap investors can also focus on value, growth, or market-orientation within the small-cap universe.

---

[41] See Bernstein (1995), pp. 61–62.

[42] Morningstar replaced "blend" with "core" in 2002. Many investors, however, use "core" in the sense of *playing a central role in the portfolio*, as in the *core-satellite* approach to managing a portfolio of managers discussed later. A "market-oriented" portfolio may be appropriate for a central role but is not absolutely required for it. Because *core* adds a connotation of role unnecessarily, rather than focusing on characteristics, we prefer the more descriptive term *market oriented.*

[43] Kritzman and Page (2003).

In some equity markets, **mid-cap equity investors** have defined an investment segment focusing on middle-capitalization equities; in the United States, such investors typically focus on stocks that are between the 200th and 1,000th largest by market cap.[44] Mid-cap investors argue that the companies in this segment may be less well researched than the largest-cap companies but financially stronger and less volatile than small-cap companies.

Large-cap equity investors focus on large-cap equities. Such investors favor the relative financial stability of large-cap issues and believe that they can add value through superior analysis and insight.

Small-cap, mid-cap, and large-cap investors are frequently also classified as value, growth, or market-oriented investors within their capitalization domain.

EXAMPLE 7-4 One Style or Two?

Jeff Fujimori is responsible for the investment of a new ¥10 billion contribution to the Honshu Bank's pension fund. The mandate is to invest with active managers. The equity portion of the pension plan has a broad equity market benchmark. Discuss the advantages and disadvantages of hiring a single manager in either a growth or value style, one manager in each style, or one manager in a market-oriented style.

Solution: ***Value or growth manager (but not both).*** *Advantage*: If the investor has a position on the desirability of these equity investment styles, this choice would lead to a portfolio expressing the clear conviction of the investor. Such a portfolio has the potential for strong gains if the investor's style is favored by the market. *Disadvantages*: The choice creates tracking risk relative to the equity benchmark. Substantial underperformance may occur if the manager's style is not in favor. Furthermore, Fujimori must confirm that Honshu Bank finds it acceptable to deviate from an overall broad market orientation of the benchmark before undertaking this alternative.

Value and growth manager. *Advantage*: We would expect this choice to have lower tracking risk relative to the benchmark than investing in a single growth or value-oriented portfolio, because it does not make an overall style bet. It is a kind of barbell approach to achieving an overall market orientation, which may have the advantage of combining the expertise of two managers. *Disadvantage*: This choice may have higher overall management fees than investing in a single portfolio. The investor must rely on security selection alone to overcome the transaction costs and higher fees associated with active management.

One manager with a market-oriented style. *Advantage*: This is the simplest way to invest consistently with the equity benchmark. *Disadvantage*: Fujimori needs to confirm that the market-oriented style reflects an appropriate and consistent process that promises to add value, as opposed to an unfocused process that has averaged to a market orientation. With that qualification, no obvious disadvantages to this approach exist.

[44]See Christopherson and Greenwood (2004).

5.1.4. Techniques for Identifying Investment Styles Two major approaches to identifying style are returns-based style analysis, which relies on portfolio returns, and holdings-based style analysis (also called composition-based style analysis), which relies on an analysis of the characteristics of individual security holdings. The analyst can use the information from either technique to identify a manager's style for performance attribution purposes and/or to formulate expectations about the manager's future performance.

The first technique of style identification was Sharpe's (1988, 1992) **returns-based style analysis** (RBSA). This technique focuses on characteristics of the overall portfolio as revealed by a portfolio's realized returns. It involves regressing portfolio returns (generally monthly returns) on return series of a set of securities indices. In principle, these indices are:

- Mutually exclusive.
- Exhaustive with respect to the manager's investment universe.
- Distinct sources of risk (ideally they should not be highly correlated).[45]

Returns-based style analysis involves a constraint that the coefficients or betas on the indices are nonnegative and sum to 1.[46] That constraint permits us to interpret a beta as the portfolio's proportional exposure to the particular style (or asset class) represented by the index.[47] For example, if a portfolio had a beta of 0.75 on a large-cap value index, a beta of 0 on a large-cap growth index, a beta of 0.25 on a small-stock value index, and a beta of 0 on a small-stock growth index, we would infer that the portfolio was run as a value portfolio with some exposure to small stocks. The **factor weights** on large-cap value, large-cap growth, small-cap value, and small-cap growth indices are 75 percent, 0, 25 percent, and 0, respectively. (The factor weights are also known as **style weights** or **Sharpe style weights.**) We expect the portfolio to move 0.75 times whatever happens to large-cap value stocks (holding everything else constant) and 0.25 times whatever happens to small-cap value stocks (holding everything else constant).

The large-cap value index and the small-cap value index held in weights of 0.75 and 0.25, respectively, would constitute a natural benchmark for this portfolio, given that the overall fit of the model was excellent. Such a benchmark is sometimes referred to as the **normal portfolio** or **normal benchmark** for a manager.[48] As defined in the chapter on performance evaluation, a normal portfolio is a portfolio with exposures to sources of systematic risk that are typical for a manager, using the manager's past portfolios as a guide. A manager's normal portfolio or normal benchmark in effect represents the universe of securities from which a manager normally might select securities for his portfolio.

---

[45]Sharpe (1992), examining U.S. mutual funds, used 12 indices representing U.S. Treasury bills, intermediate-term government bonds, long-term government bonds, corporate bonds, mortgage-related securities, large-cap value stocks, large-cap growth stocks, mid-cap stocks, small-cap stocks, non-U.S. bonds, European stocks, and Japanese stocks.

[46]With this constraint, the model must be solved using quadratic programming (e .g., Solver in Microsoft Excel). It is possible to do a returns-based style analysis constraining the coefficients to sum to 1 but not constraining the coefficients to be nonnegative; that approach could capture elements such as the use of leverage (a negative coefficient on T-bills, included as an index).

[47]Furthermore, Lobosco and DiBartolomeo (1997) have shown how to calculate approximate confidence intervals for the weights.

[48]As defined in the chapter on performance evaluation, a normal portfolio is a portfolio with exposures to sources of systematic risk that are typical for a manager, using the manager's past portfolios as a guide.

EXAMPLE 7-5 The Choice of Indices in Returns-Based Style Analysis

In the example just given in the text, the style analysis used four indices. Suppose that instead we used the following three indices:

- A large-cap value index
- A large-cap growth index
- A small stock index

We find a large weight on large-cap value, no weight on large-cap growth, and a small weight on small stocks and we conclude that the portfolio was run as value portfolio with some exposure to small stocks. Critique the conclusion.

Solution: The evidence does not contradict the conclusion, but does not completely validate the value characterization. In particular, the portfolio's weight on small stocks might be explained (at least in part) by a positive weight on small-cap growth. By breaking down small stocks into small-cap value and small-cap growth and running the style analysis with four indices (including large-cap value and large-cap growth), we can remove all ambiguity.

We can use a returns-based style analysis to calculate a coefficient of determination measuring **style fit.** The quantity 1 minus the style fit equals **selection,** the fraction of return variation unexplained by style. The error term in the style analysis equation—the difference between the portfolio's return and a passive asset mix with the same style as the portfolio—represents **selection return** (the return from active security selection ability).

Example 7-6 shows the use of returns-based style analysis to independently evaluate a portfolio manager's style. In this example, Exhibit 7-13 is a **rolling style chart** showing the evolution of a portfolio's style exposures through time.

EXAMPLE 7-6 Returns-Based Style Analysis (1)

Giles Hébert is chief pension officer of Compagnie Minière de l'Ouest SA (CMO). One of Hébert's outside managers for the U.S. equity portion of his portfolio is Arizona Capital Partners (ACP). Hébert is conducting a review of ACP's performance as of mid-2003. CMO decided to pursue a large-cap growth strategy for its U.S. equity investments and selected ACP's U.S. large-cap growth strategy for the investment of part of its allocation to U.S. large-cap growth stocks. When the relationship was established, Hébert and ACP agreed that the Russell 1000 Growth Index fairly represents the investment universe of this strategy. CMO uses returns-based style analysis in evaluating its investment managers.

Hébert knows from the portfolio's custodian that, following its mandate, the portfolio has remained fully invested in U.S. equities. He thus selects the following four benchmarks as the independent variables for a returns-based style analysis:

- Russell 1000 Growth Index (R1000G)
- Russell 1000 Value Index (R1000V)
- Russell 2000 Growth Index (R2000G)
- Russell 2000 Value Index (R2000V)

Hébert includes the R1000G because it is the account's benchmark. He adds the R1000V to capture the degree to which the manager may not be adhering to a growth orientation. Finally, Hébert includes the R2000G and R2000V to capture the degree to which ACP may be failing to adhere to a large-cap orientation. Exhibit 7-12 gives the results of the returns-based style analysis. Hébert also notes the following facts:

- Exhibit 7-12 is based on the most recent three years of monthly data as of March 31, 2003.
- Exhibit 7-13 is based on rolling three-year monthly data ending March 31, 2003.
- For the data period shown in Exhibit 7-12, selection is 8.1 percent and the style fit is 91.9 percent.
- For the data period shown in Exhibit 7-12, the annualized active return is −0.38 percent and the annualized tracking risk is 6.58 percent.

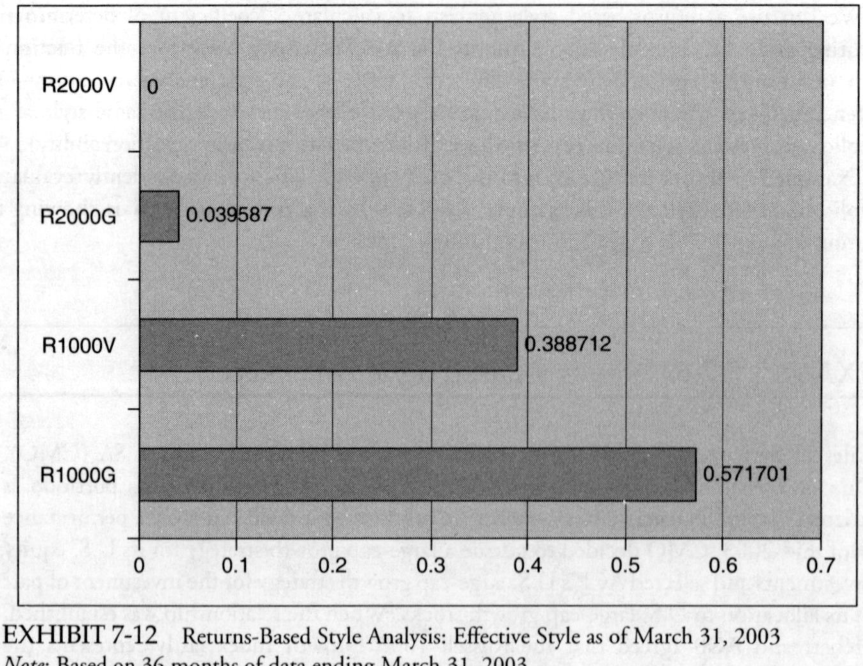

EXHIBIT 7-12 Returns-Based Style Analysis: Effective Style as of March 31, 2003
Note: Based on 36 months of data ending March 31, 2003

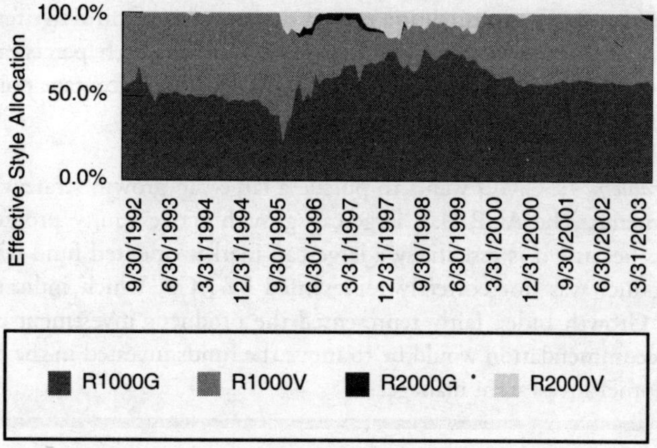

EXHIBIT 7-13 Style History: A Rolling Style Chart, September 30, 1992 to March 31, 2003

Using the information given, address the following:

1. State and justify whether the ACP product in which CMO is invested is accurately described as a U.S. large-cap growth active equity product.
2. Characterize the historical style of the ACP product and evaluate whether the historical analysis supports the answer to the previous question.
3. Calculate and interpret the information ratio of the ACP product.
4. Recommend a course of action to CMO.

Solution to 1. The ACP product cannot accurately be described as a U.S. large-cap growth active equity product. The product does indeed appear to be actively managed, because the fraction of return variation unexplained by style (selection) is 8.1 percent; the product is not merely replicating the returns on more-passive benchmarks. The very low weights on the R2000G and R2000V small-cap indices, at 4 percent and 0 respectively, also confirm that the product is essentially large-cap. Furthermore, the largest factor weight at 57.2 percent is on the manager's large-cap benchmark, the R1000G. However, the product has a substantial factor weight of 38.9 percent on large-cap value as represented by the R1000V. Considering all these facts, the portfolio appears to be an actively managed large-cap market-oriented portfolio with a growth bias.

Solution to Problem 2: As Exhibit 7-13 shows, the ACP product has generally had substantial exposure to both large-cap growth and large-cap value; the factor weight on large-cap value was greatest in the first third of the overall period, peaking in September 30, 1995 when it exceeded the weight on large-cap growth. In the middle period, the factor weight on large-cap growth increased at the expense of large-cap value; however, the weight on small-cap stocks, particularly small-cap value, increased to noticeable levels. Since the end of 2000, the style weights have been fairly close to the values shown in Exhibit 7-12. The ACP product appears to always have had a meaningful weight on value. For the most part, the ACP product has adhered to its specified large-cap orientation. Thus the historical analysis supports the conclusions reached in the previous question.

Solution to Problem 3: The information ratio is the mean historical active return divided by the tracking risk, or −0.38%/6.58% = −0.0578. For each percentage point of tracking risk, the ACP product earned approximately −0.06 percentage points of active return. Thus the portfolio's active risk has been unrewarded.

Solution to Problem 4: CMO wants to pursue a large-cap growth strategy for its U.S. equity investments. The ACP U.S. large-cap growth active equity product does not meet its needs because it is essentially a large-cap market-oriented fund with a growth bias. The product was not correctly represented by ACP, which indicated that the Russell 1000 Growth Index fairly represented the product's investment universe. An appropriate recommendation would be to move the funds invested in the ACP growth strategy to another investment manager.

Example 7-7 shows an error that can occur in returns-based style analysis.

EXAMPLE 7-7 Returns-Based Style Analysis (2)

Frank Harvey is analyzing a U.S. equity mutual fund that states the investment objective of investing for growth and income, with an orientation to mid-cap stocks within the universe of U.S.-domiciled companies. Harvey may select from the following indices for use in a returns-based style analysis:

- The S&P/Citigroup 500 Growth and Value indices, which have a large-cap orientation.
- The Russell 2000 Growth and Value indices, which have a small-cap orientation.
- The Russell 1000 Growth and Value indices, which include large-cap and mid-cap shares.
- The Russell Top 200 Growth and Value indices, which together represent the 200 largest market-cap securities in the Russell 1000 Index.
- The Russell Midcap Growth and Value indices, which together represent the 800 smallest market-cap issues in the Russell 1000 Index (the Russell Top 200 Index and the Russell Midcap Index together constitute the Russell 1000 Index).

Harvey selects the S&P/Citigroup 500 Growth and Value indices and the Russell 2000 Growth and Value indices for the style analysis.

1. Critique Harvey's selection.
2. Recommend a more appropriate selection of indices.

Solution to Problem 1: Harvey's choice omits from coverage a substantial number of stocks: those with market caps too small for the S&P 500 but too large for the Russell 2000. Many of the excluded stocks could be characterized as mid-cap. This omission is significant because Harvey should seek to confirm whether the fund being analyzed is actually oriented to mid-cap stocks as it claims to be. The selection of indices should be mutually exclusive and at least approximately exhaustive with respect to the investment manager's universe. The results of an RBSA using a faulty set of indices can be misleading.

Solution to Problem 2: The following selection of indices would be best:

- Russell Top 200 Growth
- Russell Top 200 Value
- Russell Midcap Growth
- Russell Midcap Value
- Russell 2000 Growth
- Russell 2000 Value

This selection of indices is not only exhaustive, in contrast to the one critiqued in Part 1, but also adequate for determining a distinct style weight for mid-cap issues (because it breaks out mid-cap issues via the Russell Midcap indices).

A less satisfactory selection, but an improvement over Harvey's selection, is the Russell 1000 Growth and Value indices and the Russell 2000 Growth and Value indices. This selection is exhaustive, in contrast to Harvey's selection, but would be inferior to the one recommended: It does not suffice to give a specific weight for mid-cap because the Russell 1000–based indices include both large- and mid-cap stocks.

The second major broad approach to style identification is **holdings-based style analysis,** which categorizes individual securities by their characteristics and aggregates results to reach a conclusion about the overall style of the portfolio at a given point in time. For example, the analyst may examine the following variables:

- *Valuation levels*. A value-oriented portfolio has a very clear bias toward low P/Es, low P/Bs, and high dividend yields. A growth-oriented portfolio exhibits the opposite characteristics. A market-oriented portfolio has valuations close to the market average.
- *Forecast EPS growth rate*. A growth-oriented portfolio will tend to hold companies experiencing above-average and/or increasing earnings growth rates (positive earnings momentum). Typically, trailing and forecast EPS growth rates are higher for a growth-oriented portfolio than for a value-oriented portfolio. The companies in a growth portfolio typically have lower dividend payout ratios than those in a value portfolio, because growth companies typically want to retain most of their earnings to finance future growth and expansion.
- *Earnings variability*. A value-oriented portfolio will hold companies with greater earnings variability because of the willingness to hold companies with cyclical earnings.
- *Industry sector weightings*. Industry sector weightings can provide some information on the portfolio manager's favored types of businesses and security characteristics, thus furnishing some information on style. In many markets, value-oriented portfolios tend to have larger weights in the finance and utilities sectors than growth portfolios, because of these sectors' relatively high dividend yields and often moderate valuation levels. Growth portfolios often have relatively high weights in the information technology and health care sectors, because historically these sectors have often included numerous high-growth enterprises. Industry

sector weightings must be interpreted with caution, however. Exceptions to the typical characteristics exist in most if not all sectors, and some sectors (e.g., consumer discretionary) are quite sensitive to the business cycle, possibly attracting different types of investors at different points in the cycle.

Example 7-8 illustrates the use of a holdings-based style analysis.

EXAMPLE 7-8 Do Portfolio Characteristics Match the Stated Investment Style?

Charles Simpson is a consultant analyzing a portfolio for consistency with the portfolio manager's stated value investment style. Exhibit 7-14 summarizes the characteristics of the portfolio and those of a representative market benchmark portfolio.

EXHIBIT 7-14 Simpson's Portfolio Analysis (1)

	Portfolio	Market Benchmark
Number of stocks	30	750
Weighted-average market cap	$37 billion	$45 billion
Dividend yield	3%	2.1%
P/E	15	20
P/B	1.2	2
EPS growth (5-year projected)	10%	12%
Sector		
Consumer Discretionary	18%	13%
Consumer Staples	5	10
Energy	11	9
Finance	25	20
Health Care	2	7
Industrials	10	9
Information Technology	2	7
Materials	10	8
Telecommunications	5	10
Utilities	12	7

What can Simpson infer about the firm's investment style?

Solution: Simpson can be fairly confident that the manager is following a value style. The portfolio's P/E and P/B are below those of the benchmark, but the dividend yield is above that of the benchmark, consistent with a value bias. EPS growth expectations that are slightly below average support the inference that the portfolio is not growth oriented. The sector breakdown suggests value as well. Finance and utilities tend to have relatively high dividend yield and moderate P/Es. On the other hand, sectors with a greater growth orientation, in particular health care and information technology, are underweighted. Thus the portfolio appears to follow a value discipline.

In Example 7-8, Simpson included some of the types of variables previously mentioned in the text (market capitalization and valuation ratios, such as dividend yield, P/E, P/B, and industry sector weightings) but not others (e.g., earnings variability). Such variation is typical of holdings-based style analysis. Holdings-based analysis involves a number of modeling decisions. One decision is the set of characteristics that discriminate among different styles: Analysts use a variety of sets of discriminating characteristics. The number of discriminating characteristics may run from one (such as the value of the P/B) to a large set, as in the Barra fundamental multifactor risk models, commercial models that have been used in holdings-based analysis. Besides modeling characteristics, a decision must be made on aggregating security-level information. A security may be assigned:

- To value exclusively or to growth exclusively in all instances.
- To value exclusively or to growth exclusively but only if the value of some characteristic exceeds or is less than a specified threshold value.
- In part to growth and in part to value.

Threshold values must be specified in order to make exclusive (also known as "0-1") assignments. For example, in the first-given assignment method, the market value–weighted average value of an attribute (or set of attributes) may determine the cutoff point for assigning a stock to growth or to value. To illustrate the second approach, assuming that the classification focuses on the P/E, if the P/E is below a specified value (e.g., 16.50) it would be assigned to value; if it is above a higher value (e.g., 24.50) it would be assigned to growth, and if it is in between (i.e., between 16.50 and 24.50), it would be viewed as neither value nor growth. In the description of the final assignment approach, "in part" means up to 100 percent so that the assignments to value and growth sum to 100 percent. To use the terminology of Lazzara (2004), in the first two approaches, style is viewed as a *category*; in the third approach, in which a stock can be "spread over" growth and value, style is viewed as a *quantity*.

Exhibit 7-15 contrasts the advantages and disadvantages of returns-based and holdings-based style analysis. Because of its less intense data needs, returns-based style analysis might often be performed first and suffice by itself; however, an analysis of holdings obviously can reveal important details of a manager's investment discipline. Both approaches have uses in practice.

The next section discusses the increasing variety of style indices available.

5.1.5. Equity Style Indices

Significant debate exists—and probably should—about how to divide the stock universe into growth and value components. Allocating stocks between growth and value indices can be as simple as ranking them by a single variable such as P/B, or it can involve multiple variables. The clear trend has been to construct style indices based on multiple variables.[49] Typical elements in many classification approaches include price, earnings, book value, dividends, and past and projected growth rates in these or other elements. Each element can be part of more than one factor in a multifactor growth/value stock allocation system, creating some (probably) benign redundancy. Attention to the details

[49] With the replacement of the S&P/BARRA style indices (which were based only on P/B) by the S&P/Citigroup style indices in December 2005, all major commercial style indices employ multiple factors.

EXHIBIT 7-15 Two Approaches to Style Analysis: Advantages and Disadvantages

	Advantages	Disadvantages
Returns-based style analysis	• Characterizes entire portfolio • Facilitates comparisons of portfolios • Aggregates the effect of the investment process • Different models usually give broadly similar results and portfolio characterizations • Clear theoretical basis for portfolio categorization • Requires minimal information • Can be executed quickly • Cost effective	• May be ineffective in characterizing current style • Error in specifying indices in the model may lead to inaccurate conclusions
Holdings-based style analysis	• Characterizes each position • Facilitates comparisons of individual positions • In looking at present, may capture changes in style more quickly than returns-based analysis	• Does not reflect the way many portfolio managers approach security selection • Requires specification of classification attributes for style; different specifications may give different results • More data intensive than returns-based analysis

of style index construction has increased as index publishers compete to serve and capture licensing fees from ETFs and other investment products.

Exhibit 7-16 summarizes information on some major style indices. Characteristically, all the indices in this exhibit essentially feature holding-based style analysis, focusing on individual stock or company attributes. In the exhibit, "overlap" means that some securities may be assigned in part to both value and growth. **Buffering** refers to rules for maintaining the style assignment of a stock consistent with a previous assignment when the stock has not clearly moved to a new style. Buffering reduces turnover in style classification and serves to reduce the transaction expenses of funds that track the style index.

As Exhibit 7-16 illustrates (and consistent with our earlier discussion of holdings-based style analysis), style index publishers use growth and value either as categories (no overlap) or as quantities (with overlap).[50] If MSCI, a categorizer, assigns a stock to the growth or value category, the company will be labeled as either growth or value and is never divided between the two. In contrast, index providers that treat growth and value as quantities will often assign a stock partly to growth and partly to value. This split allocation recognizes that some stocks do not fit neatly into either growth or value. Among the style index families in Exhibit 7-16, Morningstar confronts this issue most directly by explicitly distinguishing three

[50] See Lazzara (2004) for more information.

EXHIBIT 7-16 Select Style Index Families: Principal Growth/Value Allocation Criteria and Rebalancing Rules

Index Family	Criteria		Rebalancing	Comments
Dow Jones Wilshire	Projected P/E		March, September (with buffering)	Two categories (value, growth), no overlap
	Projected earnings growth			
	P/B			
	Dividend yield			
	Trailing P/E			
	Trailing earnings growth			
FTSE	Value		June and December	Two categories (value, growth).
	P/B			
	P/S			
	Dividend yield			Constituents are members of the FTSE All-World Index, and
	Price/cash flow			Value and Growth indices are calculated for the FTSE World Index, derivatives of the FTSE World Index, plus regional and country indices in the FTSE World index. Constituents showing high growth (value) characteristics are assigned to growth (value), an intermediate group is apportioned to both growth and value.
	Growth			
	3-year historical sales growth rate			
	3-year historical EPS growth rate			
	2-year forward sales growth estimate			
	2-year forward EPS growth estimate Internal growth rate (ROE × [1 − Payout ratio])			
	Long-term			
	Past book value growth			
Morningstar	Value	Weight	June, December (with buffering)	Three categories (value, core, and growth), no overlap
	Price/Projected earnings	50.0%		
	P/B	12.5		
	P/S	12.5		
	Price/Cash flow	12.5		
	Dividend yield	12.5		
		12.5		
	Growth	Weight		
	Long-term projected earnings growth	50.0%		
	Past earnings growth	12.5		
	Past sales growth	12.5		
	Past cash flow growth	12.5		
	Past book value growth	12.5		

(continued)

EXHIBIT 7-16 (*continued*)

Index Family	Criteria	Rebalancing	Comments
MSCI	Value P/B 12-month forward earnings/price Dividend yield Growth Long-term forward EPS growth rate Short-term forward EPS growth rate Long-term historical EPS growth trend Long-term historical sales per share	May, November (with buffering)	Two categories (value, growth), no overlap
Russell	P/B IBES growth estimates	Approximately June 30	Two categories (value, growth), with overlap
S&P/Citigroup World	Value Book/Price Sales/Price Cash flow/Price Dividend yield Growth 5-year average internal growth rate[51] 5-year historical EPS growth rate 5-year historical sales per share growth rate	July 1	Style Index series: Two categories (value, growth), with overlap Pure Style Index series: two categories (value, growth), no overlap

Source: www.djindexes.com, www.ftse.com, http://indexes.morningstar.com, www.msci.com, www.russell.com/US/Indexes, www.globalindices.standardandpoors.com.

mutually exclusive categories (value, core, and growth). The two-category value/growth split of other index families reflects the consideration that most active equity mandates specifying style are an order for the portfolio manager to manage according to one of these two styles (value or growth).

EXAMPLE 7-9 Returns-Based and Holdings-Based Style Analyses

John Whitney is a consultant being asked to evaluate a portfolio managed by California Investment Management. He uses proprietary software to do both returns-based and holdings-based style analysis.

[51]The internal growth rate is defined as Return on equity × Earnings retention rate.

Returns-Based Style Analysis:

- Effective style for 36 monthly periods ending June 30, 2004.
- 44.9 percent S&P/Citigroup growth.
- 55.1 percent S&P/Citigroup value.
- Style fit: 99.5 percent; Selection: 0.5 percent.

Exhibit 7-17 shows a holdings-based style analysis (based on June 30, 2004 holdings):

EXHIBIT 7-17 Holdings-Based Analysis, June 30, 2004

	Portfolio	S&P 500 Index	Difference
P/E	18.34	19.54	−1.20
P/B	2.87	2.96	−0.09
Dividend yield	1.53%	1.70%	−0.17%
Size (Market-Cap) Analysis			
Largest quintile	25.40%	24.87%	0.53%
Quintile 2	22.34	26.00	−3.66
Quintile 3	23.75	24.37	−0.62
Quintile 4	22.03	21.74	0.29
Smallest quintile	6.48	3.02	3.46

How should Whitney interpret the style analysis results from the two approaches?

Solution: The two methods offer complementary and essentially confirming views of the portfolio. The holdings-based analysis suggests a market-oriented portfolio with a very slight tilt to value (the portfolio's P/E and P/B both are slightly lower than those of S&P 500, suggesting a tilt toward value, although dividend yield is also lower, suggesting a tilt toward growth). The portfolio also seems to have a slight bias toward smaller-cap stocks relative to the S&P 500.

The returns-based analysis produces similar conclusions. The results also suggest a market orientation, with perhaps a slight leaning toward value. The style fit (R^2) is very high at 99.5 percent. Any performance difference between this portfolio and the S&P 500 can likely be attributed to the slight tilts toward value and smaller stocks.

5.1.6. The Style Box Today, the style box is probably the most popular way of, literally, looking at style. Although an early version of the style box with four component boxes appeared in Sharpe's 1992 paper (see Exhibit 7-11), his original style divisions were only between growth and value among large-cap funds and among large-cap, mid-cap, and small-cap funds on the market capitalization dimension. The most widely recognized version of the style box is probably Morningstar's because of that firm's high-profile use of the 3 × 3-style box to categorize mutual funds and, more recently, individual common stocks. The Morningstar style box, shown in Exhibit 7-18, divides a fund portfolio or stock universe by market capitalization

	VALUE	CORE	GROWTH
Large cap	2	1	13
Mid cap	3	17	60
Small cap	0	1	3

EXHIBIT 7-18 Morningstar Style Box for Vanguard Mid-Cap Growth Fund
Source: www.morningstar.com.

(large cap through mid cap to small cap, from top to bottom), and style (value through core to growth, from left to right), creating a total of nine boxes.[52] Morningstar uses holdings-based style analysis and classifies roughly one third of its stock universe as growth, one third as value, and another third as core. We see from Exhibit 7-18 that most of the value of Vanguard Mid-Cap Growth Fund is indeed centered in mid-cap growth holdings as defined by Morningstar.

Different criteria may lead to noticeably different style box characterizations for the same portfolio. The techniques used to categorize a stock or the components of a portfolio by size are relatively standard, in the size division is based on market capitalization.[53] The specifics of the techniques used to distinguish among value, growth, and (sometimes) market-oriented stocks, however, are almost as diverse as the firms selling style-based indices and financial products/services can make them. Price relative to earnings or book value or some other measure(s) typically forms the basis of value categorization and measurement, whereas historical, forecast, or implied (by market valuation) growth in earnings, sales, or dividends typically forms the basis for growth categorization. The market-oriented category is characterized by a mix of growth and value characteristics in a portfolio. The market-oriented designation usually reflects an inability to clearly categorize a stock or a portfolio as definitively growth or value in nature. In rare cases (e.g., Morningstar's style box and the Morningstar equity style indices), a technique makes a deliberate attempt to define a group of stocks as being *neither* growth *nor* value. An alternative interpretation is that the group constitutes a *blend* of growth and value characteristics.

The numbers in each box represent the percentage of this fund's portfolio value consisting of stocks that fall in that style box (using Morningstar's own index classification). For example, in the Vanguard Mid-Cap Growth Fund, 60 percent of the portfolio by market value falls in the mid-cap growth box and 17 percent falls in the mid-cap core box. All boxes except small-cap value are represented by at least one position in this Vanguard Mid-Cap Growth Fund portfolio.

5.1.7. Style Drift Professional investors view inconsistency in style, or **style drift,** as an obstacle to investment planning and risk control. Ordinarily a value manager holding what is perceived by the market to be a growth stock would have some trouble explaining that

[52] *Core* was formerly called *blend* by Morningstar.

[53] Most float-weighted indices rank companies by total capitalization before adjusting their index weightings for float.

holding to his or her clients. One stock in isolation may not be much of an issue; but if a manager is hired as a value manager and over time begins to hold stocks that would be primarily characterized as growth stocks, that manager can be said to be experiencing style drift. Investors should be concerned about style drift because they hired the investment manager (bought the mutual fund or unit trust) to achieve a particular exposure to an equity market segment—be it large-cap, mid-cap, small-cap, value, growth, or market oriented. Managers are also hired for their expertise in a given style. Consequently, when a manager begins to stray from her stated style to the style currently in favor, the investor understandably should worry—the investor may no longer be getting exposure to the particular style desired, and the manager may now be operating outside her area of expertise.

EXAMPLE 7-10 Style Drift or Not?

Six months later, Charles Simpson is reexamining the portfolio that he analyzed in Example 7-8. In that example, we determined that the portfolio was managed according to a value style. Exhibit 7-19 provides the portfolio's current characteristics. What can Simpson infer about consistency of the firm's investment style?

EXHIBIT 7-19 Simpson's Portfolio Analysis (2)

	Portfolio	Market Benchmark
Number of stocks	45	750
Weighted-average market cap	$46 billion	$45 billion
Dividend yield	2.0%	2.1%
P/E	19	20
P/B	1.9	2
EPS growth (5-year projected)	13%	12%
Sector		
Consumer discretionary	15%	13%
Consumer staples	8	10
Energy	11	9
Finance	22	20
Health Care	5	7
Industrials	10	9
Information technology	5	7
Materials	10	8
Telecommunications	5	10
Utilities	9	7

Solution: The portfolio's style has definitely drifted from value (in Example 7-8) to become market oriented. Looking at the valuation measures, the portfolio does not deviate much from the market benchmark. Although the sector weights still lean very slightly toward value (see the weights on finance, utilities, and information technology, and health care), the magnitudes of these biases relative to the market benchmark have decreased significantly compared with the prior period.

5.2. Socially Responsible Investing

Socially responsible investing, also called **ethical investing,** integrates ethical values and societal concerns with investment decisions. With increasing demand for SRI coming from individual investors, public pension fund sponsors, religious-affiliated groups, and others in many of the world's major markets, an increasing number of equity portfolio managers are responsible for, or have contact with, SRI mandates.

SRI commonly involves the use of stock screens involving SRI-related criteria. SRI stock screens include negative screens and positive screens. Negative SRI screens apply a set of SRI criteria to reduce an investment universe to a smaller set of securities satisfying SRI criteria. SRI criteria may include:

- Industry classification, reflecting concern for sources of revenue judged to be ethically questionable (tobacco, gaming, alcohol, and armaments are common focuses).
- Corporate practices (for example, practices relating to environmental pollution, human rights, labor standards, animal welfare, and integrity in corporate governance).

Positive SRI screens include criteria used to identify companies that have ethically desirable characteristics. Internationally, SRI portfolios most commonly employ negative screens only, a smaller number employ both negative and positive screens, and even fewer employ positive screens only.[54] The particulars of the SRI screening process should reflect the concerns and values communicated by the client.

Portfolio managers should be alert to an SRI discipline's effects on a portfolio's financial characteristics. In particular, managers should track any style biases induced by the SRI portfolio selection process. For example, applying a negative screen, the portfolio manager may exclude (because of environmental concerns) companies from basic industries and energy, which sometimes present a concentration of value stocks; as a result the portfolio could have a growth bias.[55] SRI mutual funds have been documented to have an average market-cap bias toward small-cap shares.[56] At least two benefits for the client can result from measuring and managing these style biases. First, the portfolio manager may be able to address the SRI mandate fully while neutralizing any style biases inconsistent with the client's financial objectives or risk tolerance. Second, the manager can choose an appropriate performance benchmark given an accurate picture of the SRI portfolio's style. Among the methods used to identify and measure progress toward addressing issues of style bias is returns-based style analysis.

5.3. Long–Short Investing

Whereas style investing is concerned with portfolio characteristics (low P/E, high earnings growth, etc.), long–short investing focuses on a constraint. Essentially, many investors face an investment policy and/or regulatory constraint against selling short stocks. Indeed, the constraint is so common and pervasive that many investors do not even recognize it as a constraint.

[54] See Ali and Gold (2002) and the references therein.

[55] For example, see Guerard (1997), who found a growth bias in the Domini Social Index relative to the S&P 500, and Bauer, Koedijk, and Otten (2005), who found a growth bias tendency among German, U.S., and U.K. mutual funds.

[56] See Bauer, Koedijk, and Otten and references therein.

In a traditional long-only strategy, the value added by the portfolio manager is called **alpha**—the portfolio's return in excess of its required rate of return, given its risk. Equivalently, alpha is the portfolio's return in excess of that on a risk-matched benchmark. In a market-neutral long–short strategy, however, the value added can be equal to two alphas. This is because the portfolio manager can use a given amount of capital to purchase a long position and to support a short position. One alpha can come from the long position and another from the short position. In addition, a **market-neutral strategy** is constructed to have an overall zero beta and thus show a pattern of returns expected to be uncorrelated with equity market returns. As discussed later, the alpha from such a strategy is **portable**—that is, it can be added to a variety of different systematic (beta) risk exposures.

In the basic long–short trade, known as a **pairs trade** or **pairs arbitrage,** an investor is long and short equal currency amounts of two common stocks in a single industry (long a perceived undervalued stock and short a perceived overvalued stock), and the risks are limited almost entirely to the specific company risks. Even such a simple convergence trade can go terribly wrong, however, if the value of the short position surges and the value of the long position collapses.

Probably the greatest risk associated with a long–short strategy involves leveraging. In order to magnify the difference in alphas between two stocks, long–short managers (in particular hedge fund managers) sometimes leverage their capital as much as two to three times using borrowed money. Although leverage magnifies the opportunity to earn alpha, it also magnifies the possibility that a negative short-term price move may force the manager to liquidate the positions prematurely in order to meet margin calls (requests for additional capital) or return borrowed securities.

5.3.1. Price Inefficiency on the Short Side

Some investors believe that more price inefficiency can be found on the short side of the market than the long side for several reasons.

First, many investors look only for undervalued stocks, but because of impediments to short selling, relatively few search for overvalued stocks. These impediments prevent investor pessimism from being fully expressed. For example, in order to short a stock, a short seller must borrow the shares from someone who already owns them.[57] When the original investor wants to sell, the securities loan is called and the short seller must return the stock. When many investors are willing to lend the stock, a replacement loan of stock is quickly arranged. When a stock is a popular short (e.g., many Internet stocks during the late 1990s) and few shares are available to borrow, the short seller may have to cover the loan by buying back the stock at an inopportune time.

Second, opportunities to short a stock may arise because of management fraud, "window-dressing" of accounts, or negligence. Few parallel opportunities exist on the long side because of the underlying assumption that management is honest and that the accounts are accurate. Rarely do corporate managers deliberately understate profits.

Third, sell-side analysts issue many more reports with buy recommendations than with sell recommendations.[58] One explanation for this phenomenon is related to commissions that a recommendation may generate: Although most customers may be potential buyers of a stock, only those who already own shares or who are short sellers—usually a smaller group—can sell

---

[57]Borrowing can be done in a number of ways. Institutional investors typically borrow/lend shares through securities lending programs run by custodian banks or prime brokers.

[58]See Womack (1996) and Dhiensiri, Mandelker, and Sayrak (2005) for evidence on the distribution of buy and sell recommendations.

it. Moreover, those customers who already own a stock may become angry when an analyst issues a sell recommendation because it can cause them to lose money.[59]

Fourth, sell-side analysts may be reluctant to issue negative opinions on companies' stocks for reasons other than generic ones such as that a stock has become relatively expensive. Most companies' managements have a vested interest in seeing their share price rise because of personal shareholdings and stock options. After an analyst issues a sell recommendation, therefore, he can find himself suddenly cut off from communicating with management and threatened with libel suits.[60] His employer may also face the prospect of losing highly lucrative corporate finance business.[61] Although such retaliations have occurred, they are not consistent with the Best Practice Guidelines Governing Analyst/Corporate Issue Relations sponsored by the CFA Centre for Financial Market Integrity and the National Investor Relations Institute. Furthermore, despite any such pressures, CFA Institute members and candidates are bound by the Code of Ethics and Standards of Professional Conduct, including Standard I(B) requiring independence and objectivity.[62]

Long–short strategies can make better use of a portfolio manager's information because both rising and falling stocks offer profit potential. Rather than simply avoiding a stock with a bad outlook, a long–short manager can short it, thereby earning the full performance spread.

5.3.2. Equitizing a Market-Neutral Long–Short Portfolio

A market-neutral long–short portfolio can be **equitized** (given equity market systematic risk exposure) by holding a permanent stock index futures position (rolling over contracts), giving the total portfolio full stock market exposure at all times. In carrying out this strategy, the manager may establish a long futures position with a notional value approximately equal to the value of the cash position resulting from shorting securities. Equitizing a market-neutral long–short portfolio is appropriate when the investor wants to add an equity-beta to the skill-based active return the investor hopes to receive from the long–short investment manager. The rate of return on the total portfolio equals the sum of the gains or losses on the long and short securities positions, the gain or loss on the long futures position, and any interest earned by the investor on the cash position that results from shorting securities, all divided by the portfolio equity.

Depending on carrying costs and the ability to borrow ETF shares for short selling, ETFs may be a more attractive way than futures to equitize or de-equitize a long–short alpha over a longer period than the life of a single futures contract. The general ease of borrowing ETF shares for institutional-sized short-sale transactions, as well as the fact that the fund's expense ratio lowers the expected cost of shorting, can making shorting ETFs an attractive alternative to rolling short futures contracts.[63]

A long–short spread can be transported to various asset classes. An investment with no systematic risk should earn the risk-free rate. Therefore, a market-neutral portfolio's performance should be measured against a nominally risk-free rate such as a Treasury bill

[59] Irvine (2000) provides evidence that sell-side analysts' choice to cover a security is positively related to the security's potential to generate commission revenue for their firm.

[60] Lim (2001) finds evidence consistent with this hypothesis.

[61] See Michaely and Womack (1999) and references therein.

[62] See the *Standards of Practice Handbook* (2005). Furthermore, a variety of self-regulatory organizations (e.g., the New York Stock Exchange in the United States) have issued rules for their members concerning analyst conflicts of interest.

[63] Individual investors often find it difficult to borrow a small number of ETF shares or other securities to sell short. Small stock loan transactions are often uneconomic for a brokerage firm to arrange.

return, provided the portfolio is truly market neutral rather than simply leveraged equity. If the long–short portfolio has been equitized, then it should be treated as equity, with returns benchmarked against the index underlying the equitizing instrument.

5.3.3. The Long-Only Constraint

Long–short strategies have an inherent efficiency advantage over long-only portfolios. That inherent advantage is the ability to act on negative insights that the investor may have, which can never be fully exploited in a long-only context. First, consider the example of the long-only investor whose benchmark is the FTSE 100 and whose portfolio holds 45 stocks. One way of thinking about that portfolio is to characterize each stock held relative to that stock's weight in the FTSE 100. A stock that is 4 percent of the portfolio but whose index weight is 3 percent can be said to have an active weight of 1 percent. A stock not included in the portfolio but whose index weight is 5 percent is said to have an active weight of −5 percent, and so on.

Looking at the portfolio this way, the investor can think of the portfolio as being long–short (positive active weights/negative active weights) around the FTSE 100 index. The problem with this portfolio, however, is that its maximum short position (negative active weight) in any given stock is limited by that stock's index weight. If the investor has a strong negative view on a company with a 5 percent index weight, the best she could do is not to hold it at all. On the other hand, if the investor has a very favorable view on a company with a 1 percent index weight, she can (at least theoretically) invest the entire portfolio in that company. The bottom line is that the investor's opportunity set is not symmetric.

A true long–short portfolio, built around a cash benchmark, solves this problem of symmetry. Subject to borrowing constraints and other risks outlined above, a long–short portfolio allows an investor to fully exploit both positive and negative views on a stock. One significant caveat exists, however. The investor needs to have both positive and negative insights about stocks in the investment universe. Stocks excluded from further research because they fail to pass some preliminary screen are not necessarily good candidates for shorting.

EXAMPLE 7-11 Long–Short and Market Structure

Jim Summers is being asked to investigate two alternatives for his company's pension plan. The first is a market-oriented active long-only portfolio benchmarked to the FTSE 100 index. Only moderate tracking risk with respect to the FTSE 100 is acceptable. The second alternative involves building a long–short portfolio using British stocks and then overlaying that portfolio with FTSE 100 futures. Summers is familiar with the FTSE 100 index and knows that the nine largest stocks account for slightly more than 50 percent of the index's weight. Explain a rationale for choosing a long–short strategy.

Solution: Summers recognizes that a market-oriented active manager will have some difficulty outperforming the FTSE 100 index because relatively few stocks make up such a large portion of the index's weight. He reasons that if the portfolio is to be market oriented, the investment manager will have to produce a portfolio with an average market capitalization somewhat in line with the index. The fact that only nine stocks make up half the index weight means that roughly half of the portfolio value will also need to be concentrated in these largest companies. The availability of insights concerning these nine stocks (a relatively small number) would have an important effect on the portfolio's benchmark-relative results. Summers concludes that this concentration of market value in a small number of issues will hinder the market-oriented active manager's ability to outperform the benchmark.

Summers then examines the long–short approach and quickly concludes that not only can the investment manager take equivalent long or short positions in all 100 stocks in the index, to increase the opportunity set the manager may also be able to use stocks not included in the index.

5.4. Sell Disciplines/Trading

Equity portfolios are not unchanging. Besides sales associated with rebalancing or a change in asset allocation, investors may sell stocks from their portfolios to raise needed cash or replace existing holdings with other stocks. Turnover may be related to the investment discipline. Several recognized categories of selling disciplines exist.

First, an investor can follow a strategy of substitution. In this situation, the investor is constantly looking at potential stocks to include in the portfolio and will replace an existing holding whenever a better opportunity presents itself. This strategy revolves around whether the new stock being added will have a higher risk-adjusted return than the stock it is replacing net of transaction costs and taking into account any tax consequences of the replacement. Such an approach may be called an **opportunity cost** sell discipline. Based on the portfolio manager's ongoing review of portfolio holdings, the manager may conclude that a company's business prospects will deteriorate, initiating a reduction or elimination of the position. This approach may be called a **deteriorating fundamentals** sell discipline.

Another group of sell disciplines is more rule driven. A value investor purchasing a stock based on its low P/E multiple may choose to sell if the multiple reaches its historical average. This approach may be called a **valuation-level sell discipline.** Also rule based are **down-from-cost, up-from-cost,** and **target price** sell disciplines. As an example of a down-from-cost sell discipline, the manager may decide at the time of purchase to sell any stock in the portfolio once it has declined 15 percent from its purchase price; this strategy is a kind of stop-loss measure. An up-from-cost may specify at purchase a percent or absolute gain that will trigger a sale. At the time of purchase, the manager may specify a target price, representing an estimate of intrinsic value, and the stock reaching that price triggers a sale.

The manager may use a combination of sell disciplines. Sales generate typically generate realized capital gains or losses. Thus, the implications of a sell discipline need to be evaluated on an after-tax basis for tax-sensitive investors such as private wealth investors and certain institutional investors such as insurance companies.

So how much trading in a portfolio is normal? To answer that question, we need to understand what drives the manager's stock selection. Ultimately, the nature of the ideas motivating the purchase should determine what level of turnover is reasonable. Value investors frequently have relatively low turnover; they buy cheap stocks hoping to reap a longer-term reward. Annual turnover levels for a value manager typically range from 20 percent to 80 percent.[64] Growth managers are trying to capitalize on earnings growth and stability. Company earnings are reported quarterly, semiannually, or annually, depending on the stock's country

[64]This level of turnover translates to a holding period of between 1.25 and 5 years.

of domicile. In any case, it is easy to understand that a growth portfolio would generally tend to have higher turnover than value—a range of 60 percent to several hundred percent for more short-term oriented investors.

6. SEMIACTIVE EQUITY INVESTING

Semiactive strategies (also known as *enhanced index* or *risk-controlled active* strategies) are designed for investors who want to outperform their benchmark while carefully managing their portfolio's risk exposures. An enhanced index portfolio is designed to perform better than its benchmark index without incurring much additional risk. The portfolio manager creates such a portfolio by making use of his investment insights while neutralizing the portfolio's risk characteristics inconsistent with those insights. Although tracking risk (also called *active risk*) will increase, the enhanced indexer believes that the incremental returns more than compensate for the small increase in risk. Such a portfolio is expected to perform better than the benchmark on a risk-adjusted basis. As Exhibit 7-3 showed, enhanced indexing strategies with their strict control of tracking risk have tended to have the highest information ratios.

Semiactive equity strategies come in two basic forms: derivatives based (also called synthetic) and stock based. Derivatives-based semiactive equity strategies intend to provide exposure to the desired equity market through a derivative and the enhanced return through something other than equity investments. A common and straightforward derivatives-based semiactive equity strategy is to equitize a cash portfolio and then attempt to add value by altering the duration of the underlying cash.[65] For example, one simple approach could be to vary the duration between 90-day bills (cash) and 3-year notes based on yield curve slope. When this segment of the yield curve slopes steeply, the manager should invest in longer-duration fixed income, because the higher yield compensates the investor for the increased risk. When the slope is flat, the manager should stay short because no increased yield exists for investing in longer maturities. In this way, a portfolio manager can attempt to achieve some incremental return over cash from the short-term fixed-income portfolio while obtaining equity exposure through the futures market, thereby creating an enhanced index fund.

Enhanced indexing strategies based on stock selection attempt to generate alpha by identifying stocks that will either outperform or underperform the index. Risk control is imposed in order to limit the degree of individual stock underweighting or overweighting and the portfolio's exposure to factor risks and industry concentrations. The resulting portfolio is intended to look like the benchmark in all respects except in those areas on which the manager explicitly wishes to bet.

One way of thinking about an enhanced index stock-selection strategy versus traditional active management involves considering the investment manager's frame of reference. A traditional active manager begins with a pool of investment capital, tries to identify stocks that will appreciate the most, and includes those in the portfolio. Whatever that manager's benchmark, if the manager is uninformed about a particular stock, she will not hold it in the portfolio. In an enhanced index stock selection strategy, the neutral portfolio is the

[65]To equitize is to go long sufficient futures contracts to provide equity exposure to the underlying cash investment. For example, to equitize cash using a $10 million cash portfolio with S&P 500 futures, divide $10 million by the notional value of each S&P 500 contract to determine how many long position contracts are required. (In practice, a small adjustment called "tailing" is made to this calculation to account for the time value of money on the daily futures marks received or paid. A discussion of tailing is outside the scope of this chapter.)

benchmark. If the manager has no opinion about a given stock, that manager holds the stock at its benchmark weight. Every portfolio position is evaluated relative to the benchmark weight.

How do semiactive equity managers try to generate alpha using stock selection? Mostly, they do it the same way traditional active managers do. They may look at broad themes relating to a company's valuation or growth. They may also build complex models to process vast quantities of information in their quest for alpha. But the bottom line is that these portfolio managers are essentially active managers who build portfolios with a high degree of risk control.

In addition to a high degree of risk control, another reason for the popularity of enhanced index portfolios can be explained in terms of Grinold and Kahn's **Fundamental Law of Active Management.**[66] The law states that:

$$\text{IR} \approx \text{IC}\sqrt{\text{Breadth}} \tag{7-1}$$

Translated, this means that the information ratio (IR) is approximately equal to what you know about a given investment (the **information coefficient** or IC)[67] multiplied by the square root of the investment discipline's breadth, which is defined as the number of independent, active investment decisions made each year. Therefore, a lower-breadth strategy necessarily requires more accurate insight about a given investment to produce the same IR as a strategy with higher breadth. Well-executed enhanced indexed strategies may have a relatively high combination of insight and breadth, resulting from the disciplined use of information across a wide range of securities that differ in some important respects. (Note, however, that the number of *independent* decisions available per period does not *necessarily* increase with the size of the research universe.)

EXAMPLE 7-12 Illustration of the Fundamental Law of Active Management

Gerhardt Holz is evaluating two investment managers:

- Manager A follows 500 stocks with annual forecasts and the IC for each of the forecasts is 0.03.
- Manager B follows 100 stocks with annual forecasts, and the IC for each of the forecasts is twice that of Manager A's security forecasts.

Based only on the above information, which manager should Holz select?

Solution: Manager A's breadth of 500 and IC of 0.03 translates into an information ratio of approximately $0.03\sqrt{500} = 0.67$ (on an annual basis). Manager B's breadth of 100 and IC of 0.06 translates into an information ratio of approximately $0.06\sqrt{100} = 0.60$ (on an annual basis). Based only on the information given, Holz would select Manager A.

[66] See Grinold and Kahn (2000) for a complete development.

[67] The information coefficient is more formally defined as the correlation between forecast return and actual return. In essence, it measures the effectiveness of investment insight.

A semiactive stock-selection approach has several possible limitations. The first is that any technique that generates positive alpha may become obsolete as other investors try to exploit it. A successful enhanced indexer is always innovating. Also, quantitative and mathematical models derived from analysis of historical returns and prices may be invalid in the future. Markets undergo secular changes, lessening the effectiveness of the past as a guide to the future. Markets also occasionally undergo shocks that, at least temporarily, render forecasting or risk models ineffective. Example 7-13 illustrates a comparison made in terms of alpha and tracking risk.[68]

EXAMPLE 7-13 Derivatives-Based versus Stock-Based Semiactive Strategies

Heidi Erikson is an investment officer with a large Swedish pension plan. Her supervisor is thinking about investing in an enhanced index product focused on Japanese equities benchmarked against the Index. He asks Erikson to investigate the various alternative approaches. Exhibit 7-20 presents her findings.

EXHIBIT 7-20 Semiactive Alternatives

	Expected Alpha	Tracking Risk
Stock-based semiactive	1.2%	2.7%
Derivative-based semiactive	1.0	2.1

Using the information given, address the following:

1. Contrast stock-based and derivative-based semiactive investment strategies.
2. State an appropriate quantitative criterion for evaluating alternative semiactive approaches.
3. Recommend and justify a semiactive approach for the pension plan.

Solution to Problem 1: A stock-based semiactive approach involves controlled under- and overweighting of securities relative to their index weights. This approach attempts to pick up active return through equity insights. By contrast, a derivative-based semiactive approach involves using derivatives to equitize cash and attempting to pick up active return by adjusting the duration of the fixed-income position.

Solution to Problem 2: The information ratio (IR), defined as mean active return divided by tracking risk, is the appropriate quantitative criterion for evaluating alternative active strategies because it permits comparison based on the mean active return gained for bearing a unit of active risk in each strategy.

[68] In the example, the use of alpha rather than active return in calculating the information ratio means only that the portfolio's benchmark has been matched in terms of systematic risk.

Solution to Problem 3: The stock-based semiactive strategy has an IR of 1.2/2.7 = 0.44 versus 1/2.1 = 0.48 for the derivative-based strategy. Because it has the higher information ratio, based only on the information given, Erikson should recommend using a derivative-based strategy.

7. MANAGING A PORTFOLIO OF MANAGERS

When investing a pool of assets, every investor must decide first on the overall asset allocation of the investments—which asset classes to use and how much to invest in each. The investor then needs to decide how to invest the assets within each class. Should the investor use index funds or have the money managed actively? What is the correct level of active risk? How many managers should be used?

When developing an asset allocation policy, the investor seeks an allocation to asset classes that maximizes expected total return subject to a given level of *total* risk. The framework of optimizing allocations to a group of managers (in this context, equity managers within the equity allocation) takes a parallel form, but with the investor now maximizing active return for a given level of active risk determined by his level of aversion to active risk:[69]

$$\underset{\text{by choice of managers}}{\text{Maximize}} \quad U_A = r_A - \lambda_A \sigma_A^2 \qquad (7\text{-}2)$$

where

U_A = expected utility of the active return of the manager mix
r_A = expected return of the manager mix
λ_A = the investor's trade-off between active risk and active return; measures risk aversion in active risk terms
σ_A^2 = variance of the active return

The efficient frontier specified by this objective function is drawn in active risk and active return space, because once active or semiactive managers are potentially in the mix, the investor's trade-off becomes one of active return versus active risk (the asset allocation decision determines the trade-off between total risk and return). How much active risk an investor wishes to assume determines the mix of specific managers. For example, an investor wishing to assume no active risk at all would hold an index fund. On the other hand, investors desiring a high level of active risk and active return may find their mix skewed toward some combination of higher active risk managers with little or no exposure to index funds.

[69] See Waring, Whitney, Pirone, and Castille (2000), on which this discussion is based. The objective function shown does not consider fees and other costs associated with the mix of managers. Investment management fees and custody costs also must be considered, and these will be higher for active and semiactive managers than for index funds. One way of incorporating costs into the optimization is simply to subtract them from each manager's expected returns.

EXHIBIT 7-21 Portfolio Statistics

	Expected Active Return	Expected Tracking Risk
Index	0.0%	0%
Semiactive	1.5	2
Active A	2.0	3
Active B	3.0	5
Active C	4.0	8

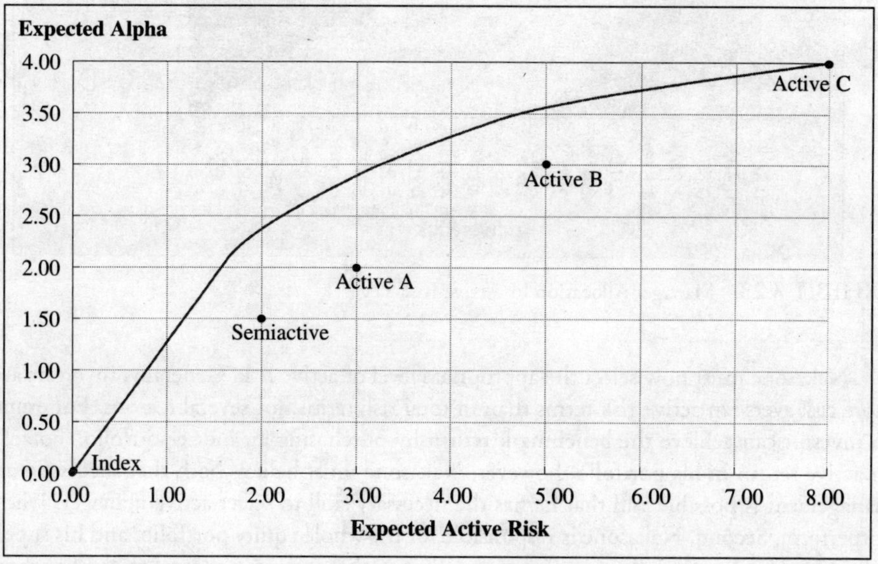

EXHIBIT 7-22 Efficient Frontier of Managers

Take the hypothetical case of Yasu Nakasone, an investment officer with the pension fund of RBG Electronics. Nakasone wants to invest ¥60 billion in Japanese equities benchmarked to TOPIX. He is considering the managers shown in Exhibit 7-21. The active managers and semiactive managers follow distinct investment styles.[70]

For his analysis, Nakasone assumes that all five managers' active returns are uncorrelated; he generates the efficient frontier in Exhibit 7-22 using a mean–variance optimizer. The question Nakasone must ask himself is how much active risk he wishes to take in the aggregate equity portfolio. The answer will help him determine the required manager mix.

In addition to generating the efficient frontier, Nakasone has also put together a "waterfall" chart (Exhibit 7-23) that breaks down manager mix for each level of active risk.

[70]Because these investment managers have different investment styles, the assumption of uncorrelated alphas made subsequently is reasonable. The model also applies if alphas are correlated, although the details will be more complex.

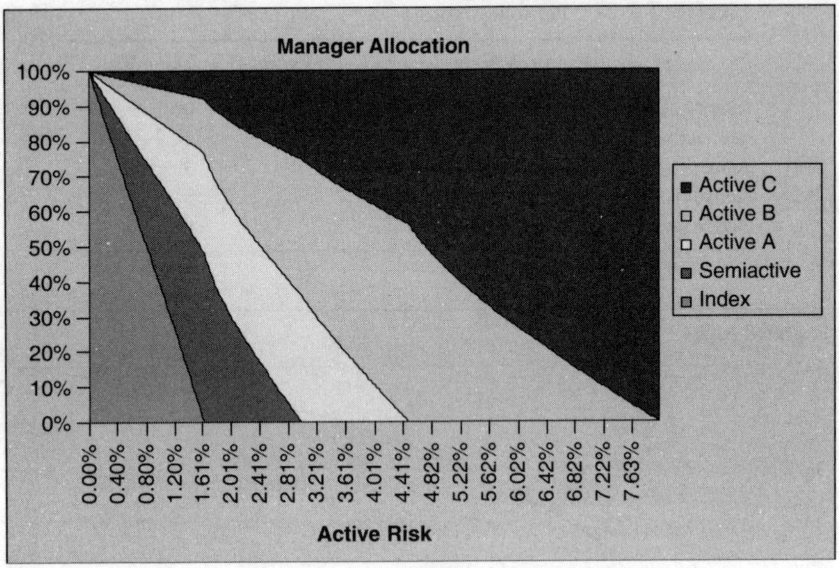

EXHIBIT 7-23 Manager Allocation by Active Risk Level

Nakasone must now select the appropriate level of active risk. Generally, investors are far more risk averse in active risk terms than in total risk terms, for several reasons. For example, an investor can achieve the benchmark return by purchasing an index portfolio. To achieve an active return in his portfolio, however, Nakasone must believe both that successful active management is possible and that he has the necessary skill to select active managers who will outperform. Second, Nakasone is responsible for the whole equity portfolio, and his superiors will judge him based on how well the overall portfolio performs relative to the benchmark. Successful active management is difficult, and many who attempt it underperform.[71] This fact produces a sort of institutional conservatism on the part of many investors. Finally, Nakasone realizes that as one moves up on the efficient frontier assuming more active risk, less manager diversification exists. For institutional investors, an overall active risk budget (target) in the range of 1.5 percent to 2.5 percent is fairly typical.[72]

Nakasone decides that he is willing to assume only 1.51 percent active risk, leading him to select the portfolio shown in Exhibit 7-24.

Despite its relatively modest level of active risk, this manager mix is expected to produce an active return of 1.92 percent, leading to a very strong IR of 1.27. The active return for the overall portfolio is a weighted average of the active returns for the individual managers.

$$\text{Portfolio active return} = \sum_{i=1}^{n} h_{Ai} r_{Ai}$$

where

h_{Ai} = weight assigned to the ith manager
r_{Ai} = active return of the ith manager

[71]The average actively managed dollar, yen, euro, etc. must necessarily underperform, per Sharpe (1991).
[72]See Waring et al. (2000).

EXHIBIT 7-24 RBG
Pension Fund Manager Mix

	Allocation
Index	8%
Semiactive	44
Active A	26
Active B	14
Active C	8

The active risk is a bit more complex. Recall that Nakasone assumes the active returns are uncorrelated. Therefore,

$$\text{Portfolio active risk} = \sqrt{\sum_{i=1}^{n} h_{Ai}^2 \sigma_{Ai}^2}$$

where

h_{Ai} = the weight assigned to the ith manager
σ_{Ai} = the active risk of the ith manager

The portfolio active risk in this case is the square root of the weighted sum of the individual managers' variances.[73]

7.1. Core Satellite

The type of portfolio that Nakasone constructed in the previous section is referred to as a **core-satellite portfolio.**[74] Specifically, 52 percent of the overall portfolio—the index and semiactive managers—constitutes the core holding, and the three active managers represent a ring of satellites around this core. When we apply the optimization shown in Equation 7-2 to a group of equity managers that includes effective indexers and/or enhanced indexers and successful active managers (as judged by information ratios), a core-satellite portfolio is a likely result.

Core-satellite portfolios can be constructed using Nakasone's rigorous approach or much more simply, as demonstrated in Example 7-14 below. In either case, the objective is to anchor a strategy with either an index portfolio or an enhanced index portfolio and to use active mangers opportunistically around that anchor to achieve an acceptable level of active return while mitigating some of the active risk associated with a portfolio consisting entirely of active managers. The index or enhanced index portfolios used in the core generally should resemble as closely as possible the investor's benchmark for the asset class. The satellite portfolios may also be benchmarked to the overall asset class benchmark, but there is greater latitude for them to have different benchmarks as well (e .g., having a growth or value focus rather than the more likely core benchmark for the asset class.)

[73]Had the active returns been correlated, the portfolio active risk equation would also have included covariance terms under the square root sign.

[74]Core-satellite is sometimes discussed as an approach to overall asset allocation in which certain asset classes are held in a passively managed core while others (believed to be inefficiently priced) are held in actively managed satellites. See Singleton (2005). The text discusses the concept in terms of allocating assets within a single asset class, another frequent usage of the term.

EXAMPLE 7-14 A Pension Fund's Information Ratio and Tracking Risk Objectives

Jim Smith manages the international equity portion of the pension portfolio of ACME Minerals, a large Australian mining company. Smith is responsible for a portfolio of A$700 million of non-Australian equities. Smith's annual compensation is related to the performance of this portfolio versus the MSCI World ex-Australia Index, the benchmark for the pension portfolio's international equity portion. He has hired the following managers with expected alphas and active risk shown (see Exhibit 7-25).

EXHIBIT 7-25 Portfolio Managers' Characteristics

	AUM (millions)	Expected Alpha	Expected Tracking Risk
Manager A	A$400	0%	0%
Manager B	100	2	4
Manager C	100	4	6
Manager D	100	4	6

All four managers' alphas are uncorrelated and are measured against the MSCI World ex-Australia benchmark.

The pension fund's trustees have stated objectives of achieving an information ratio of 0.6 or greater, with tracking risk of no more than 2 percent a year. An optimization based on Equation 7-2 results in weights on Managers A, B, C, and D of 4/7, 1/7, 1/7, and 1/7, respectively. Based only on the information given, address the following:

1. Identify the investment approach of Manager A.
2. Characterize the structure of the optimal portfolio of managers.
3. Evaluate whether the optimal portfolio of managers is expected to meet the trustees' investment objectives.

Solution to Problem 1: Because Manager A has expected tracking risk of 0 percent, we can infer that this manager is an indexer.

Solution to Problem 2: The portfolio of managers represents a core-satellite portfolio. An indexed investment (Manager A) represents more than half the portfolio's value and functions as the core. Actively managed portfolios (Managers B, C, and D) represent the satellite portfolios surrounding the core.

Solution to Problem 3: We need to calculate the expected alpha and active tracking risk for the portfolio of managers to evaluate whether this portfolio meets the trustees' information ratio and tracking risk objectives. The portfolio's expected alpha is

$$(4/7)(0\%) + (1/7)(2\%) + (1/7)(4\%) + (1/7)(4\%) = 1.43\%$$

The portfolio's tracking risk is

$$[(4/7)^2 0^2 + (1/7)^2 (4\%)^2 + (1/7)^2 (6\%)^2 + (1/7)^2 (6\%)^2]^{1/2} = 1.34\%$$

Tracking risk of 1.34 percent satisfies the trustees' objective of tracking risk of no more than 2 percent annually. The information ratio of 1.43%/1.34% = 1.07 exceeds the target of 0.6. Thus the portfolio of managers meets both the information ratio and tracking risk requirements of the trustees. Note that the tracking risk calculation used the assumption that the managers' alphas are uncorrelated.

Example 7-14 assumed that the managers under consideration were all benchmarked to the benchmark for the overall international equity allocation—that is, all of the managers are essentially broad capitalization market-oriented managers. In reality, investors often wish to consider managers that are either value or growth and perhaps specialize within a given range of market capitalization. To evaluate such managers, it is useful to divide their total active return into two components:

1. Manager's return − Manager's normal benchmark = **Manager's "true" active return**
2. Manager's normal benchmark − Investor's benchmark = **Manager's "misfit" active return**

To review, the manager's normal benchmark (normal portfolio) represents the universe of securities from which a manager normally might select securities for her portfolio. The term **investor's benchmark** refers to the benchmark the investor uses to evaluate performance of a given portfolio or asset class.

The standard deviation of "true" active return is called **manager's "true" active risk** (or "true" active risk); the standard deviation of "misfit" active return is **manager's "misfit" risk** (or "misfit" risk). The manager's total active risk, reflecting both "true" and "misfit" risk, is:

$$\text{Manager's total active risk} = [(\text{Manager's "true" active risk})^2 + (\text{Manager's "misfit" active risk})^2]^{1/2}$$

The most accurate measure of the manager's risk-adjusted performance is the IR computed as (Manager's "true" active return)/(Manager's "true" active risk).

The "true"/"misfit" distinction has two chief uses: One relates to performance appraisal, and the other relates to optimizing a portfolio of managers. We can illustrate the technically less complex of these two uses, that related to performance appraisal, using the numbers given in Exhibit 7-25 in Example 7-14, and the following additional facts:

- Manager C is a value-oriented manager.
- The MSCI World ex-Australia Value Index well represents Manager C's investment universe.
- Manager C, the MSCI World ex-Australia Index, and the MSCI World ex-Australia Value Index respectively return 12 percent, 10 percent, and 15 percent per year, for a given time period.
- Manager C's total active risk computed with respect to MSCI World ex-Australia Index is 5.5 percent annually. The manager's "misfit" risk is 4 percent annually.

Based on the second fact on page 463, the MSCI World ex-Australia Value Index is appropriate as Manager C's normal benchmark. By contrast, the MSCI World ex-Australia Index is the investor's benchmark. Although Manager C appears to outperform the asset class benchmark (12 percent versus 10 percent), in reality the manager has not done such a great job:

- The manager's "true" active return is 12% − 15% = −3%.
- The manager's "misfit" active return is 15% − 10% = 5%.

Measuring the manager's results against the normal benchmark rather than the investor's benchmark far more accurately evaluates performance. The positive "misfit" active return indicates that the manager would be expected to outperform the asset class benchmark for the simple reason that value stocks outperformed the investor's benchmark. The manager's negative "true" active return, however, indicates that the manager actually underperformed a passive investment in the normal benchmark. The manager's performance relative to the investor's benchmark reflects the sum of "true" active return and "misfit" active return and misleadingly nets to a positive value: −3% + 5% = 2%. To complete the picture, we need to calculate the manager's IR based on "true" active risk and "true" active return. Using the expression for manager's total active risk and letting X represent "true" active risk, $5.5\% = [X^2 + (4\%)^2]^{1/2}, X = 3.775\%$ is "true" active risk. The manager's "true" IR was thus quite poor: $-3\%/3.775\% = -0.7947$.

The second use of the "true"/"misfit" distinction is in optimization. By disaggregating the active risk and return into two components, it is possible to create optimal solutions that maximize total active return at every level of total active risk and that also allow for the optimal level of "misfit" risk. Although it may seem that no "misfit" risk is desired, a nonzero amount may actually be optimal, because a high level of "true" active return may more than compensate for a given level of "misfit" risk.

7.2. Completeness Fund

The Nakasone and Smith examples illustrated a rigorous approach to constructing a portfolio of managers. Some investors will construct a portfolio of active managers using an equal-weighting approach or other heuristic. Whether the active manager's normal portfolio is the overall equity benchmark or some other benchmark (especially in this latter case), the aggregate portfolio of active managers may have any number of risk exposures or biases, such as sector underweighting or overweighting, relative to the investor's overall equity benchmark. The portfolios of bottom-up stock pickers often evidence industry concentrations as an outcome of their stock selection processes rather than intentional macro bets.

In such cases, the fund sponsor should consider establishing a completeness fund for the equity portfolio. A **completeness fund,** when added to active managers' positions, establishes an overall portfolio with approximately the same risk exposures as the investor's overall equity benchmark.[75] For example, the completeness fund may be constructed with the objective of making the overall portfolio sector and/or style neutral with respect to the benchmark while attempting to retain the value added from the active managers'

[75]Completeness funds are sometimes referred to as **dynamic completion funds** or as **bias control funds.** Tierney and Winston (1990) offer an early presentation of the rationale for this technique.

stock-selection ability. The completeness portfolio may be managed passively or semiactively. This portfolio needs to be re-estimated periodically to reflect changes in the active portfolios.

One drawback of completeness portfolios is that they essentially seek to eliminate misfit risk. As stated above, a nonzero amount of misfit risk may be optimal. In seeking to eliminate misfit risk through a completeness fund, a fund sponsor may be giving up some of the value added from the stock selection of the active managers.

7.3. Other Approaches: Alpha and Beta Separation

Another method which may be used to build a portfolio of multiple managers involves what has become known as **alpha and beta separation.** A typical long active equity portfolio provides an investor with exposure to the market (beta) as well as to the active manager's stock selection ability (alpha). As previously discussed, a market-neutral long–short strategy is a pure alpha strategy with no beta exposure.

For example, an investor might choose to hire a comparatively inexpensive index fund manager to provide beta exposure and pay explicitly for alpha by hiring a market-neutral long–short manager. The second approach adds the advantage of allowing the investor to mix and match beta and alpha in a way that long-only active management cannot accomplish. For example, an investor may need beta exposure to a relatively efficient part of the equity market (e .g., the Russell Top 200, representing the 200 largest securities in the Russell 3000) but will also want to outperform that part of the market. This may be difficult to do with long-only active management. The investor, however, may choose to hire a Russell Top 200 index fund manager and a manager that seeks to add 4 percent annual alpha by managing a long–short portfolio of Japanese equities. Assuming that the long–short portfolio is also market neutral (i.e., beta of zero with respect to the Japanese equity market) and that the long–short manager delivers on the alpha target, the strategy becomes a Russell Top 200 + 4% strategy. This is an example of **portable alpha**—that is, alpha available to be added to a variety of systematic risk exposures.

One of this approach's big advantages is that an investor can obtain the beta exposure desired while broadening the opportunity set for alpha to cover styles and even asset classes outside the beta asset class. In the example above, the long–short manager could also have been a bond manager. Alpha and beta separation allows the investor to manage the market and active risks more effectively than if dealing solely with long-only managers. In doing so, the investor can also very clearly understand the fees being paid to capture market (inexpensive) and active (costly) returns. That said, certain markets may constrain the ability to manage long–short alpha-generating strategies. Short positions may be very costly to establish in smaller or emerging markets. Also, investors need to realize that not all long–short strategies that appear to be market neutral really are. Some may have a degree of market risk.

Some investors may be explicitly precluded from investing on a long–short basis. These investors may still be able to use portable alpha, although in a less efficient way than described above. For example, assume that an investor desires S&P 500 market exposure but has identified a capable active manager of Japanese equities benchmarked to the TOPIX index. The investor can port the manager's alpha by taking a short futures position in TOPIX and a corresponding long position in S&P 500 futures.[76] The resulting portfolio is S&P 500 plus an alpha associated with the Japanese equity portfolio.

[76]The short exposure to TOPIX can be seen as a hedge of sorts and might not violate specific pension plan restrictions in the way that an explicit net short position in an equity issue would.

8. IDENTIFYING, SELECTING, AND CONTRACTING WITH EQUITY PORTFOLIO MANAGERS

Institutional and private wealth investors face critical decisions when deciding what funds (if any) to manage themselves and, second, what investment managers to engage for the funds they delegate to outside management. Frequently, investors will work with a consultant in an investment manager search. The following sections address some of the issues that investors will face in identifying, selecting, and contracting with equity managers.

8.1. Developing a Universe of Suitable Manager Candidates

The process of developing a universe of suitable manager candidates starts with a general evaluation of the large number of investment managers, and then researching and monitoring those that are worthy of further consideration. Investment consultants typically have a research staff whose job is to collect information on investment managers and to meet with them to understand the managers' investment approach and organization. Consultants employ various tools to determine which managers have talented individuals and truly add value in their investment style.

Consultants use both qualitative and quantitative factors in evaluating investment managers. The qualitative factors include the people and organizational structure, the firm's investment philosophy, the decision-making process, and the strength of its equity research. The quantitative factors include performance comparisons with benchmarks and peer groups, as well as the measured style orientation and valuation characteristics of the firm's portfolios. At all times, the investment consultant seeks consistency between a firm's *stated* philosophy and process and its *actual* practices.

8.2. The Predictive Power of Past Performance

Anyone who invests in the stock market is well aware that the best performing stock or sector in any given year is rarely the best performer in the next. In fact, one reasonable approach to investing could be simply to sell the winners and buy the losers (although many investors tend to do the opposite). The same holds true of investment performance, which is one reason why fund managers are legally required to state in their advertisements that "past performance is no guarantee of future results."

The evidence generally supports this caution. For example, the Frank Russell Company, a multimanager investment strategies firm, found that of the 81 managers who were in the top quartile of their 293 U.S. equity manager database in 1997, only 16 remained in the top quartile in 1998, and only 7 remained in 1999. None of these original top performers in 1997 was still in the top quartile in 2000, 2001, or 2002. This result does not mean that past performance goes unexamined, however. A portfolio manager who has consistently underperformed his benchmark is unlikely to be considered for an active manager role, because an active manager is expected to generate positive alpha.

Investors and their consultants place considerable weight on an equity manager's investment process and the strength of the manager's organization. A good investment record achieved by the same set of managers over a long period, following consistent investment disciplines, is more likely to indicate future satisfactory results for the client than a record with comparable statistics but an underlying history of manager turnover and shifts in investment orientation.

8.3. Fee Structures

Investors must pay attention to the management fees of the investment managers that they hire. Absent such fees, the investor would realize exactly the same alpha that the manager achieves (after transactions costs). With management fees, the investor earns a net-of-fee alpha that is smaller and possibly negative even when the manager's alpha (gross of fees) is positive. In short, the investment management fee represents a wedge between managerial skill and investor results.[77]

Fees are typically set in one of two basic ways: ad valorem and performance based. **Ad valorem fees** are calculated by multiplying a percentage by the value of assets managed (e.g., 0.60 percent on the first £50 million, and 0.45 percent on assets above £50 million). Ad valorem fees are also called assets under management (AUM) fees.

A simple **performance-based fee** is usually specified by a combination of a base fee plus sharing percentage (e .g., 0.20 percent on all assets managed plus 20 percent of any performance in excess of the benchmark return). Performance-based fees can also include other features such as fee caps and "high water marks." A **fee cap** limits the total fee paid regardless of performance and is frequently put in place to limit the portfolio manager's incentive to aim for very high returns by taking a high level of risk. A **high water mark** is a provision requiring the portfolio manager to have cumulatively generated outperformance since the last performance-based fee was paid. As an example, ABC Investments charged a performance-based fee based on its performance in 2001. In 2002, however, the firm underperformed its benchmark and could collect only the base fee. If ABC is subject to a high water mark provision, in 2003 it will need to outperform its benchmark by an amount greater than the 2002 underperformance in order to collect a performance-based fee.

Ad valorem fees have the advantage of simplicity and predictability. If a plan sponsor must budget fees in advance, an ad valorem approach makes estimation much simpler. In contrast, performance-based fees are typically quite involved, as every term of the performance-based fee must be precisely defined. But performance-based fees—particularly symmetric incentive fees that reduce as well as increase compensation—may align the plan sponsor's interests with those of the portfolio manager by spurring the manager to greater effort. The better the manager's performance, the greater the reward for both sides. For the client, the impact of poor performance is reduced by the smaller fees paid to the investment manager. On the other hand, reliance on such arrangements can create revenue volatility for the investment manager, which might present practical issues (e.g., staff retention) when the manager performs relatively poorly in a year in which its competitors have done better.[78] A one-sided performance-based fee, by contrast, conveys a call option to the investment manager whose value can be determined by option pricing methodology and whose expected net cost to the fund sponsor may be judged relative to expected fee if a strictly ad valorem compensation contract were in place.

8.4. The Equity Manager Questionnaire

A typical equity manager questionnaire examines five key areas: organization/people, philosophy/process, resources, performance, and fees. The questionnaire creates a formal basis for directly comparing different investment firms.

[77]Ennis (2005) quantifies the extent of this wedge for various fee levels and levels of managerial skill.
[78]See Arnott (2005) for a further discussion.

In the questionnaire's first section, Organization/People, the investment firm must describe the firm's organization and who will be managing the portfolio. Equity portfolio management is a people business; nothing is more important than having the right people in place. Typical questions cover such areas as the vision of the firm, its competitive advantages, and how it defines success; the organization of the group and the role of portfolio managers, traders, and analysts; the delegation of responsibility for decisions on asset allocation, portfolio construction, research, and security selection; the structure of the compensation program, with an emphasis on the manner in which talented individuals are rewarded; the background of the professionals directly involved in managing the assets, such as prior experience, education, and professional qualifications such as the CFA designation; and finally, the length of time the team has been together and the reasons for any turnover.

The second section, Philosophy/Process, asks questions about how the equity portfolio will be managed. Typical questions concern:

- The firm's investment philosophy and the market inefficiency that it is trying to capture, along with any supporting evidence for this inefficiency.
- The research process, including whether or not a top-down analysis is applied (**top-down** analysis is analysis that proceeds from the macroeconomy to the economic sector level to the industry level to the firm level).
- The risk management function, including management and monitoring of risk and risk models.
- How the firm monitors the portfolio's adherence to its stated investment style, philosophy, and process.
- The stock selection process including unique sources of information, and how the buy or sell decision is made.
- The portfolio construction process.

The third section, Resources, looks at the allocation of resources within the organization. In particular, the focus is on the research process: how and by whom research is conducted, the outputs of this research, how the research outputs are communicated, and how the research is incorporated into the portfolio construction process. In addition, there are questions addressing any quantitative models used in research and portfolio construction, and the investments that have been made in technology. Finally, the trading function is examined in terms of turnover, traders, trading strategies, and the measurement of costs.

The fourth section, Performance, asks questions about what the equity manager considers to be an appropriate benchmark (and why) and what level of excess return is appropriate. There are also questions about how performance is evaluated within the firm, including causes of dispersion in the returns of similarly managed portfolios. The firm must then normally submit monthly or quarterly returns as well as holdings, so that the evaluator can calculate performance for all candidates in the same way.

The final section deals with fees. Questions are typically about what is included in the fee, the type of fee (ad valorem or performance based), and any specific terms and conditions relating to the fees quoted.

The equity manager questionnaire is used to identify a short list of the fund managers most suitable for the sponsor's needs. This process is followed up with face-to-face interviews (and sometimes on-site visits) to better understand the fund manager and to ask additional questions raised by any responses to the questionnaire before the final selection decision.

EXAMPLE 7-15 Equity Manager Questionnaire (Excerpt)

A. Organization, Structure, and Personnel:

1. Provide a brief history of the firm, including:
   a. The month and year of the U.S. Securities and Exchange Commission (SEC) 1940 Act registration.
   b. The month and year the subject product was introduced.
   c. Ownership structure.
2. Form of ownership (if an affiliate, designate percent of parent firm's total revenue generated by your organization).
3. If the firm is a joint venture partner, identify the percentage of ownership and revenues recognized by each partner to the combined association.
4. Provide an organizational chart diagramming the relationships between the professional staff as well as the parent–subsidiary, affiliate, or joint venture entities.
5. Describe the levels (U.S. dollar amounts) of coverage for SEC-required (17g-1) fidelity bonds, errors and omissions coverage, and any other fiduciary coverage which your firm carries. List the insurance carriers supplying the coverage.
6. During the past five years, has your organization or any of its affiliates or parent, or any officer or principal been involved in any business litigation, regulatory, or legal proceedings? If so, provide a detailed explanation and indicate the current status. Also provide complete Form ADV (Parts I and II) or explain the nature of the exemption.
7. Has your firm been the subject of an audit, censure (fine), inquiry, or administrative action by the SEC, IRS, State Attorney General, or Department of Labor in the past seven years? If so, explain findings and provide a copy, as well as evidence of any changes in procedures implemented as a result of such audit.
8. Describe in detail the material developments in your organization (changes in ownership, restructuring, personnel, business, etc.) during the past three years.
9. Provide the location and function of each of your firm's offices.
10. Provide details on the financial condition of the firm (i.e ., most recent annual report filed with the SEC).
11. Investment professionals:
    a. List all senior investment professionals and portfolio managers involved with the subject product. Please also separately provide appropriate biographical information. Highlight the person(s) who would be responsible for this account.
    b. Indicate when and why any investment professionals left or joined the firm in the last three years. In which products were they involved? For personnel who have left, indicate job titles and years with the firm. Please include all additions and departures, regardless of seniority.
    c. Discuss your organization's compensation and incentive program. How are professionals evaluated and rewarded? What incentives are provided

to attract and retain superior individuals? If equity ownership is possible, on what basis is it determined and distributed? How is the departure of a shareholder treated?

d. Describe your firm's backup procedures in the event the key investment professional assigned to this account should leave the firm.

For Items 12 through 14, please provide the following information for the years ending on June 30 from 1999 through 2004 (all in $ millions and number of accounts, counting funds as one account):

12. Total assets under management—all products.
13. Total discretionary U.S. equity assets—all products.
14. Total assets in subject product—distinguish between retail and institutional.
15. Provide the names and the size of the mandate for your top five clients.
16. Provide the names and the size of your top five clients in the strategy under review.
17. List all clients (or the number and type) and asset amounts gained in the subject product during the past five years as of June 30, 2004.
18. List all clients (or the number and type) and asset amounts lost in the subject product during the past five years as of June 30, 2004.
19. Identify three clients that have terminated accounts in the subject product during the past three years that can be contacted as references. Provide the firm name, contact person and title, phone number, product name and reason for termination.
20. Provide the client name, address, phone number, contact name, title, and account type (e .g., defined benefit, defined contribution, endowment) of three accounts, who are invested in the subject product that can be contacted as references. Also indicate the length of your relationship and AUM for each reference.

B. Investment Philosophy, Policy, and Process:

1. Describe your investment philosophy for the product.

    a. What market anomaly or inefficiency are you trying to capture?
    b. Why do you believe this philosophy will be successful in the future?
    c. Provide any evidence or research that supports this belief.
    d. How has this philosophy changed over time?
    e. What are the product's shortcomings or limitations?
    f. In what market environment(s) will your product have difficulty outperforming?

2. Describe your investment decision process and valuation approaches used in regard to the following:

    a. Security selection
    b. Sector selection
    c. Portfolio construction

3. Indicate what fundamental/quantitative factors are used to analyze a stock and indicate their relative importance in the decision making process. If applicable, who developed and maintains your quantitative models?
4. Describe the techniques used to identify and control overall portfolio risk. What limits/constraints do you establish, if any?
   a. What is the market liquidity criteria applied by your firm for the companies in which it invests?
   b. Provide the typical number of securities in a portfolio of $50 million, $100 million, $1 billion, and $2 billion.
   c. Describe the use of futures, options, or other derivatives (when and how much?).
5. Describe the decision process used to make sell decisions. When would your firm deviate from its sell disciplines?
6. Over what time horizon could your strategy be expected to meet performance objectives?
7. Provide the average annual portfolio turnover for the past three years and the source of this turnover.
8. Describe your firm's policy regarding cash and cash equivalents. Would your firm accept a "fully invested" mandate?
9. Describe your firm's process for executing trades. Include answers to the following:
   a. Does your firm use electronic trading systems?
   b. What guidelines do you have pertaining to dealing/trading execution parameters/costs?
   c. How are trading costs monitored? How are these costs minimized?
   d. Describe how your firm evaluates trading execution.
   e. What is the firm's average commission (cents/share) for the product in question?
   f. Does your firm trade with an affiliate broker/dealer?
10. Submit a sample portfolio (an actual portfolio) as of June 30, 2004, that reflects the investments of the product proposed for this account.
11. Provide the following characteristics as of June 30, 2004, and for the years ending 1999 through 2003:
    a. Typical number of holdings
    b. Typical turnover rate
    c. Average market capitalization
    d. Median market capitalization
    e. P/E
    f. P/B
    g. Beta
    h. Sector limitations
    i. Highest sector weightings
    j. Tracking error
    k. Since-inception information ratio

C. Research Capabilities and Resources:

1. Explain your firm's research process as it pertains to the product.
2. Rate your firm's reliance on the following sources of research; average rating should approximate 3: (1 = *very important*, 5 = *unimportant*)

    a. Internal
    b. Broker/dealer
    c. Third-party fundamental research
    d. External economists
    e. Company visits
    f. Other (explain)

3. Describe the software packages used to manage portfolios. If owned, were they internally developed and by whom? Are they internally maintained? How long have the current systems been in place?

D. Historical Performance/Risk Factors:

1. Provide your monthly gross and net-of-fees composite performance in the subject product, since the inception of the product, in an attached Microsoft Excel spreadsheet file in the following format:

	A	B	C
1	Date	Gross Returns	Net Returns
2	12/1990	1.01	0.81
3	1/1991	−3.04	−3.24
4	2/1991	5.02	4.82
5	3/1991	12.10	11.90

2. Provide a description of composite:

    a. Number of accounts and market value of assets represented in composite as of each annual period shown.
    b. Include low/high and median return for each annual period.
    c. Is composite in compliance with AIMR Performance Presentation Standards?
    d. Has composite been verified for compliance? If not, why not?
    e. Is there a period for which composite is not in compliance?

3. What benchmark is most appropriate for evaluating the performance results of your process?

E. Fee Structure:

1. Provide a proposed fee schedule for the proposed strategy, including any breakpoints. In addition, please provide a proposed fee schedule for the various portfolio sizes of: $50 million, $100 million, and $500 million.

2. Will you certify that the fee schedule provided above is the most favorable fee schedule that the firm offers for accounts of similar size? If not, please explain why.
3. Do you offer clients performance-based fees?

Example 7-16 shows a highly simplified fee proposal. In practice, fees stated as annual rate are usually paid at regular intervals during the year, and asset valuations within a given payment interval are important. For instance, in practice an ad valorem fee of 0.50 percent a year of assets under management might be billed at the end of each quarter at a rate of 0.50%/4 = 0.125%, based on the average AUM during the quarter. Nevertheless, the principles involved would the same as those illustrated.

EXAMPLE 7-16 A Fee Proposal

Helen Warburton is evaluating a fee proposal from Buckingham Equity Investors. She has been quoted both ad valorem and performance-based fees.

Ad Valorem:

First £25 million @ 0.80 percent.

Next £25 million @ 0.60 percent.

Balance @ 0.40 percent.

The above fees are payable in advance.

Performance Based:

Base fee of 0.20% of beginning AUM plus 20% of outperformance versus the FTSE All-Share Index, to be paid annually at the end of each 12-month period.

Warburton expects to invest a £100 million lump sum, and based on Buckingham's questionnaire response, she expects the firm to outperform the FTSE All-Share by 2.50 percent gross of fees. If Warburton assumes that the FTSE All-Share returns 0 percent, what fee approach should she choose? What other considerations might she make in deciding which fee structure makes more sense?

Solution: The fees for a £100 million account given Buckingham's expected performance are:

$$\text{Ad valorem: } £550,000 = (£25 \text{ million})(0.80\%) + (£25 \text{ million})(0.60\%) + (£50 \text{ million})(0.40\%)$$

$$\text{Performance based: } £700,000 = (£100 \text{ million})(0.20\%) + (£100 \text{ million})(20\%)(2.50\%)$$

The ad valorem fee is lower assuming that Buckingham delivers its expected outperformance. Investors should consider a firm's performance history when determining which approach to choose. If Buckingham's FTSE All-Share strategy has a very high information ratio, implying a high degree of consistency in annual outperformance, Warburton might prefer using an ad valorem fee because Warburton might expect to pay higher fees over time under a performance-based fee arrangement. The reverse is true if Buckingham's history of outperformance was less consistent. (Note that in setting its fee structure, Buckingham could factor in the volatility of its outperformance. This element would make both Buckingham and Warburton indifferent to the fee structure.)

9. STRUCTURING EQUITY RESEARCH AND SECURITY SELECTION

Equity research is a necessary component of both active and semiactive investing. The security selection process varies from firm to firm, but some generalities apply.

9.1. Top-Down versus Bottom-Up Approaches

Investors focusing their research primarily on macroeconomic factors or investment themes are said to use a top-down approach. For example, an investor focused on a single country might favor certain defensive industries like consumer staples and utilities if she believes the economy may be heading into a recession. Although top-down investors build portfolios from individual stocks, they want those stocks to reflect their macro insights.

A more complex top-down example might involve a global portfolio. The investor might wish to identify:

1. Themes affecting the global economy.
2. The effect of those themes on various economic sectors and industries.
3. Any special country or currency considerations.
4. Individual stocks within the industries or economic sectors that are likely to benefit most from the global themes.

Conversely, an investor focusing on company-specific fundamentals or factors such as revenues, earnings, cash flow, or new product development is said to follow a **bottom-up** approach. This investor pays attention to company specifics when doing research and building a portfolio. For example, a value investor might screen stocks based on P/E or dividend yield. His focus is on the individual company. Bottom-up investors have little interest in the state of the economy or other macro factors but rather try to put together the best portfolio of stocks based on company-specific information.

A more complex bottom-up example might also involve a global portfolio. The investor might approach the problem by:

1. Identifying factors with which to screen the investment universe (e .g., stocks in the lowest P/E quartile that also have expected above-median earnings growth).
2. Collecting further financial information on companies passing the screen.
3. Identifying companies from this subset that may be potential investments based on other company-specific criteria.

That said, many investors use some combination of the two approaches. An investor managing a global portfolio can, for example, decide which countries to favor based on a top-down analysis but build the portfolio of stocks within each country based on a bottom-up analysis. Furthermore, some analysts use technical analysis, which attempts to predict future stock prices from the time series of their past values.

9.2. Buy-Side versus Sell-Side Research

The terms *buy side* and *sell side* refer to the source of the equity research. **Buy side** refers to those who do research with the intent of assembling a portfolio, such as investment management firms. **Sell side** refers either to independent researchers who sell their work, or to investment banks/brokerage firms that use research as a means to generate business for themselves. Sell-side research is also what most people hear on TV or read about in the newspaper. Buy-side research by its very nature is generally inaccessible to those outside of the investment firm generating the research.

Sell-side and buy-side research frequently are developed in a different manner. Sell-side research is generally organized by sector/industry with a regional delineation (e.g., U.S. autos, European telecommunications, Japanese banks, etc.). Analysts work either in teams or by themselves and produce reports on individual companies and also on the industries they cover. In addition to providing information such as earnings forecasts, sell-side analysts also rate companies as buy, hold, or sell (the nomenclature varies from firm to firm).

Because buy-side research is concerned with assembling a portfolio rather than just rating a company, decisions on buy-side research are usually made through a committee structure. An analyst may investigate a particular theme or individual company, but usually an investment committee makes the decisions. The analyst prepares a report to substantiate the idea and why it should be included in the portfolio or sold; she then uses the research to persuade the investment committee.

EXAMPLE 7-17 Top Down or Bottom Up?

Maria Ramirez is watching a financial program on television in which a unit trust portfolio manager is explaining the investment approach he uses in managing the global equity unit trust. He says, "Right now, I really like Japan. The economic growth we see there looks to us like it is solid and driven as much by consumer demand as it is by capital investment. One market that we really don't like very much is the U.K., which we are avoiding because we fear further interest rate hikes by the Bank of England." From this brief statement what can Maria conclude about the portfolio manager's research approach?

Solution: The portfolio manager is employing a top-down approach, because his comments are focused exclusively on macro factors driving the British and Japanese markets. A bottom-up investor might also have favored Japan over the United Kingdom but would have emphasized that he finds more stocks that are attractive investments in one market rather than another.

9.3. Industry Classification

Many equity research departments are organized along industry or sector lines. Given the need to do sector/industry research across many countries, it is important to have a system for like companies to be classified in the same categories. Developed by Standard & Poor's and MSCI, the Global Industry Classification Standard is one representative industry classification method that does exactly this. GICS divides stocks into:

- 10 sectors (Consumer Discretionary, Consumer Staples, Energy, Financials, Health Care, Industrials, Information Technology, Materials, Telecommunication, and Utilities).
- 24 industry groups.
- 62 industries.
- 132 subindustries.

GICS assigns a company to a particular category based on the percentage of revenue derived from each of that company's businesses. The company is then categorized into one and only one sector, industry group, industry, and subindustry. For example, Michelin is included in the Consumer Discretionary Sector, the Automobiles & Components Industry Group, the Auto Components Industry, and the Tires & Rubber Subindustry. Other classification systems include:

- The Industry Classification Benchmark, proprietary to FTSE International Ltd and Dow Jones & Co., consisting of 10 industries (Oil & Gas, Basic Materials, Industrials, Consumer Goods, Health Care, Consumer Services, Telecommunications, Utilities, Financials, and Technology), 18 supersectors, 39 sectors, and 104 subsectors.
- The highly detailed North American Industry Classification System (NAICS—pronounced "nakes"), sponsored by the U.S., Canadian, and Mexican governments.

CHAPTER 8

ALTERNATIVE INVESTMENTS PORTFOLIO MANAGEMENT

Jot K. Yau, CFA

Seattle University
Seattle, Washington
and
Strategic Options Investment Advisors Ltd
Hong Kong

Thomas Schneeweis

Alternative Investment Analytics
Amherst, Massachusetts

Thomas R. Robinson, CFA

TRRobinson and Associates
Coral Gables, Florida

Lisa R. Weiss, CFA

Black Knight Ventures, Inc.
Tampa, Florida

1. INTRODUCTION

Today, many defined-benefit (DB) pension funds, endowments, foundations, and high-net-worth individuals allocate money to alternative investments in proportions comparable to those given to traditional assets, such as bonds and common equities. In doing so, such investors may be seeking risk diversification, greater opportunities to apply active management skills, or both. Portfolio managers who understand alternative investments have a substantial advantage over those who do not.

This chapter presents six groups of alternative investments: real estate, private equity, commodities, hedge funds, managed futures, and distressed securities. These six diverse asset groups cover a wide spectrum of risk and return characteristics and are the major alternative asset classes in the portfolios of most institutional and individual investors.

This chapter focuses on the distinguishing investment characteristics of alternative investments and their potential contributions in a portfolio context. Among the questions we will address in this chapter are the following:

- What types of investments are available in each market, and what are their most important differences for an investor?
- What benchmarks are available to evaluate the performance of alternative investment managers, and what are their limitations?
- What investment strategies and portfolio roles are characteristic of each alternative investment?
- What should due diligence cover? (**Due diligence** is the investigation into the details of a potential investment, including the scrutiny of operations and management and the verification of material facts.)

The chapter is organized as follows: Section 2 introduces and presents an overview of the field of alternative investments. In Sections 3 through 8, we present the six alternative asset groups. For each group, we discuss the market for the investments; benchmarks and historical performance, with a focus on the group's record as a stand-alone investment; the portfolio role of the investments and specific strategies; and issues in performance evaluation and reporting.

2. ALTERNATIVE INVESTMENTS: DEFINITIONS, SIMILARITIES, AND CONTRASTS

Alternative investments comprise groups of investments with risk and return characteristics that differ markedly from those of traditional stock and bond investments. Common features of alternative investments include

- Relative illiquidity, which tends to be associated with a return premium as compensation.
- Diversifying potential relative to a portfolio of stocks and bonds.
- High due diligence costs for the following reasons: investment structures and strategies may be complex; evaluation may draw heavily on asset-class, business-specific, or other expertise; reporting often lacks transparency.
- Unusually difficult performance appraisal because of the complexity of establishing valid benchmarks.

In addition, many professional investors believe that alternative investment markets are informationally less efficient than the world's major equity and bond markets and offer greater scope for adding value through skill and superior information.

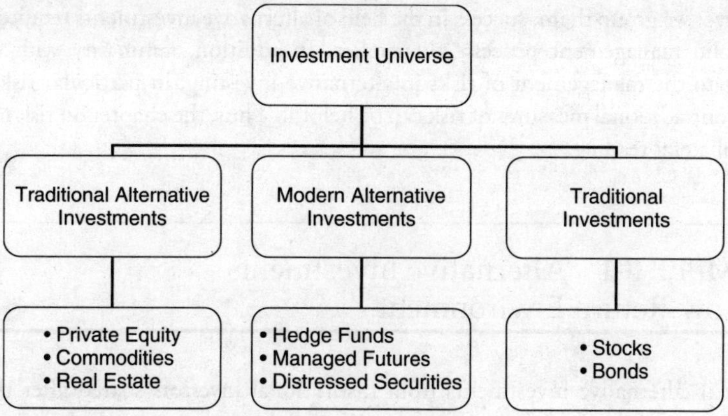

EXHIBIT 8-1 Alternative and Traditional Investments

Historically, **real estate** (ownership interests in land or structures attached to land), **private equity** (ownership interests in non-publicly-traded companies), and **commodities** (articles of commerce such as agricultural goods, metals, and petroleum) have been viewed as the primary alternatives to traditional stock and bond investments. However, in recent years, additional investments—**hedge funds** (relatively loosely regulated, pooled investment vehicles) and **managed futures** (pooled investment vehicles in futures and options on futures, frequently structured as limited partnerships)—have increasingly been considered "modern alternatives," not only to traditional investments but also to traditional *alternative* investments. The modern alternative investments are more akin to investment or trading strategies than to asset classes. Exhibit 8-1 shows alternative investments grouped according to these distinctions. In some instances, placement of an alternative investment in more than one category can be justified. For example, we discuss **distressed securities** investing separately as a distinct type of alternative investment, but it could be classified differently.[1]

The list of alternative investments discussed in this chapter is representative but by no means exhaustive. For example, some investors invest in timberland or intangibles (such as fine art), and benchmarks and professional advisory services for these and some other alternative investments have long been available.

In addition to the traditional-or-modern distinction, we can place alternative investments in three groups by the primary role they usually play in portfolios:

- Investments that primarily provide exposure to risk factors not easily accessible through traditional stock and bond investments. Real estate and (long-only) commodities might be included in this group.
- Investments that provide exposure to specialized investment strategies run by an outside manager. Hedge funds and managed futures might be placed in this category. Any value added by such investment is typically heavily dependent on the skills of the manager.
- Investments that combine features of the prior two groups. Private equity funds and distressed securities might be included in this group.

[1]Distressed securities/bankruptcy investing can be classified (1) within private equity if private debt is considered to be private equity, (2) as a subcategory of event-driven strategies under hedge funds as an alternative investment strategy, or (3) as a separate alternative investment strategy. In this chapter, we introduce it as an event-driven substrategy of hedge funds, but we discuss it separately in Section 8.

However we group them, success in the field of alternative investments requires discipline. The portfolio management process still applies. In addition, familiarity with quantitative approaches to the management of risks in alternative investing, in particular risk budgeting, and with nontraditional measures of risk can be helpful. Thus, the chapter on risk management is useful collateral reading.

EXAMPLE 8-1 Alternative Investments in a Low-Return Environment

Interest in alternative investments from institutional investors soared after the severe equity bear markets of the first years of the twenty-first century. The resulting investment environment for traditional investments was seen as "low return." Return expectations for equities were widely ratcheted down from pre-bear-market and long-term historical levels. In that environment, using the revised capital market expectations and established strategic asset allocations, many investors foresaw built-in shortfalls relative to return requirements. The problem was particularly acute for DB pension funds in countries such as Canada and the United States, where such funds have traditionally had a strong equity orientation. With declining interest rates increasing the present value of liabilities, many DB plans faced severe pressures.

The experience led a number of industry leaders to question prior investment practices in areas such as strategic asset allocation and to reexamine the role of alternative investments in meeting return objectives and, to a lesser degree perhaps, in controlling risk. Many institutional investors made new and/or higher allocations to alternative investments. Vehicles such as hedge funds proliferated to meet the demand. This trend raised issues of capacity—that is, given the market opportunities, the ability of alternative investment managers to meet performance expectations with more assets.[2] In the private wealth marketplace, alternative investments also began to be packaged and marketed to new segments, such as the "mass affluent," raising issues of suitability and appropriate due diligence processes for such investors.[3]

Who are the major investors in alternative investments? The list includes both high-net-worth individuals (who were among the pioneer investors in hedge funds) and institutional investors, although banks and insurers may face regulatory restrictions and the investment policy statements of other investors may have self-imposed limitations. The themes already mentioned play varying roles for different investors. The potential risk-diversification benefits of alternative investments have broad appeal across investor types. The possibility of enhancing

[2] See Christopher Wright, "Ripe for the Picking," *CFA Magazine*, September/October 2005, pp. 27–35. The article's title refers to the question it colorfully posed: Does alpha grow on trees, and if so, is it being overharvested?

[3] **Mass affluent** is an industry term for a segment of the private wealth marketplace that is not sufficiently wealthy to command certain individualized services (such as separately managed accounts) at many investment counseling firms. In the United States as of this writing, individuals with investable assets between US$100,000 and US$1 million would fall in this group.

returns also draws many investors to seriously consider alternative investments. Illiquidity is a limiting factor in the size of the allocation to alternative investments for investors with short investment horizons. In contrast, investors with long investment horizons, such as endowments and some DB pension funds, may be competitively well placed to earn illiquidity premiums and to make large allocations.

The costs of due diligence in alternative investments may be a limiting factor for smaller portfolios. Deutsche Bank's Equity Prime Services Group 2004 Institutional Alternative Investment Survey, with a range of respondents serving the institutional and private markets, was revealing. In the case of hedge funds, the survey found that one major investor segment, pension funds, evaluates 40 managers, on average, to make only one to three allocations per year. Another major segment, endowments, researches 90 managers, on average, to make four to six placements per year. Sixty percent of respondents took three months to complete due diligence on a hedge fund.[4] In alternative investments as in traditional investments, expenses—whether management fees or trading or operational expenses—require justification and management.

For both traditional and alternative investments, selecting active managers is a process of attempting to identify superiorly skilled or informed managers. As Example 8-2 illustrates, the set of questions the investor needs to raise in selecting active managers in any investment field has a compellingly simple logic.

EXAMPLE 8-2 How One University Endowment Evaluates Alternative Investments

The University of Virginia Investment Management Company (UVIMCO) was responsible for the investment of more than US$2.5 billion in assets as of the end of 2005. With a policy portfolio at that time giving more than a 50 percent target weighting to hedge funds, private equity, and real assets as a group, UVIMCO has accumulated considerable experience in alternative investments portfolio management. Notably, the framework of questions to which UVIMCO seeks answers applies not only to alternative investments but also to active managers in general, reflecting the unity of the investment process.[5] The chief investment officer (CIO) of UVIMCO, Christopher J. Brightman, CFA, summarized the chief points of UVIMCO's active manager selection process as follows:[6]

1. Market opportunity: What is the opportunity and why is it there? We start by studying capital markets and the types of managers operating within those markets. We identify market inefficiencies and try to understand their causes, such as regulatory structures or behavioral biases. We can rule out many broad groups of managers and strategies by simply determining that the degree of

[4]As reported by Jones (2005).

[5]UVIMCO has a focus on active management (www.virginia.edu/uvimco/IPS.htm). For investors with passive and active investment components, the first major heading in "market opportunity" might be expanded to strategy/product/market opportunity to cover, in addition to market opportunity, questions such as "Is the product what it claims to be?" that a passive investor would explore.

[6]Based on a communication of December 19, 2005.

market inefficiency necessary to support a strategy is implausible. Importantly, we consider a past history of active returns meaningless unless we understand why markets will allow those active returns to continue into the future.

2. Investment process: Who does this best and what's their edge? We identify groups of managers that seek to exploit these inefficiencies. Few, if any, important opportunities are exploited by a single manager. We study investment process and identify best practice and competitive advantages among similar managers.
3. Organization: Are all the pieces in place? Is the firm well organized and stable? Are research, trading, risk management, and operations properly staffed given the investment process and scale? Is compensation fair? Has there been turnover? What is the succession plan?
4. People: Do we trust the people? We speak at length to the principals face to face. We look for experience, intelligence, candor, and integrity. Then, we do reference checks; we speak to former bosses, colleagues, and business partners as well as current and past clients. We have real conversations with people who know the managers well and are willing to speak openly and at length. We also perform general Google and LexisNexis searches.
5. Terms and structure: Are the terms fair? Are interests aligned? Is the fund or account structured appropriately to the opportunity? How much money can or should be invested in the space? Details here vary by market, asset class, and strategy.
6. Service providers: Who supports them? We verify lawyers, auditors, prime brokers, lenders, etc. We investigate those with whom we are not familiar.
7. Documents: Read the documents! We read the prospectus or private placement memorandum. If we do not understand everything in the documents, we hire lawyers who do. We also read the audits.
8. Write-up: Prior to making a manager selection decision, we produce a formal manager recommendation discussing the above steps. The write-up ensures organized thought, informs others, and formally documents the process.

Some questions in due diligence and alternative investment selection are unique, or more acute, for advisers of private wealth clients than for institutional investors. These include:

- *Tax issues*. This is a pervasive issue in investing for individuals. In contrast to equities and bonds, with alternative investments, the adviser will frequently be dealing with partnerships and other structures that have distinct tax issues.
- *Determining suitability*. This is often more complex for an adviser to an individual client or family than for an institutional investor. The adviser often addresses multistage time horizons and liquidity needs. Client-relevant facts—for example, the time horizon—may change more suddenly than for, say, a pension fund with thousands of participants. The private client adviser also may be faced with questions of emotional as well as financial needs.
- *Communication with client*. When the adviser explores the suitability of an alternative investment with a client as part of his or her fiduciary responsibilities, the adviser will often discuss suitability with the client. The adviser then faces the difficult problem of communicating and discussing the possible role in the portfolio (and risk) of an often complex investment with a nonprofessional investor.

- *Decision risk*. As used by one authority on investing for private wealth clients, **decision risk** is the risk of changing strategies at the point of maximum loss.[7] Many advisers to private wealth clients are familiar with the issue of clients who are acutely sensitive to positions of loss at stages prior to an investment policy statement's stated time horizon(s). Of course, advisers need to do continuing evaluation of investments, but the point is that the adviser needs to evaluate whether an alternative investment not only promises to be rewarding over a given time horizon but is also acceptable at all intermediate points in time.[8] In effect, the issue relates to downside risk at all points within a time horizon and investors' reactions to it. Many alternative investments—for example, many hedge fund strategies—have complex risk characteristics. Decision risk is increased by strategies that by their nature have:
  - Frequent small positive returns but, when a large return occurs, it is more likely to be a large negative return than a large positive one[9] or
  - Extreme returns (relative to the mean return) with some unusual degree of frequency.[10]
- *Concentrated equity position of the client in a closely held company*. For some clients, ownership in a closely held company may represent a substantial part of wealth. The adviser needs to be particularly sensitive to an investment's effect on the client's risk and liquidity position. For example, is a private equity fund suitable for the investor? The issues of concentrated risk and illiquidity also arise for concentrated positions in public equities with built-in capital gains, although hedging and monetization strategies are available. (These strategies are discussed in the chapter on monitoring and rebalancing.) Although a client's residences are often viewed separately from the client's investable portfolio, a similar issue arises in real estate investment vis-à-vis wealth represented by residences. Problems of this type form an interface of suitability, tax, and asset allocation issues.

In discussing individual alternative investments, we will sometimes provide a perspective on what effect an alternative investment would have on the risk and expected return characteristics of a stock/bond portfolio in which some of the money is shifted to the alternative investment. In some cases, we can also refer to evidence on the effects of the addition of the new alternative investment to a portfolio that already includes stocks, bonds, and a different major alternative investment. This approach reflects the situation faced by many investors and is a type of exercise that can be informative.

In many cases, we give evidence based on data relating to the period 1990 to 2004.[11] *Here a caution is appropriate*: In any forward-looking exercise, the investor needs to evaluate the differences between current or forecasted economic fundamentals and those of any selected

[7] See Brunel (2004).

[8] Brunel (2003).

[9] Technically, such a strategy would be said to have *negatively skewed returns*.

[10] Technically, such a strategy would be said to have *high kurtosis*. To summarize using the language of statistics, many investors are presumed to want *positive* skewness and *moderate or low kurtosis* (the standard for moderate is the kurtosis of a normal distribution). For more details on these statistical concepts, see Chapter 3 of DeFusco (2004). In discussions of alternative investments in trade publications as well as in outlets such as the *Financial Analysts Journal* and the *Journal of Wealth Management*, the practitioner will encounter these statistical terms, which are covered in the CFA Institute's curriculum, and we will use them occasionally in this chapter.

[11] Hedge funds have reliable data going back only to 1990. We chose to be consistent on the starting point for the sake of comparability across investment types.

historical period used in the analysis. In addition, the results for any relatively short period can be affected by short-term dislocations, such as currency crises.

Overall, the 1990 to 2004 period was a time of historically low and stable or declining interest rates and inflation in the United States and many developed markets. The beginning year was recessionary in the United States. A long expansion followed in the United States and many developed countries (with the notable exception of Japan), but at least three dislocations with worldwide effects occurred.[12] In the United States and some other major markets, an exceptionally long equity bull market (1991 to 1999 inclusive) was followed by an extended bear market.[13] The year 2001 was recessionary in the United States, whereas 2002 to 2004 were recovery years. The period 1990 to 2004 covers one full business cycle for the United States and many developed markets.

EXAMPLE 8-3 Alternative Investments and Core–Satellite Investing

A way of thinking about allocating money known as **core satellite** seeks to define each investment's place in the portfolio in relation to specific investment goals or roles. A traditional core–satellite perspective places competitively priced assets, such as government bonds and/or large-capitalization stocks, in the core. Because alpha is hard to obtain with such assets, the core may be managed in a passive or risk-controlled active manner. (Informally, *alpha* is the return to skill.) In the satellite ring would go investments designed to play special roles, such as to add alpha or to diminish portfolio volatility via low correlation with the core. Alternative investments would be in the satellite ring for most investors.[14]

In a 2005 paper, Leibowitz and Bova championed an alternative position that would place alternative investments in an "alpha core" at their maximum allowable percentages and then add stocks and bonds as "swing assets" to get a portfolio that best reflected the desired balance between return and risk.[15] The traditional viewpoint takes traditional assets as the centerpiece, whereas the Leibowitz–Bova position builds the portfolio around alternative investments. The Leibowitz–Bova perspective is an example of the ferment in investment thinking mentioned in Example 8-1.

Having provided a bird's-eye view of the field of alternative investments, we use the following sections to analyze each in detail, beginning with real estate.

[12]The dislocations were the Mexican currency crisis of 1994, the Asian financial crisis of 1997, and the Russian debt crisis of 1998.

[13]U.S. equities experienced a record nine-year string of positive-return years (1991–1999), including six years (1991 and 1995 to 1999) of plus 20 percent returns. This period was followed by a post-1941 record string of three negative-return years (2000 to 2002).

[14]See Singleton (2005).

[15]In the Leibowitz–Bova approach, the term *alpha* in *alpha core* strictly refers not to a return to skill or risk-adjusted excess return, as in standard finance theory, but to a type of return–risk enhancement that may be available relative to a more traditional asset allocation approach.

3. REAL ESTATE

As one of the earliest of the traditional alternative investments, real estate plays an important role in institutional and individual investor portfolios internationally. The focus of our discussion is *equity investments* in real estate (covered in the definition given earlier). Investing in such instruments as mortgages, securitizations of mortgages, or hybrid debt/equity interests (e.g., mortgages in which the lender's interest includes participation in any appreciation of the underlying real estate) are not covered here.

3.1. The Real Estate Market

Both individual and institutional investors have had long-standing involvement in the real estate market. For centuries, individual investors have owned interests in real estate, primarily in the form of residential and agricultural properties. In the United States, institutional investors ventured into real estate in the late 1970s and early 1980s as they sought to diversify their portfolios and hedge against inflation. By the late 1980s, the performance of real estate had become lackluster as a result of volatile changes in U.S. tax policies, deregulation in the savings and loan industry, and the onset of risk-based capital regulations. These events culminated in the real estate crash of the late 1980s and early 1990s. Outside the United States, real estate investment has always been an important part of institutional as well as individual portfolios. At the beginning of the twenty-first century, individual and institutional investors continue to focus on the potential return enhancement and risk-diversification benefits of real estate investments in a portfolio of stocks, bonds, and frequently, other alternative investments.

3.1.1. Types of Real Estate Investments

Investors may participate in real estate directly and indirectly (which is sometimes called *financial ownership*). Direct ownership includes investment in residences, business (commercial) real estate, and agricultural land.

Indirect investment includes investing in:

- Companies engaged in real estate ownership, development, or management, such as homebuilders and real estate operating companies (which are in the business of owning such real estate assets as office buildings); such companies would be in the Global Industrial Classification System's (GICS) and FTSE Industry Classification Benchmark's real estate management and development subsector.
- **Real estate investment trusts** (REITs), which are publicly traded equities representing pools of money invested in real estate properties and/or real estate debt.
- **Commingled real estate funds** (CREFs), which are professionally managed vehicles for substantial commingled (i.e., pooled) investment in real estate properties.
- Separately managed accounts, which are often offered by the same real estate advisers sponsoring CREF.
- **Infrastructure funds,** which in cooperation with governmental authorities, make private investment in public infrastructure projects—such as roads, tunnels, schools, hospitals, and airports—in return for rights to specified revenue streams over a contracted period.

Investments in real estate management and development subsector shares and in REITS are both made through the public stock markets. REITs, however, unlike real estate management and development shares, essentially function as conduits to investors for the cash flows from the underlying real estate holdings. The list of markets in which REITs are available includes

Australia, Belgium, Canada, China, France, Hong Kong, Japan, the Netherlands, Singapore, South Korea, and the United States.

Equity REITs own and manage such properties as office buildings, apartment buildings, and shopping centers. Shareholders receive rental income and income from capital appreciation if the property is sold for a gain. **Mortgage REITs** own portfolios in which more than 75 percent of the assets are mortgages. Mortgage REITs lend money to builders and make loan collections; shareholders receive interest income and capital appreciation income from improvement in the prices of loans. **Hybrid REITs** operate by buying real estate and by acquiring mortgages on both commercial and residential real estate.

REITs securitize illiquid real estate assets; their shares are listed on stock exchanges and over the counter. REITs permit smaller investors to gain real estate exposure. Exchange-traded funds, mutual funds, and traded closed-end investment companies allow investors to obtain a professionally managed diversified portfolio of real estate securities with a relatively small outlay.

CREFs include open-end funds and closed-end funds (i.e., funds that are closed to new investment after an initial period). Institutional and wealthy individual investors use these private real estate funds to access the real estate expertise of a professional real estate fund manager in selecting, developing, and realizing the value of real estate properties. In contrast to open-end funds, closed-end funds are usually leveraged and have higher return objectives; they operate by opportunistically acquiring, repositioning, and disposing of properties. Individually managed separate accounts are also an important alternative for investors.

In an infrastructure investment, a private company—or, more frequently, a consortium of private companies—designs, finances, and builds the new project (e.g., a road or hospital) for public use. The consortium maintains the physical infrastructure over a period that often ranges from 25 to 30 years. The public sector (via the government) leases the infrastructure and pays the consortium an annual fee for the use of the completed project over the contracted period. Thus, the public sector avoids the need to issue debt or raise taxes to finance infrastructure development. The public sector staffs the infrastructure and ensures safety. The projects are financed through bond issuance by the consortium as well as by an equity investment. The consortium will often want to pull its equity capital out of a project for reinvestment in other projects. It can do this by selling its interest to investors through a variety of investment structures. Public/private infrastructure investment has been classified under real estate, under private equity, and also as a distinct alternative investment class. Infrastructure investment was pioneered in the United Kingdom in 1992 (as the Private Financing Initiative) and is a rapidly growing alternative investment segment in North America, Western Europe, and Asia. One estimate as of early 2006 is that in the United Kingdom alone, there are more than 700 public/private infrastructure projects totaling US$100 billion in value.[16]

3.1.2. Size of the Real Estate Market

Estimates have been made that real estate represents one third to one half of the world's wealth, although figures are hard to document. In the United States, as of the end of 2005, real estate owned by households was valued at US$19.8 trillion and represented approximately one third of total assets (tangible and financial) of U.S. households.

According to one report, U.S. real estate held in U.S. investment portfolios is estimated to be worth US$4.5 trillion.[17] According to the National Association of Real Estate Investment Trusts (NAREIT), the market capitalization of all publicly traded REITs in the United States

[16] Jacobius (2006a).

[17] See Broad (2005).

was more than US$300 billion in 2004 and the market capitalization of REITs traded in Canada was about US$13 billion in the same year.

3.2. Benchmarks and Historical Performance

In this section, we discuss the performance measurement of real estate investments by using publicly available information. Performance of private equity in real estate may vary and does not necessarily correlate closely with the benchmarks discussed here. More importantly, it has been observed that the real estate market lags behind publicly traded real estate securities.

3.2.1. Benchmarks Exhibit 8-2 shows some of the popular real estate indices for selected countries. The principal benchmark used to measure the performance of direct real estate investment in the United States is the National Council of Real Estate Investment Fiduciaries (NCREIF) Property Index. The NCREIF Index is a quarterly benchmark for real estate covering a sample of commercial properties owned by large U.S. institutions. The NCREIF Index is essentially value weighted and includes subindices grouped by real estate sector (apartment, industrial, office, and retail) and geographical region. Property appraisals largely determine the values in the NCREIF Index because real estate properties change ownership relatively infrequently. Property appraisals are also conducted infrequently (typically once a year), so appraisal-based property values exhibit remarkable inertia. Therefore, returns calculated solely on percentage changes in the index suffer from a number of deficiencies, including the tendency to underestimate volatility in underlying values.[18] However, methods have been developed to "unsmooth" or correct for this bias.[19] Recently, a transaction-based index has been developed based on NCREIF data and the use of econometrics to address the issue of infrequent market transactions.

The principal benchmark used to represent indirect investment in real estate is the index compiled by the NAREIT. Begun in 1972, the NAREIT Index is a real-time, market-cap-weighted index of all REITs actively traded on the New York Stock Exchange and American Stock Exchange. NAREIT also computes a monthly index based on month-end share prices of REITs that own and manage real estate assets, or equity REITs. NAREIT publishes several other indices, including a monthly index of REITs that specialize in acquiring various types of mortgage loans on many types of properties (mortgage REITs) and a monthly index based on share prices of hybrid REITs, which operate by buying real estate and by acquiring mortgages on both commercial and residential real estate. REIT indices are also published by various institutions, such as Standard & Poor's, Dow Jones, Wilshire Associates, and Morgan Stanley. The FTSE EPRA/NAREIT Global Real Estate Index listed in Exhibit 8-2 is an example of a global index of securitized real estate investment.

Both direct and indirect investments have significant measurement issues associated with them.

3.2.2. Historical Performance In the United States, direct and indirect real estate investments as represented by the major indices produced better risk-adjusted performance over the 1990 to 2004 period than did general stocks and commodities, as shown in Exhibit 8-3. In Exhibit 8-3, the "hedged" REIT return series has been purged of its overall equity market

[18]For details of the deficiencies, see Geltner (2000) and Geltner and Ling (2001).

[19]The approach used to unsmooth the NCREIF Index is based on the assumption that real estate returns follow a first-order autoregressive process as described in CISDM (2005a).

EXHIBIT 8-2 Selected Real Estate Benchmarks

Country	Name	Type	Begin Date	Frequency
Australia	Property Council of Australia index (PCA)	Appraisal based	1984	Quarterly
Canada	Institute of Canadian Real Estate Investment Managers (ICREIM)/IPD Canadian Property Index	Appraisal based	1985	Quarterly
France	Investment Property Databank (IPD)	Appraisal based	1998	Quarterly and monthly
United Kingdom	IPD	Appraisal based	1980	Quarterly and monthly
United States	NCREIF Property Index	Individual properties; appraisal based	1978	Quarterly
	Transaction-Based Index (TBI) for Institutional Commercial Property Performance (MIT Center for Real Estate)	Individual properties; based on transaction prices of properties sold from the NCREIF Index database	1984	Quarterly
	S&P REIT Composite Index	REITs	1997	Daily
	NAREIT Index	REITs	1972	Real time
	Morgan Stanley REITs Index	REITs	1996	Real time
	Wilshire real estate indices	REITs and real estate operating companies	1978	Daily
	Dow Jones REIT indices	REITs	1998	Real time
World	FTSE EPRA/NAREIT Global Real Estate Index	REITs and real estate operating companies	1989	Daily

Sources: CISDM (2005a) and Hoesli, Lekander, and Witkiewicz (2003), http://web.mit.edu/cre, www.ftse.com/indices.

return component, as represented by the S&P 500 Index. Such an adjustment is meaningful only for equity REITs because mortgage and hybrid REITs have different risk characteristics. However, equity REITs represent close to 95 percent of the composition of the index.[20] GSCI is the Goldman Sachs Commodity Index, discussed further in the section on commodities.

Note that the NCREIF Index represents nonleveraged investment only. In contrast, debt often represents 50 percent or more of the capital structure of REITs, so REITs are a levered exposure to real estate. This contrast is important for understanding the higher standard

[20]The data and methodology are described in CISDM (2005).

EXHIBIT 8-3 Real Estate Performance, 1990–2004

Measure	NAREIT Index	NAREIT Index Hedged	NCREIF Index	NCREIF Index Unsmoothed	S&P 500 Index	Lehman Aggregate Bond Index	GSCI
Annualized return	12.71%	8.96%	6.14%	7.27%	10.94%	7.70%	7.08%
Annualized std. dev.	12.74%	11.93%	3.37%	8.95%	14.65%	3.91%	19.26%
Sharpe ratio	0.66	0.39	0.55	0.33	0.45	0.87	0.15
Minimum quarterly return	−14.19%	−10.16%	−5.33%	−18.55%	−17.28%	−2.87%	−17.73%
Correlation w/NAREIT	1.00	0.94	0.00	0.21	0.35	0.18	−0.04
Correlation w/NAREIT hedged	0.94	1.00	0.00	0.24	0.00	0.14	−0.01
Correlation w/NCREIF	0.00	0.00	1.00	0.71	0.01	−0.18	0.06
Correlation w/NCREIF unsmoothed	0.21	0.24	0.71	1.00	−0.01	−0.27	0.13

Note: Based on quarterly returns for stock, bond, commodity, and real estate indices; a quarterly risk-free rate based on the U.S. Treasury 30-day bill was used to compute Sharpe ratios.
Source: CISDM (2005a).

deviation of REITs compared with the unsmoothed NCREIF Index. The NCREIF Index is most representative of the performance of private real estate funds because these funds are the major contributors of data to NCREIF.

The performance properties of direct and securitized real estate investment differ significantly. REITs exhibit a relatively high return (12.71 percent) and high standard deviation (12.74 percent), whereas appraisal-based real estate returns are low (6.14 percent) with low volatility (3.37 percent). The extremely low standard deviation of NCREIF Index returns is indicative of the volatility dampening associated with smoothing because of stale valuations. After the correction for smoothing, the NCREIF Index's volatility more than doubles to 8.95 percent. However, the average return increases from 6.14 percent for the NCREIF Index to 7.27 percent for the unsmoothed NCREIF Index. The correlation between these two indices is 0.71. The correlations between the unhedged NAREIT Index and the NCREIF Index and the unsmoothed NCREIF Index are both low (0.00 and 0.21, respectively), suggesting that securitized real estate investment is a poor substitute for direct investment.

The volatility of the hedged NAREIT Index, 11.93 percent, is higher than that of the NCREIF Index unsmoothed, 8.95 percent. This suggests the presence of a residual equity component in the hedged NAREIT Index that could be related to small-cap stocks, be simply unique to REITs, or be both. Even though the hedging correction is imperfect, the hedged NAREIT Index is a more realistic representation of the underlying real estate market, with a higher correlation with the unsmoothed NCREIF Index (0.24) than without the correction.

3.2.3. Interpretation Issues When NAREIT and NCREIF indices are used as benchmarks for real estate investments or in asset allocation studies, the problems associated with the construction of the indices mentioned previously must be taken into account.[21] Importantly for performance appraisal, the NCREIF Index is not an investable index.

3.3. Real Estate: Investment Characteristics and Roles

Real estate accounts for a major portion of many individuals' wealth. For example, equity in the residential property represented close to 30 percent of the net worth in the United Kingdom in 1999.[22] For all homeowners in the United States, home equity represented 43 percent of their net worth in 2001 and is expected to be much greater today because real estate values have risen substantially since then.[23] Because of the role of residential real estate for individuals as the place in which they live, however, most advisers to private clients do not include the clients' residences as "marketable" in the sense of assets that the adviser includes in a strategic asset allocation.

3.3.1. Investment Characteristics In contrast to such alternative investments as hedge funds, which are essentially investment strategies and are similar to direct investment in commodities, real estate is an asset in itself, with some intrinsic value based on the benefits it may supply to individuals or businesses. Furthermore, investment in commercial real estate properties includes a substantial income component through rental income, which increases the stability of its returns.

A variety of investment characteristics affect the returns to real estate. The physical real estate market is characterized by relative lack of liquidity, large lot sizes, relatively high

[21] For details see Geltner (2000) and Geltner and Ling (2001).

[22] See *Social Trends*, issue 30, February 2000.

[23] See *Survey of Consumer Finances*, Federal Reserve Board, 2001.

transaction costs, heterogeneity, immobility (with the asset fixed at a location), and relatively low information transparency (so the seller often knows more than the buyer). Physical real estate has rarely been traded on a centralized exchange. These characteristics can create the market opportunity for relatively high risk-adjusted returns for investors who can obtain cost-efficient, high-quality information.

The lack of reliable, high-frequency transaction data for properties necessitates the use of appraisal-based valuations. Later, we will discuss the checkpoints that a quantitative analysis of the returns to real estate must cover when evaluating real estate return data resulting from the use of appraisals.

Various market and economic factors affect real estate. For instance, interest rates directly or indirectly affect a multitude of factors associated with the demand and supply for real estate, such as business financing costs, employment levels, savings habits, and the demand and supply for mortgage financing. Worldwide, the returns to real estate are positively correlated with changes in gross national product.[24] Population growth is, in the long term, a positive factor for real estate returns, but the real estate investor needs to research the demographics affecting the particular investment (such as migration into or out of the area and changes in the wealth profile of the locality).

Investigators have come to mixed conclusions on the inflation-hedging capabilities of real estate investment. Bond and Seiler (1998) found that U.S. residential real estate provided a significant inflation hedge in the 1969–94 period. Hoesli et al. (1997) found that U.K. real estate provided a better short-term inflation hedge than bonds but a worse hedge than stocks. Stevenson and Murray (1999) did not find evidence that Irish real estate provided a significant inflation hedge. Liu et al. (1997) found that real estate provided a worse hedge than stocks in some countries but a comparable hedge in others. Analyzing U.S. REITs specifically, Chatrath and Liang (1998) found some long-run but no short-run inflation-hedging ability.

Real estate values are affected by idiosyncratic variables, such as location. There appear to be strong continent-specific factors in real estate returns for Europe and North America.[25] The implication is that complete diversification in real estate can be achieved only by investing internationally. Nearly optimal diversification can be achieved by targeting one country from each continent.

The following is a list of the general advantages and disadvantages of direct equity real estate investing.[26] Most of the advantages and disadvantages apply to both individual and institutional investors.

Advantages

- To the extent that the law allows mortgage interest, property taxes, and other expenses to be tax deductible, taxable owners of real estate may benefit from tax subsidies.
- Mortgage loans permit most real estate borrowers to use more financial leverage than is available in most securities investing.
- Real estate investors have direct control over their property and may take action, such as expanding or modernizing, to increase the market value of the property. In contrast, an investor who owns a small position in the equity of a publicly traded company has virtually no voice in the management of the company.

---

[24] See Case, Goetzmann and Rouwenhorst (2000).

[25] See Eichholtz et al. (1998) and Eichholtz et al. (1999).

[26] In part, this list reflects Francis and Ibbotson (2001).

- Geographical diversification can be effective in reducing exposure to catastrophic risks (e.g., the risk of hurricanes or floods). The values of real estate investments in different locations can have low correlations; substantial geographical distance is often not necessary to achieve risk-reduction benefits.
- Real estate returns, on average, have relatively low volatility in comparison with returns to public equities—even after correcting for the downward bias that results from the smoothing process associated with real estate appraisals. We discuss this bias later.

Disadvantages

- Most parcels of real estate are not easy to divide into smaller pieces. As a result, when such properties are a relatively large part of an investor's total portfolio, real estate investing may involve large idiosyncratic risks for investors. Owners of single-family residences and large institutional investors that buy shopping centers may both experience this problem.
- The cost of acquiring information is high because each piece of real estate is unique.
- Real estate brokers charge high commissions relative to securities transaction fees.
- Real estate involves substantial operating and maintenance costs (e.g., for administration, leasing, repairs, and replacements) and hands-on management expertise, which are expenses or requirements not incurred by securities investors.
- Real estate investors are exposed to the risk of neighborhood deterioration, and the conditions that may lead to that are beyond the investor's control.
- Any income tax deductions that a taxable investor in real estate may benefit from are subject to political risk—they may be discontinued.

3.3.2. Roles in the Portfolio According to the *2005–2006 Russell Survey on Alternative Investing*, strategic allocations to real estate average 3.4 percent of total assets in Japan, 6.7 percent in North America, 9.8 percent in Europe, and 10.4 percent in Australia. This survey forecasted increased allocations to real estate in all these countries except Australia. Almost two-thirds of European capital and about half of North American and Australian capital is reportedly committed to direct investment in land and buildings.[27] Japan has much less capital committed to direct investment in real estate. The survey also indicates a strong home bias is revealed in real estate investments. The range of allocations is broadly consistent with what a quantitative approach to asset allocation would suggest.[28]

Because real estate may follow many economic fundamentals, real estate markets follow economic cycles. From a tactical asset allocation point of view, good forecasting of economic cycles should thus result in improved dynamic strategies for reallocating among different assets on the basis of expected stages of their respective cycles. Among the variables to focus on as systematic determinants of real estate returns are growth in consumption, real interest rates, the term structure of interest rates, and unexpected inflation.[29]

3.3.2.1. The Role of Real Estate as a Diversifier In addition to its potential to add value through active management, real estate has historically been viewed as an important diversifier. Real estate as an asset class typically responds differently from the way either stocks or bonds

[27] The survey points out that these data may be biased by the kind of respondents—namely, the larger institutions, which tend to use direct investments.

[28] For example, Kallberg and Liu (1996), using a mean–variance-optimization framework, found that a 9 percent allocation to real estate is optimal in a portfolio that includes stocks, bonds, and cash.

[29] See Ling and Naranjo (1997).

do. The reason is that, in the past, directly owned real estate was not highly correlated with the performance of other assets. For example, it was a good risk diversifier in the traditional stock and bond portfolio. Also, historically, real estate investment has experienced lower volatility than other asset classes because it is typically less affected by short-term economic conditions. Income-producing commercial real estate can be a relatively stable investment with income derived from tenants' lease payments. Thus, real estate can also be a good income enhancer.[30]

To illustrate the potential diversification benefit of real estate investments in a portfolio context, Exhibit 8-4 presents performance results using an approach that is also used in subsequent parts of this chapter and elsewhere.[31] The exhibit shows statistics for a 50 percent/50 percent U.S. stock/U.S. bond portfolio (Portfolio I), which is a simple baseline portfolio. Then the allocations to U.S. stocks and bonds are each reduced by 10 percentage points and reassigned in various ways to other asset classes; the resulting portfolios include a portfolio containing the alternative investment under discussion, in this case real estate. This method of presentation provides information on the effect of holding the alternative investment under discussion in conjunction with various other asset classes that the investor might hold. A particular investor may have a different baseline portfolio, but the investor can adapt the approach shown here to his or her needs. In Section 2, we supplied the additional cautions the reader should be aware of in evaluating an analysis based on a given historical sample. In real estate, data series extend much further back than 1990, which we have selected for the reasons of comparability discussed in Section 2.

Comparing Portfolio III (REITs, U.S. equities, and U.S. bonds) with Portfolio I (only U.S. equities and U.S bonds), one can see that the addition of REITs increases the Sharpe ratio from 0.67 to 0.79. The reason for this improvement is the high Sharpe ratio of REIT returns in the sample period coupled with their moderate correlation with S&P 500 Index returns (0.35, Exhibit 8-3). When REITs are added to a more diversified portfolio made up of assets included in Portfolio II to produce Portfolio IV, different results are observed: The Sharpe ratio is actually the same for Portfolios II and IV.

Overall, for the sample period, REITs provided some diversification benefits relative to a stock/bond portfolio, but it was relatively less effective in that role than hedge funds and commodities and did not have diversification benefits in a stock/bond portfolio to which hedge fund and commodity exposures had been added.

Direct investment in real estate as represented by unsmoothed NCREIF returns, however, provided more diversification benefit. Adding the unsmoothed NCREIF Index (20 percent) to a portfolio of stocks and bonds raised the Sharpe ratio of the portfolio from 0.67 (Portfolio I) to 0.77 (Portfolio V). This result would be expected because of the small negative correlation between unsmoothed NCREIF Index returns and the S&P 500 returns (−0.01, Exhibit 8-3) and the negative correlation between unsmoothed NCREIF Index returns and Lehman Aggregate returns (−0.27, Exhibit 8-3). As the results for Portfolio VI show, adding the unsmoothed NCREIF Index to a portfolio including hedge funds and commodities results in a slightly larger Sharpe ratio than that of Portfolio II, although adding NAREIT to such a portfolio results in the same Sharpe ratio as Portfolio II. These results may indicate that real estate is an *ex post* redundant asset in the presence of hedge funds and commodities.

---

[30] See Downs et al. (2003).

[31] See Schneeweis and Spurgin (1997a) and Ankrim and Hensel (1993). The Hedge Fund Composite Index (HFCI) is created by CISDM of the University of Massachusetts as follows: Between 1990 and 1993, it is an equally weighted portfolio of EACM 100 and HFR; since 1994, it has been an equally weighted portfolio of EACM 100, HFR, and Credit Suisse/Tremont.

EXHIBIT 8-4 Real Estate Performance in Portfolios, 1990–2004

Measure	Portfolio I	Portfolio II	Portfolio III	Portfolio IV	Portfolio V	Portfolio VI
Annualized return	9.60%	9.95%	10.34%	10.16%	9.33%	9.72%
Annualized std. dev.	7.87%	6.81%	7.62%	7.05%	6.59%	6.43%
Sharpe ratio	0.67	0.83	0.79	0.83	0.77	0.85
Minimum quarterly return	−6.45%	−5.18%	−7.99%	−5.47%	−5.35%	−4.67%
Correlation w/NAREIT Index	0.37	0.36	0.64	0.52	0.51	0.50
Correlation w/NAREIT Index hedged	0.03	0.04	0.34	0.20	0.21	0.20
Correlation w/NCREIF Index	−0.03	−0.03	−0.03	−0.03	0.16	0.06
Correlation w/NCREIF Index unsmoothed	−0.08	−0.04	0.01	−0.01	0.19	0.08

Notes: In the following listing, HFCI is the Hedge Funds Composite Index published by CISDM (Center for International Securities and Derivatives Markets) of the University of Massachusetts. It is created as follows: For the period between 1990 and 1993, it is an equally weighted portfolio of the EACM 100 and Hedge Fund Research (HFR) indices; since 1994, it has been an equally weighted portfolio of EACM 100, HFR, and Credit Suisse/Tremont hedge fund indices.

Portfolio I: 50 percent S&P 500 and 50 percent Lehman Aggregate Bond Index.

Portfolio II: 40 percent S&P 500, 40 percent Lehman Aggregate, 10 percent HFCI, and 10 percent GSCI.

Portfolio III: 40 percent S&P 500, 40 percent Lehman Aggregate, and 20 percent NAREIT.

Portfolio IV: 40 percent S&P 500, 40 percent Lehman Aggregate, 5 percent HFCI, 5 percent GSCI, and 10 percent NAREIT.

Portfolio V: 40 percent S&P 500, 40 percent Lehman Aggregate, and 20 percent NCREIF unsmoothed.

Portfolio VI: 40 percent S&P 500, 40 percent Lehman Aggregate, 5 percent HFCI, 5 percent GSCI, and 10% NCREIF unsmoothed.

Source: CISDM (2005a).

EXHIBIT 8-5 Unsmoothed Performance of Direct Real Estate Indices, 1990–2004

Measure	NCREIF Unsmoothed	Apartment	Industrial	Office	Retail
Annualized return	7.27%	9.39%	7.85%	4.59%	8.17%
Annualized std. dev.	8.95%	5.76%	10.68%	10.63%	9.65%
Sharpe ratio	0.33	0.89	0.33	0.03	0.40
Minimum quarterly return	−18.55%	−10.45%	−16.15%	−20.91%	−14.25%

Source: CISDM (2005a).

These results are consistent with evidence indicating that direct real estate investment may provide some diversification benefits to stocks and bonds[32] but benefits may disappear when hedge funds and commodities are added to the portfolio.[33]

3.3.2.2. Diversification within Real Estate Itself Investors also seek diversification by type and geography within real estate investing. Investments in different real estate sectors differ in regard to risk and return. The property types that have higher levels of embedded risk, such as large office assets, have generated lower risk-adjusted returns than other sectors and are likely to have more pronounced market cycles. Conversely, those sectors that offer higher risk-adjusted returns, such as apartments, appear to be less volatile and offer more defensive characteristics. As Exhibit 8-5 shows, apartments offered the highest risk-adjusted returns, and office assets showed low returns (4.59 percent) and high volatility (10.63 percent) in the 1990–2004 period. This suggests that targeting the apartment sector of the commercial real estate market over the last decade would have yielded better results than simply diversifying across all sectors. The higher returns of apartment real estate can be partially explained by a low correlation with inflation. In addition, to the degree that inflation results in a slowdown in the real economy, the apartment sector would be negatively correlated with inflation. Thus, the office, retail, and industrial sectors, whose returns seem to include an inflation component, have been at a relative disadvantage in the 1990s.

Overall, direct real estate investment may be able to provide an inflation hedge to some degree.

Exhibit 8-6 shows the correlation matrix of total returns for the four geographical NCREIF (unsmoothed) indices and the combined index. The correlations are high for all pairs of geographical subindices. This suggests that successful geographical diversification should take into account finer subdivisions, such as metropolitan areas or cities.

The properties of real estate return distributions are important for the portfolio manager because they provide key inputs into the asset allocation process. Many return observations in indices of direct investment tend to be close to zero as a result of the illiquid market. Equity real estate returns generally have been found not to follow a normal distribution, in U.S. markets and elsewhere, for both the direct investments[34] and indirect investments.[35] Furthermore, the

[32]See Kallberg and Liu (1996), Grauer and Hakansson (1995), and Chandrashekaran (1999).

[33]See also results in Section 4 (Commodity Investment), which are consistent with Froot (1995).

[34]See Young and Graff (1995), Miles and McCue (1984), and Hartzell, Hekman, and Miles (1986).

[35]See Lizieri and Satchell (1997), Sieler, Webb and Myer (1999), Mei and Hu (2000), and Lizieri and Ward (2000) for a review.

EXHIBIT 8-6 Correlation of Direct Real Estate Returns by U.S. Geographical Region

	Index	East	Midwest	South	West
Index	1.00				
East	0.95	1.00			
Midwest	0.91	0.88	1.00		
South	0.91	0.85	0.86	1.00	
West	0.93	0.81	0.75	0.77	1.00

Source: CISDM (2005a).

direct market exhibits a high degree of persistence in returns (positive following positive and negative following negative), whereas the indirect market does not show such persistence. The explanation for these facts is a matter of continuing investigation.[36]

3.3.2.3. Investment in Real Estate Worldwide The benefit of real estate investment internationally has been researched. Overall, the evidence indicates that investors may benefit from including domestic and nondomestic investments in real estate in their portfolios.

Real estate has been found to be an effective portfolio diversifier for seven countries (Australia, France, the Netherlands, Sweden, Switzerland, the United Kingdom, and the United States) on three continents, based on data from 1987–2001, and including both domestic and international real estate assets increases the benefits.[37] Case, Goetzmann, and Wachter (1997) concluded that international real estate diversification would have been beneficial to a U.S. investor. The correlation between property share (real estate company) returns and other common stock returns appears to have declined in both the United States and the United Kingdom, indicating the possibility of increased diversification potential for property shares.[38] Research has also suggested that U.S. REITs may be an attractive addition to domestic stocks and bonds for investors from Canada and the United Kingdom.[39] Example 8-4 shows the application of some of the facts and methods discussed in the text.

EXAMPLE 8-4 Adding Real Estate to the Strategic Asset Allocation

As CIO of The Annette Hansen Charitable Foundation (TAHCF), a U.S.-based foundation supporting medical research, Maryann Dunn will present to the trustees a recommendation that they revise the foundation's strategic asset allocation to include direct investment in real estate.

[36] See Lizieri and Ward (2000).
[37] See Hoesli, Lekander, and Witkiewiez (2003).
[38] See Brounen and Eichholtz (2003).
[39] See Mull and Soenen (1997), who studied the 1985 to 1994 period.

- The Foundation's current portfolio and strategic asset allocation is allocated 50 percent common stocks/50 percent bonds. Twelve percent of the common stock allocation (six percent of the total portfolio) is invested in REITs.
- The risk-free rate of interest is 3.5 percent.
- The forecasted inflation rate is 3 percent.
- TAHCF's overall investment objective is to preserve the real (inflation-adjusted) value of assets after spending. Its spending rate is 5 percent of 12-month average asset value.
- TAHCF's cost of earning investment returns is 20 basis points per year.
- Exhibit 8-7 shows Dunn's expectations for the current and proposed asset allocations. Dunn's expectations for direct investment are based on unsmoothed NCREIF historical data adjusted for her current economic outlook.

EXHIBIT 8-7 Forecast Data

Measure	50/50 Stocks/Bonds	45/45/10 Stocks/Bonds/U.S. Direct Real Estate Investment
Expected return	5.5%	5.9%
Std. dev. of return	11.8%	10.8%

Dunn expects opposition to her proposal to come from a trustee, Bob Enicar. Enicar has stated at a prior board meeting: "TAHCF's allocation to equity includes substantial investment in REITs. REITs typically provide risk diversification comparable to that of direct equity investments for a balanced portfolio of stocks and bonds while offering substantially more liquidity."

1. State and explain two financial justifications that Hansen could present for revising TAHCF's asset allocation to 45/45/10 stocks/bonds/U.S. direct real estate investment.
2. State and explain one disadvantage of the proposed revised strategic asset allocation.
3. Contrast unsmoothed and smoothed NCREIF indices and justify Hansen's choice of the unsmoothed NCREIF Index in formulating expectations for direct real estate investment.
4. Draft a response to Enicar's critique.

Solution to Problem 1: The financial justifications for adding direct real estate investment to the strategic asset allocation include the following:

- The Sharpe ratio of the 45/45/10 stock/bonds/U.S. direct real estate investment portfolio at $(5.9\% - 3.5\%)/10.8 = 0.222$ is greater than that of the current 50/50 stocks/bonds allocation at $(5.5\% - 3.5\%)/11.8 = 0.169$.
- Direct real estate investment's inflation-hedging qualities are consonant with TAHCF's stated concern for preserving the real purchasing power of funds.
- The revised strategic asset allocation is expected to come closer to satisfying TAHCF's investment objective than does the existing strategic asset allocation.

Solution to Problem 2: The proposed strategic asset allocation's expected return of 5.9 percent falls well short of the (1.05)(1.03)(1.0020) − 1.0 = 8.37% return objective implicit in the description of the problem.

Solution to Problem 3: The NCREIF Index is based on property appraisals rather than market values. Appraised values tend to be less volatile than market values, an effect known as smoothing. As a result of smoothing, volatility and correlations with other assets will tend to be understated, which means an overstatement of the benefits of real estate in the portfolio. Using the unsmoothed NCREIF index gives a more accurate picture of the benefits of real estate investment.

Solution to Problem 4: Enicar is correct that securitized real estate is more liquid than direct real estate investment. However, direct real estate's correlations with U.S. equities and U.S. bonds are lower than REITs' correlations, making direct real estate a stronger diversifier when added to a portfolio of stocks and bonds.

In Example 8-4, a strategic asset allocation involving direct real estate investment was reviewed that, in expectation, did not promise to fulfill the investor's return requirement. Section 4 discusses an alternative asset class that has become a popular vehicle for investors seeking high returns.

3.3.3. Other Issues Due diligence in active direct real estate investment should cover the checkpoints outlined in Example 8-2: market opportunity, investment process, organization, people, terms and structure, service providers, documents, and write-up. Within each of these headings, some checkpoints will involve investment-specific points, such as valuation methods, financing, real estate legal issues (e.g., zoning, a title check), and for taxable investors especially, tax issues.

In the next section, we discuss another major type of alternative investment, private equity.

4. PRIVATE EQUITY/VENTURE CAPITAL

Private equity is an ownership interest in a private (non-publicly-traded) company. The term *private equity* refers to any security by which equity capital is raised via a private placement rather than through a public offering. As private placements, private equity securities are not registered with a regulatory body. To qualify as private placements, securities are generally offered for sale to either institutions or high-net-worth individuals (accredited investors). Private equity investments can be made face to face with the company needing financing or indirectly through private equity funds.

A variety of investment activities can take place in the investment structures known as **private equity funds**—the pooled investment vehicles through which many investors make (indirect) investments in generally highly illiquid assets. These investment activities range from financing private businesses, to leveraged buyouts of public companies, to distressed debt investing, to the public financing of public infrastructure projects. Thus, a host of investing activities requiring distinct expertise is often gathered under the rubric of private equity. In this section, the focus is on the two historically most important fields of private equity activity: the equity financing of new or growing private companies, an activity often called **venture capital,** and the buyout of established companies via private equity funds known as buyout funds.[40] In venture capital, a company that starts out as private may eventually become publicly owned. The converse process—taking a publicly owned company private in a buyout of publicly held interests and the private purchase of a division of a public corporation, as well as buyouts of established private companies—constitutes the chief sphere of activity of buyout funds.

EXAMPLE 8-5 Private Investment in Public Entity (PIPE)

The range of activities conducted via the structure of a private equity fund evolves and grows. An example is the PIPE—private investment in public entity. If the share price of a publicly traded company has dropped significantly from its value at the time of going public, the company may seek new sources of capital via a PIPE. Through a PIPE, an investor makes a relatively large investment in a company, usually at a price less than the current market value.

On January 16, 2004, Novatel Wireless, Inc., a publicly traded company, sold 1,142,855 shares of newly issued common stock to a group of private investment firms (a PIPE). The shares included warrants entitling the investors to purchase an additional 228,565 shares at a price of US$8.833 per share. Novatel raised net capital of US$7,525,000 in the initial transaction. On February 13, 2004, Novatel filed a registration statement with the U.S. SEC that would entitle these private investors to sell their shares on the open market. At the time of the original transaction, Novatel's shares were trading for US$9. At the time the registration statement was filed, the shares were trading for US$16.48.

Source: *BusinessWeek*, 10 May 2004, pp. 118–120, and Novatel Wireless, Inc., SEC Form S-3 filed February 13, 2004.

Private equity represents an important asset class that has received increasing interest from pension plans, endowments, foundations, and corporations, and from family offices and other advisers to the private wealth market. In some countries, such as the United Kingdom, exposure to this investment type is also available through exchange-traded vehicles.

In a number of countries, including the United States, private equity is one type of alternative investment that practitioners often point to as facing serious capacity issues. The high failure rate of young businesses is an indication that the combination of winning ideas for products/services and the entrepreneurial and/or managerial skill, experience, and commitment to realize them is in limited supply at any given point in time. The venture or business that

[40]"Venture capital" is widely used to refer to early-stage financing of companies. Yet, practitioners also talk of late-stage venture capital, referring to the portion prior to exiting from the investment. According to Lerner (2000), p. 522, outside the United States, the term "venture capital" is often used as a synonym for "private equity." Confusingly, practitioners sometimes use "private equity" to refer to investment buyout funds rather than venture capital funds. In short, terminology varies, but the reader can understand the meaning from the context.

EXHIBIT 8-8 Investment Processes of (Direct) Private Equity Investment and Investment in Publicly Traded Equities

Private Equity Investments	Publicly Traded Securities
Structure and Valuation	
Deal structure and price are negotiated between the investor and company management.	Price is set in the context of the market. Deal structure is standardized. Variations typically require approval from securities regulators.
Access to Information for Investment Selection	
Investor can request access to all information, including internal projections.	Analysts can use only publicly available information to assess investment potential.
Postinvestment Activity	
Investors typically remain heavily involved in the company after the transaction by participating at the board level and through regular contact with management.	Investors typically do not sit on corporate boards or make ongoing assessments based on publicly available information and have limited access to management.

Source: Prepared by Andrew Abouchar, CFA, of Tech Capital Partners.

is in a position of strength with respect to those qualities will be scrutinizing the potential investor for qualities needed in a partner/collaborator as closely as the investor will go over the investment checkpoints.

Most professional investors have wide experience and knowledge of public equity markets. Although public and private equity investments have common elements, private equity investment involves distinct knowledge and experience. The contrast is greatest in the case of direct private equity investment, which often calls on the investor's skills as a businessperson, as Exhibit 8-8 shows.

The following section discusses some prominent characteristics of the private equity marketplace and private equity funds.

4.1. The Private Equity Market

The first question to address is why the market opportunities for private equity arise. Take the case of venture capital investment first: A closely held business is characterized by a small number of owners and is not publicly traded. Often, the owners of a closely held business are family members, but closely held businesses can also have unrelated owners. Such businesses may seek outside investors for a variety of reasons. For example, the original owners may not have adequate capital for growth or even to fund current operations. Entrepreneurs frequently lack the professional managerial skills and experience to manage the enterprise they started after it reaches a certain size. Venture capital firms may be able to supply valuable assistance in the transition to professional management.[41] The original owners may also want to diversify their wealth. For an individual investor, a closely held business can represent a significant portion of his or her overall wealth. The liquidity afforded by markets for publicly traded shares allows such investors to diversify their portfolios at lower costs. Venture capitalists also

[41] As discussed in more detail shortly, **venture capital firms** represent dedicated pools of capital providing equity or equity-linked financing to privately held companies.

can assist in the initial public offering (IPO) of shares, which permits the original owners to eventually realize public market valuations for their holdings.[42]

Formative-stage companies usually raise money through marketing an effective business plan to potentially interested parties. The business plan describes the intended products and/or services, the market that will be served, the business strategy, the dates of expected financial milestones (such as profitability to be achieved), the expected cash "burn rate," the additional rounds of financing that the company expects to need, and other relevant information.

In the case of funds raised through an agent, a document called a **private placement memorandum** may be used. This document should discuss a myriad of factors affecting the company. It should describe the company's business and competitive factors and discuss how it intends to use the proceeds from the offering. It should also contain financial statements and projections, although not necessarily audited financial statements.

4.1.1. The Demand for Venture Capital

Issuers of venture capital include the following:

- *Formative-stage companies.* This group ranges from newly formed companies, to young companies beginning product development ("start-ups"), to companies that are just beginning to sell a product. Worldwide, probably more than a million new businesses are formed every year, but venture capitalists frequently are not interested in companies at that earliest stage. In the United States, venture capitalists that do invest in formative-stage companies might be looking for companies with, for example, projected revenues in the US$10 million to US$50 million range within a five-year horizon.[43]
- *Expansion-stage companies.* This group ranges from young companies that need financing for expanding sales, to established companies with significant revenues (middle-market companies), to companies that are preparing for an IPO of stock.

The financing stages through which many private companies pass include the following:[44]

Early-stage financing:

- Seed—generally, seed money is a relatively small amount of money provided to the entrepreneur to form a company and prove that an idea has a reasonable chance of commercial success.
- Start-up—at this stage, the company has been formed and an idea has been proven but the company needs money to bring the product or idea to commercialization. This is a pre-revenue stage.
- First stage—if the company has exhausted its seed and start-up financing, the company may seek additional funds. Obviously, the company must have made progress from earlier stages to warrant an investment at this stage.

Later-stage financing: This is the financing of promising companies that need funds for expanding sales.

[42]An **initial public offering** is the initial issuance of common stock registered for public trading by a formerly private corporation.

[43]This comment supplies an idea of the stage at which venture capitalists become active; the numbers can be expected to change over time and may be different elsewhere.

[44]There is some variation in terminology. For example, after the seed and start-up stages, some practitioners distinguish Series A from Series B in reference to the series of preferred shares being issued in the transaction.

EXHIBIT 8-9 Venture Capital Timeline

	Formative-Stage Companies			Expansion-Stage Companies		
	Seed	Early Stage		Later Stage		Pre-IPO
		Start-Up	First Stage	Second Stage	Third Stage	Mezzanine
Stage characteristics	Idea incorporation, first personnel hired, prototype development	Moving into operation, initial revenues		Revenue growth		Preparation for IPO
Stage financing (buyers of private equity)	Founders, FF&F,[a] angels, venture capital	Angels, venture capital		Venture capital, strategic partners		
Purpose of financing	Supports market research and establishment of business	**Start-up financing** supports product development and initial marketing	**First-stage financing** supports such activities as initial manufacturing and sales	**Second-stage financing** supports the initial expansion of a company already producing and selling a product	**Third-stage financing** provides capital for major expansion	**Mezzanine** (bridge) **financing** provides capital to prepare for the IPO—often a mix of debt and equity

[a]FF&F = founder's friends and family. The sources of financing are listed in typical order of importance.

4.1.2. The Exit Because private equity is by definition not publicly traded, the exit (the liquidation or divestment of a private equity investment) is often difficult and is a major item of strategy. The investor can realize the value of the holding in several ways:

- Merger with another company.
- Acquisition by another company (including a private equity fund specializing in this).
- An IPO by which the company becomes publicly traded.

Of course, it is also possible that the venture will not succeed and the business will be closed without any recovery of the original investment by the equityholder. Exhibit 8-9 summarizes the venture capital timeline.

4.1.3. The Supply of Venture Capital Suppliers of venture capital include the following:

- *Angel investors.* An **angel investor** is an accredited individual investing chiefly in seed and early-stage companies, sometimes after the resources of the founder's friends and family have been exhausted. Angel investors are often the first outside investors in a company, even before a company is organized or there is a real product. The size of the investments made by angels is relatively small. However, because they are generally invested at the earliest point, such investments are among the riskiest.
- *Venture capital.* **Venture capital** (VC) refers broadly to the pools of capital managed by specialists known as **venture capitalists** who seek to identify companies that have great business opportunities but need financial, managerial, and strategic support. Venture capitalists invest alongside company managers; they often take representation on the board of directors of the company and provide significant expertise in addition to capital. An individual pool is a **venture capital fund** (VC fund). An industry of investment firms sponsors series of such funds and sometimes a variety of similarly structured vehicles taking advantage of different opportunities. These firms may be private partnerships, closely held corporations, or sometimes, publicly traded corporations. In the United Kingdom, **venture capital trusts** (VCTs), which are exchange-traded, closed-end vehicles, provide an example of other opportunities that are available.
- *Large companies.* A variety of major companies invest their own money via corporate private equity in promising young companies in the same or a related industry. The activity is known as **corporate venturing,** and the investors are often referred to as "strategic partners." Corporate venturing funds are not available to the public.

EXAMPLE 8-6 The IPO of Google

The IPO of Google, Inc., illustrates the timeline for private equity. Google was incorporated in 1998 with an initial investment of US$1 million by family, friends, and angel investors. In early 1999, Google received US$25 million in venture capital funds. The two venture capital firms that provided capital in 1999 each own about 10.2 percent of the company. In April 2004, Google filed for an IPO. The IPO date was August 19, 2004, with Morgan Stanley and Credit Suisse First Boston as the lead underwriters in an unusual (for equities) Dutch auction–style auction, which affords more access to shares by smaller investors. The offering was for approximately 19.6 million shares of Class A common stock. Of that number, approximately 4.5 million shares were from selling shareholders realizing part of the cash value of their shareholdings, including company founders Larry Page and Sergey Brin. The offering was at US$85 per share and raised about US$1.2 billion for Google and US$464 million for the selling shareholders. After the offering, about 33.6 million Class A shares and about 237.6 million privately held Class B shares were outstanding. The Class B shares, held by the founders and other executives and investors, had 10 votes per share (versus 1 vote per share for the Class A shareholders). This dual-stock structure was viewed as unusual in technology IPOs, but it had been used by media companies, such as the New York Times. It permitted insiders to maintain voting control over Google and, according to Google executives, protected the company from pressures felt by public companies to produce short-term performance. At the same time, the Class B shares were convertible to the registered Class A shares, so the investing group could access public markets to realize the cash values of their holdings in the future. The August 2004 IPO was oversubscribed, and the shares (NASDAQ: GOOG) rose about 18 percent in initial trading. On September 14, 2005, Google made a follow-on offering of about 14.2 million shares at US$295 per share that raised US$4.18 billion. On March 31, 2006, Google was added to the S&P 500.

Sources: Reuters, "Key Dates in the History of Google" and "Update: Brin, Page Lead List of Google Shareholders," both on April 29, 2004 at www.google-ipo.com.

Most investors participate in private equity through private equity funds. Among these funds, buyout funds constitute a larger segment than VC funds, as measured by assets under management or the size of capital commitments. The capital commitments to buyout funds in many years have been two to three times the size of those to VC funds.

Buyout funds may be separated into two major groups, mega-cap buyout funds and middle-market buyout funds. **Mega-cap buy-out funds** take public companies private. **Middle-market buy-out funds** purchase private companies whose revenues and profits are too small to access capital from the public equity markets. Middle-market buyout funds typically purchase established businesses, such as small privately held companies (including those that may have received venture capital support) and divisions spun off from larger companies. The buyout fund manager seeks to add value by:

- Restructuring operations and improving management.
- Opportunistically identifying and executing the purchase of companies at a discount to intrinsic value.
- Capturing any gains from the addition of debt or restructuring of existing debt.

To further their ability to add value through restructuring operations and improving management, large buyout organizations maintain a pool of experienced operating and financial executives who can be inserted into the companies if necessary or appropriate. These organizations look to cut costs and increase revenues. As the owner/managers of companies, buyout organizations have well-developed processes for installing incentive compensation systems and management reporting systems. They have experience restructuring supply chains and distribution channels. Buyout firms may explain the market opportunity as the potential to add value by substitution of a highly focused private governance model, in which expert owners have complete control, for a public governance model with dispersed ownership, conflicts of interest, and high regulatory compliance costs.

Buyout funds can realize value gains through a sale of the acquired company, an IPO, or a dividend recapitalization. A **dividend recapitalization** involves the issuance of debt to finance a special dividend to owners (sometimes refinancing existing debt in the process). Dividend recapitalizations have at times allowed buyout funds to recoup all or most of the cash used to acquire a company within two to four years of the buyout while still retaining ownership and control of the company. However, dividend recapitalization has the potential to weaken the company as a going concern by overleveraging it.

The major investors in private equity funds are public pension funds, corporate defined-benefit pension plans, endowments, foundations, and family offices. In the United States, public pension plans are currently the most important players as measured by the amount of dollars committed; they are followed by the other investors in the order listed. Endowments and foundations have among the largest allocations in their policy portfolios. Family offices are a growing influence.[45]

4.1.4. Types of Private Equity Investment

Both direct and indirect investors in private equity need to understand the basics of direct private equity investment in order to have an informed grasp of its return and risk characteristics.

Direct venture capital investment is structured as convertible preferred stock rather than common stock. The terms of the preferred stock require that the corporation pay cash equal to some multiple (e.g., 2×) of preferred shareholders' original investment before any cash can be paid on the common stock, which is the equity investment of the founders. Preferred stock is senior to common stock also in its claims on liquidation value. This financing structure mitigates the risk that the company will take on the venture capital investment and distribute it to the owners/founders. It also provides an incentive to the company to meet the return goals of the outside investors.

Investors in subsequent rounds usually have rights to cash flows that are senior to preferred stock issued in previous financing rounds. All else being equal, therefore, shares issued in later rounds are more valuable than shares issued in earlier rounds, which in turn, are more valuable than the founders' common shares. Nevertheless, the differences in value may be slight and are frequently ignored in valuation. For convertible preferred shares issued in any round, an event such as a buyout or an acquisition of the common equity at a favorable price will trigger conversion of the preferred into the common shares of the company.

Indirect investment is primarily through private equity funds, including VC funds and buyout funds. Private equity funds are usually structured as limited partnerships or limited liability companies (LLCs) with an expected life of 7 to 10 years with an option to extend the life for another 1 to 5 years.[46] The fund manager's objective is to realize the value of all portfolio investments by the fund's liquidation date. There is typically an offering period in which capital commitments are solicited.

The limited partnership and LLC forms are attractive because income and capital gains flow through to the limited partners (for the LLC, the shareholders) for tax purposes, thus avoiding the possible double taxation that can occur in the corporate form. The limited

[45] See Boyer (2005).

[46] Anson (2002a), p. 273.

partners or shareholders do not bear any liability beyond the amount of their investments. The limited partners or shareholders commit to a specific investment amount that the general partner (in an LLC, the managing director) "takes down" over time in a series of capital calls to make specific investments or to pay expenses; private equity funds usually do not maintain a pool of uninvested capital. The general partner (or the managing director) is the venture capitalist, the party selecting and advising investments. The general partner, who may be an individual or another entity (such as a corporation or partnership), also commits its own capital. In this way, the interests of the outside investors and the fund manager/general partner/managing director are closely aligned.

The LLC form, available in the Unites States and some other countries under different names and with different requirements, is a hybrid of the corporate and partnership forms. It provides investors with more influence on the fund's operations than does a limited partnership interest—in particular, more control over the raising of additional committed capital. The LLC is often the preferred form when raising funds from a relatively small group of substantial and knowledgeable investors who may want to be proactive investors.

Private equity funds of funds are also available. Such funds invest in other private equity funds. Management fees of funds-of-funds vehicles range from 0.5 percent to 2 percent of the net assets managed; these fees are on top of fees charged by the underlying funds.

In contrast to the structure of private equity funds, in venture capital, the company receiving support is organized in a corporate form because one desirable exit is a successful initial offering of shares to the public. Examples of the corporate form include the U.K. public limited company (PLC), the corporation in the United States, the *kabushiki kaisha* (K.K.) in Japan, the *sociedad anónima* in Spain, the *société anonyme* in France, and the *Gesellshaft mit beschränkter Haftung* (GmbH) in Germany. The European Union has developed a new structure, the European company or *societas Europeae* (SE), that will permit companies in the EU to operate throughout the EU under one set of rules and with a uniform management system.

The compensation to the fund manager of a private equity fund consists of a management fee plus an incentive fee. The management fee is usually a percentage of limited partner *commitments* to the fund. (If the investor has made a capital commitment of US$50 million but actually invested only US$10 million, the investor generally pays a management fee on the US$50 million committed.) Management fees are often in the 1.5 to 2.5 percent range and often scale down in the later years of a partnership to reflect a lower work load.

The fund manager's incentive fee, the **carried interest,** is the share of the private equity fund's profits that the fund manager is due once the fund has returned the outside investors' capital (which may be specified as the capital committed or the capital invested). Carried interest is usually expressed as a percentage of the total profits of the fund. A common value is 20 percent. In such a structure, the fund manager will thus receive 20 percent of the profits and distribute the remaining 80 percent of the profits to investors. In some funds, the carried interest is computed on only those profits that represent a return in excess of a hurdle rate (the hurdle rate is also known as the **preferred return**). A hurdle rate of 6 percent means that only the private equity fund's profits in excess of an annualized return of 6 percent are subject to the 20 percent carried interest. Because early investments by the fund may achieve high rates of return but later investments do poorly, private equity funds sometimes have a **claw-back provision** that specifies that money from the fund manager be returned to investors if at the end of a fund's life investors have not received back their capital contributions and contractual share of profits.

In distributing cash flows to investors and the fund manager, a private equity fund first distributes to investors their invested capital and preferred return (if any is specified). Sometimes, the fund manager is allowed to take a small percentage of early distributions.

EXHIBIT 8-10 U.S. Venture Capital Activity: MoneyTree™ Survey

Year	Investment Amount (US$)	Number of Deals
1995	7,627,158,000	1,874
1996	11,521,998,000	2,612
1997	14,799,528,000	3,185
1998	21,258,792,000	3,695
1999	54,525,275,000	5,608
2000	105,859,076,000	8,082
2001	40,582,005,000	4,600
2002	21,409,439,000	3,035
2003	18,186,857,000	2,715
2004	21,341,540,000	2,910

Source: www.pwcmoneytree.com.

Typically, following the period in which all or most distributions go to investors, there is a catch-up period in which the fund manager receives all or the major share of profits. After the fund manager has caught up to its specified share of profits according to the contract, subsequent profits are distributed according to the carried interest percentage—for example, 80 percent to investors and 20 percent to the fund manager. Some of the manager's profits may be put in an escrow account to satisfy any claw-back liability.

The investor in a private equity fund expects to receive the benefits of the general manager's ability to select worthy investments and maintain active involvement in the investments. The fund manager and the manager's team should be able to shore up weaknesses in the companies' management and assist in planning and executing a successful exit strategy that realizes the value of the investments.

4.1.5. Size of the Private Equity Market A reliable estimate of direct private equity investment worldwide is hard to obtain, but as of early 2006, approximately US$200 billion was invested in private equity VC and buyout funds worldwide via approximately 1,000 private equity vehicles.[47] In the United States, a quarterly study of venture capital activity is performed through a joint effort of PricewaterhouseCoopers, Thomson Venture Economics, and the National Venture Capital Association (NVCA). Exhibit 8-10 presents a summary of the annual results through 2004.

Pricewaterhousecoopers, Thomson Venture Economics, and the European Private Equity and Venture Capital Association collaborate on similar surveys of private equity activity across continental Europe and the United Kingdom. Exhibit 8-11 on page 508 summarizes recent investment activity of VC and buyout funds. As in the United States, 2000 marked a high point of activity.

4.2. Benchmarks and Historical Performance

As for many other alternative investment types, events that indicate the market value of a private equity investment generally occur infrequently. Typical market price–revealing events include the raising of new financing, the acquisition of the company by another company, the

[47] Goodman (2006).

EXHIBIT 8-11 Pan-European Private Equity Activity (in € billions)

Year	Venture Capital Fund Investment	Buyout Fund Investment	Total
2000	19.6	15.3	34.9
2001	13.3	11.0	24.3
2002	10.7	16.9	27.6
2003	10.7	18.4	29.1
2004	11.2	25.7	36.9

Note: Numbers for venture capital rounded to make venture capital activity and buyout activity sum to the reported totals.
Source: www.evca.com.

IPO, or failure of the business. Infrequent market pricing poses a major challenge to index construction. How can returns be calculated without market transactions?

When measuring the performance of a private equity investment, investors typically calculate an internal rate of return based on cash flows since inception of the investment and the ending valuation of the investment (the net asset value or residual value). Similarly, major venture capital benchmarks, such as Thomson Venture Economics, provide IRR estimates for private equity funds that are based on fund cash flows and valuations.

4.2.1. Benchmarks

Major benchmarks for U.S. and European private equity are those provided by Cambridge Associates and Thomson Venture Economics, who present an overall private equity index representing two major segments: VC funds and buyout funds. Custom benchmarks are also frequently used by private equity investors.

4.2.2. Historical Performance

Exhibit 8-12 gives U.S. private equity's annualized IRRs as compiled by the National Venture Capital Association and Thomson Venture Economics as of 2005. In Exhibit 8-12, "balanced VC funds" are funds that make both early-stage and late-stage investments.

Private equity returns have exhibited a low correlation with publicly traded securities, making them an attractive addition to a portfolio. However, because of a lack of observable market prices for private equity, short-term return and correlation data may be a result of stale prices. Emery (2003) showed that the correlation between venture capital and NASDAQ returns increased substantially when annual or biannual (i.e., calculated every two years)

EXHIBIT 8-12 U.S. Private Equity Returns as of September 30, 2005 (in percent)

	Venture Capital Funds						
Period	Seed/Early	Balanced	Late Stage	All	Buyout Funds	NASDAQ	S&P500
3 Year	0.4	9.3	6.1	4.9	14.7	22.4	14.7
5 Year	−13.2	−5.6	−7.7	−9.3	3.1	−10.1	−3.1
10 Year	−46.8	20.8	13.0	26.5	8.7	7.5	7.7
20 Year	20.2	14.6	13.7	16.5	13.3	12.3	11.2

Source: NVCA and Thomson Venture Economics, February 4, 2004, news release,www.nvca.com.

data were used rather than quarterly data.[48] Emery showed that venture capital returns demonstrated a 0.69 correlation with NASDAQ returns and a 0.40 correlation with S&P 500 returns based on quarterly data. When biannual data were used, the correlation was 0.93 with the NASDAQ and 0.64 with the S&P 500.

4.2.3. Interpretation Issues

The private equity investor thinks of returns in terms of IRR calculations based, generally, on estimates of the values of the investor's interest. However, the fund manager's appraisals (usually supplied on a quarterly basis) supply estimates, not a market price. Appraised values are often slow to adjust to new circumstances (use stale data) and focus only on company-specific events, so the returns may be erroneous. Furthermore, there is no generally accepted standard for appraisals.

In evaluating past records of returns of private equity funds, investors often make comparisons with funds closed in the same year (the funds' **vintage year**). This helps assure the funds are compared with other funds at a similar stage in their life cycle. The effects of vintage year on returns are known as **vintage year effects,** and include, in addition to the effects of life-cycle stage, the influence that economic conditions and market opportunities associated with a given vintage year may have on various funds' probabilities of success.

4.3. Private Equity: Investment Characteristics and Roles

Like public equity investment, but to a greater degree, private equity plays a growth role in investment portfolios. On the one hand, at the company level, the highest earnings growth rates are usually achievable early, when the markets for the company's products may be largely untapped and competition may be slight. When a promising private company comes to market, its prospective growth may be capitalized at an above-market-average multiple. On the other hand, investment in established companies via buyout funds generally involves less risk and earlier returns. The private equity investor hopes to gauge and control the risk through appropriate due diligence processes. The following section provides more details on investment characteristics.

4.3.1. Investment Characteristics

The general investment characteristics of private equity investments include the following:

- *Illiquidity*. Private equity investments are generally highly illiquid. Convertible preferred stock investments do not trade in a secondary market. Private equity fund investors have more restricted opportunities to withdraw investments from the fund than do hedge fund investors. This is natural, because the underlying investments are not liquid.
- *Long-term commitments required*. Private equity investment generally requires long-term commitments. For direct VC investments, the time horizon also can be quite uncertain.
- *Higher risk than seasoned public equity investment*. The returns to private equity investments, on average, show greater dispersion than seasoned public equity investments, although they may be roughly comparable to those of publicly traded microcap shares.[49] The risk of complete loss of investment is also higher. The failure rate of new and young businesses is high.
- *High expected IRR required*. Private equity investors target high rates of returns as compensation for the risk and illiquidity of such investments.

---

[48] See Emery (2003), pp. 43–50.
[49] See Cochrane (2004).

For venture capital investments, the following also holds:

- *Limited information.* Because new ventures operate in product or service markets that may break new ground in some way, projections concerning cash flows are often based on limited information or make many assumptions. Although this is a risk factor, it is also related to the potential for unusual profits, however, of successful ventures.

Venture capitalists often target rates of return of 25 to 30 percent or more in individual investments. Dramatic success stories of venture capital include companies such as Apple Computers, Intel Corporation, Microsoft, and Google. Many investments do not work out. For bearing the additional risks of private equity compared with public equity, the private equity fund investor targets earning a substantial premium over expected public equity returns.

The illiquidity of private equity affects the value, of course, of an investor's interest. The value that is determined by using models such as the venture capital method or discounted cash-flow method may be used as the estimate of the value for a marketable controlling interest.[50] If the owner has a minority interest and the equity interest does not have a ready market, then discounts are applied to reflect the value for a minority-interest holder with a nonmarketable interest. The discount for a minority interest reflects the lack of control that investor has over the business and distributions. Studies have indicated that minority-interest discounts can range from 20 percent to 30 percent.[51] The discount for lack of marketability (for short, marketability discount) takes account of the lack of liquidity in the investment and depends on a number of factors, such as the size of the interest and the level of dividends paid. Studies of marketability discounts have shown mean discounts in the 28 to 36 percent range.[52] If the interest to be valued is a controlling interest, only the marketability discount needs to be considered. For a majority interest, the discount for lack of marketability might reflect both the cost of going public and a discount for owning a large block of shares. Example 8-7 illustrates one possibility for the valuation of a nonmarketable minority interest. A cautionary note is that the valuation of a nonmarketable minority interest can figure in the value of an estate and the estate taxes due for deceased private wealth clients. The calculation shown is not intended as a guide to estate planning in any given jurisdiction.

EXAMPLE 8-7 A Nonmarketable Minority Interest

Brent Smith has determined that his company will make a small investment in a private company, Clark Computing. The investment will be a nonmarketable minority interest. Smith's investment banker estimates that the value of Clark equity, if it were publicly traded, would be £500 million. Smith's company's interest in Clark will be 10 percent of Clark's equity. Smith's investment banker determines that a minority interest discount of 20 percent and a marketability discount of 25 percent are appropriate. What is the value of the nonmarketable minority interest?

---

[50] The venture capital method of valuation involves discounting at a high interest rate a projected future value of the company, where the projected future value assumes the company is successful.

[51] CCH Business Valuation Guide, paragraph 2105.

[52] Ibid, paragraph 2111.

Solution: The money amounts shown are in millions of pounds sterling.

Marketable controlling interest value: (10% × 500) = 50.
Minority interest discount: (20% × 50) = −10.
Marketable minority interest: (50 − 10) = 40.
Marketability discount: (25% × 40) = −10.
Nonmarketable minority interest: (40 − 10) = 30.

Smith's investment banker values the investment at £30 million.

VC funds and buyout funds have some expected differences in return characteristics.[53]

- *Buyout funds are usually highly leveraged*. The capital raised by the fund may be 25 to 40 percent of capital used to purchase the equity of the target company, with the balance coming from debt collateralized by the target company's assets. The operating cash flows of the target company, typically an established company, are used to service the debt payments. In contrast, VC funds use no debt in obtaining their equity interests.
- *The cash flows to buyout fund investors come earlier and are often steadier than those to VC fund investors*. Because buyout funds purchase established companies, buyout fund investors usually realize returns earlier than VC fund investors, for which fund investments may still be in the cash-burning stage. The expected pattern of interim returns over the life of a successful venture capital fund has sometimes been described as a ***J*-curve,** in which early returns (e.g., over the first five or six years) are negative as the portfolio of companies burns cash but later returns accelerate as companies are exited. In general, the earlier the stage in which a fund invests in companies, the greater the risk and the potential.
- *The returns to VC fund investors are subject to greater error in measurement*. The interim return calculations of private equity funds depend not only on cash-flow transactions with the fund but also on the valuations of the portfolio companies. These valuations are subject to much less uncertainty for buyout funds investing in established companies.

Thus, venture capital investing may be expected to involve more frequent losses than buyouts in return for higher upside potential when investments are successful.

EXAMPLE 8-8 An Investment in Private Equity

The Lee Foundation was established 10 years ago to provide grants to minority- and female-owned enterprises. A well-diversified asset allocation has resulted in successful growth in the value of the foundation's investments. The trustees have thus decided to allocate US$5 million to private equity. Their objectives are to earn significantly high returns on a high-growth investment and to take an active and dominant role in

[53] Emery (2003).

control of the company in which they decide to invest. They understand that such an investment requires a high level of risk tolerance and a multiyear time horizon.

1. Evaluate the suitability of the following three potential investments, with specific reference to short- and long-term returns, sources of risk, and degree of investor control:
   a. Seed investment in a new medical device recently developed by three doctors.
   b. Venture capital trust that invests exclusively in 15 to 20 start-up companies at any given time.
   c. Second-stage (follow-on) investment in a company that successfully patented a new medical device two years ago and seeks to expand its manufacturing facilities.
2. Recommend and justify the investment that is most likely to satisfy the goals of the foundation's proposed US$5 million investment.

Solution to Problem 1:

a. The seed investment is an investment in an early-stage company with no proven "track record" or history of revenues. Therefore, there are not likely to be any immediate or short-term returns because the next stage is marketing and manufacturing this new device. If the sales of this unique device are successful, however, future long-term returns could be significant. Sources of risk include the failure of the device, future competition from other similar companies, lack of follow-on funds for marketing and manufacturing, and the possibility that the device may not receive a patent. Consequently, the level of risk is high. Because the foundation is likely to be the first outside investor, the possibility of taking an active role in the company, possibly as outside board members, is high.
b. The venture capital trust is diversified over many start-up companies and is thus probably providing some current return, with the potential for additional return in the future. Although there is considerable risk associated with start-up companies, the trust is well diversified over many companies, which mitigates the impact of risk of the failure of one or two of the start-ups. There is no outside investor control available because the trust makes all the decisions and is traded on a pubic exchange.
c. The second-stage investment is most likely already showing positive cash flow and net income because it is seeking financing to expand an existing manufacturing facility. Therefore, short-term returns may be attractive and projections probably indicate potential for additional long-term returns, although the level of these returns may be muted in comparison with a seed or start-up because some of the early money has already been made. Investors at the second stage may be able to negotiate some active control, although the founders and seed/start-up investors are probably directly involved in company decisions also.

Solution to Problem 2: The seed company is most consistent with the foundation's objectives of earning a significant return in a high-growth opportunity and having the ability to take an active role in the company. Additionally, the foundation is willing to accept a high degree of risk and a longer-term perspective for future returns.

4.3.2. Roles in the Portfolio The moderately high average correlation of private equity returns with publicly traded share returns that has been documented has an economic explanation that is at least plausible: All types of businesses have some exposure to economic and industry conditions, so correlations of public and private equity returns may be expected to be positive. Furthermore, venture capital has public equity markets as one main exit route, so returns to VC fund investors would be expected to be higher when public equity market values are advancing. Private equity bears more idiosyncratic or company-specific risk than the average seasoned public company, however, so any correlation should not be extremely high.

Private equity probably can play a moderate role as a risk diversifier. However, many investors look to private equity investment for long-term return enhancement.

Given the capacity issues already mentioned and private equity's generally high illiquidity, target allocations of 5 percent or less are commonplace. For example, in 2004, based on money already committed, Canadian public sector pension plans averaged allocations of 3.6 percent and corporate pension plans averaged 1.3 percent.[54]

Among the issues that must be addressed in formulating a strategy for private equity investment are the following:[55]

- *Ability to achieve sufficient diversification*. Suppose an investor's allocation to private equity is 5 percent. Given that institutional partnership commitments are typically not smaller than US\$5 million, a reasonably diversified portfolio (5–10 investments) means commitments totaling 5 × US\$5 million = US\$25 million to 10 × US\$5 million = US\$50 million. These amounts imply that the assets of the institutions investing in this kind of investment typically need to exceed US\$500 million (= US\$25 million ÷ 5%). For smaller investors, a private equity fund of funds is a possible diversification choice, although it involves a second layer of fees.
- *Liquidity of the position*. Direct private equity investments are inherently illiquid. Consequently, private equity funds are also illiquid. Investors in funds must be prepared to have the capital tied up for 7 to 10 years. Although a limited secondary market for private equity commitments exists, the investments trade at highly discounted prices, which makes selling the positions an unattractive proposition.
- *Provision for capital commitment*. An investor in a private equity fund makes a commitment of capital. The cash is advanced over a period of time known as the **commitment period,** which is typically five years. Therefore, the investor needs to make provisions to have cash available for future capital calls.
- *Appropriate diversification strategy*. An investor contemplating an exposure to private equity should be clear on the stand-alone risk factors of an investment and also the effect on the overall risk of the portfolio. Each private equity fund will have a different investment focus, which when combined with other funds in the portfolio, modifies the overall risk. Diversification may be across industry sectors, by stage of company development, and by location:
    - Industry sector (information technology, biotechnology, alternative energy, etc.).
    - Stage (early stage, expansion, buyout, etc.).
    - Geography (locally focused, internationally focused, etc.).

The element shared by all private equity investment is the identification of promising private businesses with committed and talented owner/managers.

[54] Based on Frank Russell Company data.

[55] Andrew Abouchar, CFA, contributed to this section.

For the many private equity investors making indirect investment, the search is for fund managers who are expert in evaluating and managing private equity investments. Indirect investment can include investment not only in newly formed private equity funds but also in secondary-market private equity fund purchases from limited partners seeking liquidity.

4.3.3. Other Issues Among the major requirements for private equity investing is careful due diligence. The framework discussed in Example 8-2 applies, of course; in particular, due diligence items for private equity can usually be placed into one of the following three bins:

1. Evaluation of prospects for market success.
2. Operational review, focusing on internal processes, such as sales management, employment contracts, internal financial controls, product engineering and development, and intellectual property management.
3. Financial/legal review, including the examination of internal financial statements, audited financial statements, auditor's management letters, prior-year budgets, documentation of past board of directors meetings, board minutes, corporate minute books, and assessment of all legal proceedings, intellectual property positions, contracts and contingent liabilities.

Some practical details and comments are as follows:

1. **Evaluation of prospects for market success:**
   - *Markets, competition, and sales prospects.* The private equity investor needs to form a judgment about the prospects for success of the company in the targeted product/service market. This review includes an evaluation of markets, competition, and sales prospects. The information in the business plan is a starting point in making such an appraisal.
   - *Management experience and capabilities.* Quality of management is often considered the single biggest factor in the success of a venture. Due diligence includes a background check on the managers and other key personnel. This should include not only references provided by the company but also independently gathered information from the investor's own sources. The investor should use all available information in assessing the management team's acumen. Moreover, the assessment of management does not stop when the initial investment is made; it is ongoing.
   - *Management's commitment.* Much of the success of a private equity company depends on its managers. Therefore, a potential investor will want to gauge how committed the managers are to the company. There are several factors to use in assessing this:
     - *Percentage ownership.* How much of the company is owned by the management team? Ownership of a large portion of the company is an indication of high commitment to the company.
     - *Compensation incentives.* If management is key to the company's success, an investor will want to ensure that the current managers' interests align with those of the shareholders through the company compensation arrangements.
   - *Cash invested.* How much cash or "skin" has management invested in the company? Investors generally regard the fact that the managers have invested a large portion of their net worth in the company as a particularly good indicator of a highly committed management team. Conversely, if the managers have invested little of their own cash

in the company, the presumption is that they are less than wholly committed to the company's success.

- *Opinion of customers.* When the company is already marketing a product or service, the investor should attempt to learn customer opinions of the company and its product or services.
- *Identity of current investors.* Current investors can give an indication of the company's future success. For example, if a company's product is a medical device dealing with the heart, it is meaningful if several leading cardiologists have already invested in the company.

2. **Operational review:**
   - *Expert validation of technology.* If the company intends to market a new technology, the investor needs to obtain expert validation that the technology is valid and represents an advance.
   - *Employment contracts.* Do key employees have contracts to ensure that they stay with the company? Do non-key employees have contracts with severance clauses that could burden the company's finances?
   - *Intellectual property.* In many companies, the ability to succeed hinges on proprietary information (formulas, processes, designs). An investor should determine whether the company holds relevant patents in such cases (or at least has applied for such patents). These patents could be a design for a machine, a new application of an existing technology, a drug, a medical device, or so on. Potential investors should have reasonable assurance that the company has the ability to conduct business without another company's infringement. Often in this area, an investor will want to consult with patent experts.
3. **Financial/legal review:**
   - *Potential for dilution of interest.* Potential investors also want to investigate the stock options that have been issued to managers and other potential means by which investor interests may be diluted and to ensure contractually that their investment will not be significantly diluted.
   - *Examination of financial statements.* Early-stage companies, in particular, may not have audited financial statements to show. Thus, investors may want to ask for tax returns or conduct their own audits of financial records.

Due diligence for private equity funds includes the managers' experience, capabilities, and commitment, the compensation arrangements, and compliance of the fund with Global Investment Performance Standards® in reporting performance. Fund selection is largely an exercise in evaluating the capabilities of the general manager's management team. Factors that should be considered include the following:

- *Historical returns generated on prior funds.*
- *Consistency of returns.* Has the team had one successful fund or many?
- *Roles and capabilities of specific individuals at the fund.* The investor will want to evaluate whether the fund manager has the needed human resources to effectively select and guide private equity investment.
- *Stability of the team.* Did the current senior personnel generate the track record of the fund manager, or has there been significant personnel turnover?

As the discussion of due diligence makes clear, many characteristics of people, structure, and costs can differentiate a set of private equity investments focused on a similar market opportunity. In contrast, different examples of a commodity, such as natural gas, have highly similar characteristics. Commodity investments are the subject of the next section.

5. COMMODITY INVESTMENTS

A **commodity** is a tangible asset that is typically relatively homogeneous in nature. Because of their relative homogeneity, commodities lend themselves to being the subject of contracts to buy and sell that have standardized terms (as in futures market contracts).[56] Commodity investments are direct or indirect investments in commodities.

The question of whether commodities represent a separate asset class has been extensively debated in both the academic and practitioner literature.[57] Practically, the question is not whether commodity investment is an asset class but whether commodity investment is appropriate for a given investor. If it is, what are the best approach to implement the investment and the appropriate allocation? In some statements of strategic asset allocations, commodities may be included under a heading of "real assets" or "real assets: resources," in which case, they may not be separately distinguished from such real investments as timberland.

Historically, commodity-linked businesses have been the major players in the cash and futures commodity markets. Individual investors in many countries have long been active in the cash markets for precious metals. In some markets, **commodity trading advisers** (CTAs, registered advisers to managed futures funds) are another active group. Historically and currently, institutional investors have been more active in financial futures markets than in commodity futures markets. Investment in publicly traded equities of commodity-linked businesses has probably been the most common approach for both individual and institutional investors to obtain exposure, albeit indirectly, to commodities. Only investment in commodities via cash and the derivatives markets constitutes alternative investing. Those markets are the focus of this treatment.

5.1. The Commodity Market

Investors can gain direct exposure to commodities in spot (cash) markets or in markets for deferred delivery, such as futures and forwards markets. Spot commodity trading can be traced back thousands of years, and commodity futures trading is at least as old as the rice futures trading in Japan several hundred years ago.

Commodity futures markets developed as a response to an economic need by suppliers and users of various agricultural and nonagricultural goods to transfer risk. Moreover, commodity futures markets tend to improve the functioning of the spot and forward markets. For instance, commodity futures may permit greater commodity production and trade because the use of futures hedges reduces the risk of holding spot inventories. By facilitating risk management and trading, commodity futures have grown to become an essential part of the production and marketing of agricultural and nonagricultural goods. Other types of commodity derivatives include options on commodity futures and swap markets.

[56]The relative homogeneity of commodities distinguishes them from tangible assets, such as fine art and other collectibles.

[57]See Huberman (1995), Strongin and Petsch (1995), Greer (1994), Froot (1995), Schneeweis and Spurgin (1997b), Geman (2005), and Erb and Harvey (2006).

Commodities futures are traded on agricultural products, metals, and energy resources. A commodity futures transaction may involve possible physical delivery (i.e., actual delivery of the underlying commodity) or may be "cash-settled," which means that no delivery takes place but a settlement in cash occurs at maturity equal to the gain that a delivery transaction would entail. Although physical delivery is possible for some futures contracts, in practice most positions in futures contracts are offset prior to maturity.

5.1.1. Types of Commodity Investments

There are two broad approaches to investing in commodities: direct and indirect. **Direct commodity investment** entails cash market purchase of physical commodities—agricultural products, metals, and crude oil—or exposure to changes in spot market values via derivatives, such as futures. Because cash market purchases involve actual possession and storage of the physical commodities and incur carrying costs (financing, insurance, and transportation) and storage costs, investors have generally preferred indirect commodity investment.

Indirect commodity investment involves the acquisition of indirect claims on commodities, such as equity in companies specializing in commodity production. As mentioned previously, indirect commodity investment was historically the principal means that most investors used to obtain exposure to commodities. There is increasing evidence, however, that indirect commodity investment—in particular, equity instruments in commodity-linked companies—does not provide effective exposure to commodity price changes.[58] To the degree that companies hedge a major portion of their commodity risk, even commodity-linked companies may not be exposed to the risk of commodity price movement.[59] This fact has been a spur to the creation of investable commodity indices and a current preference for gaining exposure to commodities through derivative markets. In some markets, such as the United States, even small investors can access the commodity markets via mutual funds or exchange-traded funds.

5.1.2. Size of the Commodity Market

With billions of dollars worth of commodities recorded by so many countries in international trade over a given year, spot commodity markets are enormous in scope and value. In the United States alone, the notional value of open interest in commodity futures was estimated at US$350 billion as of the fourth quarter of 2005, with energy futures (natural gas, crude oil, heating oil, and gasoline) the dominant segment.[60]

5.2. Benchmarks and Historical Performance[61]

Although the physical markets for commodities are not centralized, information about commodity prices is transmitted around the world through commodity-based financial products. Thus, performance of commodity investments can be evaluated by using commodity indices that form the basis for many products. The development of active markets for indexed commodity investments has been a major force in broadening investor interest in commodity investment.

5.2.1. Benchmarks

A variety of indices based on futures prices can be used as benchmarks for the performance of futures-based commodity investments. These include the Reuters

[58] See Schneeweis and Spurgin (1997a).
[59] See Chung (2000).
[60] See Barclays Capital's *The Commodity Refiner* (Fourth Quarter 2005), p. 24.
[61] This section draws on CISDM (2005b).

Jefferies/Commodity Research Bureau (RJ/CRB) Index, the Goldman Sachs Commodity Index (GSCI), the Dow Jones–AIG Commodity Index (DJ-AIGCI), and the S&P Commodity Index (S&PCI).

Commodity indices attempt to replicate the returns available to holding long positions in commodities. The DJ-AIGCI, the RJ/CRB Index, the GSCI, and the S&PCI provide returns comparable to passive long positions in listed futures contracts. Because the cost-of-carry model ensures that the return on a fully margined position in a futures contract mimics the return on an underlying spot deliverable, futures contract returns are often used as a surrogate for cash market performance. (The cost-of-carry model relates the futures price to the current spot price and the cost of holding the spot commodity.) All of these indices are considered investable.

The major indices contain different groups of underlying assets. For example, the RJ/CRB Index and the GSCI include energy (oil and gas), metals (industrial and precious), grains (corn, soybeans, and wheat), and soft commodities (cocoa, coffee, cotton, and sugar). Beyond these basic groupings, commodity indices differ widely in composition, weighting scheme, and purpose.

The commodity indices also differ in the relative emphasis placed on various commodities and the procedure used to determine the weightings in the index. A market-cap weighting scheme, so common for equity and bond market indices, cannot be carried over to indices of commodity futures. Because every long futures position has a corresponding short futures position, the market capitalization of a futures contract is always zero. The RJ/CRB Index, for example, groups commodities into four sectors and gives unequal fixed weights to a sector to reflect its perceived relative importance. The GSCI uses world-production weighting. The weights assigned to individual commodities in the GSCI are based on a five-year moving average of world production. Weights are determined each July and are made effective the following January.

Commodity index providers use either arithmetic or geometric averaging to calculate the index return from the component returns. For example, the RJ/CRB Index is based on arithmetic averaging of the monthly component returns; the GSCI is an arithmetic measure of the performance of actively traded, dollar-denominated nearby commodity futures contracts. All contracts are rolled on the fifth business day of the month prior to the expiration month of the contract. Investors attempting to replicate the GSCI must rebalance their portfolios monthly to maintain constant dollar weights.

Subindices of the GSCI are calculated for agricultural, energy, industrial, livestock, and precious metals contracts. Two versions of the indices are available: a total-return version, which assumes that capital sufficient to purchase the basket of commodities is invested at the risk-free rate, and a spot version, which tracks movements in only the futures prices.

5.2.2. Historical Performance

Exhibit 8-13 presents the monthly return, the annualized return, standard deviation of returns, Sharpe ratio, minimum monthly return, and correlations of the GSCI, S&PCI, and DJ-AIGCI with a sample of stock, bond, and hedge fund indices for the period January 1990 through December 2004. The results for the S&PCI and DJ-AIGCI differ meaningfully from the results for the GSCI, with the DJ-AIGCI showing comparable mean returns but lower volatility and the S&PCI evidencing both lower mean returns and the volatility.

The differences can be explained, at least in part, by differences in the components of the indices and different approaches to determining the weights of individual commodity futures contracts in each index. For example, the performance of energy has played the dominant role in results for the GSCI because its portfolio weights are based on the value of worldwide

EXHIBIT 8-13 Commodity Index Performance, 1990–2004

Measure	GSCI	S&PCI	DJ-AIGCI	S&P 500	Lehman Gov./ Corp. Bond	MSCI World	Lehman Global Bond
Annualized mean return	7.08%	4.78%	6.89%	10.94%	7.77%	7.08%	8.08%
Annualized std. dev.	19.26%	12.85%	11.85%	14.65%	4.46%	14.62%	5.23%
Sharpe ratio	0.15	0.04	0.22	0.45	0.78	0.19	0.72
Minimum monthly return	−14.41%	−8.97%	−7.54%	−14.46%	−4.19%	−13.32%	−3.66%
Correlation with GSCI	1.00	0.84	0.89	−0.08	0.03	−0.06	0.06
Correlation with S&PCI	0.84	1.00	0.91	0.03	0.02	0.05	0.07
Correlation with DJ-AIGCI	0.89	0.91	1.00	0.08	0.03	0.15	0.12

Note: MSCI World is the MSCI World equity index.
Source: CISDM (2005b).

EXHIBIT 8-14 Performance of GSCI Subindices, 1990–2004

Subindex	Annualized Return	Annualized Std. Dev.	Sharpe Ratio	Minimum Monthly Return
GSCI Agricultural	−2.49%	13.99%	−0.49	−10.57%
GSCI Energy	9.77	32.48	0.17	−22.14%
GSCI Industrial Metals	5.42	16.98	0.07	−12.89%
GSCI Livestock	3.58	13.75	−0.05	−12.76%
GSCI Nonenergy	1.21	9.04	−0.34	−6.27%
GSCI Precious Metals	1.66	12.68	−0.21	−11.03%

Source: CISDM (2005b).

production for each included commodity. Based on that criterion, the weight of energy-related futures has exceeded two-thirds.[62] Energy was a good performer over the period examined. The DJ-AIGCI's weights reflect primarily futures contract liquidity data as supplemented by production data, and the influence of energy on the DJ-AIGCI's results, although important, is less than for the GSCI.[63] Each index represents a somewhat distinct view of the world commodity marketplace.

On a stand-alone basis, as judged by the Sharpe ratio, commodities have underperformed U.S. and world bonds and equities (except for the DJ-AIGCI versus the MSCI World Index). In terms of the minimum monthly return, the GSCI registered −14.41 percent, which is not significantly different from the S&P 500's −14.46 percent but is higher than the minimum monthly return of either U.S. or global bonds.

The correlations of the three commodity indices with the traditional asset classes are of a similar order of magnitude and close to zero, indicating potential as risk diversifiers.

Exhibit 8-14, which presents the performance statistics for the six GSCI sector subindices, shows considerable difference in stand-alone risk and return among them (particularly between the GSCI Energy Index and the other subindices). Energy plays a major role in the positive Sharpe ratio and the high volatility of the GSCI shown in Exhibit 8-13.

Another message of Exhibit 8-14 is that one cannot think of commodities as a homogeneous market of similar investments. In data not reported, the average correlation of GSCI commodity sector returns is low.

5.2.2.1. Recent Performance (2000–2004) Exhibit 8-15 shows that during this recent period, all commodity indices outperformed U.S. and world equities but not bonds. The stand-alone comparisons with traditional asset classes appear to be time-period dependent. The consistent feature in the evidence is correlation. Although the commodities' correlations with bonds have gone up in comparison with the longer (1990 to 2004) period, the generally low correlations among commodities and traditional asset classes in Exhibit 8-15 is consistent with the evidence for the longer time period.

5.2.2.2. Commodity Index Return Components In general, the return on a commodity futures contract is not the same as the return on the underlying spot commodity. A commodity

[62]According to Erb and Harvey (2006), Table 8-2, the weight of energy-related futures in the GSCI exceeded two-thirds as of May 2004.

[63]Erb and Harvey, ibid., Table 8-4, show a weight of energy for the DJ AIGCI of less than 40 percent as of May 2004.

EXHIBIT 8-15 Recent Commodity Index Performance, 2000–2004

Measure	GSCI	S&PCI	DJ- AIGCI	S&P 500	Lehman Gov./ Corp. Bond	MSCI World	Lehman Global Bond
Annualized mean return	13.77%	10.27%	12.63%	−2.30%	8.00%	−2.05%	8.47%
Annualized std. dev.	22.10%	16.62%	13.85%	16.35%	4.76%	15.62%	6.02%
Sharpe ratio	0.50	0.06	0.72	−0.31	1.11	−0.30	0.96
Minimum monthly return	−14.41%	−8.71%	−7.54%	−10.87%	−4.19%	−10.98%	−3.66%
Correlation with GSCI	1.00	0.89	0.89	−0.05	0.05	0.00	0.10
Correlation with S&PCI	0.89	1.00	0.94	0.03	0.07	0.08	0.18
Correlation with DJ-AIGCI	0.89	0.94	1.00	0.09	0.05	0.14	0.20

Source: CISDM (2005b).

EXHIBIT 8-16 Calculation of Roll Return

(1) Contract Maturity	(2) Futures Price as of May 200X	(3) Futures Price as of April 200X	(4) Change in Spot Price	(5) = (2) – (3) – (4) Roll Return/Yield
June 200X	US$40.58	US$39.10	US$0.40	US$1.08
Sept. 200X	US$39.67	US$38.70	US$0.40	US$0.57
Dec. 200X	US$38.45	US$37.65	US$0.40	US$0.40

futures investor needs to understand, in particular, how the returns on a futures contract–based commodity index are calculated. The returns have three components: the spot return, the collateral return, and the roll return.

The **spot return** or **price return** derives from changes in commodity futures prices that come from changes in the underlying spot prices via the cost-of-carry model.[64] Because of the cost of owning and storing spot commodities, when the spot price goes up (down), so does the futures price, which gives rise to a positive (negative) return to a long futures position. The change in spot prices should be reflected in the change in the price of the futures price with the shortest time to maturity (the nearby futures contract) over the time period. Anson (2002a) noted that most of the shocks with respect to physical commodities tend to be events that reduce the current supply and cause prices to rise; thus, physical commodities have positive event risk.

Collateral return or **collateral yield** comes from the assumption that the full value of the underlying futures contract is invested to earn the risk-free interest rate—that is, that an investor long a futures contract posts 100 percent margin in the form of T-bills (in such a case the futures position is said to be **fully collateralized**). The implied yield is the collateral return.

Roll return or **roll yield** arises from rolling long futures positions forward through time. The concept is best explained through an example. Consider the data given in Exhibit 8-16, which shows a downward-sloping term structure of futures prices (i.e., the more distant the contract maturity, the lower the futures price), a situation known as **backwardation.**

A monthly roll return is computed as the change in the futures contract price over the month minus the change in the spot price over the month. Suppose an investor establishes a position in the June 200X contract in April 200X when the futures price is US$39.10. Between April 200X and May 200X, the futures price increases to US$40.58, for a gain of US$1.48, of which US$0.40 is attributable to a US$0.40 increase in the spot price (perhaps because the supply has been reduced as a result of bad weather). Note that the closer the futures contract is to maturity, the greater the roll return/yield is. In this example, the roll return on the June contract (US$1.08) is greater than the next position, the September contract (US$0.57), which is, in turn, greater than that of the December contract (US$0.40).

When the futures markets are in backwardation, a positive return will be earned from a simple buy-and-hold strategy. The positive return is earned because as the futures contract gets closer to maturity, its price must converge to that of the spot price of the commodity. Because in backwardation the spot price is greater than the futures price, the futures price must increase in value. (The opposite is true with an upward-sloping term structure of futures

[64]Recall that the cost-of-carry model is $F = Se^{(r+c-y)(T-t)}$, where F is the futures price, S is the current spot price of the underlying commodity, r is the risk-free rate of return, c is the cost of storage, y is the convenience yield, and $T - t$ is the time to maturity of the contract. For more details, see Chance (2003).

EXHIBIT 8-17 Calculation of Commodity Index Total Return

Year	GSCI Total Annual Return	GSCI Collateral Yield	GSCI Roll Return/Yield	GSCI Spot Annual Return
1970	15.1%	7.3%	2.9%	4.9%
:	:	:	:	:
2000	49.7	8.6	14.2	26.9
Average	15.3	7.6	3.0	4.7

Source: Anson (2002a).

prices, or **contango.**) All else being equal, an increase in a commodity's convenience yield (the nonmonetary benefit from owning the spot commodity) should lead to futures market conditions offering higher roll returns; the converse holds for a decline in convenience yields. (Convenience yields are discussed later.) Over the 1990 to 2004 period, there was an overall positive relationship between the mean monthly roll return and intramonth spot price volatility in the GSCI Energy and Industrial Metals subindices; because of the importance for the GSCI of the sectors associated with these subindices, the relationship held for the GSCI overall.[65] In general, the effect is more pronounced for nonperishable, storable commodities, whose convenience yield rises in periods of increased volatility because of demand and supply shocks.

Using the data in Exhibit 8-17, we can illustrate the calculation of the total return for the GSCI.

The total return on a commodity index = Collateral return + Roll return + Spot return. Thus, for 2000, the total return on the GSCI = 8.6% + 14.2% + 26.9% = 49.7%.

5.2.3. Interpretation Issues

The use of the commodity indices as benchmarks assumes that commodities are approved in the investor's investment policy statement as a distinct asset class in which the investor may invest. If commodities do not receive separate treatment but are included within some broader asset class, such as real assets, evaluation of performance should be based on a customized benchmark that reflects the other assets included in the asset class.

In interpreting historical results, such as those presented here, the investor should also be sensitive to differences in economic conditions between the historical period and current and forecasted future period.

5.3. Commodities: Investment Characteristics and Roles

Some experts are now advising investors to afford commodity investment a larger allocation in their portfolios than they have heretofore given it. (Allocations to commodities in most institutional and individual portfolios have typically been well under 5 percent.) In the following sections, we discuss the characteristics of commodities as investments.

For the reasons discussed earlier, direct investment in commodities for most investors will be via the futures markets. For investors seeking passive exposure to commodities, the liquidity of the market for futures contracts on a given commodity index will be a major consideration. The three most widely used futures contracts are those based on the GSCI, the DJ-AIGCI, and the RJ/CRB Index, with the GSCI representing approximately 85 percent of the combined open interest of these contracts as of the time of this writing.

[65]See CISDM (2005b). The findings relate to the 1990–2004 period.

5.3.1. Investment Characteristics The discussion of the historical performance of commodities highlighted the need for active investors to understand the investment characteristics of commodities on a sector- or individual-commodity level. However, there are some common themes. The chief two relate to characteristics that affect use of commodities in managing portfolio risk and serving as an inflation hedge.

5.3.1.1. Special Risk Characteristics With some consistency, commodities have tended to have correlations with equities and bonds that are unusually low even in the realm of alternative investments. But the risk characteristics of commodities are more nuanced than simple correlation statistics can reveal and indicate several attractive features of commodities. In periods of financial and economic distress, commodity prices tend to rise, potentially providing valuable diversification services in such times. Long-term growth in world demand for certain commodities in limited supply, such as petroleum-related commodities, may be a factor in their long-term trend growth.

Nevertheless, commodities are generally business-cycle sensitive. The reason commodities behave differently under different economic conditions has to do with the sources of their returns. The determinants of commodity returns include the following:

1. *Business cycle–related supply and demand*. Commodity prices are determined by the supply and demand of the underlying commodities. Because the supply and demand conditions are determined by different economic fundamentals from those affecting stocks and bonds, commodity prices are expected to be sensitive to the business cycle but have little or even negative correlation with stocks and bonds. For example, the variation in spot and futures prices of industrial metals has a strong business-cycle component.[66] Anson (2002a) suggested three reasons commodity returns have been weakly correlated with stock and bond returns. First, commodities correlate positively with inflation whereas stocks and bonds are negatively correlated with inflation. Second, commodity prices and stock/bond prices react differently in different phases of the business cycle. Commodity future prices are more affected by short-term expectations, whereas stock and bond prices are affected by long-term expectations. Finally, commodity prices tend to decline during times of a weak economy.
2. *Convenience yield*. The theory of storage splits the difference between the futures price and the spot price into three components: the forgone interest from purchasing and storing the commodity, storage costs, and the commodity's convenience yield.[67] Convenience yield reflects an embedded consumption-timing option in holding a storable commodity. Furthermore, the theory predicts an inverse relationship between the level of inventories and convenience yield: At low inventory levels, convenience yields are high, and vice versa. A related implication is that the term structure of forward price volatility generally declines with time to expiration of the futures contract—the so-called Samuelson effect. This is caused by the expectation that, although at shorter horizons mismatched supply and demand forces for the underlying commodity increase the volatility of cash prices, these forces will fall into equilibrium at longer horizons.
3. *Real options under uncertainty*. Oil futures markets are often backwardated; in these markets, futures prices are often below the current spot price. This may be caused by the existence of real options under uncertainty.[68] A **real option** is an option involving

[66] See Fama and French (1988), Schneeweis, Spurgin (1997b), and CISDM (2005b).
[67] See Kaldor (1939), Working (1948, 1949), and Telser (1958).
[68] See Litzenberger and Rabinowitz (1995).

decisions related to tangible assets or processes. In other words, producers are holding valuable real options—options to produce or not to produce—and will not exercise them unless the spot prices start to climb up. Production occurs only if discounted futures prices are below spot prices, and backwardation results if the risk of future prices is sufficiently high. A major consequence of a downward-sloping term structure of futures prices is the opportunity to capture a positive roll return as investment in expiring contracts is moved to cheaper new outstanding contracts.

The role of commodities in regard to protecting portfolio value against unexpected inflation has been a continuing theme of comments on the characteristics of commodities as investments. Among the reasons for including commodities in a portfolio are that they are:[69]

- "Natural" sources of return (i.e., related to economic fundamentals) over the long term, as discussed above.
- Providers of protection for a portfolio against unexpected inflation.

The premise that investments in physical commodities may hedge inflation is natural. The prices of some commodities, such as crude oil, may have significant links to the component costs of official price indices, and certain commodities, such as gold, have been traditionally demanded as stores of value by investors during inflationary times.

EXAMPLE 8-9 An Investment in Energy Commodities

Nancy Lopez, CIO of a university endowment fund, is reviewing investment data with the university's treasurer, Sergio Garcia. They are discussing performance of the fund's investment in oil futures. Garcia refers to Exhibit 8-18 and states: "I thought prices for futures contracts maturing in more distant months were usually higher than prices for nearer-month contracts, but this exhibit shows the opposite case. Spot prices are even higher than the futures. What is this situation called, and what is causing it?"

EXHIBIT 8-18 Futures Data

Contract Maturity	Futures Price as of July 200X	Futures Price as of June 200X	Change in Spot Price	Roll Return
Aug. 200X	US$28.90	US$27.90	US$0.35	US$?
Sep. 200X	US$28.55	US$27.65	US$0.35	US$?
Oct. 200X	US$27.88	US$27.01	US$0.35	US$?

1. Compute the roll return from the information in Exhibit 8-18.
2. Characterize the term structure of futures prices.

[69]See Strongin and Petsch (1995), who also include pricing inefficiencies (opportunities for active management), a feature that is particularly relevant to managed futures investing, which is discussed later.

3. Discuss one reason the situation shown in Exhibit 8-18 might exist.

Garcia then asks, "In this situation, it seems our investment in energy commodities can only show negative returns. Is this true? Given the recent hurricane activity, I thought our investments would be making money."

4. Recommend a futures strategy that will provide a positive return in this scenario. Justify your recommendation with reference to the roll return calculated in Part 1, and formulate your response by explaining the benefit of this strategy in an environment of a declining term structure of futures prices.

Solution to Problem 1: The roll returns are as follows:

August contract = US\$28.9 – US\$27.9 – US\$0.35 = US\$0.65.

September contract = US\$28.55 – US\$27.65 – US\$0.35 = US\$0.55.

October contract = US\$27.88 – US\$27.01 – US\$0.35 = US\$0.52.

Solution to Problem 2: The term structure of futures prices is downward sloping. The oil futures market is in backwardation.

Solution to Problem 3: Oil producers hold valuable real options to produce or not to produce. They may not exercise this option unless spot prices begin to rise. Production may occur only if futures prices are below the current spot price, which is associated with a downward-sloping term structure of futures prices.

Solution to Problem 4: When futures markets are in backwardation, a positive return will be earned from a simple buy-and-hold strategy. This occurs because as the futures contract gets closer to maturity, its price will rise to converge with the higher spot price. This increase in value produces a positive roll return, as calculated in the solution to Problem 1.

5.3.1.2. Commodities as an Inflation Hedge[70] The premise that commodities are an inflation hedge can be tested by calculating the correlation of spot GSCI returns, as well as stock, bond, and hedge fund returns, with a proxy for unexpected inflation.[71] The proxy we have used is the monthly change in the rate of inflation. For the 1990 to 2004 period, correlations were calculated by using data in months in which the change in the rate of inflation was beyond 1 standard deviation from the average change. The results are presented in the last column of Exhibit 8-19.

Stocks and bonds in Exhibit 8-19 exhibit a negative correlation with unexpected inflation (−0.23 and −0.06, respectively), as do some commodity classes (e.g., agriculture, livestock, and nonenergy). However, storable commodities directly related to the intensity of economic activity exhibit positive correlation with unexpected inflation (0.15 for precious metals and 0.46 for energy). Similarly, industrial metals have a correlation of 0.11. These results suggest

[70]There is extensive research on commodities as an inflation hedge covering a variety of time periods and markets; overall, it supports the proposition that at least some commodities or commodity index investments have value as inflation hedges. See Becker and Finnerty (2000) and references therein.

[71]Inflation was measured by changes in the U.S. Consumer Price Index.

EXHIBIT 8-19 Factor Correlations, 1990–2004

Index	S&P	Lehman Gov./Corp	Change in Credit Spread (Baa–Aaa)	Change in Term Spread	Change in Bond Volume	Change in Stock Volume	Unexpected Inflation
GSCI	−0.08	0.03	−0.09	−0.03	−0.05	−0.13	0.44
GSCI Agric.	0.18	−0.03	−0.01	0.02	0.01	0.00	−0.27
GSCI Energy	−0.11	0.03	−0.08	−0.03	−0.03	−0.09	0.46
GSCI Industrial Metals	0.21	−0.14	−0.22	0.19	0.07	−0.13	0.11
GSCI Livestock	0.01	0.01	−0.02	−0.01	−0.03	−0.03	−0.12
GSCI Nonenergy	0.20	−0.03	−0.09	0.05	−0.01	−0.08	−0.23
GSCI Precious Metals	−0.08	0.04	0.09	−0.02	−0.02	−0.06	0.15
S&P 500	1.00	0.13	−0.14	−0.05	0.00	−0.29	−0.23
Lehman Gov./Corp.	0.13	1.00	0.00	−0.96	−0.11	−0.02	−0.06
HFCI	0.59	0.17	−0.24	−0.08	−0.17	−0.35	0.19

Notes: Monthly changes in inflation beyond 1 standard deviation of the average were used to proxy for unexpected inflation. The HFCI is the Hedge Fund Composite Index computed by CISDM.
Source: CISDM (2005b).

that direct investment in energy—and, to a lesser degree, industrial and precious metals—may provide a significant inflation hedge.

As shown in Exhibit 8-19, the returns to the GSCI reflect the inflation-hedging properties of its dominant sector, energy. The broad conclusion from the time period examined, 1990–2004, is that commodity sectors differ in inflation-hedging properties, with storable commodities (such as energy) that are directly linked to the intensity of economic activity having superior inflation-hedging properties.

5.3.2. Roles in the Portfolio The principal roles that have been suggested for commodities in the portfolio are as:

- A potent portfolio risk diversifier.
- An inflation hedge, providing an expected offset to the losses to such assets as conventional debt instruments, which typically lose value during periods of unexpected inflation.[72]

There is support both in the historical record and economics for these roles. Research also indicates a link between the two roles, which suggests that most investable commodity indices provide diversification advantages to stock and bond investment primarily during periods of unexpected changes in inflation.[73] To the degree that inflation is already incorporated into the yield structure of bonds and the cash flow of companies—that is, inflation is fully anticipated—the economy may have periods of high commodity prices or price increases with positive stock and bond returns. Halpern and Warsager (1998) observed that commodity indices add their most value as inflation hedges in traditional stock and bond portfolios during periods of unexpected changes in inflation.

More ambiguous is a role of passive long-only commodity futures investments in increasing the expected return vis-à-vis a portfolio of traditional and other alternative investments. Erb and Harvey (2005) claimed that the average historical excess returns of individual commodity futures is approximately zero. They suggest that the measured positive excess return of portfolios of these futures for some time periods is a result not of a risk premium but of the portfolio weighting selected and of rebalancing to it.

Long-term investors with liabilities indexed to inflation, such as DB plans, may be able to improve their risk–return trade-off by including commodities in the portfolio.[74] For university endowments, which support the inflation-sensitive costs of operating a university, commodities can have a role as a good risk diversifier in a portfolio that needs inflation protection. The role of commodities in a private wealth client's portfolio awaits further study, but passive investment programs have generally been infrequently marketed to that group.

Below, using the methodology familiar from the section on real estate, we provide some quantitative information on the *ex post* role of commodities as a risk diversifier.

In Exhibit 8-20, the benefits of commodity investment are examined by using the GSCI (a long-only futures-based investable commodity index) in combination with equities, bonds, and hedge funds in various weights for the period January 1990 through December 2004.[75]

As presented in Exhibit 8-14 from a stand-alone perspective, whether risk-adjusted or not, commodities underperformed U.S. and world bond and equity markets during the sample

[72]See Bodie (1983), Greer (1978), Halpern and Warsager (1998), and Becker and Finnerty (2000).

[73]For example, see Halpern and Warsager (1998).

[74]See Nijman and Swinkels (2003), pp. 1–36.

[75]The GSCI futures contract has been the most active commodity index futures listed in the United States for 2004 in terms of outstanding open interest and total volume.

EXHIBIT 8-20 Commodities Performance in Portfolios, 1990–2004

Measure	Portfolio I	Portfolio II	Portfolio III	Portfolio IV	Portfolio V	Portfolio VI
Annualized return	9.64%	9.51%	9.99%	7.86%	8.07%	8.56%
Annualized std. dev.	7.94%	7.19%	6.87%	8.29%	7.55%	7.16%
Sharpe ratio	0.67	0.73	0.83	0.43	0.50	0.60
Minimum monthly return	−6.25%	−6.18%	−6.28%	−5.61%	−5.67%	−5.77%
Correlation with GSCI	−0.07	0.47	0.22	−0.03	0.48	0.24

Notes:
Portfolio I: 50 percent S&P 500, 50 percent Lehman Gov./Corp. Bond.
Portfolio II: 40 percent S&P 500, 40 percent Lehman Gov./Corp., and 20 percent GSCI.
Portfolio III: 40 percent S&P 500, 40 percent Lehman Gov./Corp., 10 percent GSCI, 10 percent HFCI.
Portfolio IV: 50 percent MSCI World, 50 percent Lehman Global Bond.
Portfolio V: 40 percent MSCI World, 40 percent Lehman Global, 20 percent GSCI.
Portfolio VI: 40 percent MSCI World, 40 percent Lehman Global, 10 percent GSCI, 10 percent HFCI.
Source: CISDM (2005b).

EXHIBIT 8-21 Recent Commodities Performance in Portfolios, 2000–2004

Measure	Portfolio I	Portfolio II	Portfolio III	Portfolio IV	Portfolio V	Portfolio VI
Annualized return	3.15%	5.66%	4.81%	3.43%	5.88%	5.03%
Annualized std. dev.	7.93%	7.60%	6.94%	8.56%	8.26%	7.57%
Sharpe ratio	0.06	0.39	0.30	0.09	0.38	0.31
Minimum monthly return	−4.36%	−5.05%	−4.12%	−4.94%	−5.40%	−4.46%
Correlation with GSCI	−0.04	0.55	0.30	0.03	0.56	0.33

Notes:
Portfolio I: 50 percent S&P 500, 50 percent Lehman Gov./Corp. Bond.
Portfolio II: 40 percent S&P 500, 40 percent Lehman Gov./Corp., 20 percent GSCI.
Portfolio III: 40 percent S&P 500, 40 percent Lehman Gov./Corp., 10 percent GSCI, 10 percent HFCI.
Portfolio IV: 50 percent MSCI World. 50 percent Lehman Global Bond.
Portfolio V: 40 percent MSCI World, 40 percent Lehman Global, 0 percent GSCI.
Portfolio VI: 40 percent MSCI World, 40 percent Lehman Global, 10 percent GSCI, 10 percent HFCI.
Source: CISDM (2005b)

period. However, the low or negative correlations of GSCI returns with returns to the S&P 500 (−0.08), Lehman Government/Corporate Bond Index (0.03), HFCI (0.09), MSCI World Index (−0.06), and Lehman Global Bond Index (0.06) suggested diversification benefits and the potential for improvement in the Sharpe ratio by including commodities. Exhibit 8-20 supports those conclusions.

Exhibit 8-21 examines the evidence for a more recent time period. When added to a U.S. portfolio of stocks and bonds, the GSCI helps reduce the standard deviation of the portfolio from 7.93 percent (Portfolio I) to 7.60 percent (Portfolio II). Additionally, risk-adjusted performance (Sharpe ratio) improves significantly from 0.06 (Portfolio I) to 0.39 (Portfolio II). Similarly, when added to a global stock/bond portfolio, the GSCI reduces volatility from 8.56 percent (Portfolio IV) to 8.26 percent (Portfolio V) and increases the Sharpe ratio from

0.09 to 0.38. Adding more assets, such as hedge funds, to the portfolio results in worse performance (Portfolio VI versus Portfolio V).

This discussion has focused on passive long-only exposures. Commodities also offer potential for active management that may involve short as well as long positions. For example, research for the United States has indicated that the benefits to adding commodity futures, particularly metals and agricultural futures (both managed and unmanaged), to a portfolio accrue almost exclusively when the U.S. Federal Reserve (the central bank) is following a restrictive monetary policy.[76] Such results suggest an active strategy based on central bank actions and monetary conditions. As another example, an investor who believes that a commodity's price reverts to the underlying production costs might implement an active long–short commodity program based on divergences from production cost value. Frequently, active programs involve momentum strategies that typically go long after recent prior returns have been positive and short after recent prior returns have been negative.

Active programs may be executed within a separately managed account or a private commodity pool. Private commodity pools will be the focus of the section on managed futures programs later in the chapter.

In the next section we discuss one of the most important types of alternative investments, the hedge fund.

6. HEDGE FUNDS

Hedge funds as a group have become a booming segment of the alternative investment market, with appeal to many segments of the private wealth and institutional investor markets. The impact of hedge funds has been broad in scope. The trading activity of hedge funds constitutes a substantial portion of trading volume in a number of traditional investment markets. Services to hedge funds, known as *prime brokerage,* have become an important and actively contested revenue source among major sell-side investment firms.[77] The competition from hedge funds has caused an increasing number of equity and bond mutual funds to seek approval from shareholders to make increased use of derivative strategies and short selling.[78]

The first hedge fund was established in the late 1940s as a long–short hedged equity vehicle. More recently, institutional investors—corporate and public pension funds, endowments and trusts, and bank trust departments—have included hedge funds as one segment of a well-diversified portfolio.

There is no precise legal or universally accepted definition of a hedge fund, and hedge funds can take many forms. Originally, hedge funds were private partnerships that took long and short equity positions to reduce net market exposure in exchange for accepting a lower rate of investment return. In other words, they were "hedged" funds. Today, the term *hedge fund* is much broader. Rather than indicating use of hedging in the portfolio, the organizational and structural characteristics of the portfolio define it as a hedge fund.

Generally, hedge funds intentionally adopt structures that permit them to be loosely regulated pooled investment vehicles, although a trend toward greater regulatory oversight is

[76] See Jensen, Mercer, and Johnson (2002).

[77] **Prime brokerage** (or **prime brokering**) is a suite of services that is often specified to include support in accounting and reporting, leveraged trade execution, financing, securities lending (related to short-selling activities), and start-up advice (for new entities).

[78] See Laise (2006), pp. D1, D2.

in motion.[79] The nature of hedge funds as private pools has permitted this investment vehicle to avoid certain reporting and other requirements, as well as some restrictions on incentive fees, that apply to many other investment vehicles. For example, unlike traditional mutual funds, most hedge fund vehicles can take aggressive long or short positions and use leverage aggressively.

Managed futures are now frequently classified as hedge funds. However, this chapter will discuss them in a separate section to give them adequate coverage.

Each hedge fund strategy is constructed to take advantage of certain market opportunities. Hedge funds use different investment strategies and thus are often classified according to investment style. There is substantial diversity in risk attributes and investment opportunities among styles, which reflects the flexibility of the hedge fund format. In general, this diversity benefits investors by increasing the range of choices among investment attributes. We will explain the diversity in more detail.

6.1. The Hedge Fund Market

The hedge fund market has experienced tremendous growth in the past 15 years and keeps evolving. The market has witnessed a proliferation of hedge funds and products offered by hedge funds. As more hedge funds with similar strategies enter the market, returns on their once-unique strategies start to shrink. Liquidity and capacity constraints have affected some hedge funds and driven some of them to become—voluntarily or involuntarily—defunct. Some have been able to return the money to their investors, but others, unfortunately, could not and did not. Nevertheless, new hedge funds continue to be established and to try their new strategies, with the successful ones being mimicked by imitators. Although many hedge funds maintain that their strategies seek "absolute returns" that require no benchmark, some institutional investors who invest in hedge funds are asking for relative performance evaluation, which requires some benchmarking.

6.1.1. Types of Hedge Fund Investments

Many style classifications of hedge funds exist; the following classification of hedge fund style will be the basis for most of our discussion. Keep in mind that industry usage applies the term *arbitrage* somewhat loosely to mean, roughly, a "low-risk" rather than a "no-risk" investment operation.

- *Equity market neutral*. Equity market-neutral managers attempt to identify overvalued and undervalued equity securities while neutralizing the portfolio's exposure to market risk by combining long and short positions. Portfolios are typically structured to be market, industry, sector, and dollar neutral. This is accomplished by holding long and short equity positions with roughly equal exposure to the related market or sector factors. The market opportunity for equity market-neutral programs comes from (1) their flexibility to take short as well as long positions in securities without regard to the securities' weights in a benchmark and (2) the existence of pockets of inefficiencies (i.e., mispricing relative to intrinsic value) in equity markets, particularly as related to overvalued securities. Because

[79]As of 2006 in the United States, the SEC requires hedge fund advisers to register with it, which subjects them to random audits, record-keeping and compliance requirements, and information filing requirements. As of early 2006, it was estimated that 15–20 percent of U.S. hedge fund advisers were exempt from SEC registration requirements (Kara Scannell, "Making Hedge Funds Less Secret," *Wall Street Journal*, February 3, 2006, pp. C1, C5).

many investors face constraints relative to shorting stocks, situations of overvaluation may be slower to correct than those of undervaluation.

- *Convertible arbitrage*. Convertible arbitrage strategies attempt to exploit anomalies in the prices of corporate convertible securities, such as convertible bonds, warrants, and convertible preferred stock. Managers in this category buy or sell these securities and then hedge part or all of the associated risks. The simplest example is buying convertible bonds and hedging the equity component of the bonds' risk by shorting the associated stock. The cash proceeds from the short sale remain with the hedge fund's prime broker but earn interest, and the hedge fund may earn an extra margin through leverage when the bonds' current yield exceeds the borrowing rate of money from the prime broker. The risks include changes in the price of the underlying stock, changes in expected volatility of the stock, changes in the level of interest rates, and changes in the credit standing of the issuer. In addition to collecting the coupon on the underlying convertible bond, convertible arbitrage strategies typically make money if the expected volatility of the underlying asset increases or if the price of the underlying asset increases rapidly. Depending on the hedge strategy, the strategy will also make money if the credit quality of the issuer improves.
- *Fixed-income arbitrage*. Managers dealing in fixed-income arbitrage attempt to identify overvalued and undervalued fixed-income securities primarily on the basis of expectations of changes in the term structure of interest rates or the credit quality of various related issues or market sectors. Fixed-income portfolios are generally neutralized against directional market movements because the portfolios combine long and short positions.
- *Distressed securities*. Portfolios of distressed securities are invested in both the debt and equity of companies that are in or near bankruptcy. Distressed debt and equity securities are fundamentally different from nondistressed securities. Most investors are unprepared for the legal difficulties and negotiations with creditors and other claimants that are common with distressed companies. Traditional investors prefer to transfer those risks to others when a company is in danger of default. Furthermore, many investors are prevented by charter from holding securities that are in default or at risk of default. Because of the relative illiquidity of distressed debt and equity, short sales are difficult, so most funds are long.
- *Merger arbitrage*. Merger arbitrage, also called *deal arbitrage,* seeks to capture the price spread between current market prices of corporate securities and their value upon successful completion of a takeover, merger, spin-off, or similar transaction involving more than one company. In merger arbitrage, the opportunity typically involves buying the stock of a target company after a merger announcement and shorting an appropriate amount of the acquiring company's stock.
- *Hedged equity*. Hedged equity strategies attempt to identify overvalued and undervalued equity securities. Portfolios are typically not structured to be market, industry, sector, and dollar neutral, and they may be highly concentrated. For example, the value of short positions may be only a fraction of the value of long positions and the portfolio may have a net long exposure to the equity market. Hedged equity is the largest of the various hedge fund strategies in terms of assets under management.[80]
- *Global macro*. Global macro strategies primarily attempt to take advantage of systematic moves in major financial and nonfinancial markets through trading in currencies, futures, and option contracts, although they may also take major positions in traditional equity and bond markets. For the most part, they differ from traditional hedge fund strategies in that

[80]The equivalent classification termed "equity long–short" represented 28.2 percent of the Credit Suisse/Tremont Hedge Fund Index as of early 2006 (www.hedgeindex.com accessed March 12, 2006).

they concentrate on major market trends rather than on individual security opportunities. Many global macro managers use derivatives, such as futures and options, in their strategies. Managed futures are sometimes classified under global macro as a result.

- *Emerging markets*. These funds focus on the emerging and less mature markets. Because short selling is not permitted in most emerging markets and because futures and options are not available, these funds tend to be long.
- *Fund of funds*. A **fund of funds** (FOF) is a fund that invests in a number of underlying hedge funds. A typical FOF invests in 10 to 30 hedge funds, and some FOFs are even more diversified. Although FOF investors can achieve diversification among hedge fund managers and strategies, they have to pay two layers of fees—one to the hedge fund manager, and the other to the manager of the FOF.[81]

There is no single standard classification system or set of labels for hedge fund strategies. One provider of hedge fund benchmarks classifies strategies into the following five broad groups:[82]

1. *Relative value* in which the manager seeks to exploit valuation discrepancies through long and short positions. This label may be used as a supercategory for, for example, equity market neutral, convertible arbitrage, and hedged equity.
2. *Event driven* in which the manager focuses on opportunities created by corporate transactions (e.g., mergers). Merger arbitrage and distressed securities would be included in this group.
3. *Equity hedge* in which the manager invests in long and short equity positions with varying degrees of equity market exposure and leverage.
4. *Global asset allocators* which are opportunistically long and short a variety of financial and/or nonfinancial assets.
5. *Short selling* in which the manager shorts equities in the expectation of a market decline.

The five most widely used hedge fund strategies, accounting for 85 to 90 percent of assets under management in the hedge fund industry as of the early 2000s, are three equity-based strategies (equity market neutral, hedged equity, and merger arbitrage), one fixed-income strategy (convertible arbitrage), and global macro, which uses all types of assets, including currencies and commodities.

The compensation structure of hedge funds comprises a percentage of net asset value (NAV) as a management fee plus an incentive fee. The management fee is also known as an "asset under management" or **AUM fee.** The management fee generally ranges from 1 percent to 2 percent. The incentive fee is a percentage of profits as specified by the terms of the investment. It has traditionally been 20 percent but has recently averaged approximately 17.5 percent.[83] Recently, roughly 50 percent of hedge funds were using a management fee of 1 percent, 1.5 percent, or 2 percent combined with an incentive fee of 20 percent.

The great majority of funds have a high-water mark provision that applies to the payment of the incentive fee. Intuitively, a **high-water mark** (HWM) is a specified net asset value level

[81]Returns on FOFs have been found to be more positively correlated with equity markets than returns on hedge funds individually; see Kat (2005, pp. 51–57).

[82]This list follows the categories established for the EACM100® Index of hedge funds by EACM Advisors LLC.

[83]As reported by Black (2005, p. 186) based on the CISDM database as of January 2004.

that a fund must exceed before performance fees are paid to the hedge fund manager. Once the first incentive fee has been paid, the highest month-end NAV establishes a high-water mark. If the NAV then falls below the HWM, no incentive fee is paid until the fund's NAV exceeds the HWM; then the incentive fee for a "1 plus 20" structure (a 1 percent management fee plus a 20 percent incentive fee) is 20 percent of the positive difference between the ending NAV and the HWM NAV. The new, higher NAV establishes a new HWM. A minority of funds also specify that no incentive fee is earned until a specified minimum rate of return (hurdle rate) is earned.

The purpose of a HWM provision is to ensure that the hedge fund manager earns an incentive fee only once for the same gain. For the hedge fund manager, the HWM is like a call option on a fraction of the increase in the value of the fund's NAV. Many hedge fund managers depend on earning the incentive fee. Given a 15 percent gain, a 1 and 20 fund would earn about 4 percent of the asset versus 1 percent if no incentive fee were earned.

Hedge fund investors also often take the opportunities offered them to withdraw capital from a fund on a losing streak. A hedge fund far under its HWM is frequently dissolved. According to Credit Suisse/Tremont, more than 20 percent of hedge funds were liquidated in 2003 after a year in which more than 70 percent of hedge funds in their database failed to earn an incentive fee.[84]

FOFs impose management fees and incentive fees. A "1.5 plus 10" structure would not be uncommon.

Much debate has surrounded the fee structures of hedge funds. One perspective is that to the extent a hedge fund investor is not paying for "beta" (exposure to systematic risk), as the investor might do with a traditional long-only mutual fund, a higher fee structure is warranted. Another rationale is that to the extent a hedge fund contributes to controlling a portfolio's downside risk, somewhat like a protective put, the fund manager should earn a premium, somewhat like an insurance premium.

All else being equal, between two similarly sized hedge funds following the same strategy, the expectation is that the fund charging the lower management fee will deliver superior performance, unless the higher fee manager in a particular case can make a convincing case that he or she can deliver future superior investment performance. Not uncommonly, hedge fund managers with superior past track records ask for and obtain higher-than-average incentive fees. The investor needs to ask whether the hedge fund manager will repeat as a winner.

Hedge funds also prescribe a minimum initial holding or **lock-up period** for investments during which no part of the investment can be withdrawn. Lock-up periods of one to three years are common. Thereafter, the fund will redeem the investments of investors only within specified exit windows—for example, quarterly after the lock-up period has ended. The rationale for these provisions is that the hedge fund manager needs to be insulated to avoid unwinding positions unfavorably. FOFs usually do not impose lock-up periods and may permit more frequent investor exits. However to offer that additional liquidity, the FOF manager must hold a cash buffer that may reduce expected returns.

6.1.2. Size of the Hedge Fund Market

According to *Forbes* magazine, almost one-quarter of the U.S. largest 1,800 pension funds, endowments, and foundations held hedge fund investments in 2003, up from 12 percent in 2000.[85] It is estimated that money under management for hedge funds grew from less than US$50 billion in 1990 to approximately

[84]Ibid.

[85]*Forbes*, May 24, 2004.

US$600 billion in 2002; the number of hedge funds increased to more than 6,000.[86] Hedge Fund Research estimated, as reported in *Forbes*, that in 2004, US$800 billion was invested in 6,300 hedge funds—900 of them less than a year old. However, 10 percent of hedge funds tracked by HedgeFund.net became defunct in that year. It is estimated that more than 8,000 hedge funds were managing more than US$1 trillion in 2005.

6.2. Benchmarks and Historical Performance

Many investors are concerned that hedge funds do not provide a means for monitoring and tracking these investments that are available for other, more traditional investments.[87] In the traditional stock and bond markets, Morningstar and Lipper provide active manager–based benchmarks of mutual fund performance. Similarly, in the alternative investment industry, CISDM (the Center for International Securities and Derivatives Markets), Hedge Fund Research (HFR), Dow Jones, Standard & Poor's, and Morgan Stanley provide monthly or daily indices that track the performance of active manager–based benchmarks of hedge fund performance.

Recently, research has also focused on developing indices for strategies (e.g., tracking portfolios) that try to separate the contribution to performance of the strategy from the contribution to performance of the manager's specific talent.[88] In most cases, evidence exists for abnormal returns based on such indices. However, investors should be cautioned that abnormal returns simply reflect that the reference benchmark is not a complete tracking portfolio for the hedge fund so the abnormal returns are simply the result of additional, nonmeasured risks.

6.2.1. Benchmarks

Hedge fund benchmarks include both monthly and daily series. In alphabetical order, a sample of monthly hedge fund indices includes the following:

- *CISDM of the University of Massachusetts*. The CISDM hedge fund and managed futures indices are based on managers reporting to the CISDM hedge fund and managed futures databases. The indices cover a broad set of hedge fund and managed futures trading strategies. Publication of returns in each style classification began in 1994 with data beginning in 1990. The broadest CISDM hedge fund index is equally weighted—the CISDM Equal Weighted Hedge Fund Index.
- *Credit Suisse/Tremont*. These indices cover more than 10 strategies and are based on a set of more than 400 funds selected from the TASS database. The Credit Suisse/Tremont Index discloses its construction methods and identifies all the funds within it. Credit Suisse/Tremont accepts only funds (not separate accounts) with a minimum of US$10 million under management and an audited statement. The Credit Suisse/Tremont Hedge Fund Index was launched in 1999 with data beginning in 1994 and is asset weighted (i.e., weights depend on assets under management).
- *EACM Advisors*. This group provides the EACM100® Index, which is an equally weighted composite of 100 hedge funds selected to be representative of five broad strategies representing 13 substrategy styles. Funds are assigned categories on the basis of how closely

[86] See SEC (2003).

[87] Siegel (2003) found it surprising, given that the inherent nature of hedge fund investing is hostile to benchmarking, that hedge funds or their clients need benchmarks.

[88] See Schneeweis and Kazemi (2001).

they match the strategy definitions. Names in the funds are not disclosed. The index is equally weighted and rebalanced annually. It was launched in 1996 with data beginning in 1990.

- *Hedge Fund Intelligence Ltd*. Hedge Fund Intelligence supplies the EuroHedge and HSBC AsiaHedge series of equally weighted indices. The EuroHedge series consists of hedge funds that are at least 50 percent managed in developed European countries or that are solely invested in developed European countries. The series began in 2002. The HSBC AsiaHedge series contains hedge funds that are at least 50 percent managed in the Asia-Pacific area or that are solely invested in the Asia-Pacific area. The series began in 1998.
- *HedgeFund.net* also called the "Tuna" indices, covers more than 30 strategies. They are equally weighted indices based on the HedgeFund.net database.
- *HFR*. This company provides equally weighted hedge fund indices based on managers reporting to the HFR database of hedge fund returns segregated into a number of categories and subcategories. FOFs are not included in the composite index but are in a separate index. The indices were launched in 1994 with data beginning in 1990. Funds are assigned to categories based on the descriptions in their offering memoranda.
- *MSCI*. These indices are classified according to five basic categories and include a composite index. Within each category, indices are segregated on the basis of asset class and geographical region. Funds included need to have a minimum of US$15 million in AUM, although there is no restriction on whether a fund is open or closed. The indices are supported by a platform that allows subscribers to access the data at a more detailed level (industry focus, fund size, open versus closed, etc.). Indices are equally weighted except at higher levels of aggregation, where both equally weighted and asset-weighted versions are available.

A sample of available daily indices includes the following:

- *Dow Jones Hedge Fund Strategy benchmarks*. These benchmarks currently cover six hedge fund strategies. Funds within each category must meet asset size, years in existence, and statistically based style purity constraints. Funds that meet these restrictions are asked to participate in the index. However, only those managers who also agree to meet reporting constraints are included. The benchmarks were launched in 2001 as the Zurich Institutional Benchmark Series. The Dow Jones indices are available in an investable form through a separate asset company not directly affiliated with Dow Jones and are approximately equally weighted.
- *HFR hedge fund indices*. These indices are based on managers reporting to HFR. The indices cover a number of categories and subcategories and were launched in 2003.
- *MSCI Hedge Invest Index*. This index is based on over 100 hedge funds that represent 24 hedge fund strategies and have weekly liquidity.[89] The MSCI Hedge Invest Index is available in an investable form through a separate asset company not directly affiliated with MSCI. The index was launched in July 2003.
- *Standard & Poor's hedge fund indices*. These indices cover three styles with three strategies each. The indices are equally weighted and are rebalanced annually. Standard & Poor's discloses the construction method and the number of funds that are in each strategy. It performs due diligence on all funds in the indices and publishes daily returns. The S&P Hedge Fund Indices are available in an investable form through a separate asset company not directly affiliated with Standard & Poor's.

[89] As of April 6, 2004.

6.2.1.1. Comparison of Major Manager-Based Hedge Fund Indices The general distinguishing feature of various hedge fund series is whether they report monthly or daily series, are investable or noninvestable, and list the actual funds used in benchmark construction. Of the current indices, only Dow Jones, Standard & Poor's, MSCI, and HFR provide a daily return series. Of these daily indices, only Dow Jones and Standard & Poor's publicly list the funds in the indices. Another important feature of the daily indices is that they are generally constructed from managed accounts of an asset manager rather than from the funds themselves.

For the monthly return series, the EACM Advisors, CISDM, HFR, and MSCI indices have many different classifications and subclassifications, whereas the Credit Suisse/Tremont and Standard & Poor's have relatively few classifications. The CISDM indices do not report a "hedge fund composite" return each month.

It is natural to want to express the performance of hedge funds with a single number. However, defining the hedge fund universe is both a difficult and unproductive exercise. There is no general agreement among institutional investors regarding which investment strategies are considered hedge fund strategies and what weights should be given to each strategy.

There are many differences in the construction of the major manager-based hedge fund indices. Principal differences are as follows:

- *Selection criteria.* Decision rules determine which hedge funds are included in the index. Examples of selection criteria include length of track record, AUM, and restrictions on new investment. For example, MSCI, Dow Jones, and Standard & Poor's have a specific rule-based processes for manager selection.
- *Style classification.* Indices have various approaches to how each hedge fund is assigned to a style-specific index and whether or not a fund that fails to satisfy the style classification methodology is excluded from the index.
- *Weighting scheme.* Indices have different schemes to determine how much weight a particular fund's return is given in the index. Common weighting schemes are equally weighting and dollar weighting on the basis of AUM. Many indices report both equal-weighted and asset-weighted versions.
- *Rebalancing scheme.* Rebalancing rules determine when assets are reallocated among the funds in an equally weighted index. For example, some funds are rebalanced monthly; others use annual rebalancing.
- *Investability.* An index may be directly or only indirectly investable. The majority of monthly manager–based hedge fund indices are not investable, whereas most of the daily hedge fund indices are investable but often in association with other financial firms.

6.2.1.2. Alpha Determination and Absolute-Return Investing Performance appraisal has emerged as a major issue in the hedge fund industry. Hedge funds have often been promoted as absolute-return vehicles. **Absolute-return vehicles** have been defined as investments that have no direct benchmark portfolios. Estimates of alpha, however, must be made relative to a benchmark portfolio.[90] Problems in alpha determination have been discussed widely; for example, differences in the selected benchmark can result in large differences in reported alpha.[91] One perspective is that all active management is about performance relative

[90] *Alpha* is defined as the return relative to an investment's expected return given a benchmark portfolio and the investment's beta with respect to the benchmark.

[91] Refer to the reading on performance evaluation for the alpha determination in traditional investments; see Schneeweis (1998) for alpha determination in hedge funds.

EXHIBIT 8-22 Hedge Fund Performance, 1990–2004

Measure	HFCI	S&P 500	Lehman Gov./Corp.	MSCI World	Lehman Global
Annualized return	13.46%	10.94%	7.77%	7.08%	8.09%
Annualized std. dev.	5.71%	14.65%	4.46%	14.62%	5.23%
Sharpe ratio	1.61	0.45	0.78	0.19	0.73
Minimum monthly return	−6.92%	−14.46%	−4.19%	−13.32%	−3.66%
Correlation with HFCI	1.00	0.59	0.16	0.56	0.04

Source: CISDM (2005c).

to some investable benchmark.[92] Another important issue in evaluating claims of alpha is whether account is being taken of all sources of systematic risk the fund may be exposed to. Alpha is the residual after returns to systematic risks have been removed. Simple models for systematic risk that have been applied to long-only equity portfolios may not be relevant for a hedge fund strategy.

The lack of a clear hedge fund benchmark, however, is not indicative of an inability to determine comparable returns for a hedge fund strategy. Hedge fund strategies within a particular style often trade similar assets with similar methodologies and are sensitive to similar market factors. Two principal means of establishing comparable portfolios are (1) using a single-factor or multifactor methodology and (2) using optimization to create tracking portfolios with similar risk and return characteristics. Kazemi and Schneeweis (2001) created passive indices, from both factors that underlie the strategy and financial instruments that are used in the strategy, to track the return of a hedge fund strategy. Their results indicate that active hedge fund management shows evidence of positive alpha relative to cited tracking portfolios.

6.2.2. Historical Performance

In this section, we provide summary information on the performance of various hedge fund strategies. Exhibit 8-22 shows the performance of a number of assets and combinations of assets (traditional assets and hedge funds) over the period 1990 to 2004.[93] These assets include CSDIM's Hedge Fund Composite Index and several measures of U.S. and global stock and bond performance.

For the entire period, the HFCI had the superior return performance relative to other traditional asset classes. During the sharp decline of the S&P 500 between mid 2000 and late 2002, the HFCI had a small but positive trend. The minimum monthly return for the HFCI for the entire period, at −6.92 percent, represents a smaller loss than that of the worst monthly return for either U.S. or world equities. The HFCI has a higher Sharpe ratio than any of the other reported assets. Note that the HFCI's correlation of 0.59 with the S&P 500 is consistent with substantial long equity market exposure as well as the potential for risk-diversification benefits (because the correlation is considerably below 1).

As Exhibit 8-23 shows, for the five-year period ending in 2004, the HFCI outperformed U.S. and world equities but not bonds. The minimum monthly return for the HFCI during the period is smaller than for all other reported asset classes.

[92] See Waring and Siegel (2005).

[93] The annual and monthly returns are presented in their nominal form. Annualized standard deviations are derived by multiplying the monthly data by the square root of 12.

EXHIBIT 8-23 Recent Hedge Fund Performance, 2000–2004

Measure	HFCI	S&P 500	Lehman Gov./Corp.	MSCI World	Lehman Global
Annualized return	6.84%	−2.30%	8.00%	−2.05%	8.51%
Annualized std. dev.	4.83%	16.35%	4.76%	15.62%	6.00%
Sharpe ratio	0.86	−0.31	1.11	−0.30	0.97
Minimum monthly return	−2.94%	−10.87%	−4.19%	−10.98%	−3.66%
Correlation with HFCI	1.00	0.52	0.11	0.60	0.21

Source: CISDM (2005c).

EXHIBIT 8-24 Performance of Hedge Fund Strategies and Traditional Assets, 1990–2004

Strategy or Index	Annual Return	Annual Standard Deviation	Sharpe Ratio	Minimum Monthly Return	Correlation w/S&P 500	Correlation w/Lehman Gov./Corp.
HFCI	13.46%	5.71%	1.61	−6.92%	0.59	0.17
Event driven	13.46	5.59	1.64	−9.37	0.59	0.07
Equity hedge	15.90	9.34	1.24	−9.70	0.64	0.10
Equity market neutral	9.24	2.50	1.98	−1.07	0.09	0.24
Merger/risk arbitrage	9.07	4.86	0.99	−8.78	0.48	0.10
Distressed securities	15.28	6.07	1.81	−9.71	0.42	0.04
Fixed-income arbitrage	7.62	3.61	0.92	−6.61	0.06	−0.06
Convertible arbitrage	10.23	3.96	1.50	−3.42	0.19	0.13
Global macro	16.98	8.38	1.51	−5.41	0.26	0.34
Short selling	−0.61	19.39	−0.25	−14.62	−0.76	−0.01
S&P 500	10.94	14.65	0.45	−14.46	1.00	0.13
Lehman Gov./Corp.	7.77	4.46	0.78	−4.19	0.13	1.00
MSCI World	7.08	14.62	0.19	−13.32	0.86	0.09
Lehman Global	8.09	5.23	0.73	−3.66	0.11	0.74

Source: CISDM (2005c).

The risk-and-return benefit of a wide range of hedge fund indices and their correlations with stock and bond indices are given in Exhibit 8-24. As the dispersion of Sharpe ratios and of correlations of hedge fund styles with stocks and bonds in Exhibit 8-24 shows, in 1990 to 2004, there was considerable variation in the risk and return characteristics among styles. As expected, those hedge fund groups whose strategies call for eliminating stock or bond market risk (e.g., equity market neutral or fixed-income arbitrage) have low correlations with, respectively, stock or bond indices. Those hedge fund strategies with equity exposure (e.g., event driven and hedged equity) have moderate correlations with the S&P 500.

Research has shown that the actual performance of hedge fund strategies depends on the market conditions affecting that strategy. As shown in Exhibit 8-25, equity-based hedge fund strategies are correlated with several equity and bond market factors. Credit-sensitive strategies (e.g., distressed securities) are correlated with similar factors (e.g., high-yield debt returns) as credit-sensitive bond instruments. Because relative-value strategies (e.g., equity market neutral) and systematic managed futures strategies (which are discussed in detail later) are sensitive to different return factors from those to which hedged equity strategies and the

EXHIBIT 8-25 Factor Correlations, 1990–2004

Hedge Fund	S&P 500	Lehman Gov/Corp.	Lehman Corp. High Yield	Stock Volatility	Bond Volatility
HFCI	0.59	0.17	0.51	−0.42	−0.13
Event driven	0.59	0.07	0.69	−0.42	−0.02
Equity hedge	0.64	0.10	0.43	−0.33	−0.04
Equity market neutral	0.09	0.24	−0.03	−0.13	−0.23
Merger/risk arbitrage	0.48	0.10	0.50	−0.31	−0.01
Distressed securities	0.42	0.04	0.70	−0.41	−0.01
Fixed-income arbitrage	0.06	−0.06	0.34	−0.36	−0.18
Convertible arbitrage	0.19	0.13	0.47	−0.12	−0.15
Global macro	0.26	0.34	0.23	−0.27	−0.26
Short selling	−0.78	−0.01	−0.50	0.20	−0.15

Notes: Stock and bond volatility was measured as, respectively, monthly volatility of daily returns of the S&P 500 and Lehman Brothers bond index.
Source: CISDM (2005c).

S&P 500 are sensitive, one expects them to have low correlations with the S&P 500 and they may be considered risk diversifiers.[94] Because equity hedge funds load on similar return factors as the S&P 500, they offer less diversification than many relative-value strategies and can be more rightly considered return enhancers.

The different sensitivities of various hedge fund strategies to various market factors result in different correlations among hedge fund strategies themselves. The correlations between various hedge fund strategies are given in Exhibit 8-26. Diversification among hedge fund strategies should therefore also reduce the volatility of hedge fund–based investment portfolios.

6.2.3. Interpretation Issues[95]

Hedge fund indices often have meaningfully different performance within a given time period. This raises the challenging question of which index is most appropriate for the investor's purposes.

Despite the differences in returns, comparable hedge fund indices appear to be sensitive to the same set of risk factors. The return differences among indices often reflect differences in the weights of different strategy groups.

The hedge fund investor should be aware of the following issues in selecting and using hedge fund indices.

6.2.3.1. Biases in Index Creation The use of manager-based hedge fund indices in performance appraisal and asset allocation is based on the premise that the indices neutrally reflect the underlying performance of the strategy. A primary concern is that most databases are self-reported; that is, the hedge fund manager chooses which databases to report to and provides the return data. Although the correlations among hedge fund indices based on similar

[94]Although some research (Schneeweis and Pescatore, 1999) has focused on CTAs as offering exposure to long volatility, unless specifically designed to capture volatility, systematic CTA strategies often make returns in periods of low-volatility in high-trend markets. Systematic commodity trading programs (e.g., CTAs) are positively correlated with various passive trend-following indices. See CISDM (2005d) and www.cisdm.som.umass.edu for information.

[95]Discussion in this section draws on Schneeweis, Kazemi, and Martin (2002).

EXHIBIT 8-26 Correlations between Hedge Fund Strategies, 1990–2004

	HFCI	Event Driven	Equity Hedge	Equity Market Neutral	Merger/ Risk Arbitrage	Distressed Securities	Fixed-Income Arbitrage	Convert. Arbitrage	Global Macro	Short Selling	S&P 500	Lehman Gov./ Corp.	MSCI World	Lehman Global
HFCI	1.00													
Event driven	0.76	1.00												
Equity hedge	0.90	0.70	1.00											
Equity market neutral	0.32	0.13	0.27	1.00										
Merger/risk arbitrage	0.52	0.82	0.50	0.06	1.00									
Distressed securities	0.66	0.87	0.56	0.14	0.57	1.00								
Fixed-income arbitrage	0.38	0.34	0.19	0.13	0.12	0.42	1.00							
Convert. arbitrage	0.47	0.55	0.34	0.15	0.35	0.56	0.37	1.00						
Global macro	0.72	0.33	0.46	0.34	0.16	0.29	0.27	0.21	1.00					
Short selling	−0.64	−0.66	−0.77	0.00	−0.50	−0.54	−0.09	−0.28	−0.18	1.00				
S&P 500	0.59	0.59	0.64	0.09	0.48	0.42	0.06	0.19	0.26	−0.78	1.00			
Lehman Gov./ Corp.	0.17	0.07	0.10	0.24	0.10	0.04	−0.06	0.13	0.34	−0.01	0.13	1.00		
MSCI World	0.56	0.54	0.62	0.07	0.42	0.39	0.09	0.17	0.24	−0.71	0.86	0.09	1.00	
Lehman Global	0.05	−0.03	0.06	0.21	0.04	−0.06	−0.16	0.00	0.19	−0.03	0.11	0.74	0.22	1.00

Source: CISDM (2005c).

strategies are generally moderately high in the period covered by Exhibit 8-26 (e.g., above 0.80), in certain cases, the correlations fall below 0.20. There are several possible explanations for low correlations between "similar strategy" indices. One is the size and age restrictions some indices impose. Another may be the weighting schemes.

Value weighting may result in a particular index taking on the return characteristics of the best-performing hedge funds in a particular time period: As top-performing funds grow from new inflows and high returns and poorly performing funds are closed, the top-performing funds represent an increasing share of the index. Fung and Hsieh (2001) pointed out that the indices that are value weighted may reflect current popularity with investors because the asset values of the various funds change as a result of asset purchases and price. Popularity may reflect the most recent results, creating a momentum effect in returns. The ability of an investor to track an index subject to momentum is problematic.

Equal-weighted indices may reflect potential diversification of hedge funds better than value-weighted indices. For funds designed to track equal-weighted indices, however, the costs of rebalancing to index weights make it difficult to create an investable form. Only recently have hedge fund indices been created that are investable. Some such indices have the express goal of tracking a comparable but noninvestable index.[96] The creation of a single, all-encompassing hedge fund index that reflects some natural, market-based equilibrium assumption as to the proper holdings of hedge funds and is appropriate for all purposes does not appear to be feasible. Many hedge fund investors use custom or negotiated benchmarks.

An appropriate benchmark reflects the particular style of an investment manager and can serve as a surrogate for the manager in studies of risk and return performance and asset allocation. Of great concern for investors is whether an index reflects the actual relative sensitivity of hedge funds to various market conditions, such that each index provides information on the true diversification benefits of the underlying hedge fund strategies. Many studies have used both single-factor and multifactor models in identifying market factors and option-like payoffs that describe the sources of hedge fund returns.[97] However, the sensitivity of various hedge fund indices to these economic factors may change over time, so the changing styles and changing assets under management (if asset-weighted) in an index may make historical results relative to that index conditional at best.

6.2.3.2. Relevance of Past Data on Performance The usefulness of historical hedge fund data is a topic of controversy. As is true for stock and bond analyses, hedge funds with similar investment styles generate similar returns, and there is little evidence of superior individual manager skill within a particular style group.[98] Research has also shown that the volatility of returns is more persistent through time than the level of returns.[99] This research shows that the best forecast of future returns is one that is consistent with prior volatility, not one that is consistent with prior returns.[100] There are a host of methodological concerns, however, with interpreting the results of such studies.

---

[96]See the Dow Jones Hedge Fund Strategy Benchmarks at www.djhedgefundindexes.com.

[97]See Fung and Hsieh (1997a) and Schneeweis and Pescatore (1999).

[98]See Bodie, Kane, and Marcus (2005) for a summary. To the degree that superior return persistence is shown, the result arises primarily from consistency among poor performers rather than superior performers; see Brown et al. (1999).

[99]See Schneeweis (1998) and Park and Staum (1998).

[100]The ability of historical data to classify managers into similar trading strategies is still an open question. Fung and Hsieh (1997a) and others have used various factor analytic programs to group managers. In contrast, various fund management companies place managers into relevant groups on the

The composition of hedge fund indices also changes greatly, so the past returns of an index reflect the performance of a different set of managers from today's or tomorrow's managers. This may be a more severe problem for value-weighted indices than for equal-weighted indices because value-weighted indices are more heavily weighted in the recent best-performing fund(s).

6.2.3.3. Survivorship Bias Survivorship bias is often raised as a major concern for investors in hedge funds. **Survivorship bias** results when managers with poor track records exit the business and are dropped from the database whereas managers with good records remain. If survivorship bias is large, then the historical return record of the average surviving manager is higher than the average return of all managers over the test period. Because a diversified portfolio would have likely consisted of funds that were destined to fail as well as funds destined to succeed, studying only survivors results in overestimation of historical returns. It is estimated that this bias is in the range of at least 1.5 to 3 percent per year.[101]

Survivorship bias varies among hedge fund strategies. For instance, survivorship bias is minor for event-driven strategies, is higher for hedged equity, and is considerable for currency funds. More importantly, for the largest hedge fund group, equity hedge funds, overestimation of historical performance because of survivorship bias has been previously reported to range from 1.5 percent to 2 percent. However, the bias may be concentrated in certain periods (e.g., following the August 1998 Long-Term Capital Management crisis). Thus, the levels of survivorship bias exhibited in past data may, depending on economic conditions and strategy, over- or underestimate future bias. Finally, data for U.S. equity hedge funds indicate that for particular hedge fund strategies, although the relative return performance of the "dead" funds was less than that of the "alive" funds, the survivorship bias may differ greatly among funds, with some nonsurvivor funds showing no return bias.

Moreover, the problem of survivorship bias may be reduced by conducting superior due diligence. For instance, one explanation for the proliferation of FOFs is that managers of these funds may be able to avoid managers destined to fail, thereby mitigating the survivorship bias problem. Investors may be willing to bear an additional layer of management fees to reduce exposure to the ill-fated managers. As a result, once the FOFs have screened funds, survivorship bias may be reduced significantly.

6.2.3.4. Stale Price Bias In asset markets, lack of security trading may lead to what is called **stale price bias.** For securities with stale prices, measured correlations may be lower than expected, and depending on the time period chosen, measured standard deviation may be higher or lower than would exist if actual prices existed.

Even in traditional asset markets, prices are often computed from factor models, appraisal values, and so on, so that reported prices do not reflect current market prices. In fact, for CTAs and many hedge fund strategies, prices reflect market-traded prices to a greater extent than in many traditional asset portfolios. There is little evidence that stale prices present a significant bias in hedge fund returns.

6.2.3.5. Backfill Bias (Inclusion Bias) Backfill bias can result when missing past return data for a component of an index are filled at the discretion of the component (e.g., a hedge

basis of direct evaluation. Future research is required to see which of the relevant methods provides the least bias.

[101] See Brown et al. (1999) and Fung and Hsieh (2000).

fund for a hedge fund index) when it joins the index. As with survivorship bias, backfill bias makes results look too good because only components with good past results will be motivated to supply them.[102] The issue of this bias has been raised particularly with respect to certain hedge fund indices.[103]

EXAMPLE 8-10 Hedge Fund Benchmarks

CBA, a large charitable organization, is planning to make an investment in one or more hedge funds. Alex Carr, CIO of CBA, is evaluating information prepared by the organization's senior analyst, Kim Park, CFA.

Carr asks Park why a U.S.-focused market-neutral long–short hedge fund CBA is considering has resisted accepting a U.S equity index as a benchmark.

1. Prepare a response to Carr's question to Park.
2. Recommend an alternative to using a stock index benchmark for a market-neutral long–short fund.
3. Discuss the impact the following factors have on index creation with respect to hedge funds:
   a. Survivorship bias
   b. Value-weighted indices
   c. Stale price bias

Solution to Problem 1: Market-neutral long–short hedge funds consider themselves to be absolute return vehicles, in that their performance should not be linked to that of the stock market. Such a fund should have effectively zero systematic risk.

Solution to Problem 2: For those hedge funds using absolute-return strategies that are indifferent to the direction of the market, a hurdle rate may be used as a standard for performance.

Solution to Problem 3:

a. Survivorship bias occurs when returns of managers who have failed or exited the market are not included in the data analyzed over a specific timeframe. This results in overestimation of historical returns in the range of 1.5 to 3.0 percent per year. The timing of survivorship bias may be concentrated during certain economic periods, which further complicates analysis of persistence of returns over shorter timeframes. A manager's investment performance reflects not only skill but the starting point of market opportunities and valuations levels—such factors constitute age effects (or vintage effects) in hedge fund performance. Over a long

[102] See Malkiel and Saha (2005) and references therein. Another bias the authors identified is end-of-life bias, which arises from the option a hedge fund has to stop reporting results. One might anticipate that predominantly poorly performing hedge funds would choose to do that.

[103] See Malkiel and Saha (2005).

horizon, the starting point should generally decrease in importance. However, hedge funds have average track records of only two to five years. Age effects make it difficult to compare the performance of hedge funds that have track records of different lengths.

b. Indices that are value weighted, as opposed to equally weighted, may take on the return characteristics of the best-performing hedge fund over a given period. These indices thus reflect the weights of popular bets by hedge fund managers, because the asset values of the various funds change as a result of asset purchases as well as price appreciation.
c. Lack of security trading leads to stale prices for those securities and can cause measured standard deviation to be over- or understated, depending on the time period being studied. This could result in measured correlations being lower than expected. This issue is not a significant concern in the creation of hedge fund indices because monthly data are used and for many hedge fund strategies, the underlying holdings are relatively liquid, so positions reflect market-traded prices.

6.3. Hedge Funds: Investment Characteristics and Roles

Hedge funds have been described as skill-based investment strategies. Skill-based investment strategies obtain returns primarily from the firm's competitive advantages in information or its interpretation. To the extent that a hedge fund's returns derive primarily from an individual manager's skill or superior depth of information, its returns may be uncorrelated or weakly correlated with the long-term return of the traditional stock and bond markets.

The investor needs to keep in mind, however, that the flip side of skill in producing investment success is market opportunity. The supply of market opportunities can and does vary for particular investment strategies as investment industry, economic, and financial market conditions evolve. To take an obvious example, the opportunities for merger arbitrage hedge funds are heavily influenced by corporate merger activities.

6.3.1. Investment Characteristics A number of empirical studies have directly assessed the return drivers of traditional and alternative investments. For instance, for traditional stocks and bonds, a common set of factors has been used to explain stock and bond returns.[104] Similarly, academic research indicates that for hedge funds, a common set of return drivers based on trading strategy factors (e.g., option-like payoffs) and location factors (e.g., payoffs from a buy-and-hold policy) help to explain returns of each strategy.[105]

Results show that, as for traditional "long-bias" stock and bond investments, the returns of some long-bias equity-based and fixed income–based hedge fund strategies are affected primarily by changes in the risk and return of the underlying stock and bond markets and should, therefore, be regarded less as portfolio return diversifiers than as portfolio return enhancers. Hedge fund strategies that attempt to be less affected by the direction of the underlying stock and bond markets (e.g., equity market neutral or bond arbitrage) may be regarded more as diversifiers for traditional stock and bond portfolios.

[104] See Fama and French (1996).

[105] See Fung and Hsieh (1997a), Schneeweis and Spurgin (1998), Schneeweis and Pescatore (1999), and Agarwal and Naik (2000).

Studies that used direct replication of underlying strategies also support market factors and option-like payoff variables (e.g., put options) as describing certain hedge fund strategies.[106] The bottom line is that analysis of the underlying factors used in trading strategies is important, given the investor's economic forecast and market expectations, when deciding which hedge funds to include in a portfolio. Investors may consider allocation to various strategies warranted by economic factors directly driving hedge fund returns and may even consider allocations to new strategies based on new economic conditions driving hedge fund returns.

6.3.2. Roles in the Portfolio[107] Hedge funds constitute a diverse set of strategies. Because the strategies are skill based, most investors will accord manager selection great scrutiny. Investors put varying emphases on style selection. For a given portfolio, the diversification benefits of adding hedge funds in different style groups can be quite distinct.

FOF investments have been popular as entry-level investments because they essentially delegate individual manager selection to the FOF manager and provide professional management. They also shorten the due diligence process to a single manager. FOFs may be diversified funds composed of various hedge fund strategies or style pure. A significant consideration is that FOF investing involves two layers of management and incentive fees.

Research indicates that an equally weighted diversified portfolio of five to seven randomly selected equity securities will result in a portfolio standard deviation similar to that of the investment population from which it is drawn. Similarly, for hedge funds, a randomly selected equal-weighted portfolio of five to seven hedge funds has a standard deviation similar to that of the population from which it is drawn.[108] Thus, as is true for equity portfolios, multimanager hedge fund portfolios may have risk levels similar to that of a larger population of hedge funds. Also important is that a portfolio of randomly selected hedge funds has a correlation in excess of 0.90 with that of a typical hedge fund benchmark. Therefore, the use of a smaller subset of hedge funds can represent the performance of the EACM 100, just as a smaller portfolio of stocks or mutual funds can represent, respectively, the performance of the S&P 500 or mutual fund indices.

6.3.2.1. The Role of Hedge Funds as Diversifiers A first caution is that, as discussed in detail in the chapter on asset allocation, the allocations produced by mean–variance optimization (MVO) are sensitive to errors in return estimates. The different historical index returns among various index providers raise a warning that basing allocations on historical hedge fund index returns in MVO may be unreliable.[109] Hedge fund strategies often have option characteristics that present a further challenge when relying on MVO.

The use of hedge fund indices in overall asset allocation is based, in part, on the assumption that FOFs created to track certain hedge fund strategies perform similarly to the benchmarks used in asset allocation analysis. In short, there are a number of issues involved in portfolio creation at the strategy level as well as among strategies. These issues include (1) persistence in historical performance, (2) portfolio rebalancing, and (3) impact of return distribution features beyond mean and standard deviation—that is, "higher moments."

---

[106] See Mitchell and Pulvino (2000).

[107] Discussion in this section draws on CISDM (2005c).

[108] See Henker (1998).

[109] It is important to note that use of historical returns in optimization modeling may not reflect expected risk and return relationships. If factor-based regression models are used to forecast expected rates of return, then the consistency of the sensitivities of various index models to factors is an issue of concern.

EXHIBIT 8-27 Hedge Fund Performance in Portfolios, 1990–2004

Measure	Portfolio I	Portfolio II	Portfolio III	Portfolio IV
Annualized return	9.64%	10.43%	7.86%	9.01%
Annualized std. dev	7.94%	7.09%	8.29%	7.28%
Sharpe ratio	0.67	0.87	0.43	0.65
Minimum Monthly Return	−6.25%	−6.39%	−5.61%	−5.87%
Correlation w/HFCI	0.59	0.69	0.51	0.62

Notes:
Portfolio I: 50 percent S&P 500, 50 percent Lehman Gov./Corp. Bond.
Portfolio II: 40 percent S&P 500, 40 percent Lehman Gov./Corp., 20 percent HFCI.
Portfolio III: 50 percent MSCI World, 50 percent Lehman Global Bond.
Portfolio IV: 40 percent MSCI World, 40 percent Lehman Global, 20 percent HFCI.
Source: CISDM (2005c).

EXHIBIT 8-28 Recent Hedge Fund Performance in Portfolios, 2000–2004

Measure	Portfolio I	Portfolio II	Portfolio III	Portfolio IV
Annualized return	3.15%	3.92%	3.45%	4.16%
Annualized std. dev	7.93%	6.94%	8.55%	7.48%
Sharpe ratio	0.06	0.18	0.09	0.19
Minimum Monthly Return	−4.36%	−3.62%	−4.94%	−4.08%
Correlation w/HFCI	0.57	0.66	0.62	0.70

Notes:
Portfolio I: 50 percent S&P 500, 50 percent Lehman Gov./Corp. Bond.
Portfolio II: 40 percent S&P 500, 40 percent Lehman Gov./Corp Bond, 20 percent HFCI.
Portfolio III: 50 percent MSCI World, 50 percent Lehman Global Bond.
Portfolio IV: 40 percent MSCI World, 40 percent Lehman Global, 20 percent HFCI.
Source: CISDM (2005c).

If one assumes that a portfolio tracks the performance of a particular index, then an investor may use hedge fund indices together with other traditional indices to improve risk–return trade-offs.

6.3.2.2. Historical Performance The benefit of including hedge funds in diversified portfolios is illustrated in Exhibit 8-27. For the 1990 to 2004 period, when the HFCI is added to U.S. stocks, bonds, or a portfolio of U.S. stocks and bonds, the risk-adjusted return improves. For instance, the Sharpe ratio of a balanced portfolio with U.S. stocks and bonds (0.67, Portfolio I) increases to 0.87 when hedge funds are added (Portfolio II). Similarly, when hedge funds are added to a balanced portfolio of world equities and bonds (Portfolio III), the Sharpe ratio increases significantly from 0.43 to 0.65 (Portfolio IV). The correlation between the HFCI and the U.S. stock/bond portfolio (Portfolio I) is 0.59 and between the HFCI and the world stock/bond portfolio (Portfolio III) is 0.51.

Hedge funds achieved historically high returns in the first half of the 1990s, which suggests that the more recent record should be examined closely. Exhibit 8-28 considers the period 2000 to 2004. The annualized return of hedge funds for this period (6.84 percent, Exhibit 8-23) is lower than for the 1990 to 2004 period (13.46 percent, Exhibit 8-22), but the benefits that hedge funds add to the portfolios are similar to those for the period that includes the early 1990s.

In interpreting data such as those in Exhibit 8-28 showing that the inclusion of hedge funds effected a mean–variance improvement, researchers such as Kat and Amin (2003) have shown that including hedge funds can also frequently lead to lower skewness and higher kurtosis, which are exactly opposite to the attributes (positive skewness and moderate kurtosis) that investors are presumed to want.

EXAMPLE 8-11 Skewness and Hedge Funds[110]

In 2002, the S&P 500 dropped by more than 20 percent and distressed debt hedge funds as a group achieved poor returns. Equity market-neutral funds also achieved poor returns, which was explained as relating to lower market liquidity.

1. Explain why distressed debt hedge funds might have performed poorly in 2002.
2. Explain how lower market liquidity might have negatively affected long–short market-neutral hedge funds.

Solution to Problem 1: Major declines in equity markets lead to widening credit spreads and, all else being equal, to capital losses on high-yield bonds. Distressed debt hedge funds are exposed to the risk of increased credit spreads and, as a result, fared poorly in 2002.

Solution to Problem 2: Maintaining market neutrality involves dynamic portfolio adjustments. Declines in market liquidity increase the cost of shorting equity markets.

The following are techniques for neutralizing negative skewness in a portfolio resulting from hedge fund positions that a portfolio manager may consider:[111]

- Adopt a mean–variance, skewness and kurtosis–aware approach to hedge fund selection. An example is given in Kat (2005), who discussed combining global macro and equity market-neutral hedge strategies with traditional assets. Global macro funds have tended to have positive skewness with only moderate correlation with equities but relatively high kurtosis and volatility; equity market-neutral strategies tend to act as volatility and kurtosis reducers in the portfolio. In other words, smart hedge fund selection may be able to reduce the problem of negative skewness.
- Invest in managed futures. Managed futures programs are generally trend following in nature, which tends to produce skewness characteristics that are opposite to those of many hedge funds.

6.3.3. Other Issues[112]

In addition to market factors affecting a broad range of investment vehicles, individual fund factors may affect expected performance. Academic and practitioner

[110] This discussion draws on Kat (2005), who also discussed a program of buying and rolling over out-of-the-money stock index put options, which tend to deliver positively skewed returns.

[111] This discussion is based on Kat (2005).

[112] Discussion in this section draws on Schneeweis, Kazemi, and Martin (2002).

research has tested various fund-specific factors—such as onshore/offshore, age, and size—on manager performance. Results from this research support the following: (1) Young funds outperform old funds on a total-return basis, or at least old funds do not outperform young ones; (2) on average, large funds underperform small funds; (3) FOFs may provide closer approximation to return estimation than indices do.[113]

Unfortunately, as in any tests of fund effects, one has the problem of disaggregating effects for a large number of funds, each with different strategies, starting periods, and so on. In fact, although it is not the purpose of this chapter to conduct a detailed analysis of each of these effects, the following discussion indicates that simple relationships between hedge fund returns and each of the aforementioned fund factors must be analyzed closely before final conclusions can be made.

- *Performance fees and lock-up impacts.* Periods of severe drawdown (e.g., 1998) may influence funds to dissolve rather than face the prospect of not earning the incentive fees because of HWM provisions. There is some evidence of an impact of lock-up periods on hedge fund performance. In the case of U.S. hedge funds, funds with quarterly lock-ups have higher returns than similar-strategy funds with monthly lock-ups.
- *Funds of funds.* FOF returns may differ from overall hedge fund performance because of various issues, including a less direct impact of survivorship bias on FOFs because hedge funds that dissolve are included in the returns of the FOFs (there still is some survivorship bias, in that FOFs may remove themselves from datasets because of, for example, poor performance). FOFs may thus provide a more accurate prediction of future fund returns than that provided by the more generic indices.

  However, classification and style drift are issues with FOFs. A number of FOFs reported as diversified by category differ greatly not only in their correlation with standard indices but also in their sensitivity to general economic factors. Investors must use factors to test "style drift" of generic FOFs.

  As a result, the use of FOFs that change over time in response to rebalancing may not fit well into strict asset allocation modeling. For instance, new FOFs (U.S. diversified FOFs) starting in the years 1992 onward were found to have lower correlations with FOFs starting in 1991 or earlier, but as years progressed, the correlations increased. This indicates that new FOFs are constructed differently from old funds. This is expected. New FOFs can be more flexible in fund selection. As time passes, however, older FOFs can redistribute cash or funds in such a way that they resemble the new fund construction. Thus, simple averaging across FOFs without taking the year of origination into account may not be appropriate.

  Over time, hedge fund correlations with hedged equity have risen and hedge fund correlations with global macro strategies have fallen, indicating an increase in FOFs' use of hedged equity and a decrease in the use of global macro. These results emphasize that FOFs may be timing one market and have become less useful in asset allocation strategies than previously because of their factor sensitivity and composition change—in contrast to more style-pure hedge fund indices or strategies.
- *Effect of fund size.* On the one hand, there are potential advantages to a hedge fund having a large asset base. The fund may be able to attract and retain more talented people than a small fund and receive more attention from, for example, its prime broker. On the other hand, a smaller fund may be more nimble. With smaller positions, the market impact cost

[113]See Howell (2001), Liang (2000), and Fung and Hsieh (2002).

of its trades may be less. Depending on the particular strategies pursued, there may be an optimal market size for the fund in relation to market opportunities available for its strategy at a given time. The investor should, following the paradigm for due diligence illustrated in Example 8-2, examine the current market opportunities in relation to the fund's size.

Research has generally supported the conclusion that, overall, larger funds have earned lower mean returns and lower risk-adjusted returns than small funds. However, the relationships of performance to fund size have been found to have exceptions according to hedge fund strategy. Because market opportunities and assets under management in a strategy change, the best advice may be to evaluate the effect of fund size on a case-by-case basis. The investor should also investigate differences in mortality rates among hedge funds by size within the strategy.

- *Age (vintage) effects.* The usual performance statistics hide the time dimension behind hedge fund performance. Investors should be sensitive to the fact that because of vintage effects, it may be difficult to compare the performance of funds with different lengths of track record. Comparisons of a fund with the performance of the median manager of the same vintage in a hedge fund's style group can be revealing.

6.3.3.1. Hedge Fund Due Diligence Hedge funds have historically been loosely regulated entities without the mandated and often standardized disclosure requirements of other investment vehicles, such as unit trusts in the United Kingdom and mutual funds in the United States. Although hedge funds typically provide an annual audited financial statement and performance review, they rarely disclose their existing portfolio positions. Possible concerns that arise from this lack of disclosure (see Anson, 2002a) include the following:

- Authenticity of the hedge fund manager's performance is doubtful if investors cannot verify the performance with a position report.
- Risk monitoring and management are difficult for investors without disclosure of trading and portfolio positions by the hedge fund manager. Without full disclosure of the holdings, investors cannot aggregate risk across their entire investment program to understand the implications at the portfolio level.

Because hedge fund operations and/or strategies may also be somewhat opaque, reducing investment risk in hedge fund investing starts with due diligence.

Again, the framework for due diligence presented in Example 8-2—covering market opportunity, investment process, organization, people, terms and structure, service providers, documents, and write-ups—applies here. The investor may interview the hedge fund and/or submit a questionnaire. The Alternative Investments Management Association provides the following due diligence checklist as a guide for investors evaluating hedge fund managers.[114] Investors should try to learn the following information:

I. Structure of the Hedge Fund

a. Legal entity: type and ownership structure
b. Name and address of hedge fund manager
c. Domicile: onshore or offshore

i. Branch offices or other locations (and their functions)

[114] See www.aima.org.

d. Regulatory registrations (e.g., investment adviser or commodity trading adviser)
e. Personnel: responsible officers and employees (including their biographies)
f. Auditors, legal counsel, and prime broker information

II. Strategy of the Hedge Fund

a. Style (e.g., event driven, global macro)
b. Instruments used under each strategy (e.g., which derivatives)
c. Benchmark, hurdle rate, high-water mark, etc.
d. Competitive niche or any uniqueness about the fund

i. The source of investment ideas or strategy
ii. How the strategy works under different market conditions
iii. Market conditions in which the strategy works best
iv. Any capacity constraint for the strategy

e. Current investments: types and positions

III. Performance Data

a. List of all funds and performance since inception.
b. Information on the performance of the funds and explanations

IV. Risk

a. What and how risks are measured and managed

i. Personnel involved

b. Specific risk-control measures, if any (e.g., position limits, derivatives, counterparty credit limits)
c. Past, current, and future use of leverage

V. Research

a. Any change in strategy in the past resulting from research findings
b. Efforts put into research for investment/trading ideas
c. Budget and personnel (internal and external) for research

VI. Administration

a. Law suits, litigations, regulatory actions against the fund or its managers
b. Significant employees and employee turnover
c. Personnel arrangement for the account: responsible account executive
d. Disaster recovery plan

VII. Legal

a. Fee structure: management and incentive fees (Is high-water mark applicable?)
b. Lock-up
c. Subscription amount: maximum and minimum
d. Drawback provision

VIII. References

a. Professional: auditor, prime broker, legal counsel
b. Existing investors

EXAMPLE 8-12 An Investor Does Due Diligence on a Hedge Fund

Alois Winkelmann is conducting due diligence on a U.S.-based hedge fund, Tricontinent Investors, for the Malvey Charitable Trust (MCT). Among the facts Winkelmann gathers are the following:

Structure: The fund employs three people—the two principals, Bryce Smith and Henrietta Duff, and an administrative assistant. Smith's prior work experience is 10 years as an equity analyst at North Country Trust Company and, prior to that, three years as an associate in a Syracuse, New York, law firm. He holds a BBA and an LLB. Duff worked for three years as an equity growth fund manager at a medium-size mutual fund complex. Prior to that, she was a corporate finance associate at a leading investment bank. Duff holds an AB in English and an MBA with a concentration in finance. The principals have at-will employment contracts. The fund's relationship with its prime broker extends back two years. The fund has used only one prime broker since it was formed. The prime broker is a prestigious firm ranked number two by prime brokerage business.

Hedge Fund Strategy:

- The fund invests in both fixed-income and equity markets.
- The fund buys U.S. 10-year Treasury notes and borrows short term abroad in markets that have particularly low interest rates to earn, currently, a positive spread.
- The fund conducts merger arbitrage involving the securities of the target and acquirer.

Legal: The fund has a 1 and 20 fee structure and a two-year lock-up period.

Based only on the information supplied, identify and discuss the risk factors in this hedge fund investment.

Solution:

- The firm is a small shop with limited management and research resources.
- Either principal could leave the firm on short notice because of the at-will nature of their employment contracts.
- The hedge fund has only a two-year track record available for evaluation.
- Neither principal has prior experience in either fixed-income investing or merger arbitrage, although Duff's investment banking experience may be somewhat relevant.
- The fixed-income strategy could become unprofitable if the U.S. dollar weakens against the currencies of the markets in which Tricontinent is borrowing short term.
- The fixed-income strategy could become less profitable or unprofitable if the spread between long-term and short-term interest rates decreases.

6.4. Performance Evaluation Concerns

The chapter on performance evaluation covers the basic concepts of performance evaluation, with components of performance measurement, performance attribution, and performance appraisal. This section provides further comments and illustrations in the context of hedge funds. In reviewing the performance of a hedge fund, some factors an investor needs to consider are:

- The returns achieved.
- Volatility, not only standard deviation but also downside volatility.
- What performance appraisal measures to use.
- Correlations (to gain information on diversification benefits in a portfolio context).
- Skewness and kurtosis because these affect risk and may qualify the conclusions drawn from a performance appraisal measure.
- Consistency, including the period specificity of performance.

6.4.1. Returns Hedge funds typically report data to hedge fund data providers monthly, and the default compounding frequency for hedge fund performance evaluation and reporting is monthly. The rate of return reported by hedge funds is the nominal monthly-holding-period return computed as follows:

$$\text{Rate of return} = [(\text{Ending value of portfolio}) - (\text{Beginning value of portfolio})]/(\text{Beginning value of portfolio})$$

These returns are typically compounded over 12 monthly periods (or 4 periods if the data are reported quarterly) to obtain the annualized rate of return. The reporting and compounding frequency can materially affect hedge funds' apparent performance for a number of reasons, including the following:

- Many hedge funds allow entry or exit to their funds quarterly or even less frequently.
- In calculating drawdowns, no compounding is typically applied to the loss.

The issues of leverage and the use of derivatives in return calculation also arise in hedge fund performance evaluation. The calculation convention followed in the hedge fund industry is to "look through" the leverage as if the asset were fully paid. Thus, as the beginning value in the above equation for rate of return, the return on a levered position is based on the amount actually paid plus any borrowing used to fund the purchase. The ending value is, of course, calculated on a consistent basis. Thus, leverage affects the weighting of an asset in the portfolio but not the return on the individual asset. The same principle of deleveraging applies to the computation of the rate of return when derivatives are included in the hedge fund portfolio.[115]

Investors sometimes examine the rolling returns to a hedge fund. The **rolling return,** *RR,* is simply the moving average of the holding-period returns for a specified period (e.g., a calendar year) that matches the investor's time horizon. For example, if the investor's time horizon is 12 months, the rolling return would be calculated using

$$RR_{n,t} = (R_t + R_{t-1} + R_{t-2} + \ldots + R_{t-n})/n$$

[115]Because derivatives require only a good faith deposit, which is interest yielding, there is no real capital investment involved. The computed rate of return under the assumption that the full value of the derivatives constitutes the investment base is, at best, a pseudo rate of return. Yau, Savanayana, and Schneeweis (1990) examined the impact of different rates of return of derivative investments based on differing computations of the rates of return and found significantly different results in portfolio optimization and hedging programs.

so

$$RR_{12,t} = (R_t + R_{t-1} + R_{t-2} + \ldots + R_{t-12})/12$$

Rolling returns provide some insight into the characteristics and qualities of returns. In particular, they show how consistent the returns are over the investment period and identify any cyclicality in the returns.

6.4.2. Volatility and Downside Volatility As in traditional investments, the standard deviation of returns is a common measure of risk in hedge fund performance. The standard deviation of hedge fund returns is computed in the usual fashion and typically based on monthly returns. The annualized standard deviation is usually computed as the standard deviation of the monthly return times the square root of 12, making the assumption of serially uncorrelated returns. The use of the standard deviation of monthly returns as a measure of risk also makes the implicit assumption that the return distribution follows the normal distribution, at least to a close approximation. As already mentioned, however, hedge funds appear to have more instances of extremely high and extremely low returns than would be expected with a normal distribution (i.e., positive excess kurtosis) and some funds also display meaningful skewness. When those conditions hold, standard deviation incorrectly represents the actual risk of a hedge fund's strategies.

Downside deviation, or semideviation, is an alternative risk measure that mitigates one critique of standard deviation, namely, that it penalizes high positive returns. Downside deviation computes deviation from a specified threshold (i.e., below a specified return, r^*); only the negative deviations are included in the calculation. The threshold can be zero (separating gains from losses) or the prevailing short-term rate or any rate chosen by the user. Semideviation uses the average monthly return as the threshold. Once the threshold is determined, the computation resembles that of the standard deviation. Using downside deviation instead of standard deviation recognizes a distinction between good and bad volatility:

$$\text{Downside deviation} = \sqrt{\frac{\sum_{i=1}^{n}[\min(r_t - r^*, 0)]^2}{n-1}}$$

where min(A,B) means "A or B, whichever is smaller."

Another popular risk measure is drawdown. As discussed in the chapter on risk management, drawdown in the field of hedge fund management is the difference between a portfolio's point of maximum net asset value (its high-water mark) and any subsequent low point (until new "high water" is reached). *Maximum* drawdown is the largest difference between a high-water point and a subsequent low.[116] A portfolio may also be said to be in a position of drawdown from a decline from a high-water mark until a new high-water mark is reached. How long this period lasts is relevant to evaluating hedge fund performance—in particular, its record of recovering from losses.

6.4.3. Performance Appraisal Measures The most extensively used industry measure to date has been the Sharpe ratio, which measures the average amount of return in excess of the risk-free rate per unit of standard deviation of return. The chapter on performance evaluation

[116]See Lhabitant (2002), p. 254.

gives a definition and a discussion, but we may present it as follows, with reference to the *ex post* performance in a given year:

$$\text{Sharpe ratio} = (\text{Annualized rate of return} - \text{Annualized risk-free rate}) / \text{Annualized standard deviation}$$

In this application, a one-year T-bill yield is usually used to determine the annualized risk-free rate.

The Sharpe ratio has a number of limitations that the hedge fund investor needs to understand:

- The Sharpe ratio is time dependent; that is, the overall Sharpe ratio increases proportionally with the square root of time. An annual Sharpe ratio will therefore be $\sqrt{12}$ bigger than a monthly Sharpe ratio if returns are serially uncorrelated.[117]
- It is not an appropriate measure of risk-adjusted performance when the investment has an asymmetrical return distribution, with either negative or positive skewness.[118]
- Illiquid holdings bias the Sharpe ratio upward.
- Sharpe ratios are overestimated when investment returns are serially correlated (i.e. returns trend), which causes a lower estimate of the standard deviation. This occurs with certain hedge fund strategies that may have a problem with stale pricing or illiquidity. Distressed securities may be an example.
- The Sharpe ratio is primarily a risk-adjusted performance measure for stand-alone investments and does not take into consideration the correlations with other assets in a portfolio.
- The Sharpe ratio has not been found to have predictive ability for hedge funds in general. Being a "winner" according to the Sharpe ratio over a past period cannot be relied on to predict future success.
- The Sharpe ratio can be gamed; that is, the reported Sharpe ratio can be increased without the investment really delivering higher risk-adjusted returns. Specifically, Spurgin (2001) showed the following means to gaming the Sharpe ratio:

    1. Lengthening the measurement interval. This will result in a lower estimate of volatility; for example, the annualized standard deviation of daily returns is generally higher than the weekly, which is, in turn, higher than the monthly.
    2. Compounding the monthly returns but calculating the standard deviation from the (not compounded) monthly returns.
    3. Writing out-of-the-money puts and calls on a portfolio. This strategy can potentially increase the return by collecting the option premium without paying off for several years. Strategies that involve taking on default risk, liquidity risk, or other forms of catastrophe risk have the same ability to report an upwardly biased Sharpe ratio. (Examples are the Sharpe ratios of market-neutral hedge funds before and after the 1998 liquidity crisis.) This is similar to trading negative skewness for a greater Sharpe ratio by improving the mean or standard deviation of the investment.[119]

[117] See Lhabitant (2004).

[118] A number of researchers insist that the Sharpe ratio should be interpreted together with the higher moments of the return distribution. For example, Brooks and Kat (2002) found that high Sharpe ratios tend to go together with negative skewness and high kurtosis.

[119] See Spurgin (2001) and Anson (2002a) for theoretical proofs and examples.

4. Smoothing of returns. Using certain derivative structures, infrequent marking to market of illiquid assets, and pricing models that understate monthly gains or losses can reduce reported volatility.
5. Getting rid of extreme returns (best and worst monthly returns each year), which increases the standard deviation. Operationally, this entails a total-return swap: One pays the best and worst returns for one's benchmark index each year, and the counterparty pays a fixed cash flow and hedges the risk in the open market. If swaps are not available, one can do it directly with options.

The **Sortino ratio** replaces standard deviation in the Sharpe ratio with downside deviation. Instead of using the mean rate of return to calculate the downside deviation, the investor's minimum acceptable return or the risk-free rate is typically used. The chapter on risk management has further comments on this measure. The Sortino ratio is

Sortino ratio = (Annualized rate of return − Annualized risk-free rate)/Downside deviation

The **gain-to-loss ratio** measures the ratio of positive returns to negative returns over a specified period of time. The higher the gain-to-loss ratio (in absolute value), the better:

Gain-to-loss ratio = (Number months with positive returns/Number months with negative returns) × (Average up-month return/Average down-month return)

In addition, two major appraisal measures based on drawdowns as indicators of risk, the Calmar ratio and the Sterling ratio, have been applied to hedge fund analysis.[120]

6.4.4. Correlations

Correlations provide information on portfolio diversification. However, correlations are most meaningful when assets' or strategies' returns are normally distributed. This fact is an additional reason to consider skewness and kurtosis.

6.4.5. Skewness and Kurtosis

To review, skewness is a measure of asymmetry in the distribution of returns. A symmetrical distribution has a skewness of zero; all else being equal, a positive value of skewness is desirable. Kurtosis evaluates the relative incidence of returns clustered near the mean return versus returns extremely far away from the mean. If one investment has higher kurtosis than another, it tends to have more instances of extreme returns.

6.4.6. Consistency

Another element in evaluating hedge funds is consistency of results. Consistency analysis is most relevant when comparing funds of the same style or strategy. It is important to look at the number of months that the strategy has had positive (or negative)

[120]The **Calmar ratio** is the compound annualized rate of return over a specified time period divided by the absolute value of maximum drawdown over the same time period. Frequently, the time horizon is set at three years (36 months), but if three years of data are not available, the available data are used. The **Sterling ratio** is the compound annualized rate of return over a specified time period divided by the average yearly maximum drawdown over the same time period less an arbitrary 10 percent. To calculate this average yearly drawdown, the data period is divided into separate 12-month periods and the maximum drawdown is calculated for each and averaged. The convention for the time horizon follows that of the Calmar ratio.

returns, the number of months that the strategy has had positive (negative) returns when the market is up (down), and the average monthly returns in up and down markets. For consistency, a fund should have a greater percentage of positive returns and less negative returns than the benchmark in all market conditions. We illustrate with the data given in Exhibit 8-29 on page 558. In computing the rolling returns, the relevant holding period for the investor is assumed to be six months. This is simply for illustration purposes. In practice, the rolling returns should match the investor's investment horizon.

Exhibit 8-30 (page 559) shows the computation of the performance statistics of a hypothetical hedge fund for 12 months from the data given in Exhibit 8-29.

7. MANAGED FUTURES

Managed futures have been used as an investment alternative since the late 1960s.[121] More recently, such institutional investors as corporate and public pension funds, endowments, trusts, and bank trust departments have been including managed futures as one segment of a well-diversified portfolio.

Managed futures are private pooled investment vehicles that can invest in cash, spot, and derivative markets for the benefit of their investors and have the ability to use leverage in a wide variety of trading strategies. Like hedge funds, managed futures programs are actively managed. Similar to hedge funds, with which they are often grouped, managed futures programs are often structured as limited partnerships open only to accredited investors (institutions and high-net-worth individuals). Compensation arrangements for managed futures programs are also similar to those of hedge funds. The primary distinguishing differences between hedge funds and managed futures is that, for the most part, managed futures trade exclusively in derivative markets (future, forward, or option markets) whereas hedge funds tend to be more active in spot markets while using futures markets for hedging. Because hedge funds often trade in individual securities whereas managed futures primarily trade market-based futures and options contracts on broader or more generic baskets of assets, one can view hedge funds as concentrating on inefficiencies in micro (security) stock and bond markets whereas managed futures look for return opportunities in macro (index) stock and bond markets. In addition, in some jurisdictions, managed futures programs have been historically more highly regulated than hedge funds.

7.1. The Managed Futures Market

Managed futures programs are an industry comprising specialist professional money managers. In the United States, such programs are run by general partners known as commodity pool operators (CPOs), who are, or have hired, professional commodity trading advisers to manage money in the pool. In the United States, both CPOs and CTAs are registered with the U.S. Commodity Futures Trading Commission and National Futures Association (a self-regulatory body).

7.1.1. Types of Managed Futures Investments

Managed futures have been described as skill-based investment strategies. Skill-based strategies obtain returns from the unique skill or strategy of the trader. Like hedge funds, managed futures have also been described as absolute-return strategies.

[121]Books that provide information on the structural and performance history of managed futures include Fox-Andrews and Meaden (1995), Peters and Warwick (1997), and Chance (1996).

EXHIBIT 8-29 Hypothetical Hedge Fund Consistency Data

Month	Hedge Fund return (%)	Index Return (%)	(HF Return - Hurdle Rate)^2	(Index Return - Hurdle Rate)^2	1+ HF Return	1+ Index Return	Rolling Six-Month Return of HF	Rolling Six-Month Return of Index
January	2.5	1.0	0.0000	0.0000	1.0250	1.0100		
February	1.5	1.3	0.0000	0.0000	1.0150	1.0130		
March	−1.0	−1.6	2.0070	4.0671	0.9900	0.9840		
April	−1.2	−2.4	2.6137	7.9338	0.9880	0.9760		
May	−1.0	−4.2	2.0070	21.3139	0.9900	0.9580		
June	0.9	2.0	0.0000	0.0000	1.0090	1.0200	0.0028	−0.0065
July	−1.0	2.5	2.0070	0.0000	0.9900	1.0250	−0.0030	−0.0040
August	0.7	−2.1	0.0000	6.3338	1.0070	0.9790	−0.0043	−0.0097
September	1.1	2.0	0.0000	0.0000	1.0110	1.0200	−0.0008	−0.0037
October	2.1	0.5	0.0000	0.0000	1.0210	1.0050	0.0047	0.0012
November	1.5	3.1	0.0000	0.0000	1.0150	1.0310	0.0088	0.0133
December	1.5	0.2	0.0000	0.0470	1.0150	1.0020	0.0098	0.0103
Sum	7.6	2.3	8.6348	39.6955				
Mean	0.63	0.19					0.0026	0.0001
Product					1.0777	1.0203		

Notes: The hurdle rate is 5 percent per year or 0.4167 percent per month. Deviation from the hurdle rate squared is computed if the fund/index return is less than the hurdle rate; otherwise, it will be equal to zero. The rolling six-month return is computed as $RR_t = (R_t + R_{t-1} + \ldots + R_{t-5})/6$.

EXHIBIT 8-30 Return and Risk Calculations

1. Return	Hedge Fund	Index
Total fund return $= [(1 + r_1)(1 + r_2) \ldots (1 + r_{12})] - 1 =$ $1.0777 - 1 = 0.0777$.		
Total index return $= 1.0203 - 1 = 0.0203$.	7.77%	2.03%
Geometric mean per year:		
Fund $= (1.0777^{1/12} - 1) \times 12 = 7.50\%$.		
Index $= (1.0203^{1/12} - 1) \times 12 = 2.02\%$.	7.50%	2.02%
Rolling six-month returns mean $=$ $(RR_{6,1} + RR_{6,2} + RR_{6,3} + RR_{6,4} + RR_{6,5} + RR_{6,6} + RR_{6,7})/7$, where $RR_{6,t} = (R_t + R_{t-1} + R_{t-2} + R_{t-3} + R_{t-4} + R_{t-5})/6$.		
Fund $= (0.0028 - 0.0030 - 0.0043 - 0.0008 + 0.0047 + 0.0088 + 0.0098)/7 = 0.0026$.		
Index $= (-0.0065 - 0.0040 - 0.0097 - 0.0037 + 0.0012 + 0.0133 + 0.0103)/7 = 0.0001$.	0.26%	0.01%
Rolling six-month returns (max)	0.98%	1.33%
Rolling six-month returns (min)	−0.43%	−0.97%
2. Risk		
Annualized standard deviation	4.62%	7.87%
Annualized downside deviation:		
Hurdle rate = 5% per year.		
Fund $= \sqrt{8.6348/(12 - 1)} \times \sqrt{12} = 3.07$.	3.07%	6.58%
3. Appraisal		
Sharpe ratio (per year) = (Return −5%)/Standard deviation:		
Fund $= (7.5 - 5)/4.62 = 0.54$.		
Index $= (2.02 - 5)/7.87 = -0.38$.	0.54	−0.38
Sortino ratio (per year) = (Return −5%)/Downside deviation:		
Fund $= (7.5 - 5)/3.07 = 0.81$.		
Index $= (2.02 - 5)/6.58 = -0.45$.	0.81	−0.45
Gain/Loss :		
Fund $= (1.475/ - 1.05) \times (8/4) = -2.82$.		
Index $= (1.575/ - 2.575) \times (8/4) = -1.22$.	−2.82	−1.22
4. Consistency		
Number of months	12	12
Number of positive months	8	8
Percentage of positive months	66.67%	66.67%
Average return in up-months	1.48%	1.58%
Number of negative months	4	4
Percentage of negative months	33.33%	33.33%
Average return in down-months	−1.05%	−2.58%
Average monthly return in index up-months :		
Fund $= (2.5 + 1.5 + 0.9 - 1.0 + 1.1 + 2.1 + 1.5 + 1.5)/8 =$ 1.263.		
Index $= (1.0 + 1.3 + 2.0 + 2.5 + 2.0 + 0.5 + 3.1 + 0.2)/8 =$ 1.575.	1.26%	1.58%
Average monthly return in index down months $=$ $(-1.0 - 1.2 - 1.0 + 0.7)/4 = -0.625$.	−0.63%	−2.58%
5. Correlation between fund and index returns—12 months		0.53

Note: The arithmetic means used in the computation of standard deviation were computed as 0.63 percent and 0.19 percent for, respectively, the fund and the index.

In addition to private commodity pools, managed futures programs are also available in separately managed accounts (sometimes known as *CTA managed accounts*). Publicly traded commodity funds open to smaller investors are also available. Managed futures programs may use a single manager or multiple managers.

Managed futures funds share the compensation structure of hedge funds consisting of a management fee plus incentive fee, with a 2 plus 20 arrangement the most common structure.

Managed futures may be classified according to investment style. They are often classified into subgroups on the basis of investment style (e.g., systematic or discretionary), markets traded (e.g., currency or financial), or trading strategy (e.g., trend following or contrarian). Managed futures are at times viewed as a subset of global macro hedge funds, in that they also attempt to take advantage of systematic moves in major financial and nonfinancial markets, primarily through trading futures and option contracts.

The trading strategies of managed futures include the following:

- *Systematic trading strategies* trade primarily according to a rule-based trading model usually based on past prices. Most systematic CTAs invest by using a trend-following program, although some trade according to a contrarian, or countertrend, program. In addition, trend-following CTAs may concentrate on short-term trends, medium-term trends, long-term trends, or a combination thereof.
- *Discretionary trading strategies* trade financial, currency, and commodity futures and options. Unlike systematic strategies, they involve portfolio manager judgment. Discretionary trading models include those based on fundamental economic data and on trader beliefs. Traders often use multiple criteria in making trading decisions.

By the markets emphasized in trading, managed futures may be classified as:

- *Financial* (trading financial futures/options, currency futures/options, and forward contracts).
- *Currency* (trading currency futures/options and forward contracts).
- *Diversified* (trading financial futures/options, currency futures/options, and forward contracts, as well as physical commodity futures/options).

  A market classification can also be used to distinguish subcategories of systematic and discretionary trading strategies.

7.1.2. Size of the Managed Futures Market Worldwide, the managed futures industry has grown from less than US\$1 billion under management in 1980 to approximately US\$130 billion under management in 2004.[122] To put this last figure in perspective, consider that the managed futures industry is probably somewhat less than 10 percent the size of the hedge fund industry as judged by assets under management.

7.2. Benchmarks and Historical Performance

The benchmarks for managed futures are similar to those for hedge funds, in that indices represent performance of a group of managers who use a similar trading strategy or style.

[122]These numbers do not include the large amount of funds traded through hedge funds (e.g., global asset allocators) or proprietary trading desks of large investment houses, insurance companies, or banks that use strategies similar to those of independent CTAs. The estimate is from Barclays Trading Group.

EXHIBIT 8-31 CTA Performance, 1990–2004

Measure	CISDM CTA$	HFCI	S&P 500	Lehman Gov./Corp.	MSCI World	Lehman Global
Annualized return	10.85%	13.46%	10.94%	7.77%	7.08%	8.09%
Annualized std. dev.	9.96%	5.71%	14.65%	4.46%	14.62%	5.23%
Sharpe ratio	0.66	1.61	0.45	0.78	0.19	0.73
Minimum monthly return	−6.00%	−6.92%	−14.46%	−4.19%	−13.32%	−3.66%
Correlation w/CTA$	1.00	0.19	−0.10	0.29	−0.11	0.27

Note: CTA$ is the dollar-weighted CTA universe.
Source: CISDM (2005d).

7.2.1. Benchmarks Investable benchmarks for actively managed derivative strategies exist. Such indices replicate the return to a mechanical, trend-following strategy in a number of financial and commodity futures markets. For example, the Mount Lucas Management Index takes both long and short positions in a number of futures markets based on a technical (moving-average) trading rule that is, in effect, an active momentum strategy.

The CISDM CTA trading strategy benchmarks are examples of benchmarks based on peer groups of CTAs. The dollar-weighted (CTA$) and equal-weighted (CTAEQ) CISDM indices reflect manager returns for all reporting managers in the CISDM database on, respectively, a dollar-weighted and equal-weighted basis. The CISDM CTA indices include indices for systematic versus discretionary strategies, for groups based on market emphasis (financial, currency, diversified), and for trend following versus contrarian. For example, the CTA trend-following index may include financial, currency, and diversified trend-following CTAs.

7.2.2. Historical Performance The performance of managed futures on an individual basis and as a group is of interest. For the 1990 to 2004 period, the annualized standard deviations of individual CTAs in the CISDM alternative investment database were, on average, comparable to the averaged annualized standard deviations of U.S. blue chip stocks.[123] As Exhibit 8-31 shows, on a portfolio basis, for the 1990 to 2004 period, the volatility of the CTA$ Index (9.96 percent) was less than that of either the S&P 500 (14.65 percent) or MSCI World Index (14.62 percent) but greater than that of U.S. or global bonds (4.46 percent and 5.23 percent, respectively). The Sharpe ratio for the CTA$ was better than those of equities but not those of bonds. Exhibit 8-32 shows that results for a more recent period (2000 to 2004) are qualitatively similar. Noteworthy is that the correlations of the CISDM CTA$ with the equity indices are slightly negative; the correlations of the CISDM CTA$ with U.S. and global bonds are similar at 0.42 and 0.46, respectively.

Exhibit 8-33 displays the correlations among CTA investment strategies, which range from moderate to highly positive. The correlation of trend-following with discretionary is among the lowest at 0.51. In general, the correlations among CTA strategies appear to be influenced by the degree to which the strategies are trend following or discretionary. The overall dollar-weighted and equal-weighted indices are highly correlated with diversified, financial,

[123]The average annualized standard deviation of the individual CTAs that have complete data for 1990 to 2004 in the CISDM database is 27.06 percent vs. 28.54 percent for the individual component stocks in the DJIA (CISDM 2005d). Annualized standard deviations are derived by multiplying the monthly data by the square root of 12.

EXHIBIT 8-32 Recent CTA Performance, 2000–2004

Measure	CISDM CTA$	HFCI	S&P 500	Lehman Gov./Corp.	MSCI World	Lehman Global
Annualized return	7.89%	6.84%	−2.30%	8.00%	−2.05%	8.51%
Annualized std. dev.	8.66%	4.83%	16.35%	4.76%	15.62%	6.00%
Sharpe ratio	0.60	0.86	−0.31	1.11	−0.30	0.97
Minimum monthly return	−5.12%	−2.94%	−10.87%	−4.19%	−10.98%	−3.66%
Correlation w/CTA$	1.00	0.18	−0.25	0.42	−0.18	0.46

Source: CISDM (2005d).

EXHIBIT 8-33 Correlations of CISDM CTA Universe Strategies, 1990–2004

	CTA$	CTAEQ	Currency	Discretionary	Diversified	Financial	Trend Following
CTA$	1.00						
CTAEQ	0.94	1.00					
Currency	0.66	0.62	1.00				
Discretionary	0.63	0.54	0.44	1.00			
Diversified	0.94	0.93	0.54	0.60	1.00		
Financial	0.93	0.88	0.59	0.47	0.84	1.00	
Trend following	0.96	0.95	0.64	0.51	0.92	0.93	1.00

Source: CISDM (2005d).

EXHIBIT 8-34 Performance of CISDM CTA Universe Strategies and Traditional Assets, 1990–2004

Strategy or Class	Return	Standard Deviation	Sharpe Ratio	Minimum Monthly Return	Correlation w/S&P 500	Correlation w/Lehman Gov./Corp.
CISDM CTA$	10.85%	9.96%	0.66	−6.00%	−0.10	0.29
CISDM CTAEQ	9.33	9.58	0.53	−5.43	−0.16	0.26
CISDM Currency	9.24	11.80	0.42	−8.17	0.05	0.15
CISDM Discretionary	11.78	6.51	1.15	−4.57	−0.05	0.21
CISDM Diversified	9.56	11.42	0.46	−7.53	−0.14	0.27
CISDM Financial	11.76	12.83	0.58	−8.56	−0.09	0.35
CISDM Trend following	11.30	16.24	0.43	−10.38	−0.16	0.29
S&P 500	10.94	14.65	0.50	−14.46	1.00	0.10
Lehman Gov./Corp.	7.77	4.46	0.80	−4.19	0.10	1.00

Source: CISDM (2005d).

and trend-following strategies and distinctly less correlated with currency and discretionary strategies.

Exhibit 8-34 complements the information that was provided in Exhibit 8-31 by adding performance information on the CTA strategies, including correlations with U.S. equity and bond indices. Across CTA strategies, correlations with U.S. equities are low and correlations with U.S. bonds are low or moderate.

7.2.3. Interpretation Issues In evaluating historical managed futures return data, the investor should be aware of the upward bias that survivorship can impart. Research has found return differences on the order of 3.5 percent between the surviving CTAs and the full sample that includes defunct CTAs.[124] The differential performance between survivor and nonsurvivor samples (on an absolute basis and a risk-adjusted basis) comes chiefly from differences in return performance in the months just prior to CTA dissolution. The ability of investment professionals to forecast which managers may not survive could result in dramatic differences in investment results.[125]

7.3. Managed Futures: Investment Characteristics and Roles

Similar to hedge funds, managed futures are active skill-based strategies that investors can examine for the potential to improve a portfolio's risk and return characteristics. In the following sections, we present more details on these investments.

7.3.1. Investment Characteristics This discussion of investment characteristics will focus on the market opportunities that may be exploited by CTAs. Derivative markets are zero-sum games.[126] As a result, the long-term return to a passively managed, unlevered futures position should be the risk-free return on invested capital less management fees and transaction costs. For derivative-based investment strategies like managed futures to produce excess returns, on average, there must be a sufficient number of hedgers or other users of the markets who systematically earn less than the risk-free rate. Hedgers, for example, may pay a risk premium to liquidity providers for the insurance they obtain. If that condition is met, managed futures may be able to earn positive excess returns (i.e., be the winning side in the zero-sum transactions).

The zero-sum nature of derivatives markets also does not restrict CTAs from attempting to conduct arbitrage when relationships are out of equilibrium. Institutional characteristics and differential carrying costs among investors may permit managed fund traders to take advantage of short-term pricing differences between theoretically identical stock, bond, futures, options, and cash market positions. CTAs may also attempt to take advantage of the opportunity of trading in trending markets.

Most actively managed derivative strategies follow momentum strategies. In equity markets, research has begun to support the notion that short-term momentum-based strategies may be able to produce excess returns; the evidence related to the market opportunity in futures markets is less well developed.[127] Government policy intervention in interest rate and currency markets may cause trending in currency and fixed-income markets. Some corporate risk management approaches may result in trading that creates short-term trending. Trading techniques based on capturing these price trends, whatever the source, may be profitable. There is also evidence that momentum trading imparts the desirable characteristic of positive skewness to managed fund returns.

Because of the ease with which futures traders take short positions, futures traders can attempt to earn positive excess returns in falling as well as rising markets. Some of the most

[124] See Fung and Hsieh (1997b) and McCarthy et al. (1996).

[125] For research in the area of manager default, see Diz (1999).

[126] The term *zero sum* refers to the fact that derivatives markets reallocate uncertain cash flows among market participants without enhancing aggregate cash flows in any way. See Gastineau and Kritzman (1999).

[127] See Lee and Swaminathan (2000) and references therein for the evidence on momentum strategies in U.S. equity markets.

EXHIBIT 8-35 Managed Futures Performance in Portfolios, 1990–2004

Measure	Portfolio I	Portfolio II	Portfolio III	Portfolio IV	Portfolio V	Portfolio VI
Annualized return	9.64%	10.43%	10.54%	7.86%	9.01%	9.26%
Annualized std. deviation	7.94%	7.09%	6.48%	8.29%	7.28%	6.65%
Sharpe ratio	0.67	0.87	0.97	0.43	0.65	0.75
Minimum monthly return	−6.25%	−6.39%	−5.21%	−5.61%	−5.87%	−4.75%
Correlation w/CISDM CTA$	−0.01	0.02	n/c	−0.01	0.02	n/c

Notes:
Portfolio I = 50 percent S&P 500, 50 percent Lehman Gov./Corp. Bond.
Portfolio II = 40 percent S&P 500, 40 percent Lehman Gov./Corp., 20 percent HFCI.
Portfolio III = 90 percent Portfolio II, 10 percent CTA$.
Portfolio IV = 50 percent MSCI World, 50 percent Lehman Global Bond.
Portfolio V = 40 percent MSCI World, 40 percent Lehman Global, 20 percent HFCI.
Portfolio VI = 90 percent Portfolio V, 10 percent CTA$.
n/c = not computed.
Source: CISDM (2005d).

impressive periods of return for CTAs have been during periods of poor performance in the equity markets (e.g., October 1987). Access to options markets permits managed futures and hedge fund traders to create positions that attempt to exploit changes in market volatility of the underlying asset (volatility being one of the determinants of option value). Such strategies are not available to investors who are restricted to using cash markets.

Because managed futures can replicate many strategies available to a cash market investor at a lower cost—and allow strategies that are unavailable to cash investors—factor models for this group must include the factors that may be unique to managed futures and hedge fund trading opportunities.[128] To the degree that different factors explain managed futures returns and stock/bond returns, managed futures may provide investors exposure to unique sources of return. The presence of such risk factors also provides an economic rationale for managed futures' diversification capabilities when added to a portfolio of equities and bonds.

7.3.2. Roles in the Portfolio As for the other alternative investments, we now offer historical evidence on the potential of managed futures as part of a portfolio. Managed futures appear to be useful in diversifying risk even in a diversified portfolio of stocks, bonds, and hedge funds.

Exhibit 8-35 shows that, for the period 1990 to 2004, managed futures would have been a valuable addition to a stock/bond/hedge fund portfolio in relation both to U.S. and global stocks and bonds. The Sharpe ratio of Portfolios III and VI, which include at least a 10 percent investment in managed futures, dominate those invested only in stocks, bonds, and hedge funds, whether the stocks and bonds are U.S. or global (see Portfolio III versus Portfolio II for the U.S. comparison and Portfolio VI versus Portfolio V for the global comparison). The portfolios with managed futures also improve on the portfolios invested only in stocks and bonds (Portfolio I for the U.S., Portfolio IV for global).

[128] For a discussion of whether managed futures returns are the natural result of market forces or are based primarily on trader skills, see Schneeweis and Spurgin (1996).

EXHIBIT 8-36 Recent Managed Futures Performance in Portfolios, 2000–2004

Measure	Portfolio I	Portfolio II	Portfolio III	Portfolio IV	Portfolio V	Portfolio VI
Annualized return	3.15%	3.92%	4.37%	3.45%	4.16%	4.58%
Annualized std. deviation	7.93%	6.94%	6.22%	8.55%	7.48%	6.81%
Sharpe ratio	0.06	0.18	0.27	0.09	0.19	0.28
Minimum monthly return	−4.36%	−3.62%	−3.07%	−4.94%	−4.08%	−3.48%
Correlation w/CTA$	−0.13	−0.10	n/c	0.00	0.02	n/c

Notes:
Portfolio I = 50 percent S&P 500, 50 percent Lehman Gov./Corp. Bond.
Portfolio II = 40 percent S&P 500, 40 percent Lehman Gov./Corp., 20 percent HFCI.
Portfolio III = 90 percent Portfolio II, 10 percent CTA$.
Portfolio IV = 50 percent MSCI World, 50 percent Lehman Global Bond.
Portfolio V = 40 percent MSCI World, 40 percent Lehman Global, 20 percent HFCI.
Portfolio VI = 90 percent Portfolio V, 10 percent CTA$.
n/c = not computed.
Source: CISDM (2005d).

Exhibit 8-36 breaks out the results for the five most recent years covered in Exhibit 8-35. For 2000–2004 also, managed futures would have provided better risk-adjusted performance than the comparison portfolios. The Sharpe ratio of an equally weighted stock and bond portfolio is 0.06, and the Sharpe ratio of an equally weighted stock and bond portfolio with a 20 percent hedge fund component is 0.18, whereas adding a 10 percent CTA allocation to the stock/bond/hedge fund portfolio resulted in a Sharpe ratio of 0.27.[129]

The performance of managed futures has also been examined in the peer-reviewed literature. The conclusions appear to be investment-vehicle dependent and, to some extent, time-period and strategy dependent. On the one hand, a number of studies found that publicly traded commodity funds have been poor investments either on a stand-alone basis or as part of a diversified portfolio.[130] On the other hand, some research has concluded that private commodity pools and CTA-based managed accounts do have value either as stand-alone investments, as part of a portfolio, or in both roles.[131] Note that many CTAs prefer not to offer their services through public or private pools, so distinctions as to investment vehicle matter in interpreting results.[132]

[129]Considerable research exists on the risk reduction benefits of managed futures. In short, the academic (Schneeweis et al., 1996) and practitioner (Schneeweis, 1996) literature has shown that the returns of managed futures have a low correlation with the returns of traditional investment vehicles, such as stocks and bonds. Recent research has shown that when managed futures returns were segmented according to whether the stock/bond market rose or fell, managed futures had a negative correlation when these cash markets posted significant negative returns and a positive correlation when these cash markets reported significant positive returns. Thus, managed futures may also offer unique asset allocation properties in differing market environments.

[130]For example, Elton et al. (1987, 1990) and Edwards and Park (1996).

[131]See Edwards and Park (1996), Edwards and Liew (1999), and McCarthy, Schneeweis, and Spurgin (1996).

[132]The value of commodity funds, in contrast to investing directly with CTAs, has been questioned by Schneeweis (1996). Schneeweis, however, also concludes that the results are strategy and time-period

It appears that an investor can fairly closely track the performance of a CTA-based managed futures index by using a small random selection of CTAs. Henker and Martin (1998) provided empirical evidence that a naively (e.g., randomly) chosen CTA portfolio replicates comparison CTA benchmark indices. They showed that a portfolio of randomly selected CTAs has a correlation in excess of 0.90 with that of a commonly cited benchmark (the Managed Account Reports dollar-weighted CTA index). Henker and Martin also showed that for CTAs, as for equity securities, a randomly selected equally weighted portfolio of 8 to 10 CTAs has a standard deviation similar to that of the population from which it is drawn.

These results, taken as a whole, suggest that the forecasted returns to a CTA-based managed futures index can be useful for determining the optimal asset allocation to managed futures when the investor will invest with a relatively limited number of CTAs.[133] Henker and Martin also concluded, as did Billingsley and Chance (1996), that fewer than 10 CTAs are needed to achieve most of the benefits of including CTAs in an existing stock and bond portfolio.

7.3.3. Other Issues Performance persistence in CTA managers has been actively debated in the academic community.[134] Although there is little evidence that a strategy of investing in winners and avoiding losers will be successful over time, there is some evidence of performance persistence. McCarthy et al. (1996), showed that the relative riskiness of a CTA—the CTA's beta with respect to an index of CTAs—is a good predictor of future relative returns.[135] Thus, past CTA performance may be valuable in forecasting CTA and multi-adviser CTA portfolios' return and risk parameters, especially at the portfolio level. In terms of public policy, public disclosure of individual CTAs as well as benchmark information may be of benefit to potential investors who want to forecast expected risk-adjusted performance of public commodity funds.

Because managed futures frequently use derivatives and leverage in their strategies, investors should conduct the same due diligence as described in the hedge fund section. Particular attention should be paid to the risk management practices of the CTA.

EXAMPLE 8-13 Adding Managed Futures to the Strategic Asset Allocation

Andrew Cassano, CIO of a large charitable organization, is meeting with his senior analyst, Lori Wood, to discuss managed futures. Wood presents Cassano with information taken from Exhibits 8-31 and 8-35.

1. Using data from these two exhibits, determine whether the addition of managed futures to a portfolio comprising world equities, global bonds, and hedge fund strategies would improve the risk/return profile of that portfolio. Justify your response with reference to two statistics provided in the exhibits.

dependent. Given that commodity funds are often multimanager in form, the benefits of commodity fund investment relative to multiple CTA investment is primarily a function of the fee structure.

[133] See also Park and Staum (1998).

[134] See Brown and Goetzmann (1995).

[135] Similar results were reported by Brorsen (1998).

EXHIBIT 8-31 (excerpted). CTA Performance, 1990–2004

Measure	CTA$	HFCI	MSCI World Index	Lehman Global Bond Index
Annualized return	10.85%	13.46%	7.08%	8.09%
Annualized std. dev.	9.96%	5.71%	14.62%	5.23%
Correlation w/CTA$	1.00	0.19	−0.11	0.27

Note: CTA$ is the dollar-weighted CISDM CTA universe
Source: CISDM (2005d).

EXHIBIT 8-35 (excerpted). Managed Futures Performance in Portfolios, 1990–2004

Measure	Portfolio I	Portfolio II	Portfolio III
Annualized return	7.86%	9.01%	9.26%
Annualized std. dev.	8.29%	7.28%	6.65%
Sharpe ratio	0.43	0.65	0.75
Minimum monthly return	−5.61%	−5.87%	−4.75%
Correlation w/CTA$	−0.01	0.02	n/a

Notes:
Portfolio I = 50 percent MSCI World, 50 percent Lehman Global Bond.
Portfolio II = 40 percent MSCI World, 40 percent Lehman Global, 20 percent HFCI.
Portfolio III = 90 percent Portfolio II, 10 percent CTA$.
Source: CISDM (2005d).

Cassano addresses Wood as follows: "You've explained why the Sharpe ratio may not be the most representative indicator of risk with respect to hedge fund strategies. Are there other statistics that could be useful as potential predictors of performance persistence for CTA managers?"

2. With respect to Cassano's question, recommend another statistic that research has shown to be a useful predictor of performance persistence among CTAs.

Cassano states: "If managed futures are a subset of hedge funds, including them in the portfolio may be redundant if we also invest in other hedge funds. We won't gain any diversification benefits."

3. Critique Cassano's statement and justify your response with reference to data in the two exhibits.

Solution to Problem 1: The Sharpe ratio for Portfolio III, which incorporates an allocation of 10 percent to managed futures, improves on the Sharpe ratio of Portfolio II. Therefore, managed futures appear to be valuable when added to a portfolio of world equities, global bonds, and hedge fund strategies. All measures of risk provided (Sharpe ratio, standard deviation, and minimum monthly return) are superior for Portfolio III.

Solution to Problem 2: Research has indicated that the relative riskiness of a CTA (i.e., the commodity trading adviser's beta with respect to an index of CTAs) is a good predictor of future relative returns. Thus, past CTA performance may be valuable in forecasting CTA and multiadviser CTA portfolios' return and risk parameters, especially at the portfolio level.

Solution to Problem 3: The correlation of the hedge fund composite with the CISDM CTA$ composite in Exhibit 8-31 is only 0.19, suggesting that combining investments in these vehicles would provide significant diversification benefits. This is also demonstrated in the low correlation of the first two portfolios with the CTA$ Index (shown in Exhibit 8-35), which indicates that the derivative trading strategies of managed futures may provide unique sources of return when compared with hedge fund strategies that have relatively high exposure to traditional equity and bond markets.

The next section discusses investment strategies based on the equity and, especially, the debt of distressed companies.

8. DISTRESSED SECURITIES

Distressed securities are the securities of companies that are in financial distress or near bankruptcy. In the United States, investing in distressed securities involves purchasing the claims of companies that have already filed for Chapter 11 (protection for reorganization) or are in immediate danger of doing so.[136] Under Chapter 11 protection, companies try to avoid Chapter 7 (protection for liquidation) through an out-of-court debt restructuring with their creditors.

Investment strategies using distressed securities exploit the fact that many investors are unable to hold below-investment-grade securities because of regulatory or investment policy restrictions. Furthermore, relatively few analysts cover distressed securities markets and bankruptcies, resulting in unresearched investment opportunities for knowledgeable investors who are prepared to do their homework. Skill in influencing management and skill in negotiation are other qualities that can be rewarded in this field.

Debt and equity are traditional asset classes. Yet, because of the special characteristics and risks of the debt and equity of distressed companies and the strategies that use them, distressed securities investing is widely viewed as an alternative investment. Contributing to this perspective is the fact that among the most active investors in the field are hedge funds and private equity funds.

8.1. The Distressed Securities Market

Distressed securities investing has a long history—in the United States, dating back to at least the 1930s, when Max L. Heine formed an investment firm specializing in selectively acquiring the debt and real estate of bankrupt railroads. Through the 1980s and early 1990s, individual professional investors, private buyout funds, and others became increasingly active in the securities (and sometimes real assets) of troubled and bankrupt companies in many industries. With the explosive growth in hedge funds, with their flexibility to take short and long positions across all markets, and an abundant supply of troubled companies, by the 2000s, distressed

[136]"Chapter" in this context refers to a section of the U.S. Bankruptcy Code.

securities investing had became well established as a set of skill-based strategies. The market opportunities for this strategy increase with higher default rates on speculative-grade bonds (which have historically averaged about 5 percent per year in the United States) and decrease with the number of distressed debt investors competing for mispriced securities.

8.1.1. Types of Distressed Securities Investments Investors may access distressed securities investing through two chief structures:

1. *Hedge fund structure*. This is the dominant type. For the hedge fund manager, it offers the advantage of being able to take in new capital on a continuing basis. The AUM fee and incentive structure, particularly when there is no hurdle rate associated with the incentive fee, may be more lucrative than with other structures. Investors generally enjoy more liquidity (that is, can withdraw capital more easily) than with other structures.
2. *Private equity fund structure*. Private equity funds have a fixed term (i.e., a mandated dissolution date) and are closed end (they close after the offering period has closed). This structure has advantages where the assets are highly illiquid or difficult to value. An NAV fee structure may be problematic when it is difficult to value assets. When assets are illiquid, hedge fund–style redemption rights may be inappropriate to offer.

There are also structures that are hybrids of the hedge fund and private equity fund structures. In addition, distressed securities investing may be conducted in traditional investment structures, such as separately managed accounts, and even in open-end investment companies (mutual funds).[137] As a result of this variety, the investor can find information about distressed securities investing in hedge fund and private equity sources and elsewhere.

Distressed securities managers may themselves invest or trade in many types of assets, including the following:

- The publicly traded debt and equity securities of the distressed company.
- Newly issued equity of a company emerging from reorganization that appears to be undervalued (**orphan equity**).
- Bank debt and trade claims, because banks and suppliers owed money by the distressed company may want to realize the cash value of their claims. When the company is in reorganization, these instruments would be bankruptcy claims.
- "Lender of last resort" notes.
- A variety of derivative instruments for hedging purposes—in particular, for hedging the market risk of a position.

8.1.2. Size of the Distressed Securities Market The appropriate measure of the size of the distressed securities marketplace is elusive. One measure would aggregate all the assets under management related to distressed securities in whatever investment structure such assets are managed. Nevertheless, the size of the high-yield bond market can give an indication of the potential supply of opportunities, because distressed debt is one part of that market—in particular, the highest-risk part. Based on a maximum quality rating of Ba1 (as determined by Moody's Investors Services), the U.S. high-yield market consisted of US$548 billion at face value and US$552 billion at market value as of the end of May 2004. This size can be compared with the market size of only US$69 billion at face value as of the end of 1991.

[137] In such traditional structures as mutual funds, long-only type investing would be expected.

EXHIBIT 8-37 Monthly Returns of High-Yield and Distressed Securities, 1990–2004

Moment	HFR Fixed-Income High-Yield Index	HFR Distressed Securities Index
Mean	0.80%	1.23%
Standard deviation	1.84%	1.77%
Skewness	−0.80	−0.68
Kurtosis	6.63	5.55

Source: www.hedgefundresearch.com.

8.2. Benchmarks and Historical Performance

Hedge fund industry data are the chief source for evaluating modern distressed securities investing.

8.2.1. Benchmarks In the context of hedge funds, distressed securities investing is often classed as a substyle of event-driven strategies. All major hedge fund indices that we discussed in the hedge fund section have a subindex for distressed securities, for example, the EACM, CISDM, and HFR indices all have distressed securities subindices. In the United States, returns to the Altman–NYU Salomon Center Defaulted Public Bond and Bank Loan Index also provide a comparison point for evaluating a long-only value strategy in distressed debt.

8.2.2. Historical Performance The returns on distressed securities investing can be quite rewarding. Exhibit 8-37 presents historical performance for distressed securities and high-yield fixed-income securities. Using the monthly HFR Distressed Securities Index for the period January 1990 to December 2004, Exhibit 8-37 shows that the return distribution for distressed securities is distinctly non-normal. In particular, it reflects significant downside risk, with a negative skewness of −0.68. The negative skewness indicates that, for distressed securities, large negative returns are more likely than large positive returns. Hence, there is a bias to the downside. In addition, the monthly return distribution displays a large degree of kurtosis (5.55). This indicates that these securities are exposed to large outlier events. The two statistics together indicate significant downside risk. Consequently, the Sharpe ratio, which is based on the normal distribution assumption, may not capture the complete risk–return trade-off of distressed securities investing.

The monthly return distribution of high-yield debt displays similar risk characteristics, with a negative skewness of −0.80 and a kurtosis of 6.63. Overall, high-yield debt investing, although producing favorable returns over the period, was subject to considerable credit and, probably, event risk. These risks were greater, however, than those observed for the distressed securities investing.

Exhibit 8-38 shows that for the same period, distressed securities outperformed all stock and bond investments with a standard deviation of 6.13 percent, compared with the S&P 500's 14.65 percent. The Sharpe ratio for the HRF Distressed Securities Index is 1.59, which is greater than the ratio for all the other assets. High mean returns with low standard deviation seem to be an attractive characteristic of this strategy. Moreover, the minimum one-month return is less negative for distressed securities than for U.S. and world equities. Low correlation with world stock and bond investments suggest that adding distressed securities to a portfolio of world stocks and bonds might increase return and reduce risk. Because returns of

EXHIBIT 8-38 Distressed Securities Performance, 1990–2004

Measure	HFR Distressed Securities	S&P 500	Lehman Global Bond	MSCI World	Lehman Gov./ Corp. Bond
Annualized return	14.76%	10.94%	8.09%	7.08%	7.77%
Annualized std. dev.	6.13%	14.65%	5.23%	14.62%	4.46%
Sharpe ratio	1.59	0.45	0.72	0.19	0.78
Minimum monthly return	−8.5%	−14.46%	−3.66%	−13.32%	−4.19%

Source: www.hedgefundresearch.com and CISDM.

distressed securities display negative skewness and high kurtosis (see Exhibit 8-37), however, risk represented by standard deviation is probably understated.

In terms of performance, this strategy depends a great deal on the business cycle and how well the economy is doing. When the economy is not doing well, bankruptcies increase and this strategy does well. An important risk factor that may not be captured by the performance data is event risk. The ability to correctly predict whether an event will occur will ensure the success of the strategy.

8.2.3. Interpretation Issues

In estimating the size of the distressed debt market, we gave figures for the high-yield debt market. Non-investment-grade or high-yield bonds are not necessarily on the brink of default; thus, they are not necessarily distressed. Distressed bonds constitute the highest credit-risk segment of the high-yield bond market.[138] Furthermore, distressed securities include distressed equities and strategies based on these instruments.

8.3. Distressed Securities: Investment Characteristics and Roles

Although certain types of distressed securities investing may be considered for risk-diversification potential, some of its typical risks are not well captured by such measures as correlation and standard deviation, which are usually the guideposts in portfolio optimization. Investors look to distressed securities investing primarily for the possibility of high returns from security selection (exploiting mispricing), activism, and other factors.

8.3.1. Investment Characteristics

The market opportunity that distressed securities investing offers to some investors arises from the problems that corporate distress poses to other investors. Many investors are barred either by regulations or by their investment policy statements from any substantial holdings in below-investment-grade debt. These investors must sell debt that has crossed the threshold from investment grade to high yield (so-called **fallen angels**). Banks and trade creditors may prefer to convert their claims to cash rather than participate as creditors in a possibly long reorganization process. Failed leveraged buyouts have also been a source of distressed securities opportunities.[139] The impetus of some investors to off-load distressed debt creates opportunities for bargain hunters.

Old equity claims may be wiped out in a reorganization, replaced by new shares issued to creditors, and sold to the public as the company emerges from reorganization. These

[138] Distressed debt has sometimes been defined arbitrarily as bonds trading at spreads of 1,000 bps or more above government bonds. See Yago and Trimbath (2003).

[139] See Anson (2002b) for a detailed discussion of leveraged buyouts and this type of opportunity.

shares may be shunned by investors and analysts, and thus be mispriced. Distressed securities may offer a fertile ground for experts in credit analysis, turnarounds, business valuation, and bankruptcy proceedings to earn returns based on their skill and experience.[140]

A common theme in distressed securities investing is that it often demands access to specialist skills and deep experience in credit analysis and business valuation. Distressed companies are potentially near the end of their life as going concerns. The investor needs to assess not only potential outcomes for the company as a going concern but also the bare-bones liquidation value of the company. The investor needs to understand the sources of the company's problems, its core business, and its financing structure. A distressed securities fund's abilities in this regard are one element in due diligence.

For a private or institutional investor investing indirectly via a hedge fund or other vehicle, this type of investment inherits the liquidity characteristics specified in the structure of the vehicle. Discussion of the types of risk involved in distressed securities investing follows an overview of strategies in the next section.

8.3.2. Roles in the Portfolio According to the 2005 Commonfund Benchmarks Study of U.S. educational endowments, overall allocation to distressed debt among the institutions surveyed was 5 percent for the year ended June 30, 2005.[141] Investors, private and institutional, are making substantial allocations to this alternative investment and need to understand the ranges of distressed securities strategies available and their risk characteristics.

From the perspective of the direct investor in distressed securities, there are a number of different strategies that may be adopted. As we discuss them, the reader should be aware that the hedge fund and private equity businesses and benchmark vendors use a variety of classifications and some differences in definition. The aim here is to convey the gist of what the various approaches involve.

8.3.2.1. Long-Only Value Investing The simplest approach involves investing in perceived undervalued distressed securities in the expectation that they will rise in value as other investors see the distressed company's prospects improve. When the distressed securities are public debt, this approach is **high-yield investing.** When the securities are orphan equities, this approach is **orphan equities investing.**

8.3.2.2. Distressed Debt Arbitrage **Distressed debt arbitrage** (or **distressed arbitrage**) involves purchasing the traded bonds of bankrupt companies and selling the common equity short. The hedge fund manager attempts to buy the debt at steep discounts. If the company's prospects worsen, the value of the company's debt and equity should decline, but the hedge fund manager hopes that the equity, in which the fund has a short position, will decline to a greater degree. Indeed, as a residual claim, the value of equity may be wiped out. If the company's prospects improve, the portfolio manager hopes that debt will appreciate at a higher rate than the equity because the initial benefits to a credit improvement accrue to bonds as the senior claim. Typically, the company will have already suspended any dividends, but debtholders will receive accrued interest. This approach has been popular with hedge funds.

[140] In fact, according to a study published by New York University's Salomon Center and the Georgetown School of Business, newly distributed stocks emanating from Chapter 11 proceedings during the 1980 to 1993 period outperformed the relevant market indices by more than 20 percent during their first 200 days of trading.

[141] See Jacobius (2006b), pp. 3, 40.

8.3.2.3. Private Equity This has also been called an "active" approach because it involves corporate activism. It has, in fact, a number of variations. The investor usually first becomes a major creditor of the target company to obtain influence on the board of directors or, if the company is already in reorganization or liquidation, on the creditor committee. The investor buys the debt at deep discounts. The investor then influences and assists in the recovery or reorganization process. The objective of this focused active involvement is to increase the value of the troubled company by deploying the company's assets more efficiently than in the past. If the investor obtains new shares in the company as part of the reorganization, the investor hopes to sell them subsequently at a profit.

A variation of the active approach is converting distressed debt to private equity in a **prepackaged bankruptcy**.[142] This type of operation is typically conducted by private equity firms. The firm (or team of firms, because the capital commitment may be major) takes a dominant position in the distressed debt of a public company. Working with the company and other creditors, the firm seeks to have a prepackaged bankruptcy in which the firm becomes the majority owner of a private company on favorable terms (the previous public equityholders losing their complete stake in the company).[143] After restoring the company to better health, the firm has a company that can be sold to private or public investors. An example discussed by Anson is the conversion in 2001 of Loews Cineplex Entertainment Corporation from a public to a private company by two buyout firms (the buyout firms subsequently sold their interest, and as of 2005, Loews is still a private company).

Distressed securities investors following an active approach will be quite proactive or aggressive in protecting and increasing the value of their claims.[144] Practitioners of the private equity approach are often referred to as *vulture* investors, and their funds as *vulture funds* or *vulture capital.* Nevertheless, if the company is turned around, other parties may benefit, and the vultures are bearing risk that presumably other investors wish to transfer to them.

EXAMPLE 8-14 Turnaround Partners

Often, distressed securities investors solicit the help of experienced executives to manage the troubled companies. In the case of the WorldCom/MCI bankruptcy, one such investor was quoted in the *Wall Street Journal,* when the investor urged Michael D. Capellas, the former chairman and CEO of Compaq Corporation, to join Worldcom Inc., as saying, "You run the business and we'll run the bankruptcy process."[145]

Investors need to assess the risks that a particular distressed securities strategy may entail. The risks may include one or more of the following:

- *Event risk.* Any number of unexpected company-specific or situation-specific risks may affect the prospects for a distressed securities investment. Because the event risk

[142] The term *prepackaged bankruptcy* refers to the case in which the debtor seeks agreement from creditors on the terms of a reorganization before filing formally for a Chapter 11 reorganization. More details are given later.

[143] See Anson (2002b). Another operation Anson discusses is private equity firms making a cash bid for the assets of a company in reorganization at a discount to perceived value.

[144] See Branch and Ray (2002).

[145] *Wall Street Journal,* April 16, 2004.

in this context is company specific, it has a low correlation with the general stock market.

- *Market liquidity risk.* Market liquidity in distressed securities is significantly less than for other securities, although the liquidity has improved in recent years. Also, market liquidity, dictated by supply and demand for such securities, can be highly cyclical in nature. This is a major risk in distressed securities investing.
- *Market risk.* The economy, interest rates, and the state of equity markets are not as important as the liquidity risks.
- *J factor risk.* Barnhill, Maxwell, and Shenkman (1999) referred to the judge's track record in adjudicating bankruptcies and restructuring as "**J factor risk.**" The judge's involvement in the proceedings and the judgments will decide the investment outcome of investing in bankruptcy. Branch and Ray (2002) noted that the judge factor is also an important variable in determining which securities, debt or equity, of a Chapter 11–protected company to invest in.

Other risks may also be present. Some are associated with the legal proceedings of a reorganization: The actions of the trustees as well as the identity of creditors can affect the investment outcome. The distressed securities investor may lack information about the other investors and their motivations. Tax issues may arise in reorganizations.[146]

A normality assumption is not appropriate in evaluating this class of strategies. It has become quite well known that the return distribution from this strategy is not normally distributed (it has negative skewness and positive kurtosis); thus, if normal distribution is assumed, risk measurement tends to underestimate the likelihood of downside returns.

Distressed securities are illiquid and almost nonmarketable at the time of purchase. As the companies turn around, values of the distressed securities may go up gradually. Typically, it takes a relatively long time for this strategy to play out; thus, valuing the holdings may be a problem. It is difficult to estimate the true market values of the distressed securities, and stale pricing is inevitable. Stale valuation makes the distressed securities appear less risky. The risk of this strategy is probably understated, and its Sharpe ratio overstated.

Whether a distressed securities investment will be successful or not depends on many factors. The outcome depends heavily on the legal process and may take years. Of course, the vulture investor's timeframe is often months, not years. The role played by vulture investors has a significant bearing on the outcome. If vulture investors do not participate in the restructuring (as in the case of MCI, where two of the vulture investors named to the board declined to take board seats) or if they decide to sell prior to the final settlement, the flood of shares into the market will create further downward pressure on the stock price. This may have a significant impact on the whole industry. Because any move by vulture investors may be heeded by other investors, they take great care not to divulge their intentions.

Thus, investing in distressed securities/bankruptcies requires legal, operational, and financial analysis. From an investment perspective, the relevant analysis involves an evaluation of the source of distress. The source could be the operations, finances, or both. This is a complex task, and each distressed situation requires a unique approach and solution. As a result, distressed investing involves company selection. In this chapter, we focus on the legal aspects.

8.3.3. Other Issues In this section, we describe the bankruptcy process to highlight how the process may affect the investment outcome and considerations that investors need to ponder.

---

[146]See Branch and Ray (2002) and Feder and Lagrange (2002) for more information.

8.3.3.1. Bankruptcy in the United States vs. Other Countries[147] For all practical purposes, the relevant legislation for distressed investment in the United States is the Bankruptcy Reform Act of 1978, which applies to all bankruptcies filed since 1 October 1979. This enactment is referred to as "The Bankruptcy *Code*," or "United States *Code*" (Branch and Ray, 2002). In the *Code*, there are several chapters of the substantive law of bankruptcy. Chapters 1, 3, and 5 generally apply to all cases, whereas Chapters 7, 9, 11, 12, and 13 provide specific treatment for particular types of cases. Of particular interest to distressed securities investors are Chapters 7 and 11, which provide specific treatments for, respectively, liquidations and reorganizations.

Branch and Ray pointed out that a U.S. Chapter 7 bankruptcy is *conceptually* (emphasis ours) similar to the bankruptcy procedures followed in most other countries. That is, when a person seeks protection under Chapter 7, that person's assets are collected and liquidated and the proceeds are distributed to creditors by an appointed bankruptcy trustee. The debtor is normally discharged from the debts that were incurred prior to bankruptcy. As in most other countries, under Chapter 7, rehabilitation of the debtor is not especially important. It is in this sense that the U.S. Chapter 7 is conceptually similar to other countries.

In contrast, Chapter 11 emphasizes rehabilitation of the debtor and provides an opportunity for the reorganization (restructuring) of the debtor. This is the distinctive feature of U.S. bankruptcy that separates it from most of the rest of the world (although a similar code exists in Canada called the Companies' Creditors Arrangement Act, or CCAA). This is where opportunity arises for distressed debt investors. In Chapter 11, the debtor (a business seeking relief and protection) retains control of its assets (which will immediately pass into a bankruptcy estate under the supervision of the court) and continues its operations. While under this protection, the debtor, now known as a "debtor-in-possession," seeks to pay off creditors (often at a discount) over a period of time according to a plan approved by the bankruptcy court. Some of the liabilities may be discharged. By filing Chapter 11, a debtor can protect its productive assets from being seized by creditors and have time to plan the turnaround of the business.

A Chapter 11 case can be initiated voluntarily by a debtor or involuntarily by certain of the debtor's creditors or their indenture trustee. The indenture trustee—typically a bank, trust company, or other secure, respected institution—is named in the indenture agreement (contract between bondholders and the bond issuer) as the bondholders' agent charged with enforcing the terms of the indenture.

A plan of reorganization is submitted to the court for approval. The plan is typically proposed by the debtor with the blessings of creditors, especially the senior creditors. In most cases, the debtor works with its creditors to formulate a plan of reorganization. This plan details how much and over what period of time the creditors will be paid. Prospective distressed securities investors should pay attention to the exclusivity period. The exclusivity period occurs at the beginning of each case. During this time (set at 120 days but often extended by the court), only the debtor can file a plan of reorganization. After the exclusivity period expires, any party with an interest in the bankruptcy can file a plan proposing how the estate's creditors are to be paid under Chapter 11. Creditors and shareholders of the debtor eventually must approve the plan and have it confirmed by the bankruptcy judge. The judge

[147]We do not intend to provide a complete treatment of the bankruptcy process but instead to provide an overview of the process so that investors can recognize the complexities involved and make intelligent investment decisions without being confused by the legal technicalities. For a detailed treatment, see Branch and Ray (2002).

can refuse to confirm a case if the plan is not proposed in good faith or if each creditor receives less than it would receive in a Chapter 7 liquidation. The judge can overrule the disapproval by some dissenting creditors, however, on economic grounds or for other considerations, such as social or legal grounds. This is commonly referred to as the *cram-down.* Thus, a cram-down is basically a compromise between the debtor and certain classes of creditors when they cannot come to an agreement on the reorganization plan. Referred to as the "impaired class," those who object to the reorganization plan are those who believe their interest in the reorganization is impaired by the proposed plan.

Put another way, an approved reorganization plan by the court of law may not necessarily make economic sense, and such an erroneous presumption may be costly to distressed investing. The uncertain nature of the outcome of legal proceedings makes analysis of such investment challenging, and it must be accompanied by extensive due diligence.[148]

8.3.3.2. Absolute Priority Rule In the United States, a reorganization plan must follow the rule of priority with respect to the order of claims by its security holders. In general, claims from senior secured debtholders (typically, bank loans) will be satisfied first. The debtor's bondholders come next. The distribution may be split between senior and subordinated bondholders. Last on the list are the debtor's shareholders.

In a cram-down in which the court overrules the objection of a dissenting class of creditors, the priority rule becomes absolute. The rule is absolute in the sense that, to be "fair and equitable" to a class of dissenting unsecured creditors, the plan must provide either that the unsecured creditors receive property of a value equal to the allowed amount of the claim or that the holder of any claim or interest junior to the dissenting class does not receive or retain any property on account of the junior claim. In other words, the classes ranked below the dissenting unsecured class must receive nothing if the dissenting class is to be crammed down. It is in this sense that the law treats the holders of claims or interest with similar legal rights fairly and equitably, even if they do not accept the proposed plan.

There is an exception to the absolute priority rule, which is referred to as the *new value exception.* In the new value exception, the debtor's shareholders seek to retain all or a portion of their equity interest by making what amounts to a capital contribution. In exchange for their contribution, they retain their interest even in the face of a dissenting vote by a senior class of creditors. The U.S. Supreme Court has held, however, that the new value exception does not permit contribution of such value without competitive bidding or some other mechanism to establish the adequacy of the contribution. Branch and Ray (2002) concluded that this ruling removes substantial uncertainty over whether or not a lower class of creditors can receive distribution under a plan of reorganization by contributing new value to the bankruptcy confirmation process. In other words, it helps reduce uncertainty in purchasing an interest in a Chapter 11 debtor.

Most of the time, holders of senior secured debts are "made whole" whereas the debtor's shareholders often receive nothing on their original equity capital. This is the residual risk that equity shareholders ultimately must bear.

8.3.3.3. Relationship between Chapter 7 and Chapter 11 Why must distressed investors pay attention to Chapter 7 filings? Chapter 11 reorganization can start from a

[148]According to Branch and Ray (2002), only one out of eight cases that file for Chapter 11 is able to reorganize successfully in the United States.

Chapter 7 filing, whether voluntarily or involuntarily. A debtor against whom an involuntary Chapter 7 is filed has a right to convert the case to a Chapter 11 proceeding. Similarly, a Chapter 7 debtor that filed a voluntary petition can convert the case to a Chapter 11, unless the case started as a Chapter 11. In addition, the court can convert a Chapter 11 case to Chapter 7 or dismiss the case for cause (e.g., the inability of the debtor to carry out a plan) at any point in the case. The latter uncertainty adds much risk to bankruptcy investors.

8.3.3.4. Prepackaged Bankruptcy Filing In a prepackaged bankruptcy filing, the debtor agrees in advance with its creditors on a plan or reorganization before it formally files for protection under Chapter 11. Creditors usually agree to make concessions in return for equity in the reorganized company. This is tantamount to obtaining advance approval of an exchange offer of public debt with less stringent requirements than those found in the public indenture. This way, a debtor expedites the bankruptcy process to emerge as a new organization.

Whether it is Chapter 7 or Chapter 11, a filing for protection under law will affect the value of the debtor. Especially under forced bankruptcy (i.e., involuntary Chapter 7 filing by creditors), its reputation is severely impaired by the stigma of being forced into bankruptcy.

EXAMPLE 8-15 Distressed Securities Investing

Gloria Richardson is CIO of a multibillion-dollar home office for the Nelson family. She is discussing the revision of the governing investment policy statement to permit the investment in distressed securities. Susan Nelson represents the family in policy matters.

Nelson states: "Distressed securities sound like a very-high-risk investment strategy because the strategy focuses on companies in bankruptcy. Is that why few investors choose to invest in distressed securities? What are the origins of distressed securities, and how are investors involved? Who researches these situations?"

1. Discuss the suitability of investing in distressed securities for buy-side (institutional) investors and evaluate the participation of sell-side analysts in researching distressed securities.

Nelson is still concerned about the downside risk of investing in distressed securities. Nelson states: "I'm a patient investor, and I want our family's philanthropic contributions to extend into perpetuity, but it seems that the strategy of investing in distressed securities has higher risk in every aspect than investing in traditional equities and bonds."

2. Judge the suitability of investing in distressed securities for the home office. Justify your response with reference to time horizon and Nelson's statement regarding risk.

Solution to Problem 1: Some buy-side investors, such as pension plans, cannot or may choose not to hold below-investment-grade securities because of the securities' relatively high risk in comparison with other asset classes. However, results suggest that institutional investors with higher risk tolerances and long time horizons may receive stable returns from distressed securities with relatively low risk in the long run.

As a result of the inability of some institutional investors to allocate funds to distressed securities, few sell-side analysts cover this area of the market. Given this limited following of distressed securities, undercovered and undervalued market opportunities exist that knowledgeable investors can exploit to earn high returns.

Solution to Problem 2: Given Nelson's statement, investing in distressed securities could provide a potentially attractive strategy for the family's home office. Because the investment time horizon is long term, there should be no inherent obstacle regarding the amount of time it may take for a distressed securities investment to work out. Additionally, Nelson is incorrect in stating that distressed securities are riskier than traditional asset classes in all respects. Although long-term returns for distressed securities show negative monthly returns for 20 percent of all months studied, the maximum 1-month and 12-month drawdowns are smaller for distressed securities than for U.S. and world equities and bonds. If Nelson understands and accepts these risks, such investments may be appropriate.

CHAPTER 9

RISK MANAGEMENT

Don M. Chance, CFA
Louisiana State University
Baton Rouge, Louisiana

Kenneth Grant
Cheyne Capital
New York, New York

John Marsland, CFA
WMG Advisors LLP
London, England

1. INTRODUCTION

Investment is an intrinsically risky activity. Indeed, risk taking is an innate characteristic of human activity and as old as humankind itself. Without risk, we have little possibility of reward. We thus need to treat risk management as a critical component of the investment process. Specifically, with regard to both individual investments and entire portfolios, we should examine and compare the full spectrum of risks and expected returns to ensure that to the greatest extent possible the exposures we assume are at all times justified by the rewards we can reasonably expect to reap. Proper identification, measurement, and control of risk are key to the process of investing, and we put our investment objectives at risk unless we commit appropriate resources to these tasks.

A portfolio manager must be familiar with risk management not only as it relates to portfolio management but also as it relates to managing an enterprise, because a portfolio manager is a responsible executive in an enterprise (his investment firm). He must also understand the risks and risk management processes of companies in which he invests. The risk management framework presented in this chapter is an inclusive one, applicable to the management of both enterprise and portfolio risk.

Although portfolio managers and enterprises may occasionally hedge their risks or engage in other risk-reducing transactions, they should not, and indeed cannot, restrict their activities to those that are risk free, as discussed in more detail later. The fact that these entities engage in risky activities raises a number of important questions:

- What is an effective process for identifying, measuring, and managing risk?
- Which risks are worth taking on a regular basis, which are worth taking on occasion, and which should be avoided altogether?
- How can our success or lack of success in risk taking be evaluated?
- What information should be reported to investors and other stakeholders concerning the risk of an enterprise or a portfolio?

The answers to these questions and many others collectively define the process of *risk management.* Over the course of this chapter, we endeavor to explain this process and some of its most important concepts. Consistent with the book's focus on portfolio management, this chapter concentrates on managing risks arising from transactions that are affected by interest rates, stock prices, commodity prices, and exchange rates. We also survey the other risks that most enterprises face and illustrates the discussion from a variety of perspectives. The chapter is organized as follows. Section 2 defines and explains a risk management framework. Section 3 discusses what constitutes good risk management. Sections 4, 5, and 6 discuss the individual steps in the risk management process.

2. RISK MANAGEMENT AS A PROCESS

We can formally define risk management as follows:

> *Risk management is a process involving the identification of exposures to risk, the establishment of appropriate ranges for exposures (given a clear understanding of an entity's objectives and constraints), the continuous measurement of these exposures (either present or contemplated), and the execution of appropriate adjustments whenever exposure levels fall outside of target ranges. The process is continuous and may require alterations in any of these activities to reflect new policies, preferences, and information.*

This definition highlights that risk management should be a *process*, not just an activity. A process is continuous and subject to evaluation and revision. Effective risk management requires the constant and consistent monitoring of exposures, with an eye toward making adjustments, whenever and wherever the situation calls for them.[1] Risk management in its totality is all at once a proactive, anticipative, and reactive process that continuously monitors and controls risk.

Exhibit 9-1 illustrates the *practical application of the process* of risk management as it applies to a hypothetical business enterprise. We see at the top that the company faces a range of financial and nonfinancial risks; moving down the exhibit, we find that the company has responded to this challenge by establishing a series of risk management policies and procedures.

[1]For brevity, we often refer to an exposure to risk or **risk exposure** (the state of being exposed to or vulnerable to a risk) as simply an *exposure.*

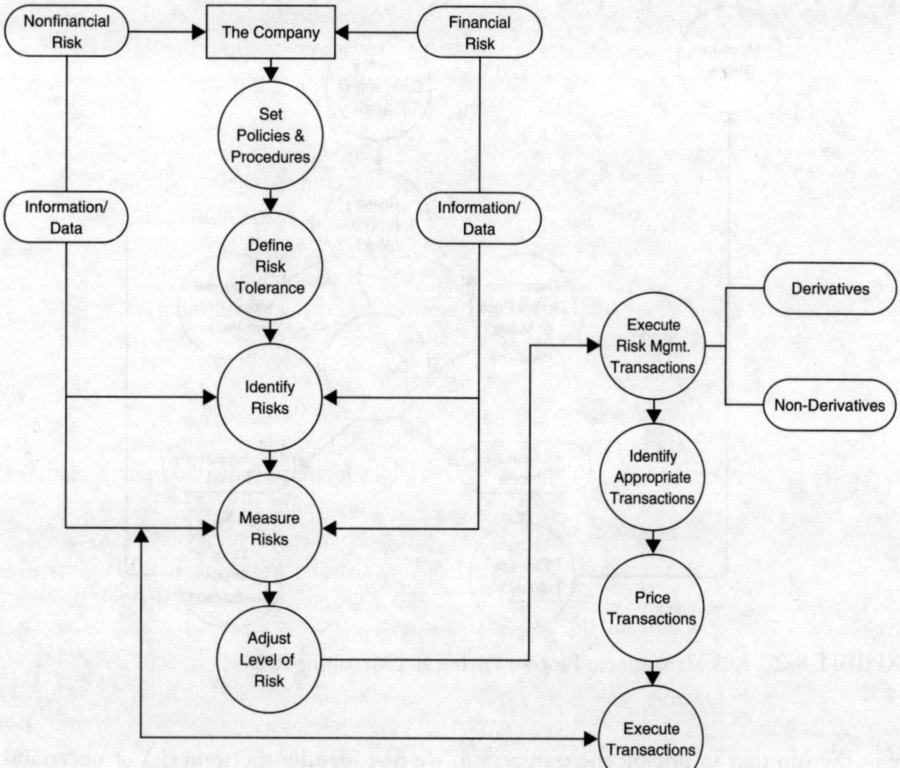

EXHIBIT 9-1 Risk Management Process: The Practice of Risk Management

First, it defines its risk tolerance, which is the level of risk it is willing and able to bear.[2] It then identifies the risks, drawing on all sources of information, and attempts to measure these risks using information or data related to all of its identified exposures. The process of risk measurement can be as simple as Exhibit 9-1 illustrates, but more often than not it involves expertise in the practice of modeling and sometimes requires complex analysis. Once the enterprise has built effective risk identification and measurement mechanisms, it is in a position to adjust its risk exposures, wherever and whenever exposures diverge from previously identified target ranges. These adjustments take the form of risk-modifying transactions (broadly understood to include the possible complete transfer of risk). The execution of risk management transactions is itself a distinct process; for portfolios, this step consists of trade identification, pricing, and execution. The process then loops around to the measurement of risk and continues in that manner, and to the constant monitoring and adjustment of the risk, to bring it into or maintain it within the desired range.

In applying the risk management process to portfolio management, managers must devote a considerable amount of attention to measuring and pricing the risks of financial transactions or positions, particularly those involving derivatives. Exhibit 9-2 illustrates this process of pricing and measuring risk, expanding on the detail given in Exhibit 9-1. In Exhibit 9-2, we

[2]An enterprise may have different risk tolerances for different types of risk in a manner that that does not readily permit averaging, so we should view risk tolerance in this context as potentially multidimensional.

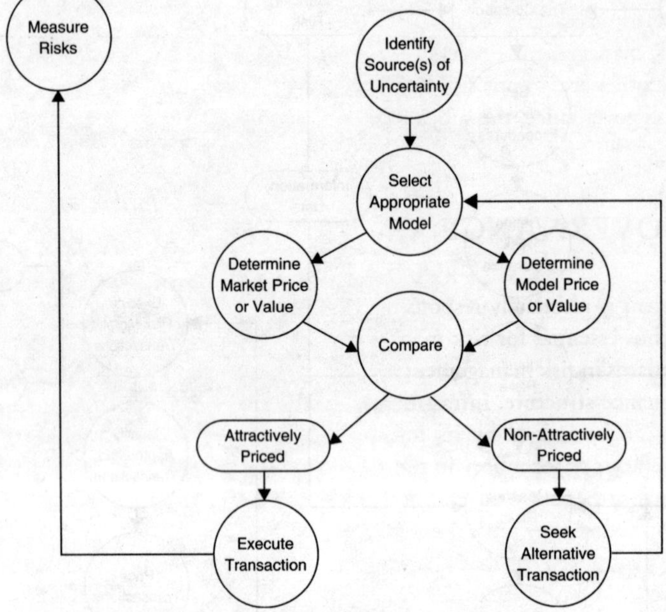

EXHIBIT 9-2 Risk Management Process: Pricing and Measuring Risk

see at the top that in pricing the transaction, we first identify the source(s) of uncertainty. Then we select the appropriate pricing model and enter our desired inputs to derive our most accurate estimate of the instrument's model value (which we hope reflects its true economic value). Next, we look to the marketplace for an indication of where we can actually execute the transaction. If the execution price is "attractive" (i.e., the market will buy the instrument from us at a price at or above, or sell it to us at a price at or below, the value indicated by our model), it fits our criteria for acceptance; if not, we should seek an alternative transaction. After executing the transaction, we would then return to the process of measuring risk.

Our discussion of Exhibit 9-1 highlighted that risk management involves adjusting levels of risk to appropriate levels, not necessarily eliminating risk altogether. It is nearly impossible to operate a successful business or investment program without taking risks. Indeed, a company that accepted no risk would not be an operating business. Corporations take risks for the purpose of generating returns that increase their owners' wealth. Corporation owners, the shareholders, risk their capital with the same objective in mind. *Companies that succeed in doing the activities they should be able to do well, however, cannot afford to fail overall because of activities in which they have no expertise.* Accordingly, many companies hedge risks that arise from areas in which they have no expertise or comparative advantage. In areas in which they do have an edge (i.e., their primary line of business), they tend to hedge only tactically. They hedge when they think they have sufficient information to suggest that a lower risk position is appropriate. They manage risk, increasing it when they perceive a competitive advantage and decreasing it when they perceive a competitive disadvantage. In essence, they attempt to efficiently allocate risk. Similarly, portfolio managers attempt to efficiently use risk to achieve their return objectives.

We have illustrated that risk management involves far more than risk reduction or hedging (one particular risk-reduction method). Risk management is a general practice that involves risk modification (e.g., risk reduction or risk expansion) as deemed necessary and appropriate by the custodians of capital and its beneficial owners.

For the risk management process to work, managers need to specify thoughtfully the business processes they use to put risk management into practice. We refer to these processes collectively as risk governance, the subject of the next section.

3. RISK GOVERNANCE

Senior management is ultimately responsible for *every* activity within an organization. Their involvement is thus essential for risk management to succeed. The process of setting overall policies and standards in risk management is called **risk governance.** Risk governance involves choices of governance structure, infrastructure, reporting, and methodology. The quality of risk governance can be judged by its transparency, accountability, effectiveness (achieving objectives), and efficiency (economy in the use of resources to achieve objectives).

Risk governance begins with choices concerning governance structure. Organizations must determine whether they wish their risk management efforts to be centralized or decentralized. Under a centralized risk management system, a company has a single risk management group that monitors and ultimately controls all of the organization's risk-taking activities. By contrast, a decentralized system places risk management responsibility on individual business unit managers. In a decentralized approach, each unit calculates and reports its exposures independently. Decentralization has the advantage of allowing the people closer to the actual risk taking to more directly manage it. Centralization permits economies of scale and allows a company to recognize the offsetting nature of distinct exposures that an enterprise might assume in its day-to-day operations. For example, suppose one subsidiary of a company buys from Japan and another subsidiary sells to Japan, with both engaged in yen-denominated transactions. Each subsidiary would perceive some foreign exchange exposure. From a centralized viewpoint, however, these risks have offsetting effects, thereby reducing the overall need to hedge.

Moreover, even when exposures to a single risk factor do not directly offset one another, enterprise-level risk estimates may be lower than those derived from individual units because of the risk-mitigating benefits of diversification. For example, one corporate division may borrow U.S. dollars at five-year maturities, and another division may fund its operation by issuing 90-day commercial paper. In theory, the corporation's overall sensitivity to rising interest rates may be less than the sum of that reported by each division, because the five-year and 90-day rate patterns are less than perfectly correlated.

In addition, centralized risk management puts the responsibility on a level closer to senior management, where we have argued it belongs. It gives an overall picture of the company's risk position, and ultimately, the overall picture is what counts. This centralized type of risk management is now called **enterprise risk management** (ERM) or sometimes firmwide risk management because its distinguishing feature is a firmwide or across-enterprise perspective.[3]

[3]The Committee of Sponsoring Organizations of the Treadway Commission defines ERM as follows: "Enterprise risk management is a process, effected by an entity's board of directors, management, and other personnel, applied in strategy setting and across the enterprise, designed to identify potential events that may affect the entity, and manage risk to be within its risk appetite, to provide reasonable assurance regarding the achievement of entity objectives." (2004, p. 2).

In ERM, an organization must consider each risk factor to which it is exposed—both in isolation and in terms of any interplay among them.

Risk governance is an element of **corporate governance** (the system of internal controls and procedures used to manage individual companies). As risk management's role in corporate governance has become better appreciated, the importance of ERM has risen proportionately. Indeed, for risk-taking entities (this means nearly the entire economic universe), it is contradictory to suggest that an organization has sound corporate governance without maintaining a clear and continuously updated understanding of its exposures at the enterprise level. Senior managers who have an adequate understanding of these factors are in a superior governance position to those who do not, and over time this advantage is almost certain to accrue to the bottom line. Therefore, the risk management system of a company that chooses a decentralized risk management approach requires a mechanism by which senior managers can inform themselves about the enterprise's overall risk exposures.

At the enterprise level, companies should control not only the sensitivity of their earnings to fluctuations in the stock market, interest rates, foreign exchange rates, and commodity prices, but also their exposures to credit spreads and default risk, to gaps in the timing match of their assets and liabilities, and to operational/systems failures, financial fraud, and other factors that can affect corporate profitability and even survival.

EXAMPLE 9-1 Some Risk Governance Concerns of Investment Firms

Regardless of the risk governance approach chosen, effective risk governance for investment firms demands that the trading function be separated from the risk management function. An individual or group that is independent of the trading function must monitor the positions taken by the traders or risk takers and price them independently. The risk manager has the responsibility for monitoring risk levels for all portfolio positions (as well as for portfolios as a whole) and executing any strategies necessary to control the level of risk. To do this, the risk manager must have timely and accurate information, authority, and independence from the trading function. That is not to say that the trading function will not need its own risk management expertise in order to allocate capital in an optimal fashion and maximize risk-adjusted profit. Ideally, the risk manager will work with the trading desks in the development of risk management specifications, such that everyone in the organization is working from a common point of reference in terms of measuring and controlling exposures.

Effective risk governance for an investment firm also requires that the back office be fully independent from the front office, so as to provide a check on the accuracy of information and to forestall collusion. (The **back office** is concerned with transaction processing, record keeping, regulatory compliance, and other administrative functions; the **front office** is concerned with trading and sales.) Besides being independent, the back office of an investment firm must have a high level of competence, training, and knowledge because failed trades, errors, and oversights can lead to significant losses that may be amplified by leverage. The back office must effectively coordinate with external service suppliers, such as the firm's **global custodian.** The global custodian effects **trade settlement** (completion of a trade wherein purchased financial instruments are transferred to the buyer and the buyer transfers money to the seller), safekeeping of assets, and the allocation of trades to individual custody accounts. Increasingly, financial institutions are seeking risk reduction with cost efficiencies through **straight-through processing** (STP) systems that obviate manual and/or duplicative intervention in the process from trade placement to settlement.

An effective ERM system typically incorporates the following steps:

1. Identify each *risk factor* to which the company is exposed.
2. Quantify each exposure's size in money terms.
3. Map these inputs into a risk estimation calculation.[4]
4. Identify overall risk exposures as well as the contribution to overall risk deriving from each risk factor.
5. Set up a process to report on these risks periodically to senior management, who will set up a committee of division heads and executives to determine capital allocations, risk limits, and risk management policies.
6. Monitor compliance with policies and risk limits.

Steps 5 and 6 help enormously in allowing an organization to quantify the magnitude and distribution of its exposures and in enabling it to use the ERM system's output to more actively align its risk profile with its opportunities and constraints on a routine, periodic basis.

As a final note, effective ERM systems always feature centralized data warehouses, where a company stores all pertinent risk information, including position and market data, in a technologically efficient manner. Depending on the organization's size and complexity, developing and maintaining a high-quality data warehouse can require a significant and continuing investment. In particular, the process of identifying and correcting errors in a technologically efficient manner can be enormously resource intensive—especially when the effort requires storing historical information on complex financial instruments. It is equally clear, however, that the return on such an investment can be significant.

4. IDENTIFYING RISKS

As indicated above, economic agents of all types assume different types of exposures on a near-continuous basis. Moreover, these risk exposures take very different forms, each of which, to varying extents, may call for customized treatment. Effective risk management demands the separation of risk exposures into specific categories that reflect their distinguishing characteristics. Once a classification framework is in place, we can move on to the next steps in the risk management process: identification, classification, and measurement.

Although the list is far from exhaustive, many company (or portfolio) exposures fall into one of the following categories: market risk (including interest rate risk, exchange rate risk, equity price risk, commodity price risk); credit risk; liquidity risk; operational risk;

[4]For example, using value at risk or another of the concepts that we will discuss later.

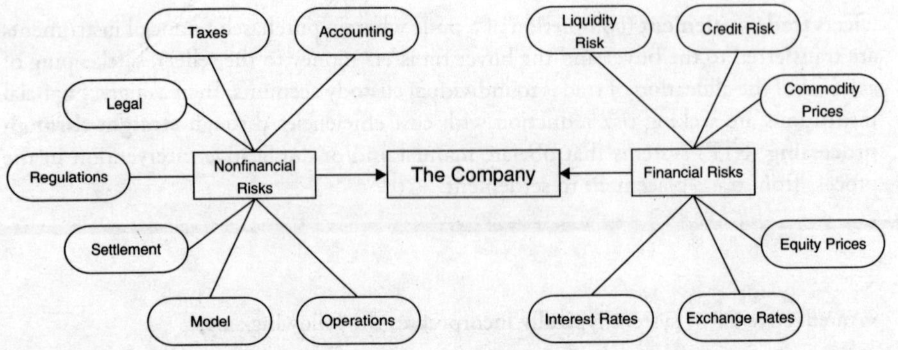

EXHIBIT 9-3 The Sources of Risk

model risk; settlement risk; regulatory risk; legal/contract risk; tax risk; accounting risk; and sovereign/political risk. These risks may be grouped into financial risks and nonfinancial risks as shown in Exhibit 9-3.[5] **Financial risk** refers to all risks derived from events in the external financial markets; **nonfinancial risk** refers to all other forms of risk.

Example 9-2 illustrates a simple analysis of risk exposures. In the example, we have detailed the subtypes of market risk; each one may pose unique issues of measurement and management.

EXAMPLE 9-2 An Analysis of Risk Exposures

Liam McNulty is the risk manager for a large multinational agricultural concern, Agripure. The company grows its own corn, wheat, and soybeans but pays large sums to third parties for pesticides, fertilizer, and other supplies. For this, it must borrow heavily to finance its purchases. Customers typically purchase Agripure's goods on credit. Moreover, Agripure buys and sells its products and raw materials worldwide, often transacting in the domestic currency of its customers and suppliers. Finally, to finance its own expansion, Agripure intends to issue stock.

Recommend and justify the risk exposures that McNulty should report as part of an enterprise risk management system for Agripure.

Solution: McNulty should report on the following risk exposures:

- Market risk, including these subtypes:
  - Commodity price risk, because Agripure has exposures in raw materials and finished products.

[5]A notable risk that could be included in a comprehensive listing (particularly as pertains to commercial enterprises) is **business risk,** defined by Ross, Westerfield, and Jordan (1993, p. 527) as "the equity risk that comes from the nature of the firm's operating activities." For example, the risk for a hotel business that arises from variability in room occupancy rates would be classified as business risk. In a later section on other risks, we also discuss two types of risks related to netting.

  - Foreign exchange risk, because it buys and sells products worldwide, often transacting in the home currency of the entity on the other side of the transaction.
  - Equity market risk, because Agripure's expansion financing is affected by the price it receives for its share issuance.
  - Interest rate risk, because Agripure has exposures in financing its raw material purchases and because its customers typically purchase their goods on credit.
- Credit risk, because Agripure's customers typically purchase their goods on credit.
- Operational risk, because as an agricultural producer Agripure is subject to weather-related risk (an external event).

In the following sections, we discuss each of these risks in detail.

4.1. Market Risk

Market risk is the risk associated with interest rates, exchange rates, stock prices, and commodity prices. It is linked to supply and demand in various marketplaces. Although we may distinguish among interest rate risk, currency risk, equity market risk, and commodity risk when discussing measurement and management issues, for example, these subtypes all have exposure to supply and demand. Much of the evolution that has taken place in the field of risk management has emanated from a desire to understand and control market risks, and we will have a good deal to say about this topic throughout the balance of this chapter.

One set of market risk takers with special requirements for market risk are defined-benefit (DB) pension funds, which manage retirement assets generally under strict regulatory regimes. Pension fund risk management necessarily concerns itself with funding the stream of promised payments to pension plan participants. Therefore, a DB plan must measure its market exposures not purely on the basis of its assets but also in terms of the risks of pension assets in relation to liabilities. Other investors as well can have strong asset/liability management concerns.[6] This has important implications for exposure measurement, risk control, capital allocation and risk budgeting, which we will address later.

4.2. Credit Risk

Apart from market risk, credit risk is the primary type of financial risk that economic agents face. **Credit risk** is the risk of loss caused by a counterparty or debtor's failure to make a payment. This definition reflects a traditional binary concept of credit risk, by and large embodied by default risk (i.e., the risk of loss associated with the nonperformance of a debtor or counterparty). For the last several years, however, credit markets have taken on more and more of the characteristics typically associated with full-scale trading markets. As this pattern has developed, the lines between credit risk and market risk have blurred as markets for credit

[6] See Chapters 3 and 5 in particular.

derivatives have developed.[7] For example, the holder of a traded credit instrument could suffer a loss as a result of a short-term supply–demand imbalance without the underlying probability of default changing. Some subset of market participants often suffers losses whether credit is improving or deteriorating because it is now quite easy to take long and short positions in credit markets. Finally, note that pricing conventions for credit typically take the form of spreads against market benchmarks, for example, government bond yields or swap rates.[8] Thus when a given credit instrument is said to be priced at 150 over, it typically means that the instrument can be purchased to yield 150 basis points over the rate on the market benchmark (e.g., the government bond with the same maturity).

Until the era of over-the-counter (OTC) derivatives, credit risk was more or less exclusively a concern in the bond and loan markets. Exchange-traded derivatives are guaranteed against credit loss. Over-the-counter derivatives, however, contain no explicit credit guaranty and, therefore, subject participants to the threat of loss if their counterparty fails to pay.

Before OTC derivatives became widely used, bond portfolio managers and bank loan officers were the primary credit risk managers. They assessed credit risk in a number of ways,[9] including the qualitative evaluation of corporate fundamentals through the review of financial statements, the calculation of credit scores, and by relying on consensus information that was and still is widely available for virtually every borrower. The synthesis of this "credit consensus" resides with rating agencies and credit bureaus, which were historically, and to some extent still are, the primary sources of information on credit quality. The proliferation and complexity of financial instruments with credit elements in the OTC derivatives market, however, has placed new demands on the understanding of credit risk. Indeed, the need to better understand credit risk has led to significant progress in developing tools to measure and manage this risk.

4.3. Liquidity Risk

Liquidity risk is the risk that a financial instrument cannot be purchased or sold without a significant concession in price because of the market's potential inability to efficiently accommodate the desired trading size.[10] In some cases, the market for a financial instrument can dry up completely, resulting in a total inability to trade an asset. This risk is present in both initiating and liquidating transactions, for both long and short positions, but can be particularly acute for liquidating transactions—especially when such liquidation is motivated by the need to reduce exposures in the wake of large losses. Those wishing to sell securities under these circumstances can find the market bereft of buyers at prices acceptable to the seller, particularly in periods of unusually high market stress. Perhaps less frequently, short sellers in need of covering losing positions are at risk to short squeezes. This situation is often

[7]A **credit derivative** is a contract in which one party has the right to claim a payment from another party in the event that a specific credit event occurs over the life of the contract.

[8]A **swap rate** is the interest rate applicable to the pay-fixed-rate side of an interest rate swap. See Chance (2003) to review the basics of swaps.

[9]Credit risk in the more general context of fixed-income securities is discussed in more detail in Fabozzi (2004a) Chapter 15. Many of the principles of credit risk analysis for fixed-income securities also apply to derivatives.

[10]Liquidity has been used in various senses. For example, **funding risk** (the risk that liabilities funding long asset positions cannot be rolled over at reasonable cost) has sometimes been referred to as a type of liquidity risk; liquidity in this sense relates to the availability of cash. One would still distinguish between market liquidity risk (discussed in the text) and funding liquidity risk.

exacerbated by the fact that for most cash instruments, short sellers establish positions by borrowing the securities in question from brokerage firms and other entities that typically can require the securities to be returned with little or no advance warning. Although derivatives can be used to effectively sell an asset or liquidate a short position, they often will not help in managing liquidity risk. If the underlying is illiquid, there is a good possibility that the universe of associated derivative instruments may also be illiquid.

For traded securities, the size of the **bid–ask spread** (the spread between the bid and ask prices), stated as a proportion of security price, is frequently used as an indicator of liquidity.[11] When markets are illiquid, dealers expect to sell at relatively high prices and buy at relatively low prices to justify their assumption of exposure to liquidity risk. However, bid–ask quotations apply only to specified, usually small size, trades, and are thus an imprecise measure of liquidity risk. Other, more complex measures of liquidity have been developed to address the issue of trading volume. For example, Amihud's (2002) illiquidity ratio measures the price impact per $1 million traded in a day, expressed in percentage terms. Note, however, that no explicit transaction volume is available for many OTC instruments. Less formally, one of the best ways to measure liquidity is through the monitoring of transaction volumes, with the obvious rule of thumb being that the greater the average transaction volume, the more liquid the instrument in question is likely to be. Historical volume patterns, however, may not repeat themselves at times when the liquidity they imply is most needed.

Liquidity risk is a serious problem and often is difficult to observe and quantify. It is not always apparent that certain securities are illiquid: Some that are liquid when purchased (or sold short) can be illiquid by the time they are sold (or repurchased to cover short positions). Valuation models rarely encompass this liquidity risk in estimating fair value. Those models that do attempt to incorporate transaction costs do so in a nonformulaic manner. Of course, these problems typically reach their apex when the markets themselves are under stress and the need for liquidity is most acute. Liquidity assessments that fail to consider the problems that might arise during periods of market stress are incomplete from a risk management perspective. For all of these reasons, liquidity risk is one of the more complex aspects of risk management.

We now turn our attention to nonfinancial risks, starting with operational risk.

4.4. Operational Risk

Operational risk, sometimes called operations risk, is the risk of loss from failures in a company's systems and procedures or from external events. These risks can arise from computer breakdowns (including bugs, viruses, and hardware problems), human error, and events completely outside of companies' control, including "acts of God" and terrorist actions.

Computer failures are quite common, but the development of backup systems and recovery procedures has reduced their impact in recent years. Technology bugs and viruses are potentially quite risky but have become more manageable with the proper personnel, software, and systems. Even the smallest business has learned to back up files and take them off the premises. Larger businesses have much more extensive computer risk management practices.

Human failures include the typically manageable unintentional errors that occur in every business, along with more critical and potentially disastrous incidences of willful misconduct.

---

[11]For example, see Amihud and Mendelson (1986). We must state the bid–ask spread as a proportion of stock price to control for differences in securities' prices.

EXAMPLE 9-3 An Operational Risk for Financial Services Companies: The Rogue Trader

Among the more prominent examples of operational risk for financial service companies is that of the so-called rogue trader: an individual who has either assumed an irresponsibly high level of risk, engaged in unauthorized transactions, or some combination of the two. The risks associated with this type of activity increase the longer it goes undetected, and often the very lack of controls that creates the opportunity for a rogue trader in the first place renders it difficult to quickly determine that a problem exists. In some extreme cases, such as an incident that occurred in the Singapore office of Barings Bank, a rogue trader can cause an entire organization to fold. The incidence of high-profile rogue trading episodes has multiplied since the early 1990s, but in nearly all of these episodes, the problem's major source was a lack of rudimentary corporate controls and oversight.[12]

Our definition of operational risk includes losses from external events. Insurance typically covers damage from fires, floods and other types of natural disasters, but insurance provides only cash compensation for losses. If a flood destroys the trading room of a bank, the monies recovered likely will not come close to paying for the loss of customers who may take their trading business elsewhere. Hence, most companies have backup facilities they can activate in such cases. The 1993 World Trade Center bombing in New York City led many companies to establish backup systems in the event of another terrorist attack, which sadly took place on a greater scale eight years later. The speed with which trading enterprises, including the New York Stock Exchange, domiciled inside or near the World Trade Center reestablished full-scale operations after such a devastating attack is but one indication of the increased importance placed on operational risk management by these enterprises.

In some cases, companies manage operational risk by using insurance contracts, which involves a transfer of risk. A few types of derivative contracts even pay off for operational losses, but the market for these has not fully developed. These instruments are essentially insurance contracts. Most companies manage operational risk, however, by monitoring their systems, taking preventive actions, and having a plan in place to respond if such events occur.

4.5. Model Risk

Model risk is the risk that a model is incorrect or misapplied; in investments, it often refers to valuation models. Model risk exists to some extent in any model that attempts to identify the fair value of financial instruments, but it is most prevalent in models used in derivatives markets.

Since the development of the seminal Black–Scholes–Merton option pricing model, both derivatives and derivative pricing models have proliferated.[13] The development of so many models has brought model risk to prominence. If an investor chooses an inappropriate model, misinterprets the results, or uses incorrect inputs, the chance of loss increases at the same time

[12]For more on the subject of operational risk in financial services companies, see Marshall (2001).
[13]See Chance (2003).

that control over risk is impaired. Therefore, investors must scrutinize and objectively validate all models they use.

4.6. Settlement (Herstatt) Risk

The payments associated with the purchase and sale of cash securities such as equities and bonds, along with cash transfers executed for swaps, forwards, options, and other types of derivatives, are referred to collectively as settlements. The process of settling a contract involves one or both parties making payments and/or transferring assets to the other. We define **settlement risk** as the risk that one party could be in the process of paying the counterparty while the counterparty is declaring bankruptcy.[14]

Most regulated futures and options exchanges are organized in such a way that they themselves (or a closely affiliated entity) act as the central counterparty to all transactions. This facility usually takes the form of a clearing house, which is backed by large and credible financial guarantees. All transactions on the exchange take place between an exchange member and the central counterparty, which removes settlement risk from the transaction. The possibility always exists, however, that the exchange member is acting in an agency capacity and/or that its end client fails to settle. Clearly in these circumstances, the responsibility falls to the exchange member to make good and bear any loss on the trade.

OTC markets, including those for bonds and derivatives, do not rely on a clearing house. Instead, they effect settlement through the execution of agreements between the actual counterparties to the transaction. With swaps and forward contracts, settlements take the form of two-way payments. Two-way payments create the problem that one party could be in the process of paying its counterparty while that counterparty is declaring bankruptcy and failing to make its payment. Netting arrangements, used in interest rate swaps and certain other derivatives, can reduce settlement risk. In such arrangements, the financial instrument is periodically marked to market (under an agreed-upon methodology) and the "loser" pays the "winner" the difference for the period. This mechanism reduces the magnitude of any settlement failures to the net payment owed plus the cost of replacing the defaulted contract. Transactions with a foreign exchange component, however (e.g., currency forwards and currency swaps, but also spot trades), do not lend themselves to netting. Furthermore, such contracts often involve two parties in different countries, increasing the risk that one party will be unaware that the other party is declaring bankruptcy. The risk has been called Herstatt risk because of a famous incident in 1974 when Bank Herstatt failed at a time when counterparties were sending money to it.

Fortunately, bankruptcy does not occur often. Furthermore, through continuously linked settlement (CLS) in which payments on foreign exchange contracts are executed simultaneously, this risk has been even further mitigated.[15]

4.7. Regulatory Risk

Regulatory risk is the risk associated with the uncertainty of how a transaction will be regulated or with the potential for regulations to change. Equities (common and preferred

---

[14]Note that settlement can also fail because of operational problems even when the counterparty is creditworthy; the risk in that case would be an operational risk.

[15]The execution takes place in a five-hour window (three hours in Asia Pacific), representing the overlapping business hours of different settlement systems. For more information, see www.cls-group.com.

stock), bonds, futures, and exchange-traded derivatives markets usually are regulated at the federal level, whereas OTC derivative markets and transactions in alternative investments (e.g., hedge funds and private equity partnerships) are much more loosely regulated. Federal authorities in most countries take the position that these latter transactions are private agreements between sophisticated parties, and as such should not be regulated in the same manner as publicly traded markets. Indeed, in some circumstances, unsophisticated investors are excluded altogether from participating in such investments.

With regard to derivatives, companies that are regulated in other ways may have their derivatives business indirectly regulated. For example, in the United States, banks are heavily regulated by federal and state banking authorities, which results in indirect regulation of their derivatives business. Beyond these de facto restrictions, however, in most countries, the government does not regulate the OTC derivatives business.[16]

Regulation is a source of uncertainty. Regulated markets are always subject to the risk that the existing regulatory regime will become more onerous, more restrictive, or more costly. Unregulated markets face the risk of becoming regulated, thereby imposing costs and restrictions where none existed previously. Regulatory risk is difficult to estimate because laws are written by politicians and regulations are written by civil servants; laws, regulations, and enforcement activities may change with changes in political parties and regulatory personnel. Both the regulations and their enforcement often reflect attitudes and philosophies that may change over time. Regulatory risk and the degree of regulation also vary widely from country to country.

Regulatory risk often arises from the arbitrage nature of derivatives and structured transactions. For example, a long position in stock accompanied by borrowing can replicate a forward contract or a futures contract. Stocks are regulated by securities regulators, and loans are typically regulated by banking oversight entities. Forward contracts are essentially unregulated. Futures contracts are regulated at the federal level in most countries, but not always by the same agency that regulates the stock market. Equivalent combinations of cash securities and derivatives thus are not always regulated in the same way or by the same regulator. Another example of inconsistent or ambiguous regulatory treatment might arise from a position spanning different geographic regions, such as the ownership of a NASDAQ-listed European-domiciled technology company in a European stock portfolio.

4.8. Legal/Contract Risk

Nearly every financial transaction is subject to some form of contract law. Any contract has two parties, each obligated to do something for the other. If one party fails to perform or believes that the other has engaged in a fraudulent practice, the contract can be abrogated. A dispute would then likely arise, which could involve litigation, especially if large losses occur. In some cases, the losing party will claim that the counterparty acted fraudulently or that the contract was illegal in the first place and, therefore, should be declared null and void. The possibility of such a claim being upheld in court creates a form of **legal/contract risk:** the possibility of loss arising from the legal system's failure to enforce a contract in which an enterprise has a financial stake.

Derivative transactions often are arranged by a dealer acting as a principal. The legal system has upheld many claims against dealers, which is not to say that the dealer has always been in the wrong but simply that dealers have sometimes put themselves into precarious

[16]Of course, contract law always applies to any such transaction.

situations. Dealers are indeed often advisers to their counterparties, giving the impression that if the dealer and counterparty enter into a contract, the counterparty expects the contract to result in a positive outcome. To avoid that misunderstanding, dealers may go to great lengths to make clear that they are the opposite party, not an adviser. Dealers also write contracts more carefully to cover the various contingencies that have been used against them in litigation. But a government or regulator might still take the legal view that a dealer has a higher duty of care for a less experienced counterparty. Contract law is in most circumstances federally or nationally governed. As such, the added possibility exists in arbitrage transactions that different laws might apply to each side of the transaction, thus adding more risk.

4.9. Tax Risk

Tax risk arises because of the uncertainty associated with tax laws. Tax law covering the ownership and transaction of financial instruments can be extremely complex, and the taxation of derivatives transactions is an area of even more confusion and uncertainty. Tax rulings clarify these matters on occasion, but on other occasions, they confuse them further. In addition, tax policy often fails to keep pace with innovations in financial instruments. When this happens, investors are left to guess what type and level of taxation will ultimately apply, creating the risk that they have guessed wrongly and could later be subject to back taxes. In some cases, transactions that appear upfront to be exempt from taxation could later be found to be taxable, thereby creating a future expense that was unanticipated (and perhaps impossible to anticipate) at the time that the transaction was executed. We noted, in discussing regulatory risk, that equivalent combinations of financial instruments are not always regulated the same way. Likewise, equivalent combinations of financial instruments are not always subject to identical tax treatment. This fact creates a tremendous burden of inconsistency and confusion, but on occasion the opportunity arises for arbitrage gains, although the tax authorities often quickly close such opportunities.

Like regulatory risk, tax risk is affected by the priorities of politicians and regulators. Many companies invest considerable resources in lobbying as well as hiring tax experts and consultants to control tax risk.

4.10. Accounting Risk

Accounting risk arises from uncertainty about how a transaction should be recorded and the potential for accounting rules and regulations to change. Accounting statements are a key, if not primary, source of information on publicly traded companies. In the United States, accounting standards are established primarily by the Financial Accounting Standards Board (FASB). Legal requirements in the area of accounting are enforced for publicly traded companies by federal securities regulators and by the primary stock exchange associated with the security. Non-U.S. domiciled companies that raise capital in the United States are also subject to these standards and laws. The law demands accurate accounting statements, and inaccurate financial reporting can subject corporations and their principals to civil and criminal litigation for fraud. In addition, the market punishes companies that do not provide accurate accounting statements, as happened for Enron and its auditor Arthur Andersen.

The International Accounting Standards Board (IASB) sets global standards for accounting. The FASB and the IASB have been working together toward convergence of accounting standards worldwide with 2005 targeted for harmonization. Historically, accounting standards have varied from country to country, with some countries requiring a higher level of disclosure than others.

EXAMPLE 9-4 Accounting Risk: The Case of Derivative Contracts

Accounting for derivative contracts has raised considerable confusion. When confusion occurs, companies run the risk that the accounting treatment for transactions could require adjustment, which could possibly lead to a need to restate earnings. Earnings restatements are almost always embarrassing for a company, because they suggest either a desire to hide information, the company's failure to fully understand material elements of its business, or some combination of the two. Restatements are very detrimental to corporate valuations because they cause investors to lose confidence in the accuracy of corporate financial disclosures. Beyond that, if negligence or intent to mislead was involved, the company could face civil and criminal liabilities as well.

Confusion over the proper accounting for derivatives gives rise to accounting as a source of risk. As with regulatory and tax risk, sometimes equivalent combinations of derivatives are not accounted for uniformly. The accounting profession typically moves to close such loopholes, but it does not move quickly and certainly does not keep pace with the pace of innovation in financial engineering, so problems nearly always remain.

The IASB in IAS 39 (International Accounting Standard No. 39) requires the inclusion of derivatives and their associated gains and losses on financial statements, as does the FASB in SFAS 133 (Statement of Financial Accounting Standard No. 133). These rulings contain some areas of confusion and inconsistency, however, affording considerable room for interpretation.[17]

Most companies deal with accounting risk by hiring personnel with the latest accounting knowledge. In addition, companies lobby and communicate actively with accounting regulatory bodies and federal regulators in efforts to modify accounting rules in a desired direction and to make them clearer. Companies have tended to fight rules requiring more disclosure, arguing that disclosure per se is not always beneficial and can involve additional costs. A trade-off exists between the rights of corporations to protect proprietary information from competitors and the need to adequately inform investors and the public. This controversy is unlikely to go away, suggesting that accounting risk will always remain.

4.11. Sovereign and Political Risks

Although they are covered indirectly above in areas such as regulatory, accounting, and tax risk, we can also isolate, and to a certain extent evaluate, the risks associated with changing political conditions in countries where portfolio managers may choose to assume exposure. Although this topic merits more discussion than can reasonably be devoted in this space, we can broadly define two types of exposures.

Sovereign risk is a form of credit risk in which the borrower is the government of a sovereign nation. Like other forms of credit risk, it has a current and a potential component, and like other forms, its magnitude has two components: the likelihood of default and

[17]Gastineau, Smith, and Todd (2001) provides excellent information on accounting for derivatives in the United States.

the estimated recovery rate. Of course, the task of evaluating sovereign risk is in some ways more complex than that of evaluating other types of credit exposure because of the additional political component involved. Like other types of borrowers, debtor nations have an asset/liability/cash-flow profile that competent analysts can evaluate. In addition to this profile, however, lenders to sovereigns (including bondholders) must consider everything from the country's willingness to meet its credit obligations (particularly in unstable political environments) to its alternative means of financing (seeking help from outside entities such as the International Monetary Fund, imposing capital controls, etc.) and other measures it might take, such as currency devaluation, to stabilize its situation.

The presence of sovereign risk is real and meaningful, and perhaps the most salient example of its deleterious effects can be found in Russia's 1998 default. This episode represented the first time in many decades that a nation of such size and stature failed to meet its obligations to its lenders. Moreover, although the country was experiencing considerable trauma at that time—in part as the result of a contagion in emerging markets—it is abundantly clear that Russia was *unwilling* rather than *unable* to meet these obligations. The end result was a global financial crisis, in which investors lost billions of dollars and the country's robust development arc was slowed down for the better part of a decade.

Political risk is associated with changes in the political environment. Political risk can take many forms, both overt (e.g., the replacement of a pro-capitalist regime with one less so) and subtle (e.g., the potential impact of a change in party control in a developed nation), and it exists in every jurisdiction where financial instruments trade.

4.12. Other Risks

Companies face nonfinancial and financial risks other than those already mentioned. **ESG risk** is the risk to a company's market valuation resulting from environmental, social, and governance factors. Environmental risk is created by the operational decisions made by the company managers, including decisions concerning the products and services to offer and the processes to use in producing those products and services. Environmental damage may lead to a variety of negative financial and other consequences. Social risk derives from the company's various policies and practices regarding human resources, contractual arrangements, and the workplace. Liability from discriminatory workplace policies and the disruption of business resulting from labor strikes are examples of this type of risk. Flaws in corporate governance policies and procedures increase governance risk, with direct and material effects on a company's value in the marketplace.

One little-discussed but very large type of risk that some investment companies face is that of performance netting risk, often referred to simply as netting risk. **Performance netting risk,** which applies to entities that fund more than one strategy, is the potential for loss resulting from the failure of fees based on net performance to fully cover contractual payout obligations to individual portfolio managers that have positive performance when other portfolio managers have losses and when there are asymmetric incentive fee arrangements with the portfolio managers. The problem is best explained through an example.

Consider a hedge fund that charges a 20 percent incentive fee of any positive returns and funds two strategies equally, each managed by independent portfolio managers (call them Portfolio Managers A and B). The hedge fund pays Portfolio Managers A and B 10 percent of any gains they achieve. Now assume that in a given year, Portfolio Manager A makes \$10 million and Portfolio Manager B loses the same amount. The net incentive fee to the hedge fund is zero because it has generated zero returns. Unless otherwise negotiated, however (and such clauses are rare), the hedge fund remains obligated to pay Portfolio Manager A $1 million. As a result, the hedge fund company has incurred a loss, despite breaking even overall in terms of returns.[18] Note that the asymmetric nature of incentive fee contracts (i.e., losses are not penalized as gains are rewarded) plays a critical role in creating the problem the hedge fund faces. Because such arrangements are effectively a call option on a percentage of profits, in some circumstances they may provide an incentive to take excessive risk (the value of a call option is positively related to the underlying's volatility). Nevertheless, such arrangements are widespread.

Performance netting risk occurs only in multistrategy, multimanager environments and only manifests itself when individual portfolio managers within a jointly managed product generate actual losses over the course of a fee-generating cycle—typically one year. Moreover, an investment entity need not be flat or down on the year to experience netting-associated losses. For any given level of net returns, its portion of fees will by definition be higher if all portfolio managers generate no worse than zero performance over the period than they would if some portfolio managers generate losses. As mentioned earlier, an asymmetric incentive fee contract must exist for this problem to arise.

Performance netting risk applies not just to hedge funds but also to banks' and broker/dealers' trading desks, commodity trading advisers, and indeed, to any environment in which individuals have asymmetric incentive fee arrangements but the entity or unit responsible for paying the fees is compensated on the basis of net results. Typically this risk is managed through a process that establishes absolute negative performance thresholds for individual accounts and aggressively cuts risk for individual portfolio managers at performance levels at, near, or below zero for the period in question.[19]

Distinct from performance netting risk, **settlement netting risk** (or again, simply netting risk) refers to the risk that a liquidator of a counterparty in default could challenge a netting arrangement so that profitable transactions are realized for the benefit of creditors.[20] Such risk is mitigated by netting agreements that can survive legal challenge.

5. MEASURING RISK

Having spent some time identifying some of the major sources of risk, both financial and nonfinancial, we now turn our attention toward the measurement of those risks. In particular, we look at some techniques for measuring market risk and credit risk. Subsequently, we briefly survey some of the issues for measuring nonfinancial risk, a very difficult area but also a very topical one—particularly after the advent of the Basel II standards on risk management for international banks, which we will discuss.

5.1. Measuring Market Risk

Market risk refers to the exposure associated with actively traded financial instruments, typically those whose prices are exposed to the changes in interest rates, exchange rates, equity prices, commodity prices, or some combination thereof.[21]

[18] The asymmetric nature of the incentive fee contract (currently typical for hedge funds) plays a critical role in this example; were the arrangement symmetric, with negative returns penalized as positive returns are rewarded, the issue discussed would disappear.

[19] For more information on this topic, see Grant (2004).

[20] See www.foa.co.uk/documentation/netting/index.jsp.

[21] The definition of market risk given here is the one used in the practice of risk management. The term market risk, however, is often used elsewhere to refer to the risk of the market as a whole, which is usually known as systematic risk. In this chapter, we define market risk as risk management professionals do.

Over the years, financial theorists have created a simple and finite set of statistical tools to describe market risk. The most widely used and arguably the most important of these is the standard deviation of price outcomes associated with an underlying asset. We usually refer to this measure as the asset's **volatility,** typically represented by the Greek letter sigma (σ). Volatility is often an adequate description of portfolio risk, particularly for those portfolios composed of instruments with linear payoffs.[22] In some applications, such as indexing, volatility relative to a benchmark is paramount. In those cases, our focus should be on the volatility of the deviation of a portfolio's returns in excess of a stated benchmark portfolio's returns, known as **active risk, tracking risk, tracking error volatility,** or by some simply as **tracking error.**

As we will see shortly, the volatility associated with individual positions, in addition to being a very useful risk management metric in its own right, can be combined with other simple statistics, such as correlations, to form the building blocks for the portfolio-based risk management systems that have become the industry standard in recent years. We cover these systems in the next section of this chapter.

A portfolio's exposure to losses because of market risk typically takes one of two forms: sensitivity to adverse movements in the value of a key variable in valuation (primary or first-order measures of risk) and risk measures associated with *changes in* sensitivities (secondary or second-order measures of risk). Primary measures of risk often reflect linear elements in valuation relationships; secondary measures often take account of curvature in valuation relationships. Each asset class (e.g., bonds, foreign exchange, equities) has specific first- and second-order measures.

Let us consider measures of primary sources of risk first. For a stock or stock portfolio, **beta** measures sensitivity to market movements and is a linear risk measure. For bonds, **duration** measures the sensitivity of a bond or bond portfolio to a small parallel shift in the yield curve and is a linear measure, as is **delta** for options, which measures an option's sensitivity to a small change in the value of its underlying. These measures all reflect the expected change in price of a financial instrument for a unit change in the value of another instrument.

Second-order measures of risk deal with the change in the price sensitivity of a financial instrument and include convexity for fixed-income portfolios and gamma for options. **Convexity** measures how interest rate sensitivity changes with changes in interest rates.[23] **Gamma** measures the delta's sensitivity to a change in the underlying's value. Delta and gamma together capture first- and second-order effects of a change in the underlying.

For options, two other major factors determine price: volatility and time to expiration, both first-order or primary effects. Sensitivity to volatility is reflected in **vega,** the change in the price of an option for a change in the underlying's volatility. Most early option-pricing models (e.g., the Black–Scholes–Merton model) assume that volatility does not change over the life of an option, but in fact, volatility does generally change. Volatility changes are sometimes easy to observe in markets: Some days are far more volatile than others. Moreover, new information affecting the value of an underlying instrument, such as pending product announcements, will discernibly affect volatility. Because of their nonlinear payoff structure, options are typically very responsive to a change in volatility. Swaps, futures, and forwards with linear payoff functions are much less sensitive to changes in volatility. Option prices are also sensitive to changes in time to expiration, as measured by **theta,** the change in price of

---

[22]The contrast is with instruments such as options that have nonlinear or piecewise linear payoffs. See Chance (2003) for more on the payoff functions of options.

[23]Convexity is covered in some detail in Fabozzi (2004a, Chapter 7).

an option associated with a one-day reduction in its time to expiration.[24] Theta, like vega, is a risk that is associated exclusively with options. Correlation is a source of risk for certain types of options—for example, options on more than one underlying (when the correlations between the underlyings' returns constitute a risk variable).[25]

Having briefly reviewed traditional notions of market risk measurement, we introduce a new topic, one that took the industry by storm: value at risk.

5.2. Value at Risk

During the 1990s, value at risk—or VaR, as it is commonly known—emerged as the financial service industry's premier risk management technique.[26] J.P. Morgan (now J.P. Morgan Chase) developed the original concept for internal use but later published the tools it had developed for managing risk (as well as related information).[27] Probably no other risk management topic has generated as much attention and controversy as has value at risk. In this section, we take an introductory look at VaR, examine an application, and look at VaR's strengths and limitations.

VaR is a probability-based measure of loss potential for a company, a fund, a portfolio, a transaction, or a strategy. It is usually expressed either as a percentage or in units of currency. Any position that exposes one to loss is potentially a candidate for VaR measurement. VaR is most widely and easily used to measure the loss from market risk, but it can also be used—subject to much greater complexity—to measure the loss from credit risk and other types of exposures.

We have noted that VaR is a probability-based measure of loss potential. This definition is very general, however, and we need something more specific. More formally: **Value at risk** is an estimate of the loss (in money terms) that we expect to be exceeded with a given level of probability over a specified time period.[28]

Readers are encouraged to think very carefully about the implications of this definition, which has a couple of important elements. First, we see that VaR is an estimate of the loss that we expect to be exceeded. Hence, it measures a minimum loss. The actual loss may be much worse without necessarily impugning the VaR model's accuracy. Second, we see that VaR is associated with a given probability. Say the VaR is €10,000,000 at a probability of 5 percent for a given time period. All else equal, if we lower the probability from 5 percent to 1 percent, the VaR will be larger in magnitude because we now are referring to a loss that we expect to be exceeded with only a 1 percent probability. Third, we see that VaR has a time element and that as such, VaRs cannot be compared directly unless they share the same time interval. There is a big difference among potential losses that are incurred daily, weekly, monthly, quarterly, or

[24] For more information on theta, see Chance (2003).

[25] For more information, see Chance (2003).

[26] The terminology *value-at-risk* is expressed in different ways. For example, sometimes hyphens are used and sometimes it is just written as "value at risk." Sometimes it is abbreviated as VAR and sometimes as VaR. Those who have studied econometrics should be alert to the fact that the letters VAR also refer to an estimation technique called Vector Autoregression, which has nothing to do with value at risk. We shall use the abbreviation "VaR."

[27] RiskMetrics Group has now spun off from J.P. Morgan and is an independent company. See www.riskmetrics.com.

[28] In the terminology of statistics, VaR with an x percent probability for a given time interval represents the xth percentile of the distribution of outcomes (ranked from worst to best) over that time period.

annually. Potential losses over longer periods should be larg[illegible] but in most instances, longer time periods will not increase ex[illegible]

Consider the following example of VaR for an investmen[illegible] portfolio is $1.5 million for one day with a probability of 0.05. [illegible] says: There is a 5 percent chance that the portfolio will lose at least [illegible] day. The emphasis here should be on the fact that the $1.5 million loss [illegible] due care, it is also possible to describe VaR as a maximum: The probab[illegible] that the portfolio will lose no more than $1.5 million in a single day. We see [illegible] perspective in the common practice of stating VaR using a confidence level: For [illegible] just given, we would say that with 95 percent confidence (or for a 95 percent confide[illegible] the VaR for a portfolio is $1.5 million for one day.[29] We prefer to express VaR in the [illegible] of a minimum loss with a given probability. This approach is a bit more conservative, because it reminds us that the loss could be worse.[30]

5.2.1. Elements of Measuring Value at Risk Although VaR has become an industry standard, it may be implemented in several forms, and establishing an appropriate VaR measure requires the user to make a number of decisions about the calculation's structure. Three important ones are picking a probability level, selecting the time period over which to measure VaR, and choosing the specific approach to modeling the loss distribution.[31]

The probability chosen is typically either 0.05 or 0.01 (corresponding to a 95 percent or 99 percent confidence level, respectively). The use of 0.01 leads to a more conservative VaR estimate, because it sets the figure at the level where there should be only a 1 percent chance that a given loss will be worse that the calculated VaR. The trade-off, however, is that the VaR risk estimate will be much larger with a 0.01 probability than it will be for a 0.05 probability. In the above example, we might have to state that the VaR is $2.1 million for one day at a probability of 0.01. The risk manager selects 0.01 or 0.05; no definitive rule exists for preferring one probability to the other. For portfolios with largely linear risk characteristics, the two probability levels will provide essentially identical information. However, the tails of the loss distribution may contain a wealth of information for portfolios that have a good deal of optionality or nonlinear risks, and in these cases risk managers may need to select the more conservative probability threshold.

The second important decision for VaR users is choosing the time period. VaR is often measured over a day, but other, longer time periods are common. Banking regulators prefer two-week period intervals. Many companies report quarterly and annual VaRs to match their performance reporting cycles. Investment banks, hedge funds, and dealers seem to prefer daily VaR, perhaps because of the high turnover in their positions. Regardless of the time interval selected, the longer the period, the greater the VaR number will be because the magnitude of potential losses varies directly with the time span over which they are measured. The individual or individuals responsible for risk management will choose the time period.

Once these primary parameters are set, one can proceed to actually obtain the VaR estimate. This procedure involves another decision: the choice of technique. The basic idea

[29]This would be referred to as 95 percent one-day VaR.

[30]For a long position, the maximum possible loss is the entire value of the portfolio. For a short position, or a portfolio with both long and short positions, it is impossible to state the maximum possible loss because at least in theory, a short faces the possibility of unlimited losses.

[31]As we will learn in this section, users can select from three basic VaR methodologies, each of which uses a slightly different algorithm to estimate exposure.

ating VaR is to identify the probability distribution characteristics of portfolio s. Consider the information in Exhibit 9-4, which is a simple probability distribution for the return on a portfolio over a specified time period. Suppose we were interested in the VaR at a probability of 0.05. We would add up the probabilities for the class intervals until we reached a cumulative probability of 0.05. Observe that the probability is 0.01 that the portfolio will lose at least 40 percent, 0.01 that the portfolio will lose between 30 percent and 40 percent, and 0.03 that the portfolio will lose between 20 percent and 30 percent. Thus, the probability is 0.05 that the portfolio will lose at least 20 percent. Because we want to express our risk measure in units of money, we would then multiply 20 percent by the portfolio's initial market value to obtain VaR. The VaR for a probability of 0.01 would be 40 percent multiplied by the market value. From a confidence-level perspective, we estimate with 99 percent confidence that our portfolio will lose no more than 40 percent of its value over the specified time period.

Exhibit 9-4 offers a simplified representation of the information necessary to estimate VaR. This method for calculating VaR is rather cumbersome, and the information is not always easy to obtain. As such, the industry has developed a set of three standardized methods for estimating VaR: the analytical or variance–covariance method, the historical method, and the Monte Carlo simulation method. We will describe and illustrate each of these in turn.

5.2.2. The Analytical or Variance–Covariance Method The analytical or variance–covariance method begins with the assumption that portfolio returns are normally distributed. Recall from your study of portfolio management that a normal distribution can be completely described by its expected value and standard deviation.

Consider the standard normal distribution, a special case of the normal distribution centered on an expected value of zero and having a standard deviation of 1.0. We can convert any outcome drawn from a nonstandard normal distribution to a standard normal value by taking the outcome of interest, subtracting its mean, and dividing the result by its standard

EXHIBIT 9-4 Sample Probability Distribution of Returns on a Portfolio

Return on Portfolio	Probability
Less than −40%	0.010
−40% to −30%	0.010
−30% to −20%	0.030
−20% to −10%	0.050
−10% to −5%	0.100
−5% to −2.5%	0.125
−2.5% to 0%	0.175
0% to 2.5%	0.175
2.5% to 5%	0.125
5% to 10%	0.100
10% to 20%	0.050
20% to 30%	0.030
30% to 40%	0.010
Greater than 40%	0.010
	1.000

deviation. The resulting value then conforms to the standard normal distribution.[32] With the standard normal distribution, 5 percent of possible outcomes are likely to be smaller than −1.65.[33] Therefore, to calculate a 5 percent VaR for a portfolio (i.e., VaR at a probability of 0.05), we would estimate its expected return and subtract 1.65 times its estimated standard deviation of returns. So, the key to using the analytical or variance–covariance method is to estimate the portfolio's expected return and standard deviation of returns. An example follows.[34]

Suppose the portfolio contains two asset classes, with 75 percent of the money invested in an asset class represented by the S&P 500 Index and 25 percent invested in an asset class represented by the NASDAQ Composite Index.[35] Recall that a portfolio's expected return is a weighted average of the expected returns of its component stocks or asset classes. A portfolio's variance can be derived using a simple quadratic formula that combines the variances and covariances of the component stocks or asset classes. For example, assume that μ_S and μ_N are the expected returns of the S&P 500 and NASDAQ, respectively; σ_S and σ_N are their standard deviations; and ρ is the correlation between the two asset classes. The expected return, μ_P, and variance, σ_P^2, of the combined positions are given as

$$\mu_P = w_S\mu_S + w_N\mu_N$$

$$\sigma_P^2 = w_S^2\sigma_S^2 + w_N^2\sigma_N^2 + 2\rho w_S w_N \sigma_S \sigma_N$$

where w indicates the percentage allocated to the respective classes. The portfolio's standard deviation is just the square root of its variance. Exhibit 9-5 on page 602 provides estimates of the portfolio's expected value and standard deviation using actual numbers, where we obtain μ_P of 0.135 and σ_P of 0.244.

Note that the example provided above is quite simplistic, involving only two assets, and thus only two variances and one covariance. As such, the calculation of portfolio variance is relatively manageable. As the number of instruments in the portfolio increases, however, the calculation components expand dramatically and the equation quickly becomes unwieldy. The important thing to remember is that in order to derive the variance for a portfolio of multiple financial instruments, all we require are the associated variances and covariances, along with the ability to calculate their quadratic relationship.

If we are comfortable with the assumption of a normal distribution and the accuracy of our estimates of the expected returns, variances, and correlations, we can confidently use the analytical-method estimate of VaR. Exhibit 9-6 illustrates the calculation of this estimate.

VaR is first expressed in terms of the return on the portfolio. With an expected return of 0.135, we move 1.65 standard deviations along the x-axis in the direction of lower returns. Each standard deviation is 0.244. Thus we would obtain $0.135 - 1.65(0.244) = -0.268$.[36]

[32] For example, suppose you were interested in knowing the probability of obtaining a return of −15 percent or less when the expected return is 12 percent and the standard deviation is 20 percent. You would calculate the standard normal value, called a "z", as $(-0.15 - 0.12)/0.20 = -1.35$. Then you would look up this value in a table or use a spreadsheet function, such as Microsoft Excel's "=normsdist()" function. In this case, the probability is 0.0885.

[33] See DeFusco, McLeavey, Pinto, and Runkle (2004, pp. 255–256).

[34] For more detailed information, see DeFusco et al. (2004, Chapter 11).

[35] The extension to three or more classes is relatively straightforward once one knows how to calculate the variance of a portfolio of more than two assets. We shall focus here on the two-asset-class case.

[36] The reader can confirm that 1.65 and 2.33 standard deviations give the correct VaR at the 5 percent and 1 percent probability levels, respectively, using the Microsoft Excel function "=normsdist()".

EXHIBIT 9-5 Estimating the Expected Return and Standard Deviation of a Portfolio Combining Two Asset Classes

	S&P 500	NASDAQ	Combined Portfolio
Percentage invested (w)	0.75	0.25	1.00
Expected annual return (μ)	0.12	0.18	0.135*
Standard deviation (σ)	0.20	0.40	0.244**
Correlation (ρ)	0.90		

*Expected return of portfolio: $\mu_P = w_S\mu_S + w_N\mu_N = 0.75(0.12) + 0.25(0.18) = 0.135$

**Standard deviation of portfolio:

$$\sigma_P^2 = w_S^2\sigma_S^2 + w_N^2\sigma_N^2 + 2\rho w_S w_N \sigma_S \sigma_N$$

$$= (0.75)^2(0.20)^2 + (0.25)^2(0.40)^2 + 2(0.90)(0.75)(0.25)(0.20)(0.40) = 0.0595$$

$$\sigma_P = (\sigma_P^2)^{1/2} = (0.0595)^{1/2} = 0.244$$

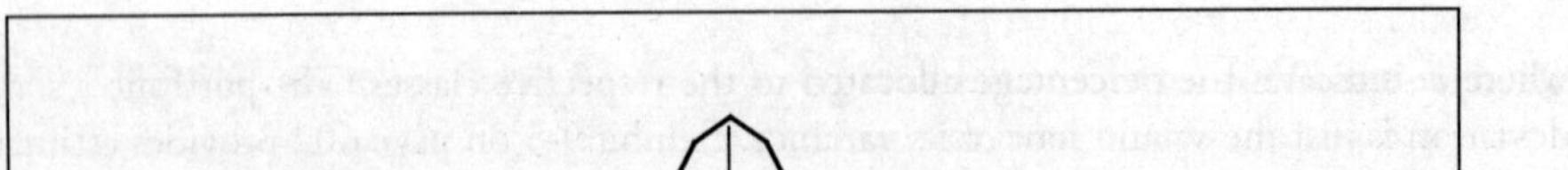

EXHIBIT 9-6 Annual VaR for a Portfolio with Expected Return of 0.135 and Standard Deviation of 0.244

At this point, VaR could be expressed as a loss of 26.8 percent. We could say that there is a 5 percent chance that the portfolio will lose at least 26.8 percent in a year. It is also customary to express VaR in terms of the portfolio's currency unit. Therefore, if the portfolio is worth $50 million, we can express VaR as $50 million(0.268) = $13.4 million.

This figure is an annual VaR. If we prefer a daily VaR, we can adjust the expected return to its daily average of approximately $0.135/250 = 0.00054$ and the standard deviation to its daily value of $0.244/\sqrt{250} = 0.01543$, which are based on the assumption of 250 trading days in a year and statistical independence between days. Then the daily VaR is $0.00054 - 1.65(0.01543) = -0.0249$. On a dollar basis, the daily VaR is \$50 million(0.0249) = \$1.245 million.

For a 1 percent VaR, we would move 2.33 standard deviations in the direction of lower returns. Thus the annual VaR would be $0.135 - 2.33(0.244) = -0.434$ or \$50 million(0.434) = \$21.7 million. The daily VaR would be $0.00054 - 2.33(0.01543) = -0.035$ or \$50 million(0.035) = \$1.75 million.

Some approaches to estimating VaR using the analytical method assume an expected return of zero. This assumption is generally thought to be acceptable for daily VaR calculations because expected daily return will indeed tend to be close to zero. Because expected returns are typically positive for longer time horizons, shifting the distribution by assuming a zero expected return will result in a larger projected loss, so the VaR estimate will be greater. Therefore, this small adjustment offers a slightly more conservative result and avoids the problem of having to estimate the expected return, a task typically much harder than that of estimating associated volatility. Another advantage of this adjustment is that it makes it easier to adjust the VaR for a different time period. For example, if the daily VaR is estimated at \$100,000, the annual VaR will be $\$100{,}000\sqrt{250} = \$1,581,139$. This simple conversion of a shorter-term VaR to a longer-term VaR (or vice versa) does not work, however, if the average return is not zero. In these cases, one would have to convert the average return and standard deviation to the different time period and compute the VaR from the adjusted average and standard deviation.

EXAMPLE 9-5 VaR with Different Probability Levels and Time Horizons

Consider a portfolio consisting of stocks as one asset class and bonds as another. The expected return on the portfolio's stock portion is 12 percent, and the standard deviation is 22 percent. The expected return on the bond portion is 5 percent, and the standard deviation is 7 percent. All of these figures are annual. The correlation between the two asset classes is 0.15. The portfolio's market value is \$150 million and is allocated 65 percent to stocks and 35 percent to bonds. Determine the VaR using the analytical method for the following cases:

1. A 5 percent yearly VaR
2. A 1 percent yearly VaR
3. A 5 percent weekly VaR
4. A 1 percent weekly VaR

Solutions: First, we must calculate the annual portfolio expected return and standard deviation. Using S to indicate stocks and B to indicate bonds, we have

$$\mu_P = w_S\mu_S + w_B\mu_B = 0.65(0.12) + 0.35(0.05) = 0.0955$$

$$\sigma_P^2 = w_S^2\sigma_S^2 + w_B^2\sigma_B^2 + 2\rho w_S w_B \sigma_S \sigma_B$$

$= (0.65)^2(0.22)^2 + (0.35)^2(0.07)^2 + 2(0.15)(0.65)(0.35)(0.22)(0.07) = 0.0221$

$\sigma_P = \sqrt{0.0221} = 0.1487$

1. For a 5 percent yearly VaR, we have $\mu_P - 1.65\sigma_P = 0.0955 - 1.65(0.1487) = -0.1499$. Then the VaR is \$150 million(0.1499) = \$22.485 million.
2. For a 1 percent yearly VaR, we have $\mu_P - 2.33\sigma_P = 0.0955 - 2.33(0.1487) = -0.251$. Then the VaR is \$150 million(0.251) = \$37.65 million.
3. For weekly VaR, we adjust the expected return to $0.0955/52 = 0.00184$ and the standard deviation to $0.1487/\sqrt{52} = 0.02062$. The 5 percent weekly VaR is then $\mu_P - 1.65\sigma = 0.00184 - 1.65(0.02062) = -0.03218$. Then the VaR is \$150 million(0.03218) = \$4.827 million.
4. The 1 percent weekly VaR is $\mu_P - 2.33\sigma_P = 0.00184 - 2.33(0.02062) = -0.0462$. Then the VaR is \$150 million(0.0462) = \$6.93 million.

The analytical or variance–covariance method's primary advantage is its simplicity. Its primary disadvantage is its reliance on several simplifying assumptions, including the normality of return distributions. In principle, there is no reason why the calculation demands a normal distribution, but if we move away from the normality assumption, we cannot rely on variance as a complete measure of risk. Distributions can deviate from normality because of skewness and kurtosis. Skewness is a measure of a distribution's deviation from the perfect symmetry (the normal distribution has a skewness of zero). A positively skewed distribution is characterized by relatively many small losses and a few extreme gains and has a long tail on its right side. A negatively skewed distribution is characterized by relatively many small gains and a few extreme losses and has a long tail on its left side. When a distribution is positively or negatively skewed, the variance–covariance method of estimating VaR will be inaccurate.

In addition, many observed distributions of returns have an abnormally large number of extreme events. This quality is referred to in statistical parlance as leptokurtosis but is more commonly called the property of fat tails.[37] Equity markets, for example, tend to have more frequent large market declines than a normal distribution would predict. Therefore, using a normality assumption to estimate VaR for a portfolio that features fat tails could understate the actual magnitude and frequency of large losses. VaR would then fail at precisely what it is supposed to do: measure the risk associated with large losses.

A related problem that surfaces with the analytical or variance–covariance method is that the normal distribution assumption is inappropriate for portfolios that contain options. The return distributions of options portfolios are often far from normal. Remember that a normal distribution has an unlimited upside and an unlimited downside. Call options have unlimited upside potential, as in a normal distribution, but their downside is a fixed value (the call's premium) and the distribution of call returns is highly skewed. Put options have a large but limited upside and a fixed downside (the put's premium), and the distribution of put returns is also highly skewed. In the same vein, covered calls and protective puts have return distributions that are sharply skewed in one direction or the other.

Therefore, when portfolios contain options, the assumption of a normal distribution to estimate VaR presents a significant problem. One common solution is to estimate the

[37] See DeFusco, McLeavey, Pinto, and Runkle (2004, Chapter 5).

option's price sensitivity using its delta. Recall that delta expresses a linear relationship between an option's price and the underlying's price (i.e., Delta = Change in option price/Change in underlying). A linear relationship lends itself more easily to treatment with a normal distribution. That is, a normally distributed random variable remains normally distributed when multiplied by a constant. In this case, the constant is the delta. The change in the option price is assumed to equal the change in the underlying price multiplied by the delta. This trick converts the normal distribution for the return on the underlying into a normal distribution for the option return. As such, the use of delta to estimate the option's price sensitivity for VaR purposes has led some to call the analytical method (or variance–covariance method) the **delta-normal method.** The use of delta is appropriate only for small changes in the underlying, however. As an alternative, some users of the delta-normal method add the second-order effect, captured by gamma. Unfortunately, as these higher-order effects are added, the relationship between the option price and the underlying's price begins to approximate the true nonlinear relationship. At that point, using a normal distribution becomes completely inappropriate. Therefore, using the analytical method could cause problems if a portfolio has options or other financial instruments that do not follow the normal distribution. Moreover, it is often difficult, if not impossible, to come up with a single second-order estimate that both is accurate and fits seamlessly into a variance/covariance VaR model.

5.2.3. The Historical Method Another widely used VaR methodology is the historical method. Using historical VaR, we calculate returns for a given portfolio using actual daily prices from a user-specified period in the recent past, graphing these returns into a histogram. From there, it becomes easy to identify the loss that is exceeded with a probability of 0.05 (or 0.01 percent, if preferred).

Consider the portfolio we have been examining, consisting of 75 percent invested in the S&P 500 and 25 percent invested in the NASDAQ Composite Index. Exhibit 9-7, a histogram, shows the daily returns on this portfolio for a recent calendar year. First, we note that the distribution is similar, but by no means identical, to that of a normal distribution. This portfolio has a few more returns slightly lower than the midpoint of the return sample than it would if its distribution were perfectly normal. With the historical method, however, we are not constrained to using the normal distribution. We simply collect the historical data and identify the return below which 5 (or 1) percent of returns fall. Although we could attempt to read this number from the histogram, it is much easier to simply rank-order the returns and determine the VaR figure from the sorted returns and the portfolio's dollar value.

The year examined here contains 248 returns. Having 5 percent of the returns in the distribution's lower tail would mean that about 12 return observations should be less than the VaR estimate. Thus the approximate VaR figure would be indicated by the 12th-worst return. A rank ordering of the data reveals that the 12th worst return is −0.0294. For a $50 million portfolio, the one-day VaR would thus be 0.0294($50 million) = $1.47 million.[38]

The historical method is also sometimes called the **historical simulation method.** This term is somewhat misleading because the approach involves not a *simulation* of the past returns but rather what *actually happened* in the past. In this context, note that a portfolio that an investor might have held in the past might not be the same as the one that investor will have in the future. When using the historical method, one must always keep in mind

[38]Technically, the VaR would fall between the 12th and 13th worst returns. Using the 13th worst return gives a more conservative VaR. Alternatively, we might average the 12th and 13th worst returns.

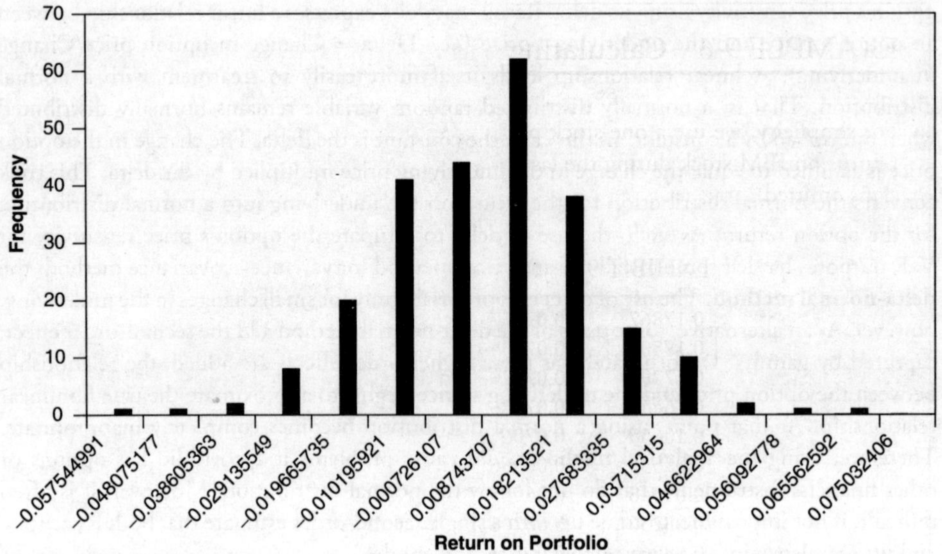

EXHIBIT 9-7 Historical Daily Returns on a Portfolio Invested 75 Percent in S&P 500 and 25 Percent in NASDAQ

that the purpose of the exercise is to apply *historical* price changes to the *current* portfolio.[39] In addition, instruments such as bonds and most derivatives behave differently at different times in their lives, and any accurate historical VaR calculation must take this into account by adjusting current bond/derivative pricing parameters to simulate their current characteristics across the period of analysis. For example, a historical VaR calculation that goes back one year for a portfolio that contains bonds that mature in the year 2027 should actually use otherwise identical bonds maturing in 2026 as proxies; these bonds are the most accurate representations of the current risk profile because they would have presented themselves one year ago in time. When a company uses a different portfolio composition to calculate its historical VaR than the one it actually had in the past, it may be more appropriate to call the method a historical simulation.

The historical method has the advantage of being **nonparametric** (i.e., involving minimal probability-distribution assumptions), enabling the user to avoid any assumptions about the type of probability distribution that generates returns. The disadvantage, however, is that this method relies completely on events of the past, and whatever distribution prevailed in the past might not hold in the future. In particular, periods of unusually large negative returns, such as the 23 percent one-day decline in the Dow Jones Industrial Average on October 19, 1987, might be questionable as an assumption for the future. This problem applies to the other types of VaR methodologies as well, however, including the analytical method and Monte Carlo simulation, both of which derive their inputs, more often than not, entirely from the historical prices associated with the securities contained in the portfolio.

---

[39] For example, in the two-asset portfolio we illustrated here, the weights were 75 percent S&P 500 and 25 percent NASDAQ. If the company were going forward with a different set of weights, it would obviously need to use the weights it planned to use in the future when calculating the VaR by the historical method.

EXAMPLE 9-6 Calculating VaR Using the Historical Method

For simplicity, we use a one-stock portfolio. Exhibit 9-8 shows the 40 worst monthly returns on IBM stock during the last 20 years, in descending order, as of 2003 (minus signs omitted):

EXHIBIT 9-8 IBM Stock: Worst Monthly Returns

0.17867	0.07237	0.05031	0.03372
0.17505	0.07234	0.04889	0.02951
0.17296	0.07220	0.04697	0.02905
0.16440	0.07126	0.04439	0.02840
0.10655	0.07064	0.04420	0.02584
0.09535	0.06966	0.04173	0.02508
0.09348	0.06465	0.04096	0.02270
0.08236	0.06266	0.03633	0.02163
0.08065	0.06204	0.03626	0.02115
0.07779	0.05304	0.03464	0.01976

For both calculations below, assume the portfolio value is \$100,000.

1. Calculate a 5 percent monthly VaR using the historical method.
2. Calculate a 1 percent monthly VaR using the historical method.

Solution: First, we note that during the last 20 years, there were 240 monthly returns. We see here only the worst 40 returns. Therefore, although we lack the entire distribution of returns, we do have enough to calculate the VaR.

1. Out of 240 returns, the 5 percent worst are the 12 worst returns. Therefore, the historical VaR would be about the 12th worst return. From the exhibit, we see that this return is -0.07234. So, the one-month VaR is $0.07234(\$100,000) = \$7,234$.
2. The 1 percent worst returns are 2.4 returns. We would probably use the second-worst return, which is -0.17505. The VaR is $0.17505(\$100,000) = \$17,505$. Alternatively, we might average the second- and third-worst returns to obtain $(-0.17505 + -0.17296)/2 = -0.17401$. Then the one-month VaR would be $0.17401(\$100,000) = \$17,401$.

The excerpt from The Goldman Sachs Group, Inc., annual report that follows in Example 9-7 shows how this investment firm reports its VaR. We see that Goldman Sachs reports average values for 5 percent daily VaR for its fiscal year using a variation of the historical simulation method. Goldman Sachs reports on VaR for interest rate, equity, currency, and commodity products, as well as for its overall trading positions (total VaR). Total VaR is less than the sum of the individual VaRs because the risks of Goldman

Sachs' positions in the various products are less than perfectly correlated. The **diversification effect** reported in the table in Example 9-7 equals the difference between the sum of the individual VaRs and total VaR. For example, for 2005, the diversification effect is $\$37 + \$34 + \$17 + \$26 - \$70 = -\$44$.

EXAMPLE 9-7 Value at Risk and the Management of Market Risk at Goldman Sachs

The following excerpt is from the 2005 Annual Report of Goldman Sachs:

> *"VaR is the potential loss in value of Goldman Sachs' trading positions due to adverse market movements over a defined time horizon with a specified confidence level.*
>
> *For the VaR numbers reported below, a one-day time horizon and a 95% confidence level were used. This means that there is a 1 in 20 chance that daily trading net revenues will fall below the expected daily trading net revenues by an amount at least as large as the reported VaR. Thus, shortfalls from expected trading net revenues on a single trading day greater than the reported VaR would be anticipated to occur, on average, about once a month. Shortfalls on a single day can exceed reported VaR by significant amounts. Shortfalls can also accumulate over a longer time horizon such as a number of consecutive trading days.*
>
> *The VaR numbers below are shown separately for interest rate, equity, currency and commodity products, as well as for our overall trading positions. The VaR numbers in each risk category include the underlying product positions and related hedges that may include positions in other product areas. For example, the hedge of a foreign exchange forward may include an interest rate futures position, and the hedge of a long corporate bond position may include a short position in the related equity.*
>
> *The modeling of the risk characteristics of our trading positions involves a number of assumptions and approximations. While management believes that these assumptions and approximations are reasonable, there is no standard methodology for estimating VaR, and different assumptions and/or approximations could produce materially different VaR estimates.*
>
> *We use historical data to estimate our VaR and, to better reflect current asset volatilities, we generally weight historical data to give greater importance to more recent observations. Given its reliance on historical data, VaR is most effective in estimating risk exposures in markets in which there are no sudden fundamental changes or shifts in market conditions. An inherent limitation of VaR is that the distribution of past changes in market risk factors may not produce accurate predictions of future market risk. Different VaR methodologies and distributional assumptions could produce a materially different VaR. Moreover, VaR calculated for a one-day time horizon does not fully capture the market risk of positions that cannot be liquidated or offset with hedges within one day. Changes in VaR between reporting periods are generally due to changes in levels of exposure, volatilities and/or correlations among asset classes.*

The following tables set forth the daily VaR:

Average Daily VaR[1] (in millions)

	Year Ended November		
Risk Categories	2005	2004	2003
Interest rates	\$37	\$36	\$38
Equity prices	34	32	27
Currency rates	17	20	18
Commodity prices	26	20	18
Diversification effect[2]	(44)	(41)	(43)
Total	\$70	\$67	\$58

[1] During the second quarter of 2004, we began to exclude from our calculation other debt portfolios that cannot be properly measured in VaR. The effect of excluding these portfolios was not material to prior periods and, accordingly, such periods have not been adjusted. For a further discussion of the market risk associated with these portfolios, see "—Other Debt Portfolios" below. [This matter is not reproduced in this excerpt.]

[2] Equals the difference between total VaR and the sum of the VaRs for the four risk categories. This effect arises because the four market risk categories are not perfectly correlated.

> *Our average daily VaR increased to \$70 million in 2005 from \$67 million in 2004. The increase was primarily due to higher levels of exposure to commodity prices, equity prices and interest rates, partially offset by reduced exposures to currency rates, as well as reduced volatilities, particularly in interest rate and equity assets.*
>
> *Our average daily VaR increased to \$67 million in 2004 from \$58 million in 2003, primarily due to higher levels of exposure to equity prices, currency rates and commodity prices, partially offset by reduced exposures to interest rates, as well as reduced volatilities, particularly in interest rates and equity assets."*

The Annual Report continues with a table giving other information about VaR, including high and low daily values.

Source: Goldman Sachs 2005 Annual Report pp. 50–52.

The next section addresses the third method of estimating VaR, Monte Carlo simulation.

5.2.4. The Monte Carlo Simulation Method The third approach to estimating VaR is Monte Carlo simulation. In general, Monte Carlo simulation produces random outcomes so we can examine what might happen given a particular set of risks. It is used widely in the sciences as well as in business to study a variety of problems. In the financial world in recent years, it has become an extremely important technique for measuring risk. Monte Carlo simulation generates random outcomes according to an assumed probability distribution and a set of input parameters. We can then analyze these outcomes to gauge the risk associated with the events in question. When estimating VaR, we use Monte Carlo simulation to produce random portfolio returns. We then assemble these returns into a summary distribution from which we can determine at which level the lower 5 percent (or 1 percent, if preferred) of return outcomes occur. We then apply this figure to the portfolio value to obtain VaR.

Monte Carlo simulation uses a probability distribution for each variable of interest and a mechanism to randomly generate outcomes according to each distribution. Our goal here is to gain a basic understanding of the technique and how to use it. Therefore, we illustrate it without explaining the full details of how to generate the random values.

Suppose we return to the example of our $50 million portfolio invested 75 percent in the S&P 500 and 25 percent in the NASDAQ Composite Index. We assume, as previously, that this portfolio should have an annual expected return of 13.5 percent and a standard deviation of 24.4 percent. We shall now conduct a Monte Carlo simulation using the normal distribution with these parameters. Keep in mind that in practice, one advantage of Monte Carlo simulation is that it does not require a normal distribution, but the normal distribution is often used and we shall stay with it for illustrative purposes.

We use a random number generator to produce a series of random values, which we then convert into a normally distributed stream of outcomes representing a rate of return for this portfolio over a period of one year. Suppose the first value it produces is a return of −21.87 percent. This rate corresponds to an end-of-year portfolio value of $39.07 million. The second random return it produces is −4.79 percent, which takes the portfolio value to $47.61 million.[40] The third random return it produces is 31.38 percent, which makes the portfolio value $65.69 million. We continue this process a large number of times, perhaps several thousand or even several million. To keep the simulation to a manageable size for illustrative purposes, we generate only 300 outcomes.

Exhibit 9-9 shows the histogram of portfolio outcomes. Notice that even though we used a normal distribution to generate the outcomes, the resulting distribution does not look entirely normal. Of course, we should be surprised if it did because we used only 300 random outcomes, a relatively small sample.

To obtain the point in the lower tail that 5 percent of the outcomes exceed, we rank order the data and find the 15th-lowest outcome, which is a portfolio value of $34.25 million, corresponding to a loss of $15.75 million. This value is higher than the annual VaR estimated using the analytical method ($13.4 million). These two values would be identical (or nearly so) if we had employed a sufficiently large sample size in the Monte Carlo simulation so that the sample VaR would converge to the true population VaR.

In Monte Carlo simulation, we can make any distributional assumption that we believe is appropriate. In many practical applications, it is inappropriate to assume a normal return distribution. In particular, for many derivatives dealers, the problems in managing the risk of these instruments are compounded by the fact that an extremely large number of random variables may affect the value of their overall position. These variables are often not normally distributed, and furthermore, they often interact with each other in complex ways. Monte Carlo simulation is often the only practical means of generating the information necessary to manage the risk. With tens of thousands of transactions on the books of most dealers, however, Monte Carlo simulation can require extensive commitments of computer resources.

5.2.5. "Surplus at Risk": VaR as It Applies to Pension Fund Portfolios

You will recall from earlier points in our discussion that pension funds face a slightly different set of challenges in the measurement of market exposures, primarily because of the fact that the

[40]The random outcomes are independent, not sequential. Each outcome thus represents a return relative to the full initial portfolio value of $50 million.

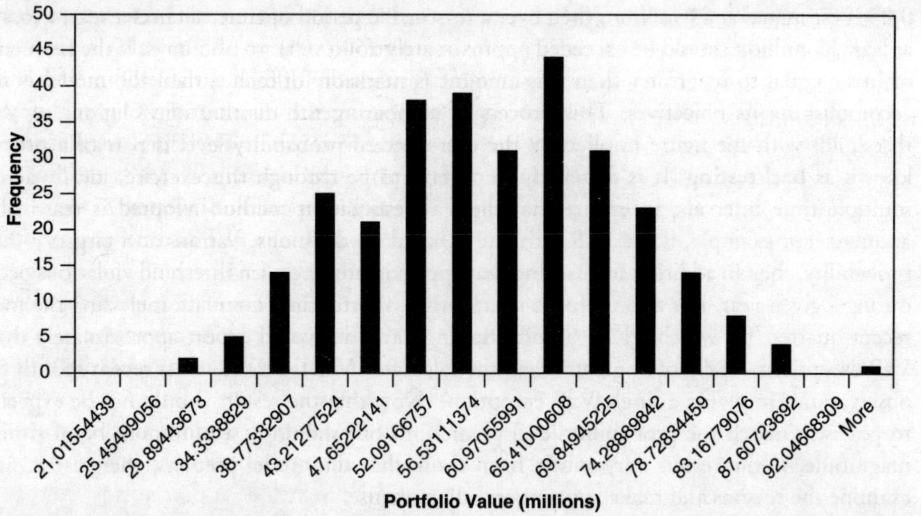

EXHIBIT 9-9 Simulated Values after One Year for a Portfolio Invested 75 Percent in S&P 500 and 25 Percent in NASDAQ

assets must fund pension obligations whose present value is itself subject to interest rate risk and other risks.[41] The difference between the value of the pension fund's assets and liabilities is referred to as the **surplus,** and it is this value that pension fund managers seek to enhance and protect. If this surplus falls into negative territory, the plan sponsor must contribute funds to make up the deficit over a period of time that is specified as part of the fund's plan.

In order to reflect this set of realities in their risk estimations, pension fund managers typically apply VaR methodologies not to their portfolio of assets but to the surplus. To do so, they simply express their liability portfolio as a set of short securities and calculate VaR on the net position. VaR handles this process quite elegantly, and once this adjustment is made, all three VaR methodologies can be applied to the task.

5.3. The Advantages and Limitations of VaR

Although value at risk has become the industry standard for risk assessment, it also has widely documented imperfections. VaR can be difficult to estimate, and different estimation methods can give quite different values. VaR can also lull one into a false sense of security by giving the impression that the risk is properly measured and under control. VaR often underestimates the magnitude and frequency of the worst returns, although this problem often derives from erroneous assumptions and models. As we discuss later, VaR for individual positions does not generally aggregate in a simple way to portfolio VaR. Also, VaR fails to incorporate positive results into its risk profile, and as such, it arguably provides an incomplete picture of overall exposures.

Users of VaR should routinely test their system to determine whether their VaR estimates prove accurate in predicting the results experienced over time. For example, if daily VaR at

41 An example of a defined benefit pension plan's obligation is the promise is to pay, for each year of service, a certain percentage of a vested participant's average salary in their final five years of service; this promise may include cost-of-living adjustments.

0.05 is estimated at $1 million, then over a reasonable period of time, such as a year, a loss of at least $1 million should be exceeded approximately 250(0.05) = 12.5 days. If the frequency of losses equal to or greater than this amount is markedly different, then the model is not accomplishing its objectives. This process of comparing the number of violations of VaR thresholds with the figure implied by the user-selected probability level is part of a process known as **backtesting.** It is extremely important to go through this exercise, ideally across multiple time intervals, to ensure that the VaR estimation method adopted is reasonably accurate. For example, if the VaR estimate is based on daily observations and targets a 0.05 probability, then in addition to ensuring that approximately a dozen threshold violations occur during a given year, it is also useful to check other, shorter time intervals, including the most recent quarter (for which, given 60-odd trading days, we would expect approximately three VaR exceptions—i.e., losses greater than the calculated VaR), and the most recent month (20 observations, implying a single VaR exception). Note that the results should not be expected to precisely match the probability level predictions but should at a minimum be of similar magnitude. If the results vary much from those that the model predicts, then users must examine the reasons and make appropriate adjustments.

An accurate VaR estimate can also be extremely difficult to obtain for complex organizations. In the simple example we used previously, VaR was driven solely by the large- and small-cap U.S. stocks. For a large international bank, however, the exposures might be to a variety of domestic and international interest rate markets, numerous exchange rates, perhaps some equity markets, and even some commodity markets. A bank could have exposure to literally thousands of risks. Consolidating the effects of these exposures into a single risk measure can be extremely difficult. Nonetheless, most large banks manage to do so and, generally, do an excellent job of managing their risk.

VaR has the attraction of quantifying the potential loss in simple terms and can be easily understood by senior management. Regulatory bodies have taken note of VaR as a risk measure, and some require that institutions provide it in their reports. In the United States, the Securities and Exchange Commission now requires publicly traded companies to report how they are managing financial risk. VaR is one acceptable method of reporting that information.

Another advantage of VaR is its versatility. Many companies use VaR as a measure of their capital at risk. They will estimate the VaR associated with a particular activity, such as a line of business, an individual asset manager, a subsidiary, or a division. Then, they evaluate performance, taking into account the VaR associated with this risky activity. In some cases, companies allocate capital based on VaR. For example, a pension fund might determine its overall acceptable VaR and then inform each asset class manager that it can operate subject to its VaR not exceeding a certain amount. The manager's goal is to earn the highest return possible given its VaR allocation. This activity is known as risk budgeting; we cover it in more detail in a later section.

In summary, VaR has notable advantages and disadvantages. Controversy and criticism have surrounded it.[42] Nevertheless, if a risk manager uses VaR with full awareness of its

[42]A well-known critic of VaR has likened its use to flying an aircraft with a potentially flawed altimeter. With an altimeter, a pilot may think he knows the correct altitude. Without an altimeter, the pilot will look out the window. Of course, this argument presumes that there are no clouds below. The probability of hitting trees or a mountain is the joint probability that the aircraft is too low and that the altimeter gives a false signal, which is less than the simple probability that the aircraft is too low. Aware of the potential for the altimeter to be flawed, the pilot will also seek information from other sources, which themselves are less than 100 percent accurate. So will the risk manager when using VaR. Both will gauge

limitations, he should definitely gain useful information about risk. Even if VaR gives an incorrect measure of the loss potential, the risk manager can take this risk measurement error into account when making the key overall decisions—provided, of course, that the magnitude of the error can be measured and adjusted for with some level of precision, e.g., through back testing a VaR method against historical data. The controversy remains, but VaR as a risk measure is unlikely to ever be completely rejected. It should not, however, be used in isolation. VaR is often paired with stress testing, discussed in a subsequent section. Remember too that no risk measure can precisely predict future losses. It is important to ensure that the inputs to the VaR calculation are as reliable as possible and relevant to the current investment mix.

5.4. Extensions and Supplements to VaR

Risk managers have developed several useful extensions and supplements to VaR. In this section, we review several of the more noteworthy.

A key concern to risk managers is the evaluation of the portfolio effect of a given risk. The ability to isolate the effect of a risk, particularly in complex portfolios with high correlation effects, is very important. We can use incremental VaR (IVaR) to investigate the effect. **Incremental VaR** measures the incremental effect of an asset on the VaR of a portfolio by measuring the difference between the portfolio's VaR while including a specified asset and the portfolio's VaR with that asset eliminated.[43] We can also use IVaR to assess the incremental effect of a subdivision on an enterprise's overall VaR. Although IVaR gives an extremely limited picture of the asset's or portfolio's contribution to risk, it nonetheless provides useful information about how adding the asset will affect the portfolio's overall risk as reflected in its VaR.

Some variations of VaR are **cash flow at risk** (CFAR) and **earnings at risk** (EAR). CFAR and EAR measure the risk to a company's cash flow or earning, respectively, instead of its market value as in the case of VaR. CFAR is the minimum cash-flow loss that we expect to be exceeded with a given probability over a specified time period. EAR is defined analogously to CFAR but measures risk to accounting earnings. CFAR and EAR can be used when a company (or portfolio of assets) generates cash flows or profits but cannot be readily valued in a publicly traded market, or when the analyst's focus is on the risk to cash flow and earnings, for example, in a valuation. CFAR and EAR can complement VaR's perspective on risk.

Another useful tool to supplement VaR is the **tail value at risk** (TVaR), also known as the **conditional tail expectation.** TVaR is defined as the VaR plus the expected loss in excess of VaR, when such excess loss occurs. For example, given a 5 percent daily VaR, TVaR might be calculated as the average of the worst 5 percent of outcomes in a simulation.

VaR developed initially as a measure for market risk, which is the risk associated with the primary market forces of interest rates, exchange rates, stock prices, and commodity prices. With some difficulty, VaR can be extended to handle credit risk, the risk that a counterparty will not pay what it owes. More-recent extensions of VaR have tended to focus on modeling assets with non-normal underlying distributions. The use of conditional normal distribution based on different regimes is a very intriguing concept, but the mathematics used in this area can be daunting.[44]

---

the risk against their tolerance for risk and take appropriate action. We look at some of these other sources of risk information in the next section.

[43] For more details, see Crouhy, Galai, and Mark (2001, Chapter 6).

[44] For an extremely entertaining tour of some of the pitfalls of traditional risk analysis and some solutions, see Osband (2002).

5.5. Stress Testing

Managers often use stress testing (a term borrowed from engineering) to supplement VaR as a risk measure. The main purpose of VaR analysis is to quantify potential losses under normal market conditions. Stress testing, by comparison, seeks to identify unusual circumstances that could lead to losses in excess of those typically expected. Clearly, different scenarios will have attached probabilities of occurring that vary from the highly likely to the almost totally improbable. It is, therefore, the natural complement to VaR analysis. Two broad approaches exist in stress testing: scenario analysis and stressing models.

5.5.1. Scenario Analysis Scenario analysis is the process of evaluating a portfolio under different states of the world. Quite often it involves designing scenarios with deliberately large movements in the key variables that affect the values of a portfolio's assets and derivatives.

One type of scenario analysis, that of **stylized scenarios,** involves simulating a movement in at least one interest rate, exchange rate, stock price, or commodity price relevant to the portfolio. These movements might range from fairly modest changes to quite extreme shifts. Many practitioners use standard sets of stylized scenarios to highlight potentially risky outcomes for the portfolio. Some organizations have formalized this process; for example, the Derivatives Policy Group recommends its members look at the following seven scenarios:

1. Parallel yield curve shifting by ±100 basis points (1 percentage point).
2. Yield curve twisting by ±25 basis points.[45]
3. Each of the four combinations of the above shifts and twists.
4. Implied volatilities changing by ±20 percent from current levels.
5. Equity index levels changing by ±10 percent.
6. Major currencies moving by ±6 percent and other currencies by ±20 percent.
7. Swap spread changing by ±20 basis points.

In 1988, the Chicago Mercantile Exchange introduced a system call SPAN to calculate collateral requirements based on their members' total portfolios of futures and options. The objective of this system was to stress portfolios under a variety of scenarios. SPAN has become a very popular system among futures and options exchanges worldwide to set margin requirements. It offers a very useful, generalized form of scenario analysis that combines elements of VaR with some specified overlay based on real-world observation of the relationship among financial instruments.

Scenario analysis is a very useful enhancement to VaR, enabling those interested in risk analysis to identify and analyze specific exposures that might affect a portfolio. The results, of course, are only as good as implied by the accuracy of the scenarios devised. One problem with the stylized scenario approach is that the shocks tend to be applied to variables in a sequential fashion. In reality, these shocks often happen at the same time, have much different correlations than normal, or have some causal relationship connecting them.

Another approach to scenario analysis involves using **actual extreme events** that have occurred in the past. Here, we might want to put our portfolio through price movements that simulate the stock market crash of October 1987; the collapse of Long-Term Capital Management in 1998; the technology stock bubble of the late 1990s; the abrupt bursting of said bubble, beginning in the spring of 2000; or the market reaction to the terrorist attacks

---

[45]A **twist** is a nonparallel movement in the yield curve. An example of a twist is a 25-bp increase in short rates and no change in long rates, which would result in a flattening of the yield curve.

of September 11, 2001. This type of scenario analysis might be particularly useful if we think that the occurrence of extreme market breaks has a higher probability than that given by the probability model or historical time period being used in developing the VaR estimate. Stress testing of actual extreme events forces one to direct attention to these outcomes.

We might also create scenarios based on **hypothetical events**—events that have never happened in the markets or market outcomes to which we attach a small probability. These types of scenarios are very difficult to analyze and may generate confusing outcomes, so it is important to carefully craft hypothetical analyses if they are to generate information that adds value to the risk management processes.

Having devised a series of appropriate scenarios, the next step in the process is to apply them to the portfolio. The key task here is to understand the instruments' sensitivities to the underlying risk factors being stressed. This process is often a complex one that demands an understanding of the portfolio's risk parameters such that we can make appropriate approximations from standardized risk characteristics such as betas, deltas, gammas, duration, and convexity. Market liquidity is often a consideration also, especially when the underlying valuation models for assets assume arbitrage-free pricing, which assumes the ability to transact in any quantity. In addition, liquidity often dries up completely in a market crisis.

5.5.2. Stressing Models

Given the difficulty in estimating the sensitivities of a portfolio's instruments to the scenarios we might design, another approach might be to use an existing model and apply shocks and perturbations to the model inputs in some mechanical way. This approach might be considered more scientific because it emphasizes a range of possibilities rather than a single set of scenarios, but it will be more computationally demanding. It is also possible to glean some idea of the likelihood of different scenarios occurring.

The simplest form of stressing model is referred to as **factor push,** the basic idea of which to is to push the prices and risk factors of an underlying model in the most disadvantageous way and to work out the combined effect on the portfolio's value. This exercise might be appropriate for a wide range of models, including option-pricing models such as Black–Scholes–Merton, multifactor equity risk models, and term structure factor models. But factor push also has its limitations and difficulties—principally the enormous model risk that occurs in assuming the underlying model will function in an extreme risk climate.

Other approaches include **maximum loss optimization**—in which we would try to optimize mathematically the risk variable that will produce the maximum loss—and **worst-case scenario analysis**—in which we can examine the worst case that we actually expect to occur.

Overall stress testing is a valuable complement to VaR analysis and can highlight weaknesses in risk management procedures.

5.6. Measuring Credit Risk

Credit risk is present when there is a positive probability that one party owing money to another will renege on the obligation (i.e., the counterparty could default). If the defaulting party has insufficient resources to cover the loss or the creditor cannot impose a claim on any assets the debtor has that are unrelated to the line of business in which the credit was extended, the creditor can suffer a loss.[46] A creditor might be able to recover some of the loss, perhaps by having the debtor sell assets and pay the creditors a portion of their claim.

[46]The personal assets of a corporation's owners are shielded from creditors by the principle of limited liability, which can also apply to certain partnerships. The law supporting limited liability is a fundamental one in most societies and supports the notion that default is a right. Indeed, option-pricing theory has been used to value this right as the option that it actually is.

Credit losses have two dimensions: the likelihood of loss and the associated amount of loss (reflecting, of course, the amount of credit outstanding and the associated recovery rate). The likelihood of loss is a probabilistic concept: In every credit-based transaction, a given probability exists that the debtor will default. When a default does occur, however, creditors are often able to recover at least a portion of their investment, and as such, it is necessary and appropriate to assess the magnitude of this recovery (i.e., the recovery rate) in order to fully understand the risk profile of the credit dynamic. In relation to data on market risk, the amount of information available on credit losses is much smaller. Credit losses occur infrequently, and as such, the empirical data set from which to draw exposure inferences is quite limited. Although some statistical data are available, historical recovery rates can be unreliable. It can be hard to predict what an asset could be sold for in bankruptcy proceedings, and claims are not always paid in the order specified by bankruptcy law.

In the risk management business, exposure must often be viewed from two different time perspectives. We must assess first the risk associated with immediate credit events and second the risk associated with events that may happen later. With respect to credit, the risk of events happening in the immediate future is called **current credit risk** (or, alternatively, **jump-to-default risk**); it relates to the risk that amounts due at the present time will not be paid. For example, some risk exists that the counterparty could default on an interest or swap payment due immediately. Assuming, however, that the counterparty is solvent and that it will make the current payment with certainty, the risk remains that the entity will default at a later date. This risk is called potential credit risk, and it can differ quite significantly from current credit risk; the relationship between the two is a complex one. A company experiencing financial difficulties at present could, with sufficient time, work out its problems and be in better financial condition at a later date. Regardless of which risk is greater, however, a creditor must assess credit risk at different points in time. In doing so, the creditor must understand how different financial instruments have different patterns of credit risk, both across instruments and across time within a given instrument. This point will be discussed later in this section.

Another element of credit risk, which blends current and potential credit risk, is the possibility that a counterparty will default on a current payment to a different creditor. Most direct lending or derivative-based credit contracts stipulate that if a borrower defaults on any outstanding credit obligations, the borrower is in default on them all (this is known as a **cross-default provision**). Creditors stipulate this condition as one means of controlling credit exposure; in particular, it allows them to act quickly to mitigate losses to counterparties unable to meet any of their obligations. For example, suppose Party A owes Party B, but no payments are due for some time. Party A, however, currently owes a payment to Party C and is unable to pay. A is, therefore, in default to Party C. Depending on what actions C takes, A may be forced into bankruptcy. If so, then B's claim simply goes into the pool of other claims on A. In that case, A has technically defaulted to B without actually having a payment due.

In a previous section, we discussed how VaR is used to measure market risk. VaR is also used, albeit with greater difficulty, to measure credit risk. This measure is sometimes called **credit VaR,** default VaR, or credit at risk. Like ordinary VaR, it reflects the minimum loss with a given probability during a period of time. A company might, for example, quote a credit VaR of €10 million for one year at a probability of 0.05 (or a confidence level of 95 percent). In other words, the company has a 5 percent chance of incurring default-related losses of at least €10 million in one year. Note that credit VaR cannot be separated from market VaR because credit risk arises from gains on market positions held. Therefore, to accurately measure credit VaR, a risk manager must focus on the upper tail of the distribution of market returns, where the return to the position is positive, in contrast to market risk VaR, which focuses on the lower tail. Suppose the 5 percent upper tail of the market risk distribution is €5 million. The credit VaR can be roughly thought of as €5 million, but this thinking assumes that the probability of loss is 100 percent and the net amount recovered in the event of a loss is zero. Further refinements incorporating more-accurate measures of the default probability and recovery rate should lead to a lower and more accurate credit VaR. In addition, the explosion of volume and liquidity in the credit derivatives market has vastly increased the amount of information available to risk managers with respect to the problem of understanding how the marketplace values credit risk on a real-time basis. Nevertheless, estimating credit VaR is more complicated than estimating market VaR because credit events are rare and recovery rates are hard to estimate. Credit risk is less easily aggregated than market risk; the correlations between the credit risks of counterparties must be considered.

In the next sections, we present the perspective of option pricing theory on credit risk and the measurement of credit risk exposures for certain derivative contracts.

5.6.1. Option-Pricing Theory and Credit Risk

Option theory enables us to better understand the nature of credit risk. In this section, we will see that the stock of a company with leverage can be viewed as a call option on its assets. This approach will lead to the result that a bond with credit risk can be viewed as a default-free bond plus an implicit short put option written by the bondholders for the stockholders.

Consider a company with assets with a market value of A_0 and debt with a face value of F. The debt is in the form of a single zero-coupon bond due at time T. The bond's market value is B_0. Thus the stock's market value is:

$$S_0 = A_0 - B_0$$

At time T, the assets will be worth A_T and the company will owe F. If $A_T \geq F$, the company will pay off its debt, leaving the amount $A_T - F$ for the stockholders. Thus S_T will be worth $A_T - F$. If the assets' value is insufficient to pay off the debt ($A_T < F$), the stockholders will discharge their obligation by turning over the assets to the bondholders. Thus the bondholders will receive A_T, which is less than their claim of F, and the stockholders will receive nothing. The company is, therefore, bankrupt. Exhibit 9-10 illustrates these results by showing the payoffs to the two suppliers of capital.

Notice that the payoffs to the stockholders resemble those of a call option in which the underlying is the assets, the exercise price is F, and the option expires at time T, the bond maturity date. Indeed, the stock of a company with a single zero-coupon bond issue is a call option on the assets.

To better understand the nature of stock as a call option, let us recall the concept of put–call parity,[47] where $p_0 + S_0 = c_0 + X/(1 + r)^T$. The put price plus the underlying price

EXHIBIT 9-10 Payoffs to the Suppliers of Capital to the Company

		Payoffs at Time T	
Source of Capital	Market Value at Time 0	$A_T < F$	$A_T \geq F$
Bondholders	B_0	A_T	F
Stockholders	S_0	0	$A_T - F$
Total	$B_0 + S_0 = A_0$	A_T	A_T

[47] See Chance (2003, Chapter 4).

EXHIBIT 9-11 Equity as a Call Option on the Value of a Company

Variable	Traditional Framework	Current Framework
Underlying	S_0 (stock)	A_0 (value of assets)
Exercise price	X	F (face value of bond)
Time to expiration	T	T (maturity of bond)
Risk-free rate	r	r
Call price	c_0	S_0 (value of stock)
Put price	p_0	p_0

equals the call price plus the present value of the exercise price. So, working this through for our own problem, we find the correspondences shown in Exhibit 9-11.

Note the last line. We see that in the traditional framework, there is a put option, which we know is an option to sell the underlying at a fixed price. In fact, we know from put-call parity that $p_0 = c_0 - S_0 + X/(1+r)^T$. The put is equivalent to a long call, a short position in the underlying stock, and a long position in a risk-free bond with face value equal to the exercise price. In the current framework, the standard expression of put-call parity is $p_0 + A_0$ (put plus underlying) $= S_0 + F/(1+r)^T$ (stock plus present value of bond principal). Turning this expression around and reversing the order of the put and bond, we obtain:

$$A_0 = S_0 + F/(1+r)^T - p_0$$

Noting, however, that by definition the asset value, A_0, equals the stock's market value, S_0, plus the bond's market value, B_0,

$$A_0 = S_0 + B_0$$

we see that the bond's market value must be equivalent to

$$B_0 = F/(1+r)^T - p_0$$

The first term on the right-hand side is equivalent to a default-free zero-coupon bond paying F at maturity. The second term is a short put. The bondholders' claim, which is subject to default, can thus be viewed as a default-free bond and a short put on the assets. In other words, the bondholders have implicitly written the stockholders a put on the assets. From the stockholders' perspective, this put is their right to fully discharge their liability by turning over the assets to the bondholders, even though those assets could be worth less than the bondholders' claim. In legal terminology, this put option is called the stockholders' right of limited liability.

The existence of this implicit put option is the difference between a default-free bond and a bond subject to default. This approach to understanding credit risk forms the basis for models that use option-pricing theory to explain credit risk premiums, probabilities of default, and the valuation of companies that use leverage. In practice, the capital structures of most companies are more complex than the one used here, but practical applications of model variants appear in the financial industry.

5.6.2. The Credit Risk of Forward Contracts

Recall that forward contracts involve commitments on the part of each party. No cash is due at the start, and no cash is paid until expiration, at which time one party owes the greater amount to the other. The party that owes the larger amount could default, leaving the other with a claim of the defaulted amount. Each party assumes the other's credit risk. Prior to expiration, no current credit risk exists, because no current payments are owed, but there is potential credit risk in connection with the payments to be made at expiration. Current credit risk arises when the contract is at its expiration. Below we will examine how potential credit risk changes during the life of the contract as the value of the underlying changes.

From the perspective of a given party, a forward contract's market value can be easily calculated as the present value of the amount owed to the party minus the present value of the amount it owes. So, the market value at a given time reflects the potential credit risk. This is another reason why the calculation of market value is important: It indicates the amount of a claim that would be subject to loss in the event of a default.

For example, look at a forward contract that expires in one year. The underlying asset price is \$100 and the risk-free interest rate is 5 percent. We can determine that the forward price is \$100(1.05) = \$105. We could then assume that three months later, the asset price is \$102. We can determine that the long forward contract's value at that time is $\$102 - \$105/(1.05)^{0.75} = \$0.7728$. This is the value to the long because the contract is a claim on the asset, which is currently worth \$102, and an obligation to pay \$105 for it in nine months. To the holder of the long position, this contract is worth \$0.7728, and to the holder of the short position, it is worth −\$0.7728.

Which party bears the potential credit risk? The long's claim is positive; the short's claim is negative. Therefore, the long currently bears the credit risk. As it stands right now, the value of the long's claim is \$0.7728. No payment is currently due, and hence no current credit risk exists, but the payments that are due later have a present value of \$0.7728. Actual default may or may not occur at expiration. Moreover, at expiration, the amount owed is unlikely to be this same amount. In fact, if the spot price falls enough, the situation will have turned around and the long could owe the short the greater amount. Nonetheless, in assessing the credit risk three months into the contract, the long's claim is \$0.7728. This claim has a probability of not being paid and also has the potential for recovery of a portion of the loss in the event of default. If the counterparty declares bankruptcy before the contract expires, the claim of the non-defaulting counterparty is the forward contract's market value at the time of the bankruptcy, assuming this value is positive. So, if the short declares bankruptcy at this time, the long has a claim worth \$0.7728. If the long declares bankruptcy, the long holds an asset worth \$0.7728.

5.6.3. The Credit Risk of Swaps A swap is similar to a series of forward contracts. The periodic payments associated with a swap imply, however, that credit risk will be present at a series of points during the contract's life. As with forward contracts, the swap's market value can be calculated at any time and reflects the present value of the amount at risk for a credit loss (i.e., the potential credit risk).

Consider, for example, the case of a plain vanilla interest rate swap with a one-year life and quarterly payments at the London Interbank Offered Rate (LIBOR). Using the term structure, we can determine that the swap has a fixed rate of 3.68 percent, leading to quarterly fixed payments of \$0.0092 per \$1 notional principal. We then can move forward 60 days into the life of the swap and, with a new term structure, we can determine that the swap's market value is \$0.0047 per \$1 notional principal. To the party that is long (i.e., paying fixed and receiving floating), the swap has a positive market value. To the counterparty, which pays floating and receives fixed, the claim has a market value of −\$0.0047.

As with a forward contract, the market value indicates the present value of the payments owed to the party minus the present value of the payments the party owes. Only 60 days into the life of a swap with quarterly payments, no payment is due for 30 more days. Thus there is no current credit risk. There is, however, potential credit risk. The market value of \$0.0047 represents the amount that is at risk of loss for default. Of course, if default occurs, it will be at a later date when the amount will probably be different. Moreover, the market value could reverse its sign. At this time, the amount owed by the short to the long is greater, but at a later date, the amount owed by the long to the short could be greater. As with forward contracts, if the party to which the value is negative defaults, the counterparty has a claim of that value. If the party to which the value is positive defaults, the defaulting party holds an asset with the positive market value. Also, the counterparty could default to someone else, thereby being forced to declare bankruptcy before a payment on this swap is due. In that case, the swap's market value at that time is either the claim of the creditor or the asset held by the bankrupt party in bankruptcy proceedings.

The credit risk of swaps can vary greatly across product types within this asset class and over a given swap's lifetime. For interest rate and equity swaps, the potential credit risk is largest during the middle period of the swap's life. During the beginning of a swap's life, typically we would assume that the credit risk is small because, presumably, the involved counterparties have performed sufficient current credit analysis on one another to be comfortable with the arrangement or otherwise they would not engage in the transaction. At the end of the life of the swap, the credit risk is diminished because most of the underlying risk has been amortized through the periodic payment process. There are fewer payments at the end of a swap than at any other time during its life; hence, the amount a party can lose because of a default is smaller. This leaves the greatest exposure during the middle period, a point at which (1) the credit profile of the counterparties may have changed for the worse and (2) the magnitude and frequency of expected payments between counterparties remain material. One exception to this pattern involves currency swaps, which often provide for the payment of the notional principal at the beginning and at the end of the life of the transaction. Because the notional principal tends to be a large amount relative to the payments, the potential for loss caused by the counterparty defaulting on the final notional principal payment is great. Thus, whereas interest rate swaps have their greatest credit risk midway during the life of the swap, currency swaps have their greatest credit risk between the midpoint and the end of the life of the swap.

5.6.4. The Credit Risk of Options

Forward contracts and swaps have bilateral default risk. Although only one party will end up making a given payment, each party could potentially be the party owing the net amount. Options, on the other hand, have unilateral credit risk. The buyer of an option pays a cash premium at the start and owes nothing more unless, under the buyer's sole discretion, he decides to exercise the option. Once the premium is paid, the seller assumes no credit risk from the buyer. Instead, credit risk accrues entirely to the buyer and can be quite significant. If the buyer exercises the option, the seller must meet certain terms embedded in the contract. If the option is a call, the seller must deliver the underlying or pay an equivalent cash settlement. If the option is a put, the seller must accept delivery of the underlying and pay for it or meet these obligations in the form of cash payments. If the seller fails to fulfill her end of the obligation, she is in default. Like forward contracts, European options have no payments due until expiration. Hence, they have no current credit risk until expiration, although significant potential credit risk exists.

Consider a European call option for which the underlying security has a price of 52.75 and a standard deviation of 0.35. The exercise price is 50, the risk-free rate is 4.88 percent continuously compounded, and the option expires in nine months. Using the Black–Scholes–Merton model, we find that the value of the option is 8.5580. The holder thus has potential credit risk represented by a present claim of 8.5580. This amount can be thought of as the amount that is at risk, even though at expiration the option will probably be worth a different amount. In fact, the option might even expire out of the money, in which case it would not matter if the short were bankrupt. If the short declares bankruptcy before expiration, the long has a claim on the value of the option under bankruptcy law.

If the option were American, the value could be greater. Moreover, with American options, current credit risk could arise if the option holder decides to exercise the option early. This alternative creates the possibility of the short defaulting before expiration.

EXAMPLE 9-8 Calculating Credit Risk Exposures

Calculate the amount at risk of a credit loss in the following situations:

1. A U.S. party goes long a forward contract on €1 denominated in dollars in which the underlying is the euro. The original term of the contract was two years, and the forward rate was \$0.90. The contract now has 18 months or 1.5 years to maturity. The spot or current exchange rate is \$0.862. The U.S. interest rate is 6 percent, and the euro interest rate is 5 percent. The interest rates are based on discrete compounding/discounting. At the point when the contract has 1.5 years remaining, the value of the contract to the long per \$1 notional principal equals the spot exchange rate, \$0.862, discounted at the international interest rate for 1.5 years, minus the forward rate, \$0.90, discounted at the domestic interest rate for 1.5 years:[48]

$$\frac{\$0.862}{(1.05)^{1.5}} - \frac{\$0.90}{(1.06)^{1.5}} = -\$0.0235$$

   Evaluate the credit risk characteristics of this situation.

2. Consider a plain vanilla interest rate swap with two months to go before the next payment. Six months after that, the swap will have its final payment. The swap fixed rate is 7 percent, and the upcoming floating payment is 6.9 percent. All payments are based on 30 days in a month and 360 days in a year. Two-month LIBOR is 7.250 percent, and eight-month LIBOR is 7.375 percent. The present value factors for two and eight months can be calculated as follows:

$$\frac{1}{1 + 0.0725(60/360)} = 0.9881$$

$$\frac{1}{1 + 0.07375(240/360)} = 0.9531$$

   The next floating payment will be $0.069(180/360) = 0.0345$. The present value of the floating payments (plus hypothetical notional principal) is $1.0345(0.9881) = 1.0222$. Given an annual rate of 7 percent, the fixed payments will be $0.07(180/360) = 0.035$. The present value of the fixed payments (plus hypothetical notional principal) is, therefore, $0.035(0.9881) + 1.035(0.9531) = 1.0210$.

[48]See Chance (2003, pp. 58–59).

Determine the amount at risk of a credit loss and state which party currently bears the risk. Assume a \$1 notional principal.

3. A dealer has sold a call option on a stock for \$35 to an investor. The option is currently worth \$46, as quoted in the market. Determine the amount at risk of a credit loss and state which party currently bears the risk.

Solution to Problem 1: The position has a negative value to the long, so the credit risk is currently borne by the short. From the short's point of view, the contract has a value of \$0.0235 per \$1 notional principal. No payments are due for 18 months, but the short's claim on the long is worth \$0.0235 more than the long's claim on the short. Therefore, this amount is the current value of the amount at risk for a credit loss. Of course, the amount could, and probably will, change over the life of the contract. The credit risk exposure might even shift to the other party.

Solution to Problem 2: The market value of the swap to the party paying fixed and receiving floating is $1.0222 - 1.0210 = 0.0012$. This value is positive to the party paying fixed and receiving floating; thus this party currently assumes the credit risk. Of course, the value will change over the life of the swap and may turn negative, meaning that the credit risk is then assumed by the party paying floating and receiving fixed.

Solution to Problem 3: All of the credit risk is borne by the investor (the owner of the call), because he will look to the dealer (the seller) for the payoff if the owner exercises the option. The current value of the amount at risk is the market price of \$46.

Derivatives' credit risk can be quite substantial, but this risk is considerably less than that faced by most lenders. When a lender makes a loan, the interest and principal are at risk. The loan principal corresponds closely to the notional principal of most derivative contracts. With the exception of currency swaps, the notional principal is never exchanged in a swap. Even with currency swaps, however, the risk is much smaller than on a loan. If a counterparty defaults on a currency swap, the amount owed to the defaulting counterparty serves as a type of collateral because the creditor is not required to pay it to the defaulting party. Therefore, the credit risk on derivative transactions tends to be quite small relative to that on loans. On forward and swap transactions, the netting of payments makes the risk extremely small relative to the notional principal and to the credit risk on a bond or loan of equivalent principal.

5.7. Liquidity Risk

One of the implicit assumptions in risk management with VaR is that positions can be liquidated when they approach or move outside pre-agreed risk limits. In practice, some assets are far more liquid than others and practitioners will often liquidity-adjust VaR estimates accordingly. Wide bid–ask spreads in proportion to price are an obvious measure of the cost of trading an illiquid instrument or underlying security. But some instruments simply trade very infrequently at any price—a far more complex problem, because infrequently quoted prices often give the statistical illusion of low or lower volatility. This dynamic is counterintuitive, because we would expect instruments that are illiquid to have a higher bid–ask spread and higher volatilities.

A famous case of underestimating liquidity risk is the failure of the hedge fund Long-Term Capital Management (LTCM) in 1998. LTCM was set up by a group of bond traders and academics and was engaged in arbitrage or relative value trading on world fixed-income markets through the use of the swap market. The total equity in the fund peaked at around $5 billion, but this amount was leveraged around 25 times (perhaps substantially more when the full impact of derivatives is considered). The BIS estimated that the notional value of the swaps entered into by LTCM was around 2.4 percent of the entire world swap market. LTCM failed to appreciate the market moves that would occur when it attempted to liquidate positions, particularly those in illiquid, emerging, fixed-income markets. The New York Federal Reserve was forced to act for fear of a global financial crisis and organized a consortium of 14 international banks to manage the assets of the fund. In the end, and after substantial financial help, LTCM's investors lost more than 90 percent of their equity.

5.8. Measuring Nonfinancial Risks

Nonfinancial risks are intrinsically very difficult to measure. Indeed, some of the nonfinancial exposures we have discussed, such as regulatory risk, tax risk, legal risk, and accounting risk, could easily be thought of as not measurable in any precise mathematical way. They are unlike market risk and the VaR concept because we usually lack an observable distribution of losses related to these factors.

Some of these risks could be thought of as more suitable for insurance than measurement and hedging. Like a flood that occurs every 50 years, they might well affect a large number of instruments or contracts. Here, it is possible to learn from best practice in the insurance industry. Insurance companies usually have sufficient assets and are capitalized to withstand these uncertain events. Where it is possible to model a source of risk, actuaries often use techniques like extreme value theory, but even these techniques are only as good as the historical data on which they are based.

5.8.1. Operational Risk

Until a few years ago, the subject of operational risk received little attention, and ideas about actually measuring operational risk were practically unheard of. But a number of well-publicized losses at financial institutions, ranging from a breakdown of internal systems to rogue employees and in some cases employee theft, have put operational risk justifiably into the forefront.

Furthermore, the explicit mention of operational risk requirements in the Basel II banking regulations has created real advantages for banks that can credibly measure their operational risks. This, in turn, has led to an explosion in the academic literature relating to the measurement of operational risk and its role in enterprise risk systems.

EXAMPLE 9-9 Basel II—A Brief Overview

The Basel banking regulations apply only to large international banks, but national governments use them as a guideline in formulating their own financial laws and regulations, so the regulations have much more widespread importance. In January 2001, the Basel Committee on Banking Supervision issued a proposal for a New Basel Capital Accord that would replace the 1988 Capital Accord. This first accord, "Basel I," was widely criticized for being too inflexible in applying an across-the-board 8 percent capital adequacy ratio that made no discrimination between a well risk-managed bank and one that was not.[49]

The Basel II proposal incorporates three mutually reinforcing pillars that allow banks and supervisors to evaluate properly the various risks that banks face:

- Pillar 1: Capital Requirements
- Pillar 2: Supervisory Review
- Pillar 3: Market Discipline

The first pillar of Basel II moves away from a blanket, one-size-fits-all approach and allows banks to develop their own mathematically based financial models. Once these internally developed techniques have been successfully demonstrated to the regulators, banks are able to progress to higher levels of risk management that within the accord are offset by reduced regulatory capital charges. Key to these higher levels of risk management are advanced systems for managing credit risk and operational risk.

The second pillar, supervisory review, requires banks to meet Basel-recommended operational risk requirements that have been tailored by their host country. "Risky" banks, whose risk management systems score lowly in the areas of market risk and operational risk, face penalties. Better-risk-managed banks will have major competitive advantages over rivals, in that, all else equal, they are likely to be subject to reduced capital requirements per unit of risk.

The third pillar says that banks must fulfill the Basel requirements for transparency and disclosing company data. A key point here is that banks must reveal more detail about their profits and losses, which may lead to a supervisory authority reviewing risk systems and changing the capital allocation under the first pillar.

6. MANAGING RISK

Having established methods for the identification and measurement of risk, we turn our attention to a critical stage of any solid risk management program: that of *managing* risk. The key components, which by now should be somewhat intuitive to you, are as follows:

- An effective risk governance model, which places overall responsibility at the senior management level, allocates resources effectively and features the appropriate separation of tasks between revenue generators and those on the control side of the business.
- Appropriate systems and technology to combine information analysis in such a way as to provide timely and accurate risk information to decision makers.
- Sufficient and suitably trained personnel to evaluate risk information and articulate it to those who need this information for the purposes of decision making.

[49] A **capital adequacy ratio** is a measure of the adequacy of capital in relation to assets. The purpose of capital is to absorb unanticipated losses with sufficient margin to permit the entity to continue as a going concern. Basel I specified a capital adequacy ratio as a percent of the credit-risk-weighted assets on the bank's balance sheet, where bank assets were divided into four broad categories. For more details, see Saunders and Cornett (2003).

A recent advertisement for the RiskMetrics Group (www.riskmetrics.com) identified the following nine principles of effective risk management:

1. *There is no return without risk.* Rewards go to those who take risks.
2. *Be transparent.* Risk should be fully understood.
3. *Seek experience.* Risk is measured and managed by people, not mathematical models.
4. *Know what you don't know.* Question the assumptions you make.
5. *Communicate.* Risk should be discussed openly.
6. *Diversify.* Multiple risks will produce more consistent rewards.
7. *Show discipline.* A consistent and rigorous approach will beat a constantly changing strategy.
8. *Use common sense.* It is better to be approximately right than to be precisely wrong.
9. *Return is only half the equation.* Decisions should be made only by considering the risk and return of the possibilities.

Risk management is in so many ways just good common business sense. It is quite remarkable, however, that commonsense rules are violated so easily and so often. But that problem is not unique to risk management.

Currently, two professional organizations are devoted to risk management. The Global Association of Risk Professionals (GARP) and the Professional Risk Managers' International Association (PRMIA) are actively involved in promoting knowledge in the field of risk management. You may wish to visit their web sites at www.garp.com and www.prmia.org.

With these principles in mind, in the following section, we will discuss the various components of a well-adapted risk-control program.

6.1. Managing Market Risk

Let us assume we have correctly identified the sources of market risk that affect our business. Further assume that we have decided on an appropriate way to measure market risk and successfully deployed the systems we need to monitor our positions and measure our risk in a timely way. The result is an appropriate firmwide VaR estimate and associated breakdown by business area. Now we must ask ourselves the following questions: How do we know how much risk is acceptable for us to take? What is the overall exposure assumption capacity for the enterprise, and how close to full capacity should we run? We already know that VaR is not a measure of the maximum possible loss but only a probabilistic guide to the minimum loss we might expect with a certain frequency over a certain time frame.

Our **enterprise risk management** system will be incomplete without a well-thought-out approach to setting appropriate **risk tolerance** levels and identifying the proper corrective behavior to take if our actual risks turn out to be significantly higher or lower than is consistent with our risk tolerance. Note here that in many circumstances, it could cause as many problems to take too little risk as to take too much risk. As we noted at the beginning of this chapter, companies are in business to take risk and taking too little risk will more than likely reduce the possible rewards; it could even make the company vulnerable to takeover. In a more extreme scenario, insufficient risk taking may lead to situations in which the expected return stands little chance of covering variable (let alone fixed) costs.

Corrective behavior in the case of excessive market risk will almost always result in the need for additional hedging or the scaling back of tradable positions. Quite often, however, liquidity and other factors will prevent perfect hedging, perhaps exacerbating risk concerns rather than mitigating them.

6.1.1. Risk Budgeting In recent years, companies and portfolio managers have begun to implement a new approach to risk management called **risk budgeting.** It focuses on questions such as, "Where do we want to take risk?" and "What is the efficient allocation of risk across various units of an organization or investment opportunities?" Risk budgeting is relevant in both an organizational and a portfolio management context.

To take an organizational perspective first, risk budgeting involves establishing objectives for individuals, groups, or divisions of an organization that take into account the allocation of an acceptable level of risk. As an example, the foreign exchange (FX) trading desk of a bank could be allocated capital of €100 million and permitted a daily VaR of €5 million. In other words, the desk is granted a budget, expressed in terms of allocated capital and an acceptable level of risk, expressed in euro amounts of VaR. In variations on this theme, instead of using VaR units an organization might allocate risk based on individual transaction size, the amount of working capital needed to support the portfolio, or the amount of losses acceptable for any given time period (e.g., one month). In any case, the innovation here is that the enterprise allocates risk capital before the fact in order to provide guidance on the acceptable amount of risky activities that a given unit can undertake.

A well-run risk-taking enterprise manages these limits carefully and constantly monitors their implementation. Any excesses are reported to management immediately for corrective action. Under this type of regime, management can compare the profits generated by each unit with the amount of capital and risk employed. So, to continue our example from above, say the FX trading desk made a quarterly profit of €20 million from its allocation. The bank's fixed-income trading desk was allocated capital of €200 million and permitted a daily VaR of €5 million; the fixed-income trading desk made €25 million in quarterly trading profits. We note that the allocated daily VaRs for the two business areas are the same, so each area has the same risk budget, and that the fixed-income desk generated better returns on the VaR allocation, but worse on the allocation of actual capital, than did the FX desk. (The FX desk shows a €20/€100 = 20% return on capital versus €25/€200 = 12.5% for the fixed-income desk.) This type of scenario is quite common and highlights the complexities of the interaction between risk management and capital allocation. Risk and capital are finite resources that must be allocated carefully.

The sum of risk budgets for individual units will typically exceed the risk budget for the organization as a whole because of the impacts of diversification. Returning to our example, let us assume that for the enterprise in question, its FX and bond trading desks engage in activities that are only weakly correlated. In this case, our present allocation of capital and risk might make perfect sense. For example, the daily VaR of the two business areas combined might be €7 million (i.e., 70 percent of the combined risk allocation for the two desks), for which we again generate a total quarterly profit of €20 million + €25 million = €45 million.

Alternatively, say the two business areas are very highly correlated (their correlation coefficient equals 1) and their combined daily VaR is €5 million + €5 million = €10 million (i.e., 100 percent of the aggregate VaR allocation across desks). The combined profit is still €20 million + €25 million = €45 million. Under these circumstances—and particularly if the bank's management believes that the correlations will remain strong—management might consider closing down the fixed-income desk to generate 0.20(€100 million + €200 million) = €60 million of returns on the (€2 million) (€5 million) = €10 million of VaR. Contrast this strategy with that of closing down the foreign exchange trading desk and allocating all of the capital and risk to the bond trading desk, which would produce 0.125(€200 million + €100 million) = €37.5 million in profit for the €10 million in VaR, representing a lower return on both capital and VaR.

A risk-budgeting perspective has also been applied to allocating funds to portfolio managers. Consider an active investor who wants to allocate funds optimally to several domestic and nondomestic equity and fixed-income investment managers. Such an investor might focus on tracking risk as the primary risk measure and decide on an overall maximum acceptable level for it, such as 200 basis points. The expected information ratio (IR) for each manager is one possible measure of each manager's ability to add value, considering the managers in isolation.[50] In this application, however, it is appropriate for the investor to adjust each manager's IR to eliminate the effect of asset class correlations; such correlation-adjusted IRs will capture each manager's incremental ability to add value in a portfolio context. Using such correlation-adjusted IRs, we can determine the optimal tracking risk allocation for each investment manager (which, intuitively, is positively related to his correlation-adjusted IR).[51]

Through these two examples, we edge toward some understanding of risk-adjusted performance measures, which we will discuss in greater detail later in the chapter. The point about risk budgeting is that it is a comprehensive methodology that empowers management to allocate capital and risk in an optimal way to the most profitable areas of a business, taking account of the correlation of returns in those business areas.

It once again bears mention that for many portfolio managers, risk budget allocations should be measured in relation to risk to the surplus—that is, the difference between the values of assets and liabilities.

EXAMPLE 9-10 A Fund Management Company and Risk Budgeting

We can readily illustrate the methodology and underlying economics of risk budgeting with the example of a fund management company. We choose, for this example, a multistrategy hedge fund, because although mutual funds and other types of institutional money managers certainly face similar risk management issues, they are often bound by strict guidelines that tie their risk budgeting to factors such as the performance of a benchmark index and other mandated fund management protocols. For example, the Vanguard family of mutual funds offers a wide range of indexed mutual funds. These funds' associated risk budgets are very narrowly defined, as the managers are called on at all times to track the underlying index very closely in terms of securities held, associated portfolio weightings, and so forth. As investor funds flow in and out of these securities, portfolio managers execute trades that do little more than reestablish this replication balance. Of course, many institutional fund products allow for much broader deviations from market benchmarks; in most cases, however, risk budgeting will be constrained by certain principles associated with benchmarking.

Hedge funds with multiple portfolio managers (as well as, in some cases, the proprietary trading divisions of banks and broker/dealers) have many fewer risk constraints than indexed mutual funds; they have more freedom, therefore, in establishing risk

[50]The information ratio is active return divided by active risk; it measures active return per unit of active risk.

[51]See Waring, Whitney, Pirone, and Castile (2000) and references therein for further reading.

budgets. Because of the absolute return (as opposed to benchmark-driven) nature of their performance, and because of issues such as performance netting risk covered earlier in this chapter, it is very much in their interest to ensure that each portfolio in the enterprise operates within a well-conceived risk budget framework. Included among the critical components of such a program might be the following:

- **Performance stopouts.** A performance stopout is the maximum amount that a given portfolio is allowed to lose in a period (e.g., a month or a year).
- **Working capital allocations.** Most funds will allocate a specific amount of working capital to each portfolio manager, both as a means of enforcing risk disciplines and also to ensure the ability to fund all operations.
- **VaR limits.** Discussed above.
- **Scenario analysis limits.** The risk manager of the fund company may establish risk limits based on the scenario analysis discussed in the preceding section. Under such an approach, the portfolio manager would be compelled to construct a portfolio such that under specified scenarios, it did not produce losses greater than certain predetermined amounts.
- **Risk factor limits.** Portfolio managers may be subject to limits on individual risk factors, as generated by a VaR analysis (e.g., VaR exposure to a certain risk cannot exceed, say, $X or X percent) or driven by linear (e.g., duration, beta) or nonlinear (e.g., convexity, gamma) risk estimation methodologies.
- **Position concentration limits.** Many risk managers seek to enforce diversification by mandating a specific maximum amount for individual positions.
- **Leverage limits.** A maximum amount of leverage in the portfolio may be specified.
- **Liquidity limits.** To help manage liquidity exposure, large funds will often also set position limits as a specified maximum percentage of daily volume, float, or open interest.

Of course, other types of limits are imposed on portfolio managers in a multistrategy environment, and by the same token, the risk-budgeting strategy of a given enterprise may include only a subset of the examples provided immediately above. Nevertheless, some subset of these limit structures is present in nearly every multistrategy fund vehicle, and it is difficult to imagine an effective risk control system that does not set limits.

6.2. Managing Credit Risk

It is important that creditors do a good job of measuring and controlling credit risk. Estimating default probabilities is difficult because of the infrequency of losses for many situations where credit risk exists. Moreover, credit losses differ considerably from losses resulting from market moves. Credit is a one-sided risk. If Party B owes Party A the amount of £1,000, B will end up paying A either £1,000 or some amount ranging from zero to £1,000. A's rate of return is certainly not normally distributed and not even symmetric. All of the risk is downside. Thus credit risk is not easily analyzed or controlled using such measures as standard deviation and VaR. Creditors need to regularly monitor the financial condition of borrowers and counterparties. In addition, they can use the risk management techniques for credit discussed next.

6.2.1. Reducing Credit Risk by Limiting Exposure Limiting the amount of exposure to a given party is the primary means of managing credit risk. Just as a bank will not lend too much money to one entity, neither will a party engage in too many derivatives transactions with one counterparty. Exactly how much exposure to a given counterparty is "too much" is still not easy to quantify. Experienced risk managers often have a good sense of when and where to limit their exposure, and they make extensive use of quantitative credit exposure measures to guide them in this process. Banks have regulatory constraints on the amount of credit risk they can assume, which are specified in terms of formulas.

6.2.2. Reducing Credit Risk by Marking to Market One device that the futures market uses to control credit risk is marking tradable positions to market. The OTC derivatives market also uses marking to market to deal with credit risk: Some OTC contracts are marked to market periodically during their lives. Recall that a forward contract or swap has a market value that is positive to one party and negative to another. When a contract calls for marking to market, the party for which the value is negative pays the market value to the party for which the value is positive. Then the fixed rate on the contract is recalculated, taking into account the new spot price, interest rate, and time to expiration.

Recall that we examined a one-year forward contract with an initial forward price of \$105. Three months later, when the asset price was \$102, its value was \$0.7728 to the long. If the contract were marked to market at that time, the short would pay the long \$0.7728. Then, the two parties would enter into a new contract expiring in nine months with a new forward price, which would be $\$102(1.05)^{0.75} = \$105.80$.

EXAMPLE 9-11 Repricing a Forward Contract

Consider a one-year forward contract established at a rate of \$105. The contract is four months into its life. The spot price is \$108, the risk-free rate is 4.25 percent, and the underlying makes no cash payments. The two parties decided at the start that they will mark the contract to market every four months. The market value of the contract is $\$108 - \$105/(1.0425)^{8/12} = \$5.873$. Determine how the cash flows and resets would work under these circumstances.

Solution: The contract is positive to the long, so the short pays the long \$5.873. The parties then reprice the contract. The new price is $\$108(1.0425)^{8/12} = \$111.04$. At this point, the forward price is reset to \$111.04. The parties will then mark to market again at the eight-month point and reset the forward price. This price will then stay in force until expiration.

OTC options usually are not marked to market because their value is always positive to one side of the transaction. Of course, one party of the option certainly bears credit risk, but marking to market is usually done only with contracts with two-way credit risk. Option credit risk is normally handled by collateral.

6.2.3. Reducing Credit Risk with Collateral The posting of collateral is a widely accepted credit exposure mitigant in both lending and derivatives transactions. One very prominent example of its use comes from futures markets, which require that all market participants post margin collateral. Beyond this, many OTC derivative markets have collateral posting provisions, with the collateral usually taking the form of cash or highly liquid, low-risk securities. A typical arrangement involves the routine, periodic posting of values sufficient to cover mark-to-market deficiencies. To illustrate, if a given derivatives contract has a positive value to Party A and a negative value to Party B, then Party B owes more than Party A, and Party B must put collateral into an account designated for this purpose. As the contract's market value changes, the amount of collateral that must be maintained will vary, increasing as the market value increases and vice versa. At some point, if the market value of the transaction changes sign (i.e., goes from positive to negative for one of the participants), the collateral position will typically reverse itself, with the entity previously posting collateral seeing a release of these assets and the other participant in the transaction experiencing a collateral obligation. In addition to market values, collateral requirements are sometimes also based on factors such as participants' credit ratings.

6.2.4. Reducing Credit Risk with Netting One of the most common features used in two-way contracts with a credit risk component, such as forwards and swaps, is netting. This process, which we have already briefly discussed, involves the reduction of all obligations owed between counterparties into a single cash transaction that eliminates these liabilities. For example, if a payment is due and Party A owes more to Party B than B owes to A, the difference between the amounts owed is calculated and Party A pays the net amount owed. This procedure, called **payment netting,** reduces the credit risk by reducing the amount of money that must be paid. If Party A owes €100,000 to Party B, which owes €40,000 to A, then the net amount owed is €60,000, which A owes to B. Without netting, B would need to send €40,000 to A, which would send €100,000 to B. Suppose B was in the process of sending its €40,000 to A but was unaware that A was in default and unable to send the €100,000 to B. If the €40,000 is received by A, B might be unable to get it back until the bankruptcy court decides what to do, which could take years. Using netting, only the €60,000 owed by A to B is at risk.

In the examples we have seen so far, netting is applied on the payment date. The concept of netting can be extended to the events and conditions surrounding a bankruptcy. Suppose A and B are counterparties to a number of derivative contracts. On some of the contracts, the market value to A is positive, while on others, the market value to B is positive. If A declares bankruptcy, the parties can use netting to solve a number of problems. If A and B agree to do so before the bankruptcy, they can net the market values of *all* of their derivative contracts to determine one overall value owed by one party to another. It could well be the case that even though A is bankrupt, B might owe more to A than A owes to B. Then, rather than B being a creditor to A, A's claim on B becomes one of A's remaining assets. This process is referred to as **closeout netting.**

During this bankruptcy process, netting plays an important role in reducing a practice known in the financial services industry as cherry picking, which in this case would involve a bankrupt company attempting to enforce contracts that are favorable to it while walking away from those that are unprofitable. In our example, without netting, A could default on the contracts in which it owes more to B than B owes to A, but B could be forced to pay up on those contracts in which it owes more to A than A owes to B.

To be supported through the bankruptcy process, however, netting must be recognized by the legal system and works best when each party's rights and obligations are specified at the time before or contemporaneous to the executions of transactions. Most, but not all, legal jurisdictions recognize netting.

6.2.5. Reducing Credit Risk with Minimum Credit Standards and Enhanced Derivative Product Companies As noted above, the first line of defense against credit risk is limiting the amount of business one party engages in with another. An important and related concept is to ensure that all credit-based business is undertaken with entities that have adequate levels of credit quality. The historical standard measures for such credit quality come from rating agencies such as Moody's Investors Service and Standard & Poor's. Some companies will not do business with an enterprise unless its rating from these agencies meets a prescribed level of credit quality. This practice can pose a problem for some derivatives dealers, most of which engage in other lines of business that expose them to a variety of other risks; for example, banks are the most common derivatives dealers. To an end user considering engaging in a derivative contract with a dealer, the potential for the dealer's other business to cause the dealer to default is a serious concern. Banks, in particular, are involved in consumer and commercial lending, which can be quite risky. In the United States, for example, we have seen banking crises involving bad loans to the real estate industry and underdeveloped countries.

The possibility that bad loans will cause a bank to default on its derivatives transactions is quite real, and credit ratings often reflect this possibility. In turn, ratings are a major determinant in business flows for banks that act as dealers. Hence, many derivatives dealers have taken action to control their exposure to rating downgrades. One such action is the formation of a type of subsidiary that is separate from the dealer's other activities. These subsidiaries are referred to as **enhanced derivatives products companies** (EDPCs), sometimes known as **special purpose vehicles** (SPVs). These companies are usually completely separate from the parent organization and are not liable for the parent's debts. They tend to be very heavily capitalized and are committed to hedging all of their derivatives positions. As a result of these features, these subsidiaries almost always receive the highest credit quality rating by the rating agencies. In the event that the parent goes bankrupt, the EDPC is not liable for the parent company's debts; if the EDPC goes under, however, the parent is liable for an amount up to its equity investment and may find it necessary to provide even more protection. Hence, an EDPC would typically have a higher credit rating than its parent. In fact, it is precisely for the purpose of obtaining the highest credit rating, and thus the most favorable financing terms with counterparties, that banks and broker dealers go through the expense of putting together EDPCs.

6.2.6. Transferring Credit Risk with Credit Derivatives Another mechanism for managing credit risk is to transfer it to another party. Credit derivatives provide mechanisms for such transfers. Credit derivatives include such contracts as credit default swaps, total return swaps, credit spread options, and credit spread forwards. These transactions are typically customized, although the wording of contract provisions is often standardized. In a **credit default swap,** the protection buyer pays the protection seller in return for the right to receive a payment from the seller in the event of a specified credit event. In a **total return swap,** the protection buyer pays the total return on a reference obligation (or basket of reference obligations) in return for floating-rate payments. If the reference obligation has a credit event, the total return on the reference obligation should fall; the total return should also fall in the event of an increase in interest rates, so the protection seller (total return receiver) in this contract is actually exposed to both credit risk and interest rate risk. A **credit spread option** is an option on the yield spread of a reference obligation and over a referenced benchmark (such as the yield on a specific default-free security of the same maturity); by contrast, a **credit spread forward** is a forward contract on a yield spread. Credit derivatives may be used not only to eliminate credit risk but also to assume credit risk. For example, an investor may be well positioned to assume a credit risk because it is uncorrelated with other credit risks in her portfolio.[52]

6.3. Performance Evaluation

In order to maximize risk-adjusted return through the capital allocation process, we must measure performance against risks assumed and budgeted at both the business unit or substrategy level and enterprise or overall portfolio level. All business activities should be evaluated against the risk taken, and a considerable body of knowledge has developed concerning the evaluation of investment performance from a risk-adjusted perspective. Traditional approaches, which take into account return against a risk penalty, are now used in other areas of business activity besides portfolio management. Some banks and service providers have developed sophisticated performance evaluation systems that account for risk, and they have marketed these systems successfully to clients. Risk-adjusted performance, as measured against sensible benchmarks, is a critically important capital allocation tool because it allows for the comparison of results in terms of homogenous units of exposure assumption. Absent these measurement tools, market participants with high risk profiles are likely to be given higher marks for positive performance than they arguably deserve because they derive more from increased exposure assumption than they do from superior portfolio management methodologies. Furthermore, most investment professionals are compensated on the basis of the performance of their portfolios, trading positions, or investment ideas, and it is appropriate to judge performance in risk-adjusted terms.

Following is a list of standard methodologies for expressing return in units of exposure assumption:

- **Sharpe ratio.** The seminal measure for risk-adjusted return, the Sharpe Ratio has become the industry standard. The traditional definition of this measure is as follows:[53]

$$\text{Sharpe ratio} = \frac{\text{Mean portfolio return} - \text{Risk-free rate}}{\text{Standard deviation of portfolio return}}$$

  The basic idea, therefore, is entirely intuitive: The Sharpe ratio is the mean return earned in excess of the risk-free rate per unit of volatility or total risk. By subtracting a risk-free rate from the mean return, we can isolate the performance associated with risk-taking activities. One elegant outcome of the calculation is that a portfolio engaging in "zero risk" investment, such as the purchase of Treasury bills for which the expected return is precisely the risk-free rate, earns a Sharpe ratio of exactly zero.

[52] For more information on credit derivatives, see Fabozzi (2004b, Chapter 9), and Chance (2003, Chapter 9).

[53] This traditional definition of the Sharpe ratio can be directly linked to the capital market line and related capital market theory concepts (see Elton, Gruber, Brown, and Goetzmann, 2003). Sharpe (1994), however, defines the Sharpe ratio as a general construct using the mean excess return in relation to a benchmark in the numerator and the standard deviation of returns in excess of the benchmark in the denominator (see the discussion of the information ratio in this book's chapter on evaluating portfolio performance for an illustration of this usage). Using the risk-free rate as the benchmark, the numerator would be as given in the text but the denominator would be the standard deviation of returns in excess of the risk-free rate (which, in practice, would infrequently result in significant discrepancies).

The Sharpe ratio calculation is the most widely used method for calculating risk-adjusted return. Nevertheless, it can be inaccurate when applied to portfolios with significant nonlinear risks, such as options positions. In part for these reasons, alternative risk-adjusted return methodologies have emerged over the years, including the following.

- **Risk-adjusted return on capital (RAROC).** This concept divides the expected return on an investment by a measure of **capital at risk,** a measure of the investment's risk that can take a number of different forms and can be calculated in a variety of ways that may have proprietary features. The company may require that an investment's expected RAROC exceed a RAROC benchmark level for capital to be allocated to it.[54]
- **Return over maximum drawdown (RoMAD).** Drawdown, in the field of hedge fund management, is defined as the difference between a portfolio's maximum point of return (known in industry parlance as its "high-water" mark), and any subsequent low point of performance. *Maximum* drawdown is the largest difference between a high-water and a subsequent low. Maximum drawdown is a preferred way of expressing the risk of a given portfolio—particularly as associated track records become longer—for investors who believe that observed loss patterns over longer periods of time are the best available proxy for actual exposure.

  Return over maximum drawdown is simply the average return in a given year that a portfolio generates, expressed as a percentage of this drawdown figure. It enables investors to ask the following question: Am I willing to accept an occasional drawdown of X percent in order to generate an average return of Y percent? An investment with $X = 10$ percent and $Y = 15$ percent (RoMAD = 1.5) would be more attractive than an investment with $X = 40$ percent and $Y = 10$ percent (RoMAD = 0.25).
- **Sortino ratio.** One school of thought concerning the measurement of risk-adjusted returns argues, with some justification, that portfolio managers should not be penalized for volatility deriving from outsized positive performance. The Sortino ratio adopts this perspective. The numerator of the Sortino ratio is the return in excess of the investor's minimum acceptable return (MAR). The denominator is the downside deviation using the MAR as the target return.[55] **Downside deviation** computes volatility using only rate of return data points below the MAR. Thus the expression for the Sortino ratio is

  $$\text{Sortino ratio} = (\text{Mean portfolio return} - \text{MAR})/\text{Downside deviation}$$

  If the MAR is set at the risk-free rate, the Sortino ratio is identical to the Sharpe ratio, save for the fact that it uses downside deviation instead of the standard deviation in the denominator. A side-by-side comparison of rankings of portfolios according to the Sharpe and Sortino ratios can provide a sense of whether outperformance may be affecting assessments of risk-adjusted performance. Taken together, the two ratios can tell a more detailed story of risk-adjusted return than either will in isolation, but the Sharpe ratio is better grounded in financial theory and analytically more tractable. Furthermore, departures from normality of returns can raise issues for the Sortino ratio as much as for the Sharpe ratio.

These approaches are only a subset of the methodologies available to investors wishing to calculate risk-adjusted returns. Each approach has both its merits and its drawbacks. Perhaps

[54] For more information on RAROC, see Saunders and Cornett (2003).

[55] Downside deviation, the term usually used in presenting the Sortino ratio, could also be called a target semideviation (using MAR as the target).

the most important lesson to bear in mind with respect to this mosaic is the critical need to understand the inputs to any method, so as to be able to interpret the results knowledgeably, with an understanding of their possible limitations.

6.4. Capital Allocation

In addition to its unquestionable value in the task of capital preservation, risk management has become a vital, if not central, component in the process of allocating capital across units of a risk-taking enterprise. The use of inputs, such as volatility/correlation analysis, risk-adjusted return calculations, scenario analysis, etc., provides the allocators of risk capital with a much more informed means of arriving at the appropriate conclusions on how best to distribute this scarce resource. The risk management inputs to the process can be used in formal, mathematical, "optimization" routines, under which enterprises input performance data into statistical programs that will then offer appropriate capital allocation combinations to make efficient use of risk. Quantitative output may simply serve as background data for qualitative decision-making processes. One way or another, however, risk management has become a vital input into the capital allocation process, and it is fair to describe this development as positive from a systemic perspective.

As part of the task of allocating capital across business units, organizations must determine how to measure such capital. Here there are multiple methodologies, and we will discuss five of them in further detail:

1. *Nominal, notional, or monetary position limits.* Under this approach, the enterprise simply defines the amount of capital that the individual portfolio or business unit can use in a specified activity, based on the actual amount of money exposed in the markets. It has the advantage of being easy to understand, and, in addition, it lends itself very nicely to the critical task of calculating a percentage-based return on capital allocated. Such limits, however, may not capture effectively the effects of correlation and offsetting risks. Furthermore, an individual may be able to work around a nominal position using other assets that can replicate a given position. For these reasons, although it is often useful to establish notional position limits, it is seldom a *sufficient* capital allocation method from a risk control perspective.
2. *VaR-based position limits.* As an alternative or supplement to notional limits, enterprises often assign a VaR limit as a proxy for allocated capital. This approach has a number of distinct advantages, most notably the fact that it allocates capital in units of estimated exposure and thus acts in greater harmony with the risk control process. This approach has potential problems as well, however. Most notably, the limit regime will be only as effective as the VaR calculation itself; when VaR is cumbersome, less than completely accurate, not well understood by traders, or some combination of the above, it is difficult to imagine it providing rational results from a capital allocation perspective. In addition, the relation between overall VaR and the VaRs of individual positions is complex and can be counterintuitive.[56] Nevertheless, VaR limits probably have an important place in any effective capital allocation scheme.

[56]For example, one cannot add the VaR of individual positions to obtain a conservative measure (i.e., maximum) of overall VaR because it is possible for the sum of the VaRs to be greater than the VaR of the combined positions.

3. *Maximum loss limits.* Irrespective of other types of limit regimes that it might have in place, it is crucial for any risk-taking enterprise to establish a maximum loss limit for each of its risk-taking units. In order to be effective, this figure must be large enough to enable the unit to achieve performance objectives but small enough to be consistent with the preservation of capital. This limit must represent a firm constraint on risk-taking activity. Nevertheless, even when risk-taking activity is generally in line with policy, management should recognize that extreme market discontinuities can cause such limits to be breached.
4. *Internal capital requirements.* Internal capital requirements specify the level of capital that management believes to be appropriate for the firm. Some regulated financial institutions, such as banks and securities firms, typically also have regulatory capital requirements that, if they are higher, overrule internal requirements. Traditionally, internal capital requirements have been specified heuristically in terms of the capital ratio (the ratio of capital to assets). Modern tools permit a more rigorous approach. If the value of assets declines by an amount that exceeds the value of capital, the firm will be insolvent. Say a 0.01 probability of insolvency over a one-year horizon is acceptable. By requiring capital to equal at least one-year aggregate VaR at the 1 percent probability level, the capital should be adequate in terms of the firm's risk tolerance. If the company can assume a normal return distribution, the required amount of capital can be stated in standard deviation units (e.g., 1.96 standard deviations would reflect a 0.025 probability of insolvency). A capital requirement based on aggregate VaR has an advantage over regulatory capital requirements in that it takes account of correlations. Furthermore, to account for extraordinary shocks, we can stress test the VaR-based recommendation.
5. *Regulatory capital requirements.* In addition, many institutions (e.g., securities firms and banks) must calculate and meet regulatory capital requirements. Wherever and whenever this is the case, it of course makes sense to allocate this responsibility to business units. Meeting regulatory capital requirements can be a difficult process, among other reasons because such requirements are sometimes inconsistent with rational capital allocation schemes that have capital preservation as a primary objective. Nevertheless, when regulations demand it, firms must include regulatory capital as part of their overall allocation process.

Depending on such factors as the type of enterprise, its corporate culture, fiduciary obligations, etc., the most effective approach to capital allocation probably involves a combination of most, if not all, of the above methodologies. The trick, of course, is to combine the appropriate ones in a rational and consistent manner that creates the proper incentives for balance between the dual objectives of profit maximization and capital preservation.

6.5. Psychological and Behavioral Considerations

Over the past several years, a body of research has emerged that seeks to model the behavioral aspects of portfolio management. This concept has important implications for risk management for two reasons. First, risk takers may behave differently at different points in the portfolio management cycle, depending on such factors as their recent performance, the risk characteristics of their portfolios, and market conditions. Second, and on a related note, risk management would improve if these dynamics could be modeled.

Although the topic merits more discussion than we can possibly include in this context, the main factor to consider from a risk management perspective is the importance of establishing a risk governance framework that anticipates the points in a cycle when the incentives of risk takers diverge from those of risk capital allocators. One prominent example (although by no means the only one) occurs when portfolio managers who are paid a percentage of their profits in a given year fall into a negative performance situation. The trader's situation does not deteriorate from a compensation perspective with incremental losses at this point (i.e., the trader is paid zero, no matter how much he loses), but of course the organization as a whole suffers from the trader's loss. Moreover, the risks at the enterprise level can be nonlinear under these circumstances because of concepts of netting risk covered earlier in this chapter. These and other behavioral issues can be handled best by risk control and governance processes that contemplate them. One such example is limit setting, which can, with some thought, easily incorporate many of these issues.[57]

[57]Those interested in studying these topics further may wish to refer to Grant (2004) and Kiev (2002).

CHAPTER 10

EXECUTION OF PORTFOLIO DECISIONS

Ananth Madhavan
Barclays Global Investors
San Francisco, California

Jack L. Treynor
Treynor Capital Management, Inc.
Palos Verdes Estates, California

Wayne H. Wagner
Plexus Group, Inc.
Los Angeles, California

1. INTRODUCTION

The investment process has been described as a three-legged stool supported equally by securities research, portfolio management, and securities trading. Of the three, trading is often the least understood and least appreciated function. As we will show, a deeper appreciation for the trading function can be a powerful help in achieving investment success.

In this chapter, we will build the knowledge and explain the concepts needed to understand how managers and traders interact with markets, choose trading strategies and tactics, and measure their success in trading. Our perspective is chiefly that of a portfolio manager (or investment adviser) whose objective is to execute portfolio decisions in the best interests of the client. The portfolio manager's agents in doing so are the firm's traders. These **buy-side traders** are the professional traders employed by investment managers or institutional investors who place the trades that execute the decisions of portfolio managers. The job of such traders is to execute the desired trades quickly, without error, and at favorable prices. Execution is the final, critical step in the interlinked investment process: *The portfolio decision is not complete until securities are bought or sold.*

A portfolio manager is not a professional trader. However, a portfolio manager does need to:

- Communicate effectively with professional traders.
- Evaluate the quality of the execution services being provided for the firm's clients.
- Take responsibility for achieving best execution on behalf of clients in his or her role as a fiduciary.

To accomplish those goals, the portfolio manager needs a grounding in:

- The market institutions within which traders work, including the different types of trading venues to which traders may direct orders.
- The measurement of trading costs.
- The tactics and strategies available to the firm's traders and the counterparties with whom they deal, including important innovations in trading technology.

The chapter is organized as follows. Section 2 presents essential information for the portfolio manager on the types of orders, the variety of market venues where orders are executed, the roles of dealers and brokers, and the evaluation of market quality. Section 3 addresses the costs of trading. The next two sections discuss topics relevant to trading strategy: the types of traders and their preferred order types (Section 4) and trade execution decisions and tactics (Section 5). Section 6 discusses serving the client's interests in trading and is followed by concluding remarks (Section 7).

2. THE CONTEXT OF TRADING: MARKET MICROSTRUCTURE

The portfolio manager needs to be familiar with **market microstructure:** the market structures and processes that affect how the manager's interest in buying or selling an asset is translated into executed trades (represented by trade prices and volumes).

Knowledge of market microstructure helps a portfolio manager understand how orders will be handled and executed. The formulation of trading strategies depends on accurate microstructure information. Such information can also help the practitioner understand the frictions that can cause asset prices to diverge from full-information expectations of value, possibly suggesting opportunities and pitfalls in trading.

The portfolio manager also needs to understand the characteristics of the major order types as he or she communicates with the trading desk on such matters as the emphasis to put on speed of execution versus price of execution. The next section presents some essential information on order types.

2.1. Order Types

Market orders and limit orders are the two major types of orders that traders use and that portfolio managers need to understand.

1. A **market order** is an instruction to execute an order promptly in the public markets at the best price available.

   For example, an order to buy 10,000 shares of BP p.l.c. directed to the London Stock Exchange (LSE) would execute at the best price available when the order reached that market. Suppose that when the order reaches the LSE, the lowest price at which a seller is ready to sell BP shares is 642p (pence) in quantity up to 8,000 shares (for a buyer, the lower the price, the better). The second-lowest price is 643p in quantity up to 6,000 shares. Thus, 8,000 shares of the market order would be **filled** (executed) at 642p and the balance of $10,000 - 8,000 = 2,000$ shares would fill at 643p.

A market order emphasizes immediacy of execution. However, a market order usually bears some degree of **price uncertainty** (uncertainty about the price at which the order will execute). In today's markets, most market orders are effectively automated from the point of origin straight through to reporting and clearing.

2. A **limit order** is an instruction to trade at the best price available but only if the price is at least as good as the limit price specified in the order. For buy orders, the trade price must not exceed the limit price, while for sell orders, the trade price must be at least as high as the limit price. An instruction always accompanies a limit order specifying when it will expire.

   Suppose that instead of the market order above, the trader places an order to buy 10,000 shares of BP p.l.c. at 641p limit (which means at a price of 641p or lower), good for one day (the order expires at the end of trading that day). Suppose that this buy order's price is higher than that of any other limit buy order for BP shares at the time. If that is the case, then 641p becomes the best available bid, or **market bid,** for BP shares. If a market sell order for 6,000 shares of BP arrives the instant after the trader's buy limit order for 10,000 shares, it will execute against that limit order. The trader will get a fill (execution) for 6,000 shares at 641p, leaving 4,000 shares of the order unfilled. At that point, favorable news on BP might reach the market. If so, the price of BP could move up sharply and not trade at or below 641p for the remainder of the day. If that is the case, at the end of the day, the trader will have 4,000 shares of his or her order unfilled and the order, which was good for one day, will expire.

   By specifying the least favorable price at which an order can execute, *a limit order emphasizes price.* However, limit orders can execute only when the market price reaches the limit price specified by the limit order. The timing of the execution, or even whether the execution happens at all, is determined by the ebb and flow of the market. Limit orders thus have **execution uncertainty.**

Each trading venue specifies the types of orders permitted and other trading protocols. The professional trader needs to know the range of order types permitted. The list of all possible kinds of orders is long, but most order types represent variations on the elemental market and limit orders.[1] Some of these order types may serve to enlist the experience, presence, and knowledge of the trader's agent (broker) in executing a trade. Others may serve to conceal the quantity of a security that the trader wants to buy or sell, or serve some other purpose. A few additional important order types are as follows:

- *Market-not-held order*. This type of order is relevant for trades placed on certain **exchanges** (regulated trading venues) where an order may be handled by an agent of the trader in executing trades (a **broker**). This variation of the market order is designed to give the agent greater discretion than a simple market order would allow. "Not held" means that the broker is not required to trade at any specific price or in any specific time interval, as would be required with a simple market order. Discretion is placed in the hands of a representative

[1] See Harris (2003) for an in-depth treatment of order types.

of the broker (such as a **floor broker**—an agent of the broker who, for certain exchanges, physically represents the trade on the exchange). The broker may choose not to participate in the flow of orders on the exchange if the broker believes he or she will be able to get a better price in subsequent trading.

- *Participate (do not initiate) order*. This is a variant of the market-not-held order. The broker is to be deliberately low-key and wait for and respond to initiatives of more active traders. Buy-side traders who use this type of order hope to capture a better price in exchange for letting the other side determine the timing of the trade.
- *Best efforts order*. This type of order gives the trader's agent even more discretion to work the order only when the agent judges market conditions to be favorable. Some degree of immediacy is implied, but not immediacy at any price.
- *Undisclosed limit order*. Also known as a *reserve, hidden,* or *iceberg order*. This is a limit order that includes an instruction not to show more than some maximum quantity of the unfilled order. For example, a trader might want to buy 200,000 shares of an issue traded on Euronext Amsterdam. The order size would represent a substantial fraction of average daily volume in the issue, and the trader is concerned that share price might move up if the full extent of his or her interest were known. The trader places an undisclosed limit order to buy the 200,000 shares, specifying that no more than 20,000 shares of the unfilled order be shown to the public at a time.
- *Market on open order*. This is a market order to be executed at the opening of the market. Similarly, a *market on close order* is a market order to be executed at the market close. These are examples of orders with an instruction for execution at a specific time. The rationale for using these two types of orders is that the opening and close in many markets provide good liquidity.

The above types of orders describe how an order to buy or sell will be presented to the market. The following describe special types of trades:

- *Principal trade*. A principal trade is a trade with a broker in which the broker commits capital to facilitate the prompt execution of the trader's order to buy or sell. Principal trades are used most frequently when the order is larger and/or more urgent than can be accommodated within the normal ebb and flow of exchange trading. A price concession provides an incentive for the broker acting as a principal in the trade.
- *Portfolio trade (or program trade, or basket trade)*. A portfolio trade involves an order that requires the execution of purchases (or sales) in a specified **basket** (list) of securities at as close to the same time as possible. For example, an S&P 500 index fund manager with new cash to invest could execute a portfolio trade to buy the S&P 500 (the shares in the S&P 500 in their index weights). Portfolio trades are often relatively low cost because the diversification implied by multiple security issues reduces the risk to the other side of the trade.

With some essential information on order types in hand, we can discuss market structures for trading.

2.2. Types of Markets

Markets are organized to provide **liquidity** (the ability to trade without delay at relatively low cost and in relatively large quantities), **transparency** (availability of timely and accurate market and trade information), and **assurity of completion** (trades settle without problems under all market conditions—**trade settlement** involves the buyer's payment for the asset purchased and the transfer of formal ownership of that asset).

In what follows, we describe the chief ways trading is organized:

- Quote-driven (or dealer) markets, in which members of the public trade with dealers rather than directly with one another.
- Order-driven markets, in which members of the public trade with one another without the intermediation of dealers.
- Brokered markets, in which the trader relies on a broker to find the other side of a desired trade.

These distinctions are valuable in understanding the dynamics of trading and price formation, although, as we discuss later, the lines between the categories are often blurry. Furthermore, markets evolve, and the portfolio manager needs to keep abreast of important new developments.

Fixed-income and equity markets have evolved very rapidly over the 1990s and early 2000s. There are many more choices as to where to trade such bonds and equities than was the case historically—a phenomenon that has been called **market fragmentation.** Another trend is the increasing amount of trading that is partly or fully automated, in the sense that the execution of a trader's order after entry requires minimal or no human intervention or trader-to-trader communication. Reflecting the concern to minimize settlement errors and costs in security markets, the settlement of the trade after execution may also be automated within a given trading system or venue (**straight through processing,** or STP).

Forward and futures markets are also in transition. For example, at the Chicago Board of Trade (CBOT, a U.S. commodities exchange), an automated trading system (e-cbot) operates alongside a type of market dating back centuries (an **open outcry auction market**). In an open outcry auction market, representatives of buyers and sellers meet at a specified location on the floor of an exchange, with voices raised ("open outcry") so they can be heard, to conduct auctions to fill customers' orders.

Alternative investment markets have also been affected by changes. For example, hedge funds (loosely regulated pooled investment vehicles) have been aggressive in exploiting advances in trading technology.

All the above developments are better understood when the structures by which trading is organized are grasped. The first type of market that we will discuss is called a quote-driven or dealer market.

2.2.1. Quote-Driven (Dealer) Markets **Quote-driven markets** rely on dealers to establish firm prices at which securities can be bought and sold. These markets are therefore also called **dealer markets,** as trades are executed with a dealer. A **dealer** (sometimes referred to as a **market maker**) is a business entity that is ready to buy an asset for inventory or sell an asset from inventory to provide the other side of an order to buy or sell the asset.

In the traditional view, market makers or dealers passively provide **immediacy** or **bridge liquidity,** the price of which is the **bid–ask spread** (the ask price minus the bid price). A dealer's (or any trader's) **bid price** (or **bid**) is the price at which he or she will buy a specified quantity of a security. A dealer's (or any trader's) **ask price** (or **ask,** or **offer price,** or **offer**) is the price at which he or she will sell a specified quantity of a security. On the principle of buying low and selling high, a dealer's ask price is greater than his bid price. The quantity associated with the bid price is often referred to the **bid size;** the quantity associated with the ask price is known as the **ask size.** From the perspective of a trader executing an order to *buy* a security from a dealer, a *lower ask* from the dealer is favorable to the trader. If the trader is executing an order to *sell* a security to a dealer, a *higher bid* from the dealer is favorable to the trader.

Suppose that a portfolio manager gives the firm's trading desk an order to buy 1,000 shares of Economical Chemical Systems, Inc. (ECSI), which is traded in a dealer market, and that three dealers (coded A, B, and C) make a market in those shares. At the time the trader views the market in ECSI on his computer screen, 10:22 a.m., the three dealers have put in the following quotes:

- Dealer A: *bid*: 98.85 for 600 shares; *ask*: 100.51 for 1,000 shares.
- Dealer B: *bid*: 98.84 for 500 shares; *ask*: 100.55 for 500 shares.
- Dealer C: *bid*: 98.82 for 700 shares; *ask*: 100.49 for 800 shares.

Thus, the bid–ask spreads of Dealers A, B, and C are, respectively,

- $100.51 - 98.85 = 1.66$
- $100.55 - 98.84 = 1.71$
- $100.49 - 98.82 = 1.67$

The trader might see the quote information organized on his screen as shown in Exhibit 10-1. In Exhibit 10-1, the bids and asks are ordered from best to worst and time-stamped. These are actually limit orders because the prices at which the dealers are ready to trade are specified. Because Exhibit 10-1 lists limit orders, it is called a **limit order book.** The **inside bid,** or **market bid,** which is the highest and best bid, is 98.85 from Dealer A. However, Dealer C is quoting the **inside ask,** or **market ask,** which is the lowest ask, at 100.49. The **inside quote,** or **market quote,** is therefore 98.85 bid, 100.49 ask. The **inside bid–ask spread,** or **market bid–ask spread** (or **inside spread** or **market spread** for short), is $100.49 - 98.85 = 1.64$, which in this case is lower than any individual dealer's spread. (**Prevailing** is also used for *inside* or *market* in all these expressions.) The trader also notes that the **midquote** (halfway between the market bid and ask prices) is $(100.49 + 98.85)/2 = 99.67$.

If the trader executes a market buy order for 1,000 shares, the trader would purchase 800 shares from Dealer C at 100.49 per share and 200 shares from Dealer A at 100.51 per share. However, in some markets, it is also possible for the trader to direct the buy order to a specific dealer—for example, Dealer A. The trader may do so for a variety of reasons. For example, the trader may believe that Dealer A is reliable in standing behind quotes but that Dealer C is not. As one example, currency markets are dealer markets, and institutions active in those markets may screen counterparties on credit criteria.

In some dealer markets, a public trader might not have real-time access to all quotes in the security as in our example; that is, the limit order book is not "open," meaning visible in real time to the public. In such **closed-book markets,** the trader would rely on a broker to locate the best ask price, paying the broker a commission. Another notable point concerns

EXHIBIT 10-1 The Limit Order Book for Economical Chemical Systems, Inc.

Bid				Ask			
Dealer	Time Entered	Price	Size	Dealer	Time Entered	Price	Size
A	10:21 a.m.	98.85	600	C	10:21 a.m.	100.49	800
B	10:21 a.m.	98.84	500	A	10:21 a.m.	100.51	1,000
C	10:19 a.m.	98.82	700	B	10:19 a.m.	100.55	500

Note: The bids are ordered from highest to lowest, while the asks are ordered from lowest to highest. These orderings are from best bid or ask to worst bid or ask.

limit orders. Historically, in dealer markets, rules would restrict a limit order from a public trader from competing with dealers' bids and asks for other public trades. In a "pure" dealer market, a dealer is a counterparty to every trade. However, in some quote-driven markets, such as the U.S. NASDAQ market for equities, public traders' limit orders are displayed and compete with dealers' bids and asks.[2]

If the portfolio manager communicated that he or she had a focus on price rather than immediacy, the trader might consider placing a limit order within the market spread—for example, an order to buy 1,000 shares at 100 limit. The trader's limit order in a market such as NASDAQ would establish a new market bid at 100, and the revised market quote would be 100 bid, 100.49 ask. If nothing else had changed, an incoming market order to sell ECSI shares would "hit" the trader's bid of 100. The trader might also hope that one of the dealers would revise the ask downward and fill part or all of the trader's order. However, it is also possible that the trader's limit order would expire unfilled.

Dealers have played important roles in bond and equity markets because *dealers can help markets operate continuously*. Bond markets, in particular, are overwhelmingly dealer markets. The explanation lies in a lack of natural liquidity for many bonds. (**Natural liquidity** is an extensive pool of investors who are aware of and have a potential interest in buying and/or selling a security.) Many bonds are extremely infrequently traded. If an investor wanted to buy such a bond, the investor might have a very long wait before the other side of the trade (an interest to sell) appeared from the public. Dealers help markets in such securities operate more nearly continuously by being ready to take the opposite side of a trade.

A study of U.S. corporate bond markets highlights the issue of lack of natural liquidity. In 2003, approximately 70,000 U.S. corporate bond issues potentially tradable in dealer markets were outstanding.[3] However, only 22,453 issues, about 23 percent of the total, traded at least *once* in 2003. Of the bonds that did trade at least once, the "active" bond issues, the median number of trades per day was less than one. Only 1 percent of active bonds traded on average more than about 22 times per day.[4] Even in the relatively frequently traded issues, an opportunity is thus created for an entity—the dealer—to "make" the market (i.e., create liquidity when no natural liquidity exists). A market is made when the dealer stands ready to provide bridge liquidity by buying stock offered by a seller and holding it until a buyer arrives, in return for earning a spread.

Similar considerations often operate in equities. For example, the London Stock Exchange has a quote-driven, competing dealer market called SEAQ for infrequently traded shares. Dealers also play important roles in markets requiring negotiation of the terms of the instrument, such as forward markets and swap markets, where otherwise finding a counterparty to the instrument would often not be feasible.

The size of the *quoted* bid–ask spread (reflecting the market quote), particularly as a proportion of the quote midpoint, is one measure of trading costs. However, the quoted bid–ask spread may be different from the spread at which a trader actually transacts. The trader's focus is therefore often on the *effective* spread.

[2]The display of public limit orders on NASDAQ followed a U.S. reform in 1997 that was triggered by a controversy about dealer collusion in setting quotes.

[3]See Edwards, Harris, and Piwowar (2004). The estimate comes from the number of U.S. corporate bonds whose trades must be reported to the TRACE (Trade Reporting and Compliance Engine) bond price reporting system, which has been operative since July 1, 2002.

[4]See Edwards et al., Table 10-2.

EXHIBIT 10-2 A Market Bid–Ask at 10:03:14 (Order Entry)

Bid Price	Bid Size	Ask Price	Ask Size
\$19.97	400	\$20.03	1,000

EXHIBIT 10-3 A Market Bid–Ask at 10:03:18 (Order Execution)

Bid Price	Bid Size	Ask Price	Ask Size
\$19.97	400	\$20.01	500

The **effective spread** is two times the deviation of the actual execution price from the midpoint of the market quote at the time an order is entered. (If parts of the order execute at different prices, the weighted-average execution price is used in computing the deviation from the midpoint.) The quoted spread is the simplest measure of round-trip transaction costs for an average-size order. The effective spread is a better representation of the true cost of a round-trip transaction because it captures both **price improvement** (i.e., execution within the quoted spread at a price such that the trader is benefited) and the tendency for larger orders to move prices (**market impact**).[5] Exhibit 10-2 gives the market bid–ask in a hypothetical common equity issue that we can use to illustrate the difference between these two kinds of spreads.

With the information in Exhibit 10-2 before him, a trader with instructions to buy 500 shares with minimal delay enters a market order for 500 shares. As the order is received in the system at 10:03:18, a dealer in the issue enters a quote of \$19.96 bid (bid size:100 shares) and \$20.01 ask (ask size: 500 shares) to improve on ("step in front of") the prior best ask price of \$20.03 and take the incoming market order. This can happen because the dealer quickly decides that the profit from the trade is satisfactory. Exhibit 10-3 shows the market bid–ask at 10:03:18, when the order executes.

Thus, 500 shares of the trader's market order execute at \$20.01, which represents a price improvement of \$0.02 relative to the market ask of \$20.03 that the trader saw when the order was entered. (The lower purchase price represents a price improvement for the buyer.)

From Exhibit 10-2 we see that the quoted bid–ask spread is \$20.03 − \$19.97 = \$0.06. The midquote is (\$20.03 + \$19.97)/2 = \$20.00. The effective spread is 2 × (\$20.01 − \$20.00) = 2 × \$0.01 = \$0.02, which is \$0.06 − \$0.02 = \$0.04 less than the quoted spread. *The price improvement has resulted in an effective spread that is lower than the quoted spread.*

The **average effective spread** is the mean effective spread (sometimes dollar weighted) over all transactions in the stock in the period under study. The average effective spread attempts to measure the liquidity of a security's market.

EXAMPLE 10-1 The Effective Spread of an Illiquid Stock

Charles McClung, portfolio manager of a Canadian small-cap equity mutual fund, is reviewing with his firm's chief trader the execution of a ticket to sell 1,000 shares of

[5]Price improvement happens when a trader improves on (or "steps in front of") the best current bid or ask price to take the other side of an incoming market order.

Alpha Company. The ticket was split into three trades executed in a single day as follows:

A. A market order to sell 200 shares was executed at a price of C$10.15. The quote that was in effect at that time was as follows:

Ask Price	Ask Size	Bid Price	Bid Size
C$10.24	200	C$10.12	300

B. A market order to sell 300 shares was executed at a price of C$10.11. The quote that was in effect at that time was as follows:

Ask Price	Ask Size	Bid Price	Bid Size
C$10.22	200	C$10.11	300

C. A market order to sell 500 shares was executed at an average price of C$10.01. The quote that was in effect at that time was as follows:

Ask Price	Ask Size	Bid Price	Bid Size
C$10.19	200	C$10.05	300

This order exceeded the quoted bid size and "walked down" the limit order book (i.e., after the market bid was used, the order made use of limit order(s) to buy at lower prices than the market bid).

1. For each of the above market orders, compute the quoted spread. Also, compute the average quoted spread for the stock for the day.
2. For each of the above, compute the effective spread. Also, compute the average effective spread and the share-volume-weighted effective spread for the stock for the day.
3. Discuss the relative magnitudes of quoted and effective spreads for each of the three orders.

Solution to Problem 1: The quoted spread is the difference between the ask and bid prices. So, for the first order, the quoted spread is C$10.24 − C$10.12 = C$0.12. Similarly, the quoted spreads for the second and third orders are C$0.11 and C$0.14, respectively. The average quoted spread is (C$0.12 + C$0.11 + C$0.14)/3 = C$0.1233.

Solution to Problem 2: Effective spread for a sell order = 2 × (Midpoint of the market at the time an order is entered − Actual execution price).

For the first order, the midpoint of the market at the time the order is entered = (C$10.12 + C$10.24)/2 = C$10.18. So, the effective spread = 2 × (C$10.18 − C$10.15) = C$0.06.

The effective spread for the second order = 2 × [(C$10.11 + C$10.22)/2 − C$10.11] = C$0.11.

The effective spread for the third order $= 2 \times [(C\$10.05 + C\$10.19)/2 - C\$10.01] = C\$0.22$.

The average effective spread $= (C\$0.06 + C\$0.11 + C\$0.22)/3 = C\$0.13$. The share-volume-weighted effective spread $= [(200 \times C\$0.06) + (300 \times C\$0.11) + (500 \times C\$0.22)]/(200 + 300 + 500) = (C\$12.00 + C\$33.00 + C\$110.00)/1,000 = C\$155.00/1,000 = C\$0.155$.

Solution to Problem 3: In the first trade, there was a price improvement because the shares were sold at a price above the bid price. Therefore, the effective spread is less than the quoted spread. In the second trade, there was no price improvement because the shares were sold at the bid price. Also, there was no impact on the execution price because the entire order was fulfilled at the quoted bid. Accordingly, the effective and quoted spreads are equal. In the third trade, the effective spread is greater than the quoted spread because the order size was greater than the bid size and the order had to walk down the limit order book, resulting in a lower average price for the sale and therefore a higher effective spread.

Empirical research confirms that effective bid–ask spreads are lower in higher-volume securities because dealers can achieve faster turnaround in inventory, which reduces their risk. Spreads are wider for riskier and less liquid securities. Later research provided a deeper understanding of trading costs by explaining variation in bid–ask spreads as part of intraday price dynamics. This research showed that market makers are not simply passive providers of immediacy but must also take an active role in price setting to rapidly turn over inventory without accumulating significant positions on one side of the market.

Price may depart from expectations of value if the dealer is long or short relative to desired (target) inventory, giving rise to transitory price movements during the day—and possibly over longer periods. This intuition drives the models of inventory control developed by, among others, Madhavan and Smidt (1993).

2.2.2. Order-Driven Markets

Order-driven markets are markets in which transaction prices are established by public limit orders to buy or sell a security at specified prices. Such markets feature trades between public investors, *usually without intermediation by designated dealers* (market makers). The limit order book shown in Exhibit 10-1 for the hypothetical Economical Chemical Systems, Inc., would also be a possible limit order book for the company if it were traded in an order-driven market, but typically with public traders replacing dealers (dealers may trade in order-driven markets but do so alongside other traders). There might be more competition for orders, because a trader does not have to transact with a dealer (as in a "pure" dealer marker). But it is also possible that a trader might be delayed in executing a trade or be unable to execute it because a dealer with an inventory of the security is not present. Orders from the public "drive," or determine, liquidity, explaining the term *order-driven markets*. In order-driven markets, a trader cannot choose with whom he or she trades because a prespecified set of rules (based on factors such as price and time of order entry) mechanically governs the execution of orders submitted to the market.

Examples of order-driven markets include the Toronto Stock Exchange for equities, the International Securities Exchange for options, and Hotspot FX for foreign exchange.

For equity markets, a worldwide trend has favored order-driven markets at the expense of quote-driven markets. Various types of order-driven markets are distinguished:

2.2.2.1. Electronic Crossing Networks Electronic crossing networks are markets in which buy and sell orders are batched (accumulated) and crossed at a specific point in time, usually in an anonymous fashion. Electronic crossing networks execute trades at prices taken from other markets. An example of a crossing network is the POSIT trading system, which matches buyers and sellers at the average of prevailing bid and ask prices at fixed points in the day. Crossing networks serve mainly institutional investors.[6]

In using crossing networks, both buyer and seller avoid the costs of dealer services (the bid–ask spread), the effects a large order can have on execution prices, and information leakage. Commissions are paid to the crossing network but are typically low. However, crossing participants cannot be guaranteed that their trades will find an opposing match: The volume in a crossing system is determined by the smallest quantity submitted.

To illustrate how trades on a crossing network are executed, we will suppose that an investment manager, coded A in Exhibit 10-4, wishes to buy 10,000 shares of a stock. At the same time, two different mutual fund traders, coded B and C, wish to sell 3,000 and 4,000 shares, respectively. The crossing of orders occurs at 12:00 P.M. on each business day. The market bid and ask prices of the stock are €30.10 and €30.16, respectively.

In this example, total volume is 7,000 shares and the execution price is at the **midquote** (halfway between the prevailing bid and ask prices) of €30.13 = (€30.10 + €30.16)/2. Both sellers have their orders executed in full, but buyer A receives a **partial fill** of 7,000 shares. The buyer has the option of sending the remaining 3,000 shares back to the crossing system for another attempt at execution at the next scheduled crossing or trying to trade this remainder in the open market. None of the participants observes the identities or original submission sizes of the others in the match pool.

Crossing networks provide no price discovery. **Price discovery** means that transaction prices adjust to equilibrate supply and demand. Because the crossing network did not provide price discovery, price could not adjust upward to uncover additional selling interest and fully satisfy trader A's demand to buy.

2.2.2.2. Auction Markets Many order-driven markets are auction markets—that is, markets in which the orders of multiple buyers compete for execution. Auction markets can be further categorized into **periodic** or **batch auction markets** (where multilateral trading

EXHIBIT 10-4 Electronic Crossing Network: Crossing of Orders at 12:00 p.m. (numerical entries are numbers of shares)

Trader Identity	Buy Orders	Sell Orders
A	10,000	
B		3,000
C		4,000

[6]In discussions of U.S. equity markets in particular, a term that is occasionally used for direct trading of securities between institutional investors is the **fourth market**; the fourth market would include trading on electronic crossing networks.

occurs at a single price at a prespecified point in time) and **continuous auction markets** (where orders can be executed at any time during the trading day). Examples of batch auction markets are the open and close of some stock exchanges and the reopening of the Tokyo Stock Exchange after the midday lunch break; at these times, orders are aggregated for execution at a single price. In contrast to electronic crossing markets, auction markets provide price discovery, lessening the problem of partial fills that we illustrated above for crossing networks.

2.2.2.3. Automated Auctions (Electronic Limit-Order Markets) These are computer-based auctions that operate continuously within the day using a specified set of rules to execute orders. **Electronic communications networks** (ECNs), such as Island and Archipelago Exchange in the United States and the Paris Bourse in France, are examples of automated auctions for equities. Like crossing networks, ECNs provide anonymity and are computer-based. In contrast to crossing networks, ECNs operate continuously and, as auction markets, provide price discovery. (Following usual practice, the acronym "ECN" is reserved to refer to electronic communications networks.)

Automated auctions have been among the fastest-growing segments in equity trading. ECNs in particular have blurred the traditional difference between order-driven markets and quote-driven dealer markets. In an ECN, it can be difficult to distinguish between participants who are regulated, professional dealers and other participants who, in effect, are also attempting to earn spread profits by providing liquidity. Hedge funds or day traders, for example, might actively supply liquidity to the market to capture the dealer-like spread profits. From the perspective of an investor, the result is added liquidity and tighter spreads.[7]

2.2.3. Brokered Markets A broker is an agent of the buy-side trader who collects a commission for skillful representation of the trade. The broker may represent the trade to dealers in the security or to the market order flow. However, the term **brokered markets** refers specifically to markets in which transactions are largely effected through a search-brokerage mechanism away from public markets.[8] Typically, these markets are important in countries where the underlying public markets (e.g., stock exchanges) are relatively small or where it is difficult to find liquidity in size. Consequently, brokered markets are mostly used for block transactions.

Brokers can help locate natural counterparties to a difficult order—for example, a block order. A **block order** is an order to sell or buy in a quantity that is large relative to the liquidity ordinarily available from dealers in the security or in other markets. The trader might use the services of a broker to carefully try to uncover the other side of the trade in return for a commission; the broker might occasionally position a portion of the block. (To **position a trade** is to take the other side of it, acting as a principal with capital at risk.) Brokers can also provide a reputational screen to protect uninformed or liquidity-motivated traders. For example, the broker might "shop the block" only to those potential counterparties that the broker believes are unlikely to **front-run** the trade (trade ahead of the initiator, exploiting privileged information about the initiator's trading intentions). These attributes of brokerage markets facilitate trading and hence add value for all parties to the transaction.

[7]For further reading on this subject, see Wagner (2004).

[8]In the United States, brokered equity markets were traditionally referred to as **upstairs markets.** The reference is to trades executed not on the floor of an exchange ("downstairs") but via communications "upstairs" in brokerage firms' offices.

EXAMPLE 10-2 Market Classifications Are Simplifications

Although it is convenient to equate the dealer function with the activities of professional market makers, many parties can and do perform parts of the dealer function. As discussed, brokerage firms' "upstairs" trading desks may commit capital to support clients' trading desires. Thus, these firms are often called broker/dealers, recognizing that they function as both brokers and dealers. Equally important, investors can compete with dealers. Buy-side traders can reduce their trading costs by providing accommodative, dealer-like services to other market participants—for example, by submitting limit orders that other participants may "hit" to fulfill liquidity needs.

2.2.4. Hybrid Markets **Hybrid markets** are combinations of the previously described market types. A good example is the New York Stock Exchange (NYSE), which offers elements of batch auction markets (e.g., the opening) and continuous auction markets (intraday trading), as well as quote-driven markets (the important role of NYSE dealers, who are known as **specialists**).

2.3. The Roles of Brokers and Dealers

Having discussed the types of markets, we now discuss the roles of brokers and dealers, because it is essential that portfolio managers and traders understand their different roles.[9]

A broker is an agent of the investor. As such, in return for a commission, the broker provides various execution services, including the following:

- *Representing the order*. The broker's primary task is to represent the order to the market. The market will accommodate, usually for a price, someone who feels he or she must trade immediately.
- *Finding the opposite side of a trade*. If interest in taking the opposite side of a trade is not currently evident in the market, it usually falls to the broker to try to locate the seller for the desired buy, or the buyer for the desired sale. Often this service requires that the broker act as a dealer and actively buy or sell shares for the broker's own account. The broker/dealer does not bear risk without compensation. Depending on the dealer's inventory position, this service may come at a high cost.
- *Supplying market information*. Market information includes the identity of buyers and sellers, the strength of buying and selling interest, and other information that is relevant to assessing the costs and risks of trading. This market intelligence, which can be provided by the broker, is very valuable to buy-side traders as they consider their trading tactics.
- *Providing discretion and secrecy*. Buy-side traders place great value on preserving the anonymity of their trading intentions. Notice, however, that such secrecy does not extend to the selected broker, whose stock in trade is the knowledge of supply and demand. That an investor is willing to trade is a very valuable piece of information the broker gains as result of his or her relationship with the trader.
- *Providing other supporting investment services*. A broker may provide a range of other services, including providing the client with financing for the use of leverage, record keeping, cash

[9]Many sell-side firms are both brokers and dealers. A given firm may deal in a security at the same time that it collects an agency commission for representing an order in it.

management, and safekeeping of securities. A particularly rich set of supporting services, often including introduction to potential clients, is provided in relationships that have come to be known as **prime brokerage.**

- *Supporting the market mechanism.* Brokerage commissions indirectly assure the continuance of the needed market facilities.

In contrast to the agency relationship of the broker with the trader, the relationship between the trader and a dealer is essentially adversarial. Like any other merchant, the dealer wants to sell merchandise at a higher price (the ask) than the purchase price (the bid). Holding trade volume constant, a dealer gains by wider bid–ask spreads while the trader gains by narrower bid–ask spreads. The dealer is wary of trading with a better-informed counterparty. Consider a portfolio manager who has concluded through new and original analysis that a bond issue currently in the portfolio has more credit risk than the rest of the market perceives. The dealer who makes a market in the company's bonds has set a bid price unaware of the fact that the bond's credit rating may be too high. The dealer's bid is too high relative to the true credit risk of the bond. The portfolio manager's trader liquidates the portfolio position in the bond issue at the dealer's bid price. The dealer's inventory in the bond issue increases, and subsequently the bond's price trends down as the rest of the market becomes aware of the bond's actual credit risk. The dealer has just experienced **adverse selection risk** (the risk of trading with a more informed trader). Dealers want to know who is active in the market, how informed traders are, and how urgent their interest in transacting with the dealer is, in order to manage profits and adverse selection risk. The tension occurs because the informed or urgent trader does not want the dealer to know those facts.

Buy-side traders are often strongly influenced by sell-side traders such as dealers (the **sell side** consists of institutions that sell services to firms such as investment managers and institutional investors). The buy-side trader may have more interaction with dealers than with other units of the trader's own firm (which might simply communicate computer files of orders). In contrast, the sell-side trader, who possesses information vital to the buy-side trader's success, is a constant verbal window on the world. Over the years, the buy-side trader may build a reservoir of trust, friendship, comfort, and goodwill with his or her sell-side counterparts. It is often necessary to rely on the sell side's reputation for integrity and its long-term desire to maintain relationships. The trader should manage the relationships with dealers, remembering that the buy-side trader's first allegiance must always be to the firm's clients, for whom the trader acts in a fiduciary capacity.

We now have an overview of how markets function and have discussed in some detail the differences between the roles of brokers and dealers. But how *well* does a market function? Does a particular trading venue deserve order flow? The next section provides some ways to think about these questions.

2.4. Evaluating Market Quality

Markets are organized to provide liquidity, transparency, and assurity of completion, so they may be judged by the degree to which they have these qualities in practice. In detail, a liquid market is one that has the following characteristics:[10]

- *The market has relatively low bid–ask spreads.* Such a market is often called **tight.** Quoted spreads and effective spreads are low. The costs of trading small amounts of an asset are themselves small. As a result, investors can trade positions without excessive loss of value.

[10]This list follows a well-known analysis and definition of liquidity by Kyle (1985).

If bid–ask spreads are high, investors cannot profitably trade on information except when the information is of great value.

- *The market is deep*. Depth means that big trades tend not to cause large price movements. As a result, the costs of trading large amounts of an asset are relatively small. Deep markets have high **quoted depth,** which is the number of shares available for purchase or sale at the quoted bid and ask prices.
- *The market is resilient*. A market is **resilient** (in the sense used here) if any discrepancies between market price and intrinsic value tend to be small and corrected quickly.

The great advantage of market liquidity is that traders and investors can trade rapidly without a major impact on price. This, in turn, makes it easy for those with relevant information to bring their insights and opinions into the price of securities. Corporations can then attract capital because investors can see that prices efficiently reflect the opportunities for profit and that they can buy and sell securities at will at relatively low cost. Liquidity adds value to the companies whose securities trade on the exchange. Investors will pay a premium for securities that possess the valuable trait of liquidity. Higher security prices enhance corporate value and lower the cost of capital.

Many factors contribute to making a market liquid:

- *Many buyers and sellers*. The presence of many buyers and sellers increases the chance of promptly locating the opposite side of a trade at a competitive price. Success breeds success in that the liquidity resulting from many buyers and sellers attracts additional participants to the market. Investors are more willing to hold shares that they can dispose of whenever they choose to do so.
- *Diversity of opinion, information, and investment needs among market participants*. If the investors in a given market are highly alike, they are likely to want to take similar investment actions and make similar trades. Diversity in the factors described above increases the chance that a buyer of a security, who might have a positive opinion about it, can find a seller, who might have a negative opinion about it or a need for cash. In general, a large pool of investors enhances diversity of opinion.
- *Convenience*. A readily accessible physical location or an easily mastered and well-thought-out electronic platform attracts investors.
- *Market integrity*. Investors who receive fair and honest treatment in the trading process will trade again. The ethical tone set by professional market operatives plays a major role in establishing this trust, as does effective regulation. For example, audits of the financial condition and regulatory compliance of brokers and dealers operating in a market increase public confidence in the market's integrity, as do procedures for the disinterested investigation of complaints about the execution of trades.

Transparency means that individuals interested in or transacting in the market can quickly, easily, and inexpensively obtain accurate information about quotes and trades (**pretrade transparency**), and that details on completed trades are quickly and accurately reported to the public (**post-trade transparency**). Without transparency, the chance that the integrity of the trading process can be compromised increases. Assurity of completion depends on **assurity of the contract** (the parties to trades are held to fulfilling their obligations). To ensure the certainty of trade completion, participating brokers or clearing entities may guarantee the trade to both buyer and seller and be subject to standards of financial strength to ensure that the guarantee has "bite."

EXAMPLE 10-3 Assessing Market Quality after a Market Structure Change

U.S. equity markets switched from price increments in sixteenths of a dollar to one-cent price increments in the first half of 2001. This decimalization of the U.S. markets has received a lot of attention. Several studies have examined the changes that have taken place on the NYSE and NASDAQ (the major dealer market for U.S. equities) as a consequence of decimalization, and some of their findings regarding the changes are as follows[11]:

1. Quoted spreads have declined from the predecimalization period to the postdecimalization period.
2. Effective spreads have declined.
3. Quoted depths have declined.

For each of the above changes, state whether it suggests an improvement or deterioration in market quality after decimalization, and justify your assertion.

Solutions:

1. This change suggests an improvement in market quality. Lower quoted spreads are consistent with lower trading costs, which suggest greater liquidity and an improvement in market quality.
2. This change also suggests an improvement in market quality. Lower effective spreads are consistent with lower trading costs, which suggest greater liquidity and an improvement in market quality. Effective spreads are a more accurate measure of trading costs than quoted spreads. One would need to examine changes in commission costs (if any) subsequent to decimalization to get a more complete picture of the changes in trading costs that resulted from decimalization.
3. Reduced quoted depths imply that large investors placing large orders are forced to split their orders more often after decimalization. Though small investors who place small orders are not likely to be affected by reduced depths, the trading costs for institutional investors could increase due to reduced depths. By itself, a decline in quoted depths after decimalization implies reduced liquidity supply and deterioration in market quality.

EXAMPLE 10-4 The Market Quality of Electronic Crossing Networks

Electronic crossing networks offer participants anonymity and low cost through the avoidance of dealer costs and the effect of large orders on execution price. For example,

[11] See Bacidore, Battalio, Jennings, and Farkas (2001), Bessembinder (2003), Chakravarty, Wood, and Van Ness (2004), and Oppenheimer and Sabherwal (2003).

a large sell order in an auction market may be interpreted as conveying negative information and cause bid prices to be revised downward, lowering execution prices. These qualities of crossing networks are particularly valuable for the large trades institutional investors often need to make. As a result of these market quality positives, electronic crossing networks have won significant market share.

Understanding and judging the available alternatives in trading is the new challenge to the buy-side trader. One of the key elements in assessing these alternatives is their costs. Effectively measuring the trading experience over time provides another valuable piece of information to the portfolio manager: On average, how much information advantage do I need to recover the hurdle-rate costs of implementing my decisions? The costs of trading are the subject of the next section.

3. THE COSTS OF TRADING

The view of investment managers on the importance of measuring and managing trading costs has evolved over time. Into the 1970s, trading was viewed as inexpensive and unimportant when contrasted to the hoped-for benefits of securities research. In those early days, portfolio managers were highly dependent on sell-side firms for investment intelligence and ideas. The traditional way to reward the broker for investment ideas was to channel the resultant trading activity to the broker.

In the early 1970s, several important trends converged to change buy-side trading forever. As pension fund assets grew, the prevailing use of fixed commission schedules for trades on exchanges created an unjustifiable bonanza for the exchange community. Buy-side investors exerted pressure to bring commission charges more in line with the cost of providing trading services. The result was a move to fully negotiated commissions, beginning in 1975 in the United States and continuing worldwide.[12] As a result, different levels of execution services could be bought for different commission charges, presenting the buy-side trader with new choices.

In addition, the first practical applications of the efficient market hypothesis (EMH) came to life in the form of index funds. Index fund managers strongly disagreed with the then-traditional view of trading as being "just a cost of doing business." Since index fund managers have no expectation of recovering trading costs through security selection, reducing these costs is a paramount goal for them. Traders are often the most "active" part of the passive management team.

As the 1980s progressed, trading processes were subjected to analytical thinking. The theory of trading costs measurement received attention. Investors continued to be concerned that trading costs were too high and exacted too great a penalty on investment performance. This concern encouraged a view that trading tactics need to be carefully designed and tailored to the investment decision with due attention paid to managing trading costs.

Today, the prevalent view is that all costs of trading are negative performance. The lower the transaction costs, the more portfolio management ideas that can be executed to add value to the portfolio. The management of transaction costs is today a leading concern of investors and many other market participants. Fund sponsors track transaction costs as part

[12]Some adoption dates for negotiated commissions were 1983 in Canada, 1986 in the United Kingdom, and 1999 in Japan.

of their responsibility to conserve assets. Investment managers do so both to document their performance in managing costs and to gain information for improving the trading function. Brokers, exchanges, and regulators are also concerned with measuring and evaluating trading costs. Transaction cost measurement not only provides feedback on the success of the trading function; today, its concepts are used in setting trading strategy. An overview of the topic is one building block for our later discussion of trading strategy.

3.1. Transaction Cost Components

Trading costs can be thought of as having two major components: explicit costs and implicit costs. **Explicit costs** are the direct costs of trading, such as broker commission costs, taxes, stamp duties, and fees paid to exchanges. They are costs for which a trader could be given a receipt. **Implicit costs,** by contrast, represent indirect trading costs. No receipt could be given for implicit costs; they are real nonetheless. Implicit costs include the following[13]:

- The bid–ask spread.
- Market impact (or price impact) is the effect of the trade on transaction prices. For example, suppose a trader splits a purchase of 400 bonds into two equal market orders when the quote for a bond is 100.297 to 100.477. The first order executes at the ask price of 100.477, after which the market quotation becomes 100.300 to 100.516. The second order is placed and executes at 100.516. The trader moved the price obtained in the second order up by 100.516 − 100.477 = 0.039, or $0.39 per thousand dollars of face value.
- Missed trade opportunity costs (or unrealized profit/loss) arise from the failure to execute a trade in a timely manner. For example, suppose a futures trader places a limit order to buy 10 contracts at a price of 99.00 (or better), good for one day, when the market quote is 99.01 to 99.04. The order does not execute, and the contract closes at 99.80. The difference (99.80 − 99.04 = $0.76) reflects the missed trade opportunity cost per contract.[14] By trading more aggressively, the trader might have avoided these costs. Missed trade opportunity costs are difficult to measure. In the example, the time frame (one day) was arbitrary, and the estimate could be quite sensitive to the time frame chosen for measurement.
- Delay costs (also called slippage) arise from the inability to complete the desired trade immediately due to its size and the liquidity of markets. Delay costs are often measured on the portion of the order carried over from one day to the next. One reason delay can be costly is that while a trade is being stretched out over time, information is leaking into the market.

Most traders measure implicit costs (i.e., costs excluding commissions) with reference to some price benchmark or reference point. We have already mentioned one price benchmark: the time-of-trade midquote (quotation midpoint), which is used to calculate the effective spread. When such precise information is lacking, the price benchmark is sometimes taken to be the **volume-weighted average price** (VWAP). The VWAP of a security is the average price at which the security traded during the day, where each trade price is weighted by the fraction of the day's volume associated with the trade. The VWAP is an appealing price benchmark because it allows the fund sponsor to identify when it transacted at a higher or lower price than

[13]Not every trade will incur each of these costs.

[14]The comparison to closing price is for illustrative purposes and only one alternative. For example, the Plexus Group calculates the missed trade opportunity costs with respect to the price of the instrument 30 days after the decision to trade was made.

the security's average trade price during the day. For example, if a buy order for 500 shares was executed at €157.25 and the VWAP for the stock for the day was €156.00, the estimated implicit cost of the order would be 500 × (€157.25 − €156.00) = €625.[15] If explicit costs were €25, the total estimated cost would be €650. Alternative price benchmarks include the opening and closing prices for a security, which use less information about prices and are less satisfactory. Although VWAP involves a data-intensive calculation, a number of vendors supply it.[16]

VWAP is less informative for trades that represent a large fraction of volume. In the extreme, if a single trading desk were responsible for all the buys in a security during a day, that desk's average price would equal VWAP and thus appear to be good, however high the prices paid. Another limitation of VWAP (and of the effective spread) is that a broker with sufficient discretion can try to "game" this measure. (To *game* a cost measure is to take advantage of a weakness in the measure, so that the value of the measure may be misleading.) Furthermore, VWAP is partly determined at any point in the day; by using weights based on volume to that point in the day, a trader can estimate the final value of VWAP. The accuracy of such an estimate would tend to increase as the close of trading approaches. By comparing the current price to that estimate, the trader can judge the chances of doing better than VWAP.

EXAMPLE 10-5 Taking Advantage of Weaknesses in Cost Measures

Reginald Smith is consulting to Apex Wealth Management on the use of transaction cost measures. Smith correctly explains to Apex's CIO:

> *"A broker who has flexibility on how aggressively to fill an order can try to game the effective spread measure by waiting for the trade to come to him—that is, by offering liquidity. The broker with a buy order can wait until an order to sell hits his bid; with a sell order, he can wait until an order to buy hits his ask. By executing buys at the bid and sells at the ask, the broker will always show negative estimated transaction costs if performance is measured by the effective spread. However, the delay costs of this approach to the client may be high. A broker with discretion on timing can also try to improve performance relative to a VWAP benchmark, because VWAP is partly determined at any point into the day. For example, if a buy order is received near the end of the day and the stock's ask price exceeds the VWAP up to that point, the broker might try to move the order into the next day, when he will be benchmarked against a fresh VWAP."*

The CIO asserts: "I see your point. Nevertheless, using the opening price as a benchmark might be much more vulnerable to gaming than using VWAP." Critique the CIO's statement.

[15]Were this a sell order, in the calculation, we would subtract the trade price from the benchmark price; in this example, we would calculate 500 × (€156.00 − €157.25) = −€625. Executing a sell order at a price above the VWAP is good.

[16]For example, Bloomberg terminals report VWAPs.

Solution: The CIO's statement is correct. In contrast to the VWAP, which is partly determined as the trading day progresses, the opening price is known with certainty at any point into the trading day, making it easier to game.

To address the possibility of gaming VWAP, VWAP could be measured over multiple days (spanning the time frame over which the order is executed), because traders would often be expected to try to execute trades within a day. However, the cost of measuring VWAP over a longer time frame is less precision in estimating trading costs.

Probably the most exact approach to cost measurement—and one not vulnerable to gaming—is the implementation shortfall approach. This approach is also attractive because it views trading from an investment management perspective: What does it cost to actuate investment decisions? This view was first articulated by Andre Perold of the Harvard Business School,[17] following ideas first put forward by Jack Treynor.[18] The approach involves a comparison of the actual portfolio with a paper portfolio, using a price benchmark that represents the price when the decision to trade is made (when the trade list is cut).

Implementation shortfall is defined as the difference between the money return on a notional or paper portfolio in which positions are established at the prevailing price when the decision to trade is made (known as the **decision price,** the **arrival price,** or the **strike price**) and the actual portfolio's return. The implementation shortfall method correctly captures all elements of transaction costs. The method takes into account not only explicit trading costs, but also the implicit costs, which are often significant for large orders.[19]

Implementation shortfall can be analyzed into four components:

1. *Explicit costs,* including commissions, taxes, and fees.
2. *Realized profit/loss,* reflecting the price movement from the decision price (usually taken to be the previous day's close)[20] to the execution price for the part of the trade executed on the day it is placed.
3. *Delay costs (slippage)*, reflecting the change in price (close-to-close price movement) over the day an order is placed when the order is not executed that day; the calculation is based on the amount of the order actually filled subsequently.
4. *Missed trade opportunity cost* (unrealized profit/loss), reflecting the price difference between the trade cancellation price and the original benchmark price based on the amount of the order that was not filled.

Market movement is a component of the last three of these costs. However, market movement is a random element for which the trader should not bear responsibility. It is now common to adjust implementation shortfall for market movements. An illustration

[17] Perold (1988).

[18] See Treynor (1987).

[19] The Plexus Group estimates that average implementation shortfall costs in 2004 for institutional traders in Asia, excluding Japan, were 153 bps, with just 22 bps from commissions. Of the implicit costs, market impact costs were 18 bps, delay costs were 84 bps, and opportunity costs from missed trades were 29 bps.

[20] The midquote at the time the decision is made is another possible benchmark price.

of the calculation of implementation shortfall might be helpful. Consider the following facts:

- On Monday, the shares of Impulse Robotics close at £10.00 per share.
- On Tuesday, before trading begins, a portfolio manager decides to buy Impulse Robotics. An order goes to the trading desk to buy 1,000 shares of Impulse Robotics at £9.98 per share or better, good for one day. The benchmark price is Monday's close at £10.00 per share. No part of the limit order is filled on Tuesday, and the order expires. The closing price on Tuesday rises to £10.05.
- On Wednesday, the trading desk again tries to buy Impulse Robotics by entering a new limit order to buy 1,000 shares at £10.07 per share or better, good for one day. That day, 700 shares are bought at £10.07 per share. Commissions and fees for this trade are £14. Shares for Impulse Robotics close at £10.08 per share on Wednesday.
- No further attempt to buy Impulse Robotics is made, and the remaining 300 shares of the 1,000 shares the portfolio manager initially specified are never bought.

The paper portfolio traded 1,000 shares on Tuesday at £10.00 per share. The return on this portfolio when the order is canceled after the close on Wednesday is the value of the 1,000 shares, now worth £10,080, less the cost of £10,000, for a net gain of £80. The real portfolio contains 700 shares (now worth $700 \times £10.08 = £7,056$), and the cost of this portfolio is $700 \times £10.07 = £7,049$, plus£14 in commissions and fees, for a total cost of £7,063. Thus, the total net gain on this portfolio is $-£7$. The implementation shortfall is the return on the paper portfolio minus the return on the actual portfolio, or $£80 - (-£7) = £87$. More commonly, the shortfall is expressed as a fraction of the total cost of the paper portfolio trade, or $£87/£10,000 = 87$ basis points.

We can break this implementation shortfall down further:

- Commissions and fees are calculated naturally as $£14/£10,000 = 0.14\%$.
- Realized profit/loss reflects the difference between the execution price and the relevant decision price (here, the closing price of the previous day). The calculation is based on the amount of the order actually filled:

$$\frac{700}{1{,}000}\left(\frac{10.07 - 10.05}{10.00}\right) = 0.14\%$$

- Delay costs reflect the price difference due to delay in filling the order. The calculation is based on the amount of the order actually filled:

$$\frac{700}{1{,}000}\left(\frac{10.05 - 10.00}{10.00}\right) = 0.35\%$$

- Missed trade opportunity cost reflects the difference between the cancellation price and the original benchmark price. The calculation is based on the amount of the order that was not filled:

$$\frac{300}{1{,}000}\left(\frac{10.08 - 10.00}{10.00}\right) = 0.24\%$$

- Implementation cost as a percent is $0.14\% + 0.14\% + 0.35\% + 0.24\% = 0.87\%$, or 87 bps.

The shortfall computation is simply reversed for sells (for sells, the return on the paper portfolio is subtracted from the return on the actual portfolio).

In this example, shortfall was positive, but this will not always be the case, especially if the effect of the return on the market is removed. To illustrate the adjustment for market

EXHIBIT 10-5 Facts on Implementation Shortfall Costs

Market Sector	Total Implementation Shortfall Costs	
	4th Quarter 2000	4th Quarter 2003
U.S. NYSE	0.88%	0.55%
U.S. NASDAQ	1.38	0.83
Europe	1.11	0.63
Emerging Markets	2.20	1.25
All Markets	1.66	0.74

Source: Plexus Group.

return using the market model, suppose that the market had risen 100 basis points (1 percent) over the period of trading and the beta of Impulse Robotics is 1.0. The market model is $\hat{R}_i = \alpha_i + \beta_i R_M$, where $\hat{R}_i$ is the predicted return on asset i, R_M is the return on the market portfolio, α_i is the average return on asset i unrelated to the market return, and β_i is the sensitivity of the return on asset i to the return on the market portfolio. In practice, with daily returns, α_i will be often very close to 0, and $\hat{R}_i \approx \beta_i R_M$. With a beta of 1.0, the predicted return on the shares would be $1.0 \times 1\% = 1\%$, and the **market-adjusted implementation shortfall** would be $0.87\% - 1.0\% = -0.13\%$. Here, the shortfall is actually negative. By contrast, pretrade cost estimates are always positive. Exhibit 10-5 lists implementation shortfall costs for various global equity market sectors.[21]

Changes in the U.S. market structure between 2000 and 2003, especially decimalization and changes in order handling rules, brought a sharp decline in the cost of trading in U.S. equity markets. However, the reduction in the costs of equity trading was widespread beyond the United States: European equity trading costs dropped from 111 bps to 63 bps, a 43 percent decrease. Emerging markets also dropped 43 percent, from 220 bps to 125 bps. The costs of implementing investment ideas were down significantly across all equity markets.

As a complement to implementation shortfall, some investment management firms measure shortfall with respect not to the above paper portfolio, but with respect to a portfolio in which all trades are transacted in expected markets and the component costs are at expected levels. This approach accounts for the anticipated cost of the trades.[22]

The application of the implementation shortfall approach is hampered when an asset trades infrequently because the decision price is then hard to determine. If the market closing price of a security is "stale"—in the sense of reflecting a trade that happened much earlier—it is not valid. The application of a benchmark price based on trading cost measures, including implementation shortfall, VWAP, and effective spread, is also compromised when a market lacks transparency (accurate price and/or quote information).

Having illustrated trade cost measurement using VWAP and implementation shortfall, we now compare these two major approaches to trade cost measurement in Exhibit 10-6. VWAP has theoretical disadvantages compared to implementation shortfall but is readily obtained and interpreted and is a useful measure of quality of execution for smaller trades in nontrending markets in particular. The portfolio manager should be familiar with both measures.

[21] Note that these transaction cost totals, particularly in the earlier period, are large enough to explain the 0.50 percent to 0.75 percent one-way transaction costs inferred from the difference between active and passive management.

[22] See Cheng (2003).

EXHIBIT 10-6 Comparison of VWAP and Implementation Shortfall

	Volume-Weighted Average Price	Implementation Shortfall
Advantages	• Easy to compute. • Easy to understand. • Can be computed quickly to assist traders during the execution. • Works best for comparing smaller trades in nontrending markets.	• Links trading to portfolio manager activity; can relate cost to the value of investment ideas. • Recognizes the trade-off between immediacy and price. • Allows attribution of costs. • Can be built into portfolio optimizers to reduce turnover and increase realized performance. • Cannot be gamed.
Disadvantages	• Does not account for costs of trades delayed or canceled. • Becomes misleading when trade is a substantial proportion of trading volume. • Not sensitive to trade size or market conditions. • Can be gamed by delaying trades.	• Requires extensive data collection and interpretation. • Imposes an unfamiliar evaluation framework on traders.

EXAMPLE 10-6 Commissions: The Most Visible Part of Transaction Costs (1)

Implementation shortfall totals can be divided into categories that define the nature of trading costs. Each component cost is as real as the other costs. Nevertheless, brokerage commissions are the most visible portion of trading costs. The dealer spreads and responses to market pressures are more difficult to gauge. The commissions, however, are printed on every ticket. For better or worse, efforts to reduce transaction costs focus first on commissions.

A good deal of attention has focused on the use of commissions to buy services other than execution services—that is, a practice known as **soft dollars** (or **soft dollar arrangements,** or **soft commissions**). Many investment managers have traditionally allocated a client's brokerage business to buy research services that aid portfolio management. In those cases, commissions pay for research received and execution, with clerical personnel assigned to the trade desk managing the commission budget. However, the practice of soft dollars makes accounting for transaction costs less exact and can be abused. CFA Institute in 1998 issued *Soft Dollar Standards* to provide disclosure standards and other guidance related to soft dollar arrangements.[23] Furthermore, individuals who are CFA Institute members or candidates have an overriding responsibility to adhere to the Code of Ethics and Standards of Professional Conduct. Standard III:

[23]See www.cfainstitute.org for any updates. As of early 2006, no substantive revisions had been made to the 1998 release.

Duties to Clients, (A) Loyalty, Prudence, and Care, specifies that CFA Institute members using soft dollars should develop policies and procedures with respect to the use of client brokerage, including soft dollars, and that those policies and procedures should reflect that members and candidates must seek best execution for their clients, among other duties.[24]

EXAMPLE 10-7 Commissions: The Most Visible Part of Transaction Costs (2)

Transaction costs can be thought of as an iceberg, with the commission being the tip visible above the water's surface. The major parts of transaction costs are unobservable. They do not appear in accounting statements, and they appear only indirectly in manager evaluations. Extensive data collection and analysis are required to gauge the size and relative importance of transaction cost components. Exhibit 10-7 illustrates the concept with numbers based on the Plexus Client Universe covering U.S. equity market transactions in 2005, with the corresponding data for 2001 given for comparison.

EXHIBIT 10-7 The Iceberg of Transaction Costs
Note: The 2001 components do not sum to exactly 142 bps due to rounding.
Source: Plexus Group, Inc.

[24]See the *Standards of Practice Handbook*, 9th ed. (Charlottesville, VA: CFA Institute, 2005). See www.cfainstitute.org for any updates.

The exhibit shows that total U.S. equity transaction costs have decreased by 91 bps from 142 bps in 2001 to 51 bps in 2005, representing a steep 64 percent decline. The most visible part of equity transaction costs—commissions—was by far the least important cost component in 2001, having already experienced long-term downward pressure. With relatively little more available to be taken out of commissions, the implicit costs of transacting came under the greatest pressure between 2001 and 2005, with missed trade opportunity costs reaching the level of commission costs. In 2005, as in 2001, implicit costs ranked from largest to smallest were delay costs, market impact, and missed trade opportunity costs. The trade that is never completed is often the most expensive trade.

Although the very long-term trend is down, the costs of equity trading can be expected to vary over time. When trading is frenzied, as it was in the Internet market of the late 1990s, costs will rise as investors become less sensitive to costs in their eagerness to participate in exciting companies and situations.

3.2. Pretrade Analysis: Econometric Models for Costs

Given posttrade shortfall estimates, we can build reliable pretrade estimates using econometric models. The theory of market microstructure suggests that trading costs are systematically related to certain factors, including the following:[25]

- Stock liquidity characteristics (e.g., market capitalization, price level, trading frequency, volume, index membership, bid–ask spread)
- Risk (e.g., the volatility of the stock's returns)
- Trade size relative to available liquidity (e.g., order size divided by average daily volume)
- Momentum (e.g., it is more costly to buy in an up market than in a down market)
- Trading style (e.g., more aggressive styles using market orders should be associated with higher costs than more passive styles using limit orders)

Given these factors, we can estimate the relation between costs and these variables using regression analysis. Since theory suggests a nonlinear relationship, we can use nonlinear methods to estimate the relationship. The key point to note is that the estimated cost function can be used in two ways:

1. To form a pretrade estimate of the cost of trading that can then be juxtaposed against the actual realized cost once trading is completed to assess execution quality, and
2. To help the portfolio manager gauge the right trade size to order in the first place.

For example, a portfolio manager may want to invest in a stock with an expected excess return target of 5 percent relative to the manager's benchmark over the intended holding period. Initially, a trade of 200,000 shares is proposed with a price currently at $10 per share. However, based on pretrade cost estimates, the cost of a 200,000-share position is 2.5 percent, so that expected round-trip transaction costs are $2 \times 2.5\% = 5\%$, which would fully erode the excess return. The optimal trade size will be much smaller than the 200,000 shares initially proposed.

[25]See Madhavan (2000, 2002).

Quantitative managers will balance three factors—return, risk, and cost—in selecting the optimal trade size. But even nonquantitative managers need to make the right choices in terms of balancing expected return against expected entry and exit costs.

EXAMPLE 10-8 An Econometric Model for Transaction Costs

Several Canadian companies' stocks are listed not only on the Toronto Stock Exchange (TSE), but also on the New York Stock Exchange (NYSE). There are no legal restrictions on cross-border ownership and trading of these stocks. Some of the clients of an American brokerage firm have occasionally asked the brokerage firm for execution of trades in some of the Canadian stocks cross-listed in the United States. These trades can be executed on either the NYSE or TSE, and the American brokerage firm has entered into an alliance with a TSE member firm to facilitate execution of trades on the TSE if desired. John Reynolds is an economist at the brokerage firm. Reynolds has identified 55 of the cross-listed Canadian companies as those in which the firm's clients typically execute trades. Reynolds observes that the implicit transaction costs for some trades in these stocks are lower on the NYSE than on the TSE, or vice versa. Reynolds has built an econometric model that can be used for pretrade assessment of the difference in the implicit costs of transacting on the two exchanges, so that traders can direct trades to the lower-cost venue. Using historic data on trade and firm characteristics and transaction costs, Reynolds developed the following model:

$$\text{Pred. } \Delta\text{Cost} = 0.25 + 1.31\ln(\text{Mkt Cap}) - 14.91(\text{U.S. Share}) + 1.64\ln(\text{Order Size}) \\ -1.40(\text{High Tech})$$

where

Pred. ΔCost = Predicted difference between the implicit transaction costs on the NYSE and TSE in basis points

Mkt Cap = Market capitalization of the company in millions of U.S. dollars

U.S. Share = Proportion (stated as a decimal) of total trading in the stock in the United States and Canada that occurs in the United States

Order Size = Number of shares ordered

High Tech is an industry dummy with a value of 1 if the company is a high-tech company and 0 otherwise.

Reynolds has also concluded that the *explicit* transaction costs for the stocks he has analyzed are lower on the NYSE than on the TSE by about 12 bps.

1. Consider an order to sell 50,000 shares of a non-high-tech company that was included in the companies analyzed by Reynolds. The company has a market capitalization of US$100 million, and the U.S. share of overall trading volume in the company is 0.30. Based on the model estimated above and the assessment of the explicit transaction costs, recommend where the order should be placed.

2. Consider an order to sell 1,000 shares of a high-tech company that was included in the companies analyzed by Reynolds. The company has a market capitalization of US$100 million, and the U.S. share of overall trading volume in the company is 0.50. Based on the model estimated above and the assessment of the explicit transaction costs, recommend where the order should be placed.

Solution to Problem 1: Pred. ΔCost $= 0.25 + 1.31 \ln(\text{Mkt Cap}) - 14.91(\text{U.S. Share}) + 1.64 \ln(\text{Order Size}) - 1.40(\text{High Tech}) = 0.25 + 1.31 \ln(100) - 14.91(0.30) + 1.64 \ln(50,000) - 1.40(0) = 19.6$ bps. The econometric model suggests that the implicit cost of executing this trade is greater on the NYSE than on the TSE by almost 20 bps. Thus, since the explicit transaction costs are lower on the NYSE by about 12 bps, the total cost of executing the trade on the TSE is expected to be less than the cost on the NYSE by almost 8 bps. The recommendation would be to direct the order to the TSE.

Solution to Problem 2: Pred. ΔCost $= 0.25 + 1.31 \ln(\text{Mkt Cap}) - 14.91(\text{U.S. Share}) + 1.64 \ln(\text{Order Size}) - 1.40(\text{High Tech}) = 0.25 + 1.31 \ln(100) - 14.91(0.50) + 1.64 \ln(1,000) - 1.40(1) = 8.8$ bps. The econometric model suggests that the implicit cost of executing this trade is greater on the NYSE than on the TSE by about 9 bps. However, since the explicit transaction costs are lower on the NYSE by about 12 bps, the total cost of executing the trade on the NYSE is expected to be less than the cost on the TSE by about 3 bps. The recommendation would be to direct the order to the NYSE.

4. TYPES OF TRADERS AND THEIR PREFERRED ORDER TYPES

Beginning with this section and continuing with Section 5, we discuss traders, trading objectives, strategies, and tactics. We first need to understand how investment style affects trading objectives. Implementation strategy and cost are direct consequences of investment management style. Some investment strategies are inherently inexpensive to implement—for example, contrarian, passive, and other "slow idea" strategies. Other strategies, particularly those based on stock price momentum or widely disseminated "news," are inherently more expensive to implement.

The success of the investment strategy depends on whether the information content of the decision process is sufficient relative to the costs of executing the strategy, including trading costs. Thus, the keystone of the buy-side trader's choice of trading strategy is the **urgency of the trade** (the importance of certainty of execution). Is the decision based on slow changes in fundamental value, valuable new information, or the need to increase cash balances? Will the value of completing the trade disappear or dissipate if it is not completed quickly?

From the portfolio manager's perspective, the key to effective trading is to realize that the portfolio decision is not complete until securities are bought or sold. Because execution is so important, market information is critical. When a trade is first seriously contemplated, the trader needs to ask: How sensitive is the security to buying or selling pressure? How much volume can be accumulated without having the price move out of the desirable range? Are there any special considerations (e.g., news, rumors, competing buyers, or anxious sellers) that make this a particularly good or particularly poor time to deal in this stock? In other words, how resilient is the market? Is the price being driven to a level at which a dealer wants to reduce or increase inventory (i.e., the dealer's layoff or buy-in position, respectively)? Armed with this tactical information, the portfolio manager fine-tunes his interest in the security.

The trader can use the answers to these questions to increase his or her awareness of market conditions and security trading behavior. The crucial function of the trading desk is to achieve the best price–time trade-off for the impending transaction given current market circumstances. This trade-off may change rapidly because of market conditions, dealer inventories, news, and changes in the portfolio manager's desires.

The above considerations regarding investment style and the urgency of the trade in particular lead to the following classification of traders according to their motivation in trading.

4.1. The Types of Traders

Traders can be classified by their motivation to trade, as follows:

Information-motivated traders trade on information that has limited value if not quickly acted upon. Accordingly, they often stress liquidity and speed of execution over securing a better price. They are likely to use market orders and rely on market makers to accommodate their desire to trade quickly. They must execute their orders before the information on which they are buying or selling becomes valueless. Information traders often trade in large blocks. Their information frequently concerns the prospects of one stock, and they seek to maximize the value of the information. Successful information-motivated traders are wary of acquiring a public reputation for astute trading, because if they did, who would wish to trade against them? Accordingly, information traders often use deceptive actions to hide their intentions.

Value-motivated traders act on value judgments based on careful, sometimes painstaking research. They trade only when the price moves into their value range. As explained earlier, they trade infrequently and are motivated only by price and value. They tend to accumulate and distribute large positions quietly over lengthy trading horizons. Value-motivated traders are ready to be patient to secure a better price.

Liquidity-motivated traders do not transact to reap profit from an information advantage of the securities involved. Rather, liquidity-motivated transactions are more a means than an end; such transactions may, for example, release cash proceeds to facilitate the purchase of another security, adjust market exposure, or fund cash needs. Lacking the information sensitivity of the information and value traders, liquidity-motivated traders tend to be natural trading counterparties to more knowledgeable traders. Thus, they need to be aware of the value their liquidity brings to knowledgeable traders.

Passive traders, acting on behalf of passive or index fund portfolio managers, similarly seek liquidity in their rebalancing transactions, but they are much more concerned with the cost of trading. They tend to use time-insensitive techniques in the hope of exchanging a lack of urgency for lower-cost execution. Passive traders have the flexibility to use lower-cost trading techniques. Because of the types of orders and markets they use, these traders resemble dealers in the sense that they allow the opposing party to determine the timing of the trade in exchange for determining the acceptable trade price.

EXHIBIT 10-8 Summary of Trading Motivations, Time Horizons, and Time vs. Price Preferences

Trader	Motivation	Trading Time Horizon	Time vs. Price Preference
Information motivated	New information	Minutes to hours	Time
Value motivated	Perceived valuation errors	Days to weeks	Price
Liquidity motivated	Invest cash or divest securities	Minutes to hours	Time
Passive	Rebalancing, investing/divesting cash	Days to weeks	Price
Dealers and day traders	Accommodation	Minutes to hours	Passive, indifferent

Other types of traders do not fit exactly into the above categories. Dealers, whose profits depend on earning bid–ask spreads, have short trading time horizons like information-motivated traders. Given that a transaction is profitable, however, they have no specific emphasis on time versus price. Arbitrageurs are sensitive to both price of execution and speed of execution as they attempt to exploit small price discrepancies between closely related assets trading in different markets. **Day traders** rapidly buy and sell stocks in the hope that the stocks will continue to rise or fall in value for the seconds or minutes they are ready to hold a position. Like dealers, they often seek to profitably accommodate the trading demands of others.

Exhibit 10-8 summarizes the attitudes toward trading displayed by the various traders in the market. In the exhibit, the final column gives the trader's emphasis on price or time (i.e., avoiding delay in execution).

This classification of traders is relevant to both equity markets and fixed-income markets.

Alternative investments tend to be characterized by infrequent trading and illiquidity; day traders are not relevant as a trader type in such markets, in general. However, the thematic differences among the major types of traders (information-motivated, value-motivated, liquidity-motivated, and passive) still have recognizable counterparts in many alternative investment markets, although the relevant time horizons are longer. For example, in real estate, information concerning planned future construction, perceived valuation errors, and the need for liquidity can motivate transactions, and some investors may seek long-term, broad, diversified exposure, corresponding roughly to the passive trader type.

4.2. Traders' Selection of Order Types

All of the orders discussed in earlier sections, as well as others discussed in advanced treatments, are used tactically by buy-side traders as warranted by market conditions and the motivations of the portfolio manager.

4.2.1. Information-Motivated Traders

Information traders believe that they need to trade immediately and often trade large quantities in specific names. Demands for high liquidity on short notice may overwhelm the ready supply of stock in the market, triggering adverse price movements as the effect of these demands reverberates through the market. Information traders may use fast action principal trades. By transacting with a dealer, the buy-side trader quickly secures execution at a guaranteed price. The major cost of these trades arises because the dealer demands a price concession to cover the inventory risks undertaken. Furthermore, information-motivated traders fear that the price may move quickly to embed the information, devaluing their information edge. They are aware that their trading often moves the market, but they believe their information justifies the increased trading cost. Accordingly, information-motivated traders may wish to disguise their anxious trading need. Where possible, they use less obvious orders, such as market orders, to disguise their trading intentions. This behavior has led information traders to be called "wolves in sheep's clothing."

4.2.2. Value-Motivated Traders

The value-motivated trader develops an independent assessment of value and waits for market prices to move into the range of that assessment. Thus, the market comes with excess inventory to the trader and presents him with attractive opportunities.

The typical value-motivated trader uses limit orders or their computerized institutional market equivalent. An attractive price is more important than timely activity. Thus, price is controlled but timing is not. Even though value-motivated traders may act quickly, they are still accommodative and pay none of the penalties of more anxious traders. As Treynor (1987) pointed out, value traders can sometimes operate as "the dealer's dealer," buying stock when dealers most want to sell stock.

4.2.3. Liquidity-Motivated Traders

The commitment or release of cash is the primary objective of liquidity-motivated traders. The types of orders used include market, market-not-held, best efforts, participate, principal trades, portfolio trades, and orders on ECNs and crossing networks. Low commissions and small impact are desirable, and liquidity traders can often tolerate somewhat more uncertainty about timely trade completion than can information-motivated traders.

Many liquidity-motivated traders believe that displaying their true liquidity-seeking nature works in their favor. When trading with a liquidity-motivated trader, dealers and other market participants can relax some of the protective measures that they use to prevent losses to informed traders.

4.2.4. Passive Traders

Low-cost trading is a strong motivation of passive traders, even though they are liquidity-motivated in their portfolio-rebalancing operations. As a result, these traders tend to favor limit orders, portfolio trades, and crossing networks. The advantages, in addition to certainty of price, are low commissions, low impact, and the possible reduction or elimination of bid–ask spread costs. The major weakness is the uncertainty of whether trades will be completed within a reasonable time frame. These orders and markets are best suited to trading that is neither large nor heavily concentrated.

5. TRADE EXECUTION DECISIONS AND TACTICS

The diversity of markets, order types, and characteristics of the particular securities that must be traded means that the task of selecting a trading strategy and promptly executing it is quite complex. In the following sub-sections, we first discuss decisions related to the handling of a trade. Then, we address objectives in trading and trading tactics, including automated trading.

5.1. Decisions Related to the Handling of a Trade

Trading costs are controllable, necessitating thoughtful approaches to trading strategies. Poor trading involving inattentive or inappropriate trading tactics leads to higher transaction costs. Conversely, good trading lowers transaction costs and improves investment performance.

A head trader thinking about how to organize his or her team needs to develop a daily strategy which balances the trading needs of the portfolio manager(s) and the condition of the market. The head trader, of course, controls neither but has to devise a strategy for trading the daily blotter. Considerations that come into play include the following:

- Small, liquidity-oriented trades can be packaged up and executed via direct market access and algorithmic trading. **Direct market access** (DMA) refers to platforms sponsored by brokers that permit buy-side traders to directly access equities, fixed income, futures, and foreign exchange markets, clearing via the broker.[26] Algorithmic trading, a type of automated electronic trading, will be discussed later. Larger trades can receive custom handling. Why waste the talent of senior traders and the most competent brokers on trades in which it is not possible to make an economically significant difference?
- Large, information-laden trades demand immediate skilled attention. Senior traders are needed to manage the tradeoff between impact and delay costs by releasing the minimum amount of information into the market that is required to get the trade done.
- In addition to best execution, the trader must be cognizant of client trading restrictions, cash balances, and brokerage allocations, if any.

Once the strategy is determined and traders are handed their assignments, the problem of best execution practice becomes tactical. Of course, trading tactics change in response to the market conditions encountered. Each trader, while working orders, should be asking the following questions:

1. What is the right trading tactic for this particular trade at this point in time?
2. Is the trade suitable for DMA or algorithmic trading, or is manual handling of the trade appropriate?
3. If a broker is used, by my experience and measurement, which broker is best suited to handle this order?
4. What is the expected vs. experienced cost for this type of trading tactic?
5. Where is the lowest-cost liquidity likely to be found?
6. If the low-cost alternatives fail, where should I go to increase the aggressiveness of the trading?
7. Is the market responding as I would expect, or are there messages that should be conveyed to portfolio management?
8. How can I find out as much as possible about the market situation while revealing as little as possible of my own unfulfilled intentions?
9. What can be done to minimize any negative tax consequences of the trade (such as earmarking specifically the lot of securities being sold so as to control their cost basis)?

The process starts with an order-by-order understanding of the urgency and size constraints. These constraints determine the appropriate processes that the desk can use. Order tactics, in turn, determine the market venues that represent the best alternative. At that point, specific order handling depends on the desk's commitments, activity by brokers currently trafficking in the name, and the desk's comfort with the specific broker or electronic venue.

In summary, the key function of trade desk organization is to prioritize trading. Good desks quickly identify the dangerous trades and assign the priority. They know how their managers

[26] As of 2004, estimates were that about a third of buy-side equity orders were executed via DMA (www.wstonline.com) in the United States.

think, in general and in relation to the specific individual trade. They attune the mix of brokers to their trading needs, often concentrating trading to increase their clout. Finally, they are constantly innovating and experimenting, trying new trade routes and refining desk processes.

5.2. Objectives in Trading and Trading Tactics

How does a trader decide which type of order to use? Earlier in this chapter, the strategic decision of the trade was identified as one of buying or selling time (deciding how much urgency to attach to trade completion). Perhaps the most common trader errors are selling time too cheaply when executing value-motivated transactions and buying time too expensively when executing information-motivated transactions. A third error, and the most serious error for a liquidity trader, is to act in a manner that evokes protective or exploitative responses from dealers and other market participants who sense an information motivation or other time-sensitive motivation.

One tactical decision faced by buy-side traders is the type of order to be used. Few portfolio managers base their investment decisions solely on value, information, or liquidity. Most managers mix strategic goals in response to client agreements, manager perceptions, and market cycles. For example, clients may require full investment in equities at all times, regardless of whether superior investment alternatives are available. Accordingly, trading tactics may at times appear inconsistent with the stated long-term strategic investment objectives. Thus, all buy-side traders need to understand, and occasionally use, the full range of trading techniques. The subsections that follow discuss a categorization of similarities and differences among various trading techniques.

5.2.1. Liquidity-at-Any-Cost Trading Focus Information traders who believe they need to trade in institutional block size with immediacy use these trading techniques. The problem, of course, is that everyone is wary of trading with an informed trader. On the other hand, dealers are mightily interested in finding out whether these anxious traders have any valuable information. Thus, these traders can usually attract brokers willing to represent their order, but often at a high commission rate or price concession.

These trades demand high liquidity on short notice. They may overwhelm the available liquidity in the market and cause prices to move when their presence is detected. Traders who use these techniques usually recognize that these methods are expensive but pay the price in order to achieve timely execution.

On occasion, urgency will place a normally nonaggressive trader into this category. A mutual fund with unusual end-of-day sales, for example, may need to liquidate security positions whatever the cost.

5.2.2. Costs-Are-Not-Important Trading Focus Market orders and the variations on this type (such as market on close) are examples of orders resulting from a costs-are-not-important focus. Some investors seldom consider using anything other than market orders when trading securities. Market orders work acceptably well for most mixes of investment strategies, in which it is difficult to assign pure information, value, or liquidity motivation. They also serve to mask trading intention, since all market orders look alike.

Traders who use market orders trust the competitive market to generate a fair price. For many orders, fair market price is a reasonable assumption. Exchanges encourage market orders and set up elaborate procedures to assure that these orders receive fair "best execution" prices. Active control of the order is not required.

Market orders work best for smaller trades and more liquid stocks. They are sometimes called "no-brainers" because they require little trading skill on the part of the buy-side trader or the broker. Because they require little effort or risk taking by market makers, they are inexpensive for a broker to execute and have been used to produce "soft dollar" commissions in exchange for broker-supplied services.

Traders who use these orders pay ordinary spreads and commissions to have their orders executed rapidly. Trade costs are accepted without question; indeed, they are seldom even considered.

The weakness of market orders is that all trader discretion is surrendered. The trader has no control over the trade, and the broker exercises only the most rudimentary cautions. The marketplace processes are viewed as sufficient to assure fair treatment. To retain discretion, such a trader may also consider using an aggressive limit order—for example, a limit buy order that improves on the best bid or a limit sell order that improves on the best ask price.

5.2.3. Need-Trustworthy-Agent Trading Focus

Buy-side traders often need to execute larger orders than the exchange can accommodate at any given moment, particularly when dealing with thinly traded issues. They recognize that their orders may create adverse impact if they are not handled carefully. Accordingly, these traders engage the services of a carefully selected floor broker to skillfully "work" such orders by placing a best efforts, market-not-held, or participate order. The advantage of these trades is that they match trading desires to interest in taking the other side of the trade as such interest is uncovered or arrives in the market. Orders are usually completed through a series of partial trades. Obviously, immediate execution is not of primary importance, so such orders are less useful for information-motivated traders.

These orders are the epitome of the agency relationship. The trader passes control of the order to the broker, who then controls when and at what price the orders execute. The trader frequently does not know how much of an order was cleared until after the market closes.

The agent, however, may serve multiple masters, including other clients and even the agent's own brokerage firm. The valuable information that a buyer or seller exists is revealed to the broker. It is difficult for the trader to know whether that information is used exclusively in the trader's best interests.

5.2.4. Advertise-to-Draw-Liquidity Trading Focus

Advertising is an explicit liquidity-enhancing technique used with initial public offerings (IPOs), secondary offerings, and **sunshine trades,** which publicly display the trading interest in advance of the actual order. If publicity attracts enough traders taking the opposite side, the trade may execute with little or no market impact.

Implied in agency orders is an authorization to do some low-level advertising on the exchange floor. Advertising lets the market know that a willing buyer or seller is around. That presence may draw out the other side of the trade. However, such an order may also bear the risk of trading in front of the order. For example, if a large block purchase order is announced, traders may take long positions in the security in the hope of realizing a profit by selling the stock at a higher price.

5.2.5. Low-Cost-Whatever-the-Liquidity Trading Focus

Limit orders are the chief example of this type of order, particularly limit orders that specify prices that are "behind the market": either a limit buy order at a price below the best bid, or a limit sell order at a price above the best ask price. The objective is to improve on the market bid or the market ask, respectively. Minimizing trading costs is the primary interest of buy-side traders who use this type of order.

There may not be a counterparty to the trader's order who is willing to trade on the terms suggested. This order type is best suited to passive and value-motivated trading situations.

The advantages of such orders are low commissions, low impact, and possibly the elimination of the market maker spread. One major weakness, of course, is execution uncertainty (the uncertainty of whether any trades will be made at all). Traders could end up "chasing the market" if the market moves away from the limit price. Furthermore, if the limit price becomes "stale" because significant new information on the security reaches the public, the trader could find that a trade has been executed before he or she has been able to revise the limit price. For example, a limit buy order specifying a price that is well below the most recent transaction price runs the risk of being executed only if major negative news relating to the security reaches the public. If that happens, the security could trade down to even lower levels.

5.2.6. Trading Technique Summary

Exhibit 10-9 summarizes the uses, costs, advantages, and weaknesses of these trading techniques.

5.3. Automated Trading

Trading strategy will vary according to the specifics of the trade and the markets in which the trade might be executed. For example, traders attempting to trade very large orders relative to typical trading volume may involve brokers to avail themselves of the brokers' network of contacts and market knowledge in locating counterparties. By contrast, traders in quote-driven markets will typically try to negotiate trades with dealers, attempting to find the best possible quotes for their trades. As noted earlier, the rapid evolution of market structure worldwide toward order-driven systems, and electronic automated auctions in particular, has important implications for the trading process. Indeed, one of the more important implications of the growth of automated venues is the rapid expansion in algorithmic trading.

Algorithmic trading refers to automated electronic trading subject to quantitative rules and user-specified benchmarks and constraints. Related, but distinct, trading strategies include using portfolio trades, in which the trader simultaneously executes a set of trades in a basket of stocks, and **smart routing,** whereby algorithms are used to intelligently route an order to the most liquid venue. The term **automated trading** is the most generic, referring to any form of trading that is not manual, including trading based on algorithms.

Estimates of automated trading usage vary widely, and some estimates put it as high as 25 percent of average share volume. Informed commentators all agree that this share is increasing, with some projecting algorithmic volume growing at a 30 to 35 percent rate per annum over the next few years.[27] This revolution raises natural questions: How do algorithmic systems work? What goes inside the "black box" of algorithmic trading? Will algorithmic systems displace human traders, or can savvy human traders infer the logic of the algorithm and profit by gaming the computer? Do algorithms always work as advertised, or do traders put too much trust in them? Are algorithms really effective in controlling transaction costs and hence adding alpha? What is the future of algorithmic trading? The following discussion sheds light on these issues and focuses on an in-depth analysis of the anatomy of algorithmic trading.

5.3.1. The Algorithmic Revolution

The rapid growth of algorithmic trading by institutional traders reflects complex regulatory and technological factors. In the United States, decimalization (the use of a minimum price increment of 0.01, for U.S. currency \$0.01) has led

[27] As of 2005, one estimate is that 15 to 20 percent of U.S. investment firms have adopted algorithmic trading. See Schmerken (2005).

EXHIBIT 10-9 Objectives in Trading

Focus	Uses	Costs	Advantages	Weaknesses
Liquidity at any cost (I must trade)	Immediate execution in institutional block size	High cost due to tipping supply/demand balance	Guarantees execution	High potential for market impact and information leakage
Need trustworthy agent (Possible hazardous trading situation)	Large-scale trades; low-level advertising	Higher commission; possible leakage of information	Hopes to trade time for improvement in price	Loses direct control of trade
Costs are not important	Certainty of execution	Pays the spread; may create impact	Competitive, market-determined price	Cedes direct control of trade; may ignore tactics with potential for lower cost
Advertise to draw liquidity	Large trades with lower information advantage	High operational and organizational costs	Market-determined price for large trades	More difficult to administer; possible leakage to front-runners
Low cost whatever the liquidity	Non-informational trading; indifferent to timing	Higher search and monitoring costs	Low commission; opportunity to trade at favorable price	Uncertainty of trading; may fail to execute and create a need to complete at a later, less desirable price

to a dramatic reduction in spreads in U.S. equities but has also reduced quoted depths. Average trade size in many U.S. markets, including the New York Stock Exchange and NASDAQ, which constitute a substantial fraction of world equity market value, has fallen dramatically.[28] For institutions with large orders, these changes greatly complicate the task of trading. Institutional orders are typically large relative to normal trading volume. *The underlying logic behind algorithmic trading is to exploit market patterns of trading volume so as to execute orders with controlled risk and costs.* This approach typically involves breaking large orders up into smaller orders that blend into the normal flow of trades in a sensible way to moderate price impact. For active equity trading desks, algorithmic or automated trading is the only recourse for efficiently handling increased volumes given increasingly smaller average trade size.

EXAMPLE 10-9 The Changing Roles of Traders

Algorithmic trading involves programming a computer to "slice and dice" a large order in a liquid security into small pieces, then meters the pieces into an automated exchange using FIX communications technology (FIX is a messaging protocol in equity markets that facilitates electronic trading).

Trading in 400-share nibbles may sound inefficient, but it is not. Due to the speed of the analytics and the connectivity, trading engines can execute many trades per minute, all without human intervention or human error. Algorithmic trading has changed the role of the trader. Today's traders have become strategists and tacticians, whereas in the past, the primary task of a trader was managing broker relationships.

Of course, the role of the broker also changes when the buy-side institution takes active control of the order. Brokers have in many cases been eliminated from trades they would have formerly been given responsibility for executing. Rather than serving as agents or dealers, brokers increasingly compete on the basis of the quality of their analytic engine.

EXAMPLE 10-10 Order Fragmentation: The Meat-Grinder Effect[29]

Plexus Group has documented a trade in Oracle Corporation (NASDAQ: ORCL) that occurred on November 21, 2002 that illustrates well both order fragmentation and electronic trading.

[28]According to the *NYSE Fact Book* (various editions), the average number of shares per trade peaked at 2,568 in June 1988 and then began to decline. The number of shares per trade remained in the low 1,000s for most of the late 1990s, falling below 1,000 shares in March of 2001, the year of decimalization, and steadily declining since. In December 2003, the average reached 433 shares per trade. Decimalization, adopted by the United States and Canada during the early 2000s, has long been the international standard in equity marketplaces.

[29]This example is based on Wagner (2003).

Before the market opening, a momentum manager sent a 1,745,640-share buy order to his trading desk, and the process unfolded as follows. The desk fed the order to Bloomberg B-Trade, one of several ECNs available to the trade desk. Trading in the issue began at 9:53 a.m. The order was small, in the sense that it was slightly less than 3 percent of Oracle's trading volume that day, and was completed in just 51 minutes in 1,014 separate executions. At times, there were up to 153 executions per minute—more than any human could handle. Average trade size was about 1,700 shares, roughly a 1,000:1 fragmentation ratio (i.e., the ratio of the size of the order to average trade size). The largest execution was roughly 64,000 shares and occurred in a cluster of rapid trading when almost 190,000 shares were executed in less than one minute. The smallest execution was for 13 shares. Seventeen percent of the executions were for 100 shares or less, and 44 percent were for less than 1,000 shares. Implementation shortfall was $0.15 per share, including $0.14 from market impact and delay and $0.01 per share commissions.

The aggressive trading strategy paid off: ORCL rose at the close to yield a trading profit for the day of 4.1 percent, or $785,538. In order for the 1,700,000-odd-share order to be executed, it had to be forced through a constriction 1,700 shares wide on average. This is the meat-grinder effect: In order for a large equity order to get done, it must often be broken up into many smaller orders.

Ever-faster trade message speed and increased volumes in automated trading systems or electronic limit order books, such as the International Securities Exchange for options and Hotspot FX for foreign exchange, have spurred the development of algorithmic systems. It is expected that the merger between the NYSE and the Archipelago Exchange will also stimulate greater use of algorithmic systems.

Automated trading requires constant monitoring to avoid taking unintentional risk. For example, if the process executes the easiest trades first, the portfolio manager might wind up later in the day with an unbalanced portfolio or unintended exposure to certain sectors or industries. Algorithmic execution systems that skillfully participate in order flow over time are well adapted to control such portfolio risks.

5.3.2. Classification of Algorithmic Execution Systems Algorithmic trading has gained considerable popularity among more sophisticated institutional traders looking for a technological solution to a complex, fast-moving, and fragmented market environment. These strategies are typically offered through algorithmic execution systems from institutional brokers, although some institutions and hedge funds have developed their own internal algorithms.

Algorithmic trading has its roots in the simple portfolio trades of the 1980s, in which large baskets of stocks were bought and sold (often as part of an index arbitrage strategy) with the push of a button. In the 1990s, automated systems such as ITG's QuantEX™ allowed for so-called rules-based trading. One example of rules-based trading is "pairs trading," in which the trading engine will automatically enter into (or exit from) a long and short position in a predesignated pair of stocks if certain conditions are met. The user can, for instance, specify a rule that calls for buying XYZ and simultaneously selling ABC if the price ratio of the two stocks crosses a certain threshold. The success of rules-based trading gave rise in the late 1990s to algorithmic trading, in which decisions regarding trading horizon, style, and even venue are

EXHIBIT 10-10 Algorithmic Trading Classification

Logical Participation Strategies			
Simple Logical Participation Strategies	Implementation Shortfall Strategies	Opportunistic Strategies	Specialized Strategies

automatically generated by a computer using specified algorithms based on specified inputs and then executed electronically. Before we delve into the details of how algorithms actually work, it is useful to develop a classification of algorithmic strategies (see Exhibit 10-10).

The most common class of algorithms in use is **logical participation strategies,** protocols for breaking up an order for execution over time.

5.3.2.1. Simple Logical Participation Strategies Institutional traders use the following simple logical participation strategies to participate in overall market volumes without being unduly visible:

- One of the most popular logical participation strategies involves breaking up an order over time according to a prespecified volume profile. The objective of this **volume-weighted average price (VWAP) strategy** is to match or improve upon the VWAP for the day.

  In a VWAP strategy, the trader attempts to match the expected volume pattern in the stock, typically over the whole day. Forecasts of the volume pattern are generally based on historical data (e.g., 21-day stock-specific or industry averages); increasingly, these forecasts are based on forward-looking volume predictors. Since the actual volume for the day is unknown before the end of the day, however, dynamic predictors are quite volatile.
- The **time-weighted average price (TWAP) strategy** is a particularly simple variant that assumes a flat volume profile and trades in proportion to time.

  The TWAP strategy breaks up the order over the day in proportion to time, which is useful in thinly traded assets whose volume patterns might be erratic. The objective here is normally to match or beat a time-weighted or equal-weighted average price. The participation strategy trades at a constant fraction of volume (usually 5 to 20 percent), attempting to blend in with market volumes. This strategy can be reactive if based on past trades or proactive if based on a dynamic forecast of incoming volume.
- Another common participation strategy is a **percentage-of-volume strategy,** in which trading takes place in proportion to overall market volume (typically at a rate of 5 to 20 percent) until the order is completed.

5.3.2.2. Implementation Shortfall Strategies Recently, a newer logical participation strategy, the so-called **implementation shortfall strategy** (or **arrival price strategy**), has gained popularity. Unlike simple logical participation strategies, implementation shortfall strategies solve for the optimal trading strategy that minimizes trading costs as measured by the implementation shortfall method.

As discussed earlier, implementation shortfall is defined as the difference between the return on a notional or paper portfolio, in which positions are executed at a price representing the prevailing price when the decision to trade is made, and the actual portfolio's return.

Implementation shortfall strategies seek to minimize implementation shortfall or overall execution costs, usually represented by a weighted average of market impact and opportunity costs. Opportunity costs are related to the risk of adverse price movements, which increases with trading horizon. Consequently, implementation shortfall strategies are typically "front-loaded"

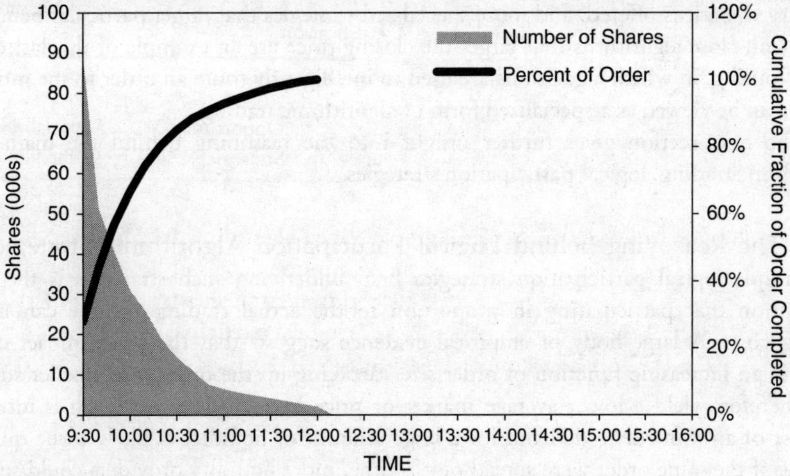

EXHIBIT 10-11 Trade Schedule for an Implementation Shortfall Strategy

in the sense of attempting to exploit market liquidity early in the trading day. Implementation shortfall strategies are especially valuable for portfolio trades, in which controlling the risk of not executing the trade list is critical. They are also useful in transition management (handing over a portfolio to a new portfolio manager), where multiperiod trading is common and there is a need for formal risk controls.

Interest in implementation shortfall strategies is also driven by an increased awareness of the limitations of traditional simple logical participation strategies using VWAP as an objective or benchmark. In addition, the objective of implementation shortfall strategies is consistent with the mean–variance framework used by many quantitative managers, a point we expand upon below. As of the date of this writing, roughly 90 percent of the value of orders traded algorithmically is executed using simple logical participation and implementation shortfall strategies. Exhibit 10-11 shows the hypothetical trade schedule for an implementation shortfall algorithmic order. Notice that the order is traded aggressively to minimize a weighted average of market impact costs and trade risk. The black line shows the cumulative fraction of the order that is complete, with the order fully complete by noon EST.

The remaining major types of algorithmic trading are opportunistic participation strategies and specialized strategies.

5.3.2.3. Opportunistic Participation Strategies Opportunistic participation strategies also involve trading over time. The opportunistic trading strategy involves passive trading combined with the opportunistic seizing of liquidity. The most common examples are pegging and discretion strategies, in which the trader who wishes to buy posts a bid, hoping others will sell to him or her, yielding negative implicit trading costs. If the bid–offer spread is sufficiently small, however, the trader might buy at the ask. This strategy typically involves using reserve or hidden orders and crossing (internally or externally) to provide additional sources of liquidity at low cost. Because trading is opportunistic, the liquidity strategy is not a true participation strategy.

5.3.2.4. Specialized Strategies Other strategies include passive order strategies, which do not necessarily guarantee execution; "hunter" strategies, which opportunistically seek liquidity when it is offered; and more specialized strategies that target particular benchmarks. Market-on-close algorithms that target the closing price are an example of this last category. Smart routing, in which algorithms are used to intelligently route an order to the most liquid venue, can be viewed as a specialized form of algorithmic trading.

The next section gives further insight into the reasoning behind the main type of algorithmic trading, logical participation strategies.

5.3.3. The Reasoning behind Logical Participation Algorithmic Strategies

To take simple logical participation strategies first, underlying such strategies is the implicit assumption that participating in proportion to the actual trading volume can minimize trading costs. A large body of empirical evidence suggests that the price impact of equity trades is an increasing function of order size. Breaking up the order into smaller sub-blocks may therefore yield a lower average market or price impact. This approach is intuitive, as the cost of an immediate demand for a large amount of liquidity is likely to be quite high, whereas if the same order were spread out in time, more liquidity providers could supply the needed opposite party, lessening the adverse price effects. Under certain assumptions (e.g., if prices are linearly related to the order size), breaking up the order in proportion to expected market liquidity yields lower market impact cost.

An implementation shortfall strategy involves minimizing a weighted average of market impact costs and missed trade opportunity costs. Missed trade opportunity cost refers to the risk of not executing a trade because of adverse price movements. A common proxy for such costs is the volatility of trade value or trade cost, which increases with trading horizon. Intuitively, the sooner an order is made available to the market, the greater the opportunity it usually has to find the opposing side of the trade. Consequently, implementation shortfall strategies are typically front-loaded, in the sense that they can involve trading significant fractions of market volume in the early periods of trading, in contrast to simple logical participation strategies.[30]

The logic for implementation shortfall strategies differs from that of the more traditional participation strategy. Recall that breaking up an order yields the lowest market impact cost. However, there is a cost to extending trade duration by breaking the order very finely, namely, risk. The implementation shortfall strategy—after the user specifies a weight on market impact cost and opportunity cost or risk—solves for the optimal trading strategy.[31] The intuition is straightforward. If the trader is very risk averse, then the strategy will trade aggressively in early periods to complete the order quickly to avoid undue risk. The more formal problem solved by the implementation shortfall algorithm can be expressed mathematically as

$$\text{Min}\{S_1, S_2, \ldots, S_T\}\text{Expected cost}(S_1, S_2, \ldots, S_T) + \lambda\text{Var}[\text{Cost}(S_1, S_2, \ldots, S_T)]$$

where T is the horizon (some algorithms actually solve for this), S_t represents the shares to be traded in trading interval (or bucket) t, λ is the weight placed on risk (aversion parameter), and Var[Cost] represents the variance of the cost of trading. The expression given is an **objective function** (a quantitative expression of the objective or goal of a process). In words, the objective function states that an implementation shortfall algorithm selects the set of trades that minimizes a quantity equal to the expected total cost of the trades and a penalty term

[30]The exception might occur when there is significant volume expected at the end of the day that the strategy takes into consideration.

[31]See, for example, Almgren and Chriss (2000/2001).

EXHIBIT 10-12 Order Management System

Symbol	Side	Size (shares)	Avg. Daily Volume	Price	Spread (%)	Urgency
ABC	B	100,000	2,000,000	55.23	0.05	Low
DEF	S	30,000	60,000	10.11	0.55	Low
GHIJ	B	25,000	250,000	23.45	0.04	High

that increases with the variance of the possible cost outcomes for the set of trades. The penalty term reflects the trader's desire for certainty as to costs.

Observe the close correspondence between this problem and the classic mean–variance portfolio optimization problem. Indeed, for a quantitative manager using a mean–variance optimization approach, it is logical to use an implementation shortfall algorithm. Implementation shortfall costs directly reduce the portfolio's return and hence are part of the expected return component in the portfolio optimization problem. Transaction costs are an integral element of portfolio performance because the variance of cost is ultimately manifested in the variance of portfolio returns, and expected costs directly reduce alpha. Although many managers do not recognize this dependence, it is quantitatively important. For example, a small-capitalization fund rebalancing daily might easily incur costs of trading of, say, 80 bps, with a standard deviation of 150 to 200 bps. On an annualized basis, these figures are large relative to the expected returns and risks of the portfolio. The implementation shortfall algorithm is thus consistent with the ultimate portfolio optimization problem.

Choosing among algorithms and setting the right parameters are difficult tasks. A simple illustration can help us understand the types of considerations that enter into selecting tactics. Exhibit 10-12 shows summary output from a trader's **order management system** (OMS) or trade blotter indicating trade size (in shares), various market attributes, and an urgency level from the portfolio manager. (A **trade blotter** is a device for entering and tracking orders to trade and trade executions.)

Which tactics are appropriate for each order? Although the first order in ABC is the largest in shares and value, it is actually the smallest as a percentage of average daily volume, and given the low spreads and low urgency level, it is ideally suited for algorithmic execution, probably with a VWAP algorithm using the entire day's liquidity. Similarly, the order in GHIJ is just 10 percent of average daily volume, but given the high urgency, an implementation shortfall algorithm might be preferred with a high urgency setting to aggressively execute the purchase. By contrast, the order in DEF is large relative to average daily volume and would likely be traded using a broker or crossing system to mitigate the large spreads.

EXAMPLE 10-11 A Trading Strategy

Charles Lee is discussing execution strategy with Rachel Katz, the head of equity trading at his investment management firm. Lee has decided to increase the position in Curzon Enterprises for growth-oriented equity accounts. Katz shows Lee Exhibit 10-13, which depicts the execution of a buy order in Curzon Enterprises that established the initial position in it. In Exhibit 10-13, the black line shows the cumulative fraction of the order that is complete as the trading day progresses, with the order fully complete by the close at 4:00 p.m. EST. The shaded area represents trading volume over half-hour intervals.

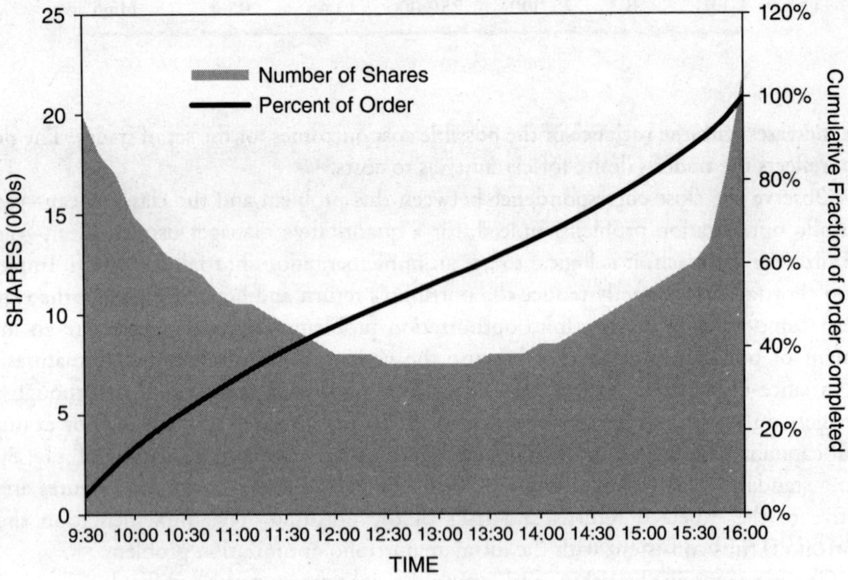

EXHIBIT 10-13 The Execution of an Order

Using the information in Exhibit 10-13, address the following:

1. Interpret the pattern of intraday trading in Curzon Enterprises.
2. Identify and evaluate the execution strategy depicted in Exhibit 10-13.

Solution to Problem 1: Trading in Curzon Enterprises follows a U shape, with highest volume at the opening and close and lowest volume at midday.

Solution to Problem 2: The exhibit depicts a VWAP algorithmic order. The execution strategy split the order up into pieces to be executed throughout the day. The curve indicating the cumulative fraction executed has a steeper slope earlier and later in the day than in midsession, indicating that the volume of orders the algorithm sent to the market was highest near the opening and the close, following the lead of the U-shaped trading volume, which indicates greatest volume at those times.

6. SERVING THE CLIENT'S INTERESTS

For the portfolio manager and buy-side trader, the effectiveness with which portfolio decisions are executed has an impact on the investment performance delivered to the client. The following sections discuss important issues related to protecting the client's interests.

6.1. CFA Institute Trade Management Guidelines

In 2002, CFA Institute published the Trade Management Guidelines[32] to offer investment managers "a framework from which to make consistently good trade-execution suggestions that, together, form a systematic, repeatable, and demonstrable approach to seeking Best Execution." The Guidelines state:

> *The concept of "Best Execution" is similar to that of "prudence" in intent and practice. Although prudence and Best Execution may be difficult to define or quantify, a general determination can be made as to whether they have been met . . . . Prudence addresses the appropriateness of holding certain securities, while Best Execution addresses the appropriateness of the methods by which securities are acquired or disposed. Security selection seeks to add value to client portfolios by evaluating future prospects; Best Execution seeks to add value by reducing frictional trading costs. These two activities go hand in hand in achieving better investment performance and in meeting standards of prudent fiduciary behavior.*

The Guidelines define best execution as "*the trading process Firms apply that seeks to maximize the value of a client's portfolio within the client's stated investment objectives and constraints.*" (Emphasis added; "Firms" refers to investment management firms.) The definition goes on to identify the four characteristics shown in the left-hand column of Exhibit 10-14. In the right-hand column, the authors amplify the thinking behind the guidelines.

EXHIBIT 10-14 Best Execution

Characteristic	Explanation
Best execution is intrinsically tied to portfolio-decision value and cannot be evaluated independently.	The purpose of trading is to capture the value of investment decisions. Thus, the definition has strong symmetry to the definition of prudent expert that guides fiduciary decisions.
Best execution is a prospective, statistical, and qualitative concept that cannot be known with certainty *ex ante*.	Trading is a negotiation, with each side of the trade having equal standing. Both buyer and seller—or their appointed agents—jointly determine what "best execution" is for every trade.
Best execution has aspects that may be measured and analyzed over time on an *ex post* basis, even though such measurement on a trade-by-trade basis may not be meaningful in isolation.	Trading occurs in a volatile environment subject to high statistical variability. One would not evaluate a card player on an individual hand; one would need to observe a sequence of hands to determine skill; similarly for traders. Despite the variability, overall trades contain some information useful in evaluating the process. By compiling trade data, one can deduce useful information about the quality of the process.
Best execution is interwoven into complicated, repetitive, and continuing practices and relationships.	Trading is a process, not an outcome. The standards are behavioral.

[32]See www.cfainstitute.org for any updates.

The Trade Management Guidelines are divided into three areas: processes, disclosures, and record keeping:

1. *Processes.* Firms should establish formal policies and procedures that have the ultimate goal of maximizing the asset value of client portfolios through best execution. A firm's policies and procedures should provide guidance to measure and manage effectively the quality of trade decisions.
2. *Disclosures.* Firms should disclose to clients and prospects (1) their general information regarding trading techniques, venues, and agents and (2) any actual or potential trading-related conflicts of interest. Such disclosure provides clients with the necessary information to help them assess a firm's ability to deliver best execution.
3. *Record keeping.* Firms should maintain proper documentation that supports (1) compliance with the firm's policies and procedures and (2) the disclosures provided to clients. In addition to aiding in the determination of best execution, the records may support a firm's broker selection practices when examined by applicable regulatory organizations.

At the time these guidelines were written, the state of the art in transaction cost measurement was such that it was not possible to specify specific methodologies for transaction cost measurement. Rather, the guidelines are a compilation of recommended practices and not standards.

In the end, best execution is primarily an exercise in serving the needs of the investment management clients. Adherence to standards of documentation and disclosure, as important as these are to ensuring best practices, is simply a means to achieving this overriding objective.[33]

6.2. The Importance of an Ethical Focus

"My word is my honor." The code of both buy-side and sell-side traders is that verbal agreements will be honored. The code is self-enforcing: Any trader who does not adhere to it quickly finds that no one is willing to deal with him.

Nonetheless, valuable information is the stock-in-trade of market participants, and the temptations are great. One of the side effects of the explosion of trading techniques and trading alternatives is that it is difficult to trace the uses to which information is being put. It is often necessary to rely on the strength of a trader's reputation and his or her avid desire to maintain and build long-term relationships.

Trading can be looked at as a "zero-sum game" in which one trader's losses are another trader's gains. The near disappearance of the brokerage commission has caused more trading costs to be implicit rather than explicit. Markets are thus becoming more adversarial and less agency-oriented, making it more difficult to align investor or buy-side interests with broker/dealer or sell-side interests.

In every case, the ethical focus for the portfolio manager and the buy-side trader must be the interests of the client. As previously mentioned, the buy-side trader acts in a fiduciary capacity, with access to the client's assets. Loyalties to the trader's own firm and relationships with sell-side traders must be consistent with the trader's fiduciary responsibilities.

[33] For further background on the subject, see Wagner and Edwards (1993), Wagner (2003), and Schwartz and Wood (2003).

7. CONCLUDING REMARKS

The ability of the sell-side system of brokers and exchanges to adapt and create solutions to investment requirements is impressive. In general, and increasingly, traders get the trading services they demand. Different order types and different venues serve investors with different motives and trading needs. In return, the broker/dealers and exchanges earn a competitive price for providing the services.

Technological advances continue to play a major role in reducing transaction costs. Faster dissemination of information, improved public access, more sophisticated analysis, and eventually the replacement of exchange floor trading by electronic trading can be expected. These efficiencies will reduce the cost of running the exchange system, but they will not necessarily reduce the cost of dealer services provided. Nor will the pressure to reduce costs and improve portfolio performance diminish.

Because of the intensity of competition and the readiness to adapt and innovate, costs continue to fall. Buy-side traders who demand the facilities and conveniences provided by the exchange community must expect to pay the costs. To reduce trading costs, an ever-evolving understanding of the trading process and its implied costs is essential. Sponsors and investment advisers may face make-or-buy decisions concerning future trading and trading-subsidized services. High-speed connectivity and algorithmic trading are clear examples of how costs can be effectively reduced by removing extraneous middlemen from the trading process.

Investors and traders are accustomed to a market that handles the duties, costs, and risks of trading. In addition, the sell side delivers an array of valuable but sometimes dimly related services without additional charge. Such services do not come free, however. In the future, pension plan sponsors and other clients will demand that portfolio managers and traders make more informed choices that reconcile trade costs with benefits received. Sponsors and other clients pay the costs of trading and are entitled to—and are increasingly demanding—a clear accounting of benefits derived.

CHAPTER 11

MONITORING AND REBALANCING

Robert D. Arnott

First Quadrant, LP
Research Affiliates, LLC
Pasadena, California

Terence E. Burns, CFA

Campion Wealth Management LLC
Vienna, Virginia

Lisa Plaxco, CFA

First Quadrant, LP
Pasadena, California

Philip Moore

Pacific Investment Consultants, LLC
Stevenson Ranch, California

1. INTRODUCTION

After a portfolio manager has worked closely with a client to document investment objectives and constraints in an investment policy statement (IPS), agreed on the strategic asset allocation that best positions the client to achieve stated objectives, and executed the strategic asset allocation through appropriate investment strategies for each asset class segment, the manager must constantly monitor and rebalance the portfolio. The need arises for several reasons.

First, clients' needs and circumstances change, and portfolio managers must respond to these changes to ensure that the portfolio reflects those changes. Life-cycle changes are expected for individual investors, so the portfolio manager must plan for these changes and respond to them when they occur. Institutional investors face changing circumstances just as commonly. A pension fund may receive a mandate from its trustees to assume less volatility. A university endowment may need to react to higher-than-anticipated inflation in faculty salaries.

Second, capital market conditions change. Portfolio managers must monitor such changes, adjust their capital market expectations appropriately, and reflect changed expectations in how the portfolio is invested. For example, if a client's return requirement is 8 percent but the strategic asset allocation promises to return on average 6.5 percent in the current climate, what changes should a portfolio manager recommend in light of the anticipated 150 bp shortfall?

Third, fluctuations in the market values of assets create differences between a portfolio's current asset allocation and its strategic asset allocation. These differences may be trivial on a daily basis; over longer periods of time, however, they can result in a significant divergence between the intended and actual allocations. When and how a portfolio manager rebalances the portfolio to the strategic asset allocation is one of the primary focuses of this chapter.

For a portfolio manager, designing and building a portfolio is only the beginning of the dynamic and interactive process that lasts for as long as she is the client's trusted advisor. As markets evolve, maintaining the alignment between a client's portfolio and his investment objectives requires constant vigilance. Therefore, monitoring and rebalancing the portfolio is one of the most important elements of the dynamic process of portfolio management.

We divide this chapter into two major sections, the first covering monitoring and the second covering rebalancing.

2. MONITORING

To monitor something means to systematically keep watch over it to collect information that is relevant to one's purpose. In investments, the purpose is to achieve investment goals. And a reality of investing is that what you don't know *can* hurt you. An overlooked fact may mean not reaching a goal. A portfolio manager should track everything affecting the client's portfolio. We can categorize most items that need to be monitored in one of three ways:

1. Investor circumstances, including wealth and constraints.
2. Market and economic changes.
3. The portfolio itself.

Monitoring investor-related factors sometimes results in changes to a client's investment policy statement, strategic asset allocation, or individual portfolio holdings. Monitoring market and economic changes sometimes results in changes to the strategic asset allocation (when they relate to long-term capital market expectations), tactical asset allocation adjustments (when they relate to shorter-term capital market expectations), changes in style and sector exposures, or adjustments in individual holdings. Monitoring the portfolio can lead to additions or deletions to holdings or to rebalancing the strategic asset allocation.

Fiduciaries need to pay particular attention to adequate monitoring in fulfilling their ethical and legal responsibilities to clients. Investment managers for individual and/or institutional separate accounts; managers of pooled funds (including mutual funds and unit trusts); and trustees of private trusts, pension plans, and charitable organizations are all fiduciaries because of their positions of trust with respect to the management of assets owned by or benefiting others. Fiduciaries have a range of ethical, reporting, auditing, disclosure, and other responsibilities to clients. But germane to this discussion, when taking investment actions, fiduciaries must consider the appropriateness and suitability of the portfolio relative to (1) the client's needs and circumstances, (2) the investment's basic characteristics, or (3) the basic characteristics of the total portfolio. These factors change over time. Only by systematic monitoring can a fiduciary secure an informed view of the appropriateness and suitability of a portfolio for a client.

The following sections provide a fuller explanation of monitoring.

2.1. Monitoring Changes in Investor Circumstances and Constraints

Each client has needs and circumstances that will most likely change over time. A successful portfolio manager makes every effort to remain sensitive to client needs and to anticipate events that might alter those needs. Periodic client meetings are an ideal time to ask whether needs, circumstances, or objectives have changed. If they have, the manager may need to revise the IPS and bring the portfolio into line with the revisions. In many cases, minor changes are needed that do not require revising the IPS. In the field of private wealth management, reviews are usually semiannual or quarterly. In institutional investing, the asset allocation review is a natural time for reviewing the range of changes in circumstance. Such reviews are often held annually. In all contacts with any type of client, however, the advisor should be alert to new client circumstances.

When a review is undertaken, what areas should be covered? Changes in investor circumstances and wealth, liquidity requirements, time horizons, legal and regulatory factors, and unique circumstances all need to be monitored.

2.1.1. Changes in Investor Circumstances and Wealth

Changes in circumstances and wealth often affect a client's investment plans. For private wealth clients, events such as changes in employment, marital status, and the birth of children may affect income, expenditures, risk exposures, and risk preferences. Each such change may affect the client's income, expected retirement income, and perhaps risk preferences. The responsibilities of marriage or children have repercussions for nearly all aspects of a client's financial situation. Such events often mark occasions to review the client's investment policy statement and overall financial plan. For institutional clients, operating performance, constituent pressures (such as demands for increased support from the beneficiaries of endowments), and changes in governance practices are among the factors that may affect income, expenditures, risk exposures, and risk preferences. A portfolio manager should communicate regularly with the client to become aware of such changes.

Wealth or net worth is one client factor that is central to investment plans. Wealth, when evaluated in the context of an investor's other circumstances, is both a measure of achieved financial success and an influence on future investment planning. Changes in wealth result from saving or spending, investment performance, and events such as gifts, donations, and inheritances. The investor's return requirements may change as a result, as financial goals recede or move closer to achievement, and risk tolerance may change too. Utility theory suggests that increases in wealth allow investors to increase their level of risk tolerance, accepting more systematic risk with its attendant expected reward. In reality, however, portfolio managers should consider only substantial and permanent changes in wealth in establishing the client's risk tolerance, even though client risk perceptions can vary quite substantially with recently experienced market performance. The portfolio manager's appraisal of a client's risk tolerance should be largely unaffected by transient changes in wealth. The investment manager thus has a difficult role to moderate some investors' desire to dramatically change asset allocations in response to market volatility. In contrast, more conservative investors may be unprepared to increase their risk tolerance even when a substantial increase in wealth suggests an increased capacity for bearing risk. Such a client's goal may become merely preserving gains that they never expected to have despite the opportunity costs. The portfolio manager should try to understand this mindset and, working within the client's comfort level, seek to restrain its excesses.

2.1.2. Changing Liquidity Requirements

When a client needs money to spend, the portfolio manager should strive to provide it. A liquidity requirement is a need for cash in excess of new contributions or savings as a consequence of some event, either anticipated or unanticipated.

Individual clients experience changes in liquidity requirements as a result of a variety of events, including unemployment, illness, court judgments, retirement, divorce, the death of a spouse, or the building or purchase of a home. Changes in liquidity requirements occur for a variety of reasons for institutional clients, such as the payment of claims by insurers or of retirement benefits by defined-benefit (DB) pension plans, or the funding of a capital project by a foundation or endowment.

The possibility of major withdrawals may constrain a portfolio manager's commitments to illiquid investments because of the costs in exiting those investments quickly. Managers who do not face major withdrawals are better positioned to earn the return premium such investments supply. Managers who do face major withdrawals near term may need to hold some part of their portfolio in liquid and low-price-risk assets such as money market instruments.

2.1.3. Changing Time Horizons

Individuals age and pension funds mature. Reducing investment risk is generally advisable as an individual moves through the life cycle and his time horizon shortens; bonds become increasingly suitable investments as this process occurs. Today's life-cycle mutual funds reflect that principle in their asset allocations. In contrast to individuals, some entities such as endowment funds have the hope of perpetual life; the passage of time in and of itself does not change their time horizon, risk budgets, or appropriate asset allocation.

Many private wealth clients have multistage time horizons. For example, a working person typically faces an accumulation stage up to retirement in which she builds wealth through saving and investment, followed by a retirement stage in which she spends wealth and ultimately bequeaths it to heirs. Accumulating funds for a child's higher education can create one or more stages before retirement. Changes in investment policy are usually needed as one time horizon (for example, reaching retirement or selling a closely-held family business) is reached and another begins.

Although some changes in time horizon are forecastable, time horizons can also shift abruptly. For instance, when the last income beneficiary of a trust dies and the **residue** (remaining funds) passes to the **remaindermen** (beneficiaries with a claim on the trust's residue), investment policy, as well as the portfolio, should be adjusted promptly. Annuitizing the benefits for older participants in a pension plan can result in an abrupt change in the plan's remaining liability stream. That should lead to an overhaul of the asset structure and rebalancing to a portfolio structure that more closely fits the new needs. The untimely death of an income-earning spouse requires immediate attention. Portfolio managers need to think about how they will respond to these changes and events and must monitor the client's circumstances for changes in time horizon. Example 11-1 addresses a change in investment horizon for an individual investor.

EXAMPLE 11-1 Monitoring a Change in Investment Horizon

William and Mary deVegh, both 32 years old, met and married when they were university students. They each embarked on promising and highly demanding executive careers after leaving college. They are hoping to retire at age 55 to travel and otherwise enjoy the fruits of their hard work. Now well established at their companies, they also want to start a family and are expecting the birth of their first child in two months. They hope the child will follow their tracks and obtain a four-year private university education. The deVeghs anticipate supporting their child through college. Assume that the deVeghs will each live to age 85.

1. Compare and contrast the deVeghs' investment time horizons prior to and immediately subsequent to the birth of their first child.
2. Interpret the challenges the birth will present to their retirement objectives and discuss approaches to meeting those challenges, including investing more aggressively.

Solution to Problem 1: Prior to the birth of their child, the deVeghs have a two-stage time horizon. The first horizon extends from age 32 up to age 55. This first time horizon could be described as an accumulation period in which the deVeghs save and invest for early retirement. The second time horizon is their retirement and is expected to extend from age 55 to age 85. After the birth of their child, they will have a three-stage time horizon. The first stage extends from age 32 through age 50, when they expect their child to enter university at age 18. During this period, the deVeghs must accumulate funds both for retirement and their child's university education. The second stage extends from age 51 up to age 55. In this period the deVeghs must anticipate disbursing substantial funds for tuition, room and board, and other expenses associated with a private university education. The third stage is retirement, expected to extend from age 55 to age 85 as before.

Solution to Problem 2: The birth of the child creates a four-year period of heavy expenses immediately prior to the deVeghs' intended retirement date. Those expenses could put their intended retirement date at risk. The most direct way to mitigate this risk is to increase the amount of money saved and to invest savings for the child's education in a tax-efficient way (tax-advantaged education saving vehicles are available in certain tax jurisdictions). Can the deVeghs mitigate their risk by increasing their risk tolerance? The need for a larger future sum of money does not in itself increase an investor's ability to take risk, although it may affect the investor's willingness to do so. There is no indication that the child's birth will be accompanied by a salary raise or other event increasing the ability to take risk. If the deVeghs' stated risk tolerance prior to the child's birth accurately reflects their ability to bear risk, investing more aggressively after the child's birth will not help them meet the challenges the event poses to their retirement objective.

2.1.4. Tax Circumstances

Taxes are certain; the form they will take and their amount in the future are uncertain. Taxable investors should make all decisions on an after-tax basis.

Managers for taxable investors must construct portfolios that deal with each client's current tax situation and take future possible tax circumstances into account. For taxable investors, holding period length and portfolio turnover rates are important because of their effect on after-tax returns. In evaluating investment strategies to meet a taxable investor's changed objective, a portfolio manager will take into account each strategy's **tax efficiency** (the proportion of the expected pretax total return that will be retained after taxes). Monitoring a client's tax situation may suggest the following actions, for example:

- Deferring the realization of income from a higher-tax year to an anticipated lower-tax year.
- Accelerating expenses to a high-tax year.
- Realizing short-term losses at year-end to offset realized short-term gains in the same year.
- Deploying assets with high unrealized gains so as to use a step-up in tax basis from original cost to market value (a break allowed investors for certain transactions in some tax jurisdictions). For example, if the client intends to make a charitable donation, making the contribution in appreciated securities may be tax advantageous in some tax jurisdictions.
- Reducing or increasing commitments to tax-exempt securities, where available.

2.1.5. Changes in Laws and Regulations

Laws and regulations create the environment in which the investor can lawfully operate, and the portfolio manager must monitor them to ensure compliance and understand how they affect the scope of the advisor's responsibility and discretion in managing client portfolios. For example, in the United States in recent years, corporate trustees have reevaluated how they manage investment portfolios for trust clients in light of the adoption of the Uniform Prudent Investor Rule (versus the traditional prudent man rule) and the Uniform Principal and Income Act.

Besides that necessity, portfolio managers should seek to grasp the implication of such legal and regulatory changes for current portfolio holdings and investment opportunities. Portfolio managers for both taxable and tax-exempt investors should monitor changes in tax regulations because such changes typically affect not only taxes but the equilibrium relationships among assets.

2.1.6. Unique Circumstances

A unique circumstance is an internal factor (other than a liquidity requirement, time horizon, or tax concern) that may constrain portfolio choice. The client may present the portfolio manager with a variety of challenges in this respect. For example, some clients direct portfolio managers to retain concentrated stock positions because of an emotional attachment to the particular holding, because the client must maintain the stock position to demonstrate his or her commitment as an officer of the company, or because the concentrated position effectively has an extremely large unrealized capital gain. Is it feasible and appropriate to hedge or monetize the position through one of several special strategies? If not, given the volatility and concentrated risk of this single holding, how should the portfolio manager allocate the balance of the client's portfolio? As a portfolio manager, what investment actions will you recommend or implement when the emotional attachment is gone, when the client is no longer an officer of the company, or when the client's heirs receive the position?

Institutional clients may have a range of special concerns. For example, a client may adopt principles of socially responsible investing (often referred to by its acronym, SRI). Endowments and public employee pension plans often have been particularly active in SRI. As an example, a fund may decide to reduce or eliminate holdings in "sin" stocks, such as gaming, alcohol, and tobacco. SRI constraints have tended to tilt a portfolio away from large companies, which introduces non-market-related risks and causes a small-capitalization stock bias. In the mid-1980s, when small-cap stocks were demonstrating a return advantage over large-cap stocks, SRI seemed a costless (even profitable) strategy. However, the client should be aware of the potential costs in adopting an SRI policy.

Institutional clients are focusing significant attention on evaluating and fostering improvements in corporate governance, believing that those efforts will in the long run enhance return and/or reduce portfolio risk. Indeed, European fund managers themselves have demanded better integration of extrafinancial issues such as corporate governance, human capital management, value creation or destruction during mergers and acquisitions, and global environment challenges in sell-side analysis.[1] Portfolio managers must respect such client concerns in evaluating the appropriateness of investments.

In Example 11-2, an investment advisor determines an appropriate investment recommendation for an inheritance and later, a new investment advisor makes changes to the client's IPS in light of dramatically changed needs. This example shows the detailed analysis and judgment that enters into revising an IPS.

EXAMPLE 11-2 Monitoring Changes in an Investor's Circumstances and Wealth[2]

John Stern, 55 years old and single, is a dentist. Stern has accumulated a $2.0 million investment portfolio with a large concentration in small-capitalization U.S. equities. Over the last five years, the portfolio has averaged 20 percent annual total return on investment. Stern does not expect to retire before age 70. His current income is more than sufficient to meet his expenses. Upon retirement, he plans to sell his dentistry practice and use the proceeds to purchase an annuity to cover his retirement cash flow needs. He has no additional long-term goals or needs.

In consultation with Stern, his investment advisor, Caroline Roppa, has drawn up an investment policy statement with the following elements. (Roppa's notes justifying each item are included.)

Elements of Stern's Investment Policy Statement:

Risk tolerance. Stern has above-average risk tolerance. *Roppa's notes*:

- Stern's present investment portfolio and his desire for large returns indicate a high *willingness* to take risk.
- His financial situation (large current asset base, ample income to cover expenses, lack of need for liquidity or cash flow, and long time horizon) indicates a high *ability* to assume risk.

Return objective. The return objective is an average total return of 10 percent or more with a focus on long-term capital appreciation. *Roppa's notes*: Stern's circumstances

[1] In 2004, four major European fund managers representing €330 billion under management announced an Enhanced Analytics Initiative in which 5 percent of brokerage commissions would be awarded on the basis of the integration of these concerns in brokerage house analysis.

[2] Adapted from the 2001 Level III CFA examination.

warrant an above-average return objective that emphasizes capital appreciation for the following reasons:

- Stern has a sizable asset base and ample income to cover his current spending; therefore, the focus should be on growing the portfolio.
- Stern's low liquidity needs and long time horizon support an emphasis on a long-term capital appreciation approach.
- Stern does not rely on the portfolio to meet living expenses.

The numerical objective of 10 percent represents an estimate of a target Stern can aim for rather than a minimum return required to meet a specific financial goal.

Liquidity. Stern's liquidity needs are low. *Roppa's notes*:

- Stern has no regular cash flow needs from the portfolio because the income from his dentistry practice meets all current spending needs.
- No large, one-time cash needs are stated. However, it could be considered appropriate to keep a small cash reserve for emergencies.

Time horizon. Stern's time horizon is long term and consists of two stages:

- The first stage consists of the time until his retirement, which he expects to be 15 years.
- The second consists of his lifetime following retirement, which could range from 10 to 20 years.

Roppa has also summarized Stern's current portfolio in Exhibit 11-1:

EXHIBIT 11-1 Summary of Stern's Current Portfolio

	Value	Percent of Total	Expected Annual Return	Expected Annual Standard Deviation
Short-term bonds	$ 200,000	10%	4.6%	1.6%
Domestic large-cap equities	600,000	30	12.4	19.5
Domestic small-cap equities	1,200,000	60	16.0	29.9
Total portfolio	$2,000,000	100	13.8	23.1

Stern expects to soon receive an inheritance of $2.0 million. Stern and Roppa sit down to discuss its investment in one of four index funds. Given Stern's already above-average risk tolerance and level of portfolio risk, Roppa and Stern have concluded that the risk tolerance description in the current IPS remains valid; they do not want to contemplate a further increase in portfolio risk. On the other hand, they do not wish to reduce expected return. Roppa is evaluating the four index funds shown in Exhibit 11-2 for their ability to produce a portfolio that will meet the following two criteria relative to the current portfolio:

- Maintain or enhance expected return.
- Maintain or reduce volatility.

Each fund is invested in an asset class that is not substantially represented in the current portfolio as shown in Exhibit 11-1. Exhibit 11-2 presents statistics on those index funds.

EXHIBIT 11-2 Index Fund Characteristics

Index Fund	Expected Annual Return	Expected Annual Standard Deviation	Correlation of Returns with Current Portfolio's Returns
Fund A	15%	25%	+0.80
Fund B	11	22	+0.60
Fund C	16	25	+0.90
Fund D	14	22	+0.65

1. Recommend the most appropriate index fund to add to Stern's portfolio. Justify your recommendation by describing how your chosen fund *best* meets both of the stated criteria. No calculations are required.

Twenty years later, Stern is meeting with his new financial advisor, Jennifer Holmstrom. Holmstrom is evaluating whether Stern's investment policy remains appropriate for his new circumstances.

- Stern is now 75 years old and retired. His spending requirements are expected to increase with the rate of general inflation, which is expected to average 3.0 percent annually.
- Stern estimates his current living expenses at $150,000 annually. An annuity, purchased with the proceeds from the sale of his dentistry practice, provides $20,000 of this amount. The annuity is adjusted for inflation annually using a national price index.
- Because of poor investment performance and a high level of spending, Stern's asset base has declined to $1,200,000 exclusive of the value of the annuity.
- Stern sold all of his small-cap investments last year and invested the proceeds in domestic bonds.
- Because his past international equity investments have performed poorly, Stern has become markedly uncomfortable with holding international equities.
- Stern plans to donate $50,000 to a charity in three months.

2. Discuss how *each* of the following components of Stern's investment policy statement should now reflect the changes in his circumstances:

   i. Risk tolerance
   ii. Return requirement
   iii. Liquidity needs
   iv. Time horizon

   Note: Your discussion should focus on, but not be limited to, the *direction* and *magnitude of change* in each component rather than on a specific numeric change.

Stern's investment portfolio at age 75 is summarized in Exhibit 11-3.

EXHIBIT 11-3 Stern's Investment Portfolio at Age 75

	Current Allocation	Expected Return	Expected Standard Deviation
Cash equivalents	2%	5%	3%
Fixed income	75	7	8
Domestic equities	10	10	16
International equities	3	12	22
Domestic real estate	10	10	17

3. Given Stern's changed circumstances, state whether the current allocation to *each* asset class should be lower, the same, or higher. Justify your response with *one* reason for *each* asset class. No calculations are required.
   i. Cash equivalents
   ii. Fixed income
   iii. Domestic equities
   iv. International equities
   v. Domestic real estate

   Note: Your response should be based only on Stern's changed circumstances and the information in Exhibit 11-3.
4. Explain one way in which Stern might seek to reduce the tension between his current return requirement and his current risk tolerance.

Solution to Problem 1: Fund D represents the single *best* addition to complement Stern's current portfolio, given the selection criteria. Fund D's expected return (14.0 percent) has the potential to increase the portfolio's return somewhat. Second, Fund D's relatively low correlation coefficient with his current portfolio (+0.65) indicates that it will provide larger diversification benefits than any of the other alternatives except Fund B. The result of adding Fund D should be a portfolio with about the same expected return and somewhat lower volatility compared to the original portfolio.

The other three funds have shortcomings in either expected return enhancement or volatility reduction through diversification:

- Fund A offers the potential for increasing the portfolio's return but is too highly correlated with other holdings to provide substantial volatility reduction through diversification.
- Fund B provides substantial volatility reduction through diversification but is expected to generate a return well below the current portfolio's return.
- Fund C has the greatest potential to increase the portfolio's return but is too highly correlated with other holdings to provide substantial volatility reduction through diversification.

Solution to Problem 2:

i. *Risk tolerance.* Stern's risk tolerance has declined as a result of investment losses and the material erosion of his asset base. His willingness to accept risk as reflected in his portfolio holdings and aversion to international equities has declined. Also, Stern's return requirement has risen sharply at the same time that assets available to generate that return are lower. Thus, Stern's ability to accept risk has also declined. Investments should emphasize less volatile securities.

ii. *Return requirement.* Stern now has a return requirement that represents an increase in both dollar and percentage terms from his return objective of 20 years earlier. In contrast to his prior situation, Stern now must use investments to meet normal living expenses.

Stern's annual expenses not covered by annuity payments total $130,000 (10.8 percent of his now reduced assets). His expenses are increasing at a rate at least as high as the 3 percent general inflation rate. To stay ahead of inflation without eroding the principal value of his portfolio, Stern needs to earn 13.8 percent. This percentage will increase to 14.3 percent after the $50,000 charitable donation occurs, because this distribution will further diminish Stern's asset base.

iii. *Liquidity needs.* Stern will require $50,000 (4.2 percent of assets) in three months for a charitable donation. In addition, Stern's need to fund a large part of his living expenses from his portfolio has created a substantial ongoing liquidity need. Investments should emphasize liquid securities in part to meet any unplanned near-term expenses without incurring substantial transaction costs.

iv. *Time horizon.* Stern is now 20 years older than when his initial investment policy was written. Assuming his life expectancy is normal, Stern's time horizon remains long term (i.e., in excess of 10 years) but shorter than when the initial policy was drafted.

Solution to Problem 3:

i. Cash equivalents should have a substantially higher weight than 2 percent. Stern requires $50,000 (4.2 percent of assets) in three months for the charitable donation. Compared with his position 20 years ago, his willingness and ability to accept volatility have decreased, his liquidity needs have increased, and his time horizon is now shorter. Stern needs a larger portion of his portfolio in low-risk, highly liquid assets.

ii. Fixed income should have a lower weight than 75 percent. Bonds are expected to provide a greater return than cash equivalents, which would help to meet Stern's return requirement. To meet additional liquidity needs and provide higher returns for expenses and inflation, however, a lower allocation is warranted.

iii. Domestic equities should have a higher weight than 10 percent. Stern requires fairly high returns and protection from inflation. Domestic equity investments would help meet those needs, but his lower ability and willingness to assume risk suggest only a moderate allocation to this somewhat volatile asset class, although higher than the current allocation.

iv. International equities should be eliminated. Although international equities may provide higher returns and diversification benefits, Stern is uncomfortable with holding international equities because of his experience with them. In the interests of respecting client wishes, Holmstrom should thus eliminate this asset class from the portfolio.

v. Domestic real estate should have a lower weight than 10 percent because of Stern's substantial liquidity requirements and reduced risk tolerance. Domestic equities have the same expected return as real estate with lower expected standard deviation and generally greater liquidity; therefore, domestic equities would be favored over domestic real estate among the higher expected return asset classes. Nevertheless, a smaller (i.e., less than 10 percent) real estate allocation could be maintained to obtain diversification benefits, to possibly generate income, and as a potential hedge against inflation.

Solution to Problem 4: Based on his current expenses of \$150,000 annually, Stern has a very high return requirement in relation to his current risk tolerance. The most direct way to reduce this tension would be to decrease annual expenses, although that might involve a change in living arrangements or lifestyle. For example, if annual expenses were cut by one-third to \$100,000, only \$80,000 would need to be supplied by investments after annuity payments. That would represent $\$80,000/\$1,200,000 = 6.7\%$ of assets, resulting in a return requirement of 9.7 percent prior to the charitable contribution. All else equal, the higher the return requirement relative to actual returns earned, the greater the need to spend principal and the greater **longevity risk** (the risk that one will outlive one's funds). Reducing expenses would mitigate that risk.

High-net-worth individuals often face the issue of concentrated stock holdings, which may be complicated by the issue of high unrealized capital gains. In Example 11-3, a change in client circumstances leads an investment advisor to search for the appropriate means to address the problem.

EXAMPLE 11-3 An Investor with a Concentrated Stock Position

Jonathan Wiese, CFA, serves as investment counsel for the Lane family. Franklin Lane, 62 years old, has a 2 million share position in Walton Energy, Inc. (WEI), an actively traded mid-cap energy company, accumulated through five years' service on its board of directors and earlier service as chief operating officer. At current market prices, the position is worth \$24 million, representing 40 percent of Lane's total portfolio of \$60 million. Another 20 percent of his portfolio is invested in other common equities, with the balance of 40 percent invested in Treasury inflation-protected and government agency securities. The cost basis of the WEI position is \$2.4 million, and the sale of the position would trigger a tax liability exceeding \$3.2 million. In the past Lane has insisted on maintaining his position in WEI shares to show his commitment to the company, but with Lane's recent retirement from WEI's board, Wiese has suggested that a portfolio review is appropriate. WEI shares are part of a mid-cap stock index, and Lane's position is substantial compared to average daily trading volume of WEI. Techniques to deal with concentrated stock positions fall under the rubric of hedging and monetization strategies. Wiese has organized several of these strategies in Exhibit 11-4, one or more of which may be appropriate to deal with Lane's concentrated position.

EXHIBIT 11-4 Hedging and Monetization Strategies

Strategy and Description	Advantages	Drawbacks
Zero-premium collar. Simultaneous purchase of puts and sale of call options on the stock. The puts are struck below and the calls are struck above the underlying's market price. The call premiums fund the cost of the puts.	• Locks in a band of values for the stock position. • Defers capital gains until stock is actually sold.	• Hedge lasts only the duration of the option's life. • Involves commissions. • Provides downside protection but gives away most of upside.
Variable prepaid forward. In effect, combines a collar with a loan against the value of the shares. When the loan comes due (often in two to four years), shares are sold to pay off the loan and part of any appreciation is shared with the lender.	• Converts 70 to 90 percent of the value of the position to cash. • Defers capital gains until stock is actually sold.	• Involves commissions and interest expenses. • Surrenders part of any appreciation in the stock.
Exchange fund. Fund into which several investors place their different share holdings in exchange for shares in the diversified fund itself. At the end of a period of time (often seven years), the fund distributes assets to shareholders pro rata.	• Diversifies holdings without triggering tax consequences.	• Expense ratio often 2 percent and other fees usually apply. • Diversification may be incomplete.
Private exchange. Shares that are a component of an index are exchanged for shares of an index mutual fund in a privately arranged transaction with the fund.	• Exchange is tax free. • Low continuing expenses. • Greatly increases diversification.	• Shares usually must be part of an index so not generally applicable. • Share position must be very substantial. • Concession to market value of shares exchanged may need to be offered. • May not be possible to arrange because fund interest may be lacking.

Note: Zero-premium collars and variable prepaid forwards may involve a tax liability; the taxation of these strategies varies across tax jurisdictions.

Lane faces no liquidity requirements, at least in the short term. At the review, Wiese and Lane agree that a 60/40 stock/bond mix remains appropriate for Lane.

1. Identify and evaluate Lane's primary investment need and the primary constraint on addressing that need.
2. Determine and justify the two strategies that most directly address the need identified in Part 1.

Solution to Problem 1: Lane's primary need is for diversification of his concentrated stock position. Having ended his last ties to WEI, Lane should be in a position to satisfy that need. The tax liability that would result from a sale of WEI stock, however, acts as a constraint on addressing that need: Selling the WEI position and investing the proceeds in a diversified stock portfolio would incur a tax liability of about $3.2 million.

Solution to Problem 2: The exchange fund and private exchange options most directly address Lane's diversification need. The zero-premium collar would hedge the value of WEI position but would not diversify Lane's equity position. Also, the zero-premium collar would essentially convert the WEI holding into a position with volatility not dissimilar to short-term bonds, over the collar's duration, changing the effective asset allocation. The variable prepaid forward would convert a large fraction of the value of the position to cash, which could then be invested in a diversified equity position; so that instrument could be used to address the diversification need. Because of the huge built-in tax liability, however, Lane would need to roll over the forward indefinitely with the attendant expenses. The exchange fund is a costly option because of its fee structure, but it does address Lane's needs more directly and on a longer-term basis. The same can be said of the private exchange option, which appears to be more cost effective than the exchange fund while achieving a similar purpose.

2.2. Monitoring Market and Economic Changes

In addition to changes in individual client circumstances, the economic and financial markets contexts of investments also require monitoring. Those contexts are not static. The economy moves through phases of expansion and contraction, each with some unique characteristics. Financial markets, which are linked to the economy and expectations of its future course, reflect the resulting changing relationships among asset classes and individual securities.[3] A portfolio manager's monitoring of market and economic conditions should be broad and inclusive. Changes in asset risk attributes, market cycles, central bank policy, and the yield curve and inflation are among the factors that need to be monitored.

2.2.1. Changes in Asset Risk Attributes

The historical record reflects that underlying mean return, volatility, and correlations of asset classes sometimes meaningfully change. An asset allocation that once promised to satisfy an investor's investment objectives may no longer do so after such a shift. If that is the case, investors will need either to adjust their asset allocations or to reconsider their investment objectives. Monitoring changes in asset risk

[3] See the chapter on capital market expectations for more information.

attributes is thus essential. Fiduciaries also owe their clients a duty to understand the risk factors in individual investments as such factors evolve.

Changes in asset risk attributes also present investment opportunities. Market prices for all assets reflect consensus perceptions of risk and reward. Changes in those perceptions produce immediate gains or losses. Successful active managers assess differences between actual risk and perceived risk of an investment and embrace that investment when the consensus view is unduly pessimistic.

Investment theoreticians and practitioners have long recognized the risk–reward tradeoff. Long-run incremental rewards are generally unattainable without incurring incremental risk. Conversely, an investor must sacrifice some return when seeking to minimize risk. Systematic risk, which diversification cannot eliminate, is the most likely type of risk to promise reward according to asset pricing theory. Although a link exists between systematic risk and return, it is less consistent than pure theory suggests. For active managers, the key to exploiting inconsistencies lies in determining when risk is already priced into an asset and when perceptions of risk deviate enough from quantifiable risk so that a courageous investor can profit from favorable mispricings and avoid the others. In equity markets historically, increasing volatility has signaled opportunity more often than not, providing buying opportunities when fear prompts others to sell.

2.2.2. Market Cycles

Investors monitor market cycles and valuation levels to form a view on the short-term risks and rewards that financial markets offer. Based on these opinions, investors may make tactical adjustments to asset allocations or adjust individual securities holdings.

Tactically, the markets' major swings present unusual opportunities to be either very right or very wrong. When things are going well, securities eventually perform too well; during economic weakness, stock prices often decline excessively. Weakness engenders an environment that may foreshadow extraordinary profits, while ebullient markets provide unusual opportunities to sell, reinvesting elsewhere. Although this point is easily illustrated by looking over our shoulders at the U.S. stock market in 1999 and 2000, it should be remembered that it was only the extremeness of the 1999 to 2000 market peak that is notable; these cycles recur nearly every decade or so. Market veterans may recall the environment of late 1974 as one of extraordinary opportunity. At one point the earnings yield of the U.S. stock market was 600 bps higher than bond yields, a difference not seen since the early 1950s. Conversely, in 1980 and 1981 and again in 1999 and 2000, bond yields exceeded earnings yields by a wide margin. That cyclical top presented another historic tactical opportunity as well as a shining example of the power and speed of mean reversion of asset-class returns. Reducing exposure to outperforming asset classes and increasing exposure to underperforming asset classes at the asset-class level—selling the stocks that had proven so comfortable and buying the bonds that the investment world seemed then to abhor—would have had a profound positive influence on total portfolio risk and return during those times.

Individual securities routinely show similar excesses. There are always securities whose issuers have either received such laudatory notices or suffered such unremitting adversity that their prices depart from reality. It is difficult to isolate those securities and then to act; only those investors suitably prepared and armed with courage will accept the challenge.

2.2.3. Central Bank Policy

Central banks wield power in the capital markets through the influence of their monetary and interest rate decisions on liquidity and interest rates. Their influence is felt in both bond and stock markets.

In bond markets, the most immediate impact of monetary policy is on money market yields rather than long-term bond yields. A central bank's influence on bond market *volatility*, however, is profound.

An example of this influence occurred in 1979, when the board of the U.S. Federal Reserve Bank under Paul Volcker changed its focus from controlling interest rates to controlling monetary growth. Previously the board had adjusted the discount rate in response to movements in the money supply, while simultaneously trying to manage that supply. Interest rates took a back seat in the board's deliberations, and T-bill rates rose from 9 percent to 14 percent in an eight-month period. The effect was dramatic. Volatility in the bond market exploded between late 1979 and mid-1982 (at which time policy was quietly reversed to combat recession). High-yielding bonds provided a compelling alternative to stocks, putting downward pressure on stock prices until the summer of 1982, when rallying bond prices and declining bond yields finally eased the pressure, making stocks again more attractive.

Turning to the stock market, "Do not fight the Fed" has been a long-standing warning from Martin Zweig—a warning that it can be problematic to invest in the market when the Fed is tightening the money supply. Jensen, Johnson, and Mercer (2000) and Conover, Jensen, Johnson, and Mercer (2005) have documented that in the United States, stock returns are on average higher during periods of expansionary monetary policy than in periods of restrictive monetary policy, as indicated by decreases and increases in the discount rate, respectively.[4]

These lessons bear repetition. Fed policy does matter and should not be ignored: Restricted credit and higher interest rates usually hurt stock returns; eased credit and lower interest rates usually enhance stock returns.

2.2.4. The Yield Curve and Inflation

The default-risk-free yield curve reflects investors' required return at various maturities. It incorporates not only individuals' time preferences for current versus future real consumption but also expected inflation and the maturity premium demanded. Yield curve changes reflect changes in bond values, and bond value changes affect equity values through the competition that bonds supply to equities. Thus investors closely monitor the yield curve.

The premium on long-term bonds over short-term bonds tends to be countercyclical (i.e., high during recessions and low at the top of expansions) because investors demand greater rewards for bearing risk during bad times. By contrast, short-term yields tend to be procyclical because central banks tend to lower short rates in an attempt to stimulate economic activity during recessions. Yield curves thus tend to become steeply upward-sloping during recessions, to flatten in the course of expansions, and to be downward sloping (inverted) before an impending recession. In the United States, for example, nearly every recession after the mid-1960s was predicted by an inverted yield curve within six quarters of the recession; only one inverted yield curve was not followed by a recession during this period.[5] Thus the evidence suggests that the yield curve contains information about future GDP growth. Theory also suggests that the yield curve reflects expectations about future inflation.

Investors monitor a number of variables to gauge opportunities in bond markets. If relative yields of lower-quality issues exceed historical norms, the prospect of higher returns

[4]The discount rate is the rate a Federal Reserve member bank pays for borrowing reserves from the Federal Reserve system. Along with open market operations (the purchase and sale of government securities by the Fed) and changes in reserve requirement, discount rate policy is one of the three tools of U.S. monetary policy.

[5]See Ang, Piazzesi, and Wei (2006).

by investing in bonds of lower quality is enhanced. Even a measure as simple as the slope of the bond market yield curve is an indicator of bond performance relative to (short-term) cash equivalents.

Looking back at the late 1970s and early 1980s and focusing on yield curve slope rather than height, the spread between bond yields and cash yields steepened, starting with a flat to mildly inverted yield curve from late 1978 through mid-1981 and increasing to a 4 percent bond risk premium by July 1982. This increased bond risk premium preceded the bond rally of August–October 1982, during which 30-year Treasuries rallied 29 percent in three months. Although it is the rise in interest rates that catalyzes subsequent stock bear markets, it is the spread between long-term and short-term rates that presages bond rallies. If the yield curve is unusually steep (i.e., if bond yields are high relative to cash equivalent yields), the outlook tends to be good for bonds. This relationship is significant when either cash yield or the inflation rate is used as a proxy for the underlying risk-free rate.[6]

This interpretation of steep yield curves is unconventional. The usual fear is that the forward curve[7] foreshadows rising yields and falling bond prices. Empirical evidence tends to refute any basis for that apprehension.

Inflation has a pervasive influence on investors' ability to achieve their financial and investment objectives. On the one hand, it affects the nominal amount of money required to purchase a given basket of goods and services. On the other hand, inflation influences returns and risk in capital markets. When inflation rises beyond expectations, bond investors face a cut in *real yield.* As nominal yields rise in turn to counteract this loss, bond prices fall. Unexpected changes in the inflation rate are highly significant to stock market returns as well.

2.3. Monitoring the Portfolio

Monitoring a portfolio is a continuous process that requires the manager to evaluate (1) events and trends affecting the prospects of individual holdings and asset classes and their suitability for attaining client objectives and (2) changes in asset values that create unintended divergences from the client's strategic asset allocation. The former tend to lead to changes in investment policy or to substitutions of individual holdings; the latter lead directly to rebalancing to the existing strategic asset allocation.

In a perfect-markets world, we could hold portfolio managers to a demanding standard: If a portfolio manager were to begin building a portfolio afresh today, would it mirror the existing portfolio? If not, he should consider changing the existing portfolio. Of course, taxes and transaction costs, discussed later, mean managers do not continuously revise portfolios. After even one day no portfolio is exactly optimal; however, the costs of adjustment may well outweigh any expected benefits from eliminating small differences between the current portfolio and the best possible one.

---

[6]T-bills and other cash instruments are not truly risk free, as they have both nonzero durations and nonzero standard deviations. Although they are generally an excellent reflection of the theoretical risk-free rate, the inflation rate can sometimes be preferable as a proxy for the risk-free rate, because it is not directly subject to manipulation by a central bank.

[7]A "forward curve" shows the incremental yield earned by going one step further out on the yield curve. Suppose a one-year bond yields 2 percent and an equivalent-credit two-year bond yields 4 percent. The two-year bond must have a one-year forward yield of approximately 6 percent during its second year in order for its two-year average yield to be 4 percent. A steep yield curve implies an expectation of rising future bond yields.

New information on economic and market conditions or on individual companies may lead a portfolio manager to take a variety of investment actions in an effort to add value for the client. The following examples offer some perspectives for the practitioner to consider as he or she translates monitoring into investment action.

EXAMPLE 11-4 How Active Managers May Use New Analysis and Information

As portfolio managers gather and analyze information that leads to capital market expectation revisions, they may attempt to add value through at least three types of portfolio actions:

1. *Tactical asset allocation.* The portfolio manager may, in the short term, adjust the target asset mix within the parameters of the investment policy statement by selling perceived overpriced asset classes and reinvesting the proceeds in perceived underpriced asset classes in an attempt to profit from perceived disequilibria. When an investor's long-term capital market expectations change, however, the manager must revisit the strategic asset allocation.
2. *Style and sector exposures.* Portfolio managers may alter investment emphasis within asset classes because of changes in capital market expectations. For example, a portfolio manager may lengthen the duration in the fixed-income allocation based on expectations of a sustained period of declining interest rates or adjust the style of the equity portfolio based on expectations that an economy is entering a period of sustained economic growth. Portfolio managers also may adjust the exposure to certain sectors back to or closer to historical weightings to reduce sector exposure relative to the index. For example, consider the impact on portfolio risk and return of reducing the exposure to the technology sector (within the large-cap U.S. equity allocation) in January 2000, when technology represented more than 31 percent of the S&P 500 Index relative to the historical average of about 17 percent.
3. *Individual security exposures.* A portfolio manager may trade an individual issue for one that seems to offer better value or reduce the exposure of a specific security as the returns of a single security begin to contribute a greater proportion of the total return than the manager believes to be appropriate.

EXAMPLE 11-5 The Characteristics of Successful Active Investors

Ironic gaps exist between the theory of revising portfolios and its practice. Some managers persist in constantly juggling the asset mix and churning portfolios in response to their basic emotions, clouded thinking, classic behavioral finance errors, and the desire to maximize fee revenue—often shrouding their "illusion of action" with marketing glitz. Clients tend to hire managers after recent success and fire them after recent disappointment. This chasing of investment performance, which reflects human nature, infrequently benefits investment results. What then are the elements of investment success?

- *Successful active investors stray from established roles.* Nature conditions us to feel that what has been working will continue to work and that failure heralds failure. In investments, experience belies this notion. Consider investment managers who scramble to find a fix when their style is out of fashion. Often they (and their clients) change their approach during a period of disappointment, just before results rebound. We see the same pattern in customers' decisions to hire and fire managers. These costly errors stem from a quest for comfort that capital markets rarely reward and a lack of discipline to remain committed to long-term strategy as defined in the investment policy statement. Investors crave the solace that companionship affords. In the investment business, when one has too much company, success is improbable.
- *Successful active investors are not swayed by the crowd.* The cultures of successful corporations and winning investors are profoundly different. Corporations, which are cooperative enterprises, prize teamwork and reward triumph while dismissing failure. The exceptional investor pursues an opposite course, staying far from the crowd and seeking opportunities in overlooked areas while avoiding excesses of the crowd. Investing in areas that are not popular while refusing to join in trends sets the successful investor apart.
- *Successful active investors are disciplined.* There is a subtle pattern in the trading of successful investors and a key ingredient of investment success—discipline. Successful investors make disciplined changes even when they are performing well, and they often are willing to endure disappointment patiently.

Opportunistic investors must steel themselves against discomfort. Only knowledge and discipline can give them the confidence needed to transact. Indeed, even then, consideration for clients (or fears of their reactions) may inhibit the profitable move. Many investors fear the consequences of acting contrary to recent market experience. Disciplined investment decision processes add value by providing an *objective* basis for having confidence in an uncomfortable investment action.

As we shall discuss in more detail later, disciplined rebalancing to the strategic asset allocation reinforces the strategy of selling high and buying low or reducing exposure to outperforming asset classes and increasing exposure to underperforming asset classes. That behavior and discipline unfortunately is at odds with human nature. When investments have performed poorly, less successful investors and portfolio managers tend to address the problem by making changes for the sake of change or by abandoning a strategy altogether! If investments are doing well, the tendency is to coast with the winning strategy. These common patterns can often make underperformance problems significantly worse (i.e., selling near the bottom) or result in forgoing some portion of handsome market gains (i.e., not selling near the top).

EXAMPLE 11-6 The Nonfinancial Costs of Portfolio Revision

When a portfolio manager revises a portfolio, he obviously incurs financial costs as detailed later in Section 3.1.2. Financial costs will indeed be a focus of the section on rebalancing. But the costs of transacting can also take nonfinancial forms. If a client grows uncomfortable with portfolio turnover she considers excessive, the portfolio manager may lose credibility and the client may limit future trading. Even if trading is timely and likely to be profitable, it may impose subjective costs that are all too real. Finance theory recognizes these costs by directing managers to focus on optimizing client satisfaction rather than maximizing return. Even the most profitable strategy or investment process is useless if the client abandons it.

3. REBALANCING THE PORTFOLIO

Monitoring and rebalancing a portfolio is similar to flying an airplane: The pilot monitors and adjusts, if necessary, the plane's altitude, speed, and direction to make sure that the plane ultimately arrives at the predetermined destination. Just as a pilot makes in-flight adjustments, so does the portfolio manager. An important question in this regard is how far off course can the plane get before the pilot must make an adjustment? In the following sections we address that issue, but we first must be clear on the scope of what we will discuss under the rubric of rebalancing.

The term *rebalancing* has been used in the literature of investing to cover a range of distinct actions including (1) adjusting the actual portfolio to the current strategic asset allocation because of price changes in portfolio holdings; (2) revisions to the investor's target asset class weights because of changes in the investor's investment objectives or constraints, or because of changes in his capital market expectations; and (3) tactical asset allocation (TAA). For pedagogical reasons and because subjects such as TAA are covered in other chapters, in this section we use "rebalancing" to refer only to the first type of action: rebalancing to the strategic asset allocation in reaction to price changes. Both individual and institutional investors need to set policy with respect to this type of action.

3.1. The Benefits and Costs of Rebalancing

Portfolio rebalancing involves a simple trade-off: the cost of rebalancing versus the cost of not rebalancing.

3.1.1. Rebalancing Benefits

Clients and their investment managers work hard to have their normal asset policy mix reflect an educated judgment of their appetite for reward and their aversion to risk. That having been done, however, the mix often drifts with the tides of day-to-day market fluctuations. If we assume that an investor's strategic asset allocation is optimal, then any divergence in the investor's portfolio from this strategic asset allocation is undesired and represents an expected utility loss to the investor. Rebalancing benefits the investor by reducing the present value of expected losses from not tracking the optimum. In theory, the basic cost of not rebalancing is this present value of expected utility losses.[8]

[8]See Leland (2000).

Equivalently, the cost of not rebalancing is the present value of expected utility losses from straying from the optimum.

There are also several practical risk management benefits to rebalancing. First, if higher-risk assets earn higher returns on average and we let the asset mix drift, higher-risk assets will tend to represent ever-larger proportions of the portfolio over time. Thus the level of portfolio risk will tend to drift upward.[9] Portfolio risk will tend to be greater than that established for the client in the investment policy statement. Rebalancing controls drift in the overall level of portfolio risk. Second, as asset mix drifts, the *types* of risk exposures drift. Rebalancing maintains the client's desired systematic risk exposures. Finally, not rebalancing may mean holding assets that have become overpriced, offering inferior future rewards. A commitment to rebalance to the strategic asset allocation offers an effective way to dissuade clients from abandoning policy at inauspicious moments. Once signed on to the concept, clients are more likely to stay the course.

Example 11-7 illustrates the benefits of disciplined rebalancing judged against the do-nothing alternative of letting asset mix drift.

EXAMPLE 11-7 An Illustration of the Benefits of Disciplined Rebalancing

Although portfolios can be rebalanced using a variety of methods that we shall soon discuss, it is important to recognize that, in comparison to letting an asset mix drift, any disciplined approach to rebalancing tends to add value over a long-term investment horizon either by enhancing portfolio returns and/or reducing portfolio risk.

For example, assume an institutional client wishes to maintain the stated policy mix of 60 percent stocks and 40 percent bonds and requires monthly rebalancing to the equilibrium 60/40 mix. That asset mix is not uncommon for North American pension funds and provides a reasonable baseline from which to quantify the likely benefits from disciplined rebalancing. Transaction costs of 10 bps on each side of a trade are assumed to be attainable using futures.

In the three decades (1973 to 2003) summarized in Exhibits 11-5 and 11-6, simple monthly rebalancing produced an average annual return of 10.22 percent versus 9.95 percent for a drifting mix, a 27 bp enhancement. Furthermore, the incremental return

EXHIBIT 11-5 Full-Period Rebalancing Results, January 1973–July 2003

	Rebalancing Return	Drifting Mix Return	Difference
Average	10.22%	9.95%	0.27%
Maximum	35.25	35.75	
Minimum	−15.71	−13.57	
Median	12.97	11.96	
Standard deviation	11.38	13.39	
Reward/risk ratio (Average/Std dev)	0.90	0.74	

[9]This type of drift will be more acute for portfolios with asset classes with dissimilar volatility and/or with low correlations.

EXHIBIT 11-6 Annual Rebalancing Results

Calendar Year	Rebalancing Return	Drifting Mix Return	Difference
1973	−10.22%	−10.19%	−0.03%
1974	−15.71	−13.57	−2.14
1975	24.87	21.66	3.21
1976	20.80	20.15	0.65
1977	−5.10	−4.62	−0.48
1978	3.28	2.51	0.77
1979	8.00	7.15	0.85
1980	16.09	15.46	0.63
1981	−1.51	−1.99	0.48
1982	29.40	28.90	0.50
1983	13.14	13.39	−0.25
1984	9.91	9.38	0.53
1985	32.41	32.29	0.12
1986	20.43	19.99	0.44
1987	2.73	1.30	1.43
1988	13.27	13.45	−0.18
1989	26.54	26.93	−0.39
1990	1.36	0.78	0.58
1991	26.26	26.74	−0.48
1992	7.64	7.55	0.09
1993	12.97	12.49	0.48
1994	−1.90	−1.36	−0.54
1995	35.25	35.75	−0.50
1996	13.58	16.23	−2.65
1997	26.38	29.00	−2.62
1998	24.45	26.60	−2.15
1999	9.12	15.72	−6.60
2000	−0.29	−6.98	6.69
2001	−5.17	−8.47	3.30
2002	−7.83	−12.88	5.05
2003 (Jan–Jul)	7.23	8.45	−1.22

involved significantly less risk. That is, the rebalanced portfolio's standard deviation during that time period was 11.38 percent versus 13.39 percent—200 bps less than that of the drifting mix!

Despite a six-year losing streak in the 1990s, annual rebalancing to the 60/40 mix outperformed a drifting mix for the January 1988 through July 2003 period, much of which constituted the largest equity bull market in U.S. history. As Exhibit 11-7 indicates, annual rebalancing produced an average incremental return of 27 bps with a standard deviation of returns that is 1.16 bps smaller than that of the drifting mix. Because rebalancing avoids the passive increases in risk that result from drifting during trending periods, it manages to reduce risk by more than 100 bps, while accumulating a modest 27 bps of additional return. As with the 1973 to 2003 time period, this translates to a reward-to-risk ratio for the rebalanced portfolio that much improves on that of the drifting mix.

EXHIBIT 11-7 Recent Rebalancing Results, January 1988 to July 2003

	Rebalancing Return	Drifting Mix Return	Difference
Average	11.29%	11.02%	0.27%
Maximum	35.25	35.75	
Minimum	−7.83	−12.88	
Median	12.97	14.78	
Standard deviation	10.01	11.17	
Reward/risk ratio	1.13	0.99	

Example 11-7 makes the point that disciplined rebalancing has tended to reduce risk while incrementally adding to returns. *Tended* means just that: It does not work in every year or even in every market cycle, but it should work over long-term investment horizons. For the two periods examined in Example 11-7 and making the assumptions therein, the incremental return was earned with turnover of just 0.9 percent per month in both periods. Historically, the benefit justifies this minimal activity. Studies such as Arnott and Lovell (1993), Plaxco and Arnott (2002), and Buetow, et al. (2002) have supported this conclusion using both historical and simulated data. Rebalancing to a fixed asset mix, because it involves both selling appreciated assets and buying depreciated assets, can be viewed as a contrarian investment discipline that can be expected to earn a positive return for supplying liquidity.

3.1.2. Rebalancing Costs

Despite its benefits, rebalancing exacts financial costs. These costs are of two types—transaction costs and, for taxable investors, tax costs.

3.1.2.1. Transaction Costs Transaction costs can never be recovered, and their cumulative erosion of value can significantly deteriorate portfolio performance. Transaction costs offset the benefits of rebalancing. Yet the true trade-off is not easy to gauge because transaction costs are difficult to measure.

Relatively illiquid investments such as private equity and real estate have become increasingly important in the portfolios of investors such as endowments and pension funds. These investments pose special challenges to rebalancing because the costs of rebalancing these investments represent a high hurdle. At the same time, the valuations given such assets often underestimate their true volatility because the valuations may be based on appraisals. If rebalancing requires reducing the value of illiquid holdings, this reduction may sometimes be accomplished through reinvestment of cash flows from them.[10] At the same time, portfolio managers cannot increase the allocations of these assets as quickly as in liquid asset markets.

Focusing on more liquid markets such as public equities, we can estimate transaction costs but only with error. There is in fact no exact answer to the question of what the transaction costs of a trade are. Transaction costs consist of more than just explicit costs such as commissions. They include implicit costs, such as those related to the bid–ask spread and market impact. Market impact is the difference between realized price and the price that *would have prevailed in the absence of the order.* That cost is inherently unobservable. In an analogy to the Heisenberg principle in physics, the process of executing a trade masks what would exist

[10] See Horvitz (2002).

without the trade taking place. Furthermore, the trades one seeks but fails to execute impose yet another tariff—an opportunity cost. This missed trade opportunity cost may be more onerous than the others, and it is equally unobservable. Trading costs take on the character of an iceberg: Commissions rise above the surface, visible to all, while the submerged leviathan encompasses the market impact of trades and the imponderable cost of the trades that never happened.

A useful analogy can be drawn from the bond market. Most bond portfolios are priced from matrix prices, which may better represent "fair value" than actual transaction prices.[11] Bond transaction prices can be too dependent on the idiosyncratic meeting of one buyer and one seller. The same curious conclusion can be drawn for equities. Actual prices are set by the marginal seller and buyer who represent not a consensus but the strongest motivation to transact at a particular point in time.[12]

Because unaffected prices are unobservable, market impact costs can never be more than indirectly estimated. Still, this is not a fatal flaw: Total transaction costs can be estimated to a useful degree of accuracy, relative to the imprecision of other financial measurements (e.g., beta, value or future internal rate of return).

3.1.2.2. Tax Costs In rebalancing, a portfolio manager sells appreciated asset classes and buys depreciated asset classes to bring the asset mix in line with target proportions. In most jurisdictions the sale of appreciated assets triggers a tax liability for taxable investors and is a cost of rebalancing for such investors.[13] The U.S. tax code distinguishes between long- and short-term capital gains based on the length of the holding period (as of 2004, holding periods greater than 12 months qualify as long-term). As of 2004 the maximum tax rates applicable to short-term and long-capital gains in the United States, 35 percent and 15 percent respectively, differed significantly. For a U.S. taxable investor, therefore, a rebalancing trade that realizes a short-term rather than long-term capital gain can be very costly. However, an appreciated asset class may contain assets with not only unrealized short- and long-term capital gains but also short- and long-term capital losses. Realizing short-term losses, long-term capital losses, long-term capital gains, and lastly short-term gains, in that order, would usually be the tax-efficient priority in selling. In contrast to the difference between long- and short-term capital gains, the value of the deferral of a long-term capital gain is generally much less in magnitude.[14]

3.2. Rebalancing Disciplines

A rebalancing discipline is a strategy for rebalancing. In practice, portfolio managers have most commonly adopted either calendar rebalancing or percentage-of-portfolio rebalancing.

[11]**Matrix prices** are prices determined by comparisons to other securities of similar credit risk and maturity.

[12]The need to outbid competitive traders suggests that market impact can even be negative. Prices would always be the same or lower without the most motivated buyer's willingness to buy. Prices similarly would always be the same or higher without the most motivated seller's willingness to sell.

[13]Some tax jurisdictions such as Jamaica, Hong Kong, and Singapore do not impose taxes on capital gains. See Ernst & Young (2005).

[14]See Horvitz (2002). The value of tax deferral of *X* years is the tax bill if the sale is today (call this *Y*) minus the present value of *Y* to be paid in *X* years, using a default-risk-free tax-exempt rate.

3.2.1. Calendar Rebalancing **Calendar rebalancing** involves rebalancing a portfolio to target weights on a periodic basis, for example, monthly, quarterly, semiannually, or annually. Quarterly rebalancing is one popular choice; the choice of rebalancing frequency is sometimes linked to the schedule of portfolio reviews.[15]

If an investor's policy portfolio has three asset classes with target proportions of 45/15/40, and his investment policy specifies rebalancing at the beginning of each month, at each rebalancing date asset proportions would be brought back to 45/15/40. Calendar rebalancing is the simplest rebalancing discipline. It does not involve continuously monitoring portfolio values within the rebalancing period. If the rebalancing frequency is adequate given the portfolio's volatility, calendar rebalancing can suffice in ensuring that the actual portfolio does not drift far away from target for long periods of time. A drawback of calendar rebalancing: It is unrelated to market behavior. On any given rebalancing date, the portfolio could be very close to or far away from optimal proportions. In the former case, the portfolio would be nearly optimal and the costs in rebalancing might swamp the benefits. In the latter case, an investor might incur unnecessarily high costs in terms of market impact by rebalancing.

3.2.2. Percentage-of-Portfolio Rebalancing **Percentage-of-portfolio rebalancing** (also called **percent range** or **interval rebalancing**) offers an alternative to calendar rebalancing. Percentage-of-portfolio rebalancing involves setting rebalancing thresholds or trigger points stated as a percentage of the portfolio's value. For example, if the target proportion for an asset class is 40 percent of portfolio value, trigger points could be at 35 percent and 45 percent of portfolio value. We would say that 35 percent to 45 percent (or 40 percent ±5 percent) is the **corridor** or **tolerance band** for the value of that asset class. The portfolio is rebalanced when an asset class's weight first passes through one of its rebalancing thresholds, or equivalently, outside the corridor.

For example, consider a three-asset class portfolio of domestic equities, international equities, and domestic bonds. The target asset proportions are 45/15/40 with respective corridors 45 percent ±4.5 percent, 15 percent ±1.5 percent, and 40 percent ±4 percent. Suppose the portfolio manager observes the actual allocation to be 50/14/36; the upper threshold (49.5 percent) for domestic equities has been breached. The asset mix would be rebalanced to 45/15/40.

Rebalancing trades can occur on any calendar date for percentage-of-portfolio rebalancing, in contrast to calendar rebalancing. Compared with calendar rebalancing (particularly at lower frequencies such as semiannual or annual), percentage-of-portfolio rebalancing can exercise tighter control on divergences from target proportions because it is directly related to market performance.

Percentage-of-portfolio rebalancing requires monitoring of portfolio values at an agreed-upon frequency in order to identify instances in which a trigger point is breached. To be implemented with greatest precision, monitoring should occur daily. Daily monitoring obviously requires having an efficient custodian, one who can accurately monitor and quickly process and communicate portfolio and asset class valuations.

[15] In practice, some portfolio managers will rebalance a portfolio just before a scheduled client meeting so the portfolio manager appears to be fulfilling his or her responsibility, although that practice may reflect more the concerns of the portfolio manager than the concerns of the client. By contrast, other portfolio managers may rebalance a portfolio just after the client meeting so the client or investment committee has the opportunity to approve the manager's actions.

An obvious and important question is: How are the corridors for asset classes determined?

Investors sometimes set ad hoc corridors. We have already illustrated example of one well-known yet ad hoc approach, based on a hypothetical portfolio of domestic equities, international equities, and domestic bonds. The corridors were set according to a formula based on a percentage of the target allocation, target ± (target allocation × P%), where P percent was 10 percent (but could be another percentage such as 5 percent). Following that formula, a corridor of 45% ± (45% × 10%) = 45% ±4.5% applied to domestic stocks, 15% ±1.5% applied to international equities, and 40% ±4% applied to domestic bonds. However, *ad hoc* approaches such this one are open to several criticisms. The approach illustrated does not account for differences in transaction costs in rebalancing these three asset classes, for example.

The literature suggests that at least five factors should play a role in setting the corridor for an asset class:

- Transaction costs.
- Risk tolerance concerning tracking risk versus the strategic asset allocation.
- Correlation with other asset classes.
- Volatility.
- Volatilities of other asset classes.

The more expensive it is to trade an asset class (or the lower its liquidity), the wider its corridor should be, because the marginal benefit in rebalancing must at least equal its marginal cost. The higher the risk tolerance (i.e., the lower the investor's sensitivity to straying from target proportions), the wider corridors can be.

Correlations also should be expected to play a role. In a two asset-class case, a higher correlation should lead to wider tolerance bands. Suppose one asset class has moved above its target allocation (so the other asset class is below its target weight). A further increase in value has an expected smaller effect on asset weights if the assets classes' returns are more highly positively correlated because the denominator in computing the asset class's weight is the sum of the values of the two asset classes. That denominator's value is likely to be higher for a given up-move of the asset class of concern if the two asset classes' returns are positively correlated. In a multi-asset-class case, all pairwise asset class correlations would need to be considered, making the interpretation of correlations complex. To expand the application of the two-asset case's intuition, one simplification involves considering the balance of a portfolio to be a single hypothetical asset and computing an asset class's correlation with it.[16]

A higher volatility should lead to a narrower corridor, all else equal. It hurts more to be a given percent off target for a more highly volatile asset class because it has a greater chance of a further large move away from target. In a two-asset case the more volatile the second asset, the more risk there is in being a given percent off target for the first asset class, all else equal. All asset classes' volatilities would affect the optimal corridor in the multi-asset-class case. Again, a simplification is to treat the balance of the portfolio as one asset. Exhibit 11-8 summarizes the discussion. (It applies to the two-asset-class case, or to the multi-asset-class case with the simplification of treating all other asset classes—the balance of the portfolio—as one asset class.)

[16]As in Masters (2003).

EXHIBIT 11-8 Factors Affecting Optimal Corridor Width

Factor	Effect on Optimal Width of Corridor (all else equal)	Intuition
Factors Positively Related to Optimal Corridor Width		
Transaction costs	The higher the transaction costs, the wider the optimal corridor.	High transaction costs set a high hurdle for rebalancing benefits to overcome.
Risk tolerance	The higher the risk tolerance, the wider the optimal corridor.	Higher risk tolerance means less sensitivity to divergences from target.
Correlation with rest of portfolio	The higher the correlation, the wider the optimal corridor.	When asset classes move in synch, further divergence from targets is less likely.
Factors Inversely Related to Optimal Corridor Width		
Asset class volatility	The higher the volatility of a given asset class, the narrower the optimal corridor.	A given move away from target is potentially more costly for a high-volatility asset class, as a further divergence becomes more likely.
Volatility of rest of portfolio	The higher this volatility, the narrower the optimal corridor.	Makes large divergences from strategic asset allocation more likely.

EXAMPLE 11-8 Tolerance Bands for an Asset Allocation

An investment committee is reviewing the following strategic asset allocation:

Domestic equities	50% ±5%
International equities	15% ±1.5%
Domestic bonds	35% ±3.5%

The committee views the above corridors as appropriate if each asset class has identical risk and transaction-cost characteristics. It now wants to account for differences among the asset classes in setting the corridors.

Evaluate the implications of the following sets of facts on the stated tolerance band (set off by italics), given an all-else-equal assumption in each case:

1. Domestic bond volatility is much lower than that of domestic or international equities, which are equal. *Tolerance band for domestic bonds.*
2. Transaction costs in international equities are 10 percent higher than those for domestic equities. *Tolerance band for international equities.*
3. Transaction costs in international equities are 10 percent higher than those for domestic equities, and international equities have a much lower correlation with domestic bonds than do domestic equities. *Tolerance band for international equities.*
4. The correlation of domestic bonds with domestic equities is higher than their correlation with international equities. *Tolerance band for domestic equities.*

5. The volatility of domestic bonds has increased. *Tolerance band for international equities.*

Solution to Problem 1: The tolerance band for domestic bonds should be wider than 35 percent ±3.5 percent.

Solution to Problem 2: The tolerance band for international equities should be wider than 15 percent ±1.5 percent.

Solution to Problem 3: Transaction costs point to widening the tolerance band for international equities, but correlations to narrowing it. The overall effect is indeterminate.

Solution to Problem 4: The tolerance band for domestic equities should be wider than 50 percent ±5 percent.

Solution to Problem 5: The tolerance band for international equities should be narrower than 15 percent ±1.5 percent.

3.2.3. Other Rebalancing Strategies

The investment literature includes rebalancing disciplines other than those discussed above. Calendar rebalancing can be combined with percentage-of-portfolio rebalancing (as described in Buetow et al.). In this approach (which may be called **calendar-and-percentage-of-portfolio rebalancing**), the manager monitors the portfolio at regular frequencies, such as quarterly. The manager then decides to rebalance based on a percentage-of-portfolio principle (has a trigger point been exceeded?). This approach mitigates the problem of incurring rebalancing costs when near the optimum that can occur in the calendar rebalancing.

McCalla (1997) describes an **equal probability rebalancing** discipline. In this discipline, the manager specifies a corridor for each asset class as a common multiple of the standard deviation of the asset class's returns. Rebalancing to the target proportions occurs when any asset class weight moves outside its corridor. In this discipline each asset class is equally likely to trigger rebalancing if the normal distribution describes asset class returns. However, equal probability rebalancing does not account for differences in transaction costs or asset correlations.

Goodsall and Plaxco (1996) and Plaxco and Arnott (2002) discuss as **tactical rebalancing** a variation of calendar rebalancing that specifies less frequent rebalancing when markets appear to be trending and more frequent rebalancing when they are characterized by reversals. This approach seeks to add value by tying rebalancing frequency to expected market conditions that most favor rebalancing to a constant mix.

3.2.4. Rebalancing to Target Weights versus Rebalancing to the Allowed Range

In the descriptions of rebalancing strategies, we have presented the standard paradigm in which a rebalancing involves adjusting asset class holdings to their target proportions. The alternative, applicable to rebalancing approaches that involve corridors, is to rebalance the asset allocation so that all asset class weights are within the allowed range but not necessarily at target weights. The rebalancing may follow a rule, such as adjusting weights halfway back to target (e.g., if an asset class's corridor is 50 percent ±5 percent and the asset class's weight is 57 percent, reducing the weight to 52.5 percent), or to some judgmentally determined set of proportions. Compared with rebalancing to target weight, rebalancing to the allowed range results in less close alignment with target proportions but lower transaction costs; it also provides some room for tactical adjustments. For example, suppose that a U.S. investor's target allocation to non-U.S. equities is 15 percent and that its weight moves above its corridor on the upside. During an expected transitory period of a depreciating U.S. dollar, the portfolio manager may want to rebalance the exposure only part way to the target proportion to take advantage of the apparent exchange rate tactical opportunity. The discipline of rebalancing to the allowed range also allows portfolio managers to better manage the weights of relatively illiquid assets.

A number of studies have contrasted rebalancing to target weights to rebalancing to the allowed range based on particular asset classes, time periods, and measures of the benefits of rebalancing. They have reached a variety of conclusions which do not permit one to state that one discipline is unqualifiedly superior to the other.

3.2.5. Setting Optimal Thresholds

The optimal portfolio rebalancing strategy should maximize the present value of the *net* benefit of rebalancing to the investor. Equivalently, the optimal strategy minimizes the present value of the sum of two costs: expected utility losses (from divergences from the optimum) and transaction costs (from rebalancing trades). Despite the apparent simplicity of the above formulations, finding the optimal strategy in a completely general context remains a complex challenge:

- If the costs of rebalancing are hard to measure, the benefits of rebalancing are even harder to quantify.
- The return characteristics of different asset classes differ from each other, and at the same time interrelationships (correlations) exist among the asset classes that a rebalancing strategy may need to reflect.
- The optimal rebalancing decisions at different points in time are linked; one decision affects another.
- Accurately reflecting transaction costs may be difficult; for example, transaction costs can be nonlinear in the size of a rebalancing trade.
- The optimal strategy is likely to change through time as prices evolve and new information becomes available.
- Rebalancing has tax implications for taxable investors.

Researchers are beginning to make headway in addressing optimal rebalancing in a general context.[17] At some future date, investors may be able to update optimal rebalancing thresholds in real time based on a lifetime utility of wealth formulation, including a transaction costs penalty component. Implementing such a system lies in the future rather than present of industry practice. If reasonable simplifying assumptions are permitted, some models are currently available to suggest specific values for optimal corridors, although no industry standard has been established yet.

3.3. The Perold–Sharpe Analysis of Rebalancing Strategies

Prior sections discussed rebalancing to a strategic asset allocation for a portfolio of many risky asset classes. That discipline of rebalancing, which can also be called a constant-mix strategy, is

[17] See Leland (2000) and Donohue and Yip (2003).

a bread-and-butter topic for investment practitioners. The following sections share the insights of Perold and Sharpe's (1988) analysis contrasting constant mix with other strategies. To make its points, the Perold–Sharpe analysis assumes a simple two-asset class setting in which just one asset class is risky. Nevertheless, the analysis throws light on the underlying features of the strategies and what market dynamics and investor attitudes to risk favor or disfavor each of them.

3.3.1. Buy-and-Hold Strategies

A buy-and-hold strategy is a passive strategy of buying an initial asset mix (e.g., 60/40 stocks/Treasury bills) and doing absolutely nothing subsequently. Whatever the market does, no adjustments are made to portfolio weights. It is a "do-nothing" strategy resulting in a drifting asset mix.

The investment in Treasury bills (bills, for short) is risk-free and for the sake of simplicity is assumed to earn a zero return; it is essentially cash. In a buy-and-hold strategy, the value of risk-free assets represents a floor for portfolio value. For instance, take €100 and invest it initially according to 60/40 stocks/cash asset allocation. If the value of the stock allocation were to fall to zero, we would still have the €40 invested in cash. Therefore, the following expression pertains:

$$\text{Portfolio value} = \text{Investment in stocks} + \text{Floor value}$$

For a 60/40 stock/cash allocation the equation is

$$\text{Portfolio value} = \text{Investment in stocks} + \text{Floor value of €40}$$

Portfolio value is a linear function of the investment in stocks (the risky asset). If the buy-and hold strategy has a floor, it is also true that there is no limit on upside potential so long as the portfolio is above the floor. The higher the initial allocation to stocks, the greater the increase (decrease) in value when stocks outperform (underperform) bills.

The amount by which portfolio value exceeds the investment in cash is the cushion (i.e., a buffer of value above the floor value). For a buy-and-hold strategy, the value of the investment in stocks moves 1:1 with the value of the cushion, as can be seen from rearranging the previous expression for portfolio value:

$$\text{Investment in stocks} = \text{Cushion} = \text{Portfolio value} - \text{Floor value} \qquad (11\text{-}1)$$

In our one-risky-asset portfolio, the portfolio return (the percent change in portfolio value over a given holding period) equals the fraction of assets in stocks multiplied by the return on stocks (under the assumption of a zero return on bills).

$$\text{Portfolio return} = (\text{Percent in stocks}) \times (\text{Return on stocks})$$

For example, if stocks earn a 10 percent return, the value of stocks rises by 6 from 60 to 66; the value of the portfolio goes up by 6 from 100 to 106 (equal to 66 + 40). For the portfolio, that represents a 6 percent return as $6/100 = 6\%$. And $6\% = 0.6 \times 10\%$.

The investor's percent allocation to stocks is directly related to stock performance. For example if stocks earn a −100 percent return, the stock/bills allocation goes from 60/40 to 0/100 (the cushion is zero, the value of the portfolio is 40, which is the amount invested in bills). If stocks earn a +100 percent return, the asset allocation goes from 60/40 to 75/25 (the value of stocks goes from 60 to 120, increasing portfolio value from 100 to 160; $120/160 = 0.75$ or 75%, which becomes the new stock allocation). A higher allocation to stocks reflects a greater risk tolerance. Therefore, a buy-and-hold strategy would work well for an investor whose risk tolerance is positively related to wealth and stock market returns.

To summarize, for a buy-and-hold strategy the following holds:

- Upside is unlimited, but portfolio value can be no lower than the allocation to bills.
- Portfolio value is a linear function of the value of stocks, and portfolio return is a linear function of the return on stocks.
- The value of stocks reflects the cushion (above floor value) 1:1.
- The implication of using this strategy is that the investor's risk tolerance is positively related to wealth and stock market returns. Risk tolerance is zero if the value of stocks declines to zero.

3.3.2. Constant-Mix Strategies What we have called rebalancing to the strategic asset allocation in prior sections is a constant-mix strategy in the terminology of Perold–Sharpe. Constant mix is a "do-something" (or "dynamic") strategy in that it reacts to market movements with trades. An investor decides, for example, that his portfolio will be 60 percent equities and 40 percent bills and rebalances to that proportion regardless of his level of wealth. In particular, the target investment in stocks in the constant-mix strategy is

$$\text{Target investment in stocks} = m \times \text{Portfolio value} \tag{11-2}$$

where m is a constant between 0 and 1 that represents the target proportion in stocks. If the equity market moves up, the actual stock proportion increases, but then it is adjusted down to m. If the equity market moves down, the actual stock proportion decreases, but then it is adjusted up to m.

Although a constant-mix strategy is "do-something," its effect is to maintain stable portfolio systematic risk characteristics over time, in contrast to a buy-and-hold strategy and the other "do-something" strategies that we will discuss shortly.

So far as returns alone are concerned, the adjustment policy of a constant-mix strategy will prove inferior to a buy-and-hold strategy if returns either move straight up, or move straight down. Strong bull and bear markets favor a buy-and-hold strategy. In the bull market case, the investor is cutting back on the shares of stock through rebalancing prior to further moves upwards. The buy-and-hold investor, by contrast, would profit by holding the number of shares constant (actually representing an increasing fraction of the portfolio invested in stocks). In the bear market case, the investor buys more shares prior to further moves down. The buy-and-hold investor does better by not changing his share holdings.

However, the constant-mix strategy tends to offer superior returns compared with buy-and hold strategies if the equities returns are characterized more by reversals than by trends. For example, suppose the corridor for equities is 60 percent ±5 percent. The stock market drops and the equity allocation falls below 55 percent; the equity allocation is rebalanced to 60 percent by selling bills and purchasing shares. The stock market then appreciates to its initial level (i.e., a return reversal occurs). The shares purchased in rebalancing under a constant-mix strategy show a gain. However, if the stock market first goes up, triggering a sale of shares and purchase of bills, and then drops back to its initial level, the constant-mix strategy also realizes a gain. Either returns reversal pattern is neutral for the buy-and-hold strategy. The constant-mix strategy is contrarian and supplies liquidity. Buying shares as stock values fall and selling shares as stock values rise are actions that supply liquidity because the investor is taking the less popular side of trades.

A constant-mix strategy is consistent with a risk tolerance that varies proportionately with wealth.[18] An investor with such risk tolerance desires to hold stocks at all levels of wealth.

---

[18]That is, with a constant-mix strategy, the amount of money invested in risky assets increases with increasing wealth, implying increasing risk tolerance. Because the amount of money held in risky assets

3.3.3. A Constant-Proportion Strategy: CPPI A constant-proportion strategy is a dynamic strategy in which the target equity allocation is a function of the value of the portfolio less a floor value for the portfolio. The following equation is used to determine equity allocation:

$$\text{Target investment in stocks} = m \times (\text{Portfolio value} - \text{Floor value}) \tag{11-3}$$

where m is a fixed constant. Constant-proportion strategies are so called because stock holdings are held to a constant proportion of the cushion. A characteristic of constant-proportion strategies is that they are consistent with a zero tolerance for risk (and hence no holdings in stocks) when the cushion is zero. Comparing Equation 11-1 with Equation 11-3, we see that a buy-and-hold strategy is a special case of a constant-proportion strategy in which $m = 1$. (For a buy-and-hold strategy, there is no distinction between the actual and target investment in stocks. The desired investment is whatever the actual level is.) When m exceeds 1, the constant-proportion strategy is called constant-proportion portfolio insurance (CPPI).[19]

CPPI is consistent with a higher tolerance for risk than a buy-and-hold strategy (when the cushion is positive), because the investor is holding a larger multiple of the cushion in stocks. Whereas a buy-and-hold strategy is do-nothing, CPPI is dynamic, requiring a manager to sell shares as stock values decline and buy shares as stock values rise. The floor in a buy-and-hold strategy is established with a fixed investment in bills; by contrast, in a CPPI strategy it is established dynamically. When stock values are trending up, the investment in stocks increases more than 1:1 with the increase in the value of stocks. The holding of bills may be minimal. When stocks are trending down, the allocation to stocks decreases more than 1:1 with the decrease in the value of stocks. The holding in bills rapidly increases until it reaches the floor value.

To manage transaction costs, a CPPI strategy requires some rules to determine when rebalancing to the stated multiple of the cushion should take place. One approach transacts when the portfolio value changes by a given percentage. At this point, the portfolio incurs transaction costs to rebalance. Because taxes can be a material consideration for taxable investors, they create a need for a rebalancing rule.

We expect a CPPI strategy to earn high returns in strong bull markets because the share purchases as the cushion increases are profitable. In a severe bear market, the sale of shares also is profitable in avoiding losses on them. By contrast, CPPI performs poorly in markets characterized more by reversals than by trends. CPPI requires a manager to sell shares after weakness and buy shares after strength; those transactions are unprofitable if drops are followed by rebounds and increases are retraced. The CPPI strategy is the just the opposite of the constant-mix strategy in using liquidity and being momentum oriented.

3.3.4. Linear, Concave, and Convex Investment Strategies A buy-and-hold strategy has been called a linear investment strategy because portfolio returns are a linear function of stock returns. The share purchases and sales involved in constant-mix and CPPI strategies introduce nonlinearities in the relationship. For constant-mix strategies, the relationship between portfolio returns and stock returns is concave; that is, portfolio return increases at a decreasing rate with positive stock returns and decreases at an increasing rate with negative

increases to maintain a constant ratio of risky assets to wealth, risk tolerance increases proportionately with wealth (constant *relative* risk tolerance or constant *relative* risk aversion).

[19]A value of m between 0 and 1 (and a floor value of zero) represents a constant-mix strategy.

EXHIBIT 11-9 Relative Return Performance of Different Strategies in Various Markets

Market Condition	Constant Mix	Buy and Hold	CPPI
Up	Underperform	Outperform	Outperform
Flat (but oscillating)	Outperform	Neutral	Underperform
Down	Underperform	Outperform	Outperform
Investment Implications			
Payoff curve	Concave	Linear	Convex
Portfolio insurance	Selling insurance	None	Buying insurance
Multiplier	$0 < m < 1$	$m = 1$	$m > 1$

stock returns.[20] In contrast, a CPPI strategy is convex. Portfolio return increases at an increasing rate with positive stock returns, and it decreases at a decreasing rate with negative stock returns.[21] Concave and convex strategies graph as mirror images of each other on either side of a buy-and-hold strategy. Convex strategies represent the purchase of portfolio insurance, concave strategies the sale of portfolio insurance. That is, convex strategies dynamically establish a floor value while concave strategies provide or sell the liquidity to convex strategies.

3.3.5. Summary of Strategies Exhibit 11-9 summarizes the prior discussion of Perold–Sharpe analysis. The multiplier refers to Equation 11-3, which integrates all the models discussed.

It is important to recognize that we have focused the discussion of performance in Exhibit 11-9 and the text on return performance, not risk (except to mention the downside risk protection in the CPPI and stock/bills buy-and-hold strategies).

Finally, the appropriateness of buy-and-hold, constant-mix, and constant-proportion portfolio insurance strategies for an investor depends on the investor's risk tolerance, the types of risk with which she is concerned (e.g., floor values or downside risk), and asset-class return expectations, as Example 11-9 illustrates.

EXAMPLE 11-9 Strategies for Different Investors

For each of the following cases, suggest the appropriate strategy:

1. Jonathan Hansen, 25 years old, has a risk tolerance that increases by 20 percent for each 20 percent increase in wealth. He wants to remain invested in equities at all times.
2. Elaine Cash has a $1 million portfolio split between stocks and money market instruments in a ratio of 70/30. Her risk tolerance increases more than proportionately with changes in wealth, and she wants to speculate on a flat market or moderate bull market.

[20]The graph of portfolio return against stock return would have an inverted saucer shape.
[21]The graph of portfolio return against stock return has a saucer shape.

3. Jeanne Roger has a €2 million portfolio. She does not want portfolio value to drop below €1 million but also does not want to incur the drag on returns of holding a large part of her portfolio in cash equivalents.

Solution to Problem 1: Given his proportional risk tolerance (constant relative risk tolerance) and desire to remain invested in equities at all times, a constant-mix strategy is appropriate for Hansen.

Solution to Problem 2: Her risk tolerance is greater than that of a constant-mix investor, yet Cash's forecasts include the possibility of a flat market in which CPPI would do poorly. A buy-and-hold strategy is appropriate for Cash.

Solution to Problem 3: The concern for downside risk suggests either a buy-and-hold strategy with €1 million in cash equivalents as a floor or dynamically providing the floor with a CPPI strategy. The buy-and-hold strategy would incur the greater cash drag, so the CPPI strategy is appropriate.

3.4. Execution Choices in Rebalancing

In our discussion of rebalancing we have skirted the important issue of transaction execution. The particulars of execution depend on the specific asset classes held, the availability of relevant derivative markets in addition to cash markets, and the tax consequences of different execution means for taxable investors. The major choices are to rebalance by selling and buying portfolio assets (cash market trades) or by overlaying derivative positions onto the portfolio (derivative trades).

3.4.1. Cash Market Trades

Cash market trades represent the most direct means of portfolio rebalancing. Such trades represent adjustment at the "retail" level of risk because they typically involve buying and selling individual security positions.[22] If the investor employs active managers, then such adjustments need to be executed with care to minimize the impact on active managers' strategies. Cash market trades generally are more costly, and slower to execute, than equivalent derivative trades. For taxable investors, however, tax considerations may favor cash market trades over derivative market trades. First, there may be no exact derivative market equivalent to a cash market trade on an after-tax basis. Second, in some tax jurisdictions such as the United States, derivative market trades may have unfavorable tax consequences relative to cash market trades.[23] In addition, even if differences in taxation are irrelevant (as in the case of tax-exempt investors), not all asset class exposures can be closely replicated using derivatives, and individual derivative markets may have liquidity limitations. To some extent, the level of granularity with which asset classes have been defined affects the availability of adequate derivative equivalents.

3.4.2. Derivative Trades

Portfolio managers can also often use derivative trades involving instruments such as futures contracts and total return swaps for rebalancing. Trades are carried

[22]An exception would be rebalancing a passive exposure through an available exchange-traded fund (ETF) or basket trade.

[23]See Horvitz (2002) for some details.

out so that the total exposure to asset classes (portfolio and derivative positions) closely mimics the effect of rebalancing by buying and selling underlying assets.

Rebalancing through derivatives markets, for the portion of the portfolio that can be closely replicated through derivative markets, has a number of major advantages:

- Lower transaction costs.
- More rapid implementation—in derivative trades one is buying and selling systematic risk exposures rather than individual security positions.
- Leaving active managers' strategies undisturbed—in contrast to cash market trades, which involve trading individual positions, derivative trades have minimal impact on active managers' strategies.[24]

Besides the possibility that an asset class exposure may not be closely replicable with available derivatives, individual derivatives markets may have liquidity limits. Many investors, including tax-exempt investors, find it appropriate to use both cash and derivative trades in rebalancing their portfolios.

4. CONCLUDING REMARKS

Managers must accord markets the respect they deserve. Implementation of portfolio strategies and tactics must be as rigorous as the investment decision process. A manager should understand his or her clients. Nothing is more important than a client's inherent tolerance for risk. Each client is unique; so should be the manager's understanding of the client's needs. When those needs change sufficiently, transaction costs assume a secondary role.

A portfolio manager must constantly monitor changes in investor circumstances, market and economic changes, and the portfolio itself, making sure that the IPS, asset allocation, and individual holdings continue to appropriately address the client's situation and investment objectives. The manager must serve as the client's champion in the investment realm, understand changes in the client's needs, and incorporate those changes into the dynamic management of the portfolio.

Legitimate chances to improve on diversified portfolios are rare. It pays to be wary of the multitude of vendors whose commercial interest argues otherwise.

A predetermined policy portfolio designed to be the continuing ideal and standard for an investor's combination of objectives, risk tolerance, and available asset classes, while hardly sacred, is the beacon one should generally steer toward.

[24]There may also be tactical advantages to using futures. For example, futures may trade cheaply in relation to the underlying cash market when the cash market is falling. See Kleidon and Whaley (1992).

CHAPTER 12

EVALUATING PORTFOLIO PERFORMANCE

Jeffery V. Bailey, CFA
Target Corporation
Minneapolis, Minnesota

Thomas M. Richards, CFA
Richards & Tierney, Inc.
Chicago, Illinois

David E. Tierney
Richards & Tierney, Inc.
Chicago, Illinois

1. INTRODUCTION

The *ex post* analysis of investment performance stands as a prominent and ubiquitous feature of modern investment management practice. Investing involves making decisions that have readily quantifiable consequences and that, at least on the surface, lend themselves to elaborate dissection and review. We broadly refer to the measurement and assessment of the outcomes of these investment management decisions as **performance evaluation.** At the institutional investor level, and to a lesser (but growing) extent on the individual investor level, a large industry has developed to satisfy the demand for performance evaluation services. Although some observers contend that performance evaluation is misguided, frequently misapplied, or simply unattainable with any reasonable degree of statistical confidence, we believe that analytic techniques representing best practices can lead to valid insights about the sources of past returns, and such insights can be useful inputs for managing an investment program.

The purpose of this chapter is to provide an overview of current performance evaluation concepts and techniques. Our focus will be on how institutional investors—both fund sponsors and investment managers—conduct performance evaluation. Individual investors tend to use variations of the performance evaluation techniques employed by institutional investors. We define fund sponsors to be owners of large pools of investable assets, such as corporate and public pension funds, endowments, and foundations. These organizations typically retain multiple investment management firms deployed across a range of asset categories. Fund sponsors have the challenge of evaluating not only the performance of the individual managers, but also the investment results within the asset categories and for their total investment programs.

In Section 2 we distinguish between the perspectives of the fund sponsor and the investment manager. Section 3 divides the broad subject of performance evaluation into three components: **performance measurement, performance attribution,** and **performance appraisal.** Under the topic of performance measurement, in Section 4 we discuss several methods of calculating portfolio performance. Section 5 introduces the concept of performance benchmarks. Turning to performance attribution, in Section 6 we consider the process of analyzing the sources of returns relative to a designated benchmark both from the total fund (fund sponsor) level and from the individual portfolio (investment manager) level. Our topic in Section 7 is performance appraisal, which deals with assessing investment skill. Section 8 addresses key issues in the practice of performance evaluation.

2. THE IMPORTANCE OF PERFORMANCE EVALUATION

Performance evaluation is important from the perspectives of both the fund sponsor and the investment manager.

2.1. The Fund Sponsor's Perspective

A typical fund sponsor would consider its investment program incomplete without a thorough and regular evaluation of the fund's performance relative to its investment objectives. Applied in a comprehensive manner, performance evaluation is more than a simple exercise in calculating rates of return. Rather, it provides an exhaustive "quality control" check, emphasizing not only the performance of the fund and its constituent parts relative to objectives, but the sources of that relative performance as well.

Performance evaluation is part of the feedback step of the investment management process. As such, it should be an integral part of a fund's investment policy and documented in its investment policy statement. As discussed in Ambachtsheer (1986) and Ellis (1985), investment policy itself is a combination of philosophy and planning. On the one hand, it expresses the fund sponsor's attitudes toward a number of important investment management issues, such as the fund's mission, the fund sponsor's risk tolerance, the fund's investment objectives, and so on. On the other hand, investment policy is a form of long-term strategic planning. It defines the specific goals that the fund sponsor expects the fund to accomplish, and it describes how the fund sponsor foresees the realization of those goals.

Investment policy gives an investment program a sense of direction and discipline. Performance evaluation enhances the effectiveness of a fund's investment policy by acting as a feedback and control mechanism. It identifies an investment program's strengths and weaknesses and attributes the fund's investment results to various key decisions. It assists the fund sponsor in reaffirming a commitment to successful investment strategies, and it helps to focus attention on poorly performing operations. Moreover, it provides evidence to fund trustees, who ultimately bear fiduciary responsibility for the fund's viability, that the investment program is being conducted in an appropriate and effective manner.

Fund sponsors are venturing into nontraditional asset categories and hiring a larger assortment of managers exhibiting unique investment styles, with the addition of hedge fund managers representing the latest and perhaps most complex example of this trend. Some fund sponsors are taking more investment decisions into their own hands, such as tactical asset allocation and style timing. Others are taking a quite different direction, giving their managers broad discretion to make asset allocation and security selection decisions. As a consequence of these developments, alert trustee boards are demanding more information from their investment staffs. The staffs, in turn, are seeking to better understand the extent of their own contributions and those of the funds' investment managers to the funds' investment results. The increased complexity of institutional investment management has brought a correspondingly greater need for sophisticated performance evaluation from the fund sponsor's perspective.

2.2. The Investment Manager's Perspective

Investment managers have various incentives to evaluate the performance of the portfolios that they manage for their clients. Virtually all fund sponsors insist that their managers offer some type of accounting of portfolio investment results. In many cases, performance evaluation conducted by the investment manager simply takes the form of reporting investment returns, perhaps presented alongside the returns of some designated benchmark. Other clients may insist on more sophisticated analyses, which the managers may produce in-house or acquire from a third party.

Some investment managers may seriously wish to investigate the effectiveness of various elements of their investment processes and examine the relative contributions of those elements. Managing investment portfolios involves a complex set of decision-making procedures. For example, an equity manager must make decisions about which stocks to hold, when to transact in those stocks, how much to allocate to various economic sectors, and how to allocate funds between stocks and cash. Numerous analysts and portfolio managers may be involved in determining a portfolio's composition. Just as in the case of the fund sponsor, performance evaluation can serve as a feedback and control loop, helping to monitor the proficiency of various aspects of the portfolio construction process.

3. THE THREE COMPONENTS OF PERFORMANCE EVALUATION

In light of the subject's importance to fund sponsors and investment managers alike, we want to consider the primary questions that performance evaluation seeks to address. In discussing performance evaluation we shall use the term *account* to refer generically to one or more portfolios of securities, managed by one or more investment management organizations. Thus, at one end of the spectrum, an account might indicate a single portfolio invested by a single manager. At the other end, an account could mean a fund sponsor's total fund, which might involve numerous portfolios invested by many different managers across multiple asset categories. In between, it might include all of a fund sponsor's assets in a particular asset category or the aggregate of all of the portfolios managed by an investment manager according to a particular mandate. The basic performance evaluation concepts are the same, regardless of the account's composition.

With the definition of an account in mind, three questions naturally arise in examining the investment performance of an account:

1. What was the account's performance?
2. Why did the account produce the observed performance?
3. Is the account's performance due to luck or skill?

In somewhat simplistic terms, these questions constitute the three primary issues of performance evaluation. The first issue is addressed by performance measurement, which calculates rates of return based on investment-related changes in an account's value over specified time periods. Performance attribution deals with the second issue. It extends the results of performance measurement to investigate both the sources of the account's performance relative to a specific investment benchmark and the importance of those sources. Finally, performance appraisal tackles the third question. It attempts to draw conclusions concerning the quality (that is, the magnitude and consistency) of the account's relative performance.

4. PERFORMANCE MEASUREMENT

To many investors, performance measurement and performance evaluation are synonymous. However, according to our classification, performance measurement is a component of performance evaluation. Performance measurement is the relatively simple procedure of calculating returns for an account. Performance evaluation, on the other hand, encompasses the broader and much more complex task of placing those investment results in the context of the account's investment objectives.

Performance measurement is the first step in the performance evaluation process. Yet it is a critical step, because to be of value, performance evaluation requires accurate and timely rate-of-return information. Therefore, we must fully understand how to compute an account's returns before advancing to more involved performance evaluation issues.

4.1. Performance Measurement without Intraperiod External Cash Flows

The rate of return on an account is the percentage change in the account's market value over some defined period of time (the evaluation period), after accounting for all external cash flows.[1] (External cash flows refer to contributions and withdrawals made to and from an account, as opposed to internal cash flows such as dividends and interest payments.) Therefore, a rate of return measures the relative change in the account's value due solely to investment-related sources, namely capital appreciation or depreciation and income. The mere addition or subtraction of assets to or from the account by the account's owner should not

[1] The evaluation period in this sense can also be called the measurement period.

affect the rate of return. Of course, in the simplest case, the account would experience no external cash flows. In that situation, the account's rate of return during evaluation period t equals the market value (MV_1) at the end of the period less the market value at the beginning of the period (MV_0), divided by the beginning market value.[2] That is,

$$r_t = \frac{MV_1 - MV_0}{MV_0} \tag{12-1}$$

Example 12-1 illustrates the use of Equation 12-1.

EXAMPLE 12-1 Rate-of-Return Calculations When There Are No External Cash Flows

Winter Asset Management manages institutional and individual accounts, including the account of the Mientkiewicz family. The Mientkiewicz account was initially valued at \$1,000,000. One month later it was worth \$1,080,000. Assuming no external cash flows and the reinvestment of all income, applying Equation 12-1, the return on the Mientkiewicz account for the month is

$$r_t = \frac{\$1,080,000 - \$1,000,000}{\$1,000,000} = 8.0\%$$

Fund sponsors occasionally (and in some cases frequently) add and subtract cash to and from their managers' accounts. These external cash flows complicate rate-of-return calculations. The rate-of-return algorithm must deal not only with the investment earnings on the initial assets in the account, but also with the earnings on any additional assets added to or subtracted from the account during the evaluation period. At the same time, the algorithm must exclude the direct impact of the external cash flows on the account's value.

An account's rate of return may still be computed in a straightforward fashion if the external cash flows occur at the beginning or the end of the measurement period when the account is valued. If a contribution is received at the start of the period, it should be added to (or, in the case of a withdrawal, subtracted from) the account's beginning value when calculating the account's rate of return for that period. The external cash flow will be invested alongside the rest of the account for the full length of the evaluation period and will have the same investment-related impact on the account's ending market value and, hence, should receive a full weighting. Thus, the account's return in the presence of an external cash flow at the beginning of the evaluation period should be calculated as

$$r_t = \frac{MV_1 - (MV_0 + CF)}{MV_0 + CF} \tag{12-2}$$

[2]From the fund sponsor's perspective, the account's market value should reflect the impact of all fees and expenses associated with investing the account's assets. Many managers report the return on accounts that they manage without including the effect of various fees and expenses. This practice is often justified based on the fact that fees vary among clients.

If a contribution is received at the end of the evaluation period, it should be subtracted from (or, in the case of a withdrawal, added to) the account's ending value. The external cash flow had no opportunity to affect the investment-related value of the account, and hence, it should be ignored.

$$r_t = \frac{(\text{MV}_1 - \text{CF}) - \text{MV}_0}{\text{MV}_0} \tag{12-3}$$

EXAMPLE 12-2 Rate-of-Return Calculations When External Cash Flows Occur at the Beginning or End of an Evaluation Period

Returning to the example of the Mientkiewicz account, assume that the account received a \$50,000 contribution at the beginning of the month. Further, the account's ending and beginning market values equal the same amounts previously stated, \$1,080,000 and \$1,000,000, respectively. Applying Equation 12-2, the rate of return for the month is therefore

$$r_t = \frac{\$1,080,000 - (\$1,000,000 + \$50,000)}{\$1,000,000 + \$50,000} = 2.86\%$$

If the contribution had occurred at month-end, using Equation 12-3, the account's return would be

$$r_t = \frac{(\$1,080,000 - \$50,000) - \$1,000,000}{\$1,000,000} = 3.00\%$$

Both returns are less than the 8 percent return reported when no external cash flows took place because we are holding the ending account value fixed at \$1,080,000. In the case of the beginning-of-period contribution, the account achieves an ending value of \$1,080,000 on a beginning value that is higher than in Example 12-1, so its return must be less than 8 percent. In the case of the end-of-period contribution, the return is lower than 8 percent because the ending value of \$1,080,000 is assumed to reflect an end-of-period contribution that is removed in calculating the return. In both instances, a portion of the account's change in value from \$1,000,000 to \$1,080,000 resulted from the contribution; in Example 12-1, by contrast, the change in value resulted entirely from positive investment performance by the account.[3]

The ease and accuracy of calculating returns when external cash flows occur, if those flows take place at the beginning or end of an evaluation period, lead to an important

[3]Note that the account's reported return was lower when the contribution took place at the start of the month than at the end. This result occurs because the account had both a positive return and proportionately more assets to invest over the month when the contribution was received at the beginning as opposed to the end. If the account's return had been negative, then, given the same ending value, a contribution at the beginning of the month would have resulted in a less negative reported return than would have resulted from a contribution that occurred at the end of the month.

practical recommendation: Whenever possible, a fund sponsor should make contributions to, or withdrawals from, an account at the end of an evaluation period (or equivalently, the beginning of the next evaluation period) when the account is valued. In the case of accounts that are valued on a daily basis, the issue is trivial. However, despite the increasing prevalence of daily valued accounts, many accounts are still valued on an audited basis once a month (or possibly less frequently), and the owners of those accounts should be aware of the potential for rate-of-return distortions caused by intraperiod external cash flows.

What does happen when external cash flows occur between the beginning and the end of an evaluation period? The simple comparison of the account's value relative to the account's beginning value must be abandoned in favor of more intricate methods.

4.2. Total Rate of Return

Interestingly, widely accepted solutions to the problem of measuring returns in the presence of intraperiod external cash flows are relatively recent developments. Prior to the 1960s, the issue received little attention, largely because the prevailing performance measures were unaffected by such flows. Performance was typically measured on an income-only basis, thus excluding the impact of capital appreciation. For example, current yield (income-to-price) and yield-to-maturity were commonly quoted return measures.

The emphasis on income-related return measures was due to several factors:

- **Portfolio management emphasis on fixed-income assets.** Particularly in the low-volatility interest rate environment that existed prior to the late 1970s, bond prices tended to be stable. Generally high allocations to fixed-income assets made income the primary source of investment-related wealth production for many investors.
- **Limited computing power.** Accurately accounting for external cash flows when calculating rates of return that include capital appreciation requires the use of computers. Access to the necessary computing resources was not readily available. The income-related return measures were simpler and could be performed by hand.
- **Less competitive investment environment.** Investors, as a whole, were less sophisticated and less demanding of accurate performance measures.

As portfolio allocations to equity securities increased, as computing costs declined, and as investors (particularly larger institutional investors) came to focus more intently on the performance of their portfolios, the demand grew for rate-of-return measures that correctly incorporated all aspects of an account's investment-related increase in wealth. This demand led to the adoption of total rate of return as the generally accepted measure of investment performance.

Total rate of return measures the increase in the investor's wealth due to both investment income (for example, dividends and interest) and capital gains (both realized and unrealized). The total rate of return implies that a dollar of wealth is equally meaningful to the investor whether that wealth is generated by the secure income from a 90-day Treasury bill or by the unrealized appreciation in the price of a share of common stock.

Acceptance of the total rate of return as the primary measure of investment performance was assured by a seminal study performed in 1968 by the Bank Administration Institute (BAI). The BAI study (which we refer to again shortly) was the first comprehensive research conducted on the issue of performance measurement. Among its many important contributions, the study strongly endorsed the use of the total rate of return as the only valid measure of investment performance. For our purposes, henceforth, it will be assumed that rate of return refers to the total rate of return, unless otherwise specified.

4.3. The Time-Weighted Rate of Return

We now return to considering the calculation of rates of return in the context of intraperiod external cash flows. To fully appreciate the issue at hand, we must think clearly about the meaning of "rate of return." In essence, the rate of return on an account is the investment-related growth rate in the account's value over the evaluation period. However, we can envision this growth rate being applied to a single dollar invested in the account at the start of the evaluation period or to an "average" amount of dollars invested in the account over the evaluation period. This subtle but important distinction leads to two different measures: the time-weighted and the money-weighted rates of return.

The **time-weighted rate of return** (TWR) reflects the compound rate of growth over a stated evaluation period of one unit of money initially invested in the account. Its calculation requires that the account be valued every time an external cash flow occurs. If no such flows take place, then the calculation of the TWR is trivial; it is simply the application of Equation 12-1, in which the change in the account's value is expressed relative to its beginning value. If external cash flows do occur, then the TWR requires computing a set of subperiod returns (with the number of subperiods equaling one plus the number of dates on which external cash flows occur). These subperiod returns must then be linked together in computing the TWR for the entire evaluation period.

EXAMPLE 12-3 Calculating Subperiod Rates of Return

Returning again to the Mientkiewicz account, let us assume that the account received two cash flows during month t: a contribution of \$30,000 on day 5 and a contribution of \$20,000 on day 16. Further, assume that we use a daily pricing system that provides us with values of the Mientkiewicz account (inclusive of the contributions) of \$1,045,000 and \$1,060,000 on days 5 and 16 of the month, respectively. We can then calculate three separate subperiod returns using the rate-of-return computation applicable to situations when external cash flows occur at the end of an evaluation period, as given by Equation 12-3:

$$\text{Subperiod 1} = \text{Days } 1 - 5$$

$$\text{Subperiod 2} = \text{Days } 6 - 16$$

$$\text{Subperiod 3} = \text{Days } 17 - 30$$

For subperiod 1:

$$\begin{aligned} r_{t,1} &= [(\$1,045,000 - \$30,000) - \$1,000,000]/\$1,000,000 \\ &= 0.0150 \\ &= 1.50\% \end{aligned}$$

For subperiod 2:

$$r_{t,2} = [(\$1,060,000 - \$20,000) - \$1,045,000]/\$1,045,000$$
$$= -0.0048$$
$$= -0.48\%$$

For subperiod 3:

$$r_{t,3} = (\$1,080,000 - \$1,060,000)/\$1,060,000$$
$$= 0.0189$$
$$= 1.89\%$$

The subperiod returns can be combined through a process called **chain-linking.** Chain-linking involves first adding 1 to the (decimal) rate of return for each subperiod to create a set of wealth relatives. A **wealth relative** can be thought of as the ending value of one unit of money (for example, one dollar) invested at each subperiod's rate of return. Next, the wealth relatives are multiplied together to produce a cumulative wealth relative for the full period, and 1 is subtracted from the result to obtain the TWR. Note that this process of chain-linking implicitly assumes that the initially invested dollar and earnings on that dollar are reinvested (or compounded) from one subperiod to the next. The cumulative wealth relative from the chain-linking of the subperiod wealth relatives can be interpreted as the ending value of one dollar invested in the account at the beginning of the evaluation period. Subtracting 1 from this wealth relative produces the TWR for the account:

$$r_{\text{twr}} = (1 + r_{t,1}) \times (1 + r_{t,2}) \times \ldots \times (1 + r_{t,n}) - 1 \qquad (12\text{-}4)$$

Note that unless the subperiods constitute a year, the time-weighted rate of return will not be expressed as an annual rate. Example 12-4 illustrates the calculation of a time-weighted rate of return.

EXAMPLE 12-4 Calculating the TWR

Continuing with the Mientkiewicz account, its TWR is

$$r_{\text{twr}} = (1 + 0.0150) \times (1 + -0.0048) \times (1 + 0.0189) - 1$$
$$= 0.0292$$
$$= 2.92\%$$

The TWR derives its name from the fact that each subperiod return within the full evaluation period receives a weight proportional to the length of the subperiod relative to the length of the full evaluation period. That relationship becomes apparent if each subperiod return is expressed as the cumulative return over smaller time units. In the Mientkiewicz account example, the return in the first subperiod is 0.015 over five days. On a daily compounded basis that return is $0.0030[= (1 + 0.015)^{1/5} - 1]$. Performing the same calculation for the other two subperiods yields the following:

$$\begin{aligned} r_{\text{twr}} &= (1 + 0.0030)^5 \times (1 + -0.0004)^{11} \times (1 + 0.0013)^{14} - 1 \\ &= 0.0292 = 2.92\% \text{ (allowing for rounding)} \end{aligned}$$

From this expression for the TWR, we can see that the subperiods 1, 2, and 3 receive compounding "weights" of 5/30, 11/30, and 14/30, respectively.

4.4. The Money-Weighted Rate of Return

The **money-weighted rate of return** (MWR) measures the compound growth rate in the value of all funds invested in the account over the evaluation period. In the corporate finance literature, the MWR goes by the name **internal rate of return,** or IRR. Of importance for performance measurement, the MWR is the growth rate that will link the ending value of the account to its beginning value plus all intermediate cash flows. With MV_1 and MV_0 the values of the account at the end and beginning of the evaluation period, respectively, in equation form the MWR is the growth rate R that solves

$$MV_1 = MV_0(1 + R)^m + CF_1(1 + R)^{m-L(1)} + \ldots + CF_n(1 + R)^{m-L(n)} \qquad (12\text{-}5)$$

where

m = number of time units in the evaluation period (for example, the number of days in the month)

CF_i = the ith cash flow

$L(i)$ = number of time units by which the ith cash flow is separated from the beginning of the evaluation period

Note that R is expressed as the return per unit of time composing the evaluation period. For example, in the case of monthly performance measurement, where the constituent time unit is one day, R would be the daily MWR of the account. Extending this thought, $[(1 + R)^m - 1]$ can be seen to be the account's MWR for the entire evaluation period, as $(1 + R)^m = (1 + r_{\text{mwr}})$. Therefore, in the case of no external cash flows, with some algebraic manipulation, Equation 12-4 reduces to Equation 12-1, the simple expression for rate of return:

$$\begin{aligned} MV_1 &= MV_0(1 + R)^m + 0 \\ (1 + R)^m &= MV_1 / MV_0 \\ (1 + r_{\text{mwr}}) &= MV_1 / MV_0 \\ r_{\text{mwr}} &= (MV_1 - MV_0) / MV_0 \\ &= r_t \end{aligned}$$

EXAMPLE 12-5 Calculating the MWR

Consider the Mientkiewicz account again. Its MWR is found by solving the following equation for R:

$$\$1,080,000 = \$1,000,000(1+R)^{30} + \$30,000(1+R)^{30-5} + \$20,000(1+R)^{30-16}$$

There exists no closed-form solution for R. That is, Equation 12-4 cannot be manipulated to isolate R on the left-hand side. Consequently, R must be solved iteratively through a trial-and-error process. In our example, we begin with an initial guess of $R = 0.001$. The right-hand side of the equation becomes \$1,081,480. Thus our initial guess is too high and must be lowered. Next try a value $R = 0.0007$. In this case the right-hand side now equals \$1,071,941. Therefore our second guess is too low.

We can continue this process. Eventually, we will arrive at the correct value for R, which for the Mientkiewicz account is 0.0009536. Remember that this value is the Mientkiewicz account's daily rate of return during the month. Expressed on a monthly basis, the MWR is 0.0290 [$= (1+0.0009536)^{30} - 1$], or 2.90%.

As one might expect, a computer is best suited to perform the repetitious task of calculating the MWR. Spreadsheet software to perform these computations is readily available.

4.5. TWR versus MWR

The MWR represents the average growth rate of all money invested in an account, while the TWR represents the growth of a single unit of money invested in the account. Consequently, the MWR is sensitive to the size and timing of external cash flows to and from the account, while the TWR is unaffected by these flows. Under "normal" conditions, these two return measures will produce similar results. In the example of the Mientkiewicz account, the MWR was 2.90 percent for the month and the TWR was 2.92 percent.

However, when external cash flows occur that are large relative to the account's value and the account's performance is fluctuating significantly during the measurement period, then the MWR and the TWR can differ materially.

EXAMPLE 12-6 When TWR and MWR Differ

Consider the Charlton account, worth \$800,000 at the beginning of the month. On Day 10 it is valued at \$1.8 million after receiving a \$1 million contribution. At the end of the month, the account is worth \$3 million. As a result, the Charlton account's MWR is 87.5 percent, while its TWR is only 66.7 percent.

For subperiod 1:

$$r_{t,1} = [(\$1,800,000 - \$1,000,000) - \$800,000]/\$800,000$$
$$= 0.0 \text{ or } 0\%$$

For subperiod 2:

$$r_{t,2} = (\$3,000,000 - \$1,800,000)/\$1,800,000$$
$$= 0.6667 \text{ or } 66.7\%$$

Then

$$r_{\text{twr}} = (1 + 0) \times (1 + 0.667) - 1$$
$$= 0.667 \text{ or } 66.7\%$$

For MWR, we need to solve:

$$\$3,000,000 = \$800,000(1 + R)^{30} + \$1,000,000(1 + R)^{30-10}$$

By trial and error, R comes out to be 0.020896. Expressed on a monthly basis, MWR is 0.859709 or 86.0%[$= (1 + 0.020896)^{30} - 1$].

If funds are contributed to an account prior to a period of strong performance (as in the case of the Charlton account in Example 12-6), then the MWR will be positively affected compared to the TWR, as a relatively large sum is invested at a high growth rate. That is, in the case of the Charlton account, a contribution was made just prior to a subperiod in which a dollar invested in the account earned 66.7 percent. In the prior subperiod the account earned 0.0 percent. Thus, on average, the account had more dollars invested earning 66.7 percent than it had dollars earning 0.0 percent, resulting in an MWR greater than the TWR. Conversely, if funds are withdrawn from the account prior to the strong performance, then the MWR will be adversely affected relative to the TWR. (The opposite conclusions hold if the external cash flow occurred prior to a period of weak performance.)

As noted, the TWR is unaffected by external cash flow activity. Valuing the account at the time of each external cash flow effectively removes the impact of those flows on the TWR. Consequently, the TWR accurately reflects how an investor would have fared over the evaluation period if he or she had placed funds in the account at the beginning of the period.

In most situations, an investment manager has little or no control over the size and timing of external cash flows into or out of his or her accounts. Therefore, practitioners generally prefer a rate-of-return measure that is not sensitive to cash flows if they want to evaluate how a manager's investment actions have affected an account's value. This consideration led the authors of the Bank Administration Institute study to recommend that the TWR be adopted as the appropriate measure of account performance. That recommendation has received almost universal acceptance since the study's publication. (Note that the Global Investment Performance Standards [GIPS®] generally require a TWR methodology.)

However, one can readily conceive of situations in which the MWR may prove useful in evaluating the returns achieved by an investment manager. The most obvious examples are those situations in which the investment manager maintains control over the timing and amount of cash flows into the account. Managers of various types of private equity investments typically operate under arrangements that permit them to call capital from their investors at the managers' discretion and ultimately to determine when the original capital, and any earnings on that capital, will be returned to investors. In these "opportunistic" situations, it is generally agreed that the MWR is the more appropriate measure of account returns.[4]

4.6. The Linked Internal Rate of Return

Despite its useful characteristics, the TWR does have an important disadvantage: It requires account valuations on every date that an external cash flow takes place. Thus, calculation of the TWR typically necessitates the ability to price a portfolio of securities on a daily basis. Although daily pricing services are becoming more common, marking an account to market daily is administratively more expensive and cumbersome, and potentially more error-prone, than traditional monthly accounting procedures. For these reasons, use of pure TWR is not yet standard practice, with the prominent exception of the mutual fund industry.[5] The MWR, on the other hand, despite its sensitivity to the size and timing of external cash flows, requires only that an account be valued at the beginning and end of the evaluation period and that the amounts and dates of any external cash flows be recorded.

The complementary advantages and disadvantages of the TWR and the MWR led the authors of the BAI study to make an important recommendation: The TWR should be approximated by calculating the MWR over reasonably frequent time intervals and then chain-linking those returns over the entire evaluation period. This process is referred to as the Linked Internal Rate of Return (LIRR) method and originally was developed by Peter Dietz (1966). The BAI study estimated that if the LIRR method were applied to an account experiencing "normal" cash flow activity, then using monthly valuations and daily dating of external cash flows, the calculated rate of return on average would fall within 4 basis points per year of the true TWR.[6] Given the inaccuracies inherent in the pricing of even the most liquid portfolios, this slight difference appears immaterial.

EXAMPLE 12-7 An Example of LIRR

Suppose, in a given month, the Mientkiewicz account's MWR is calculated each week. These MWRs are 0.021 in week 1, 0.0016 in week 2, −0.014 in week 3, and 0.018 in week 4. The LIRR is obtained by linking these rates:

$$\begin{aligned} R_{\text{LIRR}} &= (1 + 0.021) \times (1 + 0.0016) \times (1 + -0.014) \times (1 + 0.018) - 1 \\ &= 0.0265 \text{ or } 2.65\% \end{aligned}$$

[4]For a discussion of the use of the MWR as a performance measure for opportunistic investments, see Tierney and Bailey (1997).

[5]Nevertheless, for periods beginning January 1, 2010, firms will be required to value portfolios on the date of all large external cash flows to claim compliance with the GIPS standards. In the interim, the GIPS standards admit the use of acceptable daily weighted methods for estimating the time-weighted rate of return. These methods are presented in Chapter 13.

[6]Bank Administration Institute (1968, p. 22).

The BAI study concluded that only under unusual circumstances would the LIRR fail to provide an acceptable representation of the TWR. Specifically, the LIRR would fail if both large external cash flows (generally over 10 percent of the account's value) and volatile swings in subperiod performance occurred during the evaluation period. With an evaluation period as short as one month, the chances of such a joint event occurring for an account are low. Nevertheless, if it should happen, the BAI study recommended valuing the account on the date of the intramonth cash flow.

4.7. Annualized Return

For comparison purposes, rates of return are typically reported on an annualized basis. As defined here, the annualized return represents the compound average annual return earned by the account over the evaluation period. The calculation is also known as the compound growth rate or geometric mean return. An annualized return is computed by employing the same chain-linking method used to calculate linked internal rates of return, except that the product of the linking is raised to the reciprocal of the number of years covering the evaluation period (or equivalently, taking the appropriate root of the linked product, where the root is the number of years in the measurement period).

EXAMPLE 12-8 Annualized Return

If in years 1, 2, and 3 of a three-year evaluation period an account earned 2.0 percent, 9.5 percent, and – 4.7 percent, respectively, then the annualized return for the evaluation period would be:

$$r_a = [(1 + 0.02) \times (1 + 0.095) \times (1 - 0.047)]^{1/3} - 1$$
$$= 0.021 \text{ or } 2.1\%$$

If 12 quarterly returns had been available for the account instead of three yearly returns, then those quarterly returns would have been similarly linked and the cube root of the product would have been calculated to produce the account's annualized return over the three-year period.

In general, with measurement periods shorter than a full year, it is inadvisable to calculate annualized returns. Essentially, the person calculating returns is extrapolating the account's returns over a sample period to the full year. Particularly for equity accounts, returns can fluctuate significantly during the remaining time in the evaluation period, making the annualized return a potentially unrealistic estimate of the account's actual return over the full year.

4.8. Data Quality Issues

The performance measurement process is only as accurate as the inputs to the process. Often performance report users fail to distinguish between rates of return of high and low reliability. In the case of accounts invested in liquid and transparently priced securities and experiencing little external cash flow activity, the reported rates of return are likely to be highly reliable performance indicators. They will accurately reflect the experience of an investor who entered such an account at the beginning of the evaluation period and liquidated his or her investment at the end of the period. Conversely, for accounts invested in illiquid and infrequently priced assets, the underlying valuations may be suspect, thereby invalidating the reported rates of return. For example, due to the inaccuracy inherent in estimation techniques, quarterly valuations of venture capital funds typically have limited economic content. An investor may not be able to enter or leave the account at a value anywhere near the reported valuations. As a result, monthly or even annual performance measurement of such funds should be viewed with caution.

Various services exist that collect data on recent market transactions for a wide range of fixed-income and equity securities. Particularly for many thinly traded fixed-income securities, a current market price may not always be available. In that case, estimated prices may be derived based on dealer-quoted prices for securities with similar attributes (for example, a security with a similar credit rating, maturity, and economic sector). This approach is referred to as **matrix pricing.** For highly illiquid securities, reasonable estimates of market prices may be difficult or impossible to obtain. Investment managers may carry these securities at cost or the price of the last trade in those securities. It is outside the scope of this discussion to address in detail the subject of account valuation. Suffice it to say that *caveat emptor*—"let the buyer beware"—should be the motto of any user of performance measurement reports who deals with securities other than liquid stocks and bonds.

In addition to obtaining accurate account valuations and external cash flow recognition, reliable performance measurement requires appropriate data collection procedures. For example, account valuations should be reported on a trade-date, fully accrued basis. That is, the stated value of the account should reflect the impact of any unsettled trades and any income owed by or to the account but not yet paid. Such a valuation process correctly represents the best available statement of the account's position at a point in time. Other methods, such as settlement date accounting and the exclusion of accrued income, incorrectly reflect the account's market value.

5. BENCHMARKS

Performance evaluation cannot be conducted in a vacuum. By its nature, performance evaluation is a relative concept. Absolute performance numbers mean little. Even so-called "absolute return" managers should provide some sense of how alternative uses of their clients' money would have performed if exposed to similar risks. Consider how one interprets a 7 percent return on a well-diversified common stock portfolio during a given month. If you knew that the broad stock market had declined 15 percent during the month, you might be impressed. Conversely, if the market had advanced 25 percent, you might be disappointed. If we are to conduct meaningful performance evaluation, then we must develop an appropriate benchmark against which an account's performance can be compared.

5.1. Concept of a Benchmark

The *Merriam-Webster Dictionary* defines a benchmark as a "standard or point of reference in measuring or judging quality, value, etc." Applying this general definition to investment management, a benchmark is a collection of securities or risk factors and associated weights that represents the persistent and prominent investment characteristics of an asset category or manager's investment process. At the asset category level, we can think of a benchmark as the collection of securities that the fund sponsor would own if the fund sponsor were required to place all of its investments within the asset category in a single, passively managed portfolio. (In other words, the benchmark is the fund sponsor's preferred index fund for the asset category.) At the manager level, we can think of a benchmark as a passive representation of the manager's investment style, incorporating the salient investment features (such as significant exposures to particular sources of systematic risk) that consistently appear in the manager's portfolios. More metaphorically, a manager's benchmark encompasses the manager's "area" of expertise. Just as an angler has a favorite fishing hole, an investment manager also has distinct preferences for certain types of securities and risk exposures. The opportunity set that represents the manager's area of expertise may be broad or narrow, reflecting the resources and investment processes that the manager brings to bear on the portfolio selection problem.

A little algebra succinctly conveys these concepts. Begin with the simple identity of an investment manager's portfolio; that is, any portfolio is equal to itself:[7]

$$P = P$$

Now, consider an appropriately selected benchmark B. If we add and subtract B from the right-hand side of this identity, effectively adding a zero to the relationship, the result is

$$P = B + (P - B)$$

Additionally, if we define the manager's active investment judgments as being the difference between the manager's portfolio P and the benchmark B so that $A = (P - B)$, then the equation just given becomes:

$$P = B + A \tag{12-6}$$

Thus, the managed portfolio P can be viewed as a combination of (1) the benchmark B and (2) active management decisions A composed of a set of over- and underweighted positions in securities relative to the benchmark. We can extend this relationship by introducing a market index M. Adding and subtracting M from the right-hand side of Equation 12-6 gives:

$$P = M + (B - M) + A$$

The difference between the manager's benchmark portfolio and the market index $(B - M)$ can be defined as the manager's investment style S. If we let $S = (B - M)$, then the equation just given becomes:

$$P = M + S + A \tag{12-7}$$

Equation 12-7 states that a portfolio has three components: market, style, and active management.

There are several interesting applications of Equation 12-7. First, note that if the portfolio is a broad market index fund, then $S = (B - M) = 0$ (that is, no style biases) and $A = (P - B) = 0$ (that is, no active management). Consequently, Equation 12-7 reduces to $P = M$; the portfolio is equivalent to the market index.

[7]The variables used in this section can be interpreted as either rates of return or weights assigned to securities that make up a portfolio.

Second, if we define the benchmark as the market index [that is, $S = (B - M) = 0$, or no style], then Equation 12-7 reduces to Equation 12-6 and substituting M for B gives

$$P = M + A$$

Because many managers and fund sponsors have been willing to define a manager's benchmark as a broad market index (for example, the S&P 500 in the case of U.S. common stock managers), both parties are implicitly stating that they believe that the manager has no distinct investment style. However, most practitioners would agree that the vast majority of managers pursue specific investment styles. Specialization has become the hallmark of our postindustrial society, and it should not be surprising that, with respect to a subject as complex as portfolio management, many managers have chosen to focus their skills on certain segments of that subject.

EXAMPLE 12-9 Returns Due to Style and Active Management

Suppose the Mientkiewicz account earns a total return of 3.6 percent in a given month, during which the portfolio benchmark has a return of 3.8 percent and the market index has a return of 2.8 percent. Then the return due to the portfolio manager's style is

$$S = B - M = 3.8\% - 2.8\% = 1\%$$

and the return due to active management is

$$A = P - B = 3.6\% - 3.8\% = -0.2\%$$

5.2. Properties of a Valid Benchmark

Although in practice an acceptable benchmark is simply one that both the manager and the fund sponsor agree fairly represents the manager's investment process, to function effectively in performance evaluation, a benchmark should possess certain basic properties. A valid benchmark is:

- **Unambiguous.** The identities and weights of securities or factor exposures constituting the benchmark are clearly defined.
- **Investable.** It is possible to forgo active management and simply hold the benchmark.
- **Measurable.** The benchmark's return is readily calculable on a reasonably frequent basis.
- **Appropriate.** The benchmark is consistent with the manager's investment style or area of expertise.
- **Reflective of current investment opinions.** The manager has current investment knowledge (be it positive, negative, or neutral) of the securities or factor exposures within the benchmark.

- **Specified in advance.** The benchmark is specified prior to the start of an evaluation period and known to all interested parties.
- **Owned.** The investment manager should be aware of and accept accountability for the constituents and performance of the benchmark. It is encouraged that the benchmark be embedded in and integral to the investment process and procedures of the investment manager.

The failure of a benchmark to possess these properties compromises its utility as an effective investment management tool. A benchmark represents an equivalent risk opportunity cost to the fund sponsor. The properties listed merely formalize intuitive notions of what constitutes a fair and relevant performance comparison. It is interesting to observe that a number of commonly used benchmarks fail to satisfy these properties.

5.3. Types of Benchmarks

At the investment manager level, a benchmark forms the basis of a covenant between the manager and the fund sponsor. It reflects the investment style that the fund sponsor expects the manager to pursue, and it becomes the basis for evaluating the success of the manager's investment management efforts. Many different benchmarks may satisfy the criteria for an acceptable benchmark and, if agreed upon by both parties, could be implemented. In general, there are seven primary types of benchmarks in use.

1. *Absolute.* An absolute return can be a return objective. Examples include an actuarial rate-of-return assumption or a minimum return target which the fund strives to exceed. Unfortunately, absolute return objectives are not investable alternatives and do not satisfy the benchmark validity criteria.[8]
2. *Manager universes.* Consultants and fund sponsors frequently use the median manager or fund from a broad universe of managers or funds as a performance evaluation benchmark. As discussed in more detail later, a median manager benchmark fails all the tests of benchmark validity except for being measurable.
3. *Broad market indexes.* Many managers and fund sponsors use **broad market indexes** as benchmarks. Prominent examples of broad market indexes used by U.S. investors include the S&P 500, Wilshire 5000, and Russell 3000 indexes for U.S. common stocks; the Lehman Aggregate and the Citigroup Broad Investment-Grade (U.S. BIG) Bond Indexes for U.S. investment-grade debt; and the Morgan Stanley Capital International

[8]As we have used the term, a benchmark is a means to differentiate managers or fund sponsors who add value through investment insights from those who do not. In this sense, a sponsor's liabilities may also be treated as a type of benchmark. That is, institutional investors such as defined-benefit pension plan sponsors and endowment and foundation executives seek to achieve rates of return enabling them, at a minimum, to meet liabilities as they come due without making greater-than-planned additions to fund assets. (Another way to express this financial objective is to say that institutional investors seek at least to maintain a stated level of fund surplus, defined as the present value of assets less the present value of liabilities.) In terms of asset-liability management, or surplus management, the fund's investment objective may be to achieve a rate of return on assets that meets or exceeds the "return" on liabilities—that is, the percentage change in the present value of the liabilities over the evaluation period. Moreover, because a liability, or a stream of liabilities, may be considered a financial asset held short, it is possible, in principle, to construct a custom index representing the fund's liabilities and to use that index as a benchmark at the level of the total fund.

(MSCI) Europe, Australasia, and Far East (EAFE) Index for non-U.S. developed-market common stocks. Market indexes are well recognized, easy to understand, and widely available, and satisfy several properties of valid benchmarks. They are unambiguous, generally investable, and measurable, and they may be specified in advance. In certain situations, market indexes are perfectly acceptable as benchmarks, particularly as benchmarks for asset category performance or for "core" type investment approaches in which the manager selects from a universe of securities similar in composition to the benchmark. However, in other circumstances, the manager's style may deviate considerably from the style reflected in a market index. For example, assigning a micro-capitalization U.S. growth stock manager an S&P 500 benchmark clearly violates the appropriateness criterion.

4. *Style indexes.* Broad market indexes have been increasingly partitioned to create **investment style indexes** that represent specific portions of an asset category: for example, subgroups within the U.S. common stock asset category. Four popular U.S. common stock style indexes are (1) large-capitalization growth, (2) large-capitalization value, (3) small-capitalization growth, and (4) small-capitalization value. (Mid-capitalization growth and value common stock indexes are also available.) The Frank Russell Company, Standard & Poor's, and Morgan Stanley Capital International produce the most widely used U.S. common stock style indexes. International common stock style indexes are more recent developments.

   Fixed-income style indexes are produced in a similar manner. In many ways, investment-grade bonds are a more convenient asset category for developing style indexes, because the broad market indexes are easily segregated into various types of securities. For example, broad bond market indexes, such as the Lehman Aggregate for U.S. debt, can be broken up into their constituent parts, such as the Lehman Government/Credit Index, the Lehman Mortgage Index, and so on. The Lehman Aggregate can also be decomposed along the lines of maturity (or duration) and quality.

   Similar to broad market indexes, investment style indexes are often well known, easy to understand, and widely available. However, their ability to pass tests of benchmark validity can be problematic. Some style indexes contain weightings in certain securities and economic sectors that are much larger than what many managers consider prudent. Further, the definition of investment style implied in the benchmark may be ambiguous or inconsistent with the investment process of the manager being evaluated. Differing definitions of investment style at times can produce rather extreme return differentials. In 1999, the S&P Large Value Index had a return of 12.72 percent, and the Russell Large Value Index had a return of 7.35 percent. These large return differences among indexes presumably designed to represent the results of the same investment style are disconcerting. Users of style indexes should closely examine how the indexes are constructed and assess their applicability to specific managers.

5. *Factor model based.* Factor models provide a means of relating one or more systematic sources of return to the returns on an account.[9] As a result, a specified set of factor exposures could potentially be used as a **factor model–based benchmark.** The simplest form of factor model is a one-factor model, such as the familiar **market model.** In that relationship, the return on a security, or a portfolio of securities, is expressed as a linear

[9]Factor models are discussed in DeFusco, McLeavey, Pinto, and Runkle (2004) as well as in standard investment textbooks such as Sharpe, Alexander, and Bailey (1999).

function of the return on a broad market index, established over a suitably long period (for example, 60 months):

$$R_p = a_p + \beta_p R_I + \varepsilon_p \tag{12-8}$$

where R_p represents the periodic return on an account and R_I represents the periodic return on the market index.[10] The market index is used as a proxy for the underlying systematic return factor (or factors). The term ε_p is the residual, or nonsystematic, element of the relationship. The term β_p measures the sensitivity of the returns on the account to the returns on the market index; it is typically estimated by regressing the account's returns on those of the market index. The sensitivity term is called the beta of the account. Finally, the intercept a_p is the "zero factor" term, representing the expected value of R_p if the factor value was zero.

EXAMPLE 12-10 Returns from a Market Model

Consider an account with a zero-factor value of 2.0 percent and a beta of 1.5. Applying Equation 12-8, a return of 8 percent for the market index generates an expected return on the account of 14% (= 2.0% + 1.5 × 8%).

Some managers hold accounts that persistently display a beta greater than 1.0, while other managers hold accounts with betas persistently less than 1.0. Out of these patterns arises the concept of a benchmark with a "normal beta" consistent with these observed tendencies. For example, suppose that an analysis of past account returns, combined with discussions with the manager, suggests a normal beta of 1.2. This normal beta becomes the basis for the benchmark that specifies the level of return that the account would be expected to generate in the absence of any value added by active management on the part of the manager.

Incorporating multiple sources of systematic risk can enhance the richness of the factor model approach. That is, Equation 12-8 can be extended to include more than one factor. For example, a company's size, industry, growth characteristics, financial strength, and other factors may have a systematic impact on a portfolio's performance. Generalizing Equation 12-8 produces

$$R_p = a_p + b_1 F_1 + b_2 F_2 + \ldots + b_K F_K + \varepsilon_p$$

where $F_1, F_2, \ldots F_K$ represent the values of factors 1 through K, respectively. Numerous commercially available multifactor risk models have been produced. Rosenberg and

[10]Although the market model has some resemblances to the capital asset pricing model (CAPM), the market model is not an equilibrium model of asset pricing, as is the CAPM. Under a set of specific assumptions, the CAPM states that investors will act in a manner that generates a unique relationship between the beta of a security or portfolio and the return on the market portfolio. Any security or portfolio with the same beta is expected to produce the same return. The market model, on the other hand, is an empirical relationship between the return on a security or portfolio and a particular market index (as opposed to the market portfolio). See Markowitz (1984) for a discussion of this distinction.

Marathe (1975) pioneered the development of these models, and their work was extended to create performance evaluation benchmarks. The concept of a "normal beta" in a multifactor context leads to the concept of a normal portfolio. A **normal portfolio** is a portfolio with exposures to sources of systematic risk that are typical for a manager, using the manager's past portfolios as a guide.

Benchmarks based on factor exposures can be useful in performance evaluation. Because they capture the systematic sources of return that affect an account's performance, they help managers and fund sponsors better understand a manager's investment style. However, they are not always intuitive to the fund sponsor and particularly to the investment managers (who rarely think in terms of factor exposures when designing investment strategies), are not always easy to obtain, and are potentially expensive to use. In addition, they are ambiguous. We can build multiple benchmarks with the same factor exposures, but each benchmark can earn different returns. For example, we can construct two different portfolios, each with a beta of 1.2 ("normal beta"), but the portfolios can have materially different returns. Also, because the composition of a factor-based benchmark is not specified with respect to the constituent securities and their weights, we cannot verify all the validity criteria (the benchmark may not be investable, for example).

6. *Returns based*. Sharpe (1988, 1992) introduced the concept of **returns-based benchmarks.** These benchmarks are constructed using (1) the series of a manager's account returns (ideally, monthly returns going back in time as long as the investment process has been in place) and (2) the series of returns on several investment style indexes over the same period. These return series are then submitted to an allocation algorithm that solves for the combination of investment style indexes that most closely tracks the account's returns.[11]

   For example, assume that we have ten years of monthly returns of a U.S. equity mutual fund. Also, assume that we have the monthly returns of four U.S. equity style indexes—(1) large-cap growth, (2) large-cap value, (3) small-cap growth, and (4) small-cap value—over the same time period. If we submit these return series to a properly constructed allocation algorithm, we can solve for a particular set of allocation weights for the four style indexes that will track most closely the return series of the manager's actual portfolio. The returns-based benchmark is represented by these allocation weights.

   Returns-based benchmarks are generally easy to use and are intuitively appealing. They satisfy most benchmark validity criteria, including those of being unambiguous, measurable, investable, and specified in advance. Returns-based benchmarks are particularly useful in situations where the only information available is account returns. One disadvantage of returns-based benchmarks is that, like the style indexes that underlie the benchmarks, they may hold positions in securities and economic sectors that a manager might find unacceptable. Further, they require many months of observation to establish a statistically reliable pattern of style exposures. In the case of managers who rotate among style exposures, such a pattern may be impossible to discern.

7. *Custom security based*. An investment manager will typically follow an investment philosophy that causes the manager to focus its research activities on certain types of securities. The manager will select those securities that represent the most attractive investment opportunities that the research process has identified. As the financial and

[11]The ability to track the account's returns is typically measured by the standard deviation of the monthly return differences of the account and the benchmark, called the tracking error.

investment characteristics of securities will change over time, a manager's research universe will similarly evolve.

A **custom security-based benchmark** is simply a manager's research universe weighted in a particular fashion. Most managers do not use a security weighting scheme that is exactly an equal weighting across all securities or one that exactly assigns weights according to market capitalization. Consequently, a custom benchmark reflecting a particular manager's unique weighting approach can be more suitable than a published index for a fair and accurate appraisal of that manager's performance.

The overwhelming advantage of a custom security-based benchmark is that it meets all of the required benchmark properties and satisfies all of the benchmark validity criteria, making it arguably the most appropriate benchmark for performance evaluation purposes. In addition, it is a valuable tool for managers to monitor and control their investment processes and for fund sponsors to effectively allocate or budget risk across teams of investment managers. One major disadvantage is that custom security-based benchmarks are expensive to construct and maintain. In addition, as they are not composed of published indexes, the perception of a lack of transparency can be of concern.

5.4. Building Custom Security-Based Benchmarks

A valid custom security-based benchmark is the product of discussions between the client or the client's consultant and the manager and of a detailed analysis of the manager's past security holdings. The construction of such a benchmark involves the following steps:

1. Identify prominent aspects of the manager's investment process.
2. Select securities consistent with that investment process.
3. Devise a weighting scheme for the benchmark securities, including a cash position.
4. Review the preliminary benchmark and make modifications.
5. Rebalance the benchmark portfolio on a predetermined schedule.

For the purpose of custom benchmark construction, an analysis of the manager's past portfolios will identify prominent aspects of the manager's investment process. The selection of benchmark portfolio securities requires both a broad universe of potential candidates and a set of screening criteria consistent with the manager's investment process. Weighting schemes may include aspects of equal weighting and capitalization weighting, depending on the manager's investment process and client restrictions. Following these steps, a preliminary benchmark portfolio is selected. At this point, the benchmark's composition is reviewed and final modifications are made. Ultimately, keeping the benchmark portfolio current with the manager's investment process necessitates rebalancing the portfolio at regularly scheduled intervals.

These steps, though simple in appearance, constitute a complex task. A proper benchmark must make a fine distinction between the manager's "normal" or policy investment decisions and the manager's active investment judgments. Considerable resources are required, including a comprehensive security database, an efficient computer screening capability, a flexible security weighting system, and a means of maintaining the integrity of the benchmark over time.

5.5. Critique of Manager Universes as Benchmarks

Fund sponsors have a natural interest in knowing how their investment results compare to those achieved by similar institutions and how the returns earned by the managers they have selected compare to those earned by managers they might have engaged. To facilitate peer group comparisons, some consulting firms and custodial banks have developed databases or "universes" of account returns ranked in descending order. Fund sponsors often use the median account in a particular peer group as a return benchmark. For instance, the investment policy statement of a public fund might specify that the fund's objective is to perform in the top half of a certain universe of public funds, and the guidelines for a domestic large-cap equity account might state that the manager's results are expected to exceed those of the median account in a certain universe consisting of portfolios with large-cap value mandates or characteristics.

With the exception of being measurable, the median account in a typical commercially available universe does not have the properties of a valid benchmark described above. One of the most significant deficiencies is that, although the universe can be named, the median account cannot be *specified in advance*. Universe compilers can only establish the median account on an *ex post* basis, after the returns earned by all accounts have been calculated and ranked. Prior to the start of an evaluation period, neither the manager nor the fund sponsor has any knowledge of who the median manager will be at period end. In addition, different accounts will fall at the median from one evaluation period to another. For these reasons, the benchmark is not *investable* and cannot serve as a passive alternative to holding the account that is under analysis. Even after the evaluation period concludes, the identity of the median manager typically remains unknown, preventing the benchmark from satisfying the *unambiguous* property. The ambiguity of the median manager benchmark makes it impossible to verify its *appropriateness* by examining whether the investment style it represents adequately corresponds to the account being evaluated. The fund sponsor who chooses to employ universes for peer group comparisons can only rely on the compiler's representations that accounts have been rigorously screened against well-defined criteria for inclusion, the integrity of the input data is scrupulously monitored, and a uniform return calculation methodology has been used for all accounts in all periods.

One other disadvantage merits attention. Because fund sponsors terminate underperforming managers, universes are unavoidably subject to "survivor bias." Consider the hypothetical universe represented in Exhibit 12-1, where a shaded cell indicates that a particular account

								Annualized Returns At End of Year 7			
	Year 1	Year 2	Year 3	Year 4	Year 5	Year 6	Year 7	1 Year	3 Years	5 Years	7 Years
Manager 1											
Manager 2								X	X	X	X
Manager 3								X			
Manager 4								X	X		
Manager 5											
Manager 6											
Manager 7								X	X	X	X
Manager 8								X	X	X	
Manager 9								X			
Manager 10											
Observations	6	6	7	7	7	5	6	6	4	3	2

EXHIBIT 12-1 Survivor Bias in a Manager Universe

existed for a given year and an X indicates that a rate of return can be calculated for the referenced evaluation period.

In this example, there were six accounts in the universe at the end of Year 1, and there were six at the end of Year 7. They were not all the same accounts, however; in fact, only two have survived for the full period to achieve seven-year returns. The other four in the Year 1 cohort were no longer present because the sponsors reallocated funds or possibly because the managers' performance was unsatisfactory. In any event, it is likely that the two survivors were among the best-performing in the group of accounts that existed in Year 1; sponsors are naturally reluctant to dismiss strong performing managers. Because the survivors' returns were presumably high, the actual median seven-year return for this universe will be higher than the median of a hypothetical return distribution from which no accounts were removed.

Why are these deficiencies of the median manager benchmark of concern? From the perspective of performance evaluation, the question becomes, "To what is the manager expected to add value?" Without a valid reference point, superior performance remains an elusive notion. Placing above the median of a universe of investment managers or funds may be a reasonable investment *objective*, but the performance of a particular manager or fund is not a suitable performance benchmark that can be used to assess investment skill.[12]

5.6. Tests of Benchmark Quality

In many organizations, benchmarks have become an important element of the investment management process. Moreover, benchmark use has expanded beyond performance evaluation. Benchmarks are now an integral part of risk management, at both the investment manager and fund sponsor levels. Most forms of risk budgeting use benchmarks to estimate the risks to which a fund sponsor's investment program is exposed at the asset category and investment manager levels.

Given the important uses of benchmarks, it is in the interests of all parties involved (fund sponsors, consultants, and managers) to identify good benchmarks and to improve or replace poor benchmarks. Good benchmarks increase the proficiency of performance evaluation, highlighting the contributions of skillful managers. Poor benchmarks obscure manager skills. Good benchmarks enhance the capability to manage investment risk. Poor benchmarks promote inefficient manager allocations and ineffective risk management. They also increase the likelihood of unpleasant surprises, which can lead to counterproductive actions and unnecessary expense on the part of the fund sponsor.

Bailey (1992b) presents a heuristic set of benchmark quality criteria designed to distinguish good benchmarks from poor benchmarks. These criteria are based on the fundamental properties of valid benchmarks discussed previously and on a logical extension of the purposes for which benchmarks are used. Although none of the criteria alone provides a definitive indicator of benchmark quality, taken together they provide a means for evaluating alternative benchmarks.

- **Systematic biases.** Over time, there should be minimal systematic biases or risks in the benchmark relative to the account. One way to measure this criterion is to calculate the

[12]Bailey (1992a) critiques in detail the use of manager universes as benchmarks. Beyond the failure to possess the properties of a valid benchmark and the issue of survivor bias, Bailey also discusses the failure of manager universes to pass tests of benchmark quality. The tests of benchmark quality are summarized in Section 5.6.

historical beta of the account relative to the benchmark; on average, it should be close to 1.0.[13]

Potential systematic bias can also be identified through a set of correlation statistics. Consider the correlation between $A = (P - B)$ and $S = (B - M)$. The contention is that a manager's ability to identify attractive and unattractive investment opportunities should be uncorrelated with whether the manager's style is in or out of favor relative to the overall market. Accordingly, a good benchmark will display a correlation between A and S that is not statistically different from zero.

Similarly, let us define the difference between the account and the market index as $E = (P - M)$. When a manager's style (S) is in favor (out of favor) relative to the market, we expect both the benchmark and the account to outperform (underperform) the market. Therefore, a good benchmark will have a statistically significant positive correlation coefficient between S and E.

- **Tracking error.** We define tracking error as the volatility of A or $(P - B)$. A good benchmark should reduce the "noise" in the performance evaluation process. Thus, the volatility (standard deviation) of an account's returns relative to a good benchmark should be less than the volatility of the account's returns versus a market index or other alternative benchmarks. Such a result indicates that the benchmark is capturing important aspects of the manager's investment style.
- **Risk characteristics.** An account's exposure to systematic sources of risk should be similar to those of the benchmark over time.[14] The objective of a good benchmark is to reflect but not to replicate the manager's investment process. Because an active manager is constantly making bets against the benchmark, a good benchmark will exhibit risk exposures at times greater than those of the managed portfolio and at times smaller. Nevertheless, if the account's risk characteristics are always greater or always smaller than those of the benchmark, a systematic bias exists.
- **Coverage.** Benchmark coverage is defined as the proportion of a portfolio's market value that is contained in the benchmark. For example, at a point in time, all of the securities and their respective weights that are contained in the account and the benchmark can be examined. The market value of the jointly held securities as a percentage of the total market value of the portfolio is termed the coverage ratio. High coverage indicates a strong correspondence between the manager's universe of potential securities and the benchmark. Low coverage indicates that the benchmark has little relationship, on a security level, with the opportunity set generated by the manager's investment process.
- **Turnover.** Benchmark turnover is the proportion of the benchmark's market value allocated to purchases during a periodic rebalancing of the benchmark. Because the benchmark should be an investable alternative to holding the manager's actual portfolio, the

[13]The historical beta of the account relative to the benchmark is derived from a regression of the account's past returns on the past returns of the benchmark. The resulting slope of the regression line, termed the beta of the regression, indicates the sensitivity of the account's returns to those of the benchmark. Note that a benchmark may fail this test because the manager holds cash in the account, typically for transaction purposes, while the benchmark may reflect a zero cash position. If the account's beta relative to the benchmark would be 1.0 excluding the positive cash position, the overall beta of the account (including the cash position) will be less than 1.0. As a result, the account will have an unfavorable performance bias in an up market and a favorable bias in a down market. The simple solution is to hold cash in the benchmark at a level reflective of the manager's "neutral" cash position.

[14]Risk characteristics refer to factors that systematically affect the returns on many securities. We will return to the issue later in the discussion on performance attribution.

benchmark turnover should not be so excessive as to preclude the successful implementation of a passively managed portfolio.

- **Positive active positions.** An active position is an account's allocation to a security minus the corresponding weight of the same security in the benchmark. For example, assume an account has a 3 percent weighting in General Electric (GE). If the benchmark has a 2 percent weighting in GE, then the active position is 1 percent (3% − 2%). Thus, the manager will receive positive credit if GE performs well. Actively managed accounts whose investment mandates permit only long positions contain primarily securities that a manager considers to be attractive. When a good custom security-based benchmark has been built, the manager should be expected to hold largely positive active positions for actively managed long-only accounts.[15] Note that when an account is benchmarked to a published index containing securities for which a long-only manager has no investment opinion and which the manager does not own, negative active positions will arise. A high proportion of negative active positions is indicative of a benchmark that is poorly representative of the manager's investment approach.

5.7. Hedge Funds and Hedge Fund Benchmarks

Hedge funds have become increasingly popular among institutional and high-net-worth investors in recent years. Although the term *hedge fund* covers a wide range of investment strategies, there are some common threads that link these strategies. In general, **hedge funds** attempt to expose investors to a particular investment opportunity while minimizing (or hedging) other investment risks that could impact the outcome. In most cases, hedging involves both long and short investment positions.

The term *hedge fund* is believed to have originated as a description of an investment strategy developed by Alfred Winslow Jones.[16] The basic strategy involved shorting stocks that managers considered to be overvalued and using the proceeds to invest in stocks that were deemed to be undervalued. In addition, an incentive fee was established, and Jones committed his own capital to assure investors that his interests were aligned with their interests.

In essence, the Jones strategy is the same as the standard long-only strategy in that, relative to the benchmark, a long-only manager will overweight undervalued securities and underweight overvalued securities. The difference is that the long-only manager is limited to a minimum investment of zero in any security. As a result, the maximum "negative bet" that a long-only manager can place on a security that is rated as overvalued is not to hold it (a weight of zero). For example, because approximately 450 companies in the S&P 500 have weights less than 0.5 percent, a long-only manager with an S&P 500 benchmark and a negative opinion on any of these stocks would be limited to, at most, a −0.5 percent active position. By removing the zero weight constraint (that is, allowing shorting), a manager can further exploit overvalued stocks.

There are, however, performance measurement issues as well as numerous administrative and compliance issues that are created when there are short positions in an account. Recall that earlier in the chapter (Equation 12-1), we stated that an account's rate of return is equal

[15]Violations of this quality criterion often occur when a benchmark is market capitalization weighted. Because many managers do not utilize a market-capitalization weighting scheme in building their portfolios, the possibility of negative active positions can arise when a capitalization-weighted benchmark is assigned.

[16]See Koh, Lee, and Fai (2002).

to its market value (MV_1) at the end of a period less its market value at the beginning of the period (MV_0), divided by the beginning market value:

$$r_t = \frac{MV_1 - MV_0}{MV_0}$$

In theory, the net assets of a long-short portfolio could be zero; the value of the portfolio's long positions equal the value of the portfolio's short positions. In this case, the beginning market value, MV_0, would be zero and the account's rate of return would be either positive infinity or negative infinity. In the real world of long-short investing, an account will typically have a positive net asset value due to various margin and administrative requirements. However, as the net asset value gets smaller and approaches zero, the account's return will become nonsensically extreme (large positive or large negative).

To address this problem, we need to revise our performance measurement methodology. One approach would be to think in terms of performance impact, which is discussed in more detail later in the chapter. That is,

$$r_v = r_p - r_B \qquad (12\text{-}9)$$

where

r_v = value-added return
r_p = portfolio return
r_B = benchmark return

Here, the term r_v is the value-added return on a long-short portfolio where the active weights sum to zero, which is the same situation as a zero-net asset hedge fund. Although the active weights sum to zero, a return can be determined by summing the performance impacts of the n individual security positions (both long and short).

$$\sum_{i=1}^{n} w_{vi} = \left(\sum_{i=1}^{n} w_{pi} - \sum_{i=1}^{n} w_{Bi} \right) = 0; \text{ and}$$

$$r_v = \sum_{i=1}^{n} [w_{vi} \times r_i] = \sum_{i=1}^{n} [(w_{pi} - w_{Bi}) \times r_i] = \sum_{i=1}^{n} (w_{pi} \times r_i) - \sum_{i=1}^{n} (w_{Bi} \times r_i) = r_p - r_B$$

where w_{vi}, w_{pi}, and w_{Bi} are respectively the *active* weight of security i in the portfolio, the weight of security i in the portfolio, and the weight of security i in the benchmark. A return could be calculated for the period during which the individual security positions were maintained. Once an individual security position changed, the return period would end and a new return period would start.[17]

The application of benchmarks to long-only portfolios has reached a mature status. Issues regarding the quality of various benchmark designs and the concerns of overly constraining active management strategies by somehow tying performance too closely to benchmarks remain

[17]Another approach to determining a rate of return for a long-short portfolio would be to specify the numerator in Equation 12-1 as the profit and/or loss resulting from the particular hedge fund strategy. The denominator could be specified as the asset base over which the strategy applies. This could be defined as the amount of assets at risk and could be approximated by the absolute value of all the long positions plus the absolute value of all the short positions.

contentious issues. (For example, see Bernstein 2003.) Nevertheless, it is the rare fund sponsor or investment manager who does not make reference to account performance relative to some benchmark. The advent of hedge funds, however, added a new dynamic to the discussion of the use and design of benchmarks. Some practitioners eschew the use of benchmarks entirely for hedge fund managers, contending that the "absolute return" mandate associated with hedge funds implies that relative performance comparisons are meaningless.

The discussion of hedge fund benchmarks is confounded by the vagueness of the definition of hedge funds. A wide variety of active investment strategies fall under the category of hedge funds. The implications of that diversity for benchmark design are considerable. Underlying all long-only benchmark designs are references to the opportunity set available to the manager. Some hedge fund managers have very clearly definable investment universes composed of highly liquid, daily priced securities. For example, many long-short equity managers also manage long-only portfolios. The universe of securities from which they select on the short side often closely resembles the universe of securities from which they select on the long side. Given information regarding the historical returns and holdings of a long-short equity manager's long and short portfolios, we could use either returns-based or security-based benchmark building approaches to construct separate long and short benchmarks for the manager. These benchmarks could be combined in appropriate proportions to create a valid benchmark. Other hedge fund managers, such as macro hedge fund managers, take rapidly changing long-short leveraged positions in an array of asset categories ranging from equities to commodities, which present significant benchmark building challenges.

The ambiguity of hedge fund manager opportunity sets has led to the widespread use of the Sharpe ratio to evaluate hedge fund manager performance. As discussed later in this chapter, the traditional Sharpe ratio is a measure of excess returns (over a risk-free return) relative to the volatility of returns; notably, it can be calculated without reference to the manager's underlying investment universe. Typically, a hedge fund's Sharpe ratio is compared to that of a universe of other hedge funds that have investment mandates assumed to resemble those of the hedge fund under evaluation. Unfortunately, this approach is exposed to the same benchmark validity criticisms leveled against standard manager universe comparisons. Further, the standard deviation as a measure of risk (the denominator of the Sharpe ratio) is questionable when an investment strategy incorporates a high degree of optionality (skewness), as is the case for the strategies of many hedge funds.

6. PERFORMANCE ATTRIBUTION

We now move to the second phase of performance evaluation, performance attribution. Fama (1972) proposed the first approach to analyzing the sources of an account's returns. Practitioners use various forms of performance attribution, but the basic concept remains the same: a comparison of an account's performance with that of a designated benchmark and the identification and quantification of sources of differential returns. Further, a unifying mathematical relationship underlies all performance attribution approaches: Impact equals weight times return. We will return to that relationship shortly.

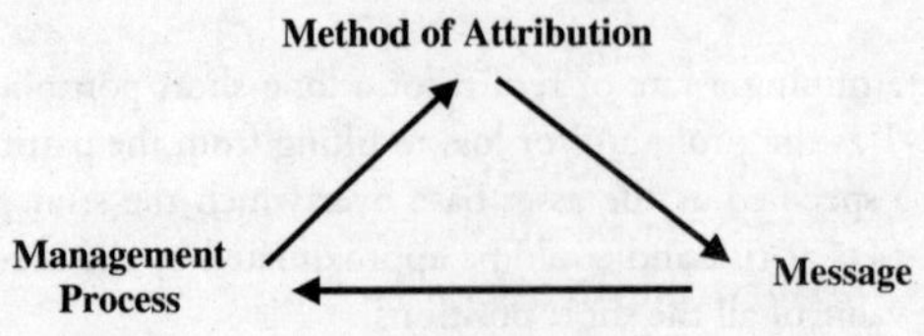

Performance attribution provides an informed look at the past. It identifies the sources of different-from-benchmark returns **(differential returns)** and their impacts on an account's performance. Presuming that one of the objectives of performance attribution is to gain insights helpful for improving the portfolio management process, that process should dictate the method of attribution. The result will be information or a message that will directly relate to the inputs that have gone into the portfolio management process.

When performance attribution is conducted in this manner, the message will either (1) *reinforce* the effectiveness of the management process or (2) cause a *rethinking* of that process.

Effective performance attribution requires an appropriate analytical framework for decomposing an account's returns relative to those of the benchmark. There is no single correct approach. The appropriate framework will depend on the context of the analysis. In particular, the appropriate framework should reflect the decision-making processes of the organizations involved.

We will consider two basic forms of performance attribution from the standpoints of the fund sponsor and the investment manager. Each form seeks to explain the sources of differential returns. We refer to the performance attribution conducted on the fund sponsor level as **macro attribution.** Performance attribution carried out on the investment manager level we call **micro attribution.** The distinction relates to the specific decision variables involved, as opposed to which organization is actually conducting the performance attribution. While it is unlikely that an investment manager would be in a position to carry out macro attribution, one can easily envision situations in which a fund sponsor may wish to conduct both macro and micro attribution.

6.1. Impact Equals Weight Times Return

A manager can have a positive impact on an account's return relative to a benchmark through two basic avenues: (1) selecting superior (or avoiding inferior) performing assets and (2) owning the superior (inferior) performing assets in greater (lesser) proportions than are held in the benchmark. This simple concept underlies all types of performance attribution. The assets themselves may be divided or combined into all sorts of categories, be they economic sectors, financial factors, or investment strategies. In the end, however, the fundamental rule prevails that impact equals (active) weight times return.

The nature of this concept is illustrated through Example 12.11.

EXAMPLE 12-11 An Analogy to the Expression for Revenue

Consider a business that sells widgets. Its total revenue is determined by the formula

$$\text{Revenue} = \text{Price} \times \text{Quantity sold}$$

This year, revenue has risen. The company wants to know why. Based on the above formula, the increase in revenues can be attributed to changes in the unit prices or quantity sold or both (perhaps offsetting to a degree). Exhibit 12-2 displays the situation in which both price and quantity sold have risen. The old revenue was equal to $P_1 \times Q_1$. The new revenue is equal to $P_2 \times Q_2$. The difference in revenues is a bit more complicated, however. It is due in part to an increase in price [$(P_2 - P_1) \times Q_1$; Area 1], in part to an increase in quantity sold [$(Q_2 - Q_1) \times P_1$; Area 2], and in part to the interaction of both variables [$(P_2 - P_1) \times (Q_2 - Q_1)$; Area 3]. Making the connection to performance attribution, the change in quantity is roughly analogous to a difference in weights between securities held in the account and the benchmark, while the change in price represents the difference in returns between securities held in the account and the benchmark.

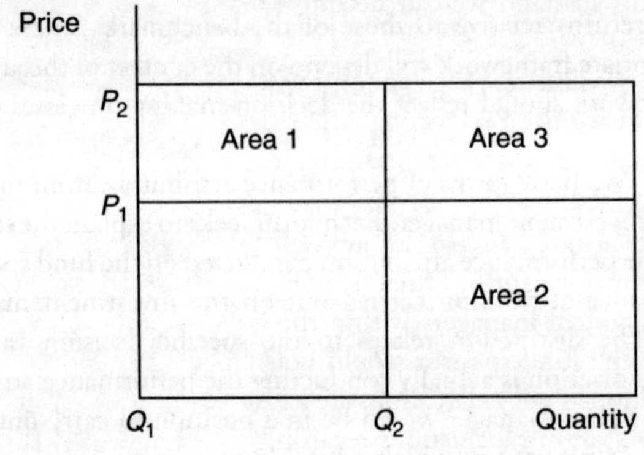

EXHIBIT 12-2 A Price–Quantity Analogy

6.2. Macro Attribution Overview

Let us assume for the moment that for a fund sponsor the term "account" refers to a total fund consisting of investments in various asset categories (for example, domestic stocks, international stocks, domestic fixed income, and so on) and that the investments are managed by various investment managers. For ease of exposition, we will call this particular account the "Fund." The fund sponsor controls a number of variables that have an impact on the performance of the Fund. For example, the fund sponsor determines the broad allocation of assets to stocks, bonds, and other types of securities. Further, because the fund sponsor retains multiple investment managers to invest the assets of the Fund, decisions must be made regarding allocations across the various investment styles offered by the managers and allocations to the individual managers themselves.

Macro attribution can be carried out solely in a rate-of-return metric. That is, the results of the analysis can be presented in terms of the effects of decision-making variables on the differential return. Most forms of macro attribution follow that approach. The analysis can be enriched by considering the impacts of the decision-making variables on the differential returns in monetary terms. Consider that it is one thing to report that a fund sponsor's active managers added, say, 0.30 percent to the Fund's performance last month. It is quite another thing to state that the 30 basis points of positive active management added US$5 million to the value of the Fund. Performance attribution expressed in a value metric (as opposed to a return metric) can make the subject more accessible not only to investment professionals, but particularly to persons not regularly exposed to the subtle issues of performance attribution. We will present examples of both approaches.

6.3. Macro Attribution Inputs

Three sets of inputs constitute the foundation of the macro attribution approach:

1. Policy allocations.
2. Benchmark portfolio returns.
3. Fund returns, valuations, and external cash flows.

With these inputs in hand we can decompose the Fund's performance from a macro perspective.

In the following, we illustrate each concept with data for a hypothetical fund sponsor, the Michigan Endowment for the Performing Arts (MEPA). We use the data for MEPA in the subsequent section to illustrate a macro performance attribution analysis.

6.3.1. Policy Allocations

As part of any effective investment program, fund sponsors should determine normal weightings (that is, policy allocations) to the asset categories within the Fund and to individual managers within the asset categories. By "normal" we mean a neutral position that the fund sponsor would hold in order to satisfy long-term investment objectives and constraints. Policy allocations are a function of the fund sponsor's risk tolerance, the fund sponsor's long-term expectations regarding the investment risks and rewards offered by various asset categories and money managers, and the liabilities that the Fund is eventually expected to satisfy.

Exhibit 12-3 displays the policy allocations of MEPA. It has divided the Fund's assets between two asset categories, with 75 percent assigned to domestic equities and 25 percent assigned to domestic fixed income. Within each asset category, MEPA has retained two active managers. It has allocated 65 percent of the domestic equities to Equity Manager 1 and the remaining 35 percent to Equity Manager 2. Similarly, the fund sponsor has assigned 55 percent of the domestic fixed income to Fixed-Income Manager 1 and 45 percent to Fixed-Income Manager 2.

6.3.2. Benchmark Portfolio Returns

We defined benchmarks earlier. Exhibit 12-4 presents the benchmarks that MEPA has selected for its two asset categories and the managers within those asset categories. The fund sponsor uses broad market indexes as the

EXHIBIT 12-3 Michigan Endowment for the Performing Arts Investment Policy Allocations

Asset Category	Policy Allocations
Domestic Equities	75.0%
Equity Manager 1	65.0
Equity Manager 2	35.0
Domestic Fixed Income	25.0
Fixed-Income Manager 1	55.0
Fixed-Income Manager 2	45.0
Total Fund	100.0%

EXHIBIT 12-4 Michigan Endowment for the Performing Arts Benchmark Assignments

Asset Category	Benchmark
Domestic Equities	S&P 500
Equity Manager 1	Large-Cap Growth Index
Equity Manager 2	Large-Cap Value Index
Domestic Fixed Income	Lehman Govt/Credit Index
Fixed-Income Manager 1	Lehman Int Govt/Credit Index
Fixed-Income Manager 2	Lehman Treasury Index

EXHIBIT 12-5 Michigan Endowment for the Performing Arts Account Valuations, Cash Flows, and Returns: June 20XX

Asset Category	Beginning Value	Ending Value	Net Cash Flows	Actual Return	Benchmark Return
Domestic Equities	$143,295,254	$148,747,228	$(1,050,000)	4.55%	4.04%
Equity Mgr 1	93,045,008	99,512,122	1,950,000	4.76	4.61
Equity Mgr 2	50,250,246	49,235,106	(3,000,000)	4.13	4.31
Domestic Fixed Income	43,124,151	46,069,371	2,000,000	2.16	2.56
Fixed-Income Mgr 1	24,900,250	25,298,754	0	1.60	1.99
Fixed-Income Mgr 2	18,223,900	20,770,617	2,000,000	2.91	2.55
Total Fund	$186,419,405	$194,816,599	$950,000	3.99%	3.94%

benchmarks for asset categories, while it uses more narrowly focused indexes to represent the managers' investment styles.[18]

6.3.3. Returns, Valuations, and External Cash Flows

Macro attribution in a return-only metric requires fund returns. These returns must be computed at the level of the individual manager to allow an analysis of the fund sponsor's decisions regarding manager selection. If macro attribution is extended to include a value-metric approach, then account valuation and external cash flow data are needed not only to calculate accurate rates of return, but also to correctly compute the value impacts of the fund sponsor's investment policy decision making.

For the month of June 20XX, Exhibit 12-5 shows the beginning and ending values, external cash flows, and the actual and benchmark returns for MEPA's total fund, asset categories, and investment managers.

With the inputs for our hypothetical fund sponsor in hand, we turn to an example of a macro performance attribution analysis in the next section.

[18]Rather than using broad market indexes as asset category benchmarks, some fund sponsors and consultants construct asset category benchmarks by weighting the managers' benchmarks in accordance with their policy allocations. Under this approach, using the data given in Exhibits 12-3 and 12-4, the blended asset category benchmark for domestic equities would consist of a 65% weighting in Large-Cap Growth Index and a 35 percent weighting in Large-Cap Value Index. However, this approach impairs the sponsor's ability to evaluate the impact of "misfit returns" or "style bias" as described later in this chapter.

6.4. Conducting a Macro Attribution Analysis

One can envision a number of different variables of interest when evaluating the fund sponsor's decision-making process. Below, we present six levels or components of investment policy decision making into which the Fund's performance might be analyzed. We do not imply that these are the only correct variables—they are simply logical extensions of a typical fund sponsor's decision-making process.

Specifically, those levels (which we later refer to as *investment strategies* for reasons to become apparent shortly) are:

1. Net contributions
2. Risk-free asset
3. Asset categories
4. Benchmarks
5. Investment managers
6. Allocation effects

Macro attribution analysis starts with the Fund's beginning-of-period and end-of-period values. Simply put, the question under consideration is: How much did each of the decision-making levels contribute, in either a return or a value metric, to the Fund's change in value over an evaluation period? Macro attribution takes an incremental approach to answering this question. Each decision-making level in the hierarchy is treated as an investment strategy, and its investment results are compared to the cumulative results of the previous levels. That is, each decision-making level represents an unambiguous, appropriate, and specified-in-advance investment alternative: in other words, a valid benchmark. The fund sponsor has the option to place all of the Fund's assets in any of the investment strategies. The strategies are ordered in terms of increasing volatility and complexity. Presumably, the fund sponsor will move to a more aggressive strategy only if it expects to earn positive incremental returns. Macro attribution calculates the incremental contribution that the choice to move to the next strategy produces.

In the previous section we gave the inputs necessary to conduct a macro performance attribution analysis for a hypothetical fund sponsor, MEPA, for the month of June 20XX. We apply the macro attribution framework just outlined to MEPA in the following discussion. Exhibit 12-6 summarizes the results.

We now examine each of the six levels in turn.

EXHIBIT 12-6 Michigan Endowment for the Performing Arts Monthly Performance Attribution: June 20XX

Decision-Making Level (Investment Alternative)	Fund Value	Incremental Return Contribution	Incremental Value Contribution
Beginning value	$186,419,405	—	—
Net contributions	187,369,405	0.00%	950,000
Risk-free asset	187,944,879	0.31	575,474
Asset category	194,217,537	3.36	6,272,658
Benchmarks	194,720,526	0.27	502,989
Investment managers	194,746,106	0.01	25,580
Allocation effects	194,816,599	0.04	70,494
Total Fund	194,816,599	3.99	8,397,194

6.4.1. Net Contributions Exhibit 12-6 indicates that the starting point of the analysis is the Fund's beginning market value. In our example, at the beginning of June 20XX, the market value of the Fund was $186,419,405. During a given month, the Fund may experience contributions and/or withdrawals. The Net Contributions investment strategy specifies that the net inflows are invested at a zero rate of return and, therefore, the Fund's value changes simply by the total amount of these flows. During June 20XX, net contributions to the Fund were a positive $950,000. Adding this amount to the Fund's beginning value produces a value of $187,369,405 for the Fund under the Net Contributions investment strategy. Although no fund sponsor would deliberately follow this investment strategy, it provides a useful baseline to begin the analysis.

6.4.2. Risk-Free Asset One highly conservative (but certainly reasonable) investment strategy open to a fund sponsor is to invest all of the Fund's assets in a risk-free asset, such as 90-day Treasury bills.[19] Assuming that the Fund's beginning value and its net external cash inflows (accounting for the dates on which those flows occur) are invested at the risk-free rate, the Fund's value will increase by an additional amount over the value achieved under the Net Contributions investment strategy with its zero rate of return. The Risk-Free Asset investment strategy, using a risk-free rate during June 20XX of 0.31 percent, produces an incremental increase in value of $575,474 ($= \$187,944,879 - 187,369,405$) over the results of the Net Contributions investment strategy, for a total fund value of $187,944,879.[20]

6.4.3. Asset Category Most fund sponsors view the Risk-Free Asset investment strategy as too risk-averse and therefore overly expensive. Instead, they choose to invest in risky assets, based on the widely held belief that, over the long run, the market rewards investors who bear systematic risk. The Asset Category investment strategy assumes that the Fund's beginning value and external cash flows are invested passively in a combination of the designated asset category benchmarks, with the specific allocation to each benchmark based on the fund sponsor's policy allocations to those asset categories.

In essence, this approach is a pure index fund approach. The Fund's value under this investment strategy will exceed or fall below the value achieved under the Risk-Free Asset investment strategy depending on whether the capital markets fulfill the expectation that risk-taking investors are rewarded. From a return-metric perspective, the incremental return contribution is

$$r_{AC} = \sum_{i=1}^{A} w_i \times (r_{Ci} - r_f) \tag{12-10}$$

where r_{AC} is the incremental return contribution of the Asset Category investment strategy, r_{Ci} is the return on the ith asset category, r_f is the risk-free return, w_i is the policy weight assigned to asset category i, and A is the number of asset categories. From a value-metric perspective, the incremental contribution of the Asset Category investment strategy is found by investing each asset category's policy proportion of the Fund's beginning value and all net external cash

[19] Alternatively, a pension fund might identify the risk-free asset as a portfolio of bonds that best hedges its liabilities.

[20] The increment of $575,474 cannot be replicated by multiplying $187,369,405 by 0.31 percent because the $950,000 net contribution (to obtain $187,369,405) was not a single, beginning-of-the-month cash flow.

inflows at the differential rate between the asset category's benchmark rate of return and the risk-free rate, and then summing across all asset categories.

In the Fund's case, investing 75 percent of the Fund's beginning value and net external cash inflows in the S&P 500 and 25 percent in the Lehman Brothers Government/Credit Bond Index (for a combined return of 3.67 percent in the month, or 3.36 percent above the risk-free rate) increases the Fund's market value by \$6,272,658 (= \$194, 217, 537 − \$187, 944, 879) over the value produced by the Risk-Free Asset investment strategy. As a result, the Fund's value totals \$194,217,537 under the Asset Category investment strategy.

It would be entirely appropriate for a fund sponsor to stop at the Asset Category investment strategy. In fact, an efficient markets proponent might view this all-passive approach as the most appropriate course of action. Nevertheless, fund sponsors typically choose to allocate their funds within an asset category among a number of active managers, most of whom pursue distinctly different investment styles. Importantly for macro attribution, when fund sponsors hire active managers, they are actually exposing their assets to two additional sources of investment returns (and risks): investment style and active management skill.

An investment manager's performance versus the broad markets is dominated by the manager's investment style. With respect to U.S. common stocks, for example, active managers cannot realistically hope to consistently add more than 2–3 percentage points (if that much) annually to their investment styles, as represented by appropriate benchmarks. Conversely, the difference in performance between investment styles can easily range from 15 to 30 percentage points per year.

6.4.4. Benchmarks The macro attribution analysis can be designed to separate the impact of the managers' investment styles (as represented by the managers' benchmarks) on the Fund's value from the effect of the managers' active management decisions. In this case, the next level of analysis assumes that the Fund's beginning value and net external cash inflows are passively invested in the aggregate of the managers' respective benchmarks. An aggregate manager benchmark return is calculated as a weighted average of the individual managers' benchmark returns. The weights used to compute the aggregate manager benchmark return are based on the fund sponsor's policy allocations to the managers. From a return-metric perspective,

$$r_{IS} = \sum_{i=1}^{A}\sum_{j=1}^{M} w_i \times w_{ij} \times (r_{Bij} - r_{Ci}) \tag{12-11}$$

where r_{IS} is the incremental return contribution of the Benchmarks strategy, r_{Bij} is the return for the jth manager's benchmark in asset category i, r_{Ci} is the return on the ith asset category, w_i is the policy weight assigned to the ith asset category, w_{ij} is the policy weight assigned to the jth manager in asset category i, and A and M are the number of asset categories and managers, respectively.[21] (Note that summed across all managers and asset categories, $w_i \times w_{ij} \times r_{Bij}$ is the aggregate manager benchmark return.) From a value-metric perspective, the incremental contribution of the Benchmarks strategy is calculated by multiplying each manager's policy proportion of the total fund's beginning value and net external cash inflows by the difference between the manager's benchmark return and the return of the manager's asset category, and then summing across all managers.

[21]Note: $\sum_{j=1}^{M} w_{ij} = 1$ for all i and $\sum_{i=1}^{A} w_i = 1$

In the case of the Fund, the aggregate manager benchmark return was 3.94 percent in June 20XX. Investing the Fund's beginning value and net external cash inflows at this aggregate manager benchmark return produces an incremental gain of $502,989 (= $194,720,526 – $194,217,537) over the Fund's value achieved under the Asset Category investment strategy. As a result, under the Investment Style investment strategy, the Fund's value grows to $194,720,526.

Paralleling the Asset Category investment strategy, the Benchmarks strategy is essentially a passively managed investment in the benchmarks of the Fund's managers. The difference in performance between the aggregate of the managers' benchmarks and the aggregate of the asset category benchmarks is termed *misfit return* or, less formally, *style bias.* In June 20XX, the Fund's misfit return was (3.94% – 3.67%), or a positive 0.27%. Although the expected value of misfit return is zero, it can be highly variable over time. That variability can be particularly large for a fund sponsor who has retained investment manager teams within the fund's various asset categories that display sizeable style biases relative to their respective asset category benchmarks. Some fund sponsors employ special risk-control strategies to keep this misfit risk within acceptable tolerances.

6.4.5. Investment Managers

In the next level of analysis, to discern the impact of the managers' active management decisions on the change in the Fund's value, macro attribution analysis calculates the value of the Fund as if its beginning value and net external cash flows were invested in the aggregate of the managers' actual portfolios. Again, the weights assigned to the managers' returns to derive the aggregate manager return will come from the policy allocations set by the fund sponsor. A relationship similar to Equation 12-11 describes the return-metric contribution of the Investment Managers strategy:

$$r_{IM} = \sum_{i=1}^{A} \sum_{j=1}^{M} w_i \times w_{ij} \times (r_{Aij} - r_{Bij}) \qquad (12\text{-}12)$$

where r_{Aij} represents the actual return on the jth manager's portfolio within asset category i and the other variables are as defined previously.

The difference in the Fund's value under the Investment Managers strategy relative to the Benchmarks strategy will depend on whether the managers, in aggregate, exceeded the return on the aggregate benchmark. In the case of the Fund, the aggregate actual return of the managers (calculated using policy weights) was 3.95 percent, as opposed to 3.94 percent return on the aggregate manager investment style benchmark. This modestly positive excess return translates into an incremental increase in the fund's value of $25,580 (= $194,746,106 – $194,720,526) over the value produced under the Benchmarks strategy, for a total value of $194,746,106 under the Investment Managers investment strategy.

It should be emphasized that macro attribution calculates the value added by the Fund's managers based on the assumption that the fund sponsor has invested in each of the managers according to the managers' policy allocations. Of course, the actual allocation to the managers will likely differ from the policy allocations. However, if we wish to correctly isolate the contributions of the various levels of fund sponsor decision making, we must distinguish between those aspects of the Fund's investment results over which the fund sponsor does and does not have control. That is, the fund sponsor sets the allocation of assets to the Fund's managers but has no influence over their investment performance. Conversely, the managers have control over their investment performance, but they do not generally determine the amount of assets placed under their management.

In examining the value added by the Fund's managers, we should assume they were funded at their respective policy allocations and ask the question, "What would the managers have contributed to the Fund's performance if the fund sponsor consistently maintained the stated policy allocations?" However, in examining the contribution of the fund sponsor, it makes sense to calculate the impact of the differences between the managers' actual and policy allocations on the Fund's performance and thus ask the question, "How did the fund sponsor's decisions to deviate from investment manager policy allocations affect the Fund's performance relative to a strategy of consistently maintaining the stated policy allocations?" The analysis performed at the Investment Managers level attempts to answer the former question. The analysis done at the Allocation Effects level begins to answer the latter question.

6.4.6. Allocation Effects

The final macro attribution component is Allocation Effects. In a sense, the Allocation Effects incremental contribution is a reconciling factor—by definition, it is the difference between the Fund's ending value and the value calculated at the Investment Managers level. If the fund sponsor had invested in all of the managers and asset categories precisely at the established policy allocations, then the Allocation Effects investment strategy's contribution would be zero. However, most fund sponsors deviate at least slightly from their policy allocations, thereby producing an allocation effect. The Fund's actual ending value was \$194,816,599, which represents a \$70,494 increase $(= \$194,816,599 - \$194,746,106)$ over the value achieved through the Investment Managers investment strategy. By implication, then, MEPA's actual weightings of the asset categories and managers versus the policy weightings contributed positively to the Fund's value in the month of June 20XX.

6.5. Micro Attribution Overview

As implied by its name, micro attribution focuses on a much narrower subject than does macro attribution. Instead of examining the performance of a total fund, micro attribution concerns itself with the investment results of individual portfolios relative to designated benchmarks. Thus, let us define the term *account* to mean a specific portfolio invested by a specific investment manager which we will refer to as the "Portfolio." The Portfolio can be formed of various types of securities. Our illustrations will initially be based on a portfolio of U.S. common stocks. We shall address fixed-income attribution in Section 6.8, below.

Over a given evaluation period, the Portfolio will produce a return that is different from the return on the benchmark. This difference is typically referred to as the manager's value-added or active return. As shown earlier in Equation 12-9, a manager's value-added can be expressed as:

$$r_v = r_p - r_B$$

Because the return on any portfolio is the weighted sum of the returns on the securities composing the portfolio, Equation 12-9 can be rewritten as

$$r_v = \sum_{i=1}^{n} w_{pi} r_i - \sum_{i=1}^{n} w_{Bi} r_i \qquad (12\text{-}13)$$

where w_{pi} and w_{Bi} are the proportions of the Portfolio and benchmark, respectively, invested in security i, r_i is the return on security i, and n is the number of securities.[22]

Rearranging the last equation demonstrates that the manager's value-added is equal to the difference in weights of the Portfolio and benchmark invested in a security times the return on that security, summed across all n securities in the Portfolio and benchmark:

$$r_v = \sum_{i=1}^{n} [(w_{pi} - w_{Bi}) \times r_i]$$

With further manipulation,[23] it can be shown that

$$r_v = \sum_{i=1}^{n} [(w_{pi} - w_{Bi}) \times (r_i - r_B)] \tag{12-14}$$

where r_B is the return on the Portfolio's benchmark.

Equation 12-14 offers the simplest form of micro performance attribution: a security-by-security attribution analysis. In this analysis, the manager's value added can be seen to come from two sources: the weights assigned to securities in the Portfolio relative to their weights in the benchmark and the returns on the securities relative to the overall return on the benchmark.

There are four cases of relative-to-benchmark weights and returns for security i to consider. Exhibit 12-7 gives those cases and their associated performance impacts versus the benchmark.

A manager can add value by overweighting (underweighting) securities that perform well (poorly) relative to the benchmark. Conversely, the manager can detract value by overweighting (underweighting) securities that perform poorly (well) relative to the benchmark.

Security-by-security micro attribution generally is unwieldy and typically provides little in the way of useful insights. The large number of securities in a well-diversified portfolio makes the impact of any individual security on portfolio returns largely uninteresting. A more productive form of micro attribution involves allocating the value-added return to various sources of systematic returns.

EXHIBIT 12-7 Relative-to-Benchmark Weights and Returns

	$w_{pi} - w_{Bi}$	$r_i - r_B$	Performance Impact versus Benchmark
1.	Positive	Positive	Positive
2.	Negative	Positive	Negative
3.	Positive	Negative	Negative
4.	Negative	Negative	Positive

[22]For simplicity we assume that the Portfolio's securities are chosen from among the securities in the benchmark. Otherwise n needs to represent the number of securities in the union of the benchmark and the Portfolio.

[23]Note that the sum of the security weights in any portfolio must equal 1.0, or, equivalently, $\sum_{i=1}^{n}(w_{pi} - w_{Bi}) = 0$. Because zero multiplied by a constant equals zero, $\sum_{i=1}^{n}(w_{pi} - w_{Bi}) \times r_B = 0$, where r_B is the known return on the benchmark (the constant). Subtracting this expression from the right-hand side of the equation just given yields $r_v = \sum_{i=1}^{n}[(w_{pi} - w_{Bi}) \times (r_i - r_B)]$.

Underlying most micro attributions is a factor model of returns. A factor model assumes that the return on a security (or portfolio of securities) is sensitive to the changes in various factors. These factors represent common elements with which security returns are correlated. Factors can be defined in a number of ways: They might be sector or industry membership variables; they might be financial variables, such as balance sheet or income statement items; or they might be macroeconomic variables, such as changes in interest rates, inflation, or economic growth.

The market model, introduced previously, relates a security's or portfolio's return to movements of a broad market index, with the exposure to that index represented by the beta of the security. Recall that Equation 12-8 provides one expression of the market model:

$$R_p = a_p + \beta_p R_I + \varepsilon_p$$

Example 12-12 illustrates the calculation of value-added (active return) relative to a one-factor model.

EXAMPLE 12-12 Active Return Relative to a One-Factor Model

Assume that the Portfolio has a zero-factor value of 1.0 percent and a beta of 1.2 at the beginning of the evaluation period. During the period, the excess return on the market index was 7%. The market model, expressed in Equation 12-8, states that the Portfolio should return 9.4 percent (= 1.0% + 1.2 × 7%). Further, assume that the Portfolio was assigned a custom benchmark with its own market model parameters, a zero-factor value of 2.0 percent and a beta of 0.8, and which thus has an expected return of 7.6 percent (= 2.0% + 0.8 × 7%). If the Portfolio's actual return was 10.9 percent, then the differential return of 3.3 percent could be attributed in part to the Portfolio's differential expected returns. That is, the Portfolio held a zero factor of 1.0 versus the 2.0 of the benchmark, while the Portfolio had a beta of 1.2 versus the benchmark's beta of 0.8. The incremental expected return of the Portfolio versus the benchmark was 1.8 percent [= (1.0% − 2.0%) + (1.2 − 0.8) × 7%]. The remaining 1.5 percent of differential return would be attributed to the investment skill of the manager.

6.6. Sector Weighting/Stock Selection Micro Attribution

Many investment managers employ analysts to research securities and portfolio managers to then build portfolios based on that research. With this investment process, managers are interested in an attribution analysis that will disaggregate the performance effects of the analysts' recommendations and the portfolio managers' decisions to over- and underweight economic sectors and industries.

We can define the returns on the Portfolio and its benchmark to be the weighted sums of their respective economic sector returns. Therefore, just as Equation 12-13 expressed the manager's value-added return as the difference between the weighted average return on the securities in the Portfolio and the benchmark, the manager's value-added return can similarly be expressed as the difference between the weighted average return on the economic sectors in the Portfolio and the benchmark:

$$r_v = \sum_{j=1}^{S} w_{pj} r_{pj} - \sum_{j=1}^{S} w_{Bj} r_{Bj} \tag{12-15}$$

w_{pj} = Portfolio weight of sector j
w_{Bj} = benchmark weight of sector j
r_{pj} = Portfolio return of sector j
r_{Bj} = benchmark return of sector j
S = number of sectors

Continuing with the example of one of MEPA's investment managers, Exhibit 12-8 shows the results of a micro attribution analysis based on partitioning a manager's value-added into a part due to skill in sector selection and a part due to skill in security selection. In this example, the return on the Portfolio for a selected one-month period was 1.12 percent. During that same month the benchmark return was 0.69 percent, generating a value-added return of 0.43 percent.

Note that this is a holdings-based or "buy-and-hold" attribution. Each sector's contribution to the total allocation and selection effects depends upon the beginning portfolio and benchmark weights in that sector and the constituent securities' returns due to price appreciation and dividend income. The buy-and-hold approach, which disregards the impact of transactions during the evaluation period, has an important practical advantage: Only the holdings and their returns need be input to the attribution system. There is, however, a disadvantage: The account's buy-and-hold return will not equal its time-weighted total return. For that reason, the attribution analysis shown above includes a reconciling item captioned "Trading and Other." In the example shown in Exhibit 12-8, "Trading and Other" is the negative 14 basis point (−0.14 percent) difference between the account's Buy/Hold return of 1.26 percent and the actual portfolio return of 1.12 percent. The imputed "trading and other" factor reflects the net impact of cash flows and security purchases and sales during the evaluation period. In actively managed accounts with high turnover, the "trading and other" factor can be significant. Where this is a concern, transaction-based attribution analysis can be employed.[24]

The value-added return can be segmented into the impact of assigning the assets of the portfolio to various economic sectors and the impact of selecting securities within those economic sectors. Equation 12-15 can be rearranged to form the following relationship:[25]

$$r_v = \underbrace{\sum_{j=1}^{S} (w_{pj} - w_{Bj})(r_{Bj} - r_B)}_{\textit{Pure Sector Allocation}} + \underbrace{\sum_{j=1}^{S} (w_{pj} - w_{Bj})(r_{pj} - r_{Bj})}_{\textit{Allocation/Selection Interaction}} + \underbrace{\sum_{j=1}^{S} w_{Bj}(r_{pj} - r_{Bj})}_{\textit{Within-Sector Selection}} \tag{12-16}$$

where S is the number of sectors and r_B is the return on the Portfolio's benchmark.

[24]See Spaulding (2003). Transaction-based attribution analysis is outside the scope of the present discussion.

[25]Equation 12-16 covers performance attribution in the single-period case. Multiperiod performance attribution, while an extension of the single-period approach, involves considerably more complexity. For a discussion of some of the issues involved in multiperiod performance attribution, see Menchero (2004) and Frongello and Bay (2002).

EXHIBIT 12-8 Results of a Micro Attribution Analysis

Economic Sectors	Portfolio Weight (%)	Sector Benchmark Weight (%)	Portfolio Return (%)	Sector Benchmark Return (%)	Performance Attribution: Pure Sector Allocation	Allocation/ Selection Interaction	Within-Sector Selection	Total Value-Added
Basic materials	5.97	5.54	−0.79	−0.67	−0.01	0.00	−0.01	−0.01
Capital goods	7.82	7.99	−3.60	−3.95	0.01	0.00	0.03	0.04
Consumer durables	2.90	2.38	0.46	−0.21	0.00	0.00	0.02	0.01
Consumer nondurables	31.78	34.75	1.92	1.97	−0.04	0.00	−0.02	−0.05
Energy	7.15	6.01	0.37	0.14	−0.01	0.00	0.01	0.01
Financial	22.47	20.91	2.92	2.05	0.02	0.01	0.18	0.22
Technology	12.14	16.02	2.00	−0.30	0.04	−0.09	0.37	0.32
Utilities	8.64	6.40	0.46	−0.37	−0.02	0.02	0.05	0.05
Cash and equivalent	1.13	0.00	0.14		−0.01	0.00	0.00	−0.01
Buy/Hold + Cash	100.00	100.00	1.26	0.69	−0.02	−0.05	0.64	0.57
Trading and Other			−0.14					−0.14
Total Portfolio			1.12	0.69				0.43

In Equation 12-16 the **Pure Sector Allocation return** equals the difference between the allocation (weight) of the Portfolio to a given sector and the Portfolio's benchmark weight for that sector, times the difference between the sector benchmark's return and the overall Portfolio's benchmark return, summed across all sectors. The pure sector allocation return assumes that within each sector the manager held the same securities as the benchmark and in the same proportions. Thus, the impact on relative performance is attributed only to the sector-weighting decisions of the manager.

EXAMPLE 12-13 The Pure Sector Allocation Return for Consumer Nondurables

Exhibit 12-8 indicates that at the beginning of the month the Portfolio had a 31.78 percent weight in consumer nondurables, while the benchmark had a 34.75 percent weight. Because the return of the benchmark consumer nondurables sector was 1.97 percent and the return of the overall benchmark was 0.69 percent, the performance impact due to the consumer nondurables sector allocation is −0.04 percent [= (31.78% − 34.75%) × (1.97% − 0.69%)]. That is, the decision to underweight a sector that performed better than the overall benchmark resulted in a negative contribution to the performance of the Portfolio relative to the overall benchmark. The Pure Sector Allocation return is typically the responsibility of the portfolio managers who determine the Portfolio's relative allocations to economic sectors and industries.

The **Within-Sector Selection return** equals the difference between the return on the Portfolio's holdings in a given sector and the return on the corresponding sector benchmark, times the weight of the benchmark in that sector, summed across all sectors. The Within-Sector Selection return implicitly assumes that the manager weights each sector in the Portfolio in the same proportion as in the overall benchmark, although *within the sector* the manager may hold securities in different-from-benchmark weights. Thus, the impact on relative performance is now attributed only to the security selection decisions of the manager.

EXAMPLE 12-14 The Within-Sector Allocation Return for Technology

Exhibit 12-8 shows that the return of the portfolio's technology sector was 2.00 percent, while the return of the benchmark's technology sector was −0.30 percent. Consequently, the performance impact of security selection within the technology sector was +0.37 percent {= 16.02% × [2.00% − (−0.30%)]}, where 16.02 percent is the weight of the benchmark's holdings in the technology sector. During the month, the Portfolio held technology stocks that in total performed better than the aggregate performance of the technology stocks contained in the sector benchmark, thereby contributing positively to the Portfolio's performance relative to the overall benchmark. The Within-Sector Selection impact is often the responsibility of the security analysts. Among the securities that they research, they are expected to identify significantly misvalued securities and recommend appropriate action.

The **Allocation/Selection Interaction return** is a more difficult concept, because it involves the joint effect of the portfolio managers' and security analysts' decisions to assign weights to both sectors and individual securities. The Allocation/Selection Interaction equals the difference between the weight of the Portfolio in a given sector and the Portfolio's benchmark for that sector, times the difference between the Portfolio's and the benchmark's returns in that sector, summed across all sectors.

EXAMPLE 12-15 The Allocation/Selection Interaction Return for Technology

Again referring to Exhibit 12-8, we can see that the Portfolio's relative underweight in the Technology sector of −3.88 percent (= 12.14% − 16.02%) and the Portfolio's positive relative performance in the Technology sector of 2.30 percent [= 2.00% − (−0.30%)] produced an Allocation/Selection Interaction effect of −0.09 percent during the month.

A decision to increase the allocation to a particular security adds not only to the weight in that security but also to the weight of the sector to which the security belongs, unless there is an offsetting adjustment to securities within that sector. Unless the portfolio manager is careful to make offsetting adjustments, security selection decisions can inadvertently drive sector-weighting decisions. In general, the Allocation/Selection Interaction impact will be relatively small if the benchmark is appropriate—that is, one that is devoid of any material systematic biases. Because the Allocation/Selection Interaction impact is often the source of some confusion and is usually the result of security selection decisions, some practitioners consolidate the Allocation/Selection Interaction impact with the Within-Sector Selection impact.

6.7. Fundamental Factor Model Micro Attribution

As we have noted, some type of factor model underlies virtually all forms of performance attribution. Economic sectors and industries represent only one potential source of common factor returns. Numerous practitioners and academics (for example, see Sharpe 1982 and Fama and French 1992) have investigated other common factor return sources. For example, with respect to common stocks, a company's size, its industry, its growth characteristics, its financial strength, and other factors seem to have an impact on account performance. Often these factors are referred to as fundamental factors. They may be combined with economic sector factors to produce multifactor models that can be used to conduct micro attribution.

As with any form of performance attribution, the exposures of the Portfolio and the benchmark to the factors of the fundamental factor model must be determined at the beginning of the evaluation period. The benchmark could be the risk exposures of a style or custom index, or it could be a set of normal factor exposures that were typical of the manager's portfolio over time. Finally, the performance of each of the factors must be determined.

EXAMPLE 12-16 Fundamental Factor Model Micro Attribution

Exhibit 12-9 provides an example of a fundamental factor model micro attribution analysis where a U.S. growth stock manager invests the Portfolio. The performance attribution example covers a one-month period, and during that time the Portfolio generated a 6.02 percent rate of return, while the normal portfolio and the market index produced returns of 5.85 percent and 6.09 percent, respectively. During this particular month, growth stocks performed less well than the market index, largely explaining why the normal portfolio (representing the manager's investment style) underperformed the return on the market index by −0.24 percent. The performance difference between the Portfolio (6.02 percent) and the normal portfolio (5.85 percent) is a measure of the portfolio manager's investment skill (0.17 percent) or value added.

EXHIBIT 12-9 Micro Attribution Using a Fundamental Factor Model

	Portfolio Exposure	Normal Exposure	Active Exposure	Active Impact	Return
Market Return					6.09%
Normal Portfolio Return					5.85
Cash Timing	2.36	0.00	2.36	−0.13	
Beta Timing	1.02	1.00	0.02	0.04	
Total Market Timing					−0.09
Growth	1.12	0.85	0.27	−0.15	
Size	−0.26	0.35	−0.61	−0.35	
Leverage	−0.33	−0.60	0.27	0.11	
Yield	−0.03	−0.12	−0.09	−0.22	
Total Fundamental Risk Factors					−0.61
Basic Industry	14.10	15.00	−0.90	0.04	
Consumer	35.61	30.00	5.61	−0.07	
Energy	8.36	5.00	3.36	0.05	
Financials	22.16	20.00	2.16	−0.02	
Technology	17.42	25.00	−7.58	0.16	
Utilities	2.35	5.00	−2.65	−0.01	
Total Economic Sectors					0.15
Specific (unexplained)					0.72
Actual Portfolio Return					6.02%

The micro attribution analysis shown in Exhibit 12-9 attributes the manager's investment skill or value-added to four primary sources: (1) market timing,

(2) exposures to fundamental factors, (3) exposures to economic sectors, and (4) a specific or unexplained return component. The market-timing component is made up of two performance impacts; one is due to the Portfolio's cash position, and the other relates to the Portfolio's beta. In the example, the combination of these two effects had a negative impact of −0.09 percent. The second primary performance attribute involves the exposures to the fundamental factors. The Portfolio's fundamental factor exposures are contrasted with "normal" fundamental factor exposures, represented by the manager's benchmark.[26] The Portfolio's actual factor exposures versus its "normal" exposures resulted in a negative return impact of −0.61 percent. Similarly, the Portfolio's economic sector allocations are contrasted with the Portfolio's "normal" allocations to produce performance attribution impacts. In this case, the active sector weights had a positive impact of 0.15 percent. Finally, the fundamental factor model was unable to explain a portion of the Portfolio's return; in this case, the Portfolio had a specific or unexplained return of +0.72 percent.[27] This specific return that cannot be explained by the factor model is attributed to the investment manager.

6.8. Fixed-Income Attribution

The sector weighting/stock selection approach to micro attribution is applicable to fixed-income as well as equity accounts. We mentioned in our remarks on fixed-income style indexes in Section 5.3 that broad fixed-income market indexes may be segregated into their constituent market segments. Accordingly, the sector weighting/stock selection equity attribution analysis can also be adapted for use with fixed-income accounts by substituting market segments such as government bonds, agency and investment-grade corporate credit bonds, high-yield bonds, and mortgage-backed securities, among others, for the economic sectors such as energy, financial, or utilities.

Nonetheless, bonds are unlike stocks, and an approach that merely isolates allocation and selection effects among bond market sectors will be of limited value in analyzing the sources of fixed-income account returns. Useful attribution analysis captures the return impact of the manager's investment decisions, and fixed-income managers weigh variables that differ in important ways from the factors considered by equity portfolio managers. In the interests of mathematical brevity, we will limit our discussion of fixed-income micro performance attribution to a conceptual overview.[28]

---

[25]Exposure to a fundamental factor in this case is measured in terms of standard deviations from the mean, where the mean is determined by the average value of the particular factor for a group of capitalization-weighted stocks.

[25]Although this type of performance attribution analysis provides valuable insights to investment practitioners, there is a serious limitation. It involves the ambiguity of the benchmark. If the benchmark is based solely on a set of exposures to investment risk factors, then the benchmark is ambiguous. That is, we can construct multiple portfolios that have the same risk characteristics, but they will not have the same investment return. For example, many portfolios might have the same beta, but they will have different investment returns. The solution to this limitation is to base the attribution analysis on the risk exposures of an appropriate benchmark portfolio, i.e., a portfolio with specified securities and weights. In this case, the benchmark portfolio will have a specific or unexplained return component. The difference between it and the portfolio's specific return is attributed to the investment manager.

[28]A more rigorous treatment of this discussion of fixed-income micro attribution can be found in Fong, Pearson, and Vasicek (1983).

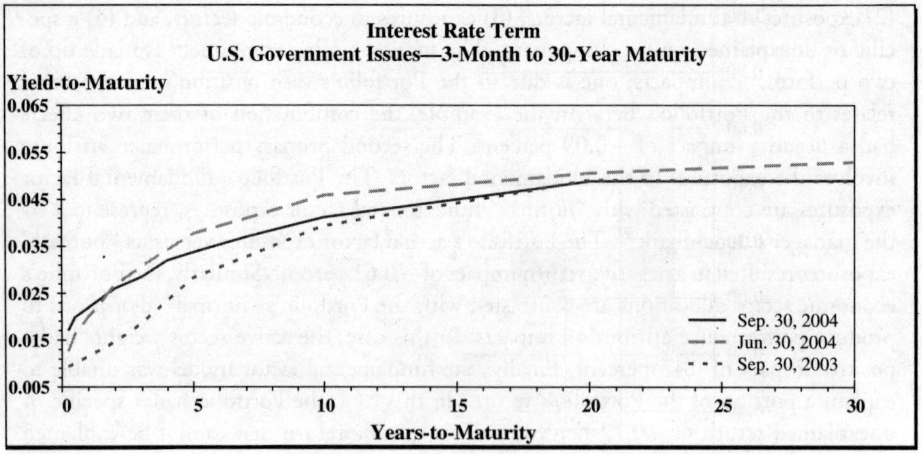

EXHIBIT 12-10 Interest Rate Term Structure U.S. Government Issue—3-Month to 30-Year Maturity

Major determinants of fixed-income results are changes in the general level of interest rates, represented by the government (default-free) yield curve, and changes in sector, credit quality, and individual security differentials, or nominal spreads, to the yield curve. As a general rule, fixed-income security prices move in the opposite direction of interest rates: If interest rates fall, bond prices rise, and vice versa. In consequence, fixed-income portfolios tend to have higher rates of return in periods of falling interest rates and, conversely, lower rates of return in periods of rising interest rates. Consider the example displayed in Exhibit 12-10, where the U.S. Treasury spot rate yield curve shifted upward across all maturities during the nine-month period ending June 30, 2004, and where the return for the Lehman Brothers U.S. Government Index for the nine-month period was −0.56 percent. Comparing the yield curves for September 30, 2004, and June 30, 2004, we see that in the third quarter of 2004 the change in the U.S. Treasury yield curve was more complex: Short-term rates rose, while the yields on government securities with terms to maturity longer than two years fell. Reflecting the decline in intermediate and long-term yields, the return on the Lehman Brothers U.S. Government Index for the three-month period was 3.11 percent.

For fixed-income securities that are subject not only to default-free yield-curve movements but also to credit risk, spread changes represent an additional source of interest rate exposure. Companies operating within the same industry face the same business environment, and the prices of the securities they issue have a general tendency to move in the same direction in response to environmental changes. All airlines, for example, are affected by changes in business and leisure travel patterns and the cost of fuel, among other economic factors. In the corporate bond market, such commonalities are reflected in sector spreads, which widen when investors require higher yields in compensation for higher perceived business risk. In addition, rating agencies evaluate the creditworthiness of corporate bond issues, and credit quality spreads vary with changes in the required yields for fixed-income securities of a given rating. Exhibit 12-11 shows the combined market-based yield effect of the spot rate yield-curve and nominal spread changes for an investor holding AA-rated 10-year industrial bonds. For example, for the nine-month period ending June 30, 2004, increases in the 10-year spot rate and the 10-year AA spread of 0.64 percent and 0.12 percent, respectively, combined to result in a total change of 0.76 percent in the yield of AA-rated 10-year industrial bonds.

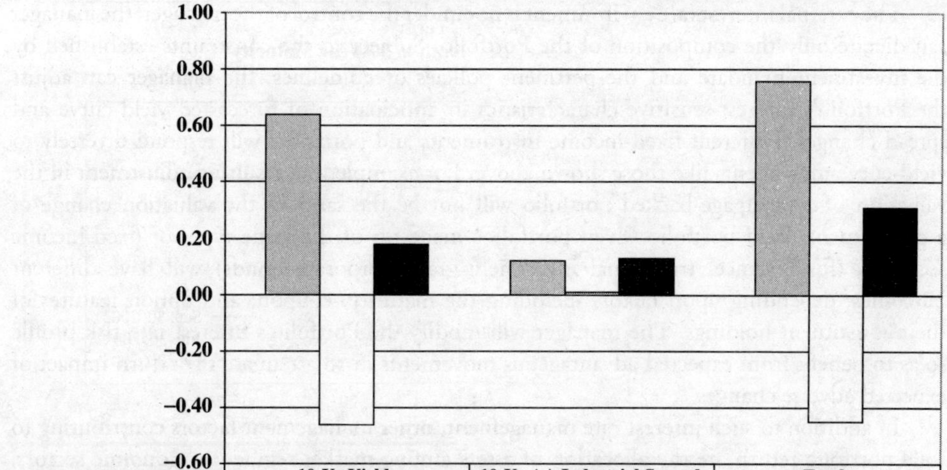

	10-Yr Yield	10-Yr AA Industrial Spread	Total
▩ 9 Mos. Ended 30 June 2004	0.64	0.12	0.76
□ 3 Mos. Ended 30 Sept 2004	−0.46	0.01	−0.45
■ 12 Mos. Ended 30 Sept 2004	0.18	0.13	0.31

EXHIBIT 12-11 Yield Curve and Nominal Spread Changes

EXHIBIT 12-12 Total Returns Data

	Total Returns	
	Lehman U.S. Government Index	Lehman AA Industrials Index
9 months ended June 30, 2004	−0.56%	−0.58%
3 months ended September 30, 2004	3.11%	3.71%
12 months ended September 30, 2004	2.52%	3.11%

Exhibit 12-12 shows the total returns of the Lehman U.S. Government and the Lehman AA Industrials Indexes for the same evaluation periods. The AA Industrials Index modestly underperformed the Government Index in the nine-month period ended June 30, 2004, when the yield curve rose and the nominal spread widened, and significantly outperformed in the subsequent quarter, when the yield curve fell and the nominal spread was essentially unchanged. In addition, of course, the spreads of individual 10-year AA-rated industrial bonds may vary from the average reflected by the sector index, and those differences, too, will be reflected in the actual performance of a specific portfolio.

The impact of interest rate and spread movements on the investment performance of a given portfolio depends upon the nature of the market changes and the interest-sensitive characteristics of the portfolio. We have already seen two types of yield-curve changes: An upward (although nonparallel) shift in the nine-month period ended June 30, 2004, and a twist in the third quarter of 2004 when short-term rates rose and long-term rates fell. Additionally, in both cases, the slope of the yield curve changed. An indicator of the slope is the difference between the 2-year and the 10-year yield-curve rates. The difference was 2.48 percent on September 30, 2003, 1.90 percent on June 30, 2004, and 1.52 percent on September 30, 2004. Thus, over this time frame, the U.S. government spot rate yield curve flattened from one measurement point to the next.

The external interest rate environment is not under the control of the manager; the manager can dictate only the composition of the Portfolio. Subject to the constraints established by the investment mandate and the pertinent policies or guidelines, the manager can adjust the Portfolio's interest-sensitive characteristics in anticipation of forecasted yield-curve and spread changes. Different fixed-income instruments and portfolios will respond diversely to yield-curve movements like those shown above. For example, the resulting adjustment in the valuation of a mortgage-backed portfolio will not be the same as the valuation change of a government bond portfolio. Even portfolios made up of the same types of fixed-income securities (for instance, traditional investment-grade corporate bonds) will have different outcomes, depending upon factors including the maturity, coupon, and option features of their constituent holdings. The manager will modify the Portfolio's interest rate risk profile so as to benefit from expected advantageous movements or to attenuate the return impact of expected adverse changes.

In addition to such interest rate management, other management factors contributing to total portfolio return are the allocation of assets among market segments, economic sectors, and quality grades, and the selection of specific securities within those categories. Trading activity during the evaluation period will also have an impact.

These sources of return are displayed in Exhibit 12-13.[29] The forward interest rates referred to in this exhibit can be calculated from the points along the spot rate government yield curve at the beginning and the end of the performance evaluation period.

The total return of a fixed-income portfolio can be attributed to the external interest rate effect, on one hand, and the management effect, on the other. The return due to the external interest rate environment is estimated from a term structure analysis of a universe of Treasury securities and can be further separated into the return from the implied forward rates (the expected return) and the difference between the actual realized return and the market implied return from the forward rates (the unexpected return). The overall external interest rate effect represents the performance of a passive, default-free bond portfolio.

The management effect is calculated by a series of repricings and provides information about how the management process affects the portfolio returns. The management effect can be decomposed into four components:

1. **Interest rate management effect.** Indicates how well the manager predicts interest rate changes. To calculate this return, each security in the portfolio is priced as if it

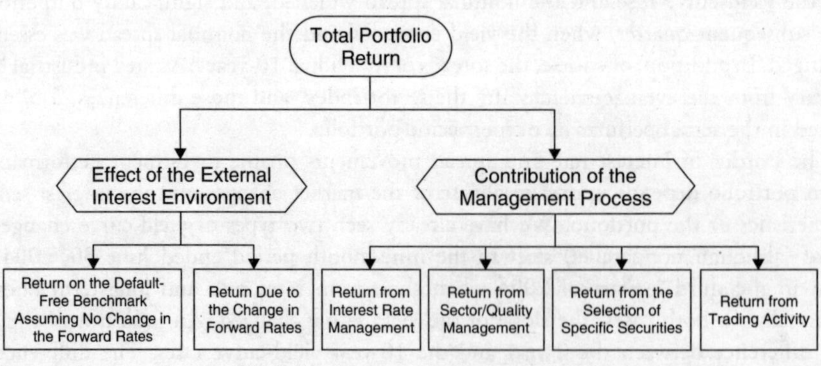

EXHIBIT 12-13 Sources of the Total Return of a Fixed-Income Portfolio

[29] Fong, Pearson, and Vasicek (1983).

were a default-free security. The interest rate management contribution is calculated by subtracting the return of the entire Treasury universe from the aggregate return of these repriced securities. The interest rate management effect can be further broken down into returns due to duration, convexity, and yield-curve shape change, as shown in Exhibit 12-14.

2. **Sector/quality effect.** Measures the manager's ability to select the "right" issuing sector and quality group. The sector/quality return is estimated by repricing each security in the portfolio using the average yield premium in its respective category. A gross return can be then calculated based on this price. The return from the sector/quality effect is calculated by subtracting the external effect and the interest rate management effect from this gross return.
3. **Security selection effect.** Measures how the return of a specific security within its sector relates to the average performance of the sector. The security selection effect for each security is the total return of a security minus all the other components. The portfolio security selection effect is the market-value weighted average of all the individual security selection effects.
4. **Trading activity.** Captures the effect of sales and purchases of bonds over a given period and is the total portfolio return minus all the other components.

Quantifying the absolute return contributions due to the management effect by means of serial portfolio repricings is data- and computation-intensive, and conducting value-added performance attribution relative to a fixed-income benchmark is still more challenging. Fixed-income investment management organizations often use commercially developed performance measurement and attribution systems. The vendor-provided systems available vary substantially in methodology and level of analytical sophistication, and selecting a system is not a trivial exercise, but most models attempt to isolate and measure the impact of environmental and management factors like those discussed here.

The output of a representative fixed-income attribution system can be demonstrated through a brief illustration. Let us consider the case of the investment officer of the Windsor Foundation, whose consultant has analyzed the performance of two of the foundation's external fixed-income managers, Broughton Asset Management and Matthews Advisors. The consultant has prepared an attribution analysis, shown in Exhibit 12-14, for a particular evaluation period.

The consultant also included in the analysis the following summary of the investment management strategies of the two firms:

- Broughton Asset Management states that its investment strategy relies on active interest rate management decisions to outperform the benchmark index. Broughton also seeks to identify individual issues that are mispriced.
- Matthews Advisors states that its investment strategy is to enhance portfolio returns by identifying undervalued sectors while maintaining a neutral interest rate exposure relative to the benchmark index. Matthews believes it is not possible to enhance returns through individual bond selection on a consistent basis.

Does the consultant's attribution analysis validate the two firms' self-descriptions of their investment strategies?

In fact, the foundation officer and the consultant can *preliminarily* conclude on the basis of the single year under review that approximately one-half of the incremental return

EXHIBIT 12-14 Performance Attribution Analysis for Two Fixed-Income Managers for the Windsor Foundation Year Ending December 31, 20XX

	Evaluation Period Returns (%)		
	Broughton Asset Management	Matthews Advisors	Bond Portfolio Benchmark
I. Interest Rate Effect			
1. Expected	0.44	0.44	0.44
2. Unexpected	0.55	0.55	0.55
Subtotal	0.99	0.99	0.99
II. Interest Rate Management Effect			
3. Duration	0.15	−0.13	0.00
4. Convexity	−0.03	−0.06	0.00
5. Yield-Curve Shape Change	0.04	0.13	0.00
Subtotal (options adjusted)	0.16	−0.06	0.00
III. Other Management Effects			
6. Sector/Quality	−0.09	1.15	0.00
7. Bond Selectivity	0.12	−0.08	0.00
8. Transaction Costs	0.00	0.00	0.00
Subtotal	0.03	1.07	0.00
IV. Trading Activity Return	0.10	0.08	0.00
V. Total Return (sum of I, II, III, and IV)	1.28	2.08	0.99

due to Broughton's management process can be attributed to relying on active interest rate management decisions. The total performance contribution for the interest rate management effect—the primary indicator of effective active interest rate management decisions in this analysis—was 16 basis points out of a total of 29 basis points due to the manager's active management process. In addition, the performance contribution for bond selectivity—here, the most direct measure of success in security selection—was 12 basis points. Therefore, nearly all of Broughton's positive performance of 29 basis points (1.28 percent versus 0.99 percent) was a result of its stated strategies of interest rate management (16 basis points) and security selection (12 basis points).

Interestingly, a substantial portion of Matthews' performance results are attributable to the firm's success in identifying undervalued sectors. The positive performance contribution for sector and quality was 1.15 percent, representing a large proportion of Matthews' return relative to the benchmark and indicating success over the evaluation period.

Fixed-income performance attribution is receiving increasing attention from plan sponsors and consultants, but it remains primarily the province of investment managers who have access to the requisite capital market data services as well as the scale of operations to justify the expense and the expertise needed to interpret the results in depth.

7. PERFORMANCE APPRAISAL

The final phase of the performance evaluation process is performance appraisal. The two preceding phases supplied information indicating how the account performed and quantifying the sources of that performance relative to a designated benchmark. Ultimately, however, fund sponsors are concerned with whether the manager of the account has displayed investment skill and whether the manager is likely to sustain that skill. The goal of performance appraisal is to provide quantitative evidence that the fund sponsor can use to make decisions about whether to retain or modify portions of its investment program.

That said, perhaps no issue elicits more frustration on the part of fund sponsors than the subject of appraising manager investment skill. The problem stems from the inherent uncertainty surrounding the outcome of active management decisions. Even the most talented managers can underperform their benchmarks during any given quarter, year, or even multiyear period due to poor luck. Conversely, ineffective managers at times may make correct decisions and outperform their benchmarks simply by good fortune. We will return to this concept later.

What do we mean by the term *investment skill?* We define **investment skill** as the ability to outperform an appropriate benchmark consistently over time. As discussed previously, a manager's returns in excess of his or her benchmark are commonly referred to as the manager's value-added return or active return. Because no manager is omniscient, every manager's value-added returns, regardless of the manager's skill, will be positive in some periods and negative in others. Nevertheless, a skillful manager should produce a larger value-added return more frequently than his or her less talented peers.

We emphasize that a skillful manager may produce a small value-added return very frequently or a larger value-added return less frequently. It is the magnitude of the value-added returns relative to the variability of value-added returns that determines a manager's skill.

When evaluating managers, many fund sponsors focus solely on the level of value-added returns produced while ignoring value-added return volatility. As a consequence, superior managers may be terminated (or not hired) and inferior managers may be retained (or hired) on the basis of statistically questionable performance data.

7.1. Risk-Adjusted Performance Appraisal Measures

Risk-adjusted performance appraisal methods can mitigate the natural fixation on rates of return. There are a number of appraisal measures that explicitly take the volatility of returns into account. A widely accepted principle of investment management theory and practice is that investors are risk averse and therefore require additional expected return to compensate for increased risk. Thus, it is not surprising that measures of performance appraisal compare returns generated by an account manager with the account's corresponding risk. Two types of risk are typically applied to deflate *ex post* returns: the account's market (or systematic) risk, as measured by its beta, and the account's total risk, as measured by its standard deviation.

Three risk-adjusted performance appraisal measures have become widely used: ***ex post* alpha** (also known as **Jensen's alpha**), the **Treynor ratio** (also known as **reward-to-volatility** or excess return to nondiversifiable risk), and the **Sharpe ratio** (also known as **reward-to-variability**). Another measure, $\mathbf{M^2}$**,** has also received some acceptance. A thorough discussion of these measures can be found in standard investment texts such as Sharpe, Alexander, and Bailey (1999), but we present a summary here. We consider these measures in their *ex post* (after the fact) form used to appraise a past record of performance.

7.1.1. Ex Post Alpha

The *ex post* alpha (also known as the *ex post* Jensen's alpha—see Jensen 1968, 1969) uses the *ex post* Security Market Line (SML) to form a benchmark for performance appraisal purposes. Recall that the capital asset pricing model (CAPM) developed by Sharpe (1966), Lintner (1965), and Mossin (1966), from which the *ex post* SML is derived, assumes that on an *ex ante* (before the fact) basis, expected account returns are a linear function of the risk-free return plus a risk premium that is based on the expected excess return on the market portfolio over the risk-free return, scaled by the amount of systematic risk (beta) assumed by the account. That is, over a single period, the *ex ante* CAPM (SML) is

$$E(R_A) = r_f + \beta_A[E(R_M) - r_f] \qquad (12\text{-}17)$$

where

$E(R_A)$ = the expected return on the account, given its beta
r_f = the risk-free rate of return (known constant for the evaluation period)
$E(R_M)$ = the expected return on the market portfolio
β_A = the account's beta or sensitivity to returns on the market portfolio, equal to the ratio of covariance to variance as $\text{Cov}(R_A, R_M)/\text{Var}(R_M)$

With data on the actual returns of (1) the account, (2) a proxy for the market portfolio (a market index), and (3) the risk-free rate, we can produce an *ex post* version of the CAPM relationship. Rearranging Equation 12-17, a simple linear regression can estimate the parameters of the following relationship:

$$R_{At} - r_{ft} = \alpha_A + \beta_A(R_{Mt} - r_{ft}) + \varepsilon_t \qquad (12\text{-}18)$$

where for period t, R_{At} is the return on the account, r_{ft} is the risk-free return, and R_{Mt} is the return on the market proxy (market index).[30] The term α_A is the intercept of the regression, β_A is the beta of the account relative to the market index, and ε is the random error term of the regression equation. The estimate of the intercept term α_A is the *ex post* alpha. We can interpret *ex post* alpha as the differential return of the account compared to the return required to compensate for the systematic risk assumed by the account during the evaluation period. The level of the manager's demonstrated skill is indicated by the sign and value of the *ex post* alpha. Left unsaid is whether the fund sponsor prefers a manager with a large (positive) but highly variable alpha to one that produces a smaller (positive) but less variable alpha.

7.1.2. Treynor Measure The Treynor measure (see Treynor 1965) is closely related to the *ex post* alpha. Like the *ex post* alpha, the Treynor measure relates an account's excess returns to the systematic risk assumed by the account. As a result, it too uses the *ex post* SML to form a benchmark, but in a somewhat different manner than the *ex post* alpha. The calculation of the Treynor ratio is:

$$T_A = \frac{\bar{R}_A - \bar{r}_f}{\hat{\beta}_A} \qquad (12\text{-}19)$$

$\bar{R}_A$ and $\bar{r}_f$ are the average values of each variable over the evaluation period. The Treynor ratio has a relatively simple visual interpretation, given that the beta of the risk-free asset is zero. The Treynor ratio is simply the slope of a line, graphed in the space of mean *ex post* returns and beta, which connects the average risk-free return to the point representing the average return and beta of the account. When viewed alongside the *ex post* SML, the account's benchmark

[30]The *ex post* alpha relationship can be expanded to incorporate other sources of risk (for example, the three-factor model developed by Fama and French). See Carhart (1997) for further discussion.

effectively becomes the slope of the *ex post* SML. Thus, a skillful manager will produce returns that result in a slope greater than the slope of the *ex post* SML.

Both the *ex post* alpha and the Treynor measure will always give the same assessment of the existence of investment skill. This correspondence is evident from the fact that any account with a positive *ex post* alpha must plot above the *ex post* SML. Therefore, the slope of a line connecting the risk-free rate to this account must be greater than the slope of the *ex post* SML, the indication of skill under the Treynor ratio.

7.1.3. Sharpe Ratio Both the *ex post* alpha and Treynor ratio compare excess returns on an account relative to the account's systematic risk. In contrast, the Sharpe ratio (see Sharpe 1966) compares excess returns to the total risk of the account, where total risk is measured by the account's standard deviation of returns. The *ex post* Sharpe ratio is traditionally given by:

$$S_A = \frac{R_A - r_f}{\hat{\sigma}_A} \qquad (12\text{-}20)$$

The benchmark in the case of the Sharpe ratio is based on the *ex post* capital market line (CML). The *ex post* CML is plotted in the space of returns and standard deviation of returns and connects the risk-free return and the point representing the mean return on the market index and its estimated standard deviation during the evaluation period. As with the Treynor ratio, a skillful manager will produce returns that place the account above the CML, and hence the slope of the line connecting the risk-free rate and the account will lie above the *ex post* CML. Such a manager is producing more average return relative to the risk-free rate per unit of volatility than is a passive investment in the market index.

7.1.4. M^2 Like the Sharpe ratio, M^2 (see Modigliani and Modigliani 1997) uses standard deviation as the measure of risk and is based on the *ex post* CML. M^2 is the mean incremental return over a market index of a hypothetical portfolio formed by combining the account with borrowing or lending at the risk-free rate so as to match the standard deviation of the market index. M^2 measures what the account would have returned if it had taken on the same total risk as the market index. To produce that benchmark, M^2 scales up or down the excess return of the account over the risk-free rate by a factor equal to the ratio of the market index's standard deviation to the account's standard deviation.

$$M_A^2 = r_f + \left(\frac{R_A - r_f}{\hat{\sigma}_A}\right)\hat{\sigma}_M \qquad (12\text{-}21)$$

Visually, we can consider a line from the average risk-free rate to the point representing the average return and standard deviation of the account. Extending (or retracing) this line to a point corresponding to the standard deviation of the market index allows us to compare the return on the account to that of the market index at the same level of risk. A skillful manager will generate an M^2 value that exceeds the return on the market index.

M^2 will evaluate the skill of a manager exactly as does the Sharpe ratio. Further, as we discussed, the Jensen's alpha and the Treynor ratio will produce the same conclusions regarding the existence of manager skill. However, it is possible for the Sharpe ratio and M^2 to identify a manager as not skillful, although the *ex post* alpha and the Treynor ratio come to the opposite conclusion. This outcome is most likely to occur in instances where the manager takes on a large amount of nonsystematic risk in the account relative to the account's systematic risk. In that case, one can see by comparing Equations 12-19 and 12-20 that while the numerator remains the same, increased nonsystematic risk will lower the Sharpe ratio but leave the Treynor ratio unaffected. As the market index, by definition, has no nonsystematic risk, the account's performance will look weaker relative to the market index under the Sharpe ratio than under the Treynor ratio (and Jensen's alpha).

7.1.5. Information Ratio The Sharpe ratio can be used to incorporate both risk-adjusted returns and a benchmark appropriate for the manager of the account under evaluation. In its traditional form, the numerator of the Sharpe ratio is expressed as the returns on the account in excess of the risk-free rate. Similarly, the denominator is expressed as the standard deviation of the difference in returns between the account and the risk-free return. However, by definition, in a single-period context the risk-free rate has no variability, and hence, the denominator can be stated as the variability in the account's returns.

Because the Sharpe ratio is based on a differential return, it represents the results of a self-financing strategy. A certain dollar amount can be viewed as being invested in the account, with this long position funded by short-selling the risk-free asset; that is, borrowing at the risk-free rate is assumed to fund the investment in the account. In order to provide a relevant context for performance appraisal using the traditional form, we must identify an appropriate benchmark and compute the Sharpe ratio for that benchmark as well as the account. A higher Sharpe ratio for the account than for the benchmark indicates superior performance.

There is no reason, however, for insisting on appraising performance in the context of borrowing at the risk-free rate to fund the investment in the account. Instead, the Sharpe ratio can be generalized to directly incorporate a benchmark appropriate to the account manager's particular investment style. Equation 12-20 can be rewritten to show the long position in the account is funded by a short position in the benchmark:

$$\mathrm{IR}_A = \frac{R_A - R_B}{\hat{\sigma}_{A-B}} \tag{12-22}$$

where $\hat{\sigma}_{A-B}$ is the standard deviation of the difference between the returns on the account and the returns on the benchmark. The Sharpe ratio in this form is commonly referred to as the **information ratio,** defined as the excess return of the account over the benchmark relative to the variability of that excess return. The numerator is often referred to as the **active return** on the account, and the denominator is referred to as the account's **active risk.** Thus, from this perspective, the information ratio measures the reward earned by the account manager per incremental unit of risk created by deviating from the benchmark's holdings.

7.1.6. Criticisms of Risk-Adjusted Performance Appraisal Methods A number of criticisms of risk-adjusted performance measures have surfaced over the years, and we will return to some of those arguments later in the discussion. Perhaps the most prominent criticisms have involved the reliance of the *ex post* alpha and the Treynor ratio on the validity of the CAPM. The CAPM has come under attack for a variety of reasons, most notably the appropriateness of its underlying assumptions and the single-index nature of the model. If assets are valued according to some other equilibrium pricing model, then beta-based performance measures may give inaccurate appraisals.

Critics (for example, Roll 1978) have also pointed to problems raised by the use of surrogates (such as the S&P 500) for the true market portfolio. Roll showed that slight changes in the market portfolio surrogate can yield significantly different performance appraisal answers.

Even those appraisal methods not tied to the CAPM face implementation problems. For example, the use of a market index or custom benchmark in the appraisal of investment performance is open to criticism in that it is difficult in most cases for the account manager to replicate precisely the benchmark's return over time (see French and Henderson 1985). Transaction costs associated with initially creating and then later rebalancing the benchmark, as well as the costs of reinvesting income flows, mean that the benchmark's reported returns overstate the performance that a passive investor in the benchmark could earn.

Stability of the parameters and the estimation error involved in the risk-adjusted appraisal measures is also an issue. Even if the assumptions underlying the appraisal measures hold true, the *ex post* calculations are merely estimates of the true parameters of the actual risk–return relationships. If the estimates are recalculated over another period, they may well show conclusions that conflict with the earlier estimates, even if those relationships are stable over time. Further, that stability cannot be taken for granted; the aggressiveness of the account manager may change rapidly over time in ways that cannot be captured by the estimation procedures.

7.2. Quality Control Charts

Conveying the essence of performance appraisal to decision makers is a difficult task. A vast quantity of data needs to be synthesized into a relatively few graphs and tables if information overload is to be avoided. Yet this summary process should not come at the expense of sound data analysis. In particular, it should not preclude a consideration of the statistical and economic significance of the performance results. One effective means of presenting performance appraisal data is through the use of **quality control charts.**

Exhibit 12-15 presents an example of a quality control chart. It illustrates the performance of an actively managed account versus a selected benchmark. The straight horizontal line emanating from the vertical axis at zero represents the performance of the benchmark. The jagged line is the portfolio's cumulative annualized performance relative to the benchmark (that is, the manager's value-added return). The funnel-shaped lines surrounding the horizontal lines form a confidence band, a statistical concept about which we will have more to say shortly. The confidence band offers a means to evaluate the statistical significance of the account's performance relative to the benchmark.

Underlying the quality control chart's construction are three assumptions concerning the likely distribution of the manager's value-added returns. The primary assumption (and one that we will subsequently test) is referred to as the null hypothesis. The null hypothesis of the quality control chart is that the manager has no investment skill; thus, the expected value-added return is zero. With respect to Exhibit 12-15, we expect that the manager's value-added return line will coincide with the benchmark line.

Of course, at the end of an evaluation period it is highly unlikely that the account's return will precisely equal that of the benchmark. The account's actual return will be either above or below the benchmark's return. The null hypothesis, however, suggests that those *ex post* differences have no directional biases and are entirely due to random chance.

Our second assumption states that the manager's value-added returns are independent from period to period and normally distributed around the expected value of zero. The third assumption is that the manager's investment process does not change from period to period. Among other things, this third assumption implies that the variability of the manager's value-added returns remains constant over time.

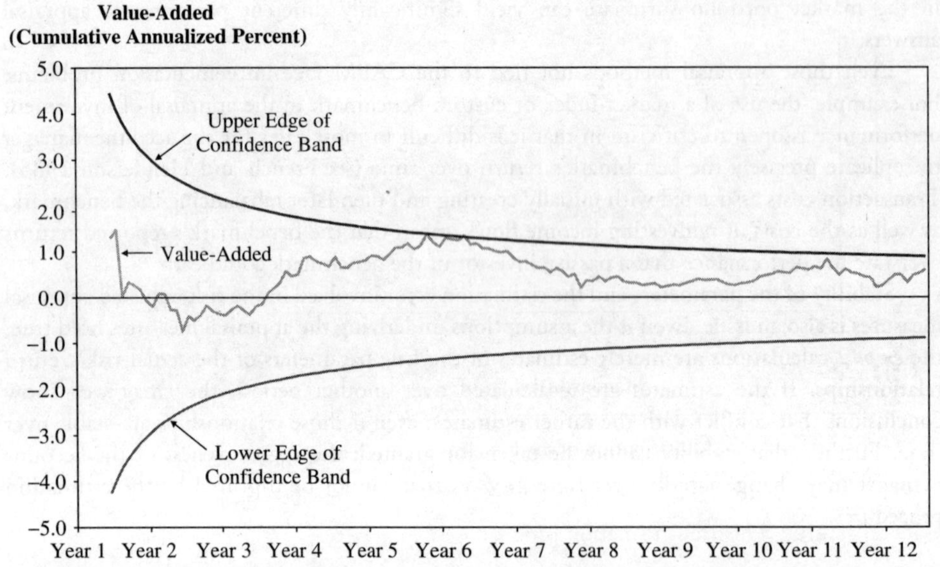

EXHIBIT 12-15 Quality Control Chart: Cumulative Annualized Value-Added Illustrating Manager Performance within Expectations

Now consider the manager whose investment results are shown in Exhibit 12-15. Employing the three assumptions described above, we can completely describe the expected distribution of the manager's value-added returns, as illustrated in Exhibit 12-16. Corresponding to our second assumption of normally distributed value-added returns, the shape of the distribution is the familiar bell-shaped curve. Under our first assumption of no skill (the null hypothesis), the center (or mean) of the distribution is located at 0 percent. Finally, given our third assumption that the manager does not alter his or her investment process over time, we can use the manager's past performance to estimate the dispersion of the value-added return distribution. That dispersion is measured by the standard deviation of the value-added returns, which in this case is an annualized 4.1 percent. We therefore expect that two-thirds of the time, the manager's annual value-added return results will be within ±4.1 percentage points of the zero mean.

Given this information, we can compute a confidence band associated with the expected distribution of the manager's value-added returns. Based on our three assumptions, the **confidence band** indicates the range in which we anticipate that the manager's value-added returns will fall a specified percentage of the time.

In our example, suppose that we wished to determine a confidence band designed to capture 80 percent of the manager's value-added return results. Based on the properties of a normal distribution, we know that 1.28 standard deviations around the mean will capture *ex ante* 80 percent of the possible outcomes associated with a normally distributed random variable. With a 4.1 percent annual standard deviation of value-added returns, the 80 percent confidence band in our example therefore covers a range from approximately −5.2 percent to approximately +5.2 percent around the manager's expected value-added return of zero.

This range, however, corresponds to only one time period: one year from the start of the analysis. To create the confidence band at other points in time, we must transform the standard deviation of the manager's value-added returns to address annualized cumulative

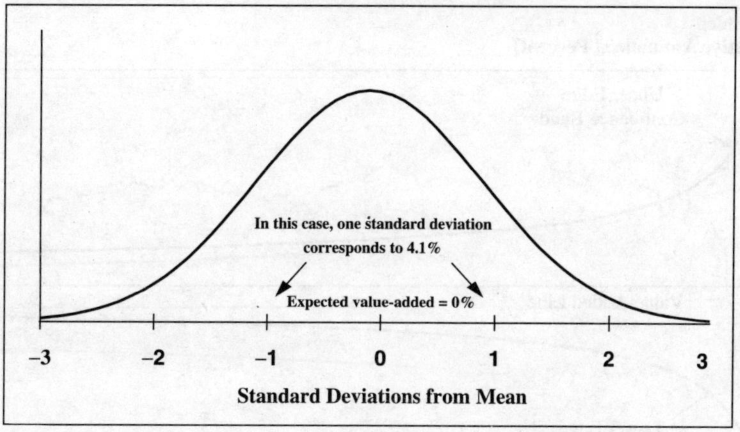

EXHIBIT 12-16 Expected Distribution of the Manager's Value Added

value-added returns. This transformation produces the funnel-shaped lines shown in Exhibit 12-15.

The standard deviation of annualized cumulative value-added returns decreases at a rate equal to the square root of time. As a result, the standard deviation of annualized cumulative value-added returns at two years is $1/\sqrt{2}$ of the one-year value, at three years it is $1/\sqrt{3}$ of the one-year value, and so on. Because the width of the confidence band depends on the standard deviation of value-added returns, as time passes, the confidence band will narrow, converging on the benchmark line.

Intuitively, that convergence means that as we collect more observations on the manager's value-added returns, the cumulative annualized results should lie closer to our expected value of zero. That is, as time passes, it becomes increasingly likely that the manager's random positive and negative value-added returns will offset one another. Therefore, the chances that the manager will produce a "large" cumulative annualized value-added return, on either side of the mean, declines over time.

7.3. Interpreting the Quality Control Chart

Statistical inference by its nature can be a baffling exercise in double negatives. For example, we do not *accept* the null hypothesis. Rather, lacking evidence to the contrary, we *fail to reject* it. Nevertheless, the equivocal nature of this type of analysis is well suited to the world of investments, where luck often masquerades as skill and skill is frequently overwhelmed by random events.

For example, do the data presented in Exhibit 12-15 tell us anything about the manager's investment skill? The answer in this case is inconclusive. Over the full period of analysis, the manager has outperformed the benchmark by about 1.0 percent per year. Based on this outcome, we might be tempted to certify the manager as being truly skillful. Before leaping to that conclusion, however, recall that our null hypothesis is that the manager has no skill. What we are really asking is, "Do the manager's performance results warrant rejecting the null hypothesis?" Remember that we assume the manager's value-added returns are normally distributed with a constant annual standard deviation of 4.1 percent. Given those assumptions, under the zero-value-added return null hypothesis, there exists a strong possibility that the manager could possess no skill and yet produce the results shown in Exhibit 12-15.

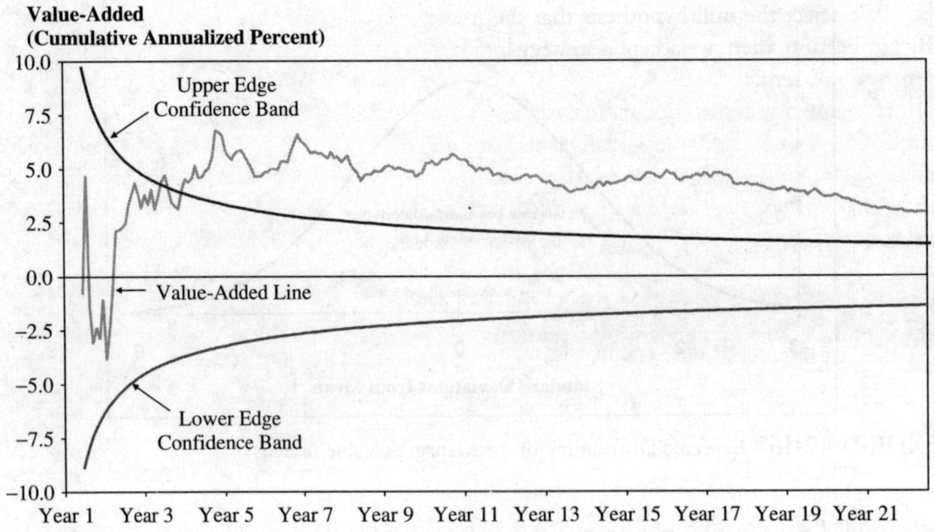

EXHIBIT 12-17 Quality Control Chart: Cumulative Annualized Value-Added Illustrating Manager Performance Significantly Greater than Benchmark

The quality control chart analysis provides a likely range of value-added return results for a manager who possesses no skill and who displays a specified level of value-added return variability. For a manager whose investment results are within that range (confidence band), we have no strong statistical evidence to indicate that our initial assumption of no skill is incorrect. Thus we are left with the rather unsatisfying statement, "We cannot reject the null hypothesis that the manager has no skill."

It may be true that the manager in Exhibit 12-15 has skill and that the 1 percent value-added return was no fluke. Unfortunately, over the limited time that we have to observe the manager, and given the variability of the manager's value-added returns, we cannot classify the manager as unambiguously skillful. Even if the manager could actually produce a 1 percent value-added return over the long run, his or her talents are obscured by the variability of his or her short-run results. That performance "noise" makes it difficult to distinguish his or her talents from those of an unskillful manager.

Now let us consider another manager who generates the value-added return series shown in Exhibit 12-17. The confidence interval is again designed to capture 80 percent of the potential value-added return outcomes for a zero-value-added return manager with a specified level of value-added return variability. In this case, the manager has breached the confidence band on the upside, outperforming the benchmark by about 5 percent per year over the evaluation period. How should we interpret this situation? One view is that the manager has no skill and was simply lucky. After all, there is a 2-in-10 chance that a zero-value-added return manager might produce results that lie somewhere outside the confidence band (actually, a 1-in-10 chance of lying above and a 1-in-10 chance of lying below the confidence band).

On the other hand, we could reject the null hypothesis. That is, there is only a 20 percent chance that a zero-value-added return manager would produce results that lie outside the confidence band. Therefore, the occurrence of such an event might indicate that our initial assumption that the manager has no skill is incorrect. Note that our statement would then be, "We reject the null hypothesis that the manager's expected value-added return is zero." By implication, then, we accept a strategy hypothesis that the manager's expected value-added return is not zero.[31]

The quality control chart analysis is similar on the downside. That is, suppose that the manager produces a cumulative negative value-added return yet lies above the lower edge of the confidence band. In that situation, we should not reject the null hypothesis that the manager's expected value-added return is zero. The manager might be a negative value-added return investor (that is, be unable to earn back his or her management fees and trading costs). On the other hand, the manager might be skillful and simply be having a poor run of investment luck. In such a case, the relatively small negative value-added return compared to the variability of that value-added return would make it difficult to reject the null hypothesis.

Conversely, piercing the confidence interval on the downside might lead us to reject the null hypothesis that the manager's expected value-added return is zero. The unstated implication is that the manager is systematically incapable of recapturing the costs of doing business and should be classified as an "underperformer."

8. THE PRACTICE OF PERFORMANCE EVALUATION

The three components of performance evaluation provide the quantitative inputs required to evaluate the investment skill of an account's manager. However, regardless of the amount of performance data compiled, the process of performance evaluation is fraught with imprecision. Performance evaluation is ultimately a forward-looking decision, and the connection between past performance and future performance is tenuous at best.[32] Indiscriminate use of quantitative data can lead to counterproductive decisions.

As a result, in evaluating investment managers, most fund sponsors follow a procedure that incorporates both quantitative and qualitative elements, with the latter typically receiving more weight than the former. For example, in selecting investment managers, many fund sponsors follow a relatively standard set of procedures. For the sake of exposition, we consider a "typical" fund sponsor. The fund sponsor has a several-person staff that carries out the fund's day-to-day operations. The fund sponsor may retain a consultant to assist in the search for new managers. The staff continually scans the marketplace for promising investment managers. The staff may become aware of a manager through such means as visits from the manager to the staff's office, attendance at various conferences, discussions with peers at other fund sponsor organizations, meetings with consulting firms, and the financial press. The staff maintains files on those managers who have attracted interest, collecting historical return data, portfolio compositions, manager investment process descriptions, and other pertinent data. Upon deciding to hire a new manager, the staff will research its files and select a group of managers for extensive review. This initial cut is an informal decision based on the staff's ongoing survey of the manager marketplace.

[31] Of course, the assumptions underlying the statistical test may not hold. For example, the manager's investment process may have become more aggressive, and hence, the variability of his value-added returns may have increased.

[32] See Carhart (1997).

EXHIBIT 12-18 Criteria for Manager Selection

Criteria	Importance
Physical	5%
• Organizational structure, size, experience, other resources	
People	25
• Investment professionals, compensation	
Process	30
• Investment philosophy, style, decision making	
Procedures	15
• Benchmarks, trading, quality control	
Performance	20
• Results relative to an appropriate benchmark	
Price	5
• Investment management fees	

The review of the "finalist" group is a much more formal and extensive process. The staff requests that each finalist submit detailed data concerning virtually all aspects of its organization and operations. We broadly group this data into six categories, as shown in Exhibit 12-18.

The staff assigns weights or relative importance to each of these criteria. Exhibit 12-18 shows one possible set of weights. The staff does not apply these criteria and weights in a mechanical manner. Its ultimate decisions are actually quite subjective. The important point is that the staff considers a broad range of quantitative and qualitative factors in arriving at a selection recommendation. No single factor dominates the decision: performance data are only one component in the ultimate evaluation decision.

In addition to collecting written information, the staff meets personally with the key decision makers from each of the finalist managers. In those meetings the staff engages in a broad discussion, the purpose of which is to focus on specific aspects of the managers' operations as highlighted by the selection criteria.

After meeting with all of the finalists, the staff compares notes and selects a manager (or managers) to recommend to the fund sponsor's investment committee, which makes the final decision. The committee members are much more performance-oriented than the staff. Nevertheless, they usually support the staff's well-researched recommendations.

8.1. Noisiness of Performance Data

The goal of evaluating prospective or existing managers is to hire or keep the best managers and to eliminate managers likely to produce inferior future results. If past performance were closely tied to future performance, then it would be desirable to rely heavily on past performance in evaluating managers. The problem is that empirical evidence generally does not support such a relationship.

The confusion results from the uncertain, or stochastic, nature of active management. Active managers are highly fallible. While we may expect a superior manager to perform well over any given time period, we will observe that the superior manager's actual performance is quite variable. Even sophisticated investors tend to focus on expected returns and ignore this risk element.

EXAMPLE 12-17 The Influence of Noise on Performance Appraisal

Suppose that we know in advance that a manager is superior and will produce an annual value-added return of 2 percent, on average. The variability of that superior performance is 5 percent per year. Our hypothetical manager has an information ratio of 0.40 (2% ÷ 5%), which by our experience is a high figure. (Hence our assertion that this manager is a superior manager.) Exhibit 12-19 shows the probability of managers outperforming their benchmarks over various evaluation periods, given the information ratios.

EXHIBIT 12-19 Probability of a Manager Outperforming a Benchmark Given Various Levels of Investment Skill

	Information Ratio					
Years	0.20	0.30	0.40	0.67	0.80	1.00
0.5	55.63%	58.40%	61.14%	68.13%	71.42%	76.02%
1.0	57.93	61.79	65.54	74.75	78.81	84.03
3.0	63.81	69.83	75.58	87.59	91.71	95.84
5.0	67.26	74.88	81.45	93.20	96.32	98.73
10.0	73.65	82.86	89.70	98.25	99.43	99.92
20.0	81.70	91.01	96.32	99.86	99.98	99.99

Perhaps surprisingly, Exhibit 12-19 shows that the manager has a one-in-four chance of underperforming the benchmark over a period as long as three years, as seen by the boxed cell in the exhibit. Remember, we have defined this manager in advance to be a superior manager. Other value-added managers with less skill than this one have a greater chance of underperforming their benchmarks over typical evaluation periods.

Most fund sponsors hire more than one manager. Consider a group of ten superior managers whose investment skills equal those of the manager in Example 12-17 (who has an information ratio of 0.40) and assume independence of decision-making processes. Exhibit 12-20 shows the probability of a given number of this group simultaneously underperforming their benchmarks over a three-year period. As we can see, a fund sponsor using a simple decision rule of firing any manager who underperforms his or her benchmark over a three-year period can expect to follow a busy manager search schedule. Moreover, these probabilities are conservatively low. Few of the fund sponsor's managers will have the investment skill with which we have endowed our hypothetical managers.

In summary, using past performance to evaluate existing managers is statistically problematic. In the long run, superior managers will outperform inferior managers. However, due to the inherent uncertainty of investment management, over typical evaluation periods (three to five years) the odds that superior managers will underperform their benchmarks (and, conversely, that inferior managers will outperform their benchmarks) are disturbingly

EXHIBIT 12-20 Probability of Superior Managers Jointly Underperforming Their Benchmarks over a Three-Year Period

Managers Below Benchmark	Probability
0	6.10%
1	19.68
2	28.59
3	24.60
4	13.90
5	5.38
6	1.45
7	0.27
8	0.03
9	0.00
10	0.00

high. Expensive, incorrect decisions may frequently result from relying on past performance to evaluate investment managers.

8.2. Manager Continuation Policy

Frequent manager firings based on recent performance might seem to be merely a waste of a fund sponsor's time if not for the expenses associated with manager transitions. Fired managers' portfolios must be converted to the hired managers' portfolios. This conversion requires buying and selling securities, which in turn involves trading costs. Making assumptions about the cost of trading securities is a tenuous business at best, because many factors influence that cost. For U.S. large-capitalization common stocks, it is reasonable to assume transaction costs of 0.50 percent (one way), and for small company stocks and stocks of companies traded in less liquid markets, those costs can be much higher. A substantial percentage of the fired manager's portfolio may need to be liquidated in the process of moving the assets to a new manager, particularly when the managers' styles are not closely similar. Moreover, this tally of the expenses of converting a manager's portfolio considers only direct monetary costs. For most fund sponsors, replacing managers involves significant time and effort.[33]

In an attempt to reduce the costs of manager turnover yet systematically act on indications of future poor performance, some fund sponsors have adopted formal, written **manager continuation policies** (MCP) to guide their manager evaluations. The purpose of an MCP is severalfold:

- To retain superior managers and to remove inferior managers, preferably before the latter can produce adverse results.
- To ensure that relevant nonperformance information is given significant weight in the evaluation process.
- To minimize manager turnover.
- To develop procedures that will be consistently applied regardless of investment committee and staff changes.

[33]The costs associated with manager hiring and firing decisions are discussed in Goyal and Wahal (2005).

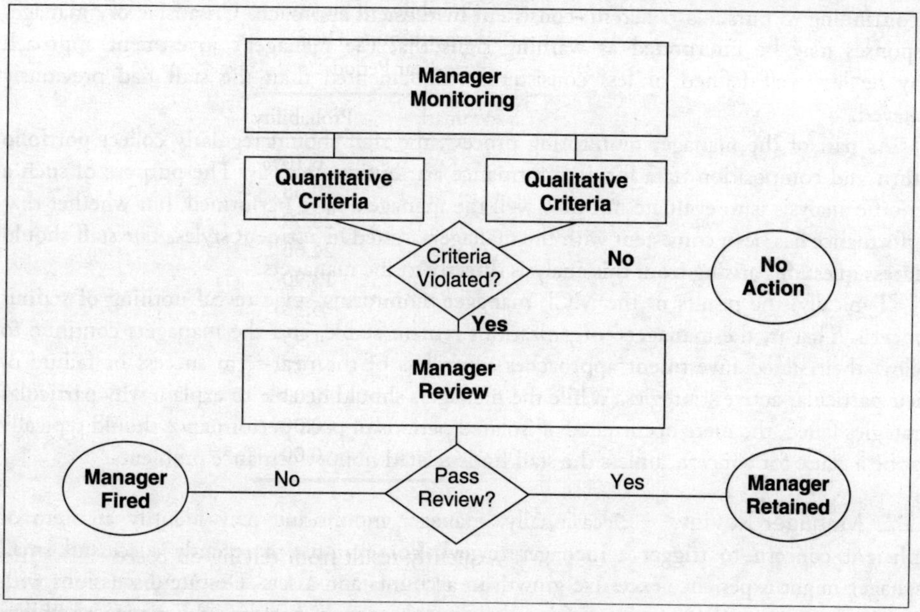

EXHIBIT 12-21 Manager Continuation Policy

An MCP can be viewed as a two-part process. The first part we refer to as **manager monitoring,** while the second part we call **manager review.** Exhibit 12-21 displays a flow chart description of an MCP.

8.2.1. Manager Monitoring

The ongoing phase of an MCP is manager monitoring. The goal of MCP manager monitoring is to identify warning signs of adverse changes in existing managers' organizations. It is a formal, documented procedure that assists fund sponsors in consistently collecting information relevant to evaluating the state of their managers' operations. The key is that the fund sponsor regularly asks the same important questions, both in written correspondence and in face-to-face meetings.

There is no firm set of appropriate manager monitoring criteria. Each fund sponsor must determine for itself the issues that are relevant to its own particular circumstances. Monitoring criteria may even vary from manager to manager. Regardless, the fund sponsor should clearly articulate its established criteria at the time a manager is hired, rather than formulate them later in a haphazard manner.

As part of the manager monitoring process, the fund sponsor periodically receives information from the managers, either in written form or through face-to-face meetings. This information is divided into two parts. The first part covers operational matters, such as personnel changes, account growth, litigation, and so on. The staff should flag significant items and discuss them in a timely manner with the respective managers.

The second part of the responses contains a discussion of the managers' investment strategies, on both a retrospective and a prospective basis. The fund sponsor should instruct the managers to explain their recent investment strategies relative to their respective benchmarks and how those strategies performed. The managers should follow this review with a discussion of their current strategies relative to the benchmark and why they believe that those strategies are appropriate. The goal of these discussions is to assure the fund sponsor that the manager is continuing to pursue a coherent, consistent investment approach. Unsatisfactory manager responses may be interpreted as warning signs that the manager's investment approach may be less well-defined or less consistently implemented than the staff had previously believed.

As part of the manager monitoring process, the staff should regularly collect portfolio return and composition data for a performance attribution analysis. The purpose of such a periodic analysis is to evaluate not how well the managers have performed, but whether that performance has been consistent with the managers' stated investment styles. The staff should address questions arising from this analysis directly to the managers.

Typically, the results of the MCP manager monitoring stage reveal nothing of serious concern. That is, the managers' organizations remain stable, and the managers continue to follow their stated investment approaches regardless of the near-term success or failure of their particular active strategies. While the managers should be able to explain why particular strategies failed, the mere occurrence of isolated periods of poor performance should typically not be a cause for concern, unless the staff finds related nonperformance problems.

8.2.2. Manager Review Occasionally, manager monitoring may identify an item of sufficient concern to trigger a manager review. For example, a recently successful small manager might experience excessive growth in accounts and assets. Despite discussions with the manager, the staff might be convinced that such growth threatens the manager's ability to produce superior returns in the future. At this point, a formal manager review becomes necessary.

The manager review closely resembles the manager selection process, in both the information considered and the comprehensiveness of the analysis. The staff should review all phases of the manager's operations, just as if the manager were being initially hired. We can view this manager review as a zero-based budgeting process (a budgeting process in which all expenditures must be justified each new period). We want to answer the question, "Would we hire the manager again today?"

As with the initial selection of a manager, the fund sponsor should collect the same comprehensive data and meet face-to-face with the manager in a formal interview setting. The manager's key personnel should attend, with the advance understanding that they must persuade the staff to "rehire" them. On conclusion of the interview, the staff should meet to compare observations, weighing the evaluation criteria in the same manner that it would if it were initially considering the manager. As part of these deliberations, the fund sponsor should also review the information that led to the manager's hiring in the first place.

The primary differences between hiring a new manager and retaining a manager under review are that the fund sponsor once had enough confidence in the manager to entrust a large sum of money to the manager's judgment and that there is a sizable cost associated with firing the manager. Thus, the fund sponsor should address the following questions:

- What has fundamentally changed in the manager's operation?
- Is the change significant?
- What are the likely ramifications of the change?
- Are the costs of firing the manager outweighed by the potential benefits?

8.3. Manager Continuation Policy as a Filter

For many reasons, investment skill does not readily lend itself to rigid "good" or "bad" interpretations. For discussion purposes, however, we will arbitrarily divide the investment manager community into three categories: positive-, zero-, and negative-value-added managers. Assume that positive-value-added managers beat their benchmarks (after all fees and expenses) by 2 percent per year, on average. Zero-value-added managers exhibit just enough skill to cover their fees and expenses and thereby match the performance of their benchmarks. Finally, negative-value-added managers lose to their benchmarks by 1 percent per year, on average, due primarily to the impact of fees and expenses.

We have no firm evidence as to how the manager community is apportioned among these three categories, although if we follow the logic of Grossman and Stiglitz (1980) and Sharpe (1994), the zero- and negative-value-added managers must predominate, with the former outnumbering the latter. Nevertheless, we speculate that out of five managers hired, a fund sponsor would be fortunate to hire two positive-value-added managers, two zero-value-added managers, and one negative-value-added manager. Therefore, in aggregate, this successful fund sponsor's managers are expected to outperform their benchmarks by 60 basis points per year, net of all costs [$0.6\% = (2\% \times 0.4) + (0\% \times 0.4) + (-1\% \times 0.2)$].

We can view a MCP as a statistical filter designed to remove negative-value-added managers and retain positive-value-added managers. Zero-value-added managers, much to the consternation of fund sponsors, always present a problem for a MCP, because they are so numerous and because they are statistically difficult to distinguish from positive- and negative-value-added managers.

We begin our MCP analysis with the null hypothesis that the managers under evaluation are at best zero-value-added managers. Then, as with any filter, two types of decision errors may occur:

- **Type I error**—keeping (or hiring) managers with zero value added. (Rejecting the null hypothesis when it is correct.)
- **Type II error**—firing (or not hiring) managers with positive value added. (Not rejecting the null hypothesis when it is incorrect.)

In implementing a MCP, the fund sponsor must determine how fine a filter to construct. A coarse filter will be conducive to Type I errors. For example, a fund sponsor may choose to overlook many violations of its manager monitoring guidelines, with the expectation that most problems experienced by managers are temporary and that they will eventually work themselves out. While this policy will avoid firing some positive-value-added managers, the fund sponsor could have identified in advance some managers who will provide mediocre long-term performance.

Conversely, a fine filter will lead the sponsor to commit more Type II errors. For example, a fund sponsor might apply its manager monitoring guidelines rigidly and automatically fire any manager who loses a key decision maker. While this policy will remove some managers whose operations will be disrupted by personnel turnover, it will also eliminate some managers possibly anticipated to recover from that turnover and to continue with superior results.

Exhibit 12-22 presents the four possible results from testing the null hypothesis that a manager has no investment skill. Referring back to the quality control chart, if in truth the manager has no skill and we reject the null hypothesis because the manager's value-added returns fall outside of the confidence band (particularly, in this case, on the upside), then we have committed a Type I error. Conversely, if the manager is indeed skillful yet we fail to reject the null hypothesis because the manager's value-added returns fall inside the confidence band, then we have committed a Type II error.

Both Type I and Type II errors are expensive. The art of a MCP is to strike a cost-effective balance between the two that avoids excessive manager turnover yet eliminates managers likely

	Reality	
	Value–Added = 0	Value–Added > 0
Reject	Type I	Correct
Do Not Reject	Correct	Type II

EXHIBIT 12-22 Null Hypothesis: Manager Has No Skill. Alternative Hypothesis: Manager Is Skillful

to produce inferior performance in the future. We can control the probabilities of committing Type I and Type II errors by adjusting the width of the confidence band within the quality control chart. For example, suppose that we widened the confidence band to encompass 95 percent of a manager's possible value-added return outcomes. Now it will be less likely than in our earlier examples that a zero-value-added return manager will generate returns that lie outside the confidence band. We thus reduce the chances of a Type I error. However, it will also now be less likely that a truly skillful manager will come to our attention by generating returns that fall outside that manager's confidence band. By continuing not to reject the null hypothesis for such a manager, we commit a Type II error.

Due to the high costs and uncertain benefits of replacing managers, it would seem advisable for fund sponsors to develop manager evaluation procedures that are tolerant toward Type I errors in order to reduce the probability of Type II errors. That is, it may be preferable to endure the discomfort of keeping several unskillful managers to avoid the expense of firing a truly superior manager. However, there is no right answer to this dilemma, and fund sponsors must undertake their own cost–benefit analyses, weighing the chances of committing one type of error versus the other. The quality control chart approach, however, provides fund sponsors with an objective framework with which to address this issue.

CHAPTER 13

GLOBAL INVESTMENT PERFORMANCE STANDARDS

Philip Lawton, CFA

CFA Institute
Charlottesville, Virginia

W. Bruce Remington, CFA

Wells Fargo
Lincoln, Nebraska

1. INTRODUCTION

The Global Investment Performance Standards (the GIPS® standards) fulfill an essential role in investment management around the world. They meet the need for consistent, globally accepted standards for investment management firms in calculating and presenting their results to potential clients.

The Standards are based on the ideals of fair representation and full disclosure of an investment management firm's performance history. Firms that claim compliance with the GIPS standards must adhere to rules governing not only rate-of-return calculations but also the way in which returns are displayed in a performance presentation. They are further required to make certain disclosures and are encouraged to make others, assisting the recipient or user in interpreting and evaluating the reported returns. Potential clients are assured that the information shown in a GIPS-compliant performance presentation reasonably reflects the results of the presenting firm's past investment decisions. They are also assured that the returns are calculated and presented on a consistent basis and that they are objectively comparable to those reported by other firms rightfully claiming compliance with the Standards.

This chapter comprehensively presents the requirements and recommendations of the 2005 version of the GIPS standards. In addition to presenting the Standards, the chapter explains the rationale and application of specific provisions, with particular attention to implementation issues. Section 2 provides background information on the need for the GIPS standards, their history, the role of the Investment Performance Council, and the objectives and key characteristics of the Standards. Section 3 covers the provisions of the GIPS standards. Section 4 describes verification, and Section 5 reviews the GIPS Advertising Guidelines enabling firms to claim compliance with the GIPS standards in advertisements that do not accommodate fully compliant performance presentations. Section 6 considers other issues relevant to the Standards.

2. BACKGROUND OF THE GIPS STANDARDS

The GIPS standards, which offer significant advantages to investors and investment management firms, evolved from earlier efforts to improve the reliability of performance information and to standardize calculation methodologies. In this part of the chapter, we will explain the benefits of the GIPS standards, recount their historical development, and introduce the governance body responsible for developing and interpreting the Standards. We will also give an overview of the GIPS standards.

2.1. The Need for Global Investment Performance Standards

In their current state, the GIPS standards are so broadly accepted and endorsed in the investment industry that it is worthwhile to recall the reasons they were developed in the first place. The total economic cost of defining, promulgating, interpreting, implementing, updating, monitoring, and validating claims of compliance with these voluntary ethical standards is substantial. Why have investment industry participants seen fit to incur such costs? What are the benefits?

To appreciate the value of industrywide performance presentation standards, consider some of the many ways in which unscrupulous employees might attempt to gather new assets by misrepresenting a firm's historical record in the Standards' absence. In communicating with a prospective client, they could:

- Present returns only for the best-performing portfolios as though those returns were fully representative of the firm's expertise in a given strategy or style.
- Base portfolio market values on their own unsubstantiated estimates of asset prices.
- Inflate returns by annualizing partial-period results.
- Select the most favorable measurement period, calculating returns from a low point to a high point.
- Present simulated returns as though they had actually been earned.
- Choose as a benchmark the particular index the selected portfolios have outperformed by the greatest margin during the preferred measurement period.
- Portray the growth of assets in the style or strategy of interest so as to mask the difference between investment returns and client contributions.
- Use the marketing department's expertise in graphic design to underplay unfavorable performance data and direct the prospect's attention to the most persuasive elements of the sales presentation.

Some of the foregoing examples are admittedly egregious abuses. They are not, however, farfetched. In the late 1980s, before performance presentation standards became widely accepted, a groundbreaking committee of the Financial Analysts Federation (a predecessor organization of CFA Institute) reported that investment advisers were "left to their own standards, which have been varied, uneven, and, in many instances, outright irresponsible and dishonest."[1] The investment management industry remains highly competitive, and people whose careers and livelihoods depend on winning new business want to communicate their firm's performance in the most favorable light (as they certainly should). The GIPS standards are ethical criteria designed simply to ensure that the firm's performance history is fairly represented and adequately disclosed. Indeed, employees who are pressured to misrepresent their firm's investment results can and should cite the GIPS standards.

Without established, well-formulated standards for investment performance measurement and presentation, the prospective client's ability to make sound decisions in selecting investment managers would be impaired. Individual investors and their advisers, as well as pension plan sponsors, foundation trustees, and other institutional investors with fiduciary responsibility for asset pools, need reliable information. The GIPS standards give them greater confidence that the returns they are shown fairly represent an investment firm's historical record. The Standards also enable them to make reasonable comparisons among different investment management firms before hiring one of them. Evaluating past returns is only one dimension of the manager selection process, but it is an important one, and the due diligence legally and ethically expected of fiduciaries cannot be satisfied without it.

The Standards' benefits to prospective clients are clear. What, if any, are the benefits to the investment management firms incurring the substantial expenses required to achieve and maintain compliance with the GIPS standards?

There is, first, an incalculable benefit to the investment management industry as a whole. The widespread acceptance of the GIPS standards contributes to the industry's credibility. The GIPS standards reassure investors about compliant firms' veracity in the area of investment performance reporting, which is highly advantageous to an industry built on trust. The development of well-founded, thoughtfully defined performance presentation standards is a great credit not only to the vision of certain professionals and organizations but, above all, to the leadership of the investment management firms that were the early adopters.

The practical benefits to individual firms facing the initial and ongoing expenses of GIPS compliance have increased over time. In some markets, the Standards are so well accepted by plan sponsors and consultants that noncompliance is a serious competitive impediment to a firm's winning new institutional business. Requests for proposals (RFPs) in manager searches routinely ask if the responding firm is in compliance with the GIPS standards and if the firm has been independently verified.[2] In addition, the global recognition the GIPS standards have gained helps the compliant firm to compete in international markets because prospective clients should value the ability to equitably compare its investment performance to that of local GIPS-compliant firms. Compliance with the GIPS standards has appropriately been characterized as the investment management firm's passport to the international marketplace.

Because the GIPS standards reflect best practices in the calculation and presentation of investment performance, firms may also realize internal benefits. In the course of implementing the Standards, they might identify opportunities to strengthen managerial controls. The discipline of reviewing portfolio guidelines and defining, documenting, and adhering to internal policies in support of compliance may generally improve the firm's oversight of investment operations. Similarly, technological enhancements designed to provide valid

[1]The Committee for Performance Presentation Standards (1987, p. 8).

[2]Competence in evaluating compliance with the GIPS standards is a major curriculum element in the Certificate in Investment Performance Measurement (CIPM) program.

calculation input data and presentation elements, such as dispersion statistics, may improve the quality of information available to the firm's investment decision makers.

Only investment **firms** may claim compliance with the GIPS standards.[3] Consultants, software houses, or third-party performance measurement providers such as custodians may not claim to be GIPS-compliant. Moreover, investment firms may claim to be compliant only on a firmwide basis (Provision II.0.A.1).[4] GIPS compliance cannot be claimed only for some of an investment firm's products, nor for specific composites.[5] A firm's claim of compliance signifies, among other things, that the firm's performance measurement data inputs, processes, and return calculation methodology conform to the prescribed guidelines and that all of the firm's fee-paying discretionary **portfolios** have been assigned to a **composite.**

2.2. The Development of Performance Presentation Standards

Investors have been keeping track of their wealth for as long as capital markets have existed. The industry standards for performance measurement and presentation as we know them today, however, have resulted from developments that began in the late 1960s and gathered speed in the 1990s.

Peter O. Dietz published his seminal work, *Pension Funds: Measuring Investment Performance*, in 1966. The Bank Administration Institute (BAI), a U.S.-based organization serving the financial services industry, subsequently formulated rate-of-return calculation guidelines based on Dietz's work.

In 1980, Wilshire Associates joined with a number of custodial banks to establish the Trust Universe Comparison Service (TUCS), a database of portfolio returns organized for use in peer group comparisons, and the members established standards for computing returns in order to ensure comparability.

The direct lineage of the current Global Investment Performance Standards starts with the voluntary guidelines for the North American marketplace defined by a committee of the Financial Analysts Federation. The Committee for Performance Presentation Standards published a report in the September/October 1987 issue of the *Financial Analysts Journal.* The committee's recommendations notably included using a time-weighted total return calculation; reporting performance before the effects of investment management fees; including cash in portfolio return calculations; reaching agreement with the client in advance on the starting date for performance measurement; selecting a risk- or style-appropriate benchmark for performance comparisons; and constructing and presenting accurate, asset-weighted composites of investment performance. The committee strongly recommended that the Financial Analysts Federation disseminate and attempt to impose performance presentation standards for investment management organizations.[6]

---

[3]The GIPS standards refer to the investment management firm claiming compliance as the FIRM. This chapter uses boldface type for terms that are defined in the GIPS glossary (Appendix E of the Global Investment Performance Standards).

[4]The GIPS standards have three major sections: I. Introduction; II. Provisions of the Global Investment Performance Standards; and III. Verification. This chapter cites the GIPS standards by giving the major section followed by subsection identifiers.

[5]A *composite* is formally defined as an "aggregation of individual portfolios representing a similar investment mandate, objective, or strategy." The construction of composites is discussed in detail in Sections 3.7–3.10, which follow.

[6]CPPS (1987, pp. 8–11).

Another milestone was the development of the Association for Investment Management and Research (AIMR) Performance Presentation Standards (AIMR-PPS®). AIMR, founded in January 1990 when the Financial Analysts Federation merged with the Institute of Chartered Financial Analysts, subsequently became CFA Institute. In 1990, as one of its first actions, the AIMR Board of Governors endorsed the AIMR-PPS standards. The Board also established the AIMR Performance Presentation Standards Implementation Committee to review the proposed Standards and to seek industry input prior to formal implementation. The AIMR-PPS standards were implemented, and the first edition of the *AIMR Performance Presentation Standards Handbook* was published in 1993.

Acting independently, the Investment Management Consultants Association (IMCA) also issued performance measurement guidelines in 1993. IMCA endorses the AIMR-PPS standards, which apply to investment firms. Updated in 1998, the IMCA standards complement the AIMR-PPS standards with guidelines for investment consultants in analyzing data obtained from investment managers in the course of manager searches as well as in reporting, monitoring, and analyzing performance results.[7]

In 1995, AIMR formed the Global Performance Presentation Standards Subcommittee, reporting to the Implementation Committee, to address international performance issues and to develop global standards for presenting investment performance. The following year, AIMR revised the AIMR-PPS standards, stipulating new requirements, such as the inclusion of accrued income in bond market values in both the numerator and the denominator of return calculations, and presenting new recommendations, such as the use of temporary accounts for significant cash flows. In 1997, AIMR released the second edition of the *AIMR Performance Presentation Standards Handbook* incorporating these and other changes.

In 1998, after circulating several preliminary drafts among industry participants, the Global PPS Subcommittee released the Global Investment Performance Standards for public comment. The AIMR Board of Governors formally endorsed the GIPS standards early in 1999 and established the Investment Performance Council (IPC) later that year to manage the further development and promulgation of the GIPS standards. (We discuss the IPC's ongoing role below.) In 2001, the AIMR-PPS standards were adopted by the AIMR Board of Governors and the IPC as the U.S. and Canadian Version of GIPS. The first edition of *The Global Investment Performance Standards (GIPS) Handbook* was published in 2002 in a loose-leaf format to accommodate changes and additions to the Standards with the passage of time.

By the end of 2004, IPC-endorsed local standards had been adopted—either verbatim in English, or in a straightforward Translation of GIPS, or in a Country Version of GIPS—in 25 countries throughout North America, Europe, Africa, and the Asia Pacific region. (We discuss translations and Country Versions of GIPS in the next section.) In 2005, the IPC issued revised Global Investment Performance Standards funded by CFA Institute and co-sponsored locally by more than 25 other key industry groups. The present chapter is based on the 2005 edition of the GIPS standards, which reflect globally applicable best practices from all regional standards.

2.3. Governance of the GIPS Standards

With the release of the GIPS standards in 1999, the Investment Performance Council (IPC) was formed to serve as the committee responsible for maintaining the Standards. It consisted of approximately 36 members from a variety of fields within the global investment industry

[7]For further information, see www.imca.org/standards.

representing 15 countries. From 1999 to 2006, the IPC focused on its principle goal: to have all countries adopt the GIPS standards as the standard for investment firms seeking to present historical investment performance.

The IPC strongly encouraged countries without an investment performance standard in place to accept the GIPS standards as the local norms, either in English or in a Translation of GIPS (TG).

Due to local regulation or to well-accepted practice, some countries were found to have additional requirements over and above those set forth in the GIPS standards. In these cases, the IPC promoted an approach designated as a "Country Version of GIPS" (CVG). The country would adopt the GIPS standards as their core standards, supplemented by additional provisions as necessary to meet local requirements. If the CVG included any differences that could not be justified on the basis of regulatory stipulations or widely recognized practice, the local sponsor (typically a professional association) was required to provide a transition plan for eliminating the differences within a specified period.

In February 2005, the IPC revised the GIPS standards and created a single global standard for investment performance reporting. The revised Standards grant all CVG-compliant firms reciprocity for periods prior to January 1, 2006, such that their CVG-compliant history will satisfy the GIPS requirement, discussed below, to show at least a five-year track record in performance presentations.

In order to facilitate involvement from all industry stakeholders and provide a necessary conduit for the collaboration of ideas and mutual engagement in the process, the IPC was transformed in 2006 into the GIPS Executive Committee (EC). Consisting of nine members, the EC serves as the effective decision-making authority for the GIPS standards. The EC created four standing subcommittees—the GIPS Council, the Interpretations Subcommittee, the Practitioners/Verifiers Subcommittee, and the Investors/Consultants Subcommittee—to support the work of the EC.

The GIPS Council works directly with all Country Sponsors in the development, promotion, and maintenance of the GIPS standards.

The Interpretations Subcommittee has the responsibility of ensuring the integrity, consistency, and applicability of the GIPS standards by providing guidance to address new issues presented by the global investment industry. Firms claiming compliance with the GIPS standards must also comply with all applicable interpretations and guidance.

The Practitioners/Verifiers Subcommittee is composed of third-party service providers, including verifiers, software developers, and custodians, that assist investment management firms in the implementation and application of the Standards. This Subcommittee provides a forum to discuss the application, implementation, and impact of the Standards. Verification, discussed below, refers to an investment firm's voluntarily engaging an independent third party to test the firm's performance measurement and composite construction procedures in order to validate the firm's claim of compliance with the GIPS standards.

The Investors/Consultants Subcommittee is composed of investors (and those representing investors), regulators and consultants from the investment industry, including clients, plan sponsors, retail investors, and others, to create a forum for the end user of investment performance information. This subcommittee will be responsible for assisting in the development and direction of the GIPS standards.

2.4. Overview of the GIPS Standards

To orient the reader, we present an outline of the Global Investment Performance Standards document in Exhibit 13-1. Section I, "Introduction," provides extensive information about

EXHIBIT 13-1 Global Investment Performance Standards

PREFACE: BACKGROUND OF THE GIPS STANDARDS

I. INTRODUCTION
   - A. Preamble: Why Is a Global Standard Needed?
   - B. Vision Statement
   - C. Objectives
   - D. Overview
   - E. Scope
   - F. Compliance
   - G. Implementing a Global Standard

II. PROVISIONS OF THE GLOBAL INVESTMENT PERFORMANCE STANDARDS
   - 0. Fundamentals of Compliance
   - 1. Input Data
   - 2. Calculation Methodology
   - 3. Composite Construction
   - 4. Disclosures
   - 5. Presentation and Reporting
   - 6. Real Estate
   - 7. Private Equity

III. VERIFICATION
   - A. Scope and Purpose of Verification
   - B. Required Verification Procedures
   - C. Detailed Examinations of Investment Performance Presentations

Appendix A: Sample GIPS-Compliant Presentations
Appendix B: Sample List and Description of Composites
Appendix C: GIPS Advertising Guidelines
Appendix D: Private Equity Valuation Principles
Appendix E: GIPS Glossary

Source: www.cfainstitute.org.

the Standards. Rather than paraphrasing and commenting on every point made in the Introduction, we will highlight certain concepts in the following paragraphs.

The vision statement in the Introduction to the Global Investment Performance Standards reads, "A global investment performance standard leads to readily accepted presentations of investment performance that (1) present performance results that are readily comparable among investment management firms without regard to geographic location, and (2) facilitate a dialogue between investment managers and their prospective clients about the critical issues of how the manager achieved performance results and determines future investment strategies" (Section I.B.5).

This statement articulates two primary goals of the GIPS standards. First, as we have seen, the establishment and acceptance of global standards enables firms to compete for new business around the world on an equal footing. This equality expands the marketplace for all investment firms by eliminating barriers to entry.

Second, global standards for performance presentation, including the requirement that a firm show each composite's investment returns alongside the returns of an appropriate benchmark, can lead to an informative discussion about the firm's investment decision-making process. The prospective client might ask, for instance, why the composite outperformed the benchmark in some periods and not in others, inviting the firm's spokespersons to explain past returns and to describe how the investment product is positioned for the future.

It must be stressed in this context that reviewing properly calculated, fully disclosed historical results does not exempt the prospective client from a thorough investigation of the candidate firm's background, resources, and capabilities for the mandate under consideration. Due diligence in selecting an investment manager includes, among many other important elements, examining a firm's regulatory history, the experience and professional credentials of its decision makers, the soundness of its investment philosophy, and the nature of its risk controls. At a minimum, however, the firm's representatives should be able to explain the sources of its past returns reasonably, credibly, and insightfully in light of the firm's investment discipline and the then-prevailing capital market environment.

The Introduction to the GIPS standards also spells out the Standards' objectives (Section I.C). Briefly paraphrased, they are to obtain worldwide acceptance of a common standard for calculating and presenting investment performance fairly, uniformly, and with full disclosure; to ensure accurate and consistent performance data for reporting, record keeping, marketing, and presentation; to promote fair, global competition for all markets without creating barriers to entry for new investment management firms; and to foster the notion of industry self-regulation on a global basis. Performance presentation standards thoughtfully and carefully designed by well-informed industry participants who are committed to the ethical principles of fairness and full disclosure may serve to limit the need for expanded regulatory intervention in this area.

In Section I.D, "Overview," the Introduction also states certain key characteristics of the GIPS standards. Among them is the proposition that the Global Investment Performance Standards are *ethical* standards intended to ensure fair representation and full disclosure of an investment firm's performance history. As ethical standards, they are voluntary. Firms that voluntarily choose to comply with the GIPS standards, however, must apply them with the goal of full disclosure and fair representation. This goal is likely to require more than bare compliance with the minimum requirements—for instance, when specific performance situations arise on which the Standards are silent or open to interpretation. In such cases, disclosures other than those required by the Standards may be necessary, and additional or supplemental information may contribute to a full explanation of the performance.

The GIPS standards apply to investment management firms, not to individuals. (We will return to the definition of the firm for the purpose of compliance with the Standards.) Relying on the integrity of input data, the Standards require firms to use certain calculation and presentation methods and to make certain disclosures. In order to promote fair representations of performance, the GIPS standards require firms to include *all* actual fee-paying, discretionary portfolios in aggregates, known as composites, defined by strategy or investment objective. The GIPS standards further require firms to show history for a minimum of five years, or since inception of the firm or composite if either has existed for less than five years. After presenting at least five years of compliant history, the firm must add annual performance each subsequent year building to a 10-year compliant track record.

The GIPS standards consist of **requirements,** which *must* be followed in order for a firm to claim compliance, and **recommendations,** which are optional but *should* be followed because they represent best practice in performance presentation. When the GIPS standards conflict with local law or regulation, the Standards obligate firms to comply with the local requirements and to make full disclosure of the conflict in the performance presentation. The GIPS standards will continue to evolve as the industry tackles additional aspects of performance measurement and recognizes the implications of new investment technologies, instruments, and strategies. For example, certain recommendations in the current version of the GIPS standards might become requirements in the future.

The Introduction additionally includes remarks on the scope of the Standards (see Section I.E). The Standards apply worldwide: Firms from any country may come into compliance with the Standards, and doing so will facilitate their participation in the investment management industry at home and abroad. Firms previously claiming compliance with an IPC-endorsed Country Version of GIPS are granted reciprocity to claim compliance with the revised GIPS Standards for historical periods prior to January 1, 2006. If the firm previously claimed compliance with a CVG, the firm must at a minimum continue to show the historical CVG-compliant track record up to 10 years, or since inception if the firm has been in existence for fewer than 10 years.

As stated in Section I.F, "Compliance," the effective date of the revised Standards is January 1, 2006. (As we will detail in addressing the provisions of the Standards, certain requirements do not take effect until specified later dates. They should be considered recommendations in the interim.) Firms must meet all the requirements set forth in the GIPS standards to claim compliance with the Standards. There can be no exceptions. Accordingly, firms must take all steps necessary to ensure that they have met all the requirements before claiming compliance with the GIPS standards. The GIPS standards acknowledge the role and value of independent third-party performance measurement and composite construction services.

Finally, Section I.G, "Implementing a Global Standard," recognizes the vital part that local sponsoring organizations play in the effective implementation and ongoing administration of the GIPS standards within their countries. Country sponsors link the GIPS EC and the local markets in which investment managers conduct their business. In addition to supporting the adoption of the Standards, country sponsors will ensure that their country's interests are taken into account as the governing body continues to develop the Standards. The GIPS standards also encourage regulators to recognize the benefit of investment management firms' voluntary compliance with standards representing global best practices, to consider enforcing sanctions on false claims of compliance with the GIPS standards as fraudulent advertising, and to advocate independent verification services.

Implementation (1)

Management Commitment. Senior management's stated commitment to the spirit and objectives of the Standards and steadfast willingness to invest the necessary time and resources are essential for a firm to achieve compliance with the GIPS standards. The implementation effort is most likely to succeed if senior management makes achieving compliance a high priority; communicates the importance of the initiative throughout the firm; oversees the preparation of a comprehensive plan; and establishes an adequate budget, with particular attention to information systems requirements.

The GIPS standards are ethical standards, and compliance is not just another marketing tool. Merely adopting the GIPS standards as a means of passing the initial screening in RFP competitions may lead the firm to take shortcuts that ultimately compromise its application of the Standards.

Some firms may wrongly assume that implementation of the GIPS standards involves "re-crunching" a few numbers and reformatting performance presentation tables. In fact, achieving compliance is a complex, challenging, and potentially expensive undertaking.

A firm must also have a high level of commitment from its investment management, operational, administrative, and sales staffs. Achieving and maintaining compliance with the

GIPS standards typically involves an investment firm's Portfolio Accounting, Market Data Services, Information Systems, Portfolio Management, Marketing, and Compliance groups, as well as the Performance Measurement team. It is a complex process for investment management organizations to define and document policies, gather and validate input data, calculate rates of return, construct and maintain meaningful composites, and present investment results wholly in compliance with the GIPS standards. Careful planning with the active participation of diverse organizational units is a critical element of the implementation project.

3. PROVISIONS OF THE GIPS STANDARDS

We turn now to the specific provisions of the GIPS standards. Section II, Provisions of the Global Investment Performance Standards, presents firmwide requirements and recommendations in subsections addressing the fundamentals of compliance, input data, calculation methodology, composite construction, disclosures, and presentation and reporting. In addition, the Standards include particular provisions for two asset classes requiring special treatment: real estate and private equity.

3.1. Fundamentals of Compliance

Section II.0, "Fundamentals of Compliance," opens with a prime requirement: The GIPS standards must be applied on a firmwide basis (Provision II.0.A.1). That is to say, firms cannot claim to be in compliance with the Standards with regard only to certain asset classes, investment strategies, products, or composites.

To comply with the GIPS standards, a firm must be an investment firm, subsidiary, or division *held out to clients or potential clients as a distinct business entity* (Provision II.0.A.2; emphasis added). The GIPS glossary entry defines a **distinct business entity** as a "unit, division, department, or office that is organizationally and functionally segregated from other units, divisions, departments, or offices and retains discretion over the assets it manages and should have autonomy over the investment decision-making process." Possible criteria for identifying a distinct business entity are the organization being a legal entity, having a distinct market or client type, or using a separate and distinct investment process. The way in which the investment management organization is held out to the public is a key factor in defining the firm. For example, if a unit of a larger company specializes in providing investment management services to private clients, and is marketed as a specialist in meeting the investment needs of high-net-worth individuals and family offices, then that organizational unit might qualify as a "firm" for the purpose of GIPS compliance. Certainly, however, the unit's entitlement to be considered a firm under the GIPS standards could be justified if it additionally were incorporated as a subsidiary and had its own dedicated financial analysts, portfolio managers, and traders located in a separate building or area of the company and reporting through a separate chain of command to the parent organization's senior management.

In view of the complexity of modern organizational structures, it may require judgment to determine if a given unit properly meets the definition of a firm. The decision has immediate and lasting practical consequences, however. Because the GIPS standards apply firmwide, the definition of the firm will determine the extent of the initial implementation and ongoing compliance activities. Furthermore, as we will see, the presentation and reporting requirements of the GIPS standards include displaying the percentage of total firm assets represented by a composite or the amount of total firm assets at the end of each annual period (Provision II.5.A.1.c). **Total firm assets** are all assets (whether or not discretionary or fee-paying) for which a firm has investment management responsibility, including assets managed by subadvisers that the firm has authority to select. The definition of the firm establishes the boundaries for determining total firm assets. In addition, subsequent changes in a firm's organization are not permitted to lead to alteration of historical composite results.

Set forth in Sections II.0.A.1–5, the requirements described above are accompanied by a recommendation in Section II.0.B that firms adopt the broadest, most meaningful definition of the firm. (Recall that the GIPS standards consist of requirements, which must be followed without exception in order for a firm to claim compliance, and recommendations, which are optional but represent best practice in performance presentation.) The Standards recommend that the scope of the definition should encompass all offices operating under the same brand regardless of their geographical location and the actual name of the individual investment management companies. We may observe that defining the firm as broadly as possible reduces the likelihood of confusion among investors and regulators over the intended applicability of a claim of compliance.

Implementation (2)

Defining the Firm. For small investment management boutiques, defining the firm may be a relatively easy task, but it can prove challenging for large firms or subsidiary companies.

Consider the case of a super-regional bank whose trust department consists of two separate and distinct divisions, Personal Trust and Institutional Trust. The personal trust division, called Eastern National Bank Personal Trust Services, offers investment management to private individuals and families. The institutional trust division, called Eastern Institutional Asset Advisors, serves tax-exempt nonprofit organizations including pension funds and charitable foundations; it does not solicit or handle noninstitutional business. Each division has its own investment management team, traders, marketing department, administrative personnel, and accounting department. After a few years of operating in this manner, the institutional investment unit decides to achieve compliance with the GIPS standards, but the personal trust department makes a business decision not to implement the Standards. The institutional investment division may nonetheless be in position to become GIPS-compliant because it holds itself out to customers as a distinct business unit, with its own autonomous investment management, research, trading, and administrative team.

Based on the information provided, the institutional trust division seems to satisfy the conditions for defining itself as a firm for the purpose of compliance with the GIPS standards. Sample language might be, "The firm is defined as Eastern Institutional Asset Advisors, the institutional asset management division of Eastern National Bank."

On the other hand, if both divisions were to use the same investment process, approved security list, style models, etc., and merely divided assets between personal and institutional accounts, then neither division alone could compellingly claim compliance. If the senior investment personnel of the personal trust division had authority to dictate the institutional trust division's investment strategy or tactical asset allocations, or to mandate the investment of institutional clients' funds in specific securities, then the institutional trust division would likely not qualify as a distinct business unit having autonomy over the investment decision-making process and discretion over the assets it manages. If the two divisions were organizationally segregated but shared the same trading desk, the institutional trust division would have to determine whether its decision-making autonomy is compromised by the trading arrangement—if the traders merely fill the portfolio manager's orders, then the institutional trust division arguably remains autonomous, but if the traders actively participate in the identification of misvalued securities, a greater impediment to the autonomy argument would exist.

Defining the firm in such a situation calls for the scrupulous exercise of professional judgment, with due attention to the ethical objectives of the Global Investment Performance Standards.

The "fundamentals of compliance" stipulate that firms must document, in writing, their policies and procedures used in establishing and maintaining compliance with all the applicable requirements of the GIPS standards (Provision II.0.A.6). We will see that in addition to the definition of the firm, the policies and procedures to be documented include but are not limited to the criteria for including portfolios in specific composites; the timing of the inclusion and exclusion of new and terminated portfolios, respectively; the firm's definition of discretion; and the treatment of cash flows. Clearly, such documentation will be useful for employees' future reference. In addition, should the firm elect to have its compliance with the GIPS standards independently verified, the verifiers will ask to see the documents articulating all pertinent policies and procedures.

A firm may claim compliance once it has satisfied all the requirements of the GIPS standards (including those we will present later in this chapter for input data, calculation methodology, composite construction, disclosures, and presentation and reporting). Sections II.0.A.7–10 of the Standards list the requirements for a compliance claim. The firm must use the exact wording of the following compliance statement: "[Name of firm] has prepared and presented this report in compliance with the Global Investment Performance Standards (GIPS®)."[8] As we have already pointed out, no exceptions to the Standards are permitted; the firm cannot represent that it is in compliance with the GIPS standards "except for" anything. Moreover, statements characterizing the calculation methodology used in a composite presentation as being in accordance or in compliance with the GIPS standards are prohibited.[9] Statements referring to the performance of a single, existing client as being "calculated in accordance with the Global Investment Performance Standards" are also prohibited except when a GIPS-compliant firm reports the performance of an individual account to the existing client. Furthermore, managers cannot evade the requirements of composite construction and performance presentation and reporting by showing a prospective client the historical record of a selected existing client and implying in any way that the record meets the GIPS standards.

Sections II.0.A.11–15 of the Standards spell out certain "fundamental responsibilities" of GIPS-compliant firms. First, firms are expected to "make every reasonable effort" to provide all prospective clients with a compliant presentation. In other words, firms cannot choose to whom they want to present GIPS-compliant performance. (The Standards clarify that a firm will have met this requirement if a prospect has received a compliant presentation within the previous 12 months.) In addition, firms must provide a list and description of all composites to any prospective client asking for such information, and they must provide upon request a

[8]The claim of compliance given here may be used only on a fully compliant performance presentation. Different wording for compliance claims in advertisements is stipulated in the GIPS Advertising Guidelines, discussed later in this chapter.

[9]It merits repeating that only investment firms can claim to be in compliance with the GIPS standards, and such claims are legitimate only if *all* the requirements have been met. Accordingly, software developers and third-party performance measurement providers may not claim compliance with the Standards.

compliant presentation for any composite listed. Discontinued composites must remain on the list for at least five years after discontinuation.

When a GIPS-compliant firm engages in joint marketing activities with other firms, the compliant firm must be distinguished from the other firms, and the marketing communication must make clear which firm is claiming compliance.

It is also among the compliant firm's fundamental responsibilities to keep abreast of developments in the GIPS standards and to comply with the most recent interpretations and updates, notably including Guidance Statements, in accordance with their effective dates.

Finally, the GIPS standards section devoted to "Fundamentals of Compliance" recommends that firms undertake verification, the review of a firm's performance measurement processes and procedures by an independent, knowledgeable third-party verifier in order to establish that a firm claiming compliance has adhered to the Standards (Sections II.0.B.2–3). The Standards make clear that a single verification report must be issued in respect to the whole firm; verification cannot be carried out for a single composite. (We will return to this point when we discuss Section III of the Global Investment Performance Standards, "Verification.") Firms that have been verified are encouraged to add a disclosure to composite presentations or advertisements concerning this fact. The verification disclosure language should read, "[Name of firm] has been verified for the periods [dates] by [name of verifier]. A copy of the verification report is available upon request."

3.2. Input Data

Before turning to time-weighted total return calculations, we will discuss the necessary input data. We observed above that accurate input data are a key characteristic of the GIPS standards. In fact, the Standards rely on the integrity of input data, because correct rates of return obviously cannot be computed from incorrect asset values and transaction records. Accurately calculated results presuppose accurate inputs.

The provisions for input data are laid out in Sections II.1.A (requirements) and II.1.B (recommendations) of the GIPS standards. The first requirement is basic: All data and information necessary to support a firm's performance presentation and to perform the required calculations must be captured and maintained. The need for a firm to obtain the inputs required for compliant rate-of-return calculations and performance presentations is self-evident, although not always easily accomplished. "Maintaining" or storing the data and information, as required by the GIPS standards, is sound business practice, similar to documenting the firm's performance-related policies and procedures. Only if the historical input data have been kept can return calculations be replicated for clients, in the event that questions arise, as well as for regulators and verifiers.

There are three central input data concepts having to do with asset valuations. First, portfolio valuations must be based on **market values,** not cost or book values (Provision II.1.A.2). Second, **trade-date accounting** is required for periods beginning January 1, 2005 (Provision II.1.A.5). Third, **accrual accounting** must be used for fixed-income securities and all other assets that accrue interest income (Provision II.1.A.6). Let us consider each of these provisions in turn.

Because market values reflect the prices at which assets could be sold in the marketplace, they represent in aggregate the portfolio's worth—its fair economic value—as of the valuation date. Cost is pertinent to performance measurement only insofar as it reflects the holding's beginning market value. Book value, an accounting convention, is also irrelevant. (Roughly speaking, a financial asset's book value is its cost adjusted for the accretion of income and the amortization of any discount or premium.) For performance measurement, as opposed to financial or tax accounting, it does not matter whether gains and losses are realized or unrealized.[10] Along with investment income, the significant factors are the magnitude and direction of change in the assets' aggregate market value over the measurement period.

Firms are expected to use the best available information in calculating performance, but valuation sources and methods vary with an asset's liquidity. In the case of frequently traded assets in developed capital markets, values reflecting recent purchase and sale transactions are readily available from recognized commercial pricing services. Valuing illiquid real assets and thinly traded securities such as private equities, however, is more complex. We will consider real estate valuation methods and the GIPS Private Equity Valuation Principles later.

A firm's judicious selection of asset-pricing sources is a key element in achieving the fair representation of investment performance. When consultants and custodial banks providing performance measurement services to institutional clients reconcile the rates of return they calculate with those reported by their clients' investment managers, valuation differences frequently are the primary cause of variances that exceed tolerance ranges. Managers sometimes challenge the custodian's valuations, contending that their daily transactional activity gives them better information about market-clearing prices than the custodian can derive secondhand from commercial market data services. Whatever the merits of this argument in specific cases, the fact remains that ascertaining the most correct asset market values is essential for the fair representation of performance. In the spirit of the GIPS standards, managers should use pricing sources and procedures that reflect objectively established market values consistently. Switching from one source to another so as to improve stated performance at the end of a reporting period is ethically indefensible. Should the firm undertake the verification process, the verifier must determine the firm's policy with regard to the market valuation of investment securities. (See "Required Verification Procedures," Section III.B.1.d.vi.)

The GIPS standards require that firms use trade-date accounting for the purpose of performance measurement for periods beginning January 1, 2005 (Provision II.1.A.5). This requirement is related to the mandatory use of market values. A portfolio manager makes purchase and sale decisions based on current market conditions. (Even holding a security may be considered an investment decision, continuously renewed, to "buy" the security, or equivalently not to sell it and reinvest the proceeds in another security, at the current market value.) The final objective of performance measurement is to quantify the value added by investment management, and the portfolio manager's determinations to buy or hold undervalued securities and to sell overvalued securities reflect her appraisal of those securities' relative attractiveness at the time of her decisions. For the purposes of the GIPS standards, under trade-date accounting the "transaction is reflected in the portfolio on the date of the purchase or sale, and not on the settlement date." Settlement—the actual exchange of a security for cash at the price agreed on when the trade was executed—may take place days later. **Settlement-date accounting** is defined as "recognizing the asset or liability on the date in which the exchange of cash, securities, and paperwork involved in a transaction is completed." If the trade and settlement dates straddle the end date of a performance measurement period, then return comparisons between portfolios that use settlement-date accounting, on one hand, and portfolios that use trade-date accounting, or benchmarks, on the other, may be invalid. The principle behind requiring trade-date accounting is to ensure that no significant lag occurs between a trade's execution and its reflection in the portfolio's performance. For compliance with the GIPS standards, the trade-date accounting requirement is considered to be satisfied

[10]Note, however, that cost or book values and realized gains and losses are pertinent for after-tax performance calculations, discussed later.

EXHIBIT 13-2 Frequency and Timing of Portfolio Valuations

For Periods...	Portfolios Must Be Valued...
Prior to January 1, 2001	At least quarterly
Between January 1, 2001, and January 1, 2010	At least monthly
Beginning January 1, 2010	On the date of all large external cash flows As of the calendar month-end or the last business day of the month[11]

provided that transactions are recorded and recognized consistently and within normal market practice, up to three days after trade date.

The GIPS standards also stipulate that accrual accounting must be used for fixed-income securities and all other assets that accrue interest income (Provision II.1.A.6). This provision is also related to the market valuation of assets. When a conventional bond is sold, it will be exchanged for cash in an amount that reflects not only the agreed-upon price of the instrument but also the seller's entitlement to interest earned but not yet paid. Similarly, for GIPS-compliant performance, interest income on an asset that is held must be recognized as it is earned versus when it is received. Accordingly, interest income earned but not yet received must be included in the market value of fixed-income securities and all other assets that accrue interest income. With respect to dividend-paying equities, the GIPS standards recommend that dividends be accrued and reflected in the securities' market values as of the ex-dividend date (Provision II.1.B.1).

In addition to the key valuation-related provisions explained above, the input data requirements of the GIPS standards specify the frequency and timing of portfolio valuations (Provisions II.1.A.3–4). Exhibit 13-2 presents the pertinent requirements.

External cash flows are cash, securities, or assets that enter or exit a portfolio. The GIPS glossary defines external cash flows as "cash, securities, or assets that enter or exit a portfolio." The Standards do not quantify "large" external cash flows; firms are required to define composite-specific amounts or percentages that constitute large external cash flows. Later in this chapter, we examine the significance of cash flows for rate-of-return calculations.

The Standards additionally require that, for periods beginning January 1, 2006, the firm's composites, and necessarily the portfolios within the composites, must have consistent beginning and ending *annual* valuation dates. Unless the composite is reported on a noncalendar fiscal year, the beginning and ending valuation dates must be at calendar year-end or on the last business day of the year (Provision II.1.A.7).

As a practical matter, the GIPS standards' input data requirements and recommendations have critically important implications for the design of a firm's performance measurement system, including its interface with the firm's portfolio accounting system. Management must be conclusively assured that portfolio valuations are performed properly and that all the data necessary for performance calculations and presentations are captured and maintained.

Implementation (3)

Input Data. Typically, the firm's portfolio accounting system is the primary source of data inputs to the performance measurement system. (The accounting system may itself have

[11] For periods before 1 January 2010, the Standards recommend but do not require that valuations be done as of calendar month-end or the last business day of the month (Standard II.1.B.3).

automated feeds from other sources, including the trading system for security transactions and external data services for market valuations.) What we may call "performance accounting"—the compilation of data inputs for rate-of-return calculations—differs from financial accounting, however, and the differences must be recognized when designing an interface between the portfolio accounting system and the performance measurement system. For instance, book values and the distinction between realized and unrealized capital gains and losses are necessary for financial accounting but inappropriate or irrelevant for before-tax performance measurement. Convertible and hybrid securities must be treated consistently across time and within composites (Provision II.3.A.6). Investment management fees may require special treatment. A net-of-fee return is defined as the gross return reduced by the **investment management fee.** If investment management fees are paid directly from the client's account, they must be treated as external cash flows for gross-of-fee return calculations; if they are not paid directly from the client's account, they must be attributed to the portfolio and deducted for net-of-fee performance calculations. In order to meet the requirements—and, optimally, the recommendations—of the GIPS standards for input data, calculation methodology, composite construction, and performance presentation and reporting, the firm must comprehensively address these and many other accounting- and system-related issues.

3.3. Calculation Methodology: Time-Weighted Total Return

The GIPS standards mandate the use of a total rate of return, called total return for short (Provision II.2.A.1). Total return is the most comprehensive and accurate expression of investment results because it reflects the change in portfolio value during the measurement period, taking into account not only income but also realized and unrealized gains and losses. (Recall from our discussion of input data that, for performance measurement, it does not matter whether gains and losses are transactionally realized. What matters is the change in market value.) In other words, total return captures both the return from investment income and the return from capital gains or losses.

In the simplest case, when no external cash flows (i.e., client-initiated additions to or withdrawals from invested assets) occur during the period, calculating total return is straightforward:

$$r_t = \frac{\text{MV}_1 - \text{MV}_0}{\text{MV}_0} \tag{13-1}$$

where r_t is the total return for period t, MV_1 is the full market value of the portfolio, including accrued income, at the end of the period; and MV_0 is the portfolio's market value, including accrued income, at the beginning of the period. (Recall that the requirement to include accrued interest income in market values of fixed-income securities appears in Provision II.1.A.6, and the recommendation that accrual accounting should be used for dividends as of the ex-dividend date appears in Provision II.1.B.1.) Equation 13-1 assumes that income received remains in the portfolio and expresses return as the ratio of the change in market value during the period to the market value at the start of the period. Despite its extreme simplicity, the total return formula shown above produces a perfectly accurate representation of investment results in a single period with no external cash flows. As we will see, this formula is also used to calculate subperiod results under the optimal "intraperiod valuation" method when external cash flows occur.

Most portfolios, of course, do have external cash flows. A pension fund, for example, routinely has additions to capital in the form of employer and employee contributions, as well as withdrawals to meet current liabilities. The fund's investment advisers, therefore, expect to see transfers into and out of the portfolios they manage on behalf of the beneficiaries. In evaluating an investment firm, the effect of such contributions and withdrawals should be removed from the return calculation because the timing and amount of external cash flows are typically controlled not by the firm but by the client (in this case, the pension plan sponsor). Because performance measurement attempts to quantify the value added by investment decisions, the GIPS standards require the use of time-weighted rates of return, or approximations to time-weighted rates of return, to eliminate the impact of external cash flows on the return calculation.

Provision II.2.A.2 specifies the use of **time-weighted rates of return** that adjust for external cash flows.[12] At a minimum, for periods beginning January 1, 2005, firms must approximate rates of return that adjust for daily weighted external cash flows, and for periods beginning January 1, 2010, firms must value portfolios on the date of all large external cash flows. (In the interim, Provision II.2.B.3 recommends that firms value portfolios on the date of all large external cash flows.) We will return to the definition of "large" external cash flows below.

The most accurate way to calculate a total return for a measurement period in which external cash flows occur is to value the portfolio whenever an external cash flow occurs, compute a subperiod return, and geometrically chain-link subperiod returns expressed in relative form according to the following formula:

$$r_{twr} = (1 + r_{t,1}) \times (1 + r_{t,2}) \times \ldots \times (1 + r_{t,n}) - 1 \qquad (13\text{-}2)$$

where r_{twr} is the time-weighted total return for the entire period and $r_{t,1}$ through $r_{t,n}$ are the subperiod returns. We explicitly point out that Provision II.2.A.2 requires periodic returns to be geometrically linked—that is, converted to relative form $(1 + r)$ and multiplied.

For example, consider a portfolio with a beginning market value of \$100,000 as of May 31, 2005, a market value of \$109,000 on June 5, 2005 (including a cash contribution of \$10,000 received that day), and an ending market value of \$110,550 on June 30, 2005. Consider that the first subperiod ends and the second begins on the cash flow date, such that the ending market value for subperiod 1 is \$99,000 (\$109,000 less the contribution of \$10,000) and the beginning market value for Subperiod 2, including the contribution, is \$109,000. The portfolio's true time-weighted return using the intraperiod valuation method is 0.41 percent, computed as follows:

$$r_{t,1} = \frac{MV_1 - MV_0}{MV_0} = \frac{(109,000 - 10,000) - 100,000}{100,000}$$

$$= \frac{99,000 - 100,000}{100,000} = -0.01$$

$$r_{t,2} = \frac{MV_1 - MV_0}{MV_0} = \frac{110,550 - 109,000}{109,000} = 0.0142$$

$$r_{twr} = (1 + r_{t,1}) \times (1 + r_{t,2}) - 1 = [1 + (-0.01)] \times (1 + 0.0142) - 1$$

$$= 1.0041 - 1 = 0.0041 = 0.41\%$$

Geometric linking, as shown here, is correct (and required by the GIPS standards) because returns are compounded and so are not additive but multiplicative.

---

[12]The GIPS glossary defines a *time-weighted rate of return* as a "calculation that computes period by period returns on an investment and removes the effects of external cash flows, which are generally client driven, and best reflects the firm's ability to manage assets according to a specified strategy or objective."

Assuming the input data are valid, the intraperiod valuation method illustrated above gives truly accurate total returns. The GIPS governance body recognizes, however, that intraperiod portfolio valuations are costly for firms in terms of both the security price data required and the systems capabilities needed to store and process the data. As noted, in the current version of the GIPS standards, portfolio valuations on the date of all large external cash flows is recommended now and will be required for periods beginning January 1, 2010. In the meantime, however, GIPS-compliant firms can use certain approximation methods to compute estimated time-weighted returns.

For periods prior to January 1, 2005, cash flows can be assumed to occur at the midpoint of the measurement period. The Original Dietz method reflects this midpoint assumption:

$$r_{Dietz} = \frac{MV_1 - MV_0 - CF}{MV_0 + (0.5 \times CF)} \tag{13-3}$$

where CF is the net external cash flow for the period.

Using the same example, the Original Dietz formula gives a return of 0.52 percent:

$$\begin{aligned} r_{Dietz} &= \frac{MV_1 - MV_0 - CF}{MV_0 + (0.5 \times CF)} \\ &= \frac{110,550 - 100,000 - 10,000}{100,000 + (0.5 \times 10,000)} = 0.0052 = 0.52\% \end{aligned}$$

A time-weighted total return calculation that adjusts for *daily* weighted cash flows is required for periods after January 1, 2005. Examples of acceptable approaches are the Modified Dietz method and the Modified Internal Rate of Return (Modified IRR) method, both of which weight each cash flow by the proportion of the measurement period it is held in the portfolio.

The formula for estimating the time-weighted rate of return using the Modified Dietz method is

$$r_{ModDietz} = \frac{MV_1 - MV_0 - CF}{MV_0 + \sum(CF_i \times w_i)} \tag{13-4}$$

where $\sum(CF_i \times w_i)$ is the sum of each cash flow multiplied by its weight and $CF = \sum CF_i$. The weight (w_i) is simply the proportion of the measurement period, in days, that each cash flow has been in the portfolio:

$$w_i = \frac{CD - D_i}{CD} \tag{13-5}$$

where CD is the total number of calendar days in the period and D_i is the number of calendar days from the beginning of the period that cash flow CF_i occurs. (Note that this formula assumes that cash flows occur at the end of the day.)[13] In our example, there is a \$10,000 contribution on June 5, so $D_i = 5$, and there are 30 days in June, so $CD = 30$. The proportion of the measurement period that the \$10,000 is in the portfolio is thus

$$\begin{aligned} w_i &= \frac{CD - D_i}{CD} = \frac{30 - 5}{30} \\ &= \frac{25}{30} = 0.83 \end{aligned}$$

[13]Cash flows can also be assumed to occur at the beginning of the day. In that case, the weight factor is adjusted to add another day to the period of time the cash flow is in the portfolio: $w_i = (CD - D_i + 1)/CD$. It is incumbent upon the firm to establish a policy to weight external cash flows consistently.

Applying the Modified Dietz formula to the same example gives a return of 0.51 percent:

$$r_{ModDietz} = \frac{MV_1 - MV_0 - CF}{MV_0 + \sum(CF_i \times w_i)}$$
$$= \frac{110,550 - 100,000 - 10,000}{100,000 + [10,000 \times (25/30)]} = 0.0051 = 0.51\%$$

The Modified or Linked IRR method is another estimation approach acceptable prior to January 1, 2010. This method determines the internal rate of return (IRR) for the period, adjusted to take into effect the timing of cash flows. The Modified IRR is the value of r that satisfies the following equation:

$$\text{Ending Market Value} = MV_1 = \sum[CF_i \times (1+r)^{w_i}] + MV_0(1+r) \qquad (13\text{-}6)$$

where the exponent, w_i, is as previously defined the ratio of the amount of time CF_i is in the portfolio to the total time in the measurement period. The equation is solved iteratively by a trial-and-error procedure, settling on the value of r that makes the series of cash flows equal to the ending market value.[14] The Modified IRR method is computationally intensive, but programs are available for solving the equation efficiently. (Some Modified IRR programs use the Modified Dietz return as an initial estimate or seed value.) Applying the Modified IRR method to the simple example used earlier in this section gives a result of 0.51 percent, the same as the rate of return found with the Modified Dietz method.

Bear in mind that approximation methods such as Modified Dietz and Modified IRR will not meet the GIPS standards for periods after January 1, 2010, when firms will be required to value portfolios on the date of all large external cash flows.

3.4. Return Calculations: External Cash Flows

In the previous section, different methodologies for calculating a rate of return from a single set of input data gave different answers. To recapitulate:

Inputs:

Market value on May 31: \$100,000

Cash flow on June 5: +\$10,000

Market value on June 5: \$109,000 (after the cash flow)

Market value on June 30: \$110,550

Solutions:

True time-weighted return: 0.41 percent

Original Dietz method: 0.52 percent

Modified Dietz method: 0.51 percent

Modified IRR method: 0.51 percent

In this particular example, the estimated rates of return given by the Modified Dietz and Modified IRR methods are nearly the same as the estimated return calculated by the Original Dietz method, which assumes that the external cash flow occurred at midmonth. The external

[14]The Modified IRR method differs from the original internal rate of return method in that the exponent is the proportion of the measurement period that each cash flow is in the portfolio. Therefore, while the original IRR is a money-weighted return, the Modified IRR approximates a time-weighted return.

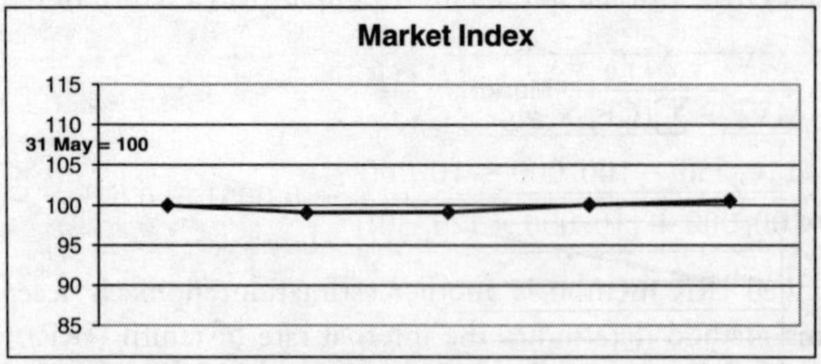

r_{twr}			r_{twr}		
	31-May Market Value	**$ 100,000**		**31-May Market Value**	**$ 100,000**
−1.00%	**5-Jun Market Value**	**$ 99,000**	**−0.93%**	**15-Jun Market Value**	**$ 99,075**
	Contribution	**$ 10,000**		**Contribution**	**$ 10,000**
	Total Market Value	**$ 109,000**		**Total Market Value**	**$ 109,075**
1.42%	**30-Jun Market Value**	**$ 110,550**	**1.35%**	**30-Jun Market Value**	**$ 110,550**
0.41%	**Modified Dietz**	**0.51%**	**0.41%**	**Modified Dietz**	**0.52%**

Source: Paula Gehr

EXHIBIT 13-3 Impact of Cash Flows in a Flat Market

cash flow causes the day-weighted estimates (0.51 percent) to vary by 10 basis points from the true time-weighted return (0.41 percent).

To appreciate the potentially distorting impact of external cash flows on estimated time-weighted rates of return, consider Exhibits 13-3 through 13-5. The exhibits depict a "market index" with a value of 100 as of May 31, and the data below each exhibit represent portfolios with a market value of $100,000 on May 31 and contributions of $10,000 received on June 5 (on the left-hand side) and June 15 (on the right-hand side). In flat and steadily rising or falling markets (illustrated in Exhibit 13-3 and Exhibit 13-4), the timing of the cash flows has a relatively modest impact on the accuracy of the estimates. We can observe this phenomenon by comparing the true time-weighted returns with those calculated using the Modified Dietz method. (Note that the Modified Dietz method is mathematically equivalent to the Original Dietz method when the cash flow occurs at the midpoint of the measurement period.) When markets are volatile, however, as illustrated in Exhibit 13-5, large external cash flows may have a material impact on the accuracy of the estimated return. The reader should work through these examples using the formulas for the true time-weighted return and the Modified Dietz method. The calculations for the first example, on the left-hand side of Exhibit 13-3, were shown above.

The GIPS standards require firms to formulate and document composite-specific policies for the treatment of external cash flows and to adhere to those policies consistently. (Provision II.2.A.2 reads in pertinent part, "External cash flows must be treated in a consistent manner with the firm's documented, composite-specific policy.") Each policy should describe the firm's methodology for computing time-weighted returns and the firm's assumptions about the timing of capital inflows and outflows. If it is the firm's rule to revalue portfolios on the date of a large external cash flow, as the GIPS standards recommend, then the firm should also state that policy.

As we have previously remarked, the Standards offer no quantitative definition of large external cash flows. Taking into account the liquidity of the market segments or asset classes and the nature of the investment strategy, firms must make their own determinations of

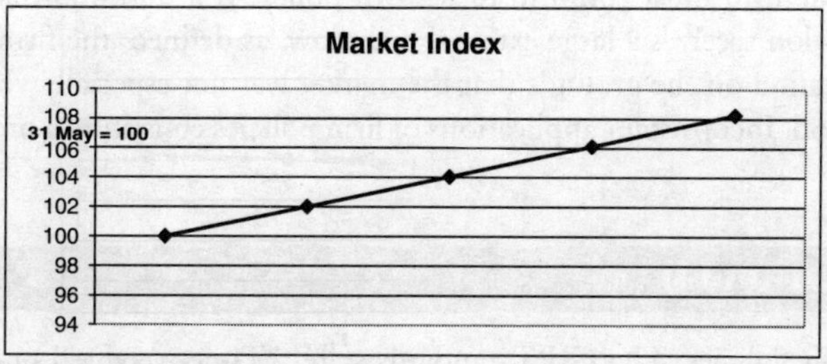

r_{twr}			r_{twr}		
	31-May Market Value	**\$ 100,000**		**31-May Market Value**	**\$ 100,000**
2.00%	**5-Jun Market Value**	**\$ 102,075**	**4.00%**	**15-Jun Market Value**	**\$ 104,000**
	Contribution	**\$ 10,000**		**Contribution**	**\$ 10,000**
	Total Market Value	**\$ 112,075**		**Total Market Value**	**\$ 114,000**
5.88%	**30-Jun Market Value**	**\$ 118,588**	**3.85%**	**30-Jun Market Value**	**\$ 118,385**
8.00%	**Modified Dietz**	**7.93%**	**8.00%**	**Modified Dietz**	**7.99%**

Source: Paula Gehr

EXHIBIT 13-4 Impact of Cash Flows in a Steadily Rising Market

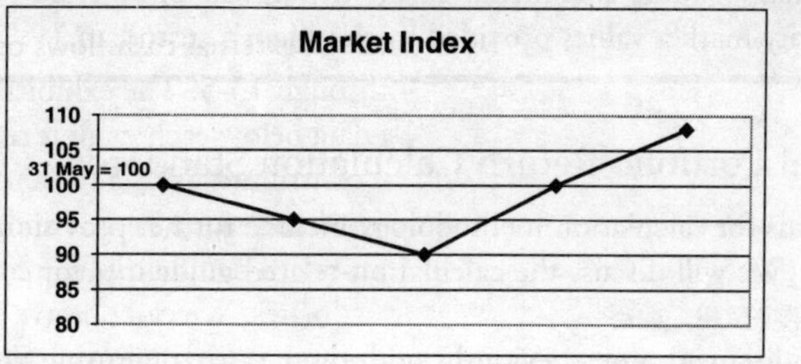

r_{twr}			r_{twr}		
	31-May Market Value	**\$ 100,000**		**31-May Market Value**	**\$ 100,000**
–5.00%	**5-Jun Market Value**	**\$ 95,000**	**–10.00%**	**15-Jun Market Value**	**\$ 90,000**
	Contribution	**\$ 10,000**		**Contribution**	**\$ 10,000**
	Total Market Value	**\$ 105,000**		**Total Market Value**	**\$ 100,000**
13.68%	**30-Jun Market Value**	**\$ 119,364**	**20.00%**	**30-Jun Market Value**	**\$ 120,000**
8.00%	**Modified Dietz**	**8.64%**	**8.00%**	**Modified Dietz**	**9.52%**

Source: Paula Gehr

EXHIBIT 13-5 Impact of Cash Flows in a Volatile Market

significance for each composite. For example, a relatively high percentage of portfolio value might be easily deployed in a developed equity market, while a lower percentage of portfolio value might be deemed the appropriate criterion for a large external cash flow in a comparatively illiquid emerging debt market.

A composite-specific policy may define a "large" external cash flow in terms of an amount or a percentage. Whatever definition a firm adopts, it must document the policy and follow it without exception. For example, if a firm defines a large external cash flow for a specific composite and states that portfolios in that composite are revalued on the date of large external cash flows, then the firm must conform to its own policy. If a portfolio that belongs to the composite in question receives a large external cash flow, as defined, the firm is not at liberty to omit the revaluation on the grounds that the market was not especially volatile during the measurement period. Inconsistent applications of firm policies constitute a breach of the GIPS standards.

Implementation (4)

Return Calculation Policies. The GIPS standards state, "Time-weighted rates of return that adjust for external cash flows must be used. Periodic returns must be geometrically linked. External cash flows must be treated in a consistent manner with the firm's documented, composite-specific policy" (excerpted from Provision II.2.A.2). The Standards also recommend, "Firms should value portfolios on the date of all large external cash flows" (Provision II.2.B.3). The following are examples of internal policy statements addressing these elements.

Portfolio return calculation methodology: "Eastern Institutional Asset Advisors employs the Modified Dietz method to compute portfolio time-weighted rates of return on a monthly basis. Returns for longer measurement periods are computed by geometrically linking the monthly returns."

Large external cash flows: "Eastern Institutional Asset Advisors revalues portfolios that belong to the Large-Cap Domestic Equity composite when capital equal to 10 percent or more of current market value is contributed or withdrawn. Intraperiod portfolio valuations are based on security market values provided by the client's custodian."

3.5. Additional Portfolio Return Calculation Standards

The GIPS standards for calculation methodology include further provisions directly affecting portfolio returns. (We will discuss the calculation-related guidelines for composites in a later section.)

The first requirement not previously addressed is that returns from cash and cash equivalents held in portfolios must be included in total return calculations (Provision II.2.A.4). One of the primary purposes of performance measurement is to enable prospective clients and, by extension, their consultants to evaluate an investment management firm's results. Within the constraints established by a client's investment policy statement (IPS), active managers often have discretion to decide what portion of a portfolio's assets to hold in cash or cash equivalents. In other words, the cash allocation decision may be under the manager's control, and thus return calculations must reflect the contribution of the cash and cash equivalents to investment results.

Consider the case of an institutional investor such as a defined-benefit pension plan sponsor. The structure of the sponsor's investment program is, generally, based on an asset allocation or, preferably, an asset/liability study identifying the optimal mix of asset classes to meet the fund's financial objectives at an acceptable level of risk. The sponsor retains investment management firms to invest the fund's assets in specific markets in accordance with the study results. For example, within the domestic equity allocation, the sponsor might hire one firm to invest a certain portion of the fund's assets in small-cap growth stocks and another firm to invest a portion in large-cap value stocks. The sponsor expects the managers to remain fully invested in their mandated market sectors at all times. The sponsor's IPS may, however, allow the managers to hold some amount (e.g., up to 5 percent of portfolio assets) in cash and cash equivalents, if only to accommodate frictional cash thrown off in the process of buying and selling securities. (The client will usually define "cash equivalents," for example, as money market instruments and fixed income securities with less than one year to maturity.) In this case, it is up to the manager to decide how much cash to hold, up to 5 percent of assets.

The total portfolio return will be higher or lower depending on how much cash the manager holds and how the equity and money markets perform relative to one another during the measurement period. A few simple scenarios based on actual historical U.S. market returns will illustrate these points. First, in a rising equity market, cash positions reduce overall portfolio returns; the higher the cash position, the lower the portfolio return. This relationship is illustrated in Exhibit 13-6, in which increasing the cash position (represented here by U.S. Treasury bills) from 1 percent to 5 percent of portfolio assets reduces the portfolio return for a three-month period by 26 basis points (0.26 percent).

In contrast, a higher cash position improves the portfolio return in a falling market. Exhibit 13-7 illustrates this result, whereby increasing the percentage of the portfolio held in cash from 1 percent to 5 percent boosts the three-month portfolio return by 11 basis points (0.11 percent).

Note that cash and cash equivalents must be included in the total return calculation even if the cash is not actually invested by the same person or group. The amount of cash available for short-term investment is more important to overall portfolio results than the money market manager's success in outperforming the short-term market. For the rising and falling equity markets described above, Exhibit 13-8 illustrates the relative impact of the portfolio manager's increasing the cash allocation from 1 percent to 5 percent and the money market trader's simultaneously achieving excess returns 50 basis points (0.5 percent) higher than Treasury bill returns. The portfolio manager's cash allocation decision has a substantially greater effect on overall portfolio returns than does the money market trader's proficiency in selecting attractive short-term investments.

The GIPS standards further require that returns be calculated after the deduction of actual—not estimated—trading expenses (Provision II.2.A.5). Trading expenses are transaction costs incurred in the purchase or sale of securities, and the performance calculation must include them because these expenses must be paid in order to execute the investment strategy.

EXHIBIT 13-6 Illustration of the Effect of Cash Holdings in Rising Markets

	1% Held in Cash		5% Held in Cash	
	Weight	Return	Weight	Return
Broad U.S. equity market index	99%	6.57%	95%	6.57%
U.S. Treasury bills	1	0.26	5	0.26
Total portfolio	100	6.51	100	6.25

EXHIBIT 13-7 Illustration of the Effect of Cash Holdings in Declining Markets

	1% Held in Cash		5% Held in Cash	
	Weight	Return	Weight	Return
Broad U.S. equity market index	99%	−2.39%	95%	−2.39%
U.S. Treasury bills	1	10.45	5	10.45
Total portfolio	100	−2.36	100	−2.25

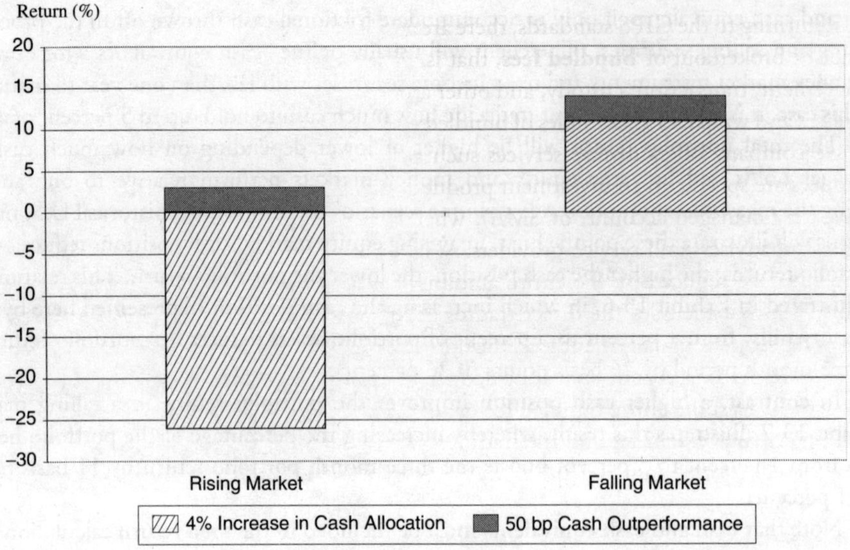

EXHIBIT 13-8 Impact of Cash on Portfolio Returns

The GIPS glossary defines **trading expenses** as the costs of buying or selling a security and notes that these costs typically take the form of brokerage commissions or spreads from either internal or external brokers. Commissions are explicit costs, generally a negotiated amount per share of common stock bought or sold, intended to compensate the broker, as the investor's agent, for arranging and settling trades. Bid–ask spreads are the difference between the price at which a dealer, acting for his firm's account, is willing to buy a security from a seller and the price at which he is willing to sell the security to a buyer. From the investor's perspective, the spread is the cost of immediacy or liquidity, and it compensates the dealer for both the cost of operations and the risk of adverse selection (the possibility that a well-informed trader has better information than the dealer has about the fundamental value of a security in the dealer's inventory).[15] Actual trading expenses are necessary input data for GIPS-compliant rate-of-return calculations.

It merits mention in this context that, as the GIPS glossary makes clear, **custody fees** should not be considered direct transaction costs, even when they are charged on a per-transaction basis. Accordingly, they are not to be included among the trading expenses required to be deducted in calculating rates of return.

From a performance measurement perspective, although transaction costs are unavoidably part of executing an investment strategy, they will naturally be higher in a portfolio with relatively greater turnover. External cash flows, whether inbound or outbound, will occasion a higher-than-normal volume of security transactions, but on an ongoing basis, a manager generally has control over portfolio turnover. A firm's trading capabilities will also affect its level of transaction costs. Although it is not a matter of compliance with the GIPS standards, the investment manager has an ethical and fiduciary responsibility to achieve best execution on behalf of clients. If a client's directed brokerage program requires the firm to channel trades through approved brokers, regular communication with the client is in order.[16]

[15]For a comprehensive treatment of these topics, the interested reader is referred to Larry Harris, *Trading and Exchanges; Market Microstructure for Practitioners* (Oxford University Press, 2003).

[16]CFA Institute addresses this and many related issues in its "Trade Management Guidelines" and "Soft Dollar Standards," available on the website at www.cfainstitute.org/standards/ethics

Returning to the GIPS standards, there are additional requirements when trading expenses cannot be broken out of **bundled fees**, that is, combined fees, which may include any mix of management, transaction, custody, and other administrative charges. The GIPS Glossary cites all-in fees and wrap fees as examples of bundled fees. All-in fee arrangements are common when a single company offers diverse services such as asset management, brokerage, and custody. Wrap fees are specific to an investment product, namely a wrap-fee account (frequently called a separately managed account, or SMA), whereby a sponsoring firm typically engages other firms as subadvisers and service providers. When trading expenses are inextricable, the gross return must be reduced by the entire amount of the bundled fee or by that portion of the bundled fee that includes the direct trading expenses. Specifically, when calculating returns gross of investment management fees, the entire bundled fee or the portion of the bundled fee that includes trading expenses must be deducted. When calculating returns net of investment management fees, the entire bundled fee or the portion(s) of the bundled fee that include the investment management fee and the trading expenses must be deducted. These requirements are presented in Provisions II.2.A.7.a–b, where it is twice reiterated that the use of estimated trading expenses is not permitted.

Finally, it remains to address a recommendation of the GIPS standards pertinent to portfolio return calculations. Standard II.2.B.1 recommends that returns be calculated net of nonreclaimable withholding taxes on dividends, interest, and capital gains. This provision applies to portfolios invested in nondomestic securities. Some countries allow certain kinds of investors to recoup a portion of withholding taxes by filing claims. Withholding taxes subject to reclamation should be accrued until such time as they are actually recovered, and withholding taxes that cannot be recovered should be treated like other transaction costs and deducted from the portfolio before returns are calculated.

3.6. Composite Return Calculation Standards

The notion of a composite is central to the GIPS standards. Because composite returns purport to convey the firm's investment results for a given strategy, style, or objective, proper composite construction is essential to achieving the Standards' ethical aims, which are fair representation and full disclosure of the firm's performance.

A composite may be thought of as a combined account composed of similar portfolios in proportion to their weights as a percent of the composite's total assets. Accordingly, the composite return is the asset-weighted average of the returns of all the individual constituent portfolios. In addition to governing the calculation methodology for portfolio returns, the GIPS standards prescribe the asset-weighting methods for composite return calculations.

Standard II.2.A.3 reads, "Composite returns must be calculated by asset-weighting the individual portfolio returns using beginning-of-period values or a method that reflects both beginning-of-period values and external cash flows." Let us explore these methods in an example. Exhibit 13-9 displays the beginning asset market values of four portfolios that, taken together, constitute a composite. The exhibit also shows the external cash flows experienced by each portfolio during the month of June. (We have seen Portfolio A before.) For completeness, the exhibit also shows each portfolio's ending market value.

Determining the percentage of total composite assets held in each portfolio at the beginning of the measurement period is straightforward. Portfolio A had a beginning market value of \$100,000, and all four portfolios combined had a beginning market value of approximately \$435,000, so the percentage held by Portfolio A is $100/434.81 = 0.23 = 23\%$.

EXHIBIT 13-9 A Composite Including Four Portfolios: Weighted External Cash Flows

	Cash Flow Weighting Factor	Portfolio ($ Thousands)				
		A	B	C	D	Total
Beginning assets (May 31)		100.00	97.40	112.94	124.47	434.81
External cash flows:						
June 5	0.83	10.00	15.00			25.00
June 8	0.73				−15.00	−15.00
June 17	0.43		−5.00			−5.00
June 24	0.20				−6.50	−6.50
June 29	0.03		−2.50		−4.00	−6.50
Ending assets (June 30)		110.55	105.20	113.30	100.50	429.55
Beginning assets + Weighted cash flows		108.30	107.63	112.94	112.10	440.97
Percent of total beginning assets		23.00%	22.40%	25.97%	28.63%	100.00%
Percent of total beginning assets + Weighted cash flows		24.56%	24.41%	25.61%	25.42%	100.00%

Note: Weighted cash flows reflect two-decimal-place precision in the weighting factors.

As we will show in a moment, under a method reflecting just beginning-of-period values, we can calculate the composite return by multiplying the individual portfolio returns by the percentage of beginning composite assets held in each portfolio and summing the products.

Determining the return impact of portfolios based on beginning assets and weighted external cash flows is a little more complex. The weighting factor, however, is already familiar from our discussion of the Modified Dietz rate-of-return calculation. Each external cash flow is weighted in proportion to percentage of the time it is held in the portfolio during the measurement period. Recall Equation 13-5:

$$w_i = \frac{\text{CD} - D_i}{\text{CD}}$$

where CD is the total number of calendar days in the period and D_i is the number of calendar days since the beginning of the period when cash flow CF_i occurs. Exhibit 13-9 showed the weighting factor computed to two decimal places with this formula for each of the days in the measurement period (the month of June) on which external cash flows occur that affect any of the portfolios in the composite. The exhibit also showed the weighted external cash flows under the two methods discussed. For the method incorporating weighted external cash flows, the sum of beginning assets and weighted external cash flows, V_p, is calculated as:

$$V_p = \text{MV}_0 + \sum(\text{CF}_i \times w_i) \tag{13-7}$$

where MV_0 is the portfolio's beginning market value and $\sum(\text{CF}_i \times w_i)$ is the sum of each portfolio's weighted external cash inflows and outflows. Note that the right-hand side in Equation 13-7 is the denominator of the Modified Dietz formula (see Equation 13-4).

The composite return is the weighted-average return of the individual portfolios that belong to that composite. Under the "beginning assets" weighting method, the composite return calculation is

$$r_C = \sum\left(r_{pi} \times \frac{MV_{0,pi}}{\sum MV_{0,pi}}\right) \tag{13-8}$$

where r_C is the composite return, r_{pi} is the return of an individual portfolio i, $MV_{0,pi}$ is the beginning market value of portfolio i, and $\sum MV_{0,pi}$ is the total beginning market value of all the individual portfolios in the composite. In other words, the composite return is the sum of the individual portfolio returns weighted in proportion to their respective percentages of aggregate beginning assets.

Under the alternate "beginning assets plus weighted cash flows" method, the return calculation uses the individual portfolios' V_P, computed above, in place of $MV_{0,p}$:

$$r_C = \sum\left(r_{pi} \times \frac{V_{pi}}{\sum V_{pi}}\right) \tag{13-9}$$

Exhibit 13-10 supplies each individual portfolio's return for the month of June and presents the composite returns resulting from these two weighting methods.

Under the "beginning assets" weighting method, the composite return shown in Exhibit 13-10 is

$$\begin{aligned} r_C &= (0.0051 \times 0.23) + (0.0028 \times 0.224) + (0.0032 \times 0.2597) + (0.0136 \times 0.2863) \\ &= 0.0065 = 0.65\% \end{aligned}$$

Similarly, the composite return under the "beginning assets plus weighted cash flows" method is

$$\begin{aligned} r_C &= (0.0051 \times 0.2456) + (0.0028 \times 0.2441) + (0.0032 \times 0.2561) + (0.0136 \times 0.2542) \\ &= 0.0062 = 0.62\% \end{aligned}$$

Mathematically astute performance analysts may already have discerned another valid way to compute composite returns under a method that correctly reflects both beginning-of-period

EXHIBIT 13-10 Composite Returns

	Percent of Beginning Assets	Percent of Beginning Assets + Weighted Cash Flows	Return for Month of June
Portfolio A	23.00%	24.56%	0.51%
Portfolio B	22.40	24.41	0.28
Portfolio C	25.97	25.61	0.32
Portfolio D	28.63	25.42	1.36
	100.00%	100.00%	
Composite Return:			
Based on beginning assets			0.65
Based on beginning assets + Weighted cash flows			0.62

values and external cash flows. Beginning assets and intraperiod external cash flows can be summed and, treating the entire composite as though it were a single portfolio, the return can be computed directly with the Modified Dietz formula. Paying attention to the direction of the cash flows, this approach can be illustrated with data from Exhibit 13-9, using Equation 13-4:

$$r_{ModDietz} = \frac{MV_1 - MV_0 - CF}{MV_0 + \sum(CF_i \times w_i)}$$

$$r_C = \frac{429.55 - 434.81 - 25 - (-15) - (-5) - (-6.5) - (-6.5)}{440.97}$$

$$= \frac{2.74}{440.97} = 0.0062 = 0.62\%$$

In the interest of ensuring that firms present composite returns with reasonable accuracy, the GIPS standards specify the required frequency of asset weighting. Provision II.2.A.6 states that for periods beginning January 1, 2006, firms must calculate composite returns by asset weighting the individual portfolio returns at least quarterly. For periods beginning January 1, 2010 composite returns must be calculated by asset weighting the individual portfolio returns at least monthly. In the meantime, Provision II.2.B.2 recommends asset weighting portfolios at least on a monthly basis. The less frequently the asset-weighting exercise is conducted, the greater the likelihood that aggregate composite returns will inaccurately reflect the constituent portfolios' performance. We will encounter this issue again, and illustrate the potential for returns to drift away from mathematically precise computations, when we discuss custom benchmark rebalancing.

3.7. Constructing Composites I—Defining Discretion

In order to prevent firms from presenting only their best-performing portfolios to prospective clients, the GIPS standards require that all of the compliant firm's actual fee-paying discretionary portfolios must be included in at least one composite. The first requirement for composite construction reads, "All actual, fee-paying, discretionary portfolios must be included in at least one composite. Although non-fee-paying discretionary portfolios may be included in a composite (with appropriate disclosures), nondiscretionary portfolios are not permitted to be included in a firm's composites" (Provision II.3.A.1).

Implementation (5)

Composite Construction: Portfolio Documentation. The GIPS standards require that all data and information necessary to support a firm's performance presentation must be captured and maintained (Provision II.1.A.1). At the outset of the implementation project, it is useful to develop a complete list of the firm's accounts. The list can then be used to check that all documentation such as investment management contracts, custody agreements, IPSs, and compliance documents are available and up to date. This exercise creates a good opportunity for managers and administrative staff to confirm that portfolios are discretionary and to verify target asset mixes, acceptable asset ranges, account size, tax status, investment restrictions, and other characteristics pertinent to the portfolios' assignment to composites. It is also advisable to conduct a formal review and update of the master account list annually. Doing so will assure that documentation is kept current and that portfolios are assigned to the correct composites, particularly if clients have modified portfolio mandates and constraints during the year. The review will also point out the need for the creation of new composites if a significant number of accounts no longer fit into existing composites or if a new investment strategy is launched.

A key term in this requirement is "discretionary." If an actual, fee-paying portfolio is discretionary, it must be included in at least one composite; if it is not discretionary, it must not be included in any composite. A portfolio is discretionary if the manager is able to implement the intended investment strategy. For example, the manager of a fully discretionary domestic mid-cap value portfolio is free to purchase any stock issued in the investor's home country that meets the pertinent market capitalization and style criteria. The firm might define mid-cap stocks as those whose market capitalization falls within a certain range. Similarly, the firm might define value stocks in terms of their price-to-earnings multiple, price-to-book ratio, dividend yield, or other characteristics intended to distinguish them from growth stocks. In line with best practice, the firm and the client will agree in advance that the portfolio's investment objective is to outperform a specified benchmark that is an appropriate measure of success in the domestic mid-cap market. For instance, the firm might construct a custom benchmark that is acceptable to the client, or the firm and the client might agree to use a commercially available index that mirrors the domestic mid-cap market.

If the client imposes restrictions on the manager's freedom to make investment decisions to buy, hold, and sell securities so as to carry out the investment strategy and achieve the portfolio's financial objectives, then the manager must consider whether the portfolio is in fact discretionary. In general, restrictions that impede the investment process to such an extent that the strategy cannot be implemented as intended may be presumed to render the portfolio nondiscretionary.

Investors commonly set forth investment restrictions in investment policy statements. In addition to articulating the investor's overall financial objectives, an IPS normally expresses a number of constraints intended to limit the investment risks to which the assets are exposed. For example, the IPS may limit an individual equity portfolio's economic sector exposure to a certain percentage of portfolio assets or a certain relationship to the comparable benchmark weight: "No portfolio shall hold more than 15 percent of assets or 125 percent of the corresponding benchmark weight, whichever is greater, in any given sector, such as consumer discretionary stocks or technology stocks." A fixed-income portfolio may be constrained to hold no securities rated below investment grade and to maintain the portfolio's weighted-average duration within a specified range, such as 75 percent to 125 percent of the benchmark duration. These restrictions are intended to preserve the portfolio from a loss in value due to inadequate sector diversification, excessive credit quality risk, or unacceptable levels of interest rate risk.

Clearly, in addition to ensuring that the benchmark is appropriate, investors must be careful to formulate constraints that achieve their intended risk-control objectives without unduly impairing the portfolio manager's ability to act on his professional judgment regarding the relative attractiveness of sectors and securities. In other words, a well-written investment IPS meets the client's need for risk mitigation while respecting the portfolio manager's discretion. The manager is well advised to discuss with the client any restrictions that are incompatible with the intended investment strategy. Upon accepting the investment management assignment, however, the portfolio manager is ethically bound by the client's stated policies. Moreover, investment management agreements often incorporate the IPS, so the portfolio manager may also be legally required to comply with properly communicated client-specified constraints.

In some cases, the client's investment constraints may significantly impinge on the portfolio manager's flexibility. A personal investor might prohibit investment in securities issued by companies operating in industries she considers socially unacceptable, such as alcohol, tobacco, or gaming. A corporate client might prohibit the sale of company stock, or a foundation might similarly ban the sale of "sentimental holdings," securities issued by the company in which its founder made a fortune. Additionally, legal restrictions may apply. For instance, a public fund might be statutorily precluded from investing in nondomestic securities. None of these constraints automatically renders a portfolio nondiscretionary. Rather, in these and other cases, the portfolio manager must determine whether or not he has discretion to execute the investment strategy. It may be appropriate to classify a portfolio as discretionary despite the presence of restrictions (such as the prohibition of alcohol, tobacco, or gaming stocks cited above) and to include it in a composite with other similarly constrained portfolios.

Recognizing that degrees of discretion exist, the firm must consider the interactions among client-directed constraints, the portfolio's strategy or style, and the investment process, notably including the financial instruments employed. For example, a client's investment policy might preclude the use of derivative securities such as futures and options. In this case, the firm must consider whether the restriction is pertinent. To take up the example of the domestic mid-cap stock portfolio again, the fact that the client prohibits the use of derivatives may be irrelevant if the manager simply buys, holds, and sells common stocks. If the use of derivative securities is central to the firm's implementation of the investment mandate, however, then the client's policy may render the portfolio nondiscretionary.

In some cases, the pattern of external cash flows might make a portfolio nondiscretionary. For example, if a client frequently makes large withdrawals, perhaps on a regular schedule, the portfolio manager might have to maintain such a high level of liquidity that she cannot truly implement the investment strategy as she does for other portfolios with a similar stated investment mandate or objective.

Implementation (6)

Defining Discretion. The Standards require that all actual fee-paying discretionary portfolios be included in at least one composite. The key words here are actual, fee paying, and discretionary. Stated in simple terms, every account that meets these criteria has to be included in at least one composite. Because discretion is one of the key variables that determine inclusion in or exclusion from a composite, a firm implementing the GIPS standards must have a clear, written definition of discretion. The "Guidance Statement on Composite Definition" defines discretion as "the ability of the firm to implement its intended strategy," and counsels, "If documented client-imposed restrictions significantly hinder the firm from fully implementing its intended strategy the firm may determine that the portfolio is nondiscretionary." The Guidance Statement, available on the CFA Institute web site, offers a starting point for the firm's internal definition of discretion. The firm's documented policy on discretion should help practitioners judge whether a specific portfolio is discretionary and decide how to handle portfolios deemed wholly or partially nondiscretionary. The firm must consistently apply its definition of discretion.

A client could insist that the manager retain specific holdings that might or might not otherwise be held in a portfolio. For example, the client could direct that legacy holdings with a low cost basis must not be sold due to the adverse tax consequences of realizing large gains. In such cases, retaining the asset in the portfolio may skew performance, and whether the impact is favorable or unfavorable, the outcome would not reflect the results of the manager's actual discretionary investment management. If holding the assets hinders the ability to implement the intended strategy, either the entire portfolio should be considered nondiscretionary and removed from the firm's composites or the individual assets should be moved to a different, nondiscretionary account and the remaining assets for which the manager has full discretion should be retained in (or added to) the composite. Alternately, the firm might include a materiality threshold in its policy, enabling it to consider a portfolio discretionary if the nondiscretionary assets consist of less than a certain percentage of portfolio assets.

3.8. Constructing Composites II—Defining Investment Strategies

Defining and constructing meaningful composites is a vital step toward achieving the ideal of fair representation and the goal of providing prospective clients with useful comparative information. Under the GIPS standards, composites must be defined according to similar investment objectives and/or strategies, and the full **composite definition** as documented in the firm's policies and procedures must be made available upon request (Provision II.3.A.2). Well-defined composites will be objectively representative of the firm's products and consistent with the firm's marketing strategy. To promote comparability, it is beneficial for firms to take into account how other firms characterize similar products.

The IPC's "Guidance Statement on Composite Definition" suggests a hierarchy that may be helpful for the firm considering how to define composites. Firms are not required to define their composites according to each level of the suggested hierarchy.

Investment Mandate
  Asset Classes
    Style or Strategy
      Benchmarks
        Risk/Return Characteristics

A composite based on the investment mandate bears a summary product or strategy description, such as "Global Equities." This may be an entirely acceptable composite definition as long as no significant strategic differences exist among the portfolios included in the composite. It is a guiding principle of composite definition that firms are not permitted to include portfolios with different investment strategies or objectives in the same composite.

A composite based on the constituent portfolios' asset class, such as "equity" or "fixed income," may also be acceptable; however, asset classes are broadly inclusive, and, because generic descriptions are not very informative, asset class composites should be offered only if they are legitimately and meaningfully representative of the firm's products.

In order to afford investors a better understanding of the nature of a composite, the firm may use an asset-class modifier indicating the composite's investment style or strategy. For example, equity portfolios may be restricted to a specific economic sector such as telecommunications stocks. Stocks issued by corporations competing in the same economic sector are presumably affected more or less the same way by exogenous factors such as changes in raw material prices, consumer demand, or the general level of interest rates.

Equity portfolios might also be actively managed to a defined style. A nine-box style matrix widely used by investment consultants in asset allocation studies and performance evaluations classifies portfolios by capitalization (large cap, midcap, and small cap) and by style (value; core, also called neutral, market oriented, or blend; and growth). In addition, some capital market index providers offer capitalization- and style-based indices. Although the construction methodologies for such indices must be carefully considered, they may serve adequately as market-based performance benchmarks for portfolios managed in conformity with these categories. Stocks assigned to one category may move more or less together, and one category may have favorable performance relative to the equity market as a whole while another category underperforms the broad market. For instance, the investment performance of portfolios managed to a small-cap growth strategy may vary considerably from the results achieved by large-cap value portfolios, depending on whether large-cap or small-cap stocks and growth or value stocks are in favor during a given measurement period.

A portfolio may be assigned to one of the style matrix categories based on the money-weighted averages of pertinent characteristics of the portfolio's holdings. For example, a portfolio holding stocks with an average market capitalization of $6 billion along with a relatively high price-to-earnings multiple, a relatively high price-to-book ratio, and a relatively low dividend yield, would likely be identified as a midcap growth portfolio. Alternately, the portfolio's monthly or quarterly return history might be regressed against the returns of pertinent capital market indices to determine which style-specific benchmarks best explain the portfolio's performance. Evaluating the comparative merits of these approaches falls outside the scope of this chapter. Suffice it to say that given the widespread acceptance of these categories, a firm may meaningfully and usefully define composites with reference to the capitalization range and the style in which the constituent portfolios are managed.

Implementation (7)

Defining Composites. One of the greatest challenges in implementing the GIPS standards is devising the set of composites that will most meaningfully represent the firm's products. The Standards require each and every actual, fee-paying, discretionary portfolio to be included in at least one composite, and composites to be defined according to similar investment objectives and/or strategies. What appears to be a straightforward exercise—defining composites and assigning portfolios to them—may prove rather difficult in practice.

A useful guideline is to build a set of composites that will accurately represent the firm's distinct investment strategies. With too few composites, a firm risks overlooking significant differences and lumping diverse portfolios together into a single, overly broad composite portfolio subject to a wide dispersion of portfolio returns. With too many composites, in addition to unnecessarily augmenting administrative expense, the firm runs the risk of creating narrowly defined groupings that are too much alike in investment strategy, contain too few accounts or assets to be useful, or compromise client confidentiality.

Assuming that the implementation team has already defined the "firm" and "discretion" and compiled a master list of portfolios, here is a common-sense strategy for reaching agreement on composite definitions.

1. Review the firm's organizational structure and investment process to see if distinctive strategies can be readily identified. For instance, an equity adviser might have units specializing in one or more active management strategies as well as index fund construction and quantitatively driven enhanced indexing.
2. Review the firm's existing marketing materials, supplemented if possible by marketing materials from competitors and by recently received RFPs. The objective is to determine how the industry defines products similar to those the firm offers.
3. Referring to the hierarchy presented in the "Guidance Statement on Composite Definition," construct a provisional framework using descriptive captions to identify possible composites.

4. Taking into account the clients' investment policies, test how well the firm's actual, fee-paying, discretionary portfolios would fit the provisional framework. The inevitable identification of exceptions—that is, the discovery that portfolios that must be included in some composite do not really fit any—will lead to the redefinition of proposed composites or the creation of new composites. Several iterations may be needed.
5. Review the proposed set of composites for compliance with the Standards.
6. Document the composite definitions in detail, and circulate the definitions for final review by all interested parties within the firm.

Of course, the most effective process for defining composites may differ from one firm to another in view of variables such as organizational structure, culture, and investment strategies, among other factors. Nonetheless, composite definitions have lasting consequences, and it is highly desirable to have a plan for reaching consensus.

Firms may also define composites based on the portfolios' benchmarks, as long as the benchmarks reflect the investment strategy and the firm has no other composites with the same characteristics. This approach is particularly appropriate if the portfolios are limited to holding stocks that are held in the index.

Finally, portfolios sharing distinctive risk/return profiles may reasonably be grouped together. For example, enhanced index funds with benchmark-specific targeted excess returns and tracking error tolerances might fall into natural groups.

Fixed-income composites can likewise be meaningfully and usefully defined in many dimensions. For example, composites might conform to asset classes or market segments such as government debt, mortgage-backed securities, convertible bonds, or high-yield bonds; investment strategies such as fundamental credit analysis, sector rotation, or interest rate anticipation; or investment styles such as indexing or core-plus. However a firm chooses to define the composites representing its investment products, they must be composed of portfolios managed in accordance with similar investment strategies or objectives.

3.9. Constructing Composites III—Including and Excluding Portfolios

The GIPS Standards governing composite construction hold that composites must include new portfolios on a timely and consistent basis after the portfolio comes under management unless specifically mandated by the client (Provision II.3.A.3). Firms are required to establish, document, and consistently apply a policy of including new portfolios in the appropriate composites on a timely basis. Preferably, new portfolios should be included as of the beginning of the next full performance measurement period after the firm receives the funds. For example, if a portfolio is funded on May 20 and the firm presents composite returns monthly, optimally the composite should include the new portfolio as of the beginning of June. It may take time to invest the assets of a new portfolio in accordance with the desired investment strategy, however, particularly when the portfolio is funded in kind (that is, with securities other than cash) and the assets have to be redeployed, or when the securities to be purchased are relatively illiquid (e.g., in emerging markets). Accordingly, the Standards give firms some discretion to determine when to add the new portfolio to a composite. In such cases, the firm should establish a policy on a composite-by-composite basis and apply it consistently to all new portfolios. In addition, firms may legitimately defer the inclusion of new portfolios in a composite on the specific instructions of a client. To cite an example, the client may indicate that assets will be deposited over an extended period, delaying the full implementation of the strategy, and the client may further state that returns are not to be calculated until the portfolio has been fully funded.

In addition to winning new business, firms routinely lose relationships. Under the GIPS standards, a firm must include a terminated portfolio in the historical record of the appropriate composite up to the last full measurement period that the portfolio was under management (Provision II.3.A.4). In many cases, the firm loses its discretion over the portfolio upon being notified of a pending termination. The client may instruct the firm to stop buying securities immediately and to commence the liquidation of holdings in preparation for an outbound cash transfer on a specified date. Alternately, the client may halt trading and transfer control of the portfolio to a transition management organization to facilitate moving assets to a new firm. When the firm being terminated thus loses its discretion over the portfolio, it should include the portfolio in the composite through the last full measurement period prior to notification of termination. To use the same example, if a firm that reports performance monthly is informed on May 20 that its management contract is being terminated effective May 31 and is instructed to stop trading forthwith, then the firm should include the portfolio in its composite through April 30. In any event, it is incumbent upon the GIPS-compliant firm to have defined and documented its policies governing the removal of terminated portfolios from composites and, of course, to apply those policies consistently.

Implementation (8)

Adding, Removing, and Switching Portfolios. GIPS-compliant firms must have written policies setting forth when portfolios may be added to or removed from composites. These policies can be either firmwide or composite-specific. For a firm that reports composite performance monthly, a firmwide policy statement could read as follows:

> *"All new portfolios funded with cash or securities on or before the 15th day of the month shall be added to the appropriate composite at the beginning of the following month. All new portfolios funded with cash or securities after the 15th day of the month shall be added to the appropriate composite at the beginning of the second month after funding. All portfolios shall be deemed 'nondiscretionary' on the date notice of termination is received and removed from the composite at the end of the month prior to notification. The historical performance record of terminated portfolios shall remain in the appropriate composite."*

For a firm that calculates composite performance quarterly and needs more time to implement its investment strategy, the following firmwide policy may be appropriate:

> *"All new portfolios funded with cash or securities on or before the 10th day of the last month of the calendar quarter shall be added to the appropriate composite at the beginning of the following quarter. All new portfolios funded with cash or securities after the 10th day of the last month of the calendar quarter shall be added to the appropriate composite at the beginning of the second quarter after funding. All portfolios shall be deemed 'nondiscretionary' on the date notice of termination is received and removed from the composite at the end of the calendar quarter prior to notification. The historical performance record of terminated portfolios shall remain in the appropriate composite."*

Policies like the samples above allow firms a reasonable amount of time to implement the strategy without delaying inclusion of the portfolio in the appropriate composite. Each firm should develop a policy that conforms to its own investment process while meeting the GIPS standards' requirement to include portfolios in composites on a timely basis. In many cases, composite-specific policies will be in order.

The firm's policy for adding or removing portfolios should also include language strictly limiting the switching of portfolios from one composite to another. Here is a sample statement for a firmwide policy:

"Portfolios shall not be moved from one composite to another unless the composite is redefined or documented changes in the client's guidelines require restructuring the portfolio in such a way that another composite becomes more appropriate. The portfolio shall be removed from the original composite at the end of the last calendar quarter before the event causing the removal occurred and shall be added to the appropriate new composite at the beginning of the next calendar quarter. The historical performance record of the portfolio shall remain in the appropriate composite."

The GIPS standards also stipulate that portfolios cannot be switched from one composite to another unless documented changes in client guidelines or the redefinition of the composite make it appropriate. The historical record of the portfolio must remain with the appropriate composite (Provision II.3.A.5). This is an important provision; if the Standards permitted firms to transfer portfolios from one composite to another at will, an unethical firm might identify and exploit opportunities to improve the reported performance of selected composites by repopulating them with the portfolios whose investment results were most advantageous during the measurement period.

The Standards spell out the only two conditions under which portfolios can be reassigned. First, a portfolio can be switched from one composite to another if the client revises the guidelines governing the investment of portfolio assets and the guideline changes are documented. For instance, a client might decide to modify the portfolio mandate from midcap value to large-cap value, or from domestic equity to global equity, with a corresponding change in the benchmark, while retaining the same investment adviser to restructure and manage the "same" portfolio in accordance with the new strategy. Or perhaps a client might decide to allow the use of derivative securities, previously prohibited, triggering a change in the investment strategy and making it suitable to assign the portfolio to a composite made up of portfolios that use derivatives. Second, a portfolio can be reassigned to another composite if the original composite is redefined in such a way that the portfolio no longer fits it. Generally, if a strategy evolves over time, it is most appropriate to create a new composite; accordingly, the redefinition of an existing composite should be a highly unusual event. (See the related disclosure requirement stated in Provision II.4.A.22, where it is also asserted that the Standards do not permit changes to composites to be applied retroactively.) To repeat, if a portfolio is switched from one composite to another as permitted in these two situations—a pertinent, documented change in the client's investment guidelines or a redefinition of the composite—the historical record of the portfolio must remain in the appropriate composite.

In the event of significant external cash flows, the GIPS standards recommend that firms use **temporary new accounts** rather than temporarily removing portfolios from composites (see Provision II.3.B.2). Firms adopting this direct approach channel incoming cash and securities to a new account that is not included in any composite until the cash has been fully invested in accordance with the intended strategy. The timing of the temporary new account's integration into the existing portfolio and the composite is governed by the firm's general or composite-specific policy on the inclusion of new portfolios. Relatedly, when the client initiates a large capital withdrawal, the firm moves cash and securities in the desired amount to a new account until it liquidates the securities. The transfer is treated as an outflow in calculating the portfolio's time-weighted total return. This theoretically appropriate means of handling large external cash flows is recommended but not required because current technology does not readily allow for the establishment of temporary new accounts. Firms may be compelled to temporarily remove portfolios from composites when large external cash flows occur. We refer the reader to the IPC's "Guidance Statement on the Treatment of Significant Cash Flows" for further information and direction on this practically important topic.

We have said that all actual portfolios that are fee-paying and discretionary must be included in at least one composite, but we have not commented on the meaning of "actual" in this context. The Standards specify that composites must include only assets under management within the defined firm. Firms are not permitted to link simulated or model portfolios with actual performance (Provision II.3.A.8). In the process of developing, testing, and refining new investment strategies, firms frequently construct model portfolios and use historical security prices to simulate their hypothetical performance in past measurement periods. Composites cannot include simulated, backtested, or model portfolios. (The "Guidance Statement on the Use of Supplemental Information" states that model, hypothetical, backtested, or simulated returns can be shown as **supplemental information** but cannot be linked to actual performance returns.) On the other hand, if the firm actually created and managed portfolios with its own seed money, it could include them from inception in appropriate composites (or, more likely, construct new composites reflecting the new strategies), subject to a presentation and reporting requirement related to the inclusion of non-fee-paying portfolios in composites (see Provision II.5.A.7, discussed later). Simply stated, only portfolios in which actual assets are invested, not hypothetical portfolios, can be included in composites.

The GIPS provisions for composite construction additionally address the issue of minimum asset levels. A firm might decide that a particular composite will not include any portfolios whose market value is below a specified level, on the grounds, for instance, that the investment strategy can be fully implemented only for portfolios above a certain size. The Standards rule that if a firm sets a minimum asset level for portfolios to be included in a composite, no portfolios below that asset level can be included in that composite. In other words, the policy, once established, must be followed consistently (Provision II.3.A.9).

The "Guidance Statement on Composite Definition" notes that portfolios may drop below a composite-specific minimum asset level because of client withdrawals or depreciation in market value. If a firm establishes a minimum asset level for a composite, it must document its policies regarding how portfolios will be treated if they fall below the minimum. The Guidance Statement recommends that firms specify in their policies the basis for evaluating portfolios against a composite's minimum asset level (for instance, a firm might use beginning market value, ending market value, or beginning market value plus cash flows, etc.). In order to curtail the movement of portfolios into and out of composites, the Guidance Statement further recommends that firms consider establishing a valuation threshold and a minimum time period for applying the policy. For example, the firm might establish a range of ±5 percent of the minimum asset level and a condition that portfolios must remain above or below the minimum asset level for at least two periods before they are added to or removed from the composite. If a portfolio is removed from a composite, its prior history must remain in the composite.

The firm must determine if the portfolio that has been removed meets any other composite definition and include it in the appropriate composite in a timely and consistent manner.

Provision II.3.A.9, mentioned earlier, also stipulates that any changes to a composite-specific minimum asset level cannot be applied retroactively. This requirement can create a problem when capital market movements cause portfolios' market values to fall below the stated minimum. For example, the total market value of the Dow Jones Wilshire 5000 Index reached a high point of approximately \$14.75 trillion on March 24, 2000. Over the period March 24, 2000, to September 30, 2002, the index had a return of −45.6 percent, representing a loss of shareholder value in excess of \$6.7 trillion. If a firm's composite had a minimum portfolio asset level of \$50 million, a portfolio initially valued at \$85 million that experienced a comparable decline in market value would no longer qualify for inclusion in the composite. Under the Standards, the portfolio would have to be removed from the composite when its market value fell below the minimum asset level. Although the magnitude of the drop in the broad U.S. equity market during this period was atypical, firms are well advised to consider the risk of having to exclude portfolios from composites with minimum asset levels. The minimum asset level can be changed prospectively, subject to disclosure (see Provision II.4.A.3), but not retroactively.

The Standards also recommend that firms should not market a composite to a prospective client whose assets are less than the composite's minimum asset level (Provision II.3.B.3). It is to be presumed that the firm has sound reasons for establishing a minimum asset level for a given strategy. Accordingly, it would be inappropriate for a firm to solicit funds from a prospect with insufficient investable assets for that particular strategy.

3.10. Constructing Composites IV—Carve-Out Segments

The GIPS standards codify the proper treatment of asset class segments "carved out" of portfolios invested in multiple asset classes.

In discussing the requirements surrounding the calculation methodology, we recognized that returns from cash and cash equivalents held in portfolios must be included in total return calculations (Provision II.2.A.4), and we examined the impact of short-term investments on equity portfolio results in "up" and "down" markets. The requirement that cash and cash equivalents be taken into account in portfolio and composite return calculations is based on the fundamental principle of fair representation: A composite that did not include cash would not fairly represent investment performance to a prospective client.

This principle carries over to the inclusion of portfolio segments in composites. Provision II.3.A.7 opens with the declaration that **carve-out** segments *excluding cash* cannot be used to represent a discretionary portfolio and, as such, cannot be included in composite returns. For example, the stock portion alone of a portfolio consisting of stocks, bonds, and cash cannot be included in an equity composite as though it were a stand-alone discretionary portfolio. The provision continues, "When a single asset class is carved out of a multiple asset class portfolio and the returns are presented as part of a single asset composite, cash must be allocated to the carve-out returns in a timely and consistent manner." In the equity segment example, a pro rata portion of the portfolio's cash position must be allotted to the stocks, and the carved-out segment return must take into account both the stocks and the temporary investments reasonably associated with them. Carve-out returns, if used at all, should be representative of the results that would realistically have been achieved in a stand-alone strategy, and as we have seen, that entails recognizing the impact of tactical and frictional cash positions.

The "Guidance Statement on the Treatment of Carve-Outs" describes two acceptable allocation methods for situations in which the carved-out segment is not managed with its

EXHIBIT 13-11 Allocating Cash to Carve-Out Segments: Data

	Actual Market Value as of May 31	Percent of Beginning Portfolio Market Value	Percent of Beginning Invested Assets	Strategic Target	June Returns
Stocks	44,609	35.0%	36.1%	37.5%	2.50%
Bonds	79,021	62.0	63.9	62.5	1.50%
Subtotal: Invested assets	123,630	97.0	100.0%	100.0%	
Cash	3,824	3.0		0.0	0.45%
Total portfolio assets	127,454	100.0%		100.0%	1.82%

own cash. Under the "beginning of period allocation" method, the cash allocation percentage for each portfolio segment is identified at the beginning of the measurement period. Under the "strategic asset allocation" method, the allocation is based on the target strategic asset mix. To see how these methods can be used to determine the cash allocation for the equity segment of a balanced portfolio, consider the data in Exhibit 13-11.

Applying the beginning-of-period allocation method, cash might be allocated to the equity segment in proportion to stocks' percentage of invested assets excluding cash.

$$\text{Equity Allocated Cash}_{\text{Beginning}} = \$3,824 \times \frac{44,609}{123,630} = \$1,380$$

Alternately, using the strategic asset allocation method, the cash position is assumed to be the difference between the portfolio's strategic and actual allocation to equities. In the example presented in Exhibit 13-11, the strategic allocation target for equities is 37.5 percent, and the actual beginning allocation to equities is 35 percent. The difference (2.5 percent of total portfolio assets) is assumed to be held in cash and cash equivalents associated with the equity segment.

$$\text{Equity Allocated Cash}_{\text{Strategic}} = \$127,454 \times (0.375 - 0.35) = \$3,186$$

Exhibit 13-12 displays the results, including the weighted segment returns for the month of June. As this example illustrates, the cash allocation method chosen and the way in which the method is implemented can substantially affect the performance calculation. Under the "beginning of period allocation" method, the equity segment return for the month is 2.44 percent (the simple arithmetic result of having 97 percent of segment assets invested in stocks with a return of 2.5 percent and 3 percent invested in cash with a return of 0.45 percent).

EXHIBIT 13-12 Allocation of Cash to Carve-Out Segments: Two Methods

	Beginning-of-Period Allocation		Strategic Asset Allocation	
Stocks	44,609	97.0%	44,609	93.3%
Allocated cash	1,380	3.0	3,186	6.7
Total equity segment assets	45,989	100.0%	47,795	100.0%
Equity segment return		2.44%		2.36%

Under the "strategic asset allocation" method, the equity segment return for the month is 8 basis points lower (2.36 percent).

It is of course illogical to conclude from this one example that the beginning-of-period allocation method will always produce a higher segment return than the strategic asset allocation method. The relative outcomes might be reversed in another case. In any event, the firm must determine which method to employ, document the policy, and apply it consistently, without regard to the *ex post* performance impact in any measurement period.

Under the GIPS standards, the allocation of cash to carved-out segments is permitted only until January 1, 2010. From that date forward, carve-out returns cannot be included in single-asset-class composite returns *unless the carve-out is actually managed separately with its own cash balance* (emphasis added; from Provision II.3.A.7). In the interim, the GIPS standards recommend that carve-out returns should not be included in single-asset-class composite returns unless the carve-outs are actually managed separately with their own cash balance (Provision II.3.B.1).

Carve-out segments are also addressed in the provisions for disclosure and for presentation and reporting. For periods prior to January 1, 2010, when a single asset class is carved out of a multiple-asset portfolio and the returns are presented as part of a single-asset composite, firms must disclose the policy used to allocate cash to the carve-out returns (see Provision II.4.A.11). In addition, beginning January 1, 2006, if a composite includes or is formed using single-asset-class carve-outs from multiple-asset-class portfolios, the presentation must include the percentage of the composite that is composed of carve-outs prospectively for each period (see Provision II.5.A.5).

Implementation (9)

Carve-Out Segments. Equilibrium Capital Advisors, a firm specializing in balanced portfolios, maintains a number of multi-class composites constructed according to strategic asset mix ranges. For example, among other multi-class composites, Equilibrium Capital Advisors has a Standard Balanced Account Composite composed of portfolios with a strategic asset allocation target of 50 percent fixed-income and 50 percent equity; a Conservative Balanced Account Composite composed of portfolios with a 65/35 fixed-income/equity strategic mix; and an Aggressive Balanced Account Composite composed of portfolios with a 20/80 fixed-income/equity strategic mix. In order to control transaction expenses by reducing the frequency of portfolio rebalancing, the target mixes are accompanied by 5 percent tolerance ranges. For instance, the Aggressive Balanced Account Composite is permitted to vary from 15/85 to 25/75 fixed-income/equity mixes. The equity segments of all the balanced composites are managed in accordance with a single strategy by the Equity Markets Group under the leadership of John Boyle, and the fixed income segments of the balanced composites as well as all cash and cash equivalent positions are managed by the Fixed Income Markets Group. Boyle wants to create a new equity composite composed of the equity segments of the multi-class portfolios. Can such a composite be constructed in compliance with the GIPS standards?

Provision II.3.B.1 recommends against constructing the composite Boyle requests. The Standard reads, "Carve-out returns should not be included in single-asset-class composite returns unless the carve-outs are actually managed separately with their own cash balance." In the case of Equilibrium Capital Advisors, it appears that the cash generated in the course of equity and fixed-income investment management is pooled, and short-term investing is conducted for the balanced portfolio as a whole. The equity segment is not managed separately with its own cash balance.

Provision II.3.A.7 states that beginning January 1, 2010, carve-out returns cannot be included in single-asset-class composite returns unless the carve-out is actually managed separately with its own cash balance. Until that time, however, the provision allows carve-out segments to be included in single asset class composites on the condition that cash is allocated to the carve-out returns in a timely and consistent manner. Accordingly, Equilibrium Capital Advisors can construct and maintain a composite composed of the equity segments of balanced portfolios until January 1, 2010. The firm must decide on an acceptable cash allocation method, document the method, and apply it consistently. The Standards expressly prohibit carve-out segments excluding cash from being included in composite returns. As noted in the text, the cash allocation method must be disclosed (Provision II.4.A.11), and beginning January 1, 2006, the percentage of the composite that is composed of carve-outs must be shown prospectively for each period in GIPS-compliant performance presentations (Provision II.5.A.5).

3.11. Disclosure Standards

The GIPS standards advance the ideals of fair representation and full disclosure. We will consider the presentation and reporting provisions shortly. Before doing so, however, we will cite the required and recommended disclosure provisions. The reader will already be familiar with most of these topics from previous sections, so we will discuss each item here only briefly. For ease of exposition, we have grouped the disclosure provisions by subject area.

Several of the provisions concern disclosures related to the GIPS-compliant firm. The definition of the *firm* used to determine the firm's total assets and firmwide compliance is a required disclosure (Provision II.4.A.1). A clear explanation of the way in which the firm is defined enables the prospective client to understand precisely which investment organization (or unit of a larger entity) is presenting results, is claiming compliance, and will be responsible for managing the client's assets if hired. If a firm is redefined, it must disclose the date and reason for the redefinition (Provision II.4.A.21).

Firms are further required to disclose all significant events that help a prospective client interpret the performance record (Provision II.4.A.19). For example, a firm must advise the prospective client if past results in a given strategy were achieved by a star portfolio manager who has left the firm, or if key members of the research team supporting the strategy have resigned. Beginning January 1, 2006, firms must disclose the use of a subadviser or subadvisers and the periods in which one or more subadvisers were used (Provision II.4.A.18).

The availability of a complete list and description of all of the firm's composites is a required disclosure (Provision II.4.A.2). This information enables prospective clients to determine if the composite they have been shown is the most appropriate for their needs and to request any other composites of interest. Note that the list must include not only all of the firm's current composites but also any that have been discontinued within the last five years (see Provision II.0.A.12). GIPS Appendix B provides a sample list and description of composites.

In addition to the foregoing firm-related requirements, the Standards make two recommendations. First, if a parent company contains multiple defined firms, each firm within the parent company is encouraged to disclose a list of the other firms contained within the parent company (Provision II.4.B.1). Second, firms that have been verified (that is, firms whose performance measurement processes and procedures have been reviewed in reference to the GIPS standards by a qualified, independent third party) should add a disclosure to their composite presentation stating that the firm has been verified and clearly indicating the periods the verification covers if not all the periods presented have been subject to firmwide verification (Provision II.4.B.3).

Other disclosure provisions concern rate-of-return calculations and **benchmarks**. Firms must disclose the currency used to express performance (Provision II.4.A.4). Firms must also disclose and describe any known inconsistencies in the exchange rates used among the portfolios within a composite and between the composite and the benchmark (Provision II.4.A.8). Firms must disclose relevant details of the treatment of withholding tax on dividends, interest income, and capital gains. If using indices that are net of taxes, the firm must disclose the tax basis of the benchmark (for example, Luxembourg based or U.S. based) versus that of the composite (Provision II.4.A.7). Firms must also disclose that **additional information** regarding policies for calculating and reporting returns in compliance with the GIPS standards is available upon request (Provision II.4.A.17). To cite obvious examples, GIPS-compliant firms should be prepared to respond to prospective clients' questions about their return calculation methodology, valuation sources, or treatment of large external cash flows. The Standards recommend, but do not require, that firms disclose when a change in a calculation methodology or valuation source results in a material impact on the performance of a composite (Provision II.4.B.2).

Numerous disclosure standards address the topic of fees. Returns must be clearly labeled as gross of fees or net of fees (Provision II.4.A.6). For reference, the GIPS glossary defines the **gross-of-fees return** as the return on assets reduced by any trading expenses incurred during the period and the **net-of-fees return** as the gross-of-fees return reduced by the investment management fee. When presenting gross-of-fees returns, firms must disclose if they deduct any other fees in addition to the direct trading expenses (Provision II.4.A.15). Similarly, when presenting net-of-fees returns, firms must disclose if any other fees are deducted in addition to the direct trading expenses and the investment management fee (Provision II.4.A.16). The firm must also disclose the **fee schedule** appropriate to the presentation (Provision II.4.A.12). As explained in the GIPS glossary, the term "fee schedule" refers to the firm's current investment management fees or bundled fees for a particular presentation. If a composite contains portfolios with bundled fees, firms must disclose the percentage of composite assets that are bundled-fee portfolios for each annual period shown in the performance presentation (Provision II.4.A.13). Firms must also disclose the various types of fees that the bundled fee includes (Provision II.4.A.14).

Some disclosure standards are pertinent to individual composites. Firms must disclose a description of the investment objectives, style, and/or strategy of the composite (Provision II.4.A.20). It is not enough merely to have a broadly indicative name such as "Growth and Income Composite," which might mean one thing to one person and something else to another; the provision requires that prospective clients be given a reasonably informative explanation, however concise, setting forth the composite's salient features. For example, a "Growth and Income Composite" composed of balanced portfolios or "accounts" managed on behalf of individuals might be described in these terms: "The Growth and Income Composite includes taxable balanced accounts with assets greater than $100,000. The accounts are managed to a strategic asset allocation target of 50 percent fixed income and 50 percent equity within a tactical range of 10 percent. The fixed income segments of the individual accounts are invested in investment-grade instruments including U.S. government and agency securities, corporate bonds, and mortgage-backed securities. The equity segments are invested in large-capitalization common stocks. The benchmark for this strategy is a blended index made up of 50 percent Lehman Aggregate Bond Index and 50 percent Standard & Poor's 500 Stock Index." Appendix B of the GIPS standards includes other examples of **composite descriptions**.

Firms must also disclose the **composite creation date** (Provision II.4.A.24), the date on which the firm first grouped the portfolios to form the composite. This is not necessarily the earliest date for which composite performance is reported. If a firm has redefined a composite, the firm must disclose the date and nature of the change. As previously noted, the Standards do not permit changes to composites to be applied retroactively (Provision II.4.A.22). Similarly, firms must disclose any changes to a composite's name (Provision II.4.A.23).

As we will see when examining the provisions of the GIPS standards related to presentation and reporting, firms must report a measure of the **dispersion** of the returns of the individual portfolios within a composite. There are different ways to convey dispersion. The disclosure standards require firms to disclose which dispersion measure they present (Provision II.4.A.26).

The preceding requirements apply to all composites. Several further requirements apply in certain cases. First, firms must disclose the minimum asset level, if any, below which portfolios are not included in a composite. Firms must also disclose any changes to the minimum asset level (Provision II.4.A.3). Second, for periods prior to January 1, 2010, when a single asset class is carved out of a multiple-asset portfolio and the returns are presented as part of a single-asset composite, firms must disclose the policy used to allocate cash to the carve-out returns (Provision II.4.A.11). Third, firms must disclose if, prior to January 1, 2010, portfolios are not valued as of calendar month-end or the last business day of the month (Provision II.4.A.25).

It is an important, albeit challenging, provision that firms must disclose the presence, use, and extent of leverage or derivatives, if material. The disclosure must include a description of the use, frequency, and characteristics of the instruments sufficient to identify risks (Provision II.4.A.5). As a practical matter, it is admittedly difficult to explain in writing the use of leverage or derivative securities and the attendant risks of their use, especially for the benefit of prospective clients who may not have been exposed previously to complex investment strategies. A clear explanation, however, will help prospective clients interpret the historical performance record and evaluate the additional risk resulting from the use of leverage or derivatives. Adequate disclosure, as required by the GIPS standards, includes a description of the investment characteristics of the financial instruments employed and an explanation of the way in which they are used.

For example, a fixed income manager might use interest rate futures contracts as an efficient and economical means of adjusting the sensitivity of corporate bond portfolios to anticipated changes in the general level of interest rates. The firm might provide the following description of its use of derivatives: "Crystal Capital routinely uses U.S. Treasury bond futures contracts to change the portfolios' modified duration. Because of their call features and credit risk, the corporate bonds held in the portfolio may experience price changes that do not closely match movements in the U.S. Treasury bond futures contracts, resulting in portfolio valuations that differ from the targeted outcome."

Finally, two disclosure provisions pertain to performance presentations. Firms must disclose if the presentation conforms with local laws and regulations that differ from the requirements of the GIPS standards. The manner in which any local laws or regulations conflict with the Standards must also be disclosed (Provision II.4.A.9). For any performance presented for periods prior to January 1, 2000, that does not comply with the GIPS standards, firms must disclose the period and the nature of noncompliance (Provision II.4.A.10.) See also Section I.F.13, "Effective Date," and Provision II.5.A.2, discussed later.

Meeting the objectives of fair representation and full disclosure may call for providing more information than the GIPS standards minimally require. Practitioners are well advised to prepare compliance checklists to ensure that the disclosure requirements and, where feasible, the recommendations of the GIPS standards are met for the firm as a whole and for each composite presented. We turn now to the provisions for presentation and reporting.

3.12. Presentation and Reporting Requirements

The ethical ideals of fair representation and full disclosure come to fruition in GIPS-compliant performance presentations. In this section, we will focus on the required elements of performance presentations prepared in accordance with the GIPS standards.

For each composite presented, the Standards require that firms show at least five years of GIPS-compliant performance (less if the firm or composite has been in existence for a shorter period), and that the GIPS-compliant performance record must then be extended each year until 10 years' results have been presented. The core elements of a GIPS-compliant performance presentation additionally include annual returns for all years; the number of portfolios (if six or more), the amount of assets in the composite, and either the percentage of the firm's total assets represented by the composite or the amount of total firm assets at the end of each period; and a measure of dispersion of individual portfolio returns if the composite contains six or more portfolios for the full year. These requirements are set forth in Provisions II.5.A.1.a–d. Some of them are straightforward; others call for more explanation.

Annual returns, required by Provision II.5.A.1.b, are normally presented for calendar years, although they may be presented for other annual periods if the composite is reported on a noncalendar fiscal year.

Provision 5.A.1.d mandates reporting a measure of dispersion of the annual returns earned by individual portfolios belonging to the composite. This important provision is intended to allow users to determine how consistently the firm implemented its strategy across the portfolios in the composite. A wide range of results should prompt the recipient of the performance presentation to inquire about possible causes of the variability of returns to individual portfolios purportedly managed in accordance with the same strategy. It may suggest, among many other possibilities, that the composite is defined too broadly to provide meaningful information.

The dispersion of the annual returns of individual portfolios within a composite can be measured and shown in various ways, and the GIPS glossary mentions several acceptable methods. Let us refer to the data in Exhibit 13-13, showing the beginning market values (in euros) and the annual rates of return earned by the 14 portfolios that were in a German Equity composite for the full year 200X. (Note that only those portfolios in the composite for the entire year are included in the calculation of a dispersion measure.) The portfolios presented in Exhibit 13-13 are arrayed in descending order of returns.

The GIPS glossary defines dispersion as "a measure of the spread of the annual returns of individual portfolios within a composite" and indicates that acceptable measures include high/low, interquartile range, and standard deviation. Using the data in Exhibit 13-13, we will consider each of these measures in turn.

The simplest method of expressing the dispersion is to disclose the highest and lowest annual returns earned by portfolios that were in the composite for the full year. In the case of the German Equity composite, the highest return was 2.66 percent and the lowest was 1.93 percent. (The high/low range—the arithmetic difference between the highest and the lowest return—might also be presented. In this case it was 0.73 percent, or 73 basis points.) The high/low disclosure is easy to understand. It has, however, a potential disadvantage. In any annual period, an outlier—that is, one portfolio with an abnormally high or low return—may be present, resulting in a measure of dispersion that is not entirely representative of the

EXHIBIT 13-13 Data for Calculation of Dispersion

Portfolio	Beginning Market Value	200X Return
A	€118,493	2.66%
B	€79,854	2.64
C	€121,562	2.53
D	€86,973	2.49
E	€105,491	2.47
F	€112,075	2.42
G	€98,667	2.38
H	€92,518	2.33
I	€107,768	2.28
J	€96,572	2.21
K	€75,400	2.17
L	€77,384	2.07
M	€31,264	1.96
N	€84,535	1.93

distribution of returns. Although they are more difficult to calculate and to interpret, other measures are statistically superior.

A second measure cited in the GIPS glossary is an interquartile range, the difference between the returns in the first and the third quartiles of the distribution. Quartiles divide the distribution of returns into quarters, such that 25 percent of the observations fall at or above the first quartile and 25 percent fall at or below the third quartile. Thus the interquartile range represents the length of the interval containing the middle 50 percent of the data. In the case of the German Equity composite, the interquartile range is approximately 36 basis points (0.36 percent).[17] Because it does not contain the extreme values, the interquartile range does not risk being skewed by outliers. Prospective clients, however, may be unfamiliar with the interquartile range as a measure of dispersion.

The standard deviation of returns to portfolios in the composite is another acceptable measure of composite dispersion.[18] As applied to composites, standard deviation measures the cross-sectional dispersion of returns to portfolios in the composite. Standard deviation for a composite in which the constituent portfolios are equally weighted is[19]

$$S_c = \sqrt{\frac{\sum_{i=1}^{n}(r_i - r_c)^2}{n-1}} \tag{13-10}$$

where r_i is the return of each individual portfolio, r_c is the equal-weighted mean or arithmetic mean return to the portfolios in the composite, and n is, as before, the number of portfolios in the composite. Applying Equation 13-10 to the portfolio data given in Exhibit 13-13,

[17] For an explanation how to calculate quartiles, see DeFusco, McLeavey, Pinto, and Runkle (2004, pp. 120–124).

[18] The GIPS glossary entry for dispersion indicates that the standard deviation of portfolio returns can be either equal weighted or asset weighted. The presentation here is limited to the equal-weighted calculation.

[19] The use of both n and $n-1$ in the denominator can be supported. If n were used in calculating the standard deviation of returns for the example presented in the text, the result would be 22 basis points (0.22 percent).

assuming equal weighting, the standard deviation proves to be 23 basis points (0.23 percent). If the individual portfolio returns are normally distributed around the mean return of 2.32 percent, then approximately two-thirds of the portfolios will have returns falling between the mean plus the standard deviation (2.32% + 0.23% = 2.55%) and the mean minus the standard deviation (2.32% − 0.23% = 2.09%).

The standard deviation of portfolio returns is a valid measure of composite dispersion. Most spreadsheet programs include statistical functions to facilitate the calculation, and many prospective clients will have at least a passing acquaintance with the concept of a standard deviation.

Note that the GIPS glossary states that measures of dispersion may include but are not limited to those introduced above (high/low, interquartile range, and standard deviation). A GIPS-compliant firm may prefer another way of expressing composite dispersion. The method chosen should, however, fairly represent the range of returns for each annual period. Recall that firms must disclose the measure of dispersion presented.

We observed in reviewing the disclosure standards that, for any performance presented for periods prior to January 1, 2000, that does not comply with the GIPS standards, the firm must disclose the period of noncompliance and the way in which the presentation fails to comply with the Standards (Provision II.4.A.10). Firms are permitted to link non-GIPS-compliant performance to their compliant history as long as the disclosure requirements are met and only compliant returns are presented for periods after January 1, 2000 (Provision II.5.A.2).

The GIPS provisions for presentation and reporting stipulate that portfolio or composite returns for periods of less than one year must not be annualized (Provision II.5.A.3). Extrapolating partial-year returns by annualizing them would amount in effect to a prediction about investment results for the rest of the year.

The "portability" of past performance is a complex subject, but Provision II.5.A.4 summarizes the explicit conditions under which performance track records of a past firm or affiliation *must* be linked to or used to represent the historical record of a new firm or new affiliation. The conditions are that (1) substantially all the investment decision makers are employed by the new firm, (2) the staff and decision-making process remain intact and independent within the new firm, *and* (3) the new firm has records that document and support the reported performance. The new firm must disclose that the performance results from the past firm are linked to the performance record of the new firm. When a firm combines with an existing firm, there is a further requirement: The performance of composites from both firms can be linked to the ongoing returns only if substantially all the assets from the past firm's composite transfer to the new firm. If a GIPS-compliant firm acquires or is acquired by a noncompliant firm, the firms are allowed one year to bring the noncompliant assets into compliance.

In our discussion of composite construction (Provision II.3.A.7) and required disclosures (Provision II.4.A.11), we mentioned the practice of "carving out" or extracting performance data on a single asset class included in a multiple-asset class strategy for inclusion in a single-asset-class composite. A related presentation and reporting requirement exists. Under Provision II.5.A.5, beginning January 1, 2006, if a composite includes or is formed using single-asset-class carve-outs from multiple-asset-class portfolios, the presentation must include the percentage of the composite that is composed of carve-outs prospectively for each period. In this context, "prospectively" means from January 1, 2006, onward. The Standards do not require firms to disclose what percentage of the composite was composed of carve-outs for historical periods.

We have previously remarked on the importance of selecting appropriate benchmarks in order to interpret historical results and to conduct meaningful performance evaluations.

We have also made note of certain benchmark-related disclosure requirements (see Provisions II.4.A.7–8). An important presentation and reporting requirement is set forth in Provision II.5.A.6: The total return for the benchmark(s) reflecting the investment strategy or mandate represented by the composite must be presented for each annual period. If no benchmark is presented, the firm must explain why none is shown. In addition, if the firm changes the benchmark used for a given composite, the firm must disclose the date of and the reason for the change.

Provision II.5.A.6 also addresses the use of custom benchmarks. For example, a firm might construct a custom security-based benchmark composed of securities that conform to the firm's investment process and the composite's strategy. Or, as another example, a firm's balanced composite might have a blended benchmark reflecting the strategic asset mix with reference to which the portfolios are managed. The benchmark in this case might be constructed by weighting well-chosen capital market indices with desirable characteristics such as asset class representativeness and investability. The provision states that if the firm uses a custom benchmark or benchmarks, the firm must describe the benchmark creation and rebalancing process.

Implementation (10)

Benchmark Presentation. Eastern Institutional Asset Advisors presents the performance of a Global Balanced Composite. The strategic asset mix of the portfolios in the composite is 50 percent U.S. equity, 10 percent international equity, 35 percent U.S. fixed-income securities, and 5 percent cash. The composite has a blended benchmark composed of capital market indices weighted in accordance with the strategic asset allocation. In compliance with Provision II.5.A.6, Eastern Institutional Asset Advisors places the following disclosure on the Global Balanced Composite's performance presentation:

> *"The benchmark for the Global Balanced Composite is composed of 50 percent S&P 500, 10 percent MSCI EAFE Index, 35 percent Lehman Aggregate Bond Index, and 5 percent U.S. Treasury bills. The benchmark is rebalanced monthly."*

The frequency of benchmark rebalancing can affect the reported returns for an annual period. Exhibit 13-14 displays one calendar year's data for the Global Balanced Composite described in Implementation (10). For the purpose of comparison, the blended benchmark return for the year is calculated first on a monthly and then on a quarterly basis.

In this example, the monthly calculation produces a blended benchmark return of −9.30 percent for the year, while the quarterly calculation (using the same input data) produces a return of −8.98 percent for the year. There is a difference of 32 basis points (0.32 percent) between the full-year benchmark returns under the two rebalancing methods. Once established, the firm must apply its benchmark rebalancing policy consistently, without regard to the *ex post* impact on the composite's relative performance in any annual period.

The final requirement of the GIPS standards for presentation and reporting to be mentioned here addresses the inclusion of non-fee-paying portfolios in composites. We saw when discussing the requirements for composite construction that all actual, fee-paying, discretionary portfolios must be included in at least one composite. Provision II.3.A.1 goes on to state that non-fee-paying discretionary portfolios may be included in a composite

EXHIBIT 13-14 Illustration of Rebalancing Policies

	Domestic Equity Index	International Equity Index	Domestic Corporate Bond Index	Cash Equivalents Index	Blended Benchmark
Blended benchmark weights	50%	10%	35%	5%	
			Monthly Rebalancing		
January	−1.46%	−3.96%	0.79%	0.15%	−0.84%
February	−1.93	0.61	0.96	0.13	−0.56
March	3.76	5.56	−1.65	0.15	1.87
April	−6.06	0.76	1.90	0.16	−2.28
May	−0.74	1.65	0.85	0.16	0.10
June	−7.12	−4.41	0.74	0.14	−3.74
July	−7.79	−9.21	1.19	0.15	−4.39
August	0.66	0.00	1.75	0.14	0.95
September	−10.87	−10.43	1.59	0.16	−5.91
October	8.80	4.87	−0.45	0.15	4.74
November	5.89	4.56	−0.02	0.16	3.40
December	−5.87	−2.86	2.08	0.12	−2.49
Linked monthly returns	−22.09%	−13.50%	10.11%	1.78%	→ **−9.30%**
			Quarterly Rebalancing		
First quarter	0.27%	2.00%	0.08%	0.43%	0.38%
Second quarter	− 13.39	− 2.09	3.53	0.46	− 5.65
Third quarter	− 17.27	− 18.68	4.60	0.45	− 8.87
Fourth quarter	8.45	6.52	1.60	0.43	5.46
Linked quarterly returns	−22.08%	−13.49%	10.11%	1.78%	→**−8.98%**

(with appropriate disclosures).[20] For example, in the interest of public service or community relations, a firm might waive the investment management fee on a charitable organization's portfolio, or a firm might use its own or its principals' capital to implement a new investment strategy. In the section of the GIPS standards devoted to presentation and reporting, Provision II.5.A.7 stipulates that if a composite contains any non-fee-paying portfolios, the firm must present, as of the end of each annual period, the percentage of the composite assets represented by the non-fee-paying portfolios.

Appendix A of the GIPS standards contains several sample GIPS-compliant performance presentations. We have reproduced one of them in Exhibit 13-15.

3.13. Presentation and Reporting Recommendations

In addition to the requirements explained above, the GIPS standards include recommended practices in presentation and reporting of investment results.

[20]Nondiscretionary portfolios, however, cannot be included in a firm's composites under the GIPS standards.

Provisions II.5.B.1.a–g recommend that certain items be presented. First, Provision II.5.B.1.a recommends that firms present composite performance gross of investment management and administrative fees and before taxes, except for nonreclaimable withholding taxes. **Administrative fees,** defined as all charges other than trading expenses and investment management fees, could include custody, accounting, consulting, and legal fees, among others. Such fees are typically not under an investment manager's control.

Provision II.5.B.1.b recommends that, in addition to the required annual returns, firms should present cumulative composite and benchmark returns for all periods. Cumulative returns are calculated by geometrically linking historical returns. For instance, using Equation 13-2 and the data given in Exhibit 13-15, we find that the composite's cumulative gross-of-fees return was 74.5 percent and the cumulative benchmark return was 68.8 percent for the 1995 to 2004 period.

EXHIBIT 13-15 Sample 1 Investment Firm Balanced Composite January 1, 1995, through December 31, 2004

Year	Gross-of-Fees Return (percent)	Net-of-Fees Return (percent)	Benchmark Return (percent)	Number of Portfolios	Internal Dispersion (percent)	Total Composite Assets (CAD million)	Total Firm Assets (CAD million)
1995	16.0	15.0	14.1	26	4.5	165	236
1996	2.2	1.3	1.8	32	2.0	235	346
1997	22.4	21.5	24.1	38	5.7	344	529
1998	7.1	6.2	6.0	45	2.8	445	695
1999	8.5	7.5	8.0	48	3.1	520	839
2000	−8.0	−8.9	−8.4	49	2.8	505	1,014
2001	−5.9	−6.8	−6.2	52	2.9	499	995
2002	2.4	1.6	2.2	58	3.1	525	1,125
2003	6.7	5.9	6.8	55	3.5	549	1,225
2004	9.4	8.6	9.1	59	2.5	575	1,290

Sample 1 Investment Firm has prepared and presented this report in compliance with the Global Investment Performance Standards (GIPS®).

Notes:

1. Sample 1 Investment Firm is a balanced portfolio investment manager that invests solely in Canadian securities. Sample 1 Investment Firm is defined as an independent investment management firm that is not affiliated with any parent organization. For the periods from 2000 through 2004, Sample 1 Investment Firm has been verified by Verification Services Inc. A copy of the verification report is available upon request. Additional Information regarding the firm's policies and procedures for calculating and reporting performance results is available upon request.
2. The composite includes all nontaxable balanced portfolios with an asset allocation of 30 percent S&P TSX and 70 percent Scotia Canadian Bond Index Fund, which allow up to a 10 percent deviation in asset allocation.
3. The benchmark: 30 percent S&P TSX; 70 percent Scotia Canadian Bond Index Fund rebalanced monthly.
4. Valuations are computed and performance reported in Canadian dollars.
5. Gross-of-fees performance returns are presented before management and custodial fees but after all trading expenses. Returns are presented net of nonreclaimable withholding taxes. Net-of-fees performance returns are calculated by deducting the highest fee of 0.25 percent from the quarterly gross composite return. The management fee schedule is as follows: 1.00 percent on first CAD25M;. 60 percent thereafter.
6. This composite was created in February 1995. A complete list and description of firm composites is available upon request.
7. For the periods 1995 and 1996 Sample 1 Investment Firm was not in compliance with the GIPS Standards because portfolios were valued annually.
8. Internal dispersion is calculated using the equal weighted standard deviation of all portfolios that were included in the composite for the entire year.

Source: Global Investment Performance Standards, 2005.

The Standards also recommend that annualized composite and benchmark returns be presented for periods greater than 12 months (Provision II.5.B.1.f). As expressed in Equation 13-11, annualized returns are calculated by taking the *n*th root of chain-linked returns, where *n* is the number of years in the period.

$$r_{ann} = \sqrt[n]{(1 + r_{t,1}) \times (1 + r_{t,2}) \times \ldots \times (1 + r_{t,N})} - 1 \qquad (13\text{-}11)$$

For instance, the sample GIPS-compliant presentation shown above covers the 10-year period 1995 through 2004. Applying Equation 13-11 to the cumulative returns calculated above, we find that the annualized gross-of-fees return for the composite during that 10-year period was approximately 5.73 percent, and the annualized return for the benchmark during the same period was approximately 5.37 percent.

The GIPS standards also recommend that performance presentations include returns for quarterly and/or shorter time periods (Provision II.5.B.1.e). We have already seen, of course, that returns for periods shorter than one year must *not* be annualized.

Recall that the standards require composite returns to be calculated on an asset-weighted basis (Provision II.2.A.3). Provision II.5.B.1.c recommends that firms present equal-weighted mean and median returns for each composite. The equal-weighted mean and the median returns for the composite portfolios may provide useful information to prospective clients, particularly if the required dispersion measure has been calculated on an equal-weighted basis.

The Standards further recommend that firms present composite-level country and sector weightings (Provision II.5.B.1.g). This information may give prospective clients a sense of each composite's diversification.

In addition, the GIPS standards suggest that firms prepare graphs and charts presenting specific information that the Standards require or recommend (Provision II.5.B.1.d). Carefully constructed graphical exhibits can convey information in a way that prospective clients find easy to grasp. Of course, the ethical ideals of fair representation and full disclosure remain in force; firms should design their graphs and charts so as to present information objectively.

We have seen that the Standards require the presentation of a measure of dispersion of portfolio returns across the composite. The GIPS standards also recommend, but do not require, the presentation of relevant composite-level risk measures. Examples of such measures cited in Provision II.5.B.2 include beta, tracking error, modified duration, the information ratio, Sharpe ratio, Treynor ratio, credit ratings, value at risk, and the volatility or variability of composite and benchmark returns over time. (Volatility might be represented by the annualized standard deviation of composite and benchmark returns during the period covered by the performance presentation if it is long enough to provide a statistically valid measure.) A discussion of the definitions, computation, applicability, and limitations of these various indicators of risk falls outside the scope of this chapter. The key point to note is that the GIPS standards advocate offering prospective clients relevant quantitative information they can use to evaluate the riskiness of the investment strategy represented by a composite.

Finally, we saw earlier that for any noncompliant performance presented for periods prior to January 1, 2000, the disclosure standards require firms to disclose the period and the nature of the noncompliance (Provision II.4.A.10). The GIPS standards for presentation and reporting encourage firms that have presented the required five years of compliant historical performance to bring any remaining portion of their historical track record into compliance with the Standards (Provision II.5.B.3). This recommendation does not relieve firms of the requirement to add annual performance on an ongoing basis to build a 10-year compliant track record.

3.14. Introduction to the Real Estate and Private Equity Provisions

The GIPS standards codify the treatment to be accorded direct real estate and private equity, two major asset classes with distinctive characteristics. In general, the GIPS standards in force for all other asset classes apply to real estate and private equity as well; however, the Standards stipulate certain exceptions to the main provisions, and set forth additional requirements and recommendations for these asset classes.

The GIPS standards for real estate and private equity override, or replace, specific provisions of the main GIPS standards for valuation. Because these types of investments (as defined below) do not trade in organized exchanges, their market values are not readily obtainable. Accordingly, the GIPS standards prescribe valuation techniques adapted to each of these asset classes. Moreover, the Standards for private equity override specific provisions for calculation methodology, fees, and the presentation and reporting of returns.

The Standards for real estate and private equity also put forward requirements and recommendations in addition to those set forth in the other sections of the Standards. For example, in the area of presentation and reporting, the provisions for real estate require that firms present total return accompanied by the component returns for income and capital appreciation. To cite another example, the provisions for private equity require that, in addition to presenting total composite assets and total firm assets, firms must disclose the total committed capital for the composite.

Real estate and private equity investments can be structured in many different ways. In order to demarcate the scope of the asset class–specific provisions, the GIPS standards specify the types of investments that are *not* considered real estate. Publicly traded real estate securities (such as real estate investment trusts, or REITs), including any listed securities issued by public companies, and commercial mortgage-backed securities (CMBSs), are subject to the general provisions rather than to the real estate provisions of the GIPS standards. Also excluded from the real estate provisions are private debt investments, including commercial and residential loans for which the expected return is solely related to contractual interest rates without any participation in the economic performance of the underlying real estate. If a portfolio holds both real estate and other types of investments that are not considered real estate, then the real estate provisions apply only to the real estate portion of the portfolio, and the carve-out provisions of the GIPS standards must also be brought to bear.

Similarly, the **private equity** provisions pertain to private equity investments other than **open-end** or **evergreen** funds, which allow for ongoing investment and redemptions. Open-end and evergreen funds remain subject to the main GIPS standards.

Real estate investing and private equity investing are highly specialized areas of expertise, and the GIPS standards governing them are necessarily complicated. In the following sections, we will consider principal concepts and major provisions of the pertinent Standards. This discussion is not an exhaustive treatment of these complex topics.

3.15. Real Estate Standards

Market values are central to calculating returns on real estate assets, and accordingly the GIPS standards for input data and disclosures include provisions related to valuation procedures. Firms are not required to determine the market value of real estate assets as frequently as they must value portfolios composed of more-liquid securities in accordance with the general provisions of the GIPS standards. At present, real estate investments must be valued at market value at least once every 12 months and, for periods beginning January 1, 2008, at least quarterly (Provision II.6.A.1). In the absence of transactions, however, managers' estimates of market values may be based on debatable assumptions. Accordingly, the Standards further require firms to have valuations conducted periodically by independent, credentialed experts. Specifically, Provision II.6.A.2 reads in part, "Real estate investments must be valued by an external **professionally designated, certified** or **licensed commercial property valuer/appraiser** at least once every 36 months." In markets where specialists with appropriate credentials are unavailable, the firm must take steps to ensure that it uses only well-qualified valuers or appraisers. Common-sense steps might include considering the appraiser's pertinent experience in the local market with the kind of properties to be independently valued.

The Standards recommend that real estate investments be valued, either internally or by an external appraiser, at least quarterly. (As noted, quarterly valuations will be required for periods beginning January 1, 2008.) They also recommend that real estate investments be valued by an external valuer or appraiser at least once every 12 months (Provisions II.6.B.1–2).

In addition to the other disclosure requirements of the GIPS standards, performance presentations for real estate investments must include disclosures about the methods, sources, and frequency of valuations. Provision II.6.A.3.c requires that firms disclose their valuation methods and procedures for real estate. For example, among other conventional approaches, the firm might capitalize the income generated by a property, using an income capitalization rate imputed or "extracted" from the market based on the net operating income and sale prices of similar properties; or the firm might base the valuation of the subject property directly on the reported sale prices of comparable nearby properties, with adjustments to reflect differences in the properties' location, features, or condition.[21] The real estate standards also require firms to disclose the source of the valuation for each period—that is, whether the valuation is prepared internally, determined by an external valuer, or obtained from a third-party manager (Provision II.6.A.3.e). The firm additionally must disclose the asset-weighted percentage of composite real estate assets valued by an **external valuation** for each period as well as the frequency with which real estate investments are valued by external valuers (Provisions II.6.A.3.f–g).

In an earlier section, we discussed the definition of *discretion* under the main GIPS standards. The GIPS provisions for disclosure associated with real estate performance presentations require firms to provide a description of discretion (Provision II.6.A.3.b). The principles we have already considered in connection with the general standards apply to real estate portfolios, which are considered discretionary if the manager has sole or primary responsibility for major investment decisions. The firm must judge whether client-imposed constraints are so restrictive as to prevent the manager from executing the desired investment strategy, thus rendering a portfolio nondiscretionary. For example, if a client motivated by tax considerations prohibits the manager from selling properties when the manager thinks their value should be realized, or if a client orders that properties be sold at a time when the manager thinks they should be held until prices improve, then the firm may conclude that the portfolio is nondiscretionary.

The Standards also include particular rate-of-return presentation and related disclosure requirements for real estate. **Total return** and its components, income return and capital return, must be presented (Provision II.6.A.4), and the calculation methodology for component returns must be disclosed (Provision II.6.A.3.a). Let us define these terms and explain the calculations.

Total return, income return, and capital return are all calculated based on **capital employed,** computed by adjusting the beginning capital for time-weighted cash flows that occur during the measurement period. Conceptually, we can adjust for weighted cash flows in the same way that we adjust beginning composite assets for external cash flows (see the

[21]These and other appraisal techniques are explained in Shilling (2002, Chapters 10 and 11).

treatment of Provision II.2.A.3). On the model of Equation 13-7, we can compute capital employed, here designated C_E, as follows:

$$C_E = C_0 + \sum(\text{CF}_i \times w_i) \tag{13-12}$$

where C_0 is the beginning capital.

The **capital return** is calculated by dividing the capital employed (C_E) into the change in market value during the measurement period minus capital expenditures (E_C) plus sale proceeds (S), as shown in Equation 13-13.

$$r_C = \frac{(\text{MV}_1 - \text{MV}_0) - E_C + S}{C_E} \tag{13-13}$$

The classification of outlays as "capital expenditures" is subject to accounting rules, but capital expenditures may broadly be characterized as costs incurred to acquire and improve real assets. In contrast to costs that are expensed immediately, capital expenditures for long-lived improvements are added to the value of the asset.

The **income return** is calculated by dividing capital employed into investment income accrued during the period (INC_A) minus nonrecoverable expenditures (E_{NR}), interest expense on debt (INT_D), and property taxes (T_P). Nonrecoverable expenditures are items not reimbursed by tenants, such as leasing and financing costs, maintenance, and major repairs. The expression for income return is:

$$r_I = \frac{\text{INC}_A - \text{E}_{NR} - \text{INT}_D - \text{T}_P}{C_E} \tag{13-14}$$

The single-period total return for real estate, then, is the sum of the component returns:

$$r_T = r_C + r_I \tag{13-15}$$

As noted, the provisions for disclosure require firms to disclose the calculation methodology for component returns (Provision II.6.A.3.a). In particular, the disclosure must indicate whether the firm calculates component returns in separate series using chain-linked time-weighted rates of return or, alternately, adjusts the returns to make the sum of the income return and the capital return equal to the total return for the periods presented. For example, Exhibit 13-16 displays a composite's income return, capital return, and total return for the four quarters of the year 200X. The full-year returns are calculated by chain-linking the quarterly returns for each series.

With this method, although the income return and the capital return added together equal the total return for each quarter, the component returns for the full year (as they will appear

EXHIBIT 13-16 Real Estate Total Return: An Illustration

	Income Return	Capital Return	Total Return
First quarter	2.15%	−0.52%	1.63%
Second quarter	2.20	0.59	2.79
Third quarter	2.17	0.75	2.92
Fourth quarter	2.10	0.91	3.01
200X	8.90	1.73	10.75

in the performance presentation) do not sum to the total return. The required disclosure on the calculation methodology will explain how the returns were chain linked. Alternatively, if the firm makes an adjustment forcing the component returns taken together to equal the total return, it must disclose that it has done so. Needless to say, the adjustment method must be set forth in the firm's internal documentation.

In addition to requiring that the capital return, income return, and total return of the composite be presented for each period (Provision II.6.A.4), the GIPS standards recommend that the capital and income segments of the appropriate real estate benchmark be presented when the data are available (Provision II.6.B.5).

The GIPS standards for real estate further recommend that firms present the **since-inception internal rate of return** (SI-IRR) for the composite (Provision II.6.B.6). We will encounter SI-IRR again in connection with the standards for private equity, where it is a required element. The internal rate of return is the discount rate that sets an investment's net present value equal to zero; expressed another way, it is the discount rate that equates the present value of an investment's cost with the present value of its benefits. The cost is the capital the client invests; the benefits are the distributions the client receives plus the asset's market value at the end of the measurement period. Mathematically, we calculate the annualized internal rate of return from the value of r that solves the following equation:

$$MV_0 = \frac{CF_1}{(1+r)^1} + \frac{CF_2}{(1+r)^2} + \cdots + \frac{MV_N}{(1+r)^N} \qquad (13\text{-}16)$$

where MV_0 represents the initial investment (the beginning market value), the terms CF_1, CF_2, and so on represent interim cash flows, and MV_N represents the ending market value. For simplicity, Equation 13-16 assumes equally spaced end-of-period cash flows. In this equation, r is a subperiod return; when annualized, it is the internal rate of return.

Of course, the investor may make more than one capital contribution. With attention to the direction (the sign) of the cash flows, we can restate the formula for the internal rate of return as follows:

$$\sum_{i=0}^{N} \frac{CF_i}{(1+r)^i} = 0 \qquad (13\text{-}17)$$

where CF_i is the cash flow for the period i and N is the total number of periods. In Equation 13-17, a negative CF_i represents a net cost or outflow to the investor and a positive CF_i represents a net distribution or inflow to the investor; CF_0 and CF_N incorporate MV_0 and MV_N, respectively, in Equation 13-17. This formulation accommodates multiple contributions (cash inflows to the portfolio) and distributions (cash outflows from the portfolio) over the entire inception-to-date timeframe. By setting the sum of the present values of cash inflows and outflows equal to zero, the equation effectively defines r as the discount rate that makes the present value of the cost equal the present value of the benefits.

An example may make the calculation more clear. Let us consider the investment from the perspective of the client who funds the real estate portfolio and receives benefits in the form of cash distributions during the measurement period and ownership of assets valued at market value as of the end of the period. For this example, Exhibit 13-17 shows the timing and amount of the quarterly cash flows. The portfolio's real estate assets are valued as of the end of the second year, so the since-inception performance measurement period is eight quarters.

The client's experience can be expressed graphically, as in Exhibit 13-18, with the ending market value displayed as a cash flow. Note that in some periods, no cash flows occur.

EXHIBIT 13-17 Data for an IRR Calculation

	Date	Quarter	Amount
Initial investment	December 31 Year 0	0	− \$150,000
Additional investment	June 30 Year 1	2	− \$100,000
Distribution received	March 31 Year 2	5	\$12,665
Distribution received	September 30 Year 2	7	\$11,130
Ending market value	December 31 Year 2	8	\$274,300

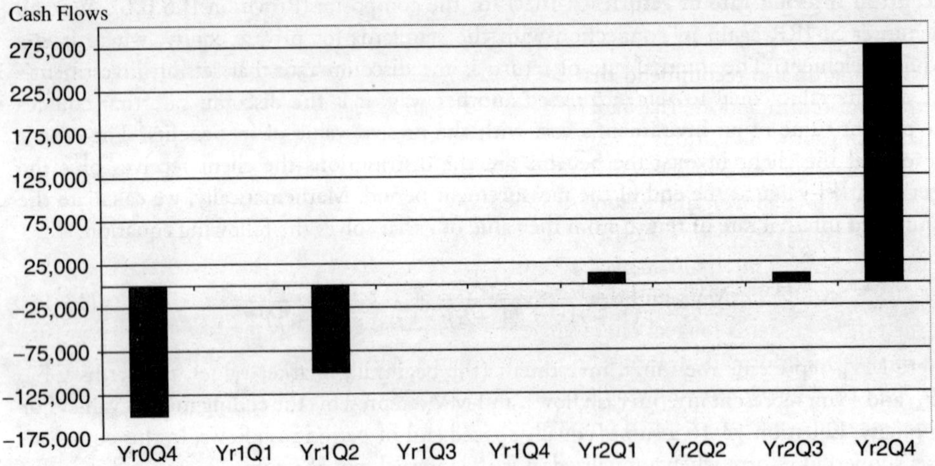

EXHIBIT 13-18

Using the data in Exhibit 13-17 as inputs to Equation 13-17, we find through an iterative trial-and-error process that the quarterly discount rate r is approximately 2.53 percent. Exhibit 13-19 demonstrates this result. The present value factor applied to each cash flow is $1/(1+r)^i$, where r is the discount rate and i is the sequential number of the subperiod. For instance, the present value factor applied to the cash distribution of \$12,665 received on March 31 of Year 2, the fifth quarter, is:

$$\frac{1}{(1+0.0253)^5} = 0.88256$$

Exhibit 13-19 shows that 2.53 percent is the quarterly discount rate that sets the sum of the present values of the cash flows from inception through the end of the measurement period equal to zero. The GIPS standards for real estate require us to annualize the since-inception internal rate of return. To annualized a quarterly return, we calculate $(1+r)^4 - 1$, so the SI-IRR earned in this example is 10.51 percent.

If the SI-IRR is shown, the firm should disclose the time period that is covered as well as the frequency of the cash flows used in the calculation (Provision II.6.B.4). The Standards further recommend that firms use quarterly cash flows at a minimum in calculating the SI-IRR (Provision II.6.B.3). In other words, CF_i should reflect the net cash flow for a period no longer than a quarter.

EXHIBIT 13-19 Demonstration That the Computed IRR is Correct

Date	Cash Flow	Period	Present Value Factor ($r = 2.53\%$)	Present Value
December 31 Year 0	(150,000)	0	1	(150,000)
June 30 Year 1	(100,000)	2	0.95126	(95,126)
March 31 Year 2	12,665	5	0.88256	11,178
September 30 Year 2	11,130	7	0.83954	9,344
December 31 Year 2	274,300	8	0.81883	224,605
Total (does not equal zero due to rounding)				1

The GIPS standards also recommend that firms present the annualized since-inception time-weighted rate of return and internal rate of return gross and net of fees. In all cases, the fees should include incentive allocations (i.e., incentive fees). The gross-of-fees and net-of-fees SI-IRRs should be presented on two bases: first, reflecting the composite's ending market value (as shown in the example above), and second, reflecting only realized cash flows—that is, excluding unrealized gains (Provisions II.6.B.7.a-b). The returns mentioned in this paragraph are especially recommended in circumstances in which the investment manager can control the timing of cash contributions to the fund.

Finally, the GIPS standards for real estate suggest that other performance measures may provide additional useful information. Provision II.6.B.7.c advises that the GIPS standards for private equity, discussed below, provide guidance on additional measures such as **investment** and **realization multiples** and ratios based on **paid-in capital.**

3.16. Private Equity Standards

The GIPS provisions for private equity use technical terms that may be unfamiliar to the performance measurement generalist. Although simplified for brevity, an overview of the private equity investment process may facilitate understanding of the Standards' requirements and recommendations. Let us take for an example a **venture capital** fund organized as a **limited partnership,** one of many investment structures used in the private equity market. A venture capital firm identifies an emerging industry, develops the fund concept, and secures commitments from investors who pledge to pay in a certain amount of capital over a certain period of time, often three to five years. In this structure, a venture capital firm will serve as **general partner,** and the investors will be **limited partners.** The general partner screens early stage companies' business plans, identifies the most promising enterprises, and conducts in-depth analysis and due diligence on the quality of their management, the legal status of their intellectual property rights, and the prospective demand for their products, among many other factors. The general partner then negotiates deals with the companies that pass scrutiny and places capital calls drawing down the limited partners' committed capital for investment in the portfolio companies. There may be multiple capital calls to meet each company's cash requirements in accordance with the terms of the deal. As the fund matures, the general partner harvests the portfolio companies (for instance, by taking them public) and distributes the proceeds to the limited partners. With this background in mind, let us turn to the GIPS standards for private equity.

Recognizing that valuations of untraded securities are critically based on business assumptions and that practitioners employ a range of valuation methods, the GIPS standards include an exposition of principles to which firms must adhere when estimating the market value of private equities (GIPS Appendix D, "Private Equity Valuation Principles"). Although they appear in an appendix, these principles are integral to the GIPS standards: Provision II.7.A.1 explicitly requires private equity investments to be valued in accordance with them.

The principles obligate firms to ensure that valuations are prepared with integrity and professionalism by individuals with appropriate experience and ability under the direction of senior management and in accordance with documented review procedures. The valuation basis must be divulged as transparently as possible in view of legal and practical constraints; for the latest period presented, the firm must clearly disclose the methodologies and key assumptions used in valuing private equity investments. The valuation basis must be logically cohesive and rigorously applied. At a minimum, valuations must recognize the impact of events that diminish an asset's value. For instance, occurrences such as defaults, legal contests, changes in management, foreign currency devaluations, or substantial deteriorations in market conditions, among many others, may adversely affect an asset's estimated market value. Private equity valuations must be prepared on a consistent and comparable basis from one period to the next; if any change to the valuation basis or method is deemed appropriate, it must be explained and its effect, if material, must be disclosed. Valuations must be prepared at least annually, but quarterly valuations are recommended (see the "Guidelines for Valuation" in GIPS Appendix D and Provision II.7.B.1).

The principles recommend that private equity investments be valued on a fair value basis. **Fair value** represents the amount or price at which an asset could be bought or sold in a current transaction between willing, knowledgeable parties. The GIPS standards set forth a hierarchy or order of fair value methodologies. In this order, the best valuation method looks to a market transaction. For example, if a new round of financing takes place for a closely held company, the arm's-length price at which an external party makes a material investment might provide a sound basis for establishing the current market value of previously issued securities. In the absence of recent market transactions, the next-best method is to use market-based multiples appropriate to the business being valued. For example, the valuation might be based on the current price-to-earnings ratio for comparable publicly traded companies engaged in the same line of business, with an appropriate discount for the limited marketability of the subject company's securities. The least preferred of the three methods in the hierarchy is to calculate the present value of risk-adjusted expected cash flows discounted at the risk-free rate. The risk-free rate is observable, so the discount rate is objectively determinable, but this method is nonetheless critically sensitive to the assumptions underlying the cash flow projections and risk adjustments.

Valuing private equity investments is a challenging assignment even for well-qualified professionals who are informed about the marketplace, knowledgeable about the issuing company's business, trained in financial statement analysis, and experienced in assessing deal structures and terms. This cursory treatment may nonetheless suffice to convey the complexity of the task. We refer the reader to GIPS Appendix D for additional considerations pertaining to the fair valuation of private equity investments.

The GIPS provisions for private equity presentation and reporting require firms to present both the net-of-fees and the gross-of-fees annualized SI-IRR of the composite for each year since inception (Provision II.7.A.20).[22] The calculation methodology provisions for private equity specify that the annualized SI-IRR must be calculated using either daily or monthly cash flows and the end-of-period valuation of the unliquidated holdings remaining in the composite portfolios. Stock **distributions** must be valued at the time of distribution (Provision II.7.A.3).

[22]We introduced the SI-IRR in connection with the GIPS standards for real estate.

Net-of-fee returns must be net of **carried interest,** representing the percentage of profits on the fund's investments that general partners receive, as well as investment management fees and **transaction expenses** (Provision II.7.A.4). For **investment advisers,** who (unlike general partners) have no role in the actual management of the portfolio companies held in the fund, *all* returns must be net of underlying partnership and/or fund fees and carried interest, and net-of-fees returns must in addition be net of the investment adviser's own fees, expenses, and carried interest (Provision II.7.A.5).

The GIPS provisions for composite construction require all closed-end private equity investments to be included in a composite defined by strategy and **vintage year** (Provision II.7.A.6). The vintage year, the year that capital is first **drawn down** or called from investors, is useful information for prospective clients who wish to establish the comparability of different composites. The Standards distinguish **direct investments** in assets (for instance, in equity securities issued by a single closely held company) from investments made through partnerships or funds, and they require that partnership and fund investments, direct investments, and open-end private equity investments be in separate composites (Provision II.7.A.7).

Specific disclosure requirements also apply for private equity. Firms must disclose the vintage year of each composite (Provision II.7.A.8) and provide a definition of the composite investment strategy (Provision II.7.A.15). In the private equity arena, the strategy may be, for instance, to make early stage investments in growing companies, to finance turnarounds of distressed companies, or to channel capital to companies operating in a particular geographic area, among other possibilities. Firms must also disclose the total **committed capital** of the composite for the most recent period (Provision II.7.A.11).

As one might expect, there are disclosure requirements pertaining to the valuation of composite assets. For the most recent period, firms must disclose the valuation methodologies employed. In addition, if any change from the prior period occurs in either the valuation basis or the valuation methodology, such a change must be disclosed (Provision II.7.A.12). As noted previously, assets must be valued in accordance with the GIPS Private Equity Valuation Principles. If the presentation complies with any local or regional valuation guidelines in addition to the GIPS principles, firms must disclose which local or regional guidelines they are required to use (Provision II.7.A.13). It must also be disclosed that the firm's valuation review procedures are available upon request (Provision II.7.A.14). Importantly, if a valuation basis other than fair value is used, firms must disclose for the most recent period presented an explanation why fair value is not applicable. Additionally, firms must disclose the number of holdings that are not fair-valued and their carrying value both in absolute amount and relative to the total fund (Provision II.7.A.17). Firms must also disclose the unrealized appreciation or depreciation of the composite for the most recent period (Provision II.7.A.10). This information about the magnitude of unrealized gains or losses will assist prospective clients in evaluating the significance of the estimated end-of-period market values used as inputs to the rate-of-return calculations.

Recall that the GIPS provisions for private equity calculation methodology require firms to use daily or monthly cash flows in computing the SI-IRR. The disclosure provisions require firms to state whether they are using daily or monthly cash flows in the SI-IRR calculation (Provision II.7.A.18).

If benchmark returns are presented, the firm must disclose the calculation methodology used for the benchmark (Provision II.7.A.16). On the other hand, if no benchmark is shown, the presentation must explain why none is provided (see Provision II.7.A.23). Also, the period-end used for a composite must be disclosed if it is not a calendar year-end (Provision II.7.A.19).

Under the general GIPS standards, discontinued composites must remain on the firm's list of composites for at least five years after discontinuation, and firms must provide a compliant presentation upon request for any composite listed (see Provisions II.0.A.12–13). For discontinued private equity composites, the final realization or liquidation date must be stated (Provision II.7.A.9). Disclosing the **final realization date** as well as the vintage date enables prospective clients to determine the time period that the fund existed, for the purpose of comparing one investment with another.

Having reviewed the valuation principles and the requirements for input data, calculation methodology, composite construction, and disclosure, we are in position to address the GIPS provisions for private equity presentation and reporting. We have already noted the requirement that the annualized gross-of-fees and net-of-fees SI-IRRs must be presented for each year since inception (Provision II.7.A.20). A benchmark reflecting the same vintage year and investment strategy may be shown (indeed, if none is shown, firms must justify the omission). If a benchmark is shown, firms must present the cumulative annualized SI-IRR of the benchmark for the same periods that composite performance is presented (Provision II.7.A.23).

Further requirements pertain to the funding status of the composite. For each period presented, firms must report cumulative paid-in capital—that is, the total payments drawn down to date from the capital committed by investors. Paid-in capital may include amounts received by the fund but not yet invested in portfolio companies; the Standards stipulate that firms must also present total current **invested capital** for each period. In addition, firms are required to report cumulative **distributions** paid out to investors in cash or stock for each period presented (Provision II.7.A.21).

Firms must also report certain multiples or ratios for each period presented. One of them is the ratio of **total value** to paid-in capital (TVPI, also called the **investment multiple**). Representing the total return of the investment although not taking time into account, TVPI gives prospective clients information about the value of the composite relative to its cost basis. For the purpose of the TVPI calculation, total value can be determined by adding distributions to date to the end-of-period **residual value** or net asset value of the fund—that is, the market value of assets less accrued investment management fees and carried interest. Firms must also report the ratio of cumulative distributions to paid-in capital (DPI, also called the **realization multiple**); the ratio of **paid-in capital to committed capital** (**PIC**); and the ratio of **residual value to paid-in capital** (**RVPI**). Listed in Provision II.7.A.22, these required statistics afford prospective clients useful information about the financial history and status of the fund. The provisions for presentation and reporting also recommend, but do not require, that firms report the average holding period of the investments (for example, the portfolio companies in a fund) over the life of the composite (Provision II.7.B.2).

The intricacies of performance presentation in compliance with the GIPS standards for private equity reflect this field's complexity. Of necessity, the introductory treatment given the subject here does not address many nuances or special circumstances that the practitioner may encounter. Further guidance may be found in a paper entitled "Private Equity Provisions for the GIPS Standards" prepared by the Venture Capital and Private Equity Subcommittee of the IPC. This resource is available on the CFA Institute web site.

4. VERIFICATION

Verification is a review of performance measurement policies, processes, and procedures by an independent third-party[23] for the purpose of establishing that a firm claiming compliance

[23]The "Guidance Statement on Verifier Independence" defines the term *independence* in the context of verification and addresses potential independence issues. It is available on the CFA Institute web site.

has adhered to the GIPS standards. Although verification can be costly and time-consuming, it may offer the firm a competitive marketing advantage by making the claim of compliance more credible. In addition, preparing for and undergoing the verification process may help the firm improve its internal operations. Verification powerfully supports the guiding principles of fair representation and full disclosure of investment performance.

The GIPS standards currently do not require firms to be verified, although verification may become mandatory at some point in the future. Nonetheless, the Standards strongly encourage firms to undergo verification. Section III of the GIPS standards reviews the scope and purpose of verification and sets forth the minimum procedures that verifiers must follow prior to issuing a verification report to the firm. The stated goal of the Investment Performance Council in presenting the verification procedures is to encourage broad acceptance of verification.

Implementation (11)

Selecting a Verification Firm. Verification is a major undertaking, and it is crucial for the investment management firm to choose an independent verifier whose resources match the firm's needs. At the outset of the selection process, the investment management firm approaching verification should consider the scope of its operations and the nature of its products. The requirements of a large investment management organization with a presence in markets around the world will differ from those of a firm operating in only a single country. Similarly, a hedge fund manager, a manager who engages in real estate or private equity investing, a quantitatively oriented manager whose investment strategies rely heavily on the use of derivative securities, or a manager who manages tax-aware portfolios for individuals may have more specialized requirements than a manager who manages funds for tax-exempt institutions such as pension plans and charitable foundations. These factors should be communicated to potential verifiers and reflected in the selection criteria.

Some organizations have standard request-for-proposal templates that can be adapted for specific purposes. The RFP should include a description of the issuing organization and a statement on the scope of the project. Firms investigating verifiers' qualifications might consider initially asking for the following information:

- A description of the verification firm, including its history, ownership, and organizational structure; a description of the performance-related services it offers; and a representative list of verification assignments completed indicating the nature of the investment management firm verified (e.g., "institutional trust division of a regional bank").
- An explanation of the firm's approach to project management, sampling, and testing.
- The roles and professional biographies of the verifiers who will be assigned to this project.
- Client references, including contact details, and information about the number of clients added and lost over some period of time (for instance, the last three years).
- The verification firm's fee schedule.
- A preliminary project plan setting forth the major tasks and estimated timeframes for completion in view of the investment management firm's organizational structure, product line, and clientele.

The reader is also referred to "Suggested Questions to Ask Prospective Verification Firms," a paper published by the IPC. This resource is available on the CFA Institute web site.

In introducing the GIPS standards, we stressed that they must be applied on a firmwide basis (Provision II.0.A.1). The standards for verification state that a verification report can be issued only with respect to the whole firm. In other words, verification cannot be carried out for a single composite (Section III.A.1). After the firm has been verified, as evidenced by a verification report, it may additionally choose to have a detailed Performance Examination conducted on one or more specific composites, but firms are expressly prohibited from stating that a particular composite presentation has been "GIPS verified" (see Section III.C).

The minimum initial period for which verification can be performed is one year of a firm's presented performance. The Standards recommend that verification cover all periods for which the firm claims GIPS compliance (Section III.A.3).

A verification report must confirm that the firm has complied with all the composite construction requirements of the GIPS standards on a firmwide basis and that the firm's processes and procedures are designed to calculate and present performance results in compliance with the GIPS standards. Without such a report from the verifier, the firm cannot state that its claim of compliance with the GIPS standards has been verified (Section III.A.4).

We have seen that a firm that does not meet all the requirements of the GIPS standards may not claim compliance; the firm cannot represent that it is in compliance with the GIPS standards "except for" certain requirements (Provision II.0.A.8). We have seen, too, that firms must document their policies and procedures in writing (Provision II.0.A.6), and they must maintain all data and information necessary to perform the required calculations and to support a performance presentation (Provision II.1.A.1). After conducting the required verification procedures summarized below, however, a verifier may conclude that the firm is not in compliance with these or other requirements of the GIPS standards. In such situations, the verifier must provide a statement to the firm explaining why it cannot issue a verification report (Section III.A.5).

The GIPS standards set forth minimum knowledge-based qualifications for verifiers. Specifically, verifiers must understand all the requirements and recommendations of the GIPS standards, including Guidance Statements and interpretations, and must adhere to any updates and clarifications published by CFA Institute and the IPC (Section III.B.1.b). In addition, verifiers must be knowledgeable about any country-specific laws and regulations that apply to the firm, and they must determine any differences between the GIPS standards and applicable country-specific laws and regulations (Section III.B.1.c).

Required preverification procedures include learning about the firm, the firm's performance-related policies, and the valuation basis for performance calculations. We will consider these requirements in turn.

First, verifiers must obtain selected samples of investment performance reports and other available information to ensure appropriate knowledge of the firm (Section III.B.1.a). This information will enable the verifiers to evaluate the firm's self-definition for the purpose of GIPS compliance.

Second, verifiers must determine the firm's assumptions, policies, and procedures for establishing and maintaining compliance with all applicable requirements of the GIPS standards. Section III.B.1.d enumerates the minimum requirements. Among other items, verifiers must receive the firm's written definition of investment discretion and the guidelines for determining whether accounts are fully discretionary; the firm's list of composite definitions, with written criteria for including accounts in each composite; and the firm's policies regarding the timeframe for including new accounts in and excluding closed accounts from composites. (The section of the GIPS standards devoted to verification uses the term "account" in place of "portfolio.") Verifiers must also determine the firm's policies related to input data, including dividend and interest income accruals and market valuations; portfolio and composite return calculation methodologies, including assumptions on the timing of external cash flows; and the presentation of composite returns. Verifiers must also obtain information on such items as the use of leverage and derivatives, investments in securities or countries that are not included in a composite's benchmark, and the timing of implied taxes on income and realized capital gains if the firm reports performance on an after-tax basis. This list is not exhaustive; indeed, the last item listed in Section III.B.1.d is "any other policies and procedures relevant to performance presentation."

Finally, prior to undertaking verification, verifiers must ensure that they understand the policies and methods used to record valuation information for the purpose of calculating performance. In particular, verifiers must determine that the firm's policy on classifying fund flows (such as interest, dividends, fees, and taxes, as well as contributions and withdrawals) will produce accurate returns in conformity with the GIPS requirements. Verifiers must confirm that the accounting treatment of investment income is appropriate; that tax payments, reclaims, and accruals are handled in a manner consistent with the desired before-tax or after-tax return calculation; that policies governing the recognition of purchases, sales, and the opening and closing of other positions are internally consistent and will produce accurate results; and that the firm's accounting for investments and derivatives is consistent with the GIPS standards. The foregoing requirements are presented in Section III.B.1.e.

Implementation (12)

Preparing for Verification. The investment management firm undertaking verification should gather the following information. The verifiers may use this information to prepare a fee estimate and a project plan, and they will need it in the course of the review.

- Sample performance presentations and marketing materials.
- All of the firm's performance-related policies, such as the firm's definition of discretion, the sources, methods, and review procedures for asset valuations, the time-weighted rate-of-return calculation methodology, the treatment of external cash flows, the computation of composite returns, etc.
- The complete list and description of composites.
- Composite definitions, including benchmarks and written criteria for including accounts.
- A list of all portfolios under management.
- All investment management agreements or contracts, and the clients' investment guidelines.
- A list of all the portfolios that have been in each composite during the verification period, the dates they were in the composites, and documentation supporting any changes to the portfolios in the composites.

The verifiers will also require historical portfolio- and composite-level performance data for sampling and testing. Other information requirements may come to light in the course of the review.

Having summarized the prerequisites for verification (the verifier's qualifications, familiarity with the firm, review of the firm's documented policies, and knowledge of the valuation basis for performance calculations), we turn now to the minimum required verification procedures.

Verifiers must first determine that the firm has been and remains appropriately defined for the purpose of GIPS compliance (Section III.B.2.a). Next, the GIPS standards for verification mandate testing of composite construction. The specific areas to be tested are set forth in Sections III.B.2.b.i–vii. Verifiers must be satisfied that the firm has defined and maintained composites according to reasonable, GIPS-compliant guidelines that have been applied consistently. Verifiers must also confirm that benchmarks are consistent with composite definitions (that is to say, the benchmark chosen for a specific composite appropriately reflects the composite's investment strategy) and that they have been consistently applied over time. Verifiers must be satisfied that the firm's list of composites is complete. In addition, verifiers must determine that all of the firm's actual discretionary fee-paying portfolios are included in at least one composite, that all accounts are included in their respective composites at all times, and that no accounts that belong in a particular composite have been excluded at any time. Verifiers must also be confident that the definition of discretion has been consistently applied over time. Section III.B.2.c requires verifiers to obtain a listing of all the firm's portfolios and to determine that selected accounts have been properly classified as discretionary or nondiscretionary in accordance with the firm's definition of discretion and the account agreements.

Verifiers must obtain a complete list of open and closed accounts for all composites for the years under examination, but they may base their compliance checks on a sample of the firm's accounts. The minimum factors to be considered when selecting sample accounts include the number of composites at the firm, the number of portfolios in each composite, and the nature of the composites. In addition, verifiers must take into account the total assets under management, the internal control structure at the firm, the number of years under examination, the computer applications used in the calculation of performance and the construction and maintenance of composites, and whether the firm uses external performance measurement services. The selection of sample accounts for testing is a critical step in the verification process. If the verifier encounters errors or discovers that the firm's record-keeping is deficient, a larger sample or additional verification procedures may be warranted (Section III.B.2.d).

Verifiers must trace selected accounts from the account agreements to the composites and confirm that the objectives articulated in the account agreement reflect the composite definition. (Verifiers must also determine that all portfolios sharing the same guidelines are included in the same composite.) For selected accounts, verifiers must confirm that the timing of the accounts' initial inclusion in their composites follows the firm's policy for new accounts, and similarly that the timing of the accounts' exclusion from the composite follows the firm's policy for closed accounts. Verifiers must furthermore determine that shifts from one composite to another are consistent with the documented guidelines of the firms' clients (Section III.B.2.e).

Verifiers must also determine whether the firm has computed performance in accordance with the methods and assumptions documented in its policies and disclosed in its presentations. In reaching this determination, verifiers should recalculate rates of return for selected accounts using an acceptable time-weighted rate of return formula as prescribed by the GIPS standards. Verifiers should also use a reasonable sample of composite calculations to test the accuracy of the asset weighting of returns, the geometric chain-linking generating annual rates of return, and the computation of the dispersion measure (Section III.B.2.f).

Verifiers must review a sample of composite presentations to ensure that they include the required information and disclosures (Section III.B.2.g).

Finally, under the GIPS standards, verifiers must maintain sufficient information to support the verification report. In particular, as part of the supporting documentation, verifiers must obtain a representation letter from the firm confirming major policies and any other representations made to the verifier during the examination (Section III.B.2.h).

5. GIPS ADVERTISING GUIDELINES

A firm may wish to claim that it complies with the GIPS standards in advertisements that do not accommodate fully compliant performance presentations. For instance, space may be limited, or the creative design and marketing message may not call for a performance presentation meeting all the requirements of the GIPS standards. To address this need, the Standards include an appendix expounding ethical standards for the advertisement of performance results. The guidelines are mandatory for firms that include a claim of GIPS compliance in their advertisements. Because the guidelines represent best practices in advertising, however, all firms are encouraged to respect them.

The GIPS Advertising Guidelines do not replace the broader GIPS standards, nor do they in any way exempt firms that claim GIPS compliance from adhering to all the required provisions of the Standards. Moreover, the guidelines do not replace laws and regulations governing performance advertisements. Firms must comply with applicable laws and regulations, and they must disclose any conflicts between the legal or regulatory requirements and the GIPS Advertising Guidelines.

Advertisements include any written or electronic materials addressed to more than one prospective or existing client. Thus "one-on-one" presentations and individual client reports are not considered advertisements. (This rule applies on a relationship basis. Presentations and reports to a single prospective or existing client are not considered advertisements despite the fact that a number of people may be in attendance, such as a board of trustees or the members of an investment committee.) The GIPS Advertising Guidelines pertain to any material disseminated more broadly to retain existing clients or solicit new clients for an adviser.

Implementation (13)

Communicating the GIPS Advertising Guidelines. Applying the GIPS Advertising Guidelines affects the work of marketing and creative staff members who may be unfamiliar with the GIPS standards. The firm's performance practitioners might conduct an educational session or workshop to present the guidelines and discuss implementation with the marketing group, including copywriters and graphic designers, and with the firm's legal or compliance officers. Here are some suggestions for presenting the guidelines and facilitating the discussion:

- Explain that the GIPS standards are ethical standards for fair representation and full disclosure of investment performance.
- Describe in general terms the domains for which Standards have been developed (fundamentals of compliance, input data, calculation methodology, composite construction, disclosures, presentation and reporting, real estate, and private equity, as well as the advertising guidelines).
- Explain how the firm is defined.
- Distribute the firm's list of composites and composite descriptions.
- Explain the relationship between the GIPS standards and the GIPS Advertising Guidelines.
- Explain how advertisements are defined for the purposes of the guidelines.

- Explain the relationship between applicable laws and regulations and the GIPS Advertising Guidelines.
- Present the requirements and recommendations of the advertising guidelines in detail as they apply to:

  1. Advertisements in which the firm claims compliance with the GIPS standards but does not present performance results.
  2. Advertisements in which the firm claims compliance with the GIPS standards and also presents performance.

- Review the sample advertisements provided in Appendix C of the Global Investment Performance Standards.
- Explain how supplemental information can be used to enhance performance presentations. (Consult the IPC's "Guidance Statement on the Use of Supplemental Information," available on the CFA Institute web site.)
- Reach agreement on compliance review procedures for new advertising materials. Because information used in advertisements subject to the guidelines is taken or derived from GIPS-compliant performance presentations, it is advisable for both a legal or compliance officer and a member of the performance measurement group to approve new advertising materials.

All advertisements that state a claim of compliance must include a description of the firm and information about how to obtain a list and description of all the firm's composites or a presentation that complies with the requirements of the GIPS standards (GIPS Advertising Guidelines B.1 and B.2). The required wording of the statement claiming compliance is: "[Name of firm] claims compliance with the Global Investment Performance Standards (GIPS®)" (Guideline B.3). We draw the reader's attention to the difference in wording between the GIPS Advertising Guidelines claim of compliance and the compliance statement that must appear on a fully compliant performance presentation: "[Name of firm] has prepared and presented this report in compliance with the Global Investment Performance Standards (GIPS®)."

All advertisements that not only state a claim of compliance but also present performance results must provide further information, as detailed below, and the relevant information must be taken or derived from a presentation that complies with the requirements of the GIPS standards. The required information includes, among other elements, a description of the strategy of the composite being advertised (Guideline B.4), an indication whether performance is shown gross of fees, net of fees, or both (Guideline B.6), and the currency used to express returns (Guideline B.8). When presenting noncompliant performance information for periods prior to January 1, 2000, in an advertisement, firms must disclose what information does not conform to the GIPS standards, explain the reasons, and identify the periods of noncompliance (Guideline B.10).

Advertisements that state a claim of compliance and present performance must also include period-to-date composite results. Returns for periods less than one year cannot be annualized. In addition to the period-to-date performance, the advertisement must also present either annualized composite returns for the one-year, three-year, and five-year periods ending as of a specified date, or five years of annual composite returns. Whichever option a firm chooses, it must clearly identify the end-of-period date. If the composite has been in existence for a period longer than one year but shorter than five years, the ad must show returns since inception. The annualized or annual returns must be calculated through the same period of time as presented in the corresponding GIPS-compliant presentation (Guideline B.5.a–b).

Advertisements asserting a claim of GIPS compliance must also present the benchmark total return for the same periods as those for which composite performance is presented. The appropriate benchmark, which must be described in the advertisement, is the same benchmark used in the corresponding GIPS-compliant presentation. If no benchmark is presented, the advertisement must disclose the reason why none is shown (Guideline B.7).

Advertisements stating compliance with the GIPS standards and presenting performance must also describe how and to what extent leverage or derivative securities are used if they are actively employed as part of the investment strategy and have a material effect on composite returns (Guideline B.9).

GIPS Appendix C, "GIPS Advertising Guidelines," includes sample advertisements with and without performance information. As the samples illustrate, it takes more space to spell out the requirements than to meet them. The guidelines recommend that firms present supplemental or additional performance information, in a manner consistent with the ethical principles of fair representation and full disclosure, on the conditions that the supplemental information must be clearly labeled as such and displayed with equal or lesser prominence than the required information. When supplemental information is presented for noncompliant periods, the advertisement must identify the periods, disclose what information is not in compliance with the GIPS standards, and explain why it is so. The reader is referred to the IPC's "Guidance Statement on the Use of Supplemental Information" for further direction.

6. OTHER ISSUES

We have finished reviewing the GIPS standards. In this part of the chapter, we will introduce after-tax performance measurement issues and calculation techniques, and we will comment on ways to keep informed about future developments affecting the application of the GIPS standards.

6.1. After-Tax Return Calculation Methodology

The GIPS standards do not require compliant firms to present after-tax returns for composites made up of portfolios managed on a tax-aware basis. Many firms engage in investment management on behalf of taxable institutions, individuals, and family offices, however, and they market tax-aware strategies to prospective clients who wish to evaluate their performance records. The interaction of complex regional tax codes with clients' varied circumstances and objectives not only renders tax-aware investing extremely arduous but also complicates performance measurement for firms subscribing to the ethical principles of fair representation and full disclosure. In this section, we will discuss major issues surrounding after-tax performance evaluation and present fundamental concepts and norms for after-tax return calculations based on standards defined for U.S.-based firms that complied with the former AIMR Performance Presentation Standards (AIMR-PPS). The AIMR-PPS after-tax provisions have been incorporated in the GIPS "Guidance Statement for Country-Specific Taxation Issues." Although country-specific tax regulations vary widely, many of the principles of after-tax performance measurement apply universally.

Let us first consider certain theoretical aspects and practical factors that make valid after-tax performance measurement, analysis, and evaluation problematic.

The timeframe in which estimated tax liabilities are assumed to be realized affects the after-tax rate of return. As we will see, a "preliquidation" calculation method (required under the section of the Guidance Statement for Country-Specific Taxation Issues subtitled "GIPS United States After-Tax Guidance") takes into account only the taxes realized during the measurement period. That is, the before-tax return is reduced by the taxes associated with investment income earned and gains and losses realized during the period. This calculation may understate the tax effect, however, because it does not recognize any tax liability or benefit for unrealized gains and losses embedded in the portfolio's ending market value. Although the securities in the portfolio are subject to future price-driven changes in market value, and the tax-aware portfolio manager will take advantage of opportunities to offset gains with losses and to defer taxes,[24] the preliquidation method entirely disregards the prospective tax effects that may result from the portfolio's currently unrealized capital gains and losses. In other words, the preliquidation method effectively assumes that unrealized capital gains are untaxed.[25]

Another calculation method assumes that all taxes on unrealized gains are immediately payable as of the end of the measurement period. (The Guidance Statement for Country-Specific Taxation Issues permits firms reporting after-tax returns to disclose this "mark-to-liquidation" return as supplemental information.) This method may overstate the tax effect, however, because in addition to disregarding future market value changes affecting the actual tax liability, it neglects the time value of money. Portfolios are generally managed on an ongoing basis, and in the normal course of events, taxable gains and losses will be realized as securities are sold, and the proceeds distributed or reinvested, at an indeterminate pace over the planning horizon.

For analytical purposes, we may derive potentially useful information from estimating the timing and amount of future tax assessments over suitably extended periods.[26] Such estimates of the portfolio's "true economic value," however, necessarily rest on debatable assumptions about future returns, among other parameters, and at present no generally accepted guidelines exist for modeling prospective tax outcomes in a manner that ensures the methodological comparability warranted for performance reporting.[27] After-tax returns uniformly calculated in accordance with the "preliquidation" and "mark-to-liquidation" methods reflect actual before-tax results achieved during the measurement period rather than projected investment experience. Given the known deficiencies of these latter methods, however, the prospective client must interpret after-tax returns with care.

We have seen that the historical cost of securities held in a portfolio is irrelevant to before-tax performance measurement, where assets are valued at market value and no distinction is made between realized and unrealized gains and losses. The taxable "cost basis" of portfolio investments is used, however, in determining tax liabilities for the purpose of after-tax return calculations. In addition, different tax regulations and rates may apply depending on the length of the holding period and the types of securities held. Clients' anticipated tax rates also vary, contingent on such factors as their level of income and the tax jurisdictions to which they belong. As a practical matter, therefore, substantially more extensive input data must be captured and managed to support reasonable after-tax performance calculations.[28]

---

[24] Existing U.S. tax law also permits the tax cost basis of securities to be "stepped up" to current market value upon the death of the owner, so heirs may avoid taxes on unrealized gains and losses in the portfolio.

[25] See Poterba (1999).

[26] Stein (1998) proposes a method for estimating a "full cost equivalent" portfolio value.

[27] The interpretive guidance in Appendix A of the "Guidance Statement for Country-Specific Taxation Issues" includes an informative treatment of the "true economic value" method in application. See Section I, "Supplemental Return Calculation Methodologies."

[28] From an implementation perspective, the input data requirements and after-tax return calculation methodology have significant implications for the development or selection of portfolio accounting and performance measurement systems. See Rogers and Price (2002) and Simpson (2003).

Implementation (14)

Anticipated Tax Rates. The GIPS standards for U.S. after-tax performance require the consistent use over time and within each composite of either the "anticipated tax rates" or the maximum tax rates applicable to each client. It is recommended that after-tax performance be calculated based on each client's "anticipated tax rates" for investment income and capital gains.

Determined in advance of the performance measurement period, the anticipated tax rates should be the tax rates that an investment manager expects a specific taxable client to face on returns generated during the prospective reporting period for each applicable tax class. The subsequent computation of the client's actual tax liability may be based on rates that prove, after the fact, to differ from the expected rates. The anticipated tax rates are appropriate for performance measurement, however, because they are the rates that guide the tax-aware portfolio manager's investment decisions. In addition, use of the anticipated tax rates enables the firm to use the same after-tax returns when reporting to individual clients and constructing composites.

Different clients will have different anticipated tax rates depending on myriad factors, typically including their income from all sources, their domicile, the types of securities in which they invest, and the details of the tax codes to which they are subject. For instance, an individual who resides in New York City is liable for U.S., New York State, and New York City income taxes, and her anticipated tax rate will differ from that of another individual holding the same assets and earning the same income elsewhere. Depending on the applicable regulations, which vary widely from one jurisdiction or tax regime to another, different rate schedules may apply to different kinds of income (e.g., ordinary income, short-term capital gains, and long-term capital gains) and to different types of securities (e.g., corporate bonds and municipal securities). In addition, taxes paid to one authority may reduce the amount payable to another. For example, income taxes paid at the state and local level may be deductible from the federal tax liability. In this case,

$$\text{Anticipated income tax rate} = \text{Federal tax rate} + [\text{State tax rate} \times (1 - \text{Federal tax rate})] + [\text{Local tax rate} \times (1 - \text{Federal tax rate})]$$

If the applicable federal, state, and local income tax rates for an individual client are estimated to be 22 percent, 5 percent, and 3 percent, respectively, and the state and local taxes are deductible from the federal taxes, then the client's anticipated income tax rate, T_{incr}, is

$$T_{incr} = 0.22 + [0.05 \times (1 - 0.22)] + [0.03 \times (1 - 0.22)]$$
$$= 0.22 + 0.039 + 0.023 = 0.282 = 28.2\%$$

The client or the investment manager may need to consult with a qualified tax accountant or attorney to determine the anticipated tax rates. The client-specific IPS or guidelines for tax-aware investment mandates should document the agreed-upon anticipated tax rates in sufficient detail to support portfolio management decisions and to facilitate the determination of valid after-tax returns. Of course, the anticipated tax rates should be periodically reviewed and updated to reflect changes in the client's circumstances.

If the client's anticipated tax rate is unknown, the section of the Guidance Statement for Country-Specific Taxation Issues subtitled "GIPS United States After-Tax Guidance" permits the use of the maximum federal tax rate (or the maximum federal, state, and local tax rates) for the specific category of investor.

Not only is calculating after-tax portfolio returns intricate, selecting or devising appropriate performance benchmarks is also difficult. Valid before-tax benchmarks have certain properties. Among other attributes, they are unambiguous, investable, measurable, specified or agreed upon in advance, and consistent with the investment strategy or style of the portfolio or composite. After-tax benchmarks should have all the desirable properties of suitable before-tax benchmarks, and one more: They should additionally reflect the client's tax status.

Financial services firms publish capital market indices representing a wide range of investment strategies and styles. Some providers calculate index returns net of withholding taxes on dividends, but at this writing none have published index returns fully reflecting imputed effects of taxation. Conceptually, given information on the constituent securities or the price and income return components, investment management firms could adjust reported before-tax index results to construct an after-tax benchmark. Adjusting standard before-tax indices is easier said than done, however. The adjustment methodology would have to incorporate the provider's rules for constructing and rebalancing the original index (e.g., whether it is equal weighted, capitalization weighted, or float weighted), the taxable turnover of securities held in the index, and issuers' corporate actions such as stock splits, as well as security-specific dividend and interest payments and price changes. A firm might formulate some simplifying assumptions to lessen the data requirements and reduce the computational intensity introduced by these factors.[29]

Alternatives to modifying standard before-tax indices include using mutual funds or exchange-traded funds as benchmarks, or developing customized shadow portfolios. Mutual funds and exchange-traded funds benchmarked to capital market indices are imperfect benchmarks because they are subject to fees, and their returns may deviate from those of the indices they emulate. The tax liabilities of mutual funds are affected by the portfolio manager's security transactions and by the collective deposit and redemption activities of shareholders. Exchange-traded funds likewise have turnover, but they do not incur taxes as a result of other investors' actions, so they may be better suited as benchmarks for after-tax performance evaluation.

Nonetheless, the investment management firm seeking a valid after-tax benchmark must address the fact that any one particular client's tax experience depends not only on the rates at which her investment income and capital gains are taxed but also the cost basis of the securities and the sequence of cash flows in her portfolio. The firm that uses custom security-based benchmarks for performance evaluation is well positioned to simulate the tax impact of external cash flows on benchmark results. Firms that use standard indices for before-tax performance evaluation can simulate the effect of client-specific cash flows on estimated after-tax benchmark returns by assuming that the benchmark pays proportionately the same capital gains taxes for withdrawals as the actual portfolio and invests contributions at the cost basis of the index at the time the contribution is made.[30] Alternately, firms can use mutual funds or exchange-traded funds to build shadow portfolios in which simulated purchases and sales are triggered by client-initiated cash flows. These approaches, however, are also data and computation intensive. Moreover, a customized shadow portfolio that works well for a single portfolio is unlikely to be useful for a composite made up of multiple client portfolios. Constructing valid benchmarks remains one of the greatest challenges in after-tax performance evaluation.

[29] Stein, Langstraat, and Narasimhan (1999) suggest a method to approximate after-tax benchmark returns.

[30] Price (2001) presents three increasingly accurate levels of approximation in constructing after-tax benchmarks from pretax indices and describes the "shadow portfolio" approach to adjusting indices for client-specific cash flows.

EXHIBIT 13-20 Data for an Illustration of After-Tax Performance Presentation

Market value as of May 31	25,000,000
Withdrawal on June 20	(2,000,000)
Market value as of June 30	24,750,000
Dividend income in June	125,000
Short-term capital gains realized in June	275,000
Long-term capital gains realized in June	2,250,000
Anticipated income tax rate	45.0%
Anticipated short-term capital gains tax rate	25.0%
Anticipated long-term capital gains tax rate	15.0%

Let us turn to the mathematics of after-tax portfolio returns. To illustrate the calculations, we will consider a U.S. equity portfolio managed by the Personal Trust Services division of Eastern National Bank for Edward Moriarty, a wealthy individual who has inquired about his portfolio's performance on an after-tax basis. The data in Exhibit 13-20 reflect activity in the Moriarty portfolio for the month of June, when the portfolio's before-tax return calculated in accordance with the Modified Dietz method was 7.19 percent. The anticipated tax rates used in this example are hypothetical. Dividends are assumed to be taxable at the ordinary income tax rate.

The GIPS provisions for U.S. after-tax performance presentation require firms to use a "preliquidation" calculation methodology reflecting the incidence of taxation on a realized basis (GIPS United States After-Tax Guidance, A.1.a). Several preliquidation alternatives were defined to parallel before-tax return calculations conforming to the main standards. The after-tax Modified Dietz method adjusts before-tax returns by reducing the numerator in the amount of realized taxes, reflecting the tax liability or benefit associated with the accrued taxable income and net realized gains or losses that occurred during the measurement period. (As noted above, preliquidation return calculation methods do not consider the tax implications of unrealized gains.) The tax liability, called "realized taxes" in the GIPS United States After-Tax Guidance, is calculated as follows:

$$T_{\text{real}} = (G_{\text{Lreal}} \times T_{\text{Lcgr}}) + (G_{\text{Sreal}} \times T_{\text{Scgr}}) + (\text{INC}_{\text{tA}} \times T_{\text{incr}}) \qquad (13\text{-}18)$$

where T_{real} is "realized taxes," G_{Lreal} is long-term capital gains realized during the period, T_{Lcgr} is the long-term capital gains tax rate, G_{Sreal} is short-term capital gains realized during the period, T_{Scgr} is the short-term capital gains tax rate, INC_{tA} is taxable income accrued during the period, and T_{incr} is the applicable income tax rate. Note that under the GIPS provisions for U.S. after-tax performance presentation, the tax liability or benefit must be recognized in the same period that the taxable event occurs, and taxes on income must be recognized on an accrual basis (GIPS United States After-Tax Guidance A.1.b–c). In addition, all calculations must consistently use either the anticipated tax rate or the maximum tax rate applicable to each client for the period for which the after-tax return is calculated (GIPS United States After-Tax Guidance A.1.e–f).

Adapting Equation 13-4, the preliquidation after-tax Modified Dietz formula can then be represented mathematically as follows:

$$r_{PLATModDietz} = \frac{\text{MV}_1 - \text{MV}_0 - \text{CF} - T_{\text{real}}}{\text{MV}_0 + \sum(\text{CF}_i \times w_i)} \qquad (13\text{-}19)$$

where $r_{PLATModDietz}$ is the preliquidation after-tax return, MV_1 is the end-of-period market value, MV_0 is the beginning market value, CF is the sum of external cash flows during the measurement period, T_{real} is the tax liability, and $\sum(CF_i \times w_i)$ is the sum of each cash flow multiplied by the proportion of the measurement period that each cash flow has been in the portfolio. The calculation of the time-weighting factor w_i is set forth in Equation 13-5. Notice that reducing the numerator by the amount of "realized taxes" is the only change from the modified Dietz formula.

The Moriarty portfolio had only one cash flow during the measurement period, a withdrawal of $2,000,000 that occurred on June 20. The corresponding end-of-day weighting factor is $(30 - 20)/30 = 0.33$. Using Equations 13-18 and 13-19, the after-tax return earned by the Moriarty portfolio in the month of June was 5.29 percent:

$$T_{real} = (2,250,000 \times 0.15) + (275,000 \times 0.25) + (125,000 \times 0.45) = 462,500$$

$$r_{PLATModDietz} = \frac{24,750,000 - 25,000,000 - (-2,000,000) - 462,500}{25,000,000 + (-2,000,000 \times 0.33)}$$

$$= 0.0529 = 5.29\%$$

Observe that the preliquidation after-tax return is equivalent to the before-tax return less the return impact of the tax liability:

$$r_{PLATModDietz} = r_{ModDietz} - \frac{T_{real}}{MV_0 + \sum(CF_i \times w_i)} \qquad (13\text{-}20)$$

This relationship is borne out in the Moriarty portfolio. The return impact of realized taxes in June precisely accounts for the 1.9 percent difference between the portfolio's before-tax return of 7.19 percent and preliquidation after-tax return of 5.29 percent:

$$\frac{462,500}{25,000,000 + (-2,000,000 \times 0.33)} = 0.019 = 1.9\%$$

The Linked Internal Rate of Return method introduced with Equation 13-6 can also be adapted to calculate the after-tax return on the preliquidation basis. In this case, the ending market value is reduced by the amount of realized taxes, and the after-tax return is the value of r that satisfies the following equation:

$$MV_1 - T_{real} = \sum[CF_i \times (1 + r)^{w_i}] + MV_0(1 + r) \qquad (13\text{-}21)$$

The third preliquidation method approved by the GIPS standards for U.S. firms can be used by firms that strike daily market valuations. In this formulation, the preliquidation after-tax return for a single day is the one-day change in market value less the tax liability, expressed as a percentage of the beginning value. (External cash flows are assumed to be captured in the beginning value.) Although daily market valuations are onerous, the after-tax return calculation is straightforward. The formula is

$$r_{PLATdv} = \frac{MV_{ED} - MV_{BD} - T_{real}}{MV_{BD}} \qquad (13\text{-}22)$$

where r_{PLATdv} is the preliquidation after-tax return with daily valuations, MV_{ED} is the market value at the end of the day (comparable to MV_1 in earlier return formulas), MV_{BD} is the market value at the beginning of the day (comparable to MV_0), and T_{real} is the tax liability as previously defined. Single-day after-tax returns can then be converted to wealth-relative form $(1 + r)$ and geometrically chain-linked to generate the time-weighted after-tax return for the measurement period.

Among the other requirements of the GIPS provisions for U.S. after-tax calculation methodology, firms must take into account taxes on income and realized capital gains regardless of whether taxes are paid from portfolio assets or from assets held outside the portfolio (GIPS United States After-Tax Guidance A.1.d). The pretax returns for composites that hold tax-exempt securities must be presented without "grossing up" tax-exempt income (GIPS United States After-Tax Guidance A.1.g)—that is, without restating tax-exempt income to a taxable-equivalent basis. Each portfolio in the composite must be given full credit for net realized losses, on the assumption that these losses will be offset by gains at a later date or in the client's other assets (GIPS United States After-Tax Guidance A.1.h).

As indicated above, the pertinent GIPS after-tax standards require U.S. firms that present after-tax returns to calculate them on a preliquidation basis but permitted firms to disclose after-tax returns calculated on a "mark-to-liquidation" basis as supplemental information. The mark-to-liquidation after-tax calculations resemble the preliquidation calculations, but they substitute "liquidation value" for the market value of assets and net cash flows in the return formula. Liquidation value is defined as market value reduced by the tax liability associated with unrealized capital gains in the portfolio. The interpretive guidance in Appendix A of the Guidance Statement for Country-Specific Taxation Issues After-Tax document shows liquidation value used in place of market value in both the numerator and the denominator of the mark-to-liquidation after-tax return formula. Some practitioners hold, however, that using the beginning liquidation value in the denominator may understate the assets at risk and lead to unreasonable results.

We have observed that performance measurement attempts to quantify the value added by a portfolio manager's investment actions. Because managers should not be held accountable for factors beyond their control, the GIPS standards exclude nondiscretionary portfolios from composites and prescribe time-weighted returns to eliminate the impact of external cash flows. Portfolio managers may be compelled to liquidate securities to meet client-directed withdrawals, however, and taxes may be realized as a result of the nondiscretionary asset sales. The GIPS recommendations for after-tax return calculation methodology permits U.S. firms to provide additional supplementary return information with an adjustment to remove the tax effect of nondiscretionary capital gains (GIPS United States After-Tax Guidance B.1.b). In effect, the adjustment adds back the hypothetical realized taxes that were not incurred at the manager's discretion.[31]

To avoid creating a perverse incentive for the portfolio manager to maximize the adjustment credit by selecting highly appreciated assets for sale, the recommended adjustment term reflects the capital gains tax that would be sustained if all the securities in the portfolio were proportionately liquidated. For this purpose, the adjustment term uses a factor called the gain ratio (GR):

$$GR = \frac{G_{real} + G_{unreal}}{MV_1 + CF_{NetOut}} \tag{13-23}$$

[31] Price (1996) presents the logic and implications of this adjustment factor.

where G_{real} is capital gains realized during the period, G_{unreal} is unrealized capital gains held in the portfolio at the end of the period, MV_1 is the ending market value, and $\text{CF}_{\text{NetOut}}$ is net client withdrawals during the period—that is, withdrawals less investment income and positive cash flows.

The adjustment factor for nondiscretionary realized taxes can then be computed as follows:

$$\text{Adjustment factor} = F = \text{CF}_{\text{NetOut}} \times T_{\text{cgr}} \times \text{GR} \tag{13-24}$$

With the adjustment factor in hand, a simple change to the preliquidation Modified Dietz after-tax return calculation (Equation 13-19) removes the effect of nondiscretionary realized taxes:

$$r_{AdjPLATModDietz} = \frac{\text{MV}_1 - \text{MV}_0 - \text{CF} - T_{\text{real}} + F}{\text{MV}_0 + \sum(\text{CF}_i \times w_i)} \tag{13-25}$$

Edward Moriarty withdrew \$2 million from his portfolio in June. Given that the tax cost basis of the portfolio was \$14.25 million at the end of the month, the portfolio's preliquidation after-tax return can be adjusted as shown below to compensate for the nondiscretionary capital gains associated with this withdrawal. Recognizing that both short-term and long-term capital gains were realized during June, we will use a weighted-average capital gains tax rate of 16.1 percent. Note that the net outflow term ($\text{CF}_{\text{NetOut}}$) represents the withdrawal less dividend income:

$$\text{GR} = \frac{(275,000 + 2,250,000) + (24,750,000 - 14,250,000)}{24,750,000 + (2,000,000 - 125,000)} = 0.4892$$

$$F = (2,000,000 - 125,000) \times 0.161 \times 0.4892 = 147,677$$

$$r_{AdjPLATModDietz} = \frac{24,750,000 - 25,000,000 - (-2,000,000) - 462,500 + 147,677}{25,000,000 + (-2,000,000 \times 0.33)}$$

$$r_{AdjPLATModDietz} = 0.059 = 5.9\%$$

Therefore, in the case of the Moriarty portfolio, the adjustment increases the preliquidation after-tax return for the month of June from 5.29 percent to 5.9 percent, an improvement of 61 basis points (0.61 percent).

There is another situation in which client actions affect after-tax returns (in this case, favorably). The client may instruct a portfolio manager to realize tax losses to offset gains realized either within the portfolio or in other assets held outside the portfolio. For the client, such "tax loss harvesting" reduces his tax liability on net capital gains. This practice is entirely consistent with the fundamental wealth management principle that investors should consider all their assets when making investment decisions. For the portfolio manager who has realized gains or who handles only a portion of the client's assets, however, the nondiscretionary directive to harvest tax losses improves reported after-tax results. One of the disclosure recommendations of the GIPS provisions for U.S. after-tax performance advises firms to disclose the percentage benefit of tax-loss harvesting for the composite if realized losses are greater than realized gains during the period (GIPS United States After-Tax Guidance B.3.b). The recommendation implicitly assumes that tax benefits not used within the portfolio in the measurement period can be used outside the portfolio or in the future. The wealth benefit derived from tax loss harvesting is computed by applying the appropriate capital gains tax rate to the net losses realized in the period; the percentage benefit may be calculated by dividing the money benefit by the simple average assets in the portfolio:

$$\text{Benefit of Tax Loss Harvesting} = B = L_{\text{net}} \times T_{\text{cgr}} \quad (13\text{-}26)$$

where L_{net} designates the amount of net losses (that is, capital losses less capital gains realized during the period) and T_{cgr} designates the applicable capital gains tax rate.

$$\text{Percent Benefit of Tax Loss Harvesting} = \frac{B}{(\text{MV}_0 + \text{MV}_1)/2} \quad (13\text{-}27)$$

where MV_0 is the beginning market value and MV_1 is the ending market value of the portfolio or composite.

With this, we conclude the introduction to after-tax return calculations for individual portfolios. It is evident even from this abbreviated presentation that after-tax performance measurement requires considerable expertise as well as extensive data and powerful technology, particularly when advancing from the portfolio to the composite level. The interpretive guidance accompanying the pertinent GIPS U.S. standards acknowledges that after-tax performance analysis is both a science and an art: "The *'scientific'* aspects are manifested in the discrete requirements and details, while the *'artisanal'* aspects recognize that cash flows, substantial Unrealized Capital Gains, and composite definitions can have a significant impact on after-tax results."[32] Supplemental information, including tax efficiency measures not presented here, can materially assist prospective clients in evaluating a firm's after-tax performance record. We refer the practitioner to the fuller treatment given after-tax performance in the GIPS standards and the guidance available on the CFA Institute web site.

6.2. Keeping Current with the GIPS Standards

At the beginning of this chapter, we surveyed the evolution of performance presentation standards, marking as particularly noteworthy events the publication of Peter Dietz's work in 1966 and the report of the Financial Analysts Federation's Committee for Performance Presentation Standards in 1987. The Global Investment Performance Standards are now fairly comprehensive and well defined, the integrated product of thoughtful contributions from many academicians and practitioners committed to the ethical ideals of fairness and honesty in reporting investment results. The revised GIPS standards issued in 2005 represent a significant advance in the globalization of performance presentation norms.

Nonetheless, the GIPS standards will continue to evolve over time to address additional aspects of performance presentation. The IPC states that it will continue to develop the GIPS standards so that they maintain their relevance within the changing investment management industry, and it has committed to evaluating the Standards every five years (Provision I.G.24).

Guidance Statements adopted by the IPC or the GIPS EC, as well as interpretations and clarifications published on the CFA Institute web site, apply to all firms that claim compliance with the GIPS standards (Provision II.0.A.15). Practitioners should visit the web site frequently in order to stay informed about requirements and recommended best practices at no cost. CFA Institute and other organizations also offer publications and conduct conferences and workshops designed to help practitioners implement and maintain compliance with the GIPS standards.

[32] Guidance Statement for Country-Specific Taxation Issues, Appendix A, "Additional Guidance on United States After-Tax Calculation and Presentation," p. 25.

APPENDIX: GIPS GLOSSARY

The following definitions are solely for the purpose of interpreting the GIPS standards.

Accrual Accounting The system of recording financial transactions as they come into existence as a legally enforceable claim, rather than when they settle.

Additional Information Information that is required or recommended under the GIPS standards and is not considered as "supplemental information" for the purposes of compliance.

Administrative Fees All fees other than the trading expenses and the investment management fee. Administrative fees include custody fees, accounting fees, consulting fees, legal fees, performance measurement fees, or other related fees. These administrative fees are typically outside the control of the investment management firm and are not included in either the gross-of-fees return or the net-of-fees return. However, there are some markets and investment vehicles where administrative fees are controlled by the firm. (See the term "bundled fee.")

Benchmark An independent rate of return (or hurdle rate) forming an objective test of the effective implementation of an investment strategy.

Bundled Fee A fee that combines multiple fees into one "bundled" fee. Bundled fees can include any combination of management, transaction, custody, and other administrative fees. Two specific examples of bundled fees are the all-in fee and the wrap fee.

All-In Fee Due to the universal banking system in some countries, asset management, brokerage, and custody are often part of the same company. This allows banks to offer a variety of choices to customers regarding how the fee will be charged. Customers are offered numerous fee models in which fees may be bundled together or charged separately. All-in fees can include any combination of investment management, trading expenses, custody, and other administrative fees.

Wrap Fee Wrap fees are specific to a particular investment product. The U.S. Securities and Exchange Commission (SEC) defines a wrap fee account (now more commonly known as a separately managed account or SMA) as "any advisory program under which a specified fee or fees not based upon transactions in a client's account is charged for investment advisory services (which may include portfolio management or advice concerning the selection of other investment advisers) and execution of client transactions." A typical separately managed account has a contract or contracts (and fee) involving a sponsor (usually a broker or independent provider) acting as the investment advisor, an investment management firm typically as the subadvisor, other services (custody, consulting, reporting, performance, manager selection, monitoring, and execution of trades), distributor, and the client (brokerage customer). Wrap fees can be all-inclusive, asset-based fees (which may include any combination of management, transaction, custody, and other administrative fees).

Capital Employed (Real Estate) The denominator of the return expressions, defined as the "weighted-average equity" (weighted-average capital) during the measurement period. Capital employed should not include any income or capital return accrued *during* the measurement period. Beginning capital is adjusted by weighting the cash flows (contributions and distributions) that occurred during the period. Cash flows are typically weighted based on the actual days the flows are in or out of the portfolio. Other weighting methods are acceptable; however, once a methodology is chosen, it should be consistently applied.

Capital Return (Real Estate) The change in the market value of the real estate investments and cash/cash equivalent assets held throughout the measurement period (ending market value less beginning market value) adjusted for all capital expenditures (subtracted) and the net proceeds from sales (added). The return is computed as a percentage of the capital employed through the measurement period. Synonyms: capital appreciation return, appreciation return.

Carried Interest (Private Equity) The profits that general partners earn from the profits of the investments made by the fund (generally 20–25%). Also known as "carry."

Carve-Out A single or multiple asset class segment of a multiple asset class portfolio.

Closed-End Fund (Private Equity) A type of investment fund where the number of investors and the total committed capital is fixed and not open for subscriptions and/or redemptions.

Committed Capital (Private Equity) Pledges of capital to a venture capital fund. This money is typically not received at once but drawn down over three to five years, starting in the year the fund is formed. Also known as "commitments."

Composite Aggregation of individual portfolios representing a similar investment mandate, objective, or strategy.

Composite Creation Date The date when the firm first groups the portfolios to create a composite. The composite creation date is not necessarily the earliest date for which performance is reported for the composite. (See composite inception date.)

Composite Definition Detailed criteria that determine the allocation of portfolios to composites. Composite definitions must be documented in the firm's policies and procedures.

Composite Description General information regarding the strategy of the composite. A description may be more abbreviated than the composite definition but includes all salient features of the composite.

Composite Inception Date The earliest date for which performance is reported for the composite. The composite inception date is not necessarily the date the portfolios are grouped together to create a composite. Instead, it is the initial date of the performance record. (See composite creation date.)

Custody Fees The fees payable to the custodian for the safekeeping of the portfolio's assets. Custody fees typically contain an asset-based portion and a transaction-based portion of the fee. The total custody fee may also include charges for additional services, including accounting, securities lending, or performance measurement. Custody fees that are charged per transaction should be included in the custody fee and not included as part of the trading expenses.

Direct Investments (Private Equity) An investment made directly in venture capital or private equity assets (i.e., not via a partnership or fund).

Dispersion A measure of the spread of the annual returns of individual portfolios within a composite. Measures may include, but are not limited to, high/low, inter-quartile range, and standard deviation (asset weighted or equal weighted).

Distinct Business Entity A unit, division, department, or office that is organizationally and functionally segregated from other units, divisions, departments, or offices and retains discretion over the assets it manages and autonomy over the investment decision-making process. Possible criteria that can be used to determine this include:

- being a legal entity
- having a distinct market or client type (e.g., institutional, retail, private client, etc.)
- using a separate and distinct investment process

Distribution (Private Equity) Cash or the value of stock disbursed to the limited partners of a venture fund.

Drawdown (Private Equity) After the total committed capital has been agreed upon between the general partner and the limited partners, the actual transfer of funds from the limited partners' to the general partners' control in as many stages as deemed necessary by the general partner is referred to as the drawdown.

Ending Market Value (Private Equity) The remaining equity that a limited partner has in a fund. Also referred to as net asset value or residual value.

Evergreen Fund (Private Equity) An open-end fund that allows for on-going investment and/or redemption by investors. Some evergreen funds reinvest profits in order to ensure the availability of capital for future investments.

Ex-Ante Before the fact. (See *ex-post.*)

Ex-Post After the fact. (See *ex-ante.*)

External Cash Flow Cash, securities, or assets that enter or exit a portfolio.

External Valuation (Real Estate) An external valuation is an assessment of market value performed by a third party who is a qualified, professionally designated, certified, or licensed commercial property valuer/appraiser. External valuations must be completed following the valuation standards of the local governing appraisal body.

Fair Value The amount at which an asset could be acquired or sold in a current transaction between willing parties in which the parties each acted knowledgeably, prudently, and without compulsion.

Fee Schedule The firm's current investment management fees or bundled fees for a particular presentation. This schedule is typically listed by asset level ranges and should be appropriate to the particular prospective client.

Final Realization Date (Private Equity) The date when a composite is fully distributed.

Firm For purposes of the GIPS standards, the term "firm" refers to the entity defined for compliance with the GIPS standards. See the term "distinct business entity."

General Partner (Private Equity) (GP) a class of partner in a partnership. The GP retains liability for the actions of the partnership. In the private equity world, the GP is the fund manager and the limited partners (LPs) are the institutional and high-net-worth investors in the partnership. The GP earns a management fee and a percentage of profits. (See the term "carried interest.")

Gross-Of-Fees Return The return on assets reduced by any trading expenses incurred during the period.

Gross-Of-Fees Return (Private Equity) The return on assets reduced by any transaction expenses incurred during the period.

Income Return (Real Estate) The investment income accrued on all assets (including cash and cash equivalents) during the measurement period net of all nonrecoverable expenditures, interest expense on debt, and property taxes. The return is computed as a percentage of the capital employed through the measurement period.

Internal Valuation (Real Estate) An internal valuation is an advisor's or underlying third-party manager's best estimate of market value based on the most current and accurate information available under the circumstances. An internal valuation could include industry practice techniques, such as discounted cash flow, sales comparison, replacement cost, or a review of all significant events (both general market and asset specific) that could have a material impact on the investment. Prudent assumptions and estimates must be used, and the process must be applied consistently from period to period, except where a change would result in better estimates of market value.

Internal Rate of Return (Private Equity) (IRR) is the annualized implied discount rate (effective compounded rate) that equates the present value of all the appropriate cash inflows (paid-in capital, such as drawdowns for net investments) associated with an investment with the sum of the present value of all the appropriate cash outflows (such as distributions) accruing from it and the present value of the unrealized residual portfolio (unliquidated holdings). For an interim cumulative return measurement, any IRR depends on the valuation of the residual assets.

Invested Capital (Private Equity) The amount of paid-in capital that has been invested in portfolio companies.

Investment Advisor (Private Equity) Any individual or institution that supplies investment advice to clients on a per fee basis. The investment advisor inherently has no role in the management of the underlying portfolio companies of a partnership/fund.

Investment Management Fee The fee payable to the investment management firm for the on-going management of a portfolio. Investment management fees are typically asset based (percentage of assets), performance based (based on performance relative to a benchmark), or a combination of the two but may take different forms as well.

Investment Multiple (TVPI Multiple) (Private Equity) The ratio of total value to paid-in-capital. It represents the total return of the investment to the original investment not taking into consideration the time invested. Total value can be found by adding the residual value and distributed capital together.

Large External Cash Flow The Standards do not contain a specified amount of cash or percentage that is considered to be a large external cash flow. Instead, firms must define the composite-specific size (amount or percentage) that constitutes a large external cash flow.

Limited Partner (Private Equity) (LP) an investor in a limited partnership. The general partner is liable for the actions of the partnership and the Limited Partners are generally protected from legal actions and any losses beyond their original investment. The limited partner receives income, capital gains, and tax benefits.

Limited Partnership (Private Equity) The legal structure used by most venture and private equity funds. Usually fixed life investment vehicles. The general partner or management firm manages the partnership using the policy laid down in a partnership agreement. The agreement also covers terms, fees, structures, and other items agreed between the limited partners and the general partner.

Market Value The current listed price at which investors buy or sell securities at a given time.

Market Value (Real Estate) The most probable price that a property should bring in a competitive and open market under all conditions requisite to a fair sale, the buyer and seller each acting prudently and knowledgeably, and assuming the price is not affected by undue stimulus. Implicit in this definition is the consummation of a sale as of a specified date and the passing of title from seller to buyer under conditions whereby:

a. Buyer and seller are typically motivated.
b. Both parties are well informed or well advised and each acting in what they consider their own best interests.
c. A reasonable time is allowed for exposure in the open market.
d. Payment is made in terms of currency or in terms of financial arrangements comparable thereto.
e. The price represents the normal consideration for the property sold unaffected by special or creative financing or sales concessions granted by anyone associated with the sale.

Must A required provision for claiming compliance with the GIPS standards. (See the term "require.")

Net-of-Fees Return The gross-of-fees return reduced by the investment management fee.

Open-End Fund (Private Equity) A type of investment fund where the number of investors and the total committed capital is not fixed (i.e., open for subscriptions and/or redemptions). (See the term "evergreen fund.")

Open Market Value (Private Equity) An opinion of the best price at which the sale of an interest in the property would have been completed unconditionally for cash consideration on the date of valuation, assuming:

a. a willing seller;
b. that prior to the date of valuation there had been a reasonable period (having regard to the nature of the property and the state of the market) for the proper marketing of the interest, for the agreement of the price and terms, and for the completion of the sale;
c. that the state of the market, level of values, and other circumstances were on any earlier assumed date of exchange of contracts the same as on the date of valuation;
d. that no account is taken of any additional bid by a prospective purchaser with a special interest; and
e. that both parties to the transaction had acted knowledgeably, prudently, and without compulsion.

Paid-In Capital (Private Equity) The amount of committed capital a limited partner has actually transferred to a venture fund. Also known as the cumulative drawdown amount.

PIC Multiple (Private Equity) The ratio of paid-in-capital to committed capital. This ratio gives prospective clients information regarding how much of the total commitments has been drawn down.

Portfolio An individually managed pool of assets. A portfolio may be a subportfolio, account, or pooled fund.

Private Equity Private equity includes, but is not limited to, organizations devoted to venture capital, leveraged buyouts, consolidations, mezzanine and distressed debt investments, and a variety of hybrids, such as venture leasing and venture factoring.

Professionally Designated, Certified, or Licensed Commercial Property Valuer/Appraiser (Real Estate) In Europe, Canada and parts of southeast Asia, the predominant professional designation is that of the Royal Institution of Chartered Surveyors (RICs). In the United States, the professional designation is Member [of the] Appraisal Institute (MAI). In addition, each state regulates real estate appraisers, and based on one's experience, body of work, and test results, is then registered, licensed, or certified.

Real Estate Real estate investments include:

- Wholly owned or partially owned properties,
- Commingled funds, property unit trusts, and insurance company separate accounts,
- Unlisted, private placement securities issued by private real estate investment trusts (REITs) and real estate operating companies (REOCs), and
- Equity-oriented debt, such as participating mortgage loans or any private interest in a property where some portion of return to the investor at the time of investment is related to the performance of the underlying real estate.

Realization Multiple (Private Equity) The realization multiple (DPI) is calculated by dividing the cumulative distributions by the paid-in-capital.

Recommend/ Recommendation Suggested provision for claiming compliance with the GIPS standards. A recommendation is considered to be best practice but is not a requirement. (See the term "should.")

Require/Requirement A provision that must be followed for compliance with the GIPS standards. (See the term "must.")

Residual Value (Private Equity) The remaining equity that a limited partner has in the fund. (The value of the investments within the fund.) Also can be referred to as ending market value or net asset value.

Residual Value to Paid-in-Capital (RVPI) (Private Equity) Residual value divided by the paid-in-capital.

Settlement Date Accounting Recognizing the asset or liability on the date when the exchange of cash, securities, and paperwork involved in a transaction is completed. Impact on performance: Between trade date and settlement date, an account does not recognize any change between the price of the transaction and the current market value. Instead, on settlement date, the total difference between the price of the transaction and the current market value is recognized on that day. (See trade date accounting.)

Should Encouraged (recommended) to follow the recommendation of the GIPS standards but not required. (See the term "recommend.")

Supplemental Information Any performance-related information included as part of a compliant performance presentation that supplements or enhances the required and/or recommended disclosure and presentation provisions of the GIPS standards.

Temporary New Account A tool that firms can use to remove the effect of significant cash flows on a portfolio. When a significant cash flow occurs in a portfolio, the firm may treat this cash flow as a "temporary new account," allowing the firm to implement the mandate of the portfolio without the impact of the cash flow on the performance of the portfolio.

Time-Weighted Rate of Return Calculation that computes period-by-period returns on an investment and removes the effects of external cash flows, which are generally client-driven, and best reflects the firm's ability to manage assets according to a specified strategy or objective.

Total Firm Assets Total firm assets are all assets for which a firm has investment management responsibility. Total firm assets include assets managed outside the firm (e.g., by subadvisors) for which the firm has asset allocation authority.

Total Return (Real Estate) The change in the market value of the portfolio, adjusted for all capital expenditures (subtracted), net proceeds from sales (added), and investment income accrued (added) during the measurement period expressed as a percentage of the capital employed in the portfolio over the measurement period.

Total Value (Private Equity) Residual value of the portfolio plus distributed capital.

Trade Date Accounting The transaction is reflected in the portfolio on the date of the purchase or sale, and not on the settlement date. Recognizing the asset or liability within at least three days of the date the transaction is entered into (Trade Date, T + 1, T + 2, or T + 3) all satisfy the trade date accounting requirement for purposes of the GIPS standards. (See settlement date accounting.)

Trading Expenses The costs of buying or selling a security. These costs typically take the form of brokerage commissions or spreads from either internal or external brokers. Custody fees charged per transaction should be considered custody fees and not direct transaction costs. Estimated trading expenses are not permitted.

Transaction Expenses (Private Equity) Include all legal, financial, advisory, and investment banking fees related to buying, selling, restructuring, and recapitalizing portfolio companies.

Venture Capital (Private Equity) Risk capital in the form of equity and/or loan capital that is provided by an investment institution to back a business venture that is expected to grow in value.

Vintage Year (Private Equity) The year that the venture capital or private equity fund or partnership first draws down or calls capital from its investors.

GLOSSARY

Absolute return objective A return objective that is independent of a reference or benchmark level of return.

Absolute-return vehicles Investments that have no direct benchmark portfolios.

Accounting risk The risk that arises from uncertainty about how a transaction should be recorded and the potential for accounting rules and regulations to change.

Accumulated benefit obligation (ABO) The present value of pension benefits, assuming the pension plan terminated immediately such that it had to provide retirement income to all beneficiaries for their years of service up to that date.

Accumulated service Years of service of a pension plan participant as of a specified date.

Active investment approach An approach to portfolio construction in which portfolio composition responds to changes in the portfolio manager's expectations concerning asset returns.

Active management An approach to investing in which the portfolio manager seeks to outperform a given benchmark portfolio.

Active return The portfolio's return in excess of the return on the portfolio's benchmark.

Active risk A synonym for tracking risk.

Active/immunization combination A portfolio with two component portfolios: an immunized portfolio that provides an assured return over the planning horizon and a second portfolio that uses an active high-return/high-risk strategy.

Active/passive combination Allocation of the core component of a portfolio to a passive strategy and the balance to an active component.

Active-lives The portion of a pension fund's liabilities associated with active workers.

Actual extreme events A type of scenario analysis used in stress testing. It involves evaluating how a portfolio would have performed given movements in interest rates, exchange rates, stock prices, or commodity prices at magnitudes such as occurred during past extreme market events (e.g., the stock market crash of October 1987).

Ad valorem fees Fees that are calculated by multiplying a percentage by the value of assets managed; also called assets under management (AUM) fees.

Adverse selection risk The risk associated with information asymmetry; in the context of trading, the risk of trading with a more informed trader.

Algorithmic trading Automated electronic trading subject to quantitative rules and user-specified benchmarks and constraints.

Allocation/selection interaction return A measure of the joint effect of weights assigned to both sectors and individual securities; the difference between the weight of the portfolio in a given sector and the portfolio's benchmark for that sector, times the difference between the portfolio's and the benchmark's returns in that sector, summed across all sectors.

Alpha Excess risk-adjusted return.

Alpha and beta separation An approach to portfolio construction that views investing to earn alpha and investing to establish systematic risk exposures as tasks that can and should be pursued separately.

Alpha research Research related to capturing excess risk-adjusted returns by a particular strategy; a way investment research is organized in some investment management firms.

Alternative investments Groups of investments with risk and return characteristics that differ markedly from those of traditional stock and bond investments.

Anchoring trap The tendency of the mind to give disproportionate weight to the first information it receives on a topic.

Angel investor An accredited individual investing chiefly in seed and early-stage companies.

Appraisal data Valuation data based on appraised rather than market values.

Ask price (or ask, offer price, offer) The price at which a dealer will sell a specified quantity of a security.

Ask size The quantity associated with the ask price.

Asset allocation reviews A periodic review of the appropriateness of a portfolio's asset allocation.

Asset covariance matrix The covariance matrix for the asset classes or markets under consideration.

Asset/liability management The management of financial risks created by the interaction of assets and liabilities.

Asset/liability management approach In the context of determining a strategic asset allocation, an asset/liability management approach involves explicitly modeling liabilities and adopting the allocation of assets that is optimal in relationship to funding liabilities.

Asset-only approach In the context of determining a strategic asset allocation, an approach that focuses on the characteristics of the assets without explicitly modeling the liabilities.

Assurity of completion In the context of trading, confidence that trades will settle without problems under all market conditions.

Assurity of the contract In the context of trading, confidence that the parties to trades will be held to fulfilling their obligations.

Asynchronism A discrepancy in the dating of observations that occurs because stale (out-of-date) data may be used in the absence of current data.

AUM fee A fee based on assets under management; an ad valorem fee.

Automated trading Any form of trading that is not manual, including trading based on algorithms.

Average effective spread A measure of the liquidity of a security's market. The mean effective spread (sometimes dollar weighted) over all transactions in the stock in the period under study.

Back office Administrative functions at an investment firm such as those pertaining to transaction processing, record keeping, and regulatory compliance.

Backtesting A method for gaining information about a model using past data. As used in reference to VAR, it is the process of comparing the number of violations of VAR thresholds over a time period with the figure implied by the user-selected probability level.

Backwardation A downward-sloping term structure of futures prices (i.e., the more distant the contract maturity, the lower the futures price).

Balance of payments An accounting of all cash flows between residents and nonresidents of a country.

Bancassurance The sale of insurance by banks.

Barbell portfolio A portfolio made up of short and long maturities relative to the investment horizon date and interim coupon payments.

Basis The difference between the cash price and the futures price.

Basis risk The risk that the basis will change in an unpredictable way.

Behavioral finance An approach to finance based on the observation that psychological variables affect and often distort individuals' investment decision making.

Benchmark Something taken as a standard of comparison; a comparison portfolio; a collection of securities or risk factors and associated weights that represents the persistent and prominent investment characteristics of an asset category or manager's investment process.

Best efforts order A type of order that gives the trader's agent discretion to execute the order only when the agent judges market conditions to be favorable.

Beta A measure of the sensitivity of a given investment or portfolio to movements in the overall market.

Beta research Research related to systematic (market) risk and return; a way investment research is organized in some investment management firms.

Bid price (or bid) The price at which a dealer will buy a specified quantity of a security.

Bid size The quantity associated with the bid price.

Bid–ask spread The difference between the current bid price and the current ask price of a security.

Binary credit options Option that provide payoffs contingent on the occurrence of a specified negative credit event.

Block order An order to sell or buy in a quantity that is large relative to the liquidity ordinarily available from dealers in the security or in other markets.

Bond-yield-plus-risk-premium method An approach to estimating the required return on equity which specifies that required return as a bond yield plus a risk premium.

Bottom-up Focusing on company-specific fundamentals or factors such as revenues, earnings, cash flow, or new product development.

Broad market indexes An index that is intended to measure the performance of an entire asset class. For example, the S&P 500 Index, Wilshire 5000, and Russell 3000 indexes for U.S. common stocks.

Broker An agent of a trader in executing trades.

Brokered markets Markets in which transactions are largely effected through a search-brokerage mechanism away from public markets.

Bubbles Episodes in which asset market prices move to extremely high levels in relation to estimated intrinsic value.

Buffering With respect to style index construction, rules for maintaining the style assignment of a stock consistent with a previous assignment when the stock has not clearly moved to a new style.

Build-up approach Synonym for the risk premium approach.

Bullet portfolio A portfolio made up of maturities that are very close to the investment horizon.

Business cycle Fluctuations in gross domestic product in relation to long-term trend growth, usually lasting 9 to 11 years.

Business risk The equity risk that comes from the nature of the firm's operating activities.

Buy side Investment management companies and other investors that use the services of brokerages.

Buy-side analysts Analysts employed by an investment manager or institutional investor.

Buy-side traders Professional traders that are employed by investment managers and institutional investors.

Calendar rebalancing Rebalancing a portfolio to target weights on a periodic basis; for example, monthly, quarterly, semiannually, or annually.

Calendar-and-percentage-of-portfolio rebalancing Monitoring a portfolio at regular frequencies, such as quarterly. Rebalancing decisions are then made based upon percentage-of-portfolio principles.

Calmar ratio The compound annualized rate of return over a specified time period divided by the absolute value of maximum drawdown over the same time period.

Cap rate With respect to options, the exercise interest rate for a cap.

Capital adequacy ratio A measure of the adequacy of capital in relation to assets.

Capital allocation line A graph line that describes the combinations of expected return and standard deviation of return available to an investor from combining an optimal portfolio of risky assets with a risk-free asset.

Capital flows forecasting approach An exchange rate forecasting approach that focuses on expected capital flows, particularly long-term flows such as equity investment and foreign direct investment.

Capital market expectations (CME) Expectations concerning the risk and return prospects of asset classes.

Caps A combination of interest rate call options designed to provide protection against interest rate increases.

Carried interest A private equity fund manager's incentive fee; the share of the private equity fund's profits that the fund manager is due once the fund has returned the outside investors' capital.

Cash balance plan A defined-benefit plan whose benefits are displayed in individual recordkeeping accounts.

Cash flow at risk A variation of value at risk that measures the risk to a company's cash flow, instead of its market value; the minimum cash flow loss expected to be exceeded with a given probability over a specified time period.

Cash flow matching An asset/liability management approach that provides the future funding of a liability stream from the coupon and matured principal payments of the portfolio. A type of dedication strategy.

Cause-and-effect relationship A relationship in which the occurrence of one event brings about the occurrence of another event.

Cautious investors Investors who are generally averse to potential losses.

Cell-matching technique (stratified sampling) A portfolio construction technique used in indexing that divides the benchmark index into cells related to the risk factors affecting the index and samples from index securities belonging to those cells.

Chain-linking A process for combining periodic returns to produce an overall time-weighted rate of return.

Cheapest-to-deliver In selecting the issue to be delivered in a Treasury futures contract, the issue that is least expensive after taking account of conversion factors.

Claw-back provision With respect to the compensation of private equity fund managers, a provision that specifies that money from the fund manager be returned to investors if, at the end of a fund's life, investors have not received back their capital contributions and contractual share of profits.

Closed-book markets Markets in which a trader does not have real-time access to all quotes in a security.

Closeout netting In a bankruptcy, a process by which multiple obligations between two counterparties are consolidated into a single overall value owed by one of the counterparties to the other.

Coincident economic indicators Economic indicators of current economic activity.

Collar The combination of a cap and a floor.

Collateral return (or collateral yield) The component of the return on a commodity futures contract that comes from the assumption that the full value of the underlying futures contract is invested to earn the risk-free interest rate.

Collateralized debt obligation A securitized pool of fixed-income assets.

Combination matching (or horizon matching) A cash flow matching technique; a portfolio is duration-matched with a set of liabilities with the added constraint that it also be cash-flow matched in the first few years, usually the first five years.

Commingled real estate funds (CREFs) Professionally managed vehicles for substantial commingled (i.e., pooled) investment in real estate properties.

Commitment period The period of time over which committed funds are advanced to a private equity fund.

Commodities Articles of commerce such as agricultural goods, metals, and petroleum; tangible assets that are typically relatively homogeneous in nature.

Commodity trading advisers Registered advisers to managed futures funds.

Completeness fund A portfolio that, when added to active managers' positions, establishes an overall portfolio with approximately the same risk exposures as the investor's overall equity benchmark.

Confidence band With reference to a quality control chart for performance evaluation, a range in which the manager's value-added returns are anticipated to fall a specified percentage of the time.

Confidence interval An interval that has a given probability of containing the parameter it is intended to estimate.

Confirming evidence trap The bias that leads individuals to give greater weight to information that supports an existing or preferred point of view than to evidence that contradicts it.

Consistent growth A growth investment substyle that focuses on companies with consistent growth having a long history of unit-sales growth, superior profitability, and predictable earnings.

Constraints (1) Restricting conditions; (2) Relating to an investment policy statement, limitations on the investor's ability to take full or partial advantage of particular investments. Such constraints are either internal (such as a client's specific liquidity needs, time horizon, and unique circumstances) or external (such as tax issues and legal and regulatory requirements).

Contango An upward-sloping term structure of futures prices.

Contingent immunization A fixed-income strategy in which immunization serves as a fall-back strategy if the actively managed portfolio does not grow at a certain rate.

Continuous auction markets Auction markets where orders can be executed at any time during the trading day.

Contrarian A value investment substyle focusing on stocks that have been beset by problems.

Conversion factors With reference to Treasury futures, the factors used for determining the invoice price of each acceptable deliverable Treasury issue against the Treasury bond futures contract.

Convexity A measure of how interest rate sensitivity changes with a change in interest rates.

Convexity adjustment An estimate of the change in price that is not explained by duration.

Core-plus A fixed-income mandate that permits the portfolio manager to add instruments with relatively high return potential to core holdings of investment-grade debt.

Core satellite A way of thinking about allocating money that seeks to define each investment's place in the portfolio in relation to specific investment goals or roles.

Core satellite portfolio A portfolio in which certain investments (often indexed or semiactive) are viewed as the core and the balance are viewed as satellite investments fulfilling specific roles.

Corner portfolio Adjacent corner portfolios define a segment of the minimum-variance frontier within which portfolios hold identical assets and the rate of change of asset weights in moving from one portfolio to another is constant.

Corner portfolio theorem In a sign-constrained mean–variance optimization, the result that the asset weights of any minimum-variance portfolio are a positive linear combination of the corresponding weights in the two adjacent corner portfolios that bracket it in terms of expected return (or standard deviation of return).

Corporate governance The system of internal controls and procedures used to define and protect the rights and responsibilities of various stakeholders.

Corporate venturing Investments by companies in promising young companies in the same or a related industry.

Country beta A measure of the sensitivity of a specified variable (e.g. yield) to a change in the comparable variable in another country.

Coverage Benchmark coverage is defined as the proportion of a portfolio's market value that is contained in the benchmark.

Covered call A strategy that involves owning an asset and writing a call on it.

Credit default swap A swap used to transfer credit risk to another party. A protection buyer pays the protection seller in return for the right to receive a payment from the seller in the event of a specified credit event.

Credit derivative A contract in which one party has the right to claim a payment from another party in the event that a specific credit event occurs over the life of the contract.

Credit event An event affecting the credit risk of a security or counterparty.

Credit forward A type of credit derivative with payoffs based on bond values or credit spreads.

Credit protection seller With respect to a credit derivative, the party that accepts the credit risk of the underlying financial asset.

Credit risk The risk of loss caused by a counterparty's or debtor's failure to make a timely payment or by the change in value of a financial instrument based on changes in default risk.

Credit spread forward A forward contract used to transfer credit risk to another party; a forward contract on a yield spread.

Credit spread option An option based on the yield spread between two securities that is used to transfer credit risk.

Credit spread risk The risk that the spread between the rate for a risky bond and the rate for a default risk-free bond may vary after the purchase of the risky bond.

Credit VaR Value at risk related to credit risk; it reflects the minimum loss due to credit exposure with a given probability during a period of time.
Credited rates Rates of interest credited to a policyholder's reserve account.
Cross hedging With respect to hedging bond investments using futures, hedging when the bond to be hedged is not identical to the bond underlying the futures contract. With respect to currency hedging, a hedging technique that uses two currencies other than the home currency.
Cross-default provision A provision stipulating that if a borrower defaults on any outstanding credit obligations, the borrower is considered to be in default on all obligations.
Currency return The percentage change in the spot exchange rate stated in terms of home currency per unit of foreign currency.
Currency risk The risk associated with the uncertainty about the exchange rate at which proceeds in the foreign currency can be converted into the investor's home currency.
Currency-hedged instruments Investment in nondomestic assets in which currency exposures are neutralized.
Current credit risk (or jump-to-default risk) The risk of credit-related events happening in the immediate future; it relates to the risk that amounts due at the present time will not be paid.
Cushion spread The difference between the minimum acceptable return and the higher possible immunized rate.
Custom security-based benchmark A custom benchmark created by weighting a manager's research universe using the manager's unique weighting approach.
Cyclical stocks The shares of companies whose earnings have above-average sensitivity to the business cycle.
Data-mining bias Bias that results from repeatedly "drilling" or searching a dataset until some statistically significant pattern is found.
Day traders Traders that rapidly buy and sell stocks in the hope that the stocks will continue to rise or fall in value for the seconds or minutes they are prepared to hold a position.
Dealer (or market maker) A business entity that is ready to buy an asset for inventory or sell an asset from inventory to provide the other side of an order.
Decision price (also called arrival price or strike price) The prevailing price when the decision to trade is made.
Decision risk The risk of changing strategies at the point of maximum loss.
Dedication strategies Specialized fixed-income strategies designed to accommodate specific funding needs of the investor.
Default risk The risk of loss if an issuer or counterparty does not fulfill its contractual obligations.
Default risk premium Compensation for the possibility that the issue of a debt instrument will fail to make a promised payment at the contracted time and in the contracted amount.
Defaultable debt Debt with some meaningful amount of credit risk.
Defined-benefit plan A pension plan that specifies the plan sponsor's obligations in terms of the benefit to plan participants.
Defined-contribution plan A pension plan that specifies the sponsor's obligations in terms of contributions to the pension fund rather than benefits to plan participants.
Deflation A decrease in the general level of prices; an increase in the purchasing power of a unit of currency.
Delay costs (or slippage) Implicit trading costs that arise from the inability to complete desired trades immediately due to order size or market liquidity.
Delivery options The quality option, the timing option, and the wild card option.
Delta A measure of an option's sensitivity to a small change in the value of the underlying security.
Delta-normal method A method of estimating value at risk that assumes asset returns are normally distributed.
Demand deposit A deposit that can be drawn upon without prior notice, such as a checking account.
Demutualizing The process of converting an insurance company from stock to mutual form.

Derivatives Contracts whose payoffs depend on the value of another asset, often called the underlying asset.

Descriptive statistics Methods for effectively summarizing data to describe important aspects of a dataset.

Deteriorating fundamentals sell discipline A sell discipline involving ongoing review of holdings in which a share issue is sold or reduced if the portfolio manager believes that the company's business prospects will deteriorate.

Differential returns Returns that deviate from a manager's benchmark.

Diffusion index An index that measures how many indicators are pointing up and how many are pointing down.

Direct commodity investment Commodity investment that involves cash market purchase of physical commodities or exposure to changes in spot market values via derivatives, such as futures.

Direct market access Platforms sponsored by brokers that permit buy-side traders to directly access equities, fixed income, futures, and foreign exchange markets, clearing via the broker.

Direct quotation Quotation in terms of domestic currency/foreign currency.

Discounted cash flow (DCF) models Valuation models that express the idea that an asset's value is the present value of its (expected) cash flows.

Disintermediation To withdraw funds from financial intermediaries for placement with other financial intermediaries offering a higher return or yield. Or, to withdraw funds from a financial intermediary for the purposes of direct investment, such as withdrawing from a mutual fund to make direct stock investments.

Distressed debt arbitrage A distressed securities investment discipline that involves purchasing the traded bonds of bankrupt companies and selling the common equity short.

Distressed securities Securities of companies that are in financial distress or near bankruptcy; the name given to various investment disciplines employing securities of companies in distress.

Diversification effect In reference to VaR across several portfolios (for example, across an entire firm), this effect equals the difference between the sum of the individual VaRs and total VaR.

Dividend recapitalization A method by which a buyout fund can realize the value of a holding; involves the issuance of debt by the holding to finance a special dividend to owners.

Dollar duration A measure of the change in portfolio value for a 100 bps change in market yields.

Downgrade risk The risk that one of the major rating agencies will lower its rating for an issuer, based on its specified rating criteria.

Downside deviation A measure of volatility using only rate of return data points below the investor's minimum acceptable return.

Downside risk Risk of loss or negative return.

Due diligence Investigation and analysis in support of an investment action or recommendation, such as the scrutiny of operations and management and the verification of material facts.

Duration A measure of the approximate sensitivity of a security to a change in interest rates (i.e., a measure of interest rate risk).

Dynamic approach With respect to strategic asset allocation, an approach that accounts for links between optimal decisions at different points in time.

Earnings at risk A variation of value at risk that measures the risk to a company's earnings, instead of its market value; measures risk to accounting earnings.

Earnings momentum A growth investment substyle that focuses on companies with earnings momentum (high quarterly year-over-year earnings growth).

Econometrics The application of quantitative modeling and analysis grounded in economic theory to the analysis of economic data.

Economic indicators Economic statistics provided by government and established private organizations that contain information on an economy's recent past activity or its current or future position in the business cycle.

Economic surplus The market value of assets minus the present value of liabilities.

Effective duration Duration adjusted to account for embedded options.

Effective spread Two times the distance between the actual execution price and the midpoint of the market quote at the time an order is entered; a measure of execution costs that captures the effects of price improvement and market impact.

Efficient frontier The graph of the set of portfolios that maximize expected return for their level of risk (standard deviation of return); the part of the minimum-variance frontier beginning with the global minimum-variance portfolio and continuing above it.

Electronic communications networks (ECNs) Computer-based auctions that operate continuously within the day using a specified set of rules to execute orders.

Emerging market debt The sovereign debt of nondeveloped countries.

Endogenous variable A variable whose values are determined within the system.

Endowments Long-term funds generally owned by operating non-profit institutions such as universities and colleges, museums, hospitals, and other organizations involved in charitable activities.

Enhanced derivatives products companies (or special purpose vehicles) A type of subsidiary separate from an entity's other activities and not liable for the parent's debts. They are often used by derivatives dealers to control exposure to ratings downgrades.

Enterprise risk management An overall assessment of a company's risk position. A centralized approach to risk management sometimes called firmwide risk management.

Equal probability rebalancing Rebalancing in which the manager specifies a corridor for each asset class as a common multiple of the standard deviation of the asset class's returns. Rebalancing to the target proportions occurs when any asset class weight moves outside its corridor.

Equal weighted In an equal-weighted index, each stock in the index is weighted equally.

Equitized Given equity market systematic risk exposure.

Equity risk premium Compensation for the additional risk of equity compared with debt.

Equity-indexed annuity A type of life annuity that provides a guarantee of a minimum fixed payment plus some participation in stock market gains, if any.

ESG risk The risk to a company's market valuation resulting from environmental, social, and governance factors.

Eurozone The region of countries using the euro as a currency.

***Ex post* alpha (or Jensen's alpha)** The average return achieved in a portfolio in excess of what would have been predicted by CAPM given the portfolio's risk level; an after-the-fact measure of excess risk-adjusted return.

Excess currency return The expected currency return in excess of the forward premium or discount.

Exchange A regulated venue for the trading of investment instruments.

Exchange fund A fund into which several investors place their different share holdings in exchange for shares in the diversified fund itself.

Exchange of futures for physicals The exchange of cash instruments for related futures contracts of equivalent value; a technique for switching or modifying exposures between cash and futures markets.

Execution uncertainty Uncertainty pertaining to the timing of execution, or if execution will even occur at all.

Exogenous shocks Events from outside the economic system that affect its course. These could be short-lived political events, changes in government policy, or natural disasters, for example.

Exogenous variable A variable whose values are determined outside the system.

Explicit transaction costs The direct costs of trading such as broker commission costs, taxes, stamp duties, and fees paid to exchanges; costs for which the trader could be given a receipt.

Externality Those consequences of a transaction (or process) that do not fall on the parties to the transaction (or process).

Factor covariance matrix The covariance matrix of factors.

Factor push A simple stress test that involves pushing prices and risk factors of an underlying model in the most disadvantageous way to estimate the impact of factor extremes on the portfolio's value.

Factor sensitivities (also called factor betas or factor loadings) In a multifactor model, the responsiveness of the dependent variable to factor movements.

Factor-model-based benchmark A benchmark that is created by relating one or more systematic sources of returns (factors or exposures) to returns of the benchmark.

Fallen angels Debt that has crossed the threshold from investment grade to high yield.

Family offices Entities, typically organized and owned by a family for its benefit, that assume responsibility for services such as financial planning, estate planning, and asset management.

Federal funds rate The interest rate on overnight loans of reserves (deposits) between U.S. Federal Reserve System member banks.

Fee cap A limit on the total fee paid regardless of performance.

Fiduciary A person or entity standing in a special relation of trust and responsibility with respect to other parties.

Financial capital As used in the text, an individual investor's investable wealth; total wealth minus human capital. Consists of assets that can be traded such as cash, stocks, bonds, and real estate.

Financial equilibrium models Models describing relationships between expected return and risk in which supply and demand are in balance.

Financial risk Risks derived from events in the external financial markets, such as changes in equity prices, interest rates, or currency exchange rates.

Fiscal policy Government activity concerning taxation and governmental spending.

Fixed annuity A type of life annuity in which periodic payments are fixed in amount.

Fixed-rate payer The party to an interest rate swap that is obligated to make periodic payments at a fixed rate.

Floating supply of shares (or free float) The number of shares outstanding that are actually available to investors.

Floating-rate payer The party to an interest rate swap that is obligated to make periodic payments based on a benchmark floating rate.

Floor broker An agent of the broker who, for certain exchanges, physically represents the trade on the exchange floor.

Floors A combination of interest rate call options designed to provide protection against interest rate decreases.

Formal tools Established research methods amenable to precise definition and independent replication of results.

Forward discount (or forward premium) The forward rate less the spot rate, divided by the spot rate; called the forward discount if negative, and forward premium if positive.

Forward hedging Hedging that involves the use of a forward contract between the foreign asset's currency and the home currency.

Foundations Typically, grant-making institutions funded by gifts and investment assets.

Fourth market A term occasionally used for direct trading of securities between institutional investors; the fourth market would include trading on electronic crossing networks.

Front office The revenue generating functions at an investment firm such as those pertaining to trading and sales.

Front-run To trade ahead of the initiator, exploiting privileged information about the initiator's trading intentions.

Full replication When every issue in an index is represented in the portfolio, and each portfolio position has approximately the same weight in the fund as in the index.

Fully funded plan A pension plan in which the ratio of the value of plan assets to the present value of plan liabilities is 100 percent or greater.

Functional (or multifunctional) duration The key rate duration.

Fund of funds A fund that invests in a number of underlying funds.

Fundamental law of active management The relation that the information ratio of a portfolio manager is approximately equal to the information coefficient multiplied by the square root of the investment discipline's breadth (the number of independent, active investment decisions made each year).

Funded status The relationship between the value of a plan's assets and the present value of its liabilities.

Funding ratio A measure of the relative size of pension assets compared to the present value of pension liabilities. Calculated by dividing the value of pension assets by the present value of pension liabilities. Also referred to as the funded ratio or funded status.

Funding risk The risk that liabilities funding long asset positions cannot be rolled over at reasonable cost.

Futures contract An enforceable contract between a buyer (seller) and an established exchange or its clearinghouse in which the buyer (seller) agrees to take (make) delivery of something at a specified price at the end of a designated period of time.

Futures price The price at which the parties to a futures contract agree to exchange the underlying.

Gain-to-loss ratio The ratio of positive returns to negative returns over a specified period of time.

Gamma A measure of the sensitivity of delta to a change in the underlying's value.

Global custodian An entity that effects trade settlement, safekeeping of assets, and the allocation of trades to individual custody accounts.

Global investable market A practical proxy for the world market portfolio consisting of traditional and alternative asset classes with sufficient capacity to absorb meaningful investment.

Global minimum-variance portfolio The portfolio on the minimum-variance frontier with small st variance of return.

Gold standard currency system A currency regime under which currency could be freely converted into gold at established rates.

Gordon (constant) growth model A version of the dividend discount model for common share value that assumes a constant growth rate in dividends.

Government structural policies Government policies that affect the limits of economic growth and incentives within the private sector.

Grinold–Kroner model An expression for the expected return on a share as the sum of an expected income return, an expected nominal earnings growth return, and an expected repricing return.

Gross domestic product (GDP) The total value of final goods and services produced in the economy during a year.

Growth in total factor productivity A component of trend growth in GDP that results from increased efficiency in using capital inputs; also known a technical progress.

Growth investment style With reference to equity investing, an investment style focused on investing in high-earnings-growth companies.

Guaranteed investment contract A debt instrument issued by insurers, usually in large denominations, that pays a guaranteed, generally fixed interest rate for a specified time period.

Hedge funds A historically loosely regulated, pooled investment vehicle that may implement various investment strategies.

Hedge ratio The ratio of the quantity of an asset being hedged to the quantity of the derivative used for hedging.

Hedged return The foreign asset return in local currency terms plus the forward discount (premium).

High yield A value investment substyle that focuses on stocks offering high dividend yield with prospects of maintaining or increasing the dividend.

High-water mark A specified net asset value level that a fund must exceed before performance fees are paid to the hedge fund manager.

High-yield investing A distressed securities investment discipline that involves investment in high-yield bonds perceived to be undervalued.

Historical simulation method The application of historical price changes to the current portfolio.

Holdings-based style analysis An approach to style analysis that categorizes individual securities by their characteristics and aggregates results to reach a conclusion about the overall style of the portfolio at a given point in time.

Human capital The present value of expected future labor income.

Hybrid markets Combinations of market types, which offer elements of batch auction markets and continuous auction markets, as well as quote-driven markets.

Hypothetical events A type of scenario analysis used in stress testing that involves the evaluation of performance given events that have never happened in the markets or market outcomes to which we attach a small probability.

Illiquidity premium Compensation for the risk of loss relative to an investment's fair value if an investment needs to be converted to cash quickly.

Immunization An asset/liability management approach that structures investments in bonds to match (offset) liabilities' weighted-average duration; a type of dedication strategy.

Immunization target rate of return The assured rate of return of an immunized portfolio, equal to the total return of the portfolio assuming no change in the term structure.

Immunized time horizon The time horizon over which a portfolio's value is immunized; equal to the portfolio duration.

Implementation shortfall The difference between the money return on a notional or paper portfolio and the actual portfolio return.

Implementation shortfall strategy (or arrival price strategy) A strategy that attempts to minimize trading costs as measured by the implementation shortfall method.

Implicit costs Indirect trading costs, such as the bid-ask spread, market impact costs, opportunity costs, and delay (slippage) costs.

Implicit transaction costs The indirect costs of trading including bid-ask spreads, the market price impacts of large trades, missed trade opportunity costs, and delay costs.

Incremental VaR A measure of the incremental effect of an asset on the value at risk of a portfolio by measuring the difference between the portfolio's VaR while including a specified asset and the portfolio's VaR with that asset eliminated.

Indexing A common passive approach to investing that involves holding a portfolio of securities designed to replicate the returns on a specified index of securities.

Indirect commodity investment Commodity investment that involves the acquisition of indirect claims on commodities, such as equity in companies specializing in commodity production.

Individualist investors Investors who have a self-assured approach to investing and investment decision making.

Inferential statistics Methods for making estimates or forecasts about a larger group from a smaller group actually observed.

Inflation An increase in the general level of prices; a decrease in the purchasing power of a unit of currency.

Inflation hedge An asset whose returns are sufficient on average to preserve purchasing power during periods of inflation.

Inflation premium Compensation for expected inflation.

Information coefficient The correlation between forecast and actual returns.

Information ratio The mean excess return of the account over the benchmark (i.e., mean active return) relative to the variability of that excess return (i.e., tracking risk); a measure of risk-adjusted performance.

Information-motivated traders Traders that seek to trade on information that has limited value if not quickly acted upon.

Infrastructure funds Funds that make private investment in public infrastructure projects in return for rights to specified revenue streams over a contracted period.

Initial public offering The initial issuance of common stock registered for public trading by a formerly private corporation.

Input uncertainty Uncertainty concerning whether the inputs are correct.

Inside ask (or market ask) The lowest available ask price.

Inside bid (or market bid) The highest available bid price.

Inside bid–ask spread (also called market bid–ask spread, inside spread, or market spread) Market ask price minus market bid price.

Inside quote (or market quote) Combination of the highest available bid price with the lowest available ask price.

Institutional investors Corporations or other legal entities that ultimately serve as financial intermediaries between individuals and investment markets.

Interest rate management effect With respect to fixed-income attribution analysis, a return component reflecting how well a manager predicts interest rate changes.

Interest rate parity A theory that the forward foreign exchange rate discount or premium over a fixed period should equal the risk-free interest rate differential between the two countries over that period.

Interest rate risk Risk related to changes in the level of interest rates.

Interest rate swap A contract between two parties (counterparties) to exchange periodic interest payments based on a specified notional amount of principal.

Interest spread With respect to banks, the average yield on earning assets minus the average percent cost of interest-bearing liabilities.

Internal rate of return The growth rate that will link the ending value of the account to its beginning value plus all intermediate cash flows; money-weighted rate of return is a synonym.

Inventory cycle A cycle measured in terms of fluctuations in inventories, typically lasting 2 to 4 years.

Investment objectives Desired investment outcomes, chiefly pertaining to return and risk.

Investment policy statement (IPS) A written document that sets out a client's return objectives and risk tolerance over a relevant time horizon, along with applicable constraints such as liquidity needs, tax considerations, regulatory requirements, and unique circumstances.

Investment skill The ability to outperform an appropriate benchmark consistently over time.

Investment strategy An investor's approach to investment analysis and security selection.

Investment style A natural grouping of investment disciplines that has some predictive power in explaining the future dispersion in returns across portfolios.

Investment style indexes Indices that represent specific portions of an asset category. For example, subgroups within the U.S. common stock asset category such as large-capitalization growth stocks.

Investor's benchmark The benchmark an investor uses to evaluate performance of a given portfolio or asset class.

J factor risk The risk associated with a judge's track record in adjudicating bankruptcies and restructuring.

J-curve The expected pattern of interim returns over the life of a successful venture capital fund in which early returns are negative as the portfolio of companies burns cash but later returns accelerate as companies are exited.

Key rate duration A method of measuring the interest rate sensitivities of a fixed-income instrument or portfolio to shifts in key points along the yield curve.

Lagging economic indicators Economic indicators of recent past economic activity.

Leading economic indicator A variable that varies with the business cycle but at a fairly consistent time interval before a turn in the business cycle.

Legal and regulatory factors External factors imposed by governmental, regulatory, or oversight authorities that constrain investment decision-making.

Legal/contract risk The possibility of loss arising from the legal system's failure to enforce a contract in which an enterprise has a financial stake; for example, if a contract is voided through litigation.

Leverage-adjusted duration gap A leverage-adjusted measure of the difference between the durations of assets and liabilities that measures a bank's overall interest rate exposure.

Liability As used in the text, a financial obligation.

Life annuity An annuity that guarantees a monthly income to the annuitant for life.

Limit order An instruction to execute an order when the best price available is at least as good as the limit price specified in the order.

Linear programming Optimization in which the objective function and constraints are linear.

Liquidity The ability to trade without delay at relatively low cost and in relatively large quantities.

Liquidity event An event giving rise to a need for cash.

Liquidity requirement A need for cash in excess of new contributions (for pension plans and endowments, for example) or savings (for individuals) at a specified point in time.

Liquidity risk Any risk of economic loss because of the need to sell relatively less liquid assets to meet liquidity requirements; the risk that a financial instrument cannot be purchased or sold without a significant concession in price because of the market's potential inability to efficiently accommodate the desired trading size.

Liquidity-motivated traders Traders that are motivated to trade based upon reasons other than an information advantage. For example, to release cash proceeds to facilitate the purchase of another security, adjust market exposure, or fund cash needs.

Locked up Said of investments that cannot be traded at all for some time.

Lock-up period A minimum initial holding period for investments during which no part of the investment can be withdrawn.

Logical participation strategies Protocols for breaking up an order for execution over time. Typically used by institutional traders to participate in overall market volumes without being unduly visible.

Longevity risk The risk of outliving one's financial resources.

Low P/E A value investment substyle that focuses on shares selling at low prices relative to current or normal earnings.

M^2 A measure of what a portfolio would have returned if it had taken on the same total risk as the market index.

Macaulay duration The percentage change in price for a percentage change in yield.

Macro attribution Performance attribution analysis conducted on the fund sponsor level.

Macro expectations Expectations concerning classes of assets.

Managed futures Pooled investment vehicles, frequently structured as limited partnerships, that invest in futures and options on futures and other instruments.

Manager continuation policies Policies adopted to guide the manager evaluations conducted by fund sponsors. The goal of manager continuation policies is to reduce the costs of manager turnover while systematically acting on indications of future poor performance.

Manager monitoring A formal, documented procedure that assists fund sponsors in consistently collecting information relevant to evaluating the state of their managers' operations; used to identify warning signs of adverse changes in existing managers' organizations.

Manager review A detailed examination of a manager that currently exists within a plan sponsor's program. The manager review closely resembles the manager selection process, in both the information considered and the comprehensiveness of the analysis. The staff should review all phases of the manager's operations, just as if the manager were being initially hired.

Mandate A set of instructions detailing the investment manager's task and how his performance will be evaluated.

Market bid The best available bid; highest price any buyer is currently willing to pay.

Market fragmentation A condition whereby a market contains no dominant group of sellers (or buyers) that are large enough to unduly influence the market.

Market impact (or price impact) The effect of the trade on transaction prices.

Market integration The degree to which there are no impediments or barriers to capital mobility across markets.

Market microstructure The market structures and processes that affect how the manager's interest in buying or selling an asset is translated into executed trades (represented by trade prices and volumes).

Market model A regression equation that specifies a linear relationship between the return on a security (or portfolio) and the return on a broad market index.

Market on open (close) order A market order to be executed at the opening (closing) of the market.

Market order An instruction to execute an order as soon as possible in the public markets at the best price available.

Market oriented With reference to equity investing, an intermediate grouping for investment disciplines that cannot be clearly categorized as value or growth.

Market resilience Condition where discrepancies between market prices and intrinsic values tend to be small and corrected quickly.

Market risk The set of risks linked to supply and demand in various marketplaces such as interest rates, exchange rates, stock prices, and commodity prices.

Market segmentation The degree to which there are some meaningful impediments to capital movement across markets.

Market timing Increasing or decreasing exposure to a market or asset class based on predictions of its performance; with reference to performance attribution, returns attributable to shorter-term tactical deviations from the strategic asset allocation.

Market-adjusted implementation shortfall The difference between the money return on a notional or paper portfolio and the actual portfolio return, adjusted using beta to remove the effect of the return on the market.

Market-not-held order A variation of the market order designed to give the agent greater discretion than a simple market order would allow. "Not held" means that the floor broker is not required to trade at any specific price or in any specific time interval.

Mass affluent An industry term for a segment of the private wealth marketplace that is not sufficiently wealthy to command certain individualized services.

Matrix prices Prices determined by comparisons to other securities of similar credit risk and maturity; the result of matrix pricing.

Matrix pricing An approach for estimating the prices of thinly traded securities based on the prices of securities with similar attributions, such as similar credit rating, maturity, or economic sector.

Maturity premium Compensation for the increased sensitivity of the market value of debt to a change in market interest rates as maturity is extended.

Maturity variance A measure of how much a given immunized portfolio differs from the ideal immunized portfolio consisting of a single pure discount instrument with maturity equal to the time horizon.

Maximum loss optimization A stress test in which we would try to optimize mathematically the risk variable that would produce the maximum loss.

Mega-cap buy-out funds A class of buyout funds that take public companies private.

Methodical investors Investors who rely on "hard facts."

Micro attribution Performance attribution analysis carried out on the investment manager level.

Micro expectations Expectations concerning individual assets.

Middle-market buy-out funds A class of buyout funds that purchase private companies whose revenues and profits are too small to access capital from the public equity markets.

Midquote The halfway point between the market bid and ask prices.

Minimum-variance frontier The graph of the set of portfolios with smallest variances of return for their levels of expected return.

Missed trade opportunity costs Unrealized profit/loss arising from the failure to execute a trade in a timely manner.

Model risk The risk that a model is incorrect or misapplied; in investments, it often refers to valuation models.

Model uncertainty Uncertainty concerning whether a selected model is correct.

Modern portfolio theory (MPT) The analysis of rational portfolio choices based on the efficient use of risk.

Monetary policy Government activity concerning interest rates and the money supply.

Money markets Markets for fixed-income securities with maturities of one year or less.

Money-weighted rate of return Same as the internal rate of return; the growth rate that will link the ending value of the account to its beginning value plus all intermediate cash flows.

Monitoring To systematically keep watch over investor circumstances (including wealth and constraints), market and economic changes, and the portfolio itself so that the client's current objectives and constraints continue to be satisfied.

Mortality risk The risk of loss of human capital in the event of premature death.

Multifactor model A model that explains a variable in terms of the values of a set of factors.

Multifactor model technique With respect to construction of an indexed portfolio, a technique that attempts to match the primary risk exposures of the indexed portfolio to those of the index.

Multiperiod Sharpe ratio A Sharpe ratio based on the investment's multiperiod wealth in excess of the wealth generated by the risk-free investment.

Mutuals With respect to insurance companies, companies that are owned by their policyholders, who share in the company's surplus earnings.

Natural liquidity An extensive pool of investors who are aware of and have a potential interest in buying and/or selling a security.

Net interest margin With respect to banks, net interest income (interest income minus interest expense) divided by average earning assets.

Net interest spread With respect to the operations of insurers, the difference between interest earned and interest credited to policyholders.

Net worth The difference between the market value of assets and liabilities.

Nominal default-free bonds Conventional bonds that have no (or minimal) default risk.

Nominal gross domestic product (nominal GDP) A money measure of the goods and services produced within a country's borders.

Nominal risk-free interest rate The sum of the real risk-free interest rate and the inflation premium.

Nominal spread The spread of a bond or portfolio above the yield of a Treasury of equal maturity.

Nonfinancial risk Risks that arise from sources other than the external financial markets, such as changes in accounting rules, legal environment, or tax rates.

Nonparametric Involving minimal probability-distribution assumptions.

Nonstationarity A property of a data series that reflects more than one set of underlying statistical properties.

Normal portfolio A portfolio with exposure to sources of systematic risk that are typical for a manager, using the manager's past portfolios as a guide.

Notional principal amount The amount specified in a swap that forms the basis for calculating payment streams.

Objective function A quantitative expression of the objective or goal of a process.

Open market operations The purchase or sale by a central bank of government securities, which are settled using reserves, to influence interest rates and the supply of credit by banks.

Open outcry auction market Public auction where representatives of buyers and sellers meet at a specified location and place verbal bids and offers.

Operational risk The risk of loss from failures in a company's systems and procedures or from external events; sometimes called operations risk.

Opportunistic participation strategies Passive trading combined with the opportunistic seizing of liquidity.

Opportunity cost sell discipline A sell discipline in which the investor is constantly looking at potential stocks to include in the portfolio and will replace an existing holding whenever a better opportunity presents itself.

Optimization With respect to portfolio construction, a procedure for determining the best portfolios according to some criterion.

Optimizer A heuristic, formula, algorithm, or program that uses risk, return, correlation, or other variables to determine the most appropriate asset allocation or asset mix for a portfolio.

Option-adjusted spread (OAS) The current spread over the benchmark yield minus that component of the spread that is attributable to any embedded optionality in the instrument.

Options on futures (futures options) Options on a designated futures contract.

Options on physicals With respect to options, exchange-traded option contracts that have cash instruments rather than futures contracts on cash instruments as the underlying.

Order-driven markets Markets in which transaction prices are established by public limit orders to buy or sell a security at specified prices.

Ordinary life insurance (also whole life insurance) A type of life insurance policy that involves coverage for the whole of the insured's life.

Orphan equities investing A distressed securities investment discipline that involves investment in orphan equities that are perceived to be undervalued.

Orphan equity Investment in the newly issued equity of a company emerging from reorganization.

Output gap The difference between the value of GDP estimated as if the economy were on its trend growth path (potential output) and the actual value of GDP.

Overall trade balance The sum of the current account (reflecting exports and imports) and the financial account (consisting of portfolio flows).

Overconfidence trap The tendency of individuals to overestimate the accuracy of their forecasts.

Pairs trade (or pairs arbitrage) A basic long–short trade in which an investor is long and short equal currency amounts of two common stocks in a single industry.

Panel method A method of capital market expectations setting that involves using the viewpoints of a panel of experts.

Partial correlation In multivariate problems, the correlation between two variables after controlling for the effects of the other variables in the system.

Partial fill Execution of a purchase or sale for fewer shares than was stipulated in the order.

Participate (do not initiate) order A variant of the market-not-held order. The broker is deliberately low-key and waits for and responds to the initiatives of more active traders.

Passive investment approach An approach to portfolio construction in which portfolio composition does not react to changes in capital market expectations; includes indexing and buy-and-hold investing.

Passive management A buy-and-hold approach to investing in which an investor does not make portfolio changes based upon short-term expectations of changing market or security performance.

Passive traders Traders that seek liquidity in their rebalancing transactions, but are much more concerned with the cost of trading.

Payment netting The reduction of all obligations owed between counterparties into a single cash transaction that eliminates these liabilities.

Pension funds Funds consisting of assets set aside to support a promise of retirement income.

Pension surplus Pension assets at market value minus the present value of pension liabilities.

Percentage-of-portfolio rebalancing Rebalancing is triggered based on set thresholds stated as a percentage of the portfolio's value.

Percentage-of-volume strategy A logical participation strategy in which trading takes place in proportion to overall market volume (typically at a rate of 5 to 20 percent) until the order is completed.

Perfect markets Markets without any frictional costs.

Performance appraisal The evaluation of portfolio performance; a quantitative assessment of a manager's investment skill.

Performance attribution A comparison of an account's performance with that of a designated benchmark and the identification and quantification of sources of differential returns.

Performance evaluation The measurement and assessment of the outcomes of investment management decisions.

Performance measurement A component of performance evaluation; the relatively simple procedure of calculating an asset's or portfolio's rate of return.

Performance netting risk For entities that fund more than one strategy and have asymmetric incentive fee arrangements with the portfolio managers, the potential for loss in cases where the net performance of the group of managers generates insufficient fee revenue to fully cover contractual payout obligations to all portfolio managers with positive performance.

Performance-based fee Fees specified by a combination of a base fee plus an incentive fee for performance in excess of a benchmark's.

Periodic (or batch) auction markets Auction markets where multilateral trading occurs at a single price at a prespecified point in time.

Permanent income hypothesis The hypothesis that consumers' spending behavior is largely determined by their long-run income expectations.

Personality typing The determination of an investor's personality type.

Plan sponsor An enterprise or organization—such as a business, labor union, municipal or state government, or not-for-profit organization—that sets up a pension plan.

Pledging requirement With respect to banks, a required collateral use of assets.

Point estimate A single-valued estimate of a quantity, as opposed to an estimate in terms of a range of values.

Policy portfolio A synonym of strategic asset allocation; the portfolio resulting from strategic asset allocation considered as a process.

Policyholder reserves With respect to an insurance company, an amount representing the estimated payments to policyholders, as determined by actuaries, based on the types and terms of the various insurance policies issued by the company.

Political risk (or geopolitical risk) The risk of war, government collapse, political instability, expropriation, confiscation, or adverse changes in taxation.

Portable Moveable. With reference to a pension plan, one in which a plan participant can move his or her share of plan assets to a new plan, subject to certain rules, vesting schedules, and possible tax penalties and payments.

Portable alpha A strategy involving the combining of multiple positions (e.g. long and short positions) so as to separate the alpha (unsystematic risk) from beta (systematic risk) in an investment.

Portfolio implementation decision The decision on how to execute the buy and sell orders of portfolio managers.

Portfolio management A process in which investment objectives and constraints are identified and specified, investment strategies are developed, portfolio composition is decided in detail, portfolio decisions are initiated by portfolio managers and implemented by traders, portfolio performance is measured and evaluated, investor and market conditions are monitored, and any necessary rebalancing is implemented.

Portfolio management process An integrated set of steps undertaken in a consistent manner to create and maintain an appropriate portfolio (combination of assets) to meet clients' stated goals.

Portfolio optimization The combining of assets to efficiently achieve a set of return and risk objectives.

Portfolio segmentation The creation of subportfolios according to the product mix for individual segments or lines of business.

Portfolio selection/composition decision The decision in which the manager integrates investment strategies with capital market expectations to select the specific assets for the portfolio.

Portfolio trade (also known as program trade or basket trade) A trade in which a number of securities are traded as a single unit.

Position a trade To take the other side of a trade, acting as a principal with capital at risk.

Positive active position An active position for which the account's allocation to a security is greater than the corresponding weight of the same security in the benchmark.

Post-trade transparency Degree to which completed trades are quickly and accurately reported to the public.

Potential output The value of GDP if the economy were on its trend growth path.

Preferred return With respect to the compensation of private equity fund managers, a hurdle rate.

Prepackaged bankruptcy A bankruptcy in which the debtor seeks agreement from creditors on the terms of a reorganization before the reorganization filing.

Present value distribution of cash flows A list showing what proportion of a portfolio's duration is attributable to each future cash flow.

Pretrade transparency Ability of individuals to quickly, easily, and inexpensively obtain accurate information about quotes and trades.

Price discovery Adjustment of transaction prices to balance supply and demand.

Price improvement Execution at a price that is better than the price quoted at the time of order placement.

Price risk The risk of fluctuations in market price.

Price uncertainty Uncertainty about the price at which an order will execute.

Price weighted With respect to index construction, an index in which each security in the index is weighted according to its absolute share price.

Priced risk Risk for which investors demand compensation.

Primary risk factors With respect to valuation, the major influences on pricing.

Prime brokerage A suite of services that is often specified to include support in accounting and reporting, leveraged trade execution, financing, securities lending (related to short-selling activities), and start-up advice (for new entities).

Principal trade A trade with a broker in which the broker commits capital to facilitate the prompt execution of the trader's order to buy or sell.

Private equity Ownership interests in non-publicly-traded companies.

Private equity funds Pooled investment vehicles investing in generally highly illiquid assets; includes venture capital funds and buyout funds.

Private exchange A method for handling undiversified positions with built-in capital gains in which shares that are a component of an index are exchanged for shares of an index mutual fund in a privately arranged transaction with the fund.

Private placement memorandum A document used to raise venture capital financing when funds are raised through an agent.

Profit-sharing plans A defined-contribution plan in which contributions are based, at least in part, on the plan sponsor's profits.

Projected benefit obligation (PBO) A measure of a pension plan's liability that reflects accumulated service in the same manner as the ABO but also projects future variables, such as compensation increases.

Prospect theory The analysis of decision making under risk in terms of choices among prospects.

Protective put A put buying strategy that establishes a minimum value for a portfolio.

Proxy hedging Hedging that involves the use of a forward contract between the home currency and a currency that is highly correlated with the foreign asset's currency.

Prudence trap The tendency to temper forecasts so that they do not appear extreme; the tendency to be overly cautious in forecasting.

Psychological profiling The determination of an investor's psychological characteristics relevant to investing, such as his or her personality type.

Public good A good that is not divisible and not excludable (a consumer cannot be denied it).

Purchasing power parity The theory that movements in an exchange rate should offset any difference in the inflation rates between two countries.

Pure sector allocation return A component of attribution analysis that relates relative returns to the manager's sector-weighting decisions. Calculated as the difference between the allocation (weight) of the portfolio to a given sector and the portfolio's benchmark weight for that sector, multiplied by the difference between the sector benchmark's return and the overall portfolio's benchmark return, summed across all sectors.

Quality control charts A graphical means of presenting performance appraisal data; charts illustrating the performance of an actively managed account versus a selected benchmark.

Quality option (or swap option) With respect to Treasury futures, the option of which acceptable Treasury issue to deliver.

Quoted depth The number of shares available for purchase or sale at the quoted bid and ask prices.

Quote-driven markets (dealer markets) Markets that rely on dealers to establish firm prices at which securities can be bought and sold.

Rate duration A fixed-income instrument's or portfolio's sensitivity to a change in key maturity, holding constant all other points along the yield curve.

Real estate Interests in land or structures attached to land.

Real estate investment trusts (REITs) Publicly traded equities representing pools of money invested in real estate properties and/or real estate debt.

Real option An option involving decisions related to tangible assets or processes.

Real risk-free interest rate The single-period interest rate for a completely risk-free security if no inflation were expected.

Rebalancing Adjusting the actual portfolio to the current strategic asset allocation because of price changes in portfolio holdings. Also: Revisions to an investor's target asset class weights because of changes in the investor's investment objectives or constraints, or because of changes in capital market expectations; or to mean tactical asset allocation.

Rebalancing ratio A quantity involved in reestablishing the dollar duration of a portfolio to a desired level, equal to the original dollar duration divided by the new dollar duration.

Rebase With reference to index construction, to change the time period used as the base of the index.

Recallability trap The tendency of forecasts to be overly influenced by events that have left a strong impression on a person's memory.

Recession A broad-based economic downturn, conventionally defined as two successive quarterly declines in gross domestic product.

Reference entity An entity, such as a bond issuer, specified in a derivatives contract.

Regime A distinct governing set of relationships.

Regulatory risk The risk associated with the uncertainty of how a transaction will be regulated or with the potential for regulations to change.

Reinvestment risk The risk of reinvesting coupon income or principal at a rate less than the original coupon or purchase rate.

Relative economic strength forecasting approach An exchange rate forecasting approach that suggests that a strong pace of economic growth in a country creates attractive investment opportunities, increasing the demand for the country's currency and causing it to appreciate.

Relative return objective A return objective stated as a return relative to the portfolio benchmark's total return.

Relative strength indicators A price momentum indicator that involves comparing a stock's performance during a specific period either to its own past performance or to the performance of some group of stocks.

Remaindermen Beneficiaries of a trust; having a claim on the residue.

Repurchase agreement A contract involving the sale of securities such as Treasury instruments coupled with an agreement to repurchase the same securities at a later date.

Repurchase yield The negative of the expected percent change in number of shares outstanding, in the Grinold–Kroner model.

Required return (or return requirement) With reference to the investment policy statement, a return objective relating to level of return that will be adequate to satisfy a need.

Resampled efficient frontier The set of resampled efficient portfolios.

Resampled efficient portfolio An efficient portfolio based on simulation.

Residue With respect to trusts, the funds remaining in a trust when the last income beneficiary dies.

Retired lives The portion of a pension fund's liabilities associated with retired workers.

Return objective An investor objective that addresses the required or desired level of returns.

Returns-based benchmarks Benchmarks that are constructed using (1) a series of a manager's account returns and (2) the series of returns on several investment style indexes over the same period. These return series are then submitted to an allocation algorithm that solves for the combination of investment style indexes that most closely tracks the account's returns.

Returns-based style analysis An approach to style analysis that focuses on characteristics of the overall portfolio as revealed by a portfolio's realized returns.

Reverse optimization A technique for reverse engineering the expected returns implicit in a diversified market portfolio.

Risk aversion The degree of an investor's inability and unwillingness to take risk.

Risk budget The desired total quantity of risk; the result of risk budgeting.

Risk budgeting The allocation of a total acceptable amount of risk to various risky activities.

Risk exposure A source of risk. Also, the state of being exposed or vulnerable to a risk.

Risk governance The process of setting overall policies and standards in risk management.

Risk objective An investor objective that addresses risk.

Risk premium approach An approach to forecasting the return of a risky asset that views its expected return as the sum of the risk-free rate of interest and one or more risk premiums.

Risk profile A detailed tabulation of the index's risk exposures.

Risk tolerance The capacity to accept risk; the level of risk an investor (or organization) is willing and able to bear.

Risk tolerance function An assessment of an investor's tolerance to risk over various levels of portfolio outcomes.

Roll return (or roll yield) The component of the return on a commodity futures contract that comes from rolling long futures positions forward through time.

Rolling return The moving average of the holding-period returns for a specified period (e.g., a calendar year) that matches the investor's time horizon.

Sample estimator A formula for assigning a unique value (a point estimate) to a population parameter.

Savings–investment imbalances forecasting approach An exchange rate forecasting approach that explains currency movements in terms of the effects of domestic savings–investment imbalances on the exchange rate.

Scenario analysis Analysis of the impact of a trade on the expected total return under different scenarios (sets of assumptions concerning relevant variables).

Secondary offering An offering after the initial public offering of securities.

Sector/quality effect In a fixed-income attribution analysis, a measure of a manager's ability to select the "right" issuing sector and quality group.

Security selection Skill in selecting individual securities within an asset class.

Security selection effect In a fixed-income attribution analysis, the residual of the security's total return after other effects are accounted for; a measure of the return due to ability in security selection.

Segmentation With respect to the management of insurance company portfolios, the notional subdivision of the overall portfolio into sub-portfolios, each of which is associated with a specified group of insurance contracts.

Sell side Broker/dealers that sell securities and make recommendations for various customers, such as investment managers and institutional investors.

Sell-side analysts Analysts employed by brokerages.

Semiactive management (also called enhanced indexing or risk-controlled active management) A variant of active management. In a semiactive portfolio, the manager seeks to outperform a given benchmark with tightly controlled risk relative to the benchmark.

Semiactive, risk-controlled active, or enhanced index approach An investment approach that seeks positive alpha while keeping tight control over risk relative to the portfolio's benchmark.

Semivariance A measure of downside risk. The average of squared deviations that fall below the mean.

Settlement date The designated date at which the parties to a trade must transact.

Settlement netting risk The risk that a liquidator of a counterparty in default could challenge a netting arrangement so that profitable transactions are realized for the benefit of creditors.

Settlement risk The risk that one party could be in the process of paying the counterparty while the counterparty is declaring bankruptcy.

Sharpe ratio (or reward-to-variability) A measure of risk-adjusted performance that compares excess returns to the total risk of the account, where total risk is measured by the account's standard deviation of returns.

Shortfall risk The risk that portfolio value will fall below some minimum acceptable level during a stated time horizon; the risk of not achieving a specified return target.

Shrinkage estimation Estimation that involves taking a weighted average of a historical estimate of a parameter and some other parameter estimate, where the weights reflect the analyst's relative belief in the estimates.

Shrinkage estimator The formula used in shrinkage estimation of a parameter.

Sign-constrained optimization An optimization that constrains asset class weights to be nonnegative and to sum to 1.

Situational profiling The categorization of individual investors by stage of life or by economic circumstance.

Smart routing The use of algorithms to intelligently route an order to the most liquid venue.

Smoothing rule With respect to spending rates, a rule that averages asset values over a period of time in order to dampen the spending rate's response to asset value fluctuation.

Socially responsible investing (ethical investing) An approach to investing that integrates ethical values and societal concerns with investment decisions.

Soft dollars (also called soft dollar arrangements or soft commissions) The use of commissions to buy services other than execution services.

Sortino ratio A performance appraisal ratio that replaces standard deviation in the Sharpe ratio with downside deviation.

Sovereign risk A form of credit risk in which the borrower is the government of a sovereign nation.

Spontaneous investors Investors who constantly readjust their portfolio allocations and holdings.

Spot return (or price return) The component of the return on a commodity futures contract that comes from changes in the underlying spot prices via the cost-of-carry model.

Spread duration The sensitivity of a non-Treasury security's price to a widening or narrowing of the spread over Treasuries.

Spread risk Risk related to changes in the spread between Treasuries and non-Treasuries.

Stale price bias Bias that arises from using prices that are stale because of infrequent trading.

Standard deviation The positive square root of variance.

Stated return desire A stated desired level of returns.

Static approach With respect to strategic asset allocation, an approach that does not account for links between optimal decisions in future time periods.

Static spread (or zero-volatility spread) The constant spread above the Treasury spot curve that equates the calculated price of the security to the market price.

Stationary A series of data for which the parameters that describe a return-generating process are stable.

Status quo trap The tendency for forecasts to perpetuate recent observations—that is, to predict no change from the recent past.

Sterling ratio The compound annualized rate of return over a specified time period divided by the average yearly maximum drawdown over the same time period less an arbitrary 10 percent.

Stock companies With respect to insurance companies, companies that have issued common equity shares.

Stock index futures Futures contracts on a specified stock index.

Straight-through processing Systems that simplify transaction processing through the minimization of manual and/or duplicative intervention in the process from trade placement to settlement.

Strategic asset allocation (1) The process of allocating money to IPS-permissible asset classes that integrates the investor's return objectives, risk tolerance, and investment constraints with long-run capital market expectations. (2) The result of the above process, also known as the policy portfolio.

Stratified sampling (representative sampling) A sampling method that guarantees that subpopulations of interest are represented in the sample.

Strike spread A spread used to determine the strike price for the payoff of a credit option.

Structural level of unemployment The level of unemployment resulting from scarcity of a factor of production.

Style drift Inconsistency in style.

Style index A securities index intended to reflect the average returns to a given style.

Stylized scenario A type of analysis often used in stress testing. It involves simulating the movement in at least one interest rate, exchange rate, stock price, or commodity price relevant to the portfolio.

Sunshine trades Public display of a transaction (usually high-volume) in advance of the actual order.

Surplus The difference between the value of assets and the present value of liabilities. With respect to an insurance company, the net difference between the total assets and total liabilities (equivalent to policyholders' surplus for a mutual insurance company and stockholders' equity for a stock company).

Surplus efficient frontier The graph of the set of portfolios that maximize expected surplus for given levels of standard deviation of surplus.

Survey method A method of capital market expectations setting that involves surveying experts.

Survivorship bias Bias that arises in a data series when managers with poor track records exit the business and are dropped from the database whereas managers with good records remain; when a data series as of a given date reflects only entities that have survived to that date.

Swap rate The interest rate applicable to the pay-fixed-rate side of an interest rate swap.

Symmetric cash flow matching A cash flow matching technique that allows cash flows occurring both before and after the liability date to be used to meet a liability; allows for the short-term borrowing of funds to satisfy a liability prior to the liability due date.

Tactical asset allocation Asset allocation that involves making short-term adjustments to asset class weights based on short-term predictions of relative performance among asset classes.

Tactical rebalancing A variation of calendar rebalancing that specifies less frequent rebalancing when markets appear to be trending and more frequent rebalancing when they are characterized by reversals.

Tail value at risk (or conditional tail expectation) The VaR plus the expected loss in excess of VaR, when such excess loss occurs.

Target covariance matrix A component of shrinkage estimation; allows the analyst to model factors that are believed to influence the data over periods longer than observed in the historical sample.

Target semivariance The average squared deviation below a target value.

Target value The value that the portfolio manager seeks to ensure; the value that the life insurance company has guaranteed the policyholder.

Tax concerns Concerns related to an investor's tax position.

Tax efficiency The proportion of the expected pretax total return that will be retained after taxes.

Tax premium Compensation for the effect of taxes on the after-tax return of an asset.

Tax risk The risk that arises because of the uncertainty associated with tax laws.

Taylor rule A rule linking a central bank's target short-term interest rate to the rate of growth of the economy and inflation.

Term life insurance A type of life insurance policy that provides coverage for a specified length of time and accumulates little or no cash values.

Theta The change in price of an option associated with a one-day reduction in its time to expiration.

Tick The smallest possible price movement of a security.

Time deposit A deposit requiring advance notice prior to a withdrawal.

Time horizon The time period associated with an investment objective.

Time-period bias Bias that occurs when results are time-period specific.

Time-series estimators Estimators that are based on lagged values of the variable being forecast; often consist of lagged values of other selected variables.

Time-weighted average price (TWAP) strategy A logical participation strategy that assumes a flat volume profile and trades in proportion to time.

Time-weighted rate of return The compound rate of growth over a stated evaluation period of one unit of money initially invested in the account.

Timing option With respect to certain futures contracts, the option that results from the ability of the short position to decide when in the delivery month actual delivery will take place.

Top-down Proceeding from the macroeconomy, to the economic sector level, to the industry level, to the firm level.

Total future liability With respect to defined-benefit pension plans, the present value of accumulated and projected future service benefits, including the effects of projected future compensation increases.

Total rate of return A measure of the increase in the investor's wealth due to both investment income (for example, dividends and interest) and capital gains (both realized and unrealized).

Total return The rate of return taking into account capital appreciation/depreciation and income. Often qualified as follows: **Nominal** returns are unadjusted for inflation; **real** returns are adjusted for inflation; **pretax** returns are returns before taxes; **post-tax** returns are returns after taxes are paid on investment income and realized capital gains.

Total return analysis Analysis of the expected effect of a trade on the portfolio's total return, given an interest rate forecast.

Total return swap A swap used to transfer credit risk and interest rate risk to another party. The protection buyer pays the total return on a reference obligation (or basket of reference obligations) in return for floating-rate payments.

Tracking risk (also called tracking error, tracking error volatility, or active risk) The standard deviation of the differences between a portfolio's and the benchmark's total returns.

Trade blotter A device for entering and tracking trade executions and orders to trade.

Trade settlement Completion of a trade wherein purchased financial instruments are transferred to the buyer and the buyer transfers money to the seller.

Trading activity In fixed-income attribution analysis, the effect of sales and purchases of bonds over a given period; the total portfolio return minus the other components determining the management effect in an attribution analysis.

Transcription errors Errors in gathering and recording data.

Transparency Availability of timely and accurate market and trade information.

Treasury spot curve The term structure of Treasury zero coupon bonds.

Treynor ratio (or reward-to-volatility) A measure of risk-adjusted performance that relates an account's excess returns to the systematic risk assumed by the account.

Turnover A measure of the rate of trading activity in a portfolio.

Twist With respect to the yield curve, a movement in contrary directions of interest rates at two maturities; a nonparallel movement in the yield curve.

Type I error With respect to manager selection, keeping (or hiring) managers with zero value-added. (Rejecting the null hypothesis when it is correct.)

Type II error With respect to manager selection, firing (or not hiring) managers with positive value-added. (Not rejecting the null hypothesis when it is incorrect.)

Unconstrained optimization Optimization that places no constraints on asset class weights except that they sum to 1. May produce negative asset weights, which implies borrowing or shorting of assets.

Underfunded plan A pension plan in which the ratio of the value of plan assets to the present value of plan liabilities is less than 100 percent.

Underlying The security underlying a derivatives contract.

Underwriting (profitability) cycle A cycle affecting the profitability of insurance companies' underwriting operations.

Undisclosed limit order (reserve, hidden, or iceberg order) A limit order that includes an instruction not to show more than some maximum quantity of the unfilled order to the public at any one time.

Unhedged return A foreign asset return stated in terms of the investor's home currency.

Unique circumstances Internal factors (other than a liquidity requirement, time horizon, or tax concern) that may constrain portfolio choices.

Universal life insurance A type of life insurance policy that provides for premium flexibility, an adjustable face amount of death benefits, and current market interest rates on the savings element.

Unrelated business income With respect to the U.S. tax code, income that is not substantially related to a foundation's charitable purposes.

Unstructured modeling Modeling without a theory on the underlying structure.

Uptick rules Trading rules that specify that a short sale must not be on a downtick relative to the last trade at a different price.

Urgency of the trade The importance of certainty of execution.

Valuation reserve With respect to insurance companies, an allowance, created by a charge against earnings, to provide for losses in the value of the assets.

Value at risk (VaR) An estimate of the loss (in money terms) that the portfolio manager expects to be exceeded with a given level of probability over a specified time period.

Value investment style With reference to equity investing, an investment style focused on paying a relatively low share price in relation to earnings or assets per share.

Value weighted (or market-capitalization weighted) With respect to index construction, an index in which each security in the index is weighted according to its market capitalization.

Value-motivated traders Traders that act on value judgments based on careful, sometimes painstaking research. They trade only when the price moves into their value range.

Variable annuity A life annuity in which the periodic payment varies depending on stock prices.

Variable life insurance (unit-linked life insurance) A type of ordinary life insurance in which death benefits and cash values are linked to the investment performance of a policyholder-selected pool of investments held in a so-called separate account.

Variable prepaid forward A monetization strategy that involves the combination of a collar with a loan against the value of the underlying shares. When the loan comes due, shares are sold to pay off the loan and part of any appreciation is shared with the lender.

Variable universal life (or flexible-premium variable life) A type of life insurance policy that combines the flexibility of universal life with the investment choice flexibility of variable life.

Variance The expected value of squared deviations from the random variable's mean; often referred to as volatility.

Vega A measure of the sensitivity of an option's price to changes in the underlying's volatility.

Venture capital The equity financing of new or growing private companies.

Venture capital firms Firms representing dedicated pools of capital for providing equity or equity-linked financing to privately held companies.

Venture capital fund A pooled investment vehicle for venture capital investing.

Venture capital trusts An exchange-traded, closed-end vehicle for venture capital investing.

Venture capitalists Specialists who seek to identify companies that have good business opportunities but need financial, managerial, and strategic support.

Vested With respect to pension benefits or assets, said of an unconditional ownership interest.

Vintage year With reference to a private equity fund, the year it closed.

Vintage year effects The effects on returns shared by private equity funds closed in the same year.

Volatility Represented by the Greek letter sigma (σ), the standard deviation of price outcomes associated with an underlying asset.

Volatility clustering The tendency for large (small) swings in prices to be followed by large (small) swings of random direction.

Volume-weighted average price The average price at which a security traded during the day, where each trade price is weighted by the fraction of the day's volume associated with the trade.

Volume-weighted average price (VWAP) strategy A logical participation strategy that involves breaking up an order over time according to a prespecified volume profile.

Wealth relative The ending value of one unit of money invested at specified rates of return.

Wild card option A provision allowing a short futures contract holder to delay delivery of the underlying.

Within-sector selection return In attribution analysis, a measure of the impact of a manager's security selection decisions relative to the holdings of the sector benchmark.

Worst-case scenario analysis A stress test in which we examine the worst case that we actually expect to occur.

Yield beta The expected relative change in two bonds.

Yield curve The relationship between yield and time to maturity.

Yield curve risk Risk related to changes in the shape of the yield curve.

Yield to worst The yield on a callable bond that assumes a bond is called at the earliest opportunity.

Zero-premium collar A hedging strategy involving the simultaneous purchase of puts and sale of call options on a stock. The puts are struck below and the calls are struck above the underlying's market price.

REFERENCES

ACLI Survey. 2003. The American Council of Life Insurers.

Agarwal, Vikas, and Narayan Naik. 2000. "Performance Evaluation of Hedge Funds with Option-Based and Buy-and-Hold Strategies." Working Paper, London Business School.

Ali, Paul Usman, and Martin Gold. 2002. "An Appraisal of Socially Responsible Investments and Implications for Trustees and Other Investment Fiduciaries." Working Paper, University of Melbourne.

Almgren, Robert, and Neil Chriss. 2000/2001. "Optimal Execution of Portfolio Transactions." *Journal of Risk.* Vol. 3: 5–39.

Ambachtsheer, Keith, Ronald Capelle, and Tom Scheibelhut. 1998. "Improving Pension Fund Performance." *Financial Analysts Journal.* Vol. 54, No. 6: 15–21.

Ambachtsheer, Keith. 1986. Pension Funds and the Bottom Line: Managing the Corporate Pension Fund as a Financial Business. Homewood, IL: Dow Jones-Irwin.

Ameriks, John, and Stephen Zeldes. 2001. "How Do Household Portfolio Shares Vary with Age?" Working Paper, Columbia University.

Amihud, Yakov, and Haim Mendelson. 1986. "Liquidity and Stock Returns." *Financial Analysts Journal.* Vol. 42, No. 3: 43–48.

Amihud, Yakov. 2002. "Illiquidity and Stock Return: Cross-Section and Time-Series Effects." *Journal of Financial Markets.* Vol. 5, No. 1: 31–56.

Amin, Gaurav, and Harry Kat. 2003. "Stocks, Bonds, and Hedge Funds." *Journal of Portfolio Management.* Vol. 29, No. 4: 113–120.

Ammann, Manuel, and Heinz Zimmerman. 2001. "Tracking Error and Tactical Asset Allocation." *Financial Analysts Journal.* Vol. 57, No. 2: 32–43.

Ang, Andrew, Monika Piazzesi, and Min Wei. 2006. "What Does the Yield Curve Tell Us about GDP Growth?" *Journal of Econometrics.* Vol. 131, No. 1/2: 359–403.

Ankrim, Ernest, and Chris Hensel. 1993. "Commodities in Asset Allocation: A Real Asset Alternative to Real Estate?" *Financial Analysts Journal.* Vol. 49, No. 3: 20–29.

Anson, Mark. 2002a. *Handbook of Alternative Assets.* New York: John Wiley & Sons.

Anson, Mark. 2002b. "A Primer on Distressed Debt Investing." *Journal of Private Equity.* Vol. 5, No. 3: 6–16.

Arnott, Robert, and Peter Bernstein. 2002. "What Premium is 'Normal'?" *Financial Analysts Journal.* Vol. 58, No. 2: 64–85.

Arnott, Robert, Jason Hsu, and Philip Moore. 2005. "Fundamental Indexation." *Financial Analysts Journal.* Vol. 61, No. 2: 83–99.

Arnott, Robert. 2005. "What Cost 'Noise'?" *Financial Analysts Journal.* Vol. 61, No. 2: 10–14.

Arnott, Robert., and Robert Lovell. 1993. "Rebalancing: Why? When? How Often?" *Journal of Investing.* Vol. 2, No. 1: 5–10.

Bacidore, Jeff, Robert Battalio, Robert Jennings, and Susan Farkas. 2001. "Changes in Order Characteristics, Displayed Liquidity, and Execution Quality on the New York Stock Exchange around the Switch to Decimal Pricing." New York Stock Exchange Working Paper 2001–02.

BAI Foundation. 1995. *Investment Portfolio Performance: Survey Results.* Chicago, IL: Bank Administration Institute.

Bailard, Thomas, David Biehl, and Ronald Kaiser. 1986. *Personal Money Management,* 5th edition. Chicago: Science Research Associates, Inc.

Bailey, Jeffery. 1992a. "Are Manager Universes Acceptable Performance Benchmarks?" *Journal of Portfolio Management*. Vol. 18, No. 3: 9–13.

Bailey, Jeffery. 1992b. "Evaluating Benchmark Quality." *Financial Analysts Journal*. Vol. 48, No. 3: 33–39.

Bank Administration Institute. 1968. *Measuring the Investment Performance of Pension Funds*. Park Ridge, IL: Bank Administration Institute.

Barnhill, Theodore, William Maxwell, and Mark Shenkman. 1999. *High Yield Bonds*. New York: McGraw-Hill.

Bauer, Rob, Kees Koedijk, and Roger Otten. 2005. "International Evidence On Ethical Mutual Fund Performance And Investment Style." *Journal of Banking and Finance*. Vol. 29, No. 7: 1751–1767.

Baumohl, Bernard. 2005. *The Secrets of Economic Indicators*. Upper Saddle River, NJ: Pearson Education, Inc.

Becker, Kent, and Joseph E. Finnerty. 2000. "Indexed Commodity Futures and the Risk and Return of Institutional Portfolios." OFOR Working Paper.

Bekaert, Geert, Robert Hodrick, and David Marshall. 2001. "Peso Problem Explanations for Term Structure Anomalies." *Journal of Monetary Economics*. Vol. 48, No. 2: 241–270.

Benninga, Simon. 2000. *Financial Modeling*. Cambridge, MA: MIT Press.

Berens, Linda. 2000. *Dynamics of Personality Type: Understanding and Applying Jung's Cognitive Processes*. Telos Publications.

Bernstein, Peter L. 1992. *Capital Ideas*. New York: The Free Press.

Bernstein, Peter L. 2003. "Points of Inflection: Investment Management Tomorrow." *Financial Analysts Journal*. Vol. 59, No. 4: 18–23.

Bernstein, Peter L. 2004. "A Do-It-Yourself Forecasting Kit Updated." *Financial Analysts Journal*. Vol. 60, No. 6: 27–32.

Bernstein, Richard. 1995. *Style Investing*. New York: John Wiley & Sons.

Bessembinder, Hendrik. 2003. "Trade Execution Costs and Market Quality after Decimalization." *Journal of Financial and Quantitative Analysis*. Vol. 38, No. 4: 747–778.

Best, Michael, and Robert Grauer. 1991. "On the Sensitivity of Mean-Variance-Efficient Portfolios to Changes in Asset Means: Some Analytical and Computational Results." *Review of Financial Studies*. Vol. 4, No. 2: 315–342.

Best's Insurance Reports. 2005. A.M. Best Company.

Bevan, Andrew, and Kurt Winkelmann. 1998. "Using the Black-Litterman Global Asset Allocation Model: Three Years of Practical Experience." *Fixed Income Research*. Goldman, Sachs & Company.

Bierwag, G.O., George Kaufman, and Alden Toevs. 1979. "Immunization for Multiple Planning Periods." Center for Capital Market Research, University of Oregon.

Billingsley, Randall, and Don Chance. 1996. "Benefits and Limitations of Diversification Among Commodity Trading Advisors." *Journal of Portfolio Management*. Vol. 23, No. 1: 65–80.

Black, Fischer, and Robert Litterman. 1991. "Asset Allocation: Combining Investor Views with Market Equilibrium." *Journal of Fixed Income*. Vol. 1, No. 2: 7–18.

Black, Fischer, and Robert Litterman. 1992. "Global Portfolio Optimization." *Financial Analysts Journal*. Vol. 48, No. 5: 28–43.

Black, Fischer. 1972. "Capital Market Equilibrium with Restricted Borrowing." *Journal of Business*. Vol. 45: 444–454.

Black, Keith H. 2005. "Designing a Long-Term Wealth Maximization Strategy for Hedge Fund Managers." *Hedge Funds*. Greg Gregoriou, Georges Hübner, Nicolas Papageorgiou, and Fabrice Rouah, eds. Hoboken, NJ: Wiley.

Blake, David, Bruce Lehmann, and Allan Timmermann. 1999. "Asset Allocation Dynamics and Pension Fund Performance." *Journal of Business*. Vol. 9: 397–421.

Blume, Marshall. 1984. "The Use of 'Alphas' to Improve Performance." *Journal of Portfolio Management*. Vol. 11, No. 1: 86–92.

Bodie, Zvi, Alex Kane, and Alan Marcus. 2001. *Investments*, 5th edition. Boston: Irwin/McGraw-Hill.

Bodie, Zvi, Alex Kane, and Alan Marcus. 2005. *Investments*, 6th edition. Boston: McGraw-Hill Irwin.

Bodie, Zvi, Robert Merton, and William Samuelson. 1992. "Labor Supply Flexibility and Portfolio Choice in a Life Cycle Model." *Journal of Economic Dynamics and Control*. Vol. 16: 427–449.

Bodie, Zvi. 1983. "Commodity Futures as a Hedge Against Inflation." *Journal of Portfolio Management,* Spring: 12–17.

Bollerslev, Tim, Robert Engle, and Daniel Nelson. 1994. "ARCH Models." *Handbook of Econometrics,* Vol. 4. Robert Engle and Daniel McFadden, eds. Amsterdam: Elsevier.

Bond, Michael, and Michael Seiler. 1998. "Real Estate Returns and Inflation: An Added Variable Approach. *Journal of Real Estate Research.* Vol. 15, No. 3: 327–338.

Boudoukh, Jacob, and Matthew Richardson. 1993. "Stock Returns and Inflation: A Long-Horizon Perspective." *American Economic Review.* Vol. 83, No. 5: 1346–1355.

Boyer, Brian. 2005. "Private Equity: A Plan Sponsor's Perspective." Presentation to CFA Society of Chicago, November 17, 2005.

Branch, Ben, and Hugh Ray. 2002. *Bankruptcy Investing: How to profit from distressed companies,* Revised edition. Washington, DC: Beard Books.

Brinson, Gary, Brian Singer, and Gilbert Beebower. 1991. "Determinants of Portfolio Performance II: An Update." *Financial Analysts Journal.* Vol. 47, No. 3: 40–48.

Brinson, Gary, Jeffrey Diermeier, and Gary Schlarbaum. 1986. "A Composite Portfolio Benchmark for Pension Plans." *Financial Analysts Journal.* Vol. 42, No. 2: 15–24.

Brinson, Gary, L. Randolph Hood, and Gilbert Beebower. 1986. "Determinants of Portfolio Performance." *Financial Analysts Journal.* Vol. 42, No. 4: 39–44.

Broad, C. 2005. "Why Invest in Real Estate: A Report from Russell Real Estate Advisors." Frank Russell Company.

Brooks, Chris, and Harry Kat. 2002. "The Statistical Properties of Hedge Fund Index Returns and Their Implications for Investors." *Journal of Alternative Investments.* Fall: 26–44.

Brorsen, B.Wade. 1998. "Performance Persistence for Managed Futures." Foundation of Managed Futures Research.

Brounen, Dirk, and Piet Eichholtz. 2003. "Property, Common Stock, and Property Shares." *Journal of Portfolio Management.* Vol. 29, No. 5: 129–137.

Brown, Stephen, and William Goetzmann. 1995. "Performance Persistence." *Journal of Finance.* Vol. 50, No. 2: 679–698.

Brown, Stephen, and William Goetzmann. 1997. "Mutual Fund Styles." *Journal of Financial Economics.* Vol. 43, No. 3: 373–399.

Brown, Stephen, William Goetzmann, and Roger Ibbotson. 1999. "Offshore Hedge Funds: Survival and Performance 1989–1995." *Journal of Business.* Vol. 72, No. 1: 91–117.

Brown, Stephen, William Goetzmann, and Stephen Ross. 1995. "Survival." *Journal of Finance.* Vol. 50: 853–873.

Brunel, Jean. 2002. *Integrated Wealth Management: The New Direction for Portfolio Managers.* New York: Institutional Investor Books.

Brunel, Jean. 2003. "A New Perspective on Hedge Funds and Hedge Fund Allocations." *Investment Counseling for Private Clients.* Charlottesville, VA: AIMR.

Brunel, Jean. 2003. "Revisiting the Asset Allocation Challenge Through a Behavioral Finance Lens." *Journal of Wealth Management.* Vol. 6, No. 2: 10–20.

Brunel, Jean. 2004. "Revisiting the Role of Hedge Funds in Diversified Portfolios." *Journal of Wealth Management.* Vol. 7, No. 3: 35–48.

Buetow, Gerald Jr., Ronald Sellers, Donald Trotter, Elaine Hunt, and Willie Whipple, Jr. 2002. "The Benefits of Rebalancing." *Journal of Portfolio Management.* Vol. 28, No. 2.

Burger, John, and Francis Warnock. 2003. "Diversification, Original Sin, and International Bond." International Finance Discussion Paper series, Board of Governors of the Federal Reserve.

Calverley, John. 2004. *Bubbles and How to Survive Them.* London: Nicholas Brealey Publishing.

Campbell, John, and Luis Viceira. 2002. *Strategic Asset Allocation: Portfolio Choice for Long-Term Investors.* Oxford University Press.

Campbell, John, and Robert Shiller. 1991. "Yield Spreads and Interest Rate Movements." *Review of Economic Studies.* Vol. 58, No. 3: 495–514.

Campbell, John, Andrew Lo, and A. Craig MacKinlay. 1997. *The Econometrics of Financial Markets.* Princeton, NJ: Princeton University Press.

Carhart, Mark. 1997. "On Persistence in Mutual Fund Performance." *Journal of Finance.* Vol. 51, No. 1: 57–82.

Cary, William, and Craig Bright. 1969. *The Law and Lore of Endowment Funds.* New York: Ford Foundation.

Case, Bradford, William Goetzmann, and K. Geert Rouwenhorst. 2000. "Global Real Estate Markets: Cycles and Fundamentals." Working Paper, National Bureau of Economic Research.

Case, Bradford, William Goetzmann, and Susan Wachter. 1997. "The Global Commercial Property Market Cycles: A Comparison Across Property Types." Presented at AREUEA 6th International Real Estate Conference, University of California at Berkeley.

Chakravarty, Sugato, Robert Wood, and Robert Van Ness. 2004. "Decimals and Liquidity: A Study of the NYSE." *Journal of Financial Research.* Vol. 27, No. 1: 75–94.

Chan, Louis, Narasimhan Jegadeesh, and Josef Lakonishok. 1999. "The Profitability of Momentum Strategies." *Financial Analysts Journal.* Vol. 55, No. 6: 80–90.

Chance, Don. 1996. *Managed Futures and Their Role in Investment Portfolios.* AIMR.

Chance, Don. 2003. *Analysis of Derivatives for the CFA® Program.* Charlottesville, VA: AIMR.

Chandrashekaran, Vinod. 1999. "Time-Series Properties and Diversification Benefits of REIT Returns." *Journal of Real Estate Research.* Vol. 17.

Chatrath, Arjun, and Youguo Liang. 1998. "REITs and Inflation: A Long-Run Perspective." *Journal of Real Estate Research.* Vol. 16, No. 3.

Chen, Honghui, Gregory Noronha, and Vijay Singal. 2006. "Index Changes and Losses to Index Fund Investors." *Financial Analysts Journal.* Vol. 62, No. 4: 31–47.

Cheng, Minder. 2003. "Pretrade Cost Analysis and Management of Implementation Shortfall." *Equity Trading: Execution and Analysis.* Charlottesville, VA: AIMR.

Chow, George, Eric Jacquier, Mark Kritzman, and Kenneth Lowry. 1999. "Optimal Portfolios in Good Times and Bad." *Financial Analysts Journal.* Vol. 55, No. 3: 65–73.

Chow, George. 1995. "Portfolio Selection Based on Return, Risk, and Relative Performance." *Financial Analysts Journal.* Vol. 51, No. 2: 54–60.

Christopherson, Jon, and C. Nola Williams. 1997. "Equity Style: What It Is and Why It Matters." *Handbook of Equity Style Management.* T. Daniel Coggin, Frank Fabozzi, and Robert Arnott, eds. New York: John Wiley & Sons.

Christopherson, Jon, and Paul Greenwood. 2004. "Equity Styles and Why They Matter." *Journal of Investment Consulting.* Vol. 1, No. 1: 21–36.

Chung, S. 2000. "Effects of Derivative Usage on Commodity-Based Corporations." Ph.D. dissertation, University of Massachusetts.

CISDM. 2005a. "The Benefits of Real Estate Investment: 2005 Update." June, CISDM, University of Massachusetts.

CISDM. 2005b. "The Benefits of Commodity Investment: 2005 Update." June, CISDM, University of Massachusetts.

CISDM. 2005c. "The Benefits of Hedge Funds: 2005 Update." June, CISDM, University of Massachusetts.

CISDM. 2005d. "The Benefits of Managed Futures: 2005 Update." June, CISDM, University of Massachusetts.

Clarke, Roger, and Mark Kritzman. 1996. *Currency Management: Concepts and Practices.* Charlottesville, VA: Research Foundation of AIMR.

Cochrane, John. 1999a. "New Facts in Finance." *Economic Perspectives.* Federal Reserve Bank of Chicago. Vol. 23, No. 3: 36–58. (Revision of NBER Working Paper 7169).

Cochrane, John. 1999b. "Portfolio Advice for a Multifactor World." *Economic Perspectives.* Federal Reserve Bank of Chicago. Vol. 23, No. 3: 59–78. (Revision of NBER Working Paper 7170).

Cochrane, John. 2004. "The Risk of Venture Capital." University of Chicago Working Paper.

Committee for Performance Presentation Standards (CPPS). 1987. "A Report on Setting Performance Presentation Standards." *Financial Analysts Journal.* Vol. 43, No. 5: 8.

Committee of Sponsoring Organizations of the Treadway Commission. 2004. *Enterprise Risk Management—Integrated Framework: Executive Summary.*

Conover, C. Mitchell, Gerald Jensen, Robert Johnson, and Jeffrey Mercer. 2005. "Is Fed Policy Still Relevant For Investors?" *Financial Analysts Journal.* Vol. 61, No. 1: 70–79.

Cox, John, Jonathan Ingersoll, Jr., and Stephen Ross. 1979. "Duration and the Measurement of Basis Risk." *Journal of Business.* Vol. 52, No. 1: 51–62.

Crouhy, Michael, Dan Galai, and Robert Mark. 2001. *Risk Management.* New York: McGraw-Hill.

Daniel, Kent, Mark Grinblatt, Sheridan Titman, and Russ Wermers. 1997. "Measuring Mutual Fund Performance With Characteristic-Based Benchmarks." *Journal of Finance.* Vol. 52, No. 3: 1035–1058.

Davis, E. Philip. 1995. *Pension Funds, Retirement-Income Security and Capital Markets: An International Perspective.* Oxford University Press.

Davis, Stephen, and Paul Willen. 2000. "Occupation-Level Income Shocks and Asset Returns: Their Covariance and Implications for Portfolio Choice." Working Paper, University of Chicago Graduate School of Business.

DeFusco, Richard, Dennis McLeavey, Jerald Pinto, and David Runkle. 2004. *Quantitative Methods for Investment Analysis,* 2nd edition. Charlottesville, VA: CFA Institute.

Denmark, Frances. 2005. "Miss Match?" *PLANSPONSOR.* April: 66–68.

Dhiensiri, Nont, Gershon Mandelker, and Akin Sayrak. 2005. "The Information Content in Analyst Recommendations." Working Paper, University of Pittsburgh.

Diebold, Francis. 2004. *Elements of Forecasting,* 3rd edition. Cincinnati, OH: Thomson/South-Western.

Diermeier, Jeffrey. 1990. "Capital Market Expectations: The Macro Factors." *Managing Investment Portfolios: A Dynamic Process,* 2nd edition. John Maginn and Donald Tuttle, eds. New York: Warren Gorham & Lamont.

Dietz, Peter. 1966. *Pension Funds: Measuring Investment Performance.* New York: The Free Press.

Dimson, Elroy, Paul Marsh, and Mike Staunton. 2002. *Triumphs of the Optimists: 101 Years of Global Investment Returns.* Princeton, NJ: Princeton University Press.

Dimson, Elroy, Paul Marsh, and Mike Staunton. 2006. *Global Investment Returns Yearbook 2006.* ABN-AMRO.

Diz, Fernando. 1999. "How do CTA's Return Distribution Characteristics Affect their Likelihood of Survival?" *Journal of Alternative Investments.* Vol. 2, No. 2: 37–41.

Downs, David, Hung-Gay Fung, Gary Patterson, and Jot Yau. 2003. "The Linkage of REIT Income- and Price-Returns with Fundamental Economic Variables." *Journal of Alternative Investments.* Vol. 6, No. 1:39–50.

Drost, Feike, and Theo Nijman. 1993. "Temporal Aggregation of GARCH Processes." *Econometrica.* Vol. 6, No. 4: 909–927.

Edwards, Amy, Lawrence Harris, and Michael Piwowar. 2004. "Corporate Bond Market Transparency and Transaction Costs." Working Paper.

Edwards, Franklin, and James Park. 1996. "Do Managed Futures Make Good Investments?" *Journal of Futures Markets.* Vol. 16, No. 5: 475–517.

Edwards, Franklin, and Jimmy Liew. 1999. "Hedge Funds Versus Managed Futures As Asset Classes." *Journal of Derivatives.* Vol. 6, No. 4: 45–64.

Eichholtz, Piet, Ronald Huisman, Kees Koedijk, and Lisa Schuin. 1998. "Continental Factors in International Real Estate Returns." *Real Estate Economics.* Vol. 23, No. 3: 493–509.

Eichholtz, Piet, Ronald Mahieu, and Peter Schotman. 1999. "Real Estate Diversification: By Country or by Continent?" Working paper, University of Maastricht and Erasmus University-Rotterdam.

Ellis, Charles. 1975. "The Loser's Game." *Financial Analysts Journal.* Reprinted in *Classics: An Investor's Anthology.* Charles D. Ellis and James R. Vertin, eds. Homewood, IL: Business One Irwin: 1989.

Ellis, Charles. 1985. *Investment Policy.* Homewood, IL: Dow Jones-Irwin.

Elton, Edwin, and Martin Gruber. 1992. "Optimal Investment Strategies with Investor Liabilities." *Journal of Banking and Finance.* Vol. 16: 869–890.

Elton, Edwin, Martin Gruber, and Jeffrey Busse. 2004. "Are Investors Rational? Choices Among Index Funds." *Journal of Finance.* Vol. 59, No. 1: 261–288.

Elton, Edwin, Martin Gruber, and Joel Rentzler. 1987. "Professionally Managed, Publicly Traded Commodity Funds." *Journal of Business.* Vol. 60, No. 2: 177–199.

Elton, Edwin, Martin Gruber, and Joel Rentzler. 1990. "The Performance of Publicly Offered Commodity Funds." *Financial Analysts Journal.* July/August: 23–30.

Elton, Edwin, Martin Gruber, Deepak Agrawal, and Christopher Mann. 2001. "Explaining the Rate Spread on Corporate Bonds." *Journal of Finance.* Vol. 56, No. 1: 247–277.

Elton, Edwin, Martin Gruber, Stephen Brown, and William Goetzmann. 2003. *Modern Portfolio Theory and Investment Analysis,* 6th edition. Hoboken, NJ: John Wiley & Sons.

Ely, David, and Kenneth Robinson. 1997. "Are Stocks a Hedge against Inflation? International Evidence using a Long-run Approach." *Journal of International Money and Finance*. Vol. 16, No. 1: 141–167.

Emery, Kenneth. 2003. "Private Equity Risk and Reward: Assessing the Stale Pricing Problem." *Journal of Private Equity*. Vol. 6, No. 2: 43–50.

Ennis, Richard. 2005. "Are Active Management Fees Too High?" *Financial Analysts Journal*. Vol. 61, No. 5: 44–51.

Erb, Claude, and Campbell Harvey. 2006. "The Strategic and Tactical Value of Commodity Futures." *Financial Analysts Journal*. Vol. 62, No. 2: 69–97.

Ernst & Young. 2005. *The Global Executive*. n.p.

Estrella, Arturo, and Frederic Mishkin. 1998. "Predicting U.S. Recessions: Financial Variables as Leading Indicators." *Review of Economics and Statistics*. Vol. 80, No. 1: 45–61.

Fabozzi, Frank J. 2004a. *Fixed Income Analysis for the Chartered Financial Analyst® Program*, 2nd edition. New Hope, PA: Frank J. Fabozzi Associates.

Fabozzi, Frank J. 2004b. *Fixed Income Readings for the Chartered Financial Analyst® Program*, 2nd edition. New Hope, PA: Frank J. Fabozzi Associates.

Fabozzi, T. Dessa, Tom Tong, and Yu Zhu. 1991. "Extensions of Dedicated Bond Portfolio Techniques." *Handbook of Fixed Income Securities*, 3rd edition. Homewood, IL: Business One Irwin.

Fama, E. and K. French. 1988. "Business Cycles and the Behavior of Metals Prices." *Journal of Finance*. Vol. 43, No. 5: 1075–1093.

Fama, Eugene, and Kenneth French. 1992. "The Cross-Section of Expected Stock Returns." *Journal of Finance*. Vol. 47, No. 2: 427–465.

Fama, Eugene, and Kenneth French. 1996. "Multifactor Explanations of Asset Pricing Anomalies." *Journal of Finance*. Vol. 51, No. 1: 55–84.

Fama, Eugene. 1972. "Components of Investment Performance." *Journal of Finance*. Vol. 27, No. 3: 551–567.

Fama, Eugene. 1976. *Foundations of Finance*. New York: Basic Books.

Feder, Warren, and Patrick Lagrange. 2002. "Considerations for Investors before Investing in Bankrupt Companies." *Journal of Private Equity*. Fall: 38–41.

Ferson, Wayne, and Rudi Schadt. 1996. "Measuring Fund Strategy and Performance in Changing Economic Conditions." *Journal of Finance*. Vol. 51, No. 2: 425–461.

Fisher, Lawrence, and Roman Weil. 1971. "Coping with Risk of Interest Rate Fluctuations: Returns to Bondholders from Naive and Optimal Strategies." *Journal of Business*. Vol. 44, No. 4: 408–431.

Fong, H. Gifford and Oldrich Vasicek. 1984. "A Risk Minimizing Strategy for Portfolio Immunization." *Journal of Finance*. Vol. 39, No. 9: 1541–1546.

Fong, H. Gifford, and Eric Tang. 1988. "Immunized Bond Portfolios in Portfolio Protection." *Journal of Portfolio Management*. Vol. 14, No. 2: 63–68.

Fong, H. Gifford, and Oldrich Vasicek. 1983. "Return Maximization for Immunized Portfolios." *Innovations in Bond Portfolio Management: Duration Analysis and Immunization*. London: JAI Press, Inc.

Fong, H. Gifford, Charles Pearson, and Oldrich Vasicek. 1983. "Bond Performance: Analyzing Sources of Return." *Journal of Portfolio Management*. Vol. 9, No. 3: 46–50.

Fox-Andrews, Mark, and Nicola Meaden. 1995. *Derivative Markets and Investment Management*. Hertfordshire, U.K.: Prentice-Hall.

Francis, Jack, and Roger Ibbotson. 2001. "Empirical Risk-Return Analysis of Real Estate Investments in the U.S., 1972–1999." *Journal of Alternative Investments*, Summer: 33–39.

French, Dan, and Glenn Henderson, Jr. 1985. "How Well Does Performance Evaluation Perform?" *Journal of Portfolio Management*. Vol. 11, No. 2: 15–18.

Friedman, Milton. 1957. *A Theory of the Consumption Function*. Princeton, NJ: Princeton University Press.

Frongello, Andrew, and Scott Bay. 2002. "Linking Single Period Attribution Results." *Journal of Performance Measurement*. Vol. 6, No. 3: 10–22.

Froot, K. 1995. "Hedging Portfolios with Real Assets." *Journal of Portfolio Management*. Summer: 60–77.

Fung, William, and David Hsieh. 1997a. "Empirical Characteristics of Dynamic Trading Strategies: The Case of Hedge Funds." *Review of Financial Studies*. Vol. 10: 275–302.

Fung, William, and David Hsieh. 1997b. "Survivor Bias and Investment Style in the Returns of CTAs." *Journal of Portfolio Management*. Fall: 30–41.

Fung, William, and David Hsieh. 2000. "Performance Characteristics of Hedge Funds and Commodity Funds: Natural vs. Spurious Biases." *Journal of Financial and Quantitative Analysis*. Vol. 35: 291–307.

Fung, William, and David Hsieh. 2001. "The Risk in Hedge Fund Strategies: Theory and Evidence from Trend Followers." *Review of Financial Studies*. Vol. 14: 313–341.

Fung, William, and David Hsieh. 2002. "Benchmarks of Hedge Fund Performance: Information Content and Measurement Biases." *Financial Analysts Journal*. January/February: 22–34.

Gastineau, Gary, and Mark Kritzman. 1999. *Dictionary of Financial Risk Management*, 3rd edition. Hoboken, NJ: John Wiley & Sons.

Gastineau, Gary, Donald Smith, and Rebecca Todd. 2001. *Risk Management, Derivatives, and Financial Analysis Under SFAS 133*. Charlottesville, VA: Research Foundation of AIMR.

Geltner, David. 2000. "Benchmarking Manager Performance Within the Private Real Estate Investment Industry." *Real Estate Finance*. Vol. 17, No. 1: 23–34.

Geltner, David, and David Ling. 2001. "Ideal Research and Benchmark Indexes in Private Real Estate: Some Conclusions from the REPI/PREA Technical Report," *Real Estate Finance*. Vol. 17, No. 4.

Geman, Helyette. 2005. *Commodities and Commodity Derivatives: Modeling and Pricing for Agriculturals, Metals and Energy*. Hoboken, NJ: John Wiley & Sons.

Goetzmann, William, and Philippe Jorion. 1999. "Re-Emerging Markets." *Journal of Financial and Quantitative Analysis*. Vol. 34, No. 1: 1–32.

Goodall, Thilo, Antonio Manzini, and Thomas Rose. 1999. "Risk Premium Project." Working Paper, UBS Global Asset Management.

Goodman, Edwin. 2006. "A culture clash could hurt high-end returns." *Financial Times*, p. 12, 7 March.

Goodsall, William, and Lisa Plaxco. 1996. "Tactical Rebalancing." First Quadrant Monograph. No. 3.

Goyal, Amit, and Sunil Wahal. 2005. "The Selection and Termination of Investment Management Firms by Plan Sponsors." Working Paper, Goizueta Business School, Emory University.

Graham, John, and Campbell Harvey. 2005. "Expectations of Equity Risk Premia, Volatility and Asymmetry from a Corporate Finance Perspective." NBER Working Paper No. 8678.

Granger, Clive. 1969. "Investigating Causal Relationships by Econometric Models and Cross-Spectral Methods." *Econometrica*. Vol. 37, No. 3: 424–438.

Grant, Kenneth. 2004. *Trading Risk: Enhanced Profitability through Risk Control*. Hoboken, NJ: John Wiley & Sons, Inc.

Grauer, Robert, and Nils Hakansson. 1995. "Gains from Diversifying into Real Estate: Three Decades of Portfolio Returns based on the Dynamic Investment Model." *Real Estate Economics*, Vol. 23, No. 1.

Greer, Robert. 1978. "Conservative Commodities: A Key Inflation Hedge." *Journal of Portfolio Management*. Summer: 26–29.

Greer, Robert. 1994. "Methods for Institutional Investment in Commodity Futures." *Journal of Derivatives*. Winter: 28–36.

Grinold, Richard, and Kenneth Kroner. 2002. "The Equity Risk Premium." *Investment Insights from Barclays Global Investors*. Vol. 5, No. 3.

Grinold, Richard, and Ronald Kahn. 1995. *Active Portfolio Management*. Chicago, IL: Probus Publications.

Grinold, Richard, and Ronald Kahn. *Active Portfolio Management*. 2000. New York: McGraw-Hill.

Grossman, Sanford, and Joseph Stiglitz. 1980. "On the Impossibility of Informationally Efficient Markets." *American Economic Review*. Vol. 70, No. 3: 393–408.

Guerard, John, Jr. "Additional Evidence On the Cost of Being Socially Responsible in Investing." *Journal of Investing*. Vol. 6, No. 4: 31–36.

Gujarati, Damodar. 2003. *Basic Econometrics*, 4th edition. New York: McGraw-Hill.

Halpern, Philip, and Randy Warsager. 1998. "The Performance of Energy and Non-Energy Based Commodity Investment Vehicles in Period of Inflation." *Journal of Alternative Assets*. Summer: 75–81.

Hamilton, James. 1994. *Time Series Analysis*. Princeton, NJ: Princeton University Press.

Hammond, John, Ralph Keeney, and Howard Raiffa. 1998. "The Hidden Traps in Decision Making." *Harvard Business Review*. Vol. 76, No. 5: 47–58.

Hanna, Sherman, and Peng Chen. 1997. "Subjective and Objective Risk Tolerance: Implications For Optimal Portfolios." *Financial Counseling and Planning*. Vol. 8.

Harris, Larry. 2003. *Trading and Exchanges*. New York: Oxford University Press.

Hartzell, David, John Hekman, and Mike Miles. 1986. "Diversification Categories in Investment Real Estate." *AREUEA Journal*. Vol. 14: 230–254.

Haugen, Robert. 1990. *Managing Institutional Assets*. New York: HarperCollins.

He, Guangliang, and Robert Litterman. 1999. "The Intuition Behind Black-Litterman Model Portfolios." *Investment Management Research*. Goldman, Sachs & Company.

Henker, Thomas. 1998. "Naïve Diversification for Hedge Funds." *Journal of Alternative Investments*. Winter 98: 33–38.

Henker, Thomas, and George Martin. 1998. "Naïve and Optimal Diversification for Managed Futures." *Journal of Alternative Investments*. Fall: 25–40.

Hill, Joanne. 2003. "Trading and Investing in 'Style' Using Futures and Exchange-Traded Funds." *The Handbook of Equity Style Management*, 3rd edition. T. Daniel Coggin, Frank Fabozzi, and Robert Arnott, eds. Hoboken, NJ: John Wiley & Sons.

Hoesli, Martin, Bryan MacGregor, George Matysiak, and Nanda Nanthakumaran. 1997. "The Short Term Inflation Hedging Characteristics of U.K. Real Estate." *Journal of Real Estate Finance and Economics*. Vol. 15, No. 1.

Hoesli, Martin, Jon Lekander, and Witold Witkiewicz. 2003. "International Evidence on Real Estate as a Portfolio Diversifier." Research Paper No. 70, FAME.

Horvitz, Jeffrey. 2002. "The Implications of Rebalancing the Investment Portfolio for the Taxable Investor." *Journal of Wealth Management*. Fall: 49–53.

Howell, Michel. 2001. "Fund Age and Performance." *Journal of Alternative Investments*. Fall: 57–60.

Huberman, Gur. 1995. "The Desirability of Investment in Commodities via Commodity Futures." *Derivatives Quarterly*. Fall: 65–67.

Ibbotson, Roger, and Gary Brinson. 1987. *Investment Markets*. New York: McGraw-Hill.

Ibbotson, Roger, and Paul Kaplan. 2000. "Does Asset Allocation Policy Explain 40, 90, or 100 Percent of Performance?" *Financial Analysts Journal*. Vol. 56, No. 1: 26–33.

Ibbotson, Roger, and Peng Chen. 2003. "Long-Run Stock Returns: Participating in the Real Economy." *Financial Analysts Journal*. Vol. 58, No. 1: 88–98.

Idzorek, Thomas. 2002. "A Step-By-Step Guide to the Black-Litterman Model." Working Paper, Stanford University.

Ilmanen, Antti, Rory Byrne, Heinz Gunasekera, and Robert Minikin. 2002 "Stocks versus bonds: Balancing expectations and reality." Schroder Salomon Smith Barney.

Ilmanen, Antti. 2003. "Expected Returns on Stocks and Bonds." *Journal of Portfolio Management*. Vol. 29, No. 2: 7–27.

IMF. 2005. *World Economic Outlook: Building Institutions*. Washington, DC: International Monetary Fund. September, p. 268.

Irvine, Paul. 2003. "Do Analysts Generate Trade for their Firms? Evidence from the Toronto Stock Exchange." *Journal of Accounting and Economics*. Vol. 30, No. 2: 209–226.

Jacobius, Arleen. 2006a. "JP Morgan Asset adds infrastructure division." *Pension & Investments*. February 6, 2006.

Jacobius, Arleen. 2006b. "Distressed debt investors await a new round of defaults." *Pensions & Investments*. March 6, 2006.

Jagannathan, Ravi, Ellen McGrattan, and Anna Scherbina. 2000. "The Declining U.S. Equity Premium." *Quarterly Review*. Federal Reserve Bank of Minnesota. Vol. 24, No. 4: 3–19.

Jensen, Gerald, Jeffrey Mercer, and Robert Johnson. 1996 "Business Conditions, Monetary Policy, and Expected Security Returns." *Journal of Financial Economics*. Vol. 40, No. 2: 213–237.

Jensen, Gerald, Jeffrey Mercer, and Robert Johnson. 2002. "Tactical Asset Allocation and Commodity Futures." *Journal of Portfolio Management*. Vol. 28, No. 4: 100–111.

Jensen, Gerald, Robert Johnson, and Jeffrey Mercer. 2000. *The Role of Monetary Policy in Investment Management*. Charlottesville, VA: Research Foundation of AIMR.

Jensen, Michael. 1968. "The Performance of Mutual Funds in the Period 1945–1964." *Journal of Finance*. Vol. 23, No. 2: 389–416.

Jensen, Michael. 1969. "Risk, the Pricing of Capital Assets, and the Evaluation of Investment Portfolios." *Journal of Business*. Vol. 42, No. 2: 167–185.

Jobson, J.D., and Bob Korkie. 1981. "Estimation for Markowitz Efficient Portfolios." *Journal of the American Statistical Association*. Vol. 75, No. 371: 544–554.

Jones, Meredith. 2005. "Investing in Hedge Funds through Multimanager Vehicles." *Hedge Funds*. Greg N Gregoriou, Georges Hübner, Nicolas Papageorgiou, and Fabrice Rouah, eds. Hoboken, NJ: John Wiley & Sons.

Jorion, Philippe. 1992. "Portfolio Optimization in Practice." *Financial Analysts Journal*. Vol. 48, No. 1: 68–74.

Jorion, Philippe. 2002. "Enhanced Index Funds and Tracking Error Optimization." Working Paper, University of California, Irvine.

Kahn, Ronald. 1997. "Fixed Income Risk." *Managing Fixed Income Portfolios*. New Hope, PA: Frank J. Fabozzi Associates.

Kahneman, Daniel, and Amos Tversky. 1979. "Prospect Theory: An Analysis of Decision Under Risk." *Econometrica*. Vol. 47, No. 2: 263–297.

Kaldor, Nicholas. 1939. "Speculation and Economic Stability." *Review of Economic Studies*. Vol. 7: 1–27.

Kallberg, Jarl, Crocker Liu, and D. Wylie Greig. 1996. "The Role of Real Estate in the Portfolio Allocation Process." *Real Estate Economics*. Vol. 24, No. 3.

Kallberg, Jarl, and Kenneth Parkinson. 1993. *Corporate Liquidity: Management and Measurement*. Homewood, IL: Irwin.

Kat, Harry. 2005. "Integrating Hedge Funds into the Traditional Portfolio." *Journal of Wealth Management*. Vol. 7, No. 4.

Kazemi, Hossein, and Thomas Schneeweis. 2001. "Traditional Asset and Alternatives Asset Allocation." CISDM/SOM Working Paper, University of Massachusetts.

Kiev, Ari. 2002. *The Psychology of Risk: Mastering Market Uncertainty*. Hoboken, NJ: John Wiley & Sons.

Kleidon, Allan, and Robert Whaley. 1992. "One Market? Stocks, Futures, and Options During October 1987." *Journal of Finance*. Vol. 7, No. 3: 851–878.

Koch, Timothy, and S. Scott MacDonald. 2003. *Bank Management*, 5th edition. Mason, OH: Thomson South-Western.

Koh, Francis, David Lee, and Phoon Kok Fai. 2002. "Investing in Hedge Funds: Risk, Return and Pitfalls." Working Paper.

Kritzman, Mark, and Sébastien Page. 2003. "The Hierarchy of Investment Choice: A Normative Interpretation." *Journal of Portfolio Management*. Vol. 29, No. 4: 11–24.

Kritzman, Mark. 1999. "Toward Defining an Asset Class." *Journal of Alternative Investments*. Vol. 1, No. 1: 79–82.

Kurz, Mordecai, Hehui Jin, and Maurizio Motolese. 2005. "Determinants of Stock Market Volatility and Risk Premia." *Annals of Finance*. Vo1.1, No. 2: 109–147.

Kurz, Mordecai. 1994. "On the Structure and Diversity of Rational Beliefs." *Economic Theory*. Vol. 8, No. 3: 877–900.

Kyle, Albert. 1985. "Continuous Auctions and Insider Trading." *Econometrica*. Vol. 53, No. 6: 1315–36.

Laise, Eleanor. 2006. "Mutual Funds Adopt Hedge-Fund Strategies." *Wall Street Journal*. February 21, 2006: D1, D2.

Lally, Martin, Melvin Roush, and Tony Van Zijl. 2004. "The Market Risk Premium in New Zealand—Survey Evidence." *INFINZ Journal*. Vol. 1: 5–12.

Lazzara, Craig. 2004. "Index Construction Issues for Exchange-Traded Funds." Available at www.etfconsultants.com/Index%20Construction%20Issues%20for%20ETFs.pdf.

Ledoit, Olivier, and Michael Wolf. 2003. "Improved Estimation of the Covariance Matrix of Stock Returns With an Application to Portfolio Selection." *Journal of Empirical Finance*. Vol. 2003, No. 5: 603–621.

Lee, Charles, and Bhaskaran Swaminathan. 2000. "Price Momentum and Trading Volume." *Journal of Finance*. Vol. 55, No. 5: 2017–2069.

Lee, Hye-Kyung, and Sherman Hanna. 1995. "Investment Portfolios and Human Wealth." *Financial Counseling and Planning*. Vol. 6.

Lee, Wei. 2000. *Theory and Methodology of Tactical Asset Allocation*. Hoboken, NJ: John Wiley & Sons.

Leibowitz, Martin, and Alfred Weinberger. 1981. "The Uses of Contingent Immunization." *Journal of Portfolio Management*. Vol. 8, No. 1: 51–55.

Leibowitz, Martin, and Anthony Bova. 2005. "Allocation Betas." *Financial Analysts Journal*. Vol. 61, No. 4: 70–82.

Leibowitz, Martin, and Roy Henriksson. 1988. "Portfolio Optimization within a Surplus Framework." *Financial Analysts Journal*. Vol. 44, No. 2: 43–51.

Leibowitz, Martin, and Roy Henriksson. 1989. "Portfolio Optimization with Shortfall Constraints: A Confidence-Limit Approach to Managing Downside Risk." *Financial Analysts Journal*. Vol. 45, No. 2: 34–41.

Leland, Hayne. 2000. "Optimal Portfolio Implementation with Transaction Costs and Capital Gains Taxes." Working Paper, University of California, Berkeley.

Lerner, Josh. 2000. *Venture Capital and Private Equity: A Casebook*. Hoboken, NJ: John Wiley & Sons, Inc.

Lhabitant, Francois-Serge. 2002. *Hedge Funds: Myths and Limits*. Hoboken, NJ: John Wiley & Sons.

Lhabitant, Francois-Serge. 2004. *Hedge Funds: Quantitative Insights*. Hoboken, NJ: John Wiley & Sons.

Liang, Bing. 2000. "Hedge Funds: The Living and the Dead." *Journal of Financial and Quantitative Analysis*. Vol. 35, No. 3: 309–326.

Life Insurance Fact Book. 1979, 1989, 2000, 2001, 2003. The American Council of Life Insurers.

Lim, Terence. 2001. "Rationality and Analysts' Forecast Bias." *Journal of Finance*. Vol. 56, No. 1: 369–385.

Ling, David, and Andy Naranjo. 1997. "Economic Risk Factors and Commercial Real Estate Returns." *Journal of Real Estate Finance and Economics*. Vol. 14, No. 3: 283–307.

Ling, David, and Andy Naranjo. 1998. "The Fundamental Determinants of Commercial Real Estate Returns." *Real Estate Finance*. Vol. 14, No. 4: 13–24.

Lintner, John. 1965. "Security Prices, Risk, and Maximal Gains from Diversification." *Journal of Finance*. Vol. 20, No. 4: 587–615.

Litterman, Robert, and Kurt Winkelmann. 1998. "Estimating Covariance Matrices." *Risk Management Series*. Goldman Sachs & Company.

Litzenberger, Robert, and Nir Rabinowitz. 1995. "Backwardation in Oil Futures Markets: Theory and Empirical Evidence." *Journal of Finance*. Vol. 50: 1517–1545.

Liu, Crocker, David Hartzell, and Martin Hoesli. 1997. "International Evidence on Real Estate Securities as an Inflation Hedge." *Real Estate Economics*. Vol. 25, No. 5.

Lizieri, Colin, and Charles Ward. 2000. "Commercial Real Estate Return Distributions: A Review of Literature and Empirical Evidence." Working Paper, University of Reading.

Lizieri, Colin, and Stephen Satchell. 1997. "Property Company Performance and Real Interest Rates: A Regime Switching Approach." *Journal of Property Research*. Vol. 14.

Lobosco, Angelo, and Dan DiBartolomeo. 1997. "Approximating the Confidence Intervals For Sharpe Style Weights." *Financial Analysts Journal*. Vol. 53, No. 4: 80–85.

Luenberger, David. 1998. *Investment Science*. New York: Oxford University Press.

Luintel, Kul, and Krishna Paudyal. 2006. "Are Common Stocks a Hedge Against Inflation?" *Journal of Financial Research*. Vol. 29 No. 1: 1–20.

Lynch, Anthony, and Richard Mendenhall. 1997. "New Evidence On Stock Price Effects Associated With Changes In The S&P 500 Index." *Journal of Business*. Vol. 70, No. 3: 351–383.

Madhavan, Ananth, and Seymour Smidt. 1993. "An Analysis of Changes in Specialist Inventories and Quotations." *Journal of Finance*. Vol. 48, No. 5: 1595–1628.

Madhavan, Ananth. 2000. "Market Microstructure: A Survey." *Journal of Financial Markets*. Vol. 3, No. 3: 205–258.

Madhavan, Ananth. 2002. "Market Microstructure: A Practitioner's Guide." *Financial Analysts Journal*. Vol. 58, No. 5: 28–42.

Malkiel, Burton, and Aleksander Radisich. 2001. "The Growth Of Index Funds And The Pricing Of Equity Securities." *Journal of Portfolio Management*. Vol. 27, No. 2: 9–21.

Malkiel, Burton, and Atanu Saha. 2005. "Hedge Funds: Risk and Return." *Financial Analysts Journal.* Vol. 61, No. 6: 80–88.

Malkiel, Burton. 1973. *A Random Walk Down Wall Street.* New York: W.W. Norton.

Malkiel, Burton. 2004. *A Random Walk Down Wall Street.* New York and London: Norton & Company.

Markowitz, Harry. 1952. "Portfolio Selection." *Journal of Finance.* Vol. 7, No. 1: 77–91.

Markowitz, Harry. 1959. *Portfolio Selection: Efficient Diversification of Investments.* New Haven, CT: Yale University Press.

Markowitz, Harry. 1984. "The Two Beta Trap." *Journal of Portfolio Management.* Vol. 10, No. 1: 12–20.

Marshall, Christopher. 2001. *Measuring and Managing Operational Risk in Financial Institutions.* Singapore: John Wiley & Sons.

Marshall, William, and Jess Yawitz. 1982. "Lower Bounds on Portfolio Performance: An Extension of the Immunization Strategy." *Journal of Financial and Quantitative Analysis.* Vol. 17, No. 1: 101–113.

Masters, Seth J. 2003. "Rebalancing." *Journal of Portfolio Management.* Vol. 29, No. 3: 52–57.

McCalla, Douglas B. 1997. "Enhancing the Efficient Frontier with Portfolio Rebalancing." *Journal of Pension Plan Investing.* Vol. 1, No. 4: 16–32.

McCarthy, David, Thomas Schneeweis, and Richard Spurgin. 1996. "Investment in CTAs: An Alternative Managed Futures Investment." *Journal of Derivatives.* Vol. 34: 36–47.

McQueen, Grant, and Steven Thorley. 1999. "Mining Fools Gold." *Financial Analysts Journal.* Vol. 55, No. 2: 61–72.

Mehra, Yash, and Jon Peterson. 2005. "Oil Prices and Consumer Spending." Federal Reserve Bank of Richmond. *Economic Quarterly.* Vol. 91, No. 3: 51–70.

Mei, Jianping, and Jiawei Hu. 2000. "Conditional Risk Premiums on Asian Real Estate Stocks." *Journal of Real Estate Finance and Economics.* Vol. 21, No. 3.

Menchero, Jose. 2004. "Multiperiod Arithmetic Attribution." *Financial Analysts Journal.* Vol. 60, No. 4: 76–91.

Merton, Robert. 1969. "Life Time Portfolio Selection Under Uncertainty: The Continuous Time Case." *Review of Economics and Statistics.* Vol. 51: 247–257.

Merton, Robert. 1973. "An Intertemporal Capital Asset Pricing Model." *Econometrica.* Vol. 41, No. 5: 867–887.

Merton, Robert. 2003. "Thoughts on the Future: Theory and Practice in Investment Management." *Financial Analysts Journal.* Vol. 59, No. 1: 17–23.

Michaely, Roni, and Kent Womack. 1999. "Conflict of Interest and the Credibility of Underwriter Analyst Recommendations," *Review of Financial Studies.* V12(Spec): 653–686.

Michaud, Richard. 1981. "Risk Policy and Long-Term Investment." *Journal of Financial and Quantitative Analysis.* Vol. 16, No. 2: 147–167.

Michaud, Richard. 1989. "The Markowitz Optimization Enigma: Is Optimized Optimal?" *Financial Analysts Journal.* Vol. 45, No. 1: 31–42.

Michaud, Richard. 1998. *Efficient Asset Management.* Boston: Harvard Business School Press.

Miles, Mike, and Tom McCue. 1984. "Diversification in the Real Estate Portfolio." *Journal of Financial Research.* Vol. 7, No. 1: 57–68.

Mitchell, Mark, and Todd PulviNo. 2000. "Characteristics of Risk in Risk Arbitrage." *Journal of Finance.* Vol. 56, No. 6: 2135–2176.

Modigliani, Franco, and Leah Modigliani. 1997. "Risk-Adjusted Performance." *Journal of Portfolio Management.* Vol. 23, No. 2: 45–54.

Mossin, Jan. 1966. "Equilibrium in a Capital Asset Market." *Econometrica.* Vol. 34, No. 4: 768–783.

Mull, Stephen, and Luc Soenen. 1997. "U.S. REITs as an Asset Class in International Investment Portfolios." *Financial Analysts Journal.* Vol. 53, No. 2: 55–61.

Nevins, Daniel. 2004. "Goals-Based Investing: Integrating Traditional and Behavioral Finance." *Journal of Wealth Management.* Vol. 6, No. 4: 8–23.

Nijman, Theo, and Lauren Swinkels. 2003. "Strategic and Tactical Allocation to Commodities for Retirement Savings Schemes." Tilburg University.

O'Neill, Jim, Dominic Wilson, and Rumi Masih. 2002. "The Equity Risk Premium from an Economics Perspective." Goldman Sachs Global Economics Paper No. 84.

Oppenheimer, Henry, and Sanjiv Sabherwal. 2003. "The Competitive Effects of U.S. Decimalization: Evidence from U.S.-Listed Canadian Stocks." *Journal of Banking & Finance.* Vol. 27, No. 9: 1883–1910.

Osband, Kent. 2002. *Iceberg Risk.* New York: Texere LLC.

Park, James, and Jeremy Staum. 1998. "Performance Persistence in Alternative Investment Industry." Working Paper, Paradigm Capital Management Inc., New York.

Perold, André F. 1988. "The Implementation Shortfall: Paper vs. Reality." *Journal of Portfolio Management.* Vol. 14, No. 3: 4–9.

Perold, André F., and William F. Sharpe. 1988. "Dynamic Strategies for Asset Allocation." *Financial Analysts Journal.* Vol. 44, No. 1: 16–27.

Peters, Carl, and Ben Warwick, ed. 1997. *The Handbook of Managed Futures.* New York: Irwin.

Phalippou, Ludovic. 2004. "What Drives the Value Premium?" Working Paper, INSEAD.

Plaxco, Lisa, and Robert Arnott. 2002. "Rebalancing a Global Policy Benchmark." *Journal of Portfolio Management.* Vol. 28, No. 2.

Poterba, James. 1999. "Unrealized Capital Gains and the Measurement of After-Tax Portfolio Performance." *Journal of Private Portfolio Management.* Vol. 1, No. 4.

Price, Lee. 1996. "Calculation and Reporting of After-Tax Performance." *Journal of Performance Measurement.* Vol. 1, No. 2.

Price, Lee. 2001. "Taxable Benchmarks: The Complexity Increases." *AIMR Conference Proceedings: Investment Counseling for Private Clients III.* No. 4.

Qian, Edward, and Stephen Gorman. 2001. "Conditional Distribution in Portfolio Theory." *Financial Analysts Journal.* Vol. 57, No. 2: 44–51.

Rapaport, Alfred, and Michael Mauboussin. 2001. *Expectations Investing: Reading Stock Prices for Better Returns.* Boston, MA: Harvard Business School Press.

Reddington, F. M. 1952. "Review of the Principles of Life Insurance Valuations." *Journal of the Institute of Actuaries.* Vol. 78: 286–340.

Reitano, Robert. 1991. "Multivariate Immunization Theory." *Transactions of the Society of Actuaries.* Vol. XLIII.

Reitano, Robert. 1992. "Non-Parallel Yield Curve Shifts and Immunization." *Journal of Portfolio Management.* Vol. 18: 36–43.

Rejda, George. 2005. *Principles of Risk Management and Insurance*, 9th edition. Boston: Addison-Wesley.

Rogers, Douglas, and Lee Price. 2002. "Challenges with Developing Portfolio Accounting Software for After-Tax Reporting." *Journal of Performance Measurement.* Vol. 6, Technology Supplement.

Roll, Richard. 1978. "Ambiguity When Performance Is Measured by the Security Market Line." *Journal of Finance.* Vol. 33, No. 4: 1051–1069.

Roll, Richard. 1992. "A Mean/Variance Analysis of Tracking Error." *Journal of Portfolio Management.* Vol. 18, No. 4: 13–22.

Roll, Richard. 2004. "Empirical TIPS." *Financial Analysts Journal.* Vol. 60, No. 1: 31–53.

Rosenberg, Barr, and Vinay Marathe. 1975. "The Prediction of Investment Risk: Systematic and Residual Risk." *Proceedings of the Seminar on the Analysis of Security Prices.* Center for Research in Security Prices, Graduate School of Business, University of Chicago.

Ross, Stephen, Randolph Westerfield, and Bradford Jordan. 1993. *Fundamentals of Corporate Finance*, 2nd edition. Homewood, IL: Irwin.

Ross, Stephen. 1999. "Adding Risks: Samuelson's Fallacy of Large Numbers Revisited." *Journal of Financial and Quantitative Analysis.* Vol. 34, No. 3: 329–339.

Roy, A.D. 1952. "Safety-First and the Holding of Assets." *Econometrica.* Vol. 20: 431–439.

Salomons, Roelof, and Henk Grootveld. 2002. "The Equity Market Risk Premium: Emerging vs. Developed Markets." University of Groningen, Research Report Vol. 4, No. 2: 121–144.

Samuelson, Paul. 1963. "Risk and Uncertainty: A Fallacy of Large Numbers." *Scientia.* Vol. 57, No. 6: 1–6.

Samuelson, Paul. 1969. "Life Time Portfolio Selection by Dynamic Stochastic Programming." *Review of Economics and Statistics.* Vol. 51: 239–246.

Samuelson, Paul. 1974. "A Challenge to Judgment." *Journal of Portfolio Management.* Vol. 1, No. 1: 17–19.

Saunders, Anthony, and Marcia Millon Cornett. 2003. *Financial Institutions Management*, 4th edition. New York: McGraw-Hill Irwin.

Scanlon, Matthew, and Carter Lyons. 2006. "The Retirement Benefits Crisis: A Survival Guide." *Journal of Investing*. Summer: 28–41.

Scherer, Bernd. 2002. "Portfolio Resampling: Review and Critique." *Financial Analysts Journal*. Vol. 58, No. 6: 98–109.

Schmerken, Ivy. 2005. "Algorithmic Trading." *Wall Street & Technology* (4 February).

Schneeweis, Thomas. 1996. *The Benefits of Managed Futures*. AIMA.

Schneeweis, Thomas. 1998. "Evidence of Superior Performance Persistence in Hedge Funds: An Empirical Comment." *Journal of Alternative Investments*. Vol. 1, No. 2:76–80.

Schneeweis, Thomas, and Hossein Kazemi. 2001. "Alternative Means of Replicating Hedge Fund Manager Performance." CISDM/SOM Working Paper, University Massachusetts.

Schneeweis, Thomas, and Joseph Pescatore, eds. 1999. *The Handbook of Alternative Investment Strategies: An Investor's Guide*. New York: Institutional Investor.

Schneeweis, Thomas, and Richard Spurgin. 1996. "Managed Futures: Nature vs. Nurture." *Barclays Newsletter*. Fall.

Schneeweis, Thomas, and Richard Spurgin. 1997a. "Comparisons of Commodity and Managed Futures Benchmark Indexes." *Journal of Derivatives*, Summer: 33–50.

Schneeweis, Thomas, and Richard Spurgin. 1997b. "Energy-Based Investment Products and Investor Asset Allocation." CISDM Working Paper, University of Massachusetts.

Schneeweis, Thomas, and Richard Spurgin. 1998. "Multi-Factor Analysis of Hedge Fund, Managed Futures, and Mutual Fund Return and Risk Characteristics." *Journal of Alternative Investments*. Vol. 1, No. 2: 1–24.

Schneeweis, Thomas, Hossein Kazemi, and George Martin. 2002. "Understanding Hedge Fund Performance: Research Issues Revisited-Part I." *Journal of Alternative Investments*. Winter: 6–22.

Schwartz, Robert, and Robert Wood. 2003. "Best Execution: A Candid Analysis." *Journal of Portfolio Management*. Vol. 29, No. 4: 37–48.

SEC. 2003. "Implications of the Growth of Hedge Funds." *SEC Staff Report*. September, Washington, D.C.

Sharpe, William, and Lawrence Tint. 1990. "Liabilities—A New Approach." *Journal of Portfolio Management*. Vol. 16, No. 2: 5–10.

Sharpe, William, Gordon Alexander, and Jeffery Bailey. 1999. *Investments*. Upper Saddle River, NJ: Prentice Hall.

Sharpe, William. 1966. "Mutual Fund Performance." *Journal of Business*. Vol. 39, No. 1: 119–138.

Sharpe, William. 1974. "Imputing Expected Security Returns From Portfolio Composition." *Journal of Financial and Quantitative Analysis*. Vol. 9, No. 3: 463–472.

Sharpe, William. 1982. "Factors in New York Stock Exchange Security Returns, 1931–1979." *Journal of Portfolio Management*. Vol. 8, No. 4: 5–19.

Sharpe, William. 1985. *AAT: Asset Allocation Tools*. New York: The Scientific Press.

Sharpe, William. 1988. "Determining a Fund's Effective Asset Mix." *Investment Management Review*. Vol. 2, No. 6: 59–69.

Sharpe, William. 1990. "Asset Allocation." *Managing Investment Portfolios: A Dynamic Process*, 2nd edition. John Maginn and Donald Tuttle, eds. Boston: Warren, Gorham, & Lamont.

Sharpe, William. 1991. "The Arithmetic of Active Management." *Financial Analysts Journal*. Vol. 47, No. 1: 7–9.

Sharpe, William. 1992. "Asset Allocation, Management Style and Performance Measurement." *Journal of Portfolio Management*. Vol. 18, No. 2: 7–19.

Sharpe, William. 1994. "The Sharpe Ratio." *Journal of Portfolio Management*. Vol. 21, No. 1: 49–59.

Sharpe, William. 2000. *Portfolio Theory and Capital Markets*. New York: McGraw-Hill.

Shefrin, Hersh, and Meir Statman. 2000. "Behavioral Portfolio Theory." *Journal of Financial and Quantitative Analysis*. June, 127–151.

Shiller, Robert. 2003. "The Invention of Inflation-Indexed Bonds in Early America." Cowles Foundation Discussion Paper No. 1442.

Shiller, Robert. 2003. *The New Financial Order: Risk in the 21st Century*. Princeton, NJ: Princeton University Press.

Shilling, James. 2002. *Real Estate*, 13th edition. Mason, OH: South-Western.

Siegel, Jeremy. 2002. *Stocks for the Long Run*, 3rd edition. New York: McGraw Hill.

Siegel, Laurence. 2003. *Benchmarks and Investment Management*. Charlotteville, VA: AIMR.

Sieler, Michael, James Webb, and F.C. Neil Myer. 1999. "Diversification Issues in Real Estate Investment." *Journal of Real Estate Literature*. Vol. 7, No. 2: 163–182.

Simpson, John. 2003. "Searching for a System to Meet Your After-Tax Performance Reporting Needs." *Journal of Performance Measurement*. Vol. 7, Performance Presentation Standards Supplement.

Singer, Brian, and Kevin Terhaar. 1997. *Economic Foundations of Capital Market Returns*. Charlottesville, VA: Research Foundation of AIMR.

Singleton, J. Clay 2005. *Core-Satellite Portfolio Management*. New-York: McGraw-Hill.

Solnik, Bruno, and Dennis McLeavey. 2004. *International Investments*, 5th edition. Boston: Pearson Addison-Wesley.

Spaulding, David. 2003. "Holdings vs. Transaction-based Attribution, an Overview." *Journal of Performance Measurement*. Vol. 8, No. 1: 52–56.

Spurgin, Richard. 2001. "How to Game Your Sharpe Ratio." *Journal of Alternative Investments*. Vol. 4, No. 3: 38–46.

Standard & Poor's. 2004. *Directory of Registered Investment Advisors*. Charlottesville, VA: Money Market Directories.

Standards of Practice Handbook. 2005. Charlottesville, VA: CFA Institute.

Staub, Renato, and Jeffrey Diermeier. 2003. "Segmentation, Illiquidity, and Returns." *Journal of Investment Management*. Vol. 1, No. 1: 135–151.

Staub, Renato. 2005. "Capital Market Assumptions." UBS white paper, February.

Staub, Renato. 2006. "Multilayer Modeling of a Market Covariance Matrix." *Journal of Portfolio Management*. Vol. 32, No. 3: 34–44.

Stein, Charles. 1956. "Inadmissibility of the Usual Estimator for the Mean of a Multivariate Normal Distribution." *Proceedings of the Third Berkeley Symposium on Mathematical Statistics and Probability*. Vol. 1: 197–206.

Stein, David, Brian Langstraat, and Premkumar Narasimhan. 1999. "Reporting After-Tax Returns: A Pragmatic Approach." *Journal of Private Portfolio Management*. Spring, 1999.

Stein, David. 1998. "Measuring and Evaluating Portfolio Performance After Taxes." *Journal of Portfolio Management*. Vol. 24, No. 2.

Stevenson, Simon, and Louis Murray. 1999. "An Examination of the Inflation Hedging Ability of Irish Real Estate." *Journal of Real Estate Portfolio Management*. Vol. 5, No. 1.

Stowe, John, Thomas Robinson, Jerald Pinto, and Dennis McLeavey. 2002. *Analysis of Equity Investments: Valuation*. Charlottesville, VA: AIMR.

Strongin, Steve, and Petsch, Melanie. 1995. "Commodity Investing: Long-Run Returns and the Function of Passive Capital." *Derivatives Quarterly*. Fall: 56–64.

Stux, Ivan. 1994. "The Active-Analytical Approach to Equity Investing." Morgan Stanley Global Equity and Derivatives Markets. June 8, 1994.

Swensen, David. 2000. *Pioneering Portfolio Management: An Unconventional Approach to Institutional Investment*. New York: Free Press.

Taylor, John. 1993. "Discretion versus Policy Rules in Practice." *Carnegie-Rochester Conference Series on Public Policy*. Vol. 39: 195–214.

Telser, Lester G. 1958. "Futures Trading and the Storage of Cotton and Wheat." *Journal of Political Economy*. Vol. 66: 134–144.

Terhaar, Kevin, Renato Staub, and Brian Singer. 2003. "The Appropriate Policy Allocation for Alternative Investments." *Journal of Portfolio Management*. Vol. 29, No. 3: 101–110.

Thomas, Lee, and Ram Willner. 1997. "Measuring the Duration Of An Internationally Diversified Bond Portfolio." *Journal of Portfolio Management*. Vol. 24, No. 1: 93–99.

Tierney, David, and Jeffery Bailey. 1997. "Opportunistic Investing." *Journal of Portfolio Management*. Vol. 23, No. 3: 69–78.

Tierney, David, and Kenneth Winston. 1990. "Defining and Using Dynamic Completeness Funds To Enhance Total Fund Efficiency." *Financial Analysts Journal*. Vol. 46, No. 4: 49–54.

Treynor, Jack. 1965. "How to Rate Management of Investment Funds." *Harvard Business Review*. Vol. 43, No. 1: 63–75.

Treynor, Jack. 1987. "The Economics of the Dealer Function." *Financial Analysts Journal.* Vol. 43, No. 6: 27–34.

Tversky, Amos. 1990. "The Psychology of Risk." *Quantifying the Market Risk Premium Phenomenon for Investment Decision-Making.* Charlottesville, VA: AIMR.

Vasicek, Oldrich, and H. Gifford Fong. "Term Structure Modeling Using Exponential Splines." *Journal of Finance.* Vol. 37, No. 22: 339–348.

Volpert, Kenneth. 2000. "Managing Indexed and Enhanced Indexed Bond Portfolios." *Fixed Income Readings for the Chartered Financial Analyst® Program.* New Hope, PA: Frank J. Fabozzi Associates.

Wagner, Wayne, and Mark Edwards. 1993. "Best Execution." *Financial Analysts Journal.* Vol. 49, No. 1: 65–71.

Wagner, Wayne. 2003. "Cost versus Liquidity: The Quest for Best Execution." *Equity Trading: Execution and Analysis.* Charlottesville, VA: AIMR.

Wagner, Wayne. 2004. "The Market Maker in the Age of the ECN." *Journal of Investment Management.* Vol. 2, No. 1.

Waring, Barton, and Laurence Siegel. 2005. "Debunking Some Myths of Active Management." *Journal of Investing.* Vol. 14, No. 2: 20–28.

Waring, Barton, Duane Whitney, John Pirone, and Charles Castille. 2000. "Optimizing Manager Structure and Budgeting Manager Risk." *Journal of Portfolio Management.* Vol. 26, No. 3: 90–104.

Waring, Barton. 2004a. "Liability-Relative Investing." *Journal of Portfolio Management.* Vol. 30, No. 4: 8–20.

Waring, Barton. 2004b. "Liability-Relative Investing II." *Journal of Portfolio Management.* Vol. 31, No. 1: 40–53.

Welch, Ivo. 2000. "Views of Financial Economists on the Equity Premium and on Professional Controversies." *Journal of Business.* Vol. 73, No. 4:501–537.

Welch, Ivo. 2001. "The Equity Premium Consensus Forecast Revisited." Cowles Foundation Discussion Paper No. 1325.

Werner, Ingrid, and Allen Kleidon. 1996. "U.K. and U.S. Trading of British Cross-Listed Stocks: An Intraday Analysis of Market Integration." *Review of Financial Studies.* Vol. 9, No. 2: 619–664.

Womack, Kent. 1996. "Do Brokerage Analysts' Recommendations Have Investment Value?" *Journal of Finance.* Vol. 51, No. 1: 137–167.

Working, Holbrook. 1948. "Theory of the Inverse Carrying Charge in Futures Markets." *Journal of Farm Economics.* 30: 1–28.

Working, H. 1949. "The Theory of the Price of Storage." *American Economic Review.* 39: 1254–1262.

Yago, Glenn, and Susanne Trimbath. 2003. *Beyond Junk Bonds: Expanding High Yield Markets.* New York: Oxford University Press.

Yau, Jot, Uttama Savanayana, and Thomas Schneeweis. 1990. "The Effect of Alternative Return Measures in Financial Futures Research." *Advances in Futures and Options Research,* Vol. 4. Frank Fabozzi, ed. Greenwich, CT: JAI Press.

Yip, Kenneth, and Christopher Donohue. 2003. "Optimal Portfolio Rebalancing With Transaction Costs." *Journal of Portfolio Management.* Vol. 29, No. 4: 49–63.

Young, Michael, and Richard Graff. 1995. "Real Estate is Not Normal: A Fresh Look at Real Estate Return Distributions." *Journal of Real Estate Finance and Economics.* Vol. 10, No. 3: 225–259.

Ziemba, William. 2003. *The Stochastic Programming Approach to Asset, Liability, and Wealth Management.* Charlottesville, VA: Research Foundation of AIMR.

Zweig, Jason. 1998. "Five Investing Lessons from America's Top Pension Fund." *Money.* (January).

ABOUT THE CFA PROGRAM

The Chartered Financial Analyst® designation (CFA®) is a globally recognized standard of excellence for measuring the competence and integrity of investment professionals. To earn the CFA charter, candidates must successfully pass through the CFA Program, a global graduate-level self-study program that combines a broad curriculum with professional conduct requirements as preparation for a wide range of investment specialties.

Anchored by a practice-based curriculum, the CFA Program is focused on the knowledge identified by professionals as essential to the investment decision-making process. This body of knowledge maintains current relevance through a regular, extensive survey of practicing CFA charterholders across the globe. The curriculum covers 10 general topic areas ranging from equity and fixed-income analysis to portfolio management to corporate finance, all with a heavy emphasis on the application of ethics in professional practice. Known for its rigor and breadth, the CFA Program curriculum highlights principles common to every market so that professionals who earn the CFA designation have a thoroughly global investment perspective and a profound understanding of the global marketplace.

www.cfainstitute.org

ABOUT THE AUTHORS

Robert D. Arnott is chairman of Research Affiliates, LLC in Pasadena, California. In 2002, he joined PIMCO, serving as a subadviser, to offer the first global asset allocation product to make active use of alternative markets. More recently, he introduced the concept of fundamental indexation. He previously developed quantitative asset management products and teams as chairman of First Quadrant, LP, global equity strategist at Salomon (now part of Citigroup), president of TSA Capital Management (now part of Analytic), and vice president at The Boston Company (now PanAgora). Mr. Arnott graduated summa cum laude from the University of California in 1977 in economics, applied mathematics, and computer science. He served as editor of the *Financial Analysts Journal* and has authored over seventy refereed articles for journals such as the *Financial Analysts Journal*, the *Journal of Portfolio Management*, and the *Harvard Business Review*. He has also served as a visiting professor of finance at UCLA, on the editorial board of the *Journal of Portfolio Management* and two other journals, and on the product advisory board of the Chicago Board Options Exchange and two other exchanges.

Jeffery V. Bailey, CFA, is director, benefits finance at Target Corporation, where he supervises the investment of the company's defined benefit and defined contribution plan assets and the funding of its nonqualified retirement plans and health and welfare plans. Formerly, Mr. Bailey was a managing partner of Richards & Tierney, Inc., a Chicago-based pension consulting firm that specializes in quantitative risk control techniques. Prior to that, he was assistant director of the Minnesota State Board of Investment, where he directed the external manager operations and developed investment policy for the Board's various funds. Mr. Bailey has published numerous articles regarding pension management. He coauthored the textbooks *Investments* and *Fundamentals of Investments* with William Sharpe and Gordon Alexander, and coauthored with David Tierney the CFA Institute Research Foundation publication *Controlling Misfit Risk in Multiple-Manager Investment Programs*. Mr. Bailey received a BA in economics from Oakland University and an MA in economics and MBA in finance from the University of Minnesota.

James W. Bronson, CFA, is vice president and senior portfolio manager at Northern Trust Corporation. He is responsible for the development and implementation of investment strategies in private client, family, and institutional portfolios. Prior to his association with Northern Trust, Mr. Bronson worked as an analyst and portfolio manager at Trust Services of America (TSA) and First National Bank of Chicago, serving both institutional and private wealth clients. Mr. Bronson holds a master's degree in finance from the University of California at Berkeley. He received his CFA charter in 1984 and has served on various committees for CFA Institute. His local affiliations include the CFA societies of Los Angeles and Orange County.

Terence E. Burns, CFA, is president and founder of Campion Wealth Management, LLC, a registered investment advisory firm located in McLean, Virginia. Mr. Burns began his investment career at Fannie Mae as a financial analyst and subsequently moved to the Association for Investment Management & Research, where he served as editor of the *CFA Digest*. He also worked as a senior portfolio manager at both Riggs & Company and Bank of America. Mr. Burns received a BS degree in finance from the University of Maryland in 1988 and an MBA from Pepperdine University in 1991. He has been a CFA charterholder since 1996, president of the Washington Society of Investment Analysts, and a Presidents

Council Representative of CFA Institute. He serves on the Editorial Advisory Board of the *Journal of Wealth Management* and as a director and treasurer of Fairfax CASA (Court Appointed Special Advocate). He also has served as an adjunct professor at Johns Hopkins University and the University of Virginia.

John P. Calverley is chief economist and strategist at American Express Bank in London, leading a team of economists providing advice to senior management and to the Bank's institutional and private clients worldwide. He edits *Economics for Investment,* the Bank's suite of publications on economic and market trends, and is a regular speaker at international conferences, seminars, and training programs. He also appears frequently on CNN, CNBC, and other TV channels. Educated at Cambridge University and Washington University, Mr. Calverley began his career at the U.K. Treasury and the Economist Intelligence Unit. He is a fellow and former chairman of the U.K. Society of Business Economists, and a council member of the European Money and Finance Forum. His books include *Investor's Guide to Economic Fundamentals* (2002) and *Bubbles and How to Survive Them* (2004).

Don M. Chance, CFA, holds the William H. Wright, Jr. Endowed Chair for Financial Services at the E.J. Ourso College of Business at Louisiana State University. He was formerly the First Union Professor of Financial Risk Management at the Pamplin College of Business at Virginia Tech. Prior to his academic career, he worked for a large southeastern bank. Professor Chance has had numerous articles published in academic and practitioner journals and has authored three books: *An Introduction to Derivatives and Risk Management,* coauthored with Robert Brooks; *Essays in Derivatives*; and *Analysis of Derivatives for the CFA® Program.* He is often quoted in the media on matters related to derivatives and risk management as well as financial markets and the economy in general. He is a frequent consultant to companies, organizations, and law firms, and has extensive instructional experience in professional training programs. His current research is primarily focused on executive stock options. He holds a PhD in finance from LSU.

Peng Chen, PhD, CFA, is managing director and chief investment officer at Ibbotson Associates, an independent consulting firm providing data, software, consulting, research, training, and presentation materials to the financial services industry, subadvisory services to asset allocation funds, and investment advice to 401K participants. Dr. Chen conducts research projects on asset allocation, portfolio risk measurement, nontraditional assets, and global financial markets. Dr. Chen contributed to the development of various Ibbotson products and services, including software, consulting services, educational services, and presentation materials. His writings have appeared in *Financial Analysts Journal, Journal of Portfolio Management, Journal of Investing, Journal of Financial Planning, Bank Securities Journal, Journal of the Association of American Individual Investors, Consumer Interest Annual,* and the *Journal of Financial Counseling and Planning.* He received the Articles of Excellence award from the Certified Financial Planner Board in 1996 and the 2003 Graham and Dodd Award from the *Financial Analysts Journal.* Dr. Chen received his bachelor's degree in industrial management engineering from Harbin Institute of Technology and his master's and doctorate in consumer economics from Ohio State University.

H. Gifford Fong is president of Gifford Fong Associates, a firm specializing in fixed-income, derivative product, and asset allocation analysis. Mr. Fong is the editor of the *Journal of Investment Management* (JOIM); founder of the JOIM Conference Series; member of the Dean's Advisory Council of the Massachusetts Institute of Technology; founding sponsor and member of the Advisory Board of the Masters in Financial Engineering program at the University of California at Berkeley; former editor of the *Financial Analysts Journal*; former member of the board of directors and program chairman of the Institute for Quantitative Research in Finance; and a contributor to a number of professional books and journals. Mr. Fong has received a number of honors, including the Institute for Quantitative Research in Finance Award and the *Financial Analysts Journal*'s Graham and Dodd Award. He serves on a number of boards of directors of nonrelated companies and nonprofit institutions. He is a graduate of the University of California, where he earned his BS, MBA., and JD (law).

Gary L. Gastineau is managing director of ETF Consultants, LLC, a firm that provides specialized exchange-traded fund and index consulting services. He is also a managing member of Managed ETFs, LLC, a firm involved in developing actively managed and improved index exchange-traded funds, and a director of Skyhawk Management, LLC, an investment management firm. Mr. Gastineau has worked as a security analyst, portfolio manager, and derivatives, index, and exchange-traded fund product developer. He is the author or coauthor of five books and numerous journal articles. He serves on the review board for the Research Foundation of CFA Institute. He is an honors graduate of both Harvard College and Harvard Business School.

Kenneth Grant is president and founder of Risk Resources, LLC. He began his career in the Chicago futures markets and, in the late 1980s, created the risk management group at the Chicago Mercantile Exchange. There, he led a project team responsible for the globalization of the SPAN Margin System—the first portfolio risk management system used on a global, institutional basis. In 1994, he moved to Société Generale as head of risk management for the North American Treasury/Capital Markets Group, eventually rising to the role of deputy director. Mr. Grant moved to the hedge fund industry in 1997, joining SAC Capital as its director of risk management and later serving as its chief investment strategist. Mr. Grant also spent two years as the head of global risk management at the Tudor Investment Corporation, and 18 months in a similar role for Cheyne Capital. Mr. Grant formed Risk Resources, LLC, in late 2004 to provide customized, diagnostic risk management services to hedge funds, banks, broker-dealers, and other capital providers. The firm has worked with over 20 companies since its inception representing investment capital in excess of $50 billion. Mr. Grant is the author of *Trading Risk: Enhanced Profitability through Risk Control* (2004), and is principal author of the Managed Funds Association's *Sound Practices for Hedge Fund Managers* (MFA, 2000, 2003, 2005). He served on the MFA's board of directors from 2000 through 2004, was a member of its executive committee (2001–2003), and was a founding member of its hedge fund advisory committee.

Larry D. Guin, DBA, CFA, is a professor of finance at Murray State University in Murray, Kentucky. A former chair of Murray State's Department of Economics and Finance, Dr. Guin teaches primarily graduate-level classes (including portfolio management, security analysis, and financial models) and is a two-time recipient of the university's highest teaching award. He received his doctorate in finance at Mississippi State University in 1979 and has been a CFA charterholder since 1984. Dr. Guin has been active with CFA Institute for over 20 years, including serving on a number of committees related to the CFA Program.

Philip Lawton, CFA, is head of the CIPM Program in the CFA and CIPM Programs Division of CFA Institute. He previously served as vice president at State Street Analytics, where he supported the investment consulting firms that belong to the Independent Consultants Cooperative, and at Citibank, where he headed U.S. performance measurement in Worldwide Securities Services. Mr. Lawton earned a PhD in the French-speaking section of the Catholic University of Louvain, Belgium, and an MA in business administration with a concentration in finance at Northeastern University. He is a member of the Society for Business Ethics.

Ananth Madhavan is the global head of trading research at Barclays Global Investors. He leads BGI's global trading research team with a focus on execution research and trading strategies across different asset classes worldwide. Dr. Madhavan also works closely with the global trading team and BGI's alpha research and product groups to design and implement trading strategies capturing liquidity-driven market opportunities. Before joining BGI in 2003, Dr. Madhavan was managing director of Research of ITG, Inc., and a member of the firm's management and executive committees. Previously, he was the Charles B. Thorton Professor of Finance at the Marshall School of Business at the University of Southern California, and assistant professor of finance at the Wharton School of the University of Pennsylvania. Dr. Madhavan is the author of numerous publications in leading academic and practitioner journals. He received his PhD in economics from Cornell University and BA from the University of Delhi, India.

John L. Maginn, CFA, is president of Maginn Associates, Inc., a financial consulting firm in Omaha, Nebraska. Mr. Maginn began his investment career at CNA Financial and subsequently joined the investment staff of Mutual of Omaha. He retired in 2000 from Mutual of Omaha, where he was executive vice president, chief investment officer, and treasurer. Mr. Maginn received his BSBA degree from Creighton University in 1961 and an MS degree in finance from the University of Minnesota in 1962. He has been a CFA charterholder since 1968, and is a past chairman of the board of governors of AIMR and the ICFA. Mr. Maginn serves on the investment committees of several endowment funds and is a director of two companies. He is also an adjunct professor at Creighton University, where he teaches an investments course in the MBA program.

John Marsland, CFA, is a senior portfolio manager and quantitative analyst at Schroder Investment Management in London. Mr. Marsland began his investment career in 1992 at UBS Philips & Drew as a U.K. economist, and subsequently moved into investment strategy and quantitative analysis. Mr. Marsland read economics at Downing College, University of Cambridge, and holds an MSc in economics from Birkbeck College, University of London. He has been a CFA charterholder since 2000. He is chairman of the special interest group for Quantitative Investment Professionals, UKSIP, and a former secretary/treasurer of the Institute for Quantitative Investment Research (Inquire UK).

Dennis W. McLeavey, CFA, is head of professional development products at CFA Institute. Previously, he served as head of curriculum development for the CFA Program. Prior to joining CFA Institute in 2000, he served on various CFA Institute committees. He is coauthor of *International Investments* with Bruno Solnik and coauthor of two CFA Institute texts, *Quantitative Methods for Investment Analysis* and *Analysis of Equity Investments: Valuation,* as well as two college texts, *Production Planning and Inventory Control* and *Operations Research for Management Decisions.* His research has been published in *Management Science* and in the *Journal of Operations Research,* and he serves as a New York Stock Exchange Arbitrator. In his academic career, he taught at the University of Western Ontario, the University of Connecticut, the University of Rhode Island where he founded a student managed fund, and Babson College. After studying economics for his bachelor's degree at the University of Western Ontario in 1968, he completed a doctorate in production management and industrial engineering at Indiana University in 1972. He earned his CFA charter in 1990.

Alan M. Meder, CFA, is a senior vice president of Duff & Phelps Investment Management Company, an investment counseling firm located in Chicago. Mr. Meder is responsible for the risk management and quantitative research areas and is also the chief financial officer of Duff & Phelps Utility and Corporate Bond Trust, Inc., and DTF Tax-Free Income, Inc. He began his career at National City Corporation and joined Duff & Phelps in 1985. Mr. Meder received his BBA degree from Cleveland State University in 1982 and an MBA degree from Baldwin-Wallace College in 1985. He has been a CFA charterholder since 1988 and has been active on CFA Institute committees. Mr. Meder is a member of the American Institute of Certified Public Accountants and the CFA Chicago Society.

Philip Moore is managing director of Pacific Investment Consultants, LLC, an investment consulting firm specializing in governance, asset allocation, and manager selection for defined benefit pension plans and other obligation-based investors. Mr. Moore began his career with Pacific Mutual Life Insurance Company (now Pacific Life), where he was senior account executive in the pension department. He has been vice president and senior consultant with the Carmack Group and vice president for product development and marketing with Research Affiliates. Mr. Moore earned a BA degree from Ohio State University and was awarded an MBA from Pepperdine University in 1983.

Andrew R. Olma, CFA, is a managing director at Barclays Global Investors. He is the head of the non-U.S. Active Equity Strategies Group in San Francisco, which he has led since 2000. His previous roles at BGI include chief investment strategist for equity index strategies and portfolio manager. Mr. Olma received an SB degree in electrical engineering from the Massachusetts Institute of Technology in 1983, and an MBA from Boston University in 1988. He has been a CFA charterholder since 1991. Mr. Olma has also previously served on the FTSE World Index Committee and currently chairs the investment committee of a charitable endowment.

Jerald E. Pinto, CFA, is director of curriculum projects in the CFA and CIPM Programs Division at CFA Institute. He is the coauthor of two textbooks used in the CFA Program, *Analysis of Equity Investments: Valuation* (2002) and *Quantitative Methods for Investment Analysis* (2001, 2004). Before coming to CFA Institute in 2002, Mr. Pinto was a consultant to corporations, foundations, and partnerships in investment planning, portfolio analysis, and quantitative analysis. He has also worked in the investment and banking industries in New York City and taught finance at New York University's Stern School of Business. He holds an MBA from Baruch College and a PhD in finance from the Stern School.

Lisa M. Plaxco, CFA, is a director and a senior member of the investment research team at First Quadrant, a global investment management firm headquartered in Pasadena, California. Ms. Plaxco's expertise extends across a broad array of strategies, implementation of passive rebalancing, global macro, asset allocation, and equity strategies. Ms. Plaxco is a frequent contributor to external research distributed by First Quadrant, as well as articles submitted to industry publications. Ms. Plaxco, who holds a BS degree from the California Institute of Technology, was an educator and a research scientist in polymer chemistry prior to entering finance. She began her work at First Quadrant in 1992 and earned her CFA designation in 2004.

W. Bruce Remington II, CFA, is vice president and senior regional investment manager with Wells Fargo Institutional Asset Advisors in Lincoln, Nebraska. Mr. Remington began his career as an operating officer with Union Pacific Railroad and, after working as an internal analyst at Union Pacific, served as an analyst and portfolio manager with a regional brokerage firm in Omaha and later with a money management firm serving high-net-worth individuals. Mr. Remington was a portfolio manager for First Commerce Investors from 1993 until the firm was acquired by Wells Fargo in 2000. He received his BS degree in labor and industrial relations from Michigan State University, and an MBA from the University of Nebraska. He has been a CFA charterholder since 1986 and is a member and past president of the CFA Society of Nebraska. Mr. Remington has been an adjunct faculty member at the University of Nebraska–Omaha since 1980.

Thomas M. Richards, CFA, is cofounder and principal of Richards & Tierney, Inc., in Chicago. Previously, Mr. Richards was with the Harris Bank where he designed and implemented the trust department's investment analytics service. Prior to joining the bank, Mr. Richards was responsible for the investment operations of a large corporate plan sponsor. Mr. Richards has published a variety of articles in pension finance literature and has been a frequent speaker at investment conferences and seminars. He has more than 30 years' experience in pension and investment management. Mr. Richards received his CFA charter in 1978. He received his AB in mathematics from Bucknell University and an MS in finance (with distinction) from Pennsylvania State University.

Thomas R. Robinson, CFA, is an associate professor of accounting and director of the Master of Professional Accounting program at the University of Miami. He also is managing director of Robinson, Desmond & Zwerner, a Florida investment advisory firm. He received a BA in conomics from the University of Pennsylvania and a master's degree and PhD from Case Western Reserve University. He is a certified public accountant (Ohio), Certified Financial Planner® certificant, and CFA charterholder. He is active locally and nationally with CFA Institute, having served on the Financial Accounting Policy Committee, among others. He is a former president and board member of CFA Miami (formerly the Miami Society of Financial Analysts). He has lectured in many cities in the United States, Canada, and Europe regarding accounting scandals and the use of financial analysis in detecting these types of financial irregularities.

Matthew H. Scanlan, CFA, serves as head of the Americas Institutional Business at Barclays Global Investors. He is responsible for managing the sales and service effort in the United States, Canada, and Latin America, focusing on the defined benefit, defined contribution, and treasury markets for corporate, public, and Taft-Hartley plans, as well as central banks, endowments, and foundations. Prior to joining BGI in 1997, Mr. Scanlan worked at Sanford C. Bernstein and Company, Inc. He also served as a senior portfolio manager at the Northern Trust Company in Chicago. He received his MM in accounting and finance from the J.L. Kellogg School at Northwestern University, and his BA in economics from the University of Southern California, where he was Phi Beta Kappa. Mr. Scanlan is a recent recipient of the CFA Institute C. Stewart Sheppard Award for contributions to the investment industry's body of knowledge. Mr. Scanlan also serves on the finance board for the Foundation of the City College of San Francisco and on the board of trustees for the Mechanics' Institute of San Francisco.

Thomas Schneeweis is Michael and Cheryl Philipp Professor of Finance at the Isenberg School of Management at the University of Massachusetts in Amherst, Massachusetts. He also serves as director of the Center for International Securities and Derivatives Markets (CISDM), a nonprofit academic research center specializing in the alternative investment area at the University of Massachusetts. He is the editor of the *Journal of Alternative Investments* and is a founding member of the Chartered Alternative Investment Analyst (CAIA) Association, a global nonprofit educational venture between CISDM and AIMA that offers the CAIA program. He is an outside trustee for the Managers Funds and is a principal in Alternative Investment Analytics, a financial consulting and education firm.

William F. Sharpe is the STANCO 25 Professor of Finance Emeritus at Stanford University's Graduate School of Business. He joined the Stanford faculty in 1970, having previously taught at the University of Washington and the University of California at Irvine. In 1996, he cofounded Financial Engines, a firm that provides online investment advice and management for individuals. Dr. Sharpe received his PhD, MA, and BA in economics from the University of California at Los Angeles. He is also the recipient of a doctor of humane letters, honoris causa, from DePaul University, a doctor honoris causa from the University of Alicante (Spain), a doctor honoris causa from the University of Vienna (Austria), and the UCLA Medal, UCLA's highest honor. In 1990, Dr. Sharpe received the Nobel Prize in economic sciences for his work on the Capital Asset Pricing Model.

Laurence B. Siegel is director of research in the investment division of the Ford Foundation in New York, where he has worked since 1994. Prior to that, he was a managing director of Ibbotson Associates, an investment consulting firm that he helped to establish in 1979. In 2005, Mr. Siegel was named research director of the Research Foundation of CFA Institute. He holds this position concurrently with his responsibilities at the Ford Foundation. Mr. Siegel chairs the investment committee of the Trust for Civil Society in Central and Eastern Europe. He serves on the investment committee of the NAACP Legal Defense Fund, and advises the boards of many other nonprofit organizations. He was a trustee of the Oberweis Emerging Growth Fund. Mr. Siegel is a member of the editorial boards of the *Journal of Portfolio Management* and the *Journal of Investing*, and is a member of the program committee of the Institute for Quantitative Research in Finance (the Q Group). He received his BA in urban studies from the University of Chicago in 1975, and his MBA in finance from the same institution in 1977.

Brian D. Singer, CFA, is head of global investment solutions and regional chief investment officer, Americas, for UBS Global Asset Management. Mr. Singer is a member of the UBS Group managing board, executive committee, and global investment committee. A member of the CFA Institute board of governors and board of trustees of the Research Foundation of CFA Institute, Mr. Singer is the recipient of a 1991 Graham and Dodd Award for Excellence from the *Financial Analysts Journal.* He holds a BA from Northwestern University and an MBA from the University of Chicago.

Jan R. Squires, CFA, is managing director, Asia Pacific operations, for CFA Institute, located in Hong Kong. He was formerly head of examination development at CFA Institute, where he was responsible for all examination products for the CFA Program. Prior to joining CFA Institute in 1999, he served the organization for more than 10 years in several volunteer and consulting capacities. Dr. Squires held several academic positions earlier in his career, receiving awards for teaching and research excellence. He also consulted extensively for a variety of clients, focusing on small business owners, financial institutions, and public agencies. He received the doctor of business administration degree in 1984 from the Darden Graduate School at the University of Virginia, and has been a CFA charterholder since 1987.

Renato Staub is a senior asset allocation and risk analyst with UBS Global Asset Management. He received an MS from the Federal Institute of Technology in Zurich (Switzerland) and a PhD from the Graduate School of Business, Economics, Law and Social Sciences in St. Gallen (Switzerland). His responsibilities include risk and valuation analysis of developed and alternative assets, which entails the building and maintenance of risk and valuation systems. He was involved in the development of alternative investments such as a global leveraged portfolio, a market-neutral portfolio, and a risk-controlled portfolio. Prior to this, he was a quantitative analyst, focusing on product development and risk analysis. Mr. Staub has published articles on asset allocation and risk-related topics in a variety of professional journals. In addition, he has presented at conferences hosted by the Q-Group, Barra, Risk Waters Group, the Society of Quantitative Analysts, and the Quantitative Work Alliance for Applied Finance, Education & Wisdom.

Dean J. Takahashi is senior director of investments for Yale University, where he helps oversee more than $18 billion of the university's endowment, pension, and charitable trust assets. Since 1986, Mr. Takahashi has been responsible for Yale's domestic, foreign, and private equity portfolios; absolute return strategies; natural resource investments; and analysis regarding asset allocation, spending policy, and long-range university finances. Mr. Takahashi is a director or investment committee member of several nonprofit charities and independent schools, and is on the advisory committee of numerous investment funds. In addition, he was formerly a board member of two NYSE-listed investment companies. Mr. Takahashi received his BA magna cum laude with distinction in economics in 1980, and a master's degree in public and private management in 1983 from Yale University, where he was a lecturer in economics and a fellow of the International Center for Finance. Mr. Takahashi teaches a senior economics seminar in Yale College and a course on endowment management at the Yale School of Management.

David E. Tierney, PhD, is cofounder and principal of Richards & Tierney, Inc., in Chicago. Formerly, Dr. Tierney was administrative manager of investments for Amoco Corporation's pension fund. He directed and coordinated the activities of the investment managers, controlled the pension fund's accounting and auditing functions, measured and analyzed the performance of the fund's investment managers, and conducted research into improved methods of pension management. For the last 20 years, Dr. Tierney has done extensive work in portfolio analysis and risk-control services. He is recognized as the originator of the "Completeness Fund" concept and quadrant mapping of portfolios. Dr. Tierney received a BS in engineering science (with distinction) from Northwestern University and an MS and PhD in applied statistics from the University of Wisconsin. In addition, he has taught at the University of Chicago Graduate School of Business.

Jack L. Treynor is president of Treynor Capital Management, Inc., in Palos Verdes Estates, California. Mr. Treynor was previously general partner and chief investment officer of Treynor-Arbit Associates, and was for many years editor of the *Financial Analysts Journal.* In addition to a book with Priest and Regan on the investment consequences of ERISA (1976), he is the author of over 70 papers, 16 of which have been anthologized. Mr. Treynor has taught the investments course at Columbia University and the University of Southern California, and has lectured in many countries. At various times he has been a trustee, general partner, or director of certain investment companies. He serves on the advisory boards of the *Financial Analysts Journal* and the *Journal of Investment Management.* He is a distinguished fellow of the Institute for Quantitative Research in Finance. Mr. Treynor majored in mathematics at Haverford College, wrote cases for a year after graduating (with distinction) from Harvard Business School, and devoted a sabbatical year to the study of economics at MIT under Franco Modigliani.

R. Charles Tschampion, CFA, is director, industry relations at CFA Institute. He retired from General Motors Asset Management in 2005, where his 28-year investment career included responsibility for portfolio strategy, asset allocation, and defined contribution plan management. Mr. Tschampion received his BS in industrial engineering in 1967 and his MBA in 1968 from Lehigh University. He has been a CFA charterholder since 1986, and is a past chair of the board of governors of AIMR and the FAF. In 2003, he received the Daniel J. Forrestal Leadership Award for Professional Ethics and Standards of Investment Practice. Mr. Tschampion cochaired the AIMR Performance Presentation Standards Implementation Committee and chaired CFA Institute task forces on corporate governance, soft dollars, and personal investing. He chairs the investment committee of the Lehigh endowment fund and is a director of two investment funds.

Wayne H. Wagner is principal of OM/NI, a partnership that consults on issues relating to securities trading and exchanges. He cofounded Plexus Group, a Los Angeles–based firm that provided trading evaluation and advisory services to money managers, brokerage firms, and pension plan sponsors. In 2006, Plexus Group became a part of ITG Solutions, Inc., for whom Mr. Wagner consults. He is author and editor of *The Complete Guide to Securities Transactions: Improving Performance and Reducing Costs,* and coauthor of a popular investment book entitled *MILLIONAIRE: The Simplest Explanation of How an Index Fund Can Turn Your Lunch Money into a Fortune.* Mr. Wagner served on the CFA Institute Blue Ribbon Task Force on Soft Dollars, the CFA Institute Best Execution Task Force, and as a regent of the Financial Analysts Seminar. He received two Graham and Dodd Awards from the *Financial Analysts Journal* for excellence in financial writing. He was a founding partner of Wilshire Associates and served as chief investment officer of Wilshire Asset Management and, earlier, participated in the design of the first index funds at Wells Fargo Bank. Mr. Wagner received an MS in statistics/management science from Stanford University, and a BBA in management science/finance from the University of Wisconsin.

Lisa Robinson Weiss, CFA, has spent nearly 30 years in investment management, having served as an analyst, portfolio manager, and investment banker for organizations including Wells Fargo, Scudder, Stevens & Clark, and USAA. Ms. Weiss is president and founder of Black Knight Ventures, an investment banking firm dedicated to private equity. In addition, she is chief investment officer for Silver Lining Capital Management, a hedge fund manager whose first fund invests in distressed debt securities. A graduate of Trinity University, she holds both a BA and an MBA and was named to Phi Beta Kappa. She was an adjunct professor at Golden Gate University, teaching an investments course in their MBA program. Ms. Weiss has been a CFA charterholder since 1981 and has served in various volunteer capacities for CFA Institute and local society chapters, including the board of directors for the San Francisco Society of Financial Analysts. In 2002, CFA Institute recognized her with the Donald L. Tuttle Award for Grading Excellence in recognition of her many years of service as a grader.

Jot Yau, PhD, CFA, is chair, MSF program director, and professor of the Department of Finance at Seattle University, where he has taught since 2001. He cofounded Strategic Options Investment Advisors Ltd., a Hong Kong–based investment advisory firm, and has served as the principal investment and commodity trading adviser since 1998. He is a member of the finance/ALCO committee of GHCU, a Seattle-based credit union. Dr. Yau has published numerous articles in scholarly and practitioner finance journals, including *Financial Analysts Journal* and *CFA Magazine.* He has served on the editorial board of *The Journal of Alternative Investments* since 2001 and as associate editor from 2001 to 2005. He worked for George Mason University, Kidder Peabody, Shearson/American Express, and Dow Chemical prior to joining Seattle University. He holds a PhD in finance from the University of Massachusetts at Amherst, and has been a CFA charterholder since 1997.

Robert G. Zielinski, CFA, is director of research of Japan Advisory, Ltd., an investment advisory firm located in Tokyo, Japan. Mr. Zielinski began his investment career in 1983 in Japan, where he worked as a banking analyst for Jardine Fleming Securities. In 1992, he moved to Thailand and then Singapore, where he conducted emerging market research. In 1998 he joined Lehman Brothers as Head of Asian Bank Research, and in 2002 moved to UBS Global Asset Management. Mr. Zielinski received his BS and MS degrees in nuclear engineering from the Massachusetts Institute of Technology, and an MBA from Harvard Business School. He has been a CFA charterholder since 1990 and is a founding director of the Japan Society of Investment Professionals. He is author of two books on Japan's stock market.

Index

Page number followed by "e" indicates Exhibit on that page; page number followed by "n" indicates Note on that page.

Q

R